2002
PEOPLE
ALMANAC

★ 2002 ★
PEOPLE
ALMANAC

CREATED AND PRODUCED BY
CADER BOOKS • NEW YORK

Cader Books
38 E. 29 Street
New York, NY 10016
www.caderbooks.com

First Edition

1 3 5 7 9 10 8 6 4 2

Printed in the United States of America

CONTENTS

TUBE 101

SONG 149

PAGES   229

STAGE   281

PEOPLE EXTRAS   305

ACKNOWLEDGMENTS

Many people and organizations have generously lent their time, resources, and expertise to help make this project possible. Special thanks go to: Academy of Recording Arts and Sciences; Frank Alkyer, *Down Beat;* Jennifer Allen, PMK; Bridget Aschenberg, ICM; Alan Axelrod; Robert Azcuy, Itsy Bitsy Productions; Michael Barson, Putnam; Anita Bedra, Reprise Records; Michelle Bega, Rogers & Cowan, Inc.; Andi Berger, PMK; Cindi Berger; Marion Billings, M/S Billings Publicity, Ltd.; Helen Blake, National Infomercial Marketing Association; Jeff Blitz, Writers Guild of America, west; Judy Boals, Berman, Boals & Flynn; Matthew Bradley, Viking; Sandy Bresler, Bresler, Kelly, and Associates; Gerry Byrne, *Variety;* Brad Cafarelli, Bragman, Nyman, Cafarelli; Fr. John Catoir, Christophers; Center for the Book, Library of Congress; Center for Media and Public Affairs; Vicki Charles, Loud Records; Marylou Chlipala, Carnegie Mellon School of Drama; Bob Christie, National Academy of Television Arts and Sciences; Robert C. Christopher, The Pulitzer Prizes; Steve Clar; Rosie Cobbe, Fraser & Dunlop; Camille Cline; Dan Cohen, Caroline Records; Sam Cohn; Ace Collins; Sarah Cooper, O. W. Toad Ltd.; Don Corathers, *Dramatics* magazine; Angela Corio, Recording Industry Association of America; Marie Costanza, NYU/Tisch Musical Theater Dept.; Kendal Culp, Random House; Louise Danton, National Academy of Television Arts and Sciences; Leslie Dart, PMK; Gary N. DaSilva; Jennifer DeGuzman, MTV; Paul Dergarabedian, Exhibitor Relations; Steve Devick, Platinum Records; Mark Dillion, Capitol Records; Joan Dim, NYU, Tisch School of the Arts; Heather Dinwiddie, American Symphony Orchestra League; Dramatists Guild; Steve Dworman, *Infomercial Marketing Report;* Marilyn Egol, RCA Victor; Allen Eichhorn; Ed Enright, *Down Beat;* Kenneth Ewing; Charmaine Ferenczi, The Tantleff Office; Ophir Finkelthal, Virgin Records; Karen Forester, Country Music Association; Diane Fortiay, Island Records; Susan Geller, Susan Geller & Associates; Heather Gifford, National Academy of Recording Artists; Debbie Gilwood; Michelle Gluckman, American Society of Magazine Editors; Bob Gregg, Paramount; Amanda Grossman, Capitol Records; Tracey Guest, Dutton Signet; Ned Hammad, *Pulse!;* Cynthia Harris, Little, Brown; Heidi, Def Jam Records; Tom Hill, Nick at Nite; Patricia Hodges, Time Warner; Hollywood Chamber of Commerce; Hollywood Foreign Press Association; Dave Howard, Hofflund/Pollone Agency; Jane Huebsch, American Symphony Orchestra League; Patrick Ingram, Bantam; Gary Ink, *Publishers Weekly;* M. Jackson, AUDELCO; A. J. Jacobs; Elizabeth Jarret; Kristin Joerg, Bantam Books; Steve Jukes, Judy Daish Associates; Susan S. Kaplan, *Billboard;* Joyce Ketay, Joyce Ketay Agency; Amanda Kimmel, Dell; John Kings, Texas Center for Writers; Pat Kingsley; Leonard Klady, *Variety;* Judy Krug, American Library Association; Amy Leavell, Capricorn Records; Marleah Leslie; Ruth Levine,

Penguin; Stacey Levitt, Rachel McCallister & Associates; Ed Limato, ICM; Elizabeth Maas, The League of American Theatres and Producers; Tracy Mann, Righteous Babe Recordings; Joe Marich; Howard Marcantel, National Academy of Cable Programming; Nicole Marti, Viking Books; Jaye Maynard, NYU; Angela Medina, Juilliard School of Drama; Gilbert Medina, William Morris Agency; Lisa Meredith, National Cable Forum; Suzanne Mikesell, *Pulse!;* Jason Mitchell, Chronicle; T. J. Mitchell, Hofflund/Pollone Agency; Jessica Morell; Jamie Morris, *Soap Opera Digest;* Nara Nahm, Pantheon; Vincent Nasso, Nielsen Media Research; The National Book Foundation; Karen Kriendler Nelson, Richard Tucker Foundation; Patricia Nicolescu, Quigley Publishing Co., Inc.; Shannon O'Boyle, *Advertising Age;* David O'Connor; Catherine Olim, PMK; Bob Palmer; Charlotte Parker, Parker Public Relations; Gilbert Parker, William Morris; Karen Pascho; Jeffrey Pasternak, Simon & Schuster; Liz Perl, Berkley; Craig Phillips, 20th Century Fox International; Aaron Pinkham; Eileen Potrock, Itsy Bitsy Productions; Ronnie Pugh, Country Music Hall of Fame; Myra Quinn, Peter Brown Agency; Joe Regal, Irene Reichbach, Harcourt-Brace; Russell & Volkening; Tom Reidy, Tuneful Productions; Jonathan S. Renes, DMB&B; Sandy Rice, PMK; Rock and Roll Hall of Fame; Sandee Richardson, *Steve Dworman's Infomercial Marketing Report;* Richard Rodzinski, Van Cliburn Competition; Bradley Roberts, *Pollstar;* Cynthia Robinson, American Library Association's Office for Intellectual Freedom; Bradley J. Rogers, *Pollstar;* Ami Roosevelt; Rachel Rosenberg, Northwestern University School of Speech; Howard Rosenstone, Rosenstone/Wender; Sheryl Rothmuller, NBC Entertainment Press and Publicity; Lucy Sabini, RCA; Heidi Schaeffer, ICM; Bill Schelble; Ken Schneider, Knopf; Mitch Schneider, Warner Brothers Records; Rachel Schnoll, Viking; Elaine Schock, RCA Records; Nancy Seltzer, Nancy Seltzer & Associates, Inc.; Greg Sharko, ATP Media Relations; John Sheehan, Center for Media and Public Affairs; Paul Shefrin, The Shefrin Company; Barry Sherman, University of Georgia; Jane Sindell, CAA; Smithsonian Institution, Division of Community Life; Robert Stein, United Talent Agency; Carol Stone, PMK; Laine Sutton, *Jeopardy!;* Jack Tantleff, The Tantleff Office; Jonathan Taylor, *Variety;* Prof. Mark Tucker, Columbia University; Terry Tuma, Yale School of Drama; Georgina Warwick, *Jeopardy!;* Rebecca Watson, Broadway Books; Kate Weaver, Avon Books; Sarah Webster, O. W. Toad Ltd.; Murray Weissman, Weissman Angellotti; Windi Wentworth, PBS; Moira Whalon; *Whitaker's Almanac;* Heather Willis, *Pulse!;* Patricia Willis, Beinecke Library, Yale University; Staci Wolfe; Lea Yardum, Weissman/Delson Communications.

STAFF

Editor in Chief
Michael Cader

Editors
Amy Woodbury, Camille Cline

Design
Charles Kreloff

Photo Research
Gina Matturri, Steve Baumgartner

Consulting Editor
Seth Godin

PEOPLE WEEKLY
Carol Wallace, Managing Editor
Nora P. McAniff, President
David Geithner, Group Business Manager
Richard Burgheim, Supervising Editor

PEOPLE Contributors
Jane Bealer, Brian Belovitch, Robert Britton, Betsy Castillo, Sal Covarrubias, Urbano DelValle, Sally Foster, Margery Frohlinger, Patricia Hustoo, Suzy Im, Terry Kelleher, Eric Levin, Amy Linden, Michael A. Lipton, Denise Lynch, Samantha Miller, Florence Nishida, James Oberman, Stan Olson, Susan Radlauer, Leah Rozen, Randy Vest, Céline Wojtala

PHOTO CREDITS

★ 2002
PEOPLE
ALMANAC

THE YEAR
IN REVIEW

JANUARY

Fox's reality TV show **Temptation Island** launches, generating almost as much controversy as the network's special from 2000, *Who Wants to Marry a Multi-Millionaire?* And the show draws more viewers for its opening than the benchmark inaugural episode of *Survivor.* Four "committed" but unmarried couples spend two weeks in a Caribbean resort off Belize, where they are separated from their mates and tempted by 26 eligible and eye-catching singles. And the grand prize is nothing more than a vacation.

Conservative and religious groups are quick to criticize the sexually charged program, and TV critics join in as well. It's revealed that one of the couples had to be booted off the show after shooting had begun when it was discovered that they had a child together—leading a North Carolina Fox affiliate to stop broadcasting the series. A station official says, "We were assured that these couples would not be married [or have] children. We reluctantly agreed to air the program with those assurances. We are not going to be a part of making light of the family institution in a 'reality' program."

In March the couple in question, Ytossie Patterson, 34, and Taheed Watson, 29, file suit in Los Angeles Superior Court against the producers of the show, claiming they were defamed when it was revealed publicly that their relationship produced a child. Patterson and Watson claim in their legal papers that the producers knew from the start that they had a child (who is 2), but decided it would be better ratings-wise to reveal that info during an episode.

Ally McBeal star **Calista Flockhart**, 36, announces that she has adopted a baby boy, Liam. She says in a statement, "I have always wanted to adopt a child, and I am overjoyed that I have been blessed with a beautiful and healthy son." The statement adds that while Flockhart, who is single, "intends on keeping her new family life very private, she has revealed that she plans on giving birth someday and may adopt another child."

Sean Combs leaves the courthouse with his mother after being found not guilty in March.

The high-profile weapons and bribery trial against rap entrepreneur **Sean Combs**, 31, begins in New York City. Police allege that they found a gun in Combs's Lincoln Navigator after he reportedly fled a shooting in a Times Square nightclub in December, 1999. They also claim that Combs attempted to bribe his driver, Wardel Fenderson, into saying that the weapon was his. Co-defendant Jamal "Shyne" Barrow, 20, is charged with attempted murder and gun possession, and Combs' bodyguard Anthony "Wolf" Jones is accused of having the loaded gun by his feet.

By Valentine's Day, Combs and one-time love **Jennifer Lopez** confirm that they have officially split. But the news is better in March, when a jury quickly acquits Combs of all charges. Barrow is found guilty of first-degree assault with depraved indifference and second-degree assault, and sentenced to 10 years in prison. Combs says afterwards, "I've changed, I've matured . . .This whole thing has made me deeper."

Former NFL player **Rae Carruth**, 26, accused of arranging the killing of his pregnant girlfriend Cherica Adams, 24, in November of 1999, is acquitted in a North Carolina courtroom of first-degree murder but found guilty of conspiracy and two other charges of shooting into an occupied vehicle and using an instrument to destroy an unborn child. Adams, who died one month after the incident (bullets were shot into her car), was seven months pregnant with the former Carolina Panther's baby. Carruth is sentenced to more than 18 years in prison.

Civil rights activist **Jesse Jackson**, 59, delivers a bombshell when he reveals that he had an extramarital affair that resulted in the birth of a daughter, Ashley, now 20 months old. "I fully accept responsibility and I am truly sorry for my actions," says the Rev. Jackson, who adds that he has provided "emotional and financial support" to the child since her birth. Jackson has been married for 38 years. "My wife, Jackie, and my children have been made aware of the child, and it has been an extremely painful, trying and difficult time for them," Jackson adds.

The mother is **Karin Stanford**, 39, who formerly ran the Washington, D.C. office of Jackson's Rainbow/PUSH Coalition. Stanford said Jackson's lawyers asked her to sign confidentiality agreements, but no money was attached to the requests. "I really need to clear up some misinformation about me," the former political science professor says. "I'm not a blackmailer. I've never received any payoff money." Jackson's spokesman confirmed that no money was offered. Stanford relocated to L.A. and sued Jackson, seeking to formalize a child support agreement. Jackson has been sending $3,000 a month to support his daughter.

PASSAGES

Married
Actor Halle Berry and singer Eric Benét, both 34, in front of a few friends on a beach in Santa Barbara, Calif.

Former *Star Trek* star William Shatner, 69, and Elizabeth J. Martin, 42, a onetime high school homecoming queen, in sleepy Lebanon, Ill.

Split
Kim Basinger, 47, files for divorce from Alec Baldwin, 42, seeking physical custody of daughter Ireland, 5 (though Baldwin would share legal custody and have visitation rights)

Shock rocker Marilyn Manson, 32, and fiancée Rose McGowan, 27, call off their impending nuptials and decide to go their separate ways

Oasis songwriter Noel Gallagher and his wife of three years, Meg Mathews, are granted a divorce on grounds of "irreconcilable breakdown arising from admitted adultery"

Former *Ally McBeal* costar Courtney Thorne-Smith, 33, and genetic scientist Andrew Conrad, separated after seven months of marriage

Farewell
My Favorite Martian star Ray Walston, 86

Singer-songwriter **Michael Bolton**, 47, loses an appeal to the U.S. Supreme Court in which he sought the reversal of an earlier $5.4 million jury ruling that his hit, "Love Is a Wonderful Thing," plagiarized parts of a song of the same name by legendary soul singers the Isley Brothers. The court rejects the appeal without any comment or dissent. In his appeal, Bolton was represented by Harvard University law professor Alan Dershowitz.

Celine Dion, 32, and her husband-manager, **René Angelil**, 26 years her senior, are the proud parents of a baby boy, René-Charles, who weighs six pounds. Dion and Angelil, married since 1994, had been trying to conceive throughout their marriage, they told PEOPLE in 2000. "I waited forever for this moment," she told the magazine. "It's like our little miracle has finally happened." Dion and Angelil credited Manhattan fertility specialist Dr. Zev Rosenwaks with Dion's in vitro fertilization procedure. Dion says in a televised interview that she has a second embryo stored at a fertility clinic and hopes to give her soon-to-be-born son a "twin."

FEBRUARY

Baywatch, the beloved bikini show that catapulted Pamela Anderson, Yasmine Bleeth and Carmen Electra to fame and re-launched David Hasselhoff's career, will jiggle off into the Hawaiian sunset after 11 years on the air. The producers announce the final episode will air in May. *Baywatch* was viewed by people in more than 100 countries at various times, making it one of the most successful TV shows internationally.

Tom Cruise, 38, and **Nicole Kidman**, 33, announce that they are separating after approximately 10 years of marriage, through their spokesman, Pat Kingsley. "Citing the difficulties inherent in divergent careers, which constantly keep them apart, they concluded that an amicable separation seems best for both of them at this time," Kingsley says. Soon thereafter, Cruise apparently surprises Kidman by quickly filing

divorce papers. Then Kidman's own publicist confirms that she suffered a miscarriage earlier in the year.

In her court papers, Kidman says that she begged Cruise not to end their marriage and was shocked when he said "he no longer wanted to live with her and wanted a divorce." One point of potential legal contention is that Cruise claims the couple split on December 21, before their 10th anniversary. Under California law, he stands to pay less in settlement costs to her if the union lasted less than a decade. But Kidman's court papers insist that, "During the balance of December and thereafter the parties were intimate; in fact respondent (Kidman) became pregnant by petitioner (Cruise)."

Then in July, Cruise apparently surprises Kidman again when he spends a week's vacation in Fiji with actor Penelope Cruz. Shortly thereafter, the divorce is granted.

Former *Survivor* castaway **Stacey Stillman** sues CBS and the executive producer of the show, Mark Burnett, claiming he rigged the show so she'd get the boot before her time. Stillman, a San Francisco attorney, claims Burnett convinced two fellow contestants to vote her off to protect 72-year-old former Navy SEAL **Rudy Boesch**, who was among the four final contestants. Boesch was the only contestant over the age of 40, and Stillman argues that Burnett fixed the vote in order to appeal to an older demographic.

"We heard about Stacey Stillman's allegations several months ago," CBS says in a statement. "They had no merit then. They have no merit now that she has packaged them into a frivolous and groundless lawsuit." The network then countersues Stillman, seeking $5 million in damages for breach of contract and defamation, citing a confidentiality agreement signed by her. (In June a judge rules that Stillman cannot be sued for breach of contract, though he allows the defamation claim against her to go forward.)

Fellow castaway **Dirk Been** files a deposition in which he reportedly says that Burnett "suggested" that he kick Stacey Stillman off the show. Though conceding that he was not manipulated by Burnett, Been ultimately did join an alliance to give Stillman the boot and to keep contestant Rudy Boesch, he says. "Instead of doing what I thought was right," says Been's deposition, "I had voted (for) Rudy—or voted against Stacey directly because of the influence of Mark Burnett."

After months of revolving suitors, the *Live With Regis* cohost position is officially filled by *All My Children* actor **Kelly Ripa**, 30. Like Regis Philbin, who does double duty as host of ABC's primetime smash hit game

show, *Who Wants to Be a Millionaire*, Ripa keeps her job on the soap. "I think it's like an ABC policy—you must work two jobs," Ripa jokes. "Between the two of us," Philbin adds, "we've got 40 percent of the schedule covered. If we go down, ABC is over."

Former money manager to the stars **Dana Giacchetto**, 38, is sentenced to a 57-month prison term after pleading guilty to charges of looting celebs' accounts. Giacchetto, a onetime trusted financial advisor whose $100 million Cassandra Fund clients included Leonardo DiCaprio, Ben Affleck, Courteney Cox Arquette and Cameron Diaz, was tearful in court as testimony revealed that he used their money (over $9 million) to pay for his personal expenses and a beyond-his-means lifestyle. Subsequently, it was disclosed that he attempted to cover up his misdeeds by shifting money between accounts. Giacchetto's lawyers claimed that their client had been abusing prescription drugs and alcohol and asked that he be considered for a drug rehabilitation program to reduce his term by a year.

Napster is dealt a serious blow by a San Francisco federal appeals court, which rules that the company must stop allowing the millions of music fans who use its Internet-based service to share

copyrighted material. The decision comes more than four months after an October hearing on the landmark copyright infringement case in which recording industry giants (including BMG, Warner, Universal, EMI, and Sony) asked that the service be ordered to stop enabling users to swap songs for free. "This is a clear victory" says Hilary Rosen, president and CEO of the Recording Industry Association of America.

PASSAGES

Married
Singer James Taylor, 52, and his girlfriend of eight years, Caroline "Kim" Smedvig, 46, in a Boston church before about 50 friends and family members

Split
General Hospital star Kristina Malandro, 38, and former co-star Jack Wagner, 41, file for divorce

Former *Cosby Show* mom Phylicia Rashad, 52, files for divorce from her husband, sportscaster Ahmad Rashad, 51

Farewells
The Queen of the West and Roy Rogers' sidekick Dale Evans, 88

Famed writer (and wife of pioneering aviator Charles Lindbergh) Anne Morrow Lindbergh, 94

Noted sex researcher Dr. William Masters, 85

Shortly thereafter, Napster and its strategic partner, Bertelsmann, offer $1 billion to the major record groups and independents to settle the copyright infringement suit—an offer that is quickly turned down, as the music powers rush to form their own paid alliances. The company tries various maneuvers to delay full compliance with the court's ruling but the order stands and increasingly, the music stops, with the service shutting down completely by July.

Charlie's Angels star **Drew Barrymore** has an angel of her own—her adopted chow-yellow Lab mix Flossie, whose barking saves the lives of Barrymore, 26, and her boyfriend (and soon-to-be-husband), comic Tom Green, 29, when a fire rips into her $3 million Beverly Hills home at 3 A.M. About 70 fire-fighters come to the scene, though too late to save the rustic 3,500-sq.-ft. house.

Race car legend **Dale Earnhardt**, 49, dies instantly of head injuries after crashing on the last turn of the last lap in Florida's Daytona 500 and slamming into a concrete wall. The NASCAR world is shocked by the death of its leading light, known as The Intimidator. (Last year, a full 25 percent of NASCAR's $1.1 billion in merchandising sales was for Earnhardt-related items.) An autopsy leads to a conclusion that the racing legend might have survived the crash if only one of his lap belts had not broken. Approximately 2,500 invited guests crowd a NASCAR farewell tribute.

Rescue workers try to help Dale Earnhardt after his Daytona crash.

MARCH

THE THREAT TO KIDNAP RUSSELL CROWE
How and why the FBI moved in to protect the *Gladiator* star

Soon-to-be Oscar winner **Russell Crowe**, whose last role was that of a kidnap-hostage negotiator in *Proof of Life*, is apparently the target of a real-life abduction plot, the FBI announces. Crowe, 36, was first told of the plot by the FBI prior to the Golden Globe Awards in January, which he attended flanked by FBI agents outfitted in tuxedos.

Melanie Chisholm, 27, better known as Sporty Spice, announces that she will no longer be performing with the Spice Girls, at one time Britain's biggest pop phenomenon since the Beatles. Instead she will focus on a solo career (she released her own album in 2000). Chisholm says, "I've not been comfortable being in the Spice Girls for probably the last two years. It doesn't really feel that natural to me anymore . . . I've grown up, and I just feel that I want to do things my own way and not compromise." Spice

20

Girls spokesman Alan Edwards later insists that the group is not disbanding. "Everyone wants to say it's over, but it isn't," he says.

Dennis the Menace, cartoonist Hank Ketcham's perennially naughty youngster, turns 50. (Heck, that must make Mr. Wilson at least 100.) Dennis's adventures began in 1951, when the kid with the cowlick appeared in the back seat of a vintage car and taunted a policeman as his parents waited nervously for a traffic ticket. The caption read: "You didn't catch us! We ran outa gas!" Ketcham retired from drawing nearly a decade ago. (Today, others draw the strip, which still appears in 1,000 newspapers.) But he does produce a week's worth of classic panels for the occasion, to commemorate the boy's journey through American culture. In June, Ketcham, 81, succumbs to heart disease and cancer.

Best-selling author **J. K. Rowling**, whose Harry Potter empire just seems to grow magically, turns a month of writing time into a donation expected to fetch more than $36 million. Her U.S. and U.K. publishers release two short paperbacks—under the pseudonyms Kennilworthy Whisp and Newt Scamander—issued to raise money for the British charity Comic Relief (a children's organization unrelated to America's Comic Relief). The books,

Whisp's *Quidditch Through the Ages* and Scamander's *Fantastic Beasts & Where to Find Them*, purport to be tomes alluded to in her boy wizard novels. (The long-awaited first Harry Potter movie is scheduled to premiere in November.)

Jerry Seinfeld appears on *Late Show with David Letterman* to perform his new act, in his first appearance doing standup on TV since his 1998 HBO special. Seinfeld, 46, has made 41 prior guest appearances on the Letterman show.

What Dennis Miller is to ABC's *Monday Night Football*, **Jason Priestley**, 31, may become to the same network's seven Indy Racing League events. The former Brandon Walsh on *Beverly Hills, 90210* signs on to provide color for the sporting programs, beginning with the Pennzoil Copper World Indy 200 at the Phoenix International Raceway. The actor is no stranger to fast cars. In 1999, he crashed his Porsche in a drunken driving accident and was sentenced to serve five days in a work-release jail program. He is also an active professional race-car driver, having competed in dozens of events over the past few years.

But for the grace of an L.A. interior designer, claims a lawsuit, there would be no Jack character on *Will & Grace*. In a lawsuit filed in

Los Angeles Superior Court, **Jack Deamer** claims that

PASSAGES

Married
Actor Lauren Holly, 37, and Francis Greco, a Canadian-born investment banker, her third husband, in Toronto

Oscar winner Tommy Lee Jones, 54, and photographer Dawn Maria Laurel, 36, his third wife, in a private ceremony in the Texas enclave of Alamo Heights

Split
Rap superstar Eminem, 28, and Kim Mathers reach a divorce agreement that gives the couple joint legal and physical custody of 5-year-old daughter Hailie Jade

Farewells
Combative talk-show host Morton Downey Jr., 68

William Hanna, 90, the groundbreaking animator who made millions laugh over more than six decades with his and partner Joseph Barbera's cartoon creations

Glenn Hughes, 50, the biker character in disco-era group The Village People

Jazz trumpeter, composer, arranger, and educator Herbie Jones, 74, a collaborator of Duke Ellington and Billy Strayhorn's

Songwriter and founding member of the '60s superstar folk-pop group the Mamas and the Papas, John Phillips, 65

he initially agreed to remain silent about being portrayed on the hit NBC sitcom, in exchange for a promise from the show's creators, Max Mutchnick and David Kohan, to buy him a house and car. So far, Deamer claims, he has yet to receive either.

When Deamer viewed the pilot of the show in 1998, say his legal papers, he was "chagrined, embarrassed, and devastated as he realized that the 'Jack' character was a thinly veiled caricature of himself...but was portrayed as being flamboyantly gay, constantly over the top, promiscuous, and irresponsible."

Nutritionist Dr. Gavin Frost declares at a conference in Australia that **Teletubbies** are turning the world's children into tubs of lard by being poor—or, rather, "fat and jolly"—role models. A representative for Itsy Bitsy Entertainment, which produces Teletubbies, is quoted as responding, "If you're going to start picking on fat things, then what's going to happen to Humpty Dumpty and Santa Claus?"

The heirs of *Gone With the Wind* author **Margaret Mitchell** file suit in Federal District Court in Atlanta to halt publication of a new novel, *The Wind Done Gone* by **Alice Randall**, that retells parts of Mitchell's epic Civil War romance from a slave's perspective. While a judge initially grants a pre-liminary injunction, in May the 11th U.S. Circuit Court of Appeals strikes it down and allows publication to go forward (though the copyright infringement suit itself is still unresolved). The book hits the *New York Times* Bestseller List shortly after its release.

APRIL

Master magician **David Copperfield**, 44, collapses while practicing a 2,000-degree Tornado of Fire trick for a televised CBS special later in the month. His publicist notes that Copperfield hadn't slept for 48 hours, and he leaves the hospital three hours after being admitted. Earlier a crew member who worked on the illusion sued the magician and his companies for more than $15,000, claiming in her court papers that she was injured when she was thrown 10 feet in the air during a rehearsal. But when it's show time, Copperfield emerges safely from the 2,000-degree vortex of fire after 30 seconds as two stagehands spray fire extinguishers on his legs. "It was exhausting, and it was scary," Copperfield tells reporters afterwards. "I felt a burning sensation in my throat."

Rosie O'Donnell celebrates the launch of her eponymous magazine with 650 friends—including Oprah Winfrey, Mary Tyler Moore, and cover girl Fran Drescher, who tells of her battle to beat uterine cancer—at Manhattan's Chelsea Piers.

Mariah Carey, 31, and her music label of more than a decade, Columbia Records, issue a joint statement that confirms that the two parties have gone their separate ways. Shortly thereafter, Carey signs with Virgin Records in a deal estimated to bring her in the range of $23.5 million per album. Carey, whose Columbia albums and singles sold more than 140 million copies worldwide, was first brought to the label by Sony Music chairman Tommy Mottola, whom she married in 1993 and divorced in 1998. Last year, Carey voiced some complaints about the way Columbia was promoting her music—or not promoting it.

In July Carey checks herself into the hospital, where she receives both medical and psychiatric care, following a grueling two-week European promotional tour and on the heels of some erratic public behavior (including her doing an impromptu striptease on MTV during an interview with Carson Daly).

Jennifer Syme, 29, a record-industry worker who was the girlfriend of *The Matrix* star **Keanu Reeves** and the mother of the couple's stillborn baby girl last year, is killed in a car accident in Los Angeles. Syme was a former assistant to filmmaker David Lynch and to controversial rocker Marilyn Manson.

Tiger Woods, 25, wins the Masters, walking away from the 18th green with tears in his eyes and heading toward his parents' open arms. Woods becomes the first player to sweep modern golf's four major championships in a row: the Masters, the U.S. Open, the British Open, and the PGA. "It will probably go down as one of the top moments in our sport," Woods says shortly after donning the green jacket, size 44 long, given to the Masters champ each year.

Kevin Olmstead, 42, a Michigan engineer and a part-time creator of academic quizzes, wins $2.18 million on an episode of ABC's *Who Wants to Be a Millionaire*, making him the biggest winner in the history of American TV. The show's usual $1 million giveaway expanded because the network had padded the kitty by

Tiger Woods celebrates his record-breaking Masters victory.

$10,000 for each show in which the grand prize was not claimed. Olmstead, a previous winner on *Jeopardy*, says the two final questions, one on the earth's circumference at the equator (24,900 miles) and another on the inventor of the first mass-produced helicopter (Igor Sikorsky), were easy. "If they had asked me who plays what on *Dawson's Creek*, I'd have been toast," Olmstead says later.

Gospel-rock vocalist **Carol Dennis**, a former backup singer for **Bob Dylan**, 60, confirms that she was secretly married to the rock icon, from 1986 to 1992 and had a daughter with him, **Desiree Gabrielle Dennis-Dylan**, now 15. The admission comes in the wake of the recent publication of British author Howard Sounes's *Down the Highway:*

The Life of Bob Dylan. The unauthorized bio contains the news of the relationship between Dennis and Dylan, though Dennis says that the book distorts the nature of their divorce and his relationship with his daughter. The decision to keep private their marriage and their daughter was a mutual one and made for the benefit of the child.

Buffy the Vampire Slayer, arguably the WB Network's biggest success ever, will leave that network starting this fall for rival UPN. The network will pay a license fee of $2.3 million per episode for the first season and $2.35 million per for the second. WB had been paying a $1.1 million license fee, say reports.

Mel Brooks's new Broadway musical ***The Producers***,

Mel Brooks celebrates a Tony record with a jubilant cast.

based on his outrageous 1968 movie comedy, opens to raves and records alike. It sparks a scramble for seats the likes of which has not been seen since 1998's ticket-buying frenzy for *The Lion King* and, generations ago, for *My Fair Lady* and *Hello, Dolly!* After receiving a record 15 Tony nominations, the show claims a record 12 trophies (beating *Dolly's!* previous mark of 10 awards).

Robert Downey Jr., 36, is arrested in suburban Los Angeles on charges of being under the influence of a controlled substance and shows traces of cocaine in his system. Shortly thereafter Downey is fired from TV's *Ally McBeal*. Downey checks himself into a detox center and prosecutors later decide to handle the infraction as a parole violation.

Downey's in court again on drug charges from last November, reduced to one misdemeanor count of drug possession and one felony count of possessing cocaine. In a plea bargain, he pleads no contest and is allowed to continue live-in drug treatment instead of jail time. Downey faces a series of fines and a court-ordered set of regulations, including random drug testing, and can go to prison for up to four years if he violates the terms of the deal. Earlier in the year, Downey's estranged wife model-actress **Deborah Falconer**, 35, filed for divorce (after six years of separation), and sought custody of their seven-year-old son, Indio.

Dennis Tito, 60, a former NASA engineer who is now a Los Angeles-based CEO of a financial consulting firm becomes the first tourist in space. Tito pays the financially strapped Russian Aviation and Space Agency $20 million to fulfill his lifelong dream of space travel. He joins two Russian astronauts for a 10-day flight, which includes a visit to the international space station.

Jenna Bush, 19, daughter of President and Laura Bush, receives a ticket for underage drinking from Austin, Texas police after officers check for minors drinking in the city's popular nightspots. (Jenna is a freshman at the University of Texas in Austin. Her twin sister, Barbara, attends Yale in Connecticut.) The first daughter was drinking beer and did not appear intoxicated, said police. She is ordered to perform community service and take a six-hour alcohol awareness course after she pleads no contest. Bush's charge is later dismissed after she meets all of the requirements of the sentencing, and the case can be expunged from her record if she is not arrested again before she turns 21.

Former *NYPD Blue* star **Andrea Thompson**, 41, who left the top-rated ABC show to become a cub reporter at an Albuquerque, N.M. television station, is tapped as the newest *CNN Headline News* anchor. Shortly thereafter, amid protests from other journalists about the appointment, nude photographs of Thompson surface on the Internet from an obscure 1986 Italian movie in which she starred called *Manhattan Gigolo* as well as from a steamy scene from the HBO comedy series *Arliss*. But Thompson makes "no apologies for the creative decisions I've made as an artist in my 20-year career."

PASSAGES

Married
Former *Suddenly Susan* star Brooke Shields, 35, and TV writer-producer Chris Henchy, 38, surprising a small group of friends and family on California's Catalina Island

Singer Tony Braxton, 34, and musician Keri Lewis, 30, in Atlanta at a ceremony officiated by former U.N. ambassador Andrew Young

Split
Director Peter Bogdanovich, 61, and Louise Hoogstraten, 32 (half-sister of his prior wife, Dorothy Stratten)

Donya Fiorentino, wife of actor Gary Oldman, files court papers seeking an end to their four-year marriage

Farewells
Pianist John Lewis, 80, who masterminded the Modern Jazz Quartet

Revolutionary punk rocker Joey Ramone, 49, of the legendary band the Ramones

Baseball Hall of Famer Willie Stargell, 61

Dutch-born guitarist **Eddie Van Halen**, 44, co-founder of the rock band that bears his name, confirms his battle with cancer. Although Van Halen does not publicly disclose where his cancer is located, his actress wife, Valerie Bertinelli, says that a lesion was removed from her husband's tongue. "I don't know why people want to know what only my wife and son and maybe my best friends have a right to know," Van Halen says. "I say to everyone else, 'Look, all I have to say is that I'm doing great.' But I'm not about to go into the details until the cancer is completely gone."

The West Wing creator **Aaron Sorkin**, 39, is arrested at the Burbank Airport and charged with two felony counts of possessing hallucinogenic mushrooms and cocaine, and a misdemeanor count of marijuana possession. After initially pleading not guilty, Sorkin changes to a guilty plea to gain admission to the "Deferred Entry of Judgement" program (and skirt nearly four years behind bars).

Cover Girl makeup model **Niki Taylor**, 26, suffers severe liver and abdominal injuries as a result of an automobile accident. Taylor's friend, James Renegar, 27, was driving, and when he looked down at his ringing cell phone he lost control of his 1993 Nissan Maxima and hit a utility pole, police said. At first in critical condition

and on a respirator for weeks, Taylor has surgery at least four times and is finally discharged from the hospital for a private rehabilitation center in June, eight weeks after the crash. The next month Taylor finally goes home to begin physical therapy.

MAY

Tina Wesson, 40, a mother and minimum-wage private nurse from Knoxville, Tenn., wins TV's favorite guessing game as the second winner on *Survivor*. Along with 36 million other viewers, Wesson learns live that she beat the heavily favored Colby Donaldson, 27, from Texas, a custom-car designer. He made the colossal mistake of selecting Wesson instead of the widely disliked Keith Famie to join him before a jury of seven previously ousted contestants who would decide the final winner. While handily beating its competition, the show attracts far fewer people than the original *Survivor* finale, which drew 51 million viewers.

Robert Blake at his wife's funeral.

Former Beatle **George Harrison**, 58, undergoes surgery to have a cancer-like sore removed from his lung at the Mayo Clinic in Minnesota. In 1998, Harrison overcame throat cancer, which he blamed on smoking. And in 1999, Harrison suffered a punctured lung when an intruder stabbed him inside his home west of London. Harrison's outlook darkens later in the year when it's revealed that he has been treated for a brain tumor with cobalt radiation therapy at a hospital in Switzerland.

Bonny Lee Bakley, 45, the wife of ex-*Baretta* star **Robert Blake**, 67, is killed by a gunshot to the head as she sits in the couple's car near a Hollywood restaurant where they had dined. A witness on the scene shortly after the murder describes for PEOPLE a near hysterical Blake pacing up and down the street, occasionally vomiting, then slumping to the ground. Blake tells police that he had left his wife alone so he could retrieve a gun he had left inside the eatery, which his attorney says the actor carried because his wife feared for her life.

Blake is under a cloud of suspicion and his house is searched by police, who seize boxes full of newspaper clippings, letters, pictures and personal effects. The case remains unsolved, and details of Bakley's con-artist past come to light.

And in the latest twist in this bizarre case, prominent L.A. attorney Barry Levin, 54, who helped defend Erik Menendez in his murder case and served as a member of Blake's legal team, takes his own life in July. He was reportedly upset over a debilitating illness, Gaucher's disease, a genetic enzyme-deficiency disorder that causes victims to bleed and bruise easily.

The original 120-foot-long, single-spaced typed scroll on which the late beat author Jack Kerouac composed *On the Road* 50 years ago is auctioned at Christie's in Manhattan for $2.4 million. The price marks a world record for a literary manuscript. The winning bidder, Jim Irsay, 41, owner of the Indianapolis Colts professional football team, says that he considers his purchase "a stewardship" of the historic work. "I wanted to make sure we kept it in the country, in America, and we give people an opportunity to enjoy it," he says.

Jeopardy host **Alex Trebek**, 59, makes headlines for shaving off his well-known mustache. But the newly-exposed gap doesn't make its TV debut until late September, when the shows being taped hit the air.

The renegade **XFL**'s co-owners, World Wrestling Federation Entertainment and NBC (which had each anted up $50 million to launch the franchise), pull the plug on the league, citing the XFL's mounting operating costs and hopeless ratings as the main reasons for dissolving the partnership. NBC Sports chairman Dick Ebersol says, "The bottom line is that we didn't deliver what they wanted to see. They came, but they just didn't come back."

Filmmaker **Woody Allen**, 65, sues his longtime producer and friend of 40 years, **Jean Doumanian**, 64, in New York State Supreme Court, charging that she cheated him out of profits from the last eight movies they made together. (Last year

they dissolved their partnership and he set up shop at DreamWorks. Both parties described the split as amicable at the time.) Allen's court papers say that because Doumanian has given him and his company no financial information, he is uncertain how much she owes him. Also named in the suit is Doumanian's financial backer and boyfriend, Jaqui Safra.

JUNE

Flamboyant pop star **Elton John**, 54, nets $2.75 million from an auction of 20 luxury classic cars from his extensive collection at Christie's. "There's obviously a lot of money to be made from second-hand cars," a delighted John exclaims. A 1993 Jaguar XJ220 fetched the most cash, nearly $331,350.

After **Cher**, 55, and a small plastic likeness of the star made a cameo appearance on *Will and Grace* last fall, doll stores and Mattel's Web sites were bombarded with

inquiries about how to buy the doll. So Mattel announces they will soon offer a Cher doll, in a lavender halter dress ensemble designed by Bob Mackie. The last time Cher was available in doll form was in 1976, when Mego offered two versions— one dressed in a pink halter dress and the other in a white halter pantsuit.

Sharon Stone, 43, sues the producers of the now defunct *Basic Instinct 2* for $14 million, after MGM film studio decided to can the much-anticipated sequel. The lawsuit alleges that *Basic Instinct 2* producers Andy Vajna and Mario Kassar had a verbal agreement with Stone guaranteeing her at least $14 million for her commitment to the sequel, even if the movie never got made. The suit alleges that Stone rejected other offers on the basis of the producers' commitments, but that they denied in December having a contract of any kind with the actor.

Later in the month, Stone's husband, *San Francisco Chronicle* Executive Editor **Phil Bronstein**, 48, is attacked by a rare 10-foot Indonesian Komodo dragon while touring the Los Angeles Zoo. The giant lizard crushes Bronstein's big toe, forcing doctors to reattach severed tendons and rebuild the casing of the toe. Afterwards Bronstein and zoo officials offer distinctly different accounts of how Bron-

---

PASSAGES

Split
An Atlanta judge quietly grants actress Jane Fonda, 63, a divorce from her husband of 10 years, CNN founder Ted Turner, 62

Farewells
British humor writer Douglas Adams, 49, author of the cult classic *The Hitch Hiker's Guide to the Galaxy*

Radio, TV and jukebox legend Perry Como, 88

Camelot court photographer Jacques Lowe, 71

Premier jazz and cabaret singer Susannah McCorkle, 55

---

stein ended up in the animal's cage without shoes on.

A kilted **Madonna** (one of six outfits she sports by French designer Jean-Paul Gaultier) kicks off her Drowned World tour in Barcelona, Spain, before 18,000 fans in a filled-to-capacity basketball stadium. The Material Mom, 42, is joined on stage by 10 dancers and two backup singers for a two-hour show. In one routine, she flies above the stage suspended by trapeze wires; in another she appears garbed as a geisha, wearing a kimono with a 52-foot train, and yet another vignette features her riding a mechanical bull. Her first concert tour in

eight years draws mostly from her two most recent albums, and is a hot ticket everywhere she visits.

Kelsey Grammer, 46, who plays sherry-swilling Seattle shrink Frasier Crane on NBC's 8-year-old sitcom *Frasier*, signs a contract extension making him the highest-salaried actor in TV history. In exchange for remaining on the show for the 2002 and 2003 seasons, he'll take home a record $1.6 million per episode. (Altogether, his two-year deal is said to be worth about $75 million.) Jerry Seinfeld, Tim Allen and *Mad About You* stars Paul Reiser and Helen Hunt all made more than $1 million in their final seasons on the air.

Madonna on her Drowned World tour.

PASSAGES

Married
Law & Order alum Angie Harmon, 28, and New York Giant Jason Sehorn, at a Texas-size bash for 400

Tom Petty, 51, and his long-time girlfriend, Dana York, in a quiet Las Vegas ceremony

Split
Former *Taxi* and *Evening Shade* star Marilu Henner, 49, and her husband of more than a decade, director Robert Lieberman, both file divorce petitions

After nearly four years together, Julia Roberts, 33, and Benjamin Bratt, 37, break up

Farewells
The musician they called the Country Gentleman, Chet Atkins, 77

Live TV comedy pioneer Imogene Coca, 92

All in the Family star Carroll O'Connor, 76

Guitar legend and one of the last remaining links to early rock and roll, John Lee Hooker, 83

Divine in comedies and searing in dramas, actor Jack Lemmon, 76

Macho two-time Oscar winner Anthony Quinn, 86

Though not in Grammer's stratosphere, **Drew Carey**, 43, negotiates a new contract for his ABC sitcom. He'll now be up to between $600,000 and $750,000 per episode. With profits from syndication thrown into the pot, Carey's deal could ultimately be worth as much as $60 million. **Ray Romano**, 43, signs for two more years of *Everybody Loves Raymond* in a reported $40 million-plus contract that will ultimately pay him roughly $800,000 per episode, with various sweeteners that could ultimately raise his fee another $100,000 per episode.

Standup comedian **Paula Poundstone**, 41, is arrested and charged with three counts of committing a lewd act on a girl under the age of 14 and one count of endangering two other girls and two boys. Poundstone's five children—three adopted ones and two more in her foster care—are placed in protective custody. (The director of Los Angeles County's Department of Children and Family Services tells the *L.A. Times* that Poundstone's charges involve the children living with her.) Poundstone was in a live-in alcohol rehabilitation program at the time she was taken into custody.
In September, she pleads no contest to felony child-endangerment and misdemeanor child-injury charges, and prosecutors drop the

three charges of lewd conduct. Prosecutors recommend that Poundstone be sentenced to five years' probation and 180 days in the rehab facility she entered in June. She says in a statement the charges were dropped "because they weren't true," but admits, "my drinking helped to create a dangerous situation."

JULY

The Liverpool Airport is renamed the Liverpool **John Lennon** Airport, with Yoko Ono, 58, watching on. This is the first time an airport in England has been named for an individual. The airport also gets a slogan: "Above us only sky," a phrase from Lennon's thematic song "Imagine."

Robert Iler, 16, who plays Tony Soprano Jr. on the HBO mob hit *The Sopranos*, is arrested near his New York apartment on robbery and drug possession charges. He was among four teens picked up by police for allegedly strong-arming two 16-year-

olds out of about $40, say authorities, who also allege that Iler had a small bag of marijuana and a water pipe in his pocket. He pleads not guilty to second-degree robbery and is released after posting $2,500 bail. Claiming innocence, Iler says: "I feel terribly embarrassed. I never ever would or did rob anyone in my life. I know that the events of the past two days have been extremely difficult for my family and friends and for that I am sorry."

Claiming he "has been frozen out of the Beach Boys," original band member **Al Jardine**, 58, files suit against former band mates **Mike Love** and **Brian Wilson** for about $4 million in L.A. Superior Court, claiming they excluded Jardine from recent concerts. Other defendants include the Carl Wilson Trust and Brother Records Inc., the corporate entity of the Beach Boys. (Carl Wilson, 51, died of lung cancer in 1998.)

Backstreet Boy heartthrob **A. J. McLean**, 23, checks himself into rehab for depression, anxiety, and alcohol abuse, as his bandmates announce on MTV's *Total Request Live* that the group is suspending its Black & Blue world tour for a month. "We didn't want to lie about it and push it under the rug and say that he was sick or broke his leg or something," Backstreeter **Kevin Richardson** says.

Robert Iler leaves the courthouse with his mother.

"It wouldn't be honest to our fans." (Band member **Nick Carter** broke his hand two days before the announcement, so he gets time to heal as well.)

A Manhattan judge paves the way for the parents of **John F. Kennedy Jr.'s** wife and sister-in-law to settle their wrongful death claim against his estate as a result of their fatal July 16, 1999, plane crash. Ann Freeman, 61, mother of Carolyn Bessette Kennedy, 33, and Lauren Bessette, 34, notified the court that she and her ex-husband, William Bessette, 63, had decided to accept a settlement offer from the Kennedy estate. The Bessette sisters and Kennedy, 38, died when a plane Kennedy was piloting crashed off Martha's Vineyard. Surrogate Renee Roth signs a decree lifting a legal bar that had blocked Freeman from settling the case because she was the administrator of her daughters' estates. JFK Jr.'s estate has been estimated to be $50 million.

Newlyweds **Brad Pitt**, 37, and **Jennifer Aniston**, 32, file a $50 million lawsuit against Italian jewelry designer Silvia Damiani and Damiani International, claiming that an agreement never to replicate their wedding rings has been breached. In their legal papers, the couple claim that the jeweler not only reproduced the rings (comprised of two concentric bands in the buyer's choice of 18 karat white or yellow gold connected by either 12 or 13 diamonds) but put them on the market via the Internet and at retail stores in Palm Desert, Calif., and Las Vegas, Nev., for $1,000 apiece.

In a statement, Damiani Group CEO Guido Damiani asserts the rings are originals owned by the company. He says, "There has never been any type of agreement or contract between Damiani and Brad Pitt and Jennifer Aniston prohibiting or limiting the marketing of the jewelry in question."

AUGUST

Ben Affleck, about to turn 29, checks himself into the popular $33,850-a-month Malibu alcohol rehabilitation center, called Promises. "Ben is a self-aware and smart man who had decided that a fuller life awaits him without alcohol," spokesman David Pollick says in a statement. Promises is where Paula Poundstone and Robert Downey Jr. reportedly have been treated.

Bill Clinton, 54, will not have to worry about his retirement. He signs a deal to write his memoirs for publisher Alfred A. Knopf, which is to be released in 2003. Newspaper accounts estimate the advance as more than $10 million, which would make it the largest ever for a non-fiction book. Asked whether or not the book will detail the Monica Lewinsky affair and the Whitewater controversy, Clinton's attorney, Robert Barnett, says that the book will be "comprehensive and candid."

The godfather of the *Star Wars* franchise, George Lucas, 57, announces the title of the fifth installment in the intergalactic fantasy series, to be released next summer: *Star Wars: Episode II—Attack of the Clones.*

New York-born, Detroit-raised R&B singer/actress **Aaliyah,** 22, dies along with eight others when a small, twin-engine Cessna bound for Miami crashes into a swamp shortly after takeoff in the Bahamas. Investigators conclude that the plane was significantly overloaded and out of balance in a preliminary report. The star had gone to the destination to shoot a music video. Born Aaliyah Haughton (her first name means "highest, most exalted one" in Arabic), the singer—who often covered her right eye with her hair—started performing professionally at age 11 as part of the Las Vegas act of her aunt, Gladys Knight. Aaliyah's single "Try Again" received a Grammy nomination for best female R&B vocalist earlier in the year, and she was due to appear in the two sequels to *The Matrix,* scheduled for release in 2003.

Fred Rogers greets youngsters for the last time on his PBS TV show, *Mister Rogers's Neighborhood,* after a run of 34 years. The episode was actually taped last December, and the show's producers hope to segue into reruns with little or no disruption for the 3- to 6-year-olds who consider the cardigan-wearing Rogers as family. Rogers, 73, says, "The general message of the neighborhood is that the truth is best. If we can share ourselves with our kids in ways that aren't frightening to them, that's the greatest gift we can give anyone—the gift of an honest self."

PASSAGES

Married
Mette-Marit Tjessem Hoiby, 28, and Norway's Crown Prince Haakon, also 28, in the Oslo Cathedral before 800 guests

Martie Seidel, 31, fiddler for the Dixie Chicks, and Gareth Maguire, 32, in a small ceremony in Kailua, Hawaii

Keely Shaye Smith, 37, and her partner of seven years and mother of their two sons, Pierce Brosnan, 49, in Ireland

Split
Screenwriter Melissa Mathison, 51, files for legal separation from Harrison Ford, 51, after 18 years of marriage

Joely Richardson, 36, daughter of Vanessa Redgrave and late director Tony Richardson, and TV producer Jamie Theakston, 30, separated, according to a spokesperson

Farewell
Christopher Hewett, 79, TV butler Mr. Belvedere

SEPTEMBER

People weekly

SEPT. 11, 2001
THE DAY THAT SHOOK AMERICA

Eclectic is the word to describe **Michael Jackson's** highly anticipated and ultimately uneven, four-hour plus concert at New York's Madison Square Garden (concertgoers paid up to $2,500 per ticket). The star roster includes **Britney Spears, Destiny's Child, Ray Charles, Liza Minnelli,** and a startlingly thin **Whitney Houston,** though it's Jackson, 43, who creates the loudest buzz, even before uttering a single note, as he makes his way to his seat, with **Elizabeth Taylor,** 69, on his arm.

The nation is stunned by **terrorist attacks on New York and Washington, D.C.** as hijacked commercial jets strike both towers at the World Trade Center in downtown Manhattan and a section of the Pentagon in the nation's capital, while a fourth hijacked jet bound for another Washington target is brought down in rural Pennsylvania. The famed twin towers both collapse, as do a number of surrounding buildings, and well over 5,000 lives are lost.

The entertainment world is temporarily silenced, as is a shocked and mournful nation. The second annual Latin Grammy awards are cancelled (the winners are not even named subsequently). The beginning of the fall television season is postponed; Broadway goes dark for two nights and even when it reopens numerous shows are imperiled by drastically reduced ticket sales. Both Major League Baseball and the National Football League suspend games, upcoming films starring Tim Allen (*Big Trouble*) and Arnold Schwarzenegger (*Collateral Damage*) are indefinitely postponed, and numerous musicians' and authors' tours are called off.

When David Letterman returns to the air almost a week later it is with deep emotion rather than laughter, and guest Dan Rather breaks into tears three times. *Politically Incorrect* leaves on open guest chair in tribute to commentator Barbara Olson, who died on one of the hijacked planes, en route to Los Angeles to appear on the show. Many stars donate personal funds and proceeds from concerts to relief efforts and to help the victims' families.

PASSAGES

Married
Geena Davis, 45, to surgeon Dr. Reza Jarrahy, 30, her fourth husband

Actor and television host David Hartman, 66, and Mary Clark Putman, 60, a homemaker

Anne Heche, 32, and cameraman Coleman "Coley" Laffoon, 27

Jennifer Lopez, 32, and choreographer Cris Judd, 32

Split
Kate Winslet, 25, and assistant movie director Jim Threapleton, 27, after less than three years of marriage and less than a year after the birth of their daughter, Mia

Farewell
South African surgeon Dr. Christiaan N. Bernard, 78, who performed the first human heart transplant in 1967

Longtime *Tonight* show producer, Fred De Cordova, 90

Teen heartthrob of the '60s, Troy Donahue, 65

Pauline Kael, 82, the feared and revered movie critic for the *New Yorker* magazine

Renowned violinist Isaac Stern, 81

SCREEN

PICKS & PANS 2001

Kids turned spies, apes and dinosaurs ruled, Dr. Dolittle and the Mummy returned, and an animated green giant tweaked fairy tales and Hollywood alike. Here's the year in film as seen by PEOPLE critic Leah Rozen and, where noted, senior writer Tom Gliatto [TG]. Asterisks mark their favorites.

ABOUT ADAM
Stuart Townsend, Kate Hudson, Frances O'Connor, Charlotte Bradley
Adam (Townsend), a businessman and conniving charmer in contemporary go-go Dublin, romances each of the three adult Owen sisters in this clumsy sex comedy. Adam may have an easy time reeling in the Owen women, but his appeal will elude viewers. (R)

*A.I.
Haley Joel Osment, Jude Law
In this futuristic *Pinocchio*, a woman and her husband adopt a boy robot that will be able to feel love for his parents. After nearly causing a drowning, his mother abandons him in a forest. Convinced that somehow he can become "real" and merit true love, he begins a journey through a series of surreal, violent adventures. Spielberg casts a mesmerizing spell with his most deeply felt movie. (PG-13) [TG]

ALONG CAME A SPIDER
Morgan Freeman, Monica Potter, Michael Wincott, Penelope Ann Miller
The daughter of a senator has been kidnapped (Miller). The perpetrator (Wincott), a publicity-seeking psycho who has spent years furtively planning his crime, deposits one of the girl's shoes in the mailbox of Alex Cross (Freeman), a top detective on the D.C. police force. The problem with *Spider* is that it's heavy on plot (yet riddled with plot holes) and light on character development. (R)

*AMERICA'S SWEETHEARTS
Julia Roberts, John Cusack, Catherine Zeta-Jones, Billy Crystal
Roberts is Kiki Harrison, the much put-upon sister of spoiled movie diva Gwen Harrison (Zeta-Jones). The task of keeping the peace between Gwen and her estranged husband, once known as America's Sweethearts, falls to Kiki and Lee Phillips (Crystal), a veteran studio publicist. *Sweethearts* is a welcome rarity, a true ensemble piece in which everyone gets a chance to shine. (PG-13)

AMERICAN OUTLAWS
Colin Farrell, Scott Caan, Ali Larter
This lamebrain western about 19th-century outlaw Jesse James (Farrell) paints him as one of the nicest guys ever to point a gun at a bank teller. James avoids pulling the trigger whenever possible, gives much of his loot to the poor, loves his ma and the feisty girl next door (Larter) and counsels young-uns against drinking too much. Farrell is still a star waiting to happen, but he can't save this one. (PG-13)

AMERICAN PIE 2
Jason Biggs, Alyson Hannigan, Seann William Scott, Chris Klein, Eugene Levy
This sequel does its daring best (or worst, take your pick) to surpass the gross-out gags of the hugely successful 1999 original. Episodic to a fault, *AP2* lurches from one mishap to another, making fools of its characters and us for watching. (R)

AMORES PERROS
Gael Garcia Bernal, Emilio Echevarria
This Mexican movie starts off with a literal bang. A Mexico City car crash slams together, then, over the next 2½ hours, disentangles three stories in which dogs are key players. As far as moviemaking goes, *Amores Perros* (loose translation: Love's a bitch) is a dazzler, fluid and sharp. At heart, though, it's softly sentimental. (R) [TG]

ANGEL EYES
Jennifer Lopez, Jim Caviezel
Jennifer Lopez and costar Caviezel are the main reasons to see *Angel Eyes*, a dopey romantic thriller that starts off promising more than it eventually delivers. Lopez plays Sharon Pogue, a cop who is saved by mystery man Catch. Soon the two have fallen in love, but both have a big secret they must share before *Eyes* is finished. Neither secret is much of a surprise. (R)

THE ANNIVERSARY PARTY
Jennifer Jason Leigh, Alan Cumming, Gwyneth Paltrow, Kevin Kline
To celebrate their anniversary, a novelist and his movie-actress wife (Cumming and Leigh) throw a bash, which turns into a bumpy night for them and their equally glamorous guests. Cowritten and codirected by Cumming and Leigh, it's the kind of project that can be self-indulgent, but here it is fairly absorbing and often funny. (R)

ANTITRUST
Ryan Phillippe, Tim Robbins, Rachael Leigh Cook, Claire Forlani
High tech doesn't equal high tension in this tedious thriller. A hotshot young programmer (Phillippe) is recruited to work at N.U.R.V., a software behemoth, where he quickly discovers that creating killer apps isn't the only lethal order of business. (PG-13)

*APOCALYPSE NOW REDUX
Martin Sheen, Marlon Brando, Robert Duvall, Frederic Forrest, Albert Hall
Coppola's brilliantly re-edited version of *Apocalypse Now* adds 49 minutes of unused footage, a monologue by Brando's crazed Colonel Kurtz, a sexual rendezvous between Playboy bunnies and G.I.s, and an extraordinary sequence in which Captain Willard (Sheen) and his men come upon a ghostly plantation still occupied by French owners. (R)

ATLANTIS: THE LOST EMPIRE
Animated, with voices by Michael J. Fox, James Garner
Hero Milo Thatch (Fox) joins forces with a ragtag group of explorers and heads deep beneath the Atlantic Ocean in search of the fabled lost continent. With all the battles and touchy-feely babble, character development and plausible plot sink without a trace. (PG)

BABY BOY
Tyrese Gibson, Ving Rhames
An unemployed father of two, Jody still lives with his mother in crime-plagued L.A. and his girlfriend is pregnant—again. There's not much new dramatically, but the cast has a strong pulse. (R)

BEAUTIFUL CREATURES
Rachel Weisz, Susan Lynch
In this black comedy, our heroines end up black-and-blue but a darn sight healthier than the low-life beaus they either beat up or do away with. Amusing for a while, it then becomes overkill, literally. (R)

BLOW
Johnny Depp, Penélope Cruz, Ray Liotta, Rachel Griffiths, Jordi Molla
This true story about the rise and fall of George Jung, a leading cocaine dealer in the 1970s, is a rush at first, but once the high wears off, it's a downer. Director Ted Demme set out to make an ambitious, cautionary epic about the intersection between the drug trade and the American Dream, but Jung proves neither complex nor charismatic enough to warrant such treatment. (R)

THE BODY
Antonio Banderas, Olivia Williams, Derek Jacobi
An unholy mess. An archeologist uncovers what could be the remains of Jesus Christ in a tomb in present-day Jerusalem. A military intelligence officer-turned-priest tries to put the kibosh on any speculation and soon the Israeli military and Palestinian terrorists are snooping around as well. The dialogue is clunky, the plotting contrived, and the acting ranges from sullenly wooden to feyly eccentric. (PG-13)

*BRIDGET JONES'S DIARY
Renee Zellweger, Colin Firth, Hugh Grant, Gemma Jones, Jim Broadbent
A hoot from start to finish. A faithful adaptation of British author Helen Fielding's highly amusing novel in diary form about a 32-year-old self-described "Singleton" who struggles to lose 20 lbs., attempts to cut back on her copious drinking and smoking and wavers between two potential suitors. Zellweger more than holds her own with her leading men, both of whom glow. (R)

THE BROTHERS
Morris Chestnut, Bill Bellamy, D.L. Hughley, Shemar Moore
The men in this likable but predictable comedy are four successful, soon-to-be-30 African-American buddies in Los Angeles, all of whom have impressive jobs (doctor, lawyer and businessman). When a dedicated bachelor announces his engagement, it throws his three pals into tizzies of romantic self-examination. *Brothers* serves as a comical mea culpa from the other side. (R)

BUBBLE BOY
Jake Gyllenhaal, Marley Shelton, Swoosie Kurtz
This misbegotten comedy is a road movie about the adventures of teenage Jimmy (Gyllenhaal), who lives in a plastic bubble because he has a deficient immune system, as he bounces across the country from California to Niagara Falls to stop the wedding of his true love (Shelton) to a boorish cad. (PG-13)

CAPTAIN CORELLI'S MANDOLIN
Nicolas Cage, Penélope Cruz, Christian Bale, John Hurt, Irene Pappas
Corelli (Cage) is an Italian army officer who arrives on the scenic Greek island of Cephallonia in 1941 as part of an Italian-German occupying force. The good captain's lust for life eventually wins over Pelagia (Cruz), the comely daughter of the island's leading doctor (Hurt). Cage and Cruz have zilch chemistry in this sappy romance. (R)

CATS & DOGS
Jeff Goldblum, Elizabeth Perkins
This convivial (if overly busy) family film contends that: 1) animals can talk and 2) there is a war going on between cats and dogs. The movie is heavy on litter box humor, and the chase and battle scenes eventually become repetitive. (PG)

THE CAVEMAN'S VALENTINE
Samuel L. Jackson, Colm Feore, Ann Magnuson, Aunjanue Ellis, Tamara Tunie

A paranoid schizophrenic who dwells in a cave in a park discovers a man's corpse frozen in a tree. The police rule the death an accident but he suspects murder and turns detective. This above-average thriller is ultimately squandered by standard-whodunit plot mechanics. The real attraction here is the full-throttle performance by Jackson. (R)

CHOCOLAT
Johnny Depp, Juliette Binoche, Lena Olin

This whimsical romantic fable tells the story of an unwed mother (Binoche) who shows up in a French village and opens a gourmet chocolate shop. Soon, half the folks in town are benefiting from the magically aphrodisiac and rejuvenating qualities of her wares while others are denouncing her. Like the rich treat it is named after, *Chocolat* is overly sweet and without nutritional value. (PG-13)

THE CLAIM
Peter Mullan, Wes Bentley

It's 1867 and the aftereffects of the Gold Rush of '49 are still being played out in the frontier mining town of Kingdom Come. An ailing, once-beautiful mother tells her daughter to call on the town's leading citizen (Mullan), a wealthy businessman, who owes both women a debt which will have devastating consequences for all of *The Claim's* major characters. *Claim* is too diffuse in both plotting and characterization to work successfully as a movie. It is, however, beautifully shot, and Mullan is moving. (R)

THE CLOSET
Daniel Auteuil, Gerard Depardieu

Auteuil is about to be eased out of his job because he is bland

and colorless. To save his career, he doctors a photo of two patrons of a gay club by pasting his own head on the photo, and sends it anonymously to the company. Overnight, he's exotic. This little farce would be completely disposable if it weren't for Depardieu. (R) [TG]

COMPANY MAN
Douglas McGrath, Sigourney Weaver

It is *Company Man's* misfortune to demonstrate that a comedy can be smart without ever actually being funny. Again and again in this slight movie about the misadventures of a bumbling CIA agent (McGrath) in Cuba during the Communist revolution, one nods in recognition at a joke but remains unmoved. (PG-13)

CRAZY/BEAUTIFUL
Kirsten Dunst, Jay Hernandez

Crazy/Beautiful seems filmed from a set of instructions ("How to Make a Boy-Meets-Girl Picture"). All it would take to breathe life into this would be a little chemistry between Dunst and Hernandez. (PG-13)

CROCODILE DUNDEE IN LOS ANGELES
Paul Hogan, Linda Kozlowski

Blunder from Down Under. In his third crack at playing reptile hunter Mick "Crocodile" Dundee, Hogan revisits the outdoorsman-in-the-city formula, relocating from the bush to L.A. with his reporter girlfriend and their 9-year-old son. This corny comedy takes as a given that everything its leathery leading man does is both charming and amusing. It ain't necessarily so. (PG)

THE CURSE OF THE JADE SCORPION
Woody Allen, Helen Hunt, Charlize Theron, Dan Aykroyd

The disheartening deceleration of Woody Allen's career continues with his latest offering, a thin caper comedy about two spatting coworkers who fall for each other while under hypnosis. *The Curse*

of the Jade Scorpion is pleasant enough and its jokes less forced than those in the writer-director-star's last film, *Small Time Crooks*, but Allen is working out of the middle drawer here. (PG-13)

*THE DEEP END
Tilda Swinton, Goran Visnjic

After her teenage son's male lover turns up dead near the family's house, a mother (Swinton) barely pauses before dumping the body in nearby Lake Tahoe. When the corpse is found, she does whatever it takes—including paying off blackmailers—to protect her son. Swinton's fierce portrait is the main reason, but not the only one, to see this taut, observant thriller. (R)

THE DISH
Sam Neill, Patrick Warburton

Long on charm if short on drama, this sweet comedy tells the true, little-known story of how a satellite dish's three-man Aussie crew and an American associate from NASA overcame technical glitches and high winds to help 600 million people around the world watch the first lunar landing live on TV. (PG-13)

*DIVIDED WE FALL
Boleslav Polivka, Anna Siskova, Jaroslav Dusek, Csongor Kassai

When the Nazis occupy a Czech village during World War II, residents no longer know whom they can trust. The problem proves particularly vexing for Josef and Marie (Polivka and Siskova) after they take in a local Jew who has escaped from a concentration camp. The couple's attempts to keep their neighbors and the Germans at bay grow ever more desperate and comic in this beautifully observed film. (PG-13)

DOWN TO EARTH
Chris Rock, Regina King, Mark Addy, Eugene Levy, Chazz Palminteri

This genial remake of 1978's

Heaven Can Wait isn't a great movie, but it shows great promise for the film future of Chris Rock, who essentially plays himself: a sharp, funny guy who doesn't mince words. (PG-13)

*DR. DOLITTLE 2
Eddie Murphy, Kristen Wilson
In this sequel, Dolittle introduces a showbiz bear named Archie into the wild, where he must learn to win the heart of a lady bear named Ava. Murphy comfortably shares the screen with a menagerie, and Murphy plays off these nonhumans with a sweet, happy ease. (PG) [TG]

DRIVEN
Sylvester Stallone, Kip Pardue, Til Schweiger, Burt Reynolds
This turgid tire opera pits a young American buck against a speedy German rival with both men chasing the same woman. Stallone's old pro, who retired after a near fatal accident a few years ago, is summoned back by a crusty team owner to counsel the rookie and back him up on the track. Stallone is more mushmouthed than ever, but for racing fans, there are vroomfuls of high-speed tableaux. (PG-13)

ENEMY AT THE GATES
Jude Law, Ed Harris, Rachel Weisz
This partially fact-based drama about a Russian sniper (Law) facing off against his German counterpart (Harris) during the siege of Stalingrad in World War II is a tale tautly told with intense performances. But the cloyingly romantic subplot serves only as filler between the snipers' duel. (R)

EVOLUTION
David Duchovny, Julianne Moore, Orlando Jones, Seann William Scott
Ivan Reitman, the director of the 1984 blockbuster *Ghostbusters* is clearly hoping magic will strike again with this movie, in which a trio of scientists wage war on alien creatures. There are amusing lines scattered throughout *Evolution*, but overall, this is an anemic effort that feels more recycled than evolved. (PG-13)

FAITHLESS
Lena Endre, Thomas Hanzon
Endre, playing an actress who embarks on a ruinous affair, not only runs the gamut of emotions; she leaps, somersaults, whirls, dives and sprints through them. It's a championship performance. Written by Ingmar Bergman and directed by Liv Ullmann, this film is marred by arty malarkey—the affair, a movie-within-a-movie, unfolds in the mind of a brooding filmmaker (Erland Josephson). (R)

15 MINUTES
Robert De Niro, Edward Burns, Melina Kanakaredes, Kelsey Grammer
The media is the message in this initially clever crime thriller set in an era where cops, criminals and the press all meet to play the fame game. A hard-drinking veteran police detective (De Niro), who's as skilled at nabbing headlines as he is at catching bad guys, teams up with a young fire department investigator (Burns) to look into a double murder and arson. (R)

FINAL FANTASY: THE SPIRITS WITHIN
Animated, with voices by Alec Baldwin, Ming-Na, Ving Rhames, James Woods
This sci-fi thriller, based on a series of bestselling video games, is set in 2065, when Earth has been invaded by soul-sucking aliens. Dr. Aki Ross (Ming-Na), a feisty scientist, joins forces with her soldier sweetie to save the planet from the extraterrestrial menace. The plot is musty and the dialogue stilted, but the look is dazzling. (PG-13)

FINDING FORRESTER
Sean Connery, Rob Brown, F. Murray Abraham, Anna Paquin, Busta Rhymes
In this likable but hokey drama, Jamal Wallace (Brown), a somber 16-year-old living in a Bronx housing project begins an unlikely friendship with a misanthropic neighbor (Connery) who shares Jamal's love for reading and writing. The teen learns his new pal is a reclusive novelist who published a single, Pulitzer-winning book back in 1953. Director Gus Van Sant covers much of the same territory he probed in *Good Will Hunting*. (PG-13)

FREDDY GOT FINGERED
Tom Green, Rip Torn, Julie Hagerty
Plot is minimal in this numbingly awful film. All the better to leave room for Green's special brand of comedy—dumb is funny, gross is even funnier, and being really nasty to one's parents is funniest of all. (R)

2001'S TOP TEN GROSSERS

Sequels and remakes are having a strong year, but *Shrek*'s originality rules the day. Here are 2001's top successes, as of Sept. 6. (Source: *Variety*)

1. Shrek
2. The Mummy Returns
3. Rush Hour 2
4. Pearl Harbor
5. Jurassic Park III
6. Planet of the Apes
7. Hannibal
8. The Fast and the Furious
9. Lara Croft: Tomb Raider
10. Cast Away

*GHOST WORLD
Thora Birch, Scarlett Johansson, Steve Buscemi, Brad Renfro

Recent high school graduates, Enid (Birch) and her best pal (Johansson) fake a response to a personal ad placed by Seymour (Buscemi), a nice-guy loser who lives in a world of old blues 78s and comic books. The girls then begin stalking him. Based on a '97 comic book by Daniel Clowes, the film is a whip-smart, coming-of-age comedy. (R)

THE GIFT
Cate Blanchett, Keanu Reeves, Greg Kinnear, Giovanni Ribisi, Katie Holmes, Hilary Swank, Michael Jeter

Annie Wilson (Blanchett), has psychic gifts and troubling dreams, including visions of the sopping wet corpse of a local glamour girl who has gone missing. But any moviegoer who has seen a few whodunits will be able to figure out who's guilty way faster than either Wilson or the local cops. (R)

THE GOLDEN BOWL
Uma Thurman, Nick Nolte, Jeremy Northam, Kate Beckinsale, Anjelica Huston, James Fox

An indigent Italian prince has just told an American of good birth but no money (Thurman) that soon he will marry another. His intended, a friend of Thurman's, is the only child of America's first billionaire. Desperate to stay close to her amour, she in turn weds her friend's courtly father. Money buys unhappiness for all involved in this plush film version of Henry James's 1904 novel about love and betrayal. (R)

GREENFINGERS
Clive Owen, Helen Mirren, David Kelly, Natasha Little

Colin Briggs (Owen) is a murderer who finds redemption in nurturing plants. Soon he is competing in England's snootiest flower show, as well as for the hand of the wallflower daughter (Little) of Georgina Woodhouse (Mirren), an amusingly flamboyant gardening guru. The slender British comedy wilts after sentimental mulch is dumped on by the truckload. (R)

HANNIBAL
Anthony Hopkins, Julianne Moore, Ray Liotta, Giancarlo Giannini

A rancid, blood-soaked disappointment. Lecter, on the loose and living in Italy, is eager to reconnect with Starling (Moore, assuming Jodie Foster's role) after 10 years. While Hannibal generates some genuine chills, its plot rambles and there's way too much gratuitous gore. (R)

*HEARTBREAKERS
Sigourney Weaver, Jennifer Love Hewitt, Gene Hackman, Ray Liotta, Jason Lee, Nora Dunn, Ricky Jay

Weaver and Hewitt play a mother-and-daughter grifter team in this uneven but still vastly enjoyable comedy. (PG-13)

HEDWIG AND THE ANGRY INCH
John Cameron Mitchell, Andrea Martin

This rock musical is about the wrath of a (would-be) woman scorned. Hedwig (Mitchell) is an East German-born, long-legged, wig-wearing lady rocker who was once a he. Or still is, sort of; the "angry inch" is what's left of Hedwig's manhood after a botched sex-change operation. With its mix of songs, comic monologues and animation, Hedwig is, like the chanteuse, unique. (R)

*THE HOUSE OF MIRTH
Gillian Anderson, Eric Stoltz, Laura Linney

An eloquent, heartbreaking work about turn-of-the century New York City society. Anderson is magnificent as Lily, the smart but self-destructive heroine of Edith Wharton's finest novel, who can't bring herself to make the moral and romantic compromises required to save herself by marrying. (PG)

IN THE MOOD FOR LOVE
Maggie Cheung, Tony Leung

In this headily erotic movie, Cheung and Leung make an exceptionally magnetic couple as neighbors who embark on a dignified, unconsummated romance after learning that their spouses are carrying on an affair. The relationship (and the movie) eventually grows more tenuous and mysterious, and the lovers' reticence finally begins to seem not so much noble as irrational. An audience is left bothered and bewildered—but mostly bewitched. (PG-13) [TG]

THE INVISIBLE CIRCUS
Cameron Diaz, Jordana Brewster, Christopher Eccleston, Blythe Danner

During a summer in the mid-'70s, an 18-year-old (Brewster) heads to Europe with a backpack filled with old postcards sent by her older sister (Diaz), who had made the same journey six years earlier and wound up dead, possibly a suicide, on a beach in Portugal. A minor coming-of-age drama as diaphanous as the gauzy shirts worn by Diaz's character. (R)

JEEPERS CREEPERS
Gina Philips, Justin Long

With his frayed duster, long hair and what appears to be a rubber face mask, the Creeper (Jonathan Breck) looks like a reject from the World Wrestling Federation. The movie's gore is moderate by current let-all-the-guts-hang-out standards, the acting is passable, and our protagonists make the now-obligatory post-*Scream* jokes contrasting their own seemingly cautious behavior with that of the apparently moronic characters in horror films. But in the end, why bother? (R)

JURASSIC PARK III

Sam Neill, Tea Leoni, William H. Macy, Alessandro Nivola, Trevor Morgan

After a plane crash, paleontologist Alan Grant (Neill) is stranded, along with an assistant and a divorced couple (Leoni and Macy) searching for their missing son, on a remote island where herds of genetically engineered dinosaurs roam. It's all competently done, but these newly minted dinos are starting to seem kind of prehistoric. (PG-13)

JOSIE AND THE PUSSYCATS

Rachael Leigh Cook, Tara Reid, Rosario Dawson, Alan Cumming, Parker Posey

Based on a comic book that was adapted in the '70s into a popular cartoon, Josie follows the misadventures of three would-be rockers. The movie is full of quick, funny gags, but Josie and her friends are lifeless characters. (PG-13) [TG]

JOE DIRT

David Spade

This is another of those extra-crude comedies—and a good, silly one, at that—but Joe, as played by Spade, is a genuine comic inspiration. Doomed to a life of indignity, he makes a half-hearted stab at improving his white-trash image and perseveres. (PG-13) [TG]

THE KING IS ALIVE

Jennifer Jason Leigh, Janet McTeer, Bruce Davison

A disparate band of contemporary European and American travelers are stranded in an African desert when their bus driver gets lost. As their situation becomes more desperate, they stage an amateur version of *King Lear*. Spurred by their roles in Shakespeare's tragedy, they begin acting out their own personal dramas. King is by turns annoying, intriguing, boring, and insightful. (R)

KINGDOM COME

Whoopi Goldberg, Jada Pinkett Smith, LL Cool J, Loretta Devine, Vivica A. Fox

From the moment Woodrow Slocumb keels over after suffering a fatal stroke at the start of the movie, his family exhibits outrageously bad behavior. As the family gathers for the funeral, husbands quarrel with wives, brother battles brother, and mother and son go at each other. The movie is gooey-soft at heart, though, so by the end differences are resolved. The fun of *Kingdom* is in watching its actors gamely stretch. (PG-13)

KISS OF THE DRAGON

Jet Li, Bridget Fonda

Filled with one bone-crushing, neck-breaking martial arts battle after another (complete with gruesome sound effects), this violent thriller allows star Jet Li to do what he does best: whup folks senseless. (R)

A KNIGHT'S TALE

Heath Ledger, Mark Addy, Shannyn Sossamon, Rufus Sewell, Alan Tudyk

When his master dies, William impersonates the older knight so that he can compete in jousts open only to those of aristocratic birth. William, it turns out, wields a mean lance, and his horseback heroics win the heart of a comely princess. What will happen when his true identity is discovered?

2000'S OVERSEAS MONEYMAKERS

American Beauty rode Oscar honors to far greater success overseas than at home, and *The Beach* was a hit on foreign shores even though it washed out in the U.S. Otherwise the traditional mix of action films and tales for children of all ages and nations were once again Hollywood's leading exports. (Source: *Variety*)

Rank	Title	Gross (in millions)
1.	Mission: Impossible 2	330
2.	Gladiator	262
3.	American Beauty	218
4.	Toy Story 2	210
5.	The Sixth Sense	187
6.	Dinosaur	181
7.	Stuart Little	154
8.	The Green Mile	150
9.	The Perfect Storm	140
10.	X-Men	137
11.	Erin Brockovich	132
12.	Gone in Sixty Seconds	129
13.	Scary Movie	120
13.	What Lies Beneath	120
15.	Hollow Man	117
16.	Charlie's Angels	114
17.	The Beach	103
18.	Sleepy Hollow	102
19.	The World Is Not Enough	95
20.	Chicken Run	94

Gleefully anachronistic, teen-centric *Tale*'s plot is plodding and its characters too one-dimensional to hold strong appeal for adult filmgoers. (PG-13)

LARA CROFT: TOMB RAIDER
Angelina Jolie
One of the advantages of high-tech action games is that they translate easily to live-action film. Not that *Raider* is a winner. The effects are blah, and the action scenes are a jumble of quick cuts. (PG-13)

LAST RESORT
Dina Korzun, Paddy Considine
In this delicate drama about the bleak lives of refugees, a Russian woman arrives in England with her son to reunite with her British fiancé. He fails to show up at the airport, she requests asylum, and is packed off to a holding center in a shabby seaside resort town. Polish-born director Pawel Pawlikowski has made a memorable movie about trying to put shattered lives back together, even when the pieces won't fit. (Not rated)

LEGALLY BLONDE
Reese Witherspoon, Luke Wilson, Selma Blair, Jennifer Coolidge
Think *Clueless* meets *The Paper Chase*. When Elle Woods's politically ambitious college beau dumps her before heading east for Harvard Law School, she manages to get into Harvard herself, hoping to win him back. *Blonde* is much like its heroine: perky but shallow. (PG-13)

L.I.E.
Paul Franklin Dano, Brian Cox
The title stands for the Long Island Expressway, a major route that borders the desperate lives of the film's smart, emotionally adrift 15-year-old hero (Dano) and the middle-aged pederast (Cox) who befriends him. Disturbing and affecting. (NC-17)

LISA PICARD IS FAMOUS
Laura Kirk, Nat DeWolf, Griffin Dunne
An aspiring actress whose only significant credit is a sexy cereal commercial, Lisa Picard (Kirk) has been singled out by a documentarian (Dunne) as his subject for a film about living on the cusp of fame. He follows her around Manhattan with his camera in this amusing mockumentary, directed by Dunne, tagging along to auditions and visits with her best bud Tate (DeWolf), another actor. (Not rated)

LUMUMBA
Eriq Ebouaney
Lumumba, about the short life of the Congo's first Prime Minister after independence from Belgium in 1960, is slashingly sharp and swift. This French-language import is a model of how to film history—a thorny, bloody chapter in history. (Not Rated) [TG]

THE LUZHIN DEFENCE
John Turturro, Emily Watson
Adapted from an early Nabokov novel, the film chronicles the troubled affair between Luzhin, a chess master who has spent his life avoiding emotional entanglements, and the sleek Natalia, an aristocratic rebel who defies her mother when she sets out to castle Luzhin. Gifted stars Turturro and Watson are well-matched, but the film is minor. (PG-13)

*MADE
Jon Favreau, Vince Vaughn, Peter Falk, Famke Janssen
What this jokey, halfhearted gangster film has going for it in a big way is the breezy, *Odd Couple* rapport between Vaughn and Favreau, who take on a job as muscle for a Mob boss. The plot is beside the point; it's the constant breaking-up and making-up between Favreau and Vaughn that's the fun. (R)

THE MAN WHO CRIED
Christina Ricci, Johnny Depp, Cate Blanchett, John Turturro
A young Jewish woman (Ricci) gets waylaid in Paris where she begins an affair with a Gypsy (Depp), rooms with a Russian gold digger, and sings at an opera house. While sumptuous, *Man* never engages emotionally or comes together as a whole. (R)

*A MATTER OF TASTE
Bernard Giraudeau, Jean-Pierre Lorit, Florence Thomassin, Charles Berling
Tycoon Frédéric Delamont hires waiter Nicolas (Lorit) to taste his food, and he soon comes to absorb and assume the older man's taste preferences in clothes, homes and women. We know from the opening scenes of this intriguing, French-language film that Nicolas will end up killing Delamont. But the draw to this taut psychological thriller is discovering what drives him to murder, and the nature of the perverse game that the older man is playing. (Not rated)

MAYBE BABY
Hugh Laurie, Joely Richardson, Adrian Lester, Rowan Atkinson, Emma Thompson, Tom Hollander
A blithe but knowing romantic comedy about infertility and the stress it causes. Laurie and Richardson are likeable as an attractive couple living the good life in London who long for a baby, however, and, despite diligent conjugal efforts and much medical help, haven't been successful. Tyro director Ben Elton, who adapted the movie from his own 1999 novel, Inconceivable, occasionally lets Baby become what the British call twee (think of *Ally McBeal*), but this is a promising debut. (R)

*MEMENTO
Guy Pearce, Carrie-Anne Moss, Joe Pantoliano
This terrific movie, about one man's quest for vengeance, does everything a thriller is supposed to do: intrigue, involve and keep you guessing. And it does it all backward. The protagonist has no short-term memory, the result of being bashed in the head by the man he believes raped and murdered his wife, the man he seeks to find and kill. Memento grows ever more complex as it unfolds, and one leaves it eager to catch it again to make sure the pieces fit and to look for clues missed the first time around. (R)

THE MEXICAN
Julia Roberts, Brad Pitt, James Gandolfini, Bob Balaban
Roberts plays a woman who insists that her live-in honey (Pitt) quit his job and head with her to Las Vegas. He can't until he fetches an antique pistol known as The Mexican from south of the border. In a huff, she heads to Vegas solo but is taken hostage en route by a hit man who is also after the gun. A determinedly quirky romantic comedy with plenty of gunplay and intrigue that adds up to no more than a tasty snack. (R)

MONKEYBONE
Brendan Fraser, Bridget Fonda
A hyperactive mess. Combining live action and animation, *Monkeybone* follows a cartoonist (Fraser) whose animated alter ego, a lascivious monkey, comes to life and torments Fraser when he lands in purgatory after a car crash. (PG-13)

MOULIN ROUGE
Nicole Kidman, Ewan McGregor, John Leguizamo, Jim Broadbent
While easy to admire for its audacious vision and lush visuals, this feverishly busy, wake-'em-and-shake-'em attempt to

revive the movie musical keeps tripping over its own aggressive flashiness. (PG-13)

THE MUMMY RETURNS
Brendan Fraser, Rachel Weisz, John Hannah, Oded Fehr, Arnold Vosloo
The sequel to 1999's *The Mummy* is so cheesy that it ought to come with a warning for the lactose-intolerant. Set in 1933, Rick (Fraser) and Evelyn (Weisz) are happily married and living in London. The tranquility is shattered when the couple are called upon to travel to Egypt to battle yet again the evil Mummy and save the world from mass destruction. (PG-13)

O
Mekhi Phifer, Julia Stiles and Josh Hartnett
Shakespeare's *Othello* plunked down in a modern high school. Works surprisingly well, with solid performances from Mekhi Phifer, Julia Stiles, and Josh Hartnett. (R)

O BROTHER, WHERE ART THOU?
George Clooney, John Turturro, Tim Blake Nelson, John Goodman, Holly Hunter, Michael Badalucco
The latest artfully wacky comedy by the brothers Coen takes as its inspiration Homer's *Odyssey*, tracking the long journey home of Ulysses Everett McGill (Clooney), an escapee from a chain gang, who is making his way back to his wife through Depression-era rural Mississippi. The movie is immensely enjoyable, but little of it stays with you afterward. (PG-13)

ONE NIGHT AT MCCOOL'S
Liv Tyler, Matt Dillon, John Goodman, Paul Reiser, Michael Douglas
There's basically one joke in this comedy, and it quickly runs out of gas: While all the men are obsessed with bedding the vampy Jewel (Tyler), all she really wants to do is redecorate her boudoir in perfect shades of pink and purple. (R)

THE OTHERS
Nicole Kidman, Fionnula Flanagan
Kidman plays Grace, a widow raising a young son and daughter inside a mansion on the island of Jersey. Someone or something is out to harm her offspring. Doors and windows are mysteriously left open, and the kids wake up screaming, saying they've had nightmare visits from a boy who claims he once lived in the house. As haunted-house movies go, the coolly elegant *Others* is a notch above most. (PG-13)

*OUR SONG
Kerry Washington, Anna Simpson, Melissa Martinez
A small, richly compelling drama that captures exactly how teenage girls talk and behave. Lanisha, Joycelyn and Maria, three 15-year olds, are spending their free time during a recent August hanging out, but by the summer's end the contours of this trio's friendship will have shifted dramatically. (R)

PEARL HARBOR
Ben Affleck, Josh Hartnett, Kate Beckinsale, Cuba Gooding Jr., Alec Baldwin
A bloated and boring collection of war-movie clichés in search of an epic. The actual, extended battle scenes are technically dazzling, but the story and dialogue that surround and accompany them are as hackneyed as that of any daytime soap opera. *Pearl* at least has the grace not to tamper with history. (PG-13)

PLANET OF THE APES
Mark Wahlberg, Tim Roth, Helena Bonham Carter, Estella Warren, Michael Clarke Duncan, Paul Giamatti
This remake looks better than the '68 film but is less filling intellectually and emotionally. Wahlberg portrays Leo Davidson, an American astronaut stranded in the future on a

planet where apes rule. You know you're in trouble when the simians—particularly Thade (Roth), an evil ape military leader, and Ari (Bonham Carter), a sympathetic chimp aristocrat—are far more compelling than any of the humans. (PG-13)

*THE PLEDGE
Jack Nicholson, Robin Wright Penn, Sam Shepard, Aaron Eckhart
Having promised the grieving mother of a molested and murdered little girl that he will find her child's killer, a veteran Reno homicide police detective (Nicholson) doggedly pursues leads more than a year after he has retired. Nicholson gives a terrific, subtle performance as a man obsessed with finding answers where none may exist. Wright Penn is equally fine as a café waitress whom he helps, and husband Sean Penn directs with great flair. (R)

*POLLOCK
Ed Harris, Marcia Gay Harden, Amy Madigan, Jeffrey Tambor
This admirably restrained biopic attempts to get at artist Jackson Pollock's essence by showing him in all his self-contradictory complexity. Pollock was insecure about his talent but also convinced that he was the greatest artist of his time. Harris is nothing short of brilliant as Pollock, nailing the painter's sinewy physicality and tortured psyche. (R)

THE PRINCESS DIARIES
Anne Hathaway, Julie Andrews, Hector Elizondo, Heather Matarazzo
Clarisse Renaldi (Andrews), the queen of Genovia, arrives in San Francisco to see if her long-lost granddaughter Mia (Hathaway) is tiara-worthy. Soon Mia is enrolled in Royalty 101, learning to differentiate between forks and submitting to a major makeover. *Diaries* is a family film with enough tart touches to balance its saccharine premise. (G)

RAT RACE
Rowan Atkinson, John Cleese, Whoopi Goldberg, Cuba Gooding Jr., Seth Green, Jon Lovitz, Breckin Meyer, Kathy Najimy, Amy Smart
Six patrons at a Las Vegas casino are selected by the owner (Cleese) to take part in a race. Each is given a key to a locker in Silver City, New Mexico, which contains $2 million. What the contestants don't know is that Cleese has set up the race for the amusement of high rollers, who are betting on which of them will get there first. This splendidly silly comedy will put a blissed-out, goofy grin on your face. (PG-13)

RECESS: SCHOOL'S OUT
Animated
Shamelessly courts its target viewers (6- to 12-year-olds) by coming out solidly in favor of summer vacations and against extending the school year. The animation is flat and uninspired, just like the plot and dialogue. (G)

THE ROAD HOME
Zhang Ziyi, Zheng Hao
Weaving the past and present together, *The Road Home* shifts gracefully between a widow's preparations for her husband's funeral and her determined pursuit as an 18-year-old villager of the shy young schoolmaster who would become her spouse. (G)

ROCK STAR
Mark Wahlberg, Jennifer Aniston, Dominic West, Timothy Spall
The breezily enjoyable *Rock Star* is a plain tale told simply, but with a winning sense of humor. It's the mid-'80s, and Chris Cole (Wahlberg) lives with his parents in working-class Pittsburgh; this heavy-metal wannabe goes from a part-time cover band to joining Steel Dragon (loosely based on Judas Priest) as vocalist, wallowing in the rock and roll life. But this is a cautionary tale about

rock's excesses, and Cole eventually discovers that his dreams of stardom were more satisfying in front of the mirror than on a real stage. (R)

RUSH HOUR 2
Jackie Chan, Chris Tucker, John Lone
In this sequel, Chan and Tucker again play cops who unite to catch international evildoers. Chan's acrobatic skills and self-deprecating humor are showcased competently, but Tucker is often boorish rather than funny. As an undercover agent, sexy Roselyn Sanchez perks things up considerably, and not just because she's in her scanties. (PG-13)

RUSSIAN DOLL
Hugo Weaving, Natalia Novikova, David Wenham
Harvey, the protagonist of this sprightly but slender romantic comedy, is most surprised when he falls for Katia, a Russian émigré facing deportation. He reluctantly agrees to marry Katia as a favor to his married buddy, with whom Katia is having an affair. *Russian Doll* finds much of its humor in the differences between Harvey and Katia, and Weaving brings an appealing gravitas to his emotionally blind detective. (R)

SAVE THE LAST DANCE
Julia Stiles, Sean Patrick Thomas
You'd have to be 15 to actually care whether two Chicago school classmates—Sara (Stiles), who's white and a would-be ballerina, and Derek (Thomas), who's black and wants to be a doctor—can overcome others' objections to their romance. There's nothing light-footed about *Dance*. (PG-13)

THE SCORE
Robert De Niro, Edward Norton, Marlon Brando, Angela Bassett
De Niro is an expert jewel thief who puts aside the rules when Max (Brando), a longtime underworld crony, offers him $4 mil-

lion to steal a jewel-encrusted 17th-century scepter. The scenes between De Niro and Brando crackle, offering a fascinating clash of acting styles. (R)

SEE SPOT RUN
David Arquette, Michael Clarke Duncan, Leslie Bibb, Paul Sorvino
Arquette plays a bachelor mailman who is babysitting a young boy. When a bullmastiff jumps into Arquette's mail truck, the pair adopt it—unaware of the dog's FBI pedigree or of the hit men who are trying to whack it. Much broad humor, including gags about human and canine flatulence, follows. (PG)

SERIES 7
Brooke Smith, Glenn Fitzgerald
Taking reality TV to a brutal extreme, six contestants on *The Contenders*, a program produced (read "enforced") by the government are armed (and required) to kill each other wherever they can—driveway, mall, field. This mercilessly dead-on satire does a brilliant job aping the visual style of reality shows. (R) [TG]

SEXY BEAST
Ben Kingsley, Ray Winstone
This stylish, often acridly funny suspense thriller tracks what happens when a British gangster's ex-colleague comes to Spain to persuade him to return to London for one last job. (R)

SHADOW MAGIC
Jared Harris, Xia Yu, Xing Yufei
When Raymond Wallace (Harris) arrives in China in 1902, he's hoping to make his fortune showing some of the earliest film footage ever shot. He has trouble attracting patrons until a Chinese man (Yu) offers to help. *Shadow Magic* is a slight, loving valentine to the power of cinema, and both Harris and Yu give heartfelt performances. (PG)

*SHADOW OF THE VAMPIRE
John Malkovich, Willem Dafoe
The premise of this bitingly amusing film is that Max Schreck (Dafoe), who played the vampire in director F. W. Murnau's 1922 horror classic *Nosferatu*, got the part because he was, in fact, among the undead. Murnau, a notorious perfectionist, seeks realism from Schreck but grows furious when the vampire gets too enthusiastic, killing off crew members in mid-shoot. *Shadow* has clever fun exploring how far an artist will go to achieve his vision, but Dafoe is the show here. (R)

*SHREK
Animated, with the voices of Mike Myers, Eddie Murphy, Cameron Diaz, John Lithgow
He is mean, green, and far from lean, but he's still the most appealing leading man to appear in movies since *Toy Story's* Woody. The movie tweaks the standard fairy tale by its tail as Shrek (a pea-soup colored, bald, hulking yet stumpy giant) and a smart-mouthed donkey, whom Shrek reluctantly allows to become his sidekick, rescue the lovely Princess Fiona from imprisonment in a castle guarded by a fire-breathing dragon. (PG)

SIGNS & WONDERS
Stellan Skarsgård, Charlotte Rampling, Deborah Kara Unger
A cryptic psychological thriller that grows increasingly dark and diffuse, *Signs & Wonders* tracks an American businessman (Skarsgård) living in Athens, as he loses his emotional bearings after ditching his wife (Rampling) for a younger coworker (Unger). Skarsgård and Rampling are both compelling, but this story wanders hither and yon until it literally falls off a cliff. (Not rated)

SILENT BOB STRIKE BACK
Jason Mewes, Kevin Smith, Shannon Elizabeth, Will Ferrell
Jay and Silent Bob are a couple of hard-core stoners who briefly graced director and screenwriter Kevin Smith's four previous movies. The two finally get starring roles in this film, which is one big, self-referential in-joke as they try to halt production of a movie about them. Only fitfully funny, it's most notable for amusing cameos by Matt Damon and Ben Affleck and for spoofing other recent movies. (R)

SNATCH
Jason Statham, Benicio Del Toro, Dennis Farina, Brad Pitt, Vinnie Jones
Director Guy Ritchie comes mighty close to rifling from *Lock, Stock and Two Smoking Barrels*, his own 1998 gangster flick, with this clever caper film about stolen jewels, fixed boxing matches and bumbling London hoods. As a mush-mouthed Gypsy pugilist, Pitt shows considerable comic skill in a minor role. (R)

SOMEONE LIKE YOU
Ashley Judd, Hugh Jackman, Greg Kinnear, Ellen Barkin, Marisa Tomei
In this overly contrived example of a romantic comedy, Judd is single and looking. Someone tries to milk laughs by having her natter on and on about the laws of animal behavior, likening men to bulls and women to cows, but her constant harping wears out its welcome long before she finally discovers that her theory is udder nonsense. (PG-13)

*SONGCATCHER
Janet McTeer, Aidan Quinn, Jane Adams, Pat Carroll
A lyrical, thoughtful movie, *Songcatcher* follows the journey of self-discovery made by a musicologist who travels deep into the Appalachian Mountains in 1907 to visit her sister. As she grows

close to the mountain folk and learns their hardscrabble ways, she comes to see that music is "as much a part of life here as the air you breathe." (PG-13)

SPY KIDS
Antonio Banderas, Carla Gugino, Alan Cumming, Tony Shaloub
Carmen and her younger brother Juni must save the day when their parents (Banderas and Gugino) are kidnapped by sinister international powermongers. Despite a busy plot and excessive reliance on special effects and hi-tech gadgetry, *Kids* is cool enough to keep non-spy kids entertained. (PG)

STARTUP.COM
Documentary
Click on this. Two former high school classmates started an Internet company, GovWorks.com, in 1998. Within a matter of months, they had 233 employees and had raised $50 million. When the dot-com bubble burst last year, so did GovWorks. *Startup.com* makes a fitting epitaph. (R)

*STATE AND MAIN
Alec Baldwin, Sarah Jessica Parker, Philip Seymour Hoffman, William H. Macy, Rebecca Pidgeon, Julia Stiles
David Mamet's amusingly snide satire about what happens when a Hollywood film company sets out to shoot a flick in a small Vermont town makes relentless fun of the filmmaking community with caustic comic work by a talented cast. (R)

SUMMER CATCH
Freddie Prinze Jr., Jessica Biel, Brittany Murphy, Matthew Lillard
This is the WB version of a baseball movie. Everyone is young, toned, sexually active and agonizes over their future. Grownups show up only as authority figures or parents, speak their piece and then vamoose so that the college-age characters can

return to figuring out their lives. Catch's homages to *Bull Durham* (scenes with panties and a promiscuous older woman) only underscore its minor-league status. (PG-13)

SWEET NOVEMBER
Charlize Theron, Keanu Reeves
A dopey tearjerker. Reeves is a workaholic who becomes the latest rehab project of Theron's—who invites uptight men (one at a time) to live and sleep with her for a month, during which she helps them loosen up and appreciate life. As the going gets hokey, he finally figures out she has a sad, secret reason for savoring each moment. (PG-13)

SWORDFISH
John Travolta, Hugh Jackman, Halle Berry, Don Cheadle, Vinnie Jones
Travolta plays a crime boss who dispatches his glamorous girlfriend to recruit one of the world's leading computer hackers (Jackman) to help him rob a bank fund. Or something like that. This technothriller starts off promisingly enough, but it's downhill in a hurry as viewers are subjected to the standard parade of pointless explosions, car chases, and gunplay. (R)

*THE TAILOR OF PANAMA
Pierce Brosnan, Jamie Lee Curtis, Geoffrey Rush, Brendan Gleeson
Brosnan plays Andy Osnard, an amoral British intelligence agent who sets about pumping Panama City's leading tailor (Rush) for the skinny on local politicos. When Osnard threatens to reveal the tailor's criminal past to his beloved wife, he finds himself telling Osnard whoppers with tragic consequences. This sophisticated international thriller brims with smarts, complex characters and cynical wit. (R)

THIRTEEN DAYS
Kevin Costner, Bruce Greenwood, Steven Culp, Dylan Baker
On one level it's an engrossing, fact-based drama; on another level it's about the making of a president. The film recounts how John F. Kennedy stood tall and maintained peace when the Soviet Union secretly installed nuclear missiles in Cuba. Greenwood nails JFK's distinctive accent and posture, and Costner enhances a strong supporting ensemble. (PG-13)

3000 MILES TO GRACELAND
Kurt Russell, Kevin Costner, Courteney Cox, Christian Slater
A dark, gratuitously violent movie in which the bad guy (Costner) teams up with his ex-prison cellmate (Russell) and three other sleazeballs to rob a casino during an Elvis impersonators' convention. Elvis would be appalled. (R)

TORTILLA SOUP
Hector Elizondo, Elizabeth Peña, Jacqueline Obradors, Tamara Mello
Don't see this food-obsessed movie, an American adaptation of director Ang Lee's Taiwanese film *Eat Drink Man Woman* (1994), with a distinctly Latin flavor, on an empty stomach. You'll never make it past the opening credits, which show one lip-smackingly tasty Mexican dish after another being lovingly prepared for a big family dinner. You know what's coming in the movie, but it is done with such gusto and style that it's as welcome as gourmet leftovers. (PG-13)

TOWN & COUNTRY
Warren Beatty, Diane Keaton, Garry Shandling, Goldie Hawn, Jenna Elfman
This misguided comedy follows the marital troubles of two long-married, wealthy Manhattan couples (Beatty and Keaton, Shandling and Hawn). Both husbands are cheating, with Beatty con-

ducting not one extramarital affair but two. Despite the cast, it's a cheerless mishmash that is as depressing to watch as it must have been to make. (R)

*TRAFFIC
Michael Douglas, Don Cheadle, Benicio Del Toro, Dennis Quaid, Catherine Zeta-Jones

Working at the top of his game and with a superior cast, director Steven Soderbergh vividly presents several distinct but interconnected stories about the morass that is the drug problem in this country today. (R)

TWO CAN PLAY THAT GAME
Vivica A. Fox, Morris Chestnut, Anthony Anderson, Bobby Brown

A predictable comedy about the war between the sexes, this trifling movie exists merely as a showcase for the fetching Fox (Soul Food). Both sides are under the impression that there's an unwritten set of rules, most of 'em harsh, that must be adhered to when dealing with an errant flame. (R)

*UNDER THE SAND
Charlotte Rampling, Bruno Cremer

In this emotionally powerful import, a French husband and his English wife are on vacation near the seaside in France. As Marie (Rampling) naps on the beach, Jean trudges off for a swim and vanishes. Did he accidentally drown? Commit suicide? Run away? In the months that follow, Marie tries to adjust to the idea that her longtime partner is gone but keeps conjuring up his image, sharing meals and a bed with a man only she can see. (NR)

*THE VISIT
Hill Harper, Billy Dee Williams, Obba Babatunde

The Visit, a moving drama about a convict trying to reconnect with his kin, accurately captures the complicated give-and-take of family relationships. (R)

THE WEDDING PLANNER
Jennifer Lopez, Matthew McConaughey, Bridgette Wilson-Sampras, Justin Chambers

Vow to miss it. The central joke of this lackluster romantic comedy is that while Mary Fiore (Lopez) spends her days making the romantic dreams of others come true, she doesn't seem able to find a match for herself. One day, a studly pediatrician (McConaughey) saves her from a runaway garbage cart in the street. The rest of *Planner* is a series of uninspired, dragged-out scenes all aimed at uniting Fiore and her medicine man. (PG-13)

WHAT'S THE WORST THAT COULD HAPPEN?
Martin Lawrence, Danny DeVito, John Leguizamo, Carmen Ejogo

When billionaire Max Fairbanks (DeVito) catches professional thief Caffrey (Lawrence) robbing his house, he calls the cops, then claims Caffrey's ring as his own. The rest of the movie is devoted to an escalating battle between the two men as the thief tries to get his ring back. As worthless as the ring it revolves around, that doesn't keep Lawrence and DeVito from having fun. (PG-13)

WHEN BRENDAN MET TRUDY
Peter McDonald, Flora Montgomery

Brendan (McDonald) is an uptight Dublin schoolteacher who is mad for the movies. When he meets Trudy (Montgomery), she agrees to go to a vintage foreign film with him but only if the movie's in color. Brendan, it seems, has much to teach this lass. Trudy, it turns out, is the one who will be doing the instructing—about life, love and the joy of stealing. (NR)

THE WIDOW OF SAINT-PIERRE
Juliette Binoche, Daniel Auteuil, Emir Kusturica

Based on a true story from 1850, residents of a remote French island off the Canadian coast questioned the wisdom of beheading a murderer (Kusturica) who had repented and sincerely reformed. This beautifully shot, affecting historical drama reminds us that the debate over the death penalty is nothing new. (R)

THE TOP 100 BOX-OFFICE FILMS OF ALL TIME

This list ranks the largest money-making movies of all time based on domestic (U.S. and Canada) box-office receipts. Figures are accurate through September 6, 2001; the newer blockbusters are still earning. (Source: *Variety*)

Rank	Film (year of release)	B.O. Gross
1.	Titanic (1997)	$600,788,188
2.	Star Wars (1977)	460,998,007
3.	Star Wars: Episode I—The Phantom Menace (1999)	430,984,033
4.	E.T., the Extra-Terrestrial (1982)	399,804,539
5.	Jurassic Park (1993)	357,067,947
6.	Forrest Gump (1994)	329,693,974
7.	The Lion King (1994)	312,855,561
8.	Return of the Jedi (1983)	309,205,079
9.	Independence Day (1996)	306,169,268
10.	The Sixth Sense (1999)	293,488,346
11.	The Empire Strikes Back (1980)	290,271,960
12.	Home Alone (1990)	285,761,243
13.	Shrek (2001)	263,046,762
14.	Dr. Seuss' How The Grinch Stole Christmas (2000)	260,044,825
15.	Jaws (1975)	260,000,000
16.	Batman (1989)	251,188,924
17.	Men in Black (1997)	250,016,330
18.	Toy Story 2 (1999)	245,852,179
19.	Raiders of the Lost Ark (1981)	242,374,454
20.	Twister (1996)	241,721,524
21.	Beverly Hills Cop (1984)	234,760,478
22.	Cast Away	229,168,596
23.	The Lost World: Jurassic Park (1997)	229,086,123
24.	Ghostbusters (1984)	220,858,490
25.	Mrs. Doubtfire (1993)	219,195,051
26.	Ghost (1990)	217,631,306
27.	Aladdin (1992)	217,350,219
28.	Saving Private Ryan (1998)	216,335,085
29.	Mission: Impossible 2 (2000)	214,343,454
30.	Back to the Future (1985)	208,242,016
31.	Austin Powers: The Spy Who Shagged Me (1999)	206,040,086
32.	Terminator 2: Judgment Day (1991)	204,843,345
33.	The Exorcist (1973; rerelease 2000)	204,671,011
34.	The Mummy Returns (2001)	201,733,280
35.	Armageddon	201,578,182
36.	Rush Hour (2001)	200,284,587
37.	Gone With the Wind (1939)	198,648,910
38.	Indiana Jones and the Last Crusade (1989)	197,171,806
39.	Pearl Harbor (2001)	196,834,083
40.	Toy Story (1995)	191,796,233
41.	Gladiator (2000)	186,870,377
42.	Dances with Wolves (1990)	184,208,848
43.	Batman Forever (1995)	184,031,112
44.	The Fugitive (1993)	183,875,760
45.	What Women Want (2000)	182,805,123
46.	The Perfect Storm (2000)	182,618,434
47.	Grease (1978)	181,513.510
48.	Liar Liar (1997)	181,410,615
49.	Mission: Impossible (1996)	180,981,866
50.	Indiana Jones and the Temple of Doom (1984)	179,870,271
51.	Pretty Woman (1990)	178,406,268
52.	Tootsie (1982)	177,200,000
53.	Top Gun (1986)	176,781,728
54.	There's Something About Mary (1998)	176,483,808
55.	Jurassic Park III (2001)	176,089,275
56.	Snow White and the Seven Dwarfs (1937)	175,263,233
57.	"Crocodile" Dundee (1986)	174,803,506
58.	Planet of the Apes (2001)	173,607,942
59.	Home Alone 2: Lost in New York (1992)	173,585,516
60.	Air Force One (1997)	172,888,056
61.	Rain Man (1988)	172,825,435
62.	Apollo 13 (1995)	172,070,496
63.	The Matrix (1999)	171,479,930
64.	Tarzan (1999)	171,010,381
65.	Three Men and a Baby (1987)	167,780,960
66.	Meet the Parents (2000)	166,225,040
67.	Close Encounters of the Third Kind (1977)	166,000,000
68.	Robin Hood: Prince of Thieves (1991)	165,493,908
69.	Hannibal (2001)	164,977,884
70.	Big Daddy (1999)	163,479,795
71.	Batman Returns (1992)	162,831,698
72.	A Bug's Life (1998)	162,798,565
73.	The Waterboy (1998)	161,487,252
74.	The Sound of Music (1965)	160,476,331
75.	The Firm (1993)	158,340,292
76.	X-Men (2000)	157,299,718
77.	Scary Movie (2000)	157,019,771
78.	Fatal Attraction (1987)	156,645,693
79.	The Sting (1972)	156,000,000
80.	What Lies Beneath (2000)	155,464,351
81.	The Mummy (1999)	155,385,488
82.	Who Framed Roger Rabbit (1988)	154,112,492
83.	Jerry Maguire (1996)	153,962,592
84.	Beverly Hills Cop II (1987)	153,665,036
85.	Gremlins (1984)	153,083,102
86.	101 Dalmatians (1961)	152,551,432
87.	Runaway Bride (1999)	152,257,409
88.	Rambo: First Blood Part II (1985)	150,415,432
89.	As Good As It Gets (1997)	148,266,088
90.	Lethal Weapon 2 (1989)	147,253,986
91.	True Lies (1994)	146,282,411
92.	Beauty and the Beast (1991)	145,863,363
93.	The Santa Clause (1994)	144,833,357
94.	Lethal Weapon 3 (1992)	144,731,527
95.	Dr. Dolittle (1998)	144,156,609
96.	Saturday Night Fever (1977)	142,500,000
97.	The Fast and the Furious (2001)	142,154,015
98.	The Jungle Book (1967)	141,843,612
99.	National Lampoon's Animal House (1978)	141,600,000
100.	Pocahontas (1995)	141,579,773

THE TOP 100 BOX-OFFICE FILMS OF 2000

The Grinch stole the crown with the lowest total for a No. 1 film since 1997, while the second *Mission* was more than fulfilled, outpacing the original, and *Scary Movie* was the surprise of the summer. (Grosses are for U.S. and Canada box office, and are limited to the calendar year; starred films earned additional income in 1999.) (Source: *Variety*)

Rank	Film	B.O. Gross	Rank	Film	B.O. Gross
1.	Dr. Seuss' How the Grinch Stole Christmas	253,367,455	51.	Men of Honor	47,512,458
2.	Mission: Impossible 2	215,409,889	52.	Miss Congeniality	46,382,671
3.	Gladiator	186,724,777	53.	The Tigger Movie	45,554,533
4.	The Perfect Storm	182,618,434	54.	Frequency	45,010,278
5.	Meet the Parents	161,325,490	55.	The Replacements	44,737,059
6.	X-Men	157,299,718	56.	Galaxy Quest	44,268,116
7.	Scary Movie	157,019,771	57.	Pokemon The Movie 2000	43,758,684
8.	What Lies Beneath	155,370,362	58.	The Family Man	43,144,370
9.	Dinosaur	137,748,063	59.	The Talented Mr. Ripley*	41,526,616
10.	Erin Brockovich	125,595,205	60.	The Beach	39,785,027
11.	Nutty Professor II: The Klumps	123,307,945	61.	The Exorcist (rerelease)	39,671,011
12.	Charlie's Angels	122,802,761	62.	Pitch Black	39,240,659
13.	Big Momma's House	117,559,438	63.	Little Nicky	38,848,624
14.	What Women Want	115,761,883	64.	The Original Kings of Comedy	38,182,790
15.	Remember the Titans	113,746,040	65.	Autumn in New York	37,752,931
16.	The Patriot	113,302,500	66.	Bedazzled	37,519,291
17.	Cast Away	109,689,440	67.	28 Days	37,163,752
18.	Chicken Run	106,834,564	68.	Keeping the Faith	37,047,880
19.	Gone In Sixty Seconds	101,648,571	69.	Toy Story 2*	37,000,922
20.	Me, Myself & Irene	90,570,999	70.	Bounce	36,675,505
21.	Space Cowboys	90,179,885	71.	Hanging Up	36,050,230
22.	Unbreakable	90,033,796	72.	Dude, Where's My Car?	35,631,910
23.	Scream 3	89,143,175	73.	Flintstones in Viva Rock Vegas	35,268,275
24.	U-571	77,122,415	74.	The Skulls	35,046,320
25.	Hollow Man	73,209,340	75.	The 6th Day	34,317,634
26.	Rugrats in Paris: The Movie	71,205,699	76.	My Dog Skip	34,134,641
27.	Shaft	70,334,258	77.	Where the Heart Is	33,772,838
28.	Disney's The Kid	69,691,949	78.	Pay It Forward	32,966,043
29.	Road Trip	68,540,777	79.	Return to Me	32,675,636
30.	Bring It On	68,353,550	80.	Almost Famous	31,961,264
31.	Rules of Engagement	61,335,550	81.	The Legend of Bagger Vance	30,695,227
32.	The Cell	61,301,011	82.	The Art of War	30,208,599
33.	Mission to Mars	60,883,407	83.	Any Given Sunday*	29,778,713
34.	Coyote Ugly	60,786,269	84.	Bless the Child	29,381,494
35.	Stuart Little*	60,632,240	85.	Proof of Life	29,053,477
36.	The Green Mile*	60,119,360	86.	The Watcher	28,946,615
37.	Snow Day	60,020,107	87.	Girl, Interrupted*	28,472,405
38.	American Beauty*	59,078,786	88.	Love & Basketball	27,459,615
39.	102 Dalmatians	58,335,959	89.	High Fidelity	27,287,137
40.	Fantasia 2000*	58,140,856	90.	Book of Shadows: Blair Witch 2	26,437,094
41.	The Whole Nine Yards	57,262,492	91.	The Adventures of Rocky and Bullwinkle	26,005,820
42.	Next Friday	57,198,675	92.	Nurse Betty	25,167,271
43.	Shanghai Noon	56,937,502	93.	Reindeer Games	23,368,995
44.	Romeo Must Die	55,973,336	94.	Titan A.E.	22,753,426
45.	The Cider House Rules*	53,343,576	95.	Boys and Girls	21,799,622
46.	Final Destination	53,331,147	96.	Magnolia*	21,691,031
47.	Vertical Limit	51,880,114	97.	Wes Craven presents Dracula 2000	21,569,567
48.	The Road to El Dorado	50,863,742	98.	Battlefield Earth	21,471,685
49.	The Emperor's New Groove	50,812,284	99.	Urban Legends: Final Cut	21,468,807
50.	The Hurricane*	50,209,689	100.	Down to You	20,069,008

THE AMERICAN FILM INSTITUTE'S TOP 100

To celebrate 100 years of movie making (1896–1996), more than 1,500 ballots were sent to leaders in the industry (and a few outsiders, including President and Mrs. Clinton) to rank the top American films. Controversial outcome? You bet. See how your favorites match up with their list. Those in bold are also among PEOPLE's movie critic Leah Rozen's list of the best (see page 55).

1. **Citizen Kane** (1941)
2. **Casablanca** (1942)
3. **The Godfather** (1972)
4. **Gone With the Wind** (1939)
5. Lawrence of Arabia (1962)
6. **The Wizard of Oz** (1939)
7. **The Graduate** (1967)
8. On the Waterfront (1954)
9. **Schindler's List** (1993)
10. Singin' in the Rain (1952)
11. It's a Wonderful Life (1946)
12. **Sunset Boulevard** (1950)
13. The Bridge on the River Kwai (1957)
14. **Some Like It Hot** (1959)
15. Star Wars (1977)
16. **All About Eve** (1950)
17. **The African Queen** (1951)
18. **Psycho** (1960)
19. **Chinatown** (1974)
20. One Flew Over the Cuckoo's Nest (1975)
21. **The Grapes of Wrath** (1940)
22. **2001: A Space Odyssey** (1968)
23. **The Maltese Falcon** (1941)
24. **Raging Bull** (1980)
25. **E.T., the Extra-Terrestrial** (1982)
26. **Dr. Strangelove** (1964)
27. Bonnie and Clyde (1967)
28. Apocalypse Now (1979)
29. Mr. Smith Goes to Washington (1939)
30. The Treasure of Sierra Madre (1948)
31. Annie Hall (1977)
32. The Godfather Part II (1974)
33. **High Noon** (1952)
34. To Kill a Mockingbird (1962)
35. **It Happened One Night** (1934)
36. Midnight Cowboy (1969)
37. **The Best Years of Our Lives** (1946)
38. **Double Indemnity** (1944)
39. Doctor Zhivago (1965)
40. North by Northwest (1959)
41. West Side Story (1961)
42. **Rear Window** (1954)
43. King Kong (1933)
44. **The Birth of a Nation** (1915)
45. A Streetcar Named Desire (1951)
46. A Clockwork Orange (1971)
47. Taxi Driver (1976)
48. **Jaws** (1975)
49. **Snow White and the Seven Dwarfs** (1937)
50. **Butch Cassidy and the Sundance Kid** (1969)
51. The Philadelphia Story (1940)
52. From Here to Eternity (1953)
53. Amadeus (1984)
54. All Quiet on the Western Front (1930)
55. **The Sound of Music** (1965)
56. M*A*S*H (1970)
57. The Third Man (1949)
58. Fantasia (1940)
59. **Rebel Without a Cause** (1955)
60. Raiders of the Lost Ark (1981)
61. Vertigo (1958)
62. Tootsie (1982)
63. Stagecoach (1939)
64. Close Encounters of the Third Kind (1977)
65. The Silence of the Lambs (1991)
66. **Network** (1976)
67. **The Manchurian Candidate** (1962)
68. An American in Paris (1951)
69. **Shane** (1953)
70. The French Connection (1971)
71. Forrest Gump (1994)
72. Ben-Hur (1959)
73. Wuthering Heights (1939)
74. **The Gold Rush** (1925)
75. Dances with Wolves (1990)
76. City Lights (1931)
77. **American Graffiti** (1973)
78. Rocky (1976)
79. The Deer Hunter (1978)
80. **The Wild Bunch** (1969)
81. Modern Times (1936)
82. Giant (1956)
83. Platoon (1986)
84. Fargo (1996)
85. Duck Soup (1933)
86. Mutiny on the Bounty (1935)
87. **Frankenstein** (1931)
88. Easy Rider (1969)
89. Patton (1970)
90. The Jazz Singer (1927)
91. My Fair Lady (1964)
92. A Place in the Sun (1951)
93. The Apartment (1960)
94. GoodFellas (1990)
95. **Pulp Fiction** (1994)
96. **The Searchers** (1956)
97. **Bringing Up Baby** (1938)
98. **Unforgiven** (1992)
99. Guess Who's Coming to Dinner (1967)
100. Yankee Doodle Dandy (1942)

THE AMERICAN FILM INSTITUTE'S TOP 100 COMEDIES

Following up on their Top 100 list (see previous page), the American Film Institute celebrated the new millennium by listing the twentieth century's top comedies. Once again, film fans found omitted favorites to be no laughing matter; the AFI's Web site reported the voting public's favorite to be the unlisted *Porky's*. As before, the bolded films below are also among PEOPLE's movie critic Leah Rozen's list of the best (see page 55).

1. **Some Like It Hot** (1959)
2. Tootsie (1982)
3. **Dr. Strangelove or: How I Learned to Stop Worrying and Love the Bomb** (1964)
4. Annie Hall (1977)
5. Duck Soup (1933)
6. Blazing Saddles (1974)
7. M*A*S*H (1970)
8. **It Happened One Night** (1934)
9. **The Graduate** (1967)
10. Airplane! (1980)
11. The Producers (1968)
12. **A Night at the Opera** (1935)
13. Young Frankenstein (1974)
14. **Bringing Up Baby** (1938)
15. The Philadelphia Story (1940)
16. **Singin' in the Rain** (1952)
17. The Odd Couple (1968)
18. **The General** (1927)
19. **His Girl Friday** (1940)
20. The Apartment (1960)
21. A Fish Called Wanda (1988)
22. Adam's Rib (1949)
23. When Harry Met Sally (1989)
24. Born Yesterday (1950)
25. **The Gold Rush** (1925)
26. Being There (1979)
27. There's Something About Mary (1998)
28. Ghostbusters (1984)
29. **This Is Spinal Tap** (1984)
30. Arsenic and Old Lace (1944)
31. Raising Arizona (1987)
32. The Thin Man (1934)
33. Modern Times (1936)
34. Groundhog Day (1993)
35. Harvey (1950)
36. National Lampoon's Animal House (1978)
37. The Great Dictator (1940)
38. City Lights (1931)
39. Sullivan's Travels (1941)
40. It's a Mad, Mad, Mad, Mad World (1963)
41. Moonstruck (1987)
42. Big (1988)
43. **American Graffiti** (1973)
44. My Man Godfrey (1936)
45. Harold and Maude (1972)
46. Manhattan (1979)
47. Shampoo (1975)
48. A Shot in the Dark (1964)
49. To Be or Not to Be (1942)
50. Cat Ballou (1965)
51. The Seven Year Itch (1955)
52. Ninotchka (1939)
53. Arthur (1981)
54. The Miracle of Morgan's Creek (1944)
55. **The Lady Eve** (1941)
56. Abbott and Costello Meet Frankenstein (1948)
57. Diner (1982)
58. It's a Gift (1934)
59. A Day at the Races (1937)
60. Topper (1937)
61. What's Up, Doc? (1972)
62. Sherlock, Jr. (1924)
63. Beverly Hills Cop (1984)
64. Broadcast News (1987)
65. Horse Feathers (1932)
66. Take the Money and Run (1969)
67. Mrs. Doubtfire (1993)
68. The Awful Truth (1937)
69. Bananas (1971)
70. Mr. Deeds Goes to Town (1936)
71. Caddyshack (1980)
72. Mr. Blandings Builds His Dream House (1948)
73. Monkey Business (1931)
74. 9 to 5 (1980)
75. She Done Him Wrong (1933)
76. Victor/Victoria (1982)
77. The Palm Beach Story (1942)
78. Road to Morocco (1942)
79. The Freshman (1925)
80. Sleeper (1973)
81. The Navigator (1924)
82. Private Benjamin (1980)
83. Father of the Bride (1950)
84. Lost in America (1985)
85. Dinner at Eight (1933)
86. City Slickers (1991)
87. Fast Times at Ridgemont High (1982)
88. Beetlejuice (1988)
89. The Jerk (1979)
90. Woman of the Year (1942)
91. The Heartbreak Kid (1972)
92. Ball of Fire (1941)
93. Fargo (1996)
94. Auntie Mame (1958)
95. Silver Streak (1976)
96. Sons of the Desert (1933)
97. **Bull Durham** (1988)
98. The Court Jester (1956)
99. The Nutty Professor (1963)
100. Good Morning, Vietnam (1987)

HOLLYWOOD'S FOOTPRINTS OF FAME

The first footprints at Grauman's Chinese Theater, as it was originally called, were made by Norma Talmadge in 1927 when, legend holds, she accidentally stepped in wet concrete outside the building. Since then over 190 stars have been immortalized, along with their hands and feet—and sometimes noses (Jimmy Durante), fists (John Wayne), and legs (Betty Grable). This year, legendary actor Anthony Hopkins became the newest member of this elite group of stars. The full Forecourt of the Stars at Mann's includes:

Abbott & Costello
Don Ameche
Julie Andrews
Edward Arnold
Fred Astaire
Gene Autry
John Barrymore
Freddie Bartholomew
Anne Baxter
Warren Beatty
Wallace Beery
Jack Benny
Edgar Bergen
Joan Blondell
Humphrey Bogart
Charles Boyer
Joe E. Brown
Yul Brynner
George Burns
Cantinflas
Eddie Cantor
Jim Carrey
Jackie Chan
Maurice Chevalier
Sean Connery
Gary Cooper
Jackie Cooper
Jeanne Crain
Joan Crawford
Bing Crosby
Tom Cruise
Robert Daly
Bebe Daniels
Linda Darnell
Marion Davies
Bette Davis
Doris Day
Olivia de Havilland
Cecil B. DeMille
The Dionne Quintuplets
Kirk Douglas
Michael Douglas
Marie Dressler
Donald Duck
Irene Dunne
Jimmie Durante
Deanna Durbin
Clint Eastwood
Nelson Eddy
Douglas Fairbanks
Alice Faye

Rhonda Fleming
Henry Fonda
Joan Fontaine
Harrison Ford
Clark Gable
Ava Gardner
Judy Garland
Greer Garson
Janet Gaynor
Richard Gere
Mel Gibson
Danny Glover
Whoopi Goldberg
Betty Grable
Cary Grant
Johnny Grant
Rosa Grauman (founder Sid
    Grauman's mother)
Sid Grauman
Tom Hanks
Ann Harding
Jean Harlow
Rex Harrison
William S. Hart
Susan Hayward
Rita Hayworth
Van Heflin
Sonja Henie
Jean Hersholt
William F. "Bill" Hertz
Charlton Heston
Bob Hope
Anthony Hopkins
Ron Howard
Rock Hudson
George Jessel
Van Johnson
Al Jolson
Danny Kaye
Michael Keaton
Gene Kelly
Deborah Kerr
Alan Ladd
Dorothy Lamour
Charles Laughton
Jack Lemmon
Mervyn LeRoy
Harold Lloyd
Sophia Loren
Myrna Loy
George Lucas

William Lundigan
Jeanette MacDonald
Ali MacGraw
Shirley MacLaine
Victor McLaglen
Steve McQueen
Fredric March
Dean Martin
Tony Martin
The Marx Brothers
James Mason
Marcello Mastroianni
Walter Matthau
Lauritz Melchior
Ray Milland
Hayley Mills
Carmen Miranda
Tom Mix
Marilyn Monroe
Colleen Moore
Eddie Murphy
George Murphy
Hildegarde Neff
Pola Negri
Paul Newman
Jack Nicholson
Jack Oakie
Margaret O'Brien
Donald O'Connor
Al Pacino
Louella Parsons
Gregory Peck
Mary Pickford
Ezio Pinza
Sidney Poitier
Dick Powell
Eleanor Powell
William Powell
Tyrone Power
Anthony Quinn
George Raft
Burt Reynolds
Debbie Reynolds
The Ritz Brothers
Edward G. Robinson
May Robson
Ginger Rogers
Roy Rogers
Mickey Rooney
Jane Russell
Rosalind Russell

Susan Sarandon
Arnold Schwarzenegger
Steven Seagal
Peter Sellers
Terry Semel
Norma Shearer
Jean Simmons
Frank Sinatra
Red Skelton
Steven Spielberg
Sylvester Stallone
Barbara Stanwyck
Star Trek crew (William
    Shatner, Leonard Nimoy,
    DeForest Kelley, James
    Doohan, Michelle Nichols,
    George Takei, Walter Koenig)
Star Wars characters
George Stevens
Jimmy Stewart
Meryl Streep
Gloria Swanson
Constance Talmadge
Norma Talmadge
Elizabeth Taylor
Robert Taylor
Shirley Temple
Danny Thomas
Gene Tierney
John Travolta
Lana Turner
Rudy Vallee
Dick Van Dyke
W. S. Van Dyke
Raoul Walsh
Denzel Washington
John Wayne
Clifton Webb
Oskar Werner
Richard Widmark
Esther Williams
Robin Williams
Bruce Willis
Jane Withers
Natalie Wood
Joanne Woodward
Monty Woolley
Jane Wyman
Diana Wynyard
Loretta Young
Robert Zemeckis

THE BIGGEST HITS, YEAR BY YEAR

Historically "rentals" (the amount of money collected by the studio), not box-office grosses, were the measure of hits. The following are the top five movies of the year based on data from *Variety*, beginning with 1939, when a Hollywood legend, *Gone With the Wind*, hit the theaters. (Figures for 1941 films, with the exception of *Sergeant York*, are rough estimates.)

1939

1. Gone With the Wind	$77,641,106
2. The Wizard of Oz	4,544,851
3. The Hunchback of Notre Dame (tie)	1,500,000
3. Jesse James (tie)	1,500,000
3. Mr. Smith Goes to Washington (tie)	1,500,000

1940

1. Fantasia	$41,660,000
2. Pinocchio	40,442,000
3. Boom Town	4,586,415
4. Rebecca (tie)	1,500,000
4. Santa Fe Trail (tie)	1,500,000

1941

1. Sergeant York	$6,135,707
2. Dive Bomber (tie)	1,500,000
2. Honky Tonk (tie)	1,500,000
2. The Philadelphia Story (tie)	1,500,000
2. A Yank in the R.A.F. (tie)	1,500,000

1942

1. Bambi	$47,265,000
2. Mrs. Miniver	5,390,009
3. Yankee Doodle Dandy	4,719,681
4. Random Harvest	4,665,501
5. Casablanca	4,145,178

1943

1. This Is the Army	$8,301,000
2. For Whom the Bell Tolls	7,100,000
3. The Outlaw	5,075,000
4. The Song of Bernadette	5,000,000
5. Stage Door Canteen	4,339,532

1944

1. Going My Way	$6,500.000
2. Meet Me in St. Louis	5,132,202
3. Since You Went Away	4,924,756
4. 30 Seconds over Tokyo	4,471,080
5. White Cliffs of Dover	4,045,250

1945

1. The Bells of St. Mary's	$8,000,000
2. Leave Her to Heaven	5,500,000
3. Spellbound	4,970,583
4. Anchors Aweigh	4,778,679
5. The Valley of Decision	4,566,374

1946

1. Song of the South	$29,228,717
2. The Best Years of Our Lives (tie)	11,300,000
2. Duel in the Sun (tie)	11,300,000
4. The Jolson Story	7,600,000
5. Blue Skies	5,700,000

1947

1. Welcome Stranger	$6,100,000
2. The Egg and I	5,500,000
3. Unconquered	5,250,000
4. Life with Father	5,057,000
5. Forever Amber	5,000,000

1948

1. The Red Shoes	$5,000,000
2. Red River	4,506,825
3. The Paleface	4,500,000
4. The Three Musketeers	4,306,876
5. Johnny Belinda	4,266,000

1949

1. Samson and Delilah	$11,500,000
2. Battleground	5,051,143
3. Jolson Sings Again (tie)	5,000,000
3. The Sands of Iwo Jima (tie)	5,000,000
5. I Was a Male War Bride	4,100,000

1950

1. Cinderella	$41,087,000
2. King Solomon's Mines	5,586,000
3. Annie Get Your Gun	4,919,394
4. Cheaper by the Dozen	4,425,000
5. Father of the Bride	4,054,405

1951

1. Quo Vadis?	$11,901,662
2. Alice in Wonderland	7,196,000
3. Show Boat	5,533,000
4. David and Bathsheba	4,720,000
5. The Great Caruso	4,531,000

1952

1. This Is Cinerama	$15,400,000
2. The Greatest Show on Earth	14,000,000
3. The Snows of Kilimanjaro	6,500,000
4. Ivanhoe	6,258,000
5. Hans Christian Andersen	6,000,000

1953

1. Peter Pan	$37,584,000
2. The Robe	17,500,000
3. From Here to Eternity	12,200,000
4. Shane	9,000,000
5. How To Marry a Millionaire	7,300,000

1954

1. White Christmas	$12,000,000
2. 20,000 Leagues Under the Sea	11,267,000
3. Rear Window	9,812,271
4. The Caine Mutiny	8,700,000
5. The Glenn Miller Story	7,590,994

1955

1. Lady and the Tramp	$40,249,000
2. Cinerama Holiday	12,000,000
3. Mister Roberts	8,500,000
4. Battle Cry	8,100,000
5. Oklahoma!	7,100,000

1956

1. The Ten Commandments	$43,000,000
2. Around the World in 80 Days	23,120,000
3. Giant	14,000,000
4. Seven Wonders of the World	12,500,000
5. The King and I	8,500,000

1957

1. The Bridge on the River Kwai	$17,195,000
2. Peyton Place	11,500,000
3. Sayonara	10,500,000
4. Old Yeller	10,050,000
5. Raintree County	5,962,839

1958

1. South Pacific	$17,500,000
2. Auntie Mame	9,300,000
3. Cat on a Hot Tin Roof	8,785,162
4. No Time for Sergeants	7,500,000
5. Gigi	7,321.423

1959

1. Ben-Hur	$36,992,088
2. Sleeping Beauty	21,998,000
3. The Shaggy Dog	12,317,000
4. Operation Petticoat	9,321,555
5. Darby O'Gill and the Little People	8,336,000

1960

1. Swiss Family Robinson	$20,178,000
2. Psycho	11,200,000
3. Spartacus	10,300,454
4. Exodus	8,331,582
5. The Alamo	7,918,776

1961

1. 101 Dalmatians	$68,648,000
2. West Side Story	19,645,570
3. The Guns of Navarone	13,000,000
4. El Cid	12,000,000
5. The Absent-Minded Professor	11,426,000

1962

1. How the West Was Won	$20,932,883
2. Lawrence of Arabia	20,310,000
3. The Longest Day	17,600,000
4. In Search of the Castaways	9,975,000
5. The Music Man	8,100,000

1963

1. Cleopatra	$26,000,000
2. It's a Mad, Mad, Mad, Mad World	20,849,786
3. Tom Jones	16,925,988
4. Irma La Douce	11,921,784
5. The Sword in the Stone	10,475,000

1964

1. Mary Poppins	$45,000,000
2. Goldfinger	22,997,706
3. The Carpetbaggers	15,500,000
4. My Fair Lady	12,000,000
5. From Russia with Love	9,924,279

1965

1. The Sound of Music	$79,975,000
2. Doctor Zhivago	47,116,811
3. Thunderball	28,621,434
4. Those Magnificent Men in Their Flying Machines	14,000,000
5. That Darn Cat	12,628,000

1966

1. Hawaii	$15,553,018
2. The Bible	15,000,000
3. Who's Afraid of Virginia Woolf?	14,500,000
4. A Man for All Seasons	12,750,000
5. Lt. Robin Crusoe, USN	10,164,000

1967

1. The Jungle Book	$60,964,000
2. The Graduate	44,090,729
3. Guess Who's Coming to Dinner	25,500,000
4. Bonnie and Clyde	22,800,000
5. The Dirty Dozen	20,403,826

1968

1. Funny Girl	$26,325,000
2. 2001: A Space Odyssey	25,521,917
3. The Odd Couple	20,000,000
4. Bullitt	19,000,000
5. Romeo and Juliet	17,473,000

1969

1. Butch Cassidy and the Sundance Kid	$46,039,000
2. The Love Bug	23,150,000
3. Midnight Cowboy	20,499,282
4. Easy Rider	19,100,000
5. Hello, Dolly!	15,200,000

1970

1. Love Story	$50,000,000
2. Airport	45,220,118
3. M*A*S*H	36,720,000
4. Patton	28,100,000
5. The Aristocats	26,462,000

1971

1. Fiddler on the Roof	$38,251,196
2. Billy Jack	32,500,000
3. The French Connection	26,315,000
4. Summer of '42	20,500,000
5. Diamonds Are Forever	19,726,829

1972

1. The Godfather	$86,691,000
2. The Poseidon Adventure	42,000,000
3. What's Up Doc?	28,000,000
4. Deliverance	22,600,000
5. Jeremiah Johnson	21,900,000

1973

1. The Exorcist	$89,000,000
2. The Sting	78,212,000
3. American Graffiti	55,128,175
4. Papillon	22,500,000
5. The Way We Were	22,457,000

1974

1. The Towering Inferno	$52,000,000
2. Blazing Saddles	47,800,000
3. Young Frankenstein	38,823,000
4. Earthquake	35,849,994
5. The Trial of Billy Jack	31,100,000

1975

1. Jaws	$129,549,325
2. One Flew over the Cuckoo's Nest	59,939,701
3. The Rocky Horror Picture Show	49,782,690
4. Shampoo	23,822,000
5. Dog Day Afternoon	22,500,000

1976

1. Rocky	$56,524,972
2. A Star Is Born	37,100,000
3. King Kong	36,915,000
4. Silver Streak	30,018,000
5. All the President's Men	30,000,000

1977

1. Star Wars	$270,918,000
2. Close Encounters of the Third Kind	82,750,000
3. Saturday Night Fever	74,100,000
4. Smokey and the Bandit	58,949,939
5. The Goodbye Girl	41,839,170

1978

1. Grease	$96,300,000
2. Superman	82,800,000
3. National Lampoon's Animal House	70,826,000
4. Every Which Way but Loose	51,900,000
5. Jaws 2	50,431,964

1979

1. Kramer vs. Kramer	$59,986,335
2. Star Trek: The Motion Picture	56,000,000
3. The Jerk	42,989,656
4. Rocky II	42,169,387
5. Alien	40,300,000

1980

1. The Empire Strikes Back	$173,814,000
2. 9 to 5	59,100,000
3. Stir Crazy	58,364,420
4. Airplane!	40,610,000
5. Any Which Way You Can	40,500,000

1981

1. Raiders of the Lost Ark	$115,598,000
2. Superman II	65,100,000
3. On Golden Pond	61,174,744
4. Arthur	42,000,000
5. Stripes	40,886,589

1982

1. E.T., the Extra-Terrestrial	$228,168,939
2. Tootsie	96,292,736
3. Rocky III	66,262,796
4. An Officer and a Gentleman	55,223,000
5. Porky's	54,000,000

1983

1. Return of the Jedi	$191,648,000
2. Terms of Endearment	50,250,000
3. Trading Places	40,600,000
4. WarGames	38,519,833
5. Superman III	37,200,000

1984

1. Ghostbusters	$130,211,324
2. Indiana Jones and the Temple of Doom	109,000,000
3. Beverly Hills Cop	108,000,000
4. Gremlins	79,500,000
5. The Karate Kid	43,432,881

1985

1. Back to the Future	$104,408,738
2. Rambo: First Blood Part II	78,919,250
3. Rocky IV	76,023,246
4. The Color Purple	47,900,000
5. Out of Africa	43,103,469

1986

1. Top Gun	$79,400,000
2. "Crocodile" Dundee	70,227,000
3. Platoon	69,742,143
4. The Karate Kid, Part II	58,362,026
5. Star Trek IV: The Voyage Home	56,820,071

1987

1. Three Men and a Baby	$81,313,000
2. Beverly Hills Cop II	80,857,776
3. Fatal Attraction	70,000,000
4. Good Morning, Vietnam	58,103,000
5. The Untouchables	36,866,530

1988

1. Rain Man	$86,813,000
2. Who Framed Roger Rabbit	81,244,000
3. Coming to America	65,000,000
4. "Crocodile" Dundee II	57,300,000
5. Twins	57,715,127

1989

1. Batman	$150,500,000
2. Indiana Jones and the Last Crusade	115,500,000
3. Lethal Weapon 2	79,500,000
4. Back to the Future Part II	72,319,630
5. Honey, I Shrunk the Kids	72,007,000

1990

1. Home Alone	$140,099,000
2. Ghost	98,200,000
3. Pretty Woman	81,905,530
4. Dances with Wolves	81,537,971
5. Teenage Mutant Ninja Turtles	67,650,000

1991

1. Terminator 2: Judgment Day	$112,500,000
2. Robin Hood: Prince of Thieves	86,000,000
3. Beauty and the Beast	69,415,000
4. Hook	65,000,000
5. City Slickers	60,750,000

1992

1. Aladdin	$111,740,683
2. Home Alone 2: Lost in New York	103,377,614
3. Batman Returns	100,100,000
4. Lethal Weapon 3	80,000,000
5. A Few Good Men	71,000,000

1993

1. Jurassic Park	$212,953,437
2. Mrs. Doubtfire	111,000,000
3. The Fugitive	97,000,000
4. The Firm	77,047,044
5. Sleepless in Seattle	64,930,137

1994

1. The Lion King	$173,057,366
2. Forrest Gump	156,000,000
3. True Lies	80,000,000
4. The Santa Clause	74,348,689
5. The Flintstones	70,753,383

1995

1. Batman Forever	$105,100,000
2. Toy Story	103,200,000
3. Apollo 13	92,642,370
4. Pocahontas	67,848,010
5. Casper	49,160,810

1996

1. Independence Day	$177,190,000
2. Twister	133,464,330
3. Mission: Impossible	93,067,933
4. Jerry Maguire	74,937,042
5. The Rock	70,600,000

1997

1. The Lost World: Jurassic Park	$130,086,760
2. Men in Black	114,110,497
3. Liar Liar	95,931,900
4. Air Force One	77,734,801
5. Batman & Robin	58,492,667

1998

1. Titanic	$324,425,520
2. Armageddon	104,806,521
3. Saving Private Ryan	89,619,599
4. There's Something About Mary	74,537,493
5. Godzilla	70,850,116

THE 100 BEST MOVIES OF ALL TIME

They are the celluloid touchstones of our inner life, the enduring echoes of various generations, and the most bittersweet of social commentaries played out 10 yards high. PEOPLE's movie critic Leah Rozen has selected 100 of the greatest, an assignment as agonizing as having to pick the 10 greatest home runs ever hit in baseball.

ADAM'S RIB (1949)
Katharine Hepburn and Spencer Tracy as married attorneys on opposite sides of an attempted murder case. The smartest and funniest of their five pairings.

THE ADVENTURES OF ROBIN HOOD (1938)
There have been other Robin Hoods, including Kevin Costner and Sean Connery, but never one as appealingly roguish as Errol Flynn. A rousing adventure.

THE AFRICAN QUEEN (1951)
In a splendidly comic and sweet romance, the mismatched Humphrey Bogart and Katharine Hepburn take a slow love boat up the river in steamy Africa.

ALL ABOUT EVE (1950)
Smart and tart. Director-writer Joseph Mankiewicz's acerbic masterpiece about theater folk, with Bette Davis at her caustic best.

AMERICAN GRAFFITI (1973)
In George Lucas's influential hit film, a group of California teenagers, including Ron Howard and Richard Dreyfuss, spend one long night in 1962 cruising in cars and goofing off.

BACK STREET (1941)
A vintage weepie about a woman who gives up everything for love. This second of three filmed versions of Fannie Hurst's potboiler shines brightly thanks to the incomparable Margaret Sullavan and Charles Boyer.

BADLANDS (1973)
Martin Sheen and Sissy Spacek play a young couple who go on an aimless killing spree in a chilling cult film by director Terence Malick.

BEAUTY AND THE BEAST (1946)
French surrealist Jean Cocteau's sophisticated version of the classic fairy tale *La Belle et la bete* is for grown-up romantics. Then again, the 1991 Disney version, a musical, is pretty swell too.

BELLE DE JOUR (1967)
Director Luis Buñuel's deliciously creepy movie about a bourgeois Paris housewife, a radiant Catherine Deneuve, who spends her days working in a brothel. Or does she?

THE BEST YEARS OF OUR LIVES (1946)
A moving drama about the domestic and occupational difficulties facing three returning World War II vets, with Fredric March, Dana Andrews, and Harold Russell, a real vet who had lost both arms in the war.

THE BICYCLE THIEF (1948)
Director Vittorio de Sica's heartbreaking drama, a linchpin of Italian neo-realism, about a workman who loses everything when his bicycle is stolen.

THE BIRTH OF A NATION (1915)
The first blockbuster. Although parts now seem irredeemably racist, director D. W. Griffith's epic Civil War drama is still a sight to behold.

BLADE RUNNER (1982)
The future as you don't want it to be. Gruff guy Harrison Ford stars in director Ridley Scott's great-looking sci-fi drama.

BRINGING UP BABY (1938)
A ditzy Katharine Hepburn sets her sights on zoology professor Cary Grant in a delightful screwball comedy. And love that tiger.

BULL DURHAM (1988)
A great romance movie disguised as a baseball picture. Susan Sarandon gets to choose between minor leaguers Kevin Costner and Tim Robbins, both of whom pitch woo her way.

BUTCH CASSIDY AND THE SUNDANCE KID (1969)
In one of the all-time cool buddy movies, Paul Newman and Robert Redford display big star charisma and charm as gallivanting outlaws.

CAGED (1949)
If you see just one women-in-prison film, make it this one. Eleanor Parker stars as the good girl gone wrong.

CASABLANCA (1942)
A kiss is still a kiss, but the ones here have real staying power. This is Hollywood movie-making at its most stylishly satisfying, with Humphrey Bogart and Ingrid Bergman.

CHINATOWN (1974)
Jack Nicholson's nose gets sliced and lots of other nasty things happen in director Roman Polanski's jaundiced thriller set in '30s Los Angeles.

CITIZEN KANE (1941)
The granddaddy of all biopics, though innovative director-star Orson Welles had to change the name from William Randolph Hearst to Charles Foster Kane. A must-see for anyone interested in movies.

THE CROWD (1928)
This silent movie, directed by King Vidor, movingly depicts the everyday life of a young white-collar worker and his wife in New

York City. It shows just how fluid and powerful the images in silent film had become right before sound took over.

DAVID COPPERFIELD (1934)
A perfect film adaptation of Charles Dickens's novel about the adventures of an orphaned youth. W. C. Fields is a hoot as Mr. Micawber.

DAY FOR NIGHT (1973)
French director François Truffaut's valentine to movie-making contains sly references and in-jokes to many of his earlier films. With Jacqueline Bisset and Jean-Pierre Léaud.

DEAD MAN WALKING (1995)
No matter where you stand on the death penalty, this powerful drama scores in telling the story of a nun (Susan Sarandon) who guides a murderer (Sean Penn) to contrition before his execution. Tim Robbins directed.

DO THE RIGHT THING (1989)
Director Spike Lee's street-smart drama about one very hot summer day in a tense Brooklyn neighborhood has plenty to say about race relations and the need for more and better communication.

DOUBLE INDEMNITY (1944)
Barbara Stanwyck, at her bad-girl best, sweet-talks Fred MacMurray into helping her kill her husband. Billy Wilder directed.

DR. STRANGELOVE… (1962)
A savagely funny black comedy, though it's a tad dated now, about the nuclear bomb and world politics. Stanley Kubrick directed and Peter Sellers and George C. Scott star.

THE EMPIRE STRIKES BACK (1980)
The best of the *Star Wars* trilogy. Stars Harrison Ford, Carrie Fisher, and Mark Hamill.

E.T., THE EXTRA-TERRESTRIAL (1982)
It may be simple-minded and sentimental, but who can resist this sweet tale of the friendship between a suburban youth and an alien marooned on Earth?

FRANKENSTEIN (1931)
Still the eeriest, and most humane, version of Mary Wollstonecraft Shelley's classic monster tale. With Boris Karloff as the big guy.

THE GENERAL (1926)
Buster Keaton, one of the comic glories of the silent era, piles on brilliant sight gag after sight gag in this Civil War comedy.

THE GODFATHER (1972)
A family drama about the troubled and violent Corleone clan. Director Francis Ford Coppola, with the help of Marlon Brando, James Caan, and a very young Al Pacino, made the ultimate gangster film.

THE GOLD RUSH (1925)
Charlie Chaplin's little tramp seeks his fortune in the Yukon. Watch for the justly famous shoe-eating scene in which Chaplin twirls shoelaces with a fork as if eating spaghetti.

GONE WITH THE WIND (1939)
This Civil War–era drama is big and long and we wouldn't change a minute of it. Except maybe the ending. But, tomorrow's another day, and maybe Rhett will come back then. With Clark Gable and Vivien Leigh.

THE GRADUATE (1968)
In a wonderfully wry comedy, Dustin Hoffman passes his first summer after college floating in his parents' pool and having a desultory affair with Anne Bancroft. Nearly 30 years later, this one still seems fresh.

THE GRAPES OF WRATH (1940)
Director John Ford's masterful adaptation of John Steinbeck's bleak novel about depression-era Oklahomans who head off for what they hope will be a better life in California. With Henry Fonda and Jane Darwell.

A HARD DAY'S NIGHT (1964)
The swinging '60s encapsulated, minus the politics. This first Beatles film is flat-out zany fun.

HIGH NOON (1952)
The Western pared to its bone. With Gary Cooper as the principled lawman who has to go it alone against the bad guys.

HIS GIRL FRIDAY (1940)
Speed is of the essence in this newspaper comedy, with Rosalind Russell and Cary Grant competing to see who can insult the other faster.

HOLIDAY INN (1942)
When Bing Crosby starts singing "White Christmas," you just know it's going to snow in time. Crosby and Fred Astaire costar in this chipper musical as the owners of a hotel where they put on shows with holiday themes.

HUD (1963)
Paul Newman as one of the screen's first anti-heroes, an amoral cowboy who brings no good to all whom he touches. With Melvyn Douglas and Patricia Neal.

INVASION OF THE BODY SNATCHERS (1955)
Low-budget, paranoid '50s sci-fi allegory about aliens taking over residents of a small town. The '78 remake can't hold a pod to it.

IT HAPPENED ONE NIGHT (1934)
Screwball comedy meets road picture in director Frank Capra's jaunty film about a runaway heiress who spars and sparks with a newspaperman. With Claudette Colbert and Clark Gable.

JAWS (1975)
Jumbo shark on the loose. Director Steven Spielberg scored his first blockbuster with this bloody thriller. Dig John Williams's carnivorous score.

THE LADY EVE (1941)

Wickedly entertaining comedy by director Preston Sturges about a con woman (Barbara Stanwyck) who hustles a youthful million-aire (Henry Fonda), only to realize almost too late that she's actually in love with the big lug.

THE LAST METRO (1980)

A moving drama about a French theatrical troupe in occupied Paris during World War II. François Truffaut directed, and Catherine Deneuve and Gérard Depardieu star.

LONE STAR (1996)

Director John Sayles's sweeping drama about fathers and sons, the past catching up to us, and cultural diversity, all crammed into the lives of folks in one small Texas border town.

LONG DAY'S JOURNEY INTO NIGHT (1962)

Playwright Eugene O'Neill's autobiographical masterpiece, brought to the screen with all the hurt showing. Katharine Hepburn digs deep as the morphine-addicted mother. Also stars Ralph Richardson and Jason Robards.

LONGTIME COMPANION (1990)

An AIDS drama about a tight-knit group of male friends in New York City in the 1980s which poignantly depicts just how devastating the disease is to both those who have it and those they leave behind.

MCCABE AND MRS. MILLER (1971)

Director Robert Altman's lyrically haunting look at how the West was wasted, with Warren Beatty as a gunfighter who sets up a brothel and Julie Christie as his opium-addicted madam.

THE MALTESE FALCON (1941)

Love that black bird. With Humphrey Bogart as private eye Sam Spade, who takes no guff from anyone, including conniving Mary Astor.

THE MANCHURIAN CANDIDATE (1962)

A sharp-witted political thriller, from which one suspects Oliver Stone learned much of what he knows. With Frank Sinatra, Laurence Harvey, and Angela Lansbury.

MEAN STREETS (1973)

Loyalty among thieves only goes so far, as a group of boyhood friends in Little Italy discover upon growing up. Martin Scors-ese's breakthrough film, with Robert De Niro and Harvey Keitel.

MILDRED PIERCE (1945)

The ultimate Joan Crawford movie. She plays a suburban divorcée who makes a fortune as a hard-working restaurateur, only to see her spoiled daughter steal her beau.

NETWORK (1976)

Biliousness raised to high art. Paddy Chayefsky's sharp satire about the influence of the media. With Peter Finch, William Holden, and Faye Dunaway.

A NIGHT AT THE OPERA (1935)

The Marx Brothers reek loony havoc when—and before and after—the fat lady sings. Also stars Margaret Dumont, the matronly butt of so many of Groucho's jokes.

NIGHTS OF CABIRIA (1957)

Italian director Federico Fellini, in directing wife Giuletta Masina in her greatest role as a hard-luck prostitute in Rome, made a near-perfect film that will have you laughing one minute, near tears the next. The musical *Sweet Charity* is based on *Cabiria*.

NOTORIOUS (1946)

Alfred Hitchcock at his perversely romantic best. Sexy and scary, with American agent Cary Grant sending lady love Ingrid Bergman to wed a covert Nazi.

PERSONA (1966)

The personalities of two women, a nurse and the mentally ill patient she is caring for, begin to overlap and mesh in Swedish filmmaker Ingmar Bergman's brooding, disturbing drama. With Liv Ullmann and Bibi Andersson.

PICNIC AT HANGING ROCK (1975)

Spooky goings-on at a girls' school in turn-of-the-century Australia when several of the students mysteriously vanish, seemingly into thin air, while at a picnic. Peter Weir directed.

PLACES IN THE HEART (1984)

A lovely movie about human frailty and redemption from director Robert Benton. Sally Field stars as a newly widowed Texas farm woman who perseveres despite hard times.

THE PLAYER (1992)

Director Robert Altman zings Hollywood in a biting satire about a studio executive who gets away with murder. Tim Robbins has the lead, but masses of other big names show up for cameos.

PSYCHO (1960)

Janet Leigh, get away from that shower. Hitchcock's scalding shocker stars Tony Perkins as a twisted hotel keeper who doesn't like his guests to check out.

PULP FICTION (1994)

Violent, amusing, and cleverly structured, director Quentin Tarantino's movie is vastly more entertaining than the horde of imitations it has spawned. With John Travolta, Bruce Willis, and Samuel L. Jackson.

THE PURPLE ROSE OF CAIRO (1984)

When the hero (Jeff Daniels) of a '30s movie steps out of the screen to begin making time with one of his biggest fans (Mia Farrow), the line between real life during the depression and movie fantasy becomes all too clear in Woody Allen's comic masterpiece.

QUEEN CHRISTINA (1937)

Greta Garbo is at her most androgynously alluring in a romanticized Hollywood biopic about a 17th-century Swedish queen. Check out Garbo's enigmatic expression in the famous final shot.

THE QUIET MAN (1952)

John Wayne and director John Ford left the Wild West behind for the greener fields of Ireland, with splendid results. In this boisterous, appealing love story, Wayne plays an American boxer who woos Irish lass Maureen O'Hara.

RAGING BULL (1980)

Director Martin Scorsese's penetrating look at the troubled life of pugilist Jake La Motta boasts one of Robert De Niro's finest performances.

RASHOMON (1950)

Truth proves elusive as four people involved each give differing accounts of a rapemurder in Japanese director Akira Kurosawa's brilliant drama.

REAR WINDOW (1954)

James Stewart and a sexy Grace Kelly star in Alfred Hitchcock's sophisticated thriller about an invalided photographer who spots a murder across his apartment courtyard.

REBEL WITHOUT A CAUSE (1955)

Alienated teens reign supreme as James Dean—who died before the movie was released—and Natalie Wood express the suffering of their generation.

ROMAN HOLIDAY (1953)

A charming romp with Audrey Hepburn at her most appealingly gamine as a princess who ditches her royal duties and takes up with Gregory Peck, an American newspaperman.

SAVING PRIVATE RYAN (1998)

War is hell, and never more so than in director Steven Spielberg's monumental film about a group of American soldiers who land in France on D-Day. Tom Hanks's final command, "Earn this," haunts us still.

SCHINDLER'S LIST (1983)

Director Steven Spielberg's powerful retelling of the story of businessman Oskar Schindler, who saved hundreds of Jews from the Nazi gas chambers during World War II. With Liam Neeson as Schindler and Ben Kingsley as his Jewish factory foreman.

THE SEARCHERS (1956)

In a multilayered Western by director John Ford, John Wayne spends years searching for his niece, Natalie Wood, after she is captured by Native Americans. One of the most influential films ever made.

SHANE (1953)

A retired gunfighter rides into town and helps out a homesteading couple and their young son. Sounds simple, but it's anything but. With Alan Ladd, Jean Arthur, and Brandon de Wilde.

THE SHOP AROUND THE CORNER (1940)

The famed "Lubitsch Touch," so named for the sophisticated comedy work of director Ernst Lubitsch, shines bright in a charming romance about two bickering shop clerks. With Jimmy Stewart and the matchless Margaret Sullavan.

SHOWBOAT (1936)

This classic musical about life aboard a Mississippi riverboat features dandy Jerome Kern tunes and a glimpse of why Paul Robeson and Helen Morgan were such electrifying performers in their day.

SINGIN' IN THE RAIN (1952)

A musical about Hollywood's awkward transition from silents to talkies, this one can't be beat, especially for Gene Kelly's singing and dancing of the damp title number.

SNOW WHITE AND THE SEVEN DWARFS (1937)

Walt Disney's first feature-length animated feature still shimmers brightly, though Snow White's brusque farewell to the dwarfs at the movie's end seems a mite ungrateful.

SOME LIKE IT HOT (1959)

The funniest movie ever made about cross-dressing. Tony Curtis and Jack Lemmon star as musicians who, after witnessing a mob hit, go undercover with an all-girl band, whose members include Marilyn Monroe. Billy Wilder directed.

THE SOUND OF MUSIC (1965)

Sure, it's sugary, but any time Julie Andrews is on screen in this Rogers and Hammerstein musical about the would-be nun who comes to stay with the Von Trapp family, all is gloriously forgiven.

SULLIVAN'S TRAVELS (1941)

A Hollywood director (Joel McCrea) rediscovers the meaning of life while traveling across America in director Preston Sturges's quick-witted comedy.

SUNSET BOULEVARD (1950)

The original. In director Billy Wilder's savage look at the underbelly of Hollywood, silent star Gloria Swanson made her big comeback playing, appropriately enough, a silent star hoping to make a comeback.

SWEET SMELL OF SUCCESS (1957)

Everyone's corrupt or corruptible in this atmospheric melodrama about nasty dealings between a Broadway press agent (Tony Curtis) and a powerful Manhattan newspaper columnist (Burt Lancaster).

TARZAN AND HIS MATE (1934)

The second of the Johnny

Weismuller films about Edgar Rice Borroughs' ape man, and the best of the series. Maureen O'Sullivan, dressed in next to nothing, makes a perky Jane.

THE TERMINATOR (1984)
Pure nihilistic fun, this sci-fi action thriller deservedly made muscleman Arnold Schwarzenegger, who plays a singularly focused android, into a big star.

THELMA AND LOUISE (1991)
Two good girls go wrong. A feminist firecracker of a movie, with strong performances by Susan Sarandon and Geena Davis. And check out the truly buff Brad Pitt.

THIS IS SPINAL TAP (1984)
This is a blast. Turn your amps up to 11 as you chuckle your way through this comic moc-umentary about a heavy metal rock group and its hangers-on. Rob Reiner directed.

TITANIC (1997)
For sheer scope and size, you gotta love it. Director James Cameron made going to the movies seem like something special again. This water-logged drama turned Leonardo DiCaprio into a household name—at least in households containing teenage girls.

TO HAVE AND HAVE NOT (1944)
Romantic sparks fly in Humprey Bogart and Lauren Bacall's first pairing, a World War II drama that borrows more than a little from *Casablanca* but boasts a comic zing all its own.

TOP HAT (1935)
Fred Astaire and Ginger Rogers dance (and sing) "Cheek to Cheek" and other great Irving Berlin tunes in their most glorious teaming. Keep an eye peeled for a young Lucille Ball in the flower shop.

2001: A SPACE ODYSSEY (1968)
Director Stanley Kubrick's

TOP FILM SOUNDTRACKS

We love to go to the movies, but a good soundtrack means we can take them home with us, too. And fans do, as this list indicates. (Source: RIAA)

Soundtrack	Sales (in millions)
The Bodyguard	17
Saturday Night Fever	15
Purple Rain	13
Forrest Gump	12
Dirty Dancing	11
Titanic	11
The Lion King	10
Top Gun	9
Footloose	8
Grease	8
Waiting to Exhale	7
The Big Chill	6
Flashdance	6
Pure Country	6
City of Angels	5
The Jazz Singer	5
Space Jam	5
Evita	5

hauntingly beautiful and enormously influential science fiction thriller. And watch out for HAL.

UNFORGIVEN (1992)
Clint Eastwood directed and stars in a mature, meditative Western about an ex–hired gun turned farmer who goes on one last killing spree.

WHITE HEAT (1949)
Jimmy Cagney at his sinister best as a gangster who can't cut his ties to his mother's apron strings. Great ending.

WHO FRAMED ROGER RABBIT (1988)
It's 'toon time as animated characters and actors interact to solve a crime in a technological bit of trickery that shows just how far animation has come since the days of Gertie the Dinosaur. 'Toon or no 'toon, Jessica Rabbit (voiced by Kathleen Turner) is vavavoom.

THE WILD BUNCH (1969)
Director Sam Peckinpah's violent tale of revenge shakes the good

ol' Western by its spurs. With William Holden, Ernest Borgnine, and Robert Ryan.

WITNESS (1985)
Cultures clash as a big-city detective (Harrison Ford) hides out among the Amish in order to protect a young Amish boy who has witnessed a murder.

THE WIZARD OF OZ (1939)
Is once a year often enough? This entertaining children's musical—assuming that the kids are old enough to sit through the flying monkeys—features stellar performances by Judy Garland, Bert Lahr, Ray Bolger, and Jack Haley.

WRITTEN ON THE WIND (1956)
So bad it's good. A steamy melodrama about a very messed-up family, directed by Douglas Sirk, the master of glossy high camp, and starring Rock Hudson, Lauren Bacall, and Dorothy Malone.

THE BRIGHTEST STARS, BY YEAR

In today's high-pressure movie business, the most valuable commodity is a star who shines so bright that he or she can "open" a movie—filling seats on the basis of pure popularity regardless of the allure of the story line. Every year since 1933, Quigley Publishing has polled more than 500 moviehouse owners nationwide to determine which stars they regarded as the surest-fire box-office draw.

1933
1. Marie Dressler
2. Will Rogers
3. Janet Gaynor
4. Eddie Cantor
5. Wallace Beery
6. Jean Harlow
7. Clark Gable
8. Mae West
9. Norma Shearer
10. Joan Crawford

1934
1. Will Rogers
2. Clark Gable
3. Janet Gaynor
4. Wallace Beery
5. Mae West
6. Joan Crawford
7. Bing Crosby
8. Shirley Temple
9. Marie Dressler
10. Norma Shearer

1935
1. Shirley Temple
2. Will Rogers
3. Clark Gable
4. Fred Astaire & Ginger Rogers
5. Joan Crawford
6. Claudette Colbert
7. Dick Powell
8. Wallace Beery
9. Joe E. Brown
10. James Cagney

1936
1. Shirley Temple
2. Clark Gable
3. Fred Astaire and Ginger Rogers
4. Robert Taylor
5. Joe E. Brown
6. Dick Powell
7. Joan Crawford
8. Claudette Colbert
9. Jeanette MacDonald
10. Gary Cooper

1937
1. Shirley Temple
2. Clark Gable
3. Robert Taylor
4. Bing Crosby
5. William Powell
6. Jane Withers
7. Fred Astaire & Ginger Rogers
8. Sonja Henie
9. Gary Cooper
10. Myrna Loy

1938
1. Shirley Temple
2. Clark Gable
3. Sonja Henie
4. Mickey Rooney
5. Spencer Tracy
6. Robert Taylor
7. Myrna Loy
8. Jane Withers
9. Alice Faye
10. Tyrone Power

1939
1. Mickey Rooney
2. Tyrone Power
3. Spencer Tracy
4. Clark Gable
5. Shirley Temple
6. Bette Davis
7. Alice Faye
8. Errol Flynn
9. James Cagney
10. Sonja Henie

1940
1. Mickey Rooney
2. Spencer Tracy
3. Clark Gable
4. Gene Autry
5. Tyrone Power
6. James Cagney
7. Bing Crosby
8. Wallace Beery
9. Bette Davis
10. Judy Garland

1941
1. Mickey Rooney
2. Clark Gable
3. Abbott & Costello
4. Bob Hope
5. Spencer Tracy
6. Gene Autry
7. Gary Cooper
8. Bette Davis
9. James Cagney
10. Spencer Tracy

1942
1. Abbott & Costello
2. Clark Gable
3. Gary Cooper
4. Mickey Rooney
5. Bob Hope
6. James Cagney
7. Gene Autry
8. Betty Grable
9. Greer Garson
10. Spencer Tracy

1943
1. Betty Grable
2. Bob Hope
3. Abbott & Costello
4. Bing Crosby
5. Gary Cooper
6. Greer Garson
7. Humphrey Bogart
8. James Cagney
9. Mickey Rooney
10. Clark Gable

1944
1. Bing Crosby
2. Gary Cooper
3. Bob Hope
4. Betty Grable
5. Spencer Tracy
6. Greer Garson
7. Humphrey Bogart
8. Abbott & Costello
9. Cary Grant
10. Bette Davis

1945
1. Bing Crosby
2. Van Johnson
3. Greer Garson
4. Betty Grable
5. Spencer Tracy
6. Humphrey Bogart (tie)
6. Gary Cooper (tie)
8. Bob Hope
9. Judy Garland
10. Margaret O'Brien

1946
1. Bing Crosby
2. Ingrid Bergman
3. Van Johnson
4. Gary Cooper
5. Bob Hope
6. Humphrey Bogart
7. Greer Garson
8. Margaret O'Brien
9. Betty Grable
10. Roy Rogers

1947
1. Bing Crosby
2. Betty Grable
3. Ingrid Bergman
4. Gary Cooper
5. Humphrey Bogart
6. Bob Hope
7. Clark Gable
8. Gregory Peck
9. Claudette Colbert
10. Alan Ladd

1948
1. Bing Crosby
2. Betty Grable
3. Abbott & Costello
4. Gary Cooper
5. Bob Hope
6. Humphrey Bogart
7. Clark Gable
8. Cary Grant
9. Spencer Tracy
10. Ingrid Bergman

1949

1. Bob Hope
2. Bing Crosby
3. Abbott & Costello
4. John Wayne
5. Gary Cooper
6. Cary Grant
7. Betty Grable
8. Esther Williams
9. Humphrey Bogart
10. Clark Gable

1950

1. John Wayne
2. Bob Hope
3. Bing Crosby
4. Betty Grable
5. James Stewart
6. Abbott & Costello
7. Clifton Webb
8. Esther Williams
9. Spencer Tracy
10. Randolph Scott

1951

1. John Wayne
2. Dean Martin & Jerry Lewis
3. Betty Grable
4. Abbott & Costello
5. Bing Crosby
6. Bob Hope
7. Randolph Scott
8. Gary Cooper
9. Doris Day
10. Spencer Tracy

1952

1. Dean Martin & Jerry Lewis
2. Gary Cooper
3. John Wayne
4. Bing Crosby
5. Bob Hope
6. James Stewart
7. Doris Day
8. Gregory Peck
9. Susan Hayward
10. Randolph Scott

1953

1. Gary Cooper
2. Dean Martin & Jerry Lewis
3. John Wayne
4. Alan Ladd
5. Bing Crosby
6. Marilyn Monroe
7. James Stewart

8. Bob Hope
9. Susan Hayward
10. Randolph Scott

1954

1. John Wayne
2. Dean Martin & Jerry Lewis
3. Gary Cooper
4. James Stewart
5. Marilyn Monroe
6. Alan Ladd
7. William Holden
8. Bing Crosby
9. Jane Wyman
10. Marlon Brando

1955

1. James Stewart
2. Grace Kelly
3. John Wayne
4. William Holden
5. Gary Cooper
6. Marlon Brando
7. Dean Martin & Jerry Lewis
8. Humphrey Bogart
9. June Allyson
10. Clark Gable

1956

1. William Holden
2. John Wayne
3. James Stewart
4. Burt Lancaster
5. Glenn Ford
6. Dean Martin & Jerry Lewis
7. Gary Cooper
8. Marilyn Monroe
9. Kim Novak
10. Frank Sinatra

1957

1. Rock Hudson
2. John Wayne
3. Pat Boone
4. Elvis Presley
5. Frank Sinatra
6. Gary Cooper
7. William Holden
8. James Stewart
9. Jerry Lewis
10. Yul Brynner

1958

1. Glenn Ford
2. Elizabeth Taylor
3. Jerry Lewis
4. Marlon Brando
5. Rock Hudson
6. William Holden
7. Brigitte Bardot
8. Yul Brynner
9. James Stewart
10. Frank Sinatra

1959

1. Rock Hudson
2. Cary Grant
3. James Stewart
4. Doris Day
5. Debbie Reynolds
6. Glenn Ford
7. Frank Sinatra
8. John Wayne
9. Jerry Lewis
10. Susan Hayward

1960

1. Doris Day
2. Rock Hudson
3. Cary Grant
4. Elizabeth Taylor
5. Debbie Reynolds
6. Tony Curtis
7. Sandra Dee
8. Frank Sinatra
9. Jack Lemmon
10. John Wayne

1961

1. Elizabeth Taylor
2. Rock Hudson
3. Doris Day
4. John Wayne
5. Cary Grant
6. Sandra Dee
7. Jerry Lewis
8. William Holden
9. Tony Curtis
10. Elvis Presley

1962

1. Doris Day
2. Rock Hudson
3. Cary Grant
4. John Wayne
5. Elvis Presley
6. Elizabeth Taylor
7. Jerry Lewis
8. Frank Sinatra
9. Sandra Dee
10. Burt Lancaster

1963

1. Doris Day
2. John Wayne
3. Rock Hudson
4. Jack Lemmon
5. Cary Grant
6. Elizabeth Taylor
7. Elvis Presley
8. Sandra Dee
9. Paul Newman
10. Jerry Lewis

1964

1. Doris Day
2. Jack Lemmon
3. Rock Hudson
4. John Wayne
5. Cary Grant
6. Elvis Presley
7. Shirley MacLaine
8. Ann-Margret
9. Paul Newman
10. Jerry Lewis

1965

1. Sean Connery
2. John Wayne
3. Doris Day
4. Julie Andrews
5. Jack Lemmon
6. Elvis Presley
7. Cary Grant
8. James Stewart
9. Elizabeth Taylor
10. Richard Burton

1966

1. Julie Andrews
2. Sean Connery
3. Elizabeth Taylor
4. Jack Lemmon
5. Richard Burton
6. Cary Grant
7. John Wayne
8. Doris Day
9. Paul Newman
10. Elvis Presley

1967

1. Julie Andrews
2. Lee Marvin
3. Paul Newman
4. Dean Martin
5. Sean Connery
6. Elizabeth Taylor
7. Sidney Poitier
8. John Wayne
9. Richard Burton
10. Steve McQueen

1968

1. Sidney Poitier
2. Paul Newman
3. Julie Andrews
4. John Wayne
5. Clint Eastwood
6. Dean Martin
7. Steve McQueen
8. Jack Lemmon
9. Lee Marvin
10. Elizabeth Taylor

1969

1. Paul Newman
2. John Wayne
3. Steve McQueen
4. Dustin Hoffman
5. Clint Eastwood
6. Sidney Poitier
7. Lee Marvin
8. Jack Lemmon
9. Katharine Hepburn
10. Barbra Streisand

1970

1. Paul Newman
2. Clint Eastwood
3. Steve McQueen
4. John Wayne
5. Elliott Gould
6. Dustin Hoffman
7. Lee Marvin
8. Jack Lemmon
9. Barbra Streisand
10. Walter Matthau

1971

1. John Wayne
2. Clint Eastwood
3. Paul Newman
4. Steve McQueen
5. George C. Scott
6. Dustin Hoffman
7. Walter Matthau
8. Ali MacGraw
9. Sean Connery
10. Lee Marvin

1972

1. Clint Eastwood
2. George C. Scott
3. Gene Hackman
4. John Wayne
5. Barbra Streisand
6. Marlon Brando
7. Paul Newman
8. Steve McQueen
9. Dustin Hoffman
10. Goldie Hawn

1973

1. Clint Eastwood
2. Ryan O'Neal
3. Steve McQueen
4. Burt Reynolds
5. Robert Redford
6. Barbra Streisand
7. Paul Newman
8. Charles Bronson
9. John Wayne
10. Marlon Brando

1974

1. Robert Redford
2. Clint Eastwood
3. Paul Newman
4. Barbra Streisand
5. Steve McQueen
6. Burt Reynolds
7. Charles Bronson
8. Jack Nicholson
9. Al Pacino
10. John Wayne

1975

1. Robert Redford
2. Barbra Streisand
3. Al Pacino
4. Charles Bronson
5. Paul Newman
6. Clint Eastwood
7. Burt Reynolds
8. Woody Allen
9. Steve McQueen
10. Gene Hackman

1976

1. Robert Redford
2. Jack Nicholson
3. Dustin Hoffman
4. Clint Eastwood
5. Mel Brooks
6. Burt Reynolds
7. Al Pacino
8. Tatum O'Neal
9. Woody Allen
10. Charles Bronson

1977

1. Sylvester Stallone
2. Barbra Streisand
3. Clint Eastwood
4. Burt Reynolds
5. Robert Redford
6. Woody Allen
7. Mel Brooks
8. Al Pacino
9. Diane Keaton
10. Robert De Niro

1978

1. Burt Reynolds
2. John Travolta
3. Richard Dreyfuss
4. Warren Beatty
5. Clint Eastwood
6. Woody Allen
7. Diane Keaton
8. Jane Fonda
9. Peter Sellers
10. Barbra Streisand

1979

1. Burt Reynolds
2. Clint Eastwood
3. Jane Fonda
4. Woody Allen
5. Barbra Streisand
6. Sylvester Stallone
7. John Travolta
8. Jill Clayburgh
9. Roger Moore
10. Mel Brooks

1980

1. Burt Reynolds
2. Robert Redford
3. Clint Eastwood
4. Jane Fonda
5. Dustin Hoffman
6. John Travolta
7. Sally Field
8. Sissy Spacek
9. Barbra Streisand
10. Steve Martin

1981

1. Burt Reynolds
2. Clint Eastwood
3. Dudley Moore
4. Dolly Parton
5. Jane Fonda
6. Harrison Ford
7. Alan Alda
8. Bo Derek
9. Goldie Hawn
10. Bill Murray

1982

1. Burt Reynolds
2. Clint Eastwood
3. Sylvester Stallone
4. Dudley Moore
5. Richard Pryor
6. Dolly Parton
7. Jane Fonda
8. Richard Gere
9. Paul Newman
10. Harrison Ford

1983

1. Clint Eastwood
2. Eddie Murphy
3. Sylvester Stallone
4. Burt Reynolds
5. John Travolta
6. Dustin Hoffman
7. Harrison Ford
8. Richard Gere
9. Chevy Chase
10. Tom Cruise

1984

1. Clint Eastwood
2. Bill Murray
3. Harrison Ford
4. Eddie Murphy
5. Sally Field
6. Burt Reynolds
7. Robert Redford
8. Prince
9. Dan Aykroyd
10. Meryl Streep

1985

1. Sylvester Stallone
2. Eddie Murphy
3. Clint Eastwood
4. Michael J. Fox
5. Chevy Chase
6. Arnold Schwarzenegger
7. Chuck Norris
8. Harrison Ford
9. Michael Douglas
10. Meryl Streep

1986

1. Tom Cruise
2. Eddie Murphy
3. Paul Hogan
4. Rodney Dangerfield
5. Bette Midler
6. Sylvester Stallone
7. Clint Eastwood
8. Whoopi Goldberg
9. Kathleen Turner
10. Paul Newman

1987

1. Eddie Murphy
2. Michael Douglas
3. Michael J. Fox
4. Arnold Schwarzenegger
5. Paul Hogan
6. Tom Cruise
7. Glenn Close
8. Sylvester Stallone
9. Cher
10. Mel Gibson

1988

1. Tom Cruise
2. Eddie Murphy
3. Tom Hanks
4. Arnold Schwarzenegger
5. Paul Hogan
6. Danny DeVito
7. Bette Midler
8. Robin Williams
9. Tom Selleck
10. Dustin Hoffman

1989

1. Jack Nicholson
2. Tom Cruise
3. Robin Williams
4. Michael Douglas
5. Tom Hanks
6. Michael J. Fox
7. Eddie Murphy
8. Mel Gibson
9. Sean Connery
10. Kathleen Turner

1990

1. Arnold Schwarzenegger
2. Julia Roberts
3. Bruce Willis
4. Tom Cruise
5. Mel Gibson
6. Kevin Costner
7. Patrick Swayze
8. Sean Connery
9. Harrison Ford
10. Richard Gere

1991

1. Kevin Costner
2. Arnold

   Schwarzenegger
3. Robin Williams
4. Julia Roberts
5. Macaulay Culkin
6. Jodie Foster
7. Billy Crystal
8. Dustin Hoffman
9. Robert De Niro
10. Mel Gibson

1992

1. Tom Cruise
2. Mel Gibson
3. Kevin Costner
4. Jack Nicholson
5. Macaulay Culkin
6. Whoopi Goldberg
7. Michael Douglas
8. Clint Eastwood
9. Steven Seagal
10. Robin Williams

1993

1. Clint Eastwood
2. Tom Cruise
3. Robin Williams
4. Kevin Costner
5. Harrison Ford
6. Julia Roberts
7. Tom Hanks
8. Mel Gibson
9. Whoopi Goldberg
10. Sylvester Stallone

1994

1. Tom Hanks
2. Jim Carrey
3. Arnold Schwarzenegger
4. Tom Cruise

5. Harrison Ford
6. Tim Allen
7. Mel Gibson
8. Jodie Foster
9. Michael Douglas
10. Tommy Lee Jones

1995

1. Tom Hanks
2. Jim Carrey
3. Brad Pitt
4. Harrison Ford
5. Robin Williams
6. Sandra Bullock
7. Mel Gibson
8. Demi Moore
9. John Travolta
10. Kevin Costner (tie)
10. Michael Douglas (tie)

1996

1. Tom Cruise (tie)
1. Mel Gibson (tie)
3. John Travolta
4. Arnold
   Schwarzenegger
5. Sandra Bullock
6. Robin Williams
7. Sean Connery
8. Harrison Ford
9. Kevin Costner
10. Michelle Pfeiffer

1997

1. Harrison Ford
2. Julia Roberts
3. Leonardo DiCaprio
4. Will Smith
5. Tom Cruise
6. Jack Nicholson

7. Jim Carrey
8. John Travolta
9. Robin Williams
10. Tommy Lee Jones

1998

1. Tom Hanks
2. Jim Carrey
3. Leonardo DiCaprio
4. Robin Williams
5. Meg Ryan
6. Mel Gibson
7. Adam Sandler
8. Eddie Murphy
9. Cameron Diaz
10. Julia Roberts

1999

1. Julia Roberts
2. Tom Hanks
3. Adam Sandler
4. Bruce Willis
5. Mike Myers
6. Tom Cruise
7. Will Smith
8. Mel Gibson
9. Meg Ryan
10. Sandra Bullock

2000

1. Tom Cruise
2. Julia Roberts
3. George Clooney
4. Eddie Murphy
5. Russell Crowe
6. Mel Gibson
7. Martin Lawrence
8. Tom Hanks
9. Jim Carrey
10. Harrison Ford

THE ALL-TIME LEADING MEN AND WOMEN

Awarding points on a descending scale of 10, PEOPLE has analyzed Quigley Publishing's yearly film stars rankings to determine the most popular screen actors of all time.

Rank	Actor	Score	Rank	Actor	Score	Rank	Actor	Score
1.	John Wayne	172	15.	Tom Hanks	60	29.	Dean Martin	
2.	Clint Eastwood	165	16.	Abbott & Costello	57		& Jerry Lewis (tie)	46
3.	Bing Crosby	111	17.	James Stewart (tie)	56	29.	Mickey Rooney (tie)	46
4.	Gary Cooper	102	17.	Harrison Ford (tie)	56	31.	Elizabeth Taylor	44
5.	Clark Gable	91	19.	Robert Redford	55	32.	Dustin Hoffman	42
6.	Burt Reynolds	90	20.	Mel Gibson	54	33.	Jack Lemmon	40
7.	Bob Hope	84	21.	Arnold Schwarzenegger	53	34.	John Travolta	37
8.	Tom Cruise	83	22.	Sylvester Stallone (tie)	50	35.	Sean Connery	36
9.	Paul Newman	76	22.	Julia Roberts (tie)	50	36.	Julie Andrews	35
10.	Doris Day	72	24.	Shirley Temple	49	37.	Humphrey Bogart (tie)	34
11.	Rock Hudson	69	25.	Barbra Streisand (tie)	48	37.	Gary Cooper (tie)	34
12.	Eddie Murphy	67	25.	Spencer Tracy (tie)	48	37.	Jack Nicholson (tie)	34
13.	Betty Grable	66	25.	Robin Williams (tie)	48	40.	Kevin Costner (tie)	33
14.	Cary Grant	62	28.	Steve McQueen	47	40.	William Holden (tie)	33
						40.	Jim Carrey (tie)	33

SUPERSTAR FILMOGRAPHIES

These filmographies list only full-length feature films to which these actors and directors contributed significantly. The lists do include some early works released directly onto video years after completion.

WOODY ALLEN
Director/screenwriter/actor

What's New, Pussycat? (screenwriter/actor, 1965)

What's Up, Tiger Lily? (director/co-screenwriter/actor, 1966)

Casino Royale (co-screenwriter/actor, 1967)

Take the Money and Run (director/co-screenwriter/actor, 1969)

Bananas (director/screenwriter/actor, 1971)

Play It Again, Sam (screenwriter/actor, 1972)

Everything You Always Wanted To Know About Sex* (*but were afraid to ask) (director/co-screenwriter/actor, 1972)

Sleeper (director/screenwriter/actor, 1973)

Love and Death (director/screenwriter/actor, 1975)

The Front (actor, 1976)

Annie Hall (director/co-screenwriter/actor, 1977; Academy Awards for best picture, best director, best original screenplay)

Interiors (director/screenwriter/ actor, 1978)

Manhattan (director/co-screenwriter/actor, 1979)

Stardust Memories (director/screenwriter/actor, 1980)

A Midsummer Night's Sex Comedy (director/screenwriter/actor, 1982)

Zelig (director/screenwriter/actor, 1983)

Broadway Danny Rose (director/screenwriter/actor, 1984)

The Purple Rose of Cairo (director/screenwriter, 1985)

Hannah and Her Sisters (director/screenwriter/actor, 1986; Academy Award for best original screenplay)

Radio Days (director/screenwriter/actor, 1987)

King Lear (actor, 1987)

September (director/screenwriter, 1987)

Another Woman (director/screenwriter, 1988)

"Oedipus Wrecks," in *New York Stories* (director/co-screenwriter/actor, 1989)

Crimes and Misdemeanors (director/screenwriter/actor, 1989)

Alice (director/screenwriter, 1990)

Scenes from a Mall (actor, 1991)

Shadows and Fog (director/screenwriter/actor, 1992)

Husbands and Wives (director/screenwriter/actor, 1992)

Manhattan Murder Mystery (director/screenwriter/actor, 1993)

Bullets over Broadway (director/co-screenwriter, 1994)

Mighty Aphrodite (director/screenwriter/actor, 1995)

Everyone Says I Love You (director/screenwriter/actor, 1996)

Deconstructing Harry (director/screenwriter/actor, 1997)

Wild Man Blues (documentary subject, 1998)

The Impostors (actor, 1998)

Antz (cartoon voice, 1998)

Celebrity (director/screenwriter/actor, 1998)

Sweet and Lowdown (director/screenwriter/actor, 1999)

Small Time Crooks (director/screenwriter/actor, 2000)

Company Man (actor, 2001)

The Curse of the Jade Scorpion (director/screenwriter/actor, 2001)

KEVIN BACON
Actor

National Lampoon's Animal House (1978)

Friday the 13th (1980)

Only When I Laugh (1981)

Forty Deuces (1982)

Diner (1982)

Enormous Changes at the Last Minute (1983)

Footloose (1984)

Quicksilver (1986)

White Water Summer (a.k.a. *Rites of Summer,* 1987)

End of the Line (1987)

Planes, Trains & Automobiles (1987)

She's Having a Baby (1988)

Criminal Law (1989)

The Big Picture (1989)

Tremors (1990)

Flatliners (1990)

Queens Logic (1991)

Pyrates (1991)

He Said, She Said (1991)

JFK (1991)

A Few Good Men (1992)

The River Wild (1994)

The Air Up There (1994)

Balto (cartoon voice, 1995)

Murder in the First (1995)

Apollo 13 (1995)

Sleepers (1996)

Losing Chase (1996)

Picture Perfect (1997)

Telling Lies in America (1997)

Digging to China (1998)

Wild Things (1998)

Stir of Echoes (1999)

My Dog Skip (2000)

Hollow Man (2000)

SANDRA BULLOCK
Actor

Who Shot Patakango? (1990)

Religion, Inc. (1990—videotape)

When the Party's Over (1992)

Who Do I Gotta Kill? (1992)

Love Potion No. 9 (1992)

The Vanishing (1993)

Fire on the Amazon (1992—videotape)

Demolition Man (1993)

The Thing Called Love (1993)

Wrestling Ernest Hemingway (1993)

Speed (1994)

While You Were Sleeping (1995)

The Net (1995)

Two If by Sea (1996)

A Time To Kill (1996)

In Love and War (1997)

Speed 2: Cruise Control (1997)

Hope Floats (1998)

Prince of Egypt (cartoon voice, 1998)

Practical Magic (1998)

Forces of Nature (1999)

Gun Shy (actor/producer, 2000)

28 Days (2000)

Miss Congeniality (2000)

NICOLAS CAGE
Actor

Fast Times at Ridgemont High (1982)

Valley Girl (1983)

Rumble Fish (1983)

Racing with the Moon (1984)

The Cotton Club (1984)

Birdy (1984)

The Boy in Blue (1986)

Peggy Sue Got Married (1986)

Raising Arizona (1987)

Moonstruck (1987)

Vampire's Kiss (1989)

Wild at Heart (1990)

Time to Kill (1990—videotape)

Fire Birds (1990)

Zandalee (1991)

Honeymoon in Vegas (1992)

Red Rock West (1992)

Amos and Andrew (1993)

Deadfall (1993)

Guarding Tess (1994)

It Could Happen to You (1994)

Trapped in Paradise (1994)

Kiss of Death (1995)

Leaving Las Vegas (1995; Academy Award for best actor)

The Rock (1996)

Con Air (1997)

Face/Off (1997)

City of Angels (1998)

Snake Eyes (1998)

8mm (1999)

Bringing Out the Dead (1999)

Gone in Sixty Seconds (2000)

The Family Man (2000)

Captain Corelli's Mandolin (2001)

JIM CARREY
Actor

Finders Keepers (1984)

Once Bitten (1985)

Peggy Sue Got Married (1986)

The Dead Pool (1988)

Pink Cadillac (1989)

Earth Girls Are Easy (1989)

High Strung (1994—videotape)

Ace Ventura: Pet Detective (1994)

The Mask (1994)

Dumb & Dumber (1994)

Batman Forever (1995)

Ace Ventura: When Nature Calls (1995)

The Cable Guy (1996)

Liar Liar (1997)

The Truman Show (1998)

Simon Birch (1998)

Man on the Moon (1999)

Me, Myself & Irene (2000)

How the Grinch Stole Christmas (2000)

GLENN CLOSE
Actor

The World According to Garp (1982)

The Big Chill (1983)

The Stone Boy (1984)

Greystoke: The Legend of Tarzan, Lord of the Apes (voice, 1984)

The Natural (1984)

Jagged Edge (1985)

Maxie (1985)

Fatal Attraction (1987)

Dangerous Liaisons (1988)

Light Years (cartoon voice, 1988)

Immediate Family (1989)

Hamlet (1990)

Reversal of Fortune (1990)

Meeting Venus (1991)

The Paper (1994)

The House of the Spirits (1994)

Mary Reilly (1996)

101 Dalmatians (1996)

Mars Attacks! (1996)

Paradise Road (1997)

Air Force One (1997)

In & Out (1997)

Cookie's Fortune (1999)

Tarzan (cartoon voice, 1999)

102 Dalmatians (2000)

SEAN CONNERY
Actor

No Road Back (1956)

Action of the Tiger (1957)

Another Time, Another Place (1958)

Hell Drivers (1957)

Time Lock (1957)

A Night to Remember (1958)

Tarzan's Greatest Adventure (1959)

Darby O'Gill and the Little People (1959)

On the Fiddle (1961)

The Frightened City (1961)

The Longest Day (1962)

Dr. No (1962)

From Russia with Love (1963)

Goldfinger (1964)

Woman of Straw (1964)

Marnie (1964)

Thunderball (1965)

The Hill (1965)

A Fine Madness (1966)

You Only Live Twice (1967)

Shalako (1968)

Bowler and Bonnet (1969, director)

The Molly Maguires (1970)

The Red Tent (1971)

The Anderson Tapes (1971)

Diamonds Are Forever (1971)

The Offence (or *Something like the Truth*, 1973)

Zardoz (1974)

Murder on the Orient Express (1974)

Ransom (1974)

The Wind and the Lion (1975)

The Man Who Would Be King (1975)

The Terrorists (1975)

Robin and Marian (1976)

The Next Man (1976)

A Bridge Too Far (1977)

The Great Train Robbery (1979)

Meteor (1979)

Cuba (1979)

Outland (1981)

Time Bandits (1981)

Wrong Is Right (1981)

G'ole (1982)

Five Days One Summer (1982)

Never Say Never Again (1983)

Sword of the Valiant (1984)

Highlander (1985)

The Name of the Rose (1986)

The Untouchables (1987; Academy Award for best supporting actor)

The Presidio (1988)

Memories of Me (1988)

Indiana Jones and the Last Crusade (1989)

Family Business (1989)

The Hunt for Red October (1990)

The Russia House (1990)

Highlander II: The Quickening (1991)

Robin Hood: Prince of Thieves (1991)

Medicine Man (1992)

Rising Sun (1993)

A Good Man in Africa (1994)

Just Cause (1995)

First Knight (1995)

Dragonheart (voice, 1996)

The Rock (1996)

The Avengers (1998)

Playing by Heart (1998)

Entrapment (1999)

Finding Forrester (2000)

KEVIN COSTNER
Actor/director/producer

Shadows Run Black (1981)

Night Shift (1982)

Stacy's Knights (1982)

The Big Chill (played corpse, all other scenes edited out, 1983)

The Gunrunner (1983)

Table for Five (1983)

Testament (1983)

American Flyers (1985)

Fandango (1985)

Silverado (1985)

Sizzle Beach, U.S.A. (1986)

No Way Out (1987)

The Untouchables (1987)

Bull Durham (1988)

Chasing Dreams (1989)

Field of Dreams (1989)

Dances with Wolves (actor/director/producer, 1990; Academy Awards for best picture, best director)

Revenge (1990)

Robin Hood: Prince of Thieves (1991)

JFK (1991)

The Bodyguard (actor/producer, 1992)

A Perfect World (1993)

Wyatt Earp (actor/producer, 1994)

Rapa Nui (co-producer, 1994)

The War (1994)

Waterworld (actor/producer, 1995)

Tin Cup (1996)

The Postman (actor/director/co-producer, 1997)

Message in a Bottle (1999)

For Love of the Game (1999)

Thirteen Days (2000)

3000 Miles to Graceland (2001)

TOM CRUISE
Actor

Endless Love (1981)

Taps (1981)

Losin' It (1983)

The Outsiders (1983)

Risky Business (1983)

All the Right Moves (1983)

Legend (1986)

Top Gun (1986)

The Color of Money (1986)

Cocktail (1988)

Rain Man (1988)

Born on the Fourth of July (1989)

Days of Thunder (1990)

Far and Away (1992)

A Few Good Men (1992)

The Firm (1993)

Interview with the Vampire (1994)

Mission: Impossible (actor/co-producer, 1996)

Jerry Maguire (1996)

Eyes Wide Shut (1999)

Magnolia (1999)

Mission: Impossible 2 (2000)

CLINT EASTWOOD
Actor/director/producer

Francis in the Navy (1955)

Lady Godiva (1955)

Never Say Goodbye (actor,1955)

Revenge of the Creature (1955)

Tarantula (1955)

The Traveling Saleslady (1956)

Star in the Dust (1956)

Escapade in Japan (1957)

Ambush at Cimarron Pass (1958)

Lafayette Escadrille (1958)

A Fistful of Dollars (1964)

For a Few Dollars More (1965)

The Good, the Bad, and the Ugly (1966)

Coogan's Bluff (1968)

Hang 'Em High (1968)

The Witches (1968)

Where Eagles Dare (1968)

Paint Your Wagon (1969)

Kelly's Heroes (1970)

Two Mules for Sister Sara (1970)

The Beguiled (1971)

Dirty Harry (1971)

Play Misty For Me (actor/director, 1971)

Joe Kidd (1972)

Breezy (1973)

High Plains Drifter (actor/director, 1973)

Magnum Force (1973)

Thunderbolt and Lightfoot (1974)

The Eiger Sanction (actor/director, 1974)

The Outlaw Josey Wales (actor/director, 1975)

The Enforcer (1976)

The Gauntlet (actor/director, 1977)

Every Which Way but Loose (1978)

Escape from Alcatraz (1979)

Any Which Way You Can (1980)

Bronco Billy (actor/director, 1980)

Firefox (actor/director/producer, 1982)

Honkytonk Man (actor/director/producer, 1982)

Sudden Impact (actor/director/producer, 1983)

City Heat (1984)

Tightrope (actor/producer, 1984)

Pale Rider (actor/director/producer, 1985)

Heartbreak Ridge (actor/director/producer, 1986)

Bird (director/producer, 1988)

The Dead Pool (actor/producer, 1988)

Pink Cadillac (1989)

The Rookie (actor/director, 1990)

White Hunter, Black Heart (actor/director/producer, 1990)

Unforgiven (actor/director/producer, 1992; Academy Awards for best director and best film)

In the Line of Fire (actor/producer, 1993)

A Perfect World (actor/director, 1993)

The Bridges of Madison County (actor/director, 1995)

Absolute Power (actor/director, 1997)

Midnight in the Garden of Good and Evil (director/co-producer, 1997)

True Crime (actor/director, 1999)

Space Cowboys (actor/director/co-producer, 2000)

HARRISON FORD
Actor

Dead Heat on a Merry-Go-Round (1966)

Luv (1967)

A Time for Killing (1967)

Journey to Shiloh (1968)

Getting Straight (1970)

American Graffiti (1973)

The Conversation (1974)

Heroes (1977)

Force 10 from Navarone (1978)

Star Wars (1977)

The Frisco Kid (1979)

Apocalypse Now (1979)

Hanover Street (1979)

The Empire Strikes Back (1980)

Raiders of the Lost Ark (1981)

Blade Runner (1982)

Return of the Jedi (1983)

Indiana Jones and the Temple of Doom (1984)

Witness (1985)

The Mosquito Coast (1986)

Frantic (1988)

Working Girl (1988)

Indiana Jones and the Last Crusade (1989)

Presumed Innocent (1990)

Regarding Henry (1991)

Patriot Games (1992)

The Fugitive (1993)

Clear and Present Danger (1994)

Sabrina (1995)

The Devil's Own (1997)

Air Force One (1997)

Six Days, Seven Nights (1998)

Random Hearts (1999)

What Lies Beneath (2000)

The Million Dollar Hotel (2001)

JODIE FOSTER
Actor/director

Napoleon and Samantha (1972)

Kansas City Bomber (1972)

Tom Sawyer (1973)

One Little Indian (1973)

Alice Doesn't Live Here Anymore (1974)

Echoes of a Summer (1976)

Bugsy Malone (1976)

Taxi Driver (1976)

The Little Girl Who Lives Down the Lane (1976)

Freaky Friday (1977)

Candleshoe (1977)

Moi, fleur bleue (1977)

Il Casotto (1977)

Carny (1980)

Foxes (1980)

O'Hara's Wife (1982)

Les Sang des autres (The Blood of Others) (1984)

The Hotel New Hampshire (1984)

Mesmerized (actor/co-producer, 1986)

Siesta (1987)

Five Corners (1988)

The Accused (1988; Academy Award for best actress)

Stealing Home (1988)

Backtrack (1989)

The Silence of the Lambs (1991; Academy Award for best actress)

Little Man Tate (actor/director, 1991)

Shadows and Fog (1992)

Sommersby (1993)

Maverick (1994)

Nell (1994)

Home for the Holidays (director, 1995)

Contact (1997)

Anna and the King (1999)

MEL GIBSON
Actor/director

Summer City (1977)

Tim (1979)

Mad Max (1979)

Attack Force Z (1981)

Gallipoli (1981)

The Road Warrior (1981)

The Year of Living Dangerously (1982)

The Bounty (1984)

Mrs. Soffel (1984)

The River (1984)

Mad Max Beyond Thunderdome (1985)

Lethal Weapon (1987)

Tequila Sunrise (1988)

Lethal Weapon 2 (1989)

Air America (1990)

Bird on a Wire (1990)

Hamlet (1990)

Forever Young (1992)

Lethal Weapon 3 (1992)

The Man Without a Face (actor/director, 1993)

Maverick (1994)

Braveheart (actor/director/producer, 1995; Academy Awards for best director and best picture)

Pocahontas (cartoon voice, 1995)

Ransom (1996)

Conspiracy Theory (1997)

Lethal Weapon 4 (1998)

Payback (1999)

Chicken Run (cartoon voice, 2000)

The Patriot (2000)

What Women Want (2000)

WHOOPI GOLDBERG
Actor

The Color Purple (1985)

Jumpin' Jack Flash (1986)

Burglar (1987)

Fatal Beauty (1987)

Clara's Heart (1988)

The Telephone (1988)

Beverly Hills Brats (1989)

Homer and Eddie (1989)

Ghost (1990; Academy Award for best supporting actress)

The Long Walk Home (1990)

Soapdish (1991)

The Player (1992)

Sarafina! (1992)

Sister Act (1992)

Made in America (1993)

Sister Act 2: Back in the Habit (1993)

Corrina, Corrina (1994)

The Lion King (cartoon voice, 1994)

The Pagemaster (cartoon voice, 1994)

The Little Rascals (1994)

Star Trek: Generations (1994)

Boys on the Side (1995)

Moonlight & Valentino (1995)

Theodore Rex (1996, video)

Eddie (1996)

Bogus (1996)

The Associate (1996)

In & Out (1997)

An Alan Smithee Film: Burn Hollywood Burn (1998)

How Stella Got Her Groove Back (1998)

The Rugrats Movie (cartoon voice, 1998)

The Deep End of the Ocean (1999)

Get Bruce (1999)

Girl, Interrupted (1999)

The Adventures of Rocky and Bullwinkle (2000)

Monkeybone (2000)

Kingdom Come (2001)

Rat Race (2001)

TOM HANKS
Actor

He Knows You're Alone (1980)

Splash (1984)

Bachelor Party (1984)

The Man with One Red Shoe (1985)

Volunteers (1985)

The Money Pit (1986)

Nothing in Common (1986)

Every Time We Say Goodbye (1986)

Dragnet (1987)

Big (1988)

Punchline (1988)

The Burbs (1989)

Turner and Hooch (1989)

Joe Versus the Volcano (1990)

The Bonfire of the Vanities (1990)

Radio Flyer (1992)

A League of Their Own (1992)

Sleepless in Seattle (1993)

Philadelphia (1993; Academy Award for best actor)

Forrest Gump (1994; Academy Award for best actor)

Apollo 13 (1995)

Toy Story (cartoon voice, 1995)

That Thing You Do! (writer/director/actor, 1996)

Saving Private Ryan (1998)

You've Got Mail (1998)

Toy Story 2 (cartoon voice, 1999)

The Green Mile (1999)

Cast Away (2000)

ANTHONY HOPKINS
Actor

The Lion in Winter (1968)

Hamlet (1969)

The Looking Glass War (1970)

When Eight Bells Toll (1971)

Young Winston (1972)

A Doll's House (1973)

The Girl From Petrovka (1974)

Juggernaut (1974)

All Creatures Great and Small (1975)

Audrey Rose (1977)

A Bridge Too Far (1977)

International Velvet (1978)

Magic (1978)

A Change of Seasons (1980)

The Elephant Man (1980)

The Bounty (1984)

The Good Father (1986)

84 Charing Cross Road (1987)

The Dawning (1988)

A Chorus of Disapproval (1987)

Desperate Hours (1990)

The Silence of the Lambs (1991; Academy Award for best actor)

Freejack (1992)

Howards End (1992)

The Efficiency Expert (1992)

Bram Stoker's Dracula (1992)

Chaplin (1992)

The Remains of the Day (1993)

Shadowlands (1993)

The Trial (1993)

The Road to Wellville (1994)

Legends of the Fall (1994)

The Innocent (1995)

Nixon (1995)

August (actor/director, 1996)

Surviving Picasso (1996)

The Edge (1997)

Amistad (1997)

The Mask of Zorro (1998)

Meet Joe Black (1998)

Instinct (1999)

Titus (1999)

Mission: Impossible 2 (2000)

How the Grinch Stole Christmas (2000)

Hannibal (2001)

HELEN HUNT
Actor

Rollercoaster (1977)

Girls Just Want to Have Fun (1985)

Trancers (a.k.a. *Future Cop*) (1985)

Peggy Sue Got Married (1986)

Project X (1987)

Stealing Home (1988)

Miles from Home (1988)

Next of Kin (1989)

The Waterdance (1992)

Only You (1992)

Bob Roberts (1992)

Mr. Saturday Night (1992)

Kiss of Death (1995)

Twister (1996)

As Good As It Gets (1997; Academy Award for best actress)

Pay It Forward (2000)

What Women Want (2000)

Cast Away (2000)

Dr. T and the Women (2000)

NICOLE KIDMAN
Actor

Bush Christmas (1983)

BMX Bandits (1983)

Archer's Adventure (1985)

The Wacky World of Wills and Burke (1985)

Windrider (1986)

Nightmaster (1987)

The Bit Part (1987)

Emerald City (1988)

Dead Calm (1989)

Days of Thunder (1990)

Flirting (1991)

Billy Bathgate (1991)

Far and Away (1992)

My Life (1993)

Malice (1993)

To Die For (1994)

Batman Forever (1995)

The Portrait of a Lady (1996)

The Peacemaker (1997)

Practical Magic (1998)

Eyes Wide Shut (1999)

Moulin Rouge (2000)

The Others (2001)

SPIKE LEE
Director/producer/screenwriter/actor

She's Gotta Have It (director/producer/screenwriter/actor, 1986)

School Daze (director/producer/screenwriter/actor, 1988)

Do the Right Thing (director/producer/screenwriter/actor, 1989)

Mo' Better Blues (director/producer/screenwriter/actor, 1990)

Lonely in America, (actor, 1990)

Jungle Fever (director/producer/screenwriter/actor, 1991)

Malcolm X (director/producer/co-screenwriter/actor, 1992)

Crooklyn (director/producer/co-screenwriter/actor, 1994)

Clockers (director/co-producer/co-screenwriter, 1995)

Girl 6 (director/producer, 1996)

Get On The Bus (director/producer, 1996)

When We Were Kings (interviewee, 1996)

4 Little Girls (director/producer, 1997)

He Got Game (director/producer/screenwriter, 1998)

Summer of Sam (director/co-producer/co-screenwriter, 1999)

The Original Kings of Comedy (director/co-producer, 2000)

Bamboozled (director/co-producer/writer, 2000)

DEMI MOORE
Actor/Producer

Choices (1981)

Parasite (1982)

Young Doctors in Love (1982)

Blame It on Rio (1984)

No Small Affair (1984)

St. Elmo's Fire (1985)

About Last Night (1986)

One Crazy Summer (1986)

Wisdom (1986)

The Seventh Sign (1988)

We're No Angels (1989)

Ghost (1990)

Mortal Thoughts (actor/co-producer, 1991)

Nothing but Trouble (1991)

The Butcher's Wife (1991)

A Few Good Men (1992)

Indecent Proposal (1993)

Disclosure (1994)

The Scarlet Letter (1995)

Now and Then (1995)

The Juror (1996)

The Hunchback of Notre Dame (cartoon voice, 1996)

Striptease (1996)

Beavis and Butt-Head Do America (cartoon voice, 1996)

Austin Powers: International Man of Mystery (co-producer, 1997)

G.I. Jane (1997)

Deconstructing Harry (1997)

Passion of Mind (2000)

JACK NICHOLSON
Actor/producer/screenwriter/director

Cry Baby Killer (1958)

Studs Lonigan (1960)

Too Soon to Love (1960)

The Wild Ride (1960)

Little Shop of Horrors (1961)

The Broken Land (1962)

The Raven (1963)

The Terror (1963)

Thunder Island (screenwriter, 1963)

Ensign Pulver (1964)

Back Door to Hell (1964)

The Fortune (1965)

Flight to Fury (actor/screenwriter, 1966)

Ride in the Whirlwind (actor/producer/screenwriter, 1966)

Hell's Angels on Wheels (1966)

The Shooting (actor/producer, 1967)

The Trip (screenwriter, 1967)

St. Valentine's Day Massacre (1967)

Head (actor/producer/screenwriter, 1968)

Psych-Out (1968)

Easy Rider (1969)

Five Easy Pieces (1970)

On a Clear Day You Can See Forever (1970)

Rebel Rousers (1970)

Carnal Knowledge (1971)

Drive, He Said (director/producer/screenwriter, 1971)

A Safe Place (1971)

The King of Marvin Gardens (1972)

The Last Detail (1973)

Chinatown (1974)

The Fortune (1975)

One Flew over the Cuckoo's Nest (1975; Academy Award for best actor)

The Passenger (1975)

Tommy (1975)

The Last Tycoon (1976)

The Missouri Breaks (1976)

Goin' South (actor/director, 1978)

The Shining (1980)

The Border (1981)

The Postman Always Rings Twice (1981)

Reds (1981)

Terms of Endearment (1983; Academy Award for best supporting actor)

Prizzi's Honor (1985)

Heartburn (1986)

Broadcast News (1987)

Ironweed (1987)

The Witches of Eastwick (1987)

Batman (1989)

The Two Jakes (actor/director, 1990)

Man Trouble (1992)

A Few Good Men (1992)

Hoffa (1992)

Wolf (1994)

The Crossing Guard (1995)

Mars Attacks! (1996)

The Evening Star (1996)

Blood and Wine (1997)

As Good As It Gets (1997; Academy Award for best actor)

The Pledge (2001)

GWYNETH PALTROW
Actor

Shout (1991)

Hook (1991)

Flesh and Bone (1993)

Malice (1993)

Mrs. Parker and the Vicious Circle (1994)

Seven (1995)

Moonlight and Valentino (1995)

Jefferson in Paris (1995)

The Pallbearer (1996)

Emma (1996)

Hard Eight (1997)

A Perfect Murder (1997)

Sliding Doors (1998)

Hush (1998)

Great Expectations (1998)

Shakespeare in Love (1998; Academy Award for best actress)

The Talented Mr. Ripley (1999)

Duets (2000)

Bounce (2000)

The Anniversary Party (2001)

MICHELLE PFEIFFER
Actor

The Hollywood Knights (1980)

Falling in Love Again (1980)

Charlie Chan and the Curse of the Dragon Queen (1981)

Grease 2 (1982)

Scarface (1983)

Into the Night (1985)

Ladyhawke (1985)

Sweet Liberty (1986)

Amazon Women on the Moon (1987)

The Witches of Eastwick (1987)

Dangerous Liaisons (1988)

Married to the Mob (1988)

Tequila Sunrise (1988)

The Fabulous Baker Boys (1989)

The Russia House (1990)

Frankie and Johnny (1991)

Batman Returns (1992)

Love Field (1992)

The Age of Innocence (1993)

Wolf (1994)

Dangerous Minds (1995)

Up Close and Personal (1996)

To Gillian on Her 37th Birthday (1996)

One Fine Day (1996)

A Thousand Acres (1997)

Prince of Egypt (cartoon voice, 1998)

William Shakespeare's A Midsummer Night's Dream (1999)

The Deep End of the Ocean (1999)

The Story of Us (1999)

What Lies Beneath (2000)

BRAD PITT
Actor

Cutting Class (1989)

Happy Together (1989)

Across the Tracks (1991)

Thelma & Louise (1991)

Johnny Suede (1991)

Cool World (1992)

A River Runs Through It (1992)

True Romance (1993)

Kalifornia (1993)

The Favor (1994)

Interview with the Vampire (1994)

Legends of the Fall (1994)

Seven (1995)

Twelve Monkeys (1995)

Sleepers (1996)

The Devil's Own (1997)

Seven Years in Tibet (1997)

Meet Joe Black (1998)

Fight Club (1999)

The Mexican (2001)

Snatch (2001)

JULIA ROBERTS
Actor

Satisfaction (1988)

Mystic Pizza (1988)

Blood Red (1989)

Steel Magnolias (1989)

Pretty Woman (1990)

Flatliners (1990)

Sleeping with the Enemy (1991)

Dying Young (1991)

Hook (1991)

The Player (1992)

The Pelican Brief (1993)

I Love Trouble (1994)

Ready to Wear (1994)

Something to Talk About (1995)

Mary Reilly (1996)

Everyone Says I Love You (1996)

My Best Friend's Wedding (1997)

Conspiracy Theory (1997)

Stepmom (1998)

Notting Hill (1999)

Runaway Bride (1999)

Erin Brockovich (2000; Academy Award for Best Actress)

The Mexican (2001)

America's Sweethearts (2001)

MEG RYAN
Actor

Rich and Famous (1981)

Amityville 3-D (1983)

Armed and Dangerous (1986)

Top Gun (1986)

Innerspace (1987)

Promised Land (1987)

D.O.A. (1988)

The Presidio (1988)

When Harry Met Sally... (1989)

Joe Versus the Volcano (1990)

The Doors (1991)

Prelude to a Kiss (1992)

Sleepless in Seattle (1993)

Flesh and Bone (1993)

When a Man Loves a Woman (1994)

I.Q. (1994)

French Kiss (actor/co-producer, 1995)

Restoration (1995)

Courage Under Fire (1996)

Addicted to Love (1997)

Anastasia (cartoon voice, 1997)

City of Angels (1998)

Hurlyburly (1998)

You've Got Mail (1998)

Hanging Up (2000)

Proof of Life (2000)

WINONA RYDER
Actor

Lucas (1986)

Square Dance (1987)

Beetlejuice (1988)

1969 (1988)

Heathers (1989)

Great Balls of Fire! (1989)

Welcome Home, Roxy Carmichael (1990)

Mermaids (1990)

Edward Scissorhands (1990)

Night on Earth (1991)

Bram Stoker's Dracula (1992)

The Age of Innocence (1993)

Reality Bites (1994)

The House of the Spirits (1994)

Little Women (1994)

How to Make an American Quilt (1995)

Boys (1996)

Looking for Richard (1996)

The Crucible (1996)

Alien Resurrection (1997)

Celebrity (1998)

Girl, Interrupted (1999)

Autumn in New York (2000)

Lost Souls (2000)

SUSAN SARANDON
Actor

Joe (1970)

Lady Liberty (a.k.a. Mortadella) (1972)

Lovin' Molly (1974)

The Front Page (1974)

The Rocky Horror Picture Show (1975)

The Great Waldo Pepper (1975)

Dragonfly (1976)

The Great Smokey Roadblock (actor/co-producer, 1976)

Checkered Flag or Crash (1977)

The Other Side of Midnight (1977)

Pretty Baby (1978)

King of the Gypsies (1978)

Something Short of Paradise (1979)

Loving Couples (1980)

Atlantic City (1981)

Tempest (1982)

The Hunger (1983)

The Buddy System (1984)

Compromising Positions (1985)

The Witches of Eastwick (1987)

Bull Durham (1988)

Sweet Hearts Dance (1988)

The January Man (1989)

A Dry White Season (1989)

White Palace (1990)

Thelma & Louise (1991)

Bob Roberts (1992)

Light Sleeper (1992)

Lorenzo's Oil (1992)

The Client (1994)

Safe Passage (1994)

Little Women (1994)

Dead Man Walking (1995)

James and the Giant Peach (cartoon voice, 1996)

Twilight (1998)

Stepmom (1998)

Anywhere But Here (1999)

Cradle Will Rock (1999)

Joe Gould's Secret (2000)

Rugrats in Paris (cartoon voice, 2000)

Cats & Dogs (voice, 2001)

ARNOLD SCHWARZENEGGER
Actor

Hercules in New York (1974)

Stay Hungry (1976)

Pumping Iron (1977)

The Villain (1979)

Conan the Barbarian (1982)

Conan the Destroyer (1984)

The Terminator (1984)

Commando (1985)

Red Sonja (1985)

Raw Deal (1986)

Predator (1987)

The Running Man (1987)

Red Heat (1988)

Twins (1988)

Total Recall (1989)

Kindergarten Cop (1990)

Terminator 2: Judgment Day (1991)

Last Action Hero (1993)

True Lies (1994)

Junior (1994)

Eraser (1996)

Jingle All the Way (1996)

Batman & Robin (1997)

End of Days (1999)

The 6th Day (2000)

Dr. Dolittle 2 (voice, 2001)

MARTIN SCORSESE
Director/producer/screen-writer

Who's That Knocking at My Door? (director/screenwriter/actor, 1969)

Street Scenes 1970 (director/actor, 1970)

Boxcar Bertha (director, 1972)

Mean Streets (director/screenwriter, 1973)

Alice Doesn't Live Here Any-more (director, 1974)

Taxi Driver (director, 1976)

New York, New York (director, 1977)

American Boy: A Profile of Steven Prince (director, 1978)

The Last Waltz (director/actor, 1978)

Raging Bull (director/actor, 1980)

The King of Comedy (direc-tor/actor, 1983)

After Hours (director, 1985)

The Color of Money (director, 1986)

The Last Temptation of Christ (director, 1988)

"Life Lessons" in New York Stories (director, 1989)

GoodFellas (director/co-screenwriter, 1990)

Made in Milan (director, 1990)

The Grifters (producer, 1990)

Cape Fear (director, 1991)

The Age of Innocence (direc-tor/co-screenwriter, 1993)

Clockers (co-producer, 1995)

Casino (director/co-screenwriter, 1995)

Kundun (director, 1997)

Bringing Out the Dead (director, 1999)

STEVEN SPIELBERG
Director/producer/screen-writer

Duel (director, telefilm, 1971; U.S. theatrical release, 1984)

The Sugarland Express (direc-tor/co-screenwriter,1974)

Jaws (director, 1975)

Close Encounters of the Third Kind (director/screenwriter, 1977)

1941 (director, 1979)

Raiders of the Lost Ark (direc-tor, 1981)

E.T., the Extra-Terrestrial (director/co-producer, 1982)

Poltergeist (co-producer/co-screenwriter, 1982)

"Kick the Can," in Twilight Zone—The Movie (director/co-producer, 1983)

Indiana Jones and the Temple of Doom (director, 1984)

The Color Purple (director/co-producer, 1985)

Empire of the Sun (director, 1987)

Always (director/co-producer, 1989)

Indiana Jones and the Last Crusade (director, 1989)

Hook (director, 1991)

An American Tail II: Fievel Goes West (co-producer, 1991)

Jurassic Park (director, 1993)

Schindler's List (director/pro-ducer, 1993; Academy Awards for best director, best picture)

The Lost World: Jurassic Park (director, 1997)

Amistad (director/co-producer, 1997)

Saving Private Ryan (direc-tor/co-producer, 1998; Academy Award for best director)

A.I.: Artificial Intelligence (director/producer/screen-writer, 2001)

SYLVESTER STALLONE
Actor/director/screenwriter

A Party at Kitty and Stud's (reissued as The Italian Stal-lion) (1970)

Bananas (1971)

The Lords of Flatbush (actor/co-screenwriter, 1974)

Capone (1975)

Death Race 2000 (1975)

Farewell, My Lovely (1975)

No Place to Hide (1975)

The Prisoner of Second Avenue (1975)

Cannonball (1976)

Rocky (actor/screenwriter/fight choreographer, 1976)

F.I.S.T. (actor/co-screenwriter, 1978)

Paradise Alley (actor/director/screenwriter, 1978)

Rocky II (actor/director/screen-writer/fight choreographer, 1979)

Victory (1981)

Nighthawks (1981)

First Blood (actor/co-screenwriter, 1982)

Rocky III (actor/director/screenwriter/fight choreogra-pher, 1982)

Staying Alive (director/co-producer/co-screenwriter, 1983)

Rhinestone (actor/co-screenwriter, 1984)

Rambo: First Blood, Part II (actor/co-screenwriter, 1985)

Rocky IV (actor/director/screenwriter, 1985)

Cobra (actor/screenwriter, 1986)

Over the Top (actor/co-screenwriter, 1987)

Rambo III (actor/co-screenwriter, 1988)

Lock Up (1989)

Tango and Cash (1989)

Rocky V (actor/screenwriter, 1990)

Oscar (1991)

Stop! or My Mom Will Shoot (1992)

Cliffhanger (actor/co-screenwriter, 1993)

Demolition Man (1993)

The Specialist (1994)

Judge Dredd (1995)

Assassins (1995)

Daylight (1996)

Cop Land (1997)

An Alan Smithee Film: Burn Hollywood Burn (1998)

Antz (cartoon voice, 1998)

Get Carter (2000)

Driven (2001)

SHARON STONE
Actor

Stardust Memories (1980)
Deadly Blessing (1981)
Bolero (1981)
Irreconcilable Differences (1984)
King Solomon's Mines (1985)
Allan Quartermain and the Lost City of Gold (1987)
Action Jackson (1988)
Above the Law (1988)
Personal Choice (a.k.a. Beyond the Stars) (1989)
Blood and Sand (1989)
Total Recall (1990)
He Said, She Said (1991)
Scissors (1991)
Year of the Gun (1991)
Basic Instinct (1992)
Where Sleeping Dogs Lie (1992)
Diary of a Hitman (1992)
Sliver (1993)
Intersection (1994)
The Specialist (1994)
The Quick and the Dead (1995)
Casino (1995)
Diabolique (1996)
Last Dance (1996)
Sphere (1998)
Antz (cartoon voice, 1998)
The Mighty (1998)
The Muse (1999)
Simpatico (1999)

MERYL STREEP
Actor

Julia (1977)
The Deer Hunter (1978)
Manhattan (1979)
The Seduction of Joe Tynan (1979)
Kramer vs. Kramer (1979; Academy Award for best supporting actress)
The French Lieutenant's Woman (1981)
Sophie's Choice (1982; Academy Award for best actress)
Still of the Night (1982)
Silkwood (1983)

Falling in Love (1984)
Plenty (1985)
Out of Africa (1985)
Heartburn (1986)
Ironweed (1987)
A Cry in the Dark (1988)
She-Devil (1989)
Postcards from the Edge (1990)
Defending Your Life (1991)
Death Becomes Her (1992)
The House of the Spirits (1994)
The River Wild (1994)
The Bridges of Madison County (1995)
Before and After (1996)
Marvin's Room (1996)
One True Thing (1998)
Antz (cartoon voice, 1998)
Dancing with Lughnasa (1998)
Music of the Heart (1999)

EMMA THOMPSON
Actor/screenwriter

Henry V (1989)
The Tall Guy (1989)
Impromptu (1990)
Dead Again (1991)
Howard's End (1992)
Peter's Friends (1992)
Much Ado About Nothing (1993)
The Remains of the Day (1993)
In the Name of the Father (1993)
Junior (1994)
Carrington (1995)
Sense and Sensibility (actor/screenwriter, 1995; Academy Award for best adapted screenplay)
The Winter Guest (1997)
Primary Colors (1998)

JOHN TRAVOLTA
Actor

The Devil's Rain (1975)
Carrie (1976)
Saturday Night Fever (1977)
Grease (1978)
Moment by Moment (1978)
Urban Cowboy (1980)

Blow Out (1981)
Staying Alive (1983)
Two of a Kind (1983)
Perfect (1985)
The Experts (1989)
Look Who's Talking (1989)
Look Who's Talking Too (1990)
Shout (1991)
Eyes of an Angel (1991)
Look Who's Talking Now (1993)
Pulp Fiction (1994)
Get Shorty (1995)
White Man's Burden (1995)
Broken Arrow (1996)
Phenomenon (1996)
Michael (1996)
Face/Off (1997)
She's So Lovely (1997)
Mad City (1997)
Primary Colors (1998)
A Civil Action (1998)
The Thin Red Line (1998)
The General's Daughter (1999)
Battlefield Earth (2000)
Lucky Numbers (2000)
Swordfish (2001)

DENZEL WASHINGTON
Actor

Carbon Copy (1981)
A Soldier's Story (1984)
Power (1986)
Cry Freedom (1987)
Glory (1989; Academy Award for best supporting actor)
For Queen and Country (1989)
Reunion (1989)
The Mighty Quinn (1989)
Mo' Better Blues (1990)
Heart Condition (1990)
Ricochet (1991)
Mississippi Masala (1991)
Malcolm X (1992)
Much Ado About Nothing (1993)
The Pelican Brief (1993)
Philadelphia (1993)
Crimson Tide (1995)
Virtuosity (1995)
Devil in a Blue Dress (1995)
Courage Under Fire (1996)
The Preacher's Wife (1996)
Fallen (1998)

He Got Game (1998)
The Siege (1998)
The Bone Collector (1999)
The Hurricane (1999)
Remember the Titans (2000)

ROBIN WILLIAMS
Actor

Can I Do It...Til I Need Glasses? (1977)
Popeye (1980)
The World According to Garp (1982)
The Survivors (1983)
Moscow on the Hudson (1984)
Seize the Day (1986)
The Best of Times (1986)
Club Paradise (1986)
Good Morning, Vietnam (1987)
The Adventures of Baron Munchausen (1989)
Dead Poets Society (1989)
Cadillac Man (1990)
Awakenings (1990)
Dead Again (1991)
Shakes the Clown (1991)
Hook (1991)
The Fisher King (1991)
FernGully: The Last Rainforest (cartoon voice, 1992)
Aladdin (cartoon voice, 1992)
Toys (1992)
Mrs. Doubtfire (1993)
Being Human (1994)
Nine Months (1994)
To Wong Foo, Thanks for Everything, Julie Newmar (1994)
Jumanji (1995)
The Birdcage (1996)
Jack (1996)
The Secret Agent (1996)
Hamlet (1996)
Fathers' Day (1997)
Flubber (1997)
Good Will Hunting (1997; Academy Award for best supporting actor)
Deconstructing Harry (1997)
What Dreams May Come (1998)
Jakob the Liar (1999)
Get Bruce (1999)
Bicentennial Man (1999)

THE TOP VIDEOS, YEAR BY YEAR

Billboard magazine has been tracking video sales since 1980 and rentals since 1982. First we bought Jane Fonda workout tapes, then cartoon classics. Now the *Austin Powers* sequel has provided another shagadelic video performance, the cartoons aren't so classic (*South Park*), and Latin music is selling big.

1980

Sales

1. The Godfather
2. Saturday Night Fever
3. Superman
4. M*A*S*H
5. The Godfather, Part II
6. Blazing Saddles
7. 10
8. Grease
9. The Sound of Music
10. Halloween

1981

Sales

1. Airplane!
2. Caddyshack
3. 9 to 5
4. Superman
5. Alien
6. Star Trek
7. Fame
8. Ordinary People
9. The Elephant Man
10. Popeye

1982

Sales

1. Clash of the Titans
2. An American Werewolf in London
3. Atlantic City
4. Stir Crazy
5. The Jazz Singer
6. The Blue Lagoon
7. Kramer vs. Kramer
8. Casablanca
9. Raging Bull
10. Jane Fonda's Workout

Rentals

1. Clash of the Titans
2. An American Werewolf in London
3. Arthur
4. Star Wars
5. Fort Apache, the Bronx
6. For Your Eyes Only
7. On Golden Pond
8. Stripes
9. The Cannonball Run
10. Superman II

1983

Sales

1. Jane Fonda's Workout
2. Star Trek II: The Wrath of Khan
3. An Officer and a Gentleman
4. The Compleat Beatles
5. Rocky III
6. Playboy Vol. I
7. Poltergeist
8. Star Wars
9. Blade Runner
10. The Road Warrior

Rentals

1. An Officer and a Gentleman
2. Star Trek II: The Wrath of Khan
3. The Road Warrior
4. Rocky III
5. Poltergeist
6. First Blood
7. Das Boot
8. Night Shift
9. Blade Runner
10. Sophie's Choice

1984

Sales

1. Jane Fonda's Workout
2. Raiders of the Lost Ark
3. Making Michael Jackson's "Thriller"
4. Flashdance
5. Duran Duran
6. Risky Business
7. 48 Hrs.
8. Do It Debbie's Way
9. Trading Places
10. The Jane Fonda Workout Challenge

Rentals

1. Raiders of the Lost Ark
2. Risky Business
3. Flashdance
4. 48 Hrs.
5. Tootsie
6. Mr. Mom
7. Sudden Impact
8. Trading Places
9. Blue Thunder
10. Making Michael Jackson's "Thriller"

1985

Sales

1. Jane Fonda's Workout
2. Jane Fonda's Prime Time Workout
3. Making Michael Jackson's "Thriller"
4. Purple Rain
5. Gone with the Wind
6. The Jane Fonda Workout Challenge
7. Raiders of the Lost Ark
8. Raquel, Total Beauty and Fitness
9. We Are the World—The Video Event
10. Wham! The Video

Rentals

1. The Karate Kid
2. The Terminator
3. Police Academy
4. Romancing the Stone
5. Revenge of the Nerds
6. The Natural
7. Starman
8. The Empire Strikes Back
9. Bachelor Party
10. Splash

1986

Sales

1. Jane Fonda's New Workout
2. Jane Fonda's Workout
3. Pinocchio
4. Beverly Hills Cop
5. The Sound of Music
6. Jane Fonda's Prime Time Workout
7. Casablanca
8. Gone With the Wind
9. The Wizard of Oz
10. The Best of John Belushi

Rentals

1. Back to the Future
2. Beverly Hills Cop
3. Prizzi's Honor
4. Witness
5. Ghostbusters
6. Rambo: First Blood Part II
7. Return of the Jedi
8. Cocoon

9. Mask
10. Gremlins

1987

Sales

1. Jane Fonda's Low Impact Aerobic Workout
2. Jane Fonda's New Workout
3. Sleeping Beauty
4. Top Gun
5. Callanetics
6. The Sound of Music
7. Kathy Smith's Body Basics
8. Indiana Jones and the Temple of Doom
9. Star Trek III: The Search for Spock
10. Star Trek II: The Wrath of Khan

Rentals

1. Short Circuit
2. Top Gun
3. Back to School
4. Indiana Jones and the Temple of Doom
5. Down and Out in Beverly Hills
6. The Color of Money
7. Ferris Bueller's Day Off
8. Stand By Me
9. Ruthless People
10. Aliens

1988

Sales

1. Lady and the Tramp
2. Callanetics
3. Jane Fonda's Low Impact Aerobic Workout
4. Star Trek IV: The Voyage Home
5. Start Up with Jane Fonda
6. An American Tail
7. Jane Fonda's New Workout
8. Pink Floyd: The Wall
9. Dirty Dancing
10. Sleeping Beauty

Rentals

1. Dirty Dancing
2. Lethal Weapon
3. Fatal Attraction

4. *The Untouchables*
5. *The Witches of Eastwick*
6. *No Way Out*
7. *Outrageous Fortune*
8. *Robocop*
9. *Stakeout*
10. *Tin Men*

1989

Sales

1. *Cinderella*
2. *E.T., the Extra-Terrestrial*
3. *Jane Fonda's Complete Workout*
4. *Moonwalker*
5. *Callanetics*
6. *Dirty Dancing*
7. *The Wizard of Oz: The 50th Anniversary Edition*
8. *Lethal Weapon*
9. *U2 Rattle and Hum*
10. *Pink Floyd: The Delicate Sound of Thunder*

Rentals

1. *Big*
2. *Die Hard*
3. *A Fish Called Wanda*
4. *Three Men and a Baby*
5. *Beetlejuice*
6. *Coming to America*
7. *Cocktail*
8. *Twins*
9. *Bull Durham*
10. *"Crocodile" Dundee II*

1990

Sales

1. *Bambi*
2. *New Kids on the Block: Hangin' Tough Live*
3. *The Little Mermaid*
4. *Lethal Weapon 2*
5. *The Wizard of Oz: The 50th Anniversary Edition*
6. *Batman*
7. *Honey, I Shrunk the Kids*
8. *The Land Before Time*
9. *Who Framed Roger Rabbit*
10. *Teenage Mutant Ninja Turtles: Cowabunga, Shredhead*

Rentals

1. *Look Who's Talking*
2. *When Harry Met Sally*
3. *Parenthood*
4. *K-9*
5. *Dead Poets Society*
6. *Steel Magnolias*

7. *Sea of Love*
8. *Turner & Hooch*
9. *Black Rain*
10. *Internal Affairs*

1991

Sales

1. *Pretty Woman*
2. *The Little Mermaid*
3. *Peter Pan*
4. *The Jungle Book*
5. *The Three Tenors in Concert*
6. *Richard Simmons: Sweatin' to the Oldies*
7. *Teenage Mutant Ninja Turtles: The Movie*
8. *The Terminator*
9. *Ducktales: The Movie*
10. *Total Recall*

Rentals

1. *Ghost*
2. *Pretty Woman*
3. *GoodFellas*
4. *Bird on a Wire*
5. *Flatliners*
6. *The Hunt for Red October*
7. *Kindergarten Cop*
8. *Total Recall*
9. *Sleeping with the Enemy*
10. *Another 48 Hrs.*

1992

Sales

1. *Fantasia*
2. *101 Dalmations*
3. *The Jungle Book*
4. *Robin Hood: Prince of Thieves*
5. *Cherfitness: A New Attitude*
6. *Fievel Goes West*
7. *1992 Playboy Video Playmate Calendar*
8. *Home Alone*
9. *The Rescuers Down Under*
10. *Playboy: Sexy Lingerie IV*

Rentals

1. *Thelma and Louise*
2. *The Silence of the Lambs*
3. *The Fisher King*
4. *City Slickers*
5. *Backdraft*
6. *Cape Fear*
7. *The Hand That Rocks the Cradle*
8. *Father of the Bride*
9. *Deceived*
10. *What About Bob?*

1993

Sales

1. *Beauty and the Beast*
2. *Pinocchio*
3. *101 Dalmatians*
4. *Playboy Celebrity Centerfold: Jessica Hahn*
5. *Sister Act*
6. *Playboy Playmate of the Year 1993: Anna Nicole Smith*
7. *Cindy Crawford/Shape Your Body Workout*
8. *Home Alone 2: Lost in New York*
9. *Disney's Sing Along Songs: Friend Like Me*
10. *Beethoven*

Rentals

1. *Sister Act*
2. *Patriot Games*
3. *Under Siege*
4. *A League of Their Own*
5. *A Few Good Men*
6. *Scent of a Woman*
7. *Unforgiven*
8. *Sneakers*
9. *Passenger 57*
10. *The Bodyguard*

1994

Sales

1. *Aladdin*
2. *Playboy Celebrity Centerfold: Dian Parkinson*
3. *Yanni: Live at the Acropolis*
4. *Free Willy*
5. *Mrs. Doubtfire*
6. *The Fugitive*
7. *The Return of Jafar*
8. *The Fox and the Hound*
9. *Ace Ventura: Pet Detective*
10. *Beauty and the Beast*

Rentals

1. *Sleepless in Seattle*
2. *Philadelphia*
3. *In the Line of Fire*
4. *The Pelican Brief*
5. *The Fugitive*
6. *The Firm*
7. *Carlito's Way*
8. *Sliver*
9. *Ace Ventura: Pet Detective*
10. *Mrs. Doubtfire*

1995

Sales

1. *The Lion King*
2. *Forrest Gump*
3. *Speed*
4. *Jurassic Park*
5. *The Mask*
6. *Playboy: The Best of Pamela Anderson*
7. *Snow White and the Seven Dwarfs*
8. *The Crow*
9. *Pink Floyd: Pulse*
10. *Yanni: Live at the Acropolis*

Rentals

1. *The Shawshank Redemption*
2. *True Lies*
3. *Disclosure*
4. *Speed*
5. *The Client*
6. *Clear and Present Danger*
7. *When a Man Loves a Woman*
8. *Dumb and Dumber*
9. *Just Cause*
10. *Outbreak*

1996

Sales

1. *Babe*
2. *Apollo 13*
3. *Pulp Fiction*
4. *Playboy: The Best of Jenny McCarthy*
5. *The Aristocats*
6. *Batman Forever*
7. *Jumanji*
8. *Pocahontas*
9. *Cinderella*
10. *Heavy Metal*

Rentals

1. *Braveheart*
2. *The Usual Suspects*
3. *Seven*
4. *Heat*
5. *Twelve Monkeys*
6. *Get Shorty*
7. *Crimson Tide*
8. *Casino*
9. *Executive Decision*
10. *The Net*

1997

Sales

1. Riverdance—The Show
2. Lord of the Dance
3. Independence Day
4. Jerry Maguire
5. 101 Dalmatians
6. Space Jam
7. Toy Story
8. Bambi
9. Star Wars Trilogy— Special Edition
10. The Hunchback of Notre Dame

Rentals

1. Fargo
2. Scream
3. Donnie Brasco
4. Sling Blade
5. Absolute Power
6. The First Wives Club
7. Sleepers
8. Phenomenon
9. Ransom
10. Jerry Maguire

1998

Sales

1. Austin Powers: International Man of Mystery
2. Hercules
3. As Good As It Gets
4. Men in Black
5. Spice World
6. The Little Mermaid: The Special Edition
7. My Best Friend's Wedding
8. Grease: 20th Anniversary Edition
9. Air Force One
10. Titanic

Rentals

1. L.A. Confidential
2. Face/Off
3. As Good As It Gets
4. Good Will Hunting
5. Devil's Advocate
6. Boogie Nights
7. The Full Monty
8. The Game
9. Wag the Dog
10. Austin Powers: International Man of Mystery

1999

Sales

1. Austin Powers: International Man of Mystery
2. Tae-Bo Workout
3. Armageddon
4. A Bug's Life
5. Blade
6. Mulan
7. The Wedding Singer
8. 'N the Mix with 'N Sync
9. You've Got Mail
10. Backstreet Boys: Homecoming—Live in Orlando

Rentals

1. Enemy of the State
2. There's Something About Mary
3. The Truman Show
4. Elizabeth
5. Ronin
6. Armageddon
7. Saving Private Ryan
8. The Siege
9. Payback
10. American History X

2000

Sales

1. The Matrix
2. Buena Vista Social Club
3. Austin Powers: The Spy Who Shagged Me
4. American Pie
5. Slipknot: Welcome to Our Neighborhood
6. Tarzan
7. South Park: Bigger, Longer & Uncut (tie)
7. Star Wars: Episode 1— The Phantom Menace (tie)
9. Sex and the City
10. Big Daddy
11. Saving Private Ryan
12. Stuart Little
13. The Sixth Sense
14. The World is Not Enough
15. Britney Spears: Time Out with Britney Spears
16. Pokemon: The First Movie
17. Mary-Kate & Ashley: Passport to Paris
18. Erin Brockovich
19. Galaxy Quest
20. The Iron Giant

Rentals

1. American Pie
2. The Matrix
3. American Beauty
4. Fight Club (tie)
4. Magnolia (tie)
6. Girl, Interrupted
7. Notting Hill
8. Erin Brockovich
9. Austin Powers: The Spy Who Shagged Me
10. Double Jeopardy
11. The General's Daughter (tie)
11. Bowfinger (tie)
11. The Whole Nine Yards (tie)
14. Dogma
15. The Green Mile
16. Arlington Road
17. Runaway Bride
18. The Sixth Sense
19. Entrapment (tie)
19. The Talented Mr. Ripley (tie)

THE ACADEMY AWARDS

	1927–28	1928–29	1929–30
Picture	*Wings*	*Broadway Melody*	*All Quiet on the Western Front*
Actor	Emil Jannings, *The Last Command; The Way of All Flesh*	Warner Baxter, *In Old Arizona*	George Arliss, *Disraeli*
Actress	Janet Gaynor, *Seventh Heaven; Street Angel; Sunrise*	Mary Pickford, *Coquette*	Norma Shearer, *The Divorcée*
Director	Frank Borzage, *Seventh Heaven;* Lewis Milestone, *Two Arabian Knights*	Frank Lloyd, *The Divine Lady; Weary River; Drag*	Lewis Milestone, *All Quiet on the Western Front*
Adapted Screenplay	Benjamin Glazer, *Seventh Heaven*	—	—
Original Story	Ben Hecht, *Underworld*	Hans Kraly, *The Patriot*	Frances Marion, *The Big House*
Cinematography	*Sunrise*	*White Shadows in the South Seas*	*With Byrd at the South Pole*
Interior Decoration	*The Dove* and *The Tempest*	*The Bridge of San Luis Rey*	*King of Jazz*
Sound	—	—	*The Big House*

OSCAR RECORDS

Most awards in any category: Walt Disney, 27 regular and six special

Most honored films: *Ben-Hur* in 1959 and *Titanic* in 1997, with 11 each, and *West Side Story* in 1961, with 10

Most nominated films: *All About Eve* and *Titanic,* with 14 each, and *Gone With the Wind, From Here to Eternity, Mary Poppins, Who's Afraid of Virginia Woolf?, Forrest Gump,* and *Shakespeare in Love,* with 13 each

Most nominated films to receive no awards: *The Turning Point* and *The Color Purple,* with 11 each

Most Best Actor awards: Spencer Tracy, Fredric March, Gary Cooper, Marlon Brando, Dustin Hoffman, Tom Hanks, and Jack Nicholson, with two each

Most Best Director awards: John Ford with four, for *The Informer, The Grapes of Wrath, How Green Was My Valley,* and *The Quiet Man*

Most Best Actress awards: Katharine Hepburn with four, for *Morning Glory, Guess Who's Coming to Dinner, The Lion in Winter,* and *On Golden Pond*

Best Actress awards for debut performances: Shirley Booth for *Come Back, Little Sheba,* Barbra Streisand for *Funny Girl,* and Marlee Matlin for *Children of a Lesser God*

First African-American Oscar winner: Hattie McDaniel, Best Supporting Actress, in *Gone With the Wind*

	1930–31	1931–32	1932–33
Picture	*Cimarron*	*Grand Hotel*	*Cavalcade*
Actor	Lionel Barrymore, *A Free Soul*	Wallace Beery, *The Champ*; Fredric March, *Dr. Jekyll and Mr. Hyde*	Charles Laughton, *The Private Life of Henry VIII*
Actress	Marie Dressler, *Min and Bill*	Helen Hayes, *The Sin of Madelon Claudet*	Katharine Hepburn, *Morning Glory*
Supporting Actor	—	—	—
Supporting Actress	—	—	—
Director	Norman Taurog, *Skippy*	Frank Borzage, *Bad Girl*	Frank Lloyd, *Cavalcade*
Adapted Screenplay/ Screenplay	Howard Estabrook, *Cimarron*	Edwin Burke, *Bad Girl*	Victor Heerman and Sarah Y. Mason, *Little Women*
Original Story	John Monk Saunders, *The Dawn Patrol*	Francis Marion, *The Champ*	Robert Lord, *One Way Passage*
Song	—	—	—
Score	—	—	—
Cinematography	*Tabu*	*Shanghai Express*	*A Farewell to Arms*
Interior Decoration	*Cimarron*	*Transatlantic*	*Cavalcade*
Film Editing	—	—	—
Sound	Paramount Studio Sound Department	Paramount Studio Sound Department	*A Farewell to Arms*
Short Films	—	*Flower and Trees* (Cartoons); *The Music Box* (Comedy); *Wrestling Swordfish* (Novelty)	*The Three Little Pigs* (Cartoons); *So This Is Harris* (Comedy); *Krakatoa* (Novelty)

POPULAR AND PRAISED

Few films claim the hearts of both the moviegoing public and the majority of the Academy of Motion Picture Arts and Sciences. In fact, only 10 of the top 100 moneymakers of all time have won best-picture Oscars. Those films are listed below, ranked in order of amount grossed. (Source: *Variety*)

1.	*Titanic*	1997
2.	*Forrest Gump*	1994
3.	*Gone With the Wind*	1939
4.	*Dances with Wolves*	1990
5.	*Rain Man*	1988
6.	*The Sound of Music*	1965
7.	*The Sting*	1973
8.	*Platoon*	1986
9.	*The Godfather*	1972
10.	*The Silence of the Lambs*	1991

1934	1935	1936	1937
It Happened One Night	Mutiny on the Bounty	The Great Ziegfeld	The Life of Emile Zola
Clark Gable, It Happened One Night	Victor McLaglen, The Informer	Paul Muni, The Story of Louis Pasteur	Spencer Tracy, Captains Courageous
Claudette Colbert, It Happened One Night	Bette Davis, Dangerous	Luise Rainer, The Great Ziegfeld	Luise Rainer, The Good Earth
—	—	Walter Brennan, Come and Get It	Joseph Schildkraut, The Life of Emile Zola
—	—	Gale Sondergaard, Anthony Adverse	Alice Brady, In Old Chicago
Frank Capra, It Happened One Night	John Ford, The Informer	Frank Capra, Mr. Deeds Goes to Town	Leo McCarey, The Awful Truth
Robert Riskin, It Happened One Night	Dudley Nichols, The Informer	Pierre Collings and Sheridan Gibney, The Story of Louis Pasteur	Heinz Herald, Geza Herczeg, and Norman Reilly Raine, The Life of Emile Zola
Arthur Caesar, Manhattan Melodrama	Ben Hecht and Charles MacArthur, The Scoundrel	Pierre Collings and Sheridan Gibney, The Story of Louis Pasteur	William A. Wellman and Robert Carson, A Star is Born
"The Continental" (The Gay Divorcée)	"Lullaby of Broadway" (Gold Diggers of 1935)	"The Way You Look Tonight" (Swing Time)	"Sweet Leilani" (Waikiki Wedding)
One Night of Love	The Informer	Anthony Adverse	100 Men and a Girl
Cleopatra	A Midsummer Night's Dream	Anthony Adverse	The Good Earth
The Merry Widow	The Dark Angel	Dodsworth	Lost Horizon
Eskimo	A Midsummer Night's Dream	Anthony Adverse	Lost Horizon
One Night of Love	Naughty Marietta	San Francisco	The Hurricane
The Tortoise and the Hare (Cartoons); La Cucaracha (Comedy); City of Wax (Novelty)	Three Orphan Kittens (Cartoons); How To Sleep (Comedy); Wings over Mt. Everest (Novelty)	Country Cousin (Cartoons); Bored of Education (One-Reel); The Public Pays (Two-Reel); Give Me Liberty (Color)	The Old Mill (Cartoons); Private Life of the Gannetts (One-Reel); Torture Money (Two-Reel); Penny Wisdom (Color)

DISNEY'S WINNING TUNES

Disney has dominated the Oscar Best Song category in recent years, winning eight times in the last 11 years. In total, the studio has won 11 times in this category; Paramount still leads with 16 wins.

Song	Film	Year
"When You Wish Upon a Star"	Pinocchio	1940
"Zip-a-Dee-Doo-Dah"	Song of the South	1947
"Chim Chim Cher-ee"	Mary Poppins	1964
"Under the Sea"	The Little Mermaid	1989
"Sooner or Later"	Dick Tracy	1990
"Beauty and the Beast"	Beauty and the Beast	1991
"A Whole New World"	Aladdin	1992
"Can You Feel the Love Tonight"	The Lion King	1994
"Colors of the Wind"	Pocahontas	1995
"You Must Love Me"	Evita	1996
"You'll Be in My Heart"	Tarzan	1999

	1938	**1939**	**1940**
Picture	*You Can't Take It with You*	*Gone With the Wind*	*Rebecca*
Actor	Spencer Tracy, *Boys Town*	Robert Donat, *Goodbye, Mr. Chips*	James Stewart, *The Philadelphia Story*
Actress	Bette Davis, *Jezebel*	Vivien Leigh, *Gone With the Wind*	Ginger Rogers, *Kitty Foyle*
Supporting Actor	Walter Brennan, *Kentucky*	Thomas Mitchell, *Stagecoach*	Walter Brennan, *The Westerner*
Supporting Actress	Fay Bainter, *Jezebel*	Hattie McDaniel, *Gone With the Wind*	Jane Darwell, *The Grapes of Wrath*
Director	Frank Capra, *You Can't Take It with You*	Victor Fleming, *Gone With the Wind*	John Ford, *The Grapes of Wrath*
Screenplay	Ian Dalrymple, Cecil Lewis, and W. P. Lipscomb, *Pygmalion*	Sidney Howard, *Gone With the Wind*	Donald Ogden Stewart, *The Philadelphia Story*
Original Screenplay/ Original Story	Eleanore Griffin and Dore Schary, *Boys Town*	Lewis R. Foster, *Mr. Smith Goes to Washington*	Preston Sturges, *The Great McGinty*; Benjamin Glazer and John S. Toldy, *Arise, My Love*
Song	"Thanks for the Memory" *(Big Broadcast of 1938)*	"Over the Rainbow" *(The Wizard of Oz)*	"When You Wish upon a Star" *(Pinocchio)*
Score/Original Score	*Alexander's Ragtime Band; The Adventures of Robin Hood*	*Stagecoach; The Wizard of Oz*	*Tin Pan Alley; Pinocchio*
Cinematography	*The Great Waltz*	*Wuthering Heights* (B&W); *Gone With the Wind* (Color)	*Rebecca* (B&W); *The Thief of Bagdad* (Color)
Interior Decoration	*The Adventures of Robin Hood*	*Gone With the Wind*	*Pride and Prejudice* (B&W); *The Thief of Bagdad* (Color)
Film Editing	*The Adventures of Robin Hood*	*Gone With the Wind*	*North West Mounted Police*
Sound	*The Cowboy and the Lady*	*When Tomorrow Comes*	*Strike Up the Band*
Special Effects	—	*The Rains Came*	*The Thief of Bagdad*
Short Films	*Ferdinand the Bull* (Cartoons); *That Mothers Might Live* (One-Reel); *Declaration of Independence* (Two-Reel)	*The Ugly Duckling* (Cartoons); *Busy Little Bears* (One-Reel); *Sons of Liberty* (Two-Reel)	*Milky Way* (Cartoons); *Quicker 'N a Wink* (One-Reel); *Teddy, the Rough Rider* (Two-Reel)
Documentaries	—	—	—

> 66 I've never actually held an Oscar before. My dad's mother has his in a goldfish bowl, or something, on the mantelpiece in New York. 99
>
> —Angelina Jolie, Best Supporting Actress, 1999

1941	1942	1943	1944
How Green Was My Valley	*Mrs. Miniver*	*Casablanca*	*Going My Way*
Gary Cooper, *Sergeant York*	James Cagney, *Yankee Doodle Dandy*	Paul Lukas, *Watch on the Rhine*	Bing Crosby, *Going My Way*
Joan Fontaine, *Suspicion*	Greer Garson, *Mrs. Miniver*	Jennifer Jones, *The Song of Bernadette*	Ingrid Bergman, *Gaslight*
Donald Crisp, *How Green Was My Valley*	Van Heflin, *Johnny Eager*	Charles Coburn, *The More the Merrier*	Barry Fitzgerald, *Going My Way*
Mary Astor, *The Great Lie*	Teresa Wright, *Mrs. Miniver*	Katina Paxinou, *For Whom the Bell Tolls*	Ethel Barrymore, *None but the Lonely Heart*
John Ford, *How Green Was My Valley*	William Wyler, *Mrs. Miniver*	Michael Curtiz, *Casablanca*	Leo McCarey, *Going My Way*
Sidney Buchman and Seton I. Miller, *Here Comes Mr. Jordan*	George Froeschel, James Hilton, Claudine West, and Arthur Wimperis, *Mrs. Miniver*	Julius J. Epstein, Philip G. Epstein, and Howard Koch, *Casablanca*	Frank Butler and Frank Cavett, *Going My Way*
Harry Segall, *Here Comes Mr. Jordan;* Herman J. Mankiewicz and Orson Welles, *Citizen Kane*	Michael Kanin and Ring Lardner Jr., *Woman of the Year;* Emeric Pressburger, *The Invaders*	Norman Krasna, *Princess O'Rourke;* William Saroyan, *The Human Comedy*	Lamar Trotti, *Wilson;* Leo McCarey, *Going My Way*
"The Last Time I Saw Paris" *(Lady Be Good)*	"White Christmas" *(Holiday Inn)*	"You'll Never Know" *(Hello, Frisco, Hello)*	"Swinging on a Star" *(Going My Way)*
All That Money Can Buy (Dramatic); *Dumbo* (Musical)	*Now, Voyager* (Dramatic or Comedy); *Yankee Doodle Dandy* (Musical)	*The Song of Bernadette* (Dramatic or Comedy); *This Is the Army* (Musical)	*Since You Went Away* (Dramatic or Comedy); *Cover Girl* (Musical)
How Green Was My Valley (B&W); *Blood and Sand* (Color)	*Mrs. Miniver* (B&W); *The Black Swan* (Color)	*The Song of Bernadette* (B&W); *The Phantom of the Opera* (Color)	*Laura* (B&W); *Wilson* (Color)
How Green Was My Valley (B&W) *Blossoms in the Dust* (Color)	*This Above All* (B&W); *My Gal Sal* (Color)	*The Song of Bernadette* (B&W); *The Phantom of the Opera* (Color)	*Gaslight* (B&W); *Wilson* (Color)
Sergeant York	*The Pride of the Yankees*	*Air Force*	*Wilson*
That Hamilton Woman	*Yankee Doodle Dandy*	*This Land Is Mine*	*Wilson*
I Wanted Wings	*Reap the Wild Wind*	*Crash Dive*	*Thirty Seconds over Tokyo*
Lend a Paw (Cartoons); *Of Pups and Puzzles* (One-Reel); *Main Street on the March* (Two-Reel)	*Der Fuehrer's Face* (Cartoons); *Speaking of Animals and Their Families* (One-Reel); *Beyond the Line of Duty* (Two-Reel)	*Yankee Doodle Mouse* (Cartoons); *Amphibious Fighters* (One-Reel); *Heavenly Music* (Two-Reel)	*Mouse Trouble* (Cartoons); *Who's Who in Animal Land* (One-Reel); *I Won't Play* (Two-Reel)
Churchill's Island	*Battle of Midway; Kokoda Front Line; Moscow Strikes Back; Prelude to War*	*December 7th* (Short); *Desert Victory* (Feature)	*With the Marines at Tarawa* (Short); *The Fighting Lady* (Feature)

	1945	1946	1947
Picture	The Lost Weekend	The Best Years of Our Lives	Gentleman's Agreement
Actor	Ray Milland, The Lost Weekend	Fredric March, The Best Years of Our Lives	Ronald Colman, A Double Life
Actress	Joan Crawford, Mildred Pierce	Olivia de Havilland, To Each His Own	Loretta Young, The Farmer's Daughter
Supporting Actor	James Dunn, A Tree Grows in Brooklyn	Harold Russell, The Best Years of Our Lives	Edmund Gwenn, Miracle on 34th Street
Supporting Actress	Anne Revere, National Velvet	Anne Baxter, The Razor's Edge	Celeste Holm, Gentleman's Agreement
Director	Billy Wilder, The Lost Weekend	William Wyler, The Best Years of Our Lives	Elia Kazan, Gentleman's Agreement
Screenplay	Charles Brackett and Billy Wilder, The Lost Weekend	Robert E. Sherwood, The Best Years of Our Lives	George Seaton, Miracle on 34th Street
Original Screenplay/ Original Story	Richard Schweizer, Marie-Louise; Charles G. Booth, The House on 92nd Street	Muriel and Sydney Box, The Seventh Veil; Clemence Dane, Vacation from Marriage	Sidney Sheldon, The Bachelor and the Bobby-Soxer; Valentine Davies, Miracle on 34th Street
Song	"It Might As Well Be Spring" (State Fair)	"On the Atchison, Topeka and Santa Fe" (The Harvey Girls)	"Zip-A-Dee-Doo-Dah" (Song of the South)
Score—Dramatic or Comedy/ Musical	Spellbound; Anchors Aweigh	The Best Years of Our Lives; The Jolson Story	A Double Life; Mother Wore Tights
Cinematography	The Picture of Dorian Gray (B&W); Leave Her to Heaven (Color)	Anna and the King of Siam (B&W); The Yearling (Color)	Great Expectations (B&W); Black Narcissus (Color)
Costume Design	—	—	—
Interior Decoration, through 1946; Art Direction—Set Decoration, from 1947	Blood on the Sun (B&W); Frenchman's Creek (Color)	Anna and the King of Siam (B&W); The Yearling (Color)	Great Expectations (B&W); Black Narcissus (Color)
Film Editing	National Velvet	The Best Years of Our Lives	Body and Soul
Sound	The Bells of St. Mary's	The Jolson Story	The Bishop's Wife
Special Effects	Wonder Man	Blithe Spirit	Green Dolphin Street
Short Films	Quiet Please (Cartoons); Stairway to Light (One-Reel); Star in the Night (Two-Reel)	The Cat Concerto (Cartoons); Facing Your Danger (One-Reel); A Boy and His Dog (Two-Reel)	Tweetie Pie (Cartoons); Goodbye Miss Turlock (One-Reel); Climbing the Matterhorn (Two-Reel)
Documentaries	Hitler Lives? (Short); The True Glory (Feature)	Seeds of Destiny (Short)	First Steps (Short); Design for Death (Feature)

> 66 I knew I wasn't going to win. I wasn't nervous in the least. It's very easy when you sing first. You have the rest of the night to relax. 99
>
> —Sting, nominee, 2000

1948	1949	1950	1951
Hamlet	*All the King's Men*	*All About Eve*	*An American in Paris*
Laurence Olivier, *Hamlet*	Broderick Crawford, *All the King's Men*	José Ferrer, *Cyrano de Bergerac*	Humphrey Bogart, *The African Queen*
Jane Wyman, *Johnny Belinda*	Olivia de Havilland, *The Heiress*	Judy Holliday, *Born Yesterday*	Vivien Leigh, *A Streetcar Named Desire*
Walter Huston, *The Treasure of the Sierra Madre*	Dean Jagger, *Twelve O'Clock High*	George Sanders, *All About Eve*	Karl Malden, *A Streetcar Named Desire*
Claire Trevor, *Key Largo*	Mercedes McCambridge, *All the King's Men*	Josephine Hull, *Harvey*	Kim Hunter, *A Streetcar Named Desire*
John Huston, *The Treasure of the Sierra Madre*	Joseph L. Mankiewicz, *A Letter to Three Wives*	Joseph L. Mankiewicz, *All About Eve*	George Stevens, *A Place in the Sun*
John Huston, *The Treasure of the Sierra Madre*	Joseph L. Mankiewicz, *A Letter to Three Wives*	Joseph L. Mankiewicz, *All About Eve*	Michael Wilson and Harry Brown, *A Place in the Sun*
Richard Schweizer and David Wechsler, *The Search*	Douglas Morrow, *The Stratton Story* (Motion Picture Story); Robert Pirosh, *Battleground* (Story and Screenplay)	Edna & Edward Anhalt, *Panic in the Streets* (Motion Picture Story); Charles Brackett, Billy Wilder, and D.M. Marshman Jr., *Sunset Boulevard* (Story and Screenplay)	Paul Dehn and James Bernard, *Seven Days to Noon* (Motion Picture Story); Alan Jay Lerner, *An American in Paris* (Story and Screenplay)
"Buttons and Bows" *(The Paleface)*	"Baby, It's Cold Outside" *(Neptune's Daughter)*	"Mona Lisa" *(Captain Carey, USA)*	"In the Cool, Cool, Cool of the Evening" *(Here Comes the Groom)*
The Red Shoes; Easter Parade	*The Heiress; On the Town*	*Sunset Boulevard; Annie Get Your Gun*	*A Place in the Sun; An American in Paris*
The Naked City (B&W); *Joan of Arc* (Color)	*Battleground* (B&W); *She Wore a Yellow Ribbon* (Color)	*The Third Man* (B&W); *King Solomon's Mines* (Color)	*A Place in the Sun* (B&W); *An American in Paris* (Color)
Hamlet (B&W); *Joan of Arc* (Color)	*The Heiress* (B&W); *Adventures of Don Juan* (Color)	*All About Eve* (B&W); *Samson and Delilah* (Color)	*A Place in the Sun* (B&W); *An American in Paris* (Color)
Hamlet (B&W); *The Red Shoes* (Color)	*The Heiress* (B&W); *Little Women* (Color)	*Sunset Boulevard* (B&W); *Samson and Delilah* (Color)	*A Streetcar Named Desire* (B&W); *An American in Paris* (Color)
The Naked City	*Champion*	*King Solomon's Mines*	*A Place in the Sun*
The Snake Pit	*Twelve O'Clock High*	*All About Eve*	*The Great Caruso*
Portrait of Jennie	*Mighty Joe Young*	*Destination Moon*	*When Worlds Collide*
The Little Orphan (Cartoons); *Symphony of a City* (One-Reel); *Seal Island* (Two-Reel)	*For Scent-imental Reasons* (Cartoons); *Aquatic House Party* (One-Reel); *Van Gogh* (Two-Reel)	*Gerald McBoing-Boing* (Cartoons); *Grandad of Races* (One-Reel); *In Beaver Valley* (Two-Reel)	*Two Mouseketeers* (Cartoons); *World of Kids* (One-Reel); *Nature's Half Acre* (Two-Reel)
Toward Independence (Short); *The Secret Land* (Feature)	*A Chance To Live* and *So Much for So Little* (Short); *Daybreak in Udi* (Feature)	*Why Korea?* (Short); *The Titan: Story of Michelangelo* (Feature)	*Benjy* (Short); *Kon-Tiki* (Feature)

> 66 We've got to do something to get people away from TV. 99
>
> —Karl Malden, 1956

	1952	1953	1954
Picture	*The Greatest Show on Earth*	*From Here to Eternity*	*On the Waterfront*
Actor	Gary Cooper, *High Noon*	William Holden, *Stalag 17*	Marlon Brando, *On the Waterfront*
Actress	Shirley Booth, *Come Back, Little Sheba*	Audrey Hepburn, *Roman Holiday*	Grace Kelly, *The Country Girl*
Supporting Actor	Anthony Quinn, *Viva Zapata!*	Frank Sinatra, *From Here to Eternity*	Edmond O'Brien, *The Barefoot Contessa*
Supporting Actress	Gloria Grahame, *The Bad and the Beautiful*	Donna Reed, *From Here to Eternity*	Eva Marie Saint, *On the Waterfront*
Director	John Ford, *The Quiet Man*	Fred Zinnemann, *From Here to Eternity*	Elia Kazan, *On the Waterfront*
Screenplay	Charles Schnee, *The Bad and the Beautiful*	Daniel Taradash, *From Here to Eternity*	George Seaton, *The Country Girl*
Story/Story and Screenplay	Frederic M. Frank, Theodore St. John, and Frank Cavett, *The Greatest Show on Earth*; T.E.B. Clarke, *The Lavender Hill Mob*	Ian McLellan Hunter, *Roman Holiday*; Charles Brackett, Walter Reisch, and Richard Breen, *Titanic*	Philip Yordan, *Broken Lance*; Budd Schulberg, *On the Waterfront*
Song	"High Noon (Do Not Forsake Me, Oh My Darlin')" *(High Noon)*	"Secret Love" *(Calamity Jane)*	"Three Coins in the Fountain" *(Three Coins in the Fountain)*
Score—Dramatic or Comedy/ Musical	*High Noon; With a Song in My Heart*	*Lili; Call Me Madam*	*The High and the Mighty; Seven Brides for Seven Brothers*
Cinematography	*The Bad and the Beautiful* (B&W); *The Quiet Man* (Color)	*From Here to Eternity* (B&W); *Shane* (Color)	*On the Waterfront* (B&W); *Three Coins in the Fountain* (Color)
Costume Design	*The Bad and the Beautiful* (B&W); *Moulin Rouge* (Color)	*Roman Holiday* (B&W); *The Robe* (Color)	*Sabrina* (B&W); *Gate of Hell* (Color)
Art Direction—Set Decoration	*The Bad and the Beautiful* (B&W); *Moulin Rouge* (Color)	*Julius Caesar* (B&W); *The Robe* (Color)	*On the Waterfront* (B&W); *20,000 Leagues Under the Sea* (Color)
Film Editing	*High Noon*	*From Here to Eternity*	*On the Waterfront*
Foreign Language Film	—	—	—
Sound	*Breaking the Sound Barrier*	*From Here to Eternity*	*The Glenn Miller Story*
Special Effects	*Plymouth Adventure*	*The War of the Worlds*	*20,000 Leagues Under the Sea*
Short Films	*Johann Mouse* (Cartoons); *Light in the Window* (One-Reel); *Water Birds* (Two-Reel)	*Toot, Whistle, Plunk and Boom* (Cartoons); *The Merry Wives of Windsor Overture* (One-Reel); *Bear Country* (Two-Reel)	*When Magoo Flew* (Cartoons); *This Mechanical Age* (One-Reel); *A Time Out of War* (Two-Reel)
Documentaries	*Neighbours* (Short); *The Sea Around Us* (Feature)	*The Alaskan Eskimo* (Short); *The Living Desert* (Feature)	*Thursday's Children* (Short); *The Vanishing Prairie* (Feature)

1955	1956	1957	1958
Marty	Around the World in 80 Days	The Bridge on the River Kwai	Gigi
Ernest Borgnine, Marty	Yul Brynner, The King and I	Alec Guinness, The Bridge on the River Kwai	David Niven, Separate Tables
Anna Magnani, The Rose Tattoo	Ingrid Bergman, Anastasia	Joanne Woodward, The Three Faces of Eve	Susan Hayward, I Want to Live!
Jack Lemmon, Mister Roberts	Anthony Quinn, Lust for Life	Red Buttons, Sayonara	Burl Ives, The Big Country
Jo Van Fleet, East of Eden	Dorothy Malone, Written on the Wind	Miyoshi Umeki, Sayonara	Wendy Hiller, Separate Tables
Delbert Mann, Marty	George Stevens, Giant	David Lean, The Bridge on the River Kwai	Vincente Minnelli, Gigi
Paddy Chayefsky, Marty	James Poe, John Farrow, and S.J. Perelman, Around the World in 80 Days (Adapted)	Pierre Boulle, The Bridge on the River Kwai (Adapted)	Alan Jay Lerner, Gigi (Adapted)
Daniel Fuchs, Love Me or Leave Me; William Ludwig and Sonya Levien, Interrupted Melody	Dalton Trumbo (aka Robert Rich), The Brave One; Albert Lamorisse, The Red Balloon (Original)	George Wells, Designing Woman	Nathan E. Douglas and Harold Jacob Smith, The Defiant Ones
"Love is a Many-Splendored Thing" (Love Is a Many-Splendored Thing)	"Whatever Will Be, Will Be (Que Será, Será)" (The Man Who Knew Too Much)	"All the Way" (The Joker Is Wild)	"Gigi" (Gigi)
Love is a Many-Splendored Thing; Oklahoma!	Around the World in 80 Days; The King and I	The Bridge on the River Kwai	The Old Man and the Sea; Gigi
The Rose Tattoo (B&W); To Catch a Thief (Color)	Somebody up There Likes Me (B&W); Around the World in 80 Days (Color)	The Bridge on the River Kwai	The Defiant Ones (B&W); Gigi (Color)
I'll Cry Tomorrow (B&W); Love Is a Many-Splendored Thing (Color)	The Solid Gold Cadillac (B&W); The King and I (Color)	Les Girls	Gigi
The Rose Tattoo (B&W); Picnic (Color)	Somebody up There Likes Me (B&W); The King and I (Color)	Sayonara	Gigi
Picnic	Around the World in 80 Days	The Bridge on the River Kwai	Gigi
—	La Strada (Italy)	The Nights of Cabiria (Italy)	My Uncle (France)
Oklahoma!	The King and I	Sayonara	South Pacific
The Bridges at Toko-Ri	The Ten Commandments	The Enemy Below	tom thumb
Speedy Gonzales (Cartoon); Survival City (One-Reel); The Face of Lincoln (Two-Reel)	Mister Magoo's Puddle Jumper (Cartoons); Crashing the Water Barrier (One-Reel); The Bespoke Overcoat (Two-Reel)	Birds Anonymous (Cartoons); The Wetback Hound (Live Action)	Knighty Knight Bugs (Cartoons); Grand Canyon (Live Action)
Men Against the Arctic (Short); Helen Keller in Her Story (Feature)	The True Story of the Civil War (Short); The Silent World (Feature)	Albert Schweitzer (Feature)	AMA Girls (Short); White Wilderness (Feature)

	1959	**1960**	**1961**
Picture	*Ben-Hur*	*The Apartment*	*West Side Story*
Actor	Charlton Heston, *Ben-Hur*	Burt Lancaster, *Elmer Gantry*	Maximilian Schell, *Judgment at Nuremburg*
Actress	Simone Signoret, *Room at the Top*	Elizabeth Taylor, *Butterfield 8*	Sophia Loren, *Two Women*
Supporting Actor	Hugh Griffith, *Ben-Hur*	Peter Ustinov, *Spartacus*	George Chakiris, *West Side Story*
Supporting Actress	Shelley Winters, *The Diary of Anne Frank*	Shirley Jones, *Elmer Gantry*	Rita Moreno, *West Side Story*
Director	William Wyler, *Ben-Hur*	Billy Wilder, *The Apartment*	Robert Wise and Jerome Robbins, *West Side Story*
Adapted Screenplay	Neil Paterson, *Room at the Top*	Richard Brooks, *Elmer Gantry*	Abby Mann, *Judgment at Nuremberg*
Story and Screenplay	Russell Rouse and Clarence Greene, story; Stanley Shapiro and Maurice Richlin, screenplay, *Pillow Talk*	Billy Wilder and I.A.L. Diamond, *The Apartment*	William Inge, *Splendor in the Grass*
Song	"High Hopes" (*A Hole in the Head*)	"Never on Sunday" (*Never on Sunday*)	"Moon River" (*Breakfast at Tiffany's*)
Score	*Ben-Hur* (Dramatic or Comedy); *Porgy and Bess* (Musical)	*Exodus* (Dramatic or Comedy); *Song Without End (The Story of Franz Liszt)* (Musical)	*Breakfast at Tiffany's* (Dramatic or Comedy); *West Side Story* (Musical)
Cinematography	*The Diary of Anne Frank* (B&W); *Ben-Hur* (Color)	*Sons and Lovers* (B&W); *Spartacus* (Color)	*The Hustler* (B&W); *West Side Story* (Color)
Costume Design	*Some Like It Hot* (B&W); *Ben-Hur* (Color)	*The Facts of Life* (B&W); *Spartacus* (Color)	*La Dolce Vita* (B&W); *West Side Story* (Color)
Art Direction—Set Decoration	*The Diary of Anne Frank* (B&W); *Ben-Hur* (Color)	*The Apartment* (B&W); *Spartacus* (Color)	*The Hustler* (B&W); *West Side Story* (Color)
Film Editing	*Ben-Hur*	*The Apartment*	*West Side Story*
Foreign Language Film	*Black Orpheus* (France)	*The Virgin Spring* (Sweden)	*Through a Glass Darkly* (Sweden)
Sound	*Ben-Hur*	*The Alamo*	*West Side Story*
Sound Effects (Editing)	—	—	—
Visual Effects	—	—	—
Special Effects	*Ben-Hur*	*The Time Machine*	*The Guns of Navarone*
Short Films	*Moonbird* (Cartoons); *The Golden Fish* (Live Action)	*Munro* (Cartoons); *Day of the Painter* (Live Action)	*Ersatz (The Substitute)* (Cartoons); *Seawards the Great Ships* (Live Action)
Documentaries	*Glass* (Short); *Serengeti Shall Not Die* (Feature)	*Giuseppina* (Short); *The Horse with the Flying Tail* (Feature)	*Project Hope* (Short); *Le Ciel et la boue (Sky Above and Mud Beneath)* (Feature)

1962	1963	1964	1965
Lawrence of Arabia	*Tom Jones*	*My Fair Lady*	*The Sound of Music*
Gregory Peck, *To Kill a Mockingbird*	Sidney Poitier, *Lilies of the Field*	Rex Harrison, *My Fair Lady*	Lee Marvin, *Cat Ballou*
Anne Bancroft, *The Miracle Worker*	Patricia Neal, *Hud*	Julie Andrews, *Mary Poppins*	Julie Christie, *Darling*
Ed Begley, *Sweet Bird of Youth*	Melvyn Douglas, *Hud*	Peter Ustinov, *Topkapi*	Martin Balsam, *A Thousand Clowns*
Patty Duke, *The Miracle Worker*	Margaret Rutherford, *The V.I.P.s*	Lila Kedrova, *Zorba the Greek*	Shelley Winters, *A Patch of Blue*
David Lean, *Lawrence of Arabia*	Tony Richardson, *Tom Jones*	George Cukor, *My Fair Lady*	Robert Wise, *The Sound of Music*
Horton Foote, *To Kill a Mockingbird*	John Osborne, *Tom Jones*	Edward Anhalt, *Beckett*	Robert Bolt, *Doctor Zhivago*
Ennio de Concini, Alfredo Giannetti, and Pietro Germi, *Divorce—Italian Style*	James R. Webb, *How the West Was Won*	S. H. Barnett, story; Peter Stone and Frank Tarloff, screenplay, *Father Goose*	Frederic Raphael, *Darling*
"Days of Wine and Roses" *(Days of Wine and Roses)*	"Call Me Irresponsible" *(Papa's Delicate Condition)*	"Chim Chim Cher-ee" *(Mary Poppins)*	"The Shadow of Your Smile" *(The Sandpiper)*
Lawrence of Arabia (Original); *The Music Man* (Adaptation)	*Tom Jones* (Original); *Irma La Douce* (Adaptation)	*Mary Poppins* (Original); *My Fair Lady* (Adaptation)	*Doctor Zhivago* (Original); *The Sound of Music* (Adaptation)
The Longest Day (B&W); *Lawrence of Arabia* (Color)	*Hud* (B&W); *Cleopatra* (Color)	*Zorba the Greek* (B&W); *My Fair Lady* (Color)	*Ship of Fools* (B&W); *Doctor Zhivago* (Color)
Whatever Happened to Baby Jane? (B&W); *The Wonderful World of the Brothers Grimm* (Color)	*8½* (B&W); *Cleopatra* (Color)	*The Night of the Iguana* (B&W); *My Fair Lady* (Color)	*Darling* (B&W); *Doctor Zhivago* (Color)
To Kill a Mockingbird (B&W); *Lawrence of Arabia* (Color)	*America America* (B&W); *Cleopatra* (Color)	*Zorba the Greek* (B&W); *My Fair Lady* (Color)	*Ship of Fools* (B&W); *Doctor Zhivago* (Color)
Lawrence of Arabia	*How the West Was Won*	*Mary Poppins*	*The Sound of Music*
Sundays and Cybèle (France)	*8½* (Italy)	*Yesterday, Today and Tomorrow* (Italy)	*The Shop on Main Street* (Czechoslovakia)
Lawrence of Arabia	*How the West Was Won*	*My Fair Lady*	*The Sound of Music*
—	*It's a Mad, Mad, Mad, Mad World*	*Goldfinger*	*The Great Race*
—	*Cleopatra*	*Mary Poppins*	*Thunderball*
The Longest Day	—	—	—
The Hole (Cartoons); *Heureux Anniversaire* (Live Action)	*The Critic* (Cartoons); *An Occurrence at Owl Creek Bridge* (Live Action)	*The Pink Phink* (Cartoons); *Casals Conducts: 1964* (Live Action)	*The Dot and the Line* (Cartoons); *The Chicken (Le Poulet)* (Live Action)
Dylan Thomas (Short); *Black Fox* (Feature)	*Chagall* (Short); *Robert Frost: A Lover's Quarrel with the World* (Feature)	*Nine from Little Rock* (Short); *Jacques-Yves Cousteau's World Without Sun* (Feature)	*To Be Alive!* (Short); *The Eleanor Roosevelt Story* (Feature)

	1966	1967	1968
Picture	*A Man for All Seasons*	*In the Heat of the Night*	*Oliver!*
Actor	Paul Scofield, *A Man for All Seasons*	Rod Steiger, *In the Heat of the Night*	Cliff Robertson, *Charly*
Actress	Elizabeth Taylor, *Who's Afraid of Virginia Woolf?*	Katharine Hepburn, *Guess Who's Coming to Dinner*	Katharine Hepburn, *The Lion in Winter;* Barbra Streisand, *Funny Girl*
Supporting Actor	Walter Matthau, *The Fortune Cookie*	George Kennedy, *Cool Hand Luke*	Jack Albertson, *The Subject Was Roses*
Supporting Actress	Sandy Dennis, *Who's Afraid of Virginia Woolf?*	Estelle Parsons, *Bonnie and Clyde*	Ruth Gordon, *Rosemary's Baby*
Director	Fred Zinnemann, *A Man for All Seasons*	Mike Nichols, *The Graduate*	Carol Reed, *Oliver!*
Adapted Screenplay	Robert Bolt, *A Man for All Seasons*	Stirling Silliphant, *In the Heat of the Night*	James Goldman, *The Lion in Winter*
Story and Screenplay	Claude Lelouch, story; Pierre Uytterhoeven and Claude Lelouch, screenplay, *A Man and a Woman*	William Rose, *Guess Who's Coming to Dinner?*	Mel Brooks, *The Producers*
Song	"Born Free" *(Born Free)*	"Talk to the Animals" *(Doctor Dolittle)*	"The Windmills of Your Mind" *(The Thomas Crown Affair)*
Score	*Born Free* (Original); *A Funny Thing Happened on the Way to the Forum* (Adaptation)	*Thoroughly Modern Millie* (Original); *Camelot* (Adaptation)	*The Lion in Winter* (Nonmusical); *Oliver!* (Musical)
Cinematography	*Who's Afraid of Virginia Woolf?* (B&W); *A Man for All Seasons*	*Bonnie and Clyde*	*Romeo and Juliet*
Costume Design	*Who's Afraid of Virginia Woolf?* (B&W); *A Man for All Seasons* (Color)	*Camelot*	*Romeo and Juliet*
Art Direction—Set Decoration	*Who's Afraid of Virginia Woolf?* (B&W); *Fantastic Voyage* (Color)	*Camelot*	*Oliver!*
Film Editing	*Grand Prix*	*In the Heat of the Night*	*Bullitt*
Foreign Language Film	*A Man and a Woman* (France)	*Closely Watched Trains* (Czechoslovakia)	*War and Peace* (U.S.S.R.)
Sound	*Grand Prix*	*In the Heat of the Night*	*Oliver!*
Sound Effects (Editing)	*Grand Prix*	*The Dirty Dozen*	—
Visual Effects	*Fantastic Voyage*	*Doctor Dolittle*	*2001: A Space Odyssey*
Short Films	*Herb Alpert and the Tijuana Brass Double Feature* (Cartoons); *Wild Wings* (Live Action)	*The Box* (Cartoons); *A Place to Stand* (Live Action)	*Winnie the Pooh and the Blustery Day* (Cartoons); *Robert Kennedy Remembered* (Live Action)
Documentaries	*A Year Toward Tomorrow* (Short); *The War Game* (Feature)	*The Redwoods* (Short); *The Anderson Platoon* (Feature)	*Why Man Creates* (Short); *Journey into Self* (Feature)

1969	1970	1971	1972
Midnight Cowboy	*Patton*	*The French Connection*	*The Godfather*
John Wayne, *True Grit*	George C. Scott, *Patton*	Gene Hackman, *The French Connection*	Marlon Brando, *The Godfather*
Maggie Smith, *The Prime of Miss Jean Brodie*	Glenda Jackson, *Women in Love*	Jane Fonda, *Klute*	Liza Minnelli, *Cabaret*
Gig Young, *They Shoot Horses, Don't They?*	John Mills, *Ryan's Daughter*	Ben Johnson, *The Last Picture Show*	Joel Grey, *Cabaret*
Goldie Hawn, *Cactus Flower*	Helen Hayes, *Airport*	Cloris Leachman, *The Last Picture Show*	Eileen Heckart, *Butterflies Are Free*
John Schlesinger, *Midnight Cowboy*	Franklin J. Schaffner, *Patton*	William Friedkin, *The French Connection*	Bob Fosse, *Cabaret*
Waldo Salt, *Midnight Cowboy*	Ring Lardner Jr., *M*A*S*H*	Ernest Tidyman, *The French Connection*	Mario Puzo and Francis Ford Coppola, *The Godfather*
William Goldman, *Butch Cassidy and the Sundance Kid*	Francis Ford Coppola and Edmund H. North, *Patton*	Paddy Chayefsky, *The Hospital*	Jeremy Larner, *The Candidate*
"Raindrops Keep Fallin' on My Head" *(Butch Cassidy and the Sundance Kid)*	"For All We Know" *(Lovers and Other Strangers)*	"Theme from *Shaft*" *(Shaft)*	"The Morning After" *(The Poseidon Adventure)*
Butch Cassidy and the Sundance Kid (Nonmusical); *Hello Dolly!* (Musical)	*Love Story* (Original Score); *Let It Be* (Original Song Score)	*Summer of '42* (Dramatic); *Fiddler on the Roof* (Adapted)	*Limelight* (Dramatic); *Cabaret* (Adapted)
Butch Cassidy and the Sundance Kid	*Ryan's Daughter*	*Fiddler on the Roof*	*Cabaret*
Anne of the Thousand Days	*Cromwell*	*Nicholas and Alexandra*	*Travels with My Aunt*
Hello Dolly!	*Patton*	*Nicholas and Alexandra*	*Cabaret*
Z	*Patton*	*The French Connection*	*Cabaret*
Z (Algeria)	*Investigation of a Citizen Above Suspicion* (Italy)	*The Garden of the Finzi-Continis* (Italy)	*The Discreet Charm of the Bourgeoisie* (France)
Hello Dolly!	*Patton*	*Fiddler on the Roof*	*Cabaret*
—	—	—	—
Marooned	*Tora! Tora! Tora!*	*Bedknobs and Broomsticks*	—
It's Tough to Be a Bird (Cartoons); *The Magic Machines* (Live Action)	*Is It Always Right To Be Right?* (Cartoons); *The Resurrection of Broncho Billy* (Live Action)	*The Crunch Bird* (Animated); *Sentinels of Silence* (Live Action)	*A Christmas Carol* (Animated); *Norman Rockwell's World...An American Dream* (Live Action)
Czechoslovakia 1968 (Short); *Arthur Rubinstein—The Love of Life* (Feature)	*Interviews with My Lai Veterans* (Short); *Woodstock* (Feature)	*Sentinels of Silence* (Short); *The Hellstrom Chronicle* (Feature)	*This Tiny World* (Short); *Marjoe* (Feature)

	1973	1974	1975
Picture	*The Sting*	*The Godfather Part II*	*One Flew over the Cuckoo's Nest*
Actor	Jack Lemmon, *Save the Tiger*	Art Carney, *Harry and Tonto*	Jack Nicholson, *One Flew over the Cuckoo's Nest*
Actress	Glenda Jackson, *A Touch of Class*	Ellen Burstyn, *Alice Doesn't Live Here Anymore*	Louise Fletcher, *One Flew over the Cuckoo's Nest*
Supporting Actor	John Houseman, *The Paper Chase*	Robert De Niro, *The Godfather Part II*	George Burns, *The Sunshine Boys*
Supporting Actress	Tatum O'Neal, *Paper Moon*	Ingrid Bergman, *Murder on the Orient Express*	Lee Grant, *Shampoo*
Director	George Roy Hill, *The Sting*	Francis Ford Coppola, *The Godfather Part II*	Milos Forman, *One Flew over the Cuckoo's Nest*
Adapted Screenplay	William Peter Blatty, *The Exorcist*	Francis Ford Coppola and Mario Puzo, *The Godfather Part II*	Lawrence Hauben and Bo Goldman, *One Flew over the Cuckoo's Nest*
Original Screenplay	David S. Ward, *The Sting*	Robert Towne, *Chinatown*	Frank Pierson, *Dog Day Afternoon*
Song	"The Way We Were" *(The Way We Were)*	"We May Never Love Like This Again" *(The Towering Inferno)*	"I'm Easy" *(Nashville)*
Score	*The Way We Were* (Original); *The Sting* (Adaptation)	*The Godfather Part II* (Original); *The Great Gatsby* (Adaptation)	*Jaws* (Original); *Barry Lyndon* (Adaptation)
Cinematography	*Cries and Whispers*	*The Towering Inferno*	*Barry Lyndon*
Costume Design	*The Sting*	*The Great Gatsby*	*Barry Lyndon*
Art Direction—Set Decoration	*The Sting*	*The Godfather Part II*	*Barry Lyndon*
Film Editing	*The Sting*	*The Towering Inferno*	*Jaws*
Foreign Language Film	*Day for Night* (France)	*Amarcord* (Italy)	*Dersu Uzala* (U.S.S.R.)
Sound	*The Exorcist*	*Earthquake*	*Jaws*
Visual Effects	—	—	—
Short Films	*Frank Film* (Animated); *The Bolero* (Live Action)	*Closed Mondays* (Animated); *One-Eyed Men Are Kings* (Live Action)	*Great* (Animated); *Angel and Big Joe* (Live Action)
Documentaries	*Princeton: A Search for Answers* (Short); *The Great American Cowboy* (Feature)	*Don't* (Short); *Hearts and Minds* (Feature)	*The End of the Game* (Short); *The Man Who Skied down Everest* (Feature)

> 66 As for me, prizes are nothing. My prize is my work. 99
> —Katharine Hepburn, 1955

1976	1977	1978	1979
Rocky	*Annie Hall*	*The Deer Hunter*	*Kramer vs. Kramer*
Peter Finch, *Network*	Richard Dreyfuss, *The Goodbye Girl*	Jon Voight, *Coming Home*	Dustin Hoffman, *Kramer vs. Kramer*
Faye Dunaway, *Network*	Diane Keaton, *Annie Hall*	Jane Fonda, *Coming Home*	Sally Field, *Norma Rae*
Jason Robards, *All the President's Men*	Jason Robards, *Julia*	Christopher Walken, *The Deer Hunter*	Melvyn Douglas, *Being There*
Beatrice Straight, *Network*	Vanessa Redgrave, *Julia*	Maggie Smith, *California Suite*	Meryl Streep, *Kramer vs. Kramer*
John G. Avildsen, *Rocky*	Woody Allen, *Annie Hall*	Michael Cimino, *The Deer Hunter*	Robert Benton, *Kramer vs. Kramer*
William Goldman, *All the President's Men*	Alvin Sargent, *Julia*	Oliver Stone, *Midnight Express*	Robert Benton, *Kramer vs. Kramer*
Paddy Chayefsky, *Network*	Woody Allen and Marshall Brickman, *Annie Hall*	Nancy Dowd, story; Waldo Salt and Robert C. Jones, screenplay, *Coming Home*	Steve Tesich, *Breaking Away*
"Evergreen" *(A Star Is Born)*	"You Light Up My Life" *(You Light Up My Life)*	"Last Dance" *(Thank God It's Friday)*	"It Goes Like It Goes" *(Norma Rae)*
The Omen (Original); *Bound for Glory* (Adaptation)	*Star Wars* (Original); *A Little Night Music* (Adaptation)	*Midnight Express* (Original); *The Buddy Holly Story* (Adaptation)	*A Little Romance* (Original); *All That Jazz* (Adaptation)
Bound for Glory	*Close Encounters of the Third Kind*	*Days of Heaven*	*Apocalypse Now*
Fellini's Casanova	*Star Wars*	*Death on the Nile*	*All That Jazz*
All the President's Men	*Star Wars*	*Heaven Can Wait*	*All That Jazz*
Rocky	*Star Wars*	*The Deer Hunter*	*All That Jazz*
Black and White in Color (Ivory Coast)	*Madame Rosa* (France)	*Get Out Your Handkerchiefs* (France)	*The Tin Drum* (Federal Republic of Germany)
All the President's Men	*Star Wars*	*The Deer Hunter*	*Apocalypse Now*
—	*Star Wars*	—	*Alien*
Leisure (Animated); *In the Region of Ice* (Live Action)	*Sand Castle* (Animated); *I'll Find a Way* (Live Action)	*Special Delivery* (Animated); *Teenage Father* (Live Action)	*Every Child* (Animated); *Board and Care* (Live Action)
Number Our Days (Short); *Harlan County, U.S.A.* (Feature)	*Gravity Is My Enemy* (Short); *Who Are the DeBolts? And Where Did They Get Nineteen Kids?* (Feature)	*The Flight of the Gossamer Condor* (Short); *Scared Straight!* (Feature)	*Paul Robeson: Tribute to an Artist* (Short); *Best Boy* (Feature)

> 66 I was just so f---ing angry to lose to Phil Collins…. My grandkids are going to be, "F--- you, Grandpa. You lost to Phil Collins. 99
>
> — Trey Parker, nominee, 1999

	1980	**1981**	**1982**
Picture	*Ordinary People*	*Chariots of Fire*	*Gandhi*
Actor	Robert De Niro, *Raging Bull*	Henry Fonda, *On Golden Pond*	Ben Kingsley, *Gandhi*
Actress	Sissy Spacek, *Coal Miner's Daughter*	Katharine Hepburn, *On Golden Pond*	Meryl Streep, *Sophie's Choice*
Supporting Actor	Timothy Hutton, *Ordinary People*	John Gielgud, *Arthur*	Louis Gossett Jr., *An Officer and a Gentleman*
Supporting Actress	Mary Steenburgen, *Melvin and Howard*	Maureen Stapleton, *Reds*	Jessica Lange, *Tootsie*
Director	Robert Redford, *Ordinary People*	Warren Beatty, *Reds*	Richard Attenborough, *Gandhi*
Adapted Screenplay	Alvin Sargent, *Ordinary People*	Ernest Thompson, *On Golden Pond*	Costa-Gavras and Donald Stewart, *Missing*
Original Screenplay	Bo Goldman, *Melvin and Howard*	Colin Welland, *Chariots of Fire*	John Briley, *Gandhi*
Song	"Fame" *(Fame)*	"Arthur's Theme (Best That You Can Do)" *(Arthur)*	"Up Where We Belong" *(An Officer and a Gentleman)*
Original Score	*Fame*	*Chariots of Fire*	*E.T., the Extra-Terrestrial; Victor/Victoria* (Song Score/Adaptation)
Cinematography	*Tess*	*Reds*	*Gandhi*
Costume Design	*Tess*	*Chariots of Fire*	*Gandhi*
Art Direction—Set Decoration	*Tess*	*Raiders of the Lost Ark*	*Gandhi*
Film Editing	*Raging Bull*	*Raiders of the Lost Ark*	*Gandhi*
Foreign Language Film	*Moscow Does Not Believe in Tears* (U.S.S.R.)	*Mephisto* (Hungary)	*Volver A Empezar (To Begin Again)* (Spain)
Sound	*The Empire Strikes Back*	*Raiders of the Lost Ark*	*Gandhi*
Sound Effects (Editing)	—	—	*E.T., the Extra-Terrestrial*
Makeup	—	*An American Werewolf in London*	*Quest for Fire*
Visual Effects	—	*Raiders of the Lost Ark*	*E.T., the Extra-Terrestrial*
Short Films	*The Fly* (Animated); *The Dollar Bottom* (Live Action)	*Crac* (Animated); *Violet* (Live Action)	*Tango* (Animated); *A Shocking Accident* (Live Action)
Documentaries	*Karl Hess: Toward Liberty* (Short); *From Mao to Mozart: Isaac Stern in China* (Feature)	*Genocide* (Short); *Close Harmony* (Feature)	*If You Love This Planet* (Short); *Just Another Missing Kid* (Feature)

1983	1984	1985	1986
Terms of Endearment	Amadeus	Out of Africa	Platoon
Robert Duvall, Tender Mercies	F. Murray Abraham, Amadeus	William Hurt, Kiss of the Spider Woman	Paul Newman, The Color of Money
Shirley MacLaine, Terms of Endearment	Sally Field, Places in the Heart	Geraldine Page, The Trip to Bountiful	Marlee Matlin, Children of a Lesser God
Jack Nicholson, Terms of Endearment	Haing S. Ngor, The Killing Fields	Don Ameche, Cocoon	Michael Caine, Hannah and Her Sisters
Linda Hunt, The Year of Living Dangerously	Peggy Ashcroft, A Passage to India	Anjelica Huston, Prizzi's Honor	Dianne Wiest, Hannah and Her Sisters
James L. Brooks, Terms of Endearment	Milos Forman, Amadeus	Sydney Pollack, Out of Africa	Oliver Stone, Platoon
James L. Brooks, Terms of Endearment	Peter Shaffer, Amadeus	Kurt Luedtke, Out of Africa	Ruth Prawer Jhabvala, A Room with a View
Horton Foote, Tender Mercies	Robert Benton, Places in the Heart	William Kelley, Pamela Wallace, and Earl W. Wallace, Witness	Woody Allen, Hannah and Her Sisters
"Flashdance...What a Feeling" (Flashdance)	"I Just Called To Say I Love You" (The Woman in Red)	"Say You, Say Me" (White Nights)	"Take My Breath Away" (Top Gun)
The Right Stuff; Yentl (Song Score/Adaptation)	A Passage to India; Purple Rain (Song Score)	Out of Africa	'Round Midnight
Fanny & Alexander	The Killing Fields	Out of Africa	The Mission
Fanny & Alexander	Amadeus	Ran	A Room with a View
Fanny & Alexander	Amadeus	Out of Africa	A Room with a View
The Right Stuff	The Killing Fields	Witness	Platoon
Fanny & Alexander (Sweden)	Dangerous Moves (Switzerland)	The Official Story (Argentina)	The Assault (The Netherlands)
The Right Stuff	Amadeus	Out of Africa	Platoon
The Right Stuff	—	Back to the Future	Aliens
—	Amadeus	Mask	The Fly
Return of the Jedi	Indiana Jones and the Temple of Doom	Cocoon	Aliens
Sundae in New York (Animated); Boys and Girls (Live Action)	Charade (Animated); Up (Live Action)	Anna & Bella (Animated); Molly's Pilgrim (Live Action)	A Greek Tragedy (Animated); Precious Images (Live Action)
Flamenco at 5:15 (Short); He Makes Me Feel Like Dancin' (Feature)	The Stone Carvers (Short); The Times of Harvey Milk (Feature)	Witness to War: Dr. Charlie Clements (Short); Broken Rainbow (Feature)	Women—For America, for the World (Short); Artie Shaw: Time Is All You've Got and Down and Out in America (Feature)

	1987	**1988**	**1989**
Picture	The Last Emperor	Rain Man	Driving Miss Daisy
Actor	Michael Douglas, Wall Street	Dustin Hoffman, Rain Man	Daniel Day-Lewis, My Left Foot
Actress	Cher, Moonstruck	Jodie Foster, The Accused	Jessica Tandy, Driving Miss Daisy
Supporting Actor	Sean Connery, The Untouchables	Kevin Kline, A Fish Called Wanda	Denzel Washington, Glory
Supporting Actress	Olympia Dukakis, Moonstruck	Geena Davis, The Accidental Tourist	Brenda Fricker, My Left Foot
Director	Bernardo Bertolucci, The Last Emperor	Barry Levinson, Rain Man	Oliver Stone, Born on the Fourth of July
Adapted Screenplay	Mark Peploe and Bernardo Bertolucci, The Last Emperor	Christopher Hampton, Dangerous Liaisons	Tom Schulman, Dead Poets Society
Original Screenplay	John Patrick Shanley, Moonstruck	Ronald Bass and Barry Morrow, Rain Man	Alfred Uhry, Driving Miss Daisy
Song	"(I've Had) The Time of My Life" (Dirty Dancing)	"Let the River Run" (Working Girl)	"Under the Sea" (The Little Mermaid)
Original Score	The Last Emperor	The Milagro Beanfield War	The Little Mermaid
Cinematography	The Last Emperor	Mississippi Burning	Glory
Costume Design	The Last Emperor	Dangerous Liaisons	Henry V
Art Direction—Set Decoration	The Last Emperor	Dangerous Liaisons	Batman
Film Editing	The Last Emperor	Who Framed Roger Rabbit	Born on the Fourth of July
Foreign Language Film	Babette's Feast (Denmark)	Pelle the Conqueror (Denmark)	Cinema Paradiso (Italy)
Sound	The Last Emperor	Bird	Glory
Sound Effects (Editing)	—	Who Framed Roger Rabbit	Indiana Jones and the Last Crusade
Makeup	Harry and the Hendersons	Beetlejuice	Driving Miss Daisy
Visual Effects	Innerspace	Who Framed Roger Rabbit	The Abyss
Short Films	The Man Who Planted Trees (Animated); Ray's Male Heterosexual Dance Hall (Live Action)	Tin Toy (Animated); The Appointments of Dennis Jennings (Live Action)	Balance (Animated); Work Experience (Live Action)
Documentaries	Young at Heart (Short); The Ten-Year Lunch: The Wit and the Legend of the Algonquin Round Table (Feature)	You Don't Have To Die (Short); Hotel Terminus: The Life and Times of Klaus Barbie (Feature)	The Johnstown Flood (Short); Common Threads: Stories from the Quilt (Feature)

> 66 This is the first time in my life I've ever worn a bow tie. I feel like a little boy. 99
> —Jude Law, 1999

1990	1991	1992	1993
Dances with Wolves	The Silence of the Lambs	Unforgiven	Schindler's List
Jeremy Irons, Reversal of Fortune	Anthony Hopkins, The Silence of the Lambs	Al Pacino, Scent of a Woman	Tom Hanks, Philadelphia
Kathy Bates, Misery	Jodie Foster, The Silence of the Lambs	Emma Thompson, Howards End	Holly Hunter, The Piano
Joe Pesci, GoodFellas	Jack Palance, City Slickers	Gene Hackman, Unforgiven	Tommy Lee Jones, The Fugitive
Whoopi Goldberg, Ghost	Mercedes Ruehl, The Fisher King	Marisa Tomei, My Cousin Vinny	Anna Paquin, The Piano
Kevin Costner, Dances with Wolves	Jonathan Demme, The Silence of the Lambs	Clint Eastwood, Unforgiven	Steven Spielberg, Schindler's List
Michael Blake, Dances with Wolves	Ted Tally, The Silence of the Lambs	Ruth Prawer Jhabvala, Howards End	Steven Zaillian, Schindler's List
Bruce Joel Rubin, Ghost	Callie Khouri, Thelma & Louise	Neil Jordan, The Crying Game	Jane Campion, The Piano
"Sooner or Later (I Always Get My Man)" (Dick Tracy)	"Beauty and the Beast" (Beauty and the Beast)	"A Whole New World" (Aladdin)	"Streets of Philadelphia" (Philadelphia)
Dances with Wolves	Beauty and the Beast	Aladdin	Schindler's List
Dances with Wolves	JFK	A River Runs Through It	Schindler's List
Cyrano de Bergerac	Bugsy	Bram Stoker's Dracula	The Age of Innocence
Dick Tracy	Bugsy	Howards End	Schindler's List
Dances with Wolves	JFK	Unforgiven	Schindler's List
Journey of Hope (Switzerland)	Mediterraneo (Italy)	Indochine (France)	Belle Epoque (Spain)
Dances with Wolves	Terminator 2: Judgment Day	The Last of the Mohicans	Jurassic Park
The Hunt for Red October	Terminator 2: Judgment Day	Bram Stoker's Dracula	Jurassic Park
Dick Tracy	Terminator 2: Judgment Day	Bram Stoker's Dracula	Mrs. Doubtfire
Total Recall	Terminator 2: Judgment Day	Death Becomes Her	Jurassic Park
Creature Comforts (Animated); The Lunch Date (Live Action)	Manipulation (Animated); Session Man (Live Action)	Mona Lisa Descending a Staircase (Animated); Omnibus (Live Action)	The Wrong Trousers (Animated); Black Rider (Live Action)
Days of Waiting (Short); American Dream (Feature)	Deadly Deception: General Electric, Nuclear Weapons and Our Environment (Short); In the Shadow of the Stars (Feature)	Educating Peter (Short); The Panama Deception (Feature)	Defending Our Lives (Short); I Am a Promise:The Children of Stanton Elementary School (Feature)

> 66 When my daughter came in and met Oscar, she immediately started talking to him. Then she decides Oscar is tired. She put Oscar in the bed and insisted he was sleepy. 99
>
> —Marcia Gay Harden, Best Supporting Actress, 2000

	1994	1995	1996
Picture	Forrest Gump	Braveheart	The English Patient
Actor	Tom Hanks, Forrest Gump	Nicolas Cage, Leaving Las Vegas	Geoffrey Rush, Shine
Actress	Jessica Lange, Blue Sky	Susan Sarandon, Dead Man Walking	Frances McDormand, Fargo
Supporting Actor	Martin Landau, Ed Wood	Kevin Spacey, The Usual Suspects	Cuba Gooding Jr., Jerry Maguire
Supporting Actress	Dianne Wiest, Bullets over Broadway	Mira Sorvino, Mighty Aphrodite	Juliette Binoche, The English Patient
Director	Robert Zemeckis, Forrest Gump	Mel Gibson, Braveheart	Anthony Minghella, The English Patient
Adapted Screenplay	Eric Roth, Forrest Gump	Emma Thompson, Sense and Sensibility	Billy Bob Thornton, Sling Blade
Original Screenplay	Roger Avary and Quentin Tarantino, Pulp Fiction	Christopher McQuarrie, The Usual Suspects	Ethan Coen & Joel Coen, Fargo
Best Song	"Can You Feel the Love Tonight" (The Lion King)	"Colors of the Wind" (Pocahontas)	"You Must Love Me" (Evita)
Original Score	The Lion King	The Postman (Il Postino)	Emma (Musical or Comedy); The English Patient (Drama)
Cinematography	Legends of the Fall	Braveheart	The English Patient
Costume Design	The Adventures of Priscilla, Queen of the Desert	Restoration	The English Patient
Art Direction—Set Decoration	The Madness of King George	Restoration	The English Patient
Film Editing	Forrest Gump	Apollo 13	The English Patient
Foreign Language Film	Burnt by the Sun	Antonia's Line	Kolya
Sound	Speed	Apollo 13	The English Patient
Sound Effects (Editing)	Speed	Braveheart	The Ghost and the Darkness
Makeup	Ed Wood	Braveheart	The Nutty Professor
Visual Effects	Forrest Gump	Babe	Independence Day
Short Films	Bob's Birthday (Animated); Franz Kafka's It's a Wonderful Life and Trevor (Live Action)	A Close Shave (Animated); Lieberman in Love (Live Action)	Quest (Animated); Dear Diary (Live Action)
Documentaries	A Time for Justice (Short); Maya Lin: A Strong Clear Vision (Feature)	One Survivor Remembers (Short); Anne Frank Remembered (Feature)	Breathing Lessons: The Life and Work of Mark O'Brien (Short); When We Were Kings (Feature)

1997	1998	1999	2000
Titanic	*Shakespeare in Love*	*American Beauty*	*Gladiator*
Jack Nicholson, *As Good As It Gets*	Roberto Benigni, *Life Is Beautiful*	Kevin Spacey, *American Beauty*	Russell Crowe, *Gladiator*
Helen Hunt, *As Good As It Gets*	Gwyneth Paltrow, *Shakespeare in Love*	Hilary Swank, *Boys Don't Cry*	Julia Roberts, *Erin Brockovich*
Robin Williams, *Good Will Hunting*	James Coburn, *Affliction*	Michael Caine, *The Cider House Rules*	Benicio Del Toro, *Traffic*
Kim Basinger, *L.A. Confidential*	Judi Dench, *Shakespeare in Love*	Angelina Jolie, *Girl, Interrupted*	Marcia Gay Harden, *Pollock*
James Cameron, *Titanic*	Steven Spielberg, *Saving Private Ryan*	Sam Mendes, *American Beauty*	Steven Soderbergh, *Traffic*
Brian Helgeland and Curtis Hanson, *L.A. Confidential*	Bill Condon, *Gods and Monsters*	John Irving, *The Cider House Rules*	Stephen Gaghan, *Traffic*
Ben Affleck and Matt Damon, *Good Will Hunting*	Marc Norman and Tom Stoppard, *Shakespeare in Love*	Alan Ball, *American Beauty*	Cameron Crowe, *Almost Famous*
"My Heart Will Go On" *(Titanic)*	"When You Believe" *(Prince of Egypt)*	"You'll Be in My Heart," *(Tarzan)*	"Things Have Changed" (Wonder Boys)
The Full Monty (Musical or Comedy); *Titanic* (Drama)	*Shakespeare in Love* (Musical or Comedy); *Life Is Beautiful* (Drama)	John Corigliano, *The Red Violin*	*Crouching Tiger, Hidden Dragon*
Titanic	*Saving Private Ryan*	*American Beauty*	*Crouching Tiger, Hidden Dragon*
Titanic	*Shakespeare in Love*	*Topsy-Turvy*	*Gladiator*
Titanic	*Shakespeare in Love*	*Sleepy Hollow*	*Crouching Tiger, Hidden Dragon*
Titanic	*Saving Private Ryan*	*The Matrix*	*Traffic*
Character	*Life Is Beautiful*	*All About My Mother*	*Crouching Tiger, Hidden Dragon*
Titanic	*Saving Private Ryan*	*The Matrix*	*Gladiator*
Titanic	*Saving Private Ryan*	*The Matrix*	*U-571*
Men in Black	*Elizabeth*	*Topsy-Turvy*	*Dr. Seuss' How The Grinch Stole Christmas*
Titanic	*What Dreams May Come*	*The Matrix*	*Gladiator*
Geri's Game (Animated); *Visas and Virtue* (Live Action)	*Bunny* (Animated); *Election Night (Valgaften)* (Live Action)	*The Old Man and the Sea* (Animated); *My Mother Dreams the Satan's Disciples in New York* (Live Action)	*Father and Daughter* (Animated); *Quiero Ser (I Want To Be...)* (Live Action)
A Story of Healing (Short); *The Long Way Home* (Feature)	*The Personals: Improvisations on Romance in the Golden Years* (Short); *The Last Days* (Feature)	*King Gimp* (Short); *One Day in September* (Feature)	*Big Mama* (Short); *Into The Arms of Strangers: Stories of the Kindertransport* (Feature)

FILM AWARDS

NATIONAL SOCIETY OF FILM CRITICS

Annual Award for Best Film

1966	Blow-Up
1967	Persona
1968	Shame
1969	Z
1970	M*A*S*H
1971	Claire's Knee
1972	The Discreet Charm of the Bourgeoisie
1973	Day for Night
1974	Scenes from a Marriage
1975	Nashville
1976	All The President's Men
1977	Annie Hall
1978	Get Out Your Handkerchiefs
1979	Breaking Away
1980	Melvin and Howard
1981	Atlantic City
1982	Tootsie
1983	Night of the Shooting Stars
1984	Stranger Than Paradise
1985	Ran
1986	Blue Velvet
1987	The Dead
1988	The Unbearable Lightness of Being
1989	Drugstore Cowboy
1990	GoodFellas
1991	Life Is Sweet
1992	Unforgiven
1993	Schindler's List
1994	Pulp Fiction
1995	Babe
1996	Breaking the Waves
1997	L.A. Confidential
1998	Out of Sight
1999	Topsy-Turvy Being John Malkovich
2000	Yi Yi (A One And A Two...)

SUNDANCE FILM FESTIVAL

GRAND JURY PRIZE

1978	Girlfriends
1979	Spirit in the Wind
1981	Heartland Gal Young Un

Dramatic

1982	Street Music
1983	Purple Haze
1984	Old Enough
1985	Blood Simple
1986	Smooth Talk
1987	Waiting for the Moon Trouble with Dick
1988	Heat and Sunlight

1989	True Love
1990	Chameleon Street
1991	Poison
1992	In the Soup
1993	Ruby in Paradise Public Access
1994	What Happened Was . . .
1995	The Brothers McMullen
1996	Welcome to the Dollhouse
1997	Sunday
1998	Slam
1999	Three Seasons
2000	Girlfight You Can Count on Me
2001	The Believer

FILMMAKERS TROPHY
Dramatic

1989	Powwow Highway
1990	House Party
1991	Privilege
1992	Zebrahead
1993	Fly By Night
1994	Clerks
1995	Angela
1996	Girls Town
1997	In the Company of Men
1998	Smoke Signals
1999	Tumbleweeds
2000	Girlfight
2001	Hedwig and the Angry Inch

AUDIENCE AWARD
Dramatic

1989	sex, lies and videotape
1990	Longtime Companion
1991	One Cup of Coffee (released as "Pastime")
1992	The Waterdance
1993	El Mariachi
1994	Spanking the Monkey
1995	Picture Bride
1996	Care of the Spitfire Grill (released as "The Spitfire Grill")
1997	Hurricane (released as "Hurricane Streets") love jones
1998	Smoke Signals
1999	Three Seasons
2000	Two Family House
2001	Hedwig and the Angry Inch

CANNES FILM FESTIVAL

Palme d'Or for Best Film

1946	La Bataille du rail (France)
1947	Antoine et Antoinette (France)
1948	No festival

1949	The Third Man (G.B.)
1950	No festival
1951	Miracle in Milan (Italy) Miss Julie (Sweden)
1952	Othello (Morocco) Two Cents Worth of Hope (Italy)
1953	Wages of Fear (France)
1954	Gate of Hell (Japan)
1955	Marty (U.S.)
1956	World of Silence (France)
1957	Friendly Persuasion (U.S.)
1958	The Cranes are Flying (U.S.S.R.)
1959	Black Orpheus (France)
1960	La Dolce Vita (Italy)
1961	Viridiana (Spain) Une Aussi longue absence (France)
1962	The Given Word (Brazil)
1963	The Leopard (Italy)
1964	The Umbrellas of Cherbourg (France)
1965	The Knack (G.B.)
1966	A Man and a Woman (France) Signore e Signori (Italy)
1967	Blow-Up (G.B.)
1968	Festival disrupted; no awards
1969	If... (G.B.)
1970	M*A*S*H (U.S.)
1971	The Go-Between (G.B.)
1972	The Working Class Goes to Paradise (Italy) The Mattei Affair (Italy)
1973	Scarecrow (U.S.) The Hireling (G.B.)
1974	The Conversation (U.S.)
1975	Chronicle of the Burning Years (Algeria)
1976	Taxi Driver (U.S.)
1977	Padre Padrone (Italy)
1978	L'Albero Degli Zoccoli (Italy)
1979	The Tin Drum (Germany) Apocalypse Now (U.S.)
1980	All That Jazz (U.S.) Kagemusha (Japan)
1981	Man of Iron (Poland)
1982	Missing (U.S.) Yol (Turkey)
1983	The Ballad of Narayama (Japan)
1984	Paris, Texas (Germany)
1985	When Father Was Away On Business (Yugoslavia)
1986	The Mission (G.B.)
1987	Under the Sun of Satan (France)
1988	Pelle the Conqueror (Denmark)
1989	sex, lies and videotape (U.S.)
1990	Wild at Heart (U.S.)
1991	Barton Fink (U.S.)
1992	The Best Intentions (Denmark)
1993	The Piano (New Zealand)

	Farewell My Concubine (Hong Kong)
1994	Pulp Fiction (U.S.)
1995	Underground (Bosnia)
1996	Secrets and Lies (G.B.)
1997	The Taste of Cherry (Iran)
	The Eel (Japan)
1998	Eternity and a Day (Greece-Italy-France)
1999	Rosetta (Belgium)
2000	Dancer in the Dark (Denmark)
2001	The Son's Room (Italy)

VENICE FILM FESTIVAL

Golden Lion [for Best Film or Best Foreign Film]

1932	No official award
1933	No festival
1934	Man of Aran (G.B.)
1935	Anna Karenina (U.S.)
1936	Der Kaiser von Kalifornien (Germany)
1937	Un Carnet debal (France)
1938	Olympia (Germany)
1939	No award given
1940	Der Postmeister (Germany)
1941	Ohm Kruger (Germany)
1942	Der grosse König (Germany)
1943	No festival
1944	No festival
1945	No festival
1946	The Southerner (U.S.)
1947	Sirena (Czechoslovakia)
1948	Hamlet (G.B.)
1949	Manon (France)
1950	Justice is Done (France)
1951	Rashomon (Japan)
1952	Forbidden Games (France)
1953	No award given
1954	Romeo and Juliet (Italy/G.B.)
1955	Ordet (Denmark)
1956	No award given
1957	Aparajito (India)
1958	Muhomatsu no Issho (Japan)
1959	Il Generale della Rovere (Italy)
1960	Le Passage du Rhin (France)
1961	Last Year at Marienbad (France)
1962	Childhood of Ivan (U.S.S.R.)
1963	Le Mani sulla città (Italy)
1964	Red Desert (Italy)
1965	Of a Thousand Delights (Italy)
1966	Battle of Algiers (Italy)
1967	Belle de Jour (France)
1968	Die Aristen in der Zirkuskuppel (Germany)

Jury and award system discontinued 1969–79

1980	Gloria (U.S.)
	Atlantic City (France/Canada)
1981	Die Bleierne Zeit (Germany)
1982	The State of Things (Germany)

1983	Prénom Carmen (France/Switzerland)
1984	Year of the Quiet Sun (Poland)
1985	Sans toit ni loi (Vagabonde) (France)
1986	Le Rayon vert (France)
1987	Au revoir, les enfants (France)
1988	The Legend of the Holy Drinker (Italy)
1989	A City of Sadness (Taiwan)
1990	Rosencrantz and Guildenstern Are Dead (G.B.)
1991	Urga (U.S.S.R./France)
1992	The Story of Qiu Ju (China)
1993	Blue (France)
	Short Cuts (U.S.)
1994	Before the Rain (Macedonia)
	Vive L'Amour (Taiwan)
1995	Cyclo (France-Vietnam)
1996	Michael Collins (Great Britain-U.S.)
1997	Hana-bi (Fireworks) (Japan)
1998	The Way We Laughed (Italy)
1999	Not One Less (China)
2000	Dayereh (The Circle) (Iran)

BERLIN FILM FESTIVAL AWARD

Golden Bear Award for Best Film

1953	The Wages of Fear (France)
1954	Hobson's Choice (G.B.)
1955	The Rats (Germany)
1956	Invitation to the Dance (G.B.)
1957	Twelve Angry Men (U.S.)
1958	The End of the Day (Sweden)
1959	The Cousins (France)
1960	Lazarillo de Tormes (Spain)
1961	La Notte (Italy)
1962	A Kind of Loving (G.B.)
1963	Oath of Obedience (Germany)
	The Devil (Italy)
1964	Dry Summer (Turkey)
1965	Alphaville (France)
1966	Cul-de-Sac (G.B.)
1967	Le Depart (Belgium)
1968	Ole Dole Duff (Sweden)
1969	Early Years (Yugoslavia)
1970	No award
1971	The Garden of the Finzi-Continis (Italy)
1972	The Canterbury Tales (Italy)
1973	Distant Thunder (India)
1974	The Apprenticeship of Duddy Kravitz (Canada)
1975	Orkobefogadas (Hungary)
1976	Buffalo Bill and the Indians (U.S.) [award declined]
1977	The Ascent (U.S.S.R.)
1978	The Trouts (Spain)
	The Words of Max (Spain)
1979	David (Germany)

1980	Heartland (U.S.)
	Palermo Oder Wolfsburg (Germany)
1981	Di Presa Di Presa (Spain)
1982	Die Sehnsucht der Veronica Voss (Germany)
1983	Ascendancy (G.B.)
	The Beehive (Spain)
1984	Love Streams (U.S.)
1985	Wetherby (G.B.)
	Die Frau und der Fremde (Germany)
1986	Stammhein (Germany)
1987	The Theme (U.S.S.R.)
1988	Red Sorghum (China)
1989	Rain Man (U.S.)
1990	Music Box (U.S.)
	Larks on a String (Czechoslovakia)
1991	House of Smiles (Italy)
1992	Grand Canyon (U.S.)
1993	The Woman from the Lake of Scented Souls (China)
	The Wedding Banquet (Taiwan/U.S.)
1994	In the Name of the Father (UK/Ireland)
1995	Live Bait (France)
1996	Sense and Sensibility (G.B.)
1997	The People vs. Larry Flynt (U.S.)
1998	Central Station (Brazil)
1999	The Thin Red Line (U.S.)
2000	Magnolia (U.S.)
2001	Intimacy (France)

INDEPENDENT SPIRIT AWARDS

These prizes are considered the Oscars of the independent film world.

Best Feature

1986	After Hours
1987	Platoon
1988	River's Edge
1989	Stand and Deliver
1990	sex, lies and videotape
1991	The Grifters
1992	Rambling Rose
1993	The Player
1994	Short Cuts
1995	Pulp Fiction
1996	Leaving Las Vegas
1997	Fargo
1998	The Apostle
1999	Election
2000	Crouching Tiger, Hidden Dragon

Best First Feature

1987	Spike Lee, director
	She's Gotta Have It
1988	Emile Ardolino, director
	Dirty Dancing

1989 Donald Petrie, director
Mystic Pizza
1990 Michael Lehmann, director
Heathers
1991 Whit Stillman, producer/director
Metropolitan
1992 Matty Rich, director
Straight Out of Brooklyn
1993 Neal Jimenez and Michael
Steinberg, directors
The Waterdance
1994 Robert Rodriguez, director
El Mariachi
1995 David O. Russell, director
Spanking the Monkey
1996 Edward Burns, director
The Brothers McMullen
1997 Billy Bob Thornton, director
Sling Blade
1998 Kasi Lemmons, director
Eve's Bayou
1999 Spike Jonze, director
Being John Malkovich
Daniel Myrick & Eduardo
Sanchez, directors
The Blair Witch Project
2000 Kenneth Lonergan, director
You Can Count On Me

Best Director

1986 Martin Scorsese
After Hours
1987 Oliver Stone
Platoon
1988 John Huston
The Dead
1989 Ramon Menendez
Stand and Deliver
1990 Steven Soderbergh
sex, lies, and videotape
1991 Charles Burnett
To Sleep with Anger
1992 Martha Coolidge
Rambling Rose
1993 Carl Franklin
One False Move
1994 Robert Altman
Short Cuts
1995 Quentin Tarantino
Pulp Fiction
1996 Mike Figgis
Leaving Las Vegas
1997 Joel Coen
Fargo
1998 Robert Duvall
The Apostle
1999 Alexander Payne
Election
2000 Ang Lee
Crouching Tiger, Hidden Dragon

Best Screenplay

1986 Horton Foote
The Trip to Bountiful
1987 Oliver Stone
Platoon
1988 Neal Jimenez
River's Edge
1989 Ramon Menendez and Tom
Musca
Stand and Deliver
1990 Gus Van Sant Jr. and Daniel Yost
Drugstore Cowboy
1991 Charles Burnett
To Sleep with Anger
1992 Gus Van Sant Jr.
My Own Private Idaho
1993 Neal Jimenez
The Waterdance
1994 Robert Altman and Frank
Barhydt
Short Cuts
1995 David O. Russell
Spanking the Monkey
1996 Christopher McQuarrie
The Usual Suspects
1997 Joel Coen and Ethan Coen
Fargo
1998 Kevin Smith
Chasing Amy
1999 Alexander Payne & Jim Taylor
Election
2000 Kenneth Lonergan
You Can Count On Me

Best Actor

1986 M. Emmet Walsh
Blood Simple
1987 James Woods
Salvador
1988 Dennis Quaid
The Big Easy
1989 Edward James Olmos
Stand and Deliver
1990 Matt Dillon
Drugstore Cowboy
1991 Danny Glover
To Sleep with Anger
1992 River Phoenix
My Own Private Idaho
1993 Harvey Keitel
Bad Lieutenant
1994 Jeff Bridges
American Heart
1995 Samuel L. Jackson
Pulp Fiction
1996 Sean Penn
Dead Man Walking
1997 William H. Macy
Fargo
1998 Robert Duvall
The Apostle

1999 Richard Farnsworth
The Straight Story
2000 Javier Bardem
Before Night Falls

Best Actress

1986 Geraldine Page
The Trip to Bountiful
1987 Isabella Rossellini
Blue Velvet
1988 Sally Kirkland
Anna
1989 Jodie Foster
Five Corners
1990 Andie MacDowell
sex, lies, and videotape
1991 Anjelica Huston
The Grifters
1992 Judy Davis
Impromptu
1993 Fairuza Balk
Gas, Food, Lodging
1994 Ashley Judd
Ruby in Paradise
1995 Linda Fiorentino
The Last Seduction
1996 Elisabeth Shue
Leaving Las Vegas
1997 Frances McDormand
Fargo
1998 Julie Christie
Afterglow
1999 Hilary Swank
Boys Don't Cry
2000 Ellen Burstyn
Requiem For A Dream

Best Supporting Actor

1988 Morgan Freeman
Street Smart
1989 Lou Diamond Phillips
Stand and Deliver
1990 Max Perlich
Drugstore Cowboy
1991 Bruce Davison
Longtime Companion
1992 David Strathairn
City of Hope
1993 Steve Buscemi
Reservoir Dogs
1994 Christopher Lloyd
Twenty Bucks
1995 Chazz Palmintieri
Bullets over Broadway
1996 Benicio Del Toro
The Usual Suspects
1997 Benecio Del Toro
Basquiat
1998 Jason Lee
Chasing Amy
1999 Steve Zahn
Happy, Texas

2000 Willem Dafoe
Shadow of the Vampire

Best Supporting Actress

1988 Anjelica Huston
The Dead
1989 Rosanna De Soto
Stand and Deliver
1990 Laura San Giacomo
sex, lies and videotape
1991 Sheryl Lee Ralph
To Sleep with Anger
1992 Diane Ladd
Rambling Rose
1993 Alfre Woodard
Passion Fish
1994 Lili Taylor
Household Saints
1995 Dianne Wiest
Bullets over Broadway
1996 Mare Winningham
Georgia
1997 Elizabeth Peña
Lone Star
1998 Debbi Morgan
Eve's Bayou
1999 Chloë Sevigny
Boys Don't Cry
2000 Zhang Ziyi
Crouching Tiger, Hidden Dragon

Best Foreign Film

1986 Kiss of the Spider Woman
1987 A Room with a View
1988 My Life as a Dog
1989 Wings of Desire
1990 My Left Foot
1991 Sweetie
1992 An Angel at My Table
1993 The Crying Game
1994 The Piano
1995 Red
1996 Before the Rain
1997 Secrets and Lies
1998 The Sweet Hereafter
1999 Run Lola Run
2000 Dancer In The Dark

MTV MOVIE AWARDS

Best Movie

1992 Terminator 2: Judgment Day
1993 A Few Good Men
1994 Menace II Society
1995 Pulp Fiction
1996 Seven
1997 Scream
1998 Titanic
1999 There's Something About Mary
2000 The Matrix
2001 Gladiator

Best Male Performance

1992 Arnold Schwarzenegger
Terminator 2: Judgment Day
1993 Denzel Washington
Malcolm X
1994 Tom Hanks
Philadelphia
1995 Brad Pitt
Interview with the Vampire
1996 Jim Carrey
Ace Ventura: When Nature Calls
1997 Tom Cruise
Jerry Maguire
1998 Leonardo DiCaprio
Titanic
1999 Jim Carrey
The Truman Show
2000 Keanu Reeves
The Matrix
2001 Tom Cruise
Mission: Impossible 2

Best Female Performance

1992 Linda Hamilton
Terminator 2: Judgment Day
1993 Sharon Stone
Basic Instinct
1994 Janet Jackson
Poetic Justice
1995 Sandra Bullock
Speed
1996 Alicia Silverstone
Clueless
1997 Claire Danes
*William Shakespeare's
Romeo and Juliet*
1998 Neve Campbell
Scream 2
1999 Cameron Diaz
There's Something About Mary
2000 Sarah Michelle Gellar
Cruel Intentions
2001 Julia Roberts
Erin Brockovich

Breakthrough Performance

1992 Edward Furlong
Terminator 2: Judgment Day
1993 Marisa Tomei
My Cousin Vinny
1994 Alicia Silverstone
The Crush
1995 Kirsten Dunst
Interview with the Vampire
1996 George Clooney
From Dusk Till Dawn
1997 Matthey McConaughey
A Time To Kill
1998 Heather Graham
Boogie Nights
1999 James Van Der Beek
Varsity Blues

Katie Holmes
Disturbing Behavior
2000 Haley Joel Osment
The Sixth Sense
Julia Stiles
10 Things I Hate About You
2001 Sean Patrick Thomas
Save the Last Dance
Erika Christensen
Traffic

Best Villain

1992 Rebecca DeMornay
The Hand That Rocks the Cradle
1993 Jennifer Jason Leigh
Single White Female
1994 Alicia Silverstone
The Crush
1995 Dennis Hopper
Speed
1996 Kevin Spacey
Seven
1997 Jim Carrey
The Cable Guy
1998 Mike Myers
*Austin Powers: International
Man of Mystery*
1999 Matt Dillon
There's Something About Mary
Stephen Dorff
Blade
2000 Mike Myers
*Austin Powers: The Spy Who
Shagged Me*
2001 Jim Carrey
*Dr. Seuss' How the Grinch Stole
Christmas*

Best On-Screen Duo

1992 Mike Myers and Dana Carvey
Wayne's World
1993 Mel Gibson and Danny Glover
Lethal Weapon 3
1994 Harrison Ford and Tommy Lee
Jones
The Fugitive
1995 Keanu Reeves and Sandra
Bullock
Speed
1996 Chris Farley and David Spade
Tommy Boy
1997 Sean Connery and Nicolas Cage
The Rock
1998 John Travolta and Nicolas Cage
Face/Off
1999 Jackie Chan and Chris Tucker
Rush Hour
2000 Mike Myers and Verne Troyer,
*Austin Powers: The Spy Who
Shagged Me*

| 2001 | Drew Barrymore, Cameron Diaz, Lucy Liu
Charlie's Angels |

Best Song

| 1992 | Bryan Adams
"(Everything I Do) I Do It For You" *(Robin Hood: Prince of Thieves)* |
| 1993 | Whitney Houston
"I Will Always Love You" *(The Bodyguard)* |
| 1994 | Michael Jackson
"Will You Be There" *(Free Willy)* |
| 1995 | Stone Temple Pilots
"Big Empty" *(The Crow)* |
| 1996 | Brandy
"Sittin' up in My Room" *(Waiting to Exhale)* |
| 1997 | Bush
"Machinehead" *(Fear)* |
| 1998 | Will Smith
"Men in Black" *(Men in Black)* |
| 1999 | Aerosmith
"I Don't Want to Miss a Thing" *(Armageddon)* |
| 2000 | "Uncle F**ka"
(South Park: Bigger, Longer, and Uncut) |

Best Kiss

| 1992 | Macaulay Culkin and Anna Chlumsky
My Girl |
| 1993 | Marisa Tomei and Christian Slater
Untamed Heart |
| 1994 | Woody Harrelson and Demi Moore
Indecent Proposal |
| 1995 | Jim Carrey and Lauren Holly
Dumb and Dumber |
| 1996 | Natasha Henstridge and Anthony Guidere
Species |
| 1997 | Will Smith and Vivica A. Fox
Independence Day |
| 1998 | Adam Sandler and Drew Barrymore
The Wedding Singer |
| 1999 | Gwyneth Paltrow and Joseph Fiennes
Shakespeare In Love |
| 2000 | Selma Blair and Sarah Michelle Gellar
Cruel Intentions |
| 2001 | Julia Stiles and Sean Patrick Thomas
Save the Last Dance |

Best Fight

| 1996 | Adam Sandler and Bob Barker
Happy Gilmore |

| 1997 | Fairuza Balk and Robin Tunney
The Craft |
| 1998 | Will Smith and Cockroach
Men in Black |
| 1999 | Ben Stiller and Puffy the Dog
There's Something About Mary |
| 2000 | Keanu Reeves and Laurence Fishburn
The Matrix |
| 2001 | Zhang Ziyi and Entire Bar
Crouching Tiger, Hidden Dragon |

DIRECTOR'S GUILD AWARDS

| 1948–49 | *A Letter to Three Wives*
Joseph Mankiewicz |
| 1949–50 | *All the King's Men*
Robert Rossen |
| 1950–51 | *All About Eve*
Joseph Mankiewicz |
| 1951 | *A Place in the Sun*
George Stevens |
| 1952 | *The Quiet Man*
John Ford |
| 1953 | *From Here to Eternity*
Fred Zinnemann |
| 1954 | *On the Waterfront*
Elia Kazan |
| 1955 | *Marty*
Delbert Mann |
| 1956 | *Giant*
George Stevens |
| 1957 | *Bridge on the River Kwai*
David Lean |
| 1958 | *Gigi*
Vincente Minnelli |
| 1959 | *Ben-Hur*
William Wyler |
| 1960 | *The Apartment*
Billy Wilder |
| 1961 | *West Side Story*
Robert Wise and Jerome Robbins |
| 1962 | *Lawrence of Arabia*
David Lean |
| 1963 | *Tom Jones*
Tony Richardson |
| 1964 | *My Fair Lady*
George Cukor |
| 1965 | *The Sound of Music*
Robert Wise |
| 1966 | *A Man for All Seasons*
Fred Zinnemann |
| 1967 | *The Graduate*
Mike Nichols |
| 1968 | *The Lion in Winter*
Anthony Harvey |
| 1969 | *Midnight Cowboy*
John Schlesinger |
| 1970 | *Patton*
Franklin J. Schaffner |

| 1971 | *The French Connection*
William Friedkin |
| 1972 | *The Godfather*
Francis Ford Coppola |
| 1973 | *The Sting*
George Roy Hill |
| 1974 | *The Godfather Part II*
Francis Ford Coppola |
| 1975 | *One Flew over the Cuckoo's Nest*
Milos Forman |
| 1976 | *Rocky*
John G. Avildsen |
| 1977 | *Annie Hall*
Woody Allen |
| 1978 | *The Deer Hunter*
Michael Cimino |
| 1979 | *Kramer vs. Kramer*
Robert Benton |
| 1980 | *Ordinary People*
Robert Redford |
| 1981 | *Reds*
Warren Beatty |
| 1982 | *Gandhi*
Richard Attenborough |
| 1983 | *Terms of Endearment*
James L. Brooks |
| 1984 | *Amadeus*
Milos Forman |
| 1985 | *The Color Purple*
Steven Spielberg |
| 1986 | *Platoon*
Oliver Stone |
| 1987 | *The Last Emperor*
Bernardo Bertolucci |
| 1988 | *Rain Man*
Barry Levinson |
| 1989 | *Born on the Fourth of July*
Oliver Stone |
| 1990 | *Dances with Wolves*
Kevin Costner |
| 1991 | *The Silence of the Lambs*
Jonathan Demme |
| 1992 | *Unforgiven*
Clint Eastwood |
| 1993 | *Schindler's List*
Steven Spielberg |
| 1994 | *Forrest Gump*
Robert Zemeckis |
| 1995 | *Apollo 13*
Ron Howard |
| 1996 | *The English Patient*
Anthony Minghella |
| 1997 | *Titanic*
James Cameron |
| 1998 | *Saving Private Ryan*
Steven Spielberg |
| 1999 | *American Beauty*
Sam Mendes |
| 2000 | *Crouching Tiger, Hidden Dragon*
Ang Lee |

TUBE

PICKS & PANS: 2000–2001

The *Weakest Link* may be the creative departments of the networks as game shows and beyond-reality programs continued to lead the prime-time schedules, even as HBO, Showtime and other cablers demonstrated that quality shows still draw viewers and buzz. PEOPLE's Terry Kelleher appraises the new and revisits some old favorites.

ALL SOULS
UPN

Surgical resident Mitchell Grace (Grayson McCouch) learned that Boston's All Souls hospital had once been home to "horrible, insane experiments" and that an off-limits part of the building is rumored to be haunted. There's little humor in this show, which can be really scary when it's not resorting to cheap gross-outs.

BANDS ON THE RUN
VH1

Tests touring groups' ability to sell tickets and souvenirs as well as play loud music. The show is raunchily watchable.

THE BEAST
ABC

In this flawed but provocative drama, World News Service reporters do their jobs in the usual way while omnipresent cameras cover all the behind-the-scenes moves for viewing over the Internet.

BOOT CAMP
Fox

Boot Camp takes the *Survivor* concept—rugged adventure as a human petri dish for conflict—and moves it to a real, unattended military base. Starting as a small troop vying for a $500,000 prize, 16 contestants submit to grueling discipline doled out by four drill instructors. Each week the "recruits" vote to discharge another weakling.

THE CHRONICLE
Sci-Fi Channel

Donald Stern, editor of the *World Chronicle*, isn't about to weigh down his supermarket tabloid with real news. But as Tucker, the new reporter discovers, *Chronicle* stories tend to be true. The premise holds promise.

CONFESSIONS
Court TV

This presentation of actual video-taped criminal confessions from police precincts and district attorneys' offices has got to be one of the most cynical, senseless and dehumanizing shows ever.

C.S.I.
CBS

The Las Vegas police officers of C.S.I. (Crime Scene Investigators) collect and analyze physical evidence, rather than chasing, punching or shooting bad guys. A droll William Petersen and dependable Marg Helgenberger head the competent cast.

CURB YOUR ENTHUSIASM
HBO

Far from an average sitcom. Trouble begins with a small misunderstanding or a seemingly harmless deception, and star Larry David maneuvers himself into an embarrassing corner. It's a peculiar place you won't want to leave.

CURSED
NBC

This sappy sitcom squanders a nifty premise: Guy goes on a blind date, spurns her; she puts a curse on him; everything proceeds to go wrong in his life. The calamities that pile up for hapless Chicago ad exec Jack Nagle (Steven Weber) are barely worth a pause on the remote.

DAG
NBC

David Alan Grier plays a Secret Service agent who protects a testy First Lady (Delta Burke) and has to put up with her smarmy chief of staff. The humor is relentlessly infantile.

DEADLINE
NBC

Oliver Platt is well-cast as Wallace Benton, a Manhattan tabloid reporter and columnist who doesn't mind twisting arms, hurting feelings and stooping to a thousand mildly unethical manipulations to get that story. But the show is often slack when it should crackle along.

THE DIVISION
Lifetime

With its premiere, *The Division* took a bold stand for the right of women to utter the same clichés men have been mouthing ever since police drama became one of TV's most reliable time-fillers.

ED
NBC

Thomas Cavanagh is by turns wry and soulful as Ed Stevens, a Manhattan lawyer who is back in his hometown, and gamely risking rejection again by courting the head cheerleader who barely knew he existed in high school and who now teaches English there. Their blossoming romance is smartly played, but there are goofier diversions in this amiable send-up of small town life.

FARSCAPE
Sci Fi Channel

American astronaut John Crichton (Ben Browder) and a bunch

of alien fugitives are taking the biomechanical spaceship Moya through the Uncharted Territories. The thickly plotted series' third season is diverting, if you can follow it.

FEAR FACTOR
NBC

Contestants vie for a $50,000 prize by attempting stunts described as "extremely dangerous." There's no purpose in watching *Fear Factor*, unless the network offers you $50,000 to endure it.

THE FIGHTING FITZGERALDS
NBC

It's the old story of the offspring failing to empty the nest. Brian Dennehy's irascible character might be designated Bunker Lite, but fortunately the star has the strength to carry this formulaic show on his back.

FIRST YEARS
NBC

First impression of this one-hour dramedy about five eager young associates at a San Francisco law firm: *Ally McBeal* Lite. But when the episodes smartly get down to business, the legal eaglets display insightful flashes of depth and feeling—a sign of this series' potential.

FRASIER
NBC

When Niles and Daphne (David Hyde Pierce and Jane Leeves) finally rode off in a Winnebago after declaring their long pent-up love for each other, viewers rejoiced. But this once-steady sitcom may now be stuck in neutral.

THE FUGITIVE
CBS

Dr. Richard Kimble, wrongly convicted of killing his wife, escapes from custody and goes off in pursuit of the one-armed man he saw at the murder scene. Meanwhile, police Lt. Philip Gerard tracks

him down. This new *Fugitive* has a very good Kimble in Tim Daly.

GARY & MIKE
UPN

Once again UPN draws a bead on its target audience of young men with this relentlessly rude, occasionally funny Claymation series about two slackers on a long road trip. But a bit of satiric intelligence glimmers through the crudity.

THE GEENA DAVIS SHOW
ABC

In this shaky star vehicle, single Teddie and widowed Max fell head over heels and got engaged after a six-week acquaintance. Teddie moves from Manhattan to Max's suburban home, foolishly convinced that being stepmother to his two children would require little thought or effort. Reality doesn't figure to be much of a factor in this mediocre sitcom.

GIDEON'S CROSSING
ABC

Dr. Ben Gideon (played with edgy intensity by Andre Braugher), the brilliant head of experimental medicine at a Boston hospital gives a few too many fiery, eloquent, commencement-style speeches about patient care, medical ethics and the meaning of life.

GILMORE GIRLS
WB

The season's nicest surprise, this one-hour dramedy explores the ties that bind Lorelai Gilmore, a small-town Connecticut innkeeper, and her 16-year-old daughter, Rory, whom Lorelai bore out of wedlock when she was 16 and has reared ever since. The show's sweetly low-key ambience is enhanced by a quirky ensemble.

GIRLFRIENDS
UPN

An African-Americanized *Sex and the City*, though the four

principals live in L.A., not Manhattan. *Girlfriends'* debt to the HBO hit is screamingly obvious.

GROSSE POINT
WB

A sitcom satire about the cast of a teen soap much like *Beverly Hills 90210*. Laughs come from the soap-within-the-sitcom's vain, stupid, ruthless young stars; bigger laughs come in the scenes from the inane soap itself.

GROUNDED FOR LIFE
Fox

It's Fox tradition to depict family life in the form of a twisted cartoon, and *Grounded for Life* comes off as edgy and derivative at the same time. Donal Logue stars as Sean Finnerty, a 32-year-old dad out of his depth.

THE HUNTRESS
USA

This second-year series about mother-and-daughter bounty hunters is loosely based on the real-life adventures of Dottie and Brandi Thorson. The plot is complicated, and the villain belongs in a comic book, but there are just enough touches of real humor here to qualify as satisfactory summer escapism.

THE CHRIS ISAAK SHOW
Showtime

A rock and roll *Larry Sanders Show*. Chris Isaak's TV venture gets off to a slow start, but later the series starts to gel, and by the fourth episode, it is firmly established that this show will be as casually engaging as the man at its center.

THE JOB
ABC

The talent of the cast, the overall quality of the writing and the genuine New York City atmosphere compensate for an occasional lapse in judgment. Denis Leary stars as Mike McNeil, a detective who smokes and drinks too much, pops pain pills as if they were breath mints and has a wife in the suburbs and a lover in town.

KRISTIN
NBC
Kristin Yancey is a frighteningly perky Oklahoman who comes to New York City with hopes of a Broadway career but takes a day job as personal assistant to a playboy real estate developer. The breakdown is 99 percent contrivance, 1 percent comedy.

LIVE WITH REGIS AND KELLY
Syndicated
Kelly Ripa, who became Regis Philbin's cohost on the syndicated morning program, displays some of the perkiness of Philbin's longtime partner, Kathie Lee Gifford, but needs to express herself more, just as Philbin needs to listen to her with both ears. But the pairing holds promise.

THE LONE GUNMEN
Fox
The pilot of this *X-Files* spinoff is what you'd call a comedy-drama, with pratfalls and some jokey dialogue balanced by the threat of catastrophe and sober talk of lost ideals. But the show eventually turns into a clumsy comedy-comedy.

MADIGAN MEN
ABC
Grandpappy Seamus (Roy Dotrice) is newly arrived in Manhattan from the Emerald Isle; his son Ben (Gabriel Byrne) is a recently separated architect warily rediscovering the dating scene; and Ben's son Luke (John C. Hensley) is a teenager with girlfriends to spare. This low-rated comedy will need the luck of the Irish to survive.

MAKING THE BAND
ABC
The five lads of O-Town seem preoccupied with career strategy, but the show occasionally offers a priceless behind-the-scenes moment.

THE MOLE
ABC
Participants are put through a number of stunts, with prize money going into a "group pot," and the main object is to identify the saboteur in their midst through a written quiz. The player who knows least about the mole is eliminated. Hardly high drama.

NORMAL, OHIO
Fox
Four years after coming out as gay and fleeing to L.A., Butch Gamble (John Goodman) is back in his Ohio hometown, hoping to mend fences. The show is shrill and graceless, with the actors screeching at each other.

OBLONGS
WB
Cartoonist Angus Oblong, co-creator of this extra-edgy animated series, says it's designed for "fans who love things that make other people squirm." While the show's robustly anti-corporate satire is applaudable, it is not for squares.

ONCE AND AGAIN
ABC
The relationship of divorced Rick (Billy Campbell) and divorced Lily (Sela Ward)—each the parent of two, and by season's end married to each other—can be lusty, frustrating, and disappointing in the same hour. But the drama's respect for the complexity of life is still impressive.

THE POWERPUFF GIRLS
Cartoon Network
Primary school superheroes Blossom, Bubbles and Buttercup exercise their powers to save the ever-embattled city of Townsville and its dithering mayor.

THE PRACTICE
ABC
Even if the characters are growing overfamiliar, creator David E. Kelley's stories about this Boston lawyer team—still in the underdog role after almost four years on the air—seems ready to resume aggressive advocacy.

PRIMETIME GLICK
Comedy Central
Showbiz interviewer Jiminy Glick (Martin Short under mounds of makeup) is the gushy master of the non sequitur and other nonsense. The heart of the program is a talk show spoof in which guest celebrities try to hold up their end of hilariously incoherent conversation.

QUEER AS FOLK
Showtime
Adapted from a British hit, this groundbreaking weekly series must be the most explicit program about gay life ever made for American TV. It trails a handful or so of hard-partying, mostly twentysomething Pittsburgh boys from bar to disco to bedroom and on to careers conducted in the glaring light of day.

SEX AND THE CITY
HBO
In its fourth season, *Sex and the City's* characterizations are deepening with the years.

SIX FEET UNDER
HBO
In this slightly ghoulish but engrossing series, weirdness, like death, is part of life. The Fisher family owns, operates, and resides in a Los Angeles funeral home. *Six Feet Under* gives us much to dig into.

SPECIAL UNIT 2
UPN
As derivative as they come. *Men in Black* and *The X-Files* are

written all over the largely tongue-in-cheek adventures of a secret Chicago police unit assigned to track strange, dangerous creatures described as missing links between man and beast.

SPIN CITY
ABC
Charlie Sheen brings his own understated rhythms and a mischievous glint to the part of new deputy mayor Charlie Crawford. His deadpan cool is refreshing.

SPY TV
NBC
In this hidden-camera comedy series, the generally predictable reactions tend to have a paltry comic payoff, and the sardonic attitude of host Michael Ian Black isn't sufficient to make the show seem all that much hipper than *Candid Camera.*

THE $TREET
Fox
The high-flying twentysomething stockbrokers of Wall Street's Balmont Stevens Inc. spout jargon with dizzying speed. But this slick series reveals that guys, too, just want to have fun after hours. Cool and cocky and filthy rich, these *Street*-smart characters just might grow on you.

SURVIVOR: THE AUSTRALIAN OUTBACK
CBS
Criticizing this ratings juggernaut is as futile as shaking your fist at a hurricane. Nevertheless, I could have survived quite nicely if the show had packed it in after last year's sojourn on Pulau Tiga.

THAT'S LIFE
CBS
Heather Paige Kent is a bartender who upsets her working-class family by enrolling in college. There are plenty of elementary ethnic stereotypes, but Kent brings so much spirit to the role of 32-year-old freshman Lydia

DeLucca that the warmed-over material sometimes seems fresh.

THAT'S MY BUSH!
Comedy Central
Creators Trey Parker and Matt Stone *(South Park)* are aiming for a presidential spoof of sitcom conventions with this comedy series set at 1600 Pennsylvania Ave. At times offensive and tasteless, the show will polarize the electorate.

THREE SISTERS
NBC
Evokes Chekhov in title only. The issue is not who wants to spend the night with these harpies but who's willing to watch them for a half hour a week.

TITANS
NBC
This anemic soap from Aaron Spelling sorely needs a slap in the face.

TRL
MTV
A fun, mindless, hour-long mix of video countdown and celebrity visits backed by an audience of screaming kids. Host Carson Daly anchors the show— upbeat but not gung ho, he is welcoming to guests without fawning, considerate to fans without being condescending.

TUCKER
NBC
An insult to the intelligence is bad enough, but this sitcom is an insult to stupidity.

WEAKEST LINK
NBC
This British rapid-fire quiz show import has contestants playing as a team before they turn on one another, but host Anne Robinson's imperious nastiness inspires an undeniable fascination.

WELCOME TO NEW YORK
CBS
Jim Gaffigan, a Lettermanesque ex-Indiana weatherman, takes a

gig on a New York City morning show and plays Middle American straight man to such strange specimens as the arrogant but insecure executive producer and an egotistical anchorman.

THE WEST WING
NBC
This White House remains a winner. President Bartlet (Martin Sheen) continues to push a liberal agenda with his staff, played by an impeccable cast.

WITCHBLADE
TNT
In this violent series, police officer Sara Pezzini wears a bracelet that glows red every so often and turns into an unbeatably versatile weapon when needed. If you're not familiar with the comic book or movie, you'll be searching for some meaning behind all the chasing, shooting and screaming.

THE X-FILES
FOX
Formerly skeptical FBI agent Dana Scully and her formerly incredulous boss Walter Skinner have both turned into True Believers as they search for the UFO that snatched Scully's partner Fox Mulder. This once-hot show is sliding toward X-tinction.

YES, DEAR
CBS
Purports to be about two young couples raising their kids in the same household, but it's really about four infantile adults cracking dumb about sex.

YOU DON'T KNOW JACK
ABC
This comedy quiz show, based on the CD-ROM game of the same name would be virtually indistinguishable from a *Saturday Night Live* game show parody if it didn't give real people the chance to win real money.

THE MOST POPULAR SHOWS ON TV

The following chart shows America's TV favorites every year beginning in 1949.
(Sources: *Variety* and, after 1949–50, Nielsen Media Research)

1949–50

1. The Texaco Star Theater — NBC
2. Toast of the Town (Ed Sullivan) — CBS
3. Arthur Godfrey's Talent Scouts — CBS
4. Fireball Fun for All — NBC
5. Philco Television Playhouse — NBC
6. Fireside Theatre — NBC
7. The Goldbergs — CBS
8. Suspense — CBS
9. The Ford Television Theater — CBS
10. Cavalcade of Stars — DUMONT

1950–51

1. The Texaco Star Theater — NBC
2. Fireside Theatre — NBC
3. Your Show of Shows — NBC
4. Philco Television Playhouse — NBC
5. The Colgate Comedy Hour — NBC
6. Gillette Cavalcade of Sports — NBC
7. Arthur Godfrey's Talent Scouts — CBS
8. Mama — CBS
9. Robert Montgomery Presents — NBC
10. Martin Kane, Private Eye — NBC
11. Man Against Crime — CBS
12. Somerset Maugham Theatre — NBC
13. Kraft Television Theatre — NBC
14. Toast of the Town (Ed Sullivan) — CBS
15. The Aldrich Family — NBC
16. You Bet Your Life — NBC
17. Armstrong Circle Theater (tie) — NBC
17. Big Town (tie) — CBS
17. Lights Out (tie) — NBC
20. The Alan Young Show — CBS

1951–52

1. Arthur Godfrey's Talent Scouts — CBS
2. The Texaco Star Theater — NBC
3. I Love Lucy — CBS
4. The Red Skelton Show — NBC
5. The Colgate Comedy Hour — NBC
6. Fireside Theatre — NBC
7. The Jack Benny Program — CBS
8. Your Show of Shows — NBC
9. You Bet Your Life — NBC
10. Arthur Godfrey and His Friends — CBS
11. Mama — CBS
12. Philco Television Playhouse — NBC
13. Amos 'n' Andy — CBS
14. Big Town — CBS
15. Pabst Blue Ribbon Bouts — CBS
16. Gillette Cavalcade of Sports — NBC
17. The Alan Young Show — CBS
18. All-Star Revue (tie) — NBC
18. Dragnet (tie) — NBC
20. Kraft Television Theatre — NBC

1952–53

1. I Love Lucy — CBS
2. Arthur Godfrey's Talent Scouts — CBS
3. Arthur Godfrey and His Friends — CBS
4. Dragnet — NBC
5. The Texaco Star Theater — NBC
6. The Buick Circus Hour — NBC
7. The Colgate Comedy Hour — NBC
8. Gangbusters — NBC
9. You Bet Your Life — NBC
10. Fireside Theatre — NBC
11. The Red Buttons Show — CBS
12. The Jack Benny Program — CBS
13. Life with Luigi — CBS
14. Pabst Blue Ribbon Bouts — CBS
15. Goodyear Television Playhouse — NBC
16. The Life of Riley — NBC
17. Mama — CBS
18. Your Show of Shows — NBC
19. What's My Line? — CBS
20. Strike It Rich — CBS

1953–54

1. I Love Lucy — CBS
2. Dragnet — NBC
3. Arthur Godfrey's Talent Scouts (tie) — CBS
3. You Bet Your Life (tie) — NBC
5. The Bob Hope Show — NBC
6. The Buick-Berle Show — NBC
7. Arthur Godfrey and His Friends — CBS
8. The Ford Television Theater — NBC
9. The Jackie Gleason Show — CBS
10. Fireside Theatre — NBC
11. The Colgate Comedy Hour (tie) — NBC
11. This Is Your Life (tie) — NBC
13. The Red Buttons Show — CBS
14. The Life of Riley — NBC
15. Our Miss Brooks — CBS
16. Treasury Men in Action — NBC
17. All-Star Revue (Martha Raye) — NBC
18. The Jack Benny Program — CBS
19. Gillette Cavalcade of Sports — NBC
20. Philco Television Playhouse — NBC

1954–55

1. I Love Lucy — CBS
2. The Jackie Gleason Show — CBS
3. Dragnet — NBC
4. You Bet Your Life — NBC
5. Toast of the Town (Ed Sullivan) — CBS
6. Disneyland — ABC
7. The Bob Hope Show — NBC
8. The Jack Benny Program — CBS
9. The Martha Raye Show — NBC
10. The George Gobel Show — NBC
11. The Ford Television Theater — NBC
12. December Bride — CBS
13. The Buick-Berle Show — NBC
14. This Is Your Life — NBC
15. I've Got a Secret — CBS
16. Two for the Money — CBS
17. Your Hit Parade — NBC
18. The Millionaire — CBS
19. General Electric Theater — CBS
20. Arthur Godfrey's Talent Scouts — CBS

1955–56

1. The $64,000 Question — CBS
2. I Love Lucy — CBS
3. The Ed Sullivan Show — CBS
4. Disneyland — ABC
5. The Jack Benny Program — CBS
6. December Bride — CBS
7. You Bet Your Life — NBC
8. Dragnet — NBC
9. I've Got a Secret — CBS
10. General Electric Theater — CBS
11. Private Secretary (tie) — CBS
11. The Ford Television
    Theater (tie) — NBC
13. The Red Skelton Show — CBS
14. The George Gobel Show — NBC
15. The $64,000 Challenge — CBS
16. Arthur Godfrey's
    Talent Scouts — CBS
17. The Lineup — CBS
18. Shower of Stars — CBS
19. The Perry Como Show — NBC
20. The Honeymooners — CBS

1956–57

1. I Love Lucy — CBS
2. The Ed Sullivan Show — CBS
3. General Electric Theater — CBS
4. The $64,000 Question — CBS
5. December Bride — CBS
6. Alfred Hitchcock Presents — CBS
7. I've Got a Secret (tie) — CBS
7. Gunsmoke (tie) — CBS
9. The Perry Como Show — NBC
10. The Jack Benny Program — CBS
11. Dragnet — NBC
12. Arthur Godfrey's
    Talent Scouts — CBS
13. The Millionaire (tie) — CBS
13. Disneyland (tie) — ABC
15. Shower of Stars — CBS
16. The Lineup — CBS
17. The Red Skelton Show — CBS
18. You Bet Your Life — NBC
19. The Life and Legend
    of Wyatt Earp — ABC
20. Private Secretary — CBS

1957–58

1. Gunsmoke — CBS
2. The Danny Thomas
   Show — CBS
3. Tales of Wells Fargo — NBC
4. Have Gun, Will Travel — CBS
5. I've Got a Secret — CBS
6. The Life and Legend
   of Wyatt Earp — ABC
7. General Electric Theater — CBS
8. The Restless Gun — NBC
9. December Bride — CBS
10. You Bet Your Life — NBC
11. Alfred Hitchcock
    Presents (tie) — CBS
11. Cheyenne (tie) — ABC
13. The Tennessee
    Ernie Ford Show — NBC
14. The Red Skelton Show — CBS
15. Wagon Train (tie) — NBC
15. Sugarfoot (tie) — ABC
15. Father Knows Best (tie) — CBS
18. Twenty-One — NBC
19. The Ed Sullivan Show — CBS
20. The Jack Benny Program — CBS

1958–59

1. Gunsmoke — CBS
2. Wagon Train — NBC
3. Have Gun, Will Travel — CBS
4. The Rifleman — ABC
5. The Danny Thomas Show — CBS
6. Maverick — ABC
7. Tales of Wells Fargo — NBC
8. The Real McCoys — ABC
9. I've Got a Secret — CBS
10. Wyatt Earp — ABC
11. The Price Is Right — NBC
12. The Red Skelton Show — CBS
13. Zane Grey Theater (tie) — CBS
13. Father Knows Best (tie) — CBS
15. The Texan — CBS
16. Wanted: Dead or Alive (tie) — CBS
16. Peter Gunn (tie) — NBC
18. Cheyenne — ABC
19. Perry Mason — CBS
20. The Tennessee
    Ernie Ford Show — NBC

1959–60

1. Gunsmoke — CBS
2. Wagon Train — NBC
3. Have Gun, Will Travel — CBS
4. The Danny Thomas Show — CBS
5. The Red Skelton Show — CBS
6. Father Knows Best (tie) — CBS
7. 77 Sunset Strip (tie) — ABC
8. The Price Is Right — NBC
9. Wanted: Dead or Alive — CBS
10. Perry Mason — CBS
11. The Real McCoys — ABC
12. The Ed Sullivan Show — CBS
13. The Bing Crosby Show — ABC
14. The Rifleman — ABC
15. The Tennessee
    Ernie Ford Show — NBC
16. The Lawman — ABC
17. Dennis the Menace — CBS
18. Cheyenne — ABC
19. Rawhide — CBS
20. Maverick — ABC

1960–61

1. Gunsmoke — CBS
2. Wagon Train — NBC
3. Have Gun, Will Travel — CBS
4. The Andy Griffith Show — CBS
5. The Real McCoys — ABC
6. Rawhide — CBS
7. Candid Camera — CBS
8. The Untouchables (tie) — ABC
8. The Price Is Right (tie) — NBC
10. The Jack Benny Program — CBS
11. Dennis the Menace — CBS
12. The Danny Thomas Show — CBS
13. My Three Sons (tie) — ABC
13. 77 Sunset Strip (tie) — ABC
15. The Ed Sullivan Show — CBS
16. Perry Mason — CBS
17. Bonanza — NBC
18. The Flintstones — ABC
19. The Red Skelton Show — CBS
20. Alfred Hitchcock
    Presents — CBS

1961–62

1.	Wagon Train	NBC
2.	Bonanza	NBC
3.	Gunsmoke	CBS
4.	Hazel	NBC
5.	Perry Mason	CBS
6.	The Red Skelton Show	CBS
7.	The Andy Griffith Show	CBS
8.	The Danny Thomas Show	CBS
9.	Dr. Kildare	NBC
10.	Candid Camera	CBS
11.	My Three Sons	ABC
12.	The Garry Moore Show	CBS
13.	Rawhide	CBS
14.	The Real McCoys	ABC
15.	Lassie	CBS
16.	Sing Along with Mitch	NBC
17.	Dennis the Menace (tie)	CBS
17.	Marshal Dillon (tie)	
	(Gunsmoke reruns)	CBS
19.	Ben Casey	ABC
20.	The Ed Sullivan Show	CBS

1962–63

1.	The Beverly Hillbillies	CBS
2.	Candid Camera (tie)	CBS
2.	The Red Skelton Show (tie)	CBS
4.	Bonanza (tie)	NBC
4.	The Lucy Show (tie)	CBS
6.	The Andy Griffith Show	CBS
7.	Ben Casey (tie)	ABC
7.	The Danny Thomas Show (tie)	CBS
9.	The Dick Van Dyke Show	CBS
10.	Gunsmoke	CBS
11.	Dr. Kildare (tie)	NBC
11.	The Jack Benny Program (tie)	CBS
13.	What's My Line?	CBS
14.	The Ed Sullivan Show	CBS
15.	Hazel	NBC
16.	I've Got a Secret	CBS
17.	The Jackie Gleason Show	CBS
18.	The Defenders	CBS
19.	The Garry Moore Show (tie)	CBS
19.	To Tell the Truth (tie)	CBS

1963–64

1.	The Beverly Hillbillies	CBS
2.	Bonanza	NBC
3.	The Dick Van Dyke Show	CBS
4.	Petticoat Junction	CBS
5.	The Andy Griffith Show	CBS
6.	The Lucy Show	CBS
7.	Candid Camera	CBS
8.	The Ed Sullivan Show	CBS
9.	The Danny Thomas Show	CBS
10.	My Favorite Martian	CBS
11.	The Red Skelton Show	CBS
12.	I've Got a Secret (tie)	CBS
12.	Lassie (tie)	CBS
12.	The Jack Benny Program (tie)	CBS
15.	The Jackie Gleason Show	CBS
16.	The Donna Reed Show	ABC
17.	The Virginian	NBC
18.	The Patty Duke Show	ABC
19.	Dr. Kildare	NBC
20.	Gunsmoke	CBS

1964–65

1.	Bonanza	NBC
2.	Bewitched	ABC
3.	Gomer Pyle, U.S.M.C.	CBS
4.	The Andy Griffith Show	CBS
5.	The Fugitive	ABC
6.	The Red Skelton Hour	CBS
7.	The Dick Van Dyke Show	CBS
8.	The Lucy Show	CBS
9.	Peyton Place (II)	ABC
10.	Combat	ABC
11.	Walt Disney's Wonderful	
	World of Color	NBC
12.	The Beverly Hillbillies	CBS
13.	My Three Sons	ABC
14.	Branded	NBC
15.	Petticoat Junction (tie)	CBS
15.	The Ed Sullivan Show (tie)	CBS
17.	Lassie	CBS
18.	The Munsters (tie)	CBS
18.	Gilligan's Island (tie)	CBS
20.	Peyton Place (V)	ABC

1965–66

1.	Bonanza	NBC
2.	Gomer Pyle, U.S.M.C.	CBS
3.	The Lucy Show	CBS
4.	The Red Skelton Hour	CBS
5.	Batman (II)	ABC
6.	The Andy Griffith Show	CBS
7.	Bewitched (tie)	ABC
7.	The Beverly Hillbillies (tie)	CBS
9.	Hogan's Heroes	CBS
10.	Batman (I)	ABC
11.	Green Acres	CBS
12.	Get Smart	NBC
13.	The Man from U.N.C.L.E.	NBC
14.	Daktari	CBS
15.	My Three Sons	CBS
16.	The Dick Van Dyke Show	CBS
17.	Walt Disney's Wonderful	
	World of Color (tie)	NBC
17.	The Ed Sullivan Show (tie)	CBS
19.	The Lawrence Welk Show (tie)	ABC
19.	I've Got a Secret (tie)	CBS

1966–67

1.	Bonanza	NBC
2.	The Red Skelton Hour	CBS
3.	The Andy Griffith Show	CBS
4.	The Lucy Show	CBS
5.	The Jackie Gleason Show	CBS
6.	Green Acres	CBS
7.	Daktari (tie)	CBS
7.	Bewitched (tie)	ABC
7.	The Beverly Hillbillies (tie)	CBS
10.	Gomer Pyle, U.S.M.C. (tie)	CBS
10.	The Virginian	NBC
10.	The Lawrence Welk Show (tie)	ABC
10.	The Ed Sullivan Show (tie)	CBS
14.	The Dean Martin Show (tie)	CBS
14.	Family Affair (tie)	CBS
16.	Smothers Brothers	
	Comedy Hour	CBS
17.	The CBS Friday Night	
	Movie (tie)	CBS
17.	Hogan's Heroes (tie)	CBS
19.	Walt Disney's Wonderful	
	World of Color	NBC
20.	Saturday Night at the	
	Movies	NBC

1967–68

1. The Andy Griffith Show — CBS
2. The Lucy Show — CBS
3. Gomer Pyle, U.S.M.C. — CBS
4. Gunsmoke (tie) — CBS
4. Family Affair (tie) — CBS
4. Bonanza (tie) — NBC
7. The Red Skelton Hour — CBS
8. The Dean Martin Show — NBC
9. The Jackie Gleason Show — CBS
10. Saturday Night at the Movies — NBC
11. Bewitched — ABC
12. The Beverly Hillbillies — CBS
13. The Ed Sullivan Show — CBS
14. The Virginian — NBC
15. The CBS Friday Night Movie (tie) — CBS
15. Green Acres (tie) — CBS
17. The Lawrence Welk Show — ABC
18. Smothers Brothers Comedy Hour — CBS
19. Gentle Ben — CBS
20. Tuesday Night at the Movies — NBC

1968–69

1. Rowan and Martin's Laugh-In — NBC
2. Gomer Pyle, U.S.M.C. — CBS
3. Bonanza — NBC
4. Mayberry R.F.D. — CBS
5. Family Affair — CBS
6. Gunsmoke — CBS
7. Julia — NBC
8. The Dean Martin Show — NBC
9. Here's Lucy — CBS
10. The Beverly Hillbillies — CBS
11. Mission: Impossible (tie) — CBS
11. Bewitched (tie) — ABC
11. The Red Skelton Hour (tie) — CBS
14. My Three Sons — CBS
15. The Glen Campbell Goodtime Hour — CBS
16. Ironside — NBC
17. The Virginian — NBC
18. The F.B.I. — ABC
19. Green Acres — CBS
20. Dragnet — NBC

1969–70

1. Rowan and Martin's Laugh-In — NBC
2. Gunsmoke — CBS
3. Bonanza — NBC
4. Mayberry R.F.D. — CBS
5. Family Affair — CBS
6. Here's Lucy — CBS
7. The Red Skelton Hour — CBS
8. Marcus Welby, M.D. — ABC
9. The Wonderful World of Disney — NBC
10. The Doris Day Show — CBS
11. The Bill Cosby Show — NBC
12. The Jim Nabors Hour — CBS
13. The Carol Burnett Show — CBS
14. The Dean Martin Show — NBC
15. My Three Sons (tie) — CBS
15. Ironside (tie) — NBC
15. The Johnny Cash Show (tie) — ABC
18. The Beverly Hillbillies — CBS
19. Hawaii Five-O — CBS
20. Glen Campbell Goodtime Hour — CBS

1970–71

1. Marcus Welby, M.D. — ABC
2. The Flip Wilson Show — NBC
3. Here's Lucy — CBS
4. Ironside — NBC
5. Gunsmoke — CBS
6. The ABC Movie of the Week — ABC
7. Hawaii Five-O — CBS
8. Medical Center — CBS
9. Bonanza — NBC
10. The F.B.I. — ABC
11. The Mod Squad — ABC
12. Adam-12 — NBC
13. Rowan and Martin's Laugh-In (tie) — NBC
13. The Wonderful World of Disney (tie) — NBC
15. Mayberry R.F.D. — CBS
16. Hee Haw — CBS
17. Mannix — CBS
18. The Men from Shiloh — NBC
19. My Three Sons — CBS
20. The Doris Day Show — CBS

1971–72

1. All in the Family — CBS
2. The Flip Wilson Show — NBC
3. Marcus Welby, M.D. — ABC
4. Gunsmoke — CBS
5. The ABC Movie of the Week — ABC
6. Sanford and Son — NBC
7. Mannix — CBS
8. Funny Face (tie) — CBS
8. Adam-12 (tie) — NBC
10. The Mary Tyler Moore Show — CBS
11. Here's Lucy — CBS
12. Hawaii Five-O — CBS
13. Medical Center — CBS
14. The NBC Mystery Movie — NBC
15. Ironside — NBC
16. The Partridge Family — ABC
17. The F.B.I. — ABC
18. The New Dick Van Dyke Show — CBS
19. The Wonderful World of Disney — NBC
20. Bonanza — NBC

1972–73

1. All in the Family — CBS
2. Sanford and Son — NBC
3. Hawaii Five-O — CBS
4. Maude — CBS
5. Bridget Loves Bernie (tie) — CBS
5. The NBC Sunday Mystery Movie (tie) — NBC
7. The Mary Tyler Moore Show (tie) — CBS
7. Gunsmoke (tie) — CBS
9. The Wonderful World of Disney — NBC
10. Ironside — NBC
11. Adam-12 — NBC
12. The Flip Wilson Show — NBC
13. Marcus Welby, M.D. — ABC
14. Cannon — CBS
15. Here's Lucy — CBS
16. The Bob Newhart Show — CBS
17. ABC Tuesday Movie of the Week — ABC
18. NFL Monday Night Football — ABC
19. The Partridge Family (tie) — ABC
19. The Waltons (tie) — CBS

1973–74

1. All in the Family — CBS
2. The Waltons — CBS
3. Sanford and Son — NBC
4. M*A*S*H — CBS
5. Hawaii Five-O — CBS
6. Maude — CBS
7. Kojak (tie) — CBS
7. The Sonny and Cher Comedy Hour (tie) — CBS
9. The Mary Tyler Moore Show (tie) — CBS
9. Cannon (tie) — CBS
11. The Six Million Dollar Man — ABC
12. The Bob Newhart Show (tie) — CBS
12. The Wonderful World of Disney (tie) — NBC
14. The NBC Sunday Mystery Movie — NBC
15. Gunsmoke — CBS
16. Happy Days — ABC
17. Good Times (tie) — CBS
17. Barnaby Jones (tie) — CBS
19. NFL Monday Night Football (tie) — ABC
19. The CBS Friday Night Movie (tie) — CBS

1974–75

1. All in the Family — CBS
2. Sanford and Son — NBC
3. Chico and the Man — NBC
4. The Jeffersons — CBS
5. M*A*S*H — CBS
6. Rhoda — CBS
7. Good Times — CBS
8. The Waltons — CBS
9. Maude — CBS
10. Hawaii Five-O — CBS
11. The Mary Tyler Moore Show — CBS
12. The Rockford Files — NBC
13. Little House on the Prairie — NBC
14. Kojak — CBS
15. Police Woman — NBC
16. S.W.A.T. — ABC
17. The Bob Newhart Show — CBS
18. The Wonderful World of Disney (tie) — NBC
18. The Rookies (tie) — ABC
20. Mannix — CBS

1975–76

1. All in the Family — CBS
2. Rich Man, Poor Man — ABC
3. Laverne and Shirley — ABC
4. Maude — CBS
5. The Bionic Woman — ABC
6. Phyllis — CBS
7. Sanford and Son (tie) — NBC
7. Rhoda (tie) — CBS
9. The Six Million Dollar Man — ABC
10. The ABC Monday Night Movie — ABC
11. Happy Days — ABC
12. One Day at a Time — CBS
13. The ABC Sunday Night Movie — ABC
14. The Waltons (tie) — CBS
14. M*A*S*H (tie) — CBS
16. Starsky and Hutch (tie) — ABC
16. Good Heavens (tie) — ABC
18. Welcome Back, Kotter — ABC
19. The Mary Tyler Moore Show — CBS
20. Kojak — CBS

1976–77

1. Happy Days — ABC
2. Laverne and Shirley — ABC
3. The ABC Monday Night Movie — ABC
4. M*A*S*H — CBS
5. Charlie's Angels — ABC
6. The Big Event — NBC
7. The Six Million Dollar Man — ABC
8. The ABC Sunday Night Movie (tie) — ABC
8. Baretta (tie) — ABC
8. One Day at a Time (tie) — CBS
11. Three's Company — ABC
12. All in the Family — CBS
13. Welcome Back, Kotter — ABC
14. The Bionic Woman — ABC
15. The Waltons (tie) — CBS
15. Little House on the Prairie (tie) — NBC
17. Barney Miller — ABC
18. 60 Minutes (tie) — CBS
18. Hawaii Five-O (tie) — CBS
20. NBC Monday Night at the Movies — NBC

1977–78

1. Laverne and Shirley — ABC
2. Happy Days — ABC
3. Three's Company — ABC
4. Charlie's Angels (tie) — ABC
4. All in the Family (tie) — CBS
6. 60 Minutes (tie) — CBS
7. Little House on the Prairie — NBC
8. M*A*S*H (tie) — CBS
8. Alice (tie) — CBS
10. One Day at a Time — CBS
11. How the West Was Won — ABC
12. Eight Is Enough — ABC
13. Soap — ABC
14. The Love Boat — ABC
15. NBC Monday Night Movie — NBC
16. NFL Monday Night Football — ABC
17. Barney Miller (tie) — ABC
17. Fantasy Island (tie) — ABC
19. The Amazing Spider-Man (tie) — CBS
19. Project U.F.O. (tie) — NBC

1978–79

1. Laverne and Shirley — ABC
2. Three's Company — ABC
3. Mork & Mindy — ABC
4. Happy Days (tie) — ABC
4. The Ropers (tie) — ABC
6. What's Happening!! (tie) — ABC
6. Alice (8:30) (tie) — CBS
8. M*A*S*H — CBS
9. One Day at a Time (Monday) — CBS
10. Taxi — ABC
11. 60 Minutes (tie) — CBS
11. Charlie's Angels (tie) — ABC
13. Angie — ABC
14. Alice (9:30) — CBS
15. All in the Family — CBS
16. WKRP in Cincinnati (tie) — CBS
16. Soap (tie) — ABC
18. Eight Is Enough — ABC
18. All in the Family — CBS
20. Barney Miller (tie) — ABC
20. CBS Sunday Night Movie (tie) — CBS

1979–80

1.	60 Minutes	CBS
2.	Three's Company	ABC
3.	That's Incredible	ABC
4.	M*A*S*H	CBS
5.	Alice	CBS
6.	Dallas	CBS
7.	Flo	CBS
8.	The Jeffersons	CBS
9.	The Dukes of Hazzard	CBS
10.	One Day at a Time	CBS
11.	WKRP in Cincinnati	CBS
12.	Goodtime Girls	ABC
13.	Archie Bunker's Place	CBS
14.	Taxi	ABC
15.	Eight Is Enough	ABC
16.	Little House on the Prairie	NBC
17.	House Calls	CBS
18.	Real People	NBC
19.	CHiPs	NBC
20.	Happy Days	ABC

1980–81

1.	Dallas	CBS
2.	60 Minutes	CBS
3.	The Dukes of Hazzard	CBS
4.	Private Benjamin	CBS
5.	M*A*S*H	CBS
6.	The Love Boat	ABC
7.	The NBC Tuesday Night Movie	NBC
8.	House Calls	CBS
9.	The Jeffersons (tie)	CBS
9.	Little House on the Prairie (tie)	NBC
11.	The Two of Us	CBS
12.	Alice	CBS
13.	Real People (tie)	NBC
13.	Three's Company (tie)	ABC
15.	The NBC Movie of the Week (tie)	NBC
15.	One Day at a Time (tie)	CBS
17.	Too Close for Comfort (tie)	ABC
17.	Magnum, P.I. (tie)	CBS
19.	Diff'rent Strokes (tie)	NBC
19.	NFL Monday Night Football (tie)	ABC

1981–82

1.	Dallas (9:00)	CBS
2.	Dallas (10:00)	CBS
3.	60 Minutes	CBS
4.	Three's Company (tie)	ABC
4.	CBS NFL Football Post 2 (tie)	CBS
6.	The Jeffersons	CBS
7.	Joanie Loves Chachi	ABC
8.	The Dukes of Hazzard (9:00)	CBS
9.	Alice (tie)	CBS
9.	The Dukes of Hazzard (8:00) (tie)	CBS
11.	The ABC Monday Night Movie (tie)	ABC
11.	Too Close for Comfort (tie)	ABC
13.	M*A*S*H	CBS
14.	One Day at a Time	CBS
15.	NFL Monday Night Football	ABC
16.	Falcon Crest	CBS
17.	Archie Bunker's Place (tie)	CBS
17.	The Love Boat (tie)	ABC
19.	Hart to Hart	ABC
20.	Trapper John, M.D.	CBS

1982–83

1.	60 Minutes	CBS
2.	Dallas	CBS
3.	M*A*S*H (tie)	CBS
3.	Magnum, P.I. (tie)	CBS
5.	Dynasty	ABC
6.	Three's Company	ABC
7.	Simon & Simon	CBS
8.	Falcon Crest	CBS
9.	NFL Monday Night Football	ABC
10.	The Love Boat	ABC
11.	One Day at a Time (Sunday)	CBS
12.	Newhart (Monday)	CBS
13.	The Jeffersons (tie)	CBS
13.	The A Team (tie)	NBC
15.	The Fall Guy (9:00)	ABC
16.	Newhart (Sunday, 9:30)	CBS
17.	The Mississippi	CBS
18.	9 to 5	ABC
19.	The Fall Guy	ABC
20.	The ABC Monday Night Movie	ABC

1983–84

1.	Dallas	CBS
2.	Dynasty	ABC
3.	The A Team	NBC
4.	60 Minutes	CBS
5.	Simon & Simon	CBS
6.	Magnum, P.I.	CBS
7.	Falcon Crest	CBS
8.	Kate & Allie	CBS
9.	Hotel	ABC
10.	Cagney & Lacey	CBS
11.	Knots Landing	CBS
12.	The ABC Sunday Night Movie (tie)	ABC
12.	The ABC Monday Night Movie (tie)	ABC
14.	TV's Bloopers & Practical Jokes	NBC
15.	AfterMASH	CBS
16.	The Fall Guy	ABC
17.	The Four Seasons	CBS
18.	The Love Boat	ABC
19.	Riptide	NBC
20.	The Jeffersons	CBS

1984–85

1.	Dynasty	ABC
2.	Dallas	CBS
3.	The Cosby Show	NBC
4.	60 Minutes	CBS
5.	Family Ties	NBC
6.	The A Team (tie)	NBC
6.	Simon & Simon (tie)	CBS
8.	Knots Landing	CBS
9.	Murder, She Wrote	CBS
10.	Falcon Crest (tie)	CBS
10.	Crazy Like a Fox (tie)	CBS
12.	Hotel	ABC
13.	Cheers	NBC
14.	Riptide (tie)	NBC
14.	Who's the Boss? (tie)	ABC
16.	Magnum, P.I.	CBS
17.	Hail to the Chief	ABC
18.	Newhart	CBS
19.	Kate & Allie	CBS
20.	The NBC Monday Night Movie	NBC

1985–86

1. The Cosby Show — NBC
2. Family Ties — NBC
3. Murder, She Wrote — CBS
4. 60 Minutes — CBS
5. Cheers — NBC
6. Dallas (tie) — CBS
6. Dynasty (tie) — ABC
6. The Golden Girls (tie) — NBC
9. Miami Vice — NBC
10. Who's the Boss? — ABC
11. Perfect Strangers — ABC
12. Night Court — NBC
13. The CBS Sunday
    Night Movie — CBS
14. Highway to Heaven (tie) — NBC
14. Kate & Allie (tie) — CBS
16. NFL Monday Night
    Football — ABC
17. Newhart — CBS
18. Knots Landing (tie) — CBS
18. Growing Pains (tie) — ABC
20. 227 — NBC

1986–87

1. The Cosby Show — NBC
2. Family Ties — NBC
3. Cheers — NBC
4. Murder, She Wrote — CBS
5. Night Court — NBC
6. The Golden Girls — NBC
7. 60 Minutes — CBS
8. Growing Pains — ABC
9. Moonlighting — ABC
10. Who's the Boss? — ABC
11. Dallas — CBS
12. Nothing in Common — NBC
13. Newhart — CBS
14. Amen — NBC
15. 227 — NBC
16. Matlock (tie) — NBC
16. CBS Sunday Night
    Movie (tie) — CBS
16. NBC Monday Night
    Movie (tie) — NBC
19. NFL Monday Night
    Football (tie) — ABC
19. Kate & Allie (tie) — CBS

1987–88

1. The Cosby Show — NBC
2. A Different World — NBC
3. Cheers — NBC
4. Growing Pains (Tuesday) — ABC
5. Night Court — NBC
6. The Golden Girls — NBC
7. Who's the Boss? — ABC
8. 60 Minutes — CBS
9. Murder, She Wrote — CBS
10. The Wonder Years — ABC
11. Alf — NBC
12. Moonlighting (tie) — ABC
12. L.A. Law (tie) — NBC
14. NFL Monday Night
    Football — ABC
15. Matlock (tie) — NBC
15. Growing Pains
    (Wednesday) (tie) — ABC
17. Amen — NBC
18. Family Ties — NBC
19. Hunter — NBC
20. The CBS Sunday
    Night Movie — CBS

1988–89

1. Roseanne (9:00) (tie) — ABC
1. The Cosby Show (tie) — NBC
3. Roseanne (8:30) (tie) — ABC
3. A Different World (tie) — NBC
5. Cheers — NBC
6. 60 Minutes — CBS
7. The Golden Girls — NBC
8. Who's the Boss? — ABC
9. The Wonder Years — ABC
10. Murder, She Wrote — CBS
11. Empty Nest — NBC
12. Anything but Love — ABC
13. Dear John — NBC
14. Growing Pains — ABC
15. Alf (tie) — NBC
15. L.A. Law (tie) — NBC
17. Matlock — NBC
18. Unsolved Mysteries (tie) — NBC
18. Hunter (tie) — NBC
20. In the Heat of the Night — NBC

1989–90

1. Roseanne — ABC
2. The Cosby Show — NBC
3. Cheers — NBC
4. A Different World — NBC
5. America's Funniest
    Home Videos — ABC
6. The Golden Girls — NBC
7. 60 Minutes — CBS
8. The Wonder Years — ABC
9. Empty Nest — NBC
10. Chicken Soup — ABC
11. NFL Monday Night Football — ABC
12. Unsolved Mysteries — NBC
13. Who's the Boss? — ABC
14. L.A. Law (tie) — NBC
14. Murder, She Wrote (tie) — CBS
16. Grand — NBC
17. In the Heat of the Night — NBC
18. Dear John — NBC
19. Coach — ABC
20. Matlock — NBC

1990–91

1. Cheers — NBC
2. 60 Minutes — CBS
3. Roseanne — ABC
4. A Different World — NBC
5. The Cosby Show — NBC
6. NFL Monday Night
    Football — ABC
7. America's Funniest
    Home Videos — ABC
8. Murphy Brown — CBS
9. America's Funniest
    People (tie) — ABC
9. Designing Women (tie) — CBS
9. Empty Nest (tie) — NBC
12. Golden Girls — NBC
13. Murder, She Wrote — CBS
14. Unsolved Mysteries — NBC
15. Full House — ABC
16. Family Matters — ABC
17. Coach (tie) — ABC
17. Matlock (tie) — NBC
19. In the Heat of the Night — NBC
20. Major Dad — CBS

1991–92

1.	60 Minutes	CBS
2.	Roseanne	ABC
3.	Murphy Brown	CBS
4.	Cheers	NBC
5.	Home Improvement	ABC
6.	Designing Women	CBS
7.	Coach	ABC
8.	Full House	ABC
9.	Murder, She Wrote (tie)	CBS
9.	Unsolved Mysteries (tie)	NBC
11.	Major Dad (tie)	CBS
11.	NFL Monday Night Football (tie)	ABC
13.	Room For Two	ABC
14.	The CBS Sunday Night Movie	CBS
15.	Evening Shade	CBS
16.	Northern Exposure	CBS
17.	A Different World	NBC
18.	The Cosby Show	NBC
19.	Wings	NBC
20.	America's Funniest Home Videos (tie)	ABC
20.	Fresh Prince of Bel Air (tie)	NBC

1992–93

1.	60 Minutes	CBS
2.	Roseanne	ABC
3.	Home Improvement	ABC
4.	Murphy Brown	CBS
5.	Murder, She Wrote	CBS
6.	Coach	ABC
7.	NFL Monday Night Football	ABC
8.	The CBS Sunday Night Movie (tie)	CBS
8.	Cheers (tie)	NBC
10.	Full House	ABC
11.	Northern Exposure	CBS
12.	Rescue: 911	CBS
13.	20/20	ABC
14.	The CBS Tuesday Night Movie (tie)	CBS
14.	Love & War (tie)	CBS
16.	Fresh Prince of Bel Air (tie)	NBC
16.	Hangin' with Mr. Cooper (tie)	ABC
16.	The Jackie Thomas Show (tie)	ABC
19.	Evening Shade	CBS
20.	Hearts Afire (tie)	CBS
20.	Unsolved Mysteries (tie)	NBC

1993–94

1.	Home Improvement	ABC
2.	60 Minutes	CBS
3.	Seinfeld	NBC
4.	Roseanne	ABC
5.	Grace Under Fire	ABC
6.	These Friends of Mine	ABC
7.	Frasier	NBC
8.	Coach (tie)	ABC
8.	NFL Monday Night Football (tie)	ABC
10.	Murder, She Wrote	CBS
11.	Murphy Brown	CBS
12.	Thunder Alley	ABC
13.	The CBS Sunday Night Movie	CBS
14.	20/20	ABC
15.	Love & War	CBS
16.	Primetime Live (tie)	ABC
16.	Wings (tie)	NBC
18.	NYPD Blue	ABC
19.	Homicide: Life on the Street	NBC
20.	Northern Exposure	CBS

1994–95

1.	Seinfeld	NBC
2.	ER	NBC
3.	Home Improvement	ABC
4.	Grace Under Fire	ABC
5.	NFL Monday Night Football	ABC
6.	60 Minutes	CBS
7.	NYPD Blue	ABC
8.	Friends	NBC
9.	Roseanne (tie)	ABC
9.	Murder, She Wrote (tie)	CBS
11.	Mad About You	NBC
12.	Madman of the People	NBC
13.	Ellen	ABC
14.	Hope & Gloria	NBC
15.	Frasier	NBC
16.	Murphy Brown	CBS
17.	20/20	ABC
18.	CBS Sunday Movie	CBS
19.	NBC Monday Night Movies	NBC
20.	Dave's World	CBS

1995–96

1.	ER	NBC
2.	Seinfeld	NBC
3.	Friends	NBC
4.	Caroline in the City	NBC
5.	NFL Monday Night Football	ABC
6.	The Single Guy	NBC
7.	Home Improvement	ABC
8.	Boston Common	NBC
9.	60 Minutes	CBS
10.	NYPD Blue	ABC
11.	Frasier (tie)	NBC
11.	20/20 (tie)	ABC
13.	Grace Under Fire	ABC
14.	Coach (tie)	ABC
14.	NBC Monday Night Movies (tie)	NBC
16.	Roseanne	ABC
17.	The Nanny	CBS
18.	Murphy Brown (tie)	CBS
18.	Primetime Live (tie)	ABC
18.	Walker, Texas Ranger (tie)	CBS

1996–97

1.	ER	NBC
2.	Seinfeld	NBC
3.	Suddenly Susan	NBC
4.	Friends (tie)	NBC
4.	The Naked Truth (tie)	NBC
6.	Fired Up	NBC
7.	NFL Monday Night Football	ABC
8.	The Single Guy	NBC
9.	Home Improvement	ABC
10.	Touched by an Angel	CBS
11.	60 Minutes	CBS
12.	20/20	ABC
13.	NYPD Blue	ABC
14.	CBS Sunday Movie	CBS
15.	Primetime Live	ABC
16.	Frasier	NBC
17.	Spin City	ABC
18.	NBC Sunday Night Movie (tie)	NBC
18.	The Drew Carey Show (tie)	ABC
20.	The X-Files	FOX

1997–98

1.	Seinfeld	NBC
2.	ER	NBC
3.	Veronica's Closet	NBC
4.	Friends	NBC
5.	NFL Monday Night Football	ABC
6.	Touched by an Angel	CBS
7.	60 Minutes	CBS
8.	Union Square	NBC
9.	CBS Sunday Movie	CBS
10.	Frasier (tie)	NBC
10.	Home Improvement (tie)	ABC
10.	Just Shoot Me (tie)	NBC
13.	Dateline NBC–Tuesday	NBC
14.	NFL Monday Showcase	ABC
15.	Dateline NBC–Monday	NBC
16.	The Drew Carey Show (tie)	ABC
16.	Fox NFL Sunday Post-Game Show (tie)	FOX
18.	20/20	ABC
19.	NYPD Blue (tie)	ABC
19.	Primetime Live (tie)	ABC
19.	The X-Files (tie)	FOX

1998–1999

1.	ER	NBC
2.	Friends	NBC
3.	Frasier	NBC
4.	NFL Monday Night Football	ABC
5.	Jesse (tie)	NBC
5.	Veronica's Closet (tie)	NBC
7.	60 Minutes	CBS
8.	Touched by an Angel	CBS
9.	CBS Sunday Movie	CBS
10.	20/20–Wednesday	ABC
11.	Home Improvement	ABC
12.	Everybody Loves Raymond	CBS
13.	NYPD Blue	ABC
14.	Law and Order	NBC
15.	The Drew Carey Show (tie)	ABC
15.	20/20–Friday (tie)	ABC
17.	Jag (tie)	CBS
17.	NFL Monday Night Showcase (tie)	ABC
17.	Providence (tie)	NBC
17.	Dateline Friday (tie)	NBC

1999–2000

1.	Who Wants to Be a Millionaire–Tuesday	ABC
2.	Who Wants to Be a Millionaire–Thursday	ABC
3.	Who Wants to Be a Millionaire–Sunday	ABC
4.	E.R.	NBC
5.	Friends	NBC
6.	NFL Monday Night Football	ABC
7.	Frasier	NBC
8.	Frasier (9:30)	NBC
9.	60 Minutes	CBS
10.	The Practice	ABC
11.	Touched by an Angel	CBS
12.	Law and Order	NBC
13.	Everybody Loves Raymond (tie)	CBS
13.	NFL Monday Showcase (tie)	ABC
15.	Jesse	NBC
16.	CBS Sunday Movie (tie)	CBS
16.	Daddio (tie)	NBC
18.	NYPD Blue (tie)	ABC
18.	Stark Raving Mad (tie)	NBC
20.	Dharma and Greg	ABC

2000-2001

1.	Survivor: The Australian Outback	CBS
2.	ER	NBC
3.	Who Wants to Be a Millionaire–Wednesday	ABC
4.	Who Wants to Be a Millionaire–Tuesday	ABC
5.	Friends	NBC
6.	NFL Monday Night Football	ABC
7.	Who Wants to Be a Millionaire–Sunday	ABC
7.	Everybody Loves Raymond (tie)	CBS
9.	Law and Order	NBC
10.	The Practice	ABC
11.	CSI	CBS
12.	Who Wants to Be a Millionaire–Thursday	ABC
12.	West Wing (tie)	NBC
14.	Will & Grace	NBC
15.	60 Minutes	CBS
16.	Cursed	NBC
16.	Becker (tie)	CBS
18.	Temptation Island	FOX
18.	Frasier (tie)	NBC
20.	Just Shoot Me	NBC

THE TOP 50 TELEVISION SHOWS

These single broadcasts drew the largest percentages of the viewing public. Perhaps the most notable thing about this honor roll is that it almost never changes any more—the viewing audience has become so fragmented that only the occasional Super Bowl can monopolize the airwaves. (Source: Nielsen Media Research)

Rank	Program	Date
1.	M*A*S*H	February 28, 1983
2.	Dallas ("Who Shot J.R.?")	November 21, 1980
3.	Roots, Part 8 (conclusion)	January 30, 1977
4.	Super Bowl XVI	January 24, 1982
5.	Super Bowl XVII	January 30, 1983
6.	Winter Olympics	February 23, 1994
7.	Super Bowl XX	January 26, 1986
8.	Gone With the Wind, Part 1	November 7, 1976
9.	Gone With the Wind, Part 2	November 8, 1976
10.	Super Bowl XII	January 15, 1978
11.	Super Bowl XIII	January 21, 1979
12.	Bob Hope Christmas Show	January 15, 1970
13.	Super Bowl XVIII (tie)	January 22, 1984
13.	Super Bowl XIX (tie)	January 20, 1985
15.	Super Bowl XIV	January 20, 1980
16.	Super Bowl XXX	January 28, 1996
17.	ABC Theater ("The Day After")	November 20, 1983
18.	Roots, Part 6 (tie)	January 28, 1977
18.	The Fugitive (tie)	August 29, 1967
20.	Super Bowl XXI	January 25, 1987
21.	Roots, Part 5	January 27, 1977
22.	Super Bowl XXVIII (tie)	January 30, 1994
22.	Cheers (tie)	May 20, 1993
24.	The Ed Sullivan Show (TV debut of The Beatles)	February 9, 1964
25.	Super Bowl XXVII	January 31, 1993
26.	Bob Hope Christmas Show	January 14, 1971
27.	Roots, Part 3	January 25, 1977
28.	Super Bowl XXXII	January 23, 1998
29.	Super Bowl XI (tie)	January 9, 1977
29.	Super Bowl XV (tie)	January 25, 1981
31.	Super Bowl VI	January 16, 1972
32.	Winter Olympics (tie)	February 25, 1994
33.	Roots, Part 2 (tie)	January 24, 1977
34.	The Beverly Hillbillies	January 8, 1964
35.	Roots, Part 4 (tie)	January 26, 1977
35.	The Ed Sullivan Show (with The Beatles) (tie)	February 16, 1964
37.	Super Bowl XXIII	January 22, 1989
38.	The 43rd Academy Awards	April 7, 1970
39.	Super Bowl XXXIV	January 30, 2000
39.	Super Bowl XXXI (tie)	January 26, 1997
41.	The Thorn Birds, Part 3	March 29, 1983
42.	The Thorn Birds, Part 4	March 30, 1983
43.	NFC championship game	January 10, 1982
44.	The Beverly Hillbillies	January 15, 1964
45.	Super Bowl VII	January 14, 1973
46.	Thorn Birds, Part 2	March 28, 1983
47.	Super Bowl IX (tie)	January 12, 1975
47.	The Beverly Hillbillies (tie)	February 26, 1964
49.	Super Bowl X (tie)	January 18, 1976
49.	Airport (tie)	November 11, 1973

MOST-WATCHED MOVIES ON TELEVISION

This list includes network prime-time feature films, both those made for theaters and those (including miniseries) made specifically for TV (*). Although *The Wizard of Oz*'s best showing misses our list at No. 34, many years of high ratings have made it, overall, the most popular movie ever shown on TV. (Source: Nielsen Media Research)

Rank	Movie	Air Date
1.	Roots, Part 8*	January 30, 1977
2.	Gone With the Wind, Part 1	November 7, 1976
3.	Gone With the Wind, Part 2	November 8, 1976
4.	The Day After*	November 20, 1983
5.	Roots, Part 6*	January 28, 1977
6.	Roots, Part 5*	January 27, 1977
7.	Roots, Part 3*	January 25, 1977
8.	Roots, Part 2*	January 24, 1977
9.	Roots, Part 4*	January 26, 1977
10.	The Thorn Birds, Part 3*	March 29, 1983
11.	The Thorn Birds, Part 4*	March 30, 1983
12.	The Thorn Birds, Part 2*	March 28, 1983
13.	Love Story (tie)	October 1, 1972
13.	Airport (tie)	November 11, 1973
13.	Roots, Part 7* (tie)	January 29, 1977
16.	The Winds of War, Part 7*	February 13, 1983
17.	Roots, Part 1	January 23, 1977
18.	The Winds of War, Part 2*	February 7, 1983
19.	The Thorn Birds, Part 1*	March 27, 1983
20.	The Godfather, Part 2	November 18, 1974
21.	Jaws	November 4, 1979
22.	The Poseidon Adventure	October 27, 1974
23.	The Birds (tie)	January 16, 1968
23.	True Grit (tie)	November 12, 1972
25.	Patton	November 19, 1972
26.	The Bridge on the River Kwai	September 25, 1966
27.	Jeremiah Johnson (tie)	January 18, 1976
27.	Helter Skelter, Part 2 (tie)*	April 2, 1976
29.	Rocky (tie)	February 4, 1979
29.	Ben-Hur (tie)	February 14, 1971

PEOPLE'S FAVORITE 50 TV STARS

The most popular TV personalities are not necessarily the most influential, but rather the sort of folks you'd like to know in real life. This year PEOPLE's Michael A. Lipton rethinks and freshens his list of tube all-stars:

TIM ALLEN

It's so nice to have a klutz around the house, but nobody could screw up as hilariously or nail the punchlines as deftly as Allen, *Home Improvement*'s hammer-handed dufus dad.

JAMES ARNESS

With his weatherbeaten face, loping gait, and laconic delivery, he stood alone as TV's last—and best—Western hero.

BEA ARTHUR

The first sitcom feminist: her foghorn voice, bristly authority, and, er, Maude-lin wit reduced mere men to spineless jellyfish.

LUCILLE BALL

Those lips (pouting ruefully), those eyes (pop-eyed with surprise), that voice ("Rick-kyyyyy!") always delivered 24-karat comedy.

JACK BENNY

Well! He got more laughs with That Look than Uncle Miltie ever did in a dress or Benny's old crony Burns did waving his cigar.

RAYMOND BURR

With his imposing baritone and X-ray eyes that penetrated the most ingenious alibis, Burr's Perry Mason never rested his defense till the guilty party (never, of course, his poor, framed client) confessed on the stand.

JOHNNY CARSON

Silver-haired, silver-tongued paterfamilias to Jay and Dave, this wise old night owl could give a hoot about returning to the throne he held for four glorious decades.

RICHARD CHAMBERLAIN

Let's see: '60s dreamboat Dr. Kildare leaves TV to Hamlet it up on the British stage, then triumphantly returns as the King of the Miniseries. There's gotta be a movie of the week here...

GEORGE CLOONEY

A Kildare for the '90s—and *ER*'s first breakout star—Clooney, more magnetic than an MRI scan, set pulses fluttering with just a cocked head, a raised brow, and a sly grin.

KATIE COURIC

She's your tomboyish kid sister all grown up, and while there's a mule-like kick to her interviews, her big heart and feisty twinkle keep her warm.

WALTER CRONKITE

America's most trusted anchor earned the nickname "Old Ironpants" through his marathon coverage of conventions, assassinations, and resignations, but it was his gosh-darn, oh-boyish enthusiasm that made him the man to watch reporting the moon shots.

PHIL DONAHUE

"Caller, are you there?" Earnest, excitable, daring, and dashing (literally, into the audience), the snow-thatched maestro of daytime talk left no taboo unturned, no trauma untreated.

DAVID DUCHOVNY

A minimalist actor with sad, basset-hound eyes and a sly-like-a-fox humor, he is the exemplar of '90s cool and cynicism.

PETER FALK

As the raincoat-rumpled detective with the frog-horn voice, Falk brought an ironic sense of mischief to his role as a regular guy besting the arrogant elites.

MICHAEL J. FOX

From *Family Ties* to *Spin City*, TV's most endearing comic actor made us love him even more for his valiant real-life battle with Parkinson's disease.

DENNIS FRANZ

The blustery, beer-bellied blue-collar joe as macho sex symbol. You got a problem with dat?

JAMES GANDOLFINI

In New Jersey mob family boss (and suburban family guy) Tony Soprano, Gandolfini essays TV's most complex characterization: the warm-hearted, cold-blooded monster you root for.

JAMES GARNER

Despite a body wracked by wear and tear, and a face etched with wisdom and woe, Garner remains TV's most credible—and comedic—action star.

JACKIE GLEASON

How sweet it was to see The Great One storm, scheme, and suffer as Ralph Kramden, the Willy Loman of bus drivers.

KELSEY GRAMMER

Portraying TV's favorite shrink, the pompous yet endearing Dr. Frasier Crane, in two hit series (*Cheers* and *Frasier*), Grammer has managed to balance his character's comic bluster with a wry, deadpan wit.

LARRY HAGMAN

So gleefully villainous, he made the viewer his grinning accomplice. We were completely in thrall of devilish J.R., TV's most hissable, kissable antihero.

ALFRED HITCHCOCK

TV transformed the film name into a household face—an erudite gargoyle whose drollery and drop-dead delivery made for a murderously marvelous one-man-show-within-the-show.

DAVID JANSSEN

A haggard, haunted underdog whose raspy voice and soulful brow served him brilliantly, whether playing fugitives or feds.

MICHAEL LANDON

From Little Joe Cartwright to big man on the prairie to angelic emissary, Landon made sentimentality a virtue, wrung drama out of decency, and rang true.

ANGELA LANSBURY

How did Cabot Cove manage to rack up the nation's highest murder rate? Ask this nebbishy doyenne of TV crimesolvers.

LASSIE

The wonder dog of our childhoods.

JAY LENO

The hardest-working man in showbiz sweated bullets to show us he is as good as—or, as his ratings would indicate, better than—Letterman.

GROUCHO MARX

An icon of '30s movie comedy, Groucho reinvented himself in the '50s as *You Bet Your Life*'s acerbic and irreverent emcee.

ELIZABETH MONTGOMERY

Sure, she bewitched us with that wiggly nose, but beyond the levity (and levitation), a serious TV-movie actress was in the wings.

MARY TYLER MOORE

She can still turn the world on with her smile. Yet for most of us, she'll always remain winsome single girl Mary Richards, her cap forever aloft, frozen in time.

LEONARD NIMOY

Who says a pointy-eared intellectual can't be a sex symbol? Star Trekkers melded their minds with Spock's and became one with the sci-fi universe.

ROSIE O'DONNELL

Okay, so she's no Oprah. But with her showbiz connections, breezy banter, and self-effacing, seat-of-the-pants wit, O'Donnell revitalized daytime talk.

JERRY ORBACH

As cynical yet shrewd Det. Lennie Briscoe, the flatfoot heart and soul of *Law & Order*, he gives this rapid-paced, city-slick crime drama the jagged edge of realism.

SARAH JESSICA PARKER

As Carrie, the spunkiest of *Sex & the City*'s man-hungry vixens, she turns Manhattan hanky-panky into a wholesome, athletic, even adventurous experience. She's never funnier than in post-coital recaps with her equally randy girlfriends.

REGIS PHILBIN

Morning TV's twinkle-eyed curmudgeon Reege blossomed into an evening superstar as the jocular host of the megahit *Who Wants to Be a Millionaire*. (Final answer: You bet your life Regis now is one, many times over.)

GILDA RADNER

The madcap heart and soul of the original *Saturday Night Live*.

DONNA REED

A suburban TV mom for the ages —smart, beautiful, and sunny.

MICHAEL RICHARDS

A maniac for all seasons: All he had to do to get laughs was walk/stagger/glide/boogie/tumble through Seinfeld's door.

THE ROCK

Can you smell what he's cooking? This cocky pro wrestler is a TV superhero for the new millennium.

FRED ROGERS

It really was a beautiful day in the neighborhood when this genial, sweet, protective grown-up first sat down 30 years ago, laced up his sneakers, and became every kid's best friend.

ROY ROGERS

The quintessential TV cowboy, tall in the saddle, handy with a six-shooter, yet for the most part, just plain Trigger-happy.

FRED SAVAGE

The joys and agonies of adolescence were wonderfully expressed in Savage's tender, perpetually wide-eyed visage.

TOM SELLECK

TV's merriest manchild, he spent his Magnum opus living out every guy's fantasies—and has a bright new career in sitcoms.

PHIL SILVERS

Ten-HUT! His Sgt. Bilko was a fast-squawking, never-balking con artist supreme who tweaked authority and energized '50s TV.

HOMER SIMPSON

Slobbus americanus, he eclipses his bratty son Bart, and has even been known to dispense pearls of Homer-spun wisdom.

SUZANNE SOMERS

A sitcom sexpot turned infomericial empress—no ifs, ands, or buttmasters about it.

DICK VAN DYKE

Limber-limbed, rubber-faced, G-rated precursor to Jim Carrey, he could trip the light fantastic (even while tripping over an ottoman).

VANNA WHITE

She turns letters—and heads—with a sensual body language all her own.

OPRAH WINFREY

So empathetic is this talk-show tsarina with her guests—and so upfront about herself it's scary—that she could be having a ball one day, and bawling the next.

HENRY WINKLER

Aaaaaaay! This retro '70s-cum-'50s sitcom star exuded the cool we all wished we'd had in our not-so-happy high school days.

PEOPLE'S 50 FORMATIVE SHOWS

The mark of all memorable series is their profound, or at least pervasive, impact on pop culture. No sooner are they on the air—like 1998's *The Sopranos*—than it's impossible to remember how we got along without them. Here are PEOPLE's shows of shows.

THE ADVENTURES OF SUPERMAN

More than 40 years later, this show starring George Reeves as the Man of Steel is still the only good superhero series TV has ever produced.

ALL IN THE FAMILY

At the heart of this epochal sitcom were the corrosive working-class prejudices of Archie Bunker, a Northern redneck. His political arguments make *Crossfire* seem tame.

AN AMERICAN FAMILY

In their time (the 1970s), the exhibitionistic Loud family opened themselves up to freakshow derision. But they paved the way for the current rage of reality-based shows and all those voyeuristic video-clip shows.

THE ANDY GRIFFITH SHOW

The precursor of the so-called rusticoms of the '60s, this quiet masterpiece had heart, humor, wisdom, and—often overlooked—an outstanding cast..

BONANZA

The Cartwrights, a larger-than-life clan, made the Ponderosa worth visiting every week.

THE BULLWINKLE SHOW

Jay Ward's kaleidoscopic, pun-crammed cartoon about a dense moose and a plucky flying squirrel delighted kids of all ages.

BURNS AND ALLEN

This iconoclastic '50s show gleefully disregarded TV tradition, including the observance of "the fourth wall." Their comic chemistry has never been duplicated.

CANDID CAMERA

"When you least expect it / You're elected / You're the star today." Alan Funt milked hilarious results from simply filming people in situations when they thought no one was watching.

CHARLIE'S ANGELS

A brilliant TV concept: staff a standard detective show with a gorgeous trio (Farrah Fawcett, Kate Jackson, and Jaclyn Smith) in sausage-skin clothing. Producer Aaron Spelling's first megahit was also his finest hour.

CHEERS

The pluperfect pinnacle of the sitcom genre.

THE COSBY SHOW

Witty, warm, and winning, the domestic experiences of the Huxtables touted family values without sermonizing.

DATELINE

A corporate bean-counter's delight, *Dateline* proves—up to four times a week!— that a steady mix of hard-edged investigative reporting and heart-tugging human interest stories can replace more expensive and riskier sitcoms and dramas.

THE DICK VAN DYKE SHOW

For the first half of the '60s, the only place on the planet funnier than the Petrie household was Rob's office at the apocryphal *Alan Brady Show.*

DRAGNET

The show's deliberately laconic style ("Just the facts, ma'am") only underscored the gritty power of its tales of cops and miscreants.

GUNSMOKE

TV's archetypal and longest-running Western.

HILL STREET BLUES

Creator Steven Bochco spiced up his precinct house gumbo with a rich mix of characters, multi-tiered narratives, wry humor and a dash of fatalism.

THE HONEYMOONERS

The antics of a bus driver and a sewer worker in a Brooklyn tenement yielded a priceless vein of American humor. Jackie Gleason and Art Carney were sublime.

JEOPARDY!

The thinking person's game show.

L.A. LAW

A powerhouse legal drama complex, unpredictable, imaginative, and always rewarding.

THE LARRY SANDERS SHOW

This sardonic backstage tour of a talk show was TV's funniest satire, perhaps because we loved to see the medium mock itself.

LEAVE IT TO BEAVER

Took the familiar family sitcom formula of the '50s and gave it a devious adolescent twist. Show stealer: Eddie Haskell.

THE MARY TYLER MOORE SHOW

A magical confluence of concept, cast, and material made this the high-water mark of '70s television.

M*A*S*H

Hands-down, the most successful series ever spun off from a feature film.

MASTERPIECE THEATRE

From *I, Claudius* to *Upstairs, Downstairs* to *The Jewel in the Crown,* this drama anthology series remains the crown jewel in PBS's lineup.

MIAMI VICE

Against a gaudy SoFlo backdrop of neon and pastels, cute cops chase after well-armed cocaine cowboys in flashy sports cars and cigarette boats. The only reason TV has ever furnished to stay home on Friday nights.

MISSION: IMPOSSIBLE

Your mission, should you decide to accept it, is to name a better adventure series than this taut, gripping espionage exercise.

NIGHTLINE

A provident opportunity to hash out the day's big news event.

THE ODD COUPLE

Opposites amuse, but never so much as in this impeccably cast, tone-perfect comedy about a pair of mismatched, middle-aged, Manhattan neo-bachelors.

THE ROCKFORD FILES

The couch potato's choice: a sly, undemanding, endlessly entertaining delight.

ROSEANNE

An adventurous, abrasive, authentic, and always amusing examination of the struggles of a working-class family.

ROUTE 66

The first dramatic series to be shot entirely on location, this '60s cross-country odyssey of two footloose do-gooders in a Corvette put prime time on the road to more sophisticated adult fare.

ROWAN AND MARTIN'S LAUGH-IN

With zany banter, double entendres, and go-go dancers (including Goldie Hawn), this late-'60s comedy cavalcade nudged TV into the age of hipsters.

ST. ELSEWHERE

Piquant and volatile, this Jack-in-the-box drama about a lesser Boston hospital ran from intense tragedy to bawdy comedy.

SATURDAY NIGHT LIVE

In a quarter-century of wildly uneven skits and ensembles, this comedy factory has churned out an endless line of comic stars.

SEINFELD

An hermetic, exquisitely maintained comedy of contemporary urban manners and mores.

SESAME STREET

This jauntily educational PBS series for pre-schoolers is culturally diverse, inventive and altogether admirable.

77 SUNSET STRIP

The most influential of the Sputnik-era private eye series was this ultra-cool conceit which starred Efrem Zimbalist Jr. and Roger Smith as a pair of suave, college-educated judo experts.

THE SIMPSONS

You'd need a shelf full of books like this *Almanac* and a crack research staff to run down all the pop culture references in a single episode of this puckish cartoon about the post-nuclear family.

60 MINUTES

The ultimate news magazine.

THE SOPRANOS

Only on cable could you get away with this profane, violent, sexy, and satiric profile of an angst-ridden, shrink-wrapped New Jersey Mafia family man—and his dysfunctional domestic clan.

STAR TREK

This notorious cult favorite was little-honored during its original '60s run but became a rerun staple and has launched a thriving industry of spin-offs.

SURVIVOR

Not since *Gilligan's Island* have such contentious castaways been thrown together—except that cranky Rudy, salty Susan, tricky Richard and company were all real contestants in the first run of a groundbreaking game show that

may signal the end of primetime as we know it.

THIRTYSOMETHING

Though dismissed by cynics as yuppie whining, this was in fact a drama of rare pathos, complexity and insight.

TODAY

The oldest, and in our book, the best of the matinal infotainment bandwagons.

THE TONIGHT SHOW

It's a tradition as comfortable as flannel pajamas: awaiting the sandman while watching Johnny's (and now Jay's) guests play musical chairs.

THE TWILIGHT ZONE

This spine-tingling supernatural anthology was penetrating, often profound, but above all, singularly spooky.

WALT DISNEY PRESENTS

Over four decades, under a variety of banners and working alternately for each of the three major networks, the Disney studio consistently turned out the tube's finest, most indelible family fare.

WILL & GRACE

The interplay between the neurotic title characters and their uninhibited sidekicks is so deft, it almost doesn't matter that this is network TV's first gay-themed hit sitcom. Almost.

THE X-FILES

"The truth is out there." Really out there. But week after week, this suspenseful series transforms paranormal and outright bizarre concepts into gripping, credible drama.

YOUR SHOW OF SHOWS

The apex of the variety show, this '50s favorite thrived on the versatile comedic talents of Sid Caesar and Imogene Coca and a stable of writers, including Mel Brooks, Larry Gelbart, Neil Simon, and Woody Allen.

SOME OF THE GOOD DIE YOUNG

Everyone remembers the long-running hits, but what about the quality shows that disappeared before they were old enough to walk? Of the countless shows that died after one season or less, here are 30 odd that PEOPLE critic Terry Kelleher misses the most.

THE ASSOCIATES
ABC, 1979
Effervescent sitcom set at a law firm. An early showcase for a major talent named Martin Short.

BEACON HILL
CBS, 1975
Derided as an expensive American imitation of *Upstairs, Downstairs,* this drama never got a chance to prove its worth.

THE BEN STILLER SHOW
Fox, 1992–93
Before he got hot on the big screen, Stiller starred in a hip half-hour sketch series with rock-bottom ratings.

THE BOB NEWHART SHOW
NBC, 1961–62
Not Newhart's first sitcom—or his second, third, or fourth. We're talking about his very first series, an acclaimed comedy-variety show that lasted just one season.

BUFFALO BILL
NBC, 1983–84
Dabney Coleman was an egotistical local TV personality in this unusually pungent sitcom. Geena Davis and Max Wright stood out in a strong supporting cast.

CALL TO GLORY
ABC, 1984–85
Craig T. Nelson starred as an Air Force officer and family man caught up in the historic events of the 1960s. Soared briefly but failed to maintain altitude.

CALUCCI'S DEPARTMENT
CBS, 1973
We still have a soft spot for this forgotten sitcom starring James Coco as the head of a New York City unemployment office. Sadly, the show got fired.

EAST SIDE, WEST SIDE
CBS, 1963–64
George C. Scott played a social worker (who later became a congressional aide) in a serious-minded drama that didn't shy away from controversial subjects.

EZ STREETS
CBS, 1996–97
Not your standard cops and crooks show, but rather a moody drama of moral ambiguity in a decaying city. In other words, it had "low ratings" written all over it.

THE FAMOUS TEDDY Z
CBS, 1989–90
Smart sitcom set at a Hollywood talent agency featured Alex Rocco's fabulous characterization of super-pushy Al Floss.

FOR THE PEOPLE
CBS, 1965
William Shatner, before *Star Trek,* starred in this classy drama about a New York City prosecutor. This line on his resumé almost makes up for *T. J. Hooker.*

FRANK'S PLACE
CBS, 1987–88
Tim Reid played a New Orleans restaurateur in a low-key comedy with some serious moments and no annoying laugh track. Too few viewers sampled this delectation.

GUN
ABC, 1997
Top-notch, Robert Altman–produced anthology that followed a gun from owner to owner. Shot blanks in the ratings.

HE & SHE
CBS, 1967–68
Real-life husband and wife Richard Benjamin and Paula Prentiss were the nominal stars, but Jack Cassidy stole the show as a vain actor with a superhero complex.

THE LAW AND MR. JONES
ABC, 1960–61
Not a Hall of Fame show, really, but James Whitmore may have been the most likable lawyer in TV history.

LIFELINE
NBC, 1978
Documentary series with a strong, simple concept: Follow one doctor each week. Twenty years later, in the age of "reality" shows, it might have been a hit.

MAX HEADROOM
ABC, 1987
Heady combination of sci-fi and TV satire. Not a smash, but quite a conversation piece.

MIDDLE AGES
CBS, 1992
Peter Riegert headed a fine ensemble cast in this short-lived drama about a group of guys on the cusp of 40.

MY WORLD AND WELCOME TO IT
NBC, 1969–70
A James Thurber–like cartoon-ist (William Windom) had Walter Mittyish dreams depicted through animation. Maybe it was too imaginative for a mass audience.

NICHOLS
NBC, 1971–72
James Garner took a laudable gamble with this offbeat Western about a reluctant sheriff trying to keep order without carrying a gun.

THE NIGHT STALKER
ABC, 1974–75
Humor and horror combined, with Darren McGavin as a rough-around-the-edges reporter covering vampires, werewolves, and other undesirables.

NOTHING SACRED
ABC, 1997–98
An unorthodox Catholic priest (Kevin Anderson) in a poor urban parish. A good idea bravely executed. No wonder it was canceled.

POLICE SQUAD!
ABC, 1982
Yes, those successful *Naked Gun* movies with Leslie Nielsen were based on a zany comedy series that ABC axed after a handful of episodes. One of the all-time least brilliant network decisions.

PROFIT
Fox, 1996
Daring drama about a frighten-ingly enterprising young man (Adrian Pasdar) clawing his way toward the top of the corporate ladder.

THE RICHARD BOONE SHOW
NBC, 1963–64
Fresh from *Have Gun Will Travel,* Boone starred in an anthology series with a regular repertory company (including Harry Morgan and Robert Blake). Will someone please resurrect this concept?

SHANNON'S DEAL
NBC, 1990 and 1991
Filmmaker John Sayles created this well-crafted series about a flawed lawyer (Jamey Sheridan).

SKAG
NBC, 1980
Gutsy drama starred Karl Malden as an old-fashioned blue-collar breadwinner trying to adjust to new realities.

SQUARE PEGS
CBS, 1982–83
Enjoyably quirky sitcom about two misfit high school girls, one of whom was the delightful Sarah Jessica Parker.

TRIALS OF O'BRIEN
CBS, 1965–66
The pre-Columbo Peter Falk was a defense lawyer with a disordered personal life in this drama with a light touch. Saturday-night viewers preferred Lawrence Welk. Go figure.

WONDERLAND
ABC, 2000
This provocative drama about the psychiatric department of a New York City hospital was committed to oblivion after just two episodes. It was disturbing and downbeat, but what did net-work execs expect?

A YEAR IN THE LIFE
NBC, 1987–88
Intelligent extended-family drama with the reliable Richard Kiley in the patriarch's role.

TRIVIAL TRIUMPHS

The answer: See below. The question? Who are *Celebrity Jeopardy!*'s all-time highest earners? These totals reflect the winnings donated to each celeb's charity or charities of choice. (P.S. Andy Richter won the 1999 tourney.) (Source: *Jeopardy!*)

Jerry Orbach	$34,000	Laura Innes	$24,400
Charles Shaughnessy	$31,800	Sam Waterston	$23,800
Andy Richter	$29,400	Jeff Greenfield	$23,000
Norman Schwarzkopf	$28,000	Peter Krause	$22,000
Jon Stewart	$28,000	Wallace Langham	$21,800
Kareem Abdul-Jabbar	$27,000	Gil Bellows	$21,200
Mark McEwen	$26,700	Michael McKean	$20,400
Bob Costas	$25,000	Robin Quivers	$19,500
Cheech Marin	$25,000	Jodi Applegate	$19,401
Thomas Gibson	$24,400	Jim Lampley	$19,200

STARS WITH SOAPY ROOTS

Ricky Martin, Usher, and Sarah Michelle Gellar are just a few of the many who were big on daytime before they became bigtime. Test your soap-opera memory against our list.

Actor	Character	Soap
Richard Dean Anderson	Dr. Jeff Webber	General Hospital
Armand Assante	Dr. Mike Powers	The Doctors
Kevin Bacon	Tim Werner	Guiding Light
Alec Baldwin	Billy Allison Aldrich	The Doctors
Bonnie Bedelia	Sandy Porter	Love of Life
Tom Berenger	Timmy Siegel	One Life to Live
Corbin Bernsen	Kenny Graham	Ryan's Hope
Yasmine Bleeth	Ryan Fenelli	Ryan's Hope
Carol Burnett	Verla Grubbs	All My Children
Ellen Burstyn	Dr. Kate Bartok	The Doctors
Kate Capshaw	Jinx Avery Mallory	The Edge of Night
Tia Carrere	Jade Soong	General Hospital
Dixie Carter	Olivia Brandeis "Brandy" Henderson	The Edge of Night
Nell Carter	Ethel Green	Ryan's Hope
Gabrielle Carteris	Tracy Julian	Another World
Shaun Cassidy	Dusty Walker	General Hospital
Lacey Chabert	Bianca Montgomery	All My Children
Jill Clayburgh	Grace Bolton	Search for Tomorrow
Dabney Coleman	Dr. Tracy Brown	Bright Promise
Courteney Cox	Bunny	As the World Turns
Ted Danson	Tim Conway	Somerset
Olympia Dukakis	Barbara Moreno	Search for Tomorrow
Morgan Fairchild	Jennifer Phillips	Search for Tomorrow
Laurence Fishburne	Joshua West	One Life to Live
Faith Ford	Julia Shearer	Another World
Vivica A. Fox	Dr. Stephanie Simmons	The Young and the Restless
Morgan Freeman	Roy Bingham	Another World
Sarah Michelle Gellar	Kendall Hart	All My Children
Thomas Gibson	Samuel R. "Sam" Fowler	Another World
Kelsey Grammer	Dr. Canard	Another World
Charles Grodin	Matt Crane	The Young Married
Larry Hagman	Ed Gibson	The Edge of Night
Mark Hamill	Kent Murray	General Hospital
David Hasselhoff	Bill "Snapper" Foster	The Young and the Restless
Anne Heche	Marley Hudson	Another World
Lauren Holly	Julie Chandler	All My Children
Kate Jackson	Daphne Harridge	Dark Shadows
James Earl Jones	Dr. Jim Frazier	Guiding Light

Actor	Character	Soap
Tommy Lee Jones	Dr. Mark Toland	One Life to Live
Raul Julia	Miguel Garcia	Love of Life
Kevin Kline	Woody Reed	Search for Tomorrow
Don Knotts	Wilbur Peabody	Search for Tomorrow
Téa Leoni	Lisa Di Napoli	Santa Barbara
Judith Light	Karen Martin	One Life to Live
Hal Linden	Larry Carter	Search for Tomorrow
Ray Liotta	Joey Perini	Another World
Ricky Martin	Miguel Morez	General Hospital
Marsha Mason	Judith Cole	Love of Life
Demi Moore	Jackie Templeton	General Hospital
Kate Mulgrew	Mary Ryan Fenelli	Ryan's Hope
Luke Perry	Ned Bates	Loving
Regis Philbin	Malachy Malone	Ryan's Hope
Phylicia Rashad	Courtney Wright	One Life to Live
Christopher Reeve	Benno ("Beanie" or "Ben") Harper	Love of Life
Ving Rhames	Czaja Carnek	Another World
Eric Roberts	Ted Bancroft	Another World
Meg Ryan	Betsy Stewart	As the World Turns
Pat Sajak	Kevin Hathaway	Days of Our Lives
Susan Sarandon	Sarah	Search for Tomorrow
Kyra Sedgwick	Julia Shearer	Another World
Tom Selleck	Jed Andrews	The Young and the Restless
Christian Slater	D. J. LaSalle	Ryan's Hope
Rick Springfield	Dr. Noah Drake	General Hospital
John Stamos	Blackie Parrish	General Hospital
Marisa Tomei	Marcy Thompson	As the World Turns
Janine Turner	Laura Templeton	General Hospital
Kathleen Turner	Nola Dancy Aldrich	The Doctors
Cicely Tyson	Martha Frazier	Guiding Light
Blair Underwood	Bobby Blue	One Life to Live
Usher	Raymond	The Bold and the Beautiful
Jack Wagner	Frisco Jones	General Hospital
Christopher Walken	Michael Bauer	Guiding Light
Sigourney Weaver	Avis Ryan	Somerset
Billy Dee Williams	Dr. Jim Frazier	Guiding Light
JoBeth Williams	Brandy Sheloo	Guiding Light
Robin Wright	Kelly Capwell	Santa Barbara

THE EMMY AWARDS

As the television industry has developed over the years, so has the business of television awards—so much so that the Emmys are now presented in two separate ceremonies to accommodate the growth of categories. The following presents a wide selection of winners in major areas throughout Emmy's history.

	1949	**1950**
Actor	—	Alan Young
Actress	—	Gertrude Berg
Drama	—	*Pulitzer Prize Playhouse*, ABC
Variety Program	—	*The Alan Young Show*, CBS
Game Show	—	*Truth or Consequences*, CBS
Children's Show	*Time for Beany*, KTLA	*Time for Beany*, KTLA

	1951	**1952**	**1953**
Actor	Sid Caesar	Thomas Mitchell	Donald O'Connor, *Colgate Comedy Hour*, NBC
Actress	Imogene Coca	Helen Hayes	Eve Arden, *Our Miss Brooks*, CBS
Drama	*Studio One*, CBS	*Robert Montgomery Presents*, NBC	*U.S. Steel Hour*, ABC
Mystery, Action, or Adventure	—	*Dragnet*, NBC	*Dragnet*, NBC
Comedy	*Red Skelton Show*, NBC	*I Love Lucy*, CBS	*I Love Lucy*, CBS
Comedian	Red Skelton, NBC	Lucille Ball, CBS; Jimmy Durante, NBC	—
Variety Program	*Your Show of Shows*, NBC	*Your Show of Shows*, NBC	*Omnibus*, CBS
Game Show	—	*What's My Line?*, CBS	*This is Your Life*, NBC; *What's My Line?*, CBS
Children's Program	—	*Time for Beany*, KTLA	*Kukla, Fran & Ollie*, NBC

	1954	**1955**	**1956**
Actor	Danny Thomas, *Make Room for Daddy*, ABC	Phil Silvers, *The Phil Silvers Show*, CBS	Robert Moss, *Father Knows Best*, NBC
Actress	Loretta Young, *The Loretta Young Show*, NBC	Lucille Ball, *I Love Lucy*, CBS	Loretta Young, *The Loretta Young Show*, NBC
Drama	*U.S. Steel Hour*, ABC	*Producers' Showcase*, NBC	*Playhouse 90*, CBS
Mystery, Action, or Adventure	*Dragnet*, NBC	*Disneyland*, ABC	—
Comedy	*Make Room for Daddy*, ABC	*The Phil Silvers Show*, CBS	—
Comedian	—	Phil Silvers, CBS; Nanette Fabray, NBC	Sid Caesar, *Caesar's Hour*, NBC; Nanette Fabray, *Caesar's Hour*, NBC
Variety Series	*Disneyland*, ABC	*The Ed Sullivan Show*, CBS	—
Game Show	*This Is Your Life*, NBC	*The $64,000 Question*, CBS	—
Children's Program	*Lassie*, CBS	*Lassie*, CBS	—

	1957	1958–59	1959–60
Drama	*Gunsmoke*, CBS	*The Alcoa Hour/Goodyear Playhouse*, NBC; *Playhouse 90*, CBS	*Playhouse 90*, CBS
Actor—Series	—	Raymond Burr, *Perry Mason*, CBS (Drama)	Robert Stack, *The Untouchables*, ABC
Actress—Series	—	Loretta Young, *The Loretta Young Show*, NBC (Drama)	Jane Wyatt, *Father Knows Best*, CBS
Supporting Actor—Series	—	Dennis Weaver, *Gunsmoke*, CBS	—
Supporting Actress—Drama Series	—	Barbara Hale, *Perry Mason*, CBS	—
Director—Drama	—	George Schaefer, *Little Moon of Aloban*, NBC; Jack Smight, *Eddie*, NBC	Robert Mulligan, *The Moon and Sixpence*, NBC
Writer—Drama	—	James Costigan, *Little Moon of Alban*, NBC; Alfred Brenner and Ken Hughes, *Eddie*, NBC	Rod Serling, *The Twilight Zone*, CBS
Comedy	*The Phil Silvers Show*, CBS	*The Jack Benny Show*, CBS	*Art Carney Special*, NBC
Actor—Comedy Series	Robert Young, *Father Knows Best*, NBC	Jack Benny, *The Jack Benny Show*, CBS	Dick Van Dyke, *The Dick Van Dyke Show*, CBS
Actress—Comedy Series	Jane Wyatt, *Father Knows Best*, NBC	Jane Wyatt, *Father Knows Best*, CBS & NBC	Jane Wyatt, *Father Knows Best*, CBS
Supporting Actor—Comedy Series	Carl Reiner, *Caesar's Hour*, NBC	Tom Poston, *The Steve Allen Show*, NBC	—
Supporting Actress—Comedy Series	Ann B. Davis, *The Bob Cummings Show*, CBS and NBC	Ann B. Davis, *The Bob Cummings Show*, NBC	—
Director—Comedy/Comedy Series	—	Peter Tewksbury, *Father Knows Best*, CBS	Ralph Levy and Bud Yorkin, *The Jack Benny Hour Specials*, CBS
Writer—Comedy/Comedy Series	Nat Hiken, Billy Friedberg, Phil Sharp, Terry Ryan, Coleman Jacoby, Arnold Rosen, Sidney Zelinko, A.J. Russell, and Tony Webster, *The Phil Silvers Show*, CBS	Sam Perrin, George Balzer, Hal Goldman, and Al Gordon, *The Jack Benny Show*, CBS	Sam Perrin, George Balzer, Hal Goldman, and Al Gordon, *The Jack Benny Show*, CBS
Variety Program	*The Dinah Shore Chevy Show*, NBC	*The Dinah Shore Chevy Show*, NBC	*The Fabulous Fifties*, CBS
Game Show	—	*What's My Line?*, CBS	—
Children's Program	—	—	*Huckleberry Hound*, SYN

	1960–61	1961–62	1962–63
Actor	Raymond Burr, *Perry Mason,* CBS	E.G. Marshall, *The Defenders,* CBS	E.G. Marshall, *The Defenders,* CBS
Actress	Barbara Stanwyck, *The Barbara Stanwyck Show,* NBC	Shirley Booth, *Hazel,* NBC	Shirley Booth, *Hazel,* NBC
Drama	*Macbeth,* NBC	*The Defenders,* CBS	*The Defenders,* CBS
Director—Drama	George Schaefer, *Macbeth,* NBC	Franklin Schaffner, *The Defenders,* CBS	Stuart Rosenberg, *The Defenders,* CBS
Writer—Drama	Rod Serling, *The Twilight Zone,* CBS	Reginald Rose, *The Defenders,* CBS	Robert Thorn, Reginald Rose, *The Defenders,* CBS
Comedy	*The Jack Benny Show,* CBS	*The Bob Newhart Show,* NBC	*The Dick Van Dyke Show,* CBS
Director—Comedy	Sheldon Leonard, *The Danny Thomas Show,* CBS	Nat Hiken, *Car 54, Where Are You?,* NBC	John Rich, *The Dick Van Dyke Show,* CBS
Writer—Comedy	Sherwood Schwartz, Dave O'Brien, Al Schwartz, Martin Ragaway, and Red Skelton, *The Red Skelton Show,* CBS	Carl Reiner, *The Dick Van Dyke Show,* CBS	Carl Reiner, *The Dick Van Dyke Show,* CBS
Variety Program	*Astaire Time,* NBC	*The Garry Moore Show,* CBS	*The Andy Williams Show,* NBC
Individual Performance—Variety or Music Program/Series	Fred Astaire, *Astaire Time,* NBC	Carol Burnett, *The Garry Moore Show,* CBS	Carol Burnett, *Julie and Carol at Carnegie Hall,* CBS; *Carol and Company,* CBS
Panel, Quiz or Audience Participation	—	—	*College Bowl,* CBS
Children's Program	*Young People's Concert: Aaron Copland's Birthday Party,* CBS	*New York Philharmonic Young People's Concerts with Leonard Bernstein,* CBS	*Walt Disney's Wonderful World of Color,* NBC

THE RATINGS CONNECTION

Having the No. 1 rated show for a season doesn't necessarily guarantee Emmy success...or does it? Here is a list of the No. 1 shows that have also won the top honors—along with those that have achieved the dubious distinction of winning the ratings race but losing the Emmy battle.

EMMY WINNERS	EMMY LOSERS
Texaco Star Theatre	Arthur Godfrey's Talent Scouts
I Love Lucy	Wagon Train
The $64,000 Question	The Beverly Hillbillies
Gunsmoke	Bonanza
Rowan and Martin's Laugh-In	The Andy Griffith Show
All in the Family	Marcus Welby, M.D.
60 Minutes	Happy Days
The Cosby Show	Laverne and Shirley
Cheers	Three's Company
Seinfeld	Dallas
ER	Dynasty
	Roseanne
	Home Improvement

	1963–64	1964–65	1965–66
Drama	The Defenders, CBS	In 1964–65 the entire award system was changed for one year, and there were no awards given in individual categories that in any way match the categories from other years.	The Fugitive, ABC
Actor—Drama Series	Jack Klugman, The Defenders, CBS		Bill Cosby, I Spy, NBC
Actress—Drama Series	Shelley Winters, Two Is The Number, NBC		Barbara Stanwyck, The Big Valley, ABC
Supporting Actor—Drama Series	Albert Parker, One Day In The Life of Ivan Denisovich, NBC	—	James Daly, Eagle in a Cage, NBC
Supporting Actress—Drama Series	Ruth White, Little Moon of Alban, NBC	—	Lee Grant, Peyton Place, ABC
Writer—Drama	Ernest Kinay, The Defenders, CBS	—	Sydney Pollack, The Game, NBC
Director—Drama	Tom Gries, East Side/West Side, CBS	—	Millard Lampell, Eagle in a Cage, NBC
Comedy	The Dick Van Dyke Show, CBS	—	The Dick Van Dyke Show, CBS
Actor—Comedy Series	Dick Van Dyke, The Dick Van Dyke Show, CBS	—	Dick Van Dyke, The Dick Van Dyke Show, CBS
Actress—Comedy Series	Mary Tyler Moore, The Dick Van Dyke Show, CBS	—	Mary Tyler Moore, The Dick Van Dyke Show, CBS
Supporting Actor—Comedy Series	—	—	Don Knotts, The Andy Griffith Show, CBS
Supp. Actress—Comedy Series	—	—	Alice Pearce, Bewitched, ABC
Director—Comedy	Jerry Paris, The Dick Van Dyke Show, CBS	—	William Asher, Bewitched, ABC
Writer—Comedy	Carl Reiner, Sam Denoff, and Bill Penky, The Dick Van Dyke Show, CBS	—	Bill Persky, Sam Denoff, The Dick Van Dyke Show, CBS
Variety Program	The Danny Kaye Show, CBS	—	The Andy Williams Show, NBC
Director—Variety or Music	Robert Scheerer, The Danny Kaye Show, CBS	—	Alan Handley, The Julie Andrews Show, NBC
Writer—Variety	—	—	Al Gordon, Hal Goldman, and Sheldon Keller, An Evening with Carol Channing, CBS
Children's Program	Discovery '63-'64, ABC	—	A Charlie Brown Christmas, CBS

WINNING TEAMS

Looking for a rare wedding gift? Consider his-and-hers Emmies: Only seven married couples have ever sported matching trophies. One duo, *St. Elsewhere*'s Daniels and Bartlett, won for playing a husband and wife onscreen.

Hume Cronyn & Jessica Tandy
William Daniels & Bonnie Bartlett
Danny DeVito & Rhea Perlman
Phil Donahue & Marlo Thomas
Alfred Lunt & Lynn Fontanne
George C. Scott & Colleen Dewhurst
Christine Lahti & Thomas Schlamme

	1966–67	1967–68	1968–69
Drama Series	*Mission: Impossible*, CBS	*Mission: Impossible*, CBS	*NET Playhouse*, NET
Actor—Drama Series	Bill Cosby, *I Spy*, NBC	Bill Cosby, *I Spy*, NBC	Carl Betz, *Judd, for the Defense*, ABC
Actress—Drama Series	Barbara Bain, *Mission: Impossible*, CBS	Barbara Bain, *Mission: Impossible*, CBS	Barbara Bain, *Mission: Impossible*, CBS
Supporting Actor—Drama	Eli Wallach, *The Poppy Is Also a Flower*, ABC	Milburn Stone, *Gunsmoke*, CBS	—
Supporting Actress—Drama	Agnes Moorehead, *The Wild, Wild West*, CBS	Barbara Anderson, *Ironside*, NBC	Susan Saint James, *The Name of the Game*, NBC
Director—Drama	Alex Segal, *Death of a Salesman*, CBS	Paul Bogart, *Dear Friends*, CBS	David Green, *The People Next Door*, CBS
Writer—Drama	Bruce Geller, *Mission: Impossible*, CBS	Loring Mandel, *Do Not Go Gentle into That Good Night*, CBS	J. P. Miller, *The People Next Door*, CBS
Comedy	*The Monkees*, NBC	*Get Smart*, NBC	*Get Smart*, NBC
Actor—Comedy Series	Don Adams, *Get Smart*, NBC	Don Adams, *Get Smart*, NBC	Don Adams, *Get Smart*, NBC
Actress—Comedy Series	Lucille Ball, *The Lucy Show*, CBS	Lucille Ball, *The Lucy Show*, CBS	Hope Lange, *The Ghost and Mrs. Muir*, NBC
Supporting Actor—Comedy Series	Don Knotts, *The Andy Griffith Show*, CBS	Werner Klemperer, *Hogan's Heroes*, CBS	Werner Klemperer, *Hogan's Heroes*, CBS
Supporting Actress—Comedy Series	Frances Bavier, *The Andy Griffith Show*, CBS	Marion Lorne, *Bewitched*, ABC	—
Director—Comedy/Comedy Series	James Frawley, *The Monkees*, NBC	Bruce Bilson, *Get Smart*, NBC	—
Writer—Comedy/Comedy Series	Buck Henry and Leonard Stern, *Get Smart*, NBC	Allan Burns and Chris Hayward, *He and She*, CBS	Alan Blye, Bob Einstein, Murray Roman, Carl Gottlieb, Jerry Music, Steve Martin, Cecil Tuck, Paul Wayne, Cy Howard, and Mason Williams, *The Smothers Brothers Comedy Hour*, CBS
Variety Program	*The Andy Williams Show*, NBC	*Rowan and Martin's Laugh-In*, NBC	*Rowan and Martin's Laugh-In*, NBC
Director—Variety or Music	Fielder Cook, *Brigadoon*, ABC	Jack Haley, Jr., *Movin' with Nancy*, NBC	—
Writer—Variety or Music	Mel Brooks, Sam Denoff, Bill Persky, Carl Reiner, and Mel Tolkin, *The Sid Caesar, Imogene Coca, Carl Reiner, Howard Morris Special*, CBS	Chris Beard, Phil Hahn, Jack Hanrahan, Coslough Johnson, Paul Keyes, Marc London, Allan Manings, David Panich, Hugh Wedlock, and Digby Wolfe, *Rowan and Martin's Laugh-In*, NBC	—
Children's Program	*Jack and the Beanstalk*, NBC	—	—

	1969–70	1970–71	1971–72
Drama	*Marcus Welby, M.D.*, ABC	*The Bold Ones: The Senator*, NBC	*Elizabeth R*, PBS
Actor—Drama Series	Robert Young, *Marcus Welby, M.D.*, ABC	Hal Holbrook, *The Bold Ones: The Senator*, NBC	Peter Falk, *Columbo*, NBC
Actress—Drama Series	Susan Hampshire, *The Forsyte Saga*, NET	Susan Hampshire, *The First Churchills*, PBS	Glenda Jackson, *Elizabeth R.*, PBS
Supporting Actor—Drama Series	James Brolin, *Marcus Welby, M.D.*, ABC	David Burns, *The Price*, NBC	Jack Warden, *Brian's Song*, ABC
Supporting Actress—Drama Series	Gail Fisher, *Mannix*, CBS	Margaret Leighton, *Hamlet*, NBC	Jenny Agutter, *The Snow Goose*, NBC
Director—Drama Series	—	Daryl Duke, *The Bold Ones: The Senator*, NBC	Alexander Singer, *The Bold Ones: The Lawyers*, NBC
Writer—Drama	Richard Levinson and William Link, *My Sweet Charlie*, NBC	Joel Oliansky, *The Bold Ones: The Senator*, NBC	Richard L. Levinson and William Link, *Columbo*, NBC
Comedy	*My World and Welcome to It*, NBC	*All in the Family*, CBS	*All in the Family*, CBS
Actor—Comedy Series	William Windom, *My World and Welcome to It*, NBC	Jack Klugman, *The Odd Couple*, ABC	Carroll O'Connor, *All in the Family*, CBS
Actress—Comedy Series	Hope Lange, *The Ghost and Mrs. Muir*, ABC	Jean Stapleton, *All in the Family*, CBS	Jean Stapleton, *All in the Family*, CBS
Supporting Actor—Comedy Series	Michael Constantine, *Room 222*, ABC	Edward Asner, *The Mary Tyler Moore Show*, CBS	Edward Asner, *The Mary Tyler Moore Show*, CBS
Supporting Actress—Comedy Series	Karen Valentine, *Room 222*, ABC	Valerie Harper, *The Mary Tyler Moore Show*, CBS	Valerie Harper, *The Mary Tyler Moore Show*, CBS; Sally Struthers, *All in the Family*, CBS
Director—Comedy Series	—	Jay Sandrich, *The Mary Tyler Moore Show*, CBS	John Rich, *All in the Family*, CBS
Writer—Comedy Series	—	James L. Brooks and Allan Burns, *The Mary Tyler Moore Show*, CBS	Burt Styler, *All in the Family*, CBS
Drama/Comedy Special	—	—	*Brian's Song*, ABC
Variety or Music Series	*The David Frost Show*, SYN	*The David Frost Show*, SYN (Talk); *The Flip Wilson Show*, NBC (Music)	*The Dick Cavett Show*, ABC (Talk), *The Carol Burnett Show*, CBS (Music)
Director—Variety or Music	—	Mark Warren, *Rowan and Martin's Laugh-In*, NBC	Art Fisher, *The Sonny & Cher Comedy Hour*, CBS
Writer—Variety or Music	—	Herbert Baker, Hal Goodman, Larry Klein, Bob Weiskopf, Bob Schiller, Norman Steinberg, and Flip Wilson, *The Flip Wilson Show*, NBC	Don Hinkley, Stan Hart, Larry Siegel, Woody Kling, Roger Beatty, Art Baer, Ben Joelson, Stan Burns, Mike Marmer, and Arnie Rosen, *The Carol Burnett Show*, CBS
Daytime Drama Series	—	—	*The Doctors*, NBC
Children's Program	*Sesame Street*, NET	*Sesame Street*, PBS	*Sesame Street*, PBS

	1972–73	**1973–74**	**1974–75**
Drama	*The Waltons*, CBS	*Upstairs, Downstairs*, PBS	*Upstairs, Downstairs*, PBS
Actor—Drama Series	Richard Thomas, *The Waltons*, CBS	Telly Savalas, *Kojak*, CBS	Robert Blake, *Baretta*, ABC
Actress—Drama Series	Michael Learned, *The Waltons*, CBS	Michael Learned, *The Waltons*, CBS	Jean Marsh, *Upstairs, Downstairs*, PBS
Supporting Actor—Drama/Drama Series	Scott Jacoby, *That Certain Summer*, ABC	Michael Moriarty, *The Glass Menagerie*, ABC	Will Geer, *The Waltons*, CBS
Supporting Actress—Drama/Drama Series	Ellen Corby, *The Waltons*, CBS	Joanna Miles, *The Glass Menagerie*, ABC	Ellen Corby, *The Waltons*, CBS
Director—Drama	Joseph Sargent, *The Marcus Nelson Murders*, CBS	John Korty, *The Autobiography of Miss Jane Pittman*, CBS	George Cukor, *Love Among the Ruins*, ABC
Director—Drama Series	Jerry Thorpe, *Kung Fu*, ABC	Robert Butler, *The Blue Knight*, NBC	Bill Bain, *Upstairs, Downstairs*, PBS
Writer—Drama Series	John McGreevey, *The Waltons*, CBS	Joanna Lee, *The Waltons*, CBS	Howard Fast, *Benjamin Franklin*, CBS
Comedy	*All in the Family*, CBS	*M*A*S*H*, CBS	*The Mary Tyler Moore Show*, CBS
Actor—Comedy Series	Jack Klugman, *The Odd Couple*, ABC	Alan Alda, *M*A*S*H*, CBS	Tony Randall, *The Odd Couple*, ABC
Actress—Comedy Series	Mary Tyler Moore, *The Mary Tyler Moore Show*, CBS	Mary Tyler Moore, *The Mary Tyler Moore Show*, CBS	Valerie Harper, *Rhoda*, CBS
Supporting Actor—Comedy Series	Ted Knight, *The Mary Tyler Moore Show*, CBS	Rob Reiner, *All in the Family*, CBS	Ed Asner, *The Mary Tyler Moore Show*, CBS
Supporting Actress—Comedy Series	Valerie Harper, *The Mary Tyler Moore Show*, CBS	Cloris Leachman, *The Mary Tyler Moore Show*, CBS	Betty White, *The Mary Tyler Moore Show*, CBS
Director—Comedy Series	Jay Sandrich, *The Mary Tyler Moore Show*, CBS	Jackie Cooper, *M*A*S*H*, CBS	Gene Reynolds, *M*A*S*H*, CBS
Writer—Comedy Series	Michael Ross, Bernie West, and Lee Kalcheim, *All in the Family*, CBS	Treva Silverman, *The Mary Tyler Moore Show*, CBS	Ed. Weinberger and Stan Daniels, *The Mary Tyler Moore Show*, CBS
Drama/Comedy Special	*A War of Children*, CBS	*The Autobiography of Miss Jane*	*Pittman*, CBS
Variety Series	*The Julie Andrews Hour*, ABC	*The Carol Burnett Show*, CBS	*The Carol Burnett Show*, CBS
Director—Variety or Music	Bill Davis, *The Julie Andrews Hour*, ABC	Dave Powers, *The Carol Burnett Show*, CBS	Dave Powers, *The Carol Burnett Show*, CBS

	1972–73	1973–74	1974–75
Writer—Variety or Music Series	Stan Hart, Larry Siegel, Gail Parent, Woody Kling, Roger Beatty, Tom Patchett, Jay Tarses, Robert Hilliard, Arnie Kogen, Bill Angelos, and Buz Kohan, *The Carol Burnett Show*, CBS	Ed Simmons, Gary Belkin, Roger Beatty, Arnie Kogen, Bill Richmond, Gene Perret, Rudy De Luca, Barry Levinson, Dick Clair, Jenna McMahon, and Barry Harman, *The Carol Burnett Show*, CBS	Ed Simmons, Gary Belkin, Roger Beatty, Arnie Kogen, Bill Richmond, Gene Perret, Rudy De Luca, Barry Levinson, Dick Clair, and Jenna McMahon, *The Carol Burnett Show*, CBS
Variety, Music, or Comedy Special	*Singer Presents Liza with a "Z,"* CBS	*Lily Tomlin*, CBS	*An Evening with John Denver*, ABC
Miniseries/Limited Series	*Tom Brown's Schooldays*, PBS	*Columbo*, NBC	*Benjamin Franklin*, CBS
Actor—Miniseries/Limited Series	Anthony Murphy, *Tom Brown's Schooldays*, PBS	William Holden, *The Blue Knight*, NBC	Peter Falk, *Columbo*, NBC
Actress—Miniseries/Limited Series	Susan Hampshire, *Vanity Fair*, PBS	Mildred Natwick, *The Snoop Sisters*, NBC	Jessica Walter, *Amy Prentiss*, NBC
Daytime Drama Series	*The Edge of Night*, CBS	*The Doctors*, NBC	*The Young and the Restless*, CBS
Actor—Daytime Drama Series	—	Macdonald Carey, *Days of Our Lives*, NBC	Macdonald Carey, *Days of Our Lives*, NBC
Actress—Daytime Drama Series	—	Elizabeth Hubbard, *The Doctors*, NBC	Susan Flannery, *Days of Our Lives*, NBC
Host—Game Show	—	Peter Marshall, *The Hollywood Squares*, NBC	Peter Marshall, *The Hollywood Squares*, NBC
Host—Talk or Service	—	Dinah Shore, *Dinah's Place*, NBC	Barbara Walters, *Today*, NBC
Game Show	—	*Password*, ABC	*Hollywood Squares*, NBC
Talk, Service or Variety Series	—	*The Merv Griffin Show*, SYN	*Dinah!*, SYN
Children's Special	—	*Marlo Thomas and Friends in Free To Be…You and Me*, ABC	*Yes, Virginia, There Is a Santa Claus*, ABC
Children's Entertainment Series	—	*Zoom*, PBS	*Star Trek*, NBC

	1975–76	1976–77	1977–78
Drama	*Police Story*, NBC	*Upstairs, Downstairs*, PBS	*The Rockford Files*, NBC
Actor—Drama Series	Peter Falk, *Columbo*, NBC	James Garner, *The Rockford Files*, NBC	Edward Asner, *Lou Grant*, CBS
Actress—Drama Series	Michael Learned, *The Waltons*, CBS	Lindsay Wagner, *The Bionic Woman*, ABC	Sada Thompson, *Family*, ABC
Supporting Actor—Drama Series	Anthony Zerbe, *Harry-O*, ABC	Gary Frank, *Family*, ABC	Robert Vaughn, *Washington: Behind Closed Doors*, ABC
Supp. Actress—Drama Series	Ellen Corby, *The Waltons*, CBS	Kristy McNichol, *Family*, ABC	Nancy Marchand, *Lou Grant*, CBS
Director—Drama Series	David Greene, *Rich Man, Poor Man*, ABC	David Greene, *Roots*, ABC	Marvin J. Chomsky, *Holocaust*, NBC
Writer—Drama Series	Sherman Yellen, *The Adams Chronicles*, PBS	Ernest Kinoy and William Blinn, *Roots*, ABC	Gerald Green, *Holocaust*, NBC
Comedy	*The Mary Tyler Moore Show*, CBS	*The Mary Tyler Moore Show*, CBS	*All in the Family*, CBS
Actor—Comedy Series	Jack Albertson, *Chico and the Man*, NBC	Carroll O'Connor, *All in the Family*, CBS	Carroll O'Connor, *All in the Family*, CBS
Actress—Comedy Series	Mary Tyler Moore, *The Mary Tyler Moore Show*, CBS	Beatrice Arthur, *Maude*, CBS	Jean Stapleton, *All in the Family*, CBS

	1975–76	**1976–77**	**1977–78**
Supporting Actor—Comedy Series	Ted Knight, *The Mary Tyler Moore Show*, CBS	Gary Burghoff, *M*A*S*H*, CBS	Rob Reiner, *All in the Family*, CBS
Supporting Actress—Comedy Series	Betty White, *The Mary Tyler Moore Show*, CBS	Mary Kay Place, *Mary Hartman, Mary Hartman*, SYN	Julie Kavner, *Rhoda*, CBS
Director—Comedy/Comedy Series	Gene Reynolds, *M*A*S*H*, CBS	Alan Alda, *M*A*S*H*, CBS	Paul Bogart, *All in the Family*, CBS
Writer—Comedy Series	David Lloyd, *The Mary Tyler Moore Show*, CBS	Allan Burns, James L. Brooks, Ed. Weinberger, Stan Daniels, David Lloyd, and Bob Ellison, *The Mary Tyler Moore Show*, CBS	Bob Weiskopf and Bob Schiller (Teleplay); Barry Harman and Harve Brosten (Story), *All in the Family*, CBS
Drama/Comedy Special	*Eleanor and Franklin*, ABC	*Eleanor and Franklin: The White House Years*, ABC	*House Years*, ABC
Variety Series	*NBC's Saturday Night*, NBC	*Van Dyke and Company*, NBC	*The Muppet Show*, SYN
Limited Series	*Upstairs, Downstairs*, PBS	*Roots*, ABC	*Holocaust*, NBC
Actor—Limited Series	Hal Holbrook, *Sandburg's Lincoln*, NBC	Christopher Plummer, *The Moneychangers*, NBC	Michael Moriarty, *Holocaust*, NBC
Actress—Limited Series	Rosemary Harris, *Notorious Women*, PBS	Patty Duke Astin, *Captains and the Kings*, NBC	Meryl Streep, *Holocaust*, NBC
Daytime Drama Series	*Another World*, NBC	*Ryan's Hope*, ABC	*Days of Our Lives*, NBC
Actor—Daytime Drama Series	Larry Haines, *Search for Tomorrow*, CBS	Val Dufour, *Search for Tomorrow*, CBS	James Pritchett, *The Doctors*, NBC
Actress—Daytime Drama Series	Helen Gallagher, *Ryan's Hope*, ABC	Helen Gallagher, *Ryan's Hope*, ABC	Laurie Heinemann, *Another World*, NBC
Host—Game Show	Allen Ludden, *Password*, ABC	Bert Convy, *Tattletales*, CBS	Richard Dawson, *Family Feud*, ABC
Host—Talk or Service Series	Dinah Shore, *Dinah!*, SYN	Phil Donahue, *Donahue*, SYN	Phil Donahue, *Donahue*, SYN
Game Show	*The $20,000 Pyramid*, ABC	*Family Feud*, ABC	*The Hollywood Squares*, NBC
Talk, Service or Variety Series	*Dinah!*, SYN	*The Merv Griffin Show*, SYN	*Donahue*, SYN
Children's Entertainment Series	*Big Blue Marble*, SYN	*Zoom*, PBS	*Captain Kangaroo*, CBS

	1978–79	1979–80	1980–81
Drama	Lou Grant, CBS	Lou Grant, CBS	Hill Street Blues, NBC
Actor—Drama Series	Ron Leibman, Kaz, CBS	Ed Asner, Lou Grant, CBS	Daniel J. Travanti, Hill Street Blues, NBC
Actress—Drama Series	Mariette Hartley, The Incredible Hulk, CBS	Barbara Bel Geddes, Dallas, CBS	Barbara Babcock, Hill Street Blues, NBC
Supporting Actor—Drama Series	Stuart Margolin, The Rockford Files, NBC	Stuart Margolin, The Rockford Files, NBC	Michael Conrad, Hill Street Blues, NBC
Supporting Actress—Drama Series	Kristy McNichol, Family, ABC	Nancy Marchand, Lou Grant, CBS	Nancy Marchand, Lou Grant, CBS
Director—Drama Series	Jackie Cooper, The White Shadow, CBS	Roger Young, Lou Grant, CBS	Robert Butler, Hill Street Blues, NBC
Writer—Drama Series	Michele Gallery, Lou Grant, CBS	Seth Freeman, Lou Grant, CBS	Michael Kozoll and Steven Bochco, Hill Street Blues, NBC
Comedy	Taxi, ABC	Taxi, ABC	Taxi, ABC
Actor—Comedy Series	Carroll O'Connor, All in the Family, CBS	Richard Mulligan, Soap, ABC	Judd Hirsch, Taxi, ABC
Actress—Comedy Series	Ruth Gordon, Taxi, ABC	Cathryn Damon, Soap, ABC	Isabel Sanford, The Jeffersons, CBS
Supporting Actor—Comedy Series	Robert Guillaume, Soap, ABC	Harry Morgan, M*A*S*H, CBS	Danny De Vito, Taxi, ABC
Supporting Actress—Comedy Series	Sally Struthers, All in the Family, CBS	Loretta Swit, M*A*S*H, CBS	Eileen Brennan, Private Benjamin, CBS
Director—Comedy Series	Noam Pitlik, Barney Miller, ABC	James Burrows, Taxi, ABC	James Burrows, Taxi, ABC
Writer—Comedy Series	Alan Alda, M*A*S*H, CBS	Bob Colleary, Barney Miller, ABC	Michael Leeson, Taxi, ABC
Drama/Comedy Special	Friendly Fire, ABC	The Miracle Worker, NBC	Playing for Time, CBS
Variety Program	Steve & Eydie Celebrate Irving Berlin, NBC	Baryshnikov on Broadway, ABC	Lily: Sold Out, CBS
Director—Variety or Music	—	Dwight Hemion, Baryshnikov on Broadway, ABC	Don Mischer, The Kennedy Center Honors: A National Celebration of the Performing Arts, CBS

	1978–79	1979–80	1980–81
Writer—Variety or Music	—	Buz Kohan, *Shirley MacLaine… Every Little Movement*, CBS	Jerry Juhl, David Odell, Chris Langham, *The Muppet Show*, SYN
Limited Series	*Roots: The Next Generations*, ABC	*Edward & Mrs. Simpson*, SYN	*Shogun*, NBC
Actor—Limited Series	Peter Strauss, *The Jericho Mile*, ABC	Powers Boothe, *Guyana Tragedy: The Story of Jim Jones*, CBS	Anthony Hopkins, *The Bunker*, CBS
Actress—Limited Series	Bette Davis, *Strangers: The Story of a Mother and Daughter*, CBS	Patty Duke Astin, *The Miracle Worker*, NBC	Vanessa Redgrave, *Playing for Time*, CBS
Supporting Actor— Limited Series or Special	Marlon Brando, *Roots: The Next Generations*, ABC	George Grizzard, *The Oldest Living Graduate*, NBC	David Warner, *Masada*, ABC
Supporting Actress— Limited Series or Special	Esther Rolle, *Summer of My German Soldier*, NBC	Mare Winningham, *Amber Waves*, ABC	Jane Alexander, *Playing for Time*, CBS
Director—Limited Series or Special	David Greene, *Friendly Fire*, ABC	Marvin J. Chomsky, *Attica*, ABC	James Goldstone, *Kent State*, NBC
Writer—Limited Series or Special	Patrick Nolan and Michael Mann, *The Jericho Mile*, ABC	David Chase, *Off the Minnesota Strip*, ABC	Arthur Miller, *Playing for Time*, CBS
Daytime Drama Series	*Ryan's Hope*, ABC	*Guiding Light*, CBS	*General Hospital*, ABC
Actor—Daytime Drama Series	Al Freeman, Jr., *One Life to Live*, ABC	Douglass Watson, *Another World*, NBC	Douglass Watson, *Another World*, NBC
Actress—Daytime Drama Series	Irene Dailey, *Another World*, NBC	Judith Light, *One Life to Live*, ABC	Judith Light, *One Life to Live*, ABC
Supporting Actor— Daytime Drama Series	Peter Hansen, *General Hospital*, ABC	Warren Burton, *All My Children*, ABC	Larry Haines, *Search for Tomorrow*, CBS
Supporting Actress— Daytime Drama Series	Suzanne Rogers, *Days of Our Lives*, NBC	Francesca James, *All My Children*, ABC	Jane Elliot, *General Hospital*, ABC
Host—Game Show	Dick Clark, *The $20,000 Pyramid*, ABC	Peter Marshall, *The Hollywood Squares*, NBC	Peter Marshall, *The Hollywood Squares*, NBC
Host—Talk or Service	Phil Donahue, *Donahue*, SYN	Phil Donahue, *Donahue*, SYN	Hugh Downs, *Over Easy*, PBS
Game Show	*The Hollywood Squares*, NBC	*The Hollywood Squares*, NBC; *The $20,000 Pyramid*, ABC	*The $20,000 Pyramid*, ABC
Talk, Service or Variety Series	*Donahue*, SYN	*Donahue*, SYN	*Donahue*, SYN
Children's Special	*Christmas Eve on Sesame Street*, PBS	—	*Donahue and Kids*, NBC
Children's Entertainment Series	*Kids Are People Too*, ABC	*Hot Hero Sandwich*, NBC	*Captain Kangaroo*, CBS

	1981–82	**1982–83**	**1983–84**
Drama	*Hill Street Blues,* NBC	*Hill Street Blues,* NBC	*Hill Street Blues,* NBC
Actor—Drama Series	Daniel J. Travanti, *Hill Street Blues,* NBC	Ed Flanders, *St. Elsewhere,* NBC	Tom Selleck, *Magnum, P.I.,* CBS
Actress—Drama Series	Michael Learned, *Nurse,* CBS	Tyne Daly, *Cagney & Lacey,* CBS	Tyne Daly, *Cagney & Lacey,* CBS
Supporting Actor—Drama Series	Michael Conrad, *Hill Street Blues,* NBC	James Coco, *St. Elsewhere,* NBC	Bruce Weitz, *Hill Street Blues,* NBC
Supporting Actress—Drama Series	Nancy Marchand, *Lou Grant,* CBS	Doris Roberts, *St. Elsewhere,* NBC	Alfre Woodard, *Hill Street Blues,* NBC
Director—Drama Series	Harry Harris, *Fame,* NBC	Jeff Bleckner, *Hill Street Blues,* NBC	Corey Allen, *Hill Street Blues,* NBC
Writer—Drama Series	Steven Bochco, Anthony Yerkovich, Jeffrey Lewis and Michael Wagner (Teleplay); Michael Kozoll, and Steven Bochco (Story), *Hill Street Blues,* NBC	David Milch, *Hill Street Blues,* NBC	John Ford Noonan (Teleplay); John Masius and Tom Fontana (Story), *St. Elsewhere,* NBC
Comedy	*Barney Miller,* ABC	*Cheers,* NBC	*Cheers,* NBC
Actor—Comedy Series	Alan Alda, *M*A*S*H,* CBS	Judd Hirsch, *Taxi,* NBC	John Ritter, *Three's Company,* ABC
Actress—Comedy Series	Carol Kane, *Taxi,* ABC	Shelley Long, *Cheers,* NBC	Jane Curtin, *Kate & Allie,* CBS
Supporting Actor—Comedy Series	Christopher Lloyd, *Taxi,* ABC	Christopher Lloyd, *Taxi,* NBC	Pat Harrington, Jr., *One Day at a Time,* CBS
Supp. Actress—Comedy Series	Loretta Swit, *M*A*S*H,* CBS	Carol Kane, *Taxi,* NBC	Rhea Perlman, *Cheers,* NBC
Director—Comedy Series	Alan Rafkin, *One Day at a Time,* CBS	James Burrows, *Cheers,* NBC	Bill Persky, *Kate & Allie,* CBS
Writer—Comedy Series	Ken Estin, *Taxi,* ABC	Glen Charles, Les Charles, *Cheers,* NBC	David Angel, *Cheers,* NBC
Drama/Comedy Special	*A Woman Called Golda,* SYN	*Special Bulletin,* NBC	*Something About Amelia,* ABC
Variety, Music, or Comedy Program	*Night of 100 Stars,* ABC	*Motown 25: Yesterday, Today, Forever,* NBC	*The 6th Annual Kennedy Center Honors: A Celebration of the Performing Arts,* CBS
Individual Performance—Variety or Music Program	—	Leontyne Price, *Live From Lincoln Center: Leontyne Price, Zubin Mehta, and the New York Philharmonic,* PBS	Cloris Leachman, *Screen Actors Guild 50th Anniversary Celebration,* CBS
Director—Variety or Music	Dwight Hemion, *Goldie and Kids Listen to Us,* ABC	Dwight Hemion, *Sheena Easton Act I,* NBC	Dwight Hemion, *Here's Television Entertainment,* NBC
Writer—Variety or Music	John Candy, Joe Flaherty, Eugene Levy, Andrea Martin, Rick Moranis, Catherine O'Hara, Dave Thomas, Dick Blasucci, Paul Flaherty, Bob Dolman, John McAndrew, Doug Steckler, M. Bert Rich, Jeffrey Barron, Michael Short, Chris Cluess, Stuart Kreisman, and Brian McConnachie, *SCTV Comedy Network,* NBC	John Candy, Joe Flaherty, Eugene Levy, Andrea Martin, Martin Short, Dick Blasucci, Paul Flaherty, John McAndrew, Doug Steckler, Bob Dolman, Michael Short, and Mary Charlotte Wilcox, *SCTV Network,* NBC	Steve O'Donnell, Gerard Mulligan, Sanford Frank, Joseph E. Toplyn, Christopher Elliott, Matt Wickline, Jeff Martin, Ted Greenberg, David Yazbek, Merrill Markoe, and David Letterman, *Late Night with David Letterman,* NBC

	1981–82	1982–83	1983–84
Limited Series	*Marco Polo*, NBC	*Nicholas Nickleby*, SYN	*Concealed Enemies*, PBS
Actor—Limited Series or Special	Mickey Rooney, *Bill*, CBS	Tommy Lee Jones, *The Executioner's Song*, NBC	Laurence Olivier, *King Lear*, SYN
Actress—Limited Series or Special	Ingrid Bergman, *A Woman Called Golda*, SYN	Barbara Stanwyck, *The Thorn Birds*, ABC	Jane Fonda, *The Dollmaker*, ABC
Supporting Actor—Limited Series or Special	Laurence Olivier, *Brideshead Revisited*, PBS	Richard Kiley, *The Thorn Birds*, ABC	Art Carney, *Terrible Joe Moran*, CBS
Supporting Actress—Limited Series or Special	Penny Fuller, *Elephant Man*, ABC	Jean Simmons, *The Thorn Birds*, ABC	Roxana Zal, *Something About Amelia*, ABC
Director—Limited Series or Special	Marvin J. Chomsky, *Inside the Third Reich*, ABC	John Erman, *Who Will Love My Children?*, ABC	Jeff Bleckner, *Concealed Enemies*, PBS
Writer—Limited Series or Special	Corey Blechman (Teleplay); Barry Morrow (Story), *Bill*, CBS	Marshall Herskovitz (Teleplay); Edward Zwick, Marshall Herskovitz (Story), *Special Bulletin*, NBC	William Hanley, *Something About Amelia*, ABC
Daytime Drama Series	*Guiding Light*, CBS	*The Young & The Restless*, CBS	*General Hospital*, ABC
Actor—Daytime Drama Series	Anthony Geary, *General Hospital*, ABC	Robert S. Woods, *One Life to Live*, ABC	Larry Bryggman, *As the World Turns*, CBS
Actress—Daytime Drama Series	Robin Strasser, *One Life To Live*, ABC	Dorothy Lyman, *All My Children*, ABC	Erika Slezak, *One Life To Live*, ABC
Supporting Actor—Daytime Drama Series	David Lewis, *General Hospital*, ABC	Darnell Williams, *All My Children*, ABC	Justin Deas, *As the World Turns*, CBS
Supporting Actress—Daytime Drama Series	Dorothy Lyman, *All My Children*, ABC	Louise Shaffer, *Ryan's Hope*, ABC	Judi Evans, *The Guiding Light*, CBS
Host—Game Show	Bob Barker, *The Price Is Right*, CBS	Betty White, *Just Men!*, NBC	Bob Barker, *The Price Is Right*, CBS
Host—Talk or Service	Phil Donahue, *Donahue*, SYN	Phil Donahue, *Donahue*, SYN	Gary Collins, *Hour Magazine*, SYN
Game Show	*Password Plus*, NBC	*The New $25,000 Pyramid*, CBS	*The $25,000 Pyramid*, CBS
Talk or Service Series	*The Richard Simmons Show*, SYN	*This Old House*, PBS	*Woman to Woman*, SYN
Children's Special	*The Wave*, ABC	*Big Bird in China*, NBC	*He Makes Me Feel Like Dancin'*, NBC
Children's Series	*Captain Kangaroo*, CBS	*Smurfs*, NBC	*Captain Kangaroo*, CBS

	1984–85	1985–86	1986–87
Drama	*Cagney and Lacey,* CBS	*Cagney & Lacey,* CBS	*L. A. Law,* NBC
Actor—Drama Series	William Daniels, *St. Elsewhere,* NBC	William Daniels, *St. Elsewhere,* NBC	Bruce Willis, *Moonlighting,* ABC
Actress—Drama Series	Tyne Daly, *Cagney & Lacey,* CBS	Sharon Gless, *Cagney & Lacey,* CBS	Sharon Gless, *Cagney & Lacey,* CBS
Supporting Actor—Drama Series	Edward James Olmos, *Miami Vice,* NBC	John Karlen, *Cagney & Lacey,* CBS	John Hillerman, *Magnum, P.I.,* CBS
Supporting Actress—Drama Series	Betty Thomas, *Hill Street Blues,* NBC	Bonnie Bartlett, *St. Elsewhere,* NBC	Bonnie Bartlett, *St. Elsewhere,* NBC
Director—Drama Series	Karen Arthur, *Cagney & Lacey,* CBS	Georg Stanford Brown, *Cagney & Lacey,* CBS	Gregory Hoblit, *L.A. Law,* NBC
Writer—Drama Series	Patricia M. Green, *Cagney & Lacey,* CBS	Tom Fontana, John Tinker, and John Masius, *St. Elsewhere,* NBC	Steven Bochco, Terry Louise Fisher, *L.A. Law,* NBC
Comedy	*The Cosby Show,* NBC	*The Golden Girls,* NBC	*The Golden Girls,* NBC
Actor—Comedy Series	Robert Guillaume, *Benson,* ABC	Michael J. Fox, *Family Ties,* NBC	Michael J. Fox, *Family Ties,* NBC
Actress—Comedy Series	Jane Curtin, *Kate & Allie,* CBS	Betty White, *The Golden Girls,* NBC	Rue McClanahan, *The Golden Girls,* NBC
Supporting Actor—Comedy Series	John Larroquette, *Night Court,* NBC	John Larroquette, *Night Court,* NBC	John Larroquette, *Night Court,* NBC
Supporting Actress—Comedy Series	Rhea Perlman, *Cheers,* NBC	Rhea Perlman, *Cheers,* NBC	Jackée Harry, *227,* NBC
Director—Comedy Series	Jay Sandrich, *The Cosby Show,* NBC	Jay Sandrich, *The Cosby Show,* NBC	Terry Hughes, *The Golden Girls,* NBC
Writer—Comedy Series	Ed. Weinberger, Michael Leeson, *The Cosby Show,* NBC	Barry Fanaro and Mort Nathan, *The Golden Girls,* NBC	Gary David Goldberg, Alan Uger, *Family Ties,* NBC
Drama/Comedy Special	*Do You Remember Love,* CBS	*Love Is Never Silent,* NBC	*Promise,* CBS
Variety, Music, or Comedy Program	*Motown Returns to the Apollo,* NBC	*The Kennedy Center Honors: A Celebration of the Performing Arts,* CBS	*The 1987 Tony Awards,* CBS
Individual Performance—Variety or Music Program	George Hearn, *Sweeney Todd,* PBS	Whitney Houston, *The 28th Annual Grammy Awards,* CBS	Robin Williams, *A Carol Burnett Special: Carol, Carl, Whoopi & Robin,* ABC
Director—Variety or Music	Terry Hughes, *Sweeney Todd,* PBS	Waris Hussein, *Copacabana,* CBS	Don Mischer, *The Kennedy Center Honors: A Celebration of the Performing Arts,* CBS
Writer—Variety or Music	Gerard Mulligan, Sandy Frank, Joe Toplyn, Chris Elliott, Matt Wickline, Jeff Martin, Eddie Gorodetsky, Randy Cohen, Larry Jacobson, Kevin Curran, Fred Graver, Merrill Markoe, and David Letterman, *Late Night with David Letterman,* NBC	David Letterman, Steve O'Donnell, Sandy Frank, Joe Toplyn, Chris Elliott, Matt Wickline, Jeff Martin, Gerard Mulligan, Randy Cohen, Larry Jacobson, Kevin Curran, Fred Graver, and Merrill Markoe, *Late Night with David Letterman,* NBC	Steve O'Donnell, Sandy Frank, Joe Toplyn, Chris Elliott, Matt Wickline, Jeff Martin, Gerard Mulligan, Randy Cohen, Larry Jacobson, Kevin Curran, Fred Graver, Adam Resnick, and David Letterman, *Late Night with David Letterman,* NBC

	1984–85	1985–86	1986–87
Miniseries	The Jewel in the Crown, PBS	Peter the Great, NBC	A Year in the Life, NBC
Actor—Miniseries	Richard Crenna, The Rape of Richard Beck, ABC	Dustin Hoffman, Death of a Salesman, CBS	James Woods, Promise, CBS
Actress—Miniseries	Joanne Woodward, Do You Remember Love, CBS	Marlo Thomas, Nobody's Child, CBS	Gena Rowlands, The Betty Ford Story, ABC
Supporting Actor—Miniseries or Special	Karl Malden, Fatal Vision, NBC	John Malkovich, Death of a Salesman, CBS	Dabney Coleman, Sworn to Silence, ABC
Supporting Actress—Miniseries/ Limited Series or Special	Kim Stanley, Cat on a Hot Tin Roof, PBS	Colleen Dewhurst, Between Two Women, ABC	Piper Laurie, Promise, CBS
Director—Miniseries or Special	Lamont Johnson, Wallenberg: A Hero's Story, NBC	Joseph Sargent, Love Is Never Silent, NBC	Glenn Jordan, Promise, CBS
Writer—Miniseries or Special	Vickie Patik, Do You Remember Love, CBS	Ron Cowen and Daniel Lipman (Teleplay); Sherman Yellen (Story), An Early Frost, NBC	Richard Friedenberg (Teleplay); Kenneth Blackwell, Tennyson Flowers, and Richard Frieden-berg (Story), Promise, CBS
Daytime Drama Series	The Young and the Restless, CBS	The Young and the Restless, CBS	As the World Turns, CBS
Actor—Daytime Drama Series	Darnell Williams, All My Children, ABC	David Canary, All My Children, ABC	Larry Bryggman, As the World Turns, CBS
Actress—Daytime Drama Series	Kim Zimmer, Guiding Light, CBS	Erika Slezak, One Life To Live, ABC	Kim Zimmer, Guiding Light, CBS
Supporting Actor—Daytime Drama Series	Larry Gates, Guiding Light, CBS	John Wesley Shipp, As the World Turns, CBS	Gregg Marx, As the World Turns, CBS
Supporting Actress—Daytime Drama Series	Beth Maitland, The Young and the Restless, CBS	Leann Hunley, Days of Our Lives, NBC	Kathleen Noone, All My Children, ABC
Ingenue— Daytime Drama Series	Tracey E. Bregman, The Young and the Restless, CBS	Ellen Wheeler, Another World, NBC	Martha Byrne, As the World Turns, CBS
Younger Leading Man— Daytime Drama Series	Brian Bloom, As the World Turns, CBS	Michael E. Knight, All My Children, ABC	Michael E. Knight, All My Children, ABC
Host—Game Show	Dick Clark, The $25,000 Pyramid, CBS	Dick Clark, The $25,000 Pyramid, CBS	Bob Barker, The Price Is Right, CBS
Host—Talk or Service	Phil Donahue, Donahue, SYN	Phil Donahue, Donahue, SYN	Oprah Winfrey, The Oprah Winfrey Show, SYN
Game Show	The $25,000 Pyramid, CBS	The $25,000 Pyramid, CBS	The $25,000 Pyramid, CBS
Talk, Service or Variety Series	Donahue, SYN	Donahue, SYN	The Oprah Winfrey Show, SYN
Children's Special	Displaced Person, PBS	Anne of Green Gables, PBS	Jim Henson's The Storyteller: Hans My Hedgehog, NBC
Children's Series	Sesame Street, PBS	Sesame Street, PBS	Sesame Street, PBS

	1987–88	1988–89	1989–90
Drama	*thirtysomething*, ABC	*L.A. Law*, NBC	*L.A. Law*, NBC
Actor—Drama Series	Richard Kiley, *A Year in the Life*, NBC	Carroll O'Connor, *In the Heat of the Night*, NBC	Peter Falk, *Columbo*, ABC
Actress—Drama Series	Tyne Daly, *Cagney & Lacey*, CBS	Dana Delany, *China Beach*, ABC	Patricia Wettig, *thirtysomething*, ABC
Supporting Actor—Drama Series	Larry Drake, *L.A. Law*, NBC	Larry Drake, *L.A. Law*, NBC	Jimmy Smits, *L.A. Law*, NBC
Supporting Actress—Drama Series	Patricia Wettig, *thirtysomething*, ABC	Melanie Mayron, *thirtysomething*, ABC	Marg Helgenberger, *China Beach*, ABC
Director—Drama Series	Mark Tinker, *St. Elsewhere*, NBC	Robert Altman, *Tanner '88*, HBO	Thomas Carter, *Equal Justice*, ABC; Scott Winant, *thirtysomething*, ABC
Writer—Drama Series	Paul Haggis, Marshall Herskovitz, *thirtysomething*, ABC	Joseph Dougherty, *thirtysomething*, ABC	David E. Kelley, *L.A. Law*, NBC
Comedy	*The Wonder Years*, ABC	*Cheers*, NBC	*Murphy Brown*, CBS
Actor—Comedy Series	Michael J. Fox, *Family Ties*, NBC	Richard Mulligan, *Empty Nest*, NBC	Ted Danson, *Cheers*, NBC
Actress—Comedy Series	Beatrice Arthur, *The Golden Girls*, NBC	Candice Bergen, *Murphy Brown*, CBS	Candice Bergen, *Murphy Brown*, CBS
Supporting Actor—Comedy Series	John Larroquette, *Night Court*, NBC	Woody Harrelson, *Cheers*, NBC	Alex Rocco, *The Famous Teddy Z*, CBS
Supporting Actress—Comedy Series	Estelle Getty, *The Golden Girls*, NBC	Rhea Perlman, *Cheers*, NBC	Bebe Neuwirth, *Cheers*, NBC
Director—Comedy Series	Gregory Hoblit, *Hooperman*, ABC	Peter Baldwin, *The Wonder Years*, ABC	Michael Dinner, *The Wonder Years*, ABC
Writer—Comedy Series	Hugh Wilson, *Frank's Place*, CBS	Diane English, *Murphy Brown*, CBS	Bob Brush, *The Wonder Years*, ABC
Drama/Comedy Special	*Inherit the Wind*, NBC	*Day One*, CBS	*Caroline?*, CBS; *The Incident*,
Variety, Music, or Comedy Program	*Irving Berlin's 100th Birthday Celebration*, CBS	*The Tracey Ullman Show*, FOX	*In Living Color*, FOX
Individual Performance—Variety or Music Program	Robin Williams, *ABC Presents a Royal Gala*, ABC	Linda Ronstadt, *Canciones de Mi Padre*, PBS	Tracey Ullman, *The Best of the Tracey Ullman Show*, FOX
Director—Variety or Music	Patricia Birch and Humphrey Burton, *Celebrating Gershwin*, PBS	Jim Henson, *The Jim Henson Hour*, NBC	Dwight Hemion, *The Kennedy Center Honors: A Celebration of the Performing Arts*, CBS

	1987–88	1988–89	1989–90
Writer—Variety or Music	Jackie Mason, *Jackie Mason on Broadway*, HBO	James Downey, head writer; John Bowman, A. Whitney Brown, Gregory Daniels, Tom Davis, Al Franken, Shannon Gaughan, Jack Handey, Phil Hartman, Lorne Michaels, Mike Myers, Conan O'Brien, Bob Odenkirk, Herb Sargent, Tom Schiller, Robert Smigel, Bonnie Turner, Terry Turner, and Christine Zander, writers; George Meyer, additional sketches, *Saturday Night Live*, NBC	Billy Crystal, *Billy Crystal: Midnight Train to Moscow*, HBO; James L. Brooks, Heide Perlman, Sam Simon, Jerry Belson, Marc Flanagan, Dinah Kirgo, Jay Kogen, Wallace Wolodarsky, Ian Praiser, Marilyn Suzanne Miller, and Tracey Ullman, *The Tracey Ullman Show*, FOX
Miniseries	*The Murder of Mary Phagan*, NBC	*War and Remembrance*, ABC	*Drug Wars: The Camarena Story*, NBC
Actor—Miniseries or Special	Jason Robards, *Inherit the Wind*, NBC	James Woods, *My Name is Bill W.*, ABC	Hume Cronyn, *Age-Old Friends*, HBO
Actress—Miniseries or Special	Jessica Tandy, *Foxfire*, CBS	Holly Hunter, *Roe vs. Wade*, NBC	Barbara Hershey, *A Killing in a Small Town*, CBS
Supporting Actor—Miniseries or Special	John Shea, *Baby M*, ABC	Derek Jacobi, *The Tenth Man*, CBS	Vincent Gardenia, *Age-Old Friends*, HBO
Supporting Actress—Miniseries or Special	Jane Seymour, *Onassis: The Richest Man in the World*, ABC	Colleen Dewhurst, *Those She Left Behind*, NBC	Eva Marie Saint, *People Like Us*, NBC
Director—Miniseries or Special	Lamont Johnson, *Gore Vidal's Lincoln*, NBC	Simon Wincer, *Lonesome Dove*, CBS	Joseph Sargent, *Caroline?*, CBS
Writer—Miniseries or Special	William Hanley, *The Attic: The Hiding of Anne Frank*, CBS	Abby Mann, Robin Vote, and Ron Hutchison, *Murderers Among Us: The Simon Wiesenthal Story*, HBO	Terrence McNally, *Andre's Mother*, PBS
Daytime Drama Series	*Santa Barbara*, NBC	*Santa Barbara*, NBC	*Santa Barbara*, NBC
Actor—Daytime Drama Series	David Canary, *All My Children*, ABC	David Canary, *All My Children*, ABC	A Martinez, *Santa Barbara*, NBC
Actress—Daytime Drama Series	Helen Gallagher, *Ryan's Hope*, ABC	Marcy Walker, *Santa Barbara*, NBC	Kim Zimmer, *Guiding Light*, CBS
Supp. Actor—Daytime Drama	Justin Deas, *Santa Barbara*, NBC	Justin Deas, *Santa Barbara*, NBC	Henry Darrow, *Santa Barbara*, NBC
Supporting Actress—Daytime Drama Series	Ellen Wheeler, *All My Children*, ABC	Debbi Morgan, *All My Children*, ABC; Nancy Lee Grahn, *Santa Barbara*, NBC	Julia Barr, *All My Children*, ABC
Ingenue—Daytime Drama Series	Julianne Moore, *As the World Turns*, CBS	Kimberly McCullough, *General Hospital*, ABC	Cady McClain, *All My Children*, ABC
Younger Leading Man—Daytime Drama Series	Billy Warlock, *Days of Our Lives*, NBC	Justin Gocke, *Santa Barbara*, NBC	Andrew Kavovit, *As the World Turns*, CBS
Host—Game Show	Bob Barker, *The Price Is Right*, CBS	Alex Trebek, *Jeopardy!*, SYN	Alex Trebek, *Jeopardy!*, SYN; Bob Barker, *The Price Is Right*, CBS
Host—Talk or Service Show	Phil Donahue, *Donahue*, SYN	Sally Jessy Raphael, *Sally Jessy Raphael*, SYN	Joan Rivers, *The Joan Rivers Show*, SYN
Game Show	*The Price Is Right*, CBS	*The $25,000 Pyramid*, CBS	*Jeopardy!*, SYN
Talk, Service, or Variety Series	*The Oprah Winfrey Show*, SYN	*The Oprah Winfrey Show*, SYN	*Sally Jessy Raphael*, SYN
Children's Special	*The Secret Garden*, CBS	*Free To Be...A Family*, ABC	*A Mother's Courage: The Mary Thomas Story*, NBC
Children's Series	*Sesame Street*, PBS	*Newton's Apple*, PBS	*Reading Rainbow*, PBS

	1990–91	1991–92	1992–93
Drama	*L.A. Law*, NBC	*Northern Exposure*, CBS	*Picket Fences*, CBS
Actor—Drama Series	James Earl Jones, *Gabriel's Fire*, ABC	Christopher Lloyd, *Avonlea*, DIS	Tom Skerritt, *Picket Fences*, CBS
Actress—Drama Series	Patricia Wettig, *thirtysomething*, ABC	Dana Delany, *China Beach*, ABC	Kathy Baker, *Picket Fences*, CBS
Supporting Actor—Drama Series	Timothy Busfield, *thirtysomething*, ABC	Richard Dysart, *L.A. Law*, NBC	Chad Lowe, *Life Goes On*, ABC
Supporting Actress—Drama Series	Madge Sinclair, *Gabriel's Fire*, ABC	Valerie Mahaffey, *Northern Exposure*, CBS	Mary Alice, *I'll Fly Away*, NBC
Director—Drama Series	Thomas Carter, *Equal Justice*, ABC	Eric Laneuville, *I'll Fly Away*, NBC	Barry Levinson, *Homicide—Life on the Street*, NBC
Writer—Drama Series	David E. Kelley, *L.A. Law*, NBC	Andrew Schneider and Diane Frolov, *Northern Exposure*, CBS	Tom Fontana, *Homicide—Life on the Street*, NBC
Comedy	*Cheers*, NBC	*Murphy Brown*, CBS	*Seinfeld*, NBC
Actor—Comedy Series	Burt Reynolds, *Evening Shade*, CBS	Craig T. Nelson, *Coach*, ABC	Ted Danson, *Cheers*, NBC
Actress—Comedy Series	Kirstie Alley, *Cheers*, NBC	Candice Bergen, *Murphy Brown*, CBS	Roseanne Arnold, *Roseanne*, ABC
Supporting Actor—Comedy Series	Jonathan Winters, *Davis Rules*, ABC	Michael Jeter, *Evening Shade*, CBS	Michael Richards, *Seinfeld*, NBC
Supp. Actress—Comedy Series	Bebe Neuwirth, *Cheers*, NBC	Laurie Metcalf, *Roseanne*, ABC	Laurie Metcalf, *Roseanne*, ABC
Director—Comedy Series	James Burrows, *Cheers*, NBC	Barnet Kellman, *Murphy Brown*, CBS	Betty Thomas, *Dream On*, HBO
Writer—Comedy Series	Gary Dontzig and Steven Peterman, *Murphy Brown*, CBS	Elaine Pope and Larry Charles, *Seinfeld*, NBC	Larry David, *Seinfeld*, NBC
Variety, Music, or Comedy Program	*The 63rd Annual Academy Awards*, ABC	*The Tonight Show Starring Johnny Carson*, NBC	*Saturday Night Live*, NBC
Individual Performance—Variety or Music Program	Billy Crystal, *The 63rd Annual Academy Awards*, ABC	Bette Midler, *The Tonight Show Starring Johnny Carson*, NBC	Dana Carvey, *Saturday Night Live*, NBC
Director—Variety or Music	Hal Gurnee, *Late Night with David Letterman*, NBC	Patricia Birch, *Unforgettable with Love: Natalie Cole Sings the Songs of Nat King Cole*, PBS	Walter C. Miller, *The 1992 Tony Awards*, CBS
Writer—Variety or Music	Hal Kanter and Buz Kohan, writers; Billy Crystal, David Steinberg, Bruce Vilanch, and Robert Wuhl (Special Material), *The 63rd Annual Academy Awards*, ABC	Hal Kanter and Buz Kohan, writers); Billy Crystal, Marc Shaiman, David Steinberg, Robert Wuhl, and Bruce Vilanch, special material, *The 64rd Annual Academy Awards*, ABC	Judd Apatow, Robert Cohen, David Cross, Brent Forrester, Jeff Kahn, Bruce Kirschbaum, Bob Odenkirk, Sultan Pepper, Dino Stamatopoulos, and Ben Stiller, *The Ben Stiller Show*, FOX
Made for Television Movie	—	*Miss Rose White*: Hallmark Hall of Fame, NBC	*Barbarians at the Gate*, HBO; *Stalin*, HBO
Miniseries	*Separate but Equal*, ABC	*A Woman Named Jackie*, NBC	*Prime Suspect 2*, PBS

	1990–91	1991–92	1992–93
Actor—Miniseries or Special	John Gielgud, *Summer's Lease*, PBS	Beau Bridges, *Without Warning: The James Brady Story*, HBO	Robert Morse, *Tru*, PBS
Actress—Miniseries or Special	Lynn Whitfield, *The Josephine Baker Story*, HBO	Gena Rowlands, *Face of a Stranger*, CBS	Holly Hunter, *The Positively True Adventures of the Alleged Texas Cheerleader-Murdering Mom*, HBO
Supporting Actor—Miniseries or Special	James Earl Jones, *Heat Wave*, TNT	Hume Cronyn, *Neil Simon's Broadway Bound*, ABC	Beau Bridges, *The Positively True Adventures of the Alleged Texas Cheerleader-Murdering Mom*, HBO
Supporting Actress—Miniseries or Special	Ruby Dee, *Decoration Day*, NBC	Amanda Plummer, *Miss Rose White*, NBC	Mary Tyler Moore, *Stolen Babies*, LIF
Director—Miniseries or Special	Brian Gibson, *The Josephine Baker Story*, HBO	Daniel Petrie, *Mark Twain and Me*, DIS	James Sadwith, *Sinatra*, CBS
Writer—Miniseries or Special	Andrew Davies, *House of Cards*, PBS	John Falsey and Joshua Brand, *I'll Fly Away*, NBC	Jane Anderson, *The Positively True Adventures of the Alleged Texas Cheerleader-Murdering Mom*, HBO
Daytime Drama Series	*As the World Turns*, CBS	*All My Children*, ABC	*The Young and the Restless*, CBS
Actor—Daytime Drama Series	Peter Bergman, *The Young and the Restless*, CBS	Peter Bergman, *The Young and the Restless*, CBS	David Canary, *All My Children*, ABC
Actress—Daytime Drama Series	Finola Hughes, *General Hospital*, ABC	Erika Slezak, *One Life to Live*, ABC	Linda Dano, *Another World*, NBC
Supporting Actor—Daytime Drama Series	Bernie Barrow, *Loving*, ABC	Thom Christopher, *One Life to Live*, ABC	Gerald Anthony, *General Hospital*, ABC
Supporting Actress—Daytime Drama Series	Jess Walton, *The Young and the Restless*, CBS	Maeve Kinkead, *Guiding Light*, CBS	Ellen Parker, *Guiding Light*, CBS
Younger Actress—Daytime Drama Series	Anne Heche, *Another World*, NBC	Tricia Cast, *The Young and the Restless*, CBS	Heather Tom, *The Young and the Restless*, CBS
Younger Leading Man—Daytime Drama Series	Rick Hearst, *Guiding Light*, CBS	Kristoff St. John, *The Young and the Restless*, CBS	Monti Sharp, *Guiding Light*, CBS
Host—Game Show	Bob Barker, *The Price Is Right*, CBS	Bob Barker, *The Price Is Right*, CBS	Pat Sajak, *Wheel of Fortune*, SYN
Host—Talk or Service Show	Oprah Winfrey, *The Oprah Winfrey Show*, SYN	Oprah Winfrey, *The Oprah Winfrey Show*, SYN	Oprah Winfrey, *The Oprah Winfrey Show*, SYN
Game Show	*Jeopardy!*, SYN	*Jeopardy!*, SYN	*Jeopardy!*, SYN
Talk, Service, or Variety Series	*The Oprah Winfrey Show*, SYN	*The Oprah Winfrey Show*, SYN	*Good Morning America*, ABC
Children's Special	*You Can't Grow Home Again: A 3-2-1 Contact Extra*, PBS	*Mark Twain and Me*, DIS	*Shades of a Single Protein*, ABC
Children's Series	*Sesame Street*, PBS	*Sesame Street*, PBS	*Reading Rainbow*, PBS; *Tiny Toon Adventures*, SYN (Animated)

	1993–94	1994–95	1995–96
Drama	*Picket Fences*, CBS	*NYPD Blue*, ABC	*ER*, NBC
Actor—Drama Series	Dennis Franz, *NYPD Blue*, ABC	Mandy Patinkin, *Chicago Hope*, CBS	Dennis Franz, *NYPD Blue*, ABC
Actress—Drama Series	Sela Ward, *Sisters*, NBC	Kathy Baker, *Picket Fences*, CBS	Kathy Baker, *Picket Fences*, CBS
Supporting Actor—Drama Series	Fyvush Finkel, *Picket Fences*, CBS	Ray Walston, *Picket Fences*, CBS	Ray Walston, *Picket Fences*, CBS
Supporting Actress—Drama Series	Leigh Taylor-Young, *Picket Fences*, CBS	Julianna Margulies, *ER*, NBC	Tyne Daly, *Christy*, CBS
Director—Drama Series	Daniel Sackheim, *NYPD Blue*, ABC	Mimi Leder, *ER*, NBC	Jeremy Kagan, *Chicago Hope*, CBS
Writer—Drama Series	Ann Biderman, *NYPD Blue*, ABC	Michael Crichton, *ER*, NBC	Darin Morgan, *The X-Files*, Fox
Comedy	*Frasier*, NBC	*Frasier*, NBC	*Frasier*, NBC
Actor—Comedy Series	Kelsey Grammer, *Frasier*, NBC	Kelsey Grammer, *Frasier*, NBC	John Lithgow, *3rd Rock from the Sun*, NBC
Actress—Comedy Series	Candice Bergen, *Murphy Brown*, CBS	Candice Bergen, *Murphy Brown*, CBS	Helen Hunt, *Mad About You*, NBC
Supporting Actor—Comedy Series	Michael Richards, *Seinfeld*, NBC	David Hyde Pierce, *Frasier*, NBC	Rip Torn, *The Larry Sanders Show*, HBO
Supp. Actress—Comedy Series	Laurie Metcalf, *Roseanne*, ABC	Christine Baranski, *Cybill*, CBS	Julia Louis-Dreyfuss, *Seinfeld*, NBC
Director—Comedy Series	James Burrows, *Frasier*, NBC	David Lee, *Frasier*, NBC	Michael Lembeck, *Friends*, NBC
Writer—Comedy Series	David Angel, Peter Casey, and David Lee, *Frasier*, NBC	Chuck Ranberg, Anne Flett-Giordano, *Frasier*, NBC	Joe Keenan, Christopher Lloyd, Rob Greenberg, Jack Burditt, Chuck Ranberg, Anne Flett-Giordano, Linda Morris, and Vic Rauseo, *Frasier*, NBC
Variety, Music, or Comedy Program	*Late Show With David Letterman*, CBS	*The Tonight Show with Jay Leno*, NBC	*Dennis Miller Live*, HBO
Individual Performance—Variety or Music Program	Tracey Ullman, *Tracey Ullman Takes On New York*, HBO	Barbra Streisand, *Barbra Streisand: The Concert*, HBO	Tony Bennett, *Tony Bennett Live by Request: A Valentine Special*, A&E
Director—Variety or Music	Walter C. Miller, *The Tony Awards*, CBS	Jeff Margolis, *The 67th Annual Academy Awards*, ABC	Louis J. Horvitz, *The Kennedy Center Honors*, CBS
Writer—Variety or Music	Jeff Cesario, Mike Dugan, Eddie Feldmann, Gregory Greenberg, Dennis Miller, Kevin Rooney, *Dennis Miller Live*, HBO	Jeff Cesario, Ed Driscoll, David Feldman, Eddie Feldmann, Gregory Greenberg, Dennis Miller, Kevin Rooney, *Dennis Miller Live*, HBO	Eddie Feldmann, David Feldmann, Mike Gandolfini, Tom Hertz, Leah Krinsky, Dennis Miller, Rick Overton, *Dennis Miller Live*, HBO
Made for Television Movie	*And the Band Played On*, HBO	*Indictment: The McMartin Trial*, HBO	*Truman*, HBO
Miniseries	*Mystery: Prime Suspect 3*, PBS	*Joseph*, TNT	*Gulliver's Travels*, NBC

	1993–94	1994–95	1995–96
Actor—Miniseries or Special	Hume Cronyn, *Hallmark Hall of Fame: To Dance With the White Dog*, CBS	Raul Julia, *The Burning Season*, HBO	Alan Rickman, *Rasputin*, HBO
Actress—Miniseries or Special	Kirstie Alley, *David's Mother*, CBS	Glenn Close, *Serving in Silence: The Margarethe Cammermeyer Story*, NBC	Helen Mirren, *Prime Suspect: Scent of Darkness*, PBS
Supporting Actor—Miniseries or Special	Michael Goorjian, *David's Mother*, CBS	Donald Sutherland, *Citizen X*, HBO	Tom Hulce, *The Heidi Chronicles*, TNT
Supporting Actress—Miniseries or Special	Cicely Tyson, *Oldest Living Confederate Widow Tells All*, CBS	Judy Davis, *Serving in Silence: The Margarethe Cammemeyer Story*, NBC	Greta Scacchi, *Rasputin*, HBO
Director—Miniseries or Special	John Frankenheimer, *Against the Wall*, HBO	John Frankenheimer, *The Burning Season*, HBO	John Frankenheimer, *Andersonville*, TNT
Writer—Miniseries or Special	Bob Randall, *David's Mother*, CBS	Alison Cross, *Serving in Silence: The Margarethe Cammermeyer Story*, NBC	Simon Moore, *Gulliver's Travels*, NBC
Daytime Drama Series	*All My Children*, ABC	*General Hospital*, ABC	*General Hospital*, ABC
Actor—Daytime Drama Series	Michael Zaslow, *Guiding Light*, CBS	Justin Deas, *Guiding Light*, CBS	Charles Keating, *Another World*, NBC
Actress—Daytime Drama Series	Hillary B. Smith, *One Life to Live*, ABC	Erika Slezak, *One Life to Live*, ABC	Erika Slezak, *One Life to Live*, ABC
Supporting Actor—Daytime Drama Series	Justin Deas, *Guiding Light*, CBS	Jerry Ver Dorn, *Guiding Light*, CBS	Jerry Ver Dorn, *Guiding Light*, CBS
Supporting Actress—Daytime Drama Series	Susan Haskell, *One Life to Live*, ABC	Rena Sofer, *General Hospital*, ABC	Anna Holbrook, *Another World*, NBC
Younger Actress—Daytime Drama Series	Melissa Hayden, *Guiding Light*, CBS	Sarah Michelle Gellar, *All My Children*, ABC	Kimberly McCullough, *General Hospital*, ABC
Younger Leading Man—Daytime Drama Series	Roger Howarth, *One Life to Live*, ABC	Jonathan Jackson, *General Hospital*, ABC	Kevin Mambo, *Guiding Light*, CBS
Host—Talk or Service Show	Oprah Winfrey, *The Oprah Winfrey Show*, SYN	Oprah Winfrey, *The Oprah Winfrey Show*, SYN	Montel Williams, *The Montel Williams Show*, SYN
Game Show	*Jeopardy!*, SYN	*Jeopardy!*, SYN	*The Price Is Right*, CBS
Talk, Service, or Variety Series	*The Oprah Winfrey Show*, SYN-	*The Oprah Winfrey Show*, SYN	*The Oprah Winfrey Show*, SYN
Children's Special	*Dead Drunk: The Kevin Tunell Story*, HBO	*A Child Betrayed: The Calvin Mire Story*, HBO	*Stand Up*, CBS
Children's Series	*Sesame Street*, PBS; *Rugrats*, Nick (Animated)	*Nick News*, Nickelodeon; *Where on Earth is Carmen San Diego?*, Fox (Animated)	*Sesame Street*, PBS; *Animaniacs*, WB (Animated)

	1996–97	1997–98	1998–99
Drama	*Law & Order*, NBC	*The Practice*, ABC	*The Practice*, ABC
Actor—Drama Series	Dennis Franz, *NYPD Blue*, ABC	Andre Braugher, *Homicide: Life on the Street*, NBC	Dennis Franz, *NYPD Blue*, ABC
Actress—Drama Series	Gillian Anderson, *The X-Files*, Fox	Christine Lahti, *Chicago Hope*, CBS	Edie Falco, *The Sopranos*, HBO
Supporting Actor—Drama Series	Hector Elizondo, *Chicago Hope*, CBS	Gordon Clapp, *NYPD Blue*, ABC	Michael Badalucco, *The Practice*, ABC
Supporting Actress—Drama Series	Kim Delaney, *NYPD Blue*, ABC	Camryn Manheim, *The Practice*, ABC	Holland Taylor, *The Practice*, ABC
Director—Drama Series	Mark Tinker, *NYPD Blue*, ABC	Mark Tinker, *Brooklyn South*, CBS and Paris Barclay, *NYPD Blue*, ABC	Paris Barclay, *NYPD Blue*, ABC
Writer—Drama Series	David Milch, Stephen Gaghan, Michael R. Perry, *NYPD Blue*, ABC	Bill Clark, Nicholas Wooton, David Milch, *NYPD Blue*, ABC	James Manos, Jr., David Chase, *The Sopranos*, HBO
Comedy	*Frasier*, NBC	*Frasier*, NBC	*Ally McBeal*, FOX
Actor—Comedy Series	John Lithgow, *3rd Rock from the Sun*, NBC	Kelsey Grammer, *Frasier*, NBC	John Lithgow, *3rd Rock from the Sun*, NBC,
Actress—Comedy Series	Helen Hunt, *Mad About You*, NBC	Helen Hunt, *Mad About You*, NBC	Helen Hunt, *Mad About You*, NBC
Supporting Actor—Comedy Series	Michael Richards, *Seinfeld*, NBC	David Hyde Pierce, *Frasier*, NBC	David Hyde Pierce, *Frasier*, NBC
Supporting Actress—Comedy Series	Kristen Johnston, *3rd Rock from the Sun*, NBC	Lisa Kudrow, *Friends*, NBC	Kristen Johnston, *3rd Rock from the Sun*, NBC
Director—Comedy Series	David Lee, *Frasier*, NBC	Todd Holland, *The Larry Sanders Show*, HBO	Thomas Schlamme, *Will & Grace*, NBC
Writer—Comedy Series	Ellen DeGeneres, Mark Driscoll, Dava Savel, Tracy Newman, and Jonathan Stark, *Ellen*, ABC	Peter Tolan, Garry Shandling, *The Larry Sanders Show*, HBO	Jay Kogen, *Frasier*, NBC
Variety, Music, or Comedy Program	*Tracey Takes On...*, HBO (series) *Chris Rock: Bring the Pain*, HBO (special)	*Late Show with David Letterman*, CBS (series); *The 1997 Tony Awards* (special)	*Late Show With David Letterman*, CBS (series); *1998 Tony Awards*, CBS (special)
Individual Performance—Variety or Music Program	Bette Midler, *Bette Midler: Diva Las Vegas*, HBO	Billy Crystal, *The 70th Annual Academy Awards*, ABC	*John Leguizamo's Freak*, HBO,
Director—Variety or Music	Don Mischer, *Centennial Olympic Games, Opening Ceremonies*, NBC	Louis J. Horvitz, *The 70th Annual Academy Awards*, ABC	Paul Miller, *1998 Tony Awards*, CBS,
Writer—Variety or Music	Chris Rock, *Chris Rock: Bring the Pain*, HBO	Eddie Feldmann, Dennis Miller, David Feldman, Leah Krinsky, Jim Hanna, David Weiss, and Jose Arroyo, *Dennis Miller Live*, HBO	Tom Agna, Vernon Chatman, Louis CK, Lance Crouther, Gregory Greenberg, Ali LeRoi, Steve O'Donnell, Chris Rock, Frank Sebastiano, Chuck Sklar, Jeff Stilson, Wanda Sykes-Hall, Mike Upchurch, *The Chris Rock Show*, HBO
Made for Television Movie	*Miss Evers' Boys*, HBO	*Don King: Only in America*, HBO	*A Lesson Before Dying*, HBO
Miniseries	*Prime Suspect 5: Errors of Judgment*, PBS	*From the Earth to the Moon*, HBO	*Horatio Hornblower*, A&E

	1996–97	1997–98	1998–99
Actor—Miniseries or Special	Armand Assante, *Gotti*, HBO	Gary Sinise, *George Wallace*, TNT	Stanley Tucci, *Winchell*, HBO
Actress—Miniseries or Special	Alfre Woodard, *Miss Evers' Boys*, HBO	Ellen Barkin, *Before Women Had Wings*, ABC	Helen Mirren, *The Passion Of Ayn Rand*, SHO
Supporting Actor—Miniseries or Special	Beau Bridges, *The Second Civil War*, HBO	George C. Scott, *12 Angry Men*, SHO	Peter O'Toole, *Joan Of Arc*, CBS,
Supporting Actress—Miniseries or Special	Diana Rigg, *Rebecca*, PBS	Mare Winningham, *George Wallace*, TNT	Anne Bancroft, *Deep In My Heart*, CBS
Director—Miniseries or Special	Andrei Konchalovsky, *The Odyssey, Parts I and II*, NBC	John Frankenheimer, *George Wallace*, TNT	Allan Arkush, *The Temptations*, NBC
Writer—Miniseries or Special	Horton Foote, *William Faulkner's Old Man*, CBS	Kario Salem, *Don King: Only in America*, HBO	Ann Peacock, *A Lesson Before Dying*, HBO
Daytime Drama Series	*General Hospital*, ABC	*All My Children*, ABC	*General Hospital*, ABC
Actor—Daytime Drama Series	Justin Deas, *Guiding Light*, CBS	Eric Braeden, *The Young and the Restless*, CBS	Anthony Geary, *General Hospital*, ABC
Actress—Daytime Drama Series	Jess Walton, *The Young and the Restless*, CBS	Cynthia Watros, *Guiding Light*	Susan Lucci, *All My Children*, ABC
Supporting Actor—Daytime Drama Series	Ian Buchanan, *The Bold and the Beautiful*, CBS	Steve Burton, *General Hospital*, ABC	Stuart Damon, *General Hospital*, ABC
Supporting Actress—Daytime Drama Series	Michelle Stafford, *The Young and the Restless*, CBS	Julia Barr, *All My Children*, ABC	Sharon Case, *The Young and the Restless*, CBS
Younger Actress—Daytime Drama Series	Sarah Brown, *General Hospital*, ABC	Sarah Brown, *General Hospital*, ABC	Heather Tom, *The Young and the Restless*, CBS
Younger Leading Man—Daytime Drama Series	Kevin Mambo, *Guiding Light*, CBS	Jonathan Jackson, *General Hospital*, ABC	Jonathan Jackson, *General Hospital*, ABC
Talk Show Host	Rosie O'Donnell, *The Rosie O'Donnell Show*, SYN	Rosie O'Donnell, *The Rosie O'Donnell Show*, SYN; and Oprah Winfrey, *The Oprah Winfrey Show*, SYN (tie)	Rosie O'Donnell, *The Rosie O'Donnell Show*, SYN
Game Show	*The Price Is Right*, CBS	*Jeopardy!*, SYN	*Win Ben Stein's Money*, COM
Talk Show	*The Oprah Winfrey Show*, SYN	*The Rosie O'Donnell Show*, SYN	*The Rosie O'Donnell Show*, SYN
Children's Series	*Reading Rainbow*, PBS; *Animaniacs*, WB (Animated)	*Sesame Street*, PBS	*Sesame Street*, PBS (pre-school); *Disney Presents "Bill Nye The Science Guy,"* SYN

1999–2000

Drama	*The West Wing*, NBC
Actor—Drama Series	James Gandolfini, *The Sopranos* HBO
Actress—Drama Series	Sela Ward, *Once and Again*, ABC
Supporting Actor— Drama Series	Richard Schiff, *The West Wing*, NBC
Supporting Actress— Drama Series	Allison Janney, *The West Wing*, NBC
Director—Drama Series	Thomas Schlamme, *The West Wing*, NBC
Writer—Drama Series	Aaron Sorkin, Rick Cleveland, *The West Wing*, NBC
Comedy	*Will & Grace*, NBC
Actor—Comedy Series	Michael J. Fox, *Spin City*, ABC
Actress—Comedy Series	Patricia Heaton, *Everybody Loves Raymond*, CBS
Supporting Actor— Comedy Series	Sean Hayes, *Will & Grace*, NBC
Supporting Actress— Comedy Series	Megan Mullally, *Will & Grace*, NBC
Director—Comedy Series	Todd Holland, *Malcolm in the Middle*, FOX
Writer—Comedy Series	Linwood Boomer, *Malcolm in the Middle*, FOX
Variety, Music, or Comedy Program	*Late Show with David Letterman*, CBS (series); *Saturday Night Live: The 25th Anniversary Special*, NBC (special)
Individual Performance— Variety or Music Program	Eddie Izzard, *Eddie Izzard: Dressed to Kill*, HBO
Director—Variety or Music	Louis J. Horvitz, *72nd Annual Academy Awards*, ABC
Writer—Variety or Music	Eddie Izzard, *Eddie Izzard: Dressed to Kill*, HBO
Made for Television Movie	*Oprah Winfrey Presents: Tuesdays with Morrie*, ABC
Miniseries	*The Corner*, HBO

1999–2000

Actor—Miniseries or Movie	Jack Lemmon, *Oprah Winfrey Presents: Tuesdays with Morrie*, ABC
Actress—Miniseries or Movie	Halle Berry, *Introducing Dorothy Dandridge*, HBO
Supporting Actor—Miniseries or Movie	Hank Azaria, *Oprah Winfrey Presents: Tuesdays with Morrie*, ABC
Supporting Actress—Miniseries or Movie	Vanessa Redgrave, *If These Walls Could Talk 2*, HBO
Director—Miniseries or Movie	Charles S. Dutton, *The Corner*, HBO
Writer—Miniseries or Movie	David Simon, David Mills, *The Corner*, HBO
Daytime Drama Series	*General Hospital*, ABC
Actor—Daytime Drama Series	Anthony Geary, *General Hospital*, ABC
Actress—Daytime Drama Series	Susan Flannery, *The Bold and the Beautiful*, CBS
Supporting Actor—Daytime Drama Series	Shemar Moore, *The Young and the Restless*, CBS
Supporting Actress—Daytime Drama Series	Sarah Brown, *General Hospital*, ABC
Younger Actress—Daytime Drama Series	Camryn Grimes, *The Young and the Restless*, CBS
Younger Leading Man—Daytime Drama Series	David Tom, *The Young and the Restless*, CBS
Talk Show Host	Rosie O'Donnell, *The Rosie O'Donnell Show*, SYN
Game Show	*Who Wants to Be a Millionaire*, ABC
Talk Show	*The Rosie O'Donnell Show*, SYN
Children's Series	*Pinky, Elmira and the Brain*, WB (animated); *Disney Presents: Bill Nye The Science Guy*, SYN

SONG

PICKS & PANS 2001

Though 'N Sync reinforced their *Celebrity*, artists from Dylan (with his forty-third album) on down proved it's not just about teen tastes. Herewith the PEOPLE playlist. Asterisks denote our reviewers' "pick of the week" selections during the year.

AALIYAH
Aaliyah

PEOPLE declared "Aaliyah is evolving into her generation's Janet Jackson" before tragedy cut her life short. The pop diva, for whom trend-setting styling, intricate choreography, and innovative production mattered at least as much as her voice, delves deeper here into her signature sound, a melange of trippy hip hop and retro-'70s R&B, on this album.

THE EXPERIENCE
Yolanda Adams

Adams revels in her faith, praising her Lord with a clear-throated yet understated intensity. It's balm for the ears.

*JUST PUSH PLAY
Aerosmith

No rocking chairs needed for these irrepressible rockers. Relics simply don't rock this hard. Nor do they pack their songs with the kind of goofy puns, irresistible if sometimes predictable hooks and guitar riffs that abound here.

EVERYBODY DOESN'T
Amanda

On her debut disc of power pop, Swedish import Amanda attempts a wholesome image with several tracks that argue strongly against teen sex. But wholesome doesn't necessarily mean boring. With her no-nonsense take on teen life, this diva junior grade keeps things real.

AMERICAN HI-FI
American Hi-Fi

Former Veruca Salt skinsman Stacy Jones makes the leap from drum riser to spotlight with this witty, jumping batch of power-pop tunes.

*YOUR WOMAN
Sunshine Anderson

With a slurred, slightly off-key voice that recalls Mary J. Blige, Sunshine Anderson lets fly with a vivid, bluesy lament about bad men happening to good women in this impressive debut effort.

WHO I AM
Jessica Andrews

At 17, country singer Andrews does seem quite a bit more in control on this second album than she did on her first. And it's refreshing to hear a teen not yet traumatized by unrequited love.

ACOUSTIC SOUL
India.Arie

Mixing classic rock, folk and jazz elements, Arie forgoes the oversaturated studio-enhanced production of much of today's R&B. This stripped-down approach allows the focus to remain on her keen melodic sense, knack for storytelling, and rich, smoky alto.

OXYGEN
Avalon

One part heart-wrenching R&B balladry and two parts teen-pop, this coed Christian quartet's songs testify to the power of love and their faith in God. Ideal for parents, kids and Jessica Simpson fans alike.

THIS IS WHERE I CAME IN
Bee Gees

The Bee Gees seem adrift. Careening from electronica to music-hall plucking, they succeed best in ballads like the elegant "Loose Talk Costs Lives."

CLOSER
Better Than Ezra

The band lost one member to suicide before their first disc was released, and later their original drummer bolted from the group. Now, a year after being dropped by their former label because of creative differences, BTE weighs in with its best album yet, and it's a wonder their music has remained largely sunny. But singer-songwriter Kevin Griffin has a soaring voice and a knack for inspirational-sounding choruses.

*1ST BORN SECOND
Bilal

Add Bilal (full name Bilal Oliver) to Philly's growing list of talented neo-soul newcomers (alongside Jill Scott and Musiq Soulchild), with this impressively eclectic debut. Like D'Angelo, Maxwell, and most every other neo-soul man, Bilal shows that he has been heavily influenced by early Prince, but he also deftly dabbles in jazz, hip-hop, and gospel.

VESPERTINE
Björk

This album raises Björk's theatricality quotient, with spooky choral accompaniments, beckoning orchestral arrangements and plenty of strange-sounding electronic noises. The result has a topsy-turvy, Alice-in-Wonderland quality to it, though Björk's girlish voice and introspective lyrics make every Vespertine song fairly soothing, almost lullaby-like. By incorporating digital chatter and plainspoken truths into her vast, melodic dreamscape, the former Sugarcube mimics modern life as we know it: jarring, hard to predict, but at times exhilaratingly beautiful.

LIONS
The Black Crowes

Now best known as the dour escort of his bride Kate Hudson, Chris Robinson seems to have checked his vocal charms at the studio door on this muddled album of vaguely structured and poorly executed heavy rock songs.

FLOWERS FROM THE FIELDS OF ALABAMA
Norman Blake

With his Uncle Sam beard, Blake belongs in a Thomas Nast cartoon. His acoustic music, picked on his collection of antique guitars and mandolins, is as timelessly American.

*NO MORE DRAMA
Mary J. Blige

On Blige's fifth studio CD, the Yonkers, N.Y.-born Grammy winner continues her growth as a writer and singer. She ups the rhythmic component of her brand of blues, and in trademark style, Blige wraps her emotionally raw alto around such retro-soul ballads as "Testimony" and the string-laden "Never Been" (written and produced by Missy Elliott).

SPIRIT OF THE CENTURY
Blind Boys of Alabama

The Blind Boys craft a soul-stirring collection that revisits such church classics as "Amazing Grace," plus gospelized versions of secular songs that are spiritual in nature. The Boys sing with a passion and spirit that will make even nonbelievers say hallelujah.

TAKE OFF YOUR PANTS AND JACKET
Blink-182

On their fourth disc, the San Diego-based lads give listeners exactly what they expect: adrenaline-laced sonic gems reveling in blink's patented, potty-mouthed humor. Recommended only for adolescents of all ages.

TRIP TO THE 13TH
Bliss 66

Melding a Detroit pop rock sound with boy band looks, this teen sextet polishes rough-edged love songs like "Sooner or Later" under the tutelage of producer Glen Ballard.

BRIDGE
Blues Traveler

With the exception of "Pretty Angry (For J. Sheehan)," an ode mourning late bassist Bobby Sheehan, most of the tracks are languorous grooves that go nowhere.

BORN
Bond

Bach with a beat. This formally trained string quartet likes to add house and dance rhythms to classical melodies. The tracks range from spectacular to silly.

AT THE FOOT OF CANAL STREET
John Boutté

Mardi Gras man: The New Orleans vocalist known for his work with ¡Cubanismo! sings "A Change Is Gonna Come" in such a sweet, soulful croon, you'll swear it's Sam Cooke himself gone gumbo.

THIS IS BR549
BR549

This roots-conscious Nashville quintet's raucously contagious, garage-band energy suggests a steel-cage match between the Nitty Gritty Dirt Band and Smash Mouth. BR549 has grown into a driving studio band.

OH WHAT A WORLD
Paul Brady

Encompassing traces of folk, country and contemporary rock, *Oh What a World* has an inviting, lived-in air of ease. It is easy to understand Brady's appeal as both a performer and tunesmith: his voice is a bit rough around the edges but infused with a heartfelt passion that gives these 11 songs a deep emotional resonance.

*STEADY PULL
Jonatha Brooke

For her fourth solo album, Brooke, who has developed a cult following with her jazz-tinged, rough-edged folk sound, maintains the breezy, matter-of-fact vocal stylings of her earlier work, but takes things a step further with her simple, poignant lyrics.

STEERS & STRIPES
Brooks & Dunn

Lest anyone fear that advancing age has taken some of the scoot out of Brooks and Dunn's boots, this album has kicky, uptempo tunes, elemental country sound and a rascally honky-tonk feel. The album does show evidence of a slide toward pop, though.

BROKEN SILENCE
Foxy Brown

The rejuvenated rapper breaks a three-year silence with this uncharacteristically confessional and surprisingly heartfelt CD, which is by far her most emotionally powerful work to date.

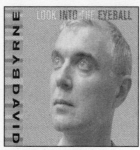

DAVID BYRNE

LOOK INTO THE EYEBALL

*LOOK INTO THE EYEBALL
David Byrne

After years of rummaging around, Byrne has re-created the art-school collage without which no undergraduate quad was complete in the mid-80s: jerky, vaguely African percussion, lyrics that might be chanted in a yoga class and singsongy melodies.

COMFORT EAGLE
Cake

This humor-fueled California quintet rarely serves up something predictable. At its best Cake achieves a laid-back vibe that mixes wildly different styles. Their musical experimentation is seriously fun—and sometimes even comforting.

FEAR OF SUCCESS
Caleb

Despite a title that would imply otherwise, this one-name singer-songwriter seems nothing but confident on this sometimes sexy ("Blue"), sometimes sinister ("Sally Doesn't Call Me Anymore") but always fearless debut.

SO BLU
Blu Cantrell

Blu (Tiffany) Cantrell takes the art of man-bashing by today's female R&B singers to a new level on her Top 5 debut single, "Hit 'Em Up Style (Oops!)." But don't judge the album by the first single—it amounts to a novelty song that doesn't do justice to Cantrell's bluesy, gospel-infused

voice. The best songs are torchy, gut-wrenching ballads on which the Providence-born chanteuse really shines.

THE PRODUCERS
Broadway Cast Recording

Nathan Lane has a voice so big he sounds like he swallowed Ethel Merman, and sidekick Matthew Broderick holds his own by channeling Jerry Lewis at his snivelingest. There is no substitute for seeing a Nazi pigeon or a chorus line of lusty old ladies wielding their walkers like a troupe of osteoporotic Fred Astaires, but this is the funniest recording since William Shatner's mangling of "Lucy in the Sky with Diamonds."

GLITTER
Mariah Carey

Those looking for signs of Mariah Carey's recent emotional breakdown in the pop diva's latest album will find a few possible clues in the short, spare ballad "Twister." The rest of this soundtrack to the semiautobiographical film starring and produced by Carey, doesn't shed much light on Carey's psyche, having been heavily inspired by the movie's setting in '80s New York City nightclubs.

TIME*SEX*LOVE*
Mary Chapin Carpenter

Pass on this. Somber verging on dreary, this navel-contemplating album sounds more like a Joan Baez project from the '60s than the work of the woman responsible for such energetic, life-affirming songs as "Down at the Twist and Shout."

REPTILE
Eric Clapton

Reptile is a chameleon, with something for old blues hands, the Unplugged set, and lite-FM fans.

TAMMY COCHRAN
Tammy Cochran

On this extraordinary first album, country songstress Cochran paints from the standard love-and-loss palette, but the lyrics have intelligence and wit, looking at a woman's romances past, present and future from a woman's point of view.

*PARACHUTES
Coldplay

This Brit-pop quartet's formula? Irrepressibly sweet lyrics set to moody hooks à la Radiohead and their Scottish counterparts, Travis.

SINCERE
MJ Cole

The latest club sound to emerge in Britain is two-step, which combines elements of house, techno, jungle, and drum-and-bass with bits of reggae and R&B. This debut collection from London-based Matt Coleman is a largely rewarding attempt to launch the phenom in the States.

WHOLE NEW YOU
Shawn Colvin

Colvin's singing remains wispy and dyspeptic, her songwriting enigmatic and abstract. Her imprecise diction at times makes it hard to understand what she's singing about, and the backgrounds are bland. It's clear that we're supposed to disapprove, but it's not clear why.

*EVERYBODY GOT THEIR SOMETHING
Nikka Costa

Costa joins the neo-soul ranks with her big gravelly alto and her sense of rhythm, effortlessly blending soul, hip-hop, and rock on sexy, hard-driving tracks. While there's not a bad track here, the subdued anthem "So Have I for You" stands out.

NIKKA COSTA

OPEN
Cowboy Junkies

On the country-rockers' eleventh album, they revisit the themes that make them the perfect mood-setters for a serial killer movie—murder, cheating, and depression—though they move slightly up-tempo on the album's brightest (a relative term) tunes.

JIMMY COZER
Jimmy Cozier

After singing backing vocals writing songs, Cozier debuts with a polished R&B album of sounds to remove clothing to. But whether this 24-year-old son of Brooklyn is complaining about his girlfriend's complaining or feeling guilty about cheating on her (in "So Much to Lose"), his suave vocals go down smoothly on ballads and dance-floor jams. This one's a soundtrack for those candlelit nights.

SHOULDA BEEN HOME
The Robert Cray Band

The 1999 Grammy winner may have polished his frets as one of the leading lights of contemporary blues, but the gifted guitarist and singer sounds like a Memphis-bred soul man on his 12th album. Cray delivers these dozen plaintive, somebody-done-somebody-wrong songs with economic guitar lines, yearning vocals and a Ginzu-sharp backing band.

*THE HOUSTON KID
Rodney Crowell

Singer-songwriter Crowell's soul-baring emotions about his troubled Texas boyhood are so intimate in these 11 songs that listening is like peeking into a diary. In a 23-year recording career that has produced 10 albums and a Grammy award, Crowell may well have achieved his masterpiece with *The Houston Kid*.

BORN TO DO IT
Craig David

David, 20, is the poster boy for England's trend of the nanosecond, a percussive and energized hybrid of R&B, reggae and techno called two-step. But it's his velvety vocals that really bring the heat to the hip shaking.

EXCITER
Depeche Mode

The revived trio sounds more easygoing, but songwriter Martin Gore still writes beautifully sad melodies better than anyone, and singer Dave Gahan delivers them in a genuinely weary-sounding baritone.

SURVIVOR
Destiny's Child

Destiny's Child steps up with strong female-empowerment themes on *Survivor*. Artistically, though, Destiny's Child needs to grow up a little. Such formulaic R&B girl-group fare as "Bootylicious" and "Sexy Daddy" aren't

nearly worthy of their gorgeous three-part harmonies.

THREE CHORD OPERA
Neil Diamond

Diamond can blast away in that Big Bertha baritone like no one else. Thirty-five years after he hit the pop charts with "Solitary Man" and "Cherry Cherry," the Tin Pan Alley vet continues to produce heroic, shirt-rending pop anthems. All 12 songs display Diamond's patented Wall of Bombast sound, which could be the product of a collaboration between Phil Spector and Andrew Lloyd Webber.

THE SAGA CONTINUES . . .
P. Diddy & The Bad Boy Family

After being acquitted on felony gun and bribery charges and splitting up with flame Jennifer Lopez earlier this year, Sean "Puffy" Combs changed his recording moniker to P. Diddy. It's new wrapping but not new rapping. P. Diddy alternates as writer, producer and performer on this compilation but is supported by a host of more capable rappers and singers.

REVELLING/RECKONING
Ani DiFranco

On this double CD, the 30-year-old singer and guitarist is backed by keyboards, bass, drums and horns as she explores the complex politics of personal relationships. At her quirky best, she errs only when she abandons subtlety.

*THE DONNAS TURN 21!
The Donnas

The anitheroine that the Donnas portray in song is a guitar-slinging, beer-swigging, stock-car and pinball-loving rock and roll party chick. The band's sound is proudly derivative, but the Donnas are no less original then the boy band to which they're most often compared: the Ramones.

IT WAS ALL A DREAM
Dream
Here we go again: four photogenic, dance-crazy California teens, sleek production numbers and a catchy bubblegum sound. But Mouseketeers these girls are not. As may be deduced by their not-that-innocent come-hither looks, the Dream team can sound decidedly adult.

LOVE AND THEFT
Bob Dylan
At 60, Bob Dylan still hasn't cleared his throat: His voice is like a stretch of unpaved road churning through sagebrush and Joshua trees. Which is to say, better than ever. This is the forty-third record of Dylan's career. May it mark the halfway point.

MISS E...SO ADDICTIVE
Missy Elliott
This effort doesn't quite reach the bar Elliott set with her two previous efforts, but it does simmer with energy. Backed with cameos by the cream of the hip-hop crop, *Miss E* proves a witty rhymer and deft singer.

SKIN
Melissa Etheridge
On this raw and revealing album of frequently wrenching breakup tunes, in which every track is infused with why-did-she-have-to-go bewilderment, Etheridge struggles to match Bob Dylan's thesaurus of pain *Blood on the Tracks*.

***SCORPION**
Eve
While she was no wilting flower on her debut album, here Eve delivers an even harder-edged manifesto. Whether demanding respect for her accomplishments or delivering homegirl boasts over blistering beats, Eve needs no help relaying her message of self-reliance and confidence.

GOOD TIME FOR A BAD ATTITUDE
Everclear
Tough times breed good rock music, which may make Everclear's new album pretty darn timely. But Alexakis is not the punk pessimist he sometimes claims to be, as much of the music is exhilirating.

ROCKIN' THE SUBURBS
Ben Folds
Prozac Nation has found its John Philip Sousa. Folds, now a solo act, plays a seductive jazz-rock piano that suggests Joe Jackson's depressed little brother. But though he can make the keys of his Baldwin seethe and snarl (the must-you-dump-me track "Gone"), he also plays as prettily as Billy Joel (the tragic "Carrying Cathy" and the mocking "The Ascent of Stan").

WILLA WAS HERE
Willa Ford
While this doesn't exactly announce the arrival of a major new talent, sassy, splashy up-tempo tracks such as "Did Ya Understand That," "Joke's on You" and "Wish" are perfect lite listening for summer vacation.

BIG BAND BLUES
Pete Fountain
While Fountain still performs at his own club in New Orleans, this is his first recording with the New Lawrence Welk Orchestra. Even though the accompanying musicians aren't the swingingest group around, Fountain, with his venerable wooden clarinet, is still a joy to hear.

STILL STANDING
Full Force
This greatest-hits set includes not only Full Force's '80s R&B classics ("Alice, I Want You Just for Me") but hits the group produced for everyone from James Brown ("Static") to Backstreet Boys ("All I Have to Give").

IN MY ARMS
Crystal Gayle
This collection of 17 original kids' tunes is a marvel of warmth, melody, and security—the kind of thing a child and his or her parents will retreat into over and over. If there is a weakness, it is that writers overdid it in the warm, fuzzy department.

DARE TO DREAM
Billy Gilman
At 13, Gilman lacks the moves of the young Michael Jackson or the pipes of LeAnn Rimes, so he must rely on a low-key, ordinary-boy charm. On this album it is successfully exploited only on "The Woman in My Life," an affecting tune about a boy's devotion to his mother. On the rest of the album Gilman plays macho, with varying success.

THE LIFE
Ginuwine
Ginuwine remains in excellent voice, but collaborates with more pedestrian producers. The result is as solid as a brick wall, but only slightly more exciting.

WHAT I LEARNED ABOUT EGO, OPINION, ART & COMMERCE
The Goo Goo Dolls
A greatest-misses collection, this sampler of the Goo Goos' first six CDs explores their indie rock roots before they super-sized their following with the made-for-Hollywood 1998 *City of Angels* weeper "Iris."

DICK'S PICKS: VOLUME 20
Grateful Dead
Five years after Deadhead Jerry Garcia's death, the band keeps on truckin', at least on disc. Two concerts from 1976 find Garcia at his plaintive best and the band at full, trippy tilt.

SUNNY BORDER BLUE
Kristin Hersh

Hersh has developed into an engaging singer with a slightly husky voice and quiet, understated style that at times evokes the softer side of Stevie Nicks. But she uses obscenities like punctuation and also tends to overdo what she calls her "oh my stupid life" songs.

CROSSING MUDDY WATERS
John Hiatt

Still haunted, it seems, by the 1985 suicide of his first wife, bluesman Hiatt infuses all 11 of these gems about busted romances and tragicomic heroes and losers with real-life humor and heartache.

HERE COME THE NOISE MAKERS
Bruce Hornsby

This new live two-CD set displays the range of Hornsby's experience and talent in several genres: jazz, prog rock, and country.

100 BROKEN WINDOWS
Idlewild

This irresistibly melancholy follow-up to '99's critically acclaimed, commercially ignored *Hope Is Important* won't have listeners disappointed. Not, that is, if they're hungry for a heaping platter of free-floating angst, with a side of seething cynicism.

ETERNAL
The Isley Brothers featuring Ronald Isley a.k.a. Mr. Biggs

The title may not be an exaggeration: These Brothers are here to stay. Since forming in the '50s, the Isleys—now reduced to just lead singer Ronald and his guitarist sibling Ernie—have churned out such R&B hits as "It's Your Thing," "That Lady (Part 1)," and "Between the Sheets," and their patented vocal-guitar interplay once again highlights their songs.

MATRIARCH OF THE BLUES
Etta James

Sounding as sexy and full of sass as she did nearly half a century ago, James proves that she is still a musical force of nature. Backed by Mike Finnigan's Hammond B3 organ, her voice modulates from bedroom purrs to barroom howls as she covers tunes by soul greats Otis Redding, Al Green, and Ray Charles.

*ALL FOR YOU
Janet

Never has Janet displayed such a broad command of the pop form as she does on this sweeping, near-73-minute opus. From percolating hip-hop to sunny soft-rock, Janet goes all over the pop planet on *All For You*.

THE DYNASTY: ROC LA FAMILIA (2000-)
Jay-Z

For every song about slurping Cristal champagne, Jay-Z has one about struggling to get out of misery. In this searing self-examination propelled by hot beats, he offers raps that sometimes sound like therapy sessions as he expresses a deep, cathartic anger.

*BLEED AMERICAN
Jimmy Eat World

Jimmy Eat World is a cross between Weezer and a more grown-up Blink-182, but with sharper guitars and profanity-free lyrics. On the title track, frontman Jim Adkins oozes just enough angst to be interesting but not so much as to be annoying.

CHAPTER 1: LOVE, PAIN AND FORGIVENESS
Syleena Johnson

The Chicago-area native probably owes some of her raw, traditional sound to her father, veteran bluesman Syl Johnson. But you can also hear shades of Chaka Khan, Randy Crawford and Tina Turner, setting Johnson apart from all of today's overproduced, ultra-glossy Destiny's Child wannabes.

*X
K-Ci & JoJo

The soulful sibs once again deliver rich, gospel-infused lead vocals, soaring harmonies and smartly crafted tunes which hearken back to the 1960s Motown heyday, and stake their claim as the best R&B singers of the hip-hop era.

SONGS IN A MINOR
Alicia Keys

Already being touted as the next Whitney Houston, Keys' breathy ballads suggest the same superstar potential on this polished first album.

AT LAST
Gladys Knight

It has been more than six years since Gladys Knight recorded her last pop-R&B album, but *At Last* makes clear that, after some four decades of recording, Knight is far from ready to call it a career.

NO NAME FACE
Lifehouse

With a debut disc of dreamy alterna-pop, this L.A. trio is hitting the big time thanks to their shimmering first single, "Hanging by a Moment."

LIL' ROMEO
Lil' Romeo

The precocious 12-year-old hip-hopper—who recently scored a

No. 1 R&B and rap single—is the son of multiplatinum No Limit Records titan Master P and the nephew of rappers C Murder and Silkk the Shocker. Seventh-grader Romeo keeps things clean and age-appropriate on his debut, rapping about cute girls, video games, fast food and other pre-pubescent obsessions. The result is PG-rated rap that is plenty safe for kids, but it doesn't make for anything like great music.

J.LO
Jennifer Lopez
The rapper-like title of Lopez's new disc reflects her desire to be down with the hip-hop crowd, but she still wants her fans to think of her as just the homegirl-next-door. Such a modest approach allows Lopez to work well within her considerable vocal limitations.

FLIGHTS OF FANCY: TRIO FASCINATION, EDITION TWO
Joe Lovano
Fresh from a Grammy win for the imaginative but straight-ahead jazz CD 52nd Street Themes, saxophonist and composer Joe Lovano returns to his more typical experimental sound on his twentieth disc as a leader. Full of freedom but never indulgent, the CD proves Lovano won't be typecast.

*MOUNTAIN SOUL
Patty Loveless
This album of bluegrass and bluegrassy tunes not only makes the songs sound good, but it also brings out an elemental, heart-felt quality heretofore absent in Loveless's singing. This album contains 14 tracks from which it is hard to pick a highlight.

EVERYDAY
Dave Matthews Band
Dave Matthews Band thrives on improvisations that blur the boundaries between rock, jazz and world music. This time out,

though, the band forgoes the rawness of its last CD for the middle of the road.

STEPHEN MALKMUS
Stephen Malkmus
The former lead singer of college rock band Pavement has shed the group's muddy-sounding guitars for a snappier, cleaner sound. While Malkmus's arch, literary-seeming lyrics are sometimes hard to decipher, the clever melodies and rhythmically complex arrangements have a sweet, adult taste.

*NOW
Maxwell
Maxwell's third studio release should come with a warning label: For Lovers Only. After 1998's more obtuse *Embrya*, *Now* finds the R&B loveman smoothly returning to the bedroom balladry that became his hallmark with his exquisite 1996 debut, *Maxwell's Urban Hang Suite*.

COMPLETE
Lila McCann
Like Reba McEntire, 19-year-old McCann has an irrepressible twang in the high end of her impressively wide-ranging voice, and she also displays the country-pop appeal of LeAnn Rimes.

*WINGSPAN
Paul McCartney
This two-disc compilation—one for hits, one mostly for songs that McCartney believes were

unjustly ignored—revisits many tracks that hold up well against his very finest Beatles compositions. Wings brought us the purest pop of pop's purest decade.

NOTHING PERSONAL
Delbert McClinton
The Texas rhythm and blues-man's impressive résumé includes giving John Lennon dressing-room harmonica lessons in the early '60s. Here the singer and multi-instrumentalist delivers a tears-and-tequila-stained CD drenched in pure Tex-Mex soul.

SET THIS CIRCUS DOWN
Tim McGraw
McGraw at his best—and worst. McGraw's vocal colorings on these 14 tracks range from mewling boy band to depressed Kurt Cobain, with too few stops in Merle Haggard country.

THE DROPPER
Medeski Martin & Wood
On this album, the improvisational jazz musicians work elements of hip-hop and the blues into the mix, but the results are somewhat disappointing. The music, while expertly performed, is not the improvisational masterpiece their fans know the group has in them.

*PRODUCTION
Mirwais
Mirwais's strength is bringing a multitextured warmth to electronica. In this dazzling French dance set, Mirwais nimbly layers rubbery disco rhythms with punctuated drum patterns and all sorts of percolating studio effects.

COME DREAM WITH ME
Jane Monheit
Jane Monheit is jazz's next sultry sweetie. She tops a pretty face with a pretty amazing voice: It's a high, clear instrument (occasionally given to unnecessary

trills) with sophisticated phrasing; but this sophomore album is a bit ballad-heavy.

*MANDY MOORE
Mandy Moore

Credit the 17-year-old singer for at least trying to stake out her own identity. Moore, with an especially savvy and diverse team of producers and songwriters, brings an off-kilter flavor to a usually formulaic genre.

MORE TEACHINGS
Morgan Heritage

In the tradition of Bob Marley and the Wailers, this familial quintet (the daughter and four sons of Jamaican singer Denroy Morgan) shy away from dance hall's exploitation of sex and violence to deliver "conscious" (read spiritual) reggae the traditional way: silky and soulful.

STRANGER THAN FICTION
Ultra Nate

This longtime club queen is no stranger to the dance charts, but rousing house tracks such as "Desire" and "Get It Up (The Feeling)" work just about as well at home as under the disco ball.

JOKO (THE LINK)
Youssou N'Dour

A great voice, in any language. On his first U.S. release in six years, West African singer N'Dour mixes elements of Senegal's percussive mbalax style with Western strains of funk and soul music. Tunes are sung alternatively in English and in Wolof.

*TROUBLE IN SHANGRI-LA
Stevie Nicks

On her first solo album since 1994, she reins in her loopy side with an assist from Sheryl Crow, who coproduces, plays guitar and sings backup on a few tracks. And though Nicks dresses like Rhiannon heading for Wicca practice on the cover photo, she keeps things real lyrically and vocally.

*CELEBRITY
'N Sync

Celebrity represents such an impressive achievement for these men among boy bands. While experimenting with edgier sounds, they also pump up their boy-band appeal with the lush five-part harmonies of "Girlfriend," "Do Your Thing" and the simply stunning ballad "Gone."

ANGEL IN THE DARK
Laura Nyro

A minor when she wrote her first major hit ("And When I Die"), Nyro, Bronx-born and street-corner-bred, honed her chops belting songs on New York City subway platforms. Seven of these unreleased tracks were recorded shortly before her 1997 death from cancer at age 49.

O-TOWN
O-Town

Having been created for television on the ABC series *Making the Band*, this prefab five has about as much musical credibility as the Monkees, or the Partridge Family. In fact, O-Town gives one new appreciation for the well-seasoned harmonies and taut teen-pop song craft of 'N Sync and Backstreet.

*CONSPIRACY OF ONE
The Offspring

Now on their sixth album, Offspring turns out more novelty songs that blend good-time

tracks with teen angst and leavening gobs of humor.

SHIVER
Jamie O'Neal

Rhythmic, expressive, a touch bluesy and subtly sexy, O'Neal is a country-pop singer poised to capture the same kind of listeners who gravitated toward Bonnie Raitt 25 years ago. The 13 tracks on this album range from romantic ballads to energetic rock turns.

THIS IS THE MOMENT
Donny Osmond

Osmond uses his still-boyish but surprisingly supple voice to deliver respectable renditions of such recent musical theater faves as "Seasons of Love" (from *Rent*), "It's Possible" (from *Seussical the Musical*), and the album's title song (from *Jekyll & Hyde*).

*PART II
Brad Paisley

It was Peter Allen who wrote that "everything old is new again." The sentiment is true in Nashville, as Brad Paisley sticks with traditions and turns in a strong version of the hymn "Old Rugged Cross"; two other stalwarts, George Jones and Buck Owens, sing on the sarcastic "Too Country."

PLEASE
Pet Shop Boys

The reissue of this 1986 dancefloor classic and five other CDs by the Brit synth-pop duo is all the excuse you need to unpack that strobe light.

*GRETCHEN PETERS
Gretchen Peters

Having already earned notable success as a songwriter, Peters (who wrote all 11 tunes) puts her prowess as a singer on display. Peters heightens the ironic effect of her songs by delivering her tart lyrics in a pleasing voice of almost girlish innocence.

BORN TO BE BLUE
Anne Phillips
This exquisite 1959 album of pop standards lacks the essential ingredient that made rock roll—a backbeat—but this reissue is a lovely reminder of how dreamy pop once was.

PAY, PACK AND FOLLOW
John Phillips
Papa John Phillips and unlikely cohorts the Rolling Stones recorded these 11 songs in 1977, and *Pay* reveals surprising melodic lucidity by all concerned. Phillips is on top of his game, and the Stones are at their twangy, country tonk best.

ODYSSEY NUMBER FIVE
Powderfinger
On their lush U.S. debut, filled with carefully crafted songs about love and loss, this Brisbane quintet show us what folks Down Under have known all along: Australians do know how to rock.

PRU
Pru
With her self-titled debut, a collection of artful, almost poetic ruminations on love, stunning R&B singer-songwriter Pru makes fetching use of her sexy, husky alto.

AMNESIAC
Radiohead
The lords of British art-rock pick up where they left off on *Kid A*. Radiohead revs up its chain saw with eerie, unpredictable blends of electronica and jazz; other songs, though, return to the more straightforward guitar rock of their earlier work.

RAMONES
Ramones
The musical Molotov cocktail that launched the punk revolution in 1976, this reissue detonates 14 sonic blasts in 29 minutes (plus bonus tracks), including "Blitzkrieg Bop" and "I

Wanna Be Your Boyfriend." You too will wanna be sedated.

BEHIND THE LIGHT
Monica Ramos
Cool jazz, warm heart. Talk about world music: On this Spanish-language CD, Ramos, a Chilean-born, classically trained harpist and singer who lives in Sweden, blends classical aesthetics with a passionate, airy beat.

THIS AIN'T A GAME
Ray J
The Game plan is to search frantically for a hit, but there isn't an obvious one on this second album from the 20-year-old younger brother of singer-actress Brandy Norwood.

THE CALLING
Dianne Reeves
On her eleventh album, the sublime jazzist pays homage to Sarah Vaughan, whom she cites as her inspiration. Revisiting nine songs associated with Vaughan as well as two new tunes written for this project, Reeves revives interest in one of jazz's greatest singers, and she establishes herself as one of her mentor's rightful heirs.

*REVEAL
R.E.M.
A lush tour de force, *Reveal* transports the band into fresh territory, where guitars take a backseat to harmonies. This pretty yet disturbing album is the musical equivalent of the film *American Beauty*.

RENAISSANCE
Lionel Richie
After a very slow period, Richie is hoping to get back in the money with *Renaissance*. He attempts to update his sound, with mixed results, but still has a way with a good old-fashioned ballad.

PETALS: THE MINNIE RIPERTON COLLECTION
Minnie Riperton
The vocal virtuoso with an ethereal five-plus-octave range died of cancer at 31 in 1979, but her savvy jazz-pop soprano soars again on this joyous two-disc set.

YELLOW BUS
Justin Roberts
Roberts is a folk-pop singer-songwriter (and former preschool teacher) who sounds a lot like James Taylor and writes with some of the same playful impulses. So while this album of songs for children is often cute, it is never silly.

CROWN ROYAL
Run DMC
It's hard to call the new Run DMC album a real Run DMC album. Every song but the bombastic title track features at least one guest artist, ranging from Nas and Method Man to Kid Rock and Fred Durst. Run DMC seems to be hoping these current hitmakers will do what the trio did for Aerosmith: revive their careers.

LOVE LETTERS
Leslie Satcher
On this performing debut by one of Nashville's most successful songwriters, Satcher approaches Emmylou Harris's rare ability to shift moods and also echoes her purity of tone and clarity of diction. She sings mostly her own material here, notably "I Will Survive," a country cousin of Gloria Gaynor's disco hit of the '70s.

LONELYLAND
Bob Schneider
This easygoing Texas-based alterna-rocker draws on country, pop, rock, blues, and even a touch of Austin rap to create a sound as broad as the Southwest.

EARL SCRUGGS AND FRIENDS
Earl Scruggs and Various Artists
The world's preeminent banjoist has rounded up Melissa Etheridge, Elton John, Vince Gill and even actors Steve Martin and Billy Bob Thornton, and at 77, Scruggs' picking is still more nimble than that of musicians 50 years his junior.

THE MAY STREET PROJECT
Shea Seger
Seger's folky funk debut melds synthesized Carnaby Street dramatics with the back-roads twang of acoustic guitars. Though musically all over the map, this *Street* is one worth getting lost on.

ALL ABOUT CHEMISTRY
Semisonic
This follow-up to 1998's *Feeling Strangely Fine* proves to be another appealing pop collection as the band adds a subtle digital latticework to the solid rhythmic foundations. With breezy melodies, laid-back guitar work and Everyguy vocals, the trio put on a fine but unassuming display of their considerable pop gifts.

IGNITION!
Brian Setzer '68 Comeback Special
Out-of-time rockabilly cat Setzer gets back to where he once belonged, with big-beat, high-speed tunes to surf, dance and drag race to.

HOTSHOT
Shaggy
Hotshot is an entertaining showcase for Shaggy's distinctive delivery and his blend of R&B, pop, and dance-hall reggae styles.

*PHANTOM MOON
Duncan Sheik
Mellow doesn't begin to describe this folkish new album from one of the most admired singer-songwriters of the last decade. Featuring songs that positively levitate on Sheik's buttery voice and quietly picked acoustic guitar, the CD occupies an otherworldly state of calm.

MILK & HONEY: 10 HITS TO BLISS
Itaal Shur
Having won a Grammy for cowriting the Santana smash "Smooth," Shur steps out on this blissful dance disc, on which retro-funk cuts such as "Feel Good" help a listener do just that.

IRRESISTIBLE
Jessica Simpson
There's nothing on Simpson's sophomore disc that is quite as irresistible as Britney Spears's *Oops!...I Did It Again* or Christina Aguilera's *What a Girl Wants*. And while Simpson is a more robust singer than Spears and a less showy one than Aguilera, her vocals aren't as distinctive.

RETURN OF DRAGON
Sisqó
This track can't quite muster that "Thong Song" magic, but even without a gimmicky novelty hit, Sisqo is still kicking, as he artfully fuses an R&B style with up-tempo rap rhythms.

LIVE IN NEW YORK CITY
Bruce Springsteen & the E Street Band
This whopping 20-song, two-CD, two-hour-and-43-minute set is filled with rousing, gospel-infused rock anthems. Among them, both "41 Shots," performed with church organ backing and chilling, liturgical vocal arrangements, and a dirgelike version of "Born in the U.S.A." assume the power of hymns. Each is a haunting interlude in the joyous, tent-revival spirit of the concerts.

FREE CITY
St. Lunatics
Front man Nelly hasn't forgotten his brothers. Like Nelly's solo album *Country Grammar*, *Free City* brims with a bass-driven, syncopated shake that celebrates girls, cars, getting paid, and living la vida Midwest.

BREAK THE CYCLE
Staind
This quartet comes into its own on this introspective follow-up to 1999's multiplatinum *Dysfunction*, which bleeds emotion on the melancholy "It's Been Awhile" and the tragic "Waste," inspired by a fan's suicide.

FIRESTARR
Fredro Starr
Former Onyx member Starr's debut solo CD has more heat than light. This profanity-laced and often mean-spirited disc is filled with B-grade gangsta rap extolling the gun-toting thug life.

HUMAN
Rod Stewart
Stewart has wisely curtailed the rusting rooster act in favor of wistful but gritty balladry. Here Rod hearkens back to the rasping, emotion-packed style of the Motown, R&B, and soul stars of the '60s that he has long emulated and delivers a satchel full of imagery-rich, slow-dance gems.

SHANGRI-LA-DEE DA
Stone Temple Pilots

Moments of surpassing beauty are not what one expects from the Pilots. Singer Scott Weiland achieves such transcendence on the achingly beautiful "A Song for Sleeping," and lilting tunes like "Days of the Week" and "Black Again" it makes you think that when he's not head-banging, he has been listening to old pop-perfect albums.

SUGAR RAY
Sugar Ray

Mark McGrath and cohorts are back with another box of radio candy. McGrath's vocals are buoyant and full of sly good humor; with 11 tracks confirming his standing as pop's latest Captain Hook, *Sugar* is sweet indeed.

DIDN'T SEE ME COMING
Keith Sweat

Now 44, Sweat's age is beginning to show a little. Here he spends much of the first half of the disc trying to prove he's as hip as any hip-hopper. But then he hits his groove with a string of trademark slow jams.

FORCE OF NATURE
Tank

The latest macho man aching to play both thug and Romeo is the R&B singer-songwriter Tank. With his baritone barely rising above conversational tone, Tank makes you feel his pain with an understated ache.

MY WORLD
Cyndi Thomson

Newcomer Cyndi Thomson may be Nashville's answer to Courtney Love. Those who like their country music with a touch of grunge should enjoy this debut album. Thomson's husky voice and earnest style are reminiscent of such introspective female rockers as Edie Brickell, Sheryl Crow and Alanis Morissette, as she sings contemplative country that rocks.

THUNDER AND ROSES
Pam Tillis

From the strident title tune to the preachy "Be A Man," Tillis keeps the intensity level at full blast. To make matters worse, a tag team of four coproducers keeps the musicians smothered in big, sweeping arrangements, even when a nice, quiet acoustic guitar might relieve some pressure.

THE INCOMPLETE GLENN TILBROOK
Glenn Tilbrook

More lush, lovely and literate pop, including a confessional about "Interviewing Randy Newman" from one of the main Squeeze men.

STANDARDS
Tortoise

Tortoises' mix of electronic, acoustic and synthesized sounds recall jazz improvisation, but with its weird pulsing beats and spacey guitars, they sound a bit like Charlie Parker meets Radiohead. *Standards* is full of twists and turns that create a pleasing whirl of textures and moods.

DROPS OF JUPITER
Train

Train, which first chugged into stations on the dial with 1999's hit "Meet Virginia," rides more of the right tracks here with a southern-roots rock sound that recalls Counting Crows.

THE INVISIBLE BAND
Travis

Tip-top jangly rock. Backed by polite guitars, deferential synthesizers and don't-mind-me percussion, front man Fran Healy's quiet tenor and delicate melodies are free to shine. They'll be about as *Invisible* as an avalanche.

MI SON
Rick Trevino

A member of the all-star group Los Super Seven, this one-time country singer mines his Mexican roots to make Tejano magic on this disc, which features band-mates Cesar Rosas on guitars and David Hidalgo on drums.

HERE AND NOW
Ike Turner & the Kings of Rhythm

Tina's splendidly talented ex rips through 11 tunes, including his 1951 hit "Rocket 88." They may not redeem his rep, but they sure do rock.

2000 WATTS
Tyrese

Neither his emote-by-numbers vocal style nor much of his material is as sculpted as actor/model Tyrese Gibson's look. Despite giving his all, Tyrese's sound is cut from typical Top 40 R&B cookie dough.

*8701
Usher

When singer-actor Usher scrapped plans to release this third album in December after some of its songs were leaked on the Internet, it may have been a blessing in disguise. The 22-year-old scrambled back to the studio and came up with the No. 1 single "U Remind Me," an old-fashioned soul ditty that in these hip-hop-happy times is as refreshing as a dip in the pool.

*LUTHER VANDROSS
Luther Vandross

With his new disc, Vandross has finally come up with a collection of songs worthy of his silky, elastic tenor. Vandross works his seductive spells on slow jams and puts his inimitable mark on sophisticated covers of such 1960s tunes as Chuck Jackson's "Any Day Now" and Dionne Warwick's "Are You There."

CALLE 54
Various Artists
A rousing turn by the late Tito Puente and a breathtaking duet of "Lagrimas Negras" by Cuban maestros Bebo Valdes on piano and Cachao on bass highlight this concert film soundtrack and homage to Latin jazz.

HOLLYWOOD GOES WILD!
Various Artists
These 11 celebs—including Brad Pitt, Russell Crowe and Johnny Depp—can be forgiven for getting in touch with their inner rockers since they are doing it for charity. (Proceeds go to the Wildlife Waystation, an animal sanctuary north of L.A.) They are also savvy enough to sing mostly original tunes.

A KNIGHT'S TALE
Various Artists
The soundtrack for Heath Ledger's hard-rocking period piece features Queen's first recording of "We Are the Champions" since Freddie Mercury's death in 1991. Brit Robbie Williams does the lead vocal honors.

MUSIC FROM MALCOLM IN THE MIDDLE
Various Artists
Call it Malcolm Pop: short, sharp and quirky, these 17 tracks, led by They Might Be Giants' show theme, "Boss of Me," proves that TV music has come a long way.

*O BROTHER, WHERE ART THOU?
Various Artists
A far cry from the layered, formulaic country sound of today, these mostly traditional, all-acoustic work and prison, church and honky-tonk tunes

are performed by a wonderful assortment of musicians.

THE OCTAVES BEYOND SILENCE PROJECT
Various Artists
The Indigo Girls, Ani DiFranco, BETTY and Me'Shell Ndegéocello are among the Liliths contributing haunting tracks to this CD benefiting female victims of political violence.

SAVE THE LAST DANCE
Various Artists
A crib sheet for keeping up with the latest in hip-hop, funk, and R&B, the soundtrack to the hit teen flick includes dance tracks by Fredro Starr and Lucy Pearl, as well as Pink's amusingly titled "You Make Me Sick."

SKETCHES OF JAMES
Various Artists
This tribute to 10 classic James Taylor songs lacks a marquee talent but turns to medium-impact names, with an emphasis on such Latin stars as Flora Purim, Oscar Castro-Neves, and Poncho Sanchez's Latin Jazz Band.

THE SOPRANOS: PEPPERS AND EGGS
Various Artists
Family favorites: Bob Dylan ("Return to Me"), Elvis Costello & the Attractions ("High Fidelity"), Otis Redding ("My Lover's Prayer"), and the Rolling Stones ("Thru and Thru") hit high notes on this spicy two-disc soundtrack.

SOUNDS ECLECTIC
Various Artists
This compilation comes from *Morning Becomes Eclectic*, on KCRW public radio in L.A., and pulls together live tracks by fans Patti Smith, Beck, Travis and Willie Nelson as well as emerging talents like badly drawn boy.

SUBSTITUTE: SONGS OF THE WHO
Various Artists
There is no sub for the real thing, but a Who's Who of Whophiles, including Pearl Jam, Sheryl Crow and Phish, wail and windmill their way through the classics.

TOMB RAIDER
Various Artists
A raucous blend of hip-hop and electronica, the soundtrack to the live-action version of the cult video game features Missy Elliott and Nelly Furtado on "Get Ur Freak On" and a rockin' remix of U2's "Elevation."

A TWIST OF MARLEY
Various Artists
Late Bob Marley's reggae canon gets jazzed by the likes of sax man Michael Brecker, guitarist Lee Ritenour, and vocalist Maxi Priest. The lilting arrangements do not blunt the master's message.

THE VERY BEST OF DR. DEMENTO
Various Artists
Everything old is new again: classic novelty tunes collected by Dr. Demento (né Barry Hansen), including faves from Tom Lehrer, Frank Zappa, and, of course, Napoleon XIV.

VIOLATOR: V2.0
Various Artists
A hip-hop family album, this follow-up to '99's No. 1 compilation reunites Violators Missy Elliott, L.L. Cool J and Busta Rhymes.

FOR THE STARS
Anne Sofie von Otter and Elvis Costello

Writer-producer Costello wisely spends most of this disc with his mouth shut, framing von Otter's floral voice with a piano here, an accordion there, some strings there. This collection, mostly covers of work by the likes of Brian Wilson and ABBA, at times results in aching beauty.

*POSES
Rufus Wainwright

Wainwright's rapier writing, rich melodies and voice full of dark, autumnal texture allow you to forgive the measured melancholia of his *Poses*. Death and despair never sounded so good.

MAROON
The Webb Brothers

The sons of Hall of Fame songwriter Jimmy Webb devote their U.S. debut to an ambitious cycle of songs. There are dissolving relationships, battles with substance abuse and depression, but the brothers turn despair into art with taut vocal harmonies and inventive, textured art-rock melodies.

WEEZER: THE GREEN ALBUM
Weezer

With their hook-laden pop and geek-rock attitude, the L.A. quartet plays off deadpan lyrics on deceptively sunny anthems. Weezer's third disc clocks in at just under 29 minutes.

TIME (THE REVELATOR)
Gillian Welch

All 10 songs are written and performed acoustically by Welch and guitarist David Rawlings, who collaborated on the *O Brother, Where Art Thou?* soundtrack. And all have a shimmering beauty rarely captured on disc.

ESSENCE
Lucinda Williams

Essence has its moments, most of them wafting on an abundance of lovely if languorous melodies. Williams is at her best here on soft but poignant tunes like "Bus to Baton Rouge" and "Broken Butterflies," the piece that ends the album.

THE W
Wu-Tang Clan

On the group's first CD in three years, the ever-inventive Wu-Tang Clan has worked out a unique act that melds everything from '60s soul music, TV themes and Afrocentric mysticism to street braggadocio. The hip-hop collective's lineup of talented rappers gives the Clan irresistible firepower.

INSIDE OUT
Trisha Yearwood

At 36, Yearwood sounds like she is reveling in the years. She certainly knows how to share the microphone, and in neither case does she have to worry about being upstaged by her partner. Yearwood also confidently tackles the blues without sounding out of her genre—or depth.

ROCKET SHIP BEACH
Dan Zanes + Friends

Formerly the hell-raising lead singer for the 1980s alt-rock group the Del Fuegos, Zanes has made an album of foot stomping kid rock with contributions from friends like Sheryl Crow and Suzanne Vega.

ROCK AND ROLL HALL OF FAME

The Rock and Roll Hall of Fame in Cleveland continues to select the greatest rock and roll musicians for inclusion. A nominee must have released a record at least 25 years prior to induction. Early Influences honors the formative figures in rock.

1986

Chuck Berry
James Brown
Ray Charles
Sam Cooke
Fats Domino
The Everly Brothers
Buddy Holly
Jerry Lee Lewis
Elvis Presley
Little Richard

Early Influences
Robert Johnson
Jimmie Rodgers
Jimmy Yancey

Nonperformer
Alan Freed
Sam Phillips

Lifetime Achievement
John Hammond

1987

The Coasters
Eddie Cochran
Bo Diddley
Aretha Franklin
Marvin Gaye
Bill Haley
B. B. King
Clyde McPhatter
Ricky Nelson
Roy Orbison
Carl Perkins
Smokey Robinson
Big Joe Turner
Muddy Waters
Jackie Wilson

Early Influences
Louis Jordan
T-Bone Walker
Hank Williams

Nonperformers
Leonard Chess
Ahmet Ertegun
Jerry Leiber and Mike Stoller
Jerry Wexler

1988

The Beach Boys
The Beatles
The Drifters
Bob Dylan
The Supremes

Early Influences
Woody Guthrie
Leadbelly
Les Paul

Nonperformer
Berry Gordy Jr.

1989

Dion
Otis Redding
The Rolling Stones
The Temptations
Stevie Wonder

Early Influences
The Ink Spots
Bessie Smith
The Soul Stirrers

Nonperformer
Phil Spector

1990

Hank Ballard
Bobby Darin
The Four Seasons
The Four Tops
The Kinks
The Platters
Simon and Garfunkel
The Who

Early Influences
Louis Armstrong
Charlie Christian
Ma Rainey

Nonperformers
Lamont Dozier
Gerry Goffin and Carole King
Brian Holland and Eddie
    Holland

1991

LaVern Baker
The Byrds
John Lee Hooker
The Impressions
Wilson Pickett
Jimmy Reed
Ike and Tina Turner

Early Influence
Howlin' Wolf

Nonperformers
Dave Bartholomew
Ralph Bass

Lifetime Achievement
Nesuhi Ertegun

1992

Bobby "Blue" Bland
Booker T. and the MG's
Johnny Cash
Jimi Hendrix Experience
The Isley Brothers
Sam and Dave
The Yardbirds

Early Influences
Elmore James
Professor Longhair

Nonperformers
Leo Fender
Doc Pomus
Bill Graham

1993

Ruth Brown
Cream
Creedence Clearwater Revival
The Doors
Etta James
Frankie Lymon and the Teenagers
Van Morrison
Sly and the Family Stone

Early Influence
Dinah Washington

Nonperformers
Dick Clark
Milt Gabler

1994

The Animals
The Band
Duane Eddy
Grateful Dead
Elton John
John Lennon
Bob Marley
Rod Stewart

Early Influence
Willie Dixon

Nonperformer
Johnny Otis

1995

The Allman Brothers Band
Al Green
Janis Joplin
Led Zeppelin
The Vandellas
Neil Young
Frank Zappa

Early Influence
The Orioles

Nonperformer
Paul Ackerman

1996

David Bowie
Gladys Knight and the Pips
Jefferson Airplane
Little Willie John
Pink Floyd
The Shirelles
The Velvet Underground

Early Influence
Pete Seeger

Nonperformer
Tom Donahue

1997

Joni Mitchell
Buffalo Springfield
The Young Rascals
Parliament/Funkadelic
The Jackson Five
The Bee Gees
Crosby, Stills and Nash

Early Influence
Bill Monroe
Mahalia Jackson

Nonperformer
Syd Nathan

1998

The Eagles
Fleetwood Mac
The Mamas and the Papas
Lloyd Price
Santana
Gene Vincent

Early Influence
J. R. Morton

Nonperformer
Allen Toussaint

1999

Billy Joel
Paul McCartney
Curtis Mayfield
Del Shannon
Dusty Springfield
Bruce Springsteen
The Staple Singers

Early Influences
Charles Brown
Bob Willis and His Texas Playboys

Nonperformer
George Martin

2000

Eric Clapton
Earth, Wind & Fire
The Lovin' Spoonful
The Moonglows
Bonnie Raitt
James Taylor

Early Influences
Nat "King" Cole
Billie Holiday

Nonperformer
Clive Davis

2001

Aerosmith
Solomon Burke
The Flamingos
Michael Jackson
Queen
Paul Simon
Steely Dan
Richie Valens

Early Influences
James Burton
Johnnie Johnson

Nonperformer
Chris Blackwell

JAZZ HALL OF FAME

Down Beat magazine, America's leading jazz publication, conducts an annual poll of both readers and critics to determine the greatest luminaries of the jazz world. The honorees:

	Readers poll	Critics poll		Readers poll	Critics poll
1952	Louis Armstrong	—	1975	Cannonball Adderley	Cecil Taylor
1953	Glenn Miller	—	1976	Woody Herman	King Oliver
1954	Stan Kenton	—	1977	Paul Desmond	Benny Carter
1955	Charlie Parker	—	1978	Joe Venuti	Rahsaan Roland Kirk
1956	Duke Ellington	—	1979	Ella Fitzgerald	Lennie Tristano
1957	Benny Goodman	—	1980	Dexter Gordon	Max Roach
1958	Count Basie	—	1981	Art Blakey	Bill Evans
1959	Lester Young	—	1982	Art Pepper	Fats Navarro
1960	Dizzy Gillespie	—	1983	Stephane Grappelli	Albert Ayler
1961	Billie Holiday	Coleman Hawkins	1984	Oscar Peterson	Sun Ra
1962	Miles Davis	Bix Beiderbecke	1985	Sarah Vaughan	Zoot Sims
1963	Thelonious Monk	Jelly Roll Morton	1986	Stan Getz	Gil Evans
1964	Eric Dolphy	Art Tatum	1987	Lionel Hampton	Johnny Dodds, Thad Jones,
1965	John Coltrane	Earl Hines			Teddy Wilson
1966	Bud Powell	Charlie Christian	1988	Jaco Pastorius	Kenny Clarke
1967	Billy Strayhorn	Bessie Smith	1989	Woody Shaw	Chet Baker
1968	Wes Montgomery	Sidney Bechet,	1990	Red Rodney	Mary Lou Williams
		Fats Waller	1991	Lee Morgan	John Carter
1969	Ornette Coleman	Pee Wee Russell,	1992	Maynard Ferguson	James P. Johnson
		Jack Teagarden	1993	Gerry Mulligan	Edward Blackwell
1970	Jimi Hendrix	Johnny Hodges	1994	Dave Brubeck	Frank Zappa
1971	Charles Mingus	Roy Eldridge,	1995	J. J. Johnson	Julius Hemphill
		Django Reinhardt	1996	Horace Silver	Artie Shaw
1972	Gene Krupa	Clifford Brown	1997	Nat King Cole	Tony Williams
1973	Sonny Rollins	Fletcher Henderson	1998	Frank Sinatra	Elvin Jones
1974	Buddy Rich	Ben Webster	1999	Milt Jackson	Betty Carter
			2000	Clark Terry	Lester Bowie

COUNTRY MUSIC HALL OF FAME

Located in Nashville along with everything else in country music, the Country Music Hall of Fame inducts its honorees each autumn. The enshrined elite:

1962 Roy Acuff
1963 (elections held but no one candidate received enough votes)
1964 Tex Ritter
1965 Ernest Tubb
1966 James R. Denny, George D. Hay, Uncle Dave Macon, Eddy Arnold
1967 Red Foley, J. L. Frank, Jim Reeves, Stephen H. Sholes
1968 Bob Wills
1969 Gene Autry
1970 Original Carter Family (A. P. Carter, Maybelle Carter, Sara Carter), Bill Monroe
1971 Arthur Edward Satherley
1972 Jimmie Davis
1973 Patsy Cline, Chet Atkins
1974 Owen Bradley, Frank "Pee Wee" King
1975 Minnie Pearl
1976 Paul Cohen, Kitty Wells

1977 Merle Travis
1978 Grandpa Jones
1979 Hubert Long, Hank Snow
1980 Connie B. Gay, Original Sons of the Pioneers, Johnny Cash
1981 Vernon Dalhart, Grant Turner
1982 Lefty Frizzell, Marty Robbins, Roy Horton
1983 Little Jimmy Dickens
1984 Ralph Peer, Floyd Tillman
1985 Lester Flatt and Earl Scruggs
1986 Wesley Rose, The Duke of Paducah
1987 Rod Brasfield
1988 Roy Rogers, Loretta Lynn
1989 Jack Stapp, Hank Thompson, Cliffie Stone
1990 Tennessee Ernie Ford
1991 Boudleaux and Felice Bryant
1992 George Jones, Frances Preston
1993 Willie Nelson

1994 Merle Haggard
1995 Roger Miller and Jo Walker-Meador
1996 Patsy Montana, Buck Owens, Ray Price
1997 Harlan Howard, Brenda Lee, Cindy Walker
1998 George Morgan, Elvis Presley, Tammy Wynette, E. W. "Bud" Wendell
1999 Dolly Parton, Johnny Bond, Conway Twitty
2000 Charlie Prodd, Faron Young
2001 Bill Anderson, The Delmore Brothers, The Everly Brothers, Don Gibson, Homer & Jethro, Waylon Jennings, The Jordanaires, Don Law, The Louvin Brothers, Ken Nelson, Webb Pierce, Sam Phillips

TOP CONCERT TOURS

These are the most successful North American tours of all time, along with year-by-year leaders since 1988. The rankings are based on grosses rather than attendance. (Source: Pollstar)

ALL TIME

Rank	Artist	Year of tour
1.	The Rolling Stones	1994
2.	Pink Floyd	1994
3.	The Rolling Stones	1989
4.	The Rolling Stones	1997
5.	U2	1997
6.	The Eagles	1994
7.	New Kids on the Block	1990
8.	U2	1992
9.	The Rolling Stones	1999
10.	The Eagles	1995
11.	Bruce Springsteen & the E St. Band	1999
12.	Barbara Streisand	1994
13.	Grateful Dead	1994
14.	'N Sync	1999
15.	Dave Matthews Band	1999
16.	Elton John/Billy Joel	1994
17.	Elton John	1998
18.	Grateful Dead	1993
19.	KISS	1996
20.	Boyz II Men	1995

1988

Rank	Artist	Cities/Shows
1.	Pink Floyd	23/35
2.	Van Halen's "Monsters of Rock"	23/26
3.	Def Leppard	94/112
4.	Grateful Dead	33/80
5.	Aerosmith	96/105
6.	Michael Jackson	19/54
7.	AC/DC	105/110
8.	Rod Stewart	82/88
9.	Rat Pack/Ultimate Event	23/41
10.	George Michael	32/46
11.	Whitesnake	83/84
12.	Bruce Springsteen & the E Street Band	21/43
13.	Robert Plant	88/92
14.	Luther Vandross/Anita Baker	26/42
15.	INXS	75/81

1989

Rank	Artist	Cities/Shows
1.	The Rolling Stones	33/60
2.	The Who	27/39
3.	Bon Jovi	129/143
4.	Grateful Dead	33/73
5.	New Kids on the Block	112/143
6.	Neil Diamond	29/69
7.	Metallica	134/140
8.	Elton John	32/47
9.	Rod Stewart	61/71
10.	Beach Boys/Chicago	57/59
11.	Poison	82/83
12.	R.E.M.	84/87
13.	Cinderella	135/136
14.	Barry Manilow	44/123
15.	George Strait	90/104

1990

Rank	Artist	Cities/Shows
1.	New Kids on the Block	122/152
2.	Billy Joel	53/95
3.	Paul McCartney	21/32
4.	Grateful Dead	27/63
5.	Janet Jackson	62/89
6.	Aerosmith	92/101
7.	M. C. Hammer	132/138
8.	Mötley Crüe	103/108
9.	Phil Collins	27/56
10.	Eric Clapton	48/57
11.	David Bowie	41/51
12.	Madonna	12/32
13.	KISS	121/121
14.	Rush	56/63
15.	Depeche Mode	32/33

1991

Rank	Artist	Cities/Shows
1.	Grateful Dead	27/76
2.	ZZ Top	85/106
3.	The Judds	116/126
4.	Rod Stewart	47/59
5.	Paul Simon	72/76
6.	Guns N' Roses	30/43
7.	Bell Biv Devoe/Johnny Gill/Keith Sweat	66/72
8.	Michael Bolton	70/103
9.	Garth Brooks	94/111
10.	Clint Black	92/100
11.	AC/DC	57/60
12.	Sting	64/81
13.	Luther Vandross	50/60
14.	Scorpions	90/93
15.	Van Halen	42/46

1992

Rank	Artist	Cities/Shows
1.	U2	61/73
2.	Grateful Dead	23/55
3.	Guns N' Roses/Metallica	25/25
4.	Neil Diamond	26/69
5.	Bruce Springsteen	36/59
6.	Genesis	24/28
7.	Elton John	32/49
8.	Metallica	87/102
9.	Eric Clapton	30/37
10.	Hammer	123/130
11.	Bryan Adams	92/94
12.	Jimmy Buffett	43/64
13.	Lollapalooza II	29/35
14.	Garth Brooks	78/79
15.	Reba McEntire	102/111

1993

Rank	Artist	Cities/Shows
1.	Grateful Dead	29/81
2.	Rod Stewart	54/68
3.	Neil Diamond	43/75
4.	Paul McCartney	23/23
5.	Bette Midler	29/71
6.	Billy Joel	22/39
7.	Garth Brooks	29/54
8.	Jimmy Buffett	32/52
9.	Reba McEntire	97/105
10.	Kenny G	82/97
11.	"Lollapalooza III"	29/34
12.	Aerosmith	61/66
13.	Clint Black/Wynonna	70/73
14.	Van Halen	32/40
15.	Alan Jackson	98/105

1994

Rank	Artist	Cities/Shows
1.	The Rolling Stones	43/60
2.	Pink Floyd	39/59
3.	The Eagles	32/54
4.	Barbra Streisand	6/22
5.	Grateful Dead	29/84
6.	Elton John/Billy Joel	14/21
7.	Aerosmith	71/76
8.	Lollapalooza IV	33/43
9.	Phil Collins	41/59
10.	Reba McEntire	96/102
11.	Bette Midler	44/54
12.	Billy Joel	40/49
13.	Michael Bolton	84/93
14.	Metallica	49/50
15.	ZZ Top	93/96

1995

Rank	Artist	Cities/Shows
1.	The Eagles	46/58
2.	Boyz II Men	133/134
3.	R.E.M.	63/81
4.	Grateful Dead	20/45
5.	Jimmy Page/Robert Plant	56/68
6.	Van Halen	85/94
7.	Tom Petty and the Heartbreakers	80/89
8.	Reba McEntire	91/101
9.	Elton John	27/41
10.	Elton John/Billy Joel	10/12
11.	Alan Jackson	95/97
12.	Jimmy Buffett	37/52
13.	Yanni	50/59
14.	Vince Gill	82/90
15.	Phish	67/79

1996

Rank	Artist	Cities/Shows
1.	KISS	75/92
2.	Garth Brooks	41/121
3.	Neil Diamond	49/72
4.	Rod Stewart	62/65
5.	Bob Seger	57/64
6.	Jimmy Buffett	28/44
7.	Reba McEntire	83/86
8.	Alanis Morissette	88/98
9.	Hootie & The Blowfish	73/80
10.	Ozzy Osbourne	100/100
11.	AC/DC	74/81
12.	Dave Matthews Band	78/81
13.	George Strait	53/58

| 14. | Sting | 51/56 |
| 15. | The Smashing Pumpkins | 68/79 |

1997

Rank	Artist	Cities/Shows
1.	The Rolling Stones	26/33
2.	U2	37/46
3.	Fleetwood Mac	40/44
4.	Metallica	65/77
5.	Brooks & Dunn/ Reba McEntire	66/69
6.	Garth Brooks	28/110
7.	Tina Turner	56/70
8.	The Artist Formerly Known As Prince	71/73
9.	Jimmy Buffett	31/44
10.	Aerosmith	60/63
11.	Phish	34/45
12.	Phil Collins	32/35
13.	Alan Jackson	66/67
14.	ZZ Top	93/94
15.	Bush	69/69

1998

Rank	Artist	Cities/Shows
1.	Elton John	52/63
2.	Dave Matthews Band	76/85
3.	Celine Dion	31/43
4.	Yanni	82/93
5.	Garth Brooks	27/99
6.	Eric Clapton	42/45
7.	Shania Twain	87/92
8.	Janet Jackson	56/60
9.	George Strait Country Music Festival	18/18
10.	The Rolling Stones	13/20
11.	Jimmy Buffett	32/44
12.	Lillith Fair	46/56
13.	Billy Joel	15/38
14.	Aerosmith	67/70
15.	Page/Plant	50/52

1999

Rank	Artist	Cities/Shows
1.	The Rolling Stones	26/34
2.	Bruce Springsteen and the E Street Band	18/54
3.	'N Sync	108/121
4.	Dave Matthews Band	47/62
5.	Shania Twain	60/62
6.	Cher	52/57
7.	Backstreet Boys	40/56
8.	Elton John	55/58

9.	George Strait Country Music Festival	17/17
10.	Bette Midler	33/34
11.	Bob Dylan/Paul Simon	40/46
12.	Phish	46/59
13.	Celine Dion	26/31
14.	Tom Petty and the Heartbreakers	53/67
15.	Jimmy Buffett	27/36

2000

Rank	Artist	Cities/Shows
1.	Tina Turner	88/95
2.	'N Sync	64/86
3.	Dave Matthews Band	43/63
4.	KISS	120/128
5.	Tim McGraw/Faith Hill	64/66
6.	Dixie Chicks	84/89
7.	Bruce Springsteen & The E Street Band	27/43
8.	Crosby, Stills, Nash & Young	35/40
9.	Metallica	19/23
10.	Britney Spears	73/81
11.	Ricky Martin	40/46
12.	Red Hot Chili Peppers	80/84
13.	Sting	54/57
14.	Barbra Streisand	2/4
15.	Creed	76/79

BILLBOARD'S TOP 10 SINGLES

Faith Hill made it three in a row for female vocalists at the top in 2000, even as Santana mounted his Grammy-dominating comeback. (Source: *Billboard*)

1946

1. "Prisoner of Love," Perry Como
2. "To Each His Own," Eddy Howard
3. "The Gypsy," Ink Spots
4. "Five Minutes More," Frank Sinatra
5. "Rumors Are Flying," Frankie Carle
6. "Oh! What It Seemed To Be," Frankie Carle
7. "Personality," Johnny Mercer & The Pied Pipers
8. "South America, Take It Away," Bing Crosby & The Andrews Sisters
9. "The Gypsy," Dinah Shore
10. "Oh! What It Seemed To Be," Frank Sinatra

1947

1. "Near You," Francis Craig
2. "Peg O' My Heart," Harmonicats
3. "Heartaches," Ted Weems
4. "Linda," Ray Noble Orchestra & Buddy Clark (tie)
4. "Smoke, Smoke, Smoke (That Cigarette)," Tex Williams (tie)
6. "I Wish I Didn't Love You So," Vaughn Monroe
7. "Peg O' My Heart," Three Suns
8. "Anniversary Song," Al Jolson
9. "Near You," Larry Green Orchestra
10. "That's My Desire," Sammy Kaye

1948

1. "Twelfth Street Rag," Pee Wee Hunt
2. "Mañana (Is Good Enough for Me)," Peggy Lee
3. "Now Is the Hour," Bing Crosby
4. "A Tree in the Meadow," Margaret Whiting
5. "My Happiness," Jon & Sandra Steele
6. "You Can't Be True, Dear," Ken Griffin & Jerry Wayne
7. "Little White Lies," Dick Haymes
8. "You Call Everybody Darlin'," Al Trace
9. "My Happiness," Pied Pipers
10. "I'm Looking Over a Four Leaf Clover," Art Mooney

1949

1. "Riders in the Sky," Vaughn Monroe Orchestra
2. "That Lucky Old Sun," Frankie Laine

3. "You're Breaking My Heart," Vic Damone
4. "Some Enchanted Evening," Perry Como
5. "Slipping Around," Jimmy Wakely & Margaret Whiting
6. "I Can Dream, Can't I?" Andrews Sisters & Gordon Jenkins
7. "Cruising Down the River," Russ Morgan Orchestra
8. "A Little Bird Told Me," Evelyn Knight & The Stardusters
9. "Mule Train," Frankie Laine
10. "Jealous Heart," Al Morgan

1950

1. "Goodnight Irene," Gordon Jenkins & The Weavers
2. "Mona Lisa," Nat King Cole
3. "Third Man Theme," Anton Karas
4. "Sam's Song," Gary & Bing Crosby
5. "Simple Melody," Gary & Bing Crosby
6. "Music, Music, Music," Teresa Brewer
7. "Third Man Theme," Guy Lombardo
8. "Chattanoogie Shoe Shine Boy," Red Foley
9. "Harbor Lights," Sammy Kaye
10. "It Isn't Fair," Sammy Kaye & Don Cornell

1951

1. "Too Young," Nat King Cole
2. "Because of You," Tony Bennett
3. "How High the Moon," Les Paul & Mary Ford
4. "Come On-A My House," Rosemary Clooney
5. "Be My Love," Mario Lanza
6. "On Top of Old Smoky," Weavers
7. "Cold, Cold Heart," Tony Bennett
8. "If," Perry Como
9. "Loveliest Night of the Year," Mario Lanza
10. "Tennessee Waltz," Patti Page

1952

1. "Blue Tango," Leroy Anderson
2. "Wheel of Fortune," Kay Starr
3. "Cry," Johnnie Ray
4. "You Belong to Me," Jo Stafford
5. "Auf Wiederseh'n, Sweetheart," Vera Lynn

6. "I Went to Your Wedding," Patti Page
7. "Half as Much," Rosemary Clooney
8. "Wish You Were Here," Eddie Fisher & Hugo Winterhalter
9. "Here in My Heart," Al Martino
10. "Delicado," Percy Faith

1953

1. "Song From Moulin Rouge," Percy Faith
2. "Vaya con Dios," Les Paul & Mary Ford
3. "Doggie in the Window," Patti Page
4. "I'm Walking Behind You," Eddie Fisher
5. "You, You, You," Ames Brothers
6. "Till I Waltz Again with You," Teresa Brewer
7. "April in Portugal," Les Baxter
8. "No Other Love," Perry Como
9. "Don't Let the Stars Get in Your Eyes," Perry Como
10. "I Believe," Frankie Laine

1954

1. "Little Things Mean a Lot," Kitty Kallen
2. "Wanted," Perry Como
3. "Hey, There," Rosemary Clooney
4. "Sh-Boom," Crew Cuts
5. "Make Love to Me," Jo Stafford
6. "Oh! My Pa-Pa," Eddie Fisher
7. "I Get So Lonely," Four Knights
8. "Three Coins in the Fountain," Four Aces
9. "Secret Love," Doris Day
10. "Hernando's Highway," Archie Bleyer

1955

1. "Cherry Pink and Apple Blossom White," Perez Prado
2. "Rock Around the Clock," Bill Haley & His Comets
3. "The Yellow Rose of Texas," Mitch Miller
4. "Autumn Leaves," Roger Williams
5. "Unchained Melody," Les Baxter
6. "The Ballad of Davy Crockett," Bill Hayes
7. "Love Is a Many-Splendored Thing," Four Aces

8. "Sincerely," McGuire Sisters
9. "Ain't That a Shame," Pat Boone
10. "Dance with Me Henry," Georgia Gibbs

1956

1. "Heartbreak Hotel," Elvis Presley
2. "Don't Be Cruel," Elvis Presley
3. "Lisbon Antigua," Nelson Riddle
4. "My Prayer," Platters
5. "The Wayward Wind," Gogi Grant
6. "Hound Dog," Elvis Presley
7. "The Poor People of Paris," Les Baxter
8. "Whatever Will Be Will Be (Que Sera Sera)," Doris Day
9. "Memories Are Made of This," Dean Martin
10. "Rock and Roll Waltz," Kay Starr

1957

1. "All Shook Up," Elvis Presley
2. "Love Letters in the Sand," Pat Boone
3. "Little Darlin'," Diamonds
4. "Young Love," Tab Hunter
5. "So Rare," Jimmy Dorsey
6. "Don't Forbid Me," Pat Boone
7. "Singing the Blues," Guy Mitchell
8. "Young Love," Sonny James
9. "Too Much," Elvis Presley
10. "Round and Round," Perry Como

1958

1. "Volare (Nel Blu Dipinto Di Blu)," Domenico Modugno
2. "All I Have To Do Is Dream"/ "Claudette," Everly Brothers
3. "Don't"/"I Beg of You," Elvis Presley
4. "Witch Doctor," David Seville
5. "Patricia," Perez Prado
6. "Sail Along Silvery Moon"/ "Raunchy," Billy Vaughn
7. "Catch a Falling Star"/"Magic Moments," Perry Como
8. "Tequila," Champs
9. "It's All in the Game," Tommy Edwards
10. "Return to Me," Dean Martin

1959

1. "The Battle of New Orleans," Johnny Horton
2. "Mack the Knife," Bobby Darin
3. "Personality," Lloyd Price
4. "Venus," Frankie Avalon
5. "Lonely Boy," Paul Anka
6. "Dream Lover," Bobby Darin

7. "The Three Bells," Browns
8. "Come Softly to Me," Fleetwoods
9. "Kansas City," Wilbert Harrison
10. "Mr. Blue," Fleetwoods

1960

1. "Theme from *A Summer Place*," Percy Faith
2. "He'll Have To Go," Jim Reeves
3. "Cathy's Clown," Everly Brothers
4. "Running Bear," Johnny Preston
5. "Teen Angel," Mark Dinning
6. "It's Now or Never," Elvis Presley
7. "Handy Man," Jimmy Jones
8. "I'm Sorry," Brenda Lee
9. "Stuck on You," Elvis Presley
10. "The Twist," Chubby Checker

1961

1. "Tossin' and Turnin'," Bobby Lewis
2. "I Fall to Pieces," Patsy Cline
3. "Michael," Highwaymen
4. "Cryin'," Roy Orbison
5. "Runaway," Del Shannon
6. "My True Story," Jive Five
7. "Pony Time," Chubby Checker
8. "Wheels," String-a-Longs
9. "Raindrops," Dee Clark
10. "Wooden Heart (Muss I Denn)," Joe Dowell

1962

1. "Stranger on the Shore," Mr. Acker Bilk
2. "I Can't Stop Loving You," Ray Charles
3. "Mashed Potato Time," Dee Dee Sharp
4. "Roses Are Red," Bobby Vinton
5. "The Stripper," David Rose
6. "Johnny Angel," Shelley Fabares
7. "Loco-motion," Little Eva
8. "Let Me In," Sensations
9. "The Twist," Chubby Checker
10. "Soldier Boy," Shirelles

1963

1. "Sugar Shack," Jimmy Gilmer & The Fireballs
2. "Surfin' USA," Beach Boys
3. "The End of the World," Skeeter Davis
4. "Rhythm of the Rain," Cascades
5. "He's So Fine," Chiffons
6. "Blue Velvet," Bobby Vinton
7. "Hey Paula," Paul & Paula
8. "Fingertips II," Little Stevie Wonder

9. "Washington Square," Village Stompers
10. "It's All Right," Impressions

1964

1. "I Want To Hold Your Hand," Beatles
2. "She Loves You," Beatles
3. "Hello, Dolly!" Louis Armstrong
4. "Oh, Pretty Woman," Roy Orbison
5. "I Get Around," Beach Boys
6. "Everybody Loves Somebody," Dean Martin
7. "My Guy," Mary Wells
8. "We'll Sing in the Sunshine," Gale Garnett
9. "Last Kiss," J. Frank Wilson & The Cavaliers
10. "Where Did Our Love Go," Supremes

1965

1. "Wooly Bully," Sam the Sham & The Pharaohs
2. "I Can't Help Myself," Four Tops
3. "(I Can't Get No) Satisfaction," Rolling Stones
4. "You Were on My Mind," We Five
5. "You've Lost That Lovin' Feelin'," Righteous Brothers
6. "Downtown," Petula Clark
7. "Help!," Beatles
8. "Can't You Hear My Heartbeat," Herman's Hermits
9. "Crying in the Chapel," Elvis Presley
10. "My Girl," Temptations

1966

1. "The Ballad of the Green Berets," S/Sgt. Barry Sadler
2. "Cherish," Association
3. "(You're My) Soul and Inspiration," Righteous Brothers
4. "Reach Out I'll Be There," Four Tops
5. "96 Tears," ? & the Mysterians
6. "Last Train to Clarksville," Monkees
7. "Monday, Monday," Mamas & the Papas
8. "You Can't Hurry Love," Supremes
9. "Poor Side of Town," Johnny Rivers
10. "California Dreamin'," Mamas & the Papas

1967

1. "To Sir with Love," Lulu
2. "The Letter," Box Tops
3. "Ode to Billie Joe," Bobby Gentry
4. "Windy," Association
5. "I'm a Believer," Monkees
6. "Light My Fire," Doors

7. "Somethin' Stupid," Nancy Sinatra & Frank Sinatra
8. "Happy Together," Turtles
9. "Groovin'," Young Rascals
10. "Can't Take My Eyes Off You," Frankie Valli

1968

1. "Hey Jude," Beatles
2. "Love Is Blue (L'Amour Est Blue)," Paul Mauriat
3. "Honey," Bobby Goldsboro
4. "(Sittin' on) The Dock of the Bay," Otis Redding
5. "People Got To Be Free," Rascals
6. "Sunshine of Your Love," Cream
7. "This Guy's in Love with You," Herb Alpert
8. "The Good, the Bad and the Ugly," Hugo Montenegro
9. "Mrs. Robinson," Simon & Garfunkel
10. "Tighten Up," Archie Bell & The Drells

1969

1. "Sugar, Sugar," Archies
2. "Aquarius/Let the Sunshine In," Fifth Dimension
3. "I Can't Get Next to You," Temptations
4. "Honky Tonk Women," Rolling Stones
5. "Everyday People," Sly & the Family Stone
6. "Dizzy," Tommy Roe
7. "Hot Fun in the Summertime," Sly & the Family Stone
8. "I'll Never Fall in Love Again," Tom Jones
9. "Build Me Up Buttercup," Foundations
10. "Crimson and Clover," Tommy James & The Shondells

1970

1. "Bridge over Troubled Water," Simon & Garfunkel
2. "(They Long To Be) Close to You," Carpenters
3. "American Woman"/"No Sugar Tonight," Guess Who
4. "Raindrops Keep Fallin' on My Head," B. J. Thomas
5. "War," Edwin Starr
6. "Ain't No Mountain High Enough," Diana Ross
7. "I'll Be There," Jackson 5
8. "Get Ready," Rare Earth
9. "Let It Be," Beatles
10. "Band of Gold," Freda Payne

1971

1. "Joy to the World," Three Dog Night
2. "Maggie May"/"Reason To Believe," Rod Stewart
3. "It's Too Late"/"I Feel the Earth Move," Carole King
4. "One Bad Apple," Osmonds
5. "How Can You Mend a Broken Heart," Bee Gees
6. "Indian Reservation," Raiders
7. "Go Away Little Girl," Donny Osmond
8. "Take Me Home, Country Roads," John Denver with Fat City
9. "Just My Imagination (Running Away with Me)," Temptations
10. "Knock Three Times," Dawn

1972

1. "The First Time Ever I Saw Your Face," Roberta Flack
2. "Alone Again (Naturally)," Gilbert O'Sullivan
3. "American Pie," Don McLean
4. "Without You," Nilsson
5. "Candy Man," Sammy Davis Jr.
6. "I Gotcha," Joe Tex
7. "Lean on Me," Bill Withers
8. "Baby Don't Get Hooked on Me," Mac Davis
9. "Brand New Key," Melanie
10. "Daddy Don't You Walk So Fast," Wayne Newton

1973

1. "Tie a Yellow Ribbon 'Round the Ole Oak Tree," Tony Orlando & Dawn
2. "Bad, Bad Leroy Brown," Jim Croce
3. "Killing Me Softly with His Song," Roberta Flack
4. "Let's Get It On," Marvin Gaye
5. "My Love," Paul McCartney & Wings
6. "Why Me," Kris Kristofferson
7. "Crocodile Rock," Elton John
8. "Will It Go Round in Circles," Billy Preston
9. "You're So Vain," Carly Simon
10. "Touch Me in the Morning," Diana Ross

1974

1. "The Way We Were," Barbra Streisand
2. "Seasons in the Sun," Terry Jacks
3. "Love's Theme," Love Unlimited Orchestra
4. "Come and Get Your Love," Redbone
5. "Dancing Machine," Jackson 5
6. "The Loco-motion," Grand Funk Railroad
7. "TSOP," MFSB

8. "The Streak," Ray Stevens
9. "Bennie and the Jets," Elton John
10. "One Hell of a Woman," Mac Davis

1975

1. "Love Will Keep Us Together," Captain & Tennille
2. "Rhinestone Cowboy," Glen Campbell
3. "Philadelphia Freedom," Elton John
4. "Before the Next Teardrop Falls," Freddy Fender
5. "My Eyes Adored You," Frankie Valli
6. "Shining Star," Earth, Wind & Fire
7. "Fame," David Bowie
8. "Laughter in the Rain," Neil Sedaka
9. "One of These Nights," Eagles
10. "Thank God I'm a Country Boy," John Denver

1976

1. "Silly Love Songs," Wings
2. "Don't Go Breaking My Heart," Elton John & Kiki Dee
3. "Disco Lady," Johnnie Taylor
4. "December, 1963 (Oh, What a Night)," Four Seasons
5. "Play That Funky Music," Wild Cherry
6. "Kiss and Say Goodbye," Manhattans
7. "Love Machine, Pt. 1," Miracles
8. "50 Ways To Leave Your Lover," Paul Simon
9. "Love Is Alive," Gary Wright
10. "A Fifth of Beethoven," Walter Murphy & The Big Apple Band

1977

1. "Tonight's the Night (Gonna Be Alright)," Rod Stewart
2. "I Just Want To Be Your Everything," Andy Gibb
3. "Best of My Love," Emotions
4. "Love Theme from *A Star Is Born* (Evergreen)," Barbra Streisand
5. "Angel in Your Arms," Hot
6. "I Like Dreamin'," Kenny Nolan
7. "Don't Leave Me This Way," Thelma Houston
8. "(Your Love Has Lifted Me) Higher and Higher," Rita Coolidge
9. "Undercover Angel," Alan O'Day
10. "Torn Between Two Lovers," Mary MacGregor

1978

1. "Shadow Dancing," Andy Gibb
2. "Night Fever," Bee Gees
3. "You Light Up My Life," Debby Boone
4. "Stayin' Alive," Bee Gees
5. "Kiss You All Over," Exile

6. "How Deep Is Your Love," Bee Gees
7. "Baby Come Back," Player
8. "Love Is Thicker Than Water," Andy Gibb
9. "Boogie Oogie Oogie," A Taste of Honey
10. "Three Times a Lady," Commodores

1979

1. "My Sharona," Knack
2. "Bad Girls," Donna Summer
3. "Le Freak," Chic
4. "Do Ya Think I'm Sexy," Rod Stewart
5. "Reunited," Peaches & Herb
6. "I Will Survive," Gloria Gaynor
7. "Hot Stuff," Donna Summer
8. "Y.M.C.A.," Village People
9. "Ring My Bell," Anita Ward
10. "Sad Eyes," Robert John

1980

1. "Call Me," Blondie
2. "Another Brick in the Wall," Pink Floyd
3. "Magic," Olivia Newton-John
4. "Rock with You," Michael Jackson
5. "Do That to Me One More Time," Captain & Tennille
6. "Crazy Little Thing Called Love," Queen
7. "Coming Up," Paul McCartney
8. "Funkytown," Lipps, Inc.
9. "It's Still Rock and Roll to Me," Billy Joel
10. "The Rose," Bette Midler

1981

1. "Bette Davis Eyes," Kim Carnes
2. "Endless Love," Diana Ross & Lionel Richie
3. "Lady," Kenny Rogers
4. "(Just Like) Starting Over," John Lennon
5. "Jessie's Girl," Rick Springfield
6. "Celebration," Kool & the Gang
7. "Kiss on My List," Daryl Hall & John Oates
8. "I Love a Rainy Night," Eddie Rabbitt
9. "9 to 5," Dolly Parton
10. "Keep On Loving You," REO Speedwagon

1982

1. "Physical," Olivia Newton-John
2. "Eye of the Tiger," Survivor
3. "I Love Rock 'n' Roll," Joan Jett & the Blackhearts
4. "Ebony and Ivory," Paul McCartney & Stevie Wonder

5. "Centerfold," The J. Geils Band
6. "Don't You Want Me," Human League
7. "Jack and Diane," John Cougar
8. "Hurts So Good," John Cougar
9. "Abracadabra," Steve Miller Band
10. "Hard To Say I'm Sorry," Chicago

1983

1. "Every Breath You Take," The Police
2. "Billie Jean," Michael Jackson
3. "Flashdance...What a Feeling," Irene Cara
4. "Down Under," Men at Work
5. "Beat It," Michael Jackson
6. "Total Eclipse of the Heart," Bonnie Tyler
7. "Maneater," Daryl Hall & John Oates
8. "Baby Come to Me," Patti Austin with James Ingram
9. "Maniac," Michael Sembello
10. "Sweet Dreams (Are Made of This)," Eurythmics

1984

1. "When Doves Cry," Prince
2. "What's Love Got To Do with It," Tina Turner
3. "Say Say Say," Paul McCartney & Michael Jackson
4. "Footloose," Kenny Loggins
5. "Against All Odds (Take a Look at Me Now)," Phil Collins
6. "Jump," Van Halen
7. "Hello," Lionel Richie
8. "Owner of a Lonely Heart," Yes
9. "Ghostbusters," Ray Parker Jr.
10. "Karma Chameleon," Culture Club

1985

1. "Careless Whisper," Wham! featuring George Michael
2. "Like a Virgin," Madonna
3. "Wake Me Up Before You Go-Go," Wham!
4. "I Want To Know What Love Is," Foreigner
5. "I Feel for You," Chaka Khan
6. "Out of Touch," Daryl Hall & John Oates
7. "Everybody Wants To Rule the World," Tears for Fears
8. "Money for Nothing," Dire Straits
9. "Crazy for You," Madonna
10. "Take on Me," a-ha

1986

1. "That's What Friends Are For," Dionne & Friends
2. "Say You, Say Me," Lionel Richie

3. "I Miss You," Klymaxx
4. "On My Own," Patti LaBelle & Michael McDonald
5. "Broken Wings," Mr. Mister
6. "How Will I Know," Whitney Houston
7. "Party All the Time," Eddie Murphy
8. "Burning Heart," Survivor
9. "Kyrie," Mr. Mister
10. "Addicted to Love," Robert Palmer

1987

1. "Walk Like an Egyptian," Bangles
2. "Alone," Heart
3. "Shake You Down," Gregory Abbott
4. "I Wanna Dance with Somebody (Who Loves Me)," Whitney Houston
5. "Nothing's Gonna Stop Us Now," Starship
6. "C'est La Vie," Robbie Nevil
7. "Here I Go Again," Whitesnake
8. "The Way It Is," Bruce Hornsby & the Range
9. "Shakedown," Bob Seger
10. "Livin' On a Prayer," Bon Jovi

1988

1. "Faith," George Michael
2. "Need You Tonight," INXS
3. "Got My Mind Set on You," George Harrison
4. "Never Gonna Give You Up," Rick Astley
5. "Sweet Child o' Mine," Guns N' Roses
6. "So Emotional," Whitney Houston
7. "Heaven Is a Place on Earth," Belinda Carlisle
8. "Could've Been," Tiffany
9. "Hands to Heaven," Breathe
10. "Roll with It," Steve Winwood

1989

1. "Look Away," Chicago
2. "My Prerogative," Bobby Brown
3. "Every Rose Has Its Thorn," Poison
4. "Straight Up," Paula Abdul
5. "Miss You Much," Janet Jackson
6. "Cold Hearted," Paula Abdul
7. "Wind Beneath My Wings," Bette Midler
8. "Girl You Know It's True," Milli Vanilli
9. "Baby, I Love Your Way/Freebird Medley," Will to Power
10. "Giving You the Best That I Got," Anita Baker

1990

1. "Hold On," Wilson Phillips
2. "It Must Have Been Love," Roxette
3. "Nothing Compares 2 U," Sinéad O'Connor

4. "Poison," Bell Biv Devoe
5. "Vogue," Madonna
6. "Vision of Love," Mariah Carey
7. "Another Day in Paradise," Phil Collins
8. "Hold On," En Vogue
9. "Cradle of Love," Billy Idol
10. "Blaze of Glory," Jon Bon Jovi

1991

1. "(Everything I Do) I Do It for You," Bryan Adams
2. "I Wanna Sex You Up," Color Me Badd
3. "Gonna Make You Sweat," C+C Music Factory
4. "Rush Rush," Paula Abdul
5. "One More Try," Timmy T.
6. "Unbelievable," EMF
7. "More Than Words," Extreme
8. "I Like the Way (The Kissing Game)," Hi-Five
9. "The First Time," Surface
10. "Baby Baby," Amy Grant

1992

1. "End of the Road," Boyz II Men
2. "Baby Got Back," Sir Mix-A-Lot
3. "Jump," Kris Kross
4. "Save the Best for Last," Vanessa Williams
5. "Baby-Baby-Baby," TLC
6. "Tears in Heaven," Eric Clapton
7. "My Lovin' (You're Never Gonna Get It)," En Vogue
8. "Under the Bridge," Red Hot Chili Peppers
9. "All 4 Love," Color Me Badd
10. "Just Another Day," Jon Secada

1993

1. "I Will Always Love You," Whitney Houston
2. "Whoomp! (There It Is)," Tag Team
3. "Can't Help Falling in Love," UB40
4. "That's the Way Love Goes," Janet Jackson
5. "Freak Me," Silk
6. "Weak," SWV
7. "If I Ever Fall in Love," Shai
8. "Dreamlover," Mariah Carey
9. "Rump Shaker," Wreckx-N-Effect
10. "Informer," Snow

1994

1. "The Sign," Ace of Base
2. "I Swear," All-4-One
3. "I'll Make Love to You," Boyz II Men
4. "The Power of Love," Celine Dion

5. "Hero," Mariah Carey
6. "Stay (I Missed You)," Lisa Loeb & Nine Stories
7. "Breathe Again," Toni Braxton
8. "All for Love," Bryan Adams/Rod Stewart/Sting
9. "All That She Wants," Ace of Base
10. "Don't Turn Around," Ace of Base

1995

1. "Gangsta's Paradise," Coolio featuring L.V.
2. "Waterfalls," TLC
3. "Creep," TLC
4. "Kiss from a Rose," Seal
5. "On Bended Knee," Boyz II Men
6. "Another Night," Real McCoy
7. "Fantasy," Mariah Carey
8. "Take a Bow," Madonna
9. "Don't Take It Personal (Just One of Dem Days)," Monica
10. "This Is How We Do It," Montell Jordan

1996

1. "Macarena (Bayside Boys Mix)," Los Del Rio
2. "One Sweet Day," Mariah Carey & Boyz II Men
3. "Because You Loved Me," Celine Dion
4. "Nobody Knows," The Tony Rich Project
5. "Always Be My Baby," Mariah Carey
6. "Give Me One Reason," Tracy Chapman
7. "Tha Crossroads," Bone Thugs-N-Harmony
8. "I Love You Always Forever," Donna Lewis
9. "You're Makin' Me High/Let It Flow," Toni Braxton
10. "Twisted," Keith Sweat

1997

1. "Candle in the Wind 1997"/"Something About the Way You Look Tonight," Elton John
2. "You Were Meant for Me"/"Foolish Games," Jewel
3. "I'll Be Missing You," Puff Daddy & Faith Evans (Featuring 112)
4. "Un-Break My Heart," Toni Braxton
5. "Can't Nobody Hold Me Down," Puff Daddy (featuring Mase)
6. "I Believe I Can Fly," R. Kelly
7. "Don't Let Go (Love)," En Vogue
8. "Return of the Mack," Mark Morrison
9. "How Do I Live," LeAnn Rimes
10. "Wannabe," Spice Girls

1998

1. "The Boy Is Mine," Brandy & Monica
2. "Too Close," Next
3. "You're Still the One," Shania Twain
4. "Candle in the Wind 1997"/"Something About the Way You Look Tonight," Elton John
5. "Been Around the World," Puff Daddy & The Family
6. "How Do I Live," LeAnn Rimes
7. "Nice & Slow," Usher
8. "No, No, No," Destiny's Child
9. "My Way," Usher
10. "My All," Mariah Carey

1999

1. "Believe," Cher
2. "No Scrubs," TLC
3. "Angel of Mind," Monica
4. "Heartbreak Hotel," Whitney Houston featuring Faith Evans and Kelly Price
5. "...Baby One More Time," Britney Spears
6. "Kiss Me," Sixpence None the Richer
7. "Genie in a Bottle," Christina Aguilera
8. "Every Morning," Sugar Ray
9. "Nobody's Supposed to Be Here," Deborah Cox
10. "Livin' La Vida Loca," Ricky Martin

2000

1. "Breathe," Faith Hill
2. "Smooth," Santana, featuring Rob Thomas
3. "Maria Maria," Santana featuring The Product G&B
4. "I Wanna Know," Joe
5. "Everything You Want," Vertical Horizon
6. "Say My Name," Destiny's Child
7. "I Knew I Loved You," Savage Garden
8. "Amazed," Lonestar
9. "Bent," Matchbox 20
10. "He Wasn't Man Enough," Toni Braxton

BILLBOARD'S TOP 10 ALBUMS

Teen favorites 'N Sync, the Backstreet Boys, and Britney Spears all *Did It Again* in 2000, joined by Christina Aguilera, with plenty of competition from Eminem's heat-seeking missile. (Source: *Billboard*)

1957

1. *My Fair Lady*, original cast
2. *Hymns*, Tennessee Ernie Ford
3. *Oklahoma!*, soundtrack
4. *Around the World in 80 Days*, soundtrack
5. *The King and I*, soundtrack
6. *Calypso*, Harry Belafonte
7. *Love Is the Thing*, Nat King Cole
8. *The Eddy Duchin Story*, soundtrack
9. *Songs of the Fabulous Fifties*, Roger Williams
10. *Film Encores*, Mantovani

1958

1. *My Fair Lady*, original cast
2. *The Music Man*, original cast
3. *Johnny's Greatest Hits*, Johnny Mathis
4. *South Pacific*, soundtrack
5. *Come Fly with Me*, Frank Sinatra
6. *Around the World in 80 Days*, soundtrack
7. *Warm*, Johnny Mathis
8. *South Pacific*, original cast
9. *Ricky*, Ricky Nelson
10. *The King and I*, soundtrack

1959

1. *Music from "Peter Gunn,"* Henry Mancini
2. *Gigi*, soundtrack
3. *South Pacific*, soundtrack
4. *From the Hungry i*, Kingston Trio
5. *The Kingston Trio at Large*, Kingston Trio
6. *Sing Along with Mitch*, Mitch Miller
7. *Inside Shelley Berman*, Shelley Berman
8. *Exotica, Vol. 1*, Martin Denny
9. *My Fair Lady*, original cast
10. *Flower Drum Song*, original cast

1960

1. *The Sound of Music*, original cast
2. *Inside Shelley Berman*, Shelley Berman
3. *The Button-Down Mind of Bob Newhart*, Bob Newhart
4. *Sixty Years of Music America Loves Best, Vol. I*, various artists
5. *Here We Go Again*, Kingston Trio
6. *Sold Out*, Kingston Trio
7. *Heavenly*, Johnny Mathis
8. *South Pacific*, soundtrack
9. *Faithfully*, Johnny Mathis
10. *Outside Shelley Berman*, Shelley Berman

1961

1. *Camelot*, original cast
2. *Great Motion Picture Themes*, various artists
3. *Never on Sunday*, soundtrack
4. *The Sound of Music*, original cast
5. *Exodus*, soundtrack
6. *Knockers Up*, Rusty Warren
7. *G.I. Blues*, Elvis Presley/soundtrack
8. *Sing Along with Mitch*, Mitch Miller
9. *Calcutta*, Lawrence Welk
10. *Tonight in Person*, Limeliters

1962

1. *West Side Story*, soundtrack
2. *Breakfast at Tiffany's*, Henry Mancini
3. *Blue Hawaii*, Elvis Presley/soundtrack
4. *West Side Story*, original cast
5. *The Sound of Music*, original cast
6. *Time Out*, Dave Brubeck
7. *Camelot*, original cast
8. *Your Twist Party*, Chubby Checker
9. *Knockers Up*, Rusty Warren
10. *Judy at Carnegie Hall*, Judy Garland

1963

1. *West Side Story*, soundtrack
2. *Peter, Paul and Mary*, Peter, Paul and Mary
3. *Moving*, Peter, Paul and Mary
4. *Joan Baez in Concert*, Joan Baez
5. *I Left My Heart in San Francisco*, Tony Bennett
6. *Moon River and Other Great Movie Themes*, Andy Williams
7. *Lawrence of Arabia*, soundtrack
8. *Days of Wine and Roses*, Andy Williams
9. *Oliver*, original cast
10. *Modern Sounds in Country and Western Music, Vol. 2*, Ray Charles

1964

1. *Hello, Dolly!*, original cast
2. *In the Wind*, Peter, Paul and Mary
3. *Honey in the Horn*, Al Hirt
4. *The Barbra Streisand Album*, Barbra Streisand
5. *West Side Story*, soundtrack
6. *Peter, Paul and Mary*, Peter, Paul & Mary
7. *The Second Barbra Streisand Album*, Barbra Streisand
8. *Meet the Beatles*, Beatles
9. *The Third Barbra Streisand Album*, Barbra Streisand
10. *Moon River and Other Great Movie Themes*, Andy Williams

1965

1. *Mary Poppins*, soundtrack
2. *Beatles '65*, Beatles
3. *The Sound of Music*, soundtrack
4. *My Fair Lady*, soundtrack
5. *Fiddler on the Roof*, original cast
6. *Goldfinger*, soundtrack
7. *Hello, Dolly!*, original cast
8. *Dear Heart*, Andy Williams
9. *Introducing Herman's Hermits*, Herman's Hermits
10. *Beatles VI*, Beatles

1966

1. *Whipped Cream and Other Delights*, Herb Alpert & the Tijuana Brass
2. *The Sound of Music*, soundtrack
3. *Going Places*, Herb Alpert & the Tijuana Brass
4. *Rubber Soul*, Beatles
5. *What Now My Love*, Herb Alpert & the Tijuana Brass
6. *If You Can Believe Your Eyes and Ears*, Mamas & the Papas
7. *Dr. Zhivago*, soundtrack
8. *Revolver*, Beatles
9. *Color Me Barbra*, Barbra Streisand
10. *Ballad of the Green Berets*, S/Sgt. Barry Sadler

1967

1. *More of the Monkees*, Monkees
2. *The Monkees*, Monkees
3. *Dr. Zhivago*, soundtrack
4. *The Sound of Music*, soundtrack
5. *The Temptations' Greatest Hits*, Temptations
6. *A Man and a Woman*, soundtrack
7. *S.R.O.*, Herb Alpert & the Tijuana Brass

8. *Whipped Cream and Other Delights,* Herb Alpert & the Tijuana Brass
9. *Going Places,* Herb Alpert & the Tijuana Brass
10. *Sgt. Pepper's Lonely Hearts Club Band,* Beatles

1968

1. *Are You Experienced?,* Jimi Hendrix Experience
2. *The Graduate,* Simon & Garfunkel/soundtrack
3. *Disraeli Gears,* Cream
4. *Magical Mystery Tour,* Beatles/soundtrack
5. *Diana Ross and the Supremes' Greatest Hits,* Diana Ross & The Supremes
6. *Sgt. Pepper's Lonely Hearts Club Band,* Beatles
7. *The Doors,* The Doors
8. *Parsley, Sage, Rosemary and Thyme,* Simon & Garfunkel
9. *Vanilla Fudge,* Vanilla Fudge
10. *Blooming Hits,* Paul Mauriat & His Orchestra

1969

1. *In-a-Gadda-Da-Vida,* Iron Butterfly
2. *Hair,* original cast
3. *Blood, Sweat and Tears,* Blood, Sweat and Tears
4. *Bayou Country,* Creedence Clearwater Revival
5. *Led Zeppelin,* Led Zeppelin
6. *Johnny Cash at Folsom Prison,* Johnny Cash
7. *Funny Girl,* soundtrack
8. *The Beatles (The White Album),* Beatles
9. *Donovan's Greatest Hits,* Donovan
10. *The Association's Greatest Hits,* Association

1970

1. *Bridge over Troubled Water,* Simon & Garfunkel
2. *Led Zeppelin II,* Led Zeppelin
3. *Chicago,* Chicago
4. *Abbey Road,* Beatles
5. *Santana,* Santana
6. *Get Ready,* Rare Earth
7. *Easy Rider,* soundtrack
8. *Butch Cassidy and the Sundance Kid,* soundtrack
9. *Joe Cocker!,* Joe Cocker
10. *Three Dog Night Was Captured Live at the Forum,* Three Dog Night

1971

1. *Jesus Christ Superstar,* various artists
2. *Tapestry,* Carole King
3. *Close to You,* Carpenters
4. *Pearl,* Janis Joplin
5. *Abraxas,* Santana
6. *The Partridge Family Album,* Partridge Family
7. *Sweet Baby James,* James Taylor
8. *Tea for the Tillerman,* Cat Stevens
9. *Greatest Hits,* Sly & the Family Stone
10. *Chicago III,* Chicago

1972

1. *Harvest,* Neil Young
2. *Tapestry,* Carole King
3. *American Pie,* Don McLean
4. *Teaser and the Firecat,* Cat Stevens
5. *Hot Rocks, 1964–71,* Rolling Stones
6. *Killer,* Alice Cooper
7. *First Take,* Roberta Flack
8. *America,* America
9. *Music,* Carole King
10. *Madman Across the Water,* Elton John

1973

1. *The World Is a Ghetto,* War
2. *Summer Breeze,* Seals & Crofts
3. *Talking Book,* Stevie Wonder
4. *No Secrets,* Carly Simon
5. *Lady Sings the Blues,* Diana Ross
6. *They Only Come Out at Night,* Edgar Winter Group
7. *I Am Woman,* Helen Reddy
8. *Don't Shoot Me, I'm Only the Piano Player,* Elton John
9. *I'm Still in Love with You,* Al Green
10. *Seventh Sojourn,* Moody Blues

1974

1. *Goodbye Yellow Brick Road,* Elton John
2. *John Denver's Greatest Hits,* John Denver
3. *Band on the Run,* Paul McCartney & Wings
4. *Innervisions,* Stevie Wonder
5. *You Don't Mess Around with Jim,* Jim Croce
6. *American Graffiti,* soundtrack
7. *Imagination,* Gladys Knight & The Pips
8. *Behind Closed Doors,* Charlie Rich
9. *The Sting,* soundtrack
10. *Tres Hombres,* ZZ Top

1975

1. *Elton John—Greatest Hits,* Elton John
2. *John Denver's Greatest Hits,* John Denver
3. *That's the Way of the World,* Earth, Wind & Fire
4. *Back Home Again,* John Denver
5. *Phoebe Snow,* Phoebe Snow
6. *Heart Like a Wheel,* Linda Ronstadt
7. *Captain Fantastic and the Brown Dirt Cowboy,* Elton John
8. *An Evening with John Denver,* John Denver
9. *AWB,* Average White Band
10. *On the Border,* Eagles

1976

1. *Frampton Comes Alive,* Peter Frampton
2. *Fleetwood Mac,* Fleetwood Mac
3. *Wings at the Speed of Sound,* Wings
4. *Greatest Hits, 1971–1975,* Eagles
5. *Chicago IX—Chicago's Greatest Hits,* Chicago
6. *The Dream Weaver,* Gary Wright
7. *Desire,* Bob Dylan
8. *A Night at the Opera,* Queen
9. *History—America's Greatest Hits,* America
10. *Gratitude,* Earth, Wind & Fire

1977

1. *Rumours,* Fleetwood Mac
2. *Songs in the Key of Life,* Stevie Wonder
3. *A Star Is Born,* Barbra Streisand/Kris Kristofferson/soundtrack
4. *Hotel California,* Eagles
5. *Boston,* Boston
6. *A New World Record,* Electric Light Orchestra
7. *Part 3,* K.C. & the Sunshine Band
8. *Silk Degrees,* Boz Scaggs
9. *Night Moves,* Bob Seger & the Silver Bullet Band
10. *Fleetwood Mac,* Fleetwood Mac

1978

1. *Saturday Night Fever,* Bee Gees/various artists/soundtrack
2. *Grease,* John Travolta/Olivia Newton-John/soundtrack
3. *Rumours,* Fleetwood Mac
4. *The Stranger,* Billy Joel
5. *Aja,* Steely Dan
6. *Feels So Good,* Chuck Mangione
7. *The Grand Illusion,* Styx
8. *Simple Dreams,* Linda Ronstadt
9. *Point of Know Return,* Kansas
10. *Slowhand,* Eric Clapton

1979

1. *52nd Street,* Billy Joel
2. *Spirits Having Flown,* Bee Gees
3. *Minute by Minute,* Doobie Brothers
4. *The Cars,* The Cars
5. *Breakfast in America,* Supertramp
6. *Live and More,* Donna Summer
7. *Pieces of Eight,* Styx
8. *Bad Girls,* Donna Summer
9. *Parallel Lines,* Blondie
10. *Blondes Have More Fun,* Rod Stewart

1980

1. *The Wall,* Pink Floyd
2. *The Long Run,* Eagles
3. *Off the Wall,* Michael Jackson
4. *Glass Houses,* Billy Joel
5. *Damn the Torpedoes,* Tom Petty & the Heartbreakers
6. *Against the Wind,* Bob Seger & the Silver Bullet Band
7. *In the Heat of the Night,* Pat Benatar
8. *Eat to the Beat,* Blondie
9. *In Through the Out Door,* Led Zeppelin
10. *Kenny,* Kenny Rogers

1981

1. *Hi Infidelity,* REO Speedwagon
2. *Double Fantasy,* John Lennon & Yoko Ono
3. *Greatest Hits,* Kenny Rogers
4. *Christopher Cross,* Christopher Cross
5. *Crimes of Passion,* Pat Benatar
6. *Paradise Theatre,* Styx
7. *Back in Black,* AC/DC
8. *Voices,* Daryl Hall & John Oates
9. *Zenyatta Mondatta,* The Police
10. *The River,* Bruce Springsteen

1982

1. *Asia,* Asia
2. *Beauty and the Beat,* The Go-Go's
3. *4,* Foreigner
4. *American Fool,* John Cougar
5. *Freeze-Frame,* The J. Geils Band
6. *Escape,* Journey
7. *Get Lucky,* Loverboy
8. *Bella Donna,* Stevie Nicks
9. *Chariots of Fire,* Vangelis/soundtrack
10. *Ghost in the Machine,* The Police

1983

1. *Thriller,* Michael Jackson
2. *Business as Usual,* Men at Work
3. *Synchronicity,* The Police
4. *H2O,* Daryl Hall & John Oates
5. *1999,* Prince
6. *Lionel Richie,* Lionel Richie

7. *Jane Fonda's Workout Record,* Jane Fonda
8. *Pyromania,* Def Leppard
9. *Kissing To Be Clever,* Culture Club
10. *Olivia's Greatest Hits, Vol. 2,* Olivia Newton-John

1984

1. *Thriller,* Michael Jackson
2. *Sports,* Huey Lewis & the News
3. *Can't Slow Down,* Lionel Richie
4. *An Innocent Man,* Billy Joel
5. *Colour by Numbers,* Culture Club
6. *1984,* Van Halen
7. *Eliminator,* ZZ Top
8. *Synchronicity,* The Police
9. *Footloose,* soundtrack
10. *Seven and the Ragged Tiger,* Duran Duran

1985

1. *Born in the U.S.A.,* Bruce Springsteen
2. *Reckless,* Bryan Adams
3. *Like a Virgin,* Madonna
4. *Make It Big,* Wham!
5. *Private Dancer,* Tina Turner
6. *No Jacket Required,* Phil Collins
7. *Beverly Hills Cop,* soundtrack
8. *Suddenly,* Billy Ocean
9. *Purple Rain,* Prince & the Revolution
10. *Songs from the Big Chair,* Tears for Fears

1986

1. *Whitney Houston,* Whitney Houston
2. *Heart,* Heart
3. *Scarecrow,* John Cougar Mellencamp
4. *Afterburner,* ZZ Top
5. *Brothers in Arms,* Dire Straits
6. *Control,* Janet Jackson
7. *Welcome to the Real World,* Mr. Mister
8. *Promise,* Sade
9. *No Jacket Required,* Phil Collins
10. *Primitive Love,* Miami Sound Machine

1987

1. *Slippery When Wet,* Bon Jovi
2. *Graceland,* Paul Simon
3. *Licensed To Ill,* Beastie Boys
4. *The Way It Is,* Bruce Hornsby & the Range
5. *Control,* Janet Jackson
6. *The Joshua Tree,* U2
7. *Fore!,* Huey Lewis & the News
8. *Night Songs,* Cinderella
9. *Rapture,* Anita Baker
10. *Invisible Touch,* Genesis

1988

1. *Faith,* George Michael
2. *Dirty Dancing,* soundtrack
3. *Hysteria,* Def Leppard
4. *Kick,* INXS
5. *Bad,* Michael Jackson
6. *Appetite for Destruction,* Guns N' Roses
7. *Out of the Blue,* Debbie Gibson
8. *Richard Marx,* Richard Marx
9. *Tiffany,* Tiffany
10. *Permanent Vacation,* Aerosmith

1989

1. *Don't Be Cruel,* Bobby Brown
2. *Hangin' Tough,* New Kids on the Block
3. *Forever Your Girl,* Paula Abdul
4. *New Jersey,* Bon Jovi
5. *Appetite for Destruction,* Guns N' Roses
6. *The Raw & the Cooked,* Fine Young Cannibals
7. *GNR Lies,* Guns N' Roses
8. *Traveling Wilburys,* Traveling Wilburys
9. *Hysteria,* Def Leppard
10. *Girl You Know It's True,* Milli Vanilli

1990

1. *Janet Jackson's Rhythm Nation 1814,* Janet Jackson
2. *...But Seriously,* Phil Collins
3. *Soul Provider,* Michael Bolton
4. *Pump,* Aerosmith
5. *Please Hammer Don't Hurt 'Em,* M.C. Hammer
6. *Forever Your Girl,* Paula Abdul
7. *Dr. Feelgood,* Mötley Crüe
8. *The End of the Innocence,* Don Henley
9. *Cosmic Thing,* The B-52's
10. *Storm Front,* Billy Joel

1991

1. *Mariah Carey,* Mariah Carey
2. *No Fences,* Garth Brooks
3. *Shake Your Money Maker,* The Black Crowes
4. *Gonna Make You Sweat,* C+C Music Factory
5. *Wilson Phillips,* Wilson Phillips
6. *To the Extreme,* Vanilla Ice
7. *Please Hammer Don't Hurt 'Em,* M.C. Hammer
8. *The Immaculate Collection,* Madonna
9. *Empire,* Queensryche
10. *I'm Your Baby Tonight,* Whitney Houston

1992

1. *Ropin' the Wind,* Garth Brooks
2. *Dangerous,* Michael Jackson

3. *Nevermind*, Nirvana
4. *Some Gave All*, Billy Ray Cyrus
5. *Achtung Baby*, U2
6. *No Fences*, Garth Brooks
7. *Metallica*, Metallica
8. *Time, Love, & Tenderness*, Michael Bolton
9. *Too Legit To Quit*, Hammer
10. *Totally Krossed Out*, Kris Kross

1993

1. *The Bodyguard*, soundtrack
2. *Breathless*, Kenny G
3. *Unplugged*, Eric Clapton
4. *janet.*, Janet Jackson
5. *Some Gave All*, Billy Ray Cyrus
6. *The Chronic*, Dr. Dre
7. *Pocket Full of Kryptonite*, Spin Doctors
8. *Ten*, Pearl Jam
9. *The Chase*, Garth Brooks
10. *Core*, Stone Temple Pilots

1994

1. *The Sign*, Ace of Base
2. *Music Box*, Mariah Carey
3. *Doggystyle*, Snoop Doggy Dogg
4. *The Lion King*, soundtrack
5. *August & Everything After*, Counting Crows
6. *VS.*, Pearl Jam
7. *Toni Braxton*, Toni Braxton
8. *janet.*, Janet Jackson
9. *Bat out of Hell II: Back into Hell*, Meat Loaf
10. *The One Thing*, Michael Bolton

1995

1. *Cracked Rear View*, Hootie & The Blowfish
2. *The Hits*, Garth Brooks
3. *II*, Boyz II Men
4. *Hell Freezes Over*, Eagles
5. *Crazysexycool*, TLC
6. *Vitalogy*, Pearl Jam
7. *Dookie*, Green Day
8. *Throwing Copper*, Live
9. *Miracles: The Holiday Album*, Kenny G
10. *The Lion King* soundtrack

1996

1. *Jagged Little Pill*, Alanis Morissette
2. *Daydream*, Mariah Carey
3. *Falling into You*, Celine Dion
4. *Waiting to Exhale*, soundtrack
5. *The Score*, Fugees
6. *The Woman in Me*, Shania Twain
7. *Fresh Horses*, Garth Brooks
8. *Anthology 1*, The Beatles
9. *Cracked Rear View*, Hootie & The Blowfish
10. *Mellon Collie and the Infinite Sadness*, The Smashing Pumpkins

1997

1. *Spice*, Spice Girls
2. *Tragic Kingdom*, No Doubt
3. *Falling into You*, Celine Dion
4. *Space Jam*, soundtrack
5. *Pieces of You*, Jewel
6. *Blue*, LeAnn Rimes
7. *Bringing Down the Horse*, The Wallflowers
8. *Life After Death*, The Notorious B.I.G.
9. *Secrets*, Toni Braxton
10. *No Way Out*, Puff Daddy & The Family

1998

1. *Titanic*, soundtrack
2. *Let's Talk About Love*, Celine Dion
3. *Sevens*, Garth Brooks
4. *Backstreet Boys*, Backstreet Boys
5. *Come On Over*, Shania Twain
6. *Yourself or Someone Like You*, Matchbox 20
7. *City of Angels*, soundtrack
8. *Big Willie Style*, Will Smith
9. *Savage Garden*, Savage Garden
10. *Spiceworld*, Spice Girls

1999

1. *Millennium*, Backstreet Boys
2. *...Baby One More Time*, Britney Spears
3. *Come On Over*, Shania Twain
4. **NSync*, 'N Sync
5. *Ricky Martin*, Ricky Martin
6. *Double Live*, Garth Brooks
7. *Americana*, The Offspring
8. *Wide Open Spaces*, Dixie Chicks
9. *Significant Other*, Limp Bizkit
10. *Fanmail*, TLC

2000

1. *No Strings Attached*, 'N Sync
2. *Supernatural*, Santana
3. *The Marshall Mathers LP*, Eminem
4. *Oops!...I Did It Again*, Britney Spears
5. *Dr. Dre—2001*, Dr. Dre
6. *Human Clay*, Creed
7. *All The Way...A Decade of Song*, Celine Dion
8. *Christina Aguilera*, Christina Aguilera
9. *Millenium*, Backstreet Boys
10. *...And Then There Was X*, DMX

THE BESTSELLING ALBUMS OF ALL TIME

The Recording Industry Association of America tracks monthly album sales and awards gold and platinum certification based on the sale of 500,000 units for gold, one million units for platinum, and two million units or more for multiplatinum. Here are the albums that top the lists, organized by category, as of September 2001.

ROCK/POP

27 million
Eagles, *Their Greatest Hits, 1971-1975*, 1977

26 million
Michael Jackson, *Thriller*, 1982

23 million
Pink Floyd, *The Wall*, 1979

22 million
Led Zeppelin, *Led Zeppelin IV*, 1971

21 million
Billy Joel, *Greatest Hits, Volumes I & II*, 1985

19 million
AC/DC, *Back in Black*, 1980
The Beatles, *The Beatles*, 1968

18 million
Fleetwood Mac, *Rumours*, 1977

17 million
Whitney Houston/various artists, *The Bodyguard* soundtrack, 1992

16 million
Alanis Morissette, *Jagged Little Pill*, 1995
The Beatles, *1967-1970*, 1993
Boston, *Boston*, 1976
Eagles, *Hotel California*, 1976
Hootie & The Blowfish, *Cracked Rear View*, 1994

15 million
The Beatles, *1962-1966*, 1993
Bee Gees/various artists, *Saturday Night Fever* soundtrack, 1977
Guns N' Roses, *Appetite for Destruction*, 1987
Elton John, *Greatest Hits*, 1974
Led Zeppelin, *Physical Graffiti*, 1975
Pink Floyd, *The Dark Side of the Moon*, 1973

Bruce Springsteen, *Born in the U.S.A.*, 1984

14 million
Backstreet Boys, *Backstreet Boys*, 1997
Meatloaf, *Bat out of Hell*, 1977
Santana, *Supernatural*, 1999

13 million
Backstreet Boys, *Millenium*, 1999
Whitney Houston, *Whitney Houston*, 1985
Prince and the Revolution, *Purple Rain*, 1984
Simon & Garfunkel, *Simon & Garfunkel's Greatest Hits*, 1972
Britney Spears, *...Baby One More Time*, 1999
Bruce Springsteen, *Bruce Springsteen & the E Street Band Live, 1975–1985*, 1986

12 million
The Beatles, *Abbey Road*, 1969
Bon Jovi, *Slippery When Wet*, 1986
Boyz II Men, *II*, 1994
Phil Collins, *No Jacket Required*, 1985
Def Leppard, *Hysteria*, 1987
Led Zeppelin, *Led Zeppelin II*, 1969
Metallica, *Metallica*, 1991
various artists, *Forrest Gump* soundtrack, 1994

11 million
The Beatles, *Sgt. Pepper's Lonely Hearts Club Band*, 1967
Jewel, *Pieces of You*, 1995
Led Zeppelin, *Houses of the Holy*, 1973
Matchbox 20, *Yourself or Someone Like You*, 1996
'N Sync, *No Strings Attached*, 2000
Pearl Jam, *Ten*, 1991
James Taylor, *Greatest Hits*, 1976
TLC, *CrazySexyCool*, 1994

various artists, *Dirty Dancing* soundtrack, 1987

10 million
Aerosmith, *Aerosmith's Greatest Hits*, 1980
Mariah Carey, *Music Box*, 1993
Mariah Carey, *Daydream*, 1995
Eagles, *Eagles' Greatest Hits Volume II*, 1982
Eric Clapton, *Unplugged*, 1992
Celine Dion, *Falling into You*, 1996
Celine Dion, *Let's Talk About Love*, 1997
Doobie Brothers, *Best of the Doobies*, 1976
Green Day, *Dookie*, 1994
Journey, *Journey's Greatest Hits*, 1988
Carole King, *Tapestry*, 1971
Led Zeppelin, *Led Zeppelin*, 1969
Madonna, *Like a Virgin*, 1984
Bob Marley and the Wailers, *Legend*, 1984
George Michael, *Faith*, 1987
'N Sync, **NSYNC*, 1998
Nirvana, *Nevermind*, 1991
No Doubt, *Tragic Kingdom*, 1995
Lionel Richie, *Can't Slow Down*, 1984
U2, *The Joshua Tree*, 1987
Van Halen, *1984*, 1984
Van Halen, *Van Halen*, 1978
various artists, *The Lion King* soundtrack, 1994
ZZ Top, *Eliminator*, 1983

9 million
Ace of Base, *The Sign*, 1993
Boyz II Men, *Cooleyhighharmony*, 1991
Mariah Carey, *Mariah Carey*, 1991
Creed, *Human Clay*, 1999
Def Leppard, *Pyromania*, 1983
John Denver, *Greatest Hits*, 1973
Dire Straits, *Brothers in Arms*, 1985
Whitney Houston, *Whitney*, 1987

Billy Joel, *The Stranger,* 1977

Journey, *Escape,* 1981

Madonna, *The Immaculate Collection,* 1990

R.E.O. Speedwagon, *Hi-Infidelity,* 1982

Britney Spears, *Oops!...I Did It Again,* 2000

Tom Petty and the Heartbreakers, *Greatest Hits,* 1993

various artists, *Footloose* soundtrack, 1984

various artists, *The Great Band Era,* 1965

various artists, *Top Gun* soundtrack, 1986

8 million

Christina Aguilera, *Christina Aguilera,* 2000

Backstreet Boys, *Black & Blue,* 2000

The Beatles, *The Beatles Anthology Volume 1,* 1995

Michael Bolton, *Time, Love and Tenderness,* 1991

Toni Braxton, *Secrets,* 1996

Toni Braxton, *Toni Braxton,* 1993

Fleetwood Mac, *Greatest Hits,* 1988

Michael Jackson, *Bad,* 1987

New Kids on the Block, *Hangin' Tough,* 1988

Olivia Newton-John/John Travolta, *Grease* soundtrack, 1972

Simon & Garfunkel, *Bridge Over Troubled Water,* 1970

Smashing Pumpkins, *Mellon Collie and the Infinite Sadness,* 1996

Steve Miller Band, *Greatest Hits 1974–1978,* 1978

U2, *Achtung Baby,* 1991

Whitesnake, *Whitesnake,* 1987

COUNTRY

18 million

Shania Twain, *Come On Over,* 1997

16 million

Garth Brooks, *No Fences,* 1990

14 million

Garth Brooks, *Double Live,* 1998

Garth Brooks, *Ropin' the Wind,* 1991

12 million

Kenny Rogers, *Greatest Hits,* 1980

Shania Twain, *The Woman in Me,* 1995

11 million

Dixie Chicks, *Wide Open Spaces,* 1998

10 million

Garth Brooks, *The Hits,* 1994

9 million

Garth Brooks, *Garth Brooks,* 1989

Patsy Cline, *Greatest Hits,* 1967

Billy Ray Cyrus, *Some Gave All,* 1992

Dixie Chicks, *Fly,* 1999

8 million

Garth Brooks, *The Chase,* 1991

Garth Brooks, *In Pieces,* 1993

6 million

Garth Brooks, *Fresh Horses,* 1995

Garth Brooks, *Sevens,* 1997

Faith Hill, *Breathe,* 1999

Alan Jackson, *A Lot About Livin' (And a Little About Love),* 1992

LeAnn Rimes, *Blue,* 1996

George Strait, *Pure Country* soundtrack, 1992

5 million

Alabama, *Alabama's Greatest Hits,* 1986

Alabama, *Mountain Music,* 1982

Brooks & Dunn, *Brand New Man,* 1991

Reba McEntire, *Greatest Hits, Vol. 2,* 1993

Vince Gill, *I Still Believe in You,* 1992

Tim McGraw, *Not a Moment Too Soon,* 1994

Bonnie Raitt, *Luck of the Draw,* 1991

Kenny Rogers, *The Gambler,* 1978

George Strait, *Strait out of the Box,* 1995

Randy Travis, *Always and Forever,* 1987

Wynonna, *Wynonna,* 1992

4 million

Alabama, *Feels So Right,* 1981

Alabama, *For the Record—41 Number One Hits,* 1998

Alabama, *Roll On,* 1984

Brooks & Dunn, *Hard Workin' Man,* 1993

Deana Carter, *Did I Shave My Legs For This?,* 1996

Vince Gill, *When Love Finds You,* 1994

Faith Hill, *Faith,* 1998

Alan Jackson, *Don't Rock the Jukebox,* 1991

Alan Jackson, *Who I Am,* 1994

Alan Jackson, *Greatest Hits Collection,* 1995

Waylon Jennings, *Greatest Hits,* 1979

Tim McGraw, *Everywhere,* 1997

Reba McEntire, *For My Broken Heart,* 1991

John Michael Montgomery, *Kickin' It Up,* 1994

Anne Murray, *Greatest Hits,* 1980

Willie Nelson, *Willie and Family Live,* 1978

Willie Nelson, *Always on My Mind,* 1982

Willie Nelson, *Stardust,* 1990

Bonnie Raitt, *Nick of Time,* 1989

LeAnn Rimes, *You Light Up My Life–Inspirational Songs,* 1997

Kenny Rogers, *Ten Years of Gold,* 1978

Kenny Rogers, *20 Greatest Hits,* 1983

Hank Williams, Jr., *Greatest Hits,* 1982

various artists, *Take Me Home Country Roads,* 1973

JAZZ

12 million

Kenny G, *Breathless,* 1992

8 million

Kenny G, *Miracles,* 1994

5 million

Kenny G, *Duotones,* 1986

4 million

Kenny G, *Silhouette,* 1988

3 million

George Benson, *Breezin',* 1984

Kenny G, *Greatest Hits,* 1997

Kenny G, *Kenny G Live,* 1989

Kenny G, *The Moment,* 1996

2 million

Miles Davis, *Kind of Blue,* 1959

Platinum

George Benson, *Give Me the Night,* 1980

George Benson, *In Flight,* 1977

George Benson, *Weekend in L.A.,* 1978

Kenny G, *Gravity,* 1985

Herbie Hancock, *Future Shock,* 1983

Bob James/David Sanborn, *Double Vision,* 1991

Al Jarreau, *Breakin' Away,* 1982

Chuck Mangione, *Feels So Good,* 1977

Spyro Gyra, *Morning Dance,* 1979

various artists, *Ken Burns' Jazz: The Story of American Music,* 2000

RAP

10 million

M.C. Hammer, *Please Hammer Don't Hurt 'Em,* 1990

Notorious B.I.G., *Life After Death,* 1997

9 million

Kid Rock, *Devil Without a Cause,* 1998

Will Smith, *Big Willie Style,* 1997

2Pac, *All Eyez On Me,* 1996

2Pac, *Greatest Hits,* 1998

8 million

Beastie Boys, *Licensed To Ill,* 1986

Eminem, *The Marshall Mathers LP,* 2000

7 million

Lauryn Hill, *The Miseducation of Lauryn Hill,* 1998

Puff Daddy and The Family, *No Way Out,* 1997

Vanilla Ice, *To the Extreme,* 1990

6 million

Dr. Dre, *Dr. Dre 2001,* 1999

Fugees, *The Score,* 1996

Nelly, *Country Grammar,* 2000

TLC, *Fanmail,* 1999

5 million

DMX, *...And Then There Was X,* 1999

Limp Bizkit, *Chocolate Starfish and the Hot Dog Flavored Water,* 2000

Salt-N-Pepa, *Very Necessary,* 1993

4 million

Arrested Development, *3 Years, 5 Months and 2 Days in the Life of...,* 1992

Bone Thugs-N-Harmony, *E. 1999 Eternal,* 1995

Bone Thugs-N-Harmony, *The Art of War,* 1997

Jay-Z, *Hard Knock Life, Volume 2,* 1998

Juvenile, *400 Degreez,* 1998

Kris Kross, *Totally Krossed Out,* 1992

Makaveli, *Don Killuminati: The 7 Day Theory,* 1996

Mase, *Harlem World,* 1997

Master P, *MP Da Last Don,* 1998

Notorious B.I.G., *Ready to Die,* 1994

Snoop Doggy Dogg, *Doggystyle,* 1993

2Pac, *R U Still Down? (Remember Me),* 1997

Wu-Tang Clan, *Wu-Tang Forever,* 1997

3 million

Beastie Boys, *Ill Communication,* 1994

Beastie Boys, *Hello Nasty,* 1998

D.J. Jazzy Jeff and The Fresh Prince, *He's the D.J., I'm the Rapper,* 1988

DMX, *It's Dark and Hell is Hot,* 1997

Dr. Dre, *The Chronic,* 1992

Eminem, *Slim Shady,* 1999

Warren G., *Regulate...G Funk Era,* 1994

Hammer, *Too Legit to Quit,* 1992

Ja Rule, *Rule 3:36,* 2001

Jay-Z, *Vol. 3...Life and Times of S. Carter,* 1999

Outkast, *Stankonia,* 2000

Run-D.M.C., *Raising Hell,* 1986

2Pac, *Until the End of Time,* 2001

CLASSICAL

11 million

Titanic soundtrack, 1997

3 million

Andrea Bocelli, *Romanza,* 1997

2 million

Benedictine Monks of Santo Domingo de Silos, *Chant,* 1994

Carreras, Domingo, Pavarotti, *The Three Tenors in Concert,* 1990

1 Million

Back to Titanic soundtrack, 1998

Andrea Bocelli, *Sacred Arias,* 1999

Andrea Bocelli, *Sogno,* 1999

Wendy Carlos, *Switched on Bach,* 1986

Carreras, Domingo, Pavarotti with Mehta, *The Three Tenors in Concert 1994,* 1994

Charlotte Church, *Dream a Dream,* 2000

Luciano Pavarotti, *O Holy Night,* London, 1985

Royal Philharmonic Orchestra, *Hooked on Classics,* 1982

Piotr Tchaikovsky performed by Van Cliburn with the RCA Symphony Orchestra/Kirill Kondrashin, *Piano Concerto No. 1 in B-flat Minor, Op. 23,* 1982

Various artists, *250 Years of Great Music—Bach to Bernstein,* 1992

THE ROCK OF AGES: PEOPLE'S FAVORITE 50

Steve Dougherty was PEOPLE's chief music writer from 1985 to 2001. Here is his list of the 50 albums he'd stock in his personal jukebox.

ATLANTIC R&B 1947–1974 (1991)
Various artists
Before they named it Rock, it was spelled R&B. A chest of pop's buried treasures.

AT THE FILMORE EAST (1979)
The Allman Brothers Band
Soulful sibs Duane and Gregg Allman unveil their new invention, Southern Rock, before a crowd of appreciative Yankees in a watershed New York City live show.

THE BAND (1969)
The Band
Rock 'n' roll's Great American Novel came with a backbeat and Robbie Robertson's story songs, as told by Richard Manuel, Levon Helm, and Rick Danko.

THE BEATLES (1968)
The Beatles
From the classic rock of the opening track to the electronica precursor "Revolution No. 9," the legendary White Album plays like a modern pop history lesson taught by four Fab profs.

ODELAY (1996)
Beck
An album from pop's beat-crazy, wordy rapping kid, Beck Hansen

(no relation to the Oklahoma teen trio), that shows off his heightened senses of rhythm and humor.

CHUCK BERRY'S GOLDEN HITS (1967)
Chuck Berry
The brown-eyed handsome man told Tchaikovsky the news: There is indeed such a thing as a three-minute masterpiece.

MERMAID AVENUE (1998)
Billy Bragg & Wilco
Brit singer Bragg and the country punks of Wilco give a posthumous present to folk icon Woodie Guthrie: a sparkling pop album of the troubadour's wondrous, and previously unsung, songs.

THE RISE AND FALL OF ZIGGY STARDUST AND THE SPIDERS FROM MARS (1972)
David Bowie
Music had never glittered quite like this before and glam rock never sounded so good again.

20 ALL-TIME GREATEST HITS! (1991)
James Brown
You'll feel good! But then, you knew that you would.

LONDON CALLING (1979)
The Clash
They pronounced rock dead,

then celebrated its resurrection on this, a double album without a lame cut in the lot.

MY AIM IS TRUE (1977)
Elvis Costello
He looked punk, acted mean, sounded nasty, and hit right on target in his album debut.

LAYLA AND OTHER ASSORTED LOVE SONGS (1970)
Derek and the Dominoes
Eric Clapton and Duane Allman. 'Nuff said.

THE CHRONIC (1992)
Dr. Dre (with Snoop Doggy Dogg)
Hip-hop's auteur and his pet rapper share their bemused family values.

BRINGING IT ALL BACK HOME (1965), **HIGHWAY 61 REVISITED** (1965), **TIME OUT OF MIND** (1997)
Bob Dylan
For all who question the lasting fuss over the rheumy rock laureate, three masterworks.

I NEVER LOVED A MAN (THE WAY I LOVE YOU) (1967)
Aretha Franklin
They invented soul so she could be queen.

Beck, *Odelay*

Nirvana, *Nevermind*

U2, *Achtung Baby*

WHAT'S GOING ON (1971)
Marvin Gaye
Motown's sex star made hearts and minds quicken with this ambitious song cycle.

ARE YOU EXPERIENCED? (1967)
Jimi Hendrix Experience
That voice. Those songs. That guitar. We're still asking, "Where did this guy come from?"

ARTHUR (DECLINE AND FALL OF THE BRITISH EMPIRE) (1969),
MUSWELL HILLBILLIES (1971)
The Kinks
Tommy without the pretensions: these are two of plaintive mod genius Ray Davies's brilliantly realized theme albums.

ORIGINAL GOLDEN HITS, VOLS. 1 AND 2 (1969)
Jerry Lee Lewis
Killer tracks from The Killer: All is forgiven.

GROOVIEST 17 ORIGINAL HITS (1959)
Little Richard
"Good Golly Miss Molly," "Tutti Fruiti," "Lucille," "Long Tall Sally," "Rip It Up." Macon, Ga.'s absolutely fabulous former dishwasher screamed 'em all to life at New Orleans's Specialty Records studio.

COURT AND SPARK (1974)
Joni Mitchell
The ultimate chick singer whips one on the boys.

MOBY GRAPE (1967)
Moby Grape
San Francisco's one-masterpiece wonder squeezed all their juice into this ignored collection.

AMERICAN BEAUTY (1970)
The Grateful Dead
Haight-Ashbury's free-form improvisational space cowboys shelve the jams and craft an aptly titled musical masterpiece.

THE BEST OF VAN MORRISON (1990)
Van Morrison
Romance for the soul.

NEVERMIND (1991)
Nirvana
Full of as much old-fashioned tube amplifier feedback as neo-

---

THE 10 MOST OVERRATED ALBUMS

For those contrarians who would rather smash discs than play them, here is a flip-side list of legendary nonlegends in the annals of rock.

SLIPPERY WHEN WET (1986)
Bon Jovi
Hair metal pin-up star Jon Bon Jovi's was the pretty face that helped sell many millions of copies of a mediocre album filled with lyric clichés and generic power chords.

4 WAY STREET (1971)
Crosby, Stills, Nash and Young
They could have used a stop sign.

THE DOORS (1967)
The Doors
As an icon, Jim Morrison can't be beat; but his great looks, leather pants, and lucrative afterlife make people forget he was a mediocre singer and pretentious poet masquerading as a rock star.

USE YOUR ILLUSION I & II (1991)
Guns N' Roses
Out the year punk pretender Axl Rose was rendered irrelevant by the real thing (Kurt Cobain), these two simultaneously released, gibberishly titled albums smelled like a teen record buyer rip-off.

UNTITLED (1971)
Led Zeppelin
The album that gave us "Stairway to Heaven" and other artifacts of arena-ready blowhard rock.

(WHAT'S THE STORY) MORNING GLORY? (1995)
Oasis
They like to compare themselves to the Beatles and Stones but prove with this album's lame lyrics and hand-me-down sound to be in the same league with neither.

ELVIS (TV SPECIAL) (1968)
Elvis Presley
The gig that was trumpeted as his

return to '50s form. Leatherclad in Vegas a year after the Summer of Love, The King was already out of touch with current culture and his music.

THE DREAM OF THE BLUE TURTLES (1985)
Sting
The Police man lured listeners with his pop status, then stung them with stingy jazz.

TOMMY (1969)
The Who
Maybe if Pete had left it to critics to call his own composition "A Rock Opera," it wouldn't make us want to gag.

MODERN R&B
Soulful self-expression is the creed of the great R&B singers of yore. Today's poor imitators, from Mariah Carey to the Backstreet Boys, caterwaul trite lyrics over clichéd arrangements to achieve the appearance, but not the true grit, of emotion. Call it artificial soul.

punk martyr Kurt Cobain's fabled rage, this is a call to get with it for all classic rock-fixated geezers who insist that the music ain't what it used to be.

TEAR THE ROOF OFF (1993)
Parliament Funkadelic
So they did, and something memorable was born.

THE SUN SESSIONS (1987),
ELVIS' GOLDEN RECORDS, VOL. 1
(1958)
Elvis Presley
Rock and roll at its best.

1999 (1982)
Prince
From when he had a name and all the critics loved him in New York, and everywhere else.

MURMUR (1983)
R.E.M.
The debut album that brought "Radio Free Europe" to the promised land. What's it about? Who knows? Who cares?

HISTORY OF OTIS REDDING (1968)
Otis Redding
The greatest soul ever told.

TIM (1985)
The Replacements
Put "Swingin' Party" on replay, never let it stop.

BEGGAR'S BANQUET (1968),
STICKY FINGERS (1971),
THE SINGLES COLLECTION (1989)
The Rolling Stones
The first two are mid-career classics. In the last, an obscure collection of mostly mono, many never released in the U.S. singles, finds the Stones paying tribute to their black American heroes.

NEVER MIND THE BOLLOCKS, HERE'S THE SEX PISTOLS (1977)
Sex Pistols
Unlistenable then, unbeatable now, it mocks, it taunts, it screams, and you can dance to it!

BACK TO MONO (1991)
Phil Spector
Actually four CDs, offering unforgettable visits by (mostly) girl groups to the little man's Great Wall of Sound.

BORN TO RUN (1975)
Bruce Springsteen
The Boss as rock and roll tradesman, redefining the exuberant yearning to get out on the highway with a guitar strapped 'cross his back.

STORYTELLER (Boxed Set, 1992)
Rod Stewart
Remember that before he turned out the lights and cuddled up to the Manilow inside him, Rod the mod was an underrated lyricist who rivaled Van Morrison in the U.K. soul crooner department.

HITSVILLE USA: THE MOTOWN SINGLES COLLECTION (1992)
The Supremes, The Four Tops, Smokey Robinson and The Miracles, The Jackson Five, The Temptations, et al.
The soundtrack of the '60s, courtesy of Detroit's big wheel, Berry Gordy. (And it's got Mary Wells and Marvin Gaye, too.)

TALKING HEADS 77 (1977)
Talking Heads
Leading the punk revolt from these shores, art school misfit David Byrne makes his bow as one of rock's strangest, and most talented, characters.

ACHTUNG BABY (1991)
U2
The Dubliners finally drop the earnest façade, as well as the endlessly repeated rhythm guitar riff that launched them and deliver a sonic treat recorded in the cold war capital of Berlin.

MEATY BEATY BIG AND BOUNCY (1971)
The Who
Known for their big productions, including the overrated *Tommy* and underrated *Quadrophenia*, the London mods rocked Top 40 radio with these high explosives.

SUMMER TEETH (1999)
Wilco
Pop go the country rockers and craft an edgy masterpiece.

CAR WHEELS ON A GRAVEL ROAD (1998)
Lucinda Williams
The Lake Charles, Louisiana, native takes listeners on a musically and emotionally rich journey through the scarred by-ways of her heartland.

AFTER THE GOLD RUSH (1970)
Neil Young
One nugget from four brilliant decades of work by the once and current rocker.

HIP-HOP RULES

Hip-hop has become such a dominant cultural and commercial force that even mainstream superstars have gotten jiggy with this once underground music. To wit:

CARLOS SANTANA Yes, he's a genius and a legend, but it was "Maria Maria," penned by Wyclef Jean that brought Carlos to the kids.

BRITNEY SPEARS/'N SYNC They (thankfully) don't rap, but these teen acts have a lot of hip-hop and R&B in their sound.

BRUCE SPRINGSTEEN The rhythm track pushing "Streets of Philadelphia" is pure hip-hop.

MADONNA An old Public Enemy beat (borrowed from James Brown) serves as the melody line for her hit "Justify My Love."

KORN/KID ROCK/LIMP BIZKIT/POD/PAPA ROACH ET AL This whole new breed of rap-meets-rock wouldn't exist without Run-DMC's "Rock Box" or "King of Rock" back in the mid-'80s.

AEROSMITH These veteran rockers were washed up and strung out until Run-DMC re-did "Walk This Way" with them in 1986.

BECK Sampling music from a variety of sources and making it your own? Hmmm, sounds like you know what.

RAP: ESSENTIAL LISTENING

From its early days in New York City to its dominance worldwide, hip-hop has become a force of nature and culture. Rap started out as a singles phenomenon and morphed into albums by the mid '80s, and certain of those albums are required listening for every fan or wannabe. Here is an admittedly subjective (and short) must-have list of rap and R&B compiled by PEOPLE reviewer Amy Linden.

THE CHRONIC (1993)
Dr. Dre
He introduced what he called The Era of G Funk with a funkadelic feel that made Compton, Calif., the center of rap and Dre a star producer.

RUN-DMC (1983)
Run-DMC
This groundbreaking group and smart record revolutionized the style (from flamboyant outfits to jeans and untied Adidas) and esthetic of rap (adding rock guitars and serious lyrics).

THE LOW END THEORY (1991)
A Tribe Called Quest
With this, its second CD, a truly visionary act made the rap-jazz connection clear and funky.

IT TAKES A NATION OF MILLIONS TO HOLD US BACK (1988)
Public Enemy
Agitprop meets sonic boom to create a CD that still reverberates.

PAID IN FULL (1986)
Eric B. and Rakim
DJ Eric B. brought the soul beats, and rapper Rakim showed why he has few peers.

DE LA SOUL IS DEAD (1991)
De La Soul
After introducing their light-hearted and whimsical style in "D.A.I.S.Y. Age," De La Soul added darkness and menace on this brilliant second album.

AMERIKKA'S MOST WANTED (1990)
Ice Cube
Cube's first solo trip was a synthesis of the rap styles of the musically esoteric East coast and the gang-fixated West coast.

READY TO DIE (1994)
The Notorious B.I.G.
A thug poet with a playa's leer, Biggie established himself as one of the greats right from this explosive debut.

PAUL'S BOUTIQUE (1989)
Beastie Boys
Adding live instrumentation to the cut-and-paste, they took sampling to dizzying and influential heights.

THE MARSHALL MATHERS LP (2000)
Eminem
Love him or hate him, this Dre protégé sold a staggering 1.75 million copies his first week and proved himself the Kurt Cobain of hip-hop, an in-your-face spokesman for disenfranchised white youth.

VOL. 2...HARD KNOCK LIFE (1998)
Jay-Z
One of the top lyricists of the '90s, Jigga broke into the mainstream with some sampling help from, of all sources, the *Annie* orphans of Broadway.

STRAIGHT OUTTA COMPTON (1989)
N.W.A.
This was the introduction of Eazy-E, Dre, and Ice Cube, not to mention the soundtrack to the subsequent L.A. riots.

GREAT ADVENTURES OF SLICK RICK (1988)
Slick Rick
He's one of rap's most beloved characters as well as its best storyteller.

CRIMINAL MINDED (1986)
Boogie Down Productions
KRS-One and the late Scott LaRock delivered a tough, literate record that was a precursor of "gangsta rap."

MAMA SAID KNOCK YOU OUT (1990)
LL Cool J
A star at 16, then washed up, LL unleashed this comeback at 21 and reaffirmed his status as rap's most poetic sex symbol.

ENTER THE WU-TANG: 36 CHAMBERS (1993)
Wu-Tang Clan
This was the introduction to the world of future solo stars Method Man, Ghostface Killah, Raekwon, and ODB aided by RZA's baroque production.

BLACKOUT! (1999)
Method Man/Redman
Two of the best team up for a smoked-out paean to the pleasures of performing stoned.

STRAIGHT OUT THE JUNGLE (1998)
Jungle Brothers
Mixing afrocentricity and house, the JBs introduced the Native Tongues movement, a hippy-esque call for a return to simpler values and nonmaterialism.

HARDCORE (1996)
Lil' Kim
Kim's full-frontal wordplay, as raunchy as it gets, changed the rules for female rappers.

FULL CLIP (1999)
Gang Starr
Underrated and underground, DJs Primer and Guru married jazz and soul to produce street-tough, rugged rhymes.

THE 50 BEST COUNTRY ALBUMS

PEOPLE's Randy Vest touts this country-album starter set, but it hurts his achy-breaky heart to leave out Webb Pierce, Ernest Tubb, Kitty Wells, Bob Wills, among many others.

THE BEST OF EDDY ARNOLD (1967)
Eddy Arnold
The Tennessee Plowboy shows his smoother side on these (mostly) '60s tracks.

THINKIN' PROBLEM (1994)
David Ball
Among a sea of hat acts, Ball's topper stands out in the crowd, thanks to this twangy tour de force.

KILLIN' TIME (1989)
Clint Black
An incredible, play-it-over-and-over-again debut that garnered Black five No. 1 singles.

NO FENCES (1990)
Garth Brooks
Pure, heartfelt songs recorded just before Garth became GARTH.

HIGH AND DRY (1991)
Marty Brown
Of all the pretenders to Hank's throne, Brown is the real deal.

COME ON COME ON (1992)
Mary Chapin Carpenter
A blissful fusion of country, folk, and rock from the "hometown girl."

I FELL IN LOVE (1990)
Carlene Carter
After years of dabbling in rock, June Carter and Carl Smith's little girl finds her roots in country.

JOHNNY CASH AT FOLSOM PRISON (1968)
Johnny Cash
Cash's live performance for a throng of inmates remains a milestone. "Folsom Prison Blues" can still evoke chills.

KING'S RECORD SHOP (1987)
Rosanne Cash
Produced by then hubby Rodney Crowell, this Grammy-winning album is right on the money.

THE PATSY CLINE STORY (1963)
Patsy Cline
Sublime sounds from country's high priestess of female vocalists.

DIAMONDS AND DIRT (1988)
Rodney Crowell
Singer-songwriter Crowell hit a home run with this critically lauded and commercially successful release.

GUITAR TOWN (1986)
Steve Earle
Rough-housin' Earle found himself a spot on country's crowded map with this inspired outing.

THE BEST OF LEFTY FRIZZELL (1991)
Lefty Frizzell
His style influenced everyone from Willie to Merle to George Jones. Here's the evidence.

WHEN I CALL YOUR NAME (1989)
Vince Gill
The sweetest pipes this side of heaven, caressing material that's just as heavenly.

CHISELED IN STONE (1987)
Vern Gosdin
A hard-edged voice that's packed with pathos.

TRIO (1987)
Emmylou Harris, Dolly Parton, Linda Ronstadt
Three distinct song stylists in a perfect, harmonious blend.

DOWN EVERY ROAD 1962–1994 (1996)
Merle Haggard
A four-disc anthology shows why the Hag is one of country's enduring legends.

HIGHWAYMAN (1985)
The Highwaymen (Johnny Cash, Waylon Jennings, Kris Kristofferson, Willie Nelson)
An inspired collaboration between some of country's elder statesmen.

ROCKIN' IN THE COUNTRY: THE BEST OF WANDA JACKSON (1990)
Wanda Jackson
From rockabilly to Nash-pop, Jackson growls and purrs up a storm.

SHE THINKS I STILL CARE: THE GEORGE JONES COLLECTION (1997)
George Jones
A two-disc set chronicling Jones's often overlooked years with the United Artists label in the '60s.

THE JUDDS (WYNONNA & NAOMI) (1984)
The Judds
Wynonna and her mater never sounded quite as honest or engaging after this memorable debut.

PICKIN' ON NASHVILLE (1989)
Kentucky Headhunters
Raucous rock from the Bluegrass State's (and Arkansas') impish, redneck sons.

SHADOWLAND (1988)
k.d. lang
Lang teams up with legendary producer Owen Bradley to create studio magic.

ANTHOLOGY 1956–80 (1991)
Brenda Lee
The songs are mostly pop, but the pipes are pure country all the way.

20 GREATEST HITS (1987)
Loretta Lynn
From givin' a carousin' hubby what-fer to wardin' off a would-be man-stealer, the coal miner's daughter is a tough lady to top.

GOLDEN HITS (1965)
Roger Miller
The King of the Road's loopy takes on booze, buffalo, and Britain.

COUNTRY MUSIC HALL OF FAME (1991)
Bill Monroe
The father of bluegrass and his mandolin. Need we say more?

LEAVE THE LIGHT ON (1989)
Lorrie Morgan
George Morgan's daughter takes center stage and stakes a claim on country's landscape.

WHY LADY WHY (1983)
Gary Morris
A voice of operatic strength surrounding some mighty sturdy songs.

JUST LIKE OLD TIMES (1992)
Heather Myles
A rousing, Bakersfield-influenced sleeper by a dynamic singer.

RED HEADED STRANGER (1975)
Willie Nelson
Bare-bones country by the genre's celebrated redneck outlaw.

WILL THE CIRCLE BE UNBROKEN (1972)
The Nitty Gritty Dirt Band
An historic summit with the likes of Roy Acuff and Mother Maybelle Carter.

THE NEW NASHVILLE CATS (1991)
Mark O'Connor
The country fiddler/classical composer is joined by some 50 heavyweight pickers on this Grammy-winning set.

'80S LADIES (1987)
K. T. Oslin
Sassy and bittersweet songs truthfully sung by a seasoned survivor.

THE BUCK OWENS COLLECTION, 1959–1990 (1992)
Buck Owens
Three CDs worth of classic tunes from the king of the Bakersfield sound and his stalwart Buckaroos.

THE COMPLETE '50S MASTERS (1992)
Elvis Presley
The King's earliest sides (8 CDs!) before Hollywood and mediocrity beckoned.

THE ESSENTIAL RAY PRICE, 1951–62 (1991)
Ray Price
Raw performances from the man once known as the "Cherokee Cowboy" who later found success crooning pop-styled ballads.

FOUR WALLS: THE LEGEND BEGINS (1991)
Jim Reeves
An early, mostly harder-edged Reeves, already showing signs of that vocal "touch of velvet."

THE ESSENTIAL MARTY ROBBINS, 1951–82 (1991)
Marty Robbins
The King of the Balladeers lends his distinct tenor to storytelling songs and country-pop.

WHAT A WOMAN WANTS TO HEAR (1991)
Dawn Sears
Shamefully overlooked powerhouse vocalist whose followup, *Nothin' but Good*, was equally as memorable.

THE ESSENTIAL CONNIE SMITH (1996)
Connie Smith
One of country's greatest female singers of the '60s, '70s, or for that matter, any decade.

STRAIT OUT OF THE BOX (1995)
George Strait
From a winning 16-year career, here are the cream of the crop.

STORMS OF LIFE (1986)
Randy Travis
With this debut album, Travis helped to restore country music's heart and soul. He's never equalled it.

THE VERY BEST OF CONWAY TWITTY (1978)
Conway Twitty
Once called "the best friend a song ever had," Twitty put his own indelible stamp on the country genre.

KEVIN WELCH (1990)
Kevin Welch
Call it alterna-country. This singer-songwriter from Oklahoma brings a poet's sensibility to his work.

THE ESSENTIAL DOTTIE WEST (1996)
Dottie West
West's husky vocals were never better than on these defining 1960s and '70s tracks.

I WONDER DO YOU THINK OF ME (1989)
Keith Whitley
The title cut alone by the late, lamented Whitley will break your heart.

40 GREATEST HITS (1978)
Hank Williams
The Daddy...the King... the Master.

ANNIVERSARY: TWENTY YEARS OF HITS (1987)
Tammy Wynette
Wynette conveys more pain in "Til I Get it Right" than most artists can in their entire repertoire.

GUITARS, CADILLACS, ETC., ETC. (1986)
Dwight Yoakam
California honky-tonk collides with Nashville tradition. A rouser of a debut.

JAZZ: ESSENTIAL LISTENING

Not encyclopedic or definitive, this is simply a list of 50 marvelous jazz albums. The recordings here date from the '20s to the '90s, and they cover a range of styles. Any jazz purist, or for that matter, impurist, will find sins of omission and commission on this list. All we—the jazz jury at PEOPLE—can say is that these albums have enriched our lives immeasurably and given us an almost embarrassing amount of pleasure. To us, these recordings are the easiest sort of listening, full of wit, passion, invention, and beauty.

Cannonball Adderly	*Live at the Jazz Workshop* (1959); reissued as *The Cannonball Adderley Quintet in San Francisco*
Louis Armstrong	*Hot Fives and Sevens,* Vol. II or III (1926–27)
Chet Baker	*My Funny Valentine* (1954)
Count Basie	*The Original American Decca Recordings* (1937–39)
Bix and Tram Beiderbecke	*The Bix Beiderbecke Story,* Vol. II (1927–28)
Art Blakey & The Jazz Messengers	*Moanin'* (1958)
Clifford Brown and Max Roach	*Clifford Brown and Max Roach* (1954–55)
Betty Carter	*Betty Carter* (1966)
Ray Charles	*The Birth of Soul: The Complete Atlantic Rhythm & Blues Recordings 1952–1959* (1991)
Nat King Cole	*Nat King Cole* (1992)
Ornette Coleman	*The Shape of Jazz to Come* (1959–60)
Ornette Coleman	*Free Jazz* (1960)
John Coltrane	*Coltrane* (1957)
John Coltrane	*A Love Supreme* (1964)
Miles Davis	*Birth of the Cool* (1957)
Miles Davis	*Milestones* (1958)
Miles Davis	*Kind of Blue* (1959)
Miles Davis	*Miles Smiles* (1966)
Miles Davis and Gil Evans	*Porgy and Bess* (1958)
Eric Dolphy	*Out to Lunch* (1964)
Duke Ellington	*The Blanton-Webster Band* (1940-42)

Duke Ellington & The Jungle Band	*Rockin' in Rhythm,* Vol. III (1929–31)
Bill Evans	*The Village Vanguard Sessions* (1961)
Art Farmer	*Something to Live For* (1987)
Ella Fitzgerald	*The Gershwin Songbook* (1959)
Ella Fitzgerald	*The Intimate Ella* (1960)
Tommy Flanagan	*Ballads and Blues* (1979)
Bill Frisell	*This Land* (1994)
Errol Garner	*Concert by the Sea* (1956/1987)
Stan Getz/Joao Gilberto	*Getz/Gilberto* (1964)
Benny Goodman	*Carnegie Hall Concert* (1938)
Charlie Haden Quartet West	*Haunted Heart* (1992)
Lionel Hampton	*The Complete Lionel Hampton* (1937–41)
Herbie Hancock	*Maiden Voyage* (1965)
Coleman Hawkins	*Body and Soul: The Complete Coleman Hawkins,* Vol. I (1929–40)
Fletcher Henderson and Don Redman	*Developing an American Orchestra, 1923–1937* (1923–37)
Billie Holiday	*The Quintessential Billie Holiday,* Vol. III, IV, or V (1937–39)
James P. Johnson	*Snowy Morning Blues* (1930, 1944)
Abbey Lincoln	*The World Is Falling Down* (1990)
Charles Mingus	*Mingus Ah Um* (1960)
Charles Mingus	*The Black Saint and the Sinner Lady* (1963)

Modern Jazz Quartet (1956/1987)	*The Complete Last Concert*	Bud Powell	*The Amazing Bud Powell*, Vol. I (1949–51)
Thelonious Monk	*The Unique Thelonious Monk* (1956)	Bud Powell	*The Genius of Bud Powell* (1951)
Thelonious Monk	*Alone in San Francisco* (1959)	Sonny Rollins	*Saxophone Colossus* (1956)
		John Scofield	*Time on My Hands* (1989)
Thelonious Monk	*Monk's Dream* (1962)	Art Tatum	*The Tatum Solo Masterpieces*, Vol. III (1953–55)
Gerry Mulligan	*What Is There to Say?* (1958–59)		
Oliver Nelson	*Blues and the Abstract Truth* (1961)	Cecil Taylor	*Unit Structures* (1966)
King Oliver	*King Oliver's Jazz Band 1923* (1923)	Sarah Vaughan and Clifford Brown	*Sarah Vaughan with Clifford Brown* (1954)
		Fats Waller	*The Joint Is Jumpin'* (1929–43)
Charlie Parker	*The Charlie Parker Story* (1945)	Lester Young	*The Complete Lester Young* (1943–44)
Charlie Parker (with Dizzy Gillespie, Max Roach, Bud Powell, and Charles Mingus)	*The Greatest Jazz Concert Ever* (1953)		

JAZZ TODAY

A new generation of stars is emerging in jazz. Steeped in tradition, technically prodigious, often daring, and always fired by the energy and passion of youth, they are a formidable lot, as varied in style as they are united in their allegiance to the verities of swing, the blues, and improvisation. Here are some standout albums by the the new school.

Geri Allen, *Twenty One* (1994)
(piano)

James Carter, *The Real Quietstorm* (1995)
(saxophone/flute/clarinet)

Paquito D'Rivera, *Come on Home* (1995)

Marty Ehrlich, *Can You Hear a Motion?* (1994)
(various instruments)

Kenny Garrett, *Triology* (1995)
(alto sax)

Javon Jackson, *For One Who Knows* (1995)
(saxophone)

Hank Jones and Charlie Haden, *Steal Away: Spirituals, Hymns, and Folk Songs* (1995)
(piano; bass)

Leroy Jones, *Mo' Cream from the Crop* (1994)
(trumpet)

Abbey Lincoln, *Who Used to Dance* (1997)

Joe Lovano, *Celebrating Sinatra* (1997)

Wynton Marsalis, *Live at the Village Vanguard* (1999)

Abbey Lincoln, *A Turtle's Dream* (1994)
(vocals)

Marcus Printup, *Song for the Beautiful Woman* (1995)
(trumpet)

Joshua Redman, *Wish* (1993)

Eric Reed, *The Swing and I* (1995)
(piano)

Poncho Sanchez, *Conga Blue* (1996)

Jacky Terrasson, *Jacky Terrasson* (1995)
(piano)

Steve Turre, *Rhythm Within* (1995)
(trombone)

Cassandra Wilson, *Blue Skies* (1988)
(vocals)

50 GREAT CLASSICAL RECORDINGS

We can't really presume to pick a classical library for all tastes, but PEOPLE's editors will hazard this tendentious consensus of outstanding recordings.

Johann Sebastian Bach	*Brandenburg Concertos*, Munich Bach Orchestra/Karl Richter
Johann Sebastian Bach	*The Well-Tempered Clavier*, BWV 846-893, Davitt Moroney
Samuel Barber	*Adagio for Strings*, Saint Louis Symphony Orchestra/Leonard Slatkin
Béla Bartók	*String Quartets Nos. 1–6*, Emerson Quartet
Ludwig van Beethoven	*Symphonies Nos. 1–9, Complete Cycles*, Berlin Philharmonic/Herbert von Karajan
Ludwig van Beethoven	*Piano Sonata in C Minor, Op. 13, "Pathétique,"* Wilhelm Kempff
Ludwig van Beethoven	*Piano Sonata in C-sharp Minor, Op. 27, No. 2, "Moonlight,"* Wilhelm Kempff
Hector Berlioz	*Symphonie fantastique*, French National Radio Orchestra/Sir Thomas Beecham
Leonard Bernstein	*Chichester Psalms*, John Paul Bogart; Camerata Singers, New York Philharmonic/Leonard Bernstein
Georges Bizet	*Carmen*, Agnes Baltsa, José Carreras; Chorus of the Paris Opéra, Berlin Philharmonic/Herbert von Karajan
Johannes Brahms	*Violin Concerto in D, Op. 77,* Itzhak Perlman; Chicago Symphony Orchestra/Carlo Maria Giulini
Benjamin Britten	*War Requiem, Op. 66*, Lorna Haywood, Anthony Rolfe Johnson, Benjamin Luxon; Atlanta Boy Choir, Atlanta Symphony Orchestra & Chorus/Robert Shaw
Frédéric Chopin	*26 Preludes*, Dmitri Alexeev
Aaron Copland	*Appalachian Spring*, New York Philharmonic/Leonard Bernstein
Claude Debussy	*Images*, Claudio Arrau
Antonín Dvořák	*Symphony No. 9 in E Minor, Op. 95, "From the New World,"* London Symphony Orchestra/István Kertész
César Franck	*Symphony in D Minor*, Berlin Radio Symphony Orchestra/Vladimir Ashkenazy
George Gershwin	*Rhapsody in Blue*, Columbia Symphony Orchestra, New York Philharmonic/Leonard Bernstein
George Gershwin	*Porgy and Bess,* Willard White, Leona Mitchell; Cleveland Orchestra & Chorus/Lorin Maazel
George Frideric Handel	*Messiah*, Heather Harper, Helen Watts, John Wakefield, John Shirley-Quirk; London Symphony Orchestra & Choir/Sir Colin Davis
Joseph Haydn	*Symphonies Nos. 93-104, "London,"* Royal Concertgebouw Orchestra/Sir Colin Davis
Joseph Haydn	*String Quartets, Op. 76, "Erdödy,"* Takács Quartet
Charles Ives	*Three Places in New England*, Boston Symphony Orchestra/Michael Tilson Thomas
Franz Liszt	*Les Préludes*, Philadelphia Orchestra/Riccardo Muti
Gustav Mahler	*Symphony No. 9 in D*, Vienna Philharmonic/Bruno Walter
Felix Mendelssohn	*Violin Concerto in E Minor, Op. 64,* Kyung Wha Chung; Montreal Symphony Orchestra/ Charles Dutoit

Wolfgang Amadeus Mozart	*Symphony No. 41 in C, K. 551, "Jupiter,"* Columbia Symphony Orchestra/Bruno Walter
Wolfgang Amadeus Mozart	*A Little Night Music, K. 525*, Prague Chamber Orchestra/Sir Charles Mackerras
Wolfgang Amadeus Mozart	*The Marriage of Figaro*, Samuel Ramey, Lucia Popp; London Opera Chorus, London Philharmonic Orchestra/Sir George Solti
Wolfgang Amadeus Mozart	*Don Giovanni*, Eberhard Wächter, Joan Sutherland, Elisabeth Schwarzkopf; Philharmonia Orchestra & Chorus/Carlo Maria Giulini
Modest Mussorgsky	*Pictures at an Exhibition*, Montreal Symphony Orchestra/Charles Dutoit
Giacomo Puccini	*La Bohème*, Mirella Freni, Luciano Pavarotti; Chorus of the Deutsche Oper Berlin, Berlin Philharmonic/Herbert von Karajan
Sergei Prokofiev	*Symphony No. 1 in D, Op. 25, "Classical,"* Berlin Philharmonic/Herbert von Karajan
Sergei Rachmaninoff	*Piano Concerto No. 2 in C Minor, Op. 18*, Vladimir Ashkenazy; London Symphony Orchestra/André Previn
Nikolai Rimsky-Korsakov	*Scheherazade, Op. 35*, Royal Concertgebouw Orchestra/Kirill Kondrashin
Gioacchino Rossini	*The Barber of Seville*, Leo Nucci, William Matteuzzi, Cecilia Bartoli; Chorus & Orchestra of the Teatro Comunale di Bologna/Giuseppe Patanè
Camille Saint-Saëns	*The Carnival of the Animals*, Montreal Symphony Orchestra, London Sinfonietta/ Charles Dutoit
Domenico Scarlatti	*Keyboard Sonatas*, Vladimir Horowitz
Arnold Schoenberg	*Verklärte Nacht (Transfigured Night), Op. 4*, Jiri Najnar, Vaclav Bernasek; Talich Quartet
Franz Schubert	*Die Schöne Müllerin, D. 795; Winterreise, D. 911*, Dietrich Fischer-Dieskau, Gerald Moore
Robert Schumann	*Op. 19, "Carnaval: Pretty Scenes on Four Notes,"* Artur Rubinstein
Dmitri Shostakovich	*Symphony No. 5 in D Minor, Op. 47*, Royal Concertgebouw Orchestra/Bernard Haitink
Jean Sibelius	*Symphony No. 5 in E-flat, Op. 82*, Boston Symphony Orchestra/Sir Colin Davis
Igor Stravinsky	*The Rite of Spring*, New York Philharmonic, Cleveland Orchestra/Pierre Boulez
Piotr Ilyich Tchaikovsky	*Symphony No. 6 in B Minor, Op. 74, "Pathétique,"* Leningrad Philharmonic/Evgeny Mravinsky
Piotr Ilyich Tchaikovsky	*Piano Concerto No. 1 in B-flat Minor, Op. 23*, Van Cliburn; RCA Symphony Orchestra/Kirill Kondrashin
Giuseppe Verdi	*Requiem*, Elisabeth Schwarzkopf, Christa Ludwig, Nicolai Gedda, Nicolai Ghiaurov; Philharmonia Orchestra & Chorus/Carlo Maria Giulini
Giuseppe Verdi	*La Traviata*, Joan Sutherland, Luciano Pavarotti; London Opera Chorus, National Philharmonic Orchestra/Richard Bonynge
Antonio Vivaldi	*Concertos for Violin, Strings, and Continuo, Op. 8, Nos. 1–4, "The Four Seasons,"* Alan Loveday; Academy of St. Martin-in-the-Fields/Sir Neville Marriner
Richard Wagner	*The Ring of the Nibelung*, Birgit Nilsson, Wolfgang Windgassen; Chorus & Orchestra of the Bayreuth Festival/Karl Böhm

CLIFFS' CLUES TO OPERA PLOTS

Opera is drama expressed musically, verbally, and visually—the ultimate experience for ears, eyes, and emotions. If you're intimidated by the prospect of sitting through three or more hours of heightened drama in a foreign language, but are intrigued by the passionate, mysterious world of divas and Don Juans, start here, with our summaries of 10 classics. (Dates given indicate the first staged production.)

THE BARBER OF SEVILLE (1782)

Composed by Gioacchino Rossini, text by Sterbini. Based on the novel by Beaumarchais. Set in Seville, Spain, in the 17th century.

Count Almaviva, a Grandee of Spain, loves Rosina, the young ward and bride-to-be of Dr. Bartolo. With the help of Figaro, the town barber and busybody, the Count enters his rival's home disguised as a drunken soldier, then as a music teacher. Having gained access to Rosina, he easily persuades her to take his hand. Almaviva then convinces a notary, procured by Bartolo for his own marriage to Rosina, to marry him to Rosina in Bartolo's absence.

LA BOHÈME (1896)

Composed by Giacomo Puccini, text by Luigi Illica and Giuseppe Giacosa. Based on the novel Scènes de la vie de Bohème *by Henri Murger. Set in Paris, France, in the 17th century.*

Rodolfo, a poet, lives in the Latin Quarter of Paris with his dear friends—a painter, a philosopher, and a musician—who defy their hunger with cheerfulness and pranks. The quartet of friends is so poor that they resort to burning Rodolfo's poetry to keep warm. But Rodolfo's heart is soon warmed by the frail and consumptive Mimi, who knocks on his door one night, her candle extinguished by a winter draft. The two fall in love, but Mimi grows weaker and weaker. Eventually, her sickness and Rodolfo's overprotectiveness drive the two apart. Mimi's last request is to return to Rodolfo's attic room, where they first met, and where she will die in his arms.

DON CARLOS (1867)

Composed by Giuseppe Verdi, text by G. Méry and C. du Locle. Based on the play by Friedrich von Schiller. Set in France and Spain, during the Spanish Inquisition.

Don Carlos, infante of Spain, is torn between a futile love for Queen Elizabeth, his stepmother, to whom he was once engaged, and a fierce desire to bring freedom to Flanders, a Protestant country under Spanish (Catholic) domain. The queen's attendant, who is deeply in love with Carlos, tells the king, untruthfully, that Carlos and Elizabeth have been unfaithful to him. Carlos is sent to death, ostensibly for demanding to be let go to Flanders. Elizabeth remains at her husband's side, and Carlos escapes his death in the last moments of the opera, saved by the King's father, who takes Carlos into the cloister.

DON GIOVANNI (1787)

Composed by Wolfgang Amadeus Mozart, text by Lorenzo da Ponte. Based on the text Il Convitato *by Giovanni Bertati. Set in Seville at the end of the 18th century.*

The insatiable lover, Don Juan, jaunts from lass to lass, breaking hearts and wreaking havoc before he is finally dragged into Hell by the statue of the Commendatore who he killed in a duel after attempting to seduce his daughter, Doña Anna.

ELEKTRA (1909)

Composed by Richard Strauss, text by Hugo von Hofmannsthal. Adapted from the play by Sophocles. Set in ancient Mycenae.

Her soul withered by grief, Elektra is bent on avenging the seven-year-old murder of her father, Agamemnon, at the hands of her mother, Klytämnestra, and her mother's lover, Aegisth. Elektra persuades her brother Orest to murder Klytämnestra and Aegisth. The murders send Elektra into a dance of joy that becomes a frenzied dance of death, ending in the explosion of her heart.

LUCIA DI LAMMERMOOR (1835)

Composed by Gaetano Donizetti, text by Salvatore Cammarano. Based on the novel The Bride of Lammermoor *by Sir Walter Scott. Set in Scotland in 1700.*

Her mother's death is slowly but inexorably driving the tragic Lucia to madness. She loves Edgardo, but their promised union is sabotaged by her brother, who forces her to marry Arturo, a wealthy man she does not love. Tormented by visions of ghosts and spirits and devastated over the loss of Edgardo, Lucia murders her groom on their wedding night, then experiences a series of hallucinations before collapsing and dying of a broken heart.

RIGOLETTO (1851)

Composed by Giuseppe Verdi, text by Francesco Maria Piave. Based on Victor Hugo's Le Roi s'amuse. *Set Mantua, Italy, in the 16th century.*

Rigoletto, a court jester, intends to have the Duke of Mantua murdered for seducing his daughter, Gilda, but brings about the murder of the girl, instead.

The first of a "romantic trilogy," *Rigoletto* is followed by *Il Trovotore* and *La Traviata*.

TOSCA (1900)

Composed by Giacomo Puccini, text by Giuseppe Giacosa and Luigi Illica. Based on the play La Tosca *by Victorien Sardou. Set in Rome, in 1800.*

Floria Tosca, a prima donna, is passionately pursued by the evil Scarpia, chief of the Roman police. Yet Tosca loves Cavaradossi, a painter and a liberal patriot. She attempts to save her lover from execution when he is accused of aiding a fugitive, by pretending to yield to Scarpia's wishes, then killing him. But her actions unwittingly help to destroy her true love, Cavaradossi.

LA TRAVIATA (1853)

Composed by Giuseppe Verdi, text by Francesco Maria Piave. Based on Alexandre Dumas's play La Tame aux Camélias. *Set in Paris and vicinity in 1850.*

Violetta, a courtesan, renounces her life of pleasure in order to be with her gentlemanly lover, Alfredo. But Alfredo's father persuades Violetta that she is a blight on his family and that she must leave Alfredo for the good of his career. She returns to her former protector, with whom Alfredo fights a duel. Alfredo is subsequently forced to flee the country, and will return only to find Violetta dying of consumption.

TRISTAN AND ISOLDE (1865)

Composed and written by Richard Wagner. Set in a ship at sea, in England, and in Ireland, in a legendary time.

Tristan is dispatched to Ireland by his uncle, King Marke, to win him Isolde's hand. Yet Tristan and Isolde have long loved one another, each believing their love to be unrequited. On board the vessel that brings them to Cornwall, they drink what they believe to be a death potion, but is in fact a love potion. King Marke later discovers them in a midnight embrace. Tristan, wounded by one of the king's knights, flees to France. Isolde follows, finds him dying, and she too dies by his side.

THE WORLD'S LARGEST OPERA HOUSES

These houses showcase the world's best singers and stand as monuments to the grandeur of opera.

Opera House	Location	Total Capacity
The Metropolitan Opera	New York, NY	4,065
Cincinnati Opera	Cincinnati, OH	3,630
Lyric Opera of Chicago	Chicago, IL	3,563
San Francisco Opera	San Francisco, CA	3,476
The Dallas Opera	Dallas, TX	3,420

THE GRAMMY AWARDS

Even more so than most award-giving bodies, the National Academy of Recording Arts and Sciences has switched, added, deleted, and renamed its various award categories on a regular basis. The following chart gathers the majority of continuing categories that honor mainstream musical achievement. This means you won't find the awards for polka or jacket liner notes, but you will find years of musical greats (and electorate gaffes) in an easy-to-follow format.

	1958	1959	1960
Record of the Year	Domenico Modugno, "Nel Blu Dipinto Di Blu (Volare)"	Bobby Darin, "Mack the Knife"	Percy Faith, "Theme from *A Summer Place*"
Album of the Year	Henry Mancini, *The Music from Peter Gunn*	Frank Sinatra, *Come Dance with Me*	Bob Newhart, *Button Down Mind*
Song of the Year	Domenico Modugno, "Nel Blu Dipinto Di Blu (Volare)"	Jimmy Driftwood, "The Battle of New Orleans"	Ernest Gold, "Theme from *Exodus*"
Pop Vocal, Female	Ella Fitzgerald, *Ella Fitzgerald Sings the Irving Berlin Song Book*	Ella Fitzgerald, "But Not for Me"	Ella Fitzgerald, *Mack the Knife, Ella in Berlin*
Pop Vocal, Male	Perry Como, "Catch a Falling Star"	Frank Sinatra, *Come Dance with Me*	Ray Charles, *Genius of Ray Charles*
New Artist	—	Bobby Darin	Bob Newhart
Pop Vocal, Duo or Group with Vocal	Louis Prima and Keely Smith, "That Old Black Magic"	Mormon Tabernacle Choir, "Battle Hymn of the Republic"	Eydie Gormé and Steve Lawrence, "We Got Us"
Rhythm and Blues Song	Champs, "Tequila"	Dinah Washington, "What a Diff'rence a Day Makes"	Ray Charles, "Let the Good Times Roll"
Jazz, Soloist	—	Ella Fitzgerald, *Ella Swings Lightly*	—
Jazz, Group	Count Basie, *Basie*	Jonah Jones, *I Dig Chicks*	André Previn, *West Side Story*
Jazz, Big Band/ Large Ensemble Performance	—	—	Henry Mancini, *The Blues and the Beat*
Folk Recording	—	Kingston Trio, *The Kingston Trio at Large*	Harry Belafonte, *Swing Dat Hammer*
Cast Show Album	*The Music Man*	*Porgy and Bess*	*The Sound of Music*
Comedy Recording (Spoken Word/Musical)	David Seville, "The Chipmunk Song"	Shelley Berman, *Inside Shelley Berman*; Homer & Jethro, *The Battle of Kookamonga*	Bob Newhart, *Button Down Mind Strikes Back*; Paul Weston and Jo Stafford, *Jonathan and Darlene Edwards in Paris*
Classical Orchestral Performance	Felix Slatkin, Hollywood Bowl Symphony, *Gaîeté Parisienne*	Charles Munch, conductor, Boston Symphony, *Debussy: Images for Orchestra*	Fritz Reiner, conductor, Chicago Symphony, *Bartók: Music for Strings, Percussion and Celeste*
Opera Recording	Roger Wagner Chorale, *Virtuoso*	Erich Leinsdorf, conductor, Vienna Philharmonic, *Mozart: The Marriage of Figaro*	Erich Leinsdorf, conductor, Rome Opera House Chorus and Orchestra, *Puccini: Turandot* (Solos: Tebaldi, Nilsson, Bjoerling, Tozzi)
Chamber Music Performance	Hollywood String Quartet, *Beethoven: Quartet 130*	Artur Rubinstein, *Beethoven: Sonata No. 21 in C, Op. 53; "Waldstein" Sonata No. 18 in E Flat, Op. 53, No. 3*	Laurindo Almeida, *Conversations with the Guitar*

	1961	**1962**	**1963**
Record of the Year	Henry Mancini, "Moon River"	Tony Bennett, "I Left My Heart in San Francisco"	Henry Mancini, "The Days of Wine and Roses"
Album of the Year	Judy Garland, *Judy at Carnegie Hall*	Vaughn Meader, *The First Family*	Barbra Streisand, *The Barbra Streisand Album*
Song of the Year	Henry Mancini and Johnny Mercer, "Moon River"	Leslie Bricusse and Anthony Newley, "What Kind of Fool Am I"	Johnny Mercer and Henry Mancini, "The Days of Wine and Roses"
(Pop) Vocal, Female	Judy Garland, *Judy at Carnegie Hall*	Ella Fitzgerald, *Ella Swings Brightly with Nelson Riddle*	Barbra Streisand, *The Barbra Streisand Album*
(Pop) Vocal, Male	Jack Jones, "Lollipops and Roses"	Tony Bennett, "I Left My Heart in San Francisco"	Jack Jones, "Wives and Lovers"
New Artist	Peter Nero	Robert Goulet	Swingle Singers
Pop Vocal, Duo or Group with Vocal	Lambert, Hendricks & Ross, *High Flying*	Peter, Paul & Mary, "If I Had a Hammer"	Peter, Paul & Mary, "Blowin' in the Wind"
Rhythm and Blues Song	Ray Charles, "Hit the Road, Jack"	Ray Charles, "I Can't Stop Loving You"	Ray Charles, "Busted"
Jazz, Soloist/Small Group	André Previn, *André Previn Plays Harold Arlen*	Stan Getz, *Desafinado*	Bill Evans, *Conversations with Myself*
Jazz, Big Band/Large Ensemble Performance	Stan Kenton, *West Side Story*	Stan Kenton, *Adventures in Jazz*	Woody Herman Band, *Encore: Woody Herman, 1963*
Contemporary Folk	Belafonte Folk Singers, *Belafonte Folk Singers at Home and Abroad*	Peter, Paul & Mary, "If I Had a Hammer"	Peter, Paul & Mary, "Blowin' in the Wind"
Cast Show Album	*How To Succeed in Business Without Really Trying*	*No Strings*	*She Loves Me*
Comedy Recording	Mike Nichols and Elaine May, *An Evening with Mike Nichols and Elaine May*	Vaughn Meader, *The First Family*	Allen Sherman, *Hello Mudduh, Hello Faddah*
Classical Album	Igor Stravinsky, conductor, Columbia Symphony, *Stravinsky Conducts, 1960: Le Sacre du Printemps; Petruchka*	Vladimir Horowitz, *Columbia Records Presents Vladimir Horowitz*	Benjamin Britten, conductor, London Symphony Orchestra and Chorus, *Britten: War Requiem*
Classical Orchestral Performance	Charles Munch, conductor, Boston Symphony, *Ravel: Daphnis et Chloe*	Igor Stravinsky, conductor, Columbia Symphony, *Stravinsky: The Firebird Ballet*	Erich Leinsdorf, conductor, Boston Symphony, *Bartók: Concerto for Orchestra*
Opera Recording	Gabriele Santini, conductor, Rome Opera Chorus and Orchestra, *Puccini: Madama Butterfly*	Georg Solti, conductor, Rome Opera House Orchestra and Chorus (Solos: Price, Vickers, Gorr, Merrill, Tozzi), *Verdi: Aïda*	Erich Leinsdorf, conductor, RCA Italiana Orchestra and Chorus (Solos: Price, Tucker, Elias), *Puccini: Madama Butterfly*
Chamber Music Performance	Jascha Heifetz, Gregor Piatigorsky, William Primrose, *Beethoven: Serenade, Op. 8; Kodaly: Duo for Violin & Cello, Op. 7*	Jascha Heifetz, Gregor Piatigorsky, William Primrose, *The Heifetz-Piatigorsky Concerts with Primrose, Pennario and Guests*	Julian Bream Consort, *An Evening of Elizabethan Music*

	1964	**1965**	**1966**
Record of the Year	Stan Getz and Astrud Gilberto, "The Girl from Ipanema"	Herb Alpert & The Tijuana Brass, "A Taste of Honey"	Frank Sinatra, "Strangers in the Night"
Album of the Year	Stan Getz and Joao Gilberto, *Getz/Gilberto*	Frank Sinatra, *September of My Years*	Frank Sinatra, *Sinatra: A Man & His Music*
Song of the Year	Jerry Herman, "Hello, Dolly!"	Paul Francis Webster and Johnny Mandel, "The Shadow of Your Smile (Love Theme from *The Sandpiper*)"	John Lennon and Paul McCartney, "Michelle"
Pop Vocal, Female	Barbra Streisand, "People"	Barbra Streisand, *My Name Is Barbra*	Eydie Gorme, "If He Walked into My Life"
Pop Vocal, Male	Louis Armstrong, "Hello, Dolly!"	Frank Sinatra, "It Was a Very Good Year"	Frank Sinatra, "Strangers in the Night"
Rock Vocal Female, Male	Petula Clark, "Downtown"	Petula Clark, "I Know a Place"; Roger Miller, "King of the Road"	Paul McCartney, "Eleanor Rigby"
New Artist	The Beatles	Tom Jones	—
Pop Vocal, Duo or Group	The Beatles, *A Hard Day's Night*	Anita Kerr Quartet, *We Dig Mancini*	Anita Kerr Quartet, "A Man and a Woman"
Rock Performance, Duo or Group with Vocal	—	Statler Brothers, "Flowers on the Wall"	The Mamas & The Papas, "Monday, Monday"
Rhythm and Blues Song	Nancy Wilson, "How Glad I Am"	James Brown, "Papa's Got a Brand New Bag"	Ray Charles, "Crying Time"
R&B Vocal	—	—	Ray Charles, "Crying Time"
R&B Duo or Group with Vocal	—	—	Ramsey Lewis, "Hold It Right There"
Country Song	Roger Miller, "Dang Me"	Roger Miller, "King of the Road"	Bill Sherrill and Glenn Sutton, "Almost Persuaded"
Country Vocal, Female	Dottie West, "Here Comes My Baby"	Jody Miller, "Queen of the House"	Jeannie Seely, "Don't Touch Me"
Country Vocal, Male	Roger Miller, "Dang Me"	Roger Miller, "King of the Road"	David Houston, "Almost Persuaded"
Jazz, Group	Stan Getz, *Getz/Gilberto*	Ramsey Lewis Trio, *The "In" Crowd*	Wes Montgomery, *Goin' Out of My Head*
Jazz, Big Band/ Large Ensemble Performance	Laurindo Almeida, *Guitar from Ipanema*	Duke Ellington Orchestra, *Ellington '66*	—
Gospel Performance, Duo, Group, Choir or Chorus	—	George Beverly Shea and Anita Ker Quartet, *Southland Favorites*	Porter Wagoner & the Blackwood Bros., *Grand Old Gospel*
Folk Recording	Gale Garnett, *We'll Sing in the Sunshine*	Harry Belafonte, Miriam Makeba, *An Evening with Belafonte/Makeba*	Cortelia Clark, *Blues in the Street*
Cast Show Album	*Funny Girl*	*On a Clear Day You Can See Forever*	*Mame*
Comedy Recording	Bill Cosby, *I Started Out as a Child*	Bill Cosby, *Why Is There Air?*	Bill Cosby, *Wonderfulness*

1964 · 1965 · 1966

	1964	1965	1966
Classical Album	Leonard Bernstein, conductor, New York Philharmonic, *Bernstein: Symphony No. 3*	Vladimir Horowitz, *Horowitz at Carnegie Hall: An Historic Return*	Morton Gould conductor, Chicago Symphony, *Ives: Symphony No. 1 in D Minor*
Classical Orchestral Performance	Erich Leinsdorf, conductor, Boston Symphony, *Mahler: Symphony No. 5 in C Sharp Minor*; Berg: *Wozzeck Excerpts*	Leopold Stokowski, conductor, American Symphony, *Ives: Symphony No. 4*	Erich Leinsdorf, conductor, Boston Symphony, *Mahler: Symphony No. 6 in A Minor*
Opera Recording	Herbert von Karajan, conductor, Vienna Philharmonic and Chorus (Solos: Price, Corelli, Merrill, Freni), *Bizet: Carmen*	Karl Bohm, conductor, Orchestra of German Opera, Berlin, (Solos: Fischer-Dieskau, Lear, Wunderlich), *Berg: Wozzeck*	Georg Solti, conductor, Vienna Philharmonic (Solos: Nilsson, Crespin, Ludwig, King, Hotter), *Wagner: Die Walküre*
Chamber Music Performance	Jascha Heifetz, Gregor Piatigorsky (Jacob Lateiner, piano), *Beethoven: Trio No. 1 in E Flat, Op. 1, No. 1*	Juilliard String Quartet, *Bartók: The Six String Quartets*	Boston Symphony Chamber Players, *Boston Symphony Chamber Players*

1967 · 1968 · 1969

	1967	1968	1969
Record of the Year	5th Dimension, "Up, Up and Away"	Simon & Garfunkel, "Mrs. Robinson"	5th Dimension, "Aquarius/Let the Sunshine In"
Album of the Year	The Beatles, *Sgt. Pepper's Lonely Hearts Club Band*	Glen Campbell, *By the Time I Get to Phoenix*	Blood, Sweat & Tears, *Blood, Sweat & Tears*
Song of the Year	Jim Webb, "Up, Up and Away"	Bobby Russell, "Little Green Apples"	Joe South, "Games People Play"
Pop Vocal, Female	Bobbie Gentry, "Ode to Billie Joe"	Dionne Warwick, "Do You Know the Way To San Jose"	Peggy Lee, "Is That All There Is"
Pop Vocal, Male	Glen Campbell, "By the Time I Get to Phoenix"	José Feliciano, "Light My Fire"	Harry Nilsson, "Everybody's Talkin"
New Artist	Bobbie Gentry	José Feliciano	Crosby, Stills & Nash
Pop Vocal	5th Dimension, "Up, Up and Away"	Simon & Garfunkel, "Mrs. Robinson"	5th Dimension, "Aquarius/Let the Sunshine In"
Rock Performance, Duo or Group	5th Dimension, "Up, Up and Away"	—	—
Rhythm and Blues Song	Aretha Franklin, "Respect"	Otis Redding and Steve Cropper, "(Sittin' On) the Dock of the Bay"	Richard Spencer, "Color Him Father"
R&B Vocal, Female	Aretha Franklin, "Respect"	Aretha Franklin, "Chain of Fools"	Aretha Franklin, "Share Your Love With Me"
R&B Vocal, Male	Lou Rawls, "Dead End Street"	Otis Redding, "(Sittin' On) the Dock of the Bay"	Joe Simon, "The Chokin' Kind"

	1967	**1968**	**1969**
R&B Duo or Group with Vocal	Sam & Dave, "Soul Man"	The Temptations, "Cloud Nine"	The Isley Brothers, "It's Your Thing"
Country Song	John Hartford, "Gentle on My Mind"	Bobby Russell, "Little Green Apples"	Shel Silverstein, "A Boy Named Sue"
Country Vocal, Female	Tammy Wynette, "I Don't Wanna Play House"	Jeannie C. Riley, "Harper Valley P.T.A."	Tammy Wynette, "Stand By Your Man"
Country Vocal, Male	Glen Campbell, "Gentle on My Mind"	Johnny Cash, "Folsom Prison Blues"	Johnny Cash, "A Boy Named Sue"
Country Performance, Duo or Group with Vocal	Johnny Cash and June Carter, "Jackson"	Flatt & Scruggs, "Foggy Mountain Breakdown"	Waylon Jennings & The Kimberlys, "MacArthur Park"
Jazz, Group	Cannonball Adderley Quintet, *Mercy, Mercy, Mercy*	Bill Evans Trio, *Bill Evans at the Montreux Jazz Festival*	Wes Montgomery, *Willow Weep For Me*
Jazz, Big Band/ Large Ensemble Performance	Duke Ellington, *Far East Suite*	Duke Ellington, *And His Mother Called Him Bill*	Quincy Jones, "Walking in Space"
Gospel Performance, Duo, Group, Choir or Chorus	Porter Wagoner & The Blackwood Bros. Quartet, *More Grand Old Gospel*	Happy Goodman Family, *The Happy Gospel of the Happy Goodmans*	Porter Wagoner & the Blackwood Bros., *In Gospel Country*
Folk Recording	John Hartford, "Gentle on My Mind"	Judy Collins, "Both Sides Now"	Joni Mitchell, *Clouds*
Cast Show Album	*Cabaret*	*Hair*	*Promises, Promises*
Comedy Recording	Bill Cosby, *Revenge*	Bill Cosby, *To Russell, My Brother, Whom I Slept With*	Bill Cosby, *The Best of Bill Cosby*
Classical Album	Pierre Boulez, conductor, Orchestra and Chorus of Paris National Opera (Solos: Berry, Strauss, Uhl, Doench), *Berg: Wozzeck;* Leonard Berstein, conductor, London Symphony, *Mahler: Symphony No. 8 in E Flat Major ("Symphony of a Thousand")*	—	Walter Carlos, *Switched-On Bach*
Classical Orchestral Performance	Igor Stravinsky, conductor, Columbia Symphony, *Stravinsky: Firebird & Petrouchka Suites*	Pierre Boulez, conductor, New Philharmonic Orchestra, *Boulez Conducts Debussy*	Pierre Boulez, conductor, Cleveland Orchestra, *Boulez Conducts Debussy, Vol. 2: "Images Pour Orchestre"*
Opera Recording	Pierre Boulez, conductor, Orchestra and Chorus of Paris National Opera (Solos: Berry, Strauss, Uhl, Doench), *Berg: Wozzeck*	Erich Leinsdorf, conductor, New Philharmonic Orchestra and Ambrosian Opera Chorus (Soloists: Price, Troyanos, Raskin, Milnes, Shirley, Flagello), *Mozart: Cosi fan tutte*	Herbert von Karajan, conductor, Berlin Philharmonic (Soloists: Thomas, Stewart, Stolze, Dernesch, Keleman, Dominguez, Gayer, Ridderbusch), *Wagner: Siegfried*
Chamber Music Performance	Ravi Shankar and Yehudi Menuhin, *West Meets East*	E. Power Biggs with Edward Tarr Brass Ensemble and Gabrieli Consort, Vittorio Negri, conductor, *Gabrieli: Canzoni for Brass, Winds, Strings & Organ*	The Philadelphia, Cleveland, and Chicago Brass Ensembles, *Gabrieli: Antiphonal Music of Gabrieli (Canzoni for Brass Choirs)*

	1970	**1971**	**1972**
Record of the Year	Simon & Garfunkel, "Bridge Over Troubled Water"	Carole King, "It's Too Late"	Roberta Flack, "The First Time Ever I Saw Your Face"
Album of the Year	Simon & Garfunkel, *Bridge Over Troubled Water*	Carole King, *Tapestry*	George Harrison and Friends (Ravi Shankar, Bob Dylan, Leon Russell, Ringo Starr, Billy Preston, Eric Clapton, Klaus Voorman, others), *The Concert for Bangladesh*
Song of the Year	Paul Simon, "Bridge Over Troubled Water"	Carole King, "You've Got a Friend"	Ewan MacColl, "The First Time Ever I Saw Your Face"
Pop Vocal, Female	Dionne Warwick, "I'll Never Fall In Love Again"	Carole King, "Tapestry"	Helen Reddy, "I Am Woman"
Pop Vocal, Male	Ray Stevens, "Everything Is Beautiful"	James Taylor, "You've Got a Friend"	Nilsson, "Without You"
New Artist	The Carpenters	Carly Simon	America
Pop Vocal, Duo or Group with Vocal	Carpenters, "Close to You"	Carpenters, *Carpenters*	Roberta Flack and Donny Hathaway, "Where Is the Love"
Rhythm and Blues Song	Ronald Dunbar, General Johnson, "Patches"	Bill Withers, "Ain't No Sunshine"	Barrett Strong and Norman Whitfield, "Papa Was a Rolling Stone"
R&B Vocal, Female	Aretha Franklin, "Don't Play That Song"	Aretha Franklin, "Bridge Over Troubled Water"	Aretha Franklin, "Young, Gifted & Black"
R&B Vocal, Male	B.B. King, "The Thrill Is Gone"	Lou Rawls, "A Natural Man"	Billy Paul, "Me and Mrs. Jones"
R&B Duo or Group with Vocal	The Delfonics, "Didn't I (Blow Your Mind This Time)"	Ike and Tina Turner, "Proud Mary"	The Temptations, "Papa Was a Rolling Stone"
Country Song	Marty Robbins, "My Woman, My Woman, My Wife"	Kris Kristofferson, "Help Me Make It Through the Night"	Ben Peters, "Kiss an Angel Good Mornin' "
Country Vocal, Female	Lynn Anderson, "Rose Garden"	Sammi Smith, "Help Me Make It Through the Night"	Donna Fargo, "Happiest Girl in the Whole U.S.A."
Country Vocal, Male	Ray Price, "For the Good Times"	Jerry Reed, "When You're Hot, You're Hot"	Charley Pride, *Charley Pride Sings Heart Songs*
Country Performance, Duo or Group with Vocal	Johnny Cash and June Carpenter, "If I Were a Carpenter"	Conway Twitty and Loretta Lynn, "After the Fire Is Gone"	The Statler Brothers, "Class of '57"
Traditional Blues Recording	T-Bone Walker, "Good Feelin' "	Muddy Waters, *They Call Me Muddy Waters*	Muddy Waters, *The London Muddy Waters Session*
Jazz, Soloist	—	Bill Evans, *The Bill Evans Album*	Gary Burton, *Alone at Last*
Jazz, Group	Bill Evans, *Alone*	Bill Evans Trio, *The Bill Evans Album*	Freddie Hubbard, *First Light*
Jazz, Big Band/ Large Ensemble Performance	Miles Davis, *Bitches Brew*	Duke Ellington, *New Orleans Suite*	Duke Ellington, *Togo Brava Suite*
Gospel Performance, Duo, Group, Choir or Chorus	Oak Ridge Boys, "Talk About the Good Times"	Charley Pride, "Let Me Live"	Blackwood Brothers, *L-O-V-E*
Cast Show Album	*Company*	*Godspell*	*Don't Bother Me, I Can't Cope*
Comedy Recording	Flip Wilson, *The Devil Made Me Buy This Dress*	Lily Tomlin, *This Is a Recording*	George Carlin, *FM & AM*

	1970	1971	1972
Classical Album	Colin Davis, conductor, Royal Opera House Orchestra and Chorus (Solos: Vickers, Veasey Lindholm), *Berlioz: Les Troyens*, Philips	Vladimir Horowitz, *Horowitz Plays Rachmaninoff*	Georg Solti, conductor, Chicago Symphony, Vienna Boys Choir, Vienna State Opera Chorus, Vienna Singverein Chorus and soloists, *Mahler: Symphony No. 8 in E Flat Major (Symphony of a Thousand)*
Classical Orchestral Performance	Pierre Boulez, conductor, Cleveland Orchestra, *Stravinsky: Le Sacre du printemps*	Carlo Maria Giulini, conductor, Chicago Symphony, *Mahler: Symphony No. 1 in D Major*	Georg Solti, conductor, Chicago Symphony, *Mahler: Symphony No. 7 in E Minor*
Opera Recording	Colin Davis, conductor, Royal Opera House Orchestra and Chorus (Solos: Vickers, Veasey, Lindholm), *Berlioz: Les Troyens*	Erich Leinsdorf, conductor, London Symphony and John Alldis Choir (Solos: Price, Domingo, Milnes, Bumbry, Raimondi), *Verdi: Aïda*	Colin Davis, conductor, BBC Symphony/Chorus of Covent Garden (Solos: Gedda, Eda-Pierre, Soyer, Berbie), *Berlioz: Benvenuto Cellini*
Chamber Music Performance	Eugene Istomin, Isaac Stern, Leonard Rose, *Beethoven: The Complete Piano Trios*	Juilliard Quartet, *Debussy: Quartet in G Minor/Ravel: Quartet in F Major*	Julian Bream and John Williams, *Julian & John*

	1973	1974	1975
Record of the Year	Roberta Flack, "Killing Me Softly with His Song"	Olivia Newton-John, "I Honestly Love You"	Captain & Tennille, "Love Will Keep Us Together"
Album of the Year	Stevie Wonder, *Innervisions*	Stevie Wonder, *Fulfillingness' First Finale*	Paul Simon, *Still Crazy After All These Years*
Song of the Year	Norman Gimbel and Charles Fox, "Killing Me Softly with His Song"	Marilyn and Alan Bergman, Marvin Hamlisch, "The Way We Were"	Stephen Sondheim, "Send In the Clowns"
Pop Vocal, Female	Roberta Flack, "Killing Me Softly with His Song"	Olivia Newton-John, "I Honestly Love You"	Janis Ian, "At Seventeen"
Pop Vocal, Male	Stevie Wonder, "You Are the Sunshine of My Life"	Stevie Wonder, *Fulfillingness' First Finale*	Paul Simon, *Still Crazy After All These Years*
New Artist	Bette Midler	Marvin Hamlisch	Natalie Cole
Pop Vocal, Duo or Group with Vocal	Gladys Knight & The Pips, "Neither One of Us (Wants To Be the First To Say Goodbye)"	Paul McCartney & Wings, "Band on the Run"	Eagles, "Lyin' Eyes"
Rhythm and Blues Song	Stevie Wonder, "Superstition"	Stevie Wonder, "Living for the City"	H. W. Casey, Richard Finch, Willie Clarke, and Betty Wright, "Where Is the Love"
R&B Vocal, Female	Aretha Franklin, "Master of Eyes"	Aretha Franklin, "Ain't Nothing Like the Real Thing"	Natalie Cole, "This Will Be"
R&B Vocal, Male	Stevie Wonder, "Superstition"	Stevie Wonder, "Boogie On Reggae Woman"	Ray Charles, "Living for the City"

1973   1974   1975

	1973	1974	1975
R&B Duo or Group with Vocal	Gladys Knight & The Pips, "Midnight Train to Georgia"	Rufus, "Tell Me Something Good"	Earth, Wind & Fire, "Shining Star"
Country Song	Kenny O'Dell, "Behind Closed Doors"	Norris Wilson and Bill Sherrill, "A Very Special Love Song"	Chips Moman and Larry Butler, "(Hey Won't You Play) Another Somebody Done Somebody Wrong Song"
Country Vocal, Female	Olivia Newton-John, "Let Me Be There "	Anne Murray, "Love Song"	Linda Ronstadt, "I Can't Help It (If I'm Still in Love with You)"
Country Vocal, Male	Charlie Rich, "Behind Closed Doors"	Ronnie Milsap, "Please Don't Tell Me How the Story Ends"	Willie Nelson, "Blue Eyes Crying in the Rain"
Country Performance, Duo or Group with Vocal	Kris Kristofferson and Rita Coolidge, "From the Bottle to the Bottom"	The Pointer Sisters, "Fairytale"	Kris Kristofferson and Rita Coolidge, "Lover Please"
Traditional Blues Recording	Doc Watson, *Then and Now*	Doc and Merle Watson, *Two Days in November*	Muddy Waters, *The Muddy Waters Woodstock Album*
Jazz, Soloist	Art Tatum, *God Is in the House*	Charlie Parker, *First Recordings!*	Dizzy Gillespie, *Oscar Peterson and Dizzy Gillespie*
Jazz, Group	Supersax, *Supersax Plays Bird*	Oscar Peterson, Joe Pass, and Niels Pedersen, *The Trio*	Return to Forever featuring Chick Corea, *No Mystery*
Jazz, Big Band/ Large Ensemble Performance	Woody Herman, *Giant Steps*	Woody Herman, *Thundering Herd*	Phil Woods with Michel Legrand & His Orchestra, *Images*
Cast Show Album	*A Little Night Music*	*Raisin*	*The Wiz*
Comedy Recording	Cheech & Chong, *Los Cochinos*	Richard Pryor, *That Nigger's Crazy*	Richard Pryor, *Is It Something I Said?*
Classical Album	Pierre Boulez, conductor, New York Philharmonic, *Bartók: Concerto for Orchestra*	Georg Solti, conductor, Chicago Symphony, *Berlioz: Symphonie Fantastique*	Georg Solti, conductor, Chicago Symphony, *Beethoven: Symphonies (9) Complete*
Classical Orchestral Performance	Pierre Boulez, conductor, New York Philharmonic, *Bartók: Concerto for Orchestra*	Georg Solti, conductor, Chicago Symphony, *Berlioz: Symphonie Fantastique*	Pierre Boulez, conductor, New York Philharmonic, *Ravel: Daphnis et Chloë*
Opera Recording	Leonard Bernstein, conductor, Metropolitan Opera Orchestra and Manhattan Opera Chorus (Solos: Horne, McCracken, Maliponte, Krause), *Bizet: Carmen*	Georg Solti, conductor, London Philharmonic (Soloists: Caballé, Domingo, Milnes, Blegen, Raimondi), *Puccini: La Bohème*	Colin Davis, conductor, Royal Opera House, Covent Garden (Solos: Caballé, Baker, Gedda, Ganzarolli, Van Allen, Cotrubas), *Mozart: Così fan tutte*
Chamber Music Performance	Gunther Schuller and New England Ragtime Ensemble, *Joplin: The Red Back Book*	Artur Rubinstein, Henryk Szeryng, and Pierre Fournier, *Brahms: Trios (complete)/ Schumann: Trio No. 1 in D Minor*	Artur Rubinstein, Henryk Szeryng, and Pierre Fournier, *Shubert: Trios Nos. 1 in B Flat Major Op. 99 & 2 in E Flat Major Op. 100*

	1976	**1977**	**1978**
Record of the Year	George Benson, "This Masquerade"	Eagles, "Hotel California"	Billy Joel, "Just the Way You Are"
Album of the Year	Stevie Wonder, *Songs in the Key of Life*	Fleetwood Mac, *Rumours*	The Bee Gees and others, *Saturday Night Fever*
Song of the Year	Bruce Johnston, "I Write the Songs"	Joe Brooks, "You Light Up My Life"; Barbra Streisand, "Love Theme from *A Star Is Born* (Evergreen)"	Billy Joel, "Just the Way You Are"
(Pop) Vocal, Female	Linda Ronstadt, *Hasten Down the Wind*	Barbra Streisand, "Love Theme from *A Star Is Born* (Evergreen)"	Anne Murray, "You Needed Me"
(Pop) Vocal, Male	Stevie Wonder, *Songs in the Key of Life*	James Taylor, "Handy Man"	Barry Manilow, "Copacabana (At the Copa)"
New Artist	Starland Vocal Band	Debby Boone	A Taste of Honey
Pop Vocal, Duo or Group with Vocal	Chicago, "If You Leave Me Now"	The Bee Gees, "How Deep Is Your Love"	The Bee Gees, *Saturday Night Fever*
Rhythm and Blues Song	Boz Scaggs and David Paich, "Lowdown"	Leo Sayer and Vini Poncia, "You Make Me Feel Like Dancing"	Paul Jabara, "Last Dance"
R&B Vocal, Female	Natalie Cole, "Sophisticated Lady (She's a Different Lady)"	Thelma Houston, "Don't Leave Me This Way"	Donna Summer, "Last Dance"
R&B Vocal, Male	Stevie Wonder, "I Wish"	Lou Rawls, *Unmistakably Lou*	George Benson, "On Broadway"
R&B Duo or Group with Vocal	Marilyn McCoo and Billy Davis, Jr., "You Don't Have To Be a Star (To Be in My Show)"	Emotions, "Best of My Love"	Earth, Wind & Fire, "All 'n All"
Country Song	Larry Gatlin, "Broken Lady"	Richard Leigh, "Don't It Make My Brown Eyes Blue"	Don Schlitz, "The Gambler"
Country Vocal, Female	Emmylou Harris, *Elite Hotel*	Crystal Gayle, "Don't It Make My Brown Eyes Blue"	Dolly Parton, *Here You Come Again*
Country Vocal, Male	Ronnie Milsap, "(I'm a) Stand by My Woman Man"	Kenny Rogers, "Lucille"	Willie Nelson, "Georgia on My Mind"
Country Performance, Duo or Group with Vocal	Amazing Rhythm Aces, "The End Is Not in Sight (The Cowboy Tune)"	The Kendalls, "Heaven's Just a Sin Away"	Waylon Jennings and Willie Nelson, "Mamas Don't Let Your Babies Grow Up To Be Cowboys"
Ethnic or Traditional Recording	John Hartford, *Mark Twang*	Muddy Waters, *Hard Again*	Muddy Waters, *I'm Ready*
Jazz, Soloist	Count Basie, *Basie & Zoot*	Oscar Peterson, *The Giants*	Oscar Peterson, *Montreux '77, Oscar Peterson Jam*
Jazz, Group	Chick Corea, *The Leprechaun*	Phil Woods, *The Phil Woods Six—Live from the Showboat*	Chick Corea, *Friends*
Jazz, Big Band/ Large Ensemble Performance	Duke Ellington, *The Ellington Suites*	Count Basie & His Orchestra, *Prime Time*	Thad Jones and Mel Lewis, *Live in Munich*
Cast Show Album	*Bubbling Brown Sugar*	*Annie*	*Ain't Misbehavin'*
Comedy Recording	Richard Pryor, *Bicentennial Nigger*	Steve Martin, *Let's Get Small*	Steve Martin, *A Wild and Crazy Guy*
Classical Album	Artur Rubinstein with Daniel Barenboim, conductor, London Philharmonic, *Beethoven: The Five Piano Concertos*	Leonard Bernstein, Vladimir Horowitz, Isaac Stern, Mstislav Rostropovich, Dietrich Fischer-Dieskau, Yehudi Menuhin, Lyndon Woodside, *Concert of the Century* (recorded live at Carnegie Hall May 18, 1976)	Itzhak Perlman with Carlo Maria Giulini, conductor, Chicago Symphony, *Brahms: Concerto for Violin in D Major*

	1976	1977	1978
Classical Orchestral Performance	Georg Solti, conductor, Chicago Symphony, *Strauss: Also Sprach Zarathustra*	Carlo Maria Giulini, conductor, Chicago Symphony, *Mahler: Symphony No. 9 in D Major*	Herbert von Karajan, conductor, Berlin Philharmonic, *Beethoven: Symphonies (9) Complete*
Opera Recording	Lorin Maazel conductor, Cleveland Orchestra and Chorus (Solos: Mitchell, White), *Gershwin: Porgy & Bess*	John De Main, conductor, Houston Grand Opera Production (Solos: Albert, Dale, Smith, Shakesnider, Lane, Brice, Smalls), *Gershwin: Porgy & Bess*	Julius Rudel, conductor, New York City Opera Orchestra and Chorus (Solos: Sills, Titus), *Lehar: The Merry Widow*
Chamber Music Performance	David Munrow, conductor, The Early Music Consort of London, *The Art of Courtly Love*	Juilliard Quartet, *Schöenberg: Quartets for Strings*	Itzhak Perlman and Vladimir Ashkenazy, *Beethoven: Sonatas for Violin and Piano*

GRAMMY AWARD RECORDS

In 1957, the newly formed National Academy of Recording Arts & Sciences first conceived of a peer award to recognize outstanding achievement in the recording field. The Grammys, named after the gramophone statuette, have since expanded from 28 categories to 98. The following artists have all set records in the annals of Grammy history:

Youngest "Album of the Year" winner:
Alanis Morissette, age 21, when *Jagged Little Pill* was named 1995's best LP

Winningest winner:
Georg Solti, the conductor of the Chicago Symphony, has won 31 awards

Winningest female:
Aretha Franklin, with 15 awards (and an uninterrupted winning streak from 1967 to 1974)

Most awards in a single year:
Michael Jackson in 1983, with seven for Album of the Year, *Thriller*; and one for *E.T., the Extra-Terrestrial* as Best Recording for Children; and Carlos Santana in 1999, with eight for Album of the Year, *Supernatural*

Most country awards:
Chet Atkins and Vince Gill with 14

Most jazz awards:
Ella Fitzgerald with 13

Most comedy awards:
Bill Cosby with 9

Most opera awards:
Leontyne Price with 13

	1979	1980	1981
Record of the Year	The Doobie Brothers, "What a Fool Believes"	Christopher Cross, "Sailing"	Kim Carnes, "Bette Davis Eyes"
Album of the Year	Billy Joel, *52nd Street*	Christopher Cross, *Christopher Cross*	John Lennon and Yoko Ono, *Double Fantasy*
Song of the Year	Kenny Loggins and Michael McDonald, "What a Fool Believes"	Christopher Cross, "Sailing"	Donna Weiss and Jackie DeShannon, "Bette Davis Eyes"
Pop Vocal, Female	Dionne Warwick, "I'll Never Love This Way Again"	Bette Midler, "The Rose"	Lena Horne, *Lena Horne: The Lady and Her Music Live on Broadway*
Pop Vocal, Male	Billy Joel, *52nd Street*	Kenny Loggins, "This Is It"	Al Jarreau, *Breakin' Away*
Rock Vocal, Female	Donna Summer, "Hot Stuff"	Pat Benatar, *Crimes of Passion*	Pat Benatar, "Fire and Ice"
Rock Vocal, Male	Bob Dylan, "Gotta Serve Somebody"	Billy Joel, *Glass Houses*	Rick Springfield, "Jessie's Girl"
New Artist	Rickie Lee Jones	Christopher Cross	Sheena Easton
Pop Vocal, Duo or Group with Vocal	The Doobie Brothers, *Minute by Minute*	Barbra Streisand and Barry Gibb, "Guilty"	The Manhattan Transfer, "Boy from New York City"
Rock Performance, Duo or Group with Vocal	The Eagles, "Heartache Tonight"	Bob Seger & the Silver Bullet Band, *Against the Wind*	The Police, "Don't Stand So Close to Me"
Rhythm and Blues Song	David Foster, Jay Graydon, and Bill Champlin, "After the Love Has Gone"	Reggie Lucas and James Mtume, "Never Knew Love Like This Before"	Bill Withers, William Salter, and Ralph MacDonald, "Just the Two of Us"
R&B Vocal, Female	Dionne Warwick, "Déjà Vu"	Stephanie Mills, "Never Knew Love Like This Before"	Aretha Franklin, "Hold On, I'm Comin' "
R&B Vocal, Male	Michael Jackson, "Don't Stop 'Til You Get Enough"	George Benson, *Give Me the Night*	James Ingram, "One Hundred Ways"
R&B Duo or Group with Vocal	Earth, Wind & Fire, "After the Love Has Gone"	Manhattans, "Shining Star"	Quincy Jones, *The Dude*
Country Song	Bob Morrison and Debbie Hupp, "You Decorated My Life"	Willie Nelson, "On the Road Again"	Dolly Parton, "9 to 5"
Country Vocal, Female	Emmylou Harris, *Blue Kentucky Girl*	Anne Murray, "Could I Have This Dance"	Dolly Parton, "9 to 5"
Country Vocal, Male	Kenny Rogers, "The Gambler"	George Jones, "He Stopped Loving Her Today"	Ronnie Milsap, "(There's) No Gettin' Over Me"
Country Performance, Duo or Group with Vocal	Charlie Daniels Band, "The Devil Went Down to Georgia"	Roy Orbison and Emmylou Harris, "That Lovin' You Feelin' Again"	Oak Ridge Boys, "Elvira"
Ethnic or Traditional Recording	Muddy Waters, *Muddy "Mississippi" Waters Live*	Dr. Isaiah Ross, Maxwell Street Jimmy, Big Joe William, Son House, Rev. Robert Wilkins, Little Brother Montgomery, and Sunnyland Slim, *Rare Blues*	B. B. King, *There Must Be a Better World Somewhere*
Jazz Vocal, Female	Ella Fitzgerald, *Fine and Mellow*	Ella Fitzgerald, *A Perfect Match/Ella & Basie*	Ella Fitzgerald, *Digital III at Montreux*
Jazz Vocal, Male	—	George Benson, "Moody's Mood"	Al Jarreau, "Blue Rondo à la Turk"
Jazz, Soloist	Oscar Peterson, *Jousts*	Bill Evans, *I Will Say Goodbye*	John Coltrane, *Bye, Bye Blackbird*

	1979	**1980**	**1981**
Jazz, Group	Gary Burton and Chick Corea, *Duet*	Bill Evans, *We Will Meet Again*	Chick Corea and Gary Burton, *Chick Corea and Gary Burton in Concert, Zurich, October 28, 1979*
Jazz, Big Band/ Large Ensemble Performance	Duke Ellington, *At Fargo, 1940 Live*	Count Basie and Orchestra, *On the Road*	Gerry Mulligan & His Orchestra, *Walk on the Water*
Jazz Fusion Performance, Vocal or Instrumental	Weather Report, *8:30*	Manhattan Transfer, "Birdland"	Grover Washington Jr., *Winelight*
Cast Show Album	*Sweeney Todd*	*Evita*	*Lena Horne: The Lady and Her Music Live on Broadway*
Comedy Recording	Robin Williams, *Reality...What a Concept*	Rodney Dangerfield, *No Respect*	Richard Pryor, *Rev. Du Rite*
Classical Album	Georg Solti, conductor, Chicago Symphony Orchestra, *Brahms: Symphonies (4) Complete*	Pierre Boulez, conductor, Orchestre d l'Opera de Paris (Solos: Stratas, Minton, Mazura, Toni Blankenheim), *Berg: Lulu*	Georg Solti, conductor, Chicago Symphony Orchestra and Chorus (Solos: Buchanan, Zakai), *Mahler: Symphony No. 2 in C Minor*
Classical Orchestral Performance	Georg Solti, conductor, Chicago Symphony, *Brahms: Symphonies (4) Complete*	Georg Solti, conductor, Chicago Symphony, *Bruckner: Symphony No. 6 in A Major*	Georg Solti, conductor, Chicago Symphony, *Mahler: Symphony No. 2 in C Minor*
Opera Recording	Colin Davis, conductor, Orchestra and Chorus of the Royal Opera House, Covent Garden (Solos: Vickers, Harper, Summers), *Britten: Peter Grimes*	Pierre Boulez, conductor, Orchestre d l'Opera de Paris (Solos: Stratas, Minton, Mazura, Blankenheim), *Berg: Lulu*	Charles Mackerras, conductor, Vienna Philharmonic (Solos: Zahradnicek, Zitek, Zidek), *Janacek: From the House of the Dead*
Chamber Music Performance	Dennis Russel Davies, conductor, St. Paul Chamber Orchestra, *Copland: Appalachian Spring*	Itzhak Perlman and Pinchas Zukerman, *Music for Two Violins* (Moszkowski: Suite for Two Violins/Shostakovich: Duets/ Prokofiev: Sonata for Two Violins)	Itzhak Perlman, Lynn Harrell, and Vladimir Ashkenazy, *Tchaikovsky: Piano Trio in A Minor*

FAMOUS LOSERS

In 200 Cher broke the Grammy jinx, but it's hard to believe that the following artists have never won a Grammy in a competitive category, although many have been nominated. Asterisks indicate that the performers have, however, belatedly received the NARAS Lifetime Achievement Award.

AC/DC	The Doors	Queen
Beach Boys	The Drifters	Cat Stevens
Chuck Berry*	The Four Tops	Diana Ross
Jackson Browne	Peter Frampton	Lawrence Welk
The Byrds	Benny Goodman*	Kitty Wells*
Patsy Cline*	Grateful Dead	The Who
Sam Cooke*	The Jackson 5	Hank Williams, Sr.*
Creedence Clearwater Revival	Janis Joplin	Neil Young
Cream	Led Zeppelin	
Bing Crosby*	Little Richard*	
Fats Domino*	Pretenders	

	1982	1983	1984
Record of the Year	Toto, "Rosanna"	Michael Jackson, "Beat It"	Tina Turner, "What's Love Got To Do with It"
Album of the Year	Toto, *Toto IV*	Michael Jackson, *Thriller*	Lionel Richie, *Can't Slow Down*
Song of the Year	Johnny Christopher, Mark James, and Wayne Thompson, "Always on My Mind"	Sting, "Every Breath You Take"	Graham Lyle and Terry Britten, "What's Love Got To Do with It"
Pop Vocal, Female	Melissa Manchester, "You Should Hear How She Talks About You"	Irene Cara, "Flashdance...What a Feeling"	Tina Turner, "What's Love got To Do with It"
Pop Vocal, Male	Lionel Richie, "Truly"	Michael Jackson, *Thriller*	Phil Collins, "Against All Odds (Take a Look at Me Now)"
Rock Vocal, Female	Pat Benatar, "Shadows of the Night"	Pat Benatar, "Love Is a Battlefield"	Tina Turner, "Better Be Good to Me"
Rock Vocal, Male	John Cougar, "Hurts So Good"	Michael Jackson, "Beat It"	Bruce Springsteen, "Dancing in the Dark"
New Artist	Men at Work	Culture Club	Cyndi Lauper
Pop Vocal, Duo or Group with Vocal	Joe Cocker and Jennifer Warnes, "Up Where We Belong"	The Police, "Every Breath You Take"	Pointer Sisters, "Jump (For My Love)"
Rock Performance, Duo or Group with Vocal	Survivor, "Eye of the Tiger"	The Police, *Synchronicity*	Prince and the Revolution, *Purple Rain*
Rhythm and Blues Song	Jay Graydon, Steve Lukather, and Bill Champlin, "Turn Your Love Around"	Michael Jackson, "Billie Jean"	Prince, "I Feel for You"
R&B Vocal, Female	Jennifer Holliday, "And I Am Telling You I'm Not Going"	Chaka Khan, *Chaka Khan*	Chaka Khan, "I Feel for You"
R&B Vocal, Male	Marvin Gaye, "Sexual Healing"	Michael Jackson, "Billie Jean"	Billy Ocean, "Caribbean Queen (No More Love on the Run)"
R&B Duo or Group with Vocal	Dazz Band, "Let It Whip"; Earth, Wind & Fire, "Wanna Be With You"	Rufus & Chaka Khan, "Ain't Nobody"	James Ingram and Michael McDonald, "Yah Mo B There"
Country Song	Johnny Christopher, Wayne Thompson, and Mark James, "Always on My Mind"	Mike Reed, "Stranger in My House"	Steve Goodman, "City of New Orleans"
Country Vocal, Female	Juice Newton, "Break It To Me Gently"	Anne Murray, "A Little Good News"	Emmylou Harris, "In My Dreams"
Country Vocal, Male	Willie Nelson, "Always on My Mind"	Lee Greenwood, "I.O.U."	Merle Haggard, "That's the Way Love Goes"
Country Performance, Group	Alabama, *Mountain Music*	Alabama, *The Closer You Get*	The Judds, "Mama He's Crazy"
Traditional Blues Recording	Clarence "Gatemouth" Brown, *Alright Again*	B. B. King, *Blues 'n' Jazz*	John Hammond, Stevie Ray Vaughan & Double Trouble, Sugar Blue, Koko Taylor & The Blues Machine, Luther "Guitar Junior" Johnson, and J. B. Hutto & The New Hawks, *Blues Explosion*
Reggae Recording	—	—	Black Uhuru, *Anthem*
Jazz Vocal, Female	Sarah Vaughan, *Gershwin Live!*	Ella Fitzgerald, *The Best Is Yet to Come*	—
Jazz Vocal, Male	Mel Torme, *An Evening with George Shearing and Mel Torme*	Mel Torme, *Top Drawer*	Joe Williams, *Nothin' but the Blues*
Jazz, Soloist	Miles Davis, *We Want Miles*	Wynton Marsalis, *Think of One*	Wynton Marsalis, *Hot House Flowers*

	1982	1983	1984
Jazz, Group	Phil Woods Quartet, *"More" Live*	The Phil Woods Quartet, *At the Vanguard*	Art Blakey & The Jazz Messengers, *New York Scene*
Jazz, Big Band/ Large Ensemble Performance	Count Basie & His Orchestra, *Warm Breeze*	Rob McConnell and The Boss Brass, *All in Good Time*	Count Basie & His Orchestra, *88 Basie Street*
Jazz Fusion Performance	Pat Metheny Group, *Offramp*	Pat Metheny Group, *Travels*	Pat Metheny Group, *First Circle*
Gospel Performance, Female	—	Amy Grant, "Ageless Medley"	Amy Grant, "Angels"
Gospel Performance, Male	—	Russ Taff, *Walls of Glass*	Michael W. Smith, *Michael W. Smith 2*
Gospel Performance, Duo, Group, Choir or Chorus	—	Sandi Patti and Larnelle Harris, "More Than Wonderful"	Debby Boone and Phil Driscoll, "Keep the Flame Burning"
Ethnic or Traditional Folk Recording	Queen Ida, *Queen Ida and the Bon Temps Zydeco Band on Tour*	Clifton Chenier & His Red Hot Louisiana Band, *I'm Here*	Elizabeth Cotten, *Elizabeth Cotten Live!*
Cast Show Album	*Dreamgirls*	*Cats (Complete Original Broadway Cast Recording)*	*Sunday in the Park with George*
Comedy Recording	Richard Pryor, *Live on the Sunset Strip*	Eddie Murphy, *Eddie Murphy: Comedian*	"Weird Al" Yankovic, "Eat It"
Classical Album	Glenn Gould, *Bach: The Goldberg Variations*	Georg Solti, conductor, Chicago Symphony, *Mahler: Symphony No. 9 in D Major*	Neville Marriner, conductor, Academy of St. Martin-in-the-Fields/Ambrosian Opera Chorus/Choristers of Westminster Abbey, *Amadeus (Original Soundtrack)*
Classical Orchestral Performance	James Levine, conductor, Chicago Symphony, *Mahler: Symphony No. 7 in E Minor (Song of the Night)*	Georg Solti, conductor, Chicago Symphony, *Mahler: Symphony No. 9 in D Major*	Leonard Slatkin, conductor, St. Louis Symphony, *Prokofiev: Symphony No. 5 in B Flat, Op. 100*
Opera Recording	Pierre Boulez, conductor, Bayreuth Festival Orchestra (Solos: Jones, Altmeyer, Wenkel, Hofmann, Jung, Jerusalem, Zednik, McIntyre, Salminen, Becht), *Wagner: Der Ring des Nibelungen*	James Levine, conductor, The Metropolitan Opera Orchestra and Chorus (Solos: Stratas, Domingo, MacNeill), *Verdi: La Traviata*	Lorin Maazel, conductor, Orchestre National de France/Choeurs et Maitrise de Radio France (Solos: Johnson, Esham, Domingo, Raimondi), *Bizet: Carmen*
Chamber Music Performance	Richard Stoltzman and Richard Goode, *Brahms: The Sonatas for Clarinet & Piano, Op. 120*	Mstislav Rostropovich and Rudolph Serkin, *Brahms: Sonata for Cello & Piano in E Minor, Op. 38 & Sonata in F Major, Op. 99*	Juilliard String Quartet, *Beethoven: The Late String Quartets*

	1985	**1986**	**1987**
Record of the Year	USA for Africa, "We Are the World"	Steve Winwood, "Higher Love"	Paul Simon, "Graceland"
Album of the Year	Phil Collins, *No Jacket Required*	Paul Simon, *Graceland*	U2, *The Joshua Tree*
Song of the Year	Michael Jackson and Lionel Richie, "We Are the World"	Burt Bacharach and Carole Bayer Sager, "That's What Friends Are For"	James Horner, Barry Mann, and Cynthia Weil, "Somewhere Out There"
Pop Vocal, Female	Whitney Houston, "Saving All My Love for You"	Barbra Streisand, *The Broadway Album*	Whitney Houston, "I Wanna Dance with Somebody (Who Loves Me)"
Pop Vocal, Male	Phil Collins, *No Jacket Required*	Steve Winwood, "Higher Love"	Sting, *Bring on the Night*
Rock Vocal, Female	Tina Turner, "One of the Living"	Tina Turner, "Back Where You Started"	—
Rock Vocal, Male	Don Henley, "The Boys of Summer"	Robert Palmer, "Addicted to Love"	Bruce Springsteen, *Tunnel of Love*
New Artist	Sade	Bruce Hornsby and the Range	Jody Watley
Pop Vocal, Duo or Group with Vocal	USA for Africa, "We Are the World"	Dionne Warwick & Friends featuring Elton John, Gladys Knight, and Stevie Wonder, "That's What Friends Are For"	Bill Medley and Jennifer Warnes, "(I've Had) The Time of My Life"
Rock Performance, Group	Dire Straits, "Money for Nothing"	Eurythmics, "Missionary Man"	U2, *The Joshua Tree*
New Age Recording	—	Andreas Vollenweider, *Down to the Moon*	Yusef Lateef, *Yusef Lateef's Little Symphony*
Rhythm and Blues Song	Narada Michael Walden and Jeffrey Cohen, "Freeway of Love"	Anita Baker, Louis A. Johnson, Gary Bias, "Sweet Love"	Bill Withers, "Lean on Me"
R&B Vocal, Female	Aretha Franklin, "Freeway of Love"	Anita Baker, *Rapture*	Aretha Franklin, *Aretha*
R&B Vocal, Male	Stevie Wonder, *In Square Circle*	James Brown, "Living in America"	Smokey Robinson, "Just To See Her"
R&B Duo or Group with Vocal	Commodores, "Nightshift"	Prince & The Revolution, "Kiss"	Aretha Franklin and George Michael, "I Knew You Were Waiting (For Me)"
Country Song	Jimmy L. Webb, "Highwayman"	Jamie O'Hara, "Grandpa (Tell Me 'Bout the Good Old Days)"	Paul Overstreet and Don Schlitz, *Forever and Ever, Amen*
Country Vocal, Female	Rosanne Cash, "I Don't Know Why You Don't Want Me"	Reba McEntire, "Whoever's in New England"	K. T. Oslin, "80's Ladies"
Country Vocal, Male	Ronnie Milsap, "Lost in the Fifties Tonight (In the Still of the Night)"	Ronnie Milsap, *Lost in the Fifties Tonight*	Randy Travis, *Always & Forever*
Country Performance, Duo or Group with Vocal	The Judds, *Why Not Me*	The Judds, "Grandpa (Tell Me 'Bout the Good Old Days)"	Dolly Parton, Linda Ronstadt, and Emmylou Harris, *Trio*
Country Vocal, Collaboration	—	—	Ronnie Milsap and Kenny Rogers, "Make No Mistake, She's Mine"
Traditional Blues Recording	B. B. King, "My Guitar Sings the Blues"	Albert Collins, Robert Cray, and Johnny Copeland, *Showdown*	Professor Longhair, *Houseparty New Orleans Style*
Contemporary Blues	—	—	Robert Cray Band, *Strong Persuader*

	1985	1986	1987
Reggae Recording	Jimmy Cliff, *Cliff Hanger*	Steel Pulse, *Babylon the Bandit*	Peter Tosh, *No Nuclear War*
Jazz Vocal, Female	Cleo Laine, *Cleo at Carnegie, the 10th Anniversary Concert*	Diane Schuur, *Timeless*	Diane Schuur, *Diane Schuur & The Count Basie Orchestra*
Jazz Vocal, Male	Jon Hendricks and Bobby McFerrin, "Another Night in Tunisia"	Bobby McFerrin, " 'Round Midnight"	Bobby McFerrin, "What Is This Thing Called Love"
Jazz, Soloist	Wynton Marsalis, *Black Codes from the Underground*	Miles Davis, *Tutu*	Dexter Gordon, *The Other Side of 'Round Midnight*
Jazz, Group	Wynton Marsalis Group, *Black Codes from the Underground*	Wynton Marsalis, *J Mood*	Wynton Marsalis, *Marsalis Standard Time, Volume I*
Jazz, Big Band/ Large Ensemble Performance	John Barry and Bob Wilber, *The Cotton Club*	The Tonight Show Band with Doc Severinsen, *The Tonight Show Band with Doc Severinsen*	The Duke Ellington Orchestra, conducted by Mercer Ellington, *Digital Duke*
Jazz Fusion Performance, Vocal or Instrumental	David Sanborn, *Straight to the Heart*	Bob James and David Sanborn, *Double Vision*	Pat Metheny Group, *Still Life (Talking)*
Gospel Performance, Female	Amy Grant, *Unguarded*	Sandi Patti, *Morning Like This*	Deniece Williams, "I Believe in You"
Gospel Performance, Male	Larnelle Harris, "How Excellent Is Thy Name"	Philip Bailey, *Triumph*	Larnelle Harris, *The Father Hath Provided*
Gospel Performance, Duo, Group, Choir or Chorus	Larnelle Harris and Sandi Patti, "I've Just Seen Jesus"	Sandi Patti & Deniece Williams, "They Say"	Mylon LeFevre & Broken Heart, *Crack the Sky*
Traditional Folk Recording	Rockin' Sidney, "My Toot Toot"	Doc Watson, *Riding the Midnight Train*	Ladysmith Black Mambazo, *Shaka Zulu*
Contemporary Folk Recording	—	Arlo Guthrie, John Hartford, Richie Havens, Bonnie Koloc, Nitty Gritty Dirt Band, John Prine and others, *Tribute to Steve Goodman*	Steve Goodman, *Unfinished Business*
Cast Show Album	*West Side Story*	*Follies in Concert*	*Les Misérables*
Comedy Recording	Whoopi Goldberg, *Whoopi Goldberg*	Bill Cosby, *Those of You With or Without Children, You'll Understand*	Robin Williams, *A Night at the Met*
Classical Album	Robert Shaw, conductor, Atlanta Symphony Orchestra and Chorus, (Solo: Aler) *Berlioz: Requiem*	Vladimir Horowitz, *Horowitz: The Studio Recordings, New York 1985*	Vladimir Horowitz, *Horowitz in Moscow*
Classical Orchestral Performance	Robert Shaw, conductor, Atlanta Symphony Orchestra, *Fauré: Pelléas et Mélisande*	Georg Solti, conductor, Chicago Symphony Orchestra, *Liszt: A Faust Symphony*	Georg Solti, conductor, Chicago Symphony Orchestra, *Beethoven: Symphony No. 9 in D Minor*
Opera Recording	Georg Solti, conductor, Chicago Symphony Orchestra and Chorus (Solos: Mazura, Langridge), *Schoenberg: Moses und Aaron*	John Mauceri, conductor, New York City Opera Chorus and Orchestra (Solos: Mills, Clement, Eisler, Lankston, Castle, Reeve, Harrold, Billings), *Bernstein: Candide*	James Levine, conductor, Vienna Philharmonic (Solos: Tomowa-Sintow, Battle, Baltsa, Lakes, Prey), *R. Strauss: Ariadne auf Naxos*
Chamber Music Performance	Emanuel Ax and Yo-Yo Ma, *Brahms: Cello and Piano Sonatas in E Major & F Major*	Yo-Yo Ma and Emanuel Ax, *Beethoven: Cello & Piano Sonata No. 4 in C and Variations*	Itzhak Perlman, Lynn Harrell, and Vladimir Ashkenazy, *Beethoven: The Complete Piano Trios*

	1988	1989	1990
Record of the Year	Bobby McFerrin, "Don't Worry, Be Happy"	Bette Midler, "Wind Beneath My Wings"	Phil Collins, "Another Day in Paradise"
Album of the Year	George Michael, *Faith*	Bonnie Raitt, *Nick of Time*	Quincy Jones, *Back on the Block*
Song of the Year	Bobby McFerrin, "Don't Worry, Be Happy"	Larry Henley and Jeff Silbar, "Wind Beneath My Wings"	Julie Gold, "From a Distance"
Pop Vocal, Female	Tracy Chapman, "Fast Car"	Bonnie Raitt, "Nick of Time"	Mariah Carey, "Vision of Love"
Pop Vocal, Male	Bobby McFerrin, "Don't Worry, Be Happy"	Michael Bolton, "How Am I Supposed to Live Without You"	Roy Orbison, "Oh, Pretty Woman"
Rock Vocal, Female	Tina Turner, *Tina Live in Europe*	Bonnie Raitt, *Nick of Time*	Alannah Myles, "Black Velvet"
Rock Vocal, Male	Robert Palmer, "Simply Irresistible"	Don Henley, *The End of the Innocence*	Eric Clapton, "Bad Love"
New Artist	Tracy Chapman	No award (Milli Vanilli)	Mariah Carey
Pop Vocal, Duo or Group with Vocal	The Manhattan Transfer, *Brasil*	Linda Ronstadt and Aaron Neville, "Don't Know Much"	Linda Ronstadt with Aaron Neville, "All My Life"
Rock Performance, Duo or Group with Vocal	U2, "Desire"	Traveling Wilburys, *Traveling Wilburys, Volume I*	Aerosmith, "Janie's Got a Gun"
New Age Recording	Shadowfax, *Folksongs for a Nuclear Village*	Peter Gabriel, *Passion (Music from The Last Temptation of Christ)*	Mark Isham, *Mark Isham*
Hard Rock	Jethro Tull, *Crest of a Knave*	Living Colour, "Cult of Personality"	Living Colour, *Time's Up*
Metal	—	Metallica, "One"	Metallica, "Stone Cold Crazy"
Alternative	—	—	Sinéad O'Connor, *I Do Not Want What I Haven't Got*
Rap Performance, Solo	D.J. Jazzy Jeff & The Fresh Prince, "Parents Just Don't Understand"	Young MC, "Bust a Move"	M.C. Hammer, "U Can't Touch This"
Rap Performance by a Duo or Group	—	—	Ice-T, Melle Mel, Big Daddy Kane, Kool Moe Dee, and Quincy Jones III, "Back on the Block"
Rhythm and Blues Song	Anita Baker, Skip Scarborough, and Randy Holland, "Giving You the Best That I Got"	Kenny Gamble and Leon Huff, "If You Don't Know Me By Now"	Rick James, Alonzo Mille, and M.C. Hammer, "U Can't Touch This"
R&B Vocal, Female	Anita Baker, "Giving You the Best That I Got"	Anita Baker, *Giving You the Best That I Got*	Anita Baker, *Compositions*
R&B Vocal, Male	Terence Trent D'Arby, *Introducing the Hardline According to Terence Trent D'Arby*	Bobby Brown, "Every Little Step"	Luther Vandross, "Here and Now"
R&B Duo or Group with Vocal	Gladys Knight & The Pips, "Love Overboard"	Soul II Soul featuring Caron Wheeler, "Back to Life"	Ray Charles and Chaka Khan, "I'll Be Good to You"
Country Song	K. T. Oslin, "Hold Me"	Rodney Crowell, "After All This Time"	Jon Vezner and Don Henry, "Where've You Been"

	1988	1989	1990
Country Vocal, Female	K. T. Oslin, "Hold Me"	k.d. lang, *Absolute Torch and Twang*	Kathy Mattea, "Where've You Been"
Country Vocal, Male	Randy Travis, *Old 8 x 10*	Lyle Lovett, *Lyle Lovett and His Large Band*	Vince Gill, "When I Call Your Name"
Country Performance, Duo or Group with Vocal	The Judds, "Give a Little Love"	The Nitty Gritty Dirt Band, *Will the Circle Be Unbroken, Volume 2*	The Kentucky Headhunters, *Pickin' on Nashville*
Country Vocal, Collaboration	Roy Orbison and k.d. lang, "Crying"	Hank Williams Jr. and Hank Williams Sr., "There's a Tear in My Beer"	Chet Atkins and Mark Knopfler, "Poor Boy Blues"
Traditional Blues Recording	Willie Dixon, *Hidden Charms*	John Lee Hooker and Bonnie Raitt, "I'm in the Mood"	B.B. King, *Live at San Quentin*
Contemporary Blues	The Robert Cray Band, "Don't Be Afraid of the Dark"	Stevie Ray Vaughan & Double Trouble, *In Step*	The Vaughan Brothers, *Family Style*
Reggae Recording	Ziggy Marley & The Melody Makers, *Conscious Party*	Ziggy Marley & The Melody Makers, *One Bright Day*	Bunny Wailer, *Time Will Tell—A Tribute to Bob Marley*
Jazz Vocal, Female	Betty Carter, *Look What I Got!*	Ruth Brown, *Blues on Broadway*	Ella Fitzgerald, *All That Jazz*
Jazz Vocal, Male	Bobby McFerrin, "Brothers"	Harry Connick Jr., *When Harry Met Sally...*	Harry Connick Jr., *We Are in Love*
Jazz, Soloist	Michael Brecker, *Don't Try This at Home*	Miles Davis, *Aura*	Oscar Peterson, *The Legendary Oscar Peterson Trio Live at the Blue Note*
Jazz, Group	McCoy Tyner, Pharaoh Sanders, David Murray, Cecil McBee, and Roy Haynes, *Blues for Coltrane: A Tribute to John Coltrane*	Chick Corea Akoustic Band, *Chick Corea Akoustic Band*	Oscar Peterson Trio, *The Legendary Oscar Peterson Trio Live at the Blue Note*
Jazz, Big Band/ Large Ensemble Performance	Gil Evans & The Monday Night Orchestra, *Bud & Bird*	Miles Davis, *Aura*	George Benson featuring the Count Basie Orchestra; Frank Foster, conductor, "Basie's Bag"
Jazz Fusion Performance, Vocal or Instrumental	Yellowjackets, *Politics*	Pat Metheny Group, *Letter from Home*	Quincy Jones, "Birdland"
Gospel Performance, Female	Amy Grant, *Lead Me On*	CeCe Winans, "Don't Cry"	—
Gospel Performance, Male	Larnelle Harris, *Christmas*	BeBe Winans, "Meantime"	—
Gospel Performance, Duo, Group, Choir or Chorus	The Winans, *The Winans Live at Carnegie Hall*	Take 6, "The Savior Is Waiting"	Rev. James Cleveland, *Having Church*
Traditional Folk Recording	Various artists, *Folkways: A Vision Shared—A Tribute to Woody Guthrie and Leadbelly*	Bulgarian State Female Vocal Choir, *Le Mystère des voix bulgares, Vol. II*	Doc Watson, *On Praying Ground*
Contemporary Folk Recording	Tracy Chapman, *Tracy Chapman*	Indigo Girls, *Indigo Girls*	Shawn Colvin, *Steady On*
Cast Show Album	*Into the Woods*	*Jerome Robbins' Broadway*	*Les Misérables, The Complete Symphonic Recording*

	1988	1989	1990
Comedy Recording	Robin Williams, *Good Morning, Vietnam*	"Professor" Peter Schickele, *P.D.Q. Bach: 1712 Overture and Other Musical Assaults*	"Professor" Peter Schickele, *P.D.Q. Bach: Oedipus Tex & Other Choral Calamities*
Classical Album	Robert Shaw, conductor, Atlanta Symphony Orchestra and Chorus, *Verdi: Requiem and Operatic Choruses*	Emerson String Quartet, *Bartók: 6 String Quartets*	Leonard Bernstein, conductor, New York Philharmonic, *Ives: Symphony No. 2 (and Three Short Works)*
Classical Orchestral Performance	Robert Shaw, conductor, Atlanta Symphony Orchestra, *Rorem: String Symphony*; Louis Lane, conductor, Atlanta Symphony Orchestra, *Sunday Morning* and *Eagles*	Leonard Bernstein, conductor, New York Philharmonic, *Mahler: Sym. No. 3 in D Min.*	Leonard Bernstein, conductor, Chicago Symphony, *Shostakovich: Symphonies No. 1, Op. 10, and No. 7, Op. 60*
Opera Recording	Georg Solti, conductor, Vienna State Opera Choir & Vienna Philharmonic (Solos: Domingo, Norman, Randova, Nimsgern, Sotin, Fischer-Dieskau), *Wagner: Lohengrin*	James Levine, conductor, Metropolitan Opera Orchestra (Solos: Lakes, Moll, Morris, Norman, Behrens, Ludwig), *Wagner: Die Walküre*	James Levine, conductor, Metropolitan Opera Orchestra (Solos: Morris, Ludwig, Jerusalem, Wlaschiha, Moll, Zednik, Rootering), *Wagner: Das Rheingold*
Chamber Music Performance	Murray Perahia and Sir Georg Solti, pianos, with David Corkhill and Evelyn Glennie, percussion, *Bartók: Sonata for Two Pianos and Percussion; Brahms: Variations on a Theme by Joseph Haydn for Two Pianos*	Emerson String Quartet, *Bartók: 6 String Quartets*	Itzhak Perlman, violin; Daniel Barenboim, piano, *Brahms: The Three Violin Sonatas*

GRAMMY CHAMPS

Sir Georg Solti still reigns supreme as the National Academy of Recording Arts and Sciences' most honored musician, though Chick Corea and Emmylou Harris did join the leader's board.

Sir Georg Solti	31	James Mallinson	12
Quincy Jones	26	Paul McCartney	
Vladimir Horowitz	25	(including The Beatles and Wings)	13
Pierre Boulez	23	Pat Metheny (including Pat Metheny Group)	13
Stevie Wonder	21	Leontyne Price	13
Henry Mancini	20	Ray Charles	12
Leonard Bernstein	17	Thomas Z. Shepard	12
John T. Williams	17	Duke Ellington	11
Aretha Franklin	15	Roger Miller	11
Itzhak Perlman	15	Chick Corea	10
Paul Simon (including Simon & Garfunkel)	15	Kenneth "Babyface" Edmonds	10
Chet Atkins	14	Emmylou Harris	10
Eric Clapton	14	Linda Ronstadt	10
David Foster	14	George Harrison	
Vince Gill	14	(including The Beatles	
Robert Shaw (including Robert Shaw Chorale)	14	and Travelling Wilburys)	10
Sting (including The Police)	14	Bobby McFerrin	10
Ella Fitzgerald	13	Alan Menken	10
Michael Jackson	13	Artur Rubinstein	10
Yo-Yo Ma	13	Robert Woods	10

	1991	1992	1993
Record of the Year	Natalie Cole (with Nat "King" Cole), "Unforgettable"	Eric Clapton, "Tears in Heaven"	Whitney Houston, "I Will Always Love You"
Album of the Year	Natalie Cole, Unforgettable	Eric Clapton, Unplugged	Whitney Houston and others, The Bodyguard—Original Soundtrack
Song of the Year	Irving Gordon, "Unforgettable"	Eric Clapton and Will Jennings, "Tears in Heaven"	Alan Menken and Tim Rice, "A Whole New World"
Pop Vocal, Female	Bonnie Raitt, "Something to Talk About"	k.d. lang, "Constant Craving"	Whitney Houston, "I Will Always Love You"
Pop Vocal, Male	Michael Bolton, "When a Man Loves a Woman"	Eric Clapton, "Tears in Heaven"	Sting, "If I Ever Lose My Faith In You"
Rock Vocal, Female	Bonnie Raitt, Luck of the Draw	Melissa Etheridge, "Ain't It Heavy"	—
Rock Vocal, Male	—	Eric Clapton, Tears in Heaven	—
Rock Song/ Rock Vocal Performance, Solo	Sting, "Soul Cages"	Eric Clapton and Jim Gordon, "Layla"	Meat Loaf, "I'd Do Anything for Love (But I Won't Do That)"
New Artist	Mark Cohn	Arrested Development	Toni Braxton
Pop Vocal, Duo or Group with Vocal	R.E.M., "Losing My Religion"	Celine Dion and Peabo Bryson, "Beauty and the Beast"	Peabo Bryson and Regina Belle, "A Whole New World"
Rock Performance, Duo or Group with Vocal	Bonnie Raitt and Delbert McClinton, "Good Man, Good Woman"	U2, Achtung Baby	Aerosmith, "Living on the Edge"
New Age Recording	Mannheim Steamroller, Fresh Aire 7	Enya, Sheperd Moons	Paul Winter Consort, Spanish Angel
Hard Rock	Van Halen, For Unlawful Carnal Knowledge	Red Hot Chili Peppers, "Give It Away"	Stone Temple Pilots, "Plush"
Metal	Metallica, Metallica	Nine Inch Nails, "Wish"	Ozzy Ozbourne, "I Don't Want To Change the World"
Alternative	R.E.M., Out of Time	Tom Waits, Bone Machine	U2, Zooropa
Rap Performance, Solo	L.L. Cool J, "Mama Said Knock You Out"	Sir Mix-A-Lot, "Baby Got Back"	Dr. Dre, "Let Me Ride"
Rap Performance by a Duo or Group	D.J. Jazzy Jeff & The Fresh Prince, "Summertime"	Arrested Development, "Tennessee"	Digable Planets, "Rebirth of Slick (Cool Like Dat)"
Rhythm and Blues Song	Luther Vandross, Marcus Miller, and Teddy Vann, "Power of Love/Love Power"	L.A. Reid, Babyface, and Daryl Simmons, "End of the Road"	Janet Jackson, James Harris III, and Terry Lewis, "That's the Way Love Goes"
R&B Vocal, Female	Patti LaBelle, Burnin'; Lisa Fischer; "How Can I Ease the Pain"	Chaka Khan, The Woman I Am	Toni Braxton, "Another Sad Love Song"
R&B Vocal, Male	Luther Vandross, Power of Love	Al Jarreau, Heaven and Earth	Ray Charles, "A Song For You"
R&B Duo or Group with Vocal	Boyz II Men, Cooleyhighharmony	Boyz II Men, "End of the Road"	Sade, "No Ordinary Love"
Country Song	Naomi Judd, John Jarvis, and Paul Overstreet, "Love Can Build a Bridge"	Vince Gill and John Barlow Jarvis, "I Still Believe in You"	Lucinda Williams, "Passionate Kisses"
Country Vocal, Female	Mary-Chapin Carpenter, "Down at the Twist and Shout"	Mary-Chapin Carpenter, "I Feel Lucky"	Mary-Chapin Carpenter, "Passionate Kisses"
Country Vocal, Male	Garth Brooks, Ropin' the Wind	Vince Gill, I Still Believe in You	Dwight Yoakam, "Ain't That Lonely Yet"

	1991	1992	1993
Country Performance, Duo or Group with Vocal	The Judds, "Love Can Build a Bridge"	Emmylou Harris & The Nash Ramblers, *Emmylou Harris & The Nash Ramblers at the Ryman*	Brooks & Dunn, "Hard Workin' Man"
Country Vocal, Collaboration	Steve Wariner, Ricky Skaggs, and Vince Gill, "Restless"	Travis Tritt and Marty Stuart, "The Whiskey Ain't Workin' "	Reba McEntire and Linda Davis, "Does He Love You"
Traditional Blues Recording	B. B. King, *Live at the Apollo*	Dr. John, *Goin' Back to New Orleans*	B.B. King, *Blues Summit*
Contemporary Blues	Buddy Guy, *Damn Right, I've Got the Blues*	Stevie Ray Vaughan & Double Trouble, *The Sky Is Crying*	Buddy Guy, *Feels Like Rain*
Reggae Recording	Shabba Ranks, *As Raw as Ever*	Shabba Ranks, *X-tra Naked*	Inner Circle, *Bad Boys*
Jazz, Soloist	Stan Getz, "I Remember You"	Joe Henderson, "Lush Life"	Joe Henderson, "Miles Ahead"
Jazz, Group	Oscar Peterson Trio, *Saturday Night at the Blue Note*	Branford Marsalis, *I Heard You Twice the First Time*	Joe Henderson, *So Near, So Far (Musings for Miles)*
Jazz, Big Band/ Large Ensemble Performance	Dizzy Gillespie & The United Nation Orchestra, *Live at the Royal Festival Hall*	McCoy Tyner Big Band, *The Turning Point*	Miles Davis and Quincy Jones, *Miles and Quincy Live at Montreaux*
Jazz Fusion Performance	—	Pat Metheny, *Secret Story*	—
Gospel Performance, Duo, Group, Choir or Chorus	Sounds of Blackness, *The Evolution of Gospel*	Music & Arts Seminar Mass Choir; Edwin Hawkins, choir director, *Edwin Hawkins Music & Arts Seminar Mass Choir: Recorded Live in Los Angeles*	Brooklyn Tabernacle Choir; Carol Cymbala, choir director, *Live...We Come Rejoicing*
Traditional Folk Recording	Ken Burns and John Colby, *The Civil War*	The Chieftains, *Another Country*	The Chieftains, *The Celtic Harp*
Contemporary Folk Recording	John Prine, *The Missing Years*	The Chieftains, *An Irish Evening Live at the Grand Opera House, Belfast*	Nanci Griffith, *Other Voices/Other Rooms*
Cast Show Album	*The Will Rogers Follies*	*Guys and Dolls*	*The Who's Tommy*
Comedy Recording	"Professor" Peter Schickele, *P.D.Q. Bach: WTWP Classical Talkity-Talk Radio*	"Professor" Peter Schickele, *P.D.Q. Bach: Music for an Awful Lot of Winds & Percussion*	George Carlin, *Jammin' in New York*
Classical Album	Leonard Bernstein, conductor, London Symphony Orchestra (Solos: Hadley, Anderson, Ludwig, Green, Gedda, Jones), *Bernstein: Candide*	Leonard Bernstein, conductor, Berlin Philharmonic Orchestra, *Mahler: Symphony No. 9*	Pierre Boulez, conductor, Chicago Symphony Orchestra and Chorus; John Alen John Tomlinson, baritone, *Bartók: The Wooden Prince & C*
Classical Orchestral Performance	Daniel Barenboim, conductor, Chicago Symphony Orchestra, *Corigliano: Symphony No. 1*	Leonard Bernstein, conductor, Berlin Philharmonic Orchestra, *Mahler: Symphony No. 9*	Pierre Boulez, conductor, Chicago Symphony, *Bartók: The Wooden Prince*
Opera Recording	James Levine, conductor, Metropolitan Opera Orchestra and Chorus (Solos: Behrens, Studer, Schwarz, Goldberg, Weikl, Wlaschiha, Salminen), *Wagner: Götterdämmerung*	Georg Solti conductor, Vienna Philharmonic (Solos: Domingo, Varady, Van Dam, Behrens, Runkel, Jo), *R. Strauss: Die Frau Ohne Schatten*	John Nelson, conductor, English Chamber Orchestra and Ambrosian Opera Chorus (Solos: Battle, Horne, Ramey, Aler, McNair, Chance, Mackie, Doss); *Handel: Semele*
Chamber Music Performance	Isaac Stern and Jamie Laredo, violins; Yo-Yo Ma, cello; Emanuel Ax, piano, *Brahms: Piano Quartets*	Yo-Yo Ma, cello; Emanuel Ax, piano, *Brahms: Sonatas for Cello & Piano*	Anne-Sophie Mutter, violin, and James Levine, conductor, Chicago Symphony, *Berg: Violoin Concerto/Rihm: Time Chant*

	1994	1995	1996
Record of the Year	Sheryl Crow, "All I Wanna Do"	Seal, "Kiss From a Rose"	Eric Clapton, "Change the World"
Album of the Year	Tony Bennett, *MTV Unplugged*	Alanis Morissette, *Jagged Little Pill*	Celine Dion, *Falling Into You*
Song of the Year	Bruce Springsteen, "Streets of Philadelphia"	Seal, "Kiss From a Rose"	Gordon Kennedy, Wayne Kirkpatrick & Tommy Sims, "Change the World"
Pop Vocal, Female	Sheryl Crow, "All I Wanna Do"	Annie Lennox, "No More 'I Love You's' "	Toni Braxton, "Un-Break My Heart"
Pop Vocal, Male	Elton John, "Can You Feel the Love Tonight"	Seal, "Kiss From a Rose"	Eric Clapton, "Change the World"
Rock Vocal, Female	Melissa Etheridge, "Come to My Window"	Alanis Morissette, "You Oughta Know"	Sheryl Crow, "If It Makes You Happy"
Rock Vocal, Male	Bruce Springsteen, "Streets of Philadelphia"	Tom Petty, "You Don't Know How It Feels"	Beck, "Where It's At"
Rock Song/ Rock Vocal Performance, Solo	Bruce Springsteen, "Streets of Philadelphia"	Glen Ballard and Alanis Morissette, "You Oughta Know"	Tracy Chapman, "Give Me One Reason"
New Artist	Sheryl Crow	Hootie & The Blowfish	LeAnn Rimes
Pop Vocal, Duo or Group with Vocal	All-4-One, "I Swear"	Hootie & The Blowfish, "Let Her Cry"	The Beatles, "Free As a Bird"
Rock Performance, Duo or Group with Vocal	Aerosmith, "Crazy"	Blues Traveler, "Run-Around"	Dave Matthews Band, "So Much To Say"
New Age Recording	Paul Winter, "Prayer for the Wild Thing"	George Winston, *Forest*	Enya, *The Memory of Trees*
Hard Rock	Soundgarden, "Black Hole Sun"	Pearl Jam, "Spin the Black Circle"	The Smashing Pumpkins, "Bullet with Butterfly Wings"
Metal	Soundgarden, "Spoonman"	Nine Inch Nails, "Happiness in Slavery"	Rage Against the Machine, "Tire Me"
Alternative	Green Day, *Dookie*	Nirvana, *MTV Unplugged in New York*	Beck, *Odelay*
Rap Performance, Solo	Queen Latifah, "U.N.I.T.Y."	Coolio, "Gangsta's Paradise"	L.L. Cool J, "Hey Lover"
Rap Performance by a Duo or Group	Salt-N-Pepa, "None of Your Business"	Method Man Featuring Mary J. Blige, "I'll Be There for You"/ "You're All I Need to Get By"	Bone Thugs-N-Harmony, "Tha Crossroads"
Rhythm and Blues Song	Babyface, "I'll Make Love to You"	Stevie Wonder, "For Your Love"	Babyface, "Exhale (Shoop Shoop)"
R&B Vocal, Female	Toni Braxton, "Breathe Again"	Anita Baker, "I Apologize"	Toni Braxton, "You're Makin' Me High"
R&B Vocal, Male	Babyface, "When Can I See You"	Stevie Wonder, "For Your Love"	Luther Vandross, "Your Secret Love"
R&B Duo or Group with Vocal	Boyz II Men, "I'll Make Love to You"	TLC, "Creep"	The Fugees, "Killing Me Softly"
Country Song	Gary Baker and Frank J. Myers, "I Swear"	Vince Gill, "Go Rest High on That Mountain"	Bill Mack, "Blue"
Country Vocal, Female	Mary Chapin Carpenter, "Shut Up and Kiss Me"	Alison Krauss, "Baby, Now That I've Found You"	LeAnn Rimes, "Blue"
Country Vocal, Male	Vince Gill, "When Love Finds You"	Vince Gill, "Go Rest High on That Mountain"	Vince Gill, "Worlds Apart"

	1994	1995	1996
Country Performance, Duo or Group with Vocal	Asleep at the Wheel with Lyle Lovett, "Blues for Dixie"	The Mavericks, "Here Comes the Rain"	Brooks & Dunn, "My Maria"
Country Vocal, Collaboration	Aaron Neville and Trisha Yearwood, "I Fall to Pieces"	Shenandoah & Alison Krauss, "Somewhere in the Vicinity of the Heart"	Vince Gill featuring Alison Krauss & Union Station, "High Lonesome Sound"
Traditional Blues Recording	Eric Clapton, *From the Cradle*	John Lee Hooker, *Chill Out*	James Cotton, *Deep in the Blues*
Contemporary Blues	Pops Staples, *Father Father*	Buddy Guy, *Slippin' In*	Keb' Mo', *Just Like You*
Reggae Recording	Bunny Wailer, *Crucial! Roots Classics*	Shaggy, *Boombastic*	Bunny Wailer, *Hall of Fame—A Tribute to Bob Marley's 50th Anniversary*
Jazz, Soloist	Benny Carter, "Prelude to a Kiss"	Lena Horne, *An Evening With Lena Horne* (vocals); Michael Brecker, *Impressions* (instrumental)	Cassandra Wilson, *New Moon Daughter* (vocals); Michael Brecker, "Cabin Fever" (instrumental)
Jazz, Group/ Jazz, Instrumental Performance, Individual or Group	Ron Carter, Herbie Hancock, Wallace Roney, Wayne Shorter & Tony Williams, *A Tribute to Miles*	McCoy Tyner Trio Featuring Michael Brecker, *Infinity*	Michael Brecker, *Tales from the Hudson*
Jazz, Big Band/ Large Ensemble Performance	McCoy Tyner Big Band, *Journey*	GRP All-Star Big Band & Tom Scott, "All Blues"	Count Basie Orchestra (with The New York Voices), *Live at Manchester Craftsmen's Guild*
Contemporary Jazz Performance	—	Pat Metheny Group, *We Live Here*	Wayne Shorter, *High Life*
Gospel Performance, Duo, Group, Choir or Chorus	The Thompson Community Singers, Rev. Milton Brunson, choir director, *Through God's Eyes* and The Love Fellowship Crusade Choir, Hezekiah Walker, choir director, *Live in Atlanta at Morehouse College* (tie)	The Brooklyn Tabernacle Choir, *Praise Him…Live!*	Shirley Caesar's Outreach Convention Choir, *Just a Word*
Traditional Folk Recording	Bob Dylan, *World Gone Wrong*	Ramblin' Jack Elliott, *South Coast*	Pete Seeger, *Pete*
Contemporary Folk Recording	Johnny Cash, *American Recordings*	Emmylou Harris, *Wrecking Ball*	Bruce Springsteen, *The Ghost of Tom Joad*
Cast Show Album	*Passion*	*Smokey Joe's Cafe—The Songs of Leiber and Stoller*	*Riverdance*
Comedy Recording	Sam Kinison, *Live From Hell*	Jonathan Winters, *Crank Calls*	Al Franken, *Rush Limbaugh Is a Big Fat Idiot*
Classical Album	Pierre Boulez, conductor, Chicago Symphony Orchestra, *Bartok: Concerto for Orch.; Four Orchestral Pieces, Op. 12*	Pierre Boulez, conductor, Cleveland Orchestra and Chorus, *Debussy: La Mer; Nocturnes; Jeux, etc.*	Leonard Slatkin, conductor, various Artists, *Corigliano: Of Rage and Remembrance*
Classical Orchestral Performance	Pierre Boulez, conductor, Chicago Symphony Orchestra, *Bartok: Concerto for Orch.; Four Orchestral Pieces, Op. 12*	Pierre Boulez, conductor, Cleveland Orchestra and Chorus, *Debussy: La Mer; Nocturnes; Jeux, etc.*	Michael Tilson Thomas, conductor, San Francisco Symphony, *Prokofiev: Romeo and Juliet (Scenes from the Ballet)*
Opera Recording	Kent Nagano, conductor, Orchestra and Chorus of Opera de Lyon (Solos: Cheryl Struder, Jerry Hadley, Samuel Ramey, Kenn Chester), *Floyd: Susannah*	Charles Dutoit, conductor, Montreal Symphony Orchestra & Chorus, *Berlioz: Les Troyens*	Richard Hickox, conductor, Opera London, London Symphony Chorus, City of London Sinfonia (Solos: Philip Langridge, Alan Opie, Janice Watson), *Britten: Peter Grimes*
Chamber Music Performance	Daniel Barenboim, piano; Dale Clevenger, horn; Larry Combs, clarinet (Chicago Symphony), Daniele Damiano, bassoon; Hansjorg Schellenberger, oboe (Berlin Philharmonic), *Beethoven/Mozart: Quintets*	Emanuel Ax, piano; Yo-Yo Ma, cello; Richard Stoltzman, clarinet, *Brahms/Beethoven/Mozart: Clarinet Trios*	Cleveland Quartet, *Corigliano: String Quartet*

	1997	1998	1999
Record of the Year	Shawn Colvin, "Sunny Came Home"	Celine Dion, "My Heart Will Go On"	Santana, "Smooth"
Album of the Year	Bob Dylan, *Time Out of Mind*	Lauryn Hill, *The Miseducation Of Lauryn Hill*	Santana, *Supernatural*
Song of the Year	Shawn Colvin, "Sunny Came Home"	James Horner and Will Jennings, "My Heart Will Go On"	Itaal Shur and Rob Thomas, "Smooth"
Pop Vocal, Female	Sarah McLachlan, "Building a Mystery"	Celine Dion, "My Heart Will Go On"	Sarah McLachlan, "I Will Remember You"
Pop Vocal, Male	Elton John, "Candle in the Wind 1997"	Eric Clapton, "My Father's Eyes"	Sting, "Brand New Day"
Rock Vocal, Female	Fiona Apple, "Criminal"	Alanis Morissette, "Uninvited"	Sheryl Crow, "Sweet Child O' Mine"
Rock Vocal, Male	Bob Dylan, "Cold Irons Bound"	Lenny Kravitz, "Fly Away"	Lenny Kravitz, "American Woman"
Rock Song	Jakob Dylan, "One Headlight"	Alanis Morissette, "Uninvited"	Flea, "Scar Tissue"
New Artist	Paula Cole	Lauryn Hill	Christina Aguilera
Pop Performance, Duo or Group with Vocal	Jamiroquai, "Virtual Insanity"	The Brian Setzer Orchestra, "Jump Jive An' Wail"	Santana, "Maria Maria"
Rock Performance, Duo or Group with Vocal	The Wallflowers, "One Headlight"	Aerosmith, "Pink"	Santana, featuring Everlast, "Put Your Lights On"
New Age Album	Michael Hedges, *Oracle*	Clannad, *Landmarks*	Paul Winter and Friends, *Celtic Solstice*
Hard Rock Performance	The Smashing Pumpkins, "The End Is the Beginning Is the End"	Jimmy Page and Robert Plant, "Most High"	Metallica, "Whiskey in the Jar"
Metal Performance	Tool, *Aenema*	Metallica, "Better Than You"	Black Sabbath, "Iron Man"
Alternative Performance	Radiohead, *OK Computer*	Beastie Boys, *Hello Nasty*	Beck, *Mutations*
Rap Performance, Solo	Will Smith, "Men in Black"	Will Smith, "Gettin' Jiggy Wit It"	Eminem, "My Name Is"
Rap Performance by a Duo or Group	Puff Daddy & Faith Evans featuring 112, "I'll Be Missing You"	Beastie Boys, "Intergalactic"	The Roots & Erykah Badu, "You Got Me"
R&B Song	R. Kelly, "I Believe I Can Fly"	Lauryn Hill, "Doo Wop (That Thing)"	TLC, "No Scrubs"
R&B Vocal, Female	Erykah Badu, "On & On"	Lauryn Hill, "Doo Wop (That Thing)"	Whitney Houston, "It's Not Right But It's Okay"
R&B Vocal, Male	R. Kelly, "I Believe I Can Fly"	Stevie Wonder, "St. Louis Blues"	Barry White, "Staying Power"
R&B Performance, Duo or Group with Vocal	Blackstreet, "No Diggity"	Brandy and Monica, "The Boy Is Mine"	TLC, "No Scrubs"
Country Song	Bob Carlisle & Randy Thomas, "Butterfly Kisses"	Robert John "Mutt" Lange and Shania Twain, "You're Still the One "	Robert John "Mutt" Lange and Shania Twain, "Come on Over"
Country Vocal, Female	Trisha Yearwood, "How Do I Live"	Shania Twain, "You're Still the One"	Shania Twain, "Man! I Feel Like a Woman"
Country Vocal, Male	Vince Gill, "Pretty Little Adriana"	Vince Gill, "If You Ever Have Forever in Mind"	George Jones, "Choices"
Country Performance, Duo or Group with Vocal	Allison Krauss & Union Station, "Looking in the Eyes of Love"	Dixie Chicks, "There's Your Trouble"	Dixie Chicks, "Ready to Run"

	1997	**1998**	**1999**
Country Vocal, Collaboration	Trisha Yearwood & Garth Brooks, "In Another's Eyes"	Clint Black, Joe Diffie, Merle Haggard, Emmylou Harris, Alison Krauss, Patty Loveless, Earl Scruggs, Ricky Skaggs, Marty Stuart, Pam Tillis, Randy Travis, Travis Tritt, and Dwight Yoakam, *Same Old Train*	Emmylou Harris, Linda Ronstadt, and Dolly Parton, *After the Gold Rush*
Traditional Blues Album	John Lee Hooker, *Don't Look Back*	Otis Rush, *Any Place I'm Going*	B.B. King, *Blues on the Bayou*
Contemporary Blues Album	Taj Mahal, *Senor Blues*	Keb' Mo', *Slow Down*	Robert Cray Band, *Take Your Shoes Off*
Reggae Album	Ziggy Marley & The Melody Makers, *Fallen Is Babylon*	Sly and Robbie, *Friends*	Burning Spear, *Calling Rastafari*
Jazz, Soloist	Dee Dee Bridgewater, *Dear Ella* (vocals); Doc Cheatham & Nicholas Payton, "Stardust" (instrumental)	Shirley Horn, *I Remember Miles* (vocals); Chick Corea and Gary Burton, "Rhumbata" (instrumental)	Diana Krall, *When I Look in Your Eyes* (vocals); Wayne Shorter, "In Walked Wayne" (instrumental)
Jazz, Instrumental Performance, Individual or Group	Charlie Haden & Pat Metheny, *Beyond the Missouri Sky*	Herbie Hancock, *Gershwin's World*	Gary Burton, Chick Corea, Pat Metheny, Roy Haynes, and Dave Holland, *Like Minds*
Jazz, Large Ensemble Performance	Joe Henderson Big Band, *Joe Henderson Big Band*	Count Basie Orchestra; Grover Mitchell, Director, *Count Plays Duke*	The Bob Florence Limited Edition, *Serendipity 18*
Contemporary Jazz Performance	Randy Brecker, *Into the Sun*	Pat Metheny Group, *Imaginary Day*	David Sanborn, *Inside*
Gospel Album	dc Talk, *Welcome to the Freak Show: dc Talk* (rock); Jars of Clay, *Much Afraid* (pop/contemp.); The Fairfield Four, *I Couldn't Hear Nobody Pray* (trad. soul); Take 6, *Brothers* (contemp. soul); God's Property, *God's Property from Kirk Franklin's Nu Nation* (choir/chorus)	Ashley Cleveland, *You Are There* (rock); Deniece Williams, *This Is My Song* (pop/contemp); Cissy Houston, *He Leadeth Me* (trad. soul); Kirk Franklin, *The Nu Nation Project* (contemp. soul); The Associates; O'Landa Draper, Choir Director, *Reflections* (choir/chorus)	Rebecca St. James, *Pray* (rock); Steven Curtis Chapman, *Speechless* (pop/contemp.); Shirley Caesar, *Christmas with Shirley Caesar* (trad. soul); Yolanda Adams, *Mountain High...Valley Low* (contemp. soul); Brooklyn Tabernacle Choir, *High and Lifted*
Traditional Folk Album	BeauSoleil, *L'Amour ou La Folie*	The Chieftains with Various Artists, *Long Journey Home*	June Carter Cash, *Press On*
Contemporary Folk Album	Bob Dylan, *Time Out of Mind*	Lucinda Williams, *Car Wheels on a Gravel Road*	Tom Waits, *Mule Variations*
Cast Show Album	*Chicago: The Musical*	*The Lion King*	*Annie Get Your Gun*
Comedy Album	Chris Rock, *Roll with the New*	Mel Brooks & Carl Reiner, *The 2000 Year Old Man in the Year 2000*	Chris Rock, *Bigger and Blacker*
Classical Album	Yo-Yo Ma, violincello; David Zinman, conductor, Philadelphia Orchestra, *Premieres—Cello Concertos (Works of Danielpour, Kirchner, Rouse)*	Robert Shaw, conductor, Atlanta Sym. Orch. Cho.; Atlanta Sym. Orch., *Barber: Prayers of Kierkegaard/Vaughan Williams: Dona Nobis Pacem/Bartok: Cantata Profana*	Michael Tilson Thomas, conductor, San Francisco Sym. Orch., *Stravinsky: Firebird; The Rite of Spring; Persephone*
Classical Orchestral Performance	Pierre Boulez, conductor, The Cleveland Orchestra, The Cleveland Orchestra Chorus, *Berlioz: Symphonie Fantastique; Tristia*	Pierre Boulez, conductor, Chicago Sym. Orch, *Mahler: Sym. No. 9*	Michael Tilson Thomas, conductor, San Francisco Sym. Orch., *Stravinsky: Firebird; The Rite of Spring; Persephone*
Opera Recording	Sir Georg Solti, conductor; Ben Heppner, Herbert Lippert, Karita Mattila, Alan Opie, Rene Pape, Iris Vermillion, Chicago Symphony Chorus, Chicago Symphony Orchestra, *Wagner: Die Meistersinger Von Nurnberg*	Pierre Boulez, conductor; Jessye Norman; Laszlo Polgar; Chicago Symphony Orchestra, *Bartók: Bluebeard's Castle*	John Eliot Gardiner, conductor; Ian Bostridge; Bryn Terfel; Anne Sofie von Otter; Deborah York; London Symphony Orchestra *Stravinsky: The Rake's Progress*
Chamber Music Performance	Emerson String Quartet, *Beethoven: The String Quartets*	André Previn, piano; Gil Shaham, violin, *American Scenes*	Anne Sophie Mutter, violin; Lambert Orkis, piano; *Beethoven: The Violin Sonatas*

2000

Record of the Year	U2, "Beautiful Day"
Album of the Year	Steely Dan, *Two Against Nature*
Song of the Year	U2, "Beautiful Day"
Pop Vocal, Female	Macy Gray, "I Try"
Pop Vocal, Male	Sting, "She Walks This Earth (Soberana Rosa)"
Rock Vocal, Female	Sheryl Crow, "There Goes The Neighborhood"
Rock Vocal, Male	Lenny Kravitz, "Again"
Rock Song	Scott Stapp and Mark Tremonti, "With Arms Wide Open"
New Artist	Shelby Lynne
Pop Performance, Duo or Group with Vocal	Steely Dan, "Cousin Dupree"
Rock Performance, Duo or Group with Vocal	U2, "Beautiful Day"
New Age Album	Kitaro, *Thinking of You*
Hard Rock Performance	Rage Against the Machine, "Guerrilla Radio"
Metal Performance	Deftones, *Elite*
Alternative Performance	Radiohead, *Kid A*
Rap Performance, Solo	Eminem, "The Real Slim Shady"
Rap Performance by a Duo or Group	Dr. Dre featuring Eminem, "Forgot About Dre"
R&B Song	Destiny's Child, "Say My Name"
R&B Vocal, Female	Toni Braxton, "He Wasn't Man Enough"
R&B Vocal, Male	D'Angelo, "Untitled (How Does It Feel)"
R&B Performance, Duo or Group with Vocal	Destiny's Child, "Say My Name"
Country Song	Mark D. Sanders & Tia Sillers, "I Hope You Dance"
Country Vocal, Female	Faith Hill, "Breathe"
Country Vocal, Male	Johnny Cash, "Solitary Man"
Country Performance, Duo or Group with Vocal	Cherokee Maiden, "Asleep at the Wheel"

ALL THE REST

Ninety-eight categories strong (and that's not even counting the Latin Grammys), here are all the other Grammy winners from 2000.

Best Pop Collaboration with Vocals: "Is You Is Or Is You Ain't (My Baby)," B.B. King & Dr. John

Best Pop Instrumental Performance: "Caravan," The Brian Setzer Orchestra

Best Dance Recording: "Who Let the Dogs Out," Baha Men

Best Pop Album: *Two Against Nature*, Steely Dan

Best Traditional Pop Vocal Performance: *Both Sides Now*, Joni Mitchell

Best Rock Instrumental Performance: "The Call of Ktulu" Metallica with Michael Kamen conducting the San Francisco Symphony Orchestra

Best Rock Album: *There Is Nothing Left to Lose*, Foo Fighters

Best R&B Album: *Voodoo*, D'Angelo

Best Traditional R&B Vocal Performance: *Ear-Resistible*, The Temptations

Best Rap Album: *The Marshall Mathers LP*, Eminem

Best Country Instrumental Performance: "Leaving Cottondale," Alison Brown with Bela Fleck

Best Country Album: *Breathe*, Faith Hill

Best Bluegrass Album: *The Grass is Blue*, Dolly Parton

Best Latin Jazz Performance: *Live at The Village Vanguard*, Chucho Valdes

Best Latin Pop Performance: *Shakira - MTV Unplugged*, Shakira

Best Latin Rock/Alternative Performance: *Uno*, La Ley

Best Tropical Latin Performance: *Alma Caribena*, Gloria Estefan

Best Mexican-American Music Performance: *Por Una Mujer Bonita*, Pepe Aguilar

Best Tejano Music Performance: *¿Que Es Musica Tejana?*, The Legends

Best World Music Album: *Joao Voz E Violao*, Joao Gilberto

Best Polka Album: *Touched by a Polka*, Jimmy Sturr

Best Musical Album for Children: *Woody's Roundup featuring Riders In the Sky*, Riders In the Sky

Best Spoken Word Album for Children: *Harry Potter and The Goblet of Fire (J. K. Rowling)*, Jim Dale

Best Spoken Word Album: *The Measure of a Man*, Sidney Poitier

Best Instrumental Composition: "Theme from *Angela's Ashes*," John Williams

Best Instrumental Composition Written for a Motion Picture or for Television: *American Beauty*, Thomas Newman

Best Song Written for a Motion Picture or for Television: "When She Loved Me" (from *Toy Story 2*), Randy Newman

Best Instrumental Arrangement: "Spain for Sextet & Orchestra," Chick Corea, arranger

Best Instrumental Arrangement Accompanying Vocal(s): "Both Sides Now," Vince Mendoza, arranger

Best Recording Package: *Music*, Kevin Reagan, art director

(continued on following page)

2000

Country Vocal, Collaboration	Faith Hill & Tim McGraw, "Let's Make Love"
Traditional Blues Album	B.B. King & Eric Clapton, *Riding With the King*
Contemporary Blues Album	Taj Mahal & The Phantom Blues Band, *Shoutin' In Key*
Reggae Album	Beenie Man, *Art and Life*
Jazz, Soloist	Dianne Reeves, *In The Moment - Live in Concert* (vocals); Pat Metheny, "(Go) Get It" (instrumental)
Jazz, Instrumental Performance, Individual or Group	Branford Marsalis Quartet, *Contemporary Jazz*
Jazz, Large Ensemble Performance	Joe Lovano, *52nd Street Themes*
Contemporary Jazz Performance	Bela Fleck & The Flecktones, *Outbound*
Gospel Album	Petra, *Double Take* (rock); Jars of Clay, *If I Left the Zoo* (pop/contemp.); Shirley Caesar, *You Can Make It* (trad. soul); Mary Mary, *Thankful* (contemp. soul); Brooklyn Tabernacle Choir, *Live - God is Working* (choir/chorus)
Traditional Folk Album	Dave Alvin, *Public Domain - Songs From the Wild Land*
Contemporary Folk Album	Emmylou Harris, *Red Dirt Girl*
Cast Show Album	*Elton John and Tim Rice's Aida*
Comedy Album	George Carlin, *Braindroppings*
Classical Album	Emerson String Quartet, *Shostakovich: The String Quartets*
Classical Orchestral Performance	Sir Simon Rattle, conductor; Berliner Philharmonic, *Mahler: Symphony No. 10*
Opera Recording	Kent Nagano, Kim Begley, Dietrich Fischer-Dieskau, Dietrich Henschel, Markus Hollop, Eva Jenis, Torsten Kerl, Orchestra de l'Opera National de Lyon, *Busoni: Doktor Faust*
Chamber Music Performance	Emerson String Quartet, *Shostakovich: The String Quartets*

Best Boxed Recording Package: *Miles Davis & John Coltrane: The Complete Columbia Recordings 1955-1961*, Frank Harkins and Arnold Levine, art directors

Best Album Notes: *Miles Davis & John Coltrane: The Complete Columbia Recordings 1955-1961*

Best Historical Album: *Louis Armstrong: The Complete Hot Five and Hot Seven Recordings*

Best Engineered Album, Non-Classical: *Two Against Nature*

Producer of the Year, Non-Classical: Dr. Dre

Remixer of the Year, Non-Classical: Hex Hector

Best Engineered Album, Classical: *Dvorak: Requiem, Op. 89; Sym. No. 9, Op. 95 "From the New World"*

Producer of the Year, Classical: Steven Epstein

Best Choral Performance: *Penderecki: Credo*

Best Instrumental Soloist(s) Performance (with Orchestra): "Maw: Violin Concerto" Joshua Bell, violin; Roger Norrington, conductor (London Phil. Orchestra)

Best Instrumental Soloist Performance (without Orchestra): *Dreams of a World* (Works of Lauro, Ruiz-Pipo, Duarte, etc.), Sharon Isbin, guitar

Best Small Ensemble Performance (with or without Conductor): *Shadow Dances* (Stravinsky Miniatures—Tango; Suite No. 1; Octet, etc.), Orpheus Chamber Orch.

Best Classical Vocal Performance: *The Vivaldi Album*, Cecilia Bartoli, mezzo soprano

Best Classical Contemporary Composition: "Crumb: Star-Child" George Crumb, composer (Joseph Alessi, trombone; Susan Narucki, soprano

Best Classical Crossover Album: *Appalachian Journey* (1B; Misty Moonlight Waltz; Indecision, etc.), Yo-Yo Ma, cello; Edgar Meyer, double bass; Mark O'Connor, violin; Alison Krauss, fiddle & vocals; James Taylor, vocals

Best Short Form Music Video: *Learn to Fly*, Foo Fighters

Best Long Form Music Video: *Gimme Some Truth—The Making of John Lennon's Imagine Album*, John Lennon

MTV VIDEO MUSIC AWARDS

BEST VIDEO OF THE YEAR

1984	The Cars	You Might Think
1985	Don Henley	The Boys of Summer
1986	Dire Straits	Money for Nothing
1987	Peter Gabriel	Sledgehammer
1988	INXS	Need You Tonight/Mediate
1989	Neil Young	This Note's for You
1990	Sinead O'Connor	Nothing Compares 2 U
1991	R.E.M.	Losing My Religion
1992	Van Halen	Right Now
1993	Pearl Jam	Jeremy
1994	Aerosmith	Cryin'
1995	TLC	Waterfalls
1996	The Smashing Pumpkins	Tonight, Tonight
1997	Jamiroquai	Virtual Insanity
1998	Madonna	Ray of Light
1999	Lauryn Hill	Doo Wop (That Thing)
2000	Eminem	The Real Slim Shady
2001	Christina Aguilera, Lil' Kim, Mya, Pink, featuring Missy "Misdemeanor" Elliott	Lady Marmalade

BEST MALE VIDEO

1984	David Bowie	China Girl
1985	Bruce Springsteen	I'm on Fire
1986	Robert Palmer	Addicted to Love
1987	Peter Gabriel	Sledgehammer
1988	Prince	U Got the Look
1989	Elvis Costello	Veronica
1990	Don Henley	The End of the Innocence
1991	Chris Isaak	Wicked Game (Concept)
1992	Eric Clapton	Tears in Heaven (Performance)
1993	Lenny Kravitz	Are You Gonna Go My Way
1994	Tom Petty and the Heartbreakers	Mary Jane's Last Dance
1995	Tom Petty and the Heartbreakers	You Don't Know How It Feels
1996	Beck	Where It's At
1997	Beck	The Devil's Haircut
1998	Will Smith	Just the Two of Us
1999	Will Smith	Miami
2000	Eminem	The Real Slim Shady
2001	Moby, featuring Gwen Stefani	South Side

BEST FEMALE VIDEO

1984	Cyndi Lauper	Girls Just Want To Have Fun
1985	Tina Turner	What's Love Got To Do with It
1986	Whitney Houston	How Will I Know
1987	Madonna	Papa Don't Preach
1988	Suzanne Vega	Luka
1989	Paula Abdul	Straight Up
1990	Sinead O'Connor	Nothing Compares 2 U
1991	Janet Jackson	Love Will Never Do Without You
1992	Annie Lennox	Why
1993	k.d. lang	Constant Craving
1994	Janet Jackson	If

1995	Madonna	Take a Bow
1996	Alanis Morissette	Ironic
1997	Jewel	You Were Meant for Me
1998	Madonna	Ray of Light
1999	Lauryn Hill	Doo Wop (That Thing)
2000	Aaliyah	Try Again
2001	Eve featuring Gwen Stefani	Let Me Blow Ya Mind

BEST CONCEPT VIDEO

1984	Herbie Hancock	Rockit
1985	Glenn Frey	Smuggler's Blues
1986	a-ha	Take On Me
1987	Peter Gabriel/ Stephen Johnson	Sledgehammer
1988	Pink Floyd	Learning to Fly

BEST GROUP VIDEO

1984	ZZ Top	Legs
1985	USA for Africa	We Are the World
1986	Dire Straits	Money for Nothing
1987	Talking Heads	Wild Wild Life
1988	INXS	Need You Tonight/Mediate
1989	Living Colour	Cult of Personality
1990	The B-52's	Love Shack
1991	R.E.M.	Losing My Religion
1992	U2	Even Better Than the Real Thing
1993	Pearl Jam	Jeremy
1994	Aerosmith	Cryin'
1995	TLC	Waterfalls
1996	Foo Fighters	Big Me
1997	No Doubt	Don't Speak
1998	Backstreet Boys	Everybody (Backstreet's Back)
1999	TLC	No Scrubs
2000	Blink-182	All the Small Things
2001	'N Sync	Pop

BEST NEW ARTIST IN A VIDEO

1984	Eurythmics	Sweet Dreams (Are Made of This)
1985	'Til Tuesday	Voices Carry
1986	a-ha	Take On Me
1987	Crowded House	Don't Dream It's Over
1988	Guns N' Roses	Welcome to the Jungle
1989	Living Colour	Cult of Personality
1990	Michael Penn	No Myth
1991	Jesus Jones	Right Here, Right Now
1992	Nirvana	Smells Like Teen Spirit
1993	Stone Temple Pilots	Plush
1994	Counting Crows	Mr. Jones
1995	Hootie & The Blowfish	Hold My Hand
1996	Alanis Morissette	Ironic
1997	Fiona Apple	Sleep to Dream
1998	Natalie Imbruglia	Torn
1999	Eminem	My Name Is
2000	Macy Gray	I Try
2001	Alicia Keys	Fallin'

BEST RAP VIDEO

Year	Artist	Song
1989	D.J. Jazzy Jeff & The Fresh Prince	Parents Just Don't Understand
1990	M.C. Hammer	U Can't Touch This
1991	L.L. Cool J	Mama Said Knock You Out
1992	Arrested Development	Tennessee
1993	Arrested Development	People Everyday
1994	Snoop Doggy Dogg	Doggy Dogg World
1995	Dr. Dre	Keep Their Heads Ringin'
1996	Coolio featuring LV	Gangsta's Paradise
1997	The Notorious B.I.G.	Hypnotize
1998	Will Smith	Gettin' Jiggy Wit It
1999	Jay-Z featuring Ja Rule/Amil-lion	Can I Get a...
2000	Dr. Dre featuring Eminem	Forgot About Dre
2001	Nelly	Ride Wit Me

BEST DANCE VIDEO

1989	Paula Abdul	Straight Up
1990	M.C. Hammer	U Can't Touch This
1991	C+C Music Factory	Gonna Make You Sweat (Everybody Dance Now)
1992	Prince & the New Power Generation	Cream
1993	En Vogue	Free Your Mind
1994	Salt-N-Pepa w/ En Vogue	Whatta Man
1995	Michael and Janet Jackson	Scream
1996	Coolio	1, 2, 3, 4 (Sumpin' New)
1997	Spice Girls	Wannabe
1998	Prodigy	Smack My Bitch Up
1999	Ricky Martin	Livin' la Vida Loca
2000	Jennifer Lopez	Waiting for Tonight
2001	'N Sync	Pop

BEST METAL/HARD ROCK VIDEO

1989	Guns N' Roses	Sweet Child o' Mine
1990	Aerosmith	Janie's Got a Gun
1991	Aerosmith	The Other Side
1992	Metallica	Enter Sandman
1993	Pearl Jam	Jeremy
1994	Soundgarden	Black Hole Sun
1995	White Zombie	More Human Than Human
1996	Metallica	Until It Sleeps
1997	Aerosmith	Falling in Love (Is Hard on the Knees)
1998	Aerosmith	Pink
1999	Korn	Freak on a Leash
2000	Limp Bizkit	Break Stuff
2001	Limp Bizkit	Rollin

BEST R&B VIDEO

1993	En Vogue	Free Your Mind
1994	Salt-N-Pepa w/ En Vogue	Whatta Man
1995	TLC	Waterfalls
1996	The Fugees	Killing Me Softly
1997	Puff Daddy and the Family	I'll Be Missing You
1998	Wyclef Jean featuring Refugee Allstars	Gone 'Till November
1999	Lauryn Hill	Doo Wop (That Thing)
2000	Destiny's Child	Say My Name
2001	Destiny's Child	Survivor

BEST POP VIDEO

1999	Ricky Martin	Livin' la Vida Loca
2000	'N Sync	Bye, Bye, Bye
2001	'N Sync	Pop

BEST VIDEO FROM A FILM

1987	Talking Heads	Wild Wild Life [True Stories]
1988	Los Lobos	La Bamba [La Bamba]
1989	U2 with B.B. King	When Love Comes to Town [U2 Rattle and Hum]
1990	Billy Idol	Cradle of Love [The Adventures of Ford Fairlaine]
1991	Chris Isaak	Wicked Game [Wild at Heart]
1992	Queen	Bohemian Rhapsody [Wayne's World]
1993	Alice in Chains	Would? [Singles]
1994	Bruce Springsteen	Streets of Philadelphia [Philadelphia]
1995	Seal	Kiss from a Rose [Batman Forever]
1996	Coolio	Gangsta's Paradise [Dangerous Minds]
1997	Will Smith	Men in Black [Men in Black]
1998	Aerosmith	I Don't Want to Miss a Thing [Armageddon]
1999	Madonna	Beautiful Stranger [Austin Powers: The Spy Who Shagged Me]
2000	Aaliyah	Try Again [Romeo Must Die]
2001	Christina Aguilera, Lil' Kim, Mya, Pink, featuring Missy "Misdemeanor" Elliott	Lady Marmalade [Moulin Rouge]

BEST CHOREOGRAPHY IN A VIDEO

1994	Salt-N-Pepa w/ En Vogue	Whatta Man
1995	Michael and Janet Jackson	Scream
1996	Bjork	It's Oh So Quiet
1997	Beck	The New Pollution
1998	Madonna	Ray of Light
1999	Fatboy Slim	Praise You
2000	'N Sync	Bye Bye Bye
2001	Fatboy Slim	Weapon of Choice

BEST ALTERNATIVE VIDEO

1991	Jane's Addiction	Been Caught Stealing
1992	Nirvana	Smells Like Teen Spirit
1993	Nirvana	In Bloom (Version 1—Dresses)
1994	Nirvana	Heart-Shaped Box
1995	Weezer	Buddy Holly
1996	The Smashing Pumpkins	1979
1997	Sublime	What I Got
1998	Green Day	Time of Your Life (Good Riddance)

BEST SPECIAL EFFECTS IN A VIDEO

1984	Herbie Hancock	Rockit
1985	Tom Petty & the Heartbreakers	Don't Come Around Here No More
1986	a-ha	Take On Me
1987	Peter Gabriel	Sledgehammer
1988	Squeeze	Hourglass
1989	Michael Jackson	Leave Me Alone
1990	Tears For Fears	Sowing the Seeds of Love
1991	Faith No More	Falling to Pieces
1992	U2	Even Better Than the Real Thing
1993	Peter Gabriel	Steam
1994	Peter Gabriel	Kiss That Frog
1995	The Rolling Stones	Love Is Strong
1996	The Smashing Pumpkins	Tonight, Tonight
1997	Jamiroquai	Virtual Insanity
1998	Madonna	Frozen
1999	Garbage	Special
2000	Bjork	All Is Full of Love
2001	Robbie Williams	RockDJ

BEST DIRECTION IN A VIDEO

1984	ZZ Top	Sharp Dressed Man
1985	Don Henley	The Boys of Summer
1986	a-ha	Take On Me
1987	Peter Gabriel	Sledgehammer
1988	George Michael	Father Figure
1989	Madonna	Express Yourself
1990	Madonna	Vogue
1991	R.E.M.	Losing My Religion
1992	Van Halen	Right Now
1993	Pearl Jam	Jeremy
1994	R.E.M.	Everybody Hurts
1995	Weezer	Buddy Holly
1996	The Smashing Pumpkins	Tonight, Tonight
1997	Beck	The New Pollution
1998	Madonna	Ray of Light
1999	Fatboy Slim	Praise You
2000	Red Hot Chili Peppers	Californication
2001	Fatboy Slim	Weapon of Choice

BREAKTHROUGH VIDEO

1988	INXS	Need You Tonight/Mediate
1989	Art of Noise, featuring Tom Jones	Kiss
1990	Tears for Fears	Sowing the Seeds of Love
1991	R.E.M.	Losing My Religion
1992	Red Hot Chili Peppers	Give It Away
1993	Los Lobos	Kiko & The Lavender Moon
1994	R.E.M.	Everybody Hurts
1995	Weezer	Buddy Holly
1996	The Smashing Pumpkins	Tonight, Tonight
1997	Jamiroquai	Virtual Insanity
1998	Prodigy	Smack My Bitch Up
1999	Fatboy Slim	Praise You
2000	Bjork	All Is Full of Love
2001	Fatboy Slim	Weapon of Choice

VIDEO VANGUARD AWARD

1984	The Beatles, David Bowie, Richard Lester
1985	David Byrne, Kevin Godley and Lol Creme, Russell Mulcahy
1986	Madonna and Zbigniew Rybeznski
1987	Julien Temple and Peter Gabriel
1988	Michael Jackson
1989	George Michael
1990	Janet Jackson
1991	Bon Jovi, Wayne Isham
1992	Guns N' Roses
1993	no award given
1994	Tom Petty
1995	R.E.M.
1996	no award given
1997	Mark Romanek, L.L. Cool J
1998	The Beastie Boys
2001	U2

VIEWER'S CHOICE AWARD

1984	Michael Jackson	Thriller
1985	USA for Africa	We Are the World
1986	a-ha	Take On Me
1987	U2	With or Without You
1988	INXS	Need You Tonight/Mediate
1989	Madonna	Like a Prayer
1990	Aerosmith	Janie's Got a Gun
1994	Aerosmith	Cryin'
1995	TLC	Waterfalls
1996	Bush	Glycerine
1997	Prodigy	Breathe
1998	Puff Daddy & The Family featuring The Lox, Lil' Kim, The Notorious B.I.G., and fuzzbubble	It's All About the Benjamins (Rock Remix)
1999	Backstreet Boys	I Want It That Way
2000	'N Sync	Bye, Bye, Bye
2001	'N Sync	Pop

THE COUNTRY MUSIC ASSOCIATION AWARDS

	1967	1968	1969
Entertainer	Eddy Arnold	Glen Campbell	Johnny Cash
Song	Dallas Frazier, "There Goes My Everything"	Bobby Russell, "Honey"	Bob Ferguson, "Carroll County Accident"
Female Vocalist	Loretta Lynn	Tammy Wynette	Tammy Wynette
Male Vocalist	Jack Greene	Glen Campbell	Johnny Cash
Album	Jack Greene, *There Goes My Everything*	Johnny Cash, *Johnny Cash at Folsom Prison*	Johnny Cash, *Johnny Cash at San Quentin Prison*
Single	Jack Greene, "There Goes My Everything"	Jeannie C. Riley, "Harper Valley P.T.A."	Johnny Cash, "A Boy Named Sue"
Vocal Group	The Stoneman Family	Porter Wagoner and Dolly Parton	Johnny Cash and June Carter
Musician	Chet Atkins	Chet Atkins	Chet Atkins

	1970	1971	1972
Entertainer	Merle Haggard	Charley Pride	Loretta Lynn
Song	Kris Kristofferson, "Sunday Morning Coming Down"	Freddie Hart, "Easy Loving"	Freddie Hart, "Easy Loving"
Female Vocalist	Tammy Wynette	Lynn Anderson	Loretta Lynn
Male Vocalist	Merle Haggard	Charley Pride	Charley Pride
Album	Merle Haggard, *Okie from Muskogee*	Ray Price, *I Won't Mention It Again*	Merle Haggard, *Let Me Tell You About a Song*
Single	Merle Haggard, "Okie From Muskogee"	Sammi Smith, "Help Me Make It Through the Night"	Donna Fargo, "The Happiest Girl in the Whole U.S.A."
Vocal Group	The Glaser Brother	The Osborne Brothers	The Statler Brothers
Vocal Duo	Porter Wagoner and Dolly Parton	Porter Wagoner and Dolly Parton	Conway Twitty and Loretta Lynn
Musician	Jerry Reed	Jerry Reed	Charlie McCoy

	1973	**1974**	**1975**
Entertainer	Roy Clark	Charlie Rich	John Denver
Song	Kenny O'Dell, "Behind Closed Doors"	Don Wayne, "Country Bumpkin"	John Denver, "Back Home Again"
Female Vocalist	Loretta Lynn	Olivia Newton-John	Dolly Parton
Male Vocalist	Charlie Rich	Ronnie Milsap	Waylon Jennings
Album	Charlie Rich, *Behind Closed Doors*	Charlie Rich, *A Very Special Love Song*	Ronnie Milsap, *A Legend in My Time*
Single	Charlie Rich, "Behind Closed Doors"	Cal Smith, "Country Bumpkin"	Freddy Fender, "Before the Next Teardrop Falls"
Vocal Group	The Statler Brothers	The Statler Brothers	The Statler Brothers
Vocal Duo	Conway Twitty and Loretta Lynn	Conway Twitty and Loretta Lynn	Conway Twitty and Loretta Lynn
Musician	Charlie McCoy	Don Rich	Johnny Gimble

	1976	**1977**	**1978**
Entertainer	Mel Tillis	Ronnie Milsap	Dolly Parton
Song	Larry Weiss, "Rhinestone Cowboy"	Roger Bowling & Hal Bynum, "Lucille"	Richard Leigh, "Don't It Make My Brown Eyes Blue"
Female Vocalist	Dolly Parton	Crystal Gayle	Crystal Gayle
Male Vocalist	Ronnie Milsap	Ronnie Milsap	Don Williams
Album	Waylon Jennings, Willie Nelson, Tompall Glaser, Jessi Colter, *Wanted—The Outlaws*	Ronnie Milsap, *Ronnie Milsap Live*	Ronnie Milsap, *It Was Almost Like a Song*
Single	Waylon Jennings & Willie Nelson, "Good Hearted Woman"	Kenny Rogers, "Lucille"	The Kendalls, "Heaven's Just a Sin Away"
Vocal Group	The Statler Brothers	The Statler Brothers	The Oak Ridge Boys
Vocal Duo	Waylon Jennings & Willie Nelson	Jim Ed Brown & Helen Cornelius	Kenny Rogers and Dottie West
Musician	Hargus "Pig" Robbins	Roy Clark	Roy Clark

	1979	1980	1981
Entertainer	Willie Nelson	Barbara Mandrell	Barbara Mandrell
Song	Don Schlitz, "The Gambler"	Bobby Braddock & Curly Putman, "He Stopped Loving Her Today"	Bobby Braddock & Curly Putman, "He Stopped Loving Her Today"
Female Vocalist	Barbara Mandrell	Emmylou Harris	Barbara Mandrell
Male Vocalist	Kenny Rogers	George Jones	George Jones
Album	Kenny Rogers, *The Gambler*	Original Motion Picture Soundtrack, *Coal Miner's Daughter*	Don Williams, *I Believe in You*
Single	Charlie Daniels Band, "The Devil Went Down to Georgia"	George Jones, "He Stopped Loving Her Today"	Oak Ridge Boys, "Elvira"
Vocal Group	The Statler Brothers	The Statler Brothers	Alabama
Horizon Award	—	—	Terri Gibbs
Vocal Duo	Kenny Rogers and Dottie West	Moe Bandy and Joe Stampley	David Frizzell and Shelly West
Musician	Charlie Daniels	Roy Clark	Chet Atkins

	1982	1983	1984
Entertainer	Alabama	Alabama	Alabama
Song	Johnny Christopher, Wayne Carson, Mark James, "Always On My Mind"	Johnny Christopher, Wayne Carson, Mark James, "Always On My Mind"	Larry Henley, Jeff Silbar, "Wind Beneath My Wings"
Female Vocalist	Janie Fricke	Janie Fricke	Reba McEntire
Male Vocalist	Ricky Skaggs	Lee Greenwood	Lee Greenwood
Album	Willie Nelson, *Always on My Mind*	Alabama, *The Closer You Get*	Anne Murray, *A Little Good News*
Single	Willie Nelson, "Always on My Mind"	John Anderson, "Swingin'"	Anne Murray, "A Little Good News"
Vocal Group	Alabama	Alabama	The Statler Brothers
Horizon Award	Ricky Skaggs	John Anderson	The Judds
Vocal Duo	David Frizzell and Shelly West	Merle Haggard and Willie Nelson	Willie Nelson & Julio Iglesias
Musician	Chet Atkins	Chet Atkins	Chet Atkins

1985 | 1986 | 1987

	1985	1986	1987
Entertainer	Ricky Skaggs	Reba McEntire	Hank Williams Jr.
Song	Lee Greenwood, "God Bless the USA"	Paul Overstreet, Don Schlitz, "On the Other Hand"	Paul Overstreet, Don Schlitz, "Forever and Ever, Amen"
Female Vocalist	Reba McEntire	Reba McEntire	Reba McEntire
Male Vocalist	George Strait	George Strait	Randy Travis
Album	George Strait, *Does Fort Worth Ever Cross Your Mind*	Ronnie Milsap, *Lost in the Fifties Tonight*	Randy Travis, *Always and Forever*
Single	The Judds, "Why Not Me"	Dan Seals, "Bop"	Randy Travis, "Forever and Ever, Amen"
Vocal Group	The Judds	The Judds	The Judds
Horizon Award	Sawyer Brown	Randy Travis	Holly Dunn
Vocal Duo	Anne Murray and Dave Loggins	Dan Seals and Marie Osmond	Ricky Skaggs and Sharon White
Musician	Chet Atkins	Johnny Gimble	Johnny Gimble
Music Video	Hank Williams Jr., *All My Rowdy Friends Are Comin' Over Tonight*	George Jones, *Who's Gonna Fill Their Shoes*	Hank Williams Jr., *My Name Is Bocephus*

1988 | 1989 | 1990

	1988	1989	1990
Entertainer	Hank Williams Jr.	George Strait	George Strait
Song	K.T. Oslin, "80's Ladies"	Max D. Barnes, Vern Gosdin, "Chiseled in Stone"	Jon Vezner, Don Henry, "Where've You Been"
Female Vocalist	K.T. Oslin	Kathy Mattea	Kathy Mattea
Male Vocalist	Randy Travis	Ricky Van Shelton	Clint Black
Album	Hank Williams Jr., *Born to Boogie*	Nitty Gritty Dirt Band, *Will the Circle Be Unbroken, Vol. II*	Kentucky HeadHunters, *Pickin' on Nashville*
Single	Kathy Mattea, "Eighteen Wheels and a Dozen Roses"	Keith Whitley, "I'm No Stranger to the Rain"	Vince Gill, "When I Call Your Name"
Vocal Group	Highway 101	Highway 101	Kentucky HeadHunters
Vocal Event	Dolly Parton, Emmylou Harris, Linda Ronstadt, *Trio*	Hank Williams Jr., Hank Williams Sr.	Lorrie Morgan, Keith Whitley
Horizon Award	Ricky Van Shelton	Clint Black	Garth Brooks
Vocal Duo	The Judds	The Judds	The Judds
Musician	Chet Atkins	Johnny Gimble	Johnny Gimble
Music Video	—	Hank Williams Jr., Hank Williams Sr., *There's a Tear in My Beer*	Garth Brooks, *The Dance*

1991 | 1992 | 1993

	1991	1992	1993
Entertainer	Garth Brooks	Garth Brooks	Vince Gill
Song	Vince Gill, Tim DuBois, "When I Call Your Name"	Vince Gill, Max D. Barnes, "Look at Us"	Vince Gill, John Barlow Jarvis, "I Still Believe in You"
Female Vocalist	Tanya Tucker	Mary-Chapin Carpenter	Mary-Chapin Carpenter
Male Vocalist	Vince Gill	Vince Gill	Vince Gill
Album	Garth Brooks, *No Fences*	Garth Brooks, *Ropin' the Wind*	Vince Gill, *I Still Believe in You*
Single	Garth Brooks, "Friends in Low Places"	Billy Ray Cyrus, "Achy Breaky Heart"	Alan Jackson, "Chattahoochee"
Vocal Group	Kentucky HeadHunters	Diamond Rio	Diamond Rio
Vocal Event	Mark O'Connor & The New Nashville Cats (featuring Vince Gill, Ricky Skaggs, and Steve Wariner)	Marty Stuart, Travis Tritt	George Jones with Vince Gill, Mark Chesnutt, Garth Brooks, Travis Tritt, Joe Diffie, Alan Jackson, Pam Tillis, T. Graham Brown, Patty Loveless, Clint Black, *I Don't Need Your Rockin' Chair*
Horizon Award	Travis Tritt	Suzy Bogguss	Mark Chesnutt
Vocal Duo	The Judds	Brooks & Dunn	Brooks & Dunn
Musician	Mark O'Connor	Mark O'Connor	Mark O'Connor
Music Video	Garth Brooks, *The Thunder Rolls*	Alan Jackson, *Midnight in Montgomery*	Alan Jackson, *Chattahoochee*

1994 | 1995 | 1996

	1994	1995	1996
Entertainer	Vince Gill	Alan Jackson	Brooks & Dunn
Song	Alan Jackson, Jim McBride, "Chattahoochee"	Gretchen Peters, "Independence Day"	Vince Gill, "Go Rest High on That Mountain"
Female Vocalist	Pam Tillis	Alison Krauss	Patty Loveless
Male Vocalist	Vince Gill	Vince Gill	George Strait
Album	*Common Thread: The Songs of the Eagles*	Patty Loveless, *When Fallen Angels Fly*	George Strait, *Blue Clear Sky*
Single	John Michael Montgomery, "I Swear"	Alison Krauss and the Union Station, "When You Say Nothing at All"	George Strait, "Check Yes or No"
Vocal Group	Diamond Rio	The Mavericks	The Mavericks
Vocal Event	Reba McEntire with Linda Davis, "Does He Love You"	Shenandoah with Alison Krauss, "Somewhere in the Vicinity of the Heart"	Dolly Parton with Vince Gill, "I Will Always Love You"
Horizon Award	John Michael Montgomery	Alison Krauss	Bryan White
Vocal Duo	Brooks & Dunn	Brooks & Dunn	Brooks & Dunn
Musician	Mark O'Connor	Mark O'Connor	Mark O'Connor
Music Video	Martina McBride, *Independence Day*	The Tractors, *Baby Likes to Rock It*	Junior Brown, *My Wife Thinks You're Dead*

	1997	1998	1999
Entertainer	Garth Brooks	Garth Brooks	Shania Twain
Song	Matraca Berg, Gary Harrison, "Strawberry Wine"	Billy Kirsch, Steve Wariner, "Holes in the Floor of Heaven"	Annie Roboff, Robin Lerner, Beth Nielsen Chapman, "This Kiss"
Female Vocalist	Trisha Yearwood	Trisha Yearwood	Martina McBride
Male Vocalist	George Strait	George Strait	Tim McGraw
Album	George Strait, *Carrying Your Love With Me*	Tim McGraw, *Everywhere*	Tim McGraw, *A Place in the Sun*
Single	Deana Carter, "Strawberry Wine"	"Holes in the Floor of Heaven," Steve Wariner	"Wide Open Spaces," Dixie Chicks
Vocal Group	Diamond Rio	Dixie Chicks	Dixie Chicks
Vocal Event	Tim McGraw with Faith Hill, "It's Your Love"	Patty Loveless with George Jones, "You Don't Seem to Miss Me"	Vince Gill and Patty Loveless, "My Kind of Woman/My Kind of Man"
Horizon Award	LeAnn Rimes	Dixie Chicks	Jo Dee Messina
Vocal Duo	Brooks & Dunn	Brooks & Dunn	Brooks & Dunn
Musician	Brent Mason	Brent Mason	Randy Scruggs
Music Video	Kathy Mattea, *455 Rocket*	Faith Hill, *This Kiss*	Dixie Chicks, "Wide Open Spaces"

	2000
Entertainer	Dixie Chicks
Song	Lee Ann Womack with Sons of the Desert, "I Hope You Dance"
Female Vocalist	Faith Hill
Male Vocalist	Tim McGraw
Album	Dixie Chicks, *Fly*
Single	Lee Ann Womack with the Sons of the Desert, "I Hope You Dance"
Group	Dixie Chicks
Vocal Event	George Strait and Alan Jackson, "Murder on Music Row"
Horizon Award	Brad Paisley
Duo	Montgomery Gentry
Musician	Hargus "Pig" Robbins
Music Video	Dixie Chicks, *Goodbye Earl*

PAGES

PICKS & PANS 2001

Live-in swamis, letters from dead wives, and the chance to relive any three weeks are just a few of the gripping plot points of this year's Picks, with the very best noted by stars. Pans, can also be found in the collection, but are mercifully far fewer.

FICTION

HORNITO
Mike Albo

The 31-year-old author, raised in Virginia, has written a gay coming-of-age novel that's rip-roaringly funny and sympathetic. The title refers to a type of volcano.

THE HERO'S WALK
Anita Rau Badami

Sripathi Rao is a ne'er-do-well Indian ad copywriter in his late 50s who is forced to take care of his orphaned 7-year-old Canadian granddaughter. In a twisty tale of shifting perspectives and resonant prose, Hero makes old values seem new again.

THE FLORABAMA LADIES' AUXILIARY & SEWING CIRCLE
Lois Battle

The local mill has shut up shop, leaving its female employees jobless and demoralized. Enter Bonnie Cullman, whose new job as a career counselor gives her the chance to help the seamstresses find work as she works on finding herself. *Florabama* is an often humorous and well-tailored tale of determined women.

NEVER CHANGE
Elizabeth Berg

Myra, 51, is a nurse who finds herself caring for Chip, a former high school crush. Time for teen fantasies finally to be fulfilled.

A PERFECT ARRANGEMENT
Suzanne Berne

Mirella Cook-Goldman's life is a mess. The babysitter just quit, her husband can't pick up the slack, and she might be pregnant again. When nanny Randi Gill shows up with glowing recommendations, Mirella believes her prayers have been answered, but the cracks in Cook-Goldman's marriage begin to widen. Berne nails the messy domesticity that resides where Martha Stewart fails to tread.

SCARLET FEATHER
Maeve Binchy

Dublin cooking-school classmates Cathy Scarlet and Tom Feather dream of starting their own catering business, *Scarlet Feather*. Business that first year is full of tribulations, as Binchy seems eager to toss in myriad characters and subplots.

IN THE FOREST OF HARM
Sallie Bissell

Atlanta prosecutor Mary Crow has just convicted her sixth murderer and heads to the mountainous forests of her childhood with her two best girlfriends from law school. Hot on their trail is the vengeful brother of the man Mary just sent to jail. The women's journey of survival—with Mary as both hunter and prey—propels this solid page-turner.

BELOVED STRANGER
Clare Boylan

This novel concerns an ordinary couple—married for 50 years—whose lives are wrenched out of shape when the husband suddenly becomes manic-depressive.

THE TRIUMPH OF KATIE BYRNE
Barbara Taylor Bradford

Katie Byrne, who narrowly escaped an attack that left one best friend dead and the other in a coma, spends the next decade haunted by the tragedy—and the fear that the killer might come back for her—even as she launches a glamorous acting career. Alas, the two story lines don't really mesh.

YEAR OF WONDERS: A NOVEL OF THE PLAGUE
Geraldine Brooks

A mining accident kills Anna Frith's husband and the plague takes her two sons. But there will be little time for grieving once the rector's wife recruits Anna, teaching her to read and to help prepare herbal remedies to treat the ever-increasing number of victims. A former war correspondent, Brooks subtly reveals how ignorance, hatred and mistrust can be as deadly as any virus.

ENVY
Sandra Brown

New York City book editor Maris Matherly-Reed is desperate to find hot new writers. Trawling through the slush pile of unsolicited manuscripts, she finds one—but comes to wish she hadn't. The intriguing novel is by a mysterious writer named P.M.E. who gives no address or phone number and doesn't seem to want to be found. But what looked like reticence from the writer was really part of his plan to lure Matherly-Reed into his web of revenge against the man who sentenced him to life in a wheelchair 14 years before—a man she knows very well.

YOU ONLY DIE TWICE
Edna Buchanan

A freshly deceased body of Kaithlin Jordan washes up on shore 10 years after she was supposedly murdered, and her husband is about to be executed for the crime. Buchanan has devised a classically molded whodunit with many twists and turns.

BITTERROOT
James Lee Burke
Billy Bob Holland, lawyer and ex-Texas Ranger, takes on a Montana mining company whose nasty doings are in sharp contrast to the beautiful scenery.

IN SUNLIGHT, IN A BEAUTIFUL GARDEN
Kathleen Cambor
A large cast swirls through this evocative, if flawed, first novel set against the Johnstown Flood, which killed more than 2,000 on Memorial Day, 1889. One can almost hear the rustle of petticoats, the sound of the (doomed) crowds lining the Johnstown Memorial Day parade route and, most ominously, the water rampaging across the earth.

CARRY ME ACROSS THE WATER
Ethan Canin
August Kleinman nears the end of his life sad and alone; he is also consumed by memories of an encounter with a Japanese soldier in a cave during World War II. Kleinman's journey of self-discovery is so well-written that it's a trip worth taking.

THE TIN COLLECTORS
Stephen J. Cannell
The title of this latest suspense novel from the noted TV writer and producer refers to the LAPD's Internal Affairs agents who go after a cop's badge if he messes up. Det. Shane Scully has, and how: He has shot his ex-partner.

THE FOURTH ANGEL
Suzanne Chazin
Newly appointed New York City Fire Marshal Georgia Skeehan must capture a sophisticated and diabolical arsonist fond of firing off quotes from the Book of Revelations before he torches

buildings. In this debut, Chazin dazzles with her knowledge of pyrotechnics and comes up with plot twists aplenty.

ECHO BURNING
Lee Child
Mexican-American Carmen Greer desperately wants a man—to murder her husband. A violent story as sweltering as the El Paso sun, Child keeps the action graphic and the tension high.

ON THE STREET WHERE YOU LIVE
Mary Higgins Clark
Hours after Emily moves into her new house, contractors find the body of a young woman buried in her yard. Soon other women are turning up dead, and Emily decides to investigate. Clark's style and penchant for plot surprises make the reader want to settle in.

*TELL NO ONE
Harlan Coben
David Beck is getting mail from his dead wife. Eight years after her murder, Beck thinks he's the victim of a sick joke, except for the emailed clues only she could provide. Hit men, a serial killer, and FBI agents on his trail soon have Beck trying to stitch everything together. Coben has crafted a gripping, pulse-pounding beach read.

*HEARSE OF A DIFFERENT COLOR
Tim Cockey
Hitchcock Sewell, an undertaker with an insatiable curiosity, is interested in the case of Helen Waggoner, a murdered beauty whose body shows up on the steps of his business during a blizzard. A most entertaining ride that recalls the TV series *Homicide*.

MIAMI TWILIGHT
Tom Coffey
Doherty is an ordinary guy whose contact with a client sucks him into an underworld where nothing is what it seems, unless, of course, you've read

this kind of book before. Coffey has written a traditional noir and, unfortunately, a ploddingly generic one.

HOLLYWOOD WIVES: THE NEW GENERATION
Jackie Collins
Sex. Scheming. More sex. Eighteen years after she hit the bestseller lists with *Hollywood Wives*, Collins takes another look at love and lust in La-La Land. Though sometimes sordid and often just plain silly, *Wives* still manages to make marital melodrama fun.

*A DARKNESS MORE THAN NIGHT
Michael Connelly
In this thoughtful new thriller, former FBI profiler Terry McCaleb thinks he has gotten crime fighting out of his system, until an old colleague wants to brainstorm about the investigation of a bizarre murder that implicates an officer McCaleb knows and admires.

DARK HOLLOW
John Connolly
Ex-cop Charlie "Bird" Parker, the shattered antihero of Connolly's first novel, has left New York City for Maine, but trouble has his forwarding address. When a

woman is found dead, a search for her thuggish ex turns into a hunt for far more unusual quarry: a serial killer who is back in business after 40 dormant years.

LAYER CAKE
J. J. Connolly

Can't wait for the next cockney caper filmed by Mr. Madonna, Guy Ritchie? This tangy and tangled trip through the London underworld is being made into Ritchie's next, *The Mole*.

SHARPE'S FORTRESS
Bernard Cornwell

Starring British officer Richard Sharpe (a kind of Indiana Jones), this novel, the sixteenth in a series, is a zippy joyride.

BEING DEAD
Jim Crace

A married couple's gruesome end marks the beginning of this unusual love story, the winner of this year's National Book Critics Circle Award for fiction.

HOSTAGE
Robert Crais

The Mob is about to make Police Chief Jeff Talley an offer he can't refuse. When a botched robbery erupts into a hostage standoff, the former L.A. SWAT negotiator panics, paralyzed by memories of the bloodbath that drove him off the squad and into sleepy suburbia. But if Talley thinks all that's at stake is a family at gunpoint, fuhged-daboutit.

A FINER END
Deborah Crombie

In this seventh tale about detectives Gemma and Duncan, the amorous duo puzzle out a mystery with pagan overtones.

FAST WOMEN
Jennifer Crusie

Nell is recently divorced and newly employed by a detective agency specializing in adultery. Intertwined with Nell's sex-and-

apartment hunting saga is a murder mystery involving diamonds, a classic Porsche, and a meat locker that hasn't been opened in seven years. The plot points are so obvious they seem to stand up and introduce themselves.

THE NEW YORK TIMES BESTSELLING AUTHOR OF *TOUGH COOKIE*

DIANE MOTT DAVIDSON

STICKS & SCONES

*STICKS AND SCONES
Diane Mott Davidson

Goldy Schulz's window is shot at, she finds a dead body, and she has to cater a luncheon. Goldy whips up dozens of theories, and suddenly everyone's a suspect. In her tenth "culinary mystery," Davidson cooks up such a complex batter that the ingredients don't blend until the very end, while the suspense factor rises higher.

*THE BLUE NOWHERE
Jeffery Deaver

In Deaver's paranoid nightmare, a game-playing psycho tries to delete as many people as possible in a week. To track him, police enlist master programmer Wyatt Gillette. Deaver keeps the excitement streaming and fills every keystroke with suspense.

SPEAKING IN TONGUES
Jeffery Deaver

From the bestselling author of *The Bone Collector* comes an

eerie tale about a therapist plotting to kidnap a patient.

OF CATS AND MEN
Nina de Gramont

These smart but not so soft and fuzzy domestic tales will give you pause about that other familiar love triangle: feisty felines, messy men—and the women who love them both.

THE BODY ARTIST
Don DeLillo

DeLillo's tightly constructed tale of fate and identity revolves around Lauren Hartke and a mysterious old man who quotes verbatim the words of Hartke's dead husband, leaving Hartke to wonder what is real and what is a fragment of her injured psyche.

CRANBERRY QUEEN
Kathleen DeMarco

After tragedy interrupts Diana Moore's self-absorption, she takes to the road and winds up in New Jersey's Pine Barrens, where she nurses her wounds amid the annual cranberry festival. Though the plot is predictable, DeMarco's sharp wit and Diana's *Bridget Jones*-style neuroses make Cranberry worth a taste.

THE SUMMERHOUSE
Jude Deveraux

A trio of friends gathering in Maine are magically given an intriguing opportunity: to relive any three weeks from their pasts.

BETWEEN LOVERS
Eric Jerome Dickey

Lust and confusion collide in this supple novel about a woman who wants it all: the man she dumped at the altar—and the sexy female lawyer she loves.

SLAMMERKIN
Emma Donoghue

The odd title is a word that means both a loose dress and a loose woman, and this novel, set in the 18th century, offers an involving tale about both.

GABRIEL'S STORY
David Anthony Durham
There are more than a few good, bad, and ugly moments to savor in this bold debut novel about a 15-year-old black Easterner's coming of age among the cowboys and homesteaders of the post-Civil War American West in the 1870s.

THE ROSE CITY
David Ebershoff
Pasadena, home of the Rose Parade, is the setting for seven perceptive short stories that demolish any notions that life in that enclave there is all sun and roses.

THE COMPANY
Arabella Edge
In this fictionalized revisit to 1629, when the Dutch East India Company's *Batavia* ran aground off the coast of Australia, Amsterdam apothecary Jeronimus Cornelisz disguises himself as a merchant and ships out for the Spice Islands. Ever the schemer, our man plots a mutiny to commandeer the *Batavia*'s vast treasures.

THE LAST REPORT ON THE MIRACLES AT LITTLE NO HORSE
Louise Erdrich
Old Father Damien has a secret: he's really a woman named Agnes DeWitt. Erdrich tells a complex and imaginative story, weaving together the mysticism of the Native American world and the raw emotions surrounding Agnes's masquerade.

THE BLACK MADONNA
Louisa Ermelino
Picture it: Little Italy, New York City, 1948. This novel, an Italian version of the *Joy Luck Club*, shows how three old ladies hew to traditions of the old country in the one they have adopted.

*SEVEN UP
Janet Evanovich
Expect a laugh per page as big-haired bounty hunter Stephanie Plum chases the depressed but gun-happy septuagenarian Eddie DeChooch in this witty, gritty seventh episode of Evanovich's popular crime series.

CAUSE CELEB
Helen Fielding
After fleeing to an African refugee camp, Rosie Richardson returns to London four years later to rally her old celebrity pals to take part in a televised appeal. The result is a searing, poignant, and at times hilarious satire of the most ludicrous elements of the Western media.

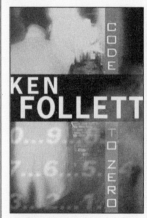

*CODE TO ZERO
Ken Follett
There is intrigue aplenty in this space-race espionage duel set in 1958. Focused, fast-moving, leavened by a few dollops of romance and no more cerebral than it has to be, this is Follett at his best.

KINGDOM OF SHADOWS
Alan Furst
James Bond minus the wise-cracks. As the Nazis slash across Europe, Nicholas Morath is a one-man resistance, dashing in and out of Hitler's jaws on various missions impossible.

MR. COMMITMENT
Mike Gayle
Gayle's second novel mines the same vein as Nick Hornby's *High Fidelity* and finds just as much comedy gold. This one centers on Benjamin Duffy, a stand-up comic forced to get serious when his longtime girlfriend asks him to marry her.

MISFORTUNE
Nancy Geary
Socialite Clio Henshaw Pratt is murdered at a posh country club in the Hamptons. Some of her peers seem less upset than if they'd run out of vermouth, but Clio's stepdaughter Frances Pratt, an assistant D.A., is sweating suspects faster than you can say "Manolo Blahnik."

A TRAITOR TO MEMORY
Elizabeth George
Detectives Thomas Lynley and Barbara Havers are searching for the link between the hit-and-run killing of Eugenie Davies and the secrets locked in the mind of her son, a celebrated violinist afflicted by his dysfunctional family and repressed memories. This mystery is entwined in a family saga that makes the Windsors look like the Cleavers.

BAD BOY
Olivia Goldsmith
Jon Delano is a computer geek whose love life reads like a disaster report; the only thing going for Jon is his best friend Tracie, who is smart, sexy and sophisticated. When Jon begs her to help rework him into a "bad boy," the novel kicks into high comic gear.

PARADISE PARK
Allegra Goodman
Narrator Sharon Spiegelman spends the 1970s and '80s wandering the Hawaiian Islands, dabbling in spiritual movements, drugs and sexual adventures.

Unfortunately, her 20 years of aimlessness stretch across the similarly meandering book.

P IS FOR PERIL
Sue Grafton

There's too little peril and too much plodding in this sixteenth installment of Grafton's much-loved alphabet mystery series. Fans of spunky P.I. Kinsey Millhone will enjoy catching up with the heroine, but the mystery of the disappearance of a doctor under investigation for Medicare fraud is less than enthralling.

MR. MAYBE
Jane Green

If money can't buy love, it still comes in handy when you want to be swathed in the Gucci and Prada labels craved by Libby Mason, who can't afford the glad rags and can't find a man. It takes her the whole book to figure out what readers know before they get past the title page: Love is more important than a society-page wedding.

A PAINTED HOUSE
John Grisham

In this middling departure from his standard fare, Grisham offers this 100 percent courtroom-free novel about Luke Chandler, a boy with "lots of secrets but no way to unload them." Grisham never quite succeeds in drawing other characters into Luke's dilemmas.

*EQUIVOCAL DEATH
Amy Gutman

Kate Paine knows that many would kill for a job like hers in the prestigious Manhattan law firm of Samson & Mills; then someone does. Circumstances suggest that the killer could well be walking Samson & Mills's halls. Gutman propels her sleuth through many hair-raising moments in this compelling first novel.

SUMMER ISLAND
Kristin Hannah

Ruby has never been able to forgive her mother Nora for abandoning her as a teen, but volunteers to care for her after Nora is badly injured in a car accident. Both women set to unpacking their anger, pride and resentment, but as the pair begin to appreciate each other, their story goes from sour to sweet.

*ANY WAY THE WIND BLOWS
E. Lynn Harris

This continuation of Harris's 2000 bestseller *Not a Day Goes By* has more lying, cheating, bed-hopping and name-calling than a year's worth of Ricki Lake. But if most of Harris's characters can't pass a mirror without falling in love, they are also surprisingly sympathetic.

BLUE DIARY
Alice Hoffman

The author of the whimsical *Practical Magic* trundles in a plot containing few surprises. But even a flawed effort by this pro makes for a satisfying read thanks to such characters as Kat, an ugly duckling who knows too well that if something looks too good to be true, it probably is.

CHALKTOWN
Melinda Haynes

Haynes's tired try at Mississippi blues is full of '50s stereotypes. A 16-year-old sets off for the community of the title, whose residents have taken to communicating by writing on chalkboards on their porches since the unsolved murder of a young woman there six years ago.

BAD HEIR DAY
Wendy Holden

As a satiric field guide to the trust-fund twentysomethings, social-climbing parents, and gold-digging singles of London, *Bad Heir Day* neatly skewers its

targets. But Holden has an unfortunate penchant for repackaged clichés and groan-inducing puns.

*HOW TO BE GOOD
Nick Hornby

Katie Carr's husband, made saintly by a gifted New Age faith healer, invites the swami to move in—and starts giving away possessions and inviting the homeless to move in. This is a surprising novel of ideas that balances spiritual, political and familial questions, and it's an exciting departure for a quietly excellent writer.

SPEAKING WITH THE ANGEL
Edited by Nick Hornby

This collection of short stories corrals such hip younger writers as Dave Eggers and Melissa Bank, plus a moonlighting actor: *The English Patient's* Colin Firth, whose contribution is a gem.

*CANDYLAND
Evan Hunter and Ed McBain

Author Evan Hunter has been slumming as celebrated crime novelist Ed McBain for more than 40 years. Now these two distinct voices have collaborated on a highly entertaining literary exercise. If Hunter provides a compelling psychological portraiture of a man falling down the rabbit hole of sex addiction, McBain easily matches his achievement with an inspired police procedural, topped off with a completely unexpected and satisfying twist at the end.

MINUTES TO BURN
Gregg Andrew Hurwitz

The Hot Zone meets *Jurassic Park* as Navy SEAL Cameron Kates, hiding a pregnancy, does battle with bizarre mutants caused by a virus.

DEAD SLEEP
Greg Iles

Jordan Glass, a combat photographer, has seen her share of

horror. But nothing prepares her for the sharp chill she feels at an exhibition of paintings in Hong Kong. The paintings are all of women who might be asleep. Or they might be dead. Most disturbing, one of the women looks just like Jordan. Following a trail that leads through the international art market and America's Vietnam legacy, Glass finds the key to the paintings and also to her family's buried secrets.

THE FOURTH HAND
John Irving
TV newsman Patrick Wallingford has a hand ripped off by a lion and finds himself in a nutty love affair with a Wisconsin woman who volunteers the hand of her husband, killed in another freak mishap, for a transplant.

THIRTYNOTHING
Lisa Jewell
Lifelong pals Digby and Nadine have not thought seriously about settling down with anyone until Digby's first love comes back into his life. At first this witty British import appears to be little more than *When Harry Met Sally* on the Thames, but Digby and Nadine's path to happiness is not in the least predictable.

GOOD COUNSEL
Tim Junkin
Jack Stanton, a hotshot D.C. trial lawyer, is a heartbeat ahead of the feds at the opening of this suspenseful novel. As Stanton holes up in a deserted home not far from where he grew up, he recalls every stumble that took him from sterling public defender to disgraced fugitive. Junkin's prose soars with a surprisingly thoughtful look at honor, loyalty and love.

DR. DEATH
Jonathan Kellerman
When Dr. Eldon Mate is found murdered, hooked up to his own euthanasia machine, the LAPD

calls in psychiatrist Alex Delaware to profile the killer. Kellerman takes the plot to a deeper level in the controversy over assisted suicide, constructing resonances without sacrificing his roller-coaster plot.

FOLLY
Laurie R. King
After losing her husband and daughter, Rae Newborn begins rebuilding a burned-down family home off the coast of Washington State, where she begins uncovering an island mystery. King has crafted a labyrinthian tale that is as haunting as it is touching.

DREAMCATCHER
Stephen King
Dreamcatcher is a creation as weird as any the master of horror has devised. A simple hunting vacation in the Maine woods takes an unplanned detour into nightmare county, with intergalactic fungus, homicidal special forces, exploding carcasses, and an alien named Mr. Gray.

CONFESSIONS OF A SHOPAHOLIC
Sophie Kinsella
Rebecca Bloomwood would sooner toss her overdue Visa bills into a Dumpster, dodge bank managers' calls or engage

in a shopping frenzy at Dolce & Gabbana than face her own spiraling money problems. But after a warning from her father, she pitches herself into a series of silly get-out-of-debt schemes, including trying to snag England's 15th-richest bachelor.

UP IN THE AIR
Walter Kirn
Ryan Bingham, corporate henchman, has one simple goal: to rack up 1 million frequent-flier miles. This stinging novel tells how he does it.

FROM THE CORNER OF HIS EYE
Dean Koontz
The bestselling author elicits as much emotion as suspense in this spooky story about a boy who loses his eyesight.

LOST & FOUND
Jayne Ann Krentz
When Cady Briggs's great-aunt, owner of a successful art gallery, dies, Cady suspects foul play and hires Mack Easton to help solve the mystery. *Lost & Found* offers a mini-education in such esoteric subjects as the market value of 16th century Italian armor, but it's the lusty ambition of grasping art-world insiders that propels this well-crafted tale.

THE JUSTUS GIRLS
Slim Lambright
The author was down on her luck when she took a $20 writing class two years ago. The result: this winning debut novel about an all-girl drill team.

JACQUELINE SUSANN'S SHADOW OF THE DOLLS
Rae Lawrence
Basing this delightfully trashy tale on a rough draft of a sequel to *Valley of the Dolls*, Lawrence has awakened all the characters from the 1966 novel. This time, they're raising children in the '90s, but not very well. This soapy, filthy setting is the most fun you can get without a prescription.

THE CONSTANT GARDENER
John le Carré

This novel begins in Kenya, where the activist wife of a British diplomat is found murdered. The truth is elusive, and husband Justin tracks his wife's friends from Italy to Germany to Canada. *The Constant Gardener* is most memorable for Justin's attempt to redeem the marriage he left untended.

MYSTIC RIVER
Dennis Lehane

The murder of Jimmy Marcus's daughter on the eve of her elopement sets the plot in motion for this shattering, suspenseful novel that combines the tension of a thriller with the dramatic inevitability of Greek tragedy.

THINKS...
David Lodge

A brilliant male scientist woos a woman poet as they argue about the heart and head in an expertly plotted campus novel.

JUNIPER TREE BURNING
Goldberry Long

Jennifer Braverman starts to crumble when her brother drowns himself. Driving to the site of the suicide, she rattles back and forth from the present to her lonely past. Entertaining but unflinching, *Burning* is a revelation of the ugliest acts we commit against ourselves and those who love us.

ELVIS AND NIXON
Jonathan Lowy

The King and the Prez met in 1970, and Lowy uses that real-life encounter as a springboard for a wild story that touches on Vietnam and Watergate.

BUMP & RUN
Mike Lupica

Steroids, crooked quarterbacks, buffoonish coaches—these are the elements that have won this novel comparisons to the pigskin classic *Semi-Tough.*

CUTOUT
Francine Mathews

When the Vice President is kidnapped, the CIA turns to Caroline Carmichael, an expert on a neo-Nazi terror group blamed for the kidnapping. Mathew's pacing is vigorous, but her plot lines tend to get tangled.

SINGING BOY
Dennis McFarland

Malcolm is driving home with his wife Sarah and their son Harry when he stops to help another motorist and is shot and killed. The novel, told from the alternating perspectives of Sarah, Harry, and Malcolm's best friend, chronicles how each suffers and how they separately fight their way back to the land of the living.

THE ICE CHILD
Elizabeth McGregor

Interconnected stories about the real 1845 voyage of Sir John Franklin from England to the Arctic form the body of this engrossing fact-based novel.

*A DAY LATE AND A DOLLAR SHORT
Terry McMillan

McMillan's back with this touching and often funny portrait of a feuding clan that needs to take the "dys" out of dysfunction. What emerges is a realistic story

of loving kin trying to find the courage to move beyond their grievances to achieve reconciliation.

BOONE'S LICK
Larry McMurtry

The narrator of McMurtry's twenty-third novel is a boy in a post-Civil War family led by feisty Mary Margaret Cecil, who hitches up the wagons on a drive from Missouri to Wyoming in search of the absentee father of her four kids. As always, McMurtry hints at the sweep of history while having some fun with details of everyday life.

THE CENTER OF THINGS
Jenny McPhee

In a sharply comic first novel, a plain-Jane tabloid writer gets obsessed with a B-movie diva while writing the ailing star's obituary.

THE FIRST COUNSEL
Brad Meltzer

When Michael Garrick, a White House lawyer, takes out the First Daughter, he soon finds himself the suspect in a high-profile murder case. *First Counsel* is fast-paced and suspenseful, but most impressive is Meltzer's knowledge of every nook of the White House. With all its grand history and mystery, the mansion comes alive.

PLAIN JANE
Fern Michaels

Part romance, part mystery, this novel is packed with enough subplots to make a reader's head spin. Psychotherapist Jane Lewis grapples with memories of the rape of a college friend, a budding romance, a menacing therapy patient, and the haunting of her southern Louisiana home.

A THEORY OF RELATIVITY
Jacquelyn Mitchard

Mitchard delivers a satisfying, delicate exploration of the ties that bind with her story about

Gordon McKenna, a 24-year-old science teacher whose sister and brother-in-law perish with her husband in a car crash. Their baby daughter is thrust into a custody case that pits Gordon against another couple amid clashing egos, legal nitpicking and misplaced blame.

FEARLESS JONES
Walter Mosley

How do you make things right after you've been beaten down, shot at, had your Nash Rambler stolen and your business torched? If you're Paris Minton, you call on a tall, guileless, Army-trained killing machine named Fearless Jones. After forays into sci-fi, essays and screenplays, Mosley again writes a mystery that rocks.

SPUTNIK SWEETHEART
Haruki Murakami

When a Japanese woman vanishes in Greece, the only clue she leaves behind is a computer file that hints at a bizarre explanation in this surreal tale of unrequited love.

LIFE AFTER DEATH
Carol Muske-Dukes

After years of lies and off-the-wall behavior from her husband, Russell, housewife Boyd Schaeffer has had it. When he leaves their daughter unattended at a playground, Boyd tells him, "Do me a favor, Russell. Die." He promptly complies, succumbing to a heart attack during a tennis match. Boyd's quest to understand what happened is a sparely told tale and her message—that a person can never know another person—is trite.

*THE BEST A MAN CAN GET
John O'Farrell

The best look into a man's mind short of a CAT scan. Michael needs some time away from his wife and two kids once and a while. During his sabbaticals he catches up on his sleep and soccer trivia in a grungy secret flat with three other boy-men. Waiting for Michael to get caught makes this an exercise in suspense as well as laughs.

FIXER CHAO
Han Ong

The Philippine-born author's satiric novel skewers the so-called Beautiful People in New York City with laser-sharp accuracy.

POTSHOT
Robert B. Parker

Parker has unleashed some formidable tough guys and *Potshot* adds five memorable supporting characters from earlier books to the mix. The plot is rustled from the *Magnificent Seven*, and the book isn't Parker's best, but Spenser and his entertaining bunch of second bananas still have plenty of appeal.

*SILENT JOE
T. Jefferson Parker

When his adopted father is ambushed and killed, amateur P.I. Joe Trona naturally investigates. He discovers that his father's well-connected acquaintances have secrets dirtier than L.A.'s air in this sun-drenched noir.

MAN AND BOY
Tony Parsons

Harry, a London TV producer, has just turned 30; his wife storms off, leaving Harry alone with their toddler son. Parsons is sad and funny, frequently in the same sentence, as he maps out the ways people who love each other can find themselves adversaries.

*1ST TO DIE
James Patterson

Four San Francisco women—a homicide inspector, a medical examiner, an assistant D.A. and a reporter—team up to catch a serial killer. While Patterson sometimes lapses into cliché, his clever twists and affecting subplots keep the pages flying.

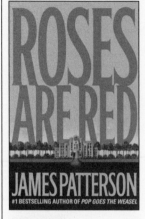

ROSES ARE RED
James Patterson

Alex Cross, the Washington D.C. forensic psychologist from books like *Jack & Jill* and *Pop Goes the Weasel*, investigates a new monster who orchestrates daring bank robberies. Fans will recognize the routine-swift pacing, but the elements are getting a mite predictable.

SUZANNE'S DIARY FOR NICHOLAS
James Patterson

Oh-so-smart Manhattan book editor Katie Wilkinson is kicking herself for being oh-so-blind: Matt, her out-of-town lover for nearly a year, has just dumped her, leaving her with a diary— written by his wife, Suzanne. Best known for Cineplex-ready mysteries, Patterson has crafted a love story as suspenseful as any thriller. Though the story is weighty with matters of birth, life and death, it's also clever, light and as welcoming as an ocean breeze.

PROTECT AND DEFEND
Richard North Patterson

The President's choice for Chief Justice secretly carries significant personal baggage, and an explosive case threatens to derail the nomination. Though too much of the plot hinges on personal secrets, this shrewd novel should make you ponder anew the ways our democracy conducts its business.

RIGHT AS RAIN
George P. Pelecanos

When a black cop is mistaken for a criminal by a white officer who kills him, the black cop's reputation is tarnished in the press. Ex-cop Derek Strange is hired to clear the dead cop's name. He hits it off with the shooter, and an uneasy friendship develops in this chilling, cold-blooded tale.

*DEATH BENEFITS
Thomas Perry

Perry takes a single case of swindling and skillfully spins from it a labyrinthine tale of murder, conspiracy and romance. The hardboiled dialogue, quirky characters and careful pacing deliver some chilling fun.

THIS HEART OF MINE
Susan Elizabeth Phillips

Molly is a struggling children's author with a bad haircut and an empty love life trying to seduce Kevin, a hotshot NFL quarterback who gets his kicks chasing bimbos. Phillips labors to create an endearingly fallible heroine here, but in the end Molly merely annoys.

SALEM FALLS
Jodi Picoult

Updating the Salem witch-hunts in soapy style with a contemporary New England setting, Picoult jumps around the viewpoints of an assortment of overwrought characters. Despite being predictable, this book is a fun brew of mystery, sex, and small-town secrets.

LOOKING BACK
Belva Plain

Cecile, Norma and Amanda are recent college roommates who reunite for Cecile's wedding to Peter. Plain's plotting arranges for the three to lunch regularly and fall out spectacularly, but this novel creaks.

THE BOTANY OF DESIRE
Michael Pollan

An apple, a potato, the tulip, and marijuana: This witty book tells the story of each from the plant's point of view.

SLIGHTLY SHADY
Amanda Quick

When the man who tried to blackmail her turns up dead, Lavinia Lake becomes an investigator. Joining forces with the volatile Tobias March, Lavinia scours London in search of the killer. Quick has spun a tense and romantic tale, and her pacing is impeccable.

THE WIND DONE GONE
Alice Randall

Believing the original story racist, Randall retells *Gone With the Wind* through the eyes of a new character, Scarlett O'Hara's mulatto half sister Cynara, an ex-slave. The book's first half is slow, and the novel is full of stereotypes, but a lyrical style and intriguing reflections on race make this rewrite deserving as well as daring.

THE MUSIC OF THE SPHERES
Elizabeth Redfern

In a period brainteaser reminiscent of Caleb Carr's *The Alienist*, civil servant Jonathan Absey pursues a savage serial killer in 18th-century London.

FATAL VOYAGE
Kathy Reichs

When forensic anthropologist Temperance Brennan investigates a plane crash site in North Carolina's Great Smoky Mountains, there are all sorts of sharp-fanged critters skulking around the debris which gnaw on a human foot that doesn't belong to any of the crash victims. The author is a forensic anthropologist, and these parts aren't lunch-hour reading, unless you're Hannibal Lecter.

DREAM COUNTRY
Luanne Rice

When their teenage daughter goes missing, Daisy and James must confront their long-buried pain and a new threat: a killer out for revenge. The plot twists feel forced, but her evocative imagery makes such flaws easy to overlook.

THE DYING ANIMAL
Phillip Roth

Turning 70, Roth's narrator, Professor David Kepesh, is still picking young women to join in a sad line of conquests stretching back to the 1960s, when he left his wife to enlist in the sexual revolution. Sexually omnivorous and occasionally brutal, Kepesh has no one to grow old with, so he hunts such prey as a beautiful 24-year-old student. Roth creeps closer to the Nobel with this searing and cold-eyed novel.

ICY SPARKS
Gwyn Hyman Rubio

The tics and curses that Icy tries to suppress are symptoms of Tourette's syndrome, a disorder that goes undiagnosed throughout Icy's trying adolescence. The relationship between Icy and her grandparents is nicely understated, but the book's overcooked symbolism grows tiresome.

THE DISCOVERY OF CHOCOLATE
James Runcie

Chocoholics not sated by *Chocolat* (book or film) will savor this novel, which sends its hero through time and space (from Vienna to Hershey, Pa.), reveling in the taste of life.

EMPIRE FALLS
Richard Russo

Miles Roby is on a losing streak: his wife of 20 years has left him, the diner he runs barely shows a profit, and everyone takes advantage of his generosity. Russo's affection for his flawed protagonists and colorful supporting characters brings this story to life.

LYING AWAKE
Mark Salzman

This spirited read thoughtfully explores a nun's crisis of faith. Sister John of the Cross finds herself blessed with miraculous visions and bedeviled by debilitating migraines. To her, the visions and headaches amount to a special relationship with God; to her doctor they suggest a form of epilepsy. But will healing Sister John's body harm her soul?

KISSING IN MANHATTAN
David Schickler

Alternately as funny and frightening as the city itself, Schickler's 11 offbeat stories are inventive, if socially stunted, visions of lonely hearts—a woman with dangerous sexual needs, a guy

who talks to elevators—desperate to only connect.

THE VENDETTA DEFENSE
Lisa Scottoline

Tony Lucia is a slight, 79-year-old Italian immigrant with broken English, a mild temperament and homing pigeons for pets. After a lifetime of fear, he has finally killed aging mobster Angelo Coluzzi, concluding a 60-year vendetta. Watching Philidelphia defense lawyer Judy Carrier turn vengeance into a plausible defense is highly entertaining.

BOY STILL MISSING
John Searles

When Dominick learns that his father's mistress is pregnant, he decides to do a secret favor for her to spite his parents, but learns a painful lesson when his efforts lead to his mother's undoing. Guilt-ridden, he embarks on a harrowing journey to uncover secrets about his family in this compelling coming-of-age tale.

RISE TO REBELLION
Jeff Shaara

The genius of this book, the story of the founding of our nation, is that the author uses the novelized voices of Washington, Adams and Franklin to tell it.

MISCONCEPTION
Robert L. Shapiro and Walt Becker

Written by one of O.J. Simpson's lawyers, this taut legal thriller culminates in a trial that threatens to overthrow Roe v. Wade.

*THE LAST TIME THEY MET
Anita Shreve

Poets Linda Fallon and Thomas Janes, ex-lovers with a turbulent past, reconnect at a book signing. The details are vague, but it looks like a happy ending is in order. Read the first 50 pages of this poignant novel and you might mistake it for a romance—but it's a mystery, and one so astonishingly well-constructed

that when you're finished you'll want to reread it at once.

ICED
Jenny Siler

Megan Gardner is an ex-con who gets herself tangled in a complex web of murder and intrigue. So much about this book is refreshing—for openers, the hit man is a woman—that despite a plot that doesn't keep pace, *Iced* remains a bracing, original tonic.

THE KILL ARTIST
Daniel Silva

The author uses his expertise as a former Middle East correspondent to concoct a heart-pounding thriller about an ex-Israeli intelligence agent and the assassination plot he must thwart.

THE BRONZE HORSEMAN
Paullina Simons

For readers who like their books doorstop size, this hefty novel (by the Russian-born author of Tully) recalls Dr. Zhivago in setting and sweep. There's no shortage of snow either.

PROOF POSITIVE
Philip Singerman

Undercover agent Roland Troy has retired to Vermont . . . but then he is drawn into solving a deliciously intriguing conspiracy.

AIDING AND ABETTING
Muriel Spark

Britain's seventh Earl of Lucan, who went missing after allegedly killing his children's nanny, has been deliciously captured in this impish comedy of manners, which imagines two fugitives, both claiming to be Lucan, as patients of a celebrated Parisian shrink.

LONE EAGLE
Danielle Steel

From their first meeting, Kate Jamison and Joe Albright can't seem to get things right, and despite their inextinguishable passion, the two manage to break each other's hearts again and again. The novel is brightly paced, but the characters' self-absorption gets tiresome.

THE CHILDREN'S WAR
J. N. Stroyar
What would today's Europe be like if the Germans had won WWII? At 1,153 pages, Stroyar's novel is not a thriller; it's pure melodrama, a tempest of personal and political passions played out against a meticulously researched alternate reality.

ALL THE FINEST GIRLS
Alexandra Styron
Novelist William Styron's daughter tries her hand at her dad's trade. Her touching novel tells of the exploration that Addy, a well-born Easterner, makes into the life of her Caribbean nanny.

THE DEATH OF VISHNU
Manil Suri
Examining odious aspects of a class-bound society, this novel, set in a multistory apartment building in Bombay, could be described as a kind of Indian *Upstairs, Downstairs*.

CANE RIVER
Lalita Tademy
Tademy cobbled together an imaginary past for four generations of her foremothers—slaves in Louisiana—and produced this strongly written first novel about determined women in seemingly hopeless situations.

*THE BONESETTER'S DAUGHTER
Amy Tan
When Ruth's mother presents her with a cache of writings about her girlhood in China, Ruth finds the key to her family history and her sense of self. Tan writes with a keen understanding of mothers and daughters that makes this book sing with emotion and insight.

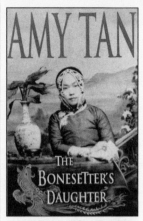

BACK WHEN WE WERE GROWNUPS
Anne Tyler
Rebecca Davitch has a full life, but not the one she expected. No longer a shy student, she's considering a new liaison with her college swain, and she hosts parties for a living. Tyler deftly finds the magic in the humdrum.

THE GARDENS OF KYOTO
Kate Walbert
In this quaintly told coming-of-age novel, middle-aged narrator Ellen recounts key moments in her life to a daughter we never come to know. Using yesteryear's untalked about topics, the narrator reminds her daughter that the world was quite a different place not so long ago.

GOOD IN BED
Jennifer Weiner
Get yourself into beach-reading mode with this lightly written debut novel about a zaftig young reporter who learns how to love her plus-size self.

*AS LONG AS SHE NEEDS ME
Nicholas Weinstock
In this light and funny first novel—written by a former publishing assistant—crass corporate politics are easy to laugh at, but the story has a sweet side, too.

LIT LIFE
Kurt Wenzel
A once-promising novelist battling writer's block hooks up with his literary hero; together, they're mercilessly lampooned in this hilarious debut novel about the publishing world.

MARTYRS' CROSSING
Amy Willentz
Middle Eastern politics rips apart personal lives in a well-reported novel that begins when a woman's 2-year-old son dies after a snafu at a border crossing in Jerusalem.

NONFICTION

DIANA'S BOYS: WILLIAM AND HARRY AND THE MOTHER THEY LOVED
Christopher Andersen
Royal snoop Christopher Andersen portrays Britain's popular young princes, William and Harry, as well-mannered, occasionally mischievous blokes. Much of *Diana's Boys* is rehashed from previous royal family chronicles, but Andersen enlivens things with a combination of personal details and fly-on-the-wall perspective.

SON OF A PREACHER MAN
Jay Bakker with Linden Gross
Televangelists Jim and Tammy Faye Bakker (now Messner) have generally been portrayed in the media as stick-figure jokes or villains. In this memoir their son Jay —a pastor whose own ministry, Revolution, targets what he calls "punks, skaters and hippies"—attempts to rehabilitate his parents' image.

THE HUMAN FACE
Brian Bates with John Cleese
Bates, a psychologist and biologist, moves from an exploration of the human face's evolution into meditations on beauty,

expressions, the purposes of vanity, and fame. Too often, though, the text cries out for the documentary on which it is based.

FAMILY: A CELEBRATION OF HUMANITY
Geoff Blackwell
This sumptuous collection of pictures pulse with the love, delight and sorrow that characterize family life. It's a coffee-table book to be savored.

A TRIP TO THE BEACH: LIVING ON ISLAND TIME IN THE CARIBBEAN
Melinda and Robert Blanchard
After selling their successful Vermont food business, Bob and Melinda Blanchard envisioned opening a little eatery in Anguilla, their favorite sleepy Caribbean island. What they got instead were a four-star restaurant, endless headaches over scarce supplies, and more hard work than they had ever imagined. As this engaging memoir, which includes some of Melinda's delectable-sounding recipes, makes clear, they loved every second of it.

A MAN'S JOURNEY TO SIMPLE ABUNDANCE
Sarah Ban Breathnach
This is a marvelous collection of 55 pithy essays by and about men. Some of the pieces are disturbing, and some surprising and the contributors include such well-regarded authors as Rick Bass, Roy Blount Jr. and Reynolds Price.

GOD SAVE THE SWEET POTATO QUEENS
Jill Conner Browne
The sassy, Mississippi-based author, whose *Sweet Potato Queens' Book of Love* was a best-seller, offers more advice on life, love and margaritas.

NO APPARENT DANGER
Victoria Bruce
Bruce thoroughly depicts the participants of the fatal expedition to the volcano Galeras in Colombia, where six foreign scientists and three Colombian hikers were killed in 1993.

ON HER OWN GROUND: THE LIFE AND TIMES OF MADAM C. J. WALKER
A'Lelia Bundles
Sarah Breedlove's great-great-granddaughter vividly recounts the rise of the washerwoman who would light the way for other black businesswomen, bankroll YMCAs and lead an antilynching campaign all the way to the White House.

THE PARROT WHO OWNS ME
Joanna Burger
In this brilliantly observed memoir, ornithologist Burger reveals what parrots can teach us. The birds express rage, jealousy, trust and even love for caretakers. Human emotions should not be excluded from animal behavior. It's an elegant idea in an unusually thoughtful book.

HAIR STORY: UNTANGLING THE ROOTS OF BLACK HAIR IN AMERICA
by Ayana D. Byrd and Lori L. Tharps
Journalists examine 600 years of cutting, straightening and braiding, from African tribes' distinctive styles to today's weaves and dreadlocks. Although sometimes repetitive, there are fascinating tidbits and anecdotes.

CLOSE TO SHORE: A TRUE STORY OF TERROR IN AN AGE OF INNOCENCE
Michael Capuzzo
In 1916 there was a series of shark attacks off the coast of New Jersey. Capuzzo makes a persuasive case that all of New Jersey's attacks that summer were the acts of a single great white shark. One of the book's greatest strengths is the painstaking research that puts the horror in context. This powerful page-turner will keep you out of the water for another year.

THE ADVERSARY
Emmanuel Carrère
French novelist Carrere launches a mesmerizing true-crime tale of an apparently ordinary man whose life mutates in a space of a few blood-splattered hours. What captivates Carrere about the murderous M. Romand is the shocking web of deception his whole life turns out to be.

WAR LETTERS
Edited by Andrew Carroll
Carroll gathered 50,000 battlefield letters from America's attics and garages by asking for them via a Dear Abby column. The nearly 200 letters here, spanning wars from Civil to Gulf, capture stench and honor, gore and affection in equal measure. No American reader can be unmoved.

AN HOUR BEFORE DAYLIGHT: MEMORIES OF A RURAL BOYHOOD
Jimmy Carter
Carter's account of his Depression-era Georgia youth makes clear that the thirty-ninth president was the sort of eager-to-please boy any parent would be proud to call son. There's plenty of warmth in Carter's account, but one can't help feeling there is too little here about young Jimmy and too much about agricultural procedures and prices.

VOICE OF AN ANGEL: MY LIFE (SO FAR)
Charlotte Church

Chronicling her rise from bubbly Welsh schoolgirl to superstar, Church amiably demonstrates that she is devoted to her art and family, not to mention her cuddly toys and shopping. This is not the voice that made her famous.

AN INVITATION TO THE WHITE HOUSE
Hillary Rodham Clinton

Senator Clinton exits with a picture-packed tome of life at 1600 Pennsylvania Ave. There are even illustrated recipes; a sorbet confection called Flora Bunda looks almost too beautiful to eat.

THE GAMES WE PLAYED
Edited by Steven A. Cohen

In this fetchingly compact volume, big name contributors ranging from Esther Williams to President Clinton offer reminiscences of childhood play.

THE PRICE OF MOTHERHOOD
Ann Crittenden

This provocative new book argues that what really hurts about motherhood isn't the delivery, but the hit to the wallet that follows.

I KNEW A WOMAN: THE EXPERIENCE OF THE FEMALE
Cortney Davis

The author, a nurse practitioner at an obstetrics-gynecological clinic in Connecticut, is a self-described poet and "caregiver." It is a dynamic tale of four composites, patients betrayed by their bodies or the bodies of others: a homeless teenager impregnated by her violent boyfriend; a victim of cervical cancer; a perennially pregnant addict; and a graphic designer undone by pain each time she has sex.

TOM DOUGLAS' SEATTLE KITCHEN
Tom Douglas

Douglas leads readers on mouth-watering tours of his favorite Seattle fish markets, butcher stores, microbreweries, and Vietnamese fast-food stands. Douglas's Seattle Kitchen features recipes from his three eateries, but many dishes require things that are hard to find unless you live in Seattle.

AUGUSTA, GONE
Martha Tod Dudman

Dudman and her daughter, who leaves home for days at a time to drop acid and snort cocaine, enter a grim subculture of parents who lock their children in restrictive schools or track them down with bounty hunters. Dudman's searing honesty speaks eloquently to our most fragile selves in a stunner of a book.

JUSTICE
Dominick Dunne

Though nonfiction, this collection of Dunne's writings about trials (O.J., the Menendez brothers, Claus von Bülow) reads like an expertly calibrated policier.

THE GIRL CODE
Diane Farr

Though a tad trite, *The Girl Code* is stacked with clever observations about relationships and cutely packaged advice. From types of dates, to wedding-party politics, the laughs are plentiful here.

WORD FREAK: HEARTBREAK, TRIUMPH, GENIUS, AND OBSESSION IN THE WORLD OF COMPETITIVE SCRABBLE PLAYERS
Stefan Fatsis

Wall Street Journal reporter Stefan Fatsis started out observing the strange and insular world of tournament Scrabble. But the game became as much of a compulsion for him as it is for the colorful cast of misfits and savants he befriended over the course of two years. Twitchy, fanatical, single-minded and spellbound characters from the upper reaches of the Scrabble universe make folks like Garry Kasparov and John McEnroe seem well-adjusted.

WALKING THE BIBLE: A JOURNEY BY LAND THROUGH THE FIVE BOOKS OF MOSES
Bruce Feiler

In an entertaining trek across the fabled lands of the Old Testament, Feiler and his guide set out to find such spots as the landing site of Noah's Ark, the ruins of Sodom and Gomorrah, and the exact place where the Israelites crossed the Red Sea on their way out of Egypt.

THE DOG LISTENER
Jan Fennell

Fennell has dedicated herself to decoding the secret language of dogs. Her program teaches you how to become the alpha wolf of your den without harsh discipline.

AN ITALIAN AFFAIR
Laura Fraser

Discarded by her husband, San Francisco journalist Fraser takes off for Italy to figure out what went wrong. She indulges in a casual fling with a Frenchman, and the pair hook up periodically in Milan, Los Angeles, London, and Casablanca. There are lush meals and heavenly settings aplenty, but the descriptions in this hybrid memoir-travelogue are often perfunctory.

AN AMERICAN FAMILY
Jon and Michael Galluccio

The gay authors, dads of three, tell of their successful real-life struggle to change a New Jersey law that forbade couples who are not officially married to adopt children.

BING CROSBY
A POCKETFUL OF DREAMS
THE EARLY YEARS
1903-1940

GARY GIDDINS

*BING CROSBY: A POCKETFUL OF DREAMS
Gary Giddins

In this fine first half of a two-part biography of the crooner and actor, Giddins packs in a lot more than most readers may want to know about Crosby, yet the author's boundless but utterly clear-eyed enthusiasm for his subject is contagious.

PARIS TO THE MOON
Adam Gopnik

Francophiles will find this collection of essays—written during the author's stay in the City of Light at the tail end of the twentieth century—*très délicieux.*

TELL ME A STORY
Don Hewitt

The executive producer of *60 Minutes* has subtitled his memoir *Fifty Years and 60 Minutes in Television*, and he shares juicy inside stories about TV news.

SEABISCUIT: AN AMERICAN LEGEND
Laura Hillenbrand

Thanks to Hillenbrand's passionate writing and fine research, readers who don't know a filly from a furlong will be captivated, and her jargon-free language makes the races—and the period—exhilarating.

WE GOTTA GET OUT OF THIS PLACE: THE TRUE, TOUGH STORY OF WOMEN IN ROCK
Gerri Hirshey

Part rock encyclopedia, part social discourse on everything from the Ronettes' beehives to Alanis Morissette's rage-infused lyrics, the book seems bent on including every female performer in history. As a result, no one gets enough time alone onstage.

BABY ER
Edward Humes

A Pulitzer Prize-winning reporter recounts the life-and-death struggles of medicine's tiniest patients—and the harrowing effect they have on doctors, nurses, mothers and fathers.

A GIRL NAMED ZIPPY
Haven Kimmel

Nicknamed for her tendency to bolt around the house, Zippy is a spunky little girl trying to puzzle through the adult world (otherwise known as 1960s Mooreland,, Ind.) in this gentle memoir.

THE PROVING GROUND
G. Bruce Knecht

Six people drowned and 55 others were plucked from the sea by rescue ships and helicopters in the famous annual day-after-Christmas yacht race between Sydney and Hobart, Australia, of 1998. Knecht navigates tricky waters here by sticking to pulse-pounding drama, leaving readers to mull the tale's moral query: At what point does blue-water trophy-chasing lapse from sport to unthinking folly?

SACRED CONNECTIONS: STORIES OF ADOPTION ESSAYS
Mary Ann Koenig, Photography by Niki Berg

Today's parents are more willing to bring adoption into the open, a trend Koenig supports with moving essays culled from interviews with adoptees.

THE OTHER GREAT DEPRESSION
Richard Lewis

For the comic star of TV's *Anything But Love*, life has been anything but funny; in this mordant book he details struggles with his "million addictions."

JOHN ADAMS
David McCullough

The tension between John Adams and Thomas Jefferson is just one of the great historical dramas played out in McCullough's engaging and thorough account of Adams. Sticking close to the diaries and letters of his principals, McCullough resists the biographer's temptation to make up dialogue, and instead points out history's quirky gaps.

FRENCH LESSONS
Peter Mayle

"Mon Dieu!" you cry, "not another Mayle book about France." Oui, but this one, subtitled *Adventures with Knife, Fork, and Corkscrew*, makes a most enjoyable repast.

CARRY ME HOME
Diane McWhorter

McWhorter revisits in fascinating detail the battle for integration and its horrifying white backlash in Birmingham, Ala., in the early '60s. The cast is huge and vivid, the story brimming with courage, drama, villains and heroes.

THE RUSSIAN WORD FOR SNOW: A TRUE STORY OF ADOPTION
Janis Cooke Newman

The author of this engrossing memoir and her husband head from their California home to Russia to adopt an infant. The couple's fight to bring Grisha home after months of dashed hopes and bureaucratic snafus vividly illustrates the perils of foreign adoption.

THE UNWANTED
Kien Nguyen

After Saigon fell to the Communists in 1975, seven-year-old Kien's fair hair and light eyes marked him for discrimination on top of the woes that befell the ravaged nation. His painfully evocative memoir is a remarkable tale of survival at all costs in which no one comes off clean, not even Kien himself.

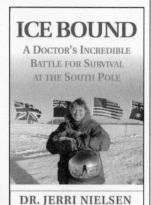

ICE BOUND
A DOCTOR'S INCREDIBLE BATTLE FOR SURVIVAL AT THE SOUTH POLE

DR. JERRI NIELSEN
with MARYANNE VOLLERS

ICE BOUND
Jerri Nielsen, with Maryanne Vollers

While serving as a doctor at the South Pole in 1999—and recovering from a painful divorce—Nielsen, then 46, discovered a lump in her breast and had to perform her own biopsy and administer chemotherapy.

FREEDOM'S DAUGHTERS
Lynne Olson

Olson puts Rosa Parks and countless other women who fought for social reforms up front in this fascinating historical account of how two movements—blacks' struggle for civil rights and women's push for equality—have combined and conflicted since the early nineteenth century.

BEHIND THE SMILE: MY JOURNEY OUT OF POSTPARTUM DEPRESSION
Marie Osmond

In this absorbing and instructive book, Marie Osmond writes that after the birth of her seventh child she "couldn't seem to stop crying." She found solace slowly: by listening to her "inner voice" and to her therapist, and asking God for help.

HOLLYWOOD MOMS
Joyce Ostin

This handsome collection offers alluring black-and-white photos of about 50 mothers with their girls. Ostin is donating 100 percent of the proceeds from this work to help fight breast cancer.

BELIEVING IT ALL: WHAT MY CHILDREN TAUGHT ME ABOUT TROUT FISHING, JELLY TOAST, AND LIFE
Marc Parent

Parent, who cared for his two toddler sons in a rural Pennsylvania farmhouse while his wife taught fifth grade, shines a welcome light on one full-time dad's world. In spare (if sometimes overly earnest) prose, Parent describes the many moments he finds himself being taught by his boys. Every parent will know what he means.

*GUNMAN'S RHAPSODY
Robert B. Parker

Parker delivers a fresh take on western marshal Wyatt Earp. Swapping his usual wisecracking for spareness, Parker makes Earp not necessarily likable—no bully but at his best behind a Colt .45. The minimalist showdown at the O.K. Corral is almost anticlimactic, but Rhapsody's psychological portrait is a sure shot.

JOHN WAYNE: THERE RODE A LEGEND
Jane Pattie

This generously illustrated coffee-table book about the Duke's 84 westerns shows why he was voted "male star of the century."

This engaging and visually absorbing volume would grace any saddlebag, east or west of the Pecos.

THE WORST-CASE SCENARIO SURVIVAL HANDBOOK: TRAVEL
Joshua Piven and David Borgenicht

In deadpan tone, Piven and Borgenicht advise how to survive a plane crash, remove a leech and escape from the trunk of a car. The scenarios owe a debt to action flick clichés, but their utter implausibility doesn't make this read any less riveting.

HAPPY TIMES
Lee Radziwill

In this photo album crossed with a memoir, Radziwill provides an up-close luxe-see into the world she shared with older sister Jacqueline Kennedy Onassis. With brief commentary, Radziwill also offers personal photos of trips, of her homes, and her own children.

FRAUD
David Rakoff

In this collection of 15 humor pieces, Canadian-born Rakoff makes clear how much he disdains the sentimentally precious. For those who share his jaundiced view, it's a laugh feast.

LOVE LETTERS OF A LIFETIME
Foreword by Dana Reeve

Laced with pain, regret, humor and honest, gushy sentiment, this is a collection of real-life love letters from more than 25 everyday couples and individuals.

COMFORT ME WITH APPLES
Ruth Reichl

In this memoir of her early years as a food writer, Reichl recalls eating whole frogs in China and grilled cockles in Thailand and documents her spicy extramarital affairs, her struggle to get pregnant, and the wackiness of her widowed mother.

BELOW ANOTHER SKY: A MOUNTAIN ADVENTURE IN SEARCH OF A LOST FATHER
Rick Ridgeway
With annoying machismo and on-your-sleeve spirituality, Ridgeway details the 1999 trek he took with a 19-year-old woman named Asia, the daughter of a friend lost 20 years ago, in search of the lost man's grave on the Himalayan peaks.

BALD IN THE LAND OF BIG HAIR
Joni Rodgers
This candid and amusing memoir recounts Rodgers's difficult cancer battle, including her wittily rendered search for a wig that won't make her look like the *Flintstones'* Betty Rubble.

*THE PRIZE WINNER OF DEFIANCE, OHIO
Terry Ryan
This delightful, inspiring memoir of the '50s presents Eisenhower-era America in prose as warm as oatmeal. The author and siblings are given their due—as is their abusive, whisky-soused dad—but the book's sturdy center is Evelyn Ryan, a woman whose can-do spirit honored her aptly named hometown.

FACING THE WIND: A TRUE STORY OF TRAGEDY AND RECONCILIATION
Julie Salamon
A devoted family man kills his wife and three children with a baseball bat, is declared not guilty by reason of insanity, and serves 2½ years in a psychiatric facility. Salamon uses that turn of events to explore the nature of sanity, responsibility and redemption.

ROBERT MITCHUM: "BABY, I DON'T CARE"
Lee Server
Offscreen Mitchum was a lot like onscreen Mitchum: he brawled, philandered, and inhaled. He was particularly obnoxious when

drunk, and such moments are cheerfully reported here.

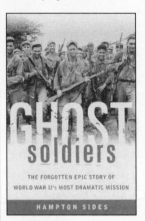

GHOST SOLDIERS
Hampton Sides
The tension is unbearable in this real-life drama of 121 soldiers of the Sixth Ranger Battalion making a desperate attempt to rescue American and British POWs from a hellish Japanese camp.

JOHN AND CAROLINE: THEIR LIVES IN PICTURES
James Spada
This photo album, published to coincide with the second anniversary of JFK Jr.'s death, spans his 38 short years. Hauntingly, the selection displays his propensity to accidents well before the July 16, 1999 plane crash that took his life.

*FIVE-FINGER DISCOUNT: A CROOKED FAMILY HISTORY
Helene Stapinski
Stapinski's debut memoir, about growing up in 1970s Jersey City, a toxic gumbo of political corruption and grifters, is by turns wry and wrenching but utterly free of self-pity.

GABORABILIA: AN ILLUSTRATED HISTORY OF THE FABULOUS, LEGENDARY GABOR SISTORS
Anthony Turtu and Donald F. Reuter
When you think of the Gabor sis-

ters, those officially ageless Hungarian queens of preen may bring to mind plumpish, overcoiffed, cop-slapping anachronisms. Surprisingly this adulatory, candy-colored scrapbook sets out not to correct that impression but to give it a big air kiss, arguing that these not-so-daffy divas wittingly and wittily strutted their female independence in the face of a straitlaced, male-dominated postwar culture.

BLACK, WHITE AND JEWISH: AUTOBIOGRAPHY OF A SHIFTING SELF
Rebecca Walker
In this unsparing autobiography, Walker, the daughter of civil rights attorney Mel Leventhal and author Alice Walker, explores her confusing childhood—shuttling between two households and two worlds. Walker masterfully illuminates differences between black and white America.

SURVIVING GALERAS
Stanley Williams and Fen Montaigne
With first-person urgency, Williams, a geology professor at Arizona State University, writes about leading an expedition to the volcano Galeras's crater at the moment it erupted.

STAY STRONG: SIMPLE LIFE LESSONS FOR TEENS
Terrie Williams
Babysitting celebrities has taught publicist Williams a lot about childish behavior. Her lessons, on topics ranging from table manners to honesty, provide sage advice for cool kids, and in hip language too.

A HISTORY OF THE WIFE
Marilyn Yalom
From Cleopatra to Puritan Anne Bradstreet to modern women, historian Marilyn Yalom shows how roles have changed for wives in this scholarly yet delectably readable volume.

FICTION AND NONFICTION BESTSELLERS

Publishers Weekly began charting the nation's top-selling hardcover fiction in 1895. The first nonfiction lists were published regularly beginning in 1917, and during World War I the trade magazine even tracked the most popular war books. (The Winston Churchill on the fiction lists, by the way, was an American novelist who died in 1947; his British statesman namesake was, of course, a bestselling and Nobel Prize–winning writer of nonfiction.) These rankings are not based on net sales figures but rather on publishers' reports of copies shipped and billed.

1900

Fiction

1. *To Have and To Hold*, Mary Johnston
2. *Red Pottage*, Mary Cholmondeley
3. *Unleavened Bread*, Robert Grant
4. *The Reign of Law*, James Lane Allen
5. *Eben Holden*, Irving Bacheller
6. *Janice Meredith*, Paul Leicester Ford
7. *The Redemption of David Corson*, Charles Frederic Goss
8. *Richard Carvel*, Winston Churchill
9. *When Knighthood Was in Flower*, Charles Major
10. *Alice of Old Vincennes*, Maurice Thompson

1901

Fiction

1. *The Crisis*, Winston Churchill
2. *Alice of Old Vincennes*, Maurice Thompson
3. *The Helmet of Navarre*, Bertha Runkle
4. *The Right of Way*, Gilbert Parker
5. *Eben Holden*, Irving Bacheller
6. *The Visits of Elizabeth*, Elinor Glyn
7. *The Puppet Crown*, Harold MacGrath
8. *Richard Yea-and-Nay*, Maurice Hewlett
9. *Graustark*, George Barr McCutcheon
10. *D'ri and I*, Irving Bacheller

1902

Fiction

1. *The Virginian*, Owen Wister
2. *Mrs. Wiggs of the Cabbage Patch*, Alice Caldwell Hegan
3. *Dorothy Vernon of Haddon Hall*, Charles Major
4. *The Mississippi Bubble*, Emerson Hough
5. *Audrey*, Mary Johnston
6. *The Right of Way*, Gilbert Parker
7. *The Hound of the Baskervilles*, A. Conan Doyle
8. *The Two Vanrevels*, Booth Tarkington
9. *The Blue Flower*, Henry van Dyke
10. *Sir Richard Calmady*, Lucas Malet

1903

Fiction

1. *Lady Rose's Daughter*, Mary Augusta Ward
2. *Gordon Keith*, Thomas Nelson Page
3. *The Pit*, Frank Norris
4. *Lovey Mary*, Alice Hegan Rice
5. *The Virginian*, Owen Wister
6. *Mrs. Wiggs of the Cabbage Patch*, Alice Hegan Rice
7. *The Mettle of the Pasture*, James Lane Allen
8. *Letters of a Self-Made Merchant to His Son*, George Horace Lorimer
9. *The One Woman*, Thomas Dixon Jr.
10. *The Little Shepherd of Kingdom Come*, John Fox Jr.

1904

Fiction

1. *The Crossing*, Winston Churchill
2. *The Deliverance*, Ellen Glasgow
3. *The Masquerader,* anonymous (Katherine Cecil Thurston)
4. *In the Bishop's Carriage*, Miriam Michelson
5. *Sir Mortimer*, Mary Johnston
6. *Beverly of Graustark*, George Barr McCutcheon
7. *The Little Shepherd of Kingdom Come*, John Fox Jr.
8. *Rebecca of Sunnybrook Farm*, Kate Douglas Wiggin
9. *My Friend Prospero*, Henry Harland
10. *The Silent Places*, Stewart Edward White

1905

Fiction

1. *The Marriage of William Ashe*, Mary Augusta Ward
2. *Sandy*, Alice Hegan Rice
3. *The Garden of Allah*, Robert Hichens
4. *The Clansman*, Thomas Dixon Jr.
5. *Nedra*, George Barr McCutcheon
6. *The Gambler*, Katherine Cecil Thurston
7. *The Masquerader*, anonymous (Katherine Cecil Thurston)
8. *The House of Mirth*, Edith Wharton
9. *The Princess Passes*, C. N. and A. M. Williamson
10. *Rose o' the River*, Kate Douglas Wiggin

1906

Fiction

1. *Coniston*, Winston Churchill
2. *Lady Baltimore*, Owen Wister
3. *The Fighting Chance*, Robert W. Chambers
4. *The House of a Thousand Candles*, Meredith Nicholson
5. *Jane Cable*, George Barr McCutcheon
6. *The Jungle*, Upton Sinclair
7. *The Awakening of Helena Ritchie*, Margaret Deland
8. *The Spoilers*, Rex Beach
9. *The House of Mirth*, Edith Wharton
10. *The Wheel of Life*, Ellen Glasgow

1907

Fiction

1. *The Lady of the Decoration*, Frances Little
2. *The Weavers*, Gilbert Parker
3. *The Port of Missing Men*, Meredith Nicholson
4. *The Shuttle*, Frances Hodgson Burnett
5. *The Brass Bowl*, Louis J. Vance
6. *Satan Sanderson*, Hallie Erminie Rives
7. *The Daughter of Anderson Crow*, George Barr McCutcheon
8. *The Younger Set*, Robert W. Chambers
9. *The Doctor*, Ralph Connor
10. *Half a Rogue*, Harold MacGrath

1908

Fiction

1. *Mr. Crewe's Career*, Winston Churchill
2. *The Barrier*, Rex Beach
3. *The Trail of the Lonesome Pine*, John Fox Jr.
4. *The Lure of the Mask*, Harold MacGrath

5. *The Shuttle*, Frances Hodgson Burnett
6. *Peter*, F. Hopkinson Smith
7. *Lewis Rand*, Mary Johnston
8. *The Black Bag*, Louis J. Vance
9. *The Man from Brodney's*, George Barr McCutcheon
10. *The Weavers*, Gilbert Parker

1909

Fiction

1. *The Inner Shrine*, anonymous (Basil King)
2. *Katrine*, Elinor Macartney Lane
3. *The Silver Horde*, Rex Beach
4. *The Man in Lower Ten*, Mary Roberts Rinehart
5. *The Trail of the Lonesome Pine*, John Fox Jr.
6. *Truxton King*, George Barr McCutcheon
7. *54-40 or Fight*, Emerson Hough
8. *The Goose Girl*, Harold MacGrath
9. *Peter*, F. Hopkinson Smith
10. *Septimus*, William J. Locke

1910

Fiction

1. *The Rosary*, Florence Barclay
2. *A Modern Chronicle*, Winston Churchill
3. *The Wild Olive*, anonymous (Basil King)
4. *Max*, Katherine Cecil Thurston
5. *The Kingdom of Slender Swords*, Hallie Erminie Rives
6. *Simon the Jester*, William J. Locke
7. *Lord Loveland Discovers America*, C. N. and A. M. Williamson
8. *The Window at the White Cat*, Mary Roberts Rinehart
9. *Molly Make-Believe*, Eleanor Abbott
10. *When a Man Marries*, Mary Roberts Rinehart

1911

Fiction

1. *The Broad Highway*, Jeffrey Farnol
2. *The Prodigal Judge*, Vaughan Kester
3. *The Winning of Barbara Worth*, Harold Bell Wright
4. *Queed*, Henry Sydnor Harrison
5. *The Harvester*, Gene Stratton Porter
6. *The Iron Woman*, Margaret Deland
7. *The Long Roll*, Mary Johnston
8. *Molly Make-Believe*, Eleanor Abbott
9. *The Rosary*, Florence Barclay
10. *The Common Law*, Robert W. Chambers

1912

Fiction

1. *The Harvester*, Gene Stratton Porter
2. *The Street Called Straight*, Basil King
3. *Their Yesterdays*, Harold Bell Wright
4. *The Melting of Molly*, Maria Thompson Daviess
5. *A Hoosier Chronicle*, Meredith Nicholson
6. *The Winning of Barbara Worth*, Harold Bell Wright
7. *The Just and the Unjust*, Vaughan Kester
8. *The Net*, Rex Beach
9. *Tante*, Anne Douglas Sedgwick
10. *Fran*, J. Breckenridge Ellis

Nonfiction

1. *The Promised Land*, Mary Antin
2. *The Montessori Method*, Maria Montessori

3. *South America*, James Bryce
4. *A New Conscience and an Ancient Evil*, Jane Addams
5. *Three Plays*, Eugène Brieux
6. *Your United States*, Arnold Bennett
7. *Creative Evolution*, Henri Bergson
8. *How to Live on Twenty-four Hours a Day*, Arnold Bennett
9. *Woman and Labor*, Olive Schreiner
10. *Mark Twain*, Albert Bigelow Paine

1913

Fiction

1. *The Inside of the Cup*, Winston Churchill
2. *V.V.'s Eyes*, Henry Sydnor Harrison
3. *Laddie*, Gene Stratton Porter
4. *The Judgment House*, Sir Gilbert Parker
5. *Heart of the Hills*, John Fox Jr.

MOST CHALLENGED (NOT BANNED) BOOKS

Books enrich our lives, but to a certain vocal part of the population they can enrage as well. While the intention of those challenging these books *was* to ban them, most of the books stayed on the shelves because of the efforts of librarians, teachers, parents, and students. Here are the most challenged books in school libraries and curriculums, in the last year, according to the American Library Association's Office for Intellectual Freedom (Jan. 1–Dec. 31, 2000) and between 1982 and 1996 according to People for the American Way.

1982–96

1. *Of Mice and Men*, John Steinbeck
2. *The Catcher in the Rye*, J. D. Salinger
3. *The Chocolate War*, Robert Cormier
4. *I Know Why the Caged Bird Sings*, Maya Angelou
5. *Scary Stories to Tell in the Dark*, Alvin Schwartz
6. *The Adventures of Huckleberry Finn*, Mark Twain
7. *More Scary Stories to Tell in the Dark*, Alvin Schwartz
8. *Go Ask Alice*, anonymous
9. *Bridge to Terabithia*, Katherine Paterson
10. *The Witches*, Roald Dahl

2000

1. The *Harry Potter* series, J. K. Rowling
2. *The Chocolate War*, Robert Cormier
3. The *Alice* series, Phyllis Reynolds Naylor
4. *Killing Mr. Griffin*, Lois Duncan
5. *Of Mice and Men*, John Steinbeck
6. *I Know Why the Caged Bird Sings*, Maya Angelou
7. *Fallen Angels*, Walter Dean Myers
8. The *Scary Stories* series, Alvin Schwartz
9. *The Terrorist*, Caroline Cooney
10. *The Giver*, Lois Lowry

6. *The Amateur Gentleman*, Jeffrey Farnol
7. *The Woman Thou Gavest Me*, Hall Caine
8. *Pollyanna*, Eleanor H. Porter
9. *The Valiants of Virginia*, Hallie Erminie Rives
10. *T. Tembarom*, Frances Hodgson Burnett

Nonfiction

1. *Crowds*, Gerald Stanley Lee
2. *Germany and the Germans*, Price Collier
3. *Zone Policeman 88*, Harry A. Franck
4. *The New Freedom*, Woodrow Wilson
5. *South America*, James Bryce
6. *Your United States*, Arnold Bennett
7. *The Promised Land*, Mary Antin
8. *Auction Bridge To-Day*, Milton C. Work
9. *Three Plays*, Eugène Brieux
10. *Psychology and Industrial Efficiency*, Hugo Munsterberg

1914

Fiction

1. *The Eyes of the World*, Harold Bell Wright
2. *Pollyanna*, Eleanor H. Porter
3. *The Inside of the Cup*, Winston Churchill
4. *The Salamander*, Owen Johnson
5. *The Fortunate Youth*, William J. Locke
6. *T. Tembarom*, Frances Hodgson Burnett
7. *Penrod*, Booth Tarkington
8. *Diane of the Green Van*, Leona Dalrymple
9. *The Devil's Garden*, W. B. Maxwell
10. *The Prince of Graustark*, George Barr McCutcheon

1915

Fiction

1. *The Turmoil*, Booth Tarkington
2. *A Far Country*, Winston Churchill
3. *Michael O'Halloran*, Gene Stratton Porter
4. *Pollyanna Grows Up*, Eleanor H. Porter
5. *K*, Mary Roberts Rinehart
6. *Jaffery*, William J. Locke
7. *Felix O'Day*, F. Hopkinson Smith
8. *The Harbor*, Ernest Poole
9. *The Lone Star Ranger*, Zane Grey
10. *Angela's Business*, Henry Sydnor Harrison

1916

Fiction

1. *Seventeen*, Booth Tarkington
2. *When a Man's a Man*, Harold Bell Wright

3. *Just David*, Eleanor H. Porter
4. *Mr. Britling Sees It Through*, H. G. Wells
5. *Life and Gabriella*, Ellen Glasgow
6. *The Real Adventure*, Henry Kitchell Webster
7. *Bars of Iron*, Ethel M. Dell
8. *Nan of Music Mountain*, Frank H. Spearman
9. *Dear Enemy*, Jean Webster
10. *The Heart of Rachael*, Kathleen Norris

1917

Fiction

1. *Mr. Britling Sees It Through*, H. G. Wells
2. *The Light in the Clearing*, Irving Bacheller
3. *The Red Planet*, William J. Locke
4. *The Road to Understanding*, Eleanor H. Porter
5. *Wildfire*, Zane Grey
6. *Christine*, Alice Cholmondeley
7. *In the Wilderness*, Robert S. Hichens
8. *His Family*, Ernest Poole
9. *The Definite Object*, Jeffrey Farnol
10. *The Hundredth Chance*, Ethel M. Dell

General Nonfiction

1. *Rhymes of a Red Cross Man*, Robert W. Service
2. *The Plattsburg Manual*, O. O. Ellis and E. B. Garey
3. *Raymond*, Sir Oliver Lodge
4. *Poems of Alan Seeger*, Alan Seeger
5. *God the Invisible King*, H. G. Wells
6. *Laugh and Live*, Douglas Fairbanks
7. *Better Meals for Less Money*, Mary Green

War Books

1. *The First Hundred Thousand*, Ian Hay
2. *My Home in the Field of Honor*, Frances W. Huard
3. *A Student in Arms*, Donald Hankey
4. *Over the Top*, Arthur Guy Empey
5. *Carry On*, Coningsby Dawson
6. *Getting Together*, Ian Hay
7. *My Second Year of the War*, Frederick Palmer
8. *The Land of Deepening Shadow*, D. Thomas Curtin
9. *Italy, France and Britain at War*, H. G. Wells
10. *The Worn Doorstep*, Margaret Sherwood

1918

Fiction

1. *The U. P. Trail*, Zane Grey

2. *The Tree of Heaven*, May Sinclair
3. *The Amazing Interlude*, Mary Roberts Rinehart
4. *Dere Mable*, Edward Streeter
5. *Oh, Money! Money!*, Eleanor H. Porter
6. *Greatheart*, Ethel M. Dell
7. *The Major*, Ralph Connor
8. *The Pawns Count*, E. Phillips Oppenheim
9. *A Daughter of the Land*, Gene Stratton Porter
10. *Sonia*, Stephen McKenna

General Nonfiction

1. *Rhymes of a Red Cross Man*, Robert W. Service
2. *Treasury of War Poetry*, G. H. Clark
3. *With the Colors*, Everard J. Appleton
4. *Recollections*, Viscount Morley
5. *Laugh and Live*, Douglas Fairbanks
6. *Mark Twain's Letters*, Albert Bigelow Paine, editor
7. *Adventures and Letters of Richard Harding Davis*, Richard Harding Davis
8. *Over Here*, Edgar Guest
9. *Diplomatic Days*, Edith O'Shaughnessy
10. *Poems of Alan Seeger*, Alan Seeger

War Books

1. *My Four Years in Germany*, James W. Gerard
2. *The Glory of the Trenches*, Coningsby Dawson
3. *Over the Top*, Arthur Guy Empey
4. *A Minstrel in France*, Harry Lauder
5. *Private Peat*, Harold R. Peat
6. *Outwitting the Hun*, Lieut. Pat O'Brien
7. *Face to Face with Kaiserism*, James W. Gerard
8. *Carry On*, Coningsby Dawson
9. *Out to Win*, Coningsby Dawson
10. *Under Fire*, Henri Barbusse

1919

Fiction

1. *The Four Horsemen of the Apocalypse*, V. Blasco Ibañez
2. *The Arrow of Gold*, Joseph Conrad
3. *The Desert of Wheat*, Zane Grey
4. *Dangerous Days*, Mary Roberts Rinehart
5. *The Sky Pilot in No Man's Land*, Ralph Connor
6. *The Re-creation of Brian Kent*, Harold Bell Wright
7. *Dawn*, Gene Stratton Porter
8. *The Tin Soldier*, Temple Bailey
9. *Christopher and Columbus*, "Elizabeth"

10. *In Secret*, Robert W. Chambers

Nonfiction
1. *The Education of Henry Adams*, Henry Adams
2. *The Years Between*, Rudyard Kipling
3. *Belgium*, Brand Whitlock
4. *The Seven Purposes*, Margaret Cameron
5. *In Flanders Fields*, John McCrae
6. *Bolshevism*, John Spargo

1920

Fiction
1. *The Man of the Forest*, Zane Grey
2. *Kindred of the Dust*, Peter B. Kyne
3. *The Re-creation of Brian Kent*, Harold Bell Wright
4. *The River's End*, James Oliver Curwood
5. *A Man for the Ages*, Irving Bacheller
6. *Mary-Marie*, Eleanor H. Porter
7. *The Portygee*, Joseph C. Lincoln
8. *The Great Impersonation*, E. Phillips Oppenheim
9. *The Lamp in the Desert*, Ethel M. Dell
10. *Harriet and the Piper*, Kathleen Norris

Nonfiction
1. *Now It Can Be Told*, Philip Gibbs
2. *The Economic Consequences of the Peace*, John M. Keynes
3. *Roosevelt's Letters to His Children*, Joseph B. Bishop, editor
4. *Theodore Roosevelt*, William Roscoe Thayer
5. *White Shadows in the South Seas*, Frederick O'Brien
6. *An American Idyll*, Cornelia Stratton Parker

1921

Fiction
1. *Main Street*, Sinclair Lewis
2. *The Brimming Cup*, Dorothy Canfield
3. *The Mysterious Rider*, Zane Grey
4. *The Age of Innocence*, Edith Wharton
5. *The Valley of Silent Men*, James Oliver Curwood
6. *The Sheik*, Edith M. Hull
7. *A Poor Wise Man*, Mary Roberts Rinehart
8. *Her Father's Daughter*, Gene Stratton Porter
9. *The Sisters-in-Law*, Gertrude Atherton
10. *The Kingdom Round the Corner*, Coningsby Dawson

Nonfiction
1. *The Outline of History*, H. G. Wells
2. *White Shadows in the South Seas*, Frederick O'Brien

3. *The Mirrors of Downing Street*, A Gentleman with a Duster (pseudonym for Harold Begbie)
4. *The Autobiography of Margot Asquith*, Margot Asquith
6. *Peace Negotiations*, Robert Lansing

1922

Fiction
1. *If Winter Comes*, A. S. M. Hutchinson
2. *The Sheik*, Edith M. Hull
3. *Gentle Julia*, Booth Tarkington
4. *The Head of the House of Coombe*, Frances Hodgson Burnett
5. *Simon Called Peter*, Robert Keable
6. *The Breaking Point*, Mary Roberts Rinehart
7. *This Freedom*, A. S. M. Hutchinson
8. *Maria Chapdelaine*, Louis Hémon
9. *To the Last Man*, Zane Grey
10. *Babbitt*, Sinclair Lewis (tie)
10. *Helen of the Old House*, Harold Bell Wright (tie)

Nonfiction
1. *The Outline of History*, H. G. Wells
2. *The Story of Mankind*, Hendrik Willem Van Loon
3. *The Americanization of Edward Bok*, Edward Bok
4. *Diet and Health*, Lulu Hunt Peters
5. *The Mind in the Making*, James Harvey Robinson
6. *The Outline of Science*, J. Arthur Thomson
7. *Outwitting Our Nerves*, Josephine A. Jackson and Helen M. Salisbury
8. *Queen Victoria*, Lytton Strachey
9. *Mirrors of Washington*, anonymous (Clinton W. Gilbert)
10. *Painted Windows*, A Gentleman with a Duster (pseudonym for Harold Begbie)

1923

Fiction
1. *Black Oxen*, Gertrude Atherton
2. *His Children's Children*, Arthur Train
3. *The Enchanted April*, "Elizabeth"
4. *Babbitt*, Sinclair Lewis
5. *The Dim Lantern*, Temple Bailey
6. *This Freedom*, A. S. M. Hutchinson
7. *The Mine with the Iron Door*, Harold Bell Wright
8. *The Wanderer of the Wasteland*, Zane Grey
9. *The Sea-Hawk*, Rafael Sabatini
10. *The Breaking Point*, Mary Roberts Rinehart

Nonfiction
1. *Etiquette*, Emily Post
2. *The Life of Christ*, Giovanni Papini
3. *The Life and Letters of Walter H. Page*, Burton J. Hendrick, editor
4. *The Mind in the Making*, James Harvey Robinson
5. *The Outline of History*, H. G. Wells
6. *Diet and Health*, Lulu Hunt Peters
7. *Self-Mastery Through Conscious Auto-Suggestion*, Emile Coué
8. *The Americanization of Edward Bok*, Edward Bok
9. *The Story of Mankind*, Hendrik Willem Van Loon
10. *A Man from Maine*, Edward Bok

1924

Fiction
1. *So Big*, Edna Ferber
2. *The Plastic Age*, Percy Marks
3. *The Little French Girl*, Anne Douglas Sedgwick
4. *The Heirs Apparent*, Philip Gibbs
5. *A Gentleman of Courage*, James Oliver Curwood
6. *The Call of the Canyon*, Zane Grey
7. *The Midlander*, Booth Tarkington
8. *The Coast of Folly*, Coningsby Dawson
9. *Mistress Wilding*, Rafael Sabatini
10. *The Homemaker*, Dorothy Canfield Fisher

Nonfiction
1. *Diet and Health*, Lulu Hunt Peters
2. *The Life of Christ*, Giovanni Papini
3. *The Boston Cooking School Cook Book*, rev. ed., Fannie Farmer, editor
4. *Etiquette*, Emily Post
5. *Ariel*, André Maurois
6. *The Cross Word Puzzle Books*, Prosper Buranelli, et al.
7. *Mark Twain's Autobiography*, Mark Twain
8. *Saint Joan*, Bernard Shaw
9. *The New Decalogue of Science*, Albert E. Wiggam
10. *The Americanization of Edward Bok*, Edward Bok

1925

Fiction
1. *Soundings*, A. Hamilton Gibbs
2. *The Constant Nymph*, Margaret Kennedy
3. *The Keeper of the Bees*, Gene Stratton Porter
4. *Glorious Apollo*, E. Barrington
5. *The Green Hat*, Michael Arlen

6. *The Little French Girl*, Anne Douglas Sedgwick
7. *Arrowsmith*, Sinclair Lewis
8. *The Perennial Bachelor*, Anne Parrish
9. *The Carolinian*, Rafael Sabatini
10. *One Increasing Purpose*, A. S. M. Hutchinson

Nonfiction

1. *Diet and Health*, Lulu Hunt Peters
2. *The Boston Cooking School Cook Book*, rev. ed., Fannie Farmer, editor
3. *When We Were Very Young*, A. A. Milne
4. *The Man Nobody Knows*, Bruce Barton
5. *The Life of Christ*, Giovanni Papini
6. *Ariel*, André Maurois
7. *Twice Thirty*, Edward Bok
8. *Twenty-five Years*, Lord Grey
9. *Anatole France Himself*, J. J. Brousson
10. *The Cross Word Puzzle Books*, Prosper Buranelli, et al.

1926

Fiction

1. *The Private Life of Helen of Troy*, John Erskine
2. *Gentlemen Prefer Blondes*, Anita Loos
3. *Sorrell and Son*, Warwick Deeping
4. *The Hounds of Spring*, Sylvia Thompson
5. *Beau Sabreur*, P. C. Wren
6. *The Silver Spoon*, John Galsworthy
7. *Beau Geste*, P. C. Wren
8. *Show Boat*, Edna Ferber
9. *After Noon*, Susan Ertz
10. *The Blue Window*, Temple Bailey

Nonfiction

1. *The Man Nobody Knows*, Bruce Barton
2. *Why We Behave Like Human Beings*, George A. Dorsey
3. *Diet and Health*, Lulu Hunt Peters
4. *Our Times*, Vol. I, Mark Sullivan
5. *The Boston Cooking School Cook Book*, rev. ed., Fannie Farmer, editor
6. *Auction Bridge Complete*, Milton C. Work
7. *The Book Nobody Knows*, Bruce Barton
8. *The Story of Philosophy*, Will Durant
9. *The Light of Faith*, Edgar A. Guest
10. *Jefferson and Hamilton*, Claude G. Bowers

1927

Fiction

1. *Elmer Gantry*, Sinclair Lewis
2. *The Plutocrat*, Booth Tarkington
3. *Doomsday*, Warwick Deeping
4. *Sorrell and Son*, Warwick Deeping
5. *Jalna*, Mazo de la Roche
6. *Lost Ecstasy*, Mary Roberts Rinehart
7. *Twilight Sleep*, Edith Wharton

8. *Tomorrow Morning*, Anne Parrish
9. *The Old Countess*, Anne Douglas Sedgwick
10. *A Good Woman*, Louis Bromfield

Nonfiction

1. *The Story of Philosophy*, Will Durant
2. *Napoleon*, Emil Ludwig
3. *Revolt in the Desert*, T. E. Lawrence
4. *Trader Horn*, Vol. I, Alfred Aloysius Horn and Ethelreda Lewis
5. *We*, Charles A. Lindbergh
6. *Ask Me Another*, Julian Spafford and Lucien Esty
7. *The Royal Road to Romance*, Richard Halliburton
8. *The Glorious Adventure*, Richard Halliburton
9. *Why We Behave Like Human Beings*, George A. Dorsey
10. *Mother India*, Katherine Mayo

1928

Fiction

1. *The Bridge of San Luis Rey*, Thornton Wilder
2. *Wintersmoon*, Hugh Walpole
3. *Swan Song*, John Galsworthy
4. *The Greene Murder Case*, S. S. Van Dine
5. *Bad Girl*, Viña Delmar
6. *Claire Ambler*, Booth Tarkington
7. *Old Pybus*, Warwick Deeping
8. *All Kneeling*, Anne Parrish
9. *Jalna*, Mazo de la Roche
10. *The Strange Case of Miss Annie Spragg*, Louis Bromfield

Nonfiction

1. *Disraeli*, André Maurois
2. *Mother India*, Katherine Mayo
3. *Trader Horn*, Vol. I, Alfred Aloysius Horn and Ethelreda Lewis
4. *Napoleon*, Emil Ludwig
5. *Strange Interlude*, Eugene O'Neill
6. *We*, Charles A. Lindbergh
7. *Count Luckner, the Sea Devil*, Lowell Thomas
8. *Goethe*, Emil Ludwig
9. *Skyward*, Richard E. Byrd
10. *The Intelligent Woman's Guide to Socialism and Capitalism*, George Bernard Shaw

1929

Fiction

1. *All Quiet on the Western Front*, Erich Maria Remarque
2. *Dodsworth*, Sinclair Lewis
3. *Dark Hester*, Anne Douglas Sedgwick

4. *The Bishop Murder Case*, S. S. Van Dine
5. *Roper's Row*, Warwick Deeping
6. *Peder Victorious*, O. E. Rölvaag
7. *Mamba's Daughters*, DuBose Heyward
8. *The Galaxy*, Susan Ertz
9. *Scarlet Sister Mary*, Julia Peterkin
10. *Joseph and His Brethren*, H. W. Freeman

Nonfiction

1. *The Art of Thinking*, Ernest Dimnet
2. *Henry the Eighth*, Francis Hackett
3. *The Cradle of the Deep*, Joan Lowell
4. *Elizabeth and Essex*, Lytton Strachey
5. *The Specialist*, Chic Sale
6. *A Preface to Morals*, Walter Lippmann
7. *Believe It or Not*, Robert L. Ripley
8. *John Brown's Body*, Stephen Vincent Benét
9. *The Tragic Era*, Claude G. Bowers
10. *The Mansions of Philosophy*, Will Durant

1930

Fiction

1. *Cimarron*, Edna Ferber
2. *Exile*, Warwick Deeping
3. *The Woman of Andros*, Thornton Wilder
4. *Years of Grace*, Margaret Ayer Barnes
5. *Angel Pavement*, J. B. Priestley
6. *The Door*, Mary Roberts Rinehart
7. *Rogue Herries*, Hugh Walpole
8. *Chances*, A. Hamilton Gibbs
9. *Young Man of Manhattan*, Katharine Brush
10. *Twenty-four Hours*, Louis Bromfield

Nonfiction

1. *The Story of San Michele*, Axel Munthe
2. *The Strange Death of President Harding*, Gaston B. Means and May Dixon Thacker
3. *Byron*, André Maurois
4. *The Adams Family*, James Truslow Adams
5. *Lone Cowboy*, Will James
6. *Lincoln*, Emil Ludwig
7. *The Story of Philosophy*, Will Durant
8. *The Outline of History*, H. G. Wells
9. *The Art of Thinking*, Ernest Dimnet
10. *The Rise of American Civilization*, Charles and Mary Beard

1931

Fiction

1. *The Good Earth*, Pearl S. Buck
2. *Shadows on the Rock*, Willa Cather
3. *A White Bird Flying*, Bess Streeter Aldrich

4. *Grand Hotel*, Vicki Baum
5. *Years of Grace*, Margaret Ayer Barnes
6. *The Road Back*, Erich Maria Remarque
7. *The Bridge of Desire*, Warwick Deeping
8. *Back Street*, Fannie Hurst
9. *Finch's Fortune*, Mazo de la Roche
10. *Maid in Waiting*, John Galsworthy

Nonfiction

1. *Education of a Princess*, Grand Duchess Marie
2. *The Story of San Michele*, Axel Munthe
3. *Washington Merry-Go-Round*, anonymous (Drew Pearson and Robert S. Allen)
4. *Boners: Being a Collection of Schoolboy Wisdom, or Knowledge as It Is Sometimes Written*, compiled by Alexander Abingdon; illustrated by Dr. Seuss
5. *Culbertson's Summary*, Ely Culbertson
6. *Contract Bridge Blue Book*, Ely Culbertson
7. *Fatal Interview*, Edna St. Vincent Millay
8. *The Epic of America*, James Truslow Adams
9. *Mexico*, Stuart Chase
10. *New Russia's Primer*, Mikhail Ilin

1932

Fiction

1. *The Good Earth*, Pearl S. Buck
2. *The Fountain*, Charles Morgan
3. *Sons*, Pearl S. Buck
4. *Magnolia Street*, Louis Golding
5. *The Sheltered Life*, Ellen Glasgow
6. *Old Wine and New*, Warwick Deeping
7. *Mary's Neck*, Booth Tarkington
8. *Magnificent Obsession*, Lloyd C. Douglas
9. *Inheritance*, Phyllis Bentley
10. *Three Loves*, A. J. Cronin

Nonfiction

1. *The Epic of America*, James Truslow Adams
2. *Only Yesterday*, Frederick Lewis Allen
3. *A Fortune to Share*, Vash Young
4. *Culbertson's Summary*, Ely Culbertson
5. *Van Loon's Geography*, Hendrik Willem Van Loon
6. *What We Live By*, Ernest Dimnet
7. *The March of Democracy*, James Truslow Adams
8. *Washington Merry-Go-Round*, anonymous (Drew Pearson and Robert S. Allen)

9. *The Story of My Life*, Clarence Darrow
10. *More Merry-Go-Round*, anonymous (Drew Pearson and Robert S. Allen)

1933

Fiction

1. *Anthony Adverse*, Hervey Allen
2. *As the Earth Turns*, Gladys Hasty Carroll
3. *Ann Vickers*, Sinclair Lewis
4. *Magnificent Obsession*, Lloyd C. Douglas
5. *One More River*, John Galsworthy
6. *Forgive Us Our Trespasses*, Lloyd C. Douglas
7. *The Master of Jalna*, Mazo de la Roche
8. *Miss Bishop*, Bess Streeter Aldrich
9. *The Farm*, Louis Bromfield
10. *Little Man, What Now?*, Hans Fallada

Nonfiction

1. *Life Begins at Forty*, Walter B. Pitkin
2. *Marie Antoinette*, Stefan Zweig
3. *British Agent*, R. H. Bruce Lockhart
4. *100,000,000 Guinea Pigs*, Arthur Kallet and F. J. Schlink
5. *The House of Exile*, Nora Waln
6. *Van Loon's Geography*, Hendrik Willem Van Loon
7. *Looking Forward*, Franklin D. Roosevelt
8. *Contract Bridge Blue Book of 1933*, Ely Culbertson
9. *The Arches of the Years*, Halliday Sutherland
10. *The March of Democracy*, Vol. II, James Truslow Adams

1934

Fiction

1. *Anthony Adverse*, Hervey Allen
2. *Lamb in His Bosom*, Caroline Miller
3. *So Red the Rose*, Stark Young
4. *Good-Bye, Mr. Chips*, James Hilton
5. *Within This Present*, Margaret Ayer Barnes
6. *Work of Art*, Sinclair Lewis
7. *Private Worlds*, Phyllis Bottome
8. *Mary Peters*, Mary Ellen Chase
9. *Oil for the Lamps of China*, Alice Tisdale Hobart
10. *Seven Gothic Tales*, Isak Dinesen

Nonfiction

1. *While Rome Burns*, Alexander Woollcott
2. *Life Begins at Forty*, Walter B. Pitkin
3. *Nijinsky*, Romola Nijinsky

4. *100,000,000 Guinea Pigs*, Arthur Kallet and F. J. Schlink
5. *The Native's Return*, Louis Adamic
6. *Stars Fell on Alabama*, Carl Carmer
7. *Brazilian Adventure*, Peter Fleming
8. *Forty-two Years in the White House*, Ike Hoover
9. *You Must Relax*, Edmund Jacobson
10. *The Life of Our Lord*, Charles Dickens

1935

Fiction

1. *Green Light*, Lloyd C. Douglas
2. *Vein of Iron*, Ellen Glasgow
3. *Of Time and the River*, Thomas Wolfe
4. *Time Out of Mind*, Rachel Field
5. *Good-Bye, Mr. Chips*, James Hilton
6. *The Forty Days of Musa Dagh*, Franz Werfel
7. *Heaven's My Destination*, Thornton Wilder
8. *Lost Horizon*, James Hilton
9. *Come and Get It*, Edna Ferber
10. *Europa*, Robert Briffault

Nonfiction

1. *North to the Orient*, Anne Morrow Lindbergh
2. *While Rome Burns*, Alexander Woollcott
3. *Life with Father*, Clarence Day
4. *Personal History*, Vincent Sheean
5. *Seven Pillars of Wisdom*, T. E. Lawrence
6. *Francis the First*, Francis Hackett
7. *Mary Queen of Scotland and the Isles*, Stefan Zweig
8. *Rats, Lice and History*, Hans Zinsser
9. *R. E. Lee*, Douglas Southall Freeman
10. *Skin Deep*, M. C. Phillips

1936

Fiction

1. *Gone with the Wind*, Margaret Mitchell
2. *The Last Puritan*, George Santayana
3. *Sparkenbroke*, Charles Morgan
4. *Drums Along the Mohawk*, Walter D. Edmonds
5. *It Can't Happen Here*, Sinclair Lewis
6. *White Banners*, Lloyd C. Douglas
7. *The Hurricane*, Charles Nordhoff and James Norman Hall
8. *The Thinking Reed*, Rebecca West
9. *The Doctor*, Mary Roberts Rinehart
10. *Eyeless in Gaza*, Aldous Huxley

Nonfiction

1. *Man the Unknown*, Alexis Carrel
2. *Wake Up and Live!*, Dorothea Brande

3. *The Way of a Transgressor*, Negley Farson
4. *Around the World in Eleven Years*, Patience, Richard, and Johnny Abbe
5. *North to the Orient*, Anne Morrow Lindbergh
6. *An American Doctor's Odyssey*, Victor Heiser
7. *Inside Europe*, John Gunther
8. *Live Alone and Like It*, Marjorie Hillis
9. *Life with Father*, Clarence Day
10. *I Write As I Please*, Walter Duranty

1937

Fiction

1. *Gone with the Wind*, Margaret Mitchell
2. *Northwest Passage*, Kenneth Roberts
3. *The Citadel*, A. J. Cronin
4. *And So—Victoria*, Vaughan Wilkins
5. *Drums Along the Mohawk*, Walter D. Edmonds
6. *The Years*, Virginia Woolf
7. *Theatre*, W. Somerset Maugham
8. *Of Mice and Men*, John Steinbeck
9. *The Rains Came*, Louis Bromfield
10. *We Are Not Alone*, James Hilton

Nonfiction

1. *How to Win Friends and Influence People*, Dale Carnegie
2. *An American Doctor's Odyssey*, Victor Heiser
3. *The Return to Religion*, Henry C. Link
4. *The Arts*, Hendrik Willem Van Loon
5. *Orchids on Your Budget*, Marjorie Hillis
6. *Present Indicative*, Noel Coward
7. *Mathematics for the Million*, Lancelot Hogben
8. *Life with Mother*, Clarence Day
9. *The Nile*, Emil Ludwig
10. *The Flowering of New England*, Van Wyck Brooks

1938

Fiction

1. *The Yearling*, Marjorie Kinnan Rawlings
2. *The Citadel*, A. J. Cronin
3. *My Son, My Son!*, Howard Spring
4. *Rebecca*, Daphne du Maurier
5. *Northwest Passage*, Kenneth Roberts
6. *All This, and Heaven Too*, Rachel Field
7. *The Rains Came*, Louis Bromfield
8. *And Tell of Time*, Laura Krey
9. *The Mortal Storm*, Phyllis Bottome
10. *Action at Aquila*, Hervey Allen

Nonfiction

1. *The Importance of Living*, Lin Yutang
2. *With Malice Toward Some*, Margaret Halsey
3. *Madame Curie*, Eve Curie
4. *Listen! The Wind*, Anne Morrow Lindbergh
5. *The Horse and Buggy Doctor*, Arthur E. Hertzler
6. *How to Win Friends and Influence People*, Dale Carnegie
7. *Benjamin Franklin*, Carl Van Doren
8. *I'm a Stranger Here Myself*, Ogden Nash
9. *Alone*, Richard E. Byrd
10. *Fanny Kemble*, Margaret Armstrong

1939

Fiction

1. *The Grapes of Wrath*, John Steinbeck
2. *All This, and Heaven Too*, Rachel Field
3. *Rebecca*, Daphne du Maurier
4. *Wickford Point*, John P. Marquand
5. *Escape*, Ethel Vance
6. *Disputed Passage*, Lloyd C. Douglas
7. *The Yearling*, Marjorie Kinnan Rawlings
8. *The Tree of Liberty*, Elizabeth Page
9. *The Nazarene*, Sholem Asch
10. *Kitty Foyle*, Christopher Morley

Nonfiction

1. *Days of Our Years*, Pierre van Paassen
2. *Reaching for the Stars*, Nora Waln
3. *Inside Asia*, John Gunther
4. *Autobiography with Letters*, William Lyon Phelps
5. *Country Lawyer*, Bellamy Partridge
6. *Wind, Sand and Stars*, Antoine de Saint-Exupéry
7. *Mein Kampf*, Adolf Hitler
8. *A Peculiar Treasure*, Edna Ferber
9. *Not Peace but a Sword*, Vincent Sheean
10. *Listen! The Wind*, Anne Morrow Lindbergh

1940

Fiction

1. *How Green Was My Valley*, Richard Llewellyn
2. *Kitty Foyle*, Christopher Morley
3. *Mrs. Miniver*, Jan Struther
4. *For Whom the Bell Tolls*, Ernest Hemingway
5. *The Nazarene*, Sholem Asch
6. *Stars on the Sea*, F. van Wyck Mason
7. *Oliver Wiswell*, Kenneth Roberts
8. *The Grapes of Wrath*, John Steinbeck
9. *Night in Bombay*, Louis Bromfield
10. *The Family*, Nina Fedorova

Nonfiction

1. *I Married Adventure*, Osa Johnson
2. *How to Read a Book*, Mortimer Adler
3. *A Smattering of Ignorance*, Oscar Levant
4. *Country Squire in the White House*, John T. Flynn
5. *Land Below the Wind*, Agnes Newton Keith
6. *American White Paper*, Joseph W. Alsop Jr. and Robert Kintnor
7. *New England: Indian Summer*, Van Wyck Brooks
8. *As I Remember Him*, Hans Zinsser
9. *Days of Our Years*, Pierre van Paassen
10. *Bet It's a Boy*, Betty B. Blunt

1941

Fiction

1. *The Keys of the Kingdom*, A. J. Cronin
2. *Random Harvest*, James Hilton
3. *This Above All*, Eric Knight
4. *The Sun Is My Undoing*, Marguerite Steen
5. *For Whom the Bell Tolls*, Ernest Hemingway
6. *Oliver Wiswell*, Kenneth Roberts
7. *H. M. Pulham, Esquire*, John P. Marquand
8. *Mr. and Mrs. Cugat*, Isabel Scott Rorick
9. *Saratoga Trunk*, Edna Ferber
10. *Windswept*, Mary Ellen Chase

Nonfiction

1. *Berlin Diary*, William L. Shirer
2. *The White Cliffs*, Alice Duer Miller
3. *Out of the Night*, Jan Valtin
4. *Inside Latin America*, John Gunther
5. *Blood, Sweat and Tears*, Winston S. Churchill
6. *You Can't Do Business with Hitler*, Douglas Miller
7. *Reading I've Liked*, Clifton Fadiman, editor
8. *Reveille in Washington*, Margaret Leech
9. *Exit Laughing*, Irvin S. Cobb
10. *My Sister and I*, Dirk van der Heide

1942

Fiction

1. *The Song of Bernadette*, Franz Werfel
2. *The Moon Is Down*, John Steinbeck
3. *Dragon Seed*, Pearl S. Buck
4. *And Now Tomorrow*, Rachel Field
5. *Drivin' Woman*, Elizabeth Pickett
6. *Windswept*, Mary Ellen Chase
7. *The Robe*, Lloyd C. Douglas
8. *The Sun Is My Undoing*, Marguerite Steen
9. *Kings Row*, Henry Bellamann

10. *The Keys of the Kingdom*, A. J. Cronin

Nonfiction

1. *See Here, Private Hargrove*, Marion Hargrove
2. *Mission to Moscow*, Joseph E. Davies
3. *The Last Time I Saw Paris*, Elliot Paul
4. *Cross Creek*, Marjorie Kinnan Rawlings
5. *Victory Through Air Power*, Major Alexander P. de Seversky
6. *Past Imperfect*, Ilka Chase
7. *They Were Expendable*, W. L. White
8. *Flight to Arras*, Antoine de Saint-Exupéry
9. *Washington Is Like That*, W. M. Kiplinger
10. *Inside Latin America*, John Gunther

1943

Fiction

1. *The Robe*, Lloyd C. Douglas
2. *The Valley of Decision*, Marcia Davenport
3. *So Little Time*, John P. Marquand
4. *A Tree Grows in Brooklyn*, Betty Smith
5. *The Human Comedy*, William Saroyan
6. *Mrs. Parkington*, Louis Bromfield
7. *The Apostle*, Sholem Asch
8. *Hungry Hill*, Daphne du Maurier
9. *The Forest and the Fort*, Hervey Allen
10. *The Song of Bernadette*, Franz Werfel

Nonfiction

1. *Under Cover*, John Roy Carlson
2. *One World*, Wendell L. Willkie
3. *Journey Among Warriors*, Eve Curie
4. *On Being a Real Person*, Harry Emerson Fosdick
5. *Guadalcanal Diary*, Richard Tregaskis
6. *Burma Surgeon*, Lt. Col. Gordon Seagrave
7. *Our Hearts Were Young and Gay*, Cornelia Otis Skinner and Emily Kimbrough
8. *U. S. Foreign Policy*, Walter Lippmann
9. *Here Is Your War*, Ernie Pyle
10. *See Here, Private Hargrove*, Marion Hargrove

1944

Fiction

1. *Strange Fruit*, Lillian Smith
2. *The Robe*, Lloyd C. Douglas
3. *A Tree Grows in Brooklyn*, Betty Smith
4. *Forever Amber*, Kathleen Winsor
5. *The Razor's Edge*, W. Somerset Maugham
6. *The Green Years*, A. J. Cronin
7. *Leave Her to Heaven*, Ben Ames Williams

8. *Green Dolphin Street*, Elizabeth Goudge
9. *A Bell for Adano*, John Hersey
10. *The Apostle*, Sholem Asch

Nonfiction

1. *I Never Left Home*, Bob Hope
2. *Brave Men*, Ernie Pyle
3. *Good Night, Sweet Prince*, Gene Fowler
4. *Under Cover*, John Roy Carlson
5. *Yankee from Olympus*, Catherine Drinker Bowen
6. *The Time for Decision*, Sumner Welles
7. *Here Is Your War*, Ernie Pyle
8. *Anna and the King of Siam*, Margaret Landon
9. *The Curtain Rises*, Quentin Reynolds
10. *Ten Years in Japan*, Joseph C. Grew

1945

Fiction

1. *Forever Amber*, Kathleen Winsor
2. *The Robe*, Lloyd C. Douglas
3. *The Black Rose*, Thomas B. Costain
4. *The White Tower*, James Ramsey Ullman
5. *Cass Timberlane*, Sinclair Lewis
6. *A Lion Is in the Streets*, Adria Locke Langley
7. *So Well Remembered*, James Hilton
8. *Captain from Castile*, Samuel Shellabarger
9. *Earth and High Heaven*, Gwethalyn Graham
10. *Immortal Wife*, Irving Stone

Nonfiction

1. *Brave Men*, Ernie Pyle
2. *Dear Sir*, Juliet Lowell
3. *Up Front*, Bill Mauldin
4. *Black Boy*, Richard Wright
5. *Try and Stop Me*, Bennett Cerf
6. *Anything Can Happen*, George and Helen Papashvily
7. *General Marshall's Report*, U.S. War Department General Staff
8. *The Egg and I*, Betty MacDonald
9. *The Thurber Carnival*, James Thurber
10. *Pleasant Valley*, Louis Bromfield

1946

Fiction

1. *The King's General*, Daphne du Maurier
2. *This Side of Innocence*, Taylor Caldwell
3. *The River Road*, Frances Parkinson Keyes
4. *The Miracle of the Bells*, Russell Janney
5. *The Hucksters*, Frederic Wakeman

6. *The Foxes of Harrow*, Frank Yerby
7. *Arch of Triumph*, Erich Maria Remarque
8. *The Black Rose*, Thomas B. Costain
9. *B.F.'s Daughter*, John P. Marquand
10. *The Snake Pit*, Mary Jane Ward

Nonfiction

1. *The Egg and I*, Betty MacDonald
2. *Peace of Mind*, Joshua L. Liebman
3. *As He Saw It*, Elliott Roosevelt
4. *The Roosevelt I Knew*, Frances Perkins
5. *Last Chapter*, Ernie Pyle
6. *Starling of the White House*, Thomas Sugrue and Col. Edmund Starling
7. *I Chose Freedom*, Victor Kravchenko
8. *The Anatomy of Peace*, Emery Reves
9. *Top Secret*, Ralph Ingersoll
10. *A Solo in Tom-Toms*, Gene Fowler

1947

Fiction

1. *The Miracle of the Bells*, Russell Janney
2. *The Moneyman*, Thomas B. Costain
3. *Gentleman's Agreement*, Laura Z. Hobson
4. *Lydia Bailey*, Kenneth Roberts
5. *The Vixens*, Frank Yerby
6. *The Wayward Bus*, John Steinbeck
7. *House Divided*, Ben Ames Williams
8. *Kingsblood Royal*, Sinclair Lewis
9. *East Side, West Side*, Marcia Davenport
10. *Prince of Foxes*, Samuel Shellabarger

Nonfiction

1. *Peace of Mind*, Joshua L. Liebman
2. *Information Please Almanac, 1947*, John Kieran, editor
3. *Inside U.S.A.*, John Gunther
4. *A Study of History*, Arnold J. Toynbee
5. *Speaking Frankly*, James F. Byrnes
6. *Human Destiny*, Pierre Lecomte du Noüy
7. *The Egg and I*, Betty MacDonald
8. *The American Past*, Roger Butterfield
9. *The Fireside Book of Folk Songs*, Margaret B. Boni, editor
10. *Together*, Katharine T. Marshall

1948

Fiction

1. *The Big Fisherman*, Lloyd C. Douglas
2. *The Naked and the Dead*, Norman Mailer
3. *Dinner at Antoine's*, Frances Parkinson Keyes
4. *The Bishop's Mantle*, Agnes Sligh Turnbull
5. *Tomorrow Will Be Better*, Betty Smith

6. *The Golden Hawk*, Frank Yerby
7. *Raintree County*, Ross Lockridge Jr.
8. *Shannon's Way*, A. J. Cronin
9. *Pilgrim's Inn*, Elizabeth Goudge
10. *The Young Lions*, Irwin Shaw

Nonfiction

1. *Crusade in Europe*, Dwight D. Eisenhower
2. *How to Stop Worrying and Start Living*, Dale Carnegie
3. *Peace of Mind*, Joshua L. Liebman
4. *Sexual Behavior in the Human Male*, A. C. Kinsey, et al.
5. *Wine, Women and Words*, Billy Rose
6. *The Life and Times of the Shmoo*, Al Capp
7. *The Gathering Storm*, Winston Churchill
8. *Roosevelt and Hopkins*, Robert E. Sherwood
9. *A Guide to Confident Living*, Norman Vincent Peale
10. *The Plague and I*, Betty MacDonald

1949

Fiction

1. *The Egyptian*, Mika Waltari
2. *The Big Fisherman*, Lloyd C. Douglas
3. *Mary*, Sholem Asch
4. *A Rage to Live*, John O'Hara
5. *Point of No Return*, John P. Marquand
6. *Dinner at Antoine's*, Frances Parkinson Keyes
7. *High Towers*, Thomas B. Costain
8. *Cutlass Empire*, Van Wyck Mason
9. *Pride's Castle*, Frank Yerby
10. *Father of the Bride*, Edward Streeter

Nonfiction

1. *White Collar Zoo*, Clare Barnes Jr.
2. *How to Win at Canasta*, Oswald Jacoby
3. *The Seven Storey Mountain*, Thomas Merton
4. *Home Sweet Zoo*, Clare Barnes Jr.
5. *Cheaper by the Dozen*, Frank B. Gilbreth Jr. and Ernestine Gilbreth Carey
6. *The Greatest Story Ever Told*, Fulton Oursler
7. *Canasta, the Argentine Rummy Game*, Ottilie H. Reilly
8. *Canasta*, Josephine Artayeta de Viel and Ralph Michael
9. *Peace of Soul*, Fulton J. Sheen
10. *A Guide to Confident Living*, Norman Vincent Peale

1950

Fiction

1. *The Cardinal*, Henry Morton Robinson
2. *Joy Street*, Frances Parkinson Keyes
3. *Across the River and into the Trees*, Ernest Hemingway
4. *The Wall*, John Hersey
5. *Star Money*, Kathleen Winsor
6. *The Parasites*, Daphne du Maurier
7. *Floodtide*, Frank Yerby
8. *Jubilee Trail*, Gwen Bristow
9. *The Adventurer*, Mika Waltari
10. *The Disenchanted*, Budd Schulberg

Nonfiction

1. *Betty Crocker's Picture Cook Book*
2. *The Baby*
3. *Look Younger, Live Longer*, Gayelord Hauser
4. *How I Raised Myself from Failure to Success in Selling*, Frank Bettger
5. *Kon-Tiki*, Thor Heyerdahl
6. *Mr. Jones, Meet the Master*, Peter Marshall
7. *Your Dream Home*, Hubbard Cobb
8. *The Mature Mind*, H. A. Overstreet
9. *Campus Zoo*, Clare Barnes Jr.
10. *Belles on Their Toes*, Frank Gilbreth Jr. and Ernestine Gilbreth Carey

1951

Fiction

1. *From Here to Eternity*, James Jones
2. *The Caine Mutiny*, Herman Wouk
3. *Moses*, Sholem Asch
4. *The Cardinal*, Henry Morton Robinson
5. *A Woman Called Fancy*, Frank Yerby
6. *The Cruel Sea*, Nicholas Monsarrat
7. *Melville Goodwin, U.S.A.*, John P. Marquand
8. *Return to Paradise*, James A. Michener
9. *The Foundling*, Cardinal Spellman
10. *The Wanderer*, Mika Waltari

Nonfiction

1. *Look Younger, Live Longer*, Gayelord Hauser
2. *Betty Crocker's Picture Cook Book*
3. *Washington Confidential*, Jack Lait and Lee Mortimer
4. *Better Homes and Gardens Garden Book*
5. *Better Homes and Gardens Handyman's Book*
6. *The Sea Around Us*, Rachel L. Carson
7. *Thorndike-Barnhart Comprehensive Desk Dictionary*, Clarence L. Barnhart, editor
8. *Pogo*, Walt Kelly

9. *Kon-Tiki*, Thor Heyerdahl
10. *The New Yorker Twenty-fifth Anniversary Album*

1952

Fiction

1. *The Silver Chalice*, Thomas B. Costain
2. *The Caine Mutiny*, Herman Wouk
3. *East of Eden*, John Steinbeck
4. *My Cousin Rachel*, Daphne du Maurier
5. *Steamboat Gothic*, Frances Parkinson Keyes
6. *Giant*, Edna Ferber
7. *The Old Man and the Sea*, Ernest Hemingway
8. *The Gown of Glory*, Agnes Sligh Turnbull
9. *The Saracen Blade*, Frank Yerby
10. *The Houses in Between*, Howard Spring

Nonfiction

1. *The Holy Bible: Revised Standard Version*
2. *A Man Called Peter*, Catherine Marshall
3. *U.S.A. Confidential*, Jack Lait and Lee Mortimer
4. *The Sea Around Us*, Rachel L. Carson
5. *Tallulah*, Tallulah Bankhead
6. *The Power of Positive Thinking*, Norman Vincent Peale
7. *This I Believe*, Edward P. Morgan, editor; Edward R. Murrow, foreword
8. *This Is Ike*, Wilson Hicks, editor
9. *Witness*, Whittaker Chambers
10. *Mr. President*, William Hillman

1953

Fiction

1. *The Robe*, Lloyd C. Douglas
2. *The Silver Chalice*, Thomas B. Costain
3. *Désirée*, Annemarie Selinko
4. *Battle Cry*, Leon M. Uris
5. *From Here to Eternity*, James Jones
6. *The High and the Mighty*, Ernest K. Gann
7. *Beyond This Place*, A. J. Cronin
8. *Time and Time Again*, James Hilton
9. *Lord Vanity*, Samuel Shellabarger
10. *The Unconquered*, Ben Ames Williams

Nonfiction

1. *The Holy Bible: Revised Standard Version*
2. *The Power of Positive Thinking*, Norman Vincent Peale
3. *Sexual Behavior in the Human Female*, Alfred C. Kinsey, et al.
4. *Angel Unaware*, Dale Evans Rogers
5. *Life Is Worth Living*, Fulton J. Sheen

6. *A Man Called Peter*, Catherine Marshall
7. *This I Believe*, Edward P. Morgan, editor; Edward R. Murrow, foreword
8. *The Greatest Faith Ever Known*, Fulton Oursler and G. A. O. Armstrong
9. *How to Play Your Best Golf*, Tommy Armour
10. *A House Is Not a Home*, Polly Adler

1954

Fiction

1. *Not as a Stranger*, Morton Thompson
2. *Mary Anne*, Daphne du Maurier
3. *Love Is Eternal*, Irving Stone
4. *The Royal Box*, Frances Parkinson Keyes
5. *The Egyptian*, Mika Waltari
6. *No Time for Sergeants*, Mac Hyman
7. *Sweet Thursday*, John Steinbeck
8. *The View from Pompey's Head*, Hamilton Basso
9. *Never Victorious, Never Defeated*, Taylor Caldwell
10. *Benton's Row*, Frank Yerby

Nonfiction

1. *The Holy Bible: Revised Standard Version*
2. *The Power of Positive Thinking*, Norman Vincent Peale
3. *Better Homes and Gardens New Cook Book*
4. *Betty Crocker's Good and Easy Cook Book*
5. *The Tumult and the Shouting*, Grantland Rice
6. *I'll Cry Tomorrow*, Lillian Roth, Gerold Frank, and Mike Connolly
7. *The Prayers of Peter Marshall*, Catherine Marshall, editor
8. *This I Believe, 2*, Raymond Swing, editor
9. *But We Were Born Free*, Elmer Davis
10. *The Saturday Evening Post Treasury*, Roger Butterfield, editor

1955

Fiction

1. *Marjorie Morningstar*, Herman Wouk
2. *Auntie Mame*, Patrick Dennis
3. *Andersonville*, MacKinlay Kantor
4. *Bonjour Tristesse*, Françoise Sagan
5. *The Man in the Gray Flannel Suit*, Sloan Wilson
6. *Something of Value*, Robert Ruark
7. *Not As a Stranger*, Morton Thompson
8. *No Time for Sergeants*, Mac Hyman
9. *The Tontine*, Thomas B. Costain
10. *Ten North Frederick*, John O'Hara

Nonfiction

1. *Gift from the Sea*, Anne Morrow Lindbergh
2. *The Power of Positive Thinking*, Norman Vincent Peale
3. *The Family of Man*, Edward Steichen
4. *A Man Called Peter*, Catherine Marshall
5. *How to Live 365 Days a Year*, John A. Schindler
6. *Better Homes and Gardens Diet Book*
7. *The Secret of Happiness*, Billy Graham
8. *Why Johnny Can't Read*, Rudolf Flesch
9. *Inside Africa*, John Gunther
10. *Year of Decisions*, Harry S Truman

1956

Fiction

1. *Don't Go Near the Water*, William Brinkley
2. *The Last Hurrah*, Edwin O'Connor
3. *Peyton Place*, Grace Metalious
4. *Auntie Mame*, Patrick Dennis
5. *Eloise*, Kay Thompson
6. *Andersonville*, MacKinlay Kantor
7. *A Certain Smile*, Françoise Sagan
8. *The Tribe That Lost Its Head*, Nicholas Monsarrat
9. *The Mandarins*, Simone de Beauvoir
10. *Boon Island*, Kenneth Roberts

Nonfiction

1. *Arthritis and Common Sense*, rev. ed., Dan Dale Alexander
2. *Webster's New World Dictionary of the American Language*, concise ed., David B. Guralnik
3. *Betty Crocker's Picture Cook Book*, 2nd. ed.
4. *Etiquette*, Frances Benton
5. *Better Homes and Gardens Barbecue Book*
6. *The Search for Bridey Murphy*, Morey Bernstein
7. *Love or Perish*, Smiley Blanton, M.D.
8. *Better Homes and Gardens Decorating Book*
9. *How to Live 365 Days a Year*, John A. Schindler
10. *The Nun's Story*, Kathryn Hulme

1957

Fiction

1. *By Love Possessed*, James Gould Cozzens
2. *Peyton Place*, Grace Metalious
3. *Compulsion*, Meyer Levin
4. *Rally Round the Flag, Boys!*, Max Shulman

5. *Blue Camellia*, Frances Parkinson Keyes
6. *Eloise in Paris*, Kay Thompson
7. *The Scapegoat*, Daphne du Maurier
8. *On the Beach*, Nevil Shute
9. *Below the Salt*, Thomas B. Costain
10. *Atlas Shrugged*, Ayn Rand

Nonfiction

1. *Kids Say the Darndest Things!*, Art Linkletter
2. *The FBI Story*, Don Whitehead
3. *Stay Alive All Your Life*, Norman Vincent Peale
4. *To Live Again*, Catherine Marshall
5. *Better Homes and Gardens Flower Arranging*
6. *Where Did You Go? Out. What Did You Do? Nothing*, Robert Paul Smith
7. *Baruch: My Own Story*, Bernard M. Baruch
8. *Please Don't Eat the Daisies*, Jean Kerr
9. *The American Heritage Book of Great Historic Places*
10. *The Day Christ Died*, Jim Bishop

1958

Fiction

1. *Doctor Zhivago*, Boris Pasternak
2. *Anatomy of a Murder*, Robert Traver
3. *Lolita*, Vladimir Nabokov
4. *Around the World with Auntie Mame*, Patrick Dennis
5. *From the Terrace*, John O'Hara
6. *Eloise at Christmastime*, Kay Thompson
7. *Ice Palace*, Edna Ferber
8. *The Winthrop Woman*, Anya Seton
9. *The Enemy Camp*, Jerome Weidman
10. *Victorine*, Frances Parkinson Keyes

Nonfiction

1. *Kids Say the Darndest Things!*, Art Linkletter
2. *'Twixt Twelve and Twenty*, Pat Boone
3. *Only in America*, Harry Golden
4. *Masters of Deceit*, Edgar Hoover
5. *Please Don't Eat the Daisies*, Jean Kerr
6. *Better Homes and Gardens Salad Book*
7. *The New Testament in Modern English*, J. P. Phillips, trans.
8. *Aku-Aku*, Thor Heyerdahl
9. *Dear Abby*, Abigail Van Buren
10. *Inside Russia Today*, John Gunther

1959

Fiction
1. *Exodus*, Leon Uris
2. *Doctor Zhivago*, Boris Pasternak
3. *Hawaii*, James Michener
4. *Advise and Consent*, Allen Drury
5. *Lady Chatterley's Lover*, D. H. Lawrence
6. *The Ugly American*, William J. Lederer and Eugene L. Burdick
7. *Dear and Glorious Physician*, Taylor Caldwell
8. *Lolita*, Vladimir Nabokov
9. *Mrs. 'Arris Goes to Paris*, Paul Gallico
10. *Poor No More*, Robert Ruark

Nonfiction
1. *'Twixt Twelve and Twenty*, Pat Boone
2. *Folk Medicine*, D. C. Jarvis
3. *For 2¢ Plain*, Harry Golden
4. *The Status Seekers*, Vance Packard
5. *Act One*, Moss Hart
6. *Charley Weaver's Letters from Mamma*, Cliff Arquette
7. *The Elements of Style*, William Strunk Jr. and E. B. White
8. *The General Foods Kitchens Cookbook*
9. *Only in America*, Harry Golden
10. *Mine Enemy Grows Older*, Alexander King

1960

Fiction
1. *Advise and Consent*, Allen Drury
2. *Hawaii*, James A. Michener
3. *The Leopard*, Giuseppe di Lampedusa
4. *The Chapman Report*, Irving Wallace
5. *Ourselves to Know*, John O'Hara
6. *The Constant Image*, Marcia Davenport
7. *The Lovely Ambition*, Mary Ellen Chase
8. *The Listener*, Taylor Caldwell
9. *Trustee from the Toolroom*, Nevil Shute
10. *Sermons and Soda-Water*, John O'Hara

Nonfiction
1. *Folk Medicine*, D. C. Jarvis
2. *Better Homes and Gardens First Aid for Your Family*
3. *The General Foods Kitchens Cookbook*
4. *May This House Be Safe from Tigers*, Alexander King
5. *Better Homes and Gardens Dessert Book*
6. *Better Homes and Gardens Decorating Ideas*

7. *The Rise and Fall of the Third Reich*, William L. Shirer
8. *The Conscience of a Conservative*, Barry Goldwater
9. *I Kid You Not*, Jack Paar
10. *Between You, Me and the Gatepost*, Pat Boone

1961

Fiction
1. *The Agony and the Ecstasy*, Irving Stone
2. *Franny and Zooey*, J. D. Salinger
3. *To Kill a Mockingbird*, Harper Lee
4. *Mila 18*, Leon Uris
5. *The Carpetbaggers*, Harold Robbins
6. *Tropic of Cancer*, Henry Miller
7. *Winnie Ille Pu*, Alexander Lenard, trans.
8. *Daughter of Silence*, Morris West
9. *The Edge of Sadness*, Edwin O'Connor
10. *The Winter of Our Discontent*, John Steinbeck

Nonfiction
1. *The New English Bible: The New Testament*
2. *The Rise and Fall of the Third Reich*, William Shirer
3. *Better Homes and Gardens Sewing Book*
4. *Casserole Cook Book*
5. *A Nation of Sheep*, William Lederer
6. *Better Homes and Gardens Nutrition for Your Family*
7. *The Making of the President, 1960*, Theodore H. White
8. *Calories Don't Count*, Dr. Herman Taller
9. *Betty Crocker's New Picture Cook Book: New Edition*
10. *Ring of Bright Water*, Gavin Maxwell

1962

Fiction
1. *Ship of Fools*, Katherine Anne Porter
2. *Dearly Beloved*, Anne Morrow Lindbergh
3. *A Shade of Difference*, Allen Drury
4. *Youngblood Hawke*, Herman Wouk
5. *Franny and Zooey*, J. D. Salinger
6. *Fail-Safe*, Eugene Burdick and Harvey Wheeler
7. *Seven Days in May*, Fletcher Knebel and Charles W. Bailey II
8. *The Prize*, Irving Wallace
9. *The Agony and the Ecstasy*, Irving Stone
10. *The Reivers*, William Faulkner

Nonfiction
1. *Calories Don't Count*, Dr. Herman Taller
2. *The New English Bible: The New Testament*
3. *Better Homes and Gardens Cook Book: New Edition*
4. *O Ye Jigs & Juleps!*, Virginia Cary Hudson
5. *Happiness Is a Warm Puppy*, Charles M. Schulz
6. *The Joy of Cooking: New Edition*, Irma S. Rombauer and Marion Rombauer Becker
7. *My Life in Court*, Louis Nizer
8. *The Rothschilds*, Frederic Morton
9. *Sex and the Single Girl*, Helen Gurley Brown
10. *Travels with Charley*, John Steinbeck

1963

Fiction
1. *The Shoes of the Fisherman*, Morris L. West
2. *The Group*, Mary McCarthy
3. *Raise High the Roof Beam, Carpenters, and Seymour—An Introduction*, J. D. Salinger
4. *Caravans*, James A. Michener
5. *Elizabeth Appleton*, John O'Hara
6. *Grandmother and the Priests*, Taylor Caldwell
7. *City of Night*, John Rechy
8. *The Glass-Blowers*, Daphne du Maurier
9. *The Sand Pebbles*, Richard McKenna
10. *The Battle of the Villa Fiorita*, Rumer Godden

Nonfiction
1. *Happiness Is a Warm Puppy*, Charles M. Schulz
2. *Security Is a Thumb and a Blanket*, Charles M. Schulz
3. *J.F.K.: The Man and the Myth*, Victor Lasky
4. *Profiles in Courage: Inaugural Edition*, John F. Kennedy
5. *O Ye Jigs & Juleps!*, Virginia Cary Hudson
6. *Better Homes and Gardens Bread Cook Book*
7. *The Pillsbury Family Cookbook*
8. *I Owe Russia $1200*, Bob Hope
9. *Heloise's Housekeeping Hints*
10. *Better Homes and Gardens Baby Book*

1964

Fiction

1. *The Spy Who Came in from the Cold*, John le Carré
2. *Candy*, Terry Southern and Mason Hoffenberg
3. *Herzog*, Saul Bellow
4. *Armageddon*, Leon Uris
5. *The Man*, Irving Wallace
6. *The Rector of Justin*, Louis Auchincloss
7. *The Martyred*, Richard E. Kim
8. *You Only Live Twice*, Ian Fleming
9. *This Rough Magic*, Mary Stewart
10. *Convention*, Fletcher Knebel and Charles W. Bailey II

Nonfiction

1. *Four Days*, American Heritage and United Press International
2. *I Need All the Friends I Can Get*, Charles M. Schulz
3. *Profiles in Courage: Memorial Edition*, John F. Kennedy

4. *In His Own Write*, John Lennon
5. *Christmas Is Together-Time*, Charles M. Schulz
6. *A Day in the Life of President Kennedy*, Jim Bishop
7. *The Kennedy Wit*, compiled by Bill Adler
8. *A Moveable Feast*, Ernest Hemingway
9. *Reminiscences*, General Douglas MacArthur
10. *The John F. Kennedys*, Mark Shaw

1965

Fiction

1. *The Source*, James A. Michener
2. *Up the Down Staircase*, Bel Kaufman
3. *Herzog*, Saul Bellow
4. *The Looking Glass War*, John le Carré
5. *The Green Berets*, Robin Moore
6. *Those Who Love*, Irving Stone
7. *The Man with the Golden Gun*, Ian Fleming
8. *Hotel*, Arthur Hailey
9. *The Ambassador*, Morris West

10. *Don't Stop the Carnival*, Herman Wouk

Nonfiction

1. *How to Be a Jewish Mother*, Dan Greenburg
2. *A Gift of Prophecy*, Ruth Montgomery
3. *Games People Play*, Eric Berne, M.D.
4. *World Aflame*, Billy Graham
5. *Happiness Is a Dry Martini*, Johnny Carson
6. *Markings*, Dag Hammarskjöld
7. *A Thousand Days*, Arthur Schlesinger Jr.
8. *My Shadow Ran Fast*, Bill Sands
9. *Kennedy*, Theodore C. Sorensen
10. *The Making of the President, 1964*, Theodore H. White

1966

Fiction

1. *Valley of the Dolls*, Jacqueline Susann
2. *The Adventurers*, Harold Robbins
3. *The Secret of Santa Vittoria*, Robert Crichton

LITERATURE GOES TO THE MOVIES

It's no secret that many movies, both good and bad, are based on books. This list presents a small sampling of unusual, delightful, and surprising books by leading writers that were turned into well-known movies. (The dates after the titles indicate the year of the film version's release.)

American Hero (released as *Wag the Dog*, 1997), Larry Beinhart

Awakenings (1990), Oliver Sacks

The Blue Angel (1930, 1959), Heinrich Mann

The Body Snatcher (1945), Robert Louis Stevenson

Breakfast at Tiffany's (1961), Truman Capote

Burning Patience (released as *Il Postino (The Postman)*, 1995), Antonio Skarmeta

Chitty, Chitty, Bang, Bang (1968), Ian Fleming

The Death and Life of Dith Pran (released as *The Killing Fields*, 1984), Sidney Schanberg

Deliverance (1972), James Dickey

Do Androids Dream of Electric Sheep? (released as *Blade Runner*, 1982), Philip K. Dick

Donnie Brasco: My Undercover Life in the Mafia (released as *Donnie Brasco*, 1997), Joseph D. Pistone with Richard Woodley

Don't Look Now (1971), Daphne du Maurier

Dream Story (released as *Eyes Wide Shut*, 1999), Arthur Schnitzler

The Executioners (released as *Cape Fear*, 1962, 1991), J. D. MacDonald

The Grifters (1990), Jim Thompson

The Hamlet (originally *The Long, Hot Summer*, 1957) William Faulkner

Jumanji (1995), Chris Van Allsburg

The Killer Angels (released as *Gettysburg*, 1993), Michael Shaara

L.A. Confidential (1997), James Ellroy

The Last Picture Show (1971), Larry McMurtry

Legends of the Fall (1994), Jim Harrison

Lost Moon (released as *Apollo 13*, 1995), Jim Lovell and Jeffrey Kluger

The Magnificent Ambersons (1942), Booth Tarkington

The Maltese Falcon (1941; also released as *Satan Met a Lady*, 1937), Dashiell Hammett

Mildred Pierce (1945), James M. Cain

The Natural (1984), Bernard Malamud

The Postman Always Rings Twice (1946, 1981), James M. Cain

Psycho (1960), Robert Bloch

Rum Punch (released as *Jackie Brown*, 1997), Elmore Leonard

The Seven Pillars of Wisdom (released as *Lawrence of Arabia*, 1962), T. E. Lawrence

Seven Years in Tibet (1997), Heinrich Harrar

Starship Troopers (1997), Robert A. Heinlein

Tales from the South Pacific (produced as the musical *South Pacific* and later released as a film, 1958), James Michener

The Turn of the Screw (released as *The Innocents*, 1961), Henry James

Two Hours to Doom (released as *Dr. Strangelove*, 1964), Peter George

4. *Capable of Honor*, Allen Drury
5. *The Double Image*, Helen MacInnes
6. *The Fixer*, Bernard Malamud
7. *Tell No Man*, Adela Rogers St. Johns
8. *Tai-Pan*, James Clavell
9. *The Embezzler*, Louis Auchincloss
10. *All in the Family*, Edwin O'Connor

Nonfiction

1. *How to Avoid Probate*, Norman F. Dacey
2. *Human Sexual Response*, William Howard Masters and Virginia E. Johnston
3. *In Cold Blood*, Truman Capote
4. *Games People Play*, Eric Berne, M.D.
5. *A Thousand Days*, Arthur M. Schlesinger Jr.
6. *Everything but Money*, Sam Levenson
7. *The Random House Dictionary of the English Language*
8. *Rush to Judgment*, Mark Lane
9. *The Last Battle*, Cornelius Ryan
10. *Phyllis Diller's Housekeeping Hints*, Phyllis Diller

1967

Fiction

1. *The Arrangement*, Elia Kazan
2. *The Confessions of Nat Turner*, William Styron (tie)
2. *The Chosen*, Chaim Potok (tie)
4. *Topaz*, Leon Uris
5. *Christy*, Catherine Marshall
6. *The Eighth Day*, Thornton Wilder
7. *Rosemary's Baby*, Ira Levin
8. *The Plot*, Irving Wallace
9. *The Gabriel Hounds*, Mary Stewart
10. *The Exhibitionist*, Henry Sutton

Nonfiction

1. *Death of a President*, William Manchester
2. *Misery Is a Blind Date*, Johnny Carson
3. *Games People Play*, Eric Berne, M.D.
4. *Stanyan Street and Other Sorrows*, Rod McKuen
5. *A Modern Priest Looks at His Outdated Church*, Father James Kavanaugh
6. *Everything but Money*, Sam Levenson
7. *Our Crowd*, Stephen Birmingham
8. *Edgar Cayce—The Sleeping Prophet*, Jess Stearn (tie)
8. *Better Homes and Gardens Favorite Ways with Chicken* (tie)
8. *Phyllis Diller's Marriage Manual*, Phyllis Diller (tie)

1968

Fiction

1. *Airport*, Arthur Hailey
2. *Couples*, John Updike
3. *The Salzburg Connection*, Helen MacInnes
4. *A Small Town in Germany*, John Le Carré
5. *Testimony of Two Men*, Taylor Caldwell
6. *Preserve and Protect*, Allen Drury
7. *Myra Breckinridge*, Gore Vidal
8. *Vanished*, Fletcher Knebel
9. *Christy*, Catherine Marshall
10. *The Tower of Babel*, Morris L. West

Nonfiction

1. *Better Homes and Gardens New Cook Book*
2. *The Random House Dictionary of the English Language: College Edition*, Laurence Urdang, editor
3. *Listen to the Warm*, Rod McKuen
4. *Between Parent and Child*, Haim G. Ginott
5. *Lonesome Cities*, Rod McKuen
6. *The Doctor's Quick Weight Loss Diet*, Erwin M. Stillman and Samm Sinclair Baker
7. *The Money Game*, Adam Smith
8. *Stanyan Street and Other Sorrows*, Rod McKuen
9. *The Weight Watcher's Cook Book*, Jean Nidetch
10. *Better Homes and Gardens Eat and Stay Slim*

1969

Fiction

1. *Portnoy's Complaint*, Philip Roth
2. *The Godfather*, Mario Puzo
3. *The Love Machine*, Jacqueline Susann
4. *The Inheritors*, Harold Robbins
5. *The Andromeda Strain*, Michael Crichton
6. *The Seven Minutes*, Irving Wallace
7. *Naked Came the Stranger*, Penelope Ashe
8. *The Promise*, Chaim Potok
9. *The Pretenders*, Gwen Davis
10. *The House on the Strand*, Daphne du Maurier

Nonfiction

1. *American Heritage Dictionary of the English Language*, William Morris, editor
2. *In Someone's Shadow*, Rod McKuen
3. *The Peter Principle*, Laurence J. Peter and Raymond Hull

4. *Between Parent and Teenager*, Dr. Haim G. Ginott
5. *The Graham Kerr Cookbook*, The Galloping Gourmet
6. *The Selling of the President, 1968*, Joe McGinniss
7. *Miss Craig's 21-Day Shape-Up Program for Men and Women*, Marjorie Craig
8. *My Life and Prophecies*, Jeane Dixon with René Noorbergen
9. *Linda Goodman's Sun Signs*, Linda Goodman
10. *Twelve Years of Christmas*, Rod McKuen

1970

Fiction

1. *Love Story*, Erich Segal
2. *The French Lieutenant's Woman*, John Fowles
3. *Islands in the Stream*, Ernest Hemingway
4. *The Crystal Cave*, Mary Stewart
5. *Great Lion of God*, Taylor Caldwell
6. *QB VII*, Leon Uris
7. *The Gang That Couldn't Shoot Straight*, Jimmy Breslin
8. *The Secret Woman*, Victoria Holt
9. *Travels with My Aunt*, Graham Greene
10. *Rich Man, Poor Man*, Irwin Shaw

Nonfiction

1. *Everything You Always Wanted to Know About Sex but Were Afraid to Ask*, David Reuben, M.D.
2. *The New English Bible*
3. *The Sensuous Woman*, "J"
4. *Better Homes and Gardens Fondue and Tabletop Cooking*
5. *Up the Organization*, Robert Townsend
6. *Ball Four*, Jim Bouton
7. *American Heritage Dictionary of the English Language*, William Morris
8. *Body Language*, Julius Fast
9. *In Someone's Shadow*, Rod McKuen
10. *Caught in the Quiet*, Rod McKuen

1971

Fiction

1. *Wheels*, Arthur Hailey
2. *The Exorcist*, William P. Blatty
3. *The Passions of the Mind*, Irving Stone
4. *The Day of the Jackal*, Frederick Forsyth
5. *The Betsy*, Harold Robbins
6. *Message from Malaga*, Helen MacInnes

7. *The Winds of War*, Herman Wouk
8. *The Drifters*, James A. Michener
9. *The Other*, Thomas Tryon
10. *Rabbit Redux*, John Updike

Nonfiction

1. *The Sensous Man*, "M"
2. *Bury My Heart at Wounded Knee*, Dee Brown
3. *Better Homes and Gardens Blender Cook Book*
4. *I'm O.K., You're O.K.*, Thomas Harris
5. *Any Woman Can!*, David Reuben, M.D.
6. *Inside the Third Reich*, Albert Speer
7. *Eleanor and Franklin*, Joseph P. Lash
8. *Wunnerful, Wunnerful!*, Lawrence Welk
9. *Honor Thy Father*, Gay Talese
10. *Fields of Wonder*, Rod McKuen

1972

Fiction

1. *Jonathan Livingston Seagull*, Richard Bach
2. *August, 1914*, Alexander Solzhenitsyn
3. *The Odessa File*, Frederick Forsyth
4. *The Day of the Jackal*, Frederick Forsyth
5. *The Word*, Irving Wallace
6. *The Winds of War*, Herman Wouk
7. *Captains and the Kings*, Taylor Caldwell
8. *Two from Galilee*, Marjorie Holmes
9. *My Name Is Asher Lev*, Chaim Potok
10. *Semi-Tough*, Dan Jenkins

Nonfiction

1. *The Living Bible*, Kenneth Taylor
2. *I'm O.K., You're O.K.*, Thomas Harris
3. *Open Marriage*, Nena and George O'Neill
4. *Harry S. Truman*, Margaret Truman
5. *Dr. Atkins' Diet Revolution*, Robert C. Atkins
6. *Better Homes and Gardens Menu Cook Book*
7. *The Peter Prescription*, Laurence J. Peter
8. *A World Beyond*, Ruth Montgomery
9. *Journey to Ixtlan*, Carlos Castaneda
10. *Better Homes and Gardens Low-Calorie Desserts*

1973

Fiction

1. *Jonathan Livingston Seagull*, Richard Bach
2. *Once Is Not Enough*, Jacqueline Susann
3. *Breakfast of Champions*, Kurt Vonnegut

4. *The Odessa File*, Frederick Forsyth
5. *Burr*, Gore Vidal
6. *The Hollow Hills*, Mary Stewart
7. *Evening in Byzantium*, Irwin Shaw
8. *The Matlock Paper*, Robert Ludlum
9. *The Billion Dollar Sure Thing*, Paul E. Erdman
10. *The Honorary Consul*, Graham Greene

Nonfiction

1. *The Living Bible*, Kenneth Taylor
2. *Dr. Atkins' Diet Revolution*, Robert C. Atkins
3. *I'm O.K., You're O.K.*, Thomas Harris
4. *The Joy of Sex*, Alex Comfort
5. *Weight Watchers Program Cookbook*, Jean Nidetch
6. *How to Be Your Own Best Friend*, Mildred Newman, et al.
7. *The Art of Walt Disney*, Christopher Finch
8. *Better Homes and Gardens Home Canning Cookbook*
9. *Alistair Cooke's America*, Alistair Cooke
10. *Sybil*, Flora R. Schreiber

1974

Fiction

1. *Centennial*, James A. Michener
2. *Watership Down*, Richard Adams
3. *Jaws*, Peter Benchley
4. *Tinker, Tailor, Soldier, Spy*, John le Carré
5. *Something Happened*, Joseph Heller
6. *The Dogs of War*, Frederick Forsyth
7. *The Pirate*, Harold J. Robbins
8. *I Heard the Owl Call My Name*, Margaret Craven
9. *The Seven-Per-Cent Solution*, John H. Watson, M.D., Nicholas Meyer, editor
10. *The Fan Club*, Irving Wallace

Nonfiction

1. *The Total Woman*, Marabel Morgan
2. *All the President's Men*, Carl Bernstein and Bob Woodward
3. *Plain Speaking: An Oral Biography of Harry S. Truman*, Merle Miller
4. *More Joy: A Lovemaking Companion to The Joy of Sex*, Alex Comfort
5. *Alistair Cooke's America*, Alistair Cooke
6. *Tales of Power*, Carlos A. Castaneda
7. *You Can Profit from a Monetary Crisis*, Harry Browne
8. *All Things Bright and Beautiful*, James Herriot
9. *The Bermuda Triangle*, Charles Berlitz with J. Manson Valentine

10. *The Memory Book*, Harry Lorayne and Jerry Lucas

1975

Fiction

1. *Ragtime*, E. L. Doctorow
2. *The Moneychangers*, Arthur Hailey
3. *Curtain*, Agatha Christie
4. *Looking for Mister Goodbar*, Judith Rossner
5. *The Choirboys*, Joseph Wambaugh
6. *The Eagle Has Landed*, Jack Higgins
7. *The Greek Treasure: A Biographical Novel of Henry and Sophia Schliemann*, Irving Stone
8. *The Great Train Robbery*, Michael Crichton
9. *Shogun*, James Clavell
10. *Humboldt's Gift*, Saul Bellow

Nonfiction

1. *Angels: God's Secret Agents*, Billy Graham
2. *Winning Through Intimidation*, Robert Ringer
3. *TM: Discovering Energy and Overcoming Stress*, Harold H. Bloomfield
4. *The Ascent of Man*, Jacob Bronowski
5. *Sylvia Porter's Money Book*, Sylvia Porter
6. *Total Fitness in 30 Minutes a Week*, Laurence E. Morehouse and Leonard Gross
7. *The Bermuda Triangle*, Charles Berlitz with J. Manson Valentine
8. *The Save-Your-Life Diet*, David Reuben
9. *Bring on the Empty Horses*, David Niven
10. *Breach of Faith: The Fall of Richard Nixon*, Theodore H. White

1976

Fiction

1. *Trinity*, Leon Uris
2. *Sleeping Murder*, Agatha Christie
3. *Dolores*, Jacqueline Susann
4. *Storm Warning*, Jack Higgins
5. *The Deep*, Peter Benchley
6. *1876*, Gore Vidal
7. *Slapstick: or, Lonesome No More!*, Kurt Vonnegut
8. *The Lonely Lady*, Harold Robbins
9. *Touch Not the Cat*, Mary Stewart
10. *A Stranger in the Mirror*, Sidney Sheldon

Nonfiction

1. *The Final Days*, Bob Woodward and Carl Bernstein
2. *Roots*, Alex Haley
3. *Your Erroneous Zones*, Dr. Wayne W. Dyer
4. *Passages: The Predictable Crises of Adult Life*, Gail Sheehy
5. *Born Again*, Charles W. Colson
6. *The Grass Is Always Greener over the Septic Tank*, Erma Bombeck
7. *Angels: God's Secret Agents*, Billy Graham
8. *Blind Ambition: The White House Years*, John Dean
9. *The Hite Report: A Nationwide Study of Female Sexuality*, Shere Hite
10. *The Right and the Power: The Prosecution of Watergate*, Leon Jaworski

1977

Fiction

1. *The Silmarillion*, J. R. R. Tolkien; Christopher Tolkien
2. *The Thorn Birds*, Colleen McCullough
3. *Illusions: The Adventures of a Reluctant Messiah*, Richard Bach
4. *The Honourable Schoolboy*, John le Carré
5. *Oliver's Story*, Erich Segal
6. *Dreams Die First*, Harold Robbins
7. *Beggarman, Thief*, Irwin Shaw
8. *How to Save Your Own Life*, Erica Jong
9. *Delta of Venus: Erotica*, Anaïs Nin
10. *Daniel Martin*, John Fowles

AMERICA'S POETS LAUREATE

To honor America's greatest poets, the Librarian of Congress names a poet laureate. The anointed:

Robert Penn Warren	1986–87
Richard Wilbur	1987–88
Howard Nemerov	1988–90
Mark Strand	1990–91
Joseph Brodsky	1991–92
Mona Van Duyn	1992–93
Rita Dove	1993–95
Robert Hass	1995–97
Robert Pinsky	1997–00
Stanley Kunitz	2000–01
Billy Collins	2001–

Nonfiction

1. *Roots*, Alex Haley
2. *Looking Out for #1*, Robert Ringer
3. *All Things Wise and Wonderful*, James Herriot
4. *Your Erroneous Zones*, Dr. Wayne W. Dyer
5. *The Book of Lists*, David Wallechinsky, Irving Wallace, and Amy Wallace
6. *The Possible Dream: A Candid Look at Amway*, Charles Paul Conn
7. *The Dragons of Eden: Speculations on the Evolution of Human Intelligence*, Carl Sagan
8. *The Second Ring of Power*, Carlos Castaneda
9. *The Grass Is Always Greener over the Septic Tank*, Erma Bombeck
10. *The Amityville Horror*, Jay Anson

1978

Fiction

1. *Chesapeake*, James A. Michener
2. *War and Remembrance*, Herman Wouk
3. *Fools Die*, Mario Puzo
4. *Bloodlines*, Sidney Sheldon
5. *Scruples*, Judith Krantz
6. *Evergreen*, Belva Plain
7. *Illusions: The Adventures of a Reluctant Messiah*, Richard Bach
8. *The Holcroft Covenant*, Robert Ludlum
9. *Second Generation*, Howard Fast
10. *Eye of the Needle*, Ken Follett

Nonfiction

1. *If Life Is a Bowl of Cherries—What Am I Doing in the Pits?*, Erma Bombeck
2. *Gnomes*, Wil Huygen and Rien Poortvliet
3. *The Complete Book of Running*, James Fixx
4. *Mommie Dearest*, Christina Crawford
5. *Pulling Your Own Strings*, Dr. Wayne W. Dyer
6. *RN: The Memoirs of Richard Nixon*, Richard Nixon
7. *A Distant Mirror: The Calamitous Fourteenth Century*, Barbara Tuchman
8. *Faeries*, Brian Froud and Alan Lee
9. *In Search of History: A Personal Adventure*, Theodore H. White
10. *The Muppet Show Book*, The Muppet People

1979

Fiction

1. *The Matarese Circle*, Robert Ludlum
2. *Sophie's Choice*, William Styron
3. *Overload*, Arthur Hailey

4. *Memories of Another Day*, Harold Robbins
5. *Jailbird*, Kurt Vonnegut
6. *The Dead Zone*, Stephen King
7. *The Last Enchantment*, Mary Stewart
8. *The Establishment*, Howard Fast
9. *The Third World War: August 1985*, Gen. Sir John Hackett, et al.
10. *Smiley's People*, John le Carré

Nonfiction

1. *Aunt Erma's Cope Book*, Erma Bombeck
2. *The Complete Scarsdale Medical Diet*, Herman Tarnower, M.D., and Samm Sinclair Baker
3. *How to Prosper During the Coming Bad Years*, Howard J. Ruff
4. *Cruel Shoes*, Steve Martin
5. *The Pritikin Program for Diet and Exercise*, Nathan Pritikin and Patrick McGrady Jr.
6. *White House Years*, Henry Kissinger
7. *Lauren Bacall: By Myself*, Lauren Bacall
8. *The Brethren: Inside the Supreme Court*, Bob Woodward and Scott Armstrong
9. *Restoring the American Dream*, Robert J. Ringer
10. *The Winner's Circle*, Charles Paul Conn

1980

Fiction

1. *The Covenant*, James A. Michener
2. *The Bourne Identity*, Robert Ludlum
3. *Rage of Angels*, Sidney Sheldon
4. *Princess Daisy*, Judith Krantz
5. *Firestarter*, Stephen King
6. *The Key to Rebecca*, Ken Follett
7. *Random Winds*, Belva Plain
8. *The Devil's Alternative*, Frederick Forsyth
9. *The Fifth Horseman*, Larry Collins and Dominique Lapierre
10. *The Spike*, Arnaud de Borchgrave and Robert Moss

Nonfiction

1. *Crisis Investing: Opportunities and Profits in the Coming Great Depression*, Douglas R. Casey
2. *Cosmos*, Carl Sagan
3. *Free to Choose: A Personal Statement*, Milton and Rose Friedman
4. *Anatomy of an Illness as Perceived by the Patient*, Norman Cousins
5. *Thy Neighbor's Wife*, Gay Talese
6. *The Sky's the Limit*, Dr. Wayne W. Dyer
7. *The Third Wave*, Alvin Toffler
8. *Craig Claiborne's Gourmet Diet*, Craig

Claiborne with Pierre Franey
9. *Nothing Down*, Robert Allen
10. *Shelley: Also Known as Shirley*, Shelley Winters

1981

Fiction

1. *Noble House*, James Clavell
2. *The Hotel New Hampshire*, John Irving
3. *Cujo*, Stephen King
4. *An Indecent Obsession*, Colleen McCullough
5. *Gorky Park*, Martin Cruz Smith
6. *Masquerade*, Kit Williams
7. *Goodbye, Janette*, Harold Robbins
8. *The Third Deadly Sin*, Lawrence Sanders
9. *The Glitter Dome*, Joseph Wambaugh
10. *No Time for Tears*, Cynthia Freeman

Nonfiction

1. *The Beverly Hills Diet*, Judy Mazel
2. *The Lord God Made Them All*, James Herriot
3. *Richard Simmons' Never-Say-Diet Book*, Richard Simmons
4. *A Light in the Attic*, Shel Silverstein
5. *Cosmos*, Carl Sagan
6. *Better Homes & Gardens New Cook Book*
7. *Miss Piggy's Guide to Life*, Miss Piggy as told to Henry Beard
8. *Weight Watchers 365-Day Menu Cookbook*
9. *You Can Negotiate Anything*, Herb Cohen
10. *A Few Minutes with Andy Rooney*, Andrew A. Rooney

1982

Fiction

1. *E.T., the Extra-Terrestrial Storybook*, William Kotzwinkle
2. *Space*, James A. Michener
3. *The Parsifal Mosaic*, Robert Ludlum
4. *Master of the Game*, Sidney Sheldon
5. *Mistral's Daughter*, Judith Krantz
6. *The Valley of Horses*, Jean M. Auel
7. *Different Seasons*, Stephen King
8. *North and South*, John Jakes
9. *2010: Odyssey Two*, Arthur C. Clarke
10. *The Man from St. Petersburg*, Ken Follett

Nonfiction

1. *Jane Fonda's Workout Book*, Jane Fonda
2. *Living, Loving and Learning*, Leo Buscaglia
3. *And More by Andy Rooney*, Andrew A. Rooney
4. *Better Homes & Gardens New Cookbook*

5. *Life Extension: Adding Years to Your Life and Life to Your Years—A Practical Scientific Approach*, Durk Pearson and Sandy Shaw
6. *When Bad Things Happen to Good People*, Harold S. Kushner
7. *A Few Minutes with Andy Rooney*, Andrew A. Rooney
8. *The Weight Watchers Food Plan Diet Cookbook*, Jean Nidetch
9. *Richard Simmons' Never-Say-Diet Cookbook*, Richard Simmons
10. *No Bad Dogs: The Woodhouse Way*, Barbara Woodhouse

1983

Fiction

1. *Return of the Jedi Storybook*, Joan D. Vinge, adapt.
2. *Poland*, James A. Michener
3. *Pet Sematary*, Stephen King
4. *The Little Drummer Girl*, John le Carré
5. *Christine*, Stephen King
6. *Changes*, Danielle Steel
7. *The Name of the Rose*, Umberto Eco
8. *White Gold Wielder: Book Three of The Second Chronicles of Thomas Covenant*, Stephen R. Donaldson
9. *Hollywood Wives*, Jackie Collins
10. *The Lonesome Gods*, Louis L'Amour

Nonfiction

1. *In Search of Excellence: Lessons from America's Best-Run Companies*, Thomas J. Peters and Robert H. Waterman Jr.
2. *Megatrends: Ten New Directions Transforming Our Lives*, John Naisbitt
3. *Motherhood: The Second Oldest Profession*, Erma Bombeck
4. *The One Minute Manager*, Kenneth Blanchard and Spencer Johnson
5. *Jane Fonda's Workout Book*, Jane Fonda
6. *The Best of James Herriot*, James Herriot
7. *The Mary Kay Guide to Beauty: Discovering Your Special Look*
8. *On Wings of Eagles*, Ken Follett
9. *Creating Wealth*, Robert G. Allen
10. *The Body Principal: The Exercise Program for Life*, Victoria Principal

1984

Fiction

1. *The Talisman*, Stephen King and Peter Straub
2. *The Aquitaine Progression*, Robert Ludlum
3. *The Sicilian*, Mario Puzo
4. *Love and War*, John Jakes

5. *The Butter Battle Book*, Dr. Seuss
6. *". . . And the Ladies of the Club,"* Helen Hooven Santmyer
7. *The Fourth Protocol*, Frederick Forsyth
8. *Full Circle*, Danielle Steel
9. *The Life and Hard Times of Heidi Abromowitz*, Joan Rivers
10. *Lincoln: A Novel*, Gore Vidal

Nonfiction

1. *Iacocca: An Autobiography*, Lee Iacocca with William Novak
2. *Loving Each Other*, Leo Buscaglia
3. *Eat to Win: The Sports Nutrition Bible*, Robert Haas, M.D.
4. *Pieces of My Mind*, Andrew A. Rooney
5. *Weight Watchers Fast and Fabulous Cookbook*
6. *What They Don't Teach You at Harvard Business School: Notes from a Street-Smart Executive*, Mark H. McCormack
7. *Women Coming of Age*, Jane Fonda with Mignon McCarthy
8. *Moses the Kitten*, James Herriot
9. *The One Minute Salesperson*, Spencer Johnson, M.D., and Larry Wilson
10. *Weight Watchers Quick Start Program Cookbook*, Jean Nidetch

1985

Fiction

1. *The Mammoth Hunters*, Jean M. Auel
2. *Texas*, James A. Michener
3. *Lake Wobegon Days*, Garrison Keillor
4. *If Tomorrow Comes*, Sidney Sheldon
5. *Skeleton Crew*, Stephen King
6. *Secrets*, Danielle Steel
7. *Contact*, Carl Sagan
8. *Lucky*, Jackie Collins
9. *Family Album*, Danielle Steel
10. *Jubal Sackett*, Louis L'Amour

Nonfiction

1. *Iacocca: An Autobiography*, Lee Iacocca with William Novak
2. *Yeager: An Autobiography*, Gen. Chuck Yeager and Leo Janos
3. *Elvis and Me*, Priscilla Beaulieu Presley with Sandra Harmon
4. *Fit for Life*, Harvey and Marilyn Diamond
5. *The Be-Happy Attitudes*, Robert Schuller
6. *Dancing in the Light*, Shirley MacLaine
7. *A Passion for Excellence: The Leadership Difference*, Thomas J. Peters and Nancy K. Austin
8. *The Frugal Gourmet*, Jeff Smith
9. *I Never Played the Game*, Howard Cosell with Peter Bonventre

10. *Dr. Berger's Immune Power Diet*, Stuart M. Berger, M.D.

1986

Fiction

1. *It*, Stephen King
2. *Red Storm Rising*, Tom Clancy
3. *Whirlwind*, James Clavell
4. *The Bourne Supremacy*, Robert Ludlum
5. *Hollywood Husbands*, Jackie Collins
6. *Wanderlust*, Danielle Steel
7. *I'll Take Manhattan*, Judith Krantz
8. *Last of the Breed*, Louis L'Amour
9. *The Prince of Tides*, Pat Conroy
10. *A Perfect Spy*, John le Carré

Nonfiction

1. *Fatherhood*, Bill Cosby
2. *Fit for Life*, Harvey and Marilyn Diamond
3. *His Way: The Unauthorized Biography of Frank Sinatra*, Kitty Kelley
4. *The Rotation Diet*, Martin Katahn
5. *You're Only Old Once*, Dr. Seuss
6. *Callanetics: Ten Years Younger in Ten Hours*, Callan Pinckney
7. *The Frugal Gourmet Cooks with Wine*, Jeff Smith
8. *Be Happy—You Are Loved!*, Robert H. Schuller
9. *Word for Word*, Andrew A. Rooney
10. *James Herriot's Dog Stories*, James Herriot

1987

Fiction

1. *The Tommyknockers*, Stephen King
2. *Patriot Games*, Tom Clancy
3. *Kaleidoscope*, Danielle Steel
4. *Misery*, Stephen King
5. *Leaving Home: A Collection of Lake Wobegon Stories*, Garrison Keillor
6. *Windmills of the Gods*, Sidney Sheldon
7. *Presumed Innocent*, Scott Turow
8. *Fine Things*, Danielle Steel
9. *Heaven and Hell*, John Jakes
10. *The Eyes of the Dragon*, Stephen King

Nonfiction

1. *Time Flies*, Bill Cosby
2. *Spycatcher: The Candid Autobiography of a Senior Intelligence Officer*, Peter Wright with Paul Greengrass
3. *Family: The Ties That Bind . . . and Gag!*, Erma Bombeck
4. *Veil: The Secret Wars of the CIA, 1981–1987*, Bob Woodward
5. *A Day in the Life of America*, Rick Smolan and David Cohen

6. *The Great Depression of 1990*, Ravi Batra
7. *It's All in the Playing*, Shirley MacLaine
8. *Man of the House: The Life and Political Memoirs of Speaker Tip O'Neill*, Thomas P. O'Neill Jr. with William Novak
9. *The Frugal Gourmet Cooks American*, Jeff Smith
10. *The Closing of the American Mind*, Allan Bloom

1988

Fiction

1. *The Cardinal of the Kremlin*, Tom Clancy
2. *The Sands of Time*, Sidney Sheldon
3. *Zoya*, Danielle Steel
4. *The Icarus Agenda*, Robert Ludlum
5. *Alaska*, James A. Michener
6. *Till We Meet Again*, Judith Krantz
7. *The Queen of the Damned*, Anne Rice
8. *To Be the Best*, Barbara Taylor Bradford
9. *One: A Novel*, Richard Bach
10. *Mitla Pass*, Leon Uris

Nonfiction

1. *The 8-Week Cholesterol Cure*, Robert E. Kowalski
2. *Talking Straight*, Lee Iacocca with Sonny Kleinfeld
3. *A Brief History of Time: From the Big Bang to Black Holes*, Steven W. Hawking
4. *Trump: The Art of the Deal*, Donald J. Trump with Tony Schwartz
5. *Gracie: A Love Story*, George Burns
6. *Elizabeth Takes Off*, Elizabeth Taylor
7. *Swim with the Sharks Without Being Eaten Alive*, Harvey MacKay
8. *Christmas in America*, David Cohen, editor
9. *Weight Watchers Quick Success Program Book*, Jean Nidetch
10. *Moonwalk*, Michael Jackson

1989

Fiction

1. *Clear and Present Danger*, Tom Clancy
2. *The Dark Half*, Stephen King
3. *Daddy*, Danielle Steel
4. *Star*, Danielle Steel
5. *Caribbean*, James A. Michener
6. *The Satanic Verses*, Salman Rushdie
7. *The Russia House*, John le Carré
8. *The Pillars of the Earth*, Ken Follet
9. *California Gold*, John Jakes

10. *While My Pretty One Sleeps*, Mary Higgins Clark

Nonfiction

1. *All I Really Need to Know I Learned in Kindergarten: Uncommon Thoughts on Common Things*, Robert Fulghum
2. *Wealth Without Risk: How to Develop a Personal Fortune Without Going Out on a Limb*, Charles J. Givens
3. *A Woman Named Jackie*, C. David Heymann
4. *It Was on Fire When I Lay Down on It*, Robert Fulghum
5. *Better Homes and Gardens New Cook Book*
6. *The Way Things Work*, David Macaulay
7. *It's Always Something*, Gilda Radner
8. *Roseanne: My Life as a Woman*, Roseanne Barr
9. *The Frugal Gourmet Cooks Three Ancient Cuisines: China, Greece, and Rome*, Jeff Smith
10. *My Turn: The Memoirs of Nancy Reagan*, Nancy Reagan with William Novak

1990

Fiction

1. *The Plains of Passage*, Jean M. Auel
2. *Four Past Midnight*, Stephen King
3. *The Burden of Proof*, Scott Turow
4. *Memories of Midnight*, Sidney Sheldon
5. *Message from Nam*, Danielle Steel
6. *The Bourne Ultimatum*, Robert Ludlum
7. *The Stand: The Complete and Uncut Edition*, Stephen King
8. *Lady Boss*, Jackie Collins
9. *The Witching Hour*, Anne Rice
10. *September*, Rosamunde Pilcher

Nonfiction

1. *A Life on the Road*, Charles Kuralt
2. *The Civil War*, Geoffrey C. Ward with Ric Burns and Ken Burns
3. *The Frugal Gourmet on Our Immigrant Heritage: Recipes You Should Have Gotten from Your Grandmother*, Jeff Smith
4. *Better Homes and Gardens New Cook Book*
5. *Financial Self-Defense: How to Win the Fight for Financial Freedom*, Charles J. Givens
6. *Homecoming: Reclaiming and Championing Your Inner Child*, John Bradshaw
7. *Wealth Without Risk: How to Develop a Personal Fortune Without Going Out on a Limb*, Charles J. Givens

8. *Bo Knows Bo*, Bo Jackson and Dick Schaap
9. *An American Life: An Autobiography*, Ronald Reagan
10. *Megatrends 2000: Ten New Directions for the 1990s*, John Naisbitt and Patricia Aburdene

1991

Fiction

1. *Scarlett: The Sequel to Margaret Mitchell's "Gone with the Wind,"* Alexandra Ripley
2. *The Sum of All Fears*, Tom Clancy
3. *Needful Things*, Stephen King
4. *No Greater Love*, Danielle Steel
5. *Heartbeat*, Danielle Steel
6. *The Doomsday Conspiracy*, Sidney Sheldon
7. *The Firm*, John Grisham
8. *Night Over Water*, Ken Follet
9. *Remember*, Barbara Taylor Bradford
10. *Loves Music, Loves to Dance*, Mary Higgins Clark

Nonfiction

1. *Me: Stories of My Life*, Katharine Hepburn
2. *Nancy Reagan: The Unauthorized Biography*, Kitty Kelley
3. *Uh-Oh: Some Observations from Both Sides of the Refrigerator Door*, Robert Fulghum
4. *Under Fire: An American Story*, Oliver North with William Novak
5. *Final Exit: The Practicalities of Self-Deliverance and Assisted Suicide for the Dying*, Derek Humphry
6. *When You Look Like Your Passport Photo, It's Time to Go Home*, Erma Bombeck
7. *More Wealth Without Risk*, Charles J. Givens
8. *Den of Thieves*, James B. Stewart
9. *Childhood*, Bill Cosby
10. *Financial Self-Defense*, Charles J. Givens

1992

Fiction

1. *Dolores Claiborne*, Stephen King
2. *The Pelican Brief*, John Grisham
3. *Gerald's Game*, Stephen King
4. *Mixed Blessings*, Danielle Steel
5. *Jewels*, Danielle Steel
6. *The Stars Shine Down*, Sidney Sheldon
7. *Tale of the Body Thief*, Anne Rice
8. *Mexico*, James A. Michener
9. *Waiting to Exhale*, Terry McMillan
10. *All Around the Town*, Mary Higgins Clark

Nonfiction

1. *The Way Things Ought to Be*, Rush Limbaugh
2. *It Doesn't Take a Hero: The Autobiography*, Gen. H. Norman Schwarzkopf
3. *How to Satisfy a Woman Every Time*, Naura Hayden
4. *Every Living Thing*, James Herriot
5. *A Return to Love*, Marianne Williamson
6. *Sam Walton: Made in America*, Sam Walton
7. *Diana: Her True Story*, Andrew Morton
8. *Truman*, David McCullough
9. *Silent Passage*, Gail Sheehy
10. *Sex*, Madonna

1993

Fiction

1. *The Bridges of Madison County*, Robert James Waller
2. *The Client*, John Grisham
3. *Slow Waltz at Cedar Bend*, Robert James Waller
4. *Without Remorse*, Tom Clancy
5. *Nightmares and Dreamscapes*, Stephen King
6. *Vanished*, Danielle Steel
7. *Lasher*, Anne Rice
8. *Pleading Guilty*, Scott Turow
9. *Like Water for Chocolate*, Laura Esquivel
10. *The Scorpio Illusion*, Robert Ludlum

Nonfiction

1. *See, I Told You So*, Rush Limbaugh
2. *Private Parts*, Howard Stern
3. *Seinlanguage*, Jerry Seinfeld
4. *Embraced by the Light*, Betty J. Eadie with Curtis Taylor
5. *Ageless Body, Timeless Mind*, Deepak Chopra
6. *Stop the Insanity*, Susan Powter
7. *Women Who Run with the Wolves*, Clarissa Pinkola Estes
8. *Men Are from Mars, Women Are from Venus*, John Gray
9. *The Hidden Life of Dogs*, Elizabeth Marshall Thomas
10. *And If You Play Golf, You're My Friend*, Harvey Penick with Bud Shrake

1994

Fiction

1. *The Chamber*, John Grisham
2. *Debt of Honor*, Tom Clancy
3. *The Celestine Prophecy*, James Redfield
4. *The Gift*, Danielle Steel
5. *Insomnia*, Steven King
6. *Politically Correct Bedtime Stories*, James Finn Garner

7. *Wings*, Danielle Steel
8. *Accident*, Danielle Steel
9. *The Bridges of Madison County*, Robert James Waller
10. *Disclosure*, Michael Crichton

Nonfiction

1. *In the Kitchen with Rosie*, Rosie Daley
2. *Men Are from Mars, Women Are from Venus*, John Gray
3. *Crossing the Threshold of Hope*, John Paul II.
4. *Magic Eye I*, N.E. Thing Enterprises
5. *The Book of Virtues*, William J. Bennett
6. *Magic Eye II*, N.E. Thing Enterprises
7. *Embraced by the Light*, Betty J. Eadie with Curtis Taylor
8. *Don't Stand Too Close to a Naked Man*, Tim Allen
9. *Couplehood*, Paul Reiser
10. *Magic Eye III*, N.E. Thing Enterprises

1995

Fiction

1. *The Rainmaker*, John Grisham
2. *The Lost World*, Michael Crichton
3. *Five Days in Paris*, Danielle Steel
4. *The Christmas Box*, Richard Paul Evans
5. *Lightning*, Danielle Steel
6. *The Celestine Prophecy*, James Redfield
7. *Rose Madder*, Stephen King
8. *Silent Night*, Mary Higgins Clark
9. *Politically Correct Holiday Stories*, James Finn Garner
10. *The Horse Whisperer*, Nicholas Evans

Nonfiction

1. *Men Are from Mars, Women Are from Venus*, John Gray
2. *My American Journey*, Colin Powell with Joseph Perisco
3. *Miss America*, Howard Stern
4. *The Seven Spiritual Laws of Success*, Deepak Chopra
5. *The Road Ahead*, Bill Gates
6. *Charles Kuralt's America*, Charles Kuralt
7. *Mars and Venus in the Bedroom*, John Gray
8. *To Renew America*, Newt Gingrich
9. *My Point...and I Do Have One*, Ellen DeGeneres
10. *The Moral Compass*, William J. Bennett

1996

Fiction

1. *The Runaway Jury*, John Grisham
2. *Executive Orders*, Tom Clancy

3. *Desperation*, Stephen King
4. *Airframe*, Michael Crichton
5. *The Regulators*, Richard Bachman
6. *Malice*, Danielle Steel
7. *Silent Honor*, Danielle Steel
8. *Primary Colors*, anonymous
9. *Cause of Death*, Patricia Cornwell
10. *The Tenth Insight*, James Redfield

Nonfiction

1. *Make the Connection*, Oprah Winfrey and Bob Greene
2. *Men Are from Mars, Women Are from Venus*, John Gray
3. *The Dilbert Principle*, Scott Adams
4. *Simple Abundance*, Sarah Ban Breathnach
5. *The Zone*, Barry Sears with Bill Lawren
6. *Bad As I Wanna Be*, Dennis Rodman
7. *In Contempt*, Christopher Darden
8. *A Reporter's Life*, Walter Cronkite
9. *Dogbert's Top Secret Management Handbook*, Scott Adams
10. *My Sergei: A Love Story*, Ekaterina Gordeeva with E. M. Swift

1997

Fiction

1. *The Partner*, John Grisham
2. *Cold Mountain*, Charles Frazier
3. *The Ghost*, Danielle Steel
4. *The Ranch*, Danielle Steel
5. *Special Delivery*, Danielle Steel
6. *Unnatural Exposure*, Patricia Cornwell
7. *The Best Laid Plans*, Sidney Sheldon
8. *Pretend You Don't See Her*, Mary Higgins Clark
9. *Cat & Mouse*, James Patterson
10. *Hornet's Nest*, Patricia Cornwell

Nonfiction

1. *Angela's Ashes*, Frank McCourt
2. *Simple Abundance*, Sarah Ban Breathnach
3. *Midnight in the Garden of Good and Evil*, John Berendt
4. *The Royals*, Kitty Kelley
5. *Joy of Cooking*, Irma S. Rombauer, Marion Rombauer Becker, and Ethan Becker
6. *Diana: Her True Story*, Andrew Morton
7. *Into Thin Air*, Jon Krakauer
8. *Conversations with God, Book I*, Neale Donald Walsch
9. *Men Are from Mars, Women Are from Venus*, John Gray
10. *Eight Weeks to Optimum Health*, Andrew Weil

1998

Fiction

1. *The Street Lawyer*, John Grisham
2. *Rainbow Six*, Tom Clancy
3. *Bag of Bones*, Stephen King
4. *A Man in Full*, Tom Wolfe
5. *Mirror Image*, Danielle Steel
6. *The Long Road Home*, Danielle Steel
7. *The Klone and I*, Danielle Steel
8. *Point of Origin*, Patricia Cornwell
9. *Paradise*, Toni Morrison
10. *All Through the Night*, Mary Higgins Clark

Nonfiction

1. *The 9 Steps to Financial Freedom*, Suze Orman
2. *The Greatest Generation*, Tom Brokaw
3. *Sugar Busters!*, H. Leighton Steward, Morrison C. Bethea, Sam S. Andrews, and Luis A. Balart
4. *Tuesdays with Morrie*, Mitch Albom
5. *The Guinness Book of Records 1999*
6. *Talking to Heaven*, James Van Praagh
7. *Something More: Excavating Your Authentic Self*, Sarah Ban Breathnach
8. *In the Meantime*, Iyanla Vanzant
9. *A Pirate Looks at Fifty*, Jimmy Buffett
10. *If Life Is a Game These Are the Rules*, Cherie Carter-Scott, Ph.D.

1999

1. *The Testament*, John Grisham
2. *Hannibal*, Thomas Harris
3. *Assassins*, Jerry B. Jenkins & Tim LaHaye
4. *Star Wars: Episode 1, The Phantom Menace*, Terry Brooks
5. *Timeline*, Michael Crichton
6. *Hearts in Atlantis*, Stephen King
7. *Apollyon*, Jerry B. Jenkins & Tim LaHaye
8. *The Girl Who Loved Tom Gordon*, Stephen King
9. *Irresistible Forces*, Danielle Steel
10. *Tara Road*, Maeve Binchy

Nonfiction

1. *Tuesdays with Morrie*, Mitch Albom
2. *The Greatest Generation*, Tom Brokaw
3. *Guinness World Records 2000: Millennium Edition*
4. *'Tis*, Frank McCourt
5. *Who Moved My Cheese?*, Spencer Johnson
6. *The Courage to Be Rich*, Suze Orman
7. *The Greatest Generation Speaks*, Tom Brokaw
8. *Sugar Busters!*, H. Leighton Steward,

Morrison C. Bethea, Sam S. Andrews and Luis A. Balart
9. *The Art of Happiness*, the Dalai Lama and Howard C. Cutler
10. *The Century*, Peter Jennings & Todd Brewster

2000

Fiction

1. *The Brethren*, John Grisham
2. *The Mark: The Beast Rules the World*, Jerry B. Jenkins and Tim LaHaye
3. *The Bear and the Dragon*, Tom Clancy
4. *The Indwelling: The Beast Takes Possession*, Jerry B. Jenkins and Tim LaHaye
5. *The Last Precinct*, Patricia Cornwell
6. *Journey*, Danielle Steel
7. *The Rescue*, Nicholas Sparks
8. *Roses Are Red*, James Patterson
9. *Cradle and All*, James Patterson
10. *The House on Hope Street*, Danielle Steel

Nonfiction

1. *Who Moved My Cheese?*, Spencer Johnson
2. *Guinness World Records 2001*
3. *Body for Life*, Bill Phillips
4. *Tuesdays with Morrie*, Mitch Albom
5. *The Beatles Anthology*, The Beatles
6. *The O'Reilly Factor*, Bill O'Reilly
7. *Relationship Rescue*, Phillip C. McGraw
8. *The Millionaire Mind*, Thomas J. Stanley
9. *Ten Things I Wish I'd Known—Before I Went Out into the Real World*, Maria Shriver
10. *Eating Well for Optimum Health*, Andrew Weil, M.D.

THE PEOPLE BOOKSHELF

PEOPLE hasn't been reviewing books long enough to hazard a best-of-the-century list, but here are the books we loved the most over the years.

FICTION

Absolute Power, David Baldacci

The Accidental Tourist, Anne Tyler

All the Pretty Horses, Cormac McCarthy

Amy and Isabelle, Elizabeth Strout

Anagrams, Lorrie Moore

Anton the Dove Fancier, Bernard Gotfryd

August, Judith Rossner

Be Cool, Elmore Leonard

Bee Season, Myla Goldberg

Before and After, Rosellen Brown

Beloved, Toni Morrison

Birds of America, Lorrie Moore

Birdy, William Wharton

Blonde, Joyce Carol Oates

The Blooding, Joseph Wambaugh

The Blue Afternoon, William Boyd

Blue Angel, Francine Prose

Body and Soul, Frank Conroy

The Bonfire of the Vanities, Tom Wolfe

Breathing Lessons, Anne Tyler

Bridget Jones's Diary, Helen Fielding

Cat's Eye, Margaret Atwood

Clockers, Richard Price

The Cloister Walk, Kathleen Norris

Cold Mountain, Charles Frazier

Collaborators, Janet Kauffman

The Collected Stories, Isaac Bashevis Singer

The Color Purple, Alice Walker

Come to Grief, Dick Francis

A Confederacy of Dunces, John Kennedy Toole

Damascus Gate, Robert Stone

Dinner at the Homesick Restaurant, Anne Tyler

The Dragons of Eden, Carl Sagan

Dutch Shea Jr., John Gregory Dunne

East Is East, T. Coraghessan Boyle

Ellis Island, Mark Helprin

Enchantment, Daphne Merkin

Eye of the Needle, Ken Follett

Fanny, Erica Jong

The Farming of Bones, Edwidge Danticat

Final Payments, Mary Gordon

The Firm, John Grisham

The First Man in Rome, Colleen McCullough

For Love, Sue Miller

Foreign Affairs, Alison Lurie

A Gesture Life, Chang-Rae Lee

Get Shorty, Elmore Leonard

The Girls' Guide to Hunting and Fishing, by Melissa Bank

The Glass House, Laura Furman

The God of Small Things, Arundhati Roy

Gone, Baby, Gone, Dennis Lehane

The Good Mother, Sue Miller

Gorky Park, Martin Cruz Smith

The Green Mile, Stephen King

Happy to Be There, Garrison Keillor

Harry Potter and the Goblet of Fire, J.K. Rowling

Her First American, Lore Segal

The Honourable Schoolboy, John Le Carré

The House of the Spirits, Isabel Allende

Illumination Night, Abbie Hoffman

An Indecent Obsession, Colleen McCollough

Independence Day, Richard Ford

Juneteenth, Ralph Ellison

Kolymsky Heights, Lionel Davidson

Krik? Krak!, Edwidge Danticat

Labrava, Elmore Leonard

Lake Wobegon Days, Garrison Keillor

Lancelot, Walker Percy

A Lesson Before Dying, Ernest J. Gaines

The Liar's Club, Mary Karr

Libra, Don DeLillo

A Light in the Attic, Shel Silverstein

Life Its Ownself, Dan Jenkins

Love in the Time of Cholera, Gabriel García Márquez

The Love Letter, Cathleen Schine

Machine Dreams, Jayne Anne Phillips

The Mambo Kings Play Songs of Love, Oscar Hijuelos

A Man in Full, Tom Wolfe

A Map of the World, Jane Hamilton

Maus: A Survivor's Tale, II: And Here My Troubles Begin, Art Spiegelman

Me and My Baby View the Eclipse, Lee Smith

Memoirs of an Invisible Man, H. F. Saint

Monkeys, Susan Minot

Monsignor Quixote, Graham Greene

More Die of Heartbreak, Saul Bellow

Music for Chameleons, Truman Capote

The Natural Man, Ed McClanahan

Noble House, James Clavell

Owning Jolene, Shelby Hearon

The Palace Thief, Ethan Canin

Patrimony, Philip Roth

Perfume, Patrick Süskind

Plainsong, Kent Haruf

Poodle Springs, Raymond Chandler and Robert B. Parker

The Pope of Greenwich Village, Vincent Park

Presumed Innocent, Scott Turow

The Progress of Love, Alice Munro

Quinn's Book, William Kennedy

Rabbit at Rest, John Updike

The Robber Bride, Margaret Atwood

Roger's Version, John Updike

Rose, Martin Cruz Smith

The Russia House, John Le Carré

Salvador, Joan Didion

The Secret History, Donna Tartt

Seventh Heaven, Alice Hoffman

She's Come Undone, Wally Lamb

The Sicilian, Mario Puzo

Sick Puppy, Carl Hiaasen

Smilla's Sense of Snow, Peter Hoeg

A Soldier of the Great War, Mark Helprin

Sophie's Choice, William Styron

Stormy Weather, Carl Hiaasen

Talking to the Dead, Sylvia Watanabe

Tooth Imprints on a Corn Dog, Mark Leyner

Tracks, Louise Erdrich

The Tree of Life, Hugh Nissenson

True Confessions, John Gregory Dunne

The Twenty-Seventh City, Jonathan Franzen

Typical American, Gish Jen
Underworld, Don Delillo
Waiting to Exhale, Terry McMillan
The White Hotel, D. M. Thomas
White Teeth, Zadie Smith
Who Will Run the Frog Hospital?, Lorrie Moore
Winter's Tale, Mark Helprin
World's Fair, E. L. Doctorow
The Yellow Wind, David Grossman

NONFICTION

All Over But the Shoutin', Rick Bragg
American Caesar, William Manchester
American Prospects, Joel Sternfeld
Backlash, Susan Faludi
Best Intentions, Robert Sam Anson
The Best of Dear Abby, Abigail Van Buren
Blood Sport, James B. Stewart
Blue Highways, William Least Heat Moon
The Bookmakers's Daughter, Shirley Abbott
The Box: An Oral History of Television 1920–61, Jeff Kisseloff
Cameraworks, David Hockney
The Chimpanzees of Gombe, Jane Goodall
A Civil Action, Jonathan Harr
Colored People: A Memoir, Henry Louis Gates Jr.
The Culture of Narcissism, Christopher Lasch
Dave Barry Is Not Making This Up, Dave Barry
Dave Barry Slept Here, Dave Barry
Den of Thieves, James B. Stewart
The Devil's Candy, Julie Salamon
Diana in Search of Herself, Sally Bedell Smith
A Distant Mirror, Barbara Tuchman
Dreaming: Hard Luck and Good Times in America, Carolyn See
The Duke of Deception, Geoffrey Wolff
Edie, Jean Stein, edited with George Plimpton
Edith Sitwell, Victoria Glendinning
The Fatal Shore, Robert Hughes
Fatal Vision, Joe McGinniss
Fatherhood, Bill Cosby
Flags of Our Fathers, James Bradley
The Forbidden Experiment, Roger Shattuck

Fungus the Bogeyman, Raymond Briggs
Gal, Ruthie Bolton
Georgiana: Duchess of Devonshire, Amanda Foreman
The Girl I Left Behind, Jane O'Reilly
The Glass House, Laura Furman
Goldwyn: A Biography, A. Scott Berg
A Good Life, Ben Bradlee
"The Good War," Studs Terkel
A Heartbreaking Work of Staggering Genius, Dave Eggers
The Hidden Life of Dogs, Elizabeth Marshall
Home Before Dark, Susan Cheever
Hometown, Peter Davis
The Hot Zone, Richard Preston
House, Tracy Kidder
I Dream a World, Brian Lanker
In and Out of the Garden, Sara Midda
In Contempt, Christopher Darden
Ingrid Bergman: My Story, Ingrid Bergman and Alan Burgess
Inside Edge: A Revealing Journey into the Secret World of Figure Skating, Christine Brennan
Into the Wild, Jon Krakauer
Into Thin Air, Jon Krakauer
Jackie Robinson: A Biography, Arnold Rampersad
January Sun, Richard Stengel
The Kennedys: An American Dream, Peter Collier and David Horowitz
Kissinger, Walter Isaacson
The Knife and Gun Club, Eugene Richards
The Last Lion, William Manchester
Laura Z.: A Life, Laura Z. Hobson
Lauren Bacall: By Myself, Lauren Bacall
Lenin's Tomb, David Remnick
A Life of Picasso, John Richardson
Lindbergh, A. Scott Berg
Little League Confidential, Bill Geist
The Lives of John Lennon, Albert Goldman
Loitering with Intent, Peter O'Toole
Maida Heatter's Book of Great Chocolate Desserts, Maida Heatter
The Man Who Mistook His Wife for a Hat, Oliver Sacks
Means of Ascent, Robert A. Caro
The Medusa and the Snail, Lewis Thomas
Midair, Frank Conroy

The Million Dollar Mermaid, Esther Williams and Digby Diehl
Miss Manners' Guide to Excruciatingly Correct Behavior, Judith Martin
Mister Rogers Talks with Parents, Fred Rogers and Barry Head
Moonshine, Alec Wilkinson
The Non-Runner's Book, Vic Ziegel and Lewis Grossberger
No Ordinary Time, Doris Kearns Goodwin
On Boxing, Joyce Carol Oates
On Photography, Susan Sontag
Outrage, Vincent Bugliosi
Pablo Picasso: A Retrospective, edited by William Rubin
Payback, Joe Klein
Personal History, Katharine Graham
Photoportraits, Henri Cartier-Bresson
President Kennedy, Richard Reeves
The Ragman's Son, Kirk Douglas
The Rise of Theodore Roosevelt, Edmund Morris
A Rumor of War, Philip Caputo
Saul Steinberg, Harold Rosenberg
Serpentine, Thomas Thompson
Side Effects, Woody Allen
The Sketchbooks of Picasso, Pablo Picasso
The Snow Leopard, Peter Mathiessen
The Spirit Catches You and You Fall Down, Anne Fadiman
The Story of English, Robert McCrum, William Cran, and Robert MacNeil
Still Me, Christopher Reeve
Sylvia Plachy's Unguided Tour, Sylvia Plachy
The Teamsters, Steven Brill
Thank You for Smoking, Christopher Buckley
Traveling Mercies, Anne Lamott
Truman, David McCullough
A Vast Conspiracy, Jeffrey Toobin
What Falls Away, Mia Farrow
Why Are They Weeping?, photographed by David C. Turnley and written by Alan Cowell
Woman: An Intimate Geography. Natalie Angier
Workers, Sebastião Salgado
A Writer's Beginnings, Eudora Welty
The Years of Lyndon Johnson: The Path to Power, Robert A. Caro

BOOKS OF THE CENTURY

To commemorate the New York Public Library's 100th anniversary, the librarians of this venerable institution identified books that, from their varying perspectives, have played defining roles in the making of the 20th century. Included are books that influenced the course of events, for good and for bad; books that interpreted new worlds; and books that simply delighted millions of patrons.

LANDMARKS OF MODERN LITERATURE

The Three Sisters, Anton Chekhov (1901)

Remembrance of Things Past, Marcel Proust (1913-27)

Tender Buttons, Gertrude Stein (1914)

The Metamorphosis, Franz Kafka (1915)

Renascence and Other Poems, Edna St. Vincent Millay (1917)

The Wild Swans at Coole, William Butler Yeats (1917)

Six Characters in Search of an Author, Luigi Pirandello (1921)

The Waste Land, T. S. Eliot (1922)

Ulysses, James Joyce (1922)

The Magic Mountain, Thomas Mann (1924)

The Great Gatsby, F. Scott Fitzgerald (1925)

To the Lighthouse, Virginia Woolf (1927)

Gypsy Ballads, Frederico García Lorca (1928)

Native Son, Richard Wright (1940)

The Age of Anxiety: A Baroque Eclogue, W. H. Auden (1947)

Invisible Man, Ralph Ellison (1952)

Lolita, Vladimir Nabokov (1955)

Fictions, Jorge Luis Borges (1944; 2nd augmented edition 1956)

One Hundred Years of Solitude, Gabriel García Márquez (1967)

Song of Solomon, Toni Morrison (1977)

PROTEST AND PROGRESS

The Battle with the Slum, Jacob Ritts (1902)

The Souls of Black Folk, W. E. B. Du Bois (1903)

The Jungle, Upton Sinclair (1906)

Twenty Years at Hull-House, Jane Addams (1910)

The House on Henry Street, Lillian Wald (1915)

The Autobiography of Lincoln Steffens, Lincoln Steffens (1931)

U.S.A., John Dos Passos (1937)

The Grapes of Wrath, John Steinbeck (1939)

Let Us Now Praise Famous Men, James Agee and Walker Evans (1941)

Strange Fruit, Lillian Smith (1944)

Growing Up Absurd, Paul Goodman (1960)

The Fire Next Time, James Baldwin (1963)

The Autobiography of Malcolm X, Malcolm X (1965)

And the Band Played On, Randy Shilts (1987)

There Are No Children Here, Alex Kotlowitz (1991)

POPULAR CULTURE & MASS ENTERTAINMENT

Dracula, Bram Stoker (1897)

The Turn of the Screw, Henry James (1898)

The Hound of the Baskervilles, Arthur Conan Doyle (1902)

Tarzan of the Apes, Edgar Rice Burroughs (1912)

Riders of the Purple Sage, Zane Grey (1912)

The Mysterious Affair at Styles, Agatha Christie (1920)

How to Win Friends and Influence People, Dale Carnegie (1936)

Gone with the Wind, Margaret Mitchell (1936)

The Big Sleep, Raymond Chandler (1939)

The Day of the Locust, Nathanael West (1939)

Peyton Place, Grace Metalious (1956)

The Cat in the Hat, Dr. Seuss (1957)

Stranger in a Strange Land, Robert A. Heinlein (1961)

Catch-22, Joseph Heller (1961)

In Cold Blood: A True Account of a Multiple Murder and Its Consequences, Truman Capote (1965)

Ball Four: My Life and Times Throwing the Knuckleball in the Big Leagues, Jim Bouton (1970)

Carrie, Stephen King (1974)

The Bonfire of the Vanities, Tom Wolfe (1987)

WOMEN RISE

The Age of Innocence, Edith Wharton (1920)

Woman Suffrage and Politics: The Inner Story of the Suffrage Movement, Carrie Chapman Catt and Nettie Rogers Shuler (1923)

My Fight for Birth Control, Margaret Sanger (1931)

Dust Tracks on a Dirt Road, Zora Neale Hurston (1942)

The Second Sex, Simone de Beauvoir (1949)

The Golden Notebook, Doris Lessing (1962)

The Feminine Mystique, Betty Friedan (1963)

I Know Why the Caged Bird Sings, Maya Angelou (1969)

Sisterhood Is Powerful: An Anthology of Writings from the Women's Liberations Movement, edited by Robin Morgan (1970)

Against Our Will: Men, Women and Rape, Susan Brownmiller (1975)

The Color Purple, Alice Walker (1982)

ECONOMICS & TECHNOLOGY

The Theory of the Leisure Class: An Economic Study of Institutions, Thorstein Veblen (1899)

The Protestant Ethic and the Spirit of Capitalism, Max Weber (1904–1905)

The Education of Henry Adams, Henry Adams (1907)

The General Theory of Employment, Interest and Money, John Meynard Keynes (1936)

A Theory of the Consumption Function, Milton Friedman (1957)

The Affluent Society, John Kenneth Galbraith (1958)

The Death and Life of Great American Cities, Jane Jacobs (1961)

Superhighway—Super Hoax, Helen Leavitt (1970)

Small Is Beautiful: A Study of Economics As If People Mattered, E. F. Schumacher (1973)

The Whole Internet: User's Guide and Catalogue, Ed Krol (1992)

MIND & SPIRIT

Suicide: A Study in Sociology, Emile Durkheim (1897)

The Interpretation of Dreams, Sigmund Freud (1900)

Studies in the Psychology of Sex, Havelock Ellis (1901–28)

The Varieties of Religious Experience: A Study in Human Nature, Wiilliam James (1902)

The Prophet, Kahlil Gibran (1923)

Why I Am Not a Christian, Bertrand Russell (1927)

Coming of Age in Samoa, Margaret Mead (1928)

Being and Nothingness, Jean-Paul Sartre (1943)

The Common Sense Book of Baby Care, Dr. Benjamin Spock (1946)

The Holy Bible, Revised Standard Version (1952)

The Courage to Be, Paul Tillich (1952)

One Flew over the Cuckoo's Nest, Ken Kesey (1962)

The Politics of Ecstasy, Timothy Leary (1968)

On Death and Dying, Elisabeth Kübler-Ross (1969)

The Uses of Enchantment, Bruno Bettelheim (1976)

MORE BOOKS THAT SHAPE LIVES

The Library of Congress established its Center for the Book in 1977 to stimulate public interest in books, reading, and libraries. Here is its list of the 25 books that have had the greatest impact on readers' lives.

The Adventures of Huckleberry Finn, Mark Twain

Atlas Shrugged, Ayn Rand

The Autobiography of Benjamin Franklin

The Bible

The Catcher in the Rye, J. D. Salinger

Charlotte's Web, E. B. White

The Diary of a Young Girl, Anne Frank

Don Quixote, Miguel de Cervantes

Gone with the Wind, Margaret Mitchell

Hiroshima, John Hersey

How to Win Friends and Influence People, Dale Carnegie

I Know Why the Caged Bird Sings, Maya Angelou

Invisible Man, Ralph Ellison

The Little Prince, Antoine de Saint-Exupéry

Little Women, Louisa May Alcott

The Lord of the Rings, J. R. R. Tolkien

Roots, Alex Haley

The Secret Garden, Frances Hodgson Burnett

To Kill a Mockingbird, Harper Lee

Treasure Island, Robert Louis Stevenson

Walden, Henry David Thoreau

War and Peace, Leo Tolstoy

What Color Is Your Parachute? Richard Nelson Bolles

THE MODERN LIBRARY FICTION LIST

Get out your pencils and get ready to quibble. In 1999 the Modern Library released its list of the top 100 English-language novels of the century (so never mind that manuscript in progress), 59 of which happen to be available in Modern Library editions. The hue and cry was heard even in hushed libraries. Objectors noted the panel of 10 was 90% male, all white, with an average age of just under 69, and a clear distaste for the contemporary. But at least they got us talking—and reading.

Rank	Book, Author (original publication date)
1.	*Ulysses*, James Joyce (1922)
2.	*The Great Gatsby*, F. Scott Fitzgerald (1925)
3.	*A Portrait of the Artist as a Young Man*, James Joyce (1916)
4.	*Lolita*, Vladimir Nabokov (1955)
5.	*Brave New World*, Aldous Huxley (1932)
6.	*The Sound and the Fury*, William Faulkner (1929)
7.	*Catch-22*, Joseph Heller (1961)
8.	*Darkness at Noon*, Arthur Koestler (1941)
9.	*Sons and Lovers*, D. H. Lawrence (1913)
10.	*The Grapes of Wrath*, John Steinbeck (1939)
11.	*Under the Volcano*, Malcolm Lowry (1947)
12.	*The Way of All Flesh*, Samuel Butler (1903)
13.	*1984*, George Orwell (1949)
14.	*I, Claudius*, Robert Graves (1934)
15.	*To the Lighthouse*, Virginia Woolf (1927)
16.	*An American Tragedy*, Theodore Dreiser (1925)
17.	*The Heart Is a Lonely Hunter*, Carson McCullers (1940)
18.	*Slaughterhouse Five*, Kurt Vonnegut, Jr. (1969)
19.	*Invisible Man*, Ralph Ellison (1952)
20.	*Native Son*, Richard Wright (1940)
21.	*Henderson the Rain King*, Saul Bellow (1959)
22.	*Appointment in Samarra*, John O'Hara (1934)
23.	*U.S.A.* (trilogy), John Dos Passos (1936)
24.	*Winesburg, Ohio*, Sherwood Anderson (1919)
25.	*A Passage to India*, E. M. Forster (1924)
26.	*The Wings of the Dove*, Henry James (1902)
27.	*The Ambassadors*, Henry James (1903)
28.	*Tender Is the Night*, F. Scott Fitzgerald (1934)
29.	*Studs Lonigan* (trilogy), James T. Farrell (1935)
30.	*The Good Soldier*, Ford Madox Ford (1915)
31.	*Animal Farm*, George Orwell (1945)
32.	*The Golden Bowl*, Henry James (1904)
33.	*Sister Carrie*, Theodore Dreiser (1900)
34.	*A Handful of Dust*, Evelyn Waugh (1934)
35.	*As I Lay Dying*, William Faulkner (1934)
36.	*All the King's Men*, Robert Penn Warren (1946)
37.	*The Bridge of San Luis Rey*, Thornton Wilder (1927)
38.	*Howards End*, E. M. Forster (1910)
39.	*Go Tell It on the Mountain*, James Baldwin (1953)
40.	*The Heart of the Matter*, Graham Greene (1948)
41.	*Lord of the Flies*, William Golding (1954)
42.	*Deliverance*, James Dickey, (1970)
43.	*A Dance to the Music of Time* (series), Anthony Powell (1975)
44.	*Point Counter Point*, Aldous Huxley (1928)
45.	*The Sun Also Rises*, Ernest Hemingway (1926)
46.	*The Secret Agent*, Joseph Conrad (1907)
47.	*Nostromo*, Joseph Conrad (1904)
48.	*The Rainbow*, D. H. Lawrence (1915)
49.	*Women in Love*, D. H. Lawrence (1920)
50.	*Tropic of Cancer*, Henry Miller (1934)

Rank	Book, Author (original publication date)
51.	*The Naked and the Dead*, Norman Mailer (1948)
52.	*Portnoy's Complaint*, Philip Roth (1969)
53.	*Pale Fire*, Vladimir Nabokov (1962)
54.	*Light in August*, William Faulkner (1932)
55.	*On the Road*, Jack Kerouac (1957)
56.	*The Maltese Falcon*, Dashiell Hammett (1930)
57.	*Parade's End*, Ford Madox Ford (1928)
58.	*The Age of Innocence*, Edith Wharton (1920)
59.	*Zuleika Dobson*, Max Beerbohm (1911)
60.	*The Moviegoer*, Walker Percy (1961)
61.	*Death Comes for the Archbishop*, Willa Cather (1927)
62.	*From Here to Eternity*, James Jones (1951)
63.	*The Wapshot Chronicle*, John Cheever (1957)
64.	*The Catcher in the Rye*, J. D. Salinger (1951)
65.	*A Clockwork Orange*, Anthony Burgess (1962)
66.	*Of Human Bondage*, W. Somerset Maugham (1915)
67.	*Heart of Darkness*, Joseph Conrad (1902)
68.	*Main Street*, Sinclair Lewis (1920)
69.	*The House of Mirth*, Edith Wharton (1905)
70.	*The Alexandria Quartet*, Lawrence Durrell (1960)
71.	*A High Wind in Jamaica*, Richard Hughes (1929)
72.	*A House for Mr. Biswas*, V. S. Naipaul (1961)
73.	*The Day of the Locust*, Nathanael West (1939)
74.	*A Farewell to Arms*, Ernest Hemingway (1929)
75.	*Scoop*, Evelyn Waugh (1938)
76.	*The Prime of Miss Jean Brodie*, Muriel Spark (1961)
77.	*Finnegans Wake*, James Joyce (1939)
78.	*Kim*, Rudyard Kipling (1901)
79.	*A Room with a View*, E. M. Forster (1908)
80.	*Brideshead Revisited*, Evelyn Waugh (1945)
81.	*The Adventures of Augie March*, Saul Bellow (1971)
82.	*Angle of Repose*, Wallace Stegner (1971)
83.	*A Bend in the River*, V. S. Naipaul (1979)
84.	*The Death of the Heart*, Elizabeth Bowen (1938)
85.	*Lord Jim*, Joseph Conrad (1900)
86.	*Ragtime*, E. L. Doctorow (1975)
87.	*The Old Wives' Tale*, Arnold Bennett (1908)
88.	*The Call of the Wild*, Jack London (1903)
89.	*Loving*, Henry Green (1945)
90.	*Midnight's Children*, Salman Rushdie (1981)
91.	*Tobacco Road*, Erskine Caldwell (1932)
92.	*Ironweed*, William Kennedy (1983)
93.	*The Magus*, John Fowles (1966)
94.	*Wide Sargasso Sea*, Jean Rhys (1966)
95.	*Under the Net*, Iris Murdoch (1954)
96.	*Sophie's Choice*, William Styron (1979)
97.	*The Sheltering Sky*, Paul Bowles (1949)
98.	*The Postman Always Rings Twice*, James M. Cain (1934)
99.	*The Ginger Man*, J. P. Donleavy (1955)
100.	*The Magnificent Ambersons*, Booth Tarkington (1918)

THE MODERN LIBRARY NONFICTION LIST

In 2000 the Modern Library struck again, with a selection of the century's best nonfiction. The panel was slightly younger and a little more balanced for gender and race, and the final results were a tad less controversial. The primary dispute was whether these books are important to read or just plain important (case in point, Whitehead and Russell's *Principia Mathematica*). Read, and judge, for yourself.

Rank	Book, Author
1.	*The Education of Henry Adams*, Henry Adams
2.	*The Varieties of Religious Experience*, William James
3.	*Up from Slavery*, Booker T. Washington
4.	*A Room of One's Own*, Virginia Woolf
5.	*Silent Spring*, Rachel Carson
6.	*Selected Essays, 1917–1932*, T. S. Eliot
7.	*The Double Helix*, James D. Watson
8.	*Speak, Memory*, Vladimir Nabokov
9.	*The American Language*, H. L. Mencken
10.	*The General Theory of Employment, Interest, and Money*, John Maynard Keynes
11.	*The Lives of a Cell*, Lewis Thomas
12.	*The Frontier in American History*, Frederick Jackson Turner
13.	*Black Boy*, Richard Wright
14.	*Aspects of the Novel*, E. M. Forster
15.	*The Civil War*, Shelby Foote
16.	*The Guns of August*, Barbara Tuchman
17.	*The Proper Study of Mankind*, Isaiah Berlin
18.	*The Nature and Destiny of Man*, Reinhold Niebuhr
19.	*Notes of a Native Son*, James Baldwin
20.	*The Autobiography of Alice B. Toklas*, Gertrude Stein
21.	*The Elements of Style*, William Strunk and E. B. White
22.	*An American Dilemma*, Gunnar Myrdal
23.	*Principia Mathematica*, Alfred North Whitehead and Bertrand Russell
24.	*The Mismeasure of Man*, Stephen Jay Gould
25.	*The Mirror and the Lamp*, Meyer Howard Abrams
26.	*The Art of the Soluble*, Peter B. Medawar
27.	*The Ants*, Bert Hölldobler and Edward O. Wilson
28.	*A Theory of Justice*, John Rawls
29.	*Art and Illusion*, Ernest H. Gombrich
30.	*The Making of the English Working Class*, E. P. Thompson
31.	*The Souls of Black Folk*, W. E. B. Du Bois
32.	*Principia Ethica*, G. E. Moore
33.	*Philosophy and Civilization*, John Dewey
34.	*On Growth and Form*, D'Arcy Thompson
35.	*Ideas and Opinions*, Albert Einstein
36.	*The Age of Jackson*, Arthur Schlesinger Jr.
37.	*The Making of the Atomic Bomb*, Richard Rhodes
38.	*Black Lamb and Grey Falcon*, Rebecca West
39.	*Autobiographies*, W. B. Yeats
40.	*Science and Civilization in China*, Joseph Needham
41.	*Goodbye to All That*, Robert Graves
42.	*Homage to Catalonia*, George Orwell
43.	*The Autobiography of Mark Twain*, Mark Twain
44.	*Children of Crisis*, Robert Coles
45.	*A Study of History*, Arnold J. Toynbee
46.	*The Affluent Society*, John Kenneth Galbraith
47.	*Present at the Creation*, Dean Acheson
48.	*The Great Bridge*, David McCullough
49.	*Patriotic Gore*, Edmund Wilson

Rank	Book, Author
50.	*Samuel Johnson*, Walter Jackson Bate
51.	*The Autobiography of Malcolm X*, Alex Haley and Malcolm X
52.	*The Right Stuff*, Tom Wolfe
53.	*Eminent Victorians*, Lytton Strachey
54.	*Working*, Studs Terkel
55.	*Darkness Visible*, William Styron
56.	*The Liberal Imagination*, Lionel Trilling
57.	*The Second World War*, Winston Churchill
58.	*Out of Africa*, Isak Dinesen
59.	*Jefferson and His Time*, Dumas Malone
60.	*In the American Grain*, William Carlos Williams
61.	*Cadillac Desert*, Marc Reisner
62.	*The House of Morgan*, Ron Chernow
63.	*The Sweet Science*, A. J. Liebling
64.	*The Open Society and Its Enemies*, Karl Popper
65.	*The Art of Memory*, Frances A. Yates
66.	*Religion and the Rise of Capitalism*, R. H. Tawney
67.	*A Preface to Morals*, Walter Lippmann
68.	*The Gate of Heavenly Peace*, Jonathan D. Spence
69.	*The Structure of Scientific Revolutions*, Thomas S. Kuhn
70.	*The Strange Career of Jim Crow*, C. Vann Woodward
71.	*The Rise of the West*, William H. McNeill
72.	*The Gnostic Gospels*, Elaine Pagels
73.	*James Joyce*, Richard Ellmann
74.	*Florence Nightingale*, Cecil Woodham-Smith
75.	*The Great War and Modern Memory*, Paul Fussell
76.	*The City in History*, Lewis Mumford
77.	*Battle Cry of Freedom*, James M. McPherson
78.	*Why We Can't Wait*, Martin Luther King Jr.
79.	*The Rise of Theodore Roosevelt*, Edmund Morris
80.	*Studies in Iconography*, Erwin Panofsky
81.	*The Face of Battle*, John Keegan
82.	*The Strange Death of Liberal England*, George Dangerfield
83.	*Vermeer*, Lawrence Gowing
84.	*A Bright Shining Lie*, Neil Sheehan
85.	*West with the Night*, Beryl Markham
86.	*This Boy's Life*, Tobias Wolff
87.	*A Mathematician's Apology*, G. H. Hardy
88.	*Six Easy Pieces*, Richard P. Feynman
89.	*Pilgrim at Tinker Creek*, Annie Dillard
90.	*The Golden Bough*, James George Frazer
91.	*Shadow and Act*, Ralph Ellison
92.	*The Power Broker*, Robert A. Caro
93.	*The American Political Tradition*, Richard Hofstadter
94.	*The Contours of American History*, William Appleman Williams
95.	*The Promise of American Life*, Herbert Croly
96.	*In Cold Blood*, Truman Capote
97.	*The Journalist and the Murderer*, Janet Malcolm
98.	*The Taming of Chance*, Ian Hacking
99.	*Operating Instructions*, Anne Lamott
100.	*Melbourne*, Lord David Cecil

LITERARY AWARDS

NATIONAL BOOK AWARDS

Fiction

1950 Nelson Algren
The Man with the Golden Arm
1951 William Faulkner
The Collected Stories of William Faulkner
1952 James Jones
From Here to Eternity
1953 Ralph Ellison
Invisible Man
1954 Saul Bellow
The Adventures of Augie March
1955 William Faulkner
A Fable
1956 John O'Hara
Ten North Frederick
1957 Wright Morris
The Field of Vision
1958 John Cheever
The Wapshot Chronicle
1959 Bernard Malamud
The Magic Barrel
1960 Philip Roth
Goodbye, Columbus
1961 Conrad Richter
The Waters of Kronos
1962 Walker Percy
The Moviegoer
1963 J. F. Powers
Morte D'Urban
1964 John Updike
The Centaur
1965 Saul Bellow
Herzog
1966 Katherine Anne Porter
The Collected Stories of Katherine Anne Porter
1967 Bernard Malamud
The Fixer
1968 Thornton Wilder
The Eighth Day
1969 Jerzy Kosinski
Steps
1970 Joyce Carol Oates
Them
1971 Saul Bellow
Mr. Sammler's Planet
1972 Flannery O'Connor
The Complete Stories of Flannery O'Connor
1973 John Barth
Chimera
John Williams
Augustus
1974 Thomas Pynchon
Gravity's Rainbow
Isaac Bashevis Singer
A Crown of Feathers and Other Stories

1975 Robert Stone
Dog Soldiers
Thomas Williams
The Hair of Harold Roux
1976 William Gaddis
JR
1977 Wallace Stegner
The Spectator Bird
1978 Mary Lee Settle
Blood Ties
1979 Tim O'Brien
Going After Cacciato
1980 William Styron (hardcover)
Sophie's Choice
John Irving (paperback)
The World According to Garp
1981 Wright Morris (hardcover)
Plains Song
John Cheever (paperback)
The Stories of John Cheever
1982 John Updike (hardcover)
Rabbit Is Rich
William Maxwell (paperback)
So Long, See You Tomorrow
1983 Alice Walker (hardcover)
The Color Purple
Eudora Welty (paperback)
Collected Stories of Eudora Welty
1984 Ellen Gilchrist
Victory over Japan: A Book of Stories
1985 Don DeLillo
White Noise
1986 E. L. Doctorow
World's Fair
1987 Larry Heinemann
Paco's Story
1988 Pete Dexter
Paris Trout
1989 John Casey
Spartina
1990 Charles Johnson
Middle Passage
1991 Norman Rush
Mating
1992 Cormac McCarthy
All the Pretty Horses
1993 E. Annie Proulx
The Shipping News
1994 William Gaddis
A Frolic of His Own
1995 Philip Roth
Sabbath's Theater
1996 Andrea Barrett
Ship Fever and Other Stories
1997 Charles Frazier
Cold Mountain
1998 Alice McDermott
Charming Billy
1999 Ha Jin
Waiting

2000 Susan Sontag
In America

Nonfiction

1950 Ralph L. Rusk
Ralph Waldo Emerson
1951 Newton Arvin
Herman Melville
1952 Rachel Carson
The Sea Around Us
1953 Bernard A. De Voto
The Course of an Empire
1954 Bruce Catton
A Stillness at Appomattox
1955 Joseph Wood Krutch
The Measure of Man
1956 Herbert Kubly
An American in Italy
1957 George F. Kennan
Russia Leaves the War
1958 Catherine Drinker Bowen
The Lion and the Throne
1959 J. Christopher Herold
Mistress to an Age: A Life of Madame de Stael
1960 Richard Ellmann
James Joyce
1961 William L. Shirer
The Rise and Fall of the Third Reich
1962 Lewis Mumford
The City in History: Its Origins, Its Transformations and Its Prospects
1963 Leon Edel
Henry James, Vol. II: The Conquest of London. Henry James, Vol. III: The Middle Years
No general nonfiction prize awarded 1964–79
1980 Tom Wolfe (hardcover)
The Right Stuff
Peter Matthiessen (paperback)
The Snow Leopard
1981 Maxine Hong Kingston (hardcover)
China Men
Jane Kramer (paperback)
The Last Cowboy
1982 Tracy Kidder (hardcover)
The Soul of a New Machine
Victor S. Navasky (paperback)
Naming Names
1983 Fox Butterfield (hardcover)
China: Alive in the Bitter Sea
James Fallows (paperback)
National Defense
1984 Rovert V. Remini
Andrew Jackson and the Course of American Democracy, 1833–1845

1985	J. Anthony Lukas *Common Ground: A Turbulent Decade in the Lives of Three American Families*
1986	Barry Lopez *Arctic Dreams*
1987	Richard Rhodes *The Making of the Atom Bomb*
1988	Neil Sheehan *A Bright Shining Lie: John Paul Vann and America in Vietnam*
1989	Thomas L. Friedman *From Beirut to Jerusalem*
1990	Ron Chernow *The House of Morgan: An American Banking Dynasty and the Rise of Modern Finance*
1991	Orlando Patterson *Freedom*
1992	Paul Monette *Becoming a Man: Half a Life Story*
1993	Gore Vidal *United States: Essays 1952–1992*
1994	Sherwin B. Nuland *How We Die: Reflections on Life's Final Chapter*
1995	Tina Rosenberg *The Haunted Land: Facing Europe's Ghosts After Communism*
1996	James Caroll *An American Requiem*
1997	Joseph J. Ellis *American Sphinx: The Character of Thomas Jefferson*
1998	Edward Ball *Slaves in the Family*
1999	John W. Dower *Embracing Defeat: Japan in the Wake of World War II*
2000	Nathaniel Philbrick *In the Heart of the Sea: The Tragedy of the Whaleship Essex*

Poetry

1950	William Carlos Williams *Paterson: Book III and Selected Poems*
1951	Wallace Stevens *The Auroras of Autumn*
1952	Marianne Moore *Collected Poems*
1953	Archibald MacLeish *Collected Poems, 1917–1952*
1954	Conrad Aiken *Collected Poems*
1955	Wallace Stevens *The Collected Poems of Wallace Stevens*
1956	W. H. Auden *The Shield of Achilles*

1957	Richard Wilbur *Things of This World*
1958	Robert Penn Warren *Promises: Poems, 1954–1956*
1959	Theodore Roethke *Words for the Wind*
1960	Robert Lowell *Life Studies*
1961	Randall Jarrell *The Woman at the Washington Zoo*
1962	Alan Dugan *Poems*
1963	William Strafford *Traveling Through the Dark*
1964	John Crowe Ransom *Selected Poems*
1965	Theodore Roethke *The Far Field*
1966	James Dickey *Buckdancer's Choice: Poems*
1967	James Merrill *Nights and Days*
1968	Robert Bly *The Light Around the Body*
1969	John Berryman *His Toy, His Dream, His Rest*
1970	Elizabeth Bishop *The Complete Poems*
1971	Mona Van Duyn *To See, To Take*
1972	Howard Moss *Selected Poems* Frank O'Hara *The Collected Poems of Frank O'Hara*
1973	A. R. Ammons *Collected Poems, 1951–1971*
1974	Allen Ginsberg *The Fall of America: Poems of These States* Adrienne Rich *Diving into the Wreck: Poems 1971–1972*
1975	Marilyn Hacker *Presentation Piece*
1976	John Ashbery *Self-Portrait in a Convex Mirror*
1977	Richard Eberhart *Collected Poems, 1930–1976*
1978	Howard Nemerov *The Collected Poems of Howard Nemerov*
1979	James Merrill *Mirabell: Book of Numbers*
1980	Philip Levine *Ashes*
1981	Lisel Mueller *The Need to Hold Still*
1982	William Bronk *Life Supports: New and Collected Poems*
1983	Galway Kinnell *Selected Poems*

	Charles Wright *Country Music: Selected Early Poems*
1991	Philip Levine *What Work Is*
1992	Mary Oliver *New and Selected Poems*
1993	A. R. Ammons *Garbage*
1994	James Tate *A Worshipful Company of Fletchers*
1995	Stanley Kunitz *Passing Through: The Later Poems New and Selected*
1996	Hayden Carruth *Scrambled Eggs and Whiskey*
1997	William Meredith *Effort at Speech: New and Selected Poems*
1998	Gerald Stern *This Time: New and Selected Poems*
1999	Ai *Vice: New and Selected Poems*
2000	Lucille Clifton *Blessing the Boats: New and Selected Poems 1988-2000*

Young People's Literature

1996	Victor Martinez *Parrot in the Oven: Mi Vida*
1997	Han Dolan *Dancing on the Edge*
1998	Louis Sachar *Holes*
1999	Kimberly Willis Holt *When Zachary Beaver Came to Town*
2000	Gloria Whelan *Homeless Bird*

NEWBERY MEDAL BOOKS

For children's literature

1922	Hendrik van Loon *The Story of Mankind*
1923	Hugh Lofting *The Voyages of Doctor Dolittle*
1924	Charles Hawes *The Dark Frigate*
1925	Charles Finger *Tales from Silver Lands*
1926	Arthur Chrisman *Shen of the Sea*
1927	Will James *Smoky, the Cowhorse*
1928	Dhan Mukerji *Gay Neck, the Story of a Pigeon*
1929	Eric P. Kelly *The Trumpeter of Krakow*
1930	Rachel Field *Hitty, Her First Hundred Years*
1931	Elizabeth Coatsworth *The Cat Who Went to Heaven*

1932	Laura Armer
	Waterless Mountain
1933	Elizabeth Lewis
	Young Fu of the Upper Yangtze
1934	Cornelia Meigs
	Invincible Louisa
1935	Monica Shannon
	Dobry
1936	Carol Brink
	Caddie Woodlawn
1937	Ruth Sawyer
	Roller Skates
1938	Kate Seredy
	The White Stag
1939	Elizabeth Enright
	Thimble Summer
1940	James Daugherty
	Daniel Boone
1941	Armstrong Sperry
	Call It Courage
1942	Walter Edmonds
	The Matchlock Gun
1943	Elizabeth Gray
	Adam of the Road
1944	Esther Forbes
	Johnny Tremain
1945	Robert Lawson
	Rabbit Hill
1946	Lois Lenski
	Strawberry Girl
1947	Carolyn Bailey
	Miss Hickory
1948	William Pène du Bois
	The Twenty-One Balloons
1949	Marguerite Henry
	King of the Wind
1950	Marguerite de Angeli
	The Door in the Wall
1951	Elizabeth Yates
	Amos Fortune, Free Man
1952	Eleanor Estes
	Ginger Pye
1953	Ann Nolan Clark
	Secret of the Andes
1954	Joseph Krumgold
	...And Now Miguel
1955	Meindert DeJong
	The Wheel on the School
1956	Jean Lee Latham
	Carry On, Mr. Bowditch
1957	Virginia Sorenson
	Miracles on Maple Hill
1958	Harold Keith
	Rifles for Watie
1959	Elizabeth George Speare
	The Witch of Blackbird Pond
1960	Joseph Krumgold
	Onion John
1961	Scott O'Dell
	Island of the Blue Dolphins
1962	Elizabeth George Speare
	The Bronze Bow

1963	Madeleine L'Engle
	A Wrinkle in Time
1964	Emily Neville
	It's Like This, Cat
1965	Maia Wojciechowska
	Shadow of a Bull
1966	Elizabeth Borton de Trevino
	I, Juan de Pareja
1967	Irene Hunt
	Up a Road Slowly
1968	E. L. Konigsburg
	From the Mixed-Up Files of Mrs. Basil E. Frankweiler
1969	Lloyd Alexander
	The High King
1970	William H. Armstrong
	Sounder
1971	Betsy Byars
	Summer of the Swans
1972	Robert C. O'Brien
	Mrs. Frisby and the Rats of NIMH
1973	Jean Craighead George
	Julie of the Wolves
1974	Paula Fox
	The Slave Dancer
1975	Virginia Hamilton
	M. C. Higgins, the Great
1976	Susan Cooper
	The Grey King
1977	Mildred D. Taylor
	Roll of Thunder, Hear My Cry
1978	Katherine Paterson
	Bridge to Terabithia
1979	Ellen Raskin
	The Westing Game
1980	Joan W. Blos
	A Gathering of Days
1981	Katherine Paterson
	Jacob Have I Loved
1982	Nancy Willard
	A Visit to William Blake's Inn: Poems for Innocent and Experienced Travelers
1983	Cynthia Voight
	Dicey's Song
1984	Beverly Cleary
	Dear Mr. Henshaw
1985	Robin McKinley
	The Hero and the Crown
1986	Patricia MacLachlan
	Sarah, Plain and Tall
1987	Sid Fleischman
	The Whipping Boy
1988	Russell Freedman
	Lincoln: A Photobiography
1989	Paul Fleischman
	Joyful Noise: Poems for Two Voices
1990	Lois Lowry
	Number the Stars
1991	Jerry Spinelli
	Maniac Magee
1992	Phyllis Reynolds Naylor
	Shiloh

1993	Cynthia Rylant
	Missing May
1994	Lois Lowry
	The Giver
1995	Sharon Creech
	Walk Two Moons
1996	Karen Cushman
	The Midwife's Apprentice
1997	E. L. Konigsburg
	The View from Saturday
1998	Karen Hesse
	Out of Dust
1999	Louis Sachar
	Holes
2000	Christopher Paul Curtis
	Bud, Not Buddy
2001	Richard Peck
	A Year Down Yonder

CALDECOTT MEDAL BOOKS

For children's picture books

1938	Helen Dean Fish, ill. by Dorothy P. Lathrop
	Animals of the Bible
1939	Thomas Handforth
	Mei Li
1940	Ingri and Edgar Parin d'Aulaire
	Abraham Lincoln
1941	Robert Lawson
	They Were Strong and Good
1942	Robert McCloskey
	Make Way for Ducklings
1943	Virginia Lee Burton
	The Little House
1944	James Thurber, ill. by Louis Slobodkin
	Many Moons
1945	Rachel Field, ill. by Elizabeth Orton Jones
	Prayer for a Child
1946	Maude and Mishka Petersham
	The Rooster Crows
1947	Golden MacDonald, ill. by Leonard Weisgard
	The Little Island
1948	Alvin Tresselt, ill. by Roger Duvoisin
	White Snow, Bright Snow
1949	Berta and Elmer Hader
	The Big Snow
1950	Leo Politi
	Song of the Swallows
1951	Katherine Milhous
	The Egg Tree
1952	Will Lipkind, ill. by Nicolas Mordvinoff
	Finders Keepers
1953	Lynd Ward
	The Biggest Bear
1954	Ludwig Bemelmans
	Madeline's Rescue

1955 Marcia Brown
Cinderella

1956 John Langstaff, ill. by Feodor Rojankovsky
Frog Went A-Courtin'

1957 Janice Udry, ill. by Marc Simont
A Tree Is Nice

1958 Robert McCloskey
Time of Wonder

1959 Barbara Cooney
Chanticleer and the Fox

1960 Marie Hall Ets and Aurora Labastida
Nine Days to Christmas

1961 Ruth Robbins, ill. by Nicolas Sidjakov
Baboushka and the Three Kings

1962 Marcia Brown
Once a Mouse

1963 Ezra Jack Keats
The Snowy Day

1964 Maurice Sendak
Where the Wild Things Are

1965 Beatrice Schenk de Regniers, ill. by Beni Montresor
May I Bring a Friend?

1966 Sorche Nic Leodhas, ill. by Nonny Hogrogian
Always Room for One More

1967 Evaline Ness
Sam, Bangs & Moonshine

1968 Barbara Emberley, ill. by Ed Emberley
Drummer Hoff

1969 Arthur Ransome, ill. by Uri Shulevitz
The Fool of the World and the Flying Ship

1970 William Steig
Sylvester and the Magic Pebble

1971 Gail E. Haley
A Story a Story

1972 Nonny Hogrogian
One Fine Day

1973 Lafcadio Hearn, retold by Arlene Mosel, ill. by Blair Lent
The Funny Little Woman

1974 Harve Zemach, picts. by Margot Zemach
Duffy and the Devil

1975 Gerald McDermott
Arrow to the Sun

1976 Verna Aardema, picts. by Leo and Diane Dillon
Why Mosquitoes Buzz in People's Ears

1977 Margaret Musgrove, picts. by Leo and Diane Dillon
Ashanti to Zulu

1978 Peter Spier
Noah's Ark

1979 Paul Goble
The Girl Who Loved Wild Horses

1980 Donald Hall, picts. by Barbara Cooney
Ox-Cart Man

1981 Arnold Lobel
Fables

1982 Chris Van Allsburg
Jumanji

1983 Blaise Cendrars, trans. and ill. by Marcia Brown
Shadow

1984 Alice and Martin Provensen
The Glorious Flight: Across the Channel with Louis Blériot

1985 Margaret Hodges, ill. by Trina Schart Hyman
Saint George and the Dragon

1986 Chris Van Allsburg
The Polar Express

1987 Arthur Yorinks, ill. by Richard Egielski
Hey, Al

1988 Jane Yolen, ill. by John Schoenherr
Owl Moon

1989 Karen Ackerman, ill. by Stephen Gammell
Song and Dance Man

1990 Ed Young
Lon Po Po

1991 David Macaulay
Black and White

1992 David Wiesner
Tuesday

1993 Emily Arnold McCully
Mirette on the High Wire

1994 Allen Say
Grandfather's Journey

1995 Eve Bunting, ill. by David Diaz
Smoky Night

1996 Peggy Rathmann
Officer Buckle and Gloria

1997 David Wisniewski
Golem

1998 Paul O. Zelinsky
Rapunzel

1999 Mary Azarian
Snowflake Bentley

2000 Simms Taback
Joseph Had a Little Overcoat

2001 Judith St. George
So You Want to Be President?

BOLLINGEN PRIZE IN POETRY

1949 Wallace Stevens
1950 John Crowe Ransom
1951 Marianne Moore
1952 Archibald MacLeish
William Carlos Williams
1953 W. H. Auden
1954 Leonie Adams
Louise Bogan
1955 Conrad Aiken
1956 Allen Tate
1957 E. E. Cummings

1958 Theodore Roethke
1959 Delmore Schwartz
1960 Yvor Winters
1961 Richard Eberhart
John Hall Wheelock
1962 Robert Frost
1965 Horace Gregory
1967 Robert Penn Warren
1969 John Berryman
Karl Shapiro
1971 Richard Wilbur
Mona Van Duyn
1973 James Merrill
1975 A. R. Ammons
1977 David Ignatow
1979 W. S. Merwin
1981 May Swenson
Howard Nemerov
1983 Anthony E. Hecht
John Hollander
1985 John Ashbery
Fred Chappell
1987 Stanley Kunitz
1989 Edgar Bowers
1991 Laura (Riding) Jackson
Donald Justice
1993 Mark Strand
1995 Kenneth Koch
1997 Gary Snyder
1999 Robert White Creeley
2001 Louise Glück

PEN/FAULKNER AWARD

Best American work of fiction

1981 Walter Abish
How German Is It?

1982 David Bradley
The Chaneysville Incident

1983 Toby Olson
Seaview

1984 John Edgar Wideman
Sent for You Yesterday

1985 Tobias Wolff
The Barracks Thief

1986 Peter Taylor
The Old Forest

1987 Richard Wiley
Soldiers in Hiding

1988 T. Coraghessan Boyle
World's End

1989 James Salter
Dusk

1990 E. L. Doctorow
Billy Bathgate

1991 John Edgar Wideman
Philadelphia Fire

1992 Don DeLillo
Mao II

1993 E. Annie Proulx
Postcards

1994 Philip Roth
Operation Shylock

1995	David Guterson	1992	Michael Ondaatje	1920	Knut Hamsun
	Snow Falling on Cedars		*The English Patient*		Norway
1996	Richard Ford		Barry Unsworth	1921	Anatole France
	Independence Day		*Sacred Hunger*		France
1997	Gina Berriault	1993	Roddy Doyle	1922	Jacinto Benaventi y Martinez
	Women in Their Beds		*Paddy Clark Ha Ha Ha*		Spain
1998	Rafi Zabor	1994	James Kelman	1923	William Butler Yeats
	The Bear Comes Home		*How Late It Was, How Late*		Ireland
1999	Michael Cunningham	1995	Pat Barker	1924	Wladylaw Reymont
	The Hours		*The Ghost Road*		Poland
2000	Ha Jin	1996	Graham Swift	1925	George Bernard Shaw
	Waiting		*Last Orders*		Ireland
2001	Philip Roth	1997	Arundhati Roy	1926	Grazia Deledda
	The Human Stain		*The God of Small Things*		Italy
		1998	Ian McEwan	1927	Henri Bergson
			Amsterdam		France

BOOKER PRIZE
British award for fiction

		1999	J. M Coetzee	1928	Sigrid Undset
			Disgrace		Norway
1969	P. H. Newby	2000	Margaret Atwood	1929	Paul Mann
	Something to Answer For		*The Blind Assassin*		Germany
1970	Bernice Rubens			1930	Henry Sinclair Lewis
	The Elected Member				United States

NOBEL PRIZE FOR LITERATURE

1971	V. S. Naipaul	1901	Rene-Francois-Armend Prudhomme	1931	Erik Axel Karlfeldt
	In a Free State		France		Sweden
1972	John Berger	1902	Bjornstjerne Bjornson	1932	John Galsworthy
	G		Norway		Great Britain
1973	J. G. Farrell	1903	Christian Mommsen	1933	Ivan Bunin
	The Siege of Krishnapur		Germany		Russia
1974	Nadine Gordimer	1904	Jose Echegaray y Eizaguirre	1934	Luigi Pirandello
	The Conservationist		Spain		Italy
1975	Ruth Prawer Jhabvala		Frederic Mistral	1936	Eugene O'Neill
	Heat and Dust		France		United States
1976	David Storey	1905	Henryk Sienkiewicz	1937	Roger Martin du Gard
	Saville		Poland		France
1977	Paul Scott	1906	Giosue Carducci	1938	Pearl S. Buck
	Staying On		Italy		United States
1978	Iris Murdoch	1907	Joseph Rudyard Kipling	1939	Frans Sillanpaa
	The Sea, the Sea		Great Britain		Finland
1979	Penelope Fitzgerald	1908	Rudolph Eucker	1944	Johannes Jensen
	Offshore		Germany		Denmark
1980	William Golding	1909	Selma Lagerlof	1945	Gabriela Mistral
	Rites of Passage		Sweden		Chile
1981	Salman Rushdie	1910	Paul Ludwig von Heyse	1946	Herman Hesse
	Midnight's Children		Germany		Germany
1982	Thomas Keneally	1911	Maurice Maeterlinck	1947	Andre Gide
	Schindler's Ark		Belgium		France
1983	J. M. Coetzee	1912	Gerhart Hauptmann	1948	Thomas Stearns Eliot
	Life and Times of Michael K		Germany		United States
1984	Anita Brookner	1913	Sir Rabindranath Tagore		Isaac Singer
	Hotel du Lac		India		Poland
1985	Keri Hulme	1915	Roland Romain	1949	William Faulkner
	The Bone People		France		United States
1986	Kingsley Amis	1916	Carl Gustof Verner Von	1950	Bertrand Russell
	The Old Devils		Heidenstam		Great Britain
1987	Penelope Lively		Sweden	1951	Par Fabian Lagerkirst
	Moon Tiger	1917	Karl Adolph Gjellerup		Sweden
1988	Peter Carey		Denmark	1952	Francois Mauriac
	Oscar and Lucinda		Henrik Pontoppidan		France
1989	Kazuo Ishiguro		Denmark	1953	Sir Winston Churchill
	The Remains of the Day	1918	Erik Axel Karlfeldt		Great Britain
1990	A. S. Byatt		Sweden	1954	Ernest Hemingway
	Possession	1919	Carl Spitteler		United States
1991	Ben Okri		Switzerland	1955	Halldor Laxness
	The Famished Road				Iceland

1956	Juan Jimenez	1987	Joseph Brodsky	2000	The New Yorker
	Spain		Russia	2001	Time
1957	Albert Camus	1988	Naguib Mahfouz		
	France		Egypt		

1956 Juan Jimenez
Spain
1957 Albert Camus
France
1958 Boris Pasternak
Russia
1959 Salvatore Quasimodo
Italy
1960 Saint-John Perse
France
1961 Ivo Andric
Yugoslavia
1962 John Steinbeck
United States
1963 Giorgos Seferis
Greece
1964 Jean-Paul Sartre
France
1965 Mikhail Sholokov
Russia
1966 Shmuel Agnon
Austria
Leonie Sachs
Germany
1967 Miguel Asturias
Guatemala
1968 Yasunari Kawabata
Japan
1969 Samuel Beckett
Ireland
1970 Alexander Solzhenitsyn
Russia
1971 Pablo Neruda
Chile
1972 Heinrich Boll
Germany
1973 Patrick White
Australia
1974 Euyind Johnson
Sweden
1975 Eugenio Montale
Italy
1976 Saul Bellow
United States
1977 Vicente Aleixandre y Merlo
Spain
1978 Isaac Bashevis Singer
United States
1979 Odysseus Elytis
Greece
1980 Czeslaw Milosz
Poland
1981 Elias Canetti
Bulgaria
1982 Gabriel Jose García Márquez
Colombia
1983 William Golding
Great Britain
1984 Jaroslav Seifert
Czechoslovakia
1985 Claude Simon
France
1986 Wole Soyinka
Nigeria

1987 Joseph Brodsky
Russia
1988 Naguib Mahfouz
Egypt
1989 Camilo Jose Cela
Spain
1990 Octavio Paz
Mexico
1991 Nadine Gordimer
South Africa
1992 Derek Walcott
St. Lucia
1993 Toni Morrison
United States
1994 Kenzaburo Oe
Japan
1995 Seamus Heaney
Ireland
1996 Wislawa Szymborska
Poland
1997 Dario Fo
Italy
1998 José Saramago
Portugal
1999 Günter Grass
Germany
2000 Gao Xingjian
China
2001 V. S. Naipaul
England

NATIONAL MAGAZINE AWARD

Public Service/Public Interest

1970 Life
1971 The Nation
1972 Philadelphia
1973 [not awarded]
1974 Scientific American
1975 Consumer Reports
1976 Business Week
1977 Philadelphia
1978 Mother Jones
1979 New West
1980 Texas Monthly
1981 Reader's Digest
1982 The Atlantic Monthly
1983 Foreign Affairs
1984 The New Yorker
1985 The Washingtonian
1986 Science 85
1987 Money
1988 The Atlantic Monthly
1989 California
1990 Southern Exposure
1991 Family Circle
1992 Glamour
1993 The Family Therapy Network
1994 Philadelphia
1995 The New Republic
1996 Texas Monthly
1997 Fortune
1998 The Atlantic Monthly
1999 Time

2000 The New Yorker
2001 Time

Specialized Journalism

1970 Philadelphia
1971 Rolling Stone
1972 Architectural Record
1973 Psychology Today
1974 Texas Monthly
1975 Medical Economics
1976 United Mine Workers Journal
1977 Architectural Record
1978 Scientific American
1979 National Journal
1980 IEEE Spectrum

Design/Visual Excellence

1970 Look
1971 Vogue
1972 Esquire
1973 Horizon
1974 Newsweek
1975 Country Journal
National Lampoon
1976 Horticulture
1977 Rolling Stone
1978 Architectural Digest
1979 Audubon
1980 GEO
1981 Attenzione
1982 Nautical Quarterly
1983 New York
1984 House & Garden
1985 Forbes
1986 Time
1987 Elle
1988 Life
1989 Rolling Stone
1990 Esquire
1991 Condé Nast Traveler
1992 Vanity Fair
1993 Harper's Bazaar
1994 Allure
1995 Martha Stewart Living
1996 Wired
1997 I.D. Magazine
1998 Entertainment Weekly
1999 ESPN: The Magazine
2000 Fast Company
2001 Nest

Reporting (Excellence)/News Reporting

1970 The New Yorker
1971 The Atlantic Monthly
1972 The Atlantic Monthly
1973 New York
1974 The New Yorker
1975 The New Yorker
1976 Audubon
1977 Audubon
1978 The New Yorker
1979 Texas Monthly
1980 Mother Jones

1981 National Journal
1982 The Washingtonian
1983 Institutional Investor
1984 Vanity Fair
1985 Texas Monthly
1986 Rolling Stone
1987 Life
1988 Baltimore Magazine
     The Washingtonian
1989 The New Yorker
1990 The New Yorker
1991 The New Yorker
1992 The New Republic
1993 IEEE Spectrum
1994 The New Yorker
1995 The Atlantic Monthly
1996 The New Yorker
1997 Outside
1998 Rolling Stone
1999 Newsweek
2000 Vanity Fair
2001 Esquire

General Excellence
(Under 100,000 circulation)

1981 ARTnews
1982 Camera Arts
1983 Louisiana Life
1984 The American Lawyer
1985 Manhattan, inc.
1986 New England Monthly
1987 New England Monthly
1988 The Sciences
1989 The Sciences
1990 7 Days
1991 The New Republic
1992 The New Republic
1993 Lingua Franca
1994 Print
1995 I.D. Magazine
1996 The Sciences
1997 I.D. Magazine
1998 DoubleTake
1999 I.D. Magazine
2000 Nest
2001 The American Scholar

General Excellence (100,000–400,000)

1981 Audubon
1982 Rocky Mountain Magazine
1983 Harper's Magazine
1984 Outside
1985 American Heritage
1986 3-2-1 Contact
1987 Common Cause
1988 Hippocrates
1989 American Heritage
1990 Texas Monthly
1991 Interview
1992 Texas Monthly
1993 American Photo
1994 Wired
1995 Men's Journal

1996 Civilization
1997 Wired
1998 Preservation
1999 Fast Company
2000 Saveur
2001 Mother Jones

General Excellence (400,000–1,000,000)

1981 Business Week
1982 Science 81
1983 Science 82
1984 House & Garden
1985 American Health
1986 Discover
1987 Elle
1988 Fortune
1989 Vanity Fair
1990 Metropolitan Home
1991 Condé Nast Traveler
1992 Mirabella
1993 The Atlantic Monthly
1994 Health
1995 The New Yorker
1996 Outside
1997 Outside
1998 Outside
1999 Condé Nast Traveler
2000 The New Yorker
2001 The New Yorker

General Excellence (over 1,000,000)

1981 Glamour
1982 Newsweek
1983 Life
1984 National Geographic
1985 Time
1986 Money
1987 People Weekly
1988 Parents
1989 Sports Illustrated
1990 Sports Illustrated
1991 Glamour
1992 National Geographic
1993 Newsweek
1994 Business Week
1995 Entertainment Weekly
1996 Business Week
1997 Vanity Fair
1998 Rolling Stone
1999 Vanity Fair
2000 National Geographic
2001 Teen People

Essays and Criticism

1978 Esquire
1979 Life
1980 Natural History
1981 Time
1982 The Atlantic Monthly
1983 The American Lawyer
1984 The New Republic
1985 Boston
1986 The Sciences

1987 Outside
1988 Harper's Magazine
1989 Harper's Magazine
1990 Vanity Fair
1991 The Sciences
1992 The Nation
1993 The American Lawyer
1994 Harper's Magazine
1995 Harper's Magazine
1996 The New Yorker
1997 The New Yorker
1998 The New Yorker
1999 The Atlantic Monthly

Fiction

1978 The New Yorker
1979 The Atlantic Monthly
1980 Antaeus
1981 The North American Review
1982 The New Yorker
1983 The North American Review
1984 Seventeen
1985 Playboy
1986 The Georgia Review
1987 Esquire
1988 The Atlantic
1989 The New Yorker
1990 The New Yorker
1991 Esquire
1992 Story
1993 The New Yorker
1994 Harper's Magazine
1995 Story
1996 Harper's Magazine
1997 The New Yorker
1998 The New Yorker
1999 Harper's Magazine
2000 The New Yorker
2001 Zoetrope: All-Story

Single Topic Issue

1979 Progressive Architecture
1980 Scientific American
1981 Business Week
1982 Newsweek
1983 IEEE Spectrum
1984 Esquire
1985 American Heritage
1986 IEEE Spectrum
1987 Bulletin of the Atomic Scientists
1988 Life
1989 Hippocrates
1990 National Geographic
1991 The American Lawyer
1992 Business Week
1993 Newsweek
1994 Health
1995 Discover
1996 Bon Appétit
1997 Scientific American
1998 The Sciences
1999 The Oxford American

Personal Service/Service to the Individual

1974	Sports Illustrated
1975	Esquire
1976	Modern Medicine
1977	Harper's Magazine
1978	Newsweek
1979	The American Journal of Nursing
1980	Saturday Review
1982	Philadelphia
1983	Sunset
1984	New York
1985	The Washingtonian
1986	Farm Journal
1987	Consumer Reports
1988	Money
1989	Good Housekeeping
1990	Consumer Reports
1991	New York
1992	Creative Classroom
1993	Good Housekeeping
1994	Fortune
1995	SmartMoney
1996	SmartMoney
1997	Glamour
1998	Men's Journal
1999	Good Housekeeping
2000	PC Computing
2001	National Geographic Adventure

Special Interests

1986	Popular Mechanics
1987	Sports Afield
1988	Condé Nast Traveler
1989	Condé Nast Traveler
1990	Arts & Antiques
1991	New York
1992	Sports Afield
1993	Philadelphia
1994	Outside
1995	Gentlemen's Quarterly
1996	Saveur
1997	Smithsonian Magazine
1998	Entertainment Weekly
1999	PC Computing
2000	I.D. Magazine
2001	The New Yorker

Photography

1985	Life
1986	Vogue
1987	National Geographic
1988	Rolling Stone
1989	National Geographic
1990	Texas Monthly
1991	National Geographic
1992	National Geographic
1993	Harper's Bazaar
1994	Martha Stewart Living
1995	Rolling Stone
1996	Saveur
1997	National Geographic
1998	W
1999	Martha Stewart Living

2000	Vanity Fair
2001	National Geographic

Feature Writing

1988	The Atlantic Monthly
1989	Esquire
1990	The Washingtonian
1991	U.S. News & World Report
1992	Sports Illustrated
1993	The New Yorker
1994	Harper's Magazine
1995	Gentlemen's Quarterly
1996	Gentlemen's Quarterly
1997	Sports Illustrated
1998	Harper's Magazine
1999	The American Scholar
2000	Sports Illustrated
2001	Rolling Stone

Online

1997	Money
1998	The Sporting News Online
1999	Cigar Aficionado
2000	Business Week Online
2001	U.S. News Online

Interactive Design

2001	SmartMoney.com

Essays

2000	The Sciences
2001	The New Yorker

Profiles

2000	Sports Illustrated
2001	The New Yorker

Reviews and Criticism

2000	Esquire
2001	The New Yorker

PULITZER PRIZE

Fiction

1918	Ernest Poole
	His Family
1919	Booth Tarkington
	The Magnificent Ambersons
1920	No award
1921	Edith Wharton
	The Age of Innocence
1922	Booth Tarkington
	Alice Adams
1923	Willa Cather
	One of Ours
1924	Margaret Wilson
	The Able McLaughlins
1925	Edna Ferber
	So Big
1926	Sinclair Lewis (refused prize)
	Arrowsmith

1927	Louis Bromfield
	Early Autumn
1928	Thornton Wilder
	Bridge of San Luis Rey
1929	Julia M. Peterkin
	Scarlet Sister Mary
1930	Oliver LaFarge
	Laughing Boy
1931	Margaret Ayer Barnes
	Years of Grace
1932	Pearl S. Buck
	The Good Earth
1933	T. S. Stribling
	The Store
1934	Caroline Miller
	Lamb in His Bosom
1935	Josephine W. Johnson
	Now in November
1936	Harold L. Davis
	Honey in the Horn
1937	Margaret Mitchell
	Gone with the Wind
1938	John P. Marquand
	The Late George Apley
1939	Marjorie Kinnan Rawlings
	The Yearling
1940	John Steinbeck
	The Grapes of Wrath
1941	No award
1942	Ellen Glasgow
	In This Our Life
1943	Upton Sinclair
	Dragon's Teeth
1944	Martin Flavin
	Journey in the Dark
1945	John Hersey
	A Bell for Adano
1946	No award
1947	Robert Penn Warren
	All the King's Men
1948	James A. Michener
	Tales of the South Pacific
1949	James Gould Cozzens
	Guard of Honor
1950	A. B. Guthrie, Jr.
	The Way West
1951	Conrad Richter
	The Town
1952	Herman Wouk
	The Caine Mutiny
1953	Ernest Hemingway
	The Old Man and the Sea
1954	No award
1955	William Faulkner
	A Fable
1956	MacKinlay Kantor
	Andersonville
1957	No award
1958	James Agee
	A Death in the Family
1959	Robert Lewis Taylor
	The Travels of Jaimie McPheeters
1960	Allen Drury
	Advise and Consent
1961	Harper Lee
	To Kill a Mockingbird

1962 Edwin O'Connor
The Edge of Sadness
1963 William Faulkner
The Reivers
1964 No award
1965 Shirley Ann Grau
The Keepers of the House
1966 Katherine Anne Porter
The Collected Stories of Katherine Anne Porter
1967 Bernard Malamud
The Fixer
1968 William Styron
The Confessions of Nat Turner
1969 N. Scott Momaday
House Made of Dawn
1970 Jean Stafford
Collected Stories
1971 No award
1972 Wallace Stegner
Angle of Repose
1973 Eudora Welty
The Optimist's Daughter
1974 No award
1975 Michael Shaara
The Killer Angels
1976 Saul Bellow
Humboldt's Gift
1977 No award
1978 James Alan McPherson
Elbow Room
1979 John Cheever
The Stories of John Cheever
1980 Norman Mailer
The Executioner's Song
1981 John Kennedy Toole
A Confederacy of Dunces
1982 John Updike
Rabbit Is Rich
1983 Alice Walker
The Color Purple
1984 William Kennedy
Ironweed
1985 Alison Lurie
Foreign Affairs
1986 Larry McMurtry
Lonesome Dove
1987 Peter Taylor
A Summons to Memphis
1988 Toni Morrison
Beloved
1989 Anne Tyler
Breathing Lessons
1990 Oscar Hijuelos
The Mambo Kings Play Songs of Love
1991 John Updike
Rabbit at Rest
1992 Jane Smiley
A Thousand Acres
1993 Robert Olen Butler
A Good Scent from a Strange Mountain
1994 E. Annie Proulx
The Shipping News

1995 Carol Shields
The Stone Diaries
1996 Richard Ford
Independence Day
1997 Steven Millhauser
Martin Dressler: The Tale of an American Dreamer
1998 Philip Roth
American Pastoral
1999 Michael Cunningham
The Hours
2000 Jhumpa Lahiri
Interpreter of Maladies
2001 Michael Chabon
The Amazing Adventures of Kavalier and Clay

Nonfiction

1962 Theodore H. White
The Making of the President, 1960
1963 Barbara W. Tuchman
The Guns of August
1964 Richard Hofstadter
Anti-Intellectualism in American Life
1965 Howard Mumford Jones
O Strange New World
1966 Edwin Way Teale
Wandering Through Winter
1967 David Brion Davis
The Problem of Slavery in Western Culture
1968 Will Durant and Ariel Durant
Rousseau and Revolution: The Tenth and Concluding Volume of The Story of Civilization
1969 Norman Mailer
The Armies of the Night
Rene Jules Dubos
So Human an Animal
1970 Erik H. Erikson
Gandhi's Truth
1971 John Toland
The Rising Sun
1972 Barbara W. Tuchman
Stilwell and the American Experience in China, 1911–1945
1973 Robert Coles
Children of Crisis, Vols. II and III
Francis FitzGerald
Fire in the Lake: The Vietnamese and the Americans in Vietnam
1974 Ernest Becker
The Denial of Death
1975 Annie Dillard
Pilgram at Tinker Creek
1976 Robert N. Butler
Why Survive?: Being Old in America
1977 William W. Warner
Beautiful Swimmers
1978 Carl Sagan
The Dragons of Eden
1979 Edward O. Wilson
On Human Nature

1980 Douglas R. Hofstadter
Gödel, Escher, Bach: An Eternal Golden Braid
1981 Carl E. Schorske
Fin-de-Siecle Vienna: Politics and Culture
1982 Tracy Kidder
The Soul of a New Machine
1983 Susan Sheehan
Is There No Place on Earth for Me?
1984 Paul Starr
The Social Transformation of American Medicine
1985 Studs Terkel
The Good War: An Oral History of World War Two
1986 J. Anthony Lukas
Common Ground: A Turbulent Decade in the Lives of Three American Families
Joseph Lelyveld
Move Your Shadow
1987 David K. Shipler
Arab and Jew: Wounded Spirits in a Promised Land
1988 Richard Rhodes
The Making of the Atomic Bomb
1989 Neil Sheehan
A Bright Shining Lie: John Paul Vann and America in Vietnam
1990 Dale Maharidge and Michael Williamson
And Their Children After Them
1991 Bert Holdobler and Edward O. Wilson
The Ants
1992 Daniel Yergin
The Prize: The Epic Quest for Oil, Money, and Power
1993 Garry Wills
Lincoln at Gettysburg
1994 David Remnick
Lenin's Tomb
1995 Jonathan Weiner
The Beak of the Finch: A Story of Evolution in Our Time
1996 Tina Rosenberg
The Haunted Land: Facing Europe's Ghosts After Communism
1997 Richard Kluger
Ashes to Ashes: America's Hundred-Year Cigarette War, the Public Health, and the Unabashed Triumph of Philip Morris
1998 Jared Diamond
Guns, Germs, and Steel: The Fates of Human Societies
1999 John A. McPhee
Annals of the Former World
2000 John W. Dower
Embracing Defeat
2001 Herbert P. Bix
Hirohito and the Making of Modern Japan

Poetry

1918 Sara Teasdale
Love Songs
1919 Carl Sandburg
Corn Huskers
Margaret Widemer
Old Road to Paradise
1920 No award
1921 No award
1922 Edwin Arlington Robinson
Collected Poems
1923 Edna St. Vincent Millay
The Ballad of the Harp-Weaver;
A Few Figs from Thistles;
Eight Sonnets in American
Poetry, 1922; A Miscellany
1924 Robert Frost
New Hampshire: A Poem with
Notes and Grace Notes
1925 Edwin Arlington Robinson
The Man Who Died Twice
1926 Amy Lowell
What's O'Clock
1927 Leonora Speyer
Fiddler's Farewell
1928 Edwin Arlington Robinson
Tristram
1929 Stephen Vincent Benet
John Brown's Body
1930 Conrad Aiken
Selected Poems
1931 Robert Frost
Collected Poems
1932 George Dillon
The Flowering Stone
1933 Archibald MacLeish
Conquistador
1934 Robert Hillyer
Collected Verse
1935 Audrey Wurdemann
Bright Ambush
1936 Robert P. Tristram Coffin
Strange Holiness
1937 Robert Frost
A Further Range
1938 Marya Zaturenska
Cold Morning Sky
1939 John Gould Fletcher
Selected Poems
1940 Mark Van Doren
Collected Poems
1941 Leonnard Bacon
Sunderland Capture
1942 William Rose Benet
The Dust Which Is God
1943 Robert Frost
A Witness Tree
1944 Stephen Vincent Benet
Western Star

1945 Karl Shapiro
V-Letter and Other Poems
1946 No award
1947 Robert Lowell
Lord Weary's Castle
1948 W. H. Auden
The Age of Anxiety
1949 Peter Viereck
Terror and Decorum
1950 Gwendolyn Brooks
Annie Allen
1951 Carl Sandburg
Complete Poems
1952 Marianne Moore
Collected Poems
1953 Archibald MacLeish
Collected Poems 1917–1952
1954 Theodore Roethke
The Waking
1955 Wallace Stevens
Collected Poems
1956 Elizabeth Bishop
Poems, North and South
1957 Richard Wilbur
Things of This World
1958 Robert Penn Warren
Promises: Poems 1954–1956
1959 Stanley Kunitz
Selected Poems 1928–1958
1960 W. D. Snodgrass
Heart's Needle
1961 Phyllis McGinley
Times Three: Selected Verse from
Three Decades
1962 Alan Dugan
Poems
1963 William Carlos Williams
Pictures from Breughel
1964 Louis Simpson
At the End of the Open Road
1965 John Berryman
77 Dream Songs
1966 Richard Eberhart
Selected Poems
1967 Anne Sexton
Live or Die
1968 Anthony Hecht
The Hard Hours
1969 George Oppen
Of Being Numerous
1970 Richard Howard
Untitled Subjects
1971 W. S. Merwin
The Carrier of Ladders
1972 James Wright
Collected Poems
1973 Maxine Kumin
Up Country

1974 Robert Lowell
The Dolphin
1975 Gary Snyder
Turtle Island
1976 John Ashbery
Self-Portrait in a Convex Mirror
1977 James Merrill
Divine Comedies
1978 Howard Nemerov
Collected Poems
1979 Robert Penn Warren
Now and Then
1980 Donald Justice
Selected Poems
1981 James Schuyler
The Morning of the Poem
1982 Sylvia Plath
The Collected Poems
1983 Galway Kinnell
Selected Poems
1984 Mary Oliver
American Primitive
1985 Carolyn Kizer
Yin
1986 Henry Taylor
The Flying Change
1987 Rita Dove
Thomas and Beulah
1988 William Meredith
Partial Accounts: New and
Selected Poems
1989 Richard Wilbur
New and Collected Poems
1990 Charles Simic
The World Doesn't End
1991 Mona Van Duyn
Near Changes
1992 James Tate
Selected Poems
1993 Louise Gluck
The Wild Iris
1994 Yusef Komunyakaa
Neon Vernacular
1995 Philip Levine
The Simple Truth
1996 Jorie Graham
The Dream of the Unified Field
1997 Lisel Mueller
Alive Together
1998 Charles Wright
Black Zodiac
1999 Mark Strand
Blizzard of One
2000 C.K. Williams
Repair: Poems
2001 Stephen Dunn
Different Hours

STAGE

BROADWAY SHOWS OF THE 2001–2002 SEASON

Producers rejoiced as new shows gave audiences the *Full Monty* of excitement for the first time in a while, even as sure-thing Seussical turned into one of the biggest flops ever. (Source: *Variety*)

NEW PRODUCTIONS

The Adventures of Tom Sawyer (M)
Bells Are Ringing (M-R)
Betrayal (R)
Blast! (M-R)
A Class Act (M)
Design for Living (R)
The Dinner Party
Follies (M-R)
42nd Street (M-R)
The Full Monty (M)
The Gathering
George Gershwin Alone
Gore Vidal's The Best Man (R)
The Invention of Love
Jane Eyre (M)
Judgement at Nuremberg
King Hedley II
Macbeth (R)
The Man Who Came to Dinner (R)
One Flew Over the Cuckoo's Nest
Patti LuPone: Matters of the Heart
   (M-So-Rev)
The Producers (M)
Proof
The Rocky Horror Show (M-R)
The Search for Signs of Intelligent
   Life in the Universe (So-R)
Seussical (M)
Stones in His Pockets
The Tale of the Allergist's Wife

HOLDOVERS

Aida (M)
Annie Get Your Gun (M-R)
Beauty and the Beast (M)
Cabaret (M-R)
Chicago (M-R)
Contact (M)
Copenhagen
Dirty Blonde
Footloose (M)
Fosse (M)
The Green Bird (M)
Jekyll & Hyde (M)
Jesus Christ Superstar (M)
Kiss Me Kate (M-R)
Les Misérables (M)
The Lion King (M)
A Moon for the Misbegotten (R)
The Music Man (M-R)
The Phantom of the Opera (M)
The Real Thing (R)
Rent (M)
The Ride Down Mt. Morgan
Riverdance-On Broadway (M-Rev)
Saturday Night Fever (M)
The Scarlet Pimpernel (M)
Side Man
Smokey Joe's Cafe (M-Rev)
The Sound of Music (M-R)
Swing! (M-Rev)
Taller Than a Dwarf
The Weir
The Wild Party (M)
You're a Good Man, Charlie Brown
   (M-R)

(M) denotes musical
(R) denotes revival
(So) denotes solo performance
(Rev) denotes revue
(Sp) denotes special attraction

THAT'S SHOW BIZ

Business was up again for the Great White Way and on the road, though the touring circuit is still missing the destination blockbusters of the '90s. (Source: *Variety*)

Season	Broadway box office/ total shows during most profitable week	Road box office/ total shows during most profitable week
1982–83	$203.1 million/27 shows	$184.3 million/24 shows
1987–88	$253.5 million/21 shows	$223.0 million/24 shows
1992–93	$327.7 million/21 shows	$620.6 million/34 shows
1993–94	$356.0 million/21 shows	$687.7 million/30 shows
1994–95	$406.3 million/23 shows	$694.6 million/33 shows
1995–96	$436.1 million/28 shows	$762.3 million/27 shows
1996–97	$499.4 million/27 shows	$752.9 million/27 shows
1997–98	$557.3 million/32 shows	$794.1 million/26 shows
1998–99	$588.1 million/30 shows	$711.4 million/26 shows
1999–00	$602.6 million/36 shows	$584.5 million/23 shows
2000–01	$665.6 million/30 shows	$615.6 million/23 shows

LONGEST-RUNNING SHOWS ON BROADWAY

At press time repercussions from the World Trade Center tragedy threatened to close some of Broadway's longest-running shows. Here's the hit parade based on the number of performances as of September 2, 2000. (M) stands for musical and (R) for revival. (Source: *Variety*)

Cats (M) (1982–00)	7,485
A Chorus Line (M) (1975–90)	6,137
Les Misérables (M) (1987–)	5,967
Oh! Calcutta! (M-R) (1976–89)	5,852
The Phantom of the Opera (M) (1988–)	5,678
Miss Saigon (M) (1991–)	3,920
42nd Street (M) (1980–89)	3,486
Grease (M) (1972–80)	3,388
Fiddler on the Roof (M) (1964–72)	3,242
Life with Father (1939–47)	3,224
Tobacco Road (1933–41)	3,182
Beauty and the Beast (M) (1994–)	2,999
Hello, Dolly! (M) (1964–70)	2,844
My Fair Lady (M) (1956–62)	2,717
Annie (M) (1977–83)	2,377
Man of La Mancha (M) (1965–71)	2,328
Abie's Irish Rose (1922–27)	2,327
Rent (M) (1996–)	2,233
Oklahoma! (M) (1943–48)	2,212
Smokey Joe's Cafe (M) (1995–2000)	2,036
Chicago (M-R) (1996–)	2,002
Pippin (M) (1972–77)	1,944
South Pacific (M) (1949–54)	1,925
The Magic Show (M) (1974–78)	1,920
Deathtrap (1978–82)	1,792
Gemini (1977–81)	1,788
Harvey (1944–49)	1,775
Dancin' (M) (1978–82)	1,774
La Cage aux folles (M) (1983–87)	1,761
Hair (M) (1968–72)	1,750
The Wiz (M) (1975–79)	1,672
Born Yesterday (1946–49)	1,642
Crazy for You (1992–96)	1,622
Ain't Misbehavin' (M) (1978–82)	1,604
The Lion King (M) (1997–)	1,590
Best Little Whorehouse in Texas (M) (1978–82)	1,584
Mary, Mary (1961–64)	1,572
Evita (M) (1979–83)	1,567
Voice of the Turtle (1943–48)	1,557
Barefoot in the Park (1963–64)	1,530
Brighton Beach Memoirs (1983–86)	1,530
Dreamgirls (M) (1981–85)	1,521

Mame (M) (1966–70)	1,508
Same Time, Next Year (1976–78)	1,453
Arsenic and Old Lace (1941–44)	1,444
The Sound of Music (M) (1959–63)	1,443
Me and My Girl (M-R) (1986–89)	1,420
How to Succeed in Business Without Really Trying (M) (1961–65)	1,417
Jekyll & Hyde (1997–)	1,407
Hellzapoppin (M) (1938–41)	1,404
Cabaret (M) (1966–69)	1,400
The Music Man (M) (1957–61)	1,375
Funny Girl (M) (1964–67)	1,348
Mummenschanz (M) (1977–80)	1,326
Oh! Calcutta! (M) (1969–72)	1,314
Angel Street (1941–44)	1,295
Lightnin' (1918–21)	1,291
Promises, Promises (M) (1968–72)	1,281
The King and I (M) (1951–54)	1,246
Cactus Flower (1965–68)	1,234
Grease (M-R) (1993–98)	1,231
Torch Song Trilogy (1982–85)	1,222
Sleuth (1970–73)	1,222
1776 (M) (1969–72)	1,217
Equus (1974–77)	1,209
Sugar Babies (M) (1979–82)	1,208
Guys and Dolls (M) (1950–53)	1,200
Amadeus (1980–83)	1,181
Mister Roberts (1948–51)	1,157
Annie Get Your Gun (M) (1946–49)	1,147
Guys and Dolls (M-R) (1992–95)	1,143
The Seven Year Itch (1952–55)	1,141
Butterflies Are Free (1969–72)	1,128
Pins and Needles (M) (1937–40)	1,108
Plaza Suite (1968–70)	1,097
They're Playing Our Song (M) (1979–81)	1,082
Kiss Me, Kate (M) (1948–51)	1,070
Don't Bother Me, I Can't Cope (M) (1972–74)	1,065
The Pajama Game (M) (1954–56)	1,063
Shenandoah (M) (1975–77)	1,050
Teahouse of the August Moon (1953–56)	1,027

BROADWAY'S FAVORITES: PLACE THAT TUNE

Know the song but can't place the musical in which it originally appeared? Here is a checklist of some Great White Way melodies that linger on.

SONG	SHOW	SONG	SHOW
"Almost Like Being in Love"	Brigadoon	"The Music of the Night"	The Phantom of the Opera
"And I Am Telling You I'm Not Going"	Dreamgirls	"My Favorite Things"	The Sound of Music
"Anything You Can Do"	Annie Get Your Gun	"Oh, What a Beautiful Mornin' "	Oklahoma!
"Bali Ha'i"	South Pacific	"Ol' Man River"	Show Boat
"The Ballad of Mack the Knife"	The Threepenny Opera	"One Night in Bangkok"	Chess
"Bewitched, Bothered, and Bewildered"	Pal Joey	"On the Street Where You Live"	My Fair Lady
"A Bushel and a Peck"	Guys and Dolls	"The Quest (The Impossible Dream)"	Man of La Mancha
"Climb Ev'ry Mountain"	The Sound of Music	"Seasons of Love"	Rent
"Everything's Coming Up Roses"	Gypsy	"Seventy-Six Trombones"	The Music Man
"Getting to Know You"	The King and I	"Shall We Dance?"	The King and I
"I Am What I Am"	La Cage aux folles	"Smoke Gets in Your Eyes"	Roberta
"I Cain't Say No"	Oklahoma!	"Some Enchanted Evening"	South Pacific
"I Could Have Danced All Night"	My Fair Lady	"The Sound of Music"	The Sound of Music
"I Don't Know How to Love Him"	Jesus Christ Superstar	"Summertime"	Porgy and Bess
"I Feel Pretty"	West Side Story	"Sunrise, Sunset"	Fiddler on the Roof
"I Get a Kick Out of You"	Anything Goes	"Tea for Two"	No, No, Nanette
"I Got Plenty o' Nothin' "	Porgy and Bess	"Thank Heaven for Little Girls"	Gigi
"I Got Rhythm"	Girl Crazy	"There Is Nothin' Like a Dame"	South Pacific
"I Got the Sun in the Morning"	Annie Get Your Gun	"There's No Business Like Show Business"	Annie Get Your Gun
"I Whistle a Happy Tune"	The King and I	"This Is the Army, Mr. Jones"	This Is the Army
"If Ever I Would Leave You"	Camelot	"This is the Moment"	Jekyll & Hyde
"It Ain't Necessarily So"	Porgy and Bess	"Till There Was You"	The Music Man
"I've Grown Accustomed to Her Face"	My Fair Lady	"Tomorrow"	Annie
"Let the Sunshine In"	Hair	"Tonight"	West Side Story
"Lover, Come Back to Me"	The New Moon	"You'll Never Walk Alone"	Carousel
"Luck Be a Lady"	Guys and Dolls	"You're the Top"	Anything Goes
"Maria"	West Side Story	"We Need a Little Christmas"	Mame
"Memory"	Cats	"What I Did for Love"	A Chorus Line

SCHOOLS FOR STARS

Even some of the most talented thespians have honed their gifts in the classroom, as indicated by the alumni rolls of these five career-nurturing institutions.

CARNEGIE MELLON SCHOOL OF DRAMA

Shari Belafonte, actor
Steven Bochco, producer
Albert Brooks, actor/director
Ted Danson, actor
Iris Rainier Dart, novelist
Barbara Feldon, actor
Mark Frost, producer
Mariette Hartley, actor
Holly Hunter, actor
Jack Klugman, actor
Judith Light, actor
Burke Moses, actor
John Pasquin, director
George Peppard, actor
George Romero, director
Laura San Giacomo, actor
Ellen Travolta, actor
Michael Tucker, actor
Blair Underwood, actor
John Wells, producer

JUILLIARD SCHOOL DRAMA DIVISION

Christine Baranski, actor
Andre Braugher, actor
Kelsey Grammer, actor
William Hurt, actor
Laura Linney, actor
Patti LuPone, actor/singer
Val Kilmer, actor
Kevin Kline, actor/director
Linda Kozlowski, actor
Kelly McGillis, actor
Elizabeth McGovern, actor
Mandy Patinkin, actor/singer
Christopher Reeve, actor
Ving Rhames, actor
Kevin Spacey, actor
Jeanne Tripplehorn, actor
Robin Williams, actor

NEW YORK UNIVERSITY, TISCH SCHOOL OF THE ARTS

Alec Baldwin, actor
Barry Bostwick, actor
Joel Coen, screenwriter
Billy Crudup, actor
Kathryn Erbe, actor
Bridget Fonda, actor
Lisa Gay Hamilton, actor
Marcia Gay Harden, actor
Kristen Johnston, actor
Tony Kushner, playwright
Eriq LaSalle, actor
Spike Lee, director/screenwriter/actor
Camryn Manheim, actor
Andrew McCarthy, actor
Jerry O'Connell, actor
Adam Sandler, actor
Kevin Spacey, actor
Stephen Spinella, actor
D. B. Sweeney, actor
Skeet Ulrich, actor
George C. Wolfe, director

NORTHWESTERN UNIVERSITY SCHOOL OF SPEECH

Ann-Margret, actor/dancer
Warren Beatty, actor
Richard Benjamin, actor
Karen Black, actor
Brad Hall, actor
Charlton Heston, actor
Sherry Lansing, producer
Shelly Long, actor
Julia Louis-Dreyfus, actor
Dermot Mulroney, actor
Patricia Neal, actor
Jerry Orbach, actor
Paula Prentiss, actor
Tony Randall, actor
Tony Roberts, actor
David Schwimmer, actor
Peter Strauss, actor
Kimberly Williams, actor

YALE SCHOOL OF DRAMA

Angela Bassett, actor
Robert Brustein, director/writer
David Duchovny, actor
Christopher Durang, playwright
Charles S. Dutton, actor
Jill Eikenberry, actor
David Alan Grier, actor
John Guare, playwright
A. R. Gurney, playwright
Julie Harris, actor
Tama Janowitz, writer
Elia Kazan, director
Stacy Keach, actor
Mark Linn-Baker, actor
Santo Loquasto, set designer
Frances McDormand, actor
Paul Newman, actor
Carrie Nye, actor
Tony Shalhoub, actor
Talia Shire, actor
Meryl Streep, actor
Ted Tally, playwright/screenwriter
John Turturro, actor/director
Joan Van Ark, actor
Courtney B. Vance, actor
Wendy Wasserstein, playwright
Sigourney Weaver, actor
Edmund Wilson, writer
Henry Winkler, actor/director

MAJOR SHOWS THAT BEGAN IN REGIONAL THEATERS

Beginning in the '70s, the creative impetus in American drama began to shift away from the increasingly expensive Broadway venues and toward regional and nonprofit theaters. While most major playwrights once wrote directly for Broadway production, regional theaters have more commonly become the place of origination for America's most important plays. The following productions may have gone on to national and even international fame, but they all began in regional theaters.

American Buffalo, by David Mamet, Goodman Theater, Chicago

Angels in America, by Tony Kushner, Eureka Theatre Company, San Francisco

Annie, by Thomas Meehan, Martin Charnin, and Charles Strouse, Goodspeed Opera House, East Haddam, Connecticut

Big River, adapted by William Hauptman from Mark Twain, La Jolla Playhouse, La Jolla, California

Buried Child, by Sam Shepard, Magic Theater, San Francisco

California Suite, by Neil Simon, Hartman Theatre, Stamford, Connecticut

Children of a Lesser God, by Mark Medoff, Mark Taper Forum, Los Angeles

The Colored Museum, by George C. Wolfe, Crossroads Theatre Company, New Brunswick, New Jersey

Conversations with My Father, by Herb Gardner, Seattle Repertory Theatre

Crimes of the Heart, by Beth Henley, Actors Theatre of Louisville

Eastern Standard, by Richard Greenberg, Seattle Repertory Theatre

Fences, by August Wilson, Yale Repertory Theatre, New Haven, Connecticut

The Gin Game, by D. L. Coburn, Long Wharf Theatre, New Haven, Connecticut

Glengarry Glen Ross, by David Mamet, Goodman Theatre, Chicago

The Heidi Chronicles, by Wendy Wasserstein, Seattle Repertory Theatre

How to Succeed in Business Without Really Trying, La

BROADWAY: PRICEY, DICEY, BUT FILLING SEATS

Theater attendance picked up again, even as ticket prices raced the moon. (Source: *Variety*)

Year	Average Ticket Price	Attendance	Year	Average Ticket Price	Attendance
1975-76	$9.86	7,181,898	1988-89	32.88	7,968,273
1976-77	10.60	8,815,095	1989-90	35.24	8,039,106
1977-78	12.05	8,621,262	1990-91	36.53	7,314,138
1978-79	14.02	9,115,613	1991-92	39.69	7,365,528
1979-80	15.29	9,380,648	1992-93	41.71	7,856,727
1980-81	17.97	10,822,324	1993-94	43.87	8,116,031
1981-82	22.07	10,025,788	1994-95	44.92	9,044,763
1982-83	25.07	8,102,262	1995-96	46.06	9,468,210
1983-84	28.68	7,898,765	1996-97	48.40	10,318,217
1984-85	29.06	7,156,683	1997-98	49.39	11,283,378
1985-86	29.20	6,527,498	1998-99	50.68	11,605,278
1986-87	29.74	6,968,277	1999-2000	53.02	11,365,309
1987-88	31.65	8,142,722	2000-20001	55.75	11,937,962

Jolla Playhouse, La Jolla, California

I'm Not Rappaport, by Herb Gardner, Seattle Repertory Theatre

In the Belly of the Beast, adapted by Adrian Hall from Jack Henry Abbott, Trinity Repertory Company, Providence, Rhode Island

Into the Woods, by James Lapine and Stephen Sondheim, Old Globe Theatre, San Diego

Jekyll & Hyde, by Frank Wildhorn, Alley Theatre, Houston, Texas

Jelly's Last Jam, by George C. Wolfe, Jelly Roll Morton, and Susan Birkenhead, Mark Taper Forum, Los Angeles

Joe Turner's Come and Gone, by August Wilson, Yale Repertory Theatre, New Haven, Connecticut

Love Letters, by A. R. Gurney, Long Wharf Theatre, New Haven, Connecticut

Ma Rainey's Black Bottom, by August Wilson, Yale Repertory Theatre, New Haven, Connecticut

Master Class, by Terrence McNally, Philadelphia Theater Company, Pennsylvania

"Master Harold"…and the Boys, by Athol Fugard, Yale Repertory Theatre, New Haven, Connecticut

'Night, Mother, by Marsha Norman, American Repertory Theatre, Cambridge, Massachusetts

Prelude to a Kiss, by Craig Lucas, South Coast Repertory, Costa Mesa, California

Quilters, by Molly Newman and Barbara Damashek, Denver Center Theatre Company

Streamers, by David Rabe, Long Wharf Theatre, New Haven, Connecticut

Twilight, by Anna Deavere Smith, Mark Taper Forum, Los Angeles, California

True West, by Sam Shepard, Steppenwolf Theatre Company, Chicago

Two Trains Running, by August Wilson, Yale Repertory Theatre, New Haven, Connecticut

The Wake of Jamey Foster, by Beth Henley, Hartford Stage Company, Hartford, Connecticut

The Who's "Tommy," by Pete Townshend and Wayne Cilento, La Jolla Playhouse, La Jolla, California

THE TONY AWARDS

	1947	1948	1949
Actor (Dramatic)	Fredric March, *Years Ago*; José Ferrer, *Cyrano de Bergerac*	Basil Rathbone, *The Heiress*; Henry Fonda, *Mister Roberts*; Paul Kelly, *Command Decision*	Rex Harrison, *Anne of the Thousand Days*
Actress (Dramatic)	Helen Hayes, *Happy Birthday*; Ingrid Bergman, *Joan of Lorraine*	Jessica Tandy, *A Streetcar Named Desire*; Judith Anderson, *Medea*; Katharine Cornell, *Antony and Cleopatra*	Martita Hunt, *The Madwoman of Chaillot*
Supporting Actor (Dramatic)	—	—	Arthur Kennedy, *Death of a Salesman*
Supporting Actress (Dramatic)	Patricia Neal, *Another Part of the Forest*	—	Shirley Booth, *Goodbye, My Fancy*
Play	—	*Mister Roberts*	*Death of a Salesman*
Actor (Musical)	—	Paul Hartman, *Angel in the Wings*	Ray Bolger, *Where's Charley?*
Actress (Musical)	—	Grace Hartman, *Angel in the Wings*	Nanette Fabray, *Love Life*
Supporting Actor (Musical)	David Wayne, *Finian's Rainbow*	—	—
Supporting Actress (Musical)	—	—	—
Musical	—	—	*Kiss Me Kate*
Director	Elia Kazan, *All My Sons*	—	Elia Kazan, *Death of a Salesman*
Score	—	—	Cole Porter, *Kiss Me Kate*
Author (Dramatic)	—	Thomas Heggen and Joshua Logan, *Mister Roberts*	Arthur Miller, *Death of a Salesman*
Author (Musical)	—		Bella and Samuel Spewack, *Kiss Me Kate*
Scenic Designer	—	Horace Armistead, *The Medium*	Jo Mielziner, *Sleepy Hollow; Summer and Smoke; Anne of the Thousand Days; Death of a Salesman; South Pacific*
Costume Designer	—	—	Lemuel Ayers, *Kiss Me Kate*
Choreographer	Agnes de Mille, *Brigadoon*; Michael Kidd, *Finian's Rainbow*	Jerome Robbins, *High Button Shoes*	Gower Champion, *Lend an Ear*
Producer (Dramatic)	—	Leland Hayward, *Mister Roberts*	Kermit Bloomgarden and Walter Fried, *Death of a Salesman*
Producer (Musical)	—	—	Saint-Subber and Lemuel Ayers, *Kiss Me Kate*
Conductor and Musical Director	—	—	Max Meth, *As the Girls Go*
Stage Technician	—	George Gebhardt; George Pierce	—

1950	1951	1952	1953
Sydney Blackmer, *Come Back, Little Sheba*	Claude Rains, *Darkness at Noon*	Jose Ferrer, *The Shrike*	Tom Ewell, *The Seven Year Itch*
Shirley Booth, *Come Back, Little Sheba*	Uta Hagen, *The Country Girl*	Julie Harris, *I Am a Camera*	Shirley Booth, *Time of the Cuckoo*
—	Eli Wallach, *The Rose Tattoo*	John Cromwell, *Point of No Return*	John Williams, *Dial M for Murder*
—	Maureen Stapleton, *The Rose Tattoo*	Marian Winters, *I Am a Camera*	Beatrice Straight, *The Crucible*
The Cocktail Party	*The Rose Tattoo*	*The Fourposter*	*The Crucible*
Ezio Pinza, *South Pacific*	Robert Alda, *Guys and Dolls*	Phil Silvers, *Top Banana*	Thomas Mitchell, *Hazel Flagg*
Mary Martin, *South Pacific*	Ethel Merman, *Call Me Madam*	Gertrude Lawrence, *The King and I*	Rosalind Russell, *Wonderful Town*
Myron McCormick, *South Pacific*	Russell Nype, *Call Me Madam*	Yul Brynner, *The King and I*	Hiram Sherman, *Two's Company*
Juanita Hall, *South Pacific*	Isabel Bigley, *Guys and Dolls*	Helen Gallagher, *Pal Joey*	Sheila Bond, *Wish You Were Here*
South Pacific	*Guys and Dolls*	*The King and I*	*Wonderful Town*
Joshua Logan, *South Pacific*	George S. Kaufman, *Guys and Dolls*	Jose Ferrer, *The Shrike; The Fourposter; Stalag 17*	Joshua Logan, *Picnic*
Richard Rodgers, *South Pacific*	Frank Loesser, *Guys and Dolls*	—	Leonard Bernstein, *Wonderful Town*
T.S. Eliot, *The Cocktail Party*	Tennessee Williams, *The Rose Tattoo*	—	Arthur Miller, *The Crucible*
Oscar Hammerstein II and Joshua Logan, *South Pacific*	Jo Swerling and Abe Burrows, *Guys and Dolls*	—	Joseph Fields and Jerome Chodorov, *Wonderful Town*
Jo Mielziner, *The Innocents*	Boris Aronson, *The Rose Tattoo; The Country Girl; Season in the Sun*	Jo Mielziner, *The King and I*	Raoul Pene du Bois, *Wonderful Town*
Aline Bernstein, *Regina*	Miles White, *Bless You All*	Irene Sharaff, *The King and I*	Miles White, *Hazel Flagg*
Helen Tamiris, *Touch and Go*	Michael Kidd, *Guys and Dolls*	Robert Alton, *Pal Joey*	Donald Saddler, *Wonderful Town*
Gilbert Miller, *The Cocktail Party*	Cheryl Crawford, *The Rose Tattoo*	—	Kermit Bloomgarden, *The Crucible*
Richard Rodgers, Oscar Hammerstein II, Leland Hayward, and Joshua Logan, *South Pacific*	Cy Feuer and Ernest H. Martin, *Guys and Dolls*	—	Robert Fryer, *Wonderful Town*
Maurice Abravanel, *Regina*	Lehman Engel, *The Consul*	Max Meth, *Pal Joey*	Lehman Engel, *Wonderful Town; Gilbert and Sullivan Season*
Joe Lynn, master propertyman, *Miss Liberty*	Richard Raven, *The Autumn Garden*	Peter Feller, master carpenter, *Call Me Madam*	Abe Kurnit, *Wish You Were Here*

	1954	1955	1956
Actor (Dramatic)	David Wayne, *The Teahouse of the August Moon*	Alfred Lunt, *Quadrille*	Paul Muni, *Inherit the Wind*
Actress (Dramatic)	Audrey Hepburn, *Ondine*	Nancy Kelly, *The Bad Seed*	Julie Harris, *The Lark*
Featured/Supporting Actor (Dramatic)	John Kerr, *Tea and Sympathy*	Francis L. Sullivan, *Witness for the Prosecution*	Ed Begley, *Inherit the Wind*
Featured/Supporting Actress (Dramatic)	Jo Van Fleet, *The Trip to Bountiful*	Patricia Jessel, *Witness for the Prosecution*	Una Merkel, *The Ponder Heart*
Play	*The Teahouse of the August Moon*	*The Desperate Hours*	*The Diary of Anne Frank*
Actor (Musical)	Alfred Drake, *Kismet*	Walter Slezak, *Fanny*	Ray Walston, *Damn Yankees*
Actress (Musical)	Dolores Gray, *Carnival in Flanders*	Mary Martin, *Peter Pan*	Gwen Verdon, *Damn Yankees*
Featured/Supporting Actor Role (Musical)	Harry Belafonte, *John Murray Anderson's Almanac*	Cyril Ritchard, *Peter Pan*	Russ Brown, *Damn Yankees*
Featured/Supporting Actress (Musical)	Gwen Verdon, *Can-Can*	Carol Haney, *The Pajama Game*	Lotte Lenya, *The Threepenny Opera*
Musical	*Kismet*	*The Pajama Game*	*Damn Yankees*
Director	Alfred Lunt, *Ondine*	Robert Montgomery, *The Desperate Hours*	Tyrone Guthrie, *The Matchmaker; Six Characters in Search of an Author; Tamburlaine the Great*
Director (Dramatic)	—	—	—
Director (Musical)	—	—	—
Score	Alexander Borodin, *Kismet*	Richard Adler and Jerry Ross, *The Pajama Game*	Richard Adler and Jerry Ross, *Damn Yankees*
Author (Dramatic)	John Patrick, *The Teahouse of the August Moon*	Joseph Hayes, *The Desperate Hours*	Frances Goodrich and Albert Hackett, *The Diary of Anne Frank*
Author (Musical)	Charles Lederer and Luther Davis, *Kismet*	George Abbott and Richard Bissell, *The Pajama Game*	George Abbott and Douglass Wallop, *Damn Yankees*
Scenic Designer	Peter Larkin, *Ondine; The Teahouse of the August Moon*	Oliver Messel, *House of Flowers*	Peter Larkin, *Inherit the Wind; No Time for Sergeants*
Costume Designer	Richard Whorf, *Ondine*	Cecil Beaton, *Quadrille*	Alvin Colt, *The Lark/Phoenix '55/Pipe Dream*
Choreographer	Michael Kidd, *Can-Can*	Bob Fosse, *The Pajama Game*	Bob Fosse, *Damn Yankees*
Producer (Dramatic)	Maurice Evans and George Schaefer, *The Teahouse of the August Moon*	Howard Erskine and Joseph Hayes, *The Desperate Hours*	Kermit Bloomgarden, *The Diary of Anne Frank*
Producer (Musical)	Charles Lederer, *Kismet*	Frederick Brisson, Robert Griffith, and Harold S. Prince, *The Pajama Game*	Frederick Brisson, Robert Griffith, Harold S. Prince in association with Albert B. Taylor, *Damn Yankees*
Conductor and Musical Director	Louis Adrian, *Kismet*	Thomas Schippers, *The Saint of Bleecker Street*	Hal Hastings, *Damn Yankees*
Stage Technician	John Davis, *Picnic*	Richard Rodda, *Peter Pan*	Harry Green, electrician and sound man, *The Middle of the Night; Damn Yankees*

1957

Fredric March, *Long Day's Journey into Night*

Margaret Leighton, *Separate Tables*

Frank Conroy, *The Potting Shed*

Peggy Cass, *Auntie Mame*

Long Day's Journey into Night

Rex Harrison, *My Fair Lady*

Judy Holliday, *Bells Are Ringing*

Sydney Chaplin, *Bells Are Ringing*

Edith Adams, *Li'l Abner*

My Fair Lady

Moss Hart, *My Fair Lady*

—

—

Frederick Loewe, *My Fair Lady*

Eugene O'Neill, *Long Day's Journey into Night*

Alan Jay Lerner, *My Fair Lady*

Oliver Smith, *A Clearing in the Woods; Candide; Auntie Mame; My Fair Lady; Eugenia; A Visit to a Small Planet*

Cecil Beaton, *Little Glass Clock/ My Fair Lady*

Michael Kidd, *Li'l Abner*

Leigh Connell, Theodore Mann, and Jose Quintero, *Long Day's Journey into Night*

Herman Levin, *My Fair Lady*

Franz Allers, *My Fair Lady*

Howard McDonald (posthumous), carpenter, *Major Barbara*

1958

Ralph Bellamy, *Sunrise at Campobello*

Helen Hayes, *Time Remembered*

Henry Jones, *Sunrise at Campobello*

Anne Bancroft, *Two for the Seesaw*

Sunrise at Campobello

Robert Preston, *The Music Man*

Gwen Verdon, *New Girl in Town;* Thelma Ritter, *New Girl in Town*

David Burns, *The Music Man*

Barbara Cook, *The Music Man*

The Music Man

—

Vincent J. Donehue, *Sunrise at Campobello*

—

Meredith Willson, *The Music Man*

Dore Schary, *Sunrise at Campobello*

Meredith Willson and Franklin Lacey, *The Music Man*

Oliver Smith, *West Side Story*

Motley, *The First Gentleman*

Jerome Robbins, *West Side Story*

Lawrence Langner, Theresa Helburn, Armina Marshall, and Dore Schary, *Sunrise at Campobello*

Kermit Bloomgarden, Herbert Greene, Frank Productions, *The Music Man*

Herbert Greene, *The Music Man*

Harry Romar, *Time Remembered*

1959

Jason Robards Jr., *The Disenchanted*

Gertrude Berg, *A Majority of One*

Charlie Ruggles, *The Pleasure of His Company*

Julie Newmar, *The Marriage-Go-Round*

J.B.

Richard Kiley, *Redhead*

Gwen Verdon, *Redhead*

Russell Nype, *Goldilocks;* cast of *La Plume de ma tante*

Pat Stanley, *Goldilocks;* cast of *La Plume de ma tante*

Redhead

Elia Kazan, *J.B.*

—

—

Albert Hague, *Redhead*

Archibald MacLeish, *J.B.*

Herbert and Dorothy Fields, Sidney Sheldon, and David Shaw, *Redhead*

Donald Oenslager, *A Majority of One*

Robert Ter-Arutunian, *Redhead*

Bob Fosse, *Redhead*

Alfred de Liagre, Jr., *J.B.*

Robert Fryer and Lawrence Carr, *Redhead*

Salvatore Dell'Isola, *Flower Drum Song*

Sam Knapp, *The Music Man*

1960

Melvyn Douglas, *The Best Man*

Anne Bancroft, *The Miracle Worker*

Roddy McDowall, *The Fighting Cock*

Anne Revere, *Toys in the Attic*

The Miracle Worker

Jackie Gleason, *Take Me Along*

Mary Martin, *The Sound of Music*

Tom Bosley, *Fiorello!*

Patricia Neway, *The Sound of Music*

Fiorello!

—

Arthur Penn, *The Miracle Worker*

George Abbott, *Fiorello!*

Jerry Bock, *Fiorello!;* Richard Rodgers, *The Sound of Music*

William Gibson, *The Miracle Worker*

Jerome Weidman and George Abbott, *Fiorello!;* Howard Lindsay and Russel Crouse, *The Sound of Music*

Howard Bey, *Toys in the Attic* (Dramatic); Oliver Smith, *The Sound of Music* (Musical)

Cecil Beaton, *Saratoga*

Michael Kidd, *Destry Rides Again*

Fred Coe, *The Miracle Worker*

Robert Griffith and Harold Prince, *Fiorello!;* Leland Hayward and Richard Halliday, *The Sound of Music*

Frederick Dvonch, *The Sound of Music*

John Walters, chief carpenter, *The Miracle Worker*

	1961	1962	1963
Actor (Dramatic)	Zero Mostel, *Rhinoceros*	Paul Scofield, *A Man for All Seasons*	Arthur Hill, *Who's Afraid of Virginia Woolf?*
Actress (Dramatic)	Joan Plowright, *A Taste of Honey*	Margaret Leighton, *Night of the Iguana*	Uta Hagen, *Who's Afraid of Virginia Woolf?*
Featured/Supporting Actor (Dramatic)	Martin Gabel, *Big Fish, Little Fish*	Walter Matthau, *A Shot in the Dark*	Alan Arkin, *Enter Laughing*
Featured/Supporting Actress (Dramatic)	Colleen Dewhurst, *All the Way Home*	Elizabeth Ashley, *Take Her, She's Mine*	Sandy Dennis, *A Thousand Clowns*
Play	*Becket*	*A Man for All Seasons*	*Who's Afraid of Virginia Woolf?*
Actor (Musical)	Richard Burton, *Camelot*	Robert Morse, *How to Succeed in Business Without Really Trying*	Zero Mostel, *A Funny Thing Happened on the Way to the Forum*
Actress (Musical)	Elizabeth Seal, *Irma La Douce*	Anna Maria Alberghetti, *Carnival*	Vivien Leigh, *Tovarich*
Featured/Supporting Actor (Musical)	Dick Van Dyke, *Bye, Bye Birdie*	Charles Nelson Reilly, *How to Succeed in Business Without Really Trying*	David Burns, *A Funny Thing Happened on the Way to the Forum*
Featured/Supporting Actress (Musical)	Tammy Grimes, *The Unsinkable Molly Brown*	Phyllis Newman, *Subways Are for Sleeping*	Anna Quayle, *Stop the World—I Want to Get Off*
Musical	*Bye, Bye Birdie*	*How to Succeed in Business Without Really Trying*	*A Funny Thing Happened on the Way to the Forum*
Director (Dramatic)	John Gielgud, *Big Fish, Little Fish*	Noel Willman, *A Man for All Seasons*	Alan Schneider, *Who's Afraid of Virginia Woolf?*
Director (Musical)	Gower Champion, *Bye, Bye Birdie*	Abe Burrows, *How to Succeed in Business Without Really Trying*	George Abbott, *A Funny Thing Happened on the Way to the Forum*
Score	—	Richard Rodgers, *No Strings*	Lionel Bart, *Oliver!*
Author (Dramatic)	Jean Anouilh, *Becket*	Robert Bolt, *A Man for All Seasons*	—
Author (Musical)	Michael Stewart, *Bye, Bye Birdie*	Abe Burrows, Jack Weinstock, and Willie Gilbert, *How to Succeed in Business Without Really Trying*	Burt Shevelove and Larry Gelbart, *A Funny Thing Happened on the Way to the Forum*
Scenic Designer	Oliver Smith, *Becket* (Dramatic); Oliver Smith, *Camelot* (Musical)	Will Steven Armstrong, *Carnival*	Sean Kenny, *Oliver!*
Costume Designer	Motley, *Becket;* Adrian and Tony Duquette, *Camelot*	Lucinda Ballard, *The Gay Life*	Anthony Powell, *The School for Scandal*
Choreographer	Gower Champion, *Bye, Bye Birdie*	Agnes de Mille, *Kwamina;* Joe Layton, *No Strings*	Bob Fosse, *Little Me*
Producer (Dramatic)	David Merrick, *Becket*	Robert Whitehead and Roger L. Stevens, *A Man for All Seasons*	Richard Barr and Clinton Wilder, Theatre 1963, *Who's Afraid of Virginia Woolf?*
Producer (Musical)	Edward Padula, *Bye, Bye Birdie*	Cy Feuer and Ernest Martin, *How to Succeed in Business Without Really Trying*	Harold Prince, *A Funny Thing Happened on the Way to the Forum*
Conductor and Musical Director	Franz Allers, *Camelot*	Elliot Lawrence, *How to Succeed in Business Without Really Trying*	Donald Pippin, *Oliver!*
Stage Technician	Teddy Van Bemmel, *Becket*	Michael Burns, *A Man for All Seasons*	—

1964	1965	1966	1967
Alec Guinness, *Dylan*	Walter Matthau, *The Odd Couple*	Hal Holbrook, *Mark Twain Tonight!*	Paul Rogers, *The Homecoming*
Sandy Dennis, *Any Wednesday*	Irene Worth, *Tiny Alice*	Rosemary Harris, *The Lion in Winter*	Beryl Reid, *The Killing of Sister George*
Hume Cronyn, *Hamlet*	Jack Albertson, *The Subject Was Roses*	Patrick Magee, *Marat/Sade*	Ian Holm, *The Homecoming*
Barbara Loden, *After the Fall*	Alice Ghostley, *The Sign in Sidney Brustein's Window*	Zoe Caldwell, *Slapstick Tragedy*	Marian Seldes, *A Delicate Balance*
Luther	*The Subject Was Roses*	*Marat/Sade*	*The Homecoming*
Bert Lahr, *Foxy*	Zero Mostel, *Fiddler on the Roof*	Richard Kiley, *Man of La Mancha*	Robert Preston, *I Do! I Do!*
Carol Channing, *Hello, Dolly!*	Liza Minnelli, *Flora, the Red Menace*	Angela Lansbury, *Mame*	Barbara Harris, *The Apple Tree*
Jack Cassidy, *She Loves Me*	Victor Spinetti, *Oh, What a Lovely War!*	Frankie Michaels, *Mame*	Joel Grey, *Cabaret*
Tessie O'Shea, *The Girl Who Came to Supper*	Maria Karnilova, *Fiddler on the Roof*	Beatrice Arthur, *Mame*	Peg Murray, *Cabaret*
Hello, Dolly!	*Fiddler on the Roof*	*Man of La Mancha*	*Cabaret*
Mike Nichols, *Barefoot in the Park*	Mike Nichols, *Luv; The Odd Couple*	Peter Brook, *Marat/Sade*	Peter Hall, *The Homecoming*
Gower Champion, *Hello, Dolly!*	Jerome Robbins, *Fiddler on the Roof*	Albert Marre, *Man of La Mancha*	Harold Prince, *Cabaret*
Jerry Herman, *Hello, Dolly!*	Jerry Bock and Sheldon Harnick, *Fiddler on the Roof*	Mitch Leigh and Joe Darion, *Man of La Mancha*	John Kander and Fred Ebb, *Cabaret*
John Osborne, *Luther*	Neil Simon, *The Odd Couple*	—	—
Michael Stewart, *Hello, Dolly!*	Joseph Stein, *Fiddler on the Roof*	—	—
Oliver Smith, *Hello, Dolly!*	Oliver Smith, *Baker Street; Luv; The Odd Couple*	Howard Bay, *Man of La Mancha*	Boris Aronson, *Cabaret*
Freddy Wittop, *Hello, Dolly!*	Patricia Zipprodt, *Fiddler on the Roof*	Gunilla Palmstierna-Weiss, *Marat/Sade*	Patricia Zipprodt, *Cabaret*
Gower Champion, *Hello, Dolly!*	Jerome Robbins, *Fiddler on the Roof*	Bob Fosse, *Sweet Charity*	Ronald Field, *Cabaret*
Herman Shumlin, *The Deputy*	Claire Nichtern, *Luv*	—	—
David Merrick, *Hello, Dolly!*	Harold Prince, *Fiddler on the Roof*	—	—
Shepard Coleman, *Hello, Dolly!*	—	—	—
—	—	—	—

	1968	1969	1970
Actor (Dramatic)	Martin Balsam, *You Know I Can't Hear You When the Water's Running*	James Earl Jones, *The Great White Hope*	Fritz Weaver, *Child's Play*
Actress (Dramatic)	Zoe Caldwell, *The Prime of Miss Jean Brodie*	Julie Harris, *Forty Carats*	Tammy Grimes, *Private Lives*
Featured/Supporting Actor (Dramatic)	James Patterson, *The Birthday Party*	Al Pacino, *Does a Tiger Wear a Necktie?*	Ken Howard, *Child's Play*
Featured/Supporting Actress (Dramatic)	Zena Walker, *Joe Egg*	Jane Alexander, *The Great White Hope*	Blythe Danner, *Butterflies Are Free*
Play	*Rosencrantz and Guildenstern Are Dead*	*The Great White Hope*	*Borstal Boy*
Actor (Musical)	Robert Goulet, *The Happy Time*	Jerry Orbach, *Promises, Promises*	Cleavon Little, *Purlie*
Actress (Musical)	Leslie Uggams, *Hallelujah, Baby!*; Patricia Routledge, *Darling of the Day*	Angela Lansbury, *Dear World*	Lauren Bacall, *Applause*
Featured/Supporting Actor (Musical)	Hiram Sherman, *How Now, Dow Jones*	Ronald Holgate, *1776*	Rene Auberjonois, *Coco*
Featured/Supporting Actress (Musical)	Lillian Hayman, *Hallelujah, Baby!*	Marian Mercer, *Promises, Promises*	Melba Moore, *Purlie*
Musical	*Hallelujah, Baby!*	*1776*	*Applause*
Director (Dramatic)	Mike Nichols, *Plaza Suite*	Peter Dews, *Hadrian VII*	Joseph Hardy, *Child's Play*
Director (Musical)	Gower Champion, *The Happy Time*	Peter Hunt, *1776*	Ron Field, *Applause*
Book (Musical)	—	—	—
Score	Jule Styne, Betty Comden, and Adolph Green, *Hallelujah, Baby!*	—	—
Scenic Designer	Desmond Heeley, *Rosencrantz and Guildenstern Are Dead*	Boris Aronson, *Zorba*	Howard Bay, *Cry for Us All*; Jo Mielziner, *Child's Play*
Costume Designer	Desmond Heeley, *Rosencrantz and Guildenstern Are Dead*	Louden Sainthill, *Canterbury Tales*	Cecil Beaton, *Coco*
Lighting Designer	—	—	Jo Mielziner, *Child's Play*
Choreographer	Gower Champion, *The Happy Time*	Joe Layton, *George M!*	Ron Field, *Applause*
Producer (Dramatic)	The David Merrick Arts Foundation, *Rosencrantz and Guildenstern Are Dead*	—	—
Producer (Musical)	Albert Selden, Hal James, Jane C. Nusbaum, and Harry Rigby, *Hallelujah, Baby!*	—	—

1971	1972	1973	1974
Brian Bedford, *The School for Wives*	Cliff Gorman, *Lenny*	Alan Bates, *Butley*	Michael Moriarty, *Find Your Way Home*
Maureen Stapleton, *The Gingerbread Lady*	Sada Thompson, *Twigs*	Julie Harris, *The Last of Mrs. Lincoln*	Colleen Dewhurst, *A Moon for the Misbegotten*
Paul Sand, *Story Theatre*	Vincent Gardenia, *The Prisoner of Second Avenue*	John Lithgow, *The Changing Room*	Ed Flanders, *A Moon for the Misbegotten*
Rae Allen, *And Miss Reardon Drinks a Little*	Elizabeth Wilson, *Sticks and Bones*	Leora Dana, *The Last of Mrs. Lincoln*	Frances Sternhagen, *The Good Doctor*
Sleuth	*Sticks and Bones*	*That Championship Season*	*The River Niger*
Hal Linden, *The Rothschilds*	Phil Silvers, *A Funny Thing Happened on the Way to the Forum* (Revival)	Ben Vereen, *Pippin*	Christopher Plummer, *Cyrano*
Helen Gallagher, *No, No, Nanette*	Alexis Smith, *Follies*	Glynis Johns, *A Little Night Music*	Virginia Capers, *Raisin*
Keene Curtis, *The Rothschilds*	Larry Blyden, *A Funny Thing Happened on the Way to the Forum* (Revival)	George S. Irving, *Irene*	Tommy Tune, *Seesaw*
Patsy Kelly, *No, No, Nanette*	Linda Hopkins, *Inner City*	Patricia Elliot, *A Little Night Music*	Janie Sell, *Over Here!*
Company	*Two Gentlemen of Verona*	*A Little Night Music*	*Raisin*
Peter Brook, *Midsummer Night's Dream*	Mike Nichols, *The Prisoner of Second Avenue*	A. J. Antoon, *That Championship Season*	Jose Quintero, *A Moon for the Misbegotten*
Harold Prince, *Company*	Harold Prince and Michael Bennett, *Follies*	Bob Fosse, *Pippin*	Harold Prince, *Candide*
George Furth, *Company*	John Guare and Mel Shapiro, *Two Gentlemen of Verona*	Hugh Wheeler, *A Little Night Music*	Hugh Wheeler, *Candide*
Stephen Sondheim, *Company*	Stephen Sondheim, *Follies*	Stephen Sondheim, *A Little Night Music*	Frederick Loewe (Music); Alan Jay Lerner (Lyrics), *Gigi*
Boris Aronson, *Company*	Boris Aronson, *Follies*	Tony Walton, *Pippin*	Franne and Eugene Lee, *Candide*
Raoul Pene du Bois, *No, No, Nanette*	Florence Klotz, *Follies*	Florence Klotz, *A Little Night Music*	Franne Lee, *Candide*
H. R. Poindexter, *Story Theatre*	Tharon Musser, *Follies*	Jules Fisher, *Pippin*	Jules Fisher, *Ulysses in Nighttown*
Donald Saddler, *No, No, Nanette*	Michael Bennett, *Follies*	Bob Fosse, *Pippin*	Michael Bennett, *Seesaw*
Helen Bonfils, Morton Gottlieb, and Michael White, *Sleuth*	—	—	—
Harold Prince, *Company*	—	—	—

	1975	1976	1977
Actor (Dramatic)	John Kani and Winston Ntshona, *Sizwe Banzi Is Dead & The Island*	John Wood, *Travesties*	Al Pacino, *The Basic Training of Pavlo Hummel*
Actress (Dramatic)	Ellen Burstyn, *Same Time, Next Year*	Irene Worth, *Sweet Bird of Youth*	Julie Harris, *The Belle of Amherst*
Featured Actor (Dramatic)	Frank Langella, *Seascape*	Edward Herrmann, *Mrs. Warren's Profession*	Jonathan Pryce, *Comedians*
Featured Actress (Dramatic)	Rita Moreno, *The Ritz*	Shirley Knight, *Kennedy's Children*	Trazana Beverley, *For Colored Girls Who Have Considered Suicide/When the Rainbow Is Enuf*
Play	*Equus*	*Travesties*	*The Shadow Box*
Actor (Musical)	John Cullum, *Shenandoah*	George Rose, *My Fair Lady*	Barry Bostwick, *The Robber Bridegroom*
Actress (Musical)	Angela Lansbury, *Gypsy*	Donna McKechnie, *A Chorus Line*	Dorothy Loudon, *Annie*
Featured Actor (Musical)	Ted Ross, *The Wiz*	Sammy Williams, *A Chorus Line*	Lenny Baker, *I Love My Wife*
Featured Actress (Musical)	Dee Dee Bridgewater, *The Wiz*	Carole Bishop, *A Chorus Line*	Delores Hall, *Your Arms Too Short to Box with God*
Musical	*The Wiz*	*A Chorus Line*	*Annie*
Director (Dramatic)	John Dexter, *Equus*	Ellis Rabb, *The Royal Family*	Gordon Davidson, *The Shadow Box*
Director (Musical)	Geoffrey Holder, *The Wiz*	Michael Bennett, *A Chorus Line*	Gene Saks, *I Love My Wife*
Book (Musical)	James Lee Barrett, *Shenandoah*	James Kirkwood and Nicholas Dante, *A Chorus Line*	Thomas Meehan, *Annie*
Score	Charlie Smalls (Music & Lyrics), *The Wiz*	Marvin Hamlisch (Music); Edward Kleban (Lyrics), *A Chorus Line*	Charles Strouse (Music); Martin Charnin (Lyrics), *Annie*
Scenic Designer	Carl Toms, *Sherlock Holmes*	Boris Aronson, *Pacific Overtures*	David Mitchell, *Annie*
Costume Designer	Geoffrey Holder, *The Wiz*	Florence Klotz, *Pacific Overtures*	Theoni V. Aldredge, *Annie;* Santo Loquasto, *The Cherry Orchard*
Lighting Designer	Neil Patrick Jampolis, *Sherlock Holmes*	Tharon Musser, *A Chorus Line*	Jennifer Tipton, *The Cherry Orchard*
Choreographer	George Faison, *The Wiz*	Michael Bennett and Bob Avian, *A Chorus Line*	Peter Gennaro, *Annie*
Reproduction of a Play or Musical	—	—	*Porgy and Bess*

1978	1979	1980	1981
Barnard Hughes, *Da*	Tom Conti, *Whose Life Is It Anyway?*	John Rubinstein, *Children of a Lesser God*	Ian McKellen, *Amadeus*
Jessica Tandy, *The Gin Game*	Constance Cummings, *Wings*; Carole Shelley, *The Elephant Man*	Phyllis Frelich, *Children of a Lesser God*	Jane Lapotaire, *Piaf*
Lester Rawlins, *Da*	Michael Gough, *Bedroom Farce*	David Rounds, *Morning's at Seven*	Brian Backer, *The Floating Light Bulb*
Ann Wedgeworth, *Chapter Two*	Joan Hickson, *Bedroom Farce*	Dinah Manoff, *I Ought to Be in Pictures*	Swoosie Kurtz, *Fifth of July*
Da	*The Elephant Man*	*Children of a Lesser God*	*Amadeus*
John Cullum, *On the Twentieth Century*	Len Cariou, *Sweeney Todd*	Jim Dale, *Barnum*	Kevin Kline, *The Pirates of Penzance*
Liza Minnelli, *The Act*	Angela Lansbury, *Sweeney Todd*	Patti LuPone, *Evita*	Lauren Bacall, *Woman of the Year*
Kevin Kline, *On the Twentieth Century*	Henderson Forsythe, *The Best Little Whorehouse in Texas*	Mandy Patinkin, *Evita*	Hinton Battle, *Sophisticated Ladies*
Nell Carter, *Ain't Misbehavin'*	Carlin Glynn, *The Best Little Whorehouse in Texas*	Priscilla Lopez, *A Day in Hollywood, a Night in the Ukraine*	Marilyn Cooper, *Woman of the Year*
Ain't Misbehavin'	*Sweeney Todd*	*Evita*	*42nd Street*
Melvin Bernhardt, *Da*	Jack Hofsiss, *The Elephant Man*	Vivian Matalon, *Morning's at Seven*	Peter Hall, *Amadeus*
Richard Maltby Jr., *Ain't Misbehavin'*	Harold Prince, *Sweeney Todd*	Harold Prince, *Evita*	Wilford Leach, *The Pirates of Penzance*
Betty Comden and Adolph Green, *On the Twentieth Century*	Hugh Wheeler, *Sweeney Todd*	Tim Rice, *Evita*	Peter Stone, *Woman of the Year*
Cy Coleman (Music); Betty Comden and Adolph Green (Lyrics), *On the Twentieth Century*	Stephen Sondheim (Music & Lyrics), *Sweeney Todd*	Andrew Lloyd Webber (Music); Tim Rice (Lyrics), *Evita*	John Kander (Music); Fred Ebb (Lyrics), *Woman of the Year*
Robin Wagner, *On the Twentieth Century*	Eugene Lee, *Sweeney Todd*	John Lee Beatty, *Talley's Folly*; David Mitchell, *Barnum*	John Bury, *Amadeus*
Edward Gorey, *Dracula*	Franne Lee, *Sweeney Todd*	Theoni V. Aldredge, *Barnum*	Willa Kim, *Sophisticated Ladies*
Jules Fisher, *Dancin'*	Roger Morgan, *The Crucifer of Blood*	David Hersey, *Evita*	John Bury, *Amadeus*
Bob Fosse, *Dancin'*	Michael Bennett and Bob Avian, *Ballroom*	Tommy Tune and Thommie Walsh, *A Day in Hollywood, a Night in the Ukraine*	Gower Champion, *42nd Street*
Dracula	—	Elizabeth I. McCann, Nelle Nugent, Ray Larsen, producers, *Morning's at Seven*	Joseph Papp, producer, *The Pirates of Penzance*

	1982	1983	1984
Actor (Dramatic)	Roger Rees, *The Life and Adventures of Nicholas Nickleby*	Harvey Fierstein, *Torch Song Trilogy*	Jeremy Irons, *The Real Thing*
Actress (Dramatic)	Zoë Caldwell, *Medea*	Jessica Tandy, *Foxfire*	Glenn Close, *The Real Thing*
Featured Actor (Dramatic)	Zakes Mokae, *"Master Harold"...and the Boys*	Matthew Broderick, *Brighton Beach Memoirs*	Joe Mantegna, *Glengarry Glen Ross*
Featured Actress (Dramatic)	Amanda Plummer, *Agnes of God*	Judith Ivey, *Steaming*	Christine Baranski, *The Real Thing*
Play	*The Life and Adventures of Nicholas Nickleby*	*Torch Song Trilogy*	*The Real Thing*
Actor (Musical)	Ben Harney, *Dreamgirls*	Tommy Tune, *My One and Only*	George Hearn, *La Cage aux folles*
Actress (Musical)	Jennifer Holliday, *Dreamgirls*	Natalia Makarova, *On Your Toes*	Chita Rivera, *The Rink*
Featured Actor (Musical)	Cleavant Derricks, *Dreamgirls*	Charles "Honi" Coles, *My One and Only*	Hinton Battle, *The Tap Dance Kid*
Featured Actress (Musical)	Liliane Montevecchi, *"Nine"*	Betty Buckley, *Cats*	Lila Kedrova, *Zorba*
Musical	*"Nine"*	*Cats*	*La Cage aux folles*
Director (Dramatic)	Trevor Nunn and John Caird, *The Life and Adventures of Nicholas Nickleby*	Gene Saks, *Brighton Beach Memoirs*	Mike Nichols, *The Real Thing*
Director (Musical)	Tommy Tune, *"Nine"*	Trevor Nunn, *Cats*	Arthur Laurents, *La Cage aux folles*
Book (Musical)	Tom Eyen, *Dreamgirls*	T. S. Eliot, *Cats*	Harvey Fierstein, *La Cage aux folles*
Score	Maury Yeston (Music & Lyrics), *"Nine"*	Andrew Lloyd Webber (Music); T. S. Eliot (Lyrics), *Cats*	Jerry Herman (Music & Lyrics), *La Cage aux folles*
Scenic Designer	John Napier and Dermot Hayes, *The Life and Adventures of Nicholas Nickleby*	Ming Cho Lee, *K2*	Tony Straiges, *Sunday in the Park with George*
Costume Designer	William Ivey Long, *"Nine"*	John Napier, *Cats*	Theoni V. Aldredge, *La Cage aux folles*
Lighting Designer	Tharon Musser, *Dreamgirls*	David Hersey, *Cats*	Richard Nelson, *Sunday in the Park with George*
Choreographer	Michael Bennett and Michael Peters, *Dreamgirls*	Thommie Walsh and Tommy Tune, *My One and Only*	Danny Daniels, *The Tap Dance Kid*
Reproduction of a Play or Musical	Barry and Fran Weissler, CBS Video Enterprises, Don Gregory, producers, *Othello*	Alfred De Liagre Jr., Roger L. Stevens, John Mauceri, Donald R. Seawell, Andre Pastoria, producers, *On Your Toes*	Robert Whitehead, Roger L. Stevens, producers, *Death of a Salesman*

1985	1986	1987	1988
Derek Jacobi, *Much Ado About Nothing*	Judd Hirsch, *I'm Not Rappaport*	James Earl Jones, *Fences*	Ron Silver, *Speed-the-Plow*
Stockard Channing, *Joe Egg*	Lily Tomlin, *The Search for Signs of Intelligent Life in the Universe*	Linda Lavin, *Broadway Bound*	Joan Allen, *Burn This*
Barry Miller, *Biloxi Blues*	John Mahoney, *The House of Blue Leaves*	John Randolph, *Broadway Bound*	B. D. Wong, *M. Butterfly*
Judith Ivey, *Hurlyburly*	Swoosie Kurtz, *The House of Blue Leaves*	Mary Alice, *Fences*	L. Scott Caldwell, *Joe Turner's Come and Gone*
Biloxi Blues	*I'm Not Rappaport*	*Fences*	*M. Butterfly*
—	George Rose, *The Mystery of Edwin Drood*	Robert Lindsay, *Me and My Girl*	Michael Crawford, *The Phantom of the Opera*
—	Bernadette Peters, *Song & Dance*	Maryann Plunkett, *Me and My Girl*	Joanna Gleason, *Into the Woods*
Ron Richardson, *Big River*	Michael Rupert, *Sweet Charity*	Michael Maguire, *Les Misérables*	Bill McCutcheon, *Anything Goes*
Leilani Jones, *Grind*	Bebe Neuwirth, *Sweet Charity*	Frances Ruffelle, *Les Misérables*	Judy Kaye, *The Phantom of the Opera*
Big River	*The Mystery of Edwin Drood*	*Les Misérables*	*The Phantom of the Opera*
Gene Saks, *Biloxi Blues*	Jerry Zaks, *The House of Blue Leaves*	Lloyd Richards, *Fences*	John Dexter, *M. Butterfly*
Des McAnuff, *Big River*	Wilford Leach, *The Mystery of Edwin Drood*	Trevor Nunn and John Caird, *Les Misérables*	Harold Prince, *The Phantom of the Opera*
William Hauptman, *Big River*	Rupert Holmes, *The Mystery of Edwin Drood*	Alain Boublil and Claude-Michel Schönberg, *Les Misérables*	James Lapine, *Into the Woods*
Roger Miller (Music & Lyrics), *Big River*	Rupert Holmes (Music & Lyrics), *The Mystery of Edwin Drood*	Claude-Michel Schönberg (Music); Herbert Kretzmer, and Alain Boublil (Lyrics), *Les Misérables*	Stephen Sondheim (Music & Lyrics), *Into the Woods*
Heidi Landesman, *Big River*	Tony Walton, *The House of Blue Leaves*	John Napier, *Les Misérables*	Maria Bjornson, *The Phantom of the Opera*
Florence Klotz, *Grind*	Patricia Zipprodt, *Sweet Charity*	John Napier, *Starlight Express*	Maria Bjornson, *The Phantom of the Opera*
Richard Riddell, *Big River*	Pat Collins, *I'm Not Rappaport*	David Hersey, *Starlight Express*	Andrew Bridge, *The Phantom of the Opera*
—	Bob Fosse, *Big Deal*	Gillian Gregory, *Me and My Girl*	Michael Smuin, *Anything Goes*
The Shubert Organization, Emanuel Azenberg, Roger Berlind, Ivan Bloch, MTM Enterprises, Inc., producers, *Joe Egg*	Jerome Minskoff, James M. Nederlander, Arthur Rubin, Joseph Harris, producers, *Sweet Charity*	Jay H. Fuchs, Steven Warnick, Charles Patsos, producers, *All My Sons*	Lincoln Center Theater, Gregory Mosher, Bernard Gersten, producers, *Anything Goes*

	1989	1990	1991
Actor (Dramatic)	Philip Bosco, *Lend Me a Tenor*	Robert Morse, *Tru*	Nigel Hawthorne, *Shadowlands*
Actress (Dramatic)	Pauline Collins, *Shirley Valentine*	Maggie Smith, *Lettice & Lovage*	Mercedes Ruehl, *Lost in Yonkers*
Featured Actor (Dramatic)	Boyd Gaines, *The Heidi Chronicles*	Charles Durning, *Cat on a Hot Tin Roof*	Kevin Spacey, *Lost in Yonkers*
Featured Actress (Dramatic)	Christine Baranski, *Rumors*	Margaret Tyzack, *Lettice & Lovage*	Irene Worth, *Lost in Yonkers*
Play	*The Heidi Chronicles*	*The Grapes of Wrath*	*Lost in Yonkers*
Actor (Musical)	Jason Alexander, *Jerome Robbins' Broadway*	James Naughton, *City of Angels*	Jonathan Pryce, *Miss Saigon*
Actress (Musical)	Ruth Brown, *Black and Blue*	Tyne Daly, *Gypsy*	Lea Salonga, *Miss Saigon*
Featured Actor (Musical)	Scott Wise, *Jerome Robbins' Broadway*	Michael Jeter, *Grand Hotel, the Musical*	Hinton Battle, *Miss Saigon*
Featured Actress (Musical)	Debbie Shapiro, *Jerome Robbins' Broadway*	Randy Graff, *City of Angels*	Daisy Eagan, *The Secret Garden*
Musical	*Jerome Robbins' Broadway*	*City of Angels*	*The Will Rogers Follies*
Director (Dramatic)	Jerry Zaks, *Lend Me a Tenor*	Frank Galati, *The Grapes of Wrath*	Jerry Zaks, *Six Degrees of Separation*
Director (Musical)	Jerome Robbins, *Jerome Robbins' Broadway*	Tommy Tune, *Grand Hotel, the Musical*	Tommy Tune, *The Will Rogers Follies*
Book (Musical)	—	Larry Gelbart, *City of Angels*	Marsha Norman, *The Secret Garden*
Score	—	Cy Coleman (Music); David Zippel (Lyrics), *City of Angels*	Cy Coleman (Music); Betty Comden and Adolph Green (Lyrics), *The Will Rogers Follies*
Scenic Designer	Santo Loquasto, *Cafe Crown*	Robin Wagner, *City of Angels*	Heidi Landesman, *The Secret Garden*
Costume Designer	Claudio Segovia, Hector Orezzoli, *Black and Blue*	Santo Loquasto, *Grand Hotel, the Musical*	Willa Kim, *The Will Rogers Follies*
Lighting Design	Jennifer Tipton, *Jerome Robbins' Broadway*	Jules Fisher, *Grand Hotel, the Musical*	Jules Fisher, *The Will Rogers Follies*
Choreographer	Cholly Atkins, Henry LeTang, Frankie Manning, Fayard Nicholas, *Black and Blue*	Tommy Tune, *Grand Hotel, the Musical*	Tommy Tune, *The Will Rogers Follies*
Reproduction of a Play or Musical	Lincoln Center Theater, Gregory Mosher, Bernard Gersten, producers, *Our Town*	Barry and Fran Weissler, Kathy Levin, Barry Brown, producers, *Gypsy*	Barry and Fran Weissler, Pace Theatrical Group, producers, *Fiddler on the Roof*

1992	1993	1994	1995
Judd Hirsch, *Conversations with My Father*	Ron Leibman, *Angels in America: Millennium Approaches*	Stephen Spinella, *Angels in America: Perestroika*	Ralph Fiennes, *Hamlet*
Glenn Close, *Death and the Maiden*	Madeline Kahn, *The Sisters Rosensweig*	Diana Rigg, *Medea*	Cherry Jones, *The Heiress*
Larry Fishburne, *Two Trains Running*	Stephen Spinella, *Angels in America: Millennium Approaches*	Jeffrey Wright, *Angels in America: Perestroika*	John Glover, *Love! Valour! Compassion!*
Brid Brennan, *Dancing at Lughnasa*	Debra Monk, *Redwood Curtain*	Jane Adams, *An Inspector Calls*	Frances Sternhagen, *The Heiress*
Dancing at Lughnasa	*Angels in America: Millennium Approaches*	*Angels in America: Perestroika*	*Love! Valour! Compassion!*
Gregory Hines, *Jelly's Last Jam*	Brent Carver, *Kiss of the Spider Woman—The Musical*	Boyd Gaines, *She Loves Me*	Matthew Broderick, *How to Succeed in Business Without Really Trying*
Faith Prince, *Guys and Dolls*	Chita Rivera, *Kiss of the Spider Woman—The Musical*	Donna Murphy, *Passion*	Glenn Close, *Sunset Boulevard*
Scott Waara, *The Most Happy Fella*	Anthony Crivello, *Kiss of the Spider Woman—The Musical*	Jarrod Emick, *Damn Yankees*	George Hearn, *Sunset Boulevard*
Tonya Pinkins, *Jelly's Last Jam*	Andrea Martin, *My Favorite Year*	Audra Ann McDonald, *Carousel*	Gretha Boston, *Show Boat*
Crazy for You	*Kiss of the Spider Woman—The Musical*	*Passion*	*Sunset Boulevard*
Patrick Mason, *Dancing at Lughnasa*	George C. Wolfe, *Angels in America: Millennium Approaches*	Stephen Daldry, *An Inspector Calls*	Gerald Gutierrez, *The Heiress*
Jerry Zaks, *Guys and Dolls*	Des McAnuff, *The Who's Tommy*	Nicholas Hynter, *Carousel*	Harold Prince, *Show Boat*
William Finn and James Lapine, *Falsettos*	Terrence McNally, *Kiss of the Spider Woman—The Musical*	James Lapine, *Passion*	Christopher Hampton and Don Black, *Sunset Boulevard*
William Finn, *Falsettos*	John Kander (Music), Fred Ebb (Lyrics), *Kiss of the Spider Woman—The Musical;* Pete Townshend (Music and Lyrics), *The Who's Tommy*	Stephen Sondheim, *Passion*	Andrew Lloyd Webber (music), Christopher Hampton and Don Black (lyrics), *Sunset Boulevard*
Tony Walton, *Guys and Dolls*	John Arnone, *The Who's Tommy*	Bob Crowley, *Carousel*	John Napier, *Sunset Boulevard*
William Ivey Long, *Crazy for You*	Florence Klotz, *Kiss of the Spider Woman—The Musical*	Ann Hould-Ward, *Beauty and the Beast*	Florence Klotz, *Show Boat*
Jules Fisher, *Jelly's Last Jam*	Chris Parry, *The Who's Tommy*	Rick Fisher, *An Inspector Calls*	Andrew Bridge, *Sunset Boulevard*
Susan Stroman, *Crazy for You*	Wayne Cilento, *The Who's Tommy*	Kenneth McMillan, *Carousel*	Susan Stroman, *Show Boat*
Dodger Productions, Roger Berlind, Jujamcyn Theaters/TV Asahi, Kardana Productions, John F. Kennedy Center for the Performing Arts, producers, *Guys and Dolls*	Roundabout Theatre Company, Todd Haimes, producers, *Anna Christie*	Noel Pearson, the Shubert Organization, Capital Cities/ABC, Joseph Harris, producers, *An Inspector Calls* (Dramatic); Lincoln Center Theater, Andre Bishop, Bernard Gersten, the Royal National Theater, Cameron Mackintosh, the Rodgers & Hammerstein Organization, producers, *Carousel* (Musical)	Lincoln Center Theater, Andre Bishop, Bernard Gersten, producers, *The Heiress* (Dramatic); Livent (U.S.) Inc., producer, *Show Boat* (Musical)

	1996	1997	1998
Actor (Dramatic)	George Grizzard, *A Delicate Balance*	Christopher Plummer, *Barrymore*	Anthony LaPaglia, *A View from the Bridge*
Actress (Dramatic)	Zoë Caldwell, *Master Class*	Janet McTeer, *A Doll's House*	Marie Mullen, *The Beauty Queen of Leenane*
Featured Actor (Dramatic)	Ruben Santiago-Hudson, *Seven Guitars*	Owen Teale, *A Doll's House*	Tom Murphy, *The Beauty Queen of Leenane*
Featured Actress (Dramatic)	Audra McDonald, *Master Class*	Lynne Thigpen, *An American Daughter*	Anna Manahan, *The Beauty Queen of Leenane*
Play	*Master Class*	*The Last Night of Ballyhoo*	*Art*
Actor (Musical)	Nathan Lane, *A Funny Thing Happened on the Way to the Forum*	James Naughton, *Chicago*	Alan Cumming, *Cabaret*
Actress (Musical)	Donna Murphy, *Passion*	Bebe Neuwirth, *Chicago*	Natasha Richardson, *Cabaret*
Featured Actor (Musical)	Wilson Jermain Heredia, *Rent*	Chuck Cooper, *The Life*	Ron Rifkin, *Cabaret*
Featured Actress (Musical)	Ann Duquesnay, *Bring in 'Da Noise, Bring in 'Da Funk*	Lillias White, *The Life*	Audra McDonald, *Ragtime*
Musical	*Rent*	*Titanic*	*The Lion King*
Director (Dramatic)	Gerald Gutierrez, *A Delicate Balance*	Anthony Page, *A Doll's House*	Garry Hynes, *The Beauty Queen of Leenane*
Director (Musical)	George C. Wolfe, *Bring in 'Da Noise, Bring in 'Da Funk*	Walter Bobbie, *Chicago*	Julie Taymor, *The Lion King*
Book (Musical)	Jonathan Larson, *Rent*	Peter Stone, *Titanic*	Terrence McNally, *Ragtime*
Score	Jonathan Larson, *Rent*	Maury Yeston, *Titanic*	Stephen Flaherty (music); Lynn Ahrens (lyrics), *Ragtime*
Scenic Designer	Brian Thomson, *The King and I*	Stewart Laing, *Titanic*	Richard Hudson, *The Lion King*
Costume Designer	Roger Kirk, *The King and I*	Judith Dolan, *Candide*	Julie Taymor, *The Lion King*
Lighting Designer	Jules Fisher and Peggy Eisenhauer, *Bring in 'Da Noise, Bring in 'Da Funk*	Ken Billington, *Chicago*	Donald Holder, *The Lion King*
Choreographer	Savion Glover, *Bring in 'Da Noise, Bring in 'Da Funk*	Ann Reinking, *Chicago*	Garth Fagan, *The Lion King*
Orchestration	—	Jonathan Tunick, *Titanic*	William David Brohn, *Ragtime*
Reproduction of a Play or Musical	Lincoln Center Theater, producer, *A Delicate Balance* (Dramatic); Dodger Productions, the John F. Kennedy Center for the Performing Arts, James M. Nederlander, Perseus Productions, John Frost, The Adelaide Festival Center, the Rodgers and Hammerstein Organization, producers, *The King and I* (Musical)	Bill Kenwright, Thelma Holt, producers, *A Doll's House* (Dramatic); Barry Weissler, Fran Weissler, Kardana Prods. Inc., producers, *Chicago* (Musical)	Roundabout Theater Co., Todd Haimes, Ellen Richard, Roger Berlind, James M. Nederlander, Nathaniel Kramer, Elizabeth Ireland McCann, Roy Gabay, Old Ivy Prods., producers, *A View from the Bridge* (Dramatic); Roundabout Theater Co., Todd Haimes, Ellen Richard, *Cabaret* (Musical)

1999	2000	2001
Brian Dennehy, *Death of a Salesman*	Stephen Dillane, *The Real Thing*	Richard Easton, *The Invention of Love*
Judi Dench, *Amy's View*	Jennifer Ehle, *The Real Thing*	Mary Louise Parker, *Proof*
Frank Wood, *Side Man*	Roy Dotrice, *A Moon for the Misbegotten*	Robert Sean Leonard, *The Invention of Love*
Elizabeth Franz, *Death of a Salesman;* Claire Bloom, *Electra*	Blair Brown, *Copenhagen*	Viola Davis, *King Hedley II*
Side Man	*Copenhagen*	*Proof*
Martin Short, *Little Me*	Brian Stokes Mitchell, *Kiss Me Kate*	Nathan Lane, *The Producers*
Bernadette Peters, *Annie Get Your Gun*	Heather Headley, *Aida*	Christine Ebersole, *42nd Street*
Roger Bart, *You're a Good Man, Charlie Brown*	Boyd Gaines, *Contact*	Gary Beach, *The Producers*
Kristin Chenoweth, *You're a Good Man, Charlie Brown*	Karen Ziemba, *Contact*	Cady Huffman, *The Producers*
Fosse	*Contact*	*The Producers*
Robert Falls, *Death of a Salesman*	Michael Blakemore, *Copenhagen*	Daniel Sullivan, *Proof*
Matthew Bourne, *Swan Lake*	Michael Blakemore, *Kiss Me Kate*	Susan Stroman, *The Producers*
Alfred Uhry, *Parade*	James Joyce's *The Dead*	Mel Brooks, *The Producers*
Jason Robert Brown, *Parade*	Elton John, *Aida*	Mel Brooks, *The Producers*
Richard Hoover, *Not About Nightingales*	Bob Crowley, *Aida*	Robin Wagner, *The Producers*
Lez Brotherston, *Swan Lake*	Martin Pakledinaz, *Kiss Me, Kate*	William Ivey Long, *The Producers*
Andrew Bridge, *Fosse*	Natasha Katz, *Aida*	Peter Kaczorowski, *The Producers*
Matthew Bourne, *Swan Lake*	Susan Stroman, *Contact*	Susan Stroman, *The Producers*
Ralph Burns & Douglas Besterman, *Fosse*	Don Sebesky, *Kiss Me, Kate*	Douglas Besterman, *The Producers*
Death of a Salesman (Dramatic); *Annie Get Your Gun* (Musical)	*The Real Thing* (Dramatic); *Kiss Me, Kate* (Musical)	*One Flew Over the Cuckoo's Nest* (Dramatic); *42nd Street* (Musical)

PEOPLE
EXTRAS

THE MOST INTRIGUING PEOPLE: 1974–PRESENT

Every December, in the Christmas double issue, the PEOPLE editors single out the 25 most intriguing people of the past year. We reprint here the complete roll of honorees, with a brief description for each, to remind readers of the notable and notorious from the past 27 years.

1974

Gerald Ford	The new president copes.
Patty Hearst	Kidnapped heiress turns terrorist.
Joe Hirshhorn	Establishes Smithsonian's new Hirshhorn Museum.
Kay Graham	Publisher of the Watergate-breaking *Washington Post* prevails.
Yasir Arafat	Addresses the United Nations.
Faye Dunaway	Stars in *Chinatown, The Towering Inferno,* and *Three Days of the Condor.*
Alexander Solzhenitsyn	Russian exile wins the Nobel.
Nelson Rockefeller	The vice president–elect gets a financial grilling from Congress.
Leon Jaworski	The Watergate prosecutor.
Erica Jong	Author scores with *Fear of Flying.*
Francis Ford Coppola	*Godfather II* confirms him as cinema's creative king.
Muhammad Ali	The champ wants another son.
Pat Nixon	The former First Lady deals stoically.
John Glenn	Could the Ohio senator be the Ike of the '70s?
Sherlock Holmes	He's the most omnipresent literary figure of 1974.
Carter Heyward	One of 11 women ordained as Episcopal priests.
Stevie Wonder	A blind artist brings soul to his music.
Alexander Calder	It seems every U.S. city must have one of his mobiles.
Charlie Finley	The fiery owner of World Series–winning Oakland A's.
Ella Grasso	The first woman to capture a governorship without inheriting it from her husband.
J. Kenneth Jamieson	Exxon's chief has big profits and big problems.
Jimmy Connors	He catches fire; his romance catches cold.
Gunnar Myrdal	Nobel Prize winner in economics.
Valerie Harper	Rhoda's a winner on her own.
Mikhail Baryshnikov	The former Kirov Ballet star defects to Toronto.

1975

Betty Ford	The president's secret weapon.
Richard Zanuck	Son of Darryl F. makes his own name coproducing *Jaws.*
Frank E. Fitzsimmons	The boss of 2.2 million Teamsters.
Charles Manson	May have influenced Squeaky Fromme in her failed assassination attempt on President Ford.
Daniel Patrick Moynihan	Fighting Irishman at the U.N. talks tough.
James Coleman	The University of Chicago professor blamed for busing says it backfired.
Indira Gandhi	After six months of rule in India, her popularity soars.
Cher Bono Allman	The new First Lady of splitsville.
Andrei Sakharov	The Nobel Peace Prize winner.
Teng Hsiao-Ping	China's tough, blunt, outspoken leader.
Patty Hearst	Was she a terrorist or a victim?
Christina Onassis	The daughter of the late shipping magnate Aristotle Onassis marries her father's rival.
Leonard Matlovich	An Air Force sergeant is discharged after admitting his homosexuality.
Dolly Parton	Nashville's new queen-in-waiting.
Fred Lynn	All-American boy dazzles baseball in his miraculous rookie year.
Frank Borman	Ex-astronaut gets Eastern Airlines off the ground.
Rosemary Rogers	The master of the erotic gothic.
Werner Erhard	The smooth guru of est.
Woody Allen	Now a triple creative threat—actor, director, and author.
Marabel Morgan	The housewife behind *The Total Woman* cashes in on the antifeminist backlash.
Jerry Brown	California loves its young governor.
Don King	A flashy ex-con turned promoter is the new lord of the rings.
Hercule Poirot	The famed Belgian detective is killed by Dame Agatha Christie after 55 years.
Anwar Sadat	Egyptian president opens the Suez Canal, closed since the Six-Day War in 1967.
Gelsey Kirkland	The prima ballerina of the American Ballet dances a triumphant *Giselle.*

1976

Jimmy Carter	He wants to be the "citizen president."
Farrah Fawcett-Majors	An "Angel" turns into a star.
Andrew Wyeth	Is he America's most popular painter? The thought grieves some critics.
Betty Williams	An anguished mother asks Ulster to give peace a chance.
Andrew Young	The first black U.S. ambassador to the U.N.
Juan Carlos I	Spain's new king empowers the people.
Linda Ronstadt	From vagabond to country rock's First Lady.
Reverend Sun Myung Moon	Troubles build for the mysterious head of the Unification Church.
Bert Jones	Pro football's man with the golden arm.
Julius Nyerere	Tanzania's superstar of African diplomacy.
Carl Sagan	Viking I's expedition to Mars thrills would-be space explorer.
Fred Silverman	TV's superprogrammer switches to ABC.
Liz Ray	After affair with Representative Wayne Hays, she brings out a book and gets religion.
C. W. McCall	His "Convoy" is the year's bestselling single.
Shere Hite	Hotly read reporter on women's sexuality.
Donald Kendall	Pepsico's chief sells his drink to Soviets.
Vivian Reed	The star of *Bubbling Brown Sugar* proves that black is beautiful on Broadway.
Ron Kovic	Disabled Vietnam veteran turned antiwar activist was *Born on the Fourth of July.*
Chevy Chase	*Saturday Night*'s stumblebum is hot.
Regine	The queen mother of the disco craze.
Har Gobind Khorana	Gives world a man-made working gene.
Nadia Comaneci	The Romanian Olympic champion.
Robert Redford	Turns producer with *All the President's Men*.
Don Shomron	Led the Entebbe raid to save 105 hostages.
King Kong	Returning, courtesy of Dino De Laurentis.

1977

Jimmy Carter	The first year at 1600: he likes it.
Diane Keaton	Woody's flaky foil is *Looking for Mr. Goodbar.*
General Omar Torrijos	Ratify the canal treaties or bring in the marines, says Panama's strongman.
Steven Ross	The chairman-impresario of Warner Communications.
Midge Costanza	The president's pipeline to the people.
Anwar Sadat and Menachem Begin	The president of Egypt and the prime minister of Israel strive for peace.
Ted Turner	Cable entrepreneur and ball team owner.
Margaret Trudeau	Runaway wife of Canada's prime minister.
Robert Byrd	A self-made fiddler calls the tunes in the world's most exclusive club.
Susanne Albrecht	A brutal murder of an old friend makes her the dark queen of German terrorism.
Lily Tomlin	Wins a Tony for her one-woman show, *Appearing Nightly.*
Billy Carter	Ad spokesman to the masses.
Anita Bryant	After a *très* un-gay year, she's still praising God and passing the orange juice.
Shaun Cassidy	*Hardy Boy* moonlights as a pop star.
Jacqueline Onassis	Quits her editor's job and gets $25 million from stepdaughter Christina Onassis.
Jasper Johns	The enigmatic master of pop art.
Toni Morrison	Flies into the literary top rank.
Dr. Robert Linn	His liquid protein diet has him in fat city.
Tracy Austin	At 14, Wimbledon's youngest invitee ever.
Rosalyn Yalow	Winner of 1977's Nobel Prize for medicine.
Reggie Jackson	Yankee hot dog turns into a hero.
Stevie Nicks	Rock singer-songwriter casts a sexy spell.
George Lucas	A new "force" in film.
Princess Caroline	Grace and Rainier's girl will wed Junot.

1978

Jimmy Carter	Negotiates peace between Egypt and Israel, and looks for antidotes to rising inflation.
Pope John Paul II	A tough, ebullient Pole remolds the papacy.
Queen Noor al-Hussein	This blue-jeaned American queen is ready for a child.
G. William Miller	Fearless chairman of the Federal Reserve.
Teng Hsiao-Ping	The tough vice-premier of China.
Brooke Shields	Three movies, beaucoup bucks, no beau.
Melvin Gottlieb	The dream this Princeton physicist pursues is limitless energy from nuclear fusion.
Louise Brown	The first test-tube baby is doing just fine.
Reverend Jim Jones	Feeling threatened, he offers a deadly communion to his followers.
John Belushi	A hard act to outgross—in every way.

PEOPLE'S COVER CHAMPS

Their fame far exceeded the usual 15 minutes. The saga of their lives held readers rapt. Here are the titleholders for the most times featured on the cover of PEOPLE.

Personality	Number of Covers
Princess Diana	52
Julia Roberts	16
Elizabeth Taylor	14
Sarah Ferguson	13
Michael Jackson	13
Jacqueline Kennedy Onassis	13
Cher	11

Jim Fixx	His *The Complete Book of Running* is a runaway bestseller.
Garry Marshall	TV writer and producer of *Laverne and Shirley*, *Happy Days*, and *Mork and Mindy*.
Arlene Blum	The biochemist who led the first all-woman expedition up Annapurna, loses two fellow climbers.
Howard Jarvis	A crusader against high property taxes sees his Proposition 13 endorsed in California
Miss Piggy	The famed Muppet pig wants it all.
Luciano Pavarotti	It's supertenor, opera's newest sex symbol.
Cheryl Tiegs	This model aims to survive in the TV jungle.
Meat Loaf	Rock's newest (and heftiest) hero.
Sir Freddie Laker	The founder of the Skytrain revolutionized air fares with cheap transatlantic flights.
Nancy Lopez	Rookie Player and Golfer of the Year.
John Travolta	A solitary new superstar, besieged by fans.
James Crosby	Brings big-time gambling to Atlantic City.
John Irving	Down-to-earth Vermonter is on the bestseller list with *The World According to Garp*.
Donna Summer	The queen of disco is softening her act.
Burt Reynolds	A star working on a new image: sensitivity.

1979

Rosalynn Carter	The First Lady skirts the charge that she is involved in government policy formation.
Aleksandr Godunov	Volatile Russian dancer defects to the U.S.
Marvin Mitchelson	The divorce lawyer introduces "palimony."
Bo Derek	This *10* is bringing sex back to films.
Lee Iacocca	Struggles valiantly to get Chrysler into gear under the threat of bankruptcy.
Sly Stallone	His *Rocky II* is the biggest movie of the year.
Megan Marshack	Former vice president Nelson Rockefeller's secretary and companion on the night of his death is back in New York.
Mani Said al-Otaiba	Poetry-writing leader of a tamer OPEC.
Joan Kennedy	Sobers up to campaign alongside Ted.
Johnny Carson	Plans to give up his 17-year reign at NBC.
Ayatollah Khomeini	Iran's ruler leads his nation toward chaos.
Tom Wolfe	*The Right Stuff* is his latest and biggest.
Joan Baez	The brave anti-warrior raises her voice for the boat people and refugees of Cambodia.
Sebastian Coe	British runner prepares for the Olympics.
Gloria Vanderbilt	Her top-grossing jeans bring a new chic.
Bruce Babbitt	The Arizona governor and Three Mile Island investigator believes nuclear power is a necessary evil.
Meryl Streep	A big year for our most intelligent actress.
Willie Stargell	The beloved Pittsburgh Pirate is voted MVP.
Pope John Paul II	A fine first year for the new pope.

Paul Volcker	The frugal chairman of the Federal Reserve.
Jesse Jackson	Offers support and often inflammatory statements around the world.
Dan Aykroyd	Brilliant actor/writer moves on to movies.
Margaret Thatcher	The first female prime minister of England.
William Webster	America's top cop de-Hooverizes the FBI.
Deborah Harry	Taking disco to a new wavelength.

1980

Ronald Reagan	He wins the presidency by a landslide.
Goldie Hawn	*Private Benjamin* liberates a beloved ding-a-ling.
Lech Walesa	An unemployed electrician turns working-class hero to Poland—and the free world.
Colonel Charlie Beckwith	Heroic commander of the failed mission to rescue American hostages in Iran.
Herbert Boyer	Makes new strides in genetic engineering.
Mary Cunningham	Blond, beautiful, and no longer at Bendix, she's looking for room at the top.
Fidel Castro	Faces a new problem: Reagan.
Mel Weinberg	Con artist sets up Abscam for the FBI.
Sugar Ray Leonard	Tough little man wins boxing championship.
Robert Redford	Superstar directs a fine debut film.
Jean Harris	Was the death of Scarsdale Diet's Dr. Tarnower an accident? Only she knows.
Stephen King	Mild down-easter finds terror is the ticket.
Grete Waitz	The swift Norwegian runner leads the pack.
Baron St. Helens	English diplomat lives on—as a volcano.
The Reverend Jerry Falwell	A TV preacher sells America on flag, family, and freedom, of sorts.
Pat Benatar	Rock finds its missing lynx.
Lee Rich	The producer behind *Dallas*.
Sonia Johnson	A Mormon feminist in the ERA battle.
Sam Shepard	Mr. Funk of off-Broadway.
Richard Pryor	Having been through the fire, he's back with a new self.
Eudora Welty	Critics bow to this master Southern writer.
Soichiro Honda	The Henry Ford of Japanese autos.
Beverly Sills	Begins bossing the New York City Opera.
Dan Rather	Can he hold Walter Cronkite's CBS audience?
Brooke Shields	Nothing comes between her and success.

1981

Ronald Reagan	Survives an assassination attempt.
Elizabeth Taylor	Claims Tony nomination for her Broadway debut.
Lech Walesa	Poland's patriarch of Solidarity.
Bradford Smith	His Voyager project took us to the planets.

PEOPLE'S MOST BEAUTIFUL PEOPLE

Every year PEOPLE faces the difficult task of choosing only 50 of the most stunning celebrities we've seen all year. Here is the face of beauty in 2001, led by new six-timer Julia Roberts, and a look at the stars who have dazzled their way onto more than one of our Most Beautiful People lists.

6-TIMERS
Tom Cruise
Michelle Pfeiffer
Julia Roberts

5-TIMERS
Halle Berry
Mel Gibson
John F. Kennedy Jr.

4-TIMERS
George Clooney
Denzel Washington

3-TIMERS
Antonio Banderas
Juliette Binoche
Kevin Costner
Faith Hill
Nicole Kidman
Jennifer Lopez
Demi Moore
Brad Pitt
Claudia Schiffer
Catherine Zeta-Jones

2-Timers
Ben Affleck
Tyra Banks
Toni Braxton
Pierce Brosnan
Sandra Bullock
Cindy Crawford
Daniel Day-Lewis
Johnny Depp
Princess Diana
Leonardo DiCaprio
Taye Diggs

Emme
Whitney Houston
Kate Hudson
Helen Hunt
Matt Lauer
Jude Law
Jared Leto
Heather Locklear
Julianne Moore
Paul Newman
Gwyneth Paltrow
Freddie Prinze Jr.
Paulina Porizkova
Jason Priestley
Rebecca Romijn-Stamos
Isabella Rossellini
Winona Ryder
Jaclyn Smith
Hunter Tylo
Meredith Vieira
Katarina Witt

2001'S PICKS
Halle Berry
Juliette Binoche
Carole Black
Ellen Burstyn
Kobe Bryant
Laura Bush
George Clooney
Katie Couric
Blythe Danner
Benicio Del Toro
Johnny Depp
Taye Diggs
Gary Dourdan
Todd English
Colin Firth
Harold Ford Jr.

Paul Goodloe
Jon Gruden
Ed Harris
Dulé Hill
Faith Hill
Kate Hudson
Hugh Jackman
Heidi Klum
Beyoncé Knowles
Jude Law
Heath Ledger
Téa Leoni
Heather Locklear
Jennifer Lopez
Evan Lowenstein
Jaron Lowenstein
Evan Lowenstein
Jaron Lowenstein
Debra Messing
Julianne Moore
Connie Nielsen
Shane Osborn
Sydney Tamiia Poitier
Jeff Probst
Carl Quintanilla
Charlotte Rampling
Kelly Ripa
Julia Roberts
Alex Rodriguez
Jill Scott
Julia Stiles
Noah Wyle
Chow Yun-Fat
Renée Zellweger
Catherine Zeta-Jones
Zhang Ziyi

Bryant Gumbel	The new *Today* show host.
Crown Prince Fahd	The Saudi heir-apparent works for peace.
Rabbit Angstrom	John Updike's fictional hero returns.
Ted Turner	Stares down the big guns of network TV.
Princess Diana	Kindergarten teacher becomes princess.
Gloria Monty	Producer of ABC's *General Hospital*.
David Stockman	Reagan's budget director is nearly done in.
Lena Horne	How does the old broad do it? With glamour.
John McEnroe	The tennis superbrat is number one.
Edgar Bronfman	Seagram's liquor baron enlivens a year of corporate merger mania.
Barbara Mandrell	A new country queen takes on TV and wins.
Thomas Sowell	Reagan's favorite black intellectual doesn't like all the attention.
Wolfgang Amadeus Mozart	After two centuries, Austria's child prodigy has become the world's favorite composer.
Tom Selleck	The modest heartthrob of *Magnum P.I.*
Mick Jagger	Finds satisfaction with rock's richest tour.
Richard Viguerie	New Right's fundraiser purges Senate of Democrats.
Nicholas Nickleby	A $100-a-seat Broadway smash by Dickens.
Sandra Day O'Connor	A woman justice's work is never done.
Harrison Ford	The new breed of action star.
Fernando Valenzuela	Mexican rookie conjures baseball magic.
Elizabeth McGovern	A talented beauty soars to stardom.

1982

Ronald Reagan	Enjoys "confinement" in the White House.
Joan Jett	Rocks latest leading lady earns her stripes.
Ariel Sharon	Defiant Israeli defense minister battles on.
Princess Stephanie	Numbed by her mother's death.
Jessica Lange	Talented beauty breaks through in *Tootsie* and *Frances*.
Herschel Walker	Georgia's got football's best running back.
Larry Gelbart	After *M*A*S*H*, he writes the hit *Tootsie*.
Margaret Thatcher	Triumphs in a nasty war in the Falklands.
Dr. William DeVries	A surgeon installs the artificial heart.
Princess Diana	Britain's darling may have newlywed blues.
Yuri Andropov	Master spy takes over Brezhnev's Kremlin.
George Wallace	Seeks blacks' votes and forgiveness.
Paolo Rossi	Leads Italy to the World Cup.
Randall Forsberg	A scholar sounds call to (freeze) arms.
Norma Kamali	Fashion's Greta Garbo.
E.T.	An alien finds his home in Hollywood.
Richard Gere	*Officer* makes a star of a movie maverick.
Sam Knox	Offers consoling facts to herpes victims.
Andrew Lloyd Webber	Broadway's hottest composer strikes all the right notes.
Evelyn Waugh	*Brideshead Revisited* is the year's TV event.

Barbra Streisand	The Brooklyn songbird directs *Yentl*.
Ted Koppel	Revolutionizes night-owl journalism.
Kiri Te Kanawa	Opera diva claims title and acts nothing like a dame.
Reverend Sun Myung Moon	The Unification Church leader is convicted of tax evasion, but he still wins converts.
Paul Newman	*The Verdict* may win him elusive Oscar gold.
Bill Agee and Mary Cunningham	The Bendix takeover didn't take, but this couple makes one merger that works.

1983

Ronald Reagan	Bombs Syrian antiaircraft nests in the mountains east of Beirut.
Debra Winger	Hollywood star scores on her own *Terms*.
Fidel Castro	The aging lion pulls in his claws.
The Cabbage Patch Kids	Glassy of eye and poker of face, this chubby horde masks a plot to take over the planet.
Jesse Jackson	His campaign breeds fusion and fission for Democrats.
William Gates	A computer software whiz makes hard cash.
Sam Shepard	Stage and screen laureate wants anonymity.
Chun Byung In	Pilot of Korean Air Lines flight 007, shot down over Soviet airspace in August.
Mr. T	The show-business maniac of the year.
Ben Lexcen	Impish Aussie wins the America's Cup.
Joan Rivers	*Tonight Show* guest host skewers guests.
Robert Mastruzzi	A demanding Bronx high school principal.
Eddie Murphy	He makes folks mad, but he's got it made.
Matthew Broderick	Buttoned-down leader of young Hollywood.
Barbara McClintock	Discoverer of "jumping genes" wins Nobel.
Harvey Fierstein	Takes theater on a gay whirl with *La Cage*.
Philip Johnson	The grand old man of architecture.
Vanessa Williams	The first black Miss America.
Richard Chamberlain	The public hails the king of miniseries.
Michael Jackson	*Thriller* makes him the biggest star in pop.
Rei Kawakubo	Designs atonal, asymmetric sad rags.
Konrad Kujau	Nearly fools world with fake Führer's diaries.
Alice Walker	*The Color Purple* brings her a Pulitzer.
Alfred Hitchcock	Five buried treasures from the master of suspense are the movie event of 1983.
Jennifer Beals	A dancing Yalie changes into a flashy star.

1984

Geraldine Ferraro	A pioneer loses the battle for vice president.
Bruce Springsteen	The Boss becomes a symbol of America.
Andrei Gromyko	The poker face of Soviet foreign policy.
José Napoleón Duarte	El Salvador's gutsy president is its hope for emerging from a nightmare civil war.

Mary Lou Retton	The Olympian is Madison Avenue's million-dollar baby.
Richard Gere	His silence marks him as an enigma.
Peter Ueberroth	Organized the L.A. Olympic Games.
Joe Kittinger	Flies the Atlantic solo in a hot-air balloon.
Farrah Fawcett	This mother-to-be's career surges.
Clint Eastwood	Reveals darker dimensions in *Tightrope*.
Betty Ford	Publicly tackles her addiction problems.
John Malkovich	A versatile young Chicago actor stars on Broadway and in film.
John Henry	Geriatric equine trots coast to coast.
Sparky Anderson	Manages the Tigers to World Series victory.
Tina Turner	A "Soul Survivor" strides back into rock.
William Kennedy	Author collects a Pulitzer and a MacArthur.
Lee Iacocca	Chrysler's blunt philosopher offers a plan to fix the economy.
Vanessa Williams	The discovery that she had posed nude forces her resignation as Miss America.
Kathleen Turner	The hottest actress since Streep.
James Baker	Reagan's ageless but his chief of staff, perhaps coincidentally, is not.
Kathleen Morris	A controversial Minnesota prosecutor fights against sexual abuse of children.
John Torrington	Discovery of a 19th-century explorer sheds new light on the chilling fate of Britain's ill-fated Franklin expedition.
Bill Murray	Star of the year's biggest box-office hit.
Baby Fae	A child with a transplanted baboon heart.
Michael Jackson	PEOPLE ran five covers on him during 1984.

1985

Bob Geldof	Raises a cry with song to save the hungry.
Joe Kennedy	Bobby's eldest son announces for the congressional seat once held by Uncle Jack.
Corazon Aquino	Philippine housewife and presidential widow rides an emotional swell to political prominence.
Steven Rosenberg	Making big steps toward a cancer cure.
Rambo	His deeds are the stuff of cinema legend.
Akira Kurosawa	Japan's feisty grand old man of the movies triumphs with *Ran*.
Nelson Mandela	Imprisoned black leader may yet save South Africa from the horror of racial war.
William Perry	308-pound surprise of the football season.
Uli Derickson	TWA Flight 847's flight attendant becomes the heroine of a hijacking.
Bernhard Goetz	NY's subway vigilante: victim or criminal?
William Hurt	Oscar favorite for *Kiss of the Spider Woman*.
Hulk Hogan	The World Wrestling Federation's heavyweight champion.
Cathleen Webb	Faked a rape that sent a man to prison.
Madonna	Rich, famous, and married to Sean Penn.

Rupert Murdoch	Now an American citizen, the publisher builds his media empire.
Dwight Gooden	Baseball's best pitcher is quiet but deadly.
Don Johnson	America's Friday night vice.
Princess Diana	Embodies dreams and looks like a princess.
Mel Fisher	Pulls 34 tons of Spanish silver from Key West.
Michael J. Fox	The boy king of Hollywood.
Mengele's Bones	Discovery of this Nazi's remains ends the intense manhunt.
Whoopi Goldberg	She's been on welfare and now she's on-screen in *The Color Purple*.
Rock Hudson	The most famous person to die of AIDS.
The Springsteens	A storybook year for Beauty and the Boss.
Gracie Mansion	A hip gallery owner brings fame to the art of Manhattan's East Village.

1986

Sarah, Duchess of York	A commoner wins a nation's heart without losing her independent personality.
Ivan Boesky	Inside tips make him a Wall Street demon.
Dr. Seuss	*You're Only Old Once!* makes oldsters hoot.
Bette Midler	Becomes a movie draw and a mother.
David Letterman	The askew host of *Late Night*.
Pat Robertson	TV preacher makes a bid to move to the White House.
Daniel Ortega	Nicaragua's president bedevils Reagan.
Raymond Hunthausen	Seattle's progressive archbishop believes he's keeping the faith.
Bob Hoskins	The Cockney Cagney is the actor of the year.
Oliver North	Reagan's marine: hero or loose cannon?
Terry Waite	Church's envoy obtains freedom for hostages in Beirut.
Paul Hogan	Makes *Crocodile Dundee* a U.S. favorite.
Howard the Duck	Turns out to be a turkey for George Lucas.
Greg LeMond	America's first Tour de France winner.
Run–D.M.C.	Rapper tells us to *Walk This Way*.
Debi Thomas	Figure-skating champion finds time to study microbiology at Stanford.
Helga	Posed for previously unknown Wyeth paintings.
Vanna White	*Wheel of Fortune*'s letter-turning bombshell rakes in endorsements and writes a book.
Beth Henley	A Mississippi playwright goes Hollywood.
Jerome P. Horwitz	Developed drug AZT now used to combat AIDS.
David Byrne	Celebrates a wacky America in *True Stories*.
William Rehnquist	The new chief justice of the Supreme Court.
Tom Cruise	The box-office *Top Gun* of 1986.
Max Headroom	A nonhuman talk-show host.
Whitney Houston	Pop's prettiest new commercial monster.

1987

Ronald Reagan — Completes his term with a Hollywood finish.

Mikhail Gorbachev — The Russian leader takes the West by storm and ushers in an age of optimism.

Baby Jessica McClure — After her rescue from a Midland, Texas well, she gets on with a normal toddler's life.

Gary Hart — Re-enters the 1988 presidential race.

Oliver North — Charms his way through the Iran-Contra hearings.

Michael Douglas — Kirk's son steps into the spotlight.

Patient Zero — French Canadian Gaetan Dugas, identified as a major transmitter of the AIDS virus.

Donald Trump — Real estate mogul emerges as an icon for the '80s.

Cher — Soars with new movie roles.

Christian Lacroix — A whimsical, chic new fashion designer.

Oprah Winfrey — Uses television to fight apartheid and racism at home.

Vincent Van Gogh — The most marketable Postimpressionist of the century.

Magic Johnson — Smiling as he leads the Lakers to the top.

The Church Lady — *Saturday Night Live*'s biting holy roller.

Princess Diana — Tests limits of acceptable royal behavior.

Donna Fawn Hahn — Rice, Hall, and Jessica: Three faces of Eve.

Bono — Rock musician struggles with hero status.

Brigitte Nielsen — Stallone's ex remains notorious for her leggy sexuality and questionable motives in love.

Tracey Ullman — Host of delightful, astonishing show on Fox.

Jerry Garcia — Singing to a new generation of Deadheads.

Glenn Close — At 40, she is a siren onscreen in *Fatal Attraction*.

Garrison Keillor — The creator of National Public Radio's *A Prairie Home Companion*.

William Casey — Reagan's CIA director dies before he can testify in Iran-Contra hearings.

Dennis Quaid — Ignites the screen in *The Big Easy*

Tammy Faye Bakker — America's most unusual makeup consumer makes herself a national joke on *Nightline*.

PEOPLE'S BEST AND WORST DRESSED

Who are the biggest fashion victors and victims? Herewith PEOPLE's halls of fame and shame and highlights from the 2001 special issue.

BEST OF ALL TIME
Fred Astaire
Warren Beatty
Coco Chanel
Bill Cosby
Tom Cruise
Princess Diana
Richard Gere
Carey Grant
Audrey Hepburn
Katharine Hepburn
Lena Horne
Peter Jennings
Grace Kelly
John F. Kennedy
Jackie Onassis
Babe Paley
Barbara Walters
The Duchess and Duke of Windsor

WORST OF ALL TIME
Mariah Carey
Pamela Anderson Lee
Tammy Faye Bakker Messner
Dolly Parton
Dennis Rodman
Roseanne
Queen Elizabeth II
Elizabeth Taylor

IN A LEAGUE OF THEIR OWN
Cher
Madonna

2001'S WINNERS AND SINNERS

Glamor Girls
Joan Allen
Jennifer Aniston
Penelope Cruz
Heather Graham
Marcia Gay Harden
Kate Hudson
Allison Janney
Ashley Judd
Nicole Kidman
Laura Linney
Jennifer Lopez
Michael Michele
Gwyneth Paltrow
Sarah Jessica Parker
Julia Roberts
Caroline Kennedy Schlossberg
Charlize Theron
Uma Thurman
Venus Williams
Michelle Yeoh
Catherine Zeta-Jones

Sharp Shooters
Benjamin Bratt
George Clooney
Taye Diggs
Cuba Gooding Jr.
Prince Harry
Hugh Jackman
Eric McCormack
Tim McGraw
Brad Pitt
Mark Wahlberg

Over the Top
Juliette Binoche
Serena Williams
Sigourney Weaver
David Boreanaz
Denise Rich
Hilary Swank
Amy Brenneman
Melissa Rivers

What a Mess
Johnny Depp
Meg Ryan
Leonardo DiCaprio
Helena Bonham Carter
Heath Ledger

1988

George Bush	The president-elect.
Jodie Foster	Makes a comeback in *The Accused*.
Roseanne Barr	A larger-than-life housewife, both on and off the small screen.
Athina Roussel	Money won't buy the love she lost with the death of her mother, Christina Onassis.
The Cyberpunk	Hackers wreak havoc on info networks.
Florence Griffith Joyner	Wins four medals as a sprinter at the Seoul Olympics.
Lisa Marie Presley	Marries a sober fellow and settles down.
Benazir Bhutto	Pakistani discovers the challenges of being the first woman to lead an Islamic nation.
Liz Taylor	Autobiography, AIDS advocacy, and addiction: another rollercoaster year for Liz.
Michelle Pfeiffer	This actress is more than just a pretty face.
Jesse Jackson	His presidential campaign shows that he is a political force to be reckoned with.
Phantom of the Opera	Beguiles us again with a vision of the tragic depths of love.
Merv Griffin	Takes over ownership of Trump's resorts.
Anne Tyler	Reclusive novelist faces an adoring public.
Orel Hershiser	Uncompromising World Series MVP pitcher.
Shi Peipu	Inspires Tony-winning play, *M. Butterfly*.
Kevin Costner	Sends hearts aflutter with *Bull Durham*.
Tracy Chapman	Serious black folk musician enjoys success.
David Hockney	His bright canvases are the talk of the art scene.
Jessica Rabbit	The hottest woman on celluloid is a 'toon.
Stephen Hawking	Unwinds mysteries of the universe in his bestselling book.
Tom Hanks	A familiar face hits the *Big* time.
Fergie	Year One with the Windsors is no fairy tale.
Mike Tyson	Heavyweight champion and husband to the beautiful Robin Givens.
Sage Volkman	Young burn survivor gets back her smile.

1989

George and Barbara Bush	George turns his gaze to domestic matters, while Barbara helps Millie write her book.
Jack Nicholson	The Joker fits him like white grease paint.
Arsenio Hall	The hippest night owl of them all.
Julio Berumen	Pluckiest survivor of the Bay Area quake.
Princess Anne	The least-liked royal turns object of desire.
Mikhail Gorbachev	Proves he's serious about *perestroika*.
Salman Rushdie	For publishing *The Satanic Verses* he now lives with the threat he'll perish.
John Goodman	The TV Barr-tender is an extra-large hit.

Gaia	The Greek goddess lends her name to the daring theory that the planet itself is alive.
Manuel Noriega	The Panamanian dictator gives American leaders fits.
Michael Milken	Junk bond entrepreneur's indictment brings an end to an era.
Paula Abdul	No longer just Janet Jackson's footwork coach, she's a song-and-dance sensation.
Deborah Gore Dean	As the HUD scandal unravels, it's clear that she saw government as a game show and helped her friends win valuable prizes.
Robert Fulghum	Author of unlikely bestseller, *All I Really Need to Know I Learned in Kindergarten*.
Madonna	Irks some Christians, splits from Sean, dallies with Warren, and gets canned by Pepsi.
Spike Lee	The director raises a ruckus—and important questions—with *Do the Right Thing*.
Ellen Barkin	Tough, vulnerable, smart, very sexy, and riveting on-screen.
Billy Crystal	Becomes a genuine sex symbol in *When Harry Met Sally*....
Pete Rose	Battles bad press, baseball commissioner A. Bartlett Giamatti, and his own demons.
Pablo Escobar	A Colombian drug lord markets death while evading an outraged citizenry.
Michelle Pfeiffer	In *The Fabulous Baker Boys* she adds a dash of hot pepper to a delicious dish.
Elizabeth Morgan	Jailed for shielding her daughter from alleged sexual abuse, she is freed at last.
Robert Mapplethorpe	The photographer rattles the art world and Jesse Helms with a shocking retrospective.
Captain Al Haynes	In crash-landing a crippled DC-10 in Iowa, he saves lives with grit and cool.
Donna Karan	High fashion's newest mogul scores with DKNY.

1990

George Bush	Faces a sea of troubles.
Sinead O'Connor	Her haunting rebel voice is heard.
Julia Roberts	The first hit female star of the '90s.
Ken Burns	Produces the 11-hour epic *The Civil War*.
Patrick Swayze	Every woman's dream of a heavenly *Ghost*.
Neil Bush	His questionable involvement with a Denver S&L puts a First Family face on the $500-billion S&L scandal.
Delta Burke	She has unkind words for her *Designing Women* producers.
Saddam Hussein	His invasion of Kuwait brings the world to the brink of war.
Michael Ovitz	The man everyone in Hollywood would like to know spins gold out of tinsel.
Nancy Cruzan	Off life support after years in a coma, she dramatizes the need for living wills.
Colin Powell	Raises the world's shield against Hussein.

Fidel Castro	The world's lone, defiant Communist.
Effi Barry	A model of decorum as husband Marion, Washington's mayor, goes up in smoke.
Dr. Anthony Fauci	America's point man in the fight against AIDS.
M.C. Hammer	Brings showbiz flash and footwork to rap.
Bart Simpson	TV's intemperate urchin gives authority figures a cow.
Nancy Ziegenmeyer	A housewife and rape victim goes public.
Nelson Mandela	He steps from the dim recesses of jail into the harsh reality of freedom.
Francis Ford Coppola	The acclaimed director stages *The Godfather, Part III*.
Keenan Ivory Wayans	His *In Living Color* brings howls of laughter and out-Foxes the network establishment.
Claudia Schiffer	A German supermodel, via Bardot.
William Styron	*Darkness Visible* helps fellow depressives.
Laura Palmer	The Girl Most Likely to Pique on *Twin Peaks*.
Bo Jackson	Hits, runs, and scores on Madison Avenue.
Princess Caroline	Monaco's First Lady copes with her husband's violent death.

1991

George and Barbara Bush	The First Couple's first concerns are war, peace, and their kids.
Jodie Foster	The first-time director commands respect with *Little Man Tate*.
Magic Johnson	Tests HIV-positive and competes against AIDS.
Julia Roberts	After a busted engagement and a box-office bust, she flies away.
Luke Perry	The hunk of *Beverly Hills 90210*.
Anita Hill	Starts a debate on sexual harassment.
Garth Brooks	Lassos the attention of all America.
Princess Diana	Surviving digs at her marriage and her AIDS activism, she turns a very regal 30.
William Kennedy Smith	He beats a charge of rape, but his famous family may never be the same again.
Terry Anderson	Emerges after seven years as a Beirut hostage.
Boris Yeltsin	Russia's new voice.
Kenneth Branagh	Goes Hollywood with *Dead Again*.
Anjelica Huston	Recovering from loss, she emerges as Morticia, the *Addams*'s coolest ghoul.
Jeffrey Dahmer	His confession could not explain why his grisly killings went so long undetected.
Elizabeth Taylor	Will altar trip No. 8 be her last?
Robert Bly	*Iron John*'s readers go ape for him.
John Singleton	*Boyz N the Hood* opens middle-class eyes.
Naomi Campbell	This diva reigns over high-fashion runways.
Axl Rose	Guns N' Roses' lead pistol.

The 4,600-Year-Old Man	Freed from an Alpine deep freeze.
Mariah Carey	Pop's queen shares her *Emotions*.
Derek Humphry	His *Final Exit* ignites debate about suicide.
Pee-Wee Herman	Loses his image at an X-rated theater.
Norman Schwarzkopf	Gulf hero faces life after the army.
Jimmy Connors	Tennis "has-been" defiantly returns.

1992

Bill Clinton	The president-elect recoups from a rough campaign.
Hillary Clinton	A savvy lawyer determined to make a difference.
Cindy Crawford	Becomes a video celebrity.
Ross Perot	Trying to crash the two major parties, he goes from can-do to quitter and back.
Denzel Washington	As *Malcolm X* he catapults to superstardom.
Princess Diana	She dumps her hubby.
Woody Allen	His breakup with Mia Farrow is ballistic.
Larry King	*Larry King Live* is the whistle-stop that White House contenders must visit this year.
Barney	Purple dino gives kid-vid a Jurassic spark.
Billy Ray Cyrus	He's raising Nashville's pulse.
Terry McMillan	Her *Waiting to Exhale* is a surprise smash.
Gregory K.	Sets legal precedents by divorcing his mom.
Desiree Washington	Scores a knockout in court over Mike Tyson.
Diane English	Makes *Murphy Brown* a single mom and herself a lightning rod.
Madonna	She bares her bod and blankets the media.
George Smoot	He finds the missing ripples that confirm the universe began with a Big Bang.
Katie Couric	She boosts the *Today* show.
Fabio	Once a fantasy figure on romance-novel covers, he actually moves and speaks.
Arthur Ashe	He brings eloquence, guts, and grace to his instructive fight against AIDS.
Dana Carvey	Whether he's doing Bush, Perot, or *Wayne*'s Garth, he's always hilariously on target.
Bernadine Healy	The first woman to head the National Institutes of Health.
Carol Moseley Braun	The first black woman to be a U.S. senator.
Henri Matisse	This glorious painter has crowds in line.
Whoopi Goldberg	More prolific than some Hollywood studios.
Sharon Stone	Shows a *Basic Instinct* for sensuality.

1993

Bill Clinton	Faces tough issues and a skeptical nation.
Hillary Rodham Clinton	Reflects on family life while heading the committee on health care reform.

Princess Diana	She still has a place in Britons' hearts.
Michael Jackson	Can't hide from allegations of child abuse.
Yasir Arafat	PLO leader makes peace with his enemy.
Oprah Winfrey	Becomes the world's highest-paid entertainer, sheds 60 pounds, and stays single.
Andrew Wiles	A Princeton prof awes math's great minds.
David Letterman	He's now the leader of the late-night pack.
Janet Reno	Wows Washington with her guts and candor.
Susan Powter	Her hot *Stop the Insanity!* suggests anger might be the best weight-loss prescription.
Howard Stern	Exposes his *Private Parts.*
Baby Jessica	Focuses us on parental rights arguments.
Lyle Lovett	Country's wry specialist in heartache and rue wins the hand of Julia Roberts.
Ol' Man River	The Mississippi inspires awe and rage.
Jerry Seinfeld	He's got TV's most buzzed-about sitcom.
Katherine Ann Power	In facing her bloody past she prompts a rethinking of '60s ideals.
Eddie Vedder	His hellbound vocals make Pearl Jam jell.
Vincent Foster	His suicide brings sadness and self-examination to Clinton's inner circle.
Sheik Omar Abdel Rahmen	A blind cleric is accused of inciting his U.S. followers to bomb and kill.
Michael Jordan	Announces a surprise retirement.
Rush Limbaugh	He bashes liberals for fun and profit.
Shannen Doherty	The feisty actress runs amok.
Tommy Lee Jones	He's a must-find in *The Fugitive.*
Lorena Bobbitt	She provokes the national imagination with an act few could view with detachment.
Tom Hanks	Three diverse, challenging roles this year.

1994

Bill Clinton	Strives to restore voter confidence.
Tim Allen	Has a hit film, book, and sitcom.
O. J. Simpson	Murder suspect of the decade.
The Pope	Delivers his message to millions in a book.
Princess Diana	She tries to resume private life amid allegations of adultery and instability.
Gerry Adams	The Sinn Fein leader calls for his Irish countrymen to lay down their arms.
Shannon Faulkner	Fights tenaciously to become the Citadel's first female cadet.
Michael Fay	In Singapore, the American teen is charged with vandalism and sentenced to a caning.
Whitney Houston	Top songstress walks a rocky path at home.
Ricki Lake	Trounces her competition, marries, and lands in jail for an anti-fur protest.
Vinton Cerf	The hearing-impaired Father of the Internet.
Michael Jordan	Basketball's king graces baseball.
Heather Locklear	Sizzling *Melrose Place* star plans marriage.
Jim Carrey	Shows off rare slapstick style.

YEAR-BY-YEAR, THE BEST- (AND WORST-) SELLING PEOPLE ISSUES

Here are the regular weekly issues that have fared best and worst at the newsstand.

	Best Seller	Worst Seller
1974	The Johnny Carsons	J. Paul Getty
1975	Cher & Gregg Allman	Liv Ullmann
1976	Cher, Gregg, & Baby	Nancy Reagan
1977	Tony Orlando's Breakdown	Julie Andrews
1978	Olivia Newton-John	Vice President & Mrs. Mondale
1979	A Readers' Poll/ 5th Anniversary	Fleetwood Mac
1980	John Lennon, A Tribute	Paul Simon
1981	Charles & Diana's Wedding	Justice Sandra Day O'Connor
1982	Princess Grace, A Tribute	*Annie,* the musical
1983	Karen Carpenter's Death First Woman in Space	Sally Ride, Amerca's
1984	Michael Jackson	How to Make Your Kid a Star
1985	The Other Life of Rock Hudson	Bisset & Godunov
1986	Andrew & Fergie's Wedding	The Raid on Libya
1987	The Follies of Fergie & Di	Michael Caine
1988	Burt & Loni's Wedding	Our American Hostages
1989	Lucy, A Tribute	Abbie Hoffman, Death of a Radical
1990	Patrick Swayze	Campus Rape
1991	Jeffrey Dahmer	Richard & Jeramie Dreyfuss
1992	Princess Diana	Betty Rollin: "I Helped My Mother Die"
1993	Julia Robert's Wedding	Hillary Clinton
1994	The Nicole Simpson Murders	Kelsey Grammer
1995	David Smith	Larry Hagman
1996	Margaux Hemingway's Death	Audrey Meadows and Gene Kelly: Tributes
1997	Goodbye Diana	The Fight Against Child Abuse
1998	Barbra's Wedding Album	Emmy's 50th Birthday
1999	J.F.K. Jr. & Carolyn Bessette Kennedy, Charmed Life/ Tragic Death	Dr. Jerri Nielsen
2000	Brad Pitt and Jennifer Aniston Wedding	Vietnam Today

Tonya Harding	Feisty figure skater slides into scandal.
Jeffrey Katzenberg	The Disney exec ditches Mickey and Pluto for Spielberg and Geffen.
Nadja Auermann	This year's supermodel.
Aldrich Ames	Rogue CIA agent caught betraying the U.S.
Christine Todd Whitman	New Jersey's new governor becomes a GOP darling.
James Redfield	*The Celestine Prophecy* breathes new life into New Age.
Andre Agassi	Tennis's reformed bad boy has Brooke in his court.
Liz Phair	Alternative rock's hottest star.
Power Rangers	Six multicultural teenage superheroes.
John Travolta	With *Pulp Fiction*, he's Hollywood's most durable comeback kid.
Newt Gingrich	Tough-talking new Speaker of the House.

1995

Bill Clinton	Takes on Bosnia and the budget.
Princess Diana	Makes stunning confession to BBC.
Christopher Reeve	Finds a new role: inspirational spokesperson.
Elizabeth Hurley	Actress, model, and Hugh Grant's better half.
Colin Powell	Decides to stay above the presidential fray.
Nicole Kidman	*To Die For* gives birth to a star.
O. J. Simpson	After the verdict, the unsettling image of a fallen idol remains.
Marcia Clark	Loses the O. J. trial but wins over the public.
Susan Smith	Sentenced to life for drowning her sons.
Jay Leno	Mr. Nice Guy becomes late night's top dog.
C. Delores Tucker	Alarmed by gangsta rap, she declares war on media giant Time Warner—and wins.
Jane Austen	Novel Brit wit makes her hot in Hollywood.
Shania Twain	A Canadian honky-tonker watches her fortunes change in Nashville.
Brad Pitt	*Seven* proves he's more than skin-deep.
Babe	The sty's no limit to a charming porker.
Louis Farrakhan	Demagogue takes a step from hate to healing.
Ted Turner	Hitches his wagon to Time Warner.
Hootie & the Blowfish	Fun-loving frat band finds sweet success.
The Unabomber	Issues another bomb, more threats, and a "manifesto."
Jennifer Aniston	Makes *Friends* and influences hairstyles.
JFK Jr.	With *George*, a political prince gets focused.
Monica Seles	A leading lady of tennis returns to court.
R. L. Stine	He gives young readers *Goosebumps*.
Selena	The late Latina takes *Tejano* mainstream.
Cal Ripken Jr.	Plays 2,131 consecutive baseball games.

1996

Rosie O'Donnell	The Queen of Nice cleans up the talk show.
Ted Kaczynski	A Harvard-educated hermit is charged as the Unabomber.
Carolyn Bessette Kennedy	She weds JFK Jr. and becomes America's most watched woman.
Dennis Rodman	Nude, lewd, and tattooed—and all Bull?
Princess Diana	Out of the palace and into the world.
George Clooney	New Batman battles stalkerazzi.
Richard Jewell	Cleared as a bombing suspect, he struggles to restore his name
Binta-Jua	A gorilla with a humanitarian streak.
Jenny McCarthy	MTV's rising star.
Christopher Reeve	Works tirelessly for the disabled.
Kathie Lee Gifford	Pushed to put an end to sweatshops.
Dilbert	Scott Adams's cartoon office drudge.
Gwyneth Paltrow	Hot new actress gets Brad Pitt too.
Marian Wright Edelman	Fighting for children's rights, she loses a White House ally.
Tom Cruise	Mission Accomplished: two blockbusters.
Alanis Morissette	The pied piper of teen angst.
Shannon Lucid	A working mom logs 188 days in space.
Brooke Shields	Comeback kid turns to comedy.
Conan O'Brien	He's the big man of the wee small hours.
Carolyn McCarthy	A victim of tragedy wins a seat in Congress.
Madonna	Is reinvented by Lourdes and Evita.
Tiger Woods	Golf gets a Gen-X superstar.
Goldie Hawn	At 51, her movie career is still golden.
Chelsea Clinton	The First Daughter takes the stage.
Bob Dole	Loses presidential bid, wins on Letterman.

1997

Princess Diana	Her sudden death becomes the year's defining event.
Bill Cosby	Copes with the slaying of his only son and the extortion trial of his would-be daughter.
Ellen DeGeneres	Reshaping TV's take on sexual identity.
Leonardo DiCaprio	In *Titanic*, he swims toward big-star status.
Kathie Lee Gifford	Adds cheating husband to her list of travails.
Rudolph W. Giuliani	The antagonistic mayor cleans up NYC.
Elton John	Mourning friends, he finds new inspiration.
Sheryl Swoopes	Basketball star is in control.
Beck	A fresh, ambitious voice in pop music.
Andrew Cunanan	A killing binge ending with the murder of Gianni Versace makes a chilling stranger an all-too-familiar face.
Michael Moore	Big Tobacco's worst headache wins billions in Medicaid costs.

Lucy Lawless	As Xena, she clears the path for powerful female role models.
Tommy Hilfiger	His bright, relaxed styles prove their cross-cultural appeal.
Frank McCourt	In childhood misery, a writer finds wisdom—and poetry.
Brenda Hoster	Blows the whistle on sexual harassment in the army.
John F. Kennedy Jr.	Successful and settled, he comes into his own.
Bobbi McCaughey	She makes history with healthy septuplets.
Madeleine Albright	Uses magnetism and muscle for diplomacy.
Drew Carey	TV's average Joe bares a long-held secret.
Bill McCartney	A onetime coach exhorts men to tackle their familial and spiritual duties.
Jewel	Folk music gets a '90s poster girl.
Joseph Hartzler	Wins a swift guilty verdict against Oklahoma bomber Timothy McVeigh.
Julia Roberts	Rediscovers her roots in romantic comedy.
Dolly	Poor little lamb—she's all a clone.
Bill Clinton	Faces a full docket of controversies.

1998

Mark McGwire	Hits 70 glorious home runs.
Cameron Diaz	Sweet center of a giddily vulgar comedy.
Kenneth Starr	He turns up the heat on Clinton so high, his own reputation gets scorched.
Lauryn Hill	Goes solo and takes hip-hop to new heights.
John Glenn	His triumphant return to space puts the country in orbit as well.
Katie Couric	Rocked by the death of her husband, Jay, she carries on with courage and strength.
Chris Rock	His edgy comic candor makes him a major player.
Edward Fugger	His quest to help you choose your baby's sex bares fruit.
Geri Halliwell	On her own, she emerges as a surprisingly admirable post–Spice Woman.
The WWII Soldier	Wins the gratitude of a new generation when brought to vivid life on the big screen.
James Brolin	Steals Barbra's heart with an easy confidence, but he'll never be Mr. Streisand.
Camryn Manheim	Triumphs as a fully rounded Emmy winner.
Judy Blume	The queen of preteen fiction hits home with grown-up fans.
David Kaczynski	A concerned brother reaches out to the Unabomber's victims.
Michael J. Fox	Courageously shares his battle with Parkinson's disease
Oprah Winfrey	She brings a *Beloved* project to completion.
Alan Greenspan	Fed chief holds the world's markets steady.

Leonardo DiCaprio	To *Titanic* fanfare, he takes a puzzling break.
Matt Drudge	This wired Walter Winchell spreads gossip that all too often becomes news.
Calista Flockhart	She faces scrutiny of body and role.
Adam Sandler	Sophomoric humor makes him head of the Hollywood class.
Joan Kroc	She quietly shares her wealth.
Emeril Legasse	The star chef is hotter than haute.
Hillary Rodham Clinton	In a difficult year, she embraces dignity.
The American People	Whether voting, viewing, or investing, we defy expectations.

1999

John F. Kennedy Jr.	He leaves the world grieving for what might have been.
Ashley Judd	Scores with *Double Jeopardy*.
Ricky Martin	Pop crowns a new king of the sexy swivel.
Serena Williams	Claims center court with beads, brilliance, and brawn.
Jesse Ventura	Wrestles political pundits to the mat as Minnesota's new governor.
Julia Roberts	The ever-Pretty Woman is Hollywood's runaway hitmaker.
Dr. Robert Atkins	Weight watchers love his low-carb diet.
George W. Bush	Aims to follow his father's footsteps.
Sara Jane Olsen	California fugitive lives an alleged double life as a Minnesota mom.
Tiger Woods	He blasts into the record books.
Bill Gates	Under attack for raking it in, he excels at giving it away.
Judge Judy	TV's supreme jurist rules with a smart mouth.
Chris Spielman	Football player leaves the game for the family he cherishes.
Jennifer Lopez	Music, movies, modeling—all her way.
David E. Kelley	With an Emmy sweep, he rules TV.
J. K. Rowling	Enchants readers with Harry Potter.
Lance Armstrong	His Tour de France makes him a hero.
JonBenet Ramsey	Becomes a symbol of judicial failure as her murder remains unsolved.
Bruce Willis	Uses his *Sixth Sense* to scare up a hit.
Mike Myers	His *Austin Powers* sequel is shagadelic.
Pokémon	They captivate kids and confound parents.
Brandi Chastain	Gives women's soccer a grand kick start.
Regis Philbin	Asks *Who Wants to Be a Millionaire* and a nation answers.
Dr. Martin Citron	Finds a chemical key that could lead to a treatment for Alzheimer's.
Hillary Clinton	Rebounds with a New York State of mind.

2000

George W. Bush	Fights to the finish for the 43rd presidency.
Michael J. Fox	Turns off his TV career to help find a cure for Parkinson's Disease.
Sarah Jessica Parker	Her naughty-but-nice routine has viewers all worked up over *Sex and the City*.
Venus Williams	Takes Wimbledon and the U.S. Open by working on her mind game.
Meg Ryan	Startles fans with a marital split and a passionate new romance.
Prince William	Britain's dashing young royal enters adulthood and makes himself heard.
Eminem	Is the defiant rapper's bestselling *LP* a poetic masterpiece or a musical hate crime?
Gloria Steinem	Enters an unlikely institution: marriage.
Steve Case	Puts America online—and sets his sights on Time Warner.
James Gandolfini	Convincingly portrays a thoroughly modern mafioso on *The Sopranos*.
Alex Rodriguez	The shortstop who'll never be caught short reigns as the richest ballplayer ever.
Renee Fleming	Hits opera's highest notes on stage, TV and a top-selling CD.
Hillary Clinton	The outgoing First Lady lines up her next job: Senator from New York.
Florida	Weathers a late hurricane season at the center of the storm over the White House.
Shawn Fleming	Sees his Napster hailed as both musical revolution and royalties ripoff.
Tiger Woods	The world's best golfer is rewriting the record books.
Ben Stiller	Makes embarrassment pay off in *Meet the Parents*.
Darva Conger	Marries a millionaire and becomes a reluctant pinup for "reality" TV.
Elian Gonzalez	Rescued from the sea, he became a child wanted by two families—and two nations.
Anna Werner	Gets the story on faulty tires and inspires a recall that saved lives.
Jennifer Aniston	Lands a sexy husband and one of TV's handsomest salaries.
The Rock	Evolves from wrestler to Renaissance man.
J. Craig Venter	Wins the race to decode the letters of the human genome.
Drew Barrymore	After a lifetime of pain, this angel karate-chops her way into calling the shots on Cloud Nine.
Richard Hatch	The man who proved the victor on *Survivor* gives new meaning to "naked ambition."

MIND YOUR E-MANNERS

Writer Samantha Miller answers readers' questions about Net dos and don'ts in PEOPLE.com's weekly Internet Manners column. Here are answers to some problems that pop up most often.

1. What's the proper salutation for business e-mail?

In today's khaki-clad office scene, we're almost all on a first-name basis, so inter-cubicle missives can start with a cheery "Hi, Bob!" "Bob:" or nothing at all. The same goes for outside contacts you're already acquainted with, unless you're a peon and they're big cheeses ("Dear Mr. Gates..."). Don't know your recipient? Stick with Mr. or Ms. Traditionalists won't bristle, and whippersnappers will be tickled.

2. How should I sign e-mail?

Like TV news anchors, Netizens love signature sign-offs. Hippies use "Peace"; gen Y, "C-ya L8R"; acronym addicts, "TTFN." ("Ta-ta for now.") Some savvy users scorn cutesiness and simply sign their names or initials. We say creativity is no crime, but be original—or you'll look as pretentious as non-Italians who double-cheek kiss a ciao.

3. Can I use e-mail to send thank-you notes for my holiday loot?

Nice try, lazybones. You think a few electrons can repay Grandma for battling the shopping-mall hordes (never mind those Amazon.com boxes in her trash)? Pick up a pen—retro is trendy! E-mail is okay for informal notes to pals and in geek enclaves like Silicon Valley, where folks e-mail wedding invitations (!). But when in doubt, write it out.

4. I got an e-mail warning me about a computer virus. Should I forward it to everyone I know?

We know you mean well. But your Net-savvy pals will cringe as if you coughed on them. Most of these scares are hoaxes that waste more time than computer solitaire. If you're worried, check with your office tech-support squad or a hoax-busting Web site like kumite.com/myths. If only the flu were as easy to avoid.

5. Can I ask for a first date via e-mail?

A casual "met you last night, wanna have dinner?" note is a fine way for the tongue-tied to break the ice—though it doesn't exactly signal a hunk of burnin' love, so hope your fun e-Valentine digs shy types. One tip: spell-check.

THE MOST BEAUTIFUL PEOPLE ON THE WEB

Every year, PEOPLE's print editors name the 50 Most Beautiful People in the World. People.com, meanwhile, asks Web surfers to nominate their own favorites. Here are those who received the most online votes in 2001.

1. James Marsters *(Buffy the Vampire Slayer)*
2. Jon Bon Jovi
3. Elizabeth Mitchell *(ER)*
4. Roy Dupuis *(La Femme Nikita)*
5. Andrea Parker *(The Pretender)*
6. Laura Innes *(ER)*
7. Jason Behr *(Roswell)*
8. Benicio Del Toro
9. Majandra Delfino *(Roswell)*
10. Benjamin Bratt

6. Why is it bad to type in all capital letters? What about all small letters?

Net tradition dictates that all caps denotes shouting: PIPE DOWN! As for the e.e. cummings mode, it's fine for speed in chat rooms, but ease up on the accelerator for e-mail.

7. How do I get my friends to stop e-mailing me lists of jokes?

Would-be Jay Lenos, listen up: This seems to be readers' top e-etiquette peeve. As for those of you who don't like being drafted into Open Mike Night, begin by trying a polite "Thanks, but no thanks." If that doesn't work, say you just don't have time. Worried about being rude? How rude are your so-called friends to clog your in-box in the first place?

8. Is it okay to send e-mail full of spelling errors?

look over emale before u sned it. its only commn curtesy. How annoying was that to read? Very—which is why the "I'm so busy I can't take time to spell-check" attitude has got to go. It's rude to recipients. They're busy too.

9. I stumbled across some intimate e-mail sent to my significant other. I believe exchanging sexy e-mail is a form of cheating. What do you think?

As any world leader would tell you, it depends on your definition of "cheating." But while a strictly cyber affair obviously isn't as bad as the real thing, it's bad enough, even if it was "just for fun"—a frequently deployed excuse that only raises disturbing questions. And don't get roped into an argument with your s.o. about whether e-dallying really is cheating. If snookums got steamy with someone else and has the gall to debate the technicalities, maybe it's time for both of you to cut your losses and head to the singles chat room.

10. When I'm sending e-mail back and forth with one person, how often should I change the subject line?

Well, if you and your steady are discussing which wedding caterer to hire and the subject still reads, "Re: Nice Meeting You," it's time to freshen it up. But using a new heading on every note can get confusing. So switch when the rest of the message no longer has anything to do with the subject—just say non to non sequiturs.

THE SEXIEST MAN ALIVE

PEOPLE has honored someone with this title beginning in 1985. Here is a look at the magazine's hunks of the year. Discerning readers will recall the drought of 1994, when no one made the honor roll.

1985
Mel Gibson

1986
Mark Harmon

1987
Harry Hamlin

1988
John F. Kennedy Jr.

1989
Sean Connery

1990
Tom Cruise

1991
Patrick Swayze

1992
Nick Nolte

1993
Richard Gere and Cindy Crawford (The Sexiest Couple Alive)

1994
No winner

1995
Brad Pitt

1996
Denzel Washington

1997
George Clooney

1998
Harrison Ford

1999
Richard Gere

2000
Brad Pitt

CYBERWORLD: 20 ESSENTIAL BOOKMARKS

Some Web sites are good for a one-time giggle, and some will have you going back again and again. PEOPLE senior writer Samantha Miller selects some of the best—the useful, the dishy, and the downright indispensable:

1. Yahoo! (www.yahoo.com)
Yahoo! breaks down the Web like a card catalog, sorting through sites by subject. It's the perfect starting point for any Web expedition—or you can stay on the site for the news stories, stock tickers, and other extras. Bonus: If you want to search the Web itself, Yahoo! puts you in the capable hands of Google, a search engine that really works.

2. Ask Jeeves (ask.com)
A different way to search the Web. Just type a question using regular language—i.e. "What is Mongolia's biggest export?"—and this plucky butler does his best to serve up sites that answer it.

3. About.com
A network of hundreds of sites dedicated to particular topics—gardening, adoption, horror movies—each run by an expert guide. A great way to get up to speed on anything, pronto.

4. Google (google.com)
The Web's best search site, bar none. Enter any word or phrase and Google will zero in on the right site in a jiffy—without the time-wasting irrelevant listings other search sites so often spout.

2001 WEBBY AWARD WINNERS

These "Oscars of the Internet," awarded to the best Web sites in a range of categories as judged by a panel of technology-world professionals, were handed out in a ceremony in San Francisco on July 18, 2001.

Activism: VolunteerMatch (www.volunteermatch.org)

Broadband: Heavy (www.heavy.com)

Commerce: Travelocity (www.travelocity.com)

Community: craigslist (www.craigslist.org)

Education: NationalGeographic.com (www.nationalgeographic.com)

Fashion: Hint Fashion Magazine (www.hintmag.com)

Film: Requiem For A Dream (www.requiemforadream.com)

Finance: Yahoo! Finance (finance.yahoo.com)

Games: 3D Groove (www.3dgroove.com)

Government & Law: Nolo Self-Help Law Center (www.nolo.com)

Health: Planned Parenthood Golden Gate (www.ppgg.org)

Humor: The Onion (www.theonion.com)

Kids: Fact Monster (www.factmonster.com)

Living: Campaign For Our Children (www.cfoc.org)

Music: sputnik7 (www.sputnik7.com)

News: [Inside] (www.inside.com)

Personal: Dancing Paul (www.dancingpaul.com)

Politics: OpenSecrets.org (www.opensecrets.org)

Print & Zines: Plastic (www.plastic.com)

Radio: BBC World Service (www.bbc.co.uk/worldservice)

Science: Plus Magazine (plus.maths.org)

Services: VolunteerMatch (www.volunteermatch.org)

Spirituality: Zen (www.do-not-zzz.com)

Sports: Swell (www.swell.com)

Travel: Expedia (www.expedia.com)

TV: PBS Online (www.pbs.org)

Weird: Peter Pan's Home Page (www.pixyland.org/peterpan)

Best Practices: Google (www.google.com)

Art: Young-Hae Chang Heavy Industries (www.yhchang.com)

Technical Achievement: Microsoft Windows Update (windowsupdate.microsoft.com)

Lifetime Achievement: Ray Tomlinson and Douglas Engelbart

5. eHow (ehow.com)

Need to know how to change a tire? How to sew on a button? How to conceal a hickey? Get it done with help from this collection of thousands of how-tos.

6. Amazon.com (www.amazon.com)

You don't have to spend, spend, spend at this ever-expanding shopping site (although it's sooo easy…). Browsing its well-written and artfully designed book, music, and video info—plus reviews from users around the world—is free.

7. eBay (eBay.com)

The one, the only—the Web's most dangerous site (for auction addicts, anyway). So what if you get carried away and overpay? It's entertainment.

8. MySimon (mysimon.com)

About to splurge on something? This site will scour the Web to see if you can get it cheaper.

9. Infospace (www.infospace.com)

National yellow pages, white pages, e-mail address directories, and more—all the better to help you track down that old buddy or lost love.

10. The Internet Movie Database (us.imdb.com)

Everything you ever wanted to know about nearly every movie ever made. Cast, crew, reviews, release dates, and more—all linked so you can play your own version of Six Degrees of Kevin Bacon.

11. ESPN.com

Whether your pleasure is baseball or roller hockey, this site dishes out more up-to-the-minute stats and scores than you can shake a stick (bat, racquet, javelin . . .) at.

12. Weather.com

A stormy paradise for weather junkies—minus the Muzak. And handy for anyone without a window office.

13. The Obscure Store and Reading Room (www.obscurestore.com)

One guy's daily roundup of wacky and/or provocative tidbits from the nation's newspapers. If a blind golfer scores a hole in one—or a crook in drag holds up a bank—this site is sure to have a link.

14. The Drudge Report (www.drudgereport.com)

See ground zero of the Monica Lewinsky mess—the snappy, salacious site of one-man gossip machine Matt Drudge.

15. Ain't It Cool News (www.aint-it-cool-news.com)

Proprietor Harry Knowles commands an army of moles who attend advance movie screenings, providing early dish and perturbing Hollywood execs.

16. The Onion (www.theonion.com)

A humor magazine that's actually funny. Long a Net pleasure, it made the big time with its bestselling book, *Our Dumb Century*.

17. Epicurious (epicurious.com)

Whether you cook or just like to eat, this foodie fave has the recipe for success, with a searchable 11,000-recipe database (chiefly taken from *Gourmet* and *Bon Appetit* magazines) and tons of tips.

18. MapQuest (www.mapquest.com)

Another great thing about the Net: enter any two places in the United States and get free personalized point-to-point driving instructions.

19. Microsoft Expedia (expedia.msn.com)

If you're picky about your travel plans—and who isn't?—it pays to book your own plane tickets. Here and on other sites (but, hey, Bill Gates really needs the money) you can shop from a full range of flights and pick your own seat assignment.

20. People.com

Head to the Web outpost of our mother magazine for daily celeb news, in-depth profiles of your favorite stars, and lots more.

MOST POPULAR WEB SITES

Ranking the popularity of Web sites is far from an exact science. One method follows the approach of TV's Nielsen ratings—following a bunch of selected surfers to see where they're clicking. For this June 2001 report, Internet measurement company Jupiter Media Metrix tracked over 60,000 computer users to determine which sites were visited most.

TOP NEWS SITES
1. MSNBC.com
2. CNN.com
3. NYTimes.com
4. ABCNews.com
5. Washingtonpost.com
6. USAToday.com
7. Slate.com
8. LATimes.com
9. Time.com
10. WSJ.com

TOP ENTERTAINMENT SITES
1. Real.com
2. About.com
3. Flowgo.com
4. Disney.com
5. Iwin.com
6. WindowsMedia.com
7. TwistedHumor.com
8. Shockwave.com
9. Sony.com
10. Warnerbros.com

TOP SEARCH SITES
1. Google.com
2. Askjeeves.com
3. Goto.com
4. Altavista.com
5. Looksmart.com

TOP PORTALS
1. Yahoo.com
2. MSN.com
3. AOL.com
4. Lycos.com
5. Netscape.com

TOP TRAVEL SITES
1. MapQuest.com
2. Expedia.com
3. Travelocity.com
4. Southwest.com
5. Delta-air.com
6. United.com
7. NWA.com
8. Secureredemption.com
9. USAir.com
10. Mapsonus.com

TOP SHOPPING SITES
1. X10.com
2. Amazon.com
3. Half.com
4. Mypoints.com
5. Bizrate.com
6. Americangreetings.com
7. Columbiahouse.com
8. Ticketmaster.com
9. BMGMusicservice.com
10. CDNow.com

TOP SPORTS SITES
1. ESPN.com
2. SportsLine.com
3. MLB.com
4. CNNSI.com
5. NBA.com
6. NFL.com
7. Sandbox.com
8. FANSonly.com
9. Sportingnews.com
10. PGATOUR.com

TOP HEALTH SITES
1. WebMD.com
2. EDiets.com
3. Drugstore.com
4. OneWorldLive.com
5. Thebreastcancersite.com
6. Dietsmart.com
7. Medscape.com
8. Dove.com
9. Walgreens.com
10. Merck-Medco.com

CYBERSPACE'S MOST WANTED

Search sites help Web crawlers find sites devoted to their favorite stars and shows. Here's what people sought out most often at Lycos (lycos.com) from January 1 through July 21, 2001:

TOP ACTRESSES

1. Pamela Anderson
2. Jennifer Lopez
3. Angelina Jolie
4. Jennifer Love Hewitt
5. Alyssa Milano
6. Jessica Alba
7. Shannon Elizabeth
8. Denise Richards
9. Nikki Cox
10. Sarah Michelle Gellar

TOP ACTORS

1. Brad Pitt
2. Russell Crowe
3. Tom Cruise
4. Josh Hartnett
5. Heath Ledger
6. Bruce Lee
7. Keanu Reeves
8. Mel Gibson
9. Ben Affleck
10. Vin Diesel

TOP MUSICIANS OR BANDS

1. Britney Spears
2. Jennifer Lopez
3. Eminem
4. 'N Sync
5. Madonna
6. Limp Bizkit
7. Christina Aguilera
8. Destiny's Child
9. Backstreet Boys
10. Metallica

TOP MOVIES

1. Pearl Harbor
2. Star Wars
3. Lord of the Rings
4. Tomb Raider
5. The Matrix
6. Titanic
7. Final Fantasy
8. Hannibal
9. The Mummy Returns
10. Crouching Tiger, Hidden Dragon

TOP TV SHOWS

1. Dragonball
2. Pokemon
3. Survivor
4. The Simpsons
5. Digimon
6. Sailor Moon
7. South Park
8. Big Brother
9. Gundam Wing
10. The Sopranos

FASHION AWARDS

CFDA AWARDS

Since 1981 the Council of Fashion Designers of America has presented annual awards to honor the best design talent. In the earlier years a single award designation was bestowed upon from five to thirteen fashion luminaries. The present categories began to take shape in 1986 with the inception of the Perry Ellis Award. Over the years a number of special awards and special categories have been added. The following list culls some of the most prominent categories and long-lived award designations over the years.

1986

Perry Ellis Award: David Cameron
Lifetime Achievement: Bill Blass and Marlene Dietrich

1987

Designer (menswear): Ronaldus Shamask
Perry Ellis Award: Marc Jacobs
Lifetime Achievement: Giorgio Armani, Horst, and Eleanor Lambert

1988

Designer (menswear): Bill Robinson
Perry Ellis Award: Isaac Mizrahi
Lifetime Achievement: Richard Avedon and Nancy Reagan

1989

Designer (womenswear): Isaac Mizrahi
Designer (menswear): Joseph Abboud
Accessory: Paloma Picasso
Perry Ellis Award: Gordon Henderson
Lifetime Achievement: Oscar de la Renta

1990

Designer (womenswear): Donna Karan
Designer (menswear): Joseph Abboud
Accessory: Manolo Blahnik
Perry Ellis Award: Christian Francis Roth
Lifetime Achievement: Martha Graham

1991

Designer (womenswear): Isaac Mizrahi
Designer (menswear): Roger Forsythe
Accessory: Karl Lagerfeld for House of Chanel
Perry Ellis Award: Todd Oldham
Lifetime Achievement: Ralph Lauren

1992

Designer (womenswear): Marc Jacobs
Designer (menswear): Donna Karan
Accessory: Chrome Hearts
Perry Ellis Award: Anna Sui
International: Gianni Versace
Lifetime Achievement: Pauline Trigère

1993

Designer (womenswear): Calvin Klein
Designer (menswear): Calvin Klein
Perry Ellis Award (womenswear): Richard Tyler
Perry Ellis Award (menswear): John Bartlett
Perry Ellis Award (accessories): Kate Spade
Lifetime Achievement: Judith Leiber and Polly Anne Mellen

1994

Designer (womenswear): Richard Tyler
Perry Ellis Award (womenswear): Victor Alfaro and Cynthia Rowley (tie)
Perry Ellis Award (menswear): Robert Freda

Perry Ellis Award (accessories): Kate Spade
Lifetime Achievement: Carrie Donova, Nonnie Moore, and Bernadine Morris

1995

Designer (womenswear): Ralph Lauren
Designer (menswear): Tommy Hilfiger
Perry Ellis Award (womenswear): Marie-Ane Oudejans for Tocca
Perry Ellis Award (menswear): Richard Tyler, Richard Bengtsson, and Edward Pavlick for Richard Edwards
Perry Ellis Award (accessories): Kate Spade
International: Tom Ford
Lifetime Achievement: Hubert de Givenchy

1996

Designer (womenswear): Donna Karan
Designer (menswear): Ralph Lauren
Designer (accessories): Elsa Peretti for Tiffany
Perry Ellis Award (womenswear): Daryl Kerrigan for Daryl K.
Perry Ellis Award (menswear): Gene Myer
Perry Ellis Award (accessories): Kari Sigerson and Miranda Morrison for Sigerson Morrison
International: Helmut Lang
Lifetime Achievement: Arnold Scaasi

1997

Designer (womenswear): Marc Jacobs
Designer (menswear): John Bartlett
Designer (accessories): Kate Spade
Perry Ellis Award (womenswear): Narciso Rodriguez
Perry Ellis Award (menswear): Sandy Dalal
International: John Galliano
Lifetime Achievement: Geoffrey Beene

1998/99

Designer (womenswear): Michael Kors
Designer (menswear): Calvin Klein
Designer (accessories): Marc Jacobs
Perry Ellis Award (womenswear): Josh Patner and Bryan Bradley for Tuleh
Perry Ellis Award (menswear): Matt Nye
Perry Ellis Award (accessories): Tony Valentine
International: Yohji Yamamoto
Lifetime Achievement: Yves Saint Laurent

2000

Designer (womenswear): Oscar de la Renta
Designer (menswear): Helmut Lang
Designer (accessories): Richard Lambertson and John Truex
Perry Ellis Award (womenswear): Miguel Adrover
Perry Ellis Award (menswear): John Varvatos
Perry Ellis Award (accessories): Dean Harris
International: Jean-Paul Gaultier
Most Stylish Dot-com: Issey Miyake's Pleats Please
Lifetime Achievement Award: Valentino

2001

Designer (womenswear): Tom Ford
Designer (menswear): John Varvatos
Designer (accessories): Reed Krakoff
Perry Ellis Award (womenswear): Nicole Noselli and Daphne Gutierrez
Perry Ellis Award (menswear): William Reid
Perry Ellis Award (accessories): Edmundo Castillo
International: Nicolas Ghesquiere
Lifetime Achievement: Calvin Klein

VH1 FASHION AWARDS

For the last six years, VH1 has bestowed fashion awards (combined with music awards in the first year), and in 1999 the channel joined forces with *Vogue* magazine in the presentation. Here are names who paraded down the presentation catwalk.

1995

Designer: Miuccia Prada
New Designer: Tom Ford for Gucci
Model (female): Shalom Harlow
Model (male): Tyson Beckford
Most Fashionable Artist: Madonna
Ongoing Life Achievement: Karl Lagerfeld
Frock 'N Rock: Gianni Versace
Catwalk to Sidewalk: Tommy Hilfiger
Stylist for a Music Video: Lori Goldstein, Madonna's "Take a Bow"

1996

Designer: Tom Ford for Gucci
Model (female): Kate Moss
Model (male): Mark Vanderloo (Hugo Boss)
Most Fashionable Artist: Elton John
Best Personal Style (female): Gwyneth Paltrow
Best Personal Style (male): Dennis Rodman

1997

Designer (womenswear): John Galliano
Designer (menswear): Helmut Lang
Model (female): Karen Elson
Model (male): Charlie Speed
Most Fashionable Artist: Beck
Best Personal Style (female): Courtney Love
Best Personal Style (male): Will Smith
Best Second Collection: Donatella Versace, for Versus
Most Stylish Music Video: Fiona Apple, "Criminal"

1998

Designer (womenswear): Marc Jacobs
Designer (menswear): Prada
Avant Garde Designer: Alexander McQueen
New Designer: Veronique Branquinho
Model (female): Carolyn Murphy
Model (male): Scott Barnhill
Most Fashionable Artist: Madonna
Best Personal Style (female): Cameron Diaz
Best Personal Style (male): Chris Rock
Photographer: Steven Meisel
Most Stylish Music Video: Janet Jackson, "Gone Till It's Gone"

1999

Designer: Tom Ford
Avant Garde Designer: Alexander McQueen
Model: Gisele Bundchen
Most Fashionable Artist (female): Jennifer Lopez
Most Fashionable Artist (male): Lenny Kravitz
Celebrity Style (female): Heather Graham
Celebrity Style (male): Rupert Everett

2000

Designer: Stella McCartney
Avant Garde Designer: Nicolas Ghesquiere
Model: Carmen Kass
Most Fashionable Artist (Female): Macy Gray
Most Fashionable Artist (Male): Enrique Iglesias
Celebrity Style (Female): Chloë Sevigny
Celebrity Style (Male): Jude Law

THE PEOPLE REGISTER

THE PEOPLE REGISTER

As always, the *Almanac* assembles essential dossiers and fascinating facts on the celebrity elite. Once again, to accommodate the new millennium's infinitely expanding galaxy of pop culture stars, we've added many glittery new names to our listing.

THE NEW REGISTRANTS:

Jessica Alba
Joan Allen
Javier Bardem
Kate Beckinsale
Jamie Bell
Jason Biggs
Björk
David Blaine
David Bowie
Gisele Bundchen
Ellen Burstyn
Jennifer Capriati
Charlotte Church
Joan Cusack
Willem Dafoe
Benicio del Toro

Robert Duvall
Missy Elliott
Will Ferrell
Colin Firth
Clare Forlani
Bryant Gumbel
Darrell Hammond
Marcia Gay Harden
Josh Hartnett
Sean Hayes
Chris Isaak
Alan Iverson
Hugh Jackman
Allison Janney
Diane Keaton
Catherine Keener
Johnny Knoxville

Beyoncé Knowles
Heath Ledger
Eric McCormack
Megan Mullaly
Thandie Newton
Julia Ormond
Jeff Probst
Busta Rhymes
Kelly Ripa
Anne Robinson
Shaggy
Julia Stiles
Amy Tan
Rob Thomas
Maura Tierney
Estella Warren
Lucinda Williams

BEN AFFLECK

Birthplace: Berkeley, CA
Birthdate: 8/15/72
Occupation: Actor, screenwriter
Education: Attended University of Vermont and Occidental College
Debut: (Film) *Mystic Pizza*, 1988
Signature: *Good Will Hunting*, 1997
Facts: Became friends with Matt Damon in elementary school. By high school, the pair held "business meeting lunches" in the cafeteria to plot their future acting careers.

Wrote *Good Will Hunting* with Damon out of frustration when they weren't getting many acting jobs. Eventually sold the script to Miramax for $800,000.

Owns vintage Ms. Pac-Man and Millipede video arcade games.

Owns 5 motorcycles.
Infamy: Checked himself into a rehabilitation facility for alcohol dependency in 2001 (his father is reportedly a recovering alcoholic).
Famous Relative: Casey Affleck, actor, brother
Major Award: Oscar, Best Original Screenplay, *Good Will Hunting*, 1997
Quote: "I feel like fame is wasted on me. I already feel like I don't want to have sex five times a day. It's kind of depressing."

CHRISTINA AGUILERA

Birthplace: Staten Island, NY
Birthdate: 12/18/80
Occupation: Singer
Education: High school
Debut: (Album) *Christina Aguilera*, 1999
Signature: "What a Girl Wants"
Facts: Born to an Ecuadoran-born army sergeant and Irish-American mother, she lived in Texas, Japan, New Jersey, and Pennsylvania.

At eight, she appeared on *Star Search*, winning runner-up for her rendition of Whitney Houston's "The Greatest Love of All."

Sang National Anthem at a Pittsburgh Steelers game at age 10.

At age 12 joined the *New Mickey Mouse Club* with Britney Spears, Justin Timberlake, J. C. Chasez, and Keri Russell.

Still sleeps with lights on because she is afraid of the dark.

Reportedly has been in relationships with Carson Daly, Eminem, and Limp Bizkit's Fred Durst.

Talent scout Ruth Imus, who claims to be her former manager filed a $7 million lawsuit against her mother and others in 2000, alleging breach of contract and accusing them of cheating her out of her share of the star's fortune.
Relationship: Jorge Santos, dancer
Major Award: Grammy, Best New Artist, 1999
Quote: "I think everybody should have a great Wonderbra. There's so many ways to enhance them, everybody does it."

JESSICA ALBA

Birthplace: Pomona, CA
Birthdate: 4/28/81
Occupation: Actor
Education: High school
Debut: (Film) *Camp Nowhere*, 1993
Signature: *Dark Angel*
Facts: Lived in Mississippi, Texas, and California for nine roving years as a child due to her father's career in the Air Force.

Is part Spanish, part Danish, part Canadian and part Italian.

Graduated high school at the age of 16.

As a teenager, she was briefly a born-again Christian.

Has performed guest roles on TV's *Love Boat: The Next Wave*, *Brooklyn South* and *Beverly Hills 90210*.

Studied martial arts and gymnastics and did weight and motorcycle training to perfect her performance in *Dark Angel*.

Worked with David Mamet and William H. Macy at their Atlantic Theater Company.
Relationship: Michael Weatherly, actor (engaged, 2001)

Quote: "I'm not going around kicking ass. But it's nice to know I can."

JASON ALEXANDER

Real Name: Jay Scott Greenspan
Birthplace: Newark, NJ
Birthdate: 9/23/59
Occupation: Actor
Education: Boston University
Debut: (Film) *The Burning*, 1981; (TV) *Senior Trip!*, 1981
Signature: *Seinfeld*
Facts: *Seinfeld* creator Larry David modeled the George character after himself.

Is an accomplished dancer and operatic tenor.
Marriage: Daena E. Title, 1979
Child: Gabriel, 1992; Noah, 1996
Major Awards: Tony, Best Actor, *Jerome Robbins' Broadway*, 1989; Grammy, Best Cast Show Album, *Jerome Robbins' Broadway* (with others), 1989
Quote: "I started losing my hair when I was a wee kid of 16."

JOAN ALLEN

Birthplace: Rochelle, IL
Birthdate: 8/20/56
Occupation: Actor
Education: Attended Eastern Illinois University; Northern Illinois University
Debut: (Off-Broadway) *And a Nightingale Sang*, 1983; (Film) *Compromising Positions*, 1985; (TV) *Evergreen*, 1985; (Broadway) *Burn This*, 1987
Signature: *Nixon*, 1996
Facts: Was rejected for her high school's cheerleading squad, so she auditioned for the school play and found her career.

Befriended fellow actor John Malkovich in college and joined him in Chicago's Steppenwolf Theater in 1978.

Has a pet miniature parrot.

Nominated three times for Academy Awards for her roles in *Nixon*, *The Crucible* and *The Contender*.

Original job: Secretary
Marriage: Peter Friedman, 1990
Child: Sadie, 1994
Major Award: Tony, Lead Actress in a Play, *Burn This*, 1988
Quote: "I think it's hard to be glamorous and be taken seriously in the U.S."

TIM ALLEN

Real Name: Tim Allen Dick
Birthplace: Denver, CO
Birthdate: 6/13/53
Occupation: Comedian, actor
Education: Western Michigan University
Debut: (TV) *Showtime Comedy Club All-Stars II*
Signature: *Home Improvement*
Facts: Has nine brothers and sisters.

Appeared in Mr. Goodwrench commercials.

Provided the voice for Buzz Lightyear in *Toy Story*, 1995.

Paid $2 million for 26 acres of Michigan campground with the intention of keeping it in its natural, undeveloped state.
Infamy: He served 28 months in jail in 1978 for attempting to sell cocaine.

Pled guilty to impaired driving in 1997. When stopped by police, Allen failed four sobriety tests, including counting backward and reciting the alphabet.
Original Job: Creative director for an advertising agency
Marriage: Laura Deibel, 1978 (separated, 1999)
Child: Kady, 1990

WOODY ALLEN

Real Name: Allen Stewart Konigsberg; legal name Heywood Allen
Birthplace: Brooklyn, NY
Birthdate: 12/1/35
Occupation: Actor, director, writer
Education: New York University, City College of New York
Debut: (Film) *What's New Pussycat?*,

1965 [see page 64 for a complete filmography]
Signature: *Annie Hall*, 1977
Facts: Played clarinet every Monday night at Michael's Pub in Manhattan. Missed the Academy Awards ceremony for *Annie Hall* because it was on a Monday night. Now plays at the Café Carlyle.

Among his many neuroses: won't take showers if the drain is in the middle.

Was suspended from New York University for inattention to his work.

His daughters are both named after jazz greats.
Infamy: After details became known of his affair with Soon-Yi, Mia Farrow's oldest adopted daughter, Farrow accused him of sexual abuse of her younger children. In 1993, he was denied custody of their adopted children, Dylan (since renamed Malone) and Moses, and biological son Satchel (since renamed Seamus).

After Allen adopted a daughter with wife Soon-Yi, Farrow commented: "I don't know how the courts permitted this, especially in light of a judge not allowing Mr. Allen to see his own children."

Sued longtime producer Jean Doumanian and others in 2001, charging that she cheated him out of profits from the last eight movies they made together.
Original Job: During high school, he supplied comic snippets to newspaper columnists Walter Winchell and Earl Wilson; he later became a hired gag-writer on a retainer of $25 a week.
Marriages: Harlene Rosen (divorced), Louise Lasser (divorced); Soon-Yi Previn, 1997
Children: Moses,1978 (adopted); Malone, 1985 (originally Dylan, changed to Eliza, changed again; adopted); Seamus, 1987 (formerly Satchel); (with Mia Farrow). Bechet Dumaine, 1998 (adopted); Manzie Tio, 2000 (adopted)
Major Awards: Oscar, Best Director, *Annie Hall*, 1977; Oscar, Best Original Screenplay, *Annie Hall*,

1977; Oscar, Best Original Screenplay, *Hannah and Her Sisters,* 1986
Quote: "I've never had an audience in any medium."

TORI AMOS

Real Name: Myra Ellen Amos
Birthdate: 8/22/63
Occupation: Singer, songwriter
Education: High school
Debut: (Album) *Y Kant Tori Read?*, 1988
Signature: "Crucify," 1992
Facts: She started playing the piano at age three. At age 5 she won a scholarship to study piano in a conservatory in Baltimore but was kicked out by age 11 for refusing to practice.

Father was an evangelical preacher, a fact that figures heavily into her sex-laden lyrics in songs like "Leather" and "God."
Original Job: Piano player in Los Angeles lounges
Marriage: Mark Hawley, 1998
Child: daughter, 2000 (name not released at press time)
Quote: "I have vivid memories of being a prostitute in another life."

GILLIAN ANDERSON

Birthplace: Chicago, IL
Birthdate: 8/9/68
Occupation: Actor
Education: DePaul University
Debut: (Stage) *Absent Friends*, 1991
Signature: *The X-Files*
Facts: Lived in London during her childhood.

As a teenager smitten by British punk rock, she spiked her hair, pierced her nose, put a safety pin through her cheek, and dated a rock musician almost a decade her senior.

To hide her pregnancy, Anderson wore bulky trench coats and took three episodes off during an alleged alien abduction.

Believes in UFOs, ESP, and other paranormal phenomena.

Thousands of male fans have

formed an online Gillian Anderson Testosterone Brigade.

Has raised about $250,000 for the nonprofit Neurofibromatosis Inc., by auctioning off X-Files memorablilia on the Web. The disease affects 100,000 Americans, including her 19-year-old brother, Aaron.

Marriage: Clyde Klotz, 1994 (separated, 1996); Rodney Rowland (relationship)

Child: Piper, 1994

Major Award: Emmy, Best Actress in a Drama Series, *The X-Files*, 1997

PAMELA ANDERSON

Birthplace: Comox, Canada
Birthdate: 7/1/67
Occupation: Actor
Education: High school
Debut: (TV) *Home Improvement*, 1991; (Film) *Barb Wire*, 1995
Signature: *V.I.P*
Facts: Got her first commercial job after her image was projected on a giant scoreboard screen at a Canadian football game in 1989.

Says her mother encouraged her to pose for her several *Playboy* covers, telling her it was a compliment (8 in all—a record).

Writes fairy tales and poetry and regularly keeps a dream diary.

Married Mötley Crüe drummer Tommy Lee in Cancun, Mexico, in 1995 wearing a tiny white bikini. (Lee wore white Bermuda shorts.)

Lost a court request to halt distribution of a homemade video showing her and then-husband Tommy Lee having sex; the two claim the tape was stolen from their home.

Filed for divorce from Lee on grounds of spousal abuse. He spent 3 months in jail for kicking her and was put on probation.

In 1999, had her silicone breast implants removed, going from a size 34 D to a 34 C. (Surgery revealed that the implants had been leaking.)

Shared a New Year's drink with Lee in 2000 which resulted in an exten-

sion of his probation until May 2003 for violating his parole.

Original Job: Beer company spokesmodel

Marriage: Tommy Lee (1995; divorced, 1998; remarried, 1999; separated, 2000); Markus Schenkenburg, model (relationship)

Child: Brandon Thomas, 1996; Dylan Jagger, 1997

Quote: "Tommy has been fixed. Actually, he has been neutered or spayed. What do you call it?"

JULIE ANDREWS

Birthplace: Walton-on-Thames, England
Birthdate: 10/1/35
Occupation: Actor, singer
Education: High school
Debut: (Stage) *Starlight Roof*, 1947; (Film) *Mary Poppins*, 1964
Signature: *Mary Poppins*
Facts: By age 8, had a fully formed adult throat and a four-octave voice.

The 1965 film *The Sound of Music*, in which she played Maria Von Trapp, was the highest-grossing film of its day.

She and husband Edwards adopted two Vietnamese girls during the war.

Under married name Julie Edwards, wrote two children's books in the 1970s, *Mandy* and *The Last of the Really Great Whangdoodles*.

Before starring in *Victor/Victoria*, was last on Broadway 33 years ago.

Rejected her 1996 Tony award nomination for best actress for *Victor/Victoria* because the show was snubbed in all other categories.

Surgery to remove noncancerous throat nodules in June 1997 has silenced her professional singing voice. In 1999, she filed a negligence complaint against Dr. Scott M. Kessler and Dr. Jeffrey D. Libin, claiming she wasn't informed that the surgery carried the risk of permanent hoarseness and "irreversible loss of vocal quality." The

suit was settled for undisclosed terms in 2000.

Infamy: Tried to shed *Mary Poppins* image by baring her breasts in 1981's *S.O.B.*

Original Job: Toured from age 12 with mother and alcoholic stepfather in a vaudeville act.

Marriages: Tony Walton, 1959 (divorced, 1968); Blake Edwards, 1969

Children: Emma, 1962 (with Tony Walton). Jennifer (stepdaughter); Geoffrey (stepson); Amy Leigh, 1974 (adopted); Joanna Lynne, 1975 (adopted).

Major Award: Oscar, Best Actress, *Mary Poppins*, 1964

MAYA ANGELOU

Real Name: Margueritte Annie Johnson
Birthplace: St. Louis, MO
Birthdate: 4/4/28
Occupation: Writer, actor, singer, dancer
Education: California Labor School
Debut: (Film) *Calypso Heatwave*, 1957
Signature: *I Know Why the Caged Bird Sings*, 1979
Facts: Nicknamed "Maya" by her brother, who called her "My" or "Mine."

At age 7, she was raped by her mother's boyfriend. Sever al days after her testimony at the trial, her assailant was found dead—killed by her uncles. She blamed herself for the death and did not speak for the next five years.

Tried to join the army in the late 1940s, but was turned down after a security check revealed that the California Labor School was listed as subversive.

Has received over 30 honorary degrees.

Read the inaugural poem at President Clinton's inauguration ceremony.

Infamy: In the late 1950s, she worked as a madam, managing two prostitutes in San Diego. Her guilty conscience caused her to quit after only a short stint.

Original job: The first black—and the first female—streetcar conductor in San Francisco at age 16.

Marriages: Tosh Angelou (divorced, c. 1952); Vusumze Make (divorced); Paul Du Feu, 1973 (divorced, 1981)

Child: Guy Johnson, 1945

Major Award: Grammy, Best Spoken Word Recording, *On the Pulse of Morning,* 1993

JENNIFER ANISTON

Birthplace: Sherman Oaks, CA

Birthdate: 2/11/69

Occupation: Actor

Education: High School of Performing Arts

Debut: (TV movie) *Camp Cucamonga,* 1990

Signature: *Friends*

Facts: Actor Telly Savalas was her godfather.

Like her *Friends* character, Aniston worked as a waitress after graduating from school.

The rail-thin Aniston actually used to be fat. When she realized that was keeping her from landing acting parts, she went on the Nutri/System diet and lost 30 pounds.

Because of her often-emulated shag, she was dubbed America's First Hairdo by *Rolling Stone* magazine.

In 2000, along with *Friends* costars, received a salary increase from $125,000 to $750,000 per episode.

Infamy: Caused a stir in 1996 when she posed nude in *Rolling Stone.*

In 2000, sued *High Society* and *Celebrity Skin* for publishing pictures of her while she sunbathed topless in her backyard.

Marriage: Brad Pitt, 2000

Famous Relative: John Aniston, actor, father

MARC ANTHONY

Real Name: Antonio Marco Muniz

Birthplace: East Harlem, New York City

Birthdate: 9/16/69

Occupation: Salsa singer

Education: High school

Debut: (Album) *When the Night Is Over,* 1991; (Film) *Hackers,* 1995; (Broadway) *The Capeman,* 1998

Signature: *Contra la Corriente (Against the Flood),* 1997

Facts: Was discovered at age 12 by commercial producer David Harris.

First exposed to salsa music in his family's kitchen, where his father would play with a salsa band.

Changed his name not only because his listeners were primarily English-speaking but also because there was a known Mexican singer with the same name.

His first solo salsa album, *Otra nota,* which included "El ultimo beso," a song written by his father, went gold five months after its release in 1992.

Rejecting the typical flashy salsa dress, he often wears a pair of jeans, a T-shirt, and a baseball cap on stage.

During his performances, he always pays a tribute to the Puerto Rican flag.

Original Job: Backup singer for TV commercials

Marriage: Dayanara Torres, 2000

Child: Arianna, 1994 (with Debbie Rosado); Cristian Anthony Muniz, 2001

Famous Relative: Felipe Muniz, Puerto Rican jibaro guitarist, father

Quote: "I still don't know how to pick up panties in front of thousands of people and be cool about it. I gotta call Tom Jones and ask his advice."

FIONA APPLE

Real Name: Fiona Apple McAfee Maggart

Birthplace: New York, NY

Birthdate: 9/13/77

Occupation: Singer-songwriter

Education: High school

Debut: (Album) *Tidal,* 1996

Signature: "Criminal," 1997

Facts: Named after a character in *Brigadoon.*

A rape by a stranger at age 12 precipitated years of therapy and inspired the lyrics to her song "Sullen Girl."

After her parents divorced, she lived with her mother and sister in New York City. Leaving school to join her father in Los Angeles, she finished her high school requirements through a correspondence course.

Lack of a driver's education course has kept her from earning her diploma. She still doesn't have a driver's license.

Regarded as a loner in high school and was nicknamed "Dog" by classmates.

Began taking piano lessons when she was about 8 years old and debuted an original composition at her first recital.

At age 18, she produced a demo tape for a publicist and was instantly signed by a manager.

Follows a vegetarian diet and her typical preperformance meal is split pea soup.

Infamy: Used profanity at the 1997 *MTV Video Music Awards* show.

Relationship: Paul Thomas Anderson, writer-director

Famous Relative: Brandon Maggart, actor, father; Diana McAfee, singer, dancer, mother

Major Awards: Grammy, Best Rock Vocal—Female, "Criminal," 1997

Quote: "If I'm going to end up a role model, then I'd rather not end up being the kind of role model that pretends to be perfect and pretends that she always has the right thing to say."

CHRISTINA APPLEGATE

Birthplace: Los Angeles, CA
Birthdate: 11/25/71
Occupation: Actor
Debut: (TV) *Days of Our Lives,* 1971; (Film) *Jaws of Satan,* 1979
Signature: *Married...With Children*
Facts: When she was 3 months old, she appeared in her mother's arms on *Days of Our Lives.*

During her period of "image-experimentation," she appeared on a poster wearing battered cut-offs and a black leather vest with nothing underneath. A falcon is sitting on one arm and a snake is wrapped around the other.

Bought her first house when she was 11 years old, using her investment money.

Her mother, poor and at one time on food stamps, took her along on casting calls.

She has 3 tattoos.
Relationship: Jonathan Schaech, actor (1998)
Famous Relative: Nancy Priddy, actor, mother
Quote: "As a kid, I was pretty wild. Now I think I'm boring."

GIORGIO ARMANI

Birthplace: Piacenza, Italy
Birthdate: 7/11/34
Occupation: Fashion designer
Facts: Entered medical school but after two years decided to join the military.

Designed uniforms for the Italian Air Force (1980).
Original Job: Medical assistant for Italian military, window dresser in a Milan department store
Major Awards: Neiman-Marcus Award, Distinguished Service in the Field of Fashion, 1979; Cutty Sark Award, Outstanding International Designer, 1981

COURTENEY COX ARQUETTE

Birthplace: Birmingham, AL
Birthdate: 6/15/64
Occupation: Actor
Education: Mt. Vernon College (Washington, DC)
Debut: (TV) *Misfits of Science,* 1985; (Film) *Down Twisted,* 1987
Signature: *Friends*
Facts: Discovered in 1984 Brian De Palma video "Dancing in the Dark" with Bruce Springsteen.

Played Michael J. Fox's girlfriend on *Family Ties* and Jim Carrey's love interest in *Ace Ventura: Pet Detective.*

Had LASIK eye surgery (to correct nearsightedness).

In 2000, along with *Friends* costars, received a salary increase from $125,000 to $750,000 per episode.
Original Job: Model
Marriage: David Arquette, 1999
Famous Relatives: Patricia Arquette, sister-in-law, actor; Rosanna Arquette, sister-in-law, actor

ROWAN ATKINSON

Birthplace: Newcastle-upon-Tyne, England
Birthdate: 1/6/55
Occupation: Actor, comedian, writer
Education: Newcastle University, Oxford University
Debut: (Stage) *Beyond a Joke,* 1978; (TV) BBC series *Not the Nine O'Clock News,* 1979; (Film) *Bean,* 1997
Signature: Mr. Bean
Facts: Earned a B.S. in electrical engineering but was rejected for a job at the BBC. Later earned a masters degree in computer engineering.

His middle name is Sebastian.

In elementary school, his fellow students referred to him as "Moon Man," "Doopie," and "Zoonie."

He drives go-carts, collects classic sports cars, and has written for automobile magazines.

His one-man Broadway show closed after only 14 performances.

He met his wife on the set of *The Black Adder;* she was a make-up artist at the time.

In 1994, he won raves for his well-known comical cameo as the misspeaking vicar in *Four Weddings and a Funeral.*

He is very protective of his private life and reveals very little about his family in interviews.
Original Job: Actor
Marriage: Sunetra Sastry, 1990
Children: Two children
Quote: "I am essentially a rather quiet, dull person who just happens to be a performer."

STEVE AUSTIN

Real Name: Steven Williams
Birthplace: Austin, TX
Birthdate: 12/18/64
Occupation: Wrestler
Education: Attended University of North Texas
Facts: Dropped out of school in 1987, a few credits short of a degree in physical education.

Began wrestling in 1989 for $20 per day.

Known as "Stone Cold" Steve Austin, he once shouted in a fight against Bible-quoting Jake "The Snake" Roberts, "Talk about your psalms, talk about John 3:16; Austin 3:16 says I just whipped your [butt]!" Since then, he sells some 1 million self-designed T-shirts each month, with his Austin 3:16 logo.

Before he married Jeannie Clark, she was his valet, Lady Blossom.

His stats are listed at 6' 2", 252 pounds.

He wrestles 180 shows a year.

Suffered a spinal injury in 1997 after wrestler Owen Hart landed on his head in a "tombstone piledriver," which left him unsure of his future with the WWF.

In 2000, he underwent spinal surgery to remove bone spurs in his neck vertebrae from years of body slamming.
Original Job: Loaded trucks at a freight terminal
Marriage: Jeannie Clark (separated)

Children: Jade, 1981 (step-daughter); Stephanie, 1992; Cassidy, 1996

Quote: "A lot of people relate to me. Look, I dumped my boss on his head. I think that everybody would like to do that."

DAN AYKROYD

Birthplace: Ottawa, Canada
Birthdate: 7/1/52
Occupation: Actor, writer
Education: Carleton University
Debut: (TV) *Saturday Night Live*, 1975; (Film) *1941*, 1979
Signature: *Ghostbusters*, 1984
Facts: His grandfather was a Mountie.

Was expelled for delinquency from St. Pious X Preparatory Seminary.

Had a cameo role in *Indiana Jones and the Temple of Doom*, 1984.

A police buff, he rides an Ontario Provincial Police motorcycle, collects police badges, sometimes rides shotgun with detectives in squad cars, and owns, in partnership with several Toronto police officers, a Toronto bar called Crooks.

He is very interested in the supernatural and has an extensive collection of books on the subject. He admits, "I've never seen a full apparition, but I once saw what could be termed ectoplasmic light, and that scared the hell out of me."

Co-founder of the House of Blues restaurant/music club chain.

Original Job: Stand-up comedian
Marriage: Donna Dixon, 1983
Children: Danielle Alexandra, 1989; Belle Kingston, 1993; Stella Irene Augustus, 1998
Major Award: Emmy, Best Writing in a Comedy, Variety, or Music Series, *Saturday Night Live*, 1977

BURT BACHARACH

Birthplace: Kansas City, MO
Birthdate: 5/12/28
Occupation: Songwriter, composer, producer, arranger

Education: Attended Mannes College of Music, New York City
Debut: (First No. 1 hit) "The Story of My Life," 1957; (First film as composer of theme song) *The Sad Sack*, 1957
Signature: "I'll Never Fall in Love Again," 1960
Facts: He toured army bases as a concert pianist from 1950 to 1952.

Following army service, he was accompanist for Polly Bergen, Georgia Gibbs, the Ames Brothers, Imogene Coca, Joel Grey, and Paula Stewart.

Once he's left the recording studio, he does not want to hear the record again.

Unwillingly studied piano during childhood to please his mother.

As a child, he attempted to grow taller and fulfill his dream of becoming a football player by eating jars of peanut butter.

In 1957, he met lyricist Hal David and began years of collaboration—some 150 songs—and No. 1 hits, including "Magic Moments" (Perry Como, 1958).

Bacharach and David teamed with Dionne Warwick in 1962, and they had 39 chart records in 10 years, eight of which made it to the Top 10.

He cowrote with Carole Bayer Sager the Grammy-winning song "That's What Friends Are For," which became the popular anthem for the struggle against AIDS.

By the mid-1990s, his music enjoyed a revival, and five of his songs were used in the 1997 film *My Best Friend's Wedding*.

Bacharach now enjoys breeding and racing thoroughbred race horses.

Original Jobs: Pianist
Marriages: Paula Stewart (divorced); Angie Dickinson, 1965 (divorced, 1981); Carole Bayer Sager, 1981 (divorced, c. 1991); Jane Hanson, 1991
Children: Lea Nikki, 1966 (with Dickinson). Cristopher Elton, c. 1986 (adopted); Oliver, c. 1993; Raleigh,

c. 1996 (with Sager)
Famous Relative: Bert Bacharach, men's fashion columnist and author, father
Major Awards: Grammy Award, Best Instrumental Arrangement, "Alfie," 1967; Academy Award, Best Original Music Score, *Butch Cassidy and the Sundance Kid*, 1969; Academy Award, Best Original Song, "Raindrops Keep Fallin' on My Head," *Butch Cassidy and the Sundance Kid*, 1969; Grammy Award, Best Original Score Written for Motion Picture, *Butch Cassidy and the Sundance Kid*, 1969; Grammy Award, Best Score from an Original Cast Album, *Promises, Promises*, 1969; Emmy Award, Outstanding Single Program, Variety or Musical, *Singer Presents Burt Bacharach*, 1970/71; Academy Award, Best Song, "Best That You Can Do," *Arthur*, 1984; Grammy Award, Song of the Year, "That's What Friends Are For," 1986; Grammy Award, Pop Collaboration With Vocals, "I Still Have That Other Girl" (with Elvis Costello), 1999
Quote: "With technology today, you can make perfect garage music, but when you peel it back, maybe what's missing is melody."

KEVIN BACON

Birthplace: Philadelphia, PA
Birthdate: 7/8/58
Occupation: Actor
Education: Manning St. Actor's Theatre, Circle in the Square Theater School
Debut: (Film) *National Lampoon's Animal House*, 1978 [see page 64 for a complete filmography]
Signature: *Footloose*, 1984
Facts: Nervous about Bacon's sex appeal, Paramount's Dawn Steel took his photo around the studio when casting *Footloose* asking everyone, "Is this guy f--kable?" (Obviously he was; he got the teen idol part in the 1984 film.)

For *Murder in the First*, went on a 600 calorie-a-day diet, shaved his head, and wore uncomfortable contacts that completely covered his eyes. When filming the "dungeon" scenes, he put crickets in his hair (to simulate lice) and got welts from being hit with a leather blackjack.

In 1994, formed band the Bacon Brothers with Emmy-winning composer, older brother Michael.
Marriage: Kyra Sedgwick, 1988
Children: Travis, 1989; Sosie Ruth, 1992
Famous Relatives: Michael Bacon, composer, brother
Quote: "My groupies are now between 40 and 50. But that's cool. I'll take them where I can get them."

ERYKAH BADU

Real Name: Erica Wright
Birthplace: Dallas, TX
Birthdate: 2/26/71
Occupation: Singer, songwriter
Education: Attended Grambling State University
Debut: (Album) *Baduizm*, 1997; (Film) *The Cider House Rules*, 1999
Signature: *Baduizm*
Facts: As a teen, wanted to change her "slave name"; when her mother objected, respelled her first name, with the *y* symbolizing "origin" and the *kah*, ancient Egyptian for "pure inner light." Later changed her surname, choosing a riff she favored.

Is influenced by "mathematics," a type of numerology that equates numbers with personal growth and self-knowledge.

Formed the group Erykah Free with cousin Robert "Free" Bradford, but she alone was signed by a label. To symbolize his presence, she began lighting a candle at her concerts.

Gave birth to son, Seven (named because that number cannot be divided by anything but itself), in a planned home birth.
Original Jobs: Teacher, waiter
Relationship: Andre "Dre" Benjamin
Child: Seven Sirius, 1997
Major Awards: Grammy, Best R&B Album, *Baduizm*, 1997; Grammy, Best Female R&B Vocal Perfor-

mance, "On and On," 1997; Grammy, Best Rap Performance–Duo or Group, "You Got Me" (with the Roots), 1999

ALEC BALDWIN

Real Name: Alexander Rae Baldwin III
Birthplace: Massapequa, NY
Birthdate: 4/3/58
Occupation: Actor
Education: New York University, Lee Strasberg Theatre Institute
Debut: (TV) *The Doctors*, 1963
Signature: *The Hunt for Red October*, 1990
Facts: He is not naturally tall, dark, and handsome—he dyes his fair hair black.

Originally wanted to be a lawyer.

Was engaged to Janine Turner (*Northern Exposure*); she had the wedding dress ready and the invitations were sent out when they broke up.
Infamy: Was taken to court for assaulting a paparazzo, who had staked out the actor's house for a photo of his newborn; Baldwin's acquittal was applauded weeks later by the audience at the Oscars.
Original Job: Waiter and doorman at Studio 54
Marriage: Kim Basinger, 1993 (filed for divorce, 2001); Kristin Davis (relationship)
Child: Ireland Eliesse, 1995
Famous Relatives: Daniel Baldwin, actor, brother; William Baldwin, actor, brother; Stephen Baldwin, actor, brother

CHRISTIAN BALE

Birthplace: Pembrokeshire, Wales
Birthdate: 1/30/74
Occupation: Actor
Debut: (TV) *Anastasia: The Mystery of Anna*, 1986; (Film) *Empire of the Sun*, 1987
Signature: *American Psycho*, 2000
Facts: He began his acting career in a commercial for Pac-Man cereal in 1983.

His mother was a circus dancer;

his grandfather was a stand-up comedian and ventriloquist.

In 1987, Steven Spielberg picked Bale out of 4,000 hopefuls to star in *Empire of the Sun*.

Almost lost his role in *American Psycho* to Leonardo DiCaprio. He won the role back when DiCaprio accepted a role in *The Beach*.

In 2000 his father married Gloria Steinem.
Marriage: Sandra (Sibi) Blazic, freelance producer, 2000
Quote: "The more high-profile I get, the less I can surprise people anymore. I've managed it very well. Nobody has a clue who I am, so it's worked."

ANTONIO BANDERAS

Birthplace: Málaga, Spain
Birthdate: 8/10/60
Occupation: Actor
Education: School of Dramatic Art, Málaga, Spain
Debut: (Stage) *Los Tarantos*, 1981; (Film) *Labyrinth of Passion*, 1982
Signature: *The Mask of Zorro*, 1998
Facts: Modeled for Ralph Lauren and Gucci.

Would love to play the Hunchback of Notre Dame, but thinks he won't be able to because of his good looks.

Studied fencing with the U.S. National Olympic Team.
Original Job: Model, waiter
Marriages: Ana Leza (divorced), Melanie Griffith, 1996
Child: Estela del Carmen, 1996
Quote: "I thought to myself, 'Oh my God. How disgusting.' Then I went to the first rehearsal and it was...so easy. I didn't lose my fingers, my ear didn't fall down. Nothing happens if you're sure of who you are." (On his first kiss in a role as a homosexual, in the 1988 Almodóvar movie *Law of Desire*.)

TYRA BANKS

Birthplace: Inglewood, CA
Birthdate: 12/4/73
Occupation: Model, actor
Education: High school
Debut: (TV) *Fresh Prince of Bel Air*, 1994; (Film) *Higher Learning*, 1995
Facts: The August before she was to enroll in college, she was asked by a French modeling agent to work at the couture shows in Paris. Within a week of that first stroll, "Miss Tyra" (as the fashion cognoscenti call her) had accumulated 25 more bookings.

Became the second-ever black model (Lana Ogilvie was the first) under contract with Cover Girl Cosmetics.

Director John Singleton saw her on the cover of *Essence* and felt she'd be perfect for a part in his *Higher Learning*. He arranged for an audition, and during the drawn-out casting process they fell in love for a spell.
Relationship: Craig Taylor

JAVIER BARDEM

Birthplace: Las Palmas, Spain
Birthdate: 3/1/69
Occupation: Actor, producer
Debut: (Film) *The Ages of Lulu*, 1990
Signature: *Before Night Falls*, 2000
Facts: A superstar in his native Spain, he comes from a large family of actors.

He is a hypochondriac.

Does not know how to drive a car.

Was the first Spaniard to receive an Academy Award Best Actor nomination, for his role in *Before Night Falls*. Scored the role only after Benicio Del Toro dropped out.

Has won two Goya Awards, Spain's equivalent of the Oscars.
Original Job: Waiter
Relationship: Cristina Pales
Quote: "I have this boxer's face, I am not brown-skinned, my hair is not black. My teeth are not white. I'm not what they want me to be, and by that I mean I'm not a typical Latin person."

DREW BARRYMORE

Birthplace: Los Angeles, CA
Birthdate: 2/22/75
Occupation: Actor
Education: High school dropout
Debut: (Film) *Altered States*, 1980
Signature: *The Wedding Singer*, 1998
Facts: Starred in a TV commercial for Gainsburgers when she was 11 months old.

After drug rehabilitation, she starred in *Fifteen and Getting Straight* (1989), a TV movie about drug abuse, and wrote her own autobiography, *Little Lost Girl*, at age 14 to clear the air. Credits musician David Crosby for helping her get over drugs.
Infamy: Began drinking at age 9 and started taking drugs at 10.

In 1992, posed nude for *Interview* magazine.

In 1995, posed nude for *Playboy*.

While on the *Late Show with David Letterman* in 1995, pulled down her trousers to display tattoos on her behind, then pulled up her shirt and flashed her breasts at Letterman.

She has six tattoos.

In 2001 her main house was gutted by fire.
Marriages: Jeremy Thomas (divorced, 1994); Tom Green, 2001
Famous Relatives: John Barrymore Jr., actor and director, father; Ethel Barrymore, actor, great-aunt; Lionel Barrymore, actor, great-uncle; John Barrymore Sr., actor, grandfather
Quote: "I was born 10 years old."

MARIA BARTIROMO

Birthplace: Brooklyn, NY
Birthdate: 9/11/67
Occupation: TV financial journalist
Education: New York University
Signature: The Money Honey
Facts: She hired a speech therapist to erase her Brooklyn accent.

In her senior year of college, began work as an intern at CNN *Business News*.

In 1995, she was the first TV journalist to report live from the floor of the New York Stock Exchange.

The Maria Bartiromo Market Hairdex is a website devoted to the correlation between her hair style and the market flux.

She laughs in her sleep.
Marriage: Jonathan Steinberg, 1999
Quote: "There's no reason to believe this stuff is over your head. A woman, particularly a woman, needs to know. It's not brain surgery."

KIM BASINGER

Birthplace: Athens, GA
Birthdate: 12/8/53
Occupation: Actor
Education: University of Georgia
Debut: (Film) *Hard Country*, 1981
Signature: *9 1/2 Weeks*, 1986
Facts: Filed for bankruptcy in May 1993 after an $8.1 million verdict was rendered against her in favor of Main Line Pictures, after she dropped out of the movie *Boxing Helena*. Had to limit her monthly living expenses to $10,000 under bankruptcy plan. An appeals court later reversed the verdict, setting the stage for another trial.

Developed agoraphobia while a model.

Threw her modeling portfolio off the Brooklyn Bridge.

Was involved with Prince before marrying Alec Baldwin.
Infamy: In 1983, she appeared in an eight-page *Playboy* spread.

Bought Braselton, a town in Georgia, for $20 million in 1989, with plans to develop it into a tourist attraction. Dumped her interest in the town after she declared bankruptcy, leaving residents angry and fearful for their futures.
Original Job: Breck shampoo model, then a Ford model; pursued a singing career under the nom-de-chant Chelsea
Marriages: Ron Britton (divorced), Alec Baldwin, 1993 (filed for divorce, 2001)
Child: Ireland Eliesse, 1995

Major Award: Oscar, Best Actress, *L.A. Confidential,* 1997
Quote: On *L.A. Confidential:* "It's great to be in a movie where people come up to me and say something besides, 'Uh, what were you thinking?' "

LANCE BASS

Real Name: James Lance Lantsen Bass
Birthplace: Laurel, MS
Birthdate: 5/4/79
Occupation: Singer
Debut: (Single) "I Want You Back," 1996; (Album) *NSYNC, 1996 (American release, 1998)
Signature: *No Strings Attached,* 2000
Facts: Was a choirboy in his Baptist church.

Was recruited to join 'N Sync because his deep voice rounded out their sound.

Manages country music acts. Reportedly raised the first red flags about the group's contract with their ex-manager.

Acted on an episode of *7th Heaven.*
Infamy: When the fivesome felt they weren't getting a fair share of the money they were generating, they left RCA Records and former manager Lou Pearlman. Pearlman responded with a $150 million lawsuit; the band countersued for $25 million. The parties reached a private, out-of-court settlement, allegedly in 'N Sync's favor.
Original Job: Day care worker
Quote: "With your second album, people think, 'I guess there must be something to their music because they lasted.' "

ANGELA BASSETT

Birthplace: New York, NY
Birthdate: 8/16/58
Occupation: Actor
Education: Yale University
Debut: (Film) *F/X,* 1986
Signature: *What's Love Got to Do With It,* 1993
Facts: Helped integrate her high school, where she was on the honor roll and the cheerleading squad. Went to college on a scholarship.
Original Job: Hair stylist, photo researcher at *U.S. News and World Report*
Marriage: Courtney B. Vance, 1997

KATHY BATES

Real Name: Kathleen Doyle Bates
Birthplace: Memphis, TN
Birthdate: 6/28/48
Occupation: Actor
Education: Southern Methodist University
Debut: (Film) *Taking Off,* 1971; (Stage) *Casserole,* 1975; (TV) *The Love Boat,* 1977
Signature: *Misery,* 1990
Facts: She lost the screen roles of characters she originated on the stage (Frankie in *Frankie and Johnny in the Claire de Lune* and Lenny McGrath in *Crimes of the Heart*) to Michelle Pfeiffer and Diane Keaton.

Terrence McNally created the character Frankie (in *Frankie and Johnny in the Claire de Lune*) with her in mind.
Original Job: Singing waitress in the Catskills, cashier in the gift shop of Museum of Modern Art in New York
Marriage: Tony Campisi (divorced, 1997)
Major Award: Oscar, Best Actress, *Misery,* 1990

WARREN BEATTY

Real Name: Henry Warren Beaty
Birthplace: Richmond, VA
Birthdate: 3/30/37
Occupation: Actor, producer, director, screenwriter
Education: Northwestern University
Debut: (Film) *Splendor in the Grass,* 1961
Signature: *Shampoo,* 1975
Facts: Rejected football scholarships to go to drama school.

Is famed for his reluctance to do interviews and his tendency to pause for a minute or more before giving a yes or no answer.

The longtime womanizer broke the hearts of many famous actresses, including Natalie Wood, Leslie Caron, and Joan Collins. (Collins even had a wedding dress hanging in a wardrobe for almost a year.)

A behind-the-scenes political player and auteur of *Bulworth,* made noises about seeking the 2000 Democratic presidential nomination.
Original Job: Bricklayer, dishwasher, construction worker, piano player
Marriage: Annette Bening, 1992
Children: Kathlyn, 1992; Benjamin, 1994; Isabel, 1997; Ella Corinne, 2000
Famous Relative: Shirley MacLaine, actor, sister
Major Award: Oscar, Best Director, *Reds,* 1981.
Quote: "For me, the highest level of sexual excitement is in a monogamous relationship."

BECK

Real Name: Beck Hansen
Birthplace: Los Angeles, CA
Birthdate: 7/8/70
Occupation: Singer, songwriter
Education: High school dropout
Debut: (Album) *Mellow Gold,* 1994
Signature: *Odelay,* 1996
Facts: In 1993, making just four dollars an hour, lived in a rat-infested shed behind a house.

Mellow Gold, which includes "Loser," was recorded for $500, mostly at his friend's house.

Hung out in New York's East Village in the late '80s, where the "anti-folk scene" convinced him that there are no restrictions on subject matter for songs.

Mom was once a regular at Andy Warhol's Factory.
Original Jobs: Painting signs, moving refrigerators, taking ID photos at New York's YMCA, clerking in a video store
Relationship: Leigh Limon
Famous Relatives: Bibbe Hansen, guitarist, mother; Al Hansen, artist, grandfather
Major Awards: Grammy, Best Rock

Vocal—Male, "Where It's At," 1996; Grammy, Best Alternative Album, *Odelay,* 1996; Grammy, Best Alternative Performance, *Mutations,* 1999

VICTORIA BECKHAM

Birthplace: Goff's Oak, Hertfordshire, England
Birthdate: 4/17/74
Occupation: Singer
Education: Performing arts college in Epsom, England
Debut: (Album) *Spice,* 1996; (Movie) *Spice World,* 1997 (American release, 1998)
Signature: "Wannabe," (1996) / Posh Spice
Facts: Was nicknamed "Acne Face" as a child.

Was awarded £100,000 from British Airways after they misplaced her four matching Louis Vuitton bags.

Named her son after the city in which he was conceived.

Her lavish wedding featured a £100,000 tiara, an 18-piece orchestra, and a turkey dinner.

Made her catwalk debut in 2000.
Was the last Spice Girl to release a solo single ("Out of Your Mind").

The British Press accused her of anorexia; she denied having a weight problem.

Caused a stir by characterizing her husband as "an animal in bed."

She and her husband sued to stop the publication of a book by a former employee in 2000, but subsequently settled and allowed publication to proceed.
Marriage: David Beckham, 1999, soccer star
Child: Brooklyn David Beckham, 1999
Quote: "I'm not that desperate to be liked."

KATE BECKINSALE

Birthplace: London, England
Birthdate: 7/26/73
Occupation: Actor

Education: Attended New College, Oxford University
Debut: (TV) *Devices and Desires,* 1991; (Film) *Much Ado About Nothing,* 1993
Signature: *Pearl Harbor,* 2001
Facts: As a teenager, won the W. H. Smith Young Writers' competition twice, for her fiction and poetry.

Suffered from a nervous breakdown and anorexia at age 15. The illness followed her father's 1979 death of a heart attack and she spent several years in analysis.

At Oxford, majored in French and Russian and spent her third year abroad in Paris before dropping out to concentrate on her acting career.

Has five step-siblings.
Admits to urinating into the thermos of a director who forced her to do a nude scene in an early film.

Caused a stir when she publicly declared Gwyneth Paltrow's interpretation of the role of Emma "cowardly" for being too likeable.

Has metaphobia, the fear of throwing up.
Original Job: Waitress
Relationship: Michael Sheen
Child: Lily, 1999
Quote: "I'm not crazy about being called an ingenue. I keep getting called an English rose as well, which I find a bit annoying because my grandfather is Burmese."

JAMIE BELL

Birthplace: England
Birthdate: 3/14/86
Occupation: Actor, dancer
Education: Royal Ballet School, England
Debut: (Film) *Billy Elliott,* 2000
Signature: *Billy Elliott*
Facts: Began his dancing career at age 6.

Auditioned seven times for the role of Billy Elliott and was finally selected over more than 2,000 other boys.

Was rumored to have been considered to play Harry Potter in the film adaptation of *Harry Potter and the Sorcerer's Stone.*
Quote: "I'm a hard-mouthed northeastern lad. That's me—the Eminem of Northeast England."

GIL BELLOWS

Birthplace: Vancouver, British Columbia, Canada
Birthdate: 6/28/67
Occupation: Actor
Education: American Academy of Dramatic Arts
Debut: (Film) *The First Season* (Canadian), 1987; (TV) *Law & Order,* 1991; (Stage) *True West*
Signature: *Ally McBeal*
Facts: First appeared in several low-budget films, one-act plays, and Off-Broadway shows. In 1995, he enjoyed his first lead in the TV movie *The Silver Strand.*

Proposed to his wife on Valentine's Day.

Landed a 10-minute role in 1994's *Shawshank Redemption,* playing the pivotal part of the thief who provided information about the murder of Tim Robbins's wife.

Co-founded a small theater group called Seraphim.

His first child was born in his home; a mirror fell and shattered as the baby let out her first screams.
Original Job: Hotel doorman
Marriage: Rya Kihlstedt, actress, 1994
Child: Ava Emmanuelle, 1999

ROBERTO BENIGNI

Birthplace: Arrezzo, Tuscany, Italy
Birthdate: 10/27/52
Occupation: Actor, comedian, screenwriter, director, producer
Education: Accounting school, Prado, Italy
Debut: (U.S. Film) *Down by Law,* 1986
Signature: *Life Is Beautiful,* 1998
Facts: Originally planning to become a priest, he attended a seminary in Florence, Italy, but left when the building was damaged by a flood.

The idea for *Life Is Beautiful* came from Benigni's father, who was imprisoned in Bergen-Belsen concentration camp for two years before being liberated in 1945. His father always added humor in the telling of his story.

When he was a child, his family spent three weeks sleeping in a friend's stable.

He was discovered at age 16 by the director of an experimental theater group while delivering an improvised, satirical, political speech in a Tuscan town square.

At 19 he began acting with a theater group in Rome while doing stand-up comedy.

In 1983, *You Disturb Me* launched his career as an actor-writer-director. It was also his first of many collaborations with Nicoletta Braschi, whom he later married.

A passionate Dantista as a youth, he could recite *The Divine Comedy* by heart.

The number Benigni wears on his concentration camp uniform in *Life Is Beautiful* is the same number that his role model, Charlie Chaplin, wore in *The Great Dictator*.

Infamy: In 1980, he mocked Pope John Paul II on Italian TV, and, facing obscenity charges, was fined and given a one-year suspended sentence. Years later, he exuberantly kissed Pope John Paul II instead of his papal ring during an audience and private screening of *Life Is Beautiful*.

Original Jobs: Musician, clown, magician's assistant
Marriage: Nicoletta Braschi, actor, 1991
Major Awards: Oscars, Best Actor and Best Foreign Film, *Life Is Beautiful*, 1998
Quote: "I am so full of joy. Every organ in my body is moving in a very bad way."

ANNETTE BENING

Birthplace: Topeka, KS
Birthdate: 5/29/58
Occupation: Actor
Education: San Diego Mesa College, San Francisco State University, American Conservatory Theater, San Francisco
Debut: (Stage) *Coastal Disturbances*, 1986; (Film) *The Great Outdoors*, 1988
Signature: *American Beauty*, 1999
Fact: Originally cast as Catwoman in *Batman Returns*, she got pregnant and lost the role to Michelle Pfeiffer.
Original Job: Cook on a charter boat for a year, to pay for college
Marriages: Steve White (divorced, 1991), Warren Beatty, 1992
Children: Kathlyn, 1992; Benjamin, 1994; Isabel, 1997; Ella Corinne, 2000

TONY BENNETT

Real Name: Anthony Dominick Benedetto
Birthplace: Astoria, NY
Birthdate: 8/3/26
Occupation: Singer
Education: Manhattan's School of Industrial Art
Debut: (Album) *The Boulevard of Broken Dreams*, 1950
Signature: "I Left My Heart in San Francisco," 1962
Facts: Marched with Martin Luther King Jr. in Selma in 1965 at the urging of Harry Belafonte.

Used the name Joe Bari until Bob Hope introduced him as Tony Bennett in 1949.

Served two years as an infantryman in Europe during World War II.

An avid painter, his works have been exhibited in galleries around the country.

Had released 98 albums as of 1999.
Original Job: Singing waiter
Marriages: Patricia Beech, 1952

(divorced, 1971); Sandra Grant, 1971 (divorced, 1984)
Children: D'andrea (Danny), 1954; Daegal, 1955 (with Patricia Beech). Joanna, 1970; Antonia, 1974
Major Awards: Grammy, Best Pop Vocal—Male, "I Left My Heart in San Francisco," 1962; Grammy, Record of the Year, "I Left My Heart in San Francisco," 1962; Grammy, Album of the Year, *MTV Unplugged*, 1994; Grammy, Best Traditional Pop Vocal Performance, *MTV Unplugged*, 1994; Grammy, Best Traditional Pop Vocal Performance, *Tony Bennett on Holiday*, 1997; Grammy, Best Traditional Pop Vocal Performance, *Bennett Sings Ellington–Hot & Cool*, 1999

CANDICE BERGEN

Birthplace: Beverly Hills, CA
Birthdate: 5/9/46
Occupation: Actor, photojournalist
Education: University of Pennsylvania
Debut: (Film) *The Group*, 1966
Signature: *Murphy Brown*
Facts: Her father's puppet, Charlie McCarthy, had a bigger bedroom and more clothes than she did as a child.

As a photojournalist, was published in *Life* and *Playboy*.

Wrote a play, *The Freezer*, which is included in *Best Short Plays of 1968*.
Original Job: Model
Marriage: Louis Malle, 1981 (deceased, 1995); Marshall Rose, 2000
Child: Chloe, 1985
Famous Relative: Edgar Bergen, ventriloquist, father
Major Awards: Emmy, Best Actress in a Comedy Series, *Murphy Brown*, 1989, 1990, 1992, 1993, 1995

HALLE BERRY

Birthplace: Cleveland, OH
Birthdate: 8/14/66
Occupation: Actor
Education: Cuyahoga Community College
Debut: (TV) *Living Dolls*, 1989

Signature: *Boomerang*, 1992
Facts: Elected prom queen her senior year in high school, she was accused of stuffing the ballot box. Was forced to share the title with a "white, blond, blue-eyed, all-American girl."

Raised by her white mother after her black father left when she was four years old.

Lost 80 percent of the hearing in her left ear from an injury sustained from a physically abusive lover. (She rarely wears her hearing aid.)

Learned she was a diabetic when she collapsed in a coma while filming the TV series *Living Dolls*.

She was first runner-up in the 1986 Miss USA pageant.

Played a crackhead in Spike Lee's *Jungle Fever* (1991) and did not bathe for days to prepare for the role.
Infamy: Sued by a Chicago dentist (and former boyfriend) who claims she never repaid the $80,000 she borrowed from him. Refused to settle and, spending $50,000 defending herself, won in court.

In 2000 was indicted on charges of leaving the scene of an accident, when she struck another motorist with her car after running through a red light. After pleading no contest to charges, she was sentenced to three years probation, fined $13,500 and ordered to serve 200 hours of community service. A civil lawsuit filed by victim Hetal Raythatha was settled out of court.
Original Job: Model
Marriage: David Justice (divorced, 1996); Eric Benet, R&B singer, 2001

JESSICA BIEL

Birthplace: Ely, MN
Birthdate: 3/3/82
Occupation: Actor, model
Education: Young Actors Space, Los Angeles
Debut: (TV) *7th Heaven*, 1996; (Film) *Ulee's Gold*, 1997
Signature: *7th Heaven*
Facts: She credits her complexion to her Choctaw blood. She is German, French, English, and American Indian.

Was a teen model for two years, making her first TV commercial for Pringles potato chips.

Enjoys mountain biking, snowboarding, gymnastics, soccer and basketball.
Infamy: Posed topless in 2000 for *Gear* magazine, attempting to change her wholesome image. *7th Heaven* producer Aaron Spelling filed a $100 million lawsuit against the magazine, claiming that the magazine had defamed him by alleging that he had prevented Biel from securing film work.
Quote: "Sex is overrated. People make such a big deal out of it."

JASON BIGGS

Birthplace: Pompton Plains, NJ
Birthdate: 5/12/78
Occupation: Actor
Education: Attended New York University and Montclair State University
Debut: (Broadway) *Conversations With My Father*, 1991; (Film) *The Boy Who Cried Bitch*, 1991; (TV) *Drexell's Class*, 1991
Signature: *American Pie*, 1999
Facts: Began working in print and TV ads at the age of 5.

In 1995, received Daytime Emmy nomination for his role as troubled teen Pete Wendall on *As the World Turns*.

Played tennis on his high school team.

Lost 20 pounds after filming *American Pie* by biking, jogging, and snowboarding.
Original jobs: Retail clerk, Subway sandwich-maker
Quote: "The best thing for me is that I know I can move on and not have to do baked-goods porn for the rest of my career."

JULIETTE BINOCHE

Birthplace: Paris, France
Birthdate: 3/9/64
Occupation: Actor
Education: Attended Paris's National Conservatory of Dramatic Arts
Debut: (Film) *La Vie de famille*, 1984
Signature: *The English Patient*, 1996
Facts: A big star in France, she is known simply as "la Binoche."

Was replaced in the title role of *Lucie Aubrac* while filming was already underway; Binoche felt some of her lines were out of character and wanted to rewrite them.

Her lucrative Lancôme deal requires only 10 working days a year.

Her parents divorced when she was four; grew up shuttling between each parent and a Catholic boarding school.
Relationship: Benoit Magimel
Children: Raphael, 1993 (with Andre Halle); Hanna, 1999
Major Awards: Cesar (France's Oscar), Best Actress, *Blue*, 1994; Oscar, Best Supporting Actress, *The English Patient*, 1996

BJORK

Real Name: Björk Gudmundsdottir
Birthplace: Reykjavik, Iceland
Birthdate: 11/21/65
Occupation: Musician, actor
Debut: (Album) *Life's Too Good*, 1988 (with The Sugarcubes); (Film) *Dancer in the Dark*, 2000
Signature: *Post*, 1995
Facts: Is a practicing Buddhist.

Is a self-described anarchist.

Studied flute, piano and voice as a child.

Enrolled in classical music school at age 5 and joined her first band by 1979.

Her first solo album, 1993's *Debut,* sold more than 2.5 million copies.

Won the Best Actress award at the Cannes Film Festival in 2000 for her role in *Dancer in the Dark*.

Original Jobs: Jazz musician, producer of a heavy metal band, composer for avant-guarde dance troupes, fish factory employee
Marriage: Thor Eldon, 1986 (divorced, 1988)
Child: Sindri, 1986
Quote: "I'm so romantic. I don't know how to turn it off."

DAVID BLAINE

Birthplace: Brooklyn, NY
Birthdate: 4/4/73
Occupation: Magician
Debut: (TV) Street Magic, 1997
Facts: Began playing with cards before kindergarten.

At 16, levitated for his doctor, who immediately wanted to order tests.

Dated singer-songwriter Fiona Apple.

Stunts have included locking himself in a plexi-glass coffin under a Manhattan street for seven days and standing inside of a 6-ton Alaskan ice cube in Times Square for 61 hours and 40 minutes. His repertoire of illusions includes stigmata messages, coin-melting, pavement levitation, and the resurrection of a decapitated chicken figure.
Quote: "I have the ability to bring people to a place where they believe."

CATE BLANCHETT

Birthplace: Melbourne, Australia
Birthdate: 5/14/69
Occupation: Actor
Education: Attended Melbourne University
Debut: (TV) Police Rescue, 1994; (Film) Paradise Road, 1997; (Stage) Plenty, 1999
Signature: Elizabeth, 1998
Facts: Her father died of a heart attack when she was 10 years old.

Dropped out of college after two years to attend drama school in Sydney.

After leaving England due to an improper visa, she found a job as an extra in a boxing movie filmed in Egypt.

She bites her nails.

Director Shekhar Kapur decided that he wanted Cate for the lead role in Elizabeth based on the trailer for 1997's Oscar and Lucinda.
Marriage: Andrew Upton, 1997
Quote: "Growing up in Australia, I always bemoaned the fact that I wasn't a bronzed surfer chick."

BILLY BLANKS

Birthplace: Erie, Pennsylvania
Birthdate: 9/1/55
Occupation: Fitness expert, actor
Debut: (Film) Bloodfist, 1989
Signature: Tae-Bo fitness program
Facts: Grew up with 14 brothers and sisters.

Inspired by Bruce Lee as Kato on TV's The Green Hornet, he took karate lessons and ultimately became an international karate champion.

Has trained Paula Abdul, Brooke Shields, Shaquille O'Neal, Ashley Judd, and Carmen Electra, among others.

Has been diagnosed with dyslexia.

He developed Tae-Bo, which combines aerobics, jazz, dance, karate, and boxing, to introduce women to martial arts.

Tae-Bo is an acronym that stands for Total Awareness, Excellence, Body Obedience.

Billy Blanks World Training Center in Sherman Oaks, Calif., is the only place where the patented and copyrighted Tae-Bo is taught.

Was paid $1.5 million for his book.

By early 1999, his workout video had grossed $75 million.
Original Job: Garbage man
Marriage: Gayle Godfrey
Children: Shellie (stepdaughter); Billy Jr., 1976
Quote: "If you want to sweat, go sit in a whirlpool. I want you to get some power, I want you to feel like you can overcome anything."

MARY J. BLIGE

Birthplace: Bronx, NY
Birthdate: 1/11/71
Occupation: Singer, songwriter
Education: High school dropout
Debut: (Album) What's the 411?, 1992
Signature: "I'm Goin' Down"
Facts: Her father left the family when she was 4, leaving her mother to raise Blige and three siblings in a Yonkers, N.Y., housing project.

While hanging out with buddies at a suburban New York mall, made a karaoke-style recording of an Anita Baker song. That tape found its way to Uptown Records' CEO, who signed her to his label.

This Queen of Hip-Hop Soul has been dubbed the Aretha Franklin of Generation X.
Infamy: Developed a reputation for having an "attitude problem" after being sullen, withdrawn, and even nasty during interviews.

Sued for $1 million by her ex-managers for breach of contract, who claimed Blige was a "selfish artist" who forgot the people who worked to make her a success.
Relationship: Jodeci lead singer K-Ci (engaged)
Major Award: Grammy, Best Rap Performance by a Duo or Group, "I'll Be There for You/You're All I Need to Get By" 1995

ANDREA BOCELLI

Birthplace: Lajatico, Italy
Birthdate: 9/22/58
Occupation: Opera singer
Education: University of Pisa
Debut: (U.S.) Kennedy Center, Spring Gala, 1998
Signature: "Con te partiro," ("Time to Say Goodbye") 1995
Facts: Took piano, saxophone, and flute lessons in his youth.

Born with visually debilitating glaucoma, he was left fully blind by a brain hemorrhage at age 12 after hitting his head playing soccer.

His parents own a farm with a small vineyard from which his father still produces Chianti Bocelli.

Obtained law degree while singing professionally in piano bars; he then studied opera.

Big break came in 1992 when he recorded "Miserere" with Italian rock star Zucchero Fornaciari.

In December 1997, PBS aired an *In the Spotlight* special of "Andrea Bocelli: Romanza in Concert." He reached a huge pop audience with this concert of opera renditions in Pisa.

Loves horseback riding and skiing.

With over 20 million albums sold worldwide by early 1999, he ranks as one of the bestselling classical recording artists of all time.

Original Job: Lawyer, piano bar entertainer

Marriage: Enrica Cenzatti, 1992

Children: Amos, Matteo, 1997

Quote: "I don't feel I'm really credible enough yet as an opera singer. I still have to suffer a little while longer."

STEVEN BOCHCO

Birthplace: New York, NY

Birthdate: 12/16/43

Occupation: Producer, screenwriter

Education: Carnegie Institute of Technology

Debut: (TV) *A Fade to Black,* 1967

Signature: *NYPD Blue*

Facts: *Hill Street Blues* won 26 Emmys.

His father, Rudolph Bochco, was a child prodigy violinist who later played with orchestras in Broadway shows and with leading artists at Carnegie Hall.

Wrote material for *Ironside* and was the story editor for *Columbo.*

Turned down the presidency of CBS Entertainment in 1987.

Original Job: Assistant to the head of the story department at Universal Studios

Marriage: One prior marriage, divorced, 1966; Barbara Bosson,

1969 (divorced, 1998); Dayna Flanagan, 2000

Children: Melissa, 1970; Jesse, 1975 (with Barbara Bosson)

Famous Relative: Alan Rachins, actor, former brother-in-law

Major Awards: Emmy, Outstanding Drama Series, *Hill Street Blues,* 1981, 1982, 1983, 1984; Emmy, Outstanding Drama Series, *L.A. Law,* 1987, 1989, 1990, 1991

MICHAEL BOLTON

Real Name: Michael Bolotin

Birthplace: New Haven, CT

Birthdate: 2/26/53

Occupation: Singer, songwriter

Education: High school dropout

Debut: (EP) *Blackjack* (with Blackjack), 1979; (Album) *Michael Bolton* (solo), 1983

Facts: Wrote ballads and love songs for other artists, including Laura Branigan, Cher, The Pointer Sisters, and Barbra Streisand.

After the breakup of his band, Blackjack, he began recording solo in 1983.

In the mid '80s, he was a regular opening act for metal acts such as Ozzy Osbourne and Krokus.

A research library in the New York Medical College was dedicated to him in 1993 for his work as honorary chairman of This Close for Cancer Research.

Infamy: After a two-week trial in 1994, a jury ruled that Bolton's "Love Is a Wonderful Thing" is remarkably similar to the Isley Brothers song "Love Is a Wonderful Thing." In 2000, a federal appeals court upheld the $7 million ruling against him. (The following year the U. S. Supreme Court also upheld the ruling.) Bolton attempted to buy the Isley Brothers' publishing rights from a bankruptcy court in 2000, but he was passed over in favor of another bidder.

Marriage: Maureen McGuire, 1975 (divorced, 1991); Ashley Judd (relationship)

Children: Isa, 1975; Holly, 1977; Taryn, 1979; (with Maureen McGuire).

Major Awards: Grammy, Best Pop Vocal—Male, "How Am I Supposed to Live Without You," 1989; Grammy, Best Pop Vocal—Male, "When a Man Loves a Woman," 1991

HELENA BONHAM CARTER

Birthplace: London, England

Birthdate: 5/26/66

Occupation: Actor

Education: Attended Westminster School

Debut: (TV) *A Pattern of Roses,* 1982; (Film) *Lady Jane,* 1985

Facts: Lived with her parents until she was 30, helping care for her paralyzed father.

As a child, she wanted to be a spy because she loved *Charlie's Angels.*

At age 13, she entered a national writing contest and used the money that she won to pay for her entry into the actors' directory *Spotlight.*

Has made four films based on E. M. Forster novels (*A Room with a View; Maurice; Where Angels Fear to Tread; Howard's End*).

Famous Relatives: Herbert Henry Asquith, Britain's prime minister, 1908–1916, great-grandfather; Anthony "Puffin" Asquith, director, screenwriter, great-uncle; Lady Violet Bonham Carter, a.k.a. Baroness Asquith, grandmother

Quote: "Period movies are my destiny. I should get a few ribs taken out, because I'll be in a corset for the rest of my life."

JON BON JOVI

Real Name: John Bongiovi

Birthplace: Sayreville, NJ

Birthdate: 3/2/62

Occupation: Singer, songwriter

Education: High school

Debut: (Album) *Bon Jovi,* 1984

Signature: Bon Jovi

Facts: Polygram executives gave the band a contract with the following conditions: John Bongiovi would become Jon Bon Jovi and only he would be given a contract. The other four members of the band would become Jon Bon Jovi's employees.

His first solo album, *Blaze of Glory* (1990), was "written for and inspired by" the film *Young Guns II,* in which he had a cameo role.

Title of Bon Jovi's album, *7800° Fahrenheit,* refers to the temperature of an exploding volcano.

Infamy: Had a legal dispute with cousin Tony Bongiovi, who owned the Record Plant, a New York City recording studio, over the extent to which Tony had aided his cousin's career. In 1984, Tony brought a lawsuit against Bon Jovi, the outcome of which gave him a producer's credit, a fee, royalties from Bon Jovi's first album, a cash award, and a one percent royalty from the group's next two albums.

Original Job: Floor sweeper at the Record Plant

Marriage: Dorothea Hurley, 1989

Children: Stephanie Rose, 1993; Jesse James Louis, 1995

BONO

Real Name: Paul Hewson

Birthplace: Dublin, Ireland

Birthdate: 5/10/60

Occupation: Singer, songwriter

Education: High school

Debut: (EP) *U2:3* (with U2), 1979

Signature: U2

Facts: Got his nickname from a billboard advertising Bono Vox, a hearing aid retailer.

In November 1987, U2 opened for themselves at the L.A. Coliseum as the country-rock group The Dalton Brothers.

His efforts to reduce the debt owed by Third World nations to the major industrial powers has resulted in the forgiving of tens of billions of dollars in loans.

Infamy: Was the first winner in Grammy history to say "f--k"during its live telecast (1994).

Marriage: Ali Hewson, 1982

Children: Jordan, 1989; Eve, c. 1993; Elijah Bob, 1999; Paul Hewson, 2001

Major Awards: Grammy, Album of the Year, *The Joshua Tree,* 1987; Grammy, Best Rock Performance—Duo or Group, *The Joshua Tree,* 1987; Grammy, Best Video—Long Form, *Where the Streets Have No Name,* 1988; Grammy, Best Rock Performance—Duo or Group, "Desire," 1988; Grammy, Best Rock Performance—Duo or Group, *Achtung Baby,* 1992; Grammy, Best Alternative Performance, *Zooropa,* 1993; Grammy, Record of the Year, "Beautiful Day," 2001; Grammy, Song of the Year, "Beautiful Day," 2001; Grammy, Best Rock Performance—Duo or Group, "Beautiful Day," 2001

DAVID BOREANAZ

Birthplace: Buffalo, NY

Birthdate: 5/16/71

Occupation: Actor

Education: Ithaca College

Debut: (TV) *Married...With Children,* 1993

Signature: *Angel*

Facts: He majored in film moved to L.A. after graduation to find work behind the cameras.

College classmates called him Q-Tip Head because of his unruly hair.

Formed MoBo Films in 1999 with actor Jarrod Moses.

Was chased out of the Creative Arts Agency in 1993 for dropping by unannounced with copies of his résumé

Original Job: Props department assistant, house painter, parking attendant

Marriages: Ingrid Quinn, screenwriter, 1997 (divorced, 1999); Jaime Bergman, actor, 2001 (engaged)

Quote: "I'm a petit prince, as my sister would say."

DAVID BOWIE

Real Name: David Robert Jones

Birthplace: Brixton, England

Birthdate: 1/8/47

Education: High school

Occupation: Singer, songwriter, actor

Debut: (Album) *David Bowie,* 1967; (Film) *The Virgin Soldiers,* 1969; (Broadway) *The Elephant Man,* 1981

Signature: "Space Oddity," 1969

Facts: His left pupil was damaged after he was hit in the eye during a teenage fight, resulting in its permanent dilation and the appearance of mismatched eyes.

Formed his first band, an R&B ensemble called *Davie Jones and the King Bees,* in 1964.

Changed his name to avoid being confused with lead singer Davy Jones of *The Monkees.*

Spent two years as a member of the Lindsay Kemp Mime Troupe.

In 1972, told *Melody Maker* he was gay, spawning a cult growing around his androgynous image.

Has taken on an array of personas throughout his career including the flamboyant Ziggy Stardust, who embodied the "glitter rock" trend of the 1970s; Aladdin Sane, an elfin man decorated with an electric blue lightning bolt drawn across his face and a painted-on teardrop; and the Thin White Duke, slicking his hair back and donning white suits.

In 1996, portrayed his late friend Andy Warhol in the art-world feature film *Basquiat.*

Was a no-show to his induction into the Rock and Roll Hall of Fame in 1996.

A postmodern Renaissance man and Dadaist, he exhibited his art work during the 1990s and co-founded the art book publishing house 21 in 1997.

Original jobs: Painter, commercial artist, music producer

Marriage: Angela Barnett, 1970 (divorced, 1980); Iman, 1992

Children: Zowie (Joey) Duncan Heywood, 1971 (with Angela Barnett);

Zulekha Haywood, 1988 (stepdaughter); Alexandria Zahra Jones, 2000
Major Awards: Grammy, Best Video-Short Form, "David Bowie," 1984; Inducted into Rock and Roll Hall of Fame, 1996
Quote: "If I'd known I was going to live that long, I would have looked after myself better."

KENNETH BRANAGH

Birthplace: Belfast, Northern Ireland
Birthdate: 12/10/60
Occupation: Actor, director
Education: Royal Academy of Dramatic Arts
Debut: (Stage) *Another Country,* 1982
Signature: *Henry V,* 1989
Facts: Grew up in poverty in the shadow of a tobacco factory in Belfast.

Co-founded England's Renaissance Theater Company.

To prepare for *Henry V,* Branagh received an audience with Prince Charles to gain insight on being heir to the throne.
Marriage: Emma Thompson (divorced, 1996)

MARLON BRANDO

Birthplace: Omaha, NE
Birthdate: 4/3/24
Occupation: Actor
Education: Expelled from Shattuck Military Academy, attended New School for Social Research
Debut: (Stage) *I Remember Mama,* 1944; (Film) *The Men,* 1950
Signature: *The Godfather,* 1972
Fact: Exiled himself to his private island, Tetiaroa, near Tahiti, which he bought after filming *Mutiny on the Bounty* there in 1960.

Wrote an autobiography, *Brando: Songs My Mother Taught Me* (1994) to raise money for son Christian's legal fees, but the book was panned for omitting his many wives and lovers, the latter including Shelley Winters and Rita Moreno.

Agreed to do a cameo in *Scary Movie 2* for $2 million but then couldn't appear due to health issues.
Infamy: Son Christian killed daughter Cheyenne's boyfriend and served time for manslaughter (1990). Distraught, Cheyenne took her own life in 1995.
Original Job: Tile fitter, elevator operator
Marriages: Anna Kashfi, 1957 (divorced, 1959); Movita Castenada, 1960 (annulled); Tarita Teripia, 1966 (divorced)
Children: Christian Devi, 1958 (with Anna Kashfi). Sergio, 1960 (a.k.a. Miko; with Movita Castenada). Teihotu Teripaia, 1963. Maya Gabriella Cui, 1963 (with Marie Cui). Tarita Cheyenne, 1970 (deceased, 1995), (with Tarita Teriipaia). Rebecca, 1966; Pietra Barrett, 1970 (adopted; birth father as James Clavell). Ninna Priscilla, 1989 (with Cristina Ruiz).
Major Awards: Oscar, Best Actor, *On the Waterfront,* 1955, Oscar, Best Actor, *The Godfather,* 1972; Emmy, Best Supporting Actor in a Limited Series, *Roots,* 1979

BRANDY

Real Name: Brandy Norwood
Birthplace: McComb, MS
Birthdate: 2/11/79
Occupation: Singer, actor
Education: Pepperdine University
Debut: (Album) *Brandy,* 1994
Signature: "The Boy is Mine," 1998
Facts: From ages 12 to 14, sang backup for the R&B group Immature.

Brandy's famous braids are styled every three weeks, with fake hair extensions added for thickness, in an eight-hour process.

Before starring in UPN's *Moesha,* played the daughter in the short-lived 1993 TV comedy, *Thea.*

Her dad was choir director at their church, so as a child Brandy was always showcased as a featured singer.

Wasn't allowed to date until she was 16, but her mother/manager did provide her with a $500/week allowance.

Enjoys jelly-and-fried-egg sandwiches.
Infamy: Sued by a management and production company for $5 million for allegedly breaking an oral contract to represent her.
Relationship: Wanya Morris
Famous Relative: Ray-J, actor, singer, brother
Major Award: Grammy, R&B Performance—Duo or Group with vocal, "The Boy Is Mine" (with Monica), 1998.

BENJAMIN BRATT

Birthplace: San Francisco, CA
Birthdate: 12/16/63
Occupation: Actor
Education: University of California, Santa Barbara
Debut: (Stage) Utah Shakespeare Festival, 1987; (TV) *Knightwatch,* 1988; (Film) *Bright Angel,* 1990
Signature: *Law & Order*
Facts: He is of Peruvian and German-English lineage.

At age 5, he participated in a takeover of Alcatraz Island with his Peruvian mother and Native American activists. He has remained active on behalf of Native Americans.

Was nicknamed "Scarecrow" in high school for being too thin.

Graduated with honors from college but left the masters program at American Conservatory Theater to begin his career.

Dated Julia Roberts.
Famous Relative: George Bratt, Broadway actor, grandfather

TONI BRAXTON

Birthplace: Severn, MD
Birthdate: 10/7/66
Occupation: Singer
Education: Bowie State University
Signature: "Breathe Again," 1994

Fact: Learned to sing in a church choir. Her three sisters sing backup vocals on her albums. She and her sisters were only allowed to listen to gospel music, but she would "sneak into empty rooms to watch *Soul Train*."

Declared bankruptcy in 1998. Some observers saw the move as a tactic to dissolve her recording contract, from which she had sought legal release on grounds of a low royalty rate. Months later, she signed with LaFace Records, reportedly for nearly $20 million.

Marriage: Keri Lewis, musician, 2001

Major Awards: Grammy, Best New Artist, 1993; Grammy, Best R&B Vocal—Female, "Another Sad Love Song," 1993; Grammy, Best R&B Vocal—Female, "Breathe Again," 1994; Grammy, Best Pop Vocal—Female, "Un-break My Heart," 1996; Grammy, Best R&B Vocal—Female, "You're Makin' Me High," 1996; Grammy, Best R&B Vocal—Female, "He Wasn't Man Enough," 2001

AMY BRENNEMAN

Birthplace: New London, CT
Birthdate: 6/22/64
Occupation: Actor, producer
Education: Harvard University, 1987
Debut: (TV) *Middle Ages*, 1992; (Film) *Bye, Bye, Love*, 1995
Signature: *Judging Amy*
Facts: Graduated high school a year early and worked in France as an au pair.

Founded the Cornerstone Theater Company and traveled with the group for five years. She is currently its chairman.

In 1993, she landed the role of Officer Janice Licalsi in *NYPD Blue* and is best remembered for her nude scene with David Caruso.

Her *Judging Amy* role is based partly on her mother Frederica, now a Connecticut State Supreme Court judge.

Marriage: Bradley Silberling,

director, 1995
Child: Charlotte, 2001
Quote: "People always talk about how they don't like shooting love scenes. I really don't mind it. I don't know what that says about me."

JEFF BRIDGES

Birthplace: Los Angeles, CA
Birthdate: 12/4/49
Occupation: Actor
Education: High school, Herbert Berghof Studio
Debut: (Film) *The Company She Keeps*, 1950; (TV) *Sea Hunt*, 1957
Signature: *The Fabulous Baker Boys*, 1989
Facts: Joined the Coast Guard Reserves in 1968 to avoid the draft.

At age 16, he wrote a song included on the soundtrack of the 1969 film *John and Mary*, which starred Dustin Hoffman and Mia Farrow, and sold two compositions to Quincy Jones. To date, he has written over 200 songs.

Has exhibited his paintings and photographs in art galleries.
Infamy: In high school, developed a dependency on marijuana. He joined DAWN (Developing Adolescents Without Narcotics) and kicked the habit.
Marriage: Susan Gaston, 1977
Children: Isabelle, 1982; Jessica, 1984; Hayley, 1988
Famous Relatives: Lloyd Bridges, actor, father; Beau Bridges, actor, brother

CHRISTIE BRINKLEY

Birthplace: Malibu, CA
Birthdate: 2/2/54
Occupation: Supermodel
Education: UCLA
Debut: (Film) *National Lampoon's Vacation*, 1983
Signature: Cover Girl Cosmetics model
Facts: An avid Francophile, Brinkley transferred from her local high school to the Lycée Français in Los Angeles.

She later dropped out of college and worked at odd jobs selling ice cream, clothes, and plants to earn money for a ticket to Paris.

Designed the cover for Billy Joel's *River of Dreams* album.

Married Taubman atop a ski mountain, a symbolic acknowledgment of the helicopter crash they both survived while heli-skiing in 1994.
Original Job: Painter
Marriages: Jean Francois Allaux (divorced); Billy Joel (divorced); Rick Taubman (divorced); Peter Cook, 1996
Children: Alexa Ray, 1985 (with Billy Joel). Jack Paris, 1995 (with Ricky Taubman). Sailor Lee, 1998
Famous Relative: David Brinkley, scriptwriter, producer, father

MATTHEW BRODERICK

Birthplace: New York, NY
Birthdate: 3/21/62
Occupation: Actor
Debut: (Stage) *Torch Song Trilogy*, 1982; (Film) *Max Dugan Returns*, 1983
Signature: *Ferris Bueller's Day Off*, 1986
Fact: Was heavily influenced by father James Broderick, who played the father in the TV series *Family* and died of cancer in 1982.
Infamy: While on vacation in Northern Ireland in 1987 with his then-girlfriend, actress Jennifer Grey, Broderick suffered a broken leg when the car he was driving collided with another automobile, killing its two occupants. Broderick was acquitted of one count of manslaughter and reckless driving.
Marriage: Sarah Jessica Parker, 1997
Famous Relative: James Broderick, character actor, father
Major Awards: Tony, Best Featured Actor (Dramatic), *Brighton Beach Memoirs*, 1983; Tony, Best Actor (Musical), *How To Succeed in Business Without Really Trying*, 1995

TOM BROKAW

Birthplace: Yankton, SD
Birthdate: 2/6/40
Occupation: Anchor, correspondent, managing editor
Education: University of South Dakota
Debut: (TV) KTIV, Sioux City, IA, 1960
Signature: *NBC Nightly News*
Facts: Served as president of high school student body. Also met future wife who became Miss South Dakota in high school.

Began with NBC as their White House correspondent in 1973.

Was the only network anchor present at the collapse of the Berlin Wall in 1989.
Marriage: Meredith, 1962
Children: Jennifer, 1966; Andrea, 1968; Sarah, 1970
Major Awards: 6 News and Documentary Emmys: 4 as anchor, 1 as interviewer, 1 as managing editor

GARTH BROOKS

Real Name: Troyal Garth Brooks
Birthplace: Tulsa, OK
Birthdate: 2/7/62
Occupation: Singer, songwriter
Education: Oklahoma State University
Debut: (Album) *Garth Brooks*, 1989
Signature: *Ropin' the Wind*, 1991
Facts: In 1990 at age 28, Garth became the youngest member of Nashville's Grand Ole Opry.

Brooks met his future wife while working as a bouncer. (He threw her out for fighting.)

In 1991, *Ropin' the Wind* became the first country album ever to reach No. 1 on the *Billboard* pop chart.

The video for "The Thunder Rolls," about a cheating husband shot by his battered wife after coming home drunk, was banned by Country Music Television and The Nashville Network. Thousands of shelters for battered women in America used the video in group counseling sessions.

Brooks' half sister is his bassist, his brother handles the books, and a college roommate is one of his guitarists.

Refused the Artist of the Year title from the American Music Awards in 1996, later explaining "I just couldn't accept it, just out of the love of the fellow musicians. I think we're all one."

Took time off from music to try and play professional baseball. He joined the San Diego Padres in 1999 for spring training but did not make the team. Playing left field, Brooks went 1 for 22 at the plate.

In 2000, he joined the New York Mets for their spring training.

Wanted to buildhimself a Graceland-like museum on his 20-acre Blue Rose Estate in a Nashville suburb, but was shot down by his neighbors.
Original Job: Bouncer in a nightclub
Marriage: Sandy Mahl, 1986
Children: Taylor Mayne Pearl, 1992; August Anna, 1994; Allie Colleen, 1996
Famous Relative: Colleen Carroll, singer, mother
Major Awards: Grammy, Best Country Vocal—Male, *Ropin' the Wind*, 1991; Grammy, Best Country Vocal—Collaboration, "In Another's Eyes" (with Trisha Yearwood), 1997

JAMES L. BROOKS

Birthplace: North Bergen, NJ
Birthdate: 5/9/40
Occupation: Producer, director, actor, screenwriter
Education: New York University
Debut: (TV) *Room 222*, 1969; (Film) *Starting Over*, 1979
Signature: *The Mary Tyler Moore Show*
Facts: Founded Gracie Films, which produces *The Simpsons*, in 1984.

With fellow writer Allan Burns, created *The Mary Tyler Moore Show* in 1970.
Original Job: Copyboy for CBS News
Marriages: Marianne Catherine Morrissey (divorced), Holly Beth Holmberg, 1978 (separated, 2000)
Children: Amy Lorraine, 1971 (with Morrissey); Chloe, c. 1984; Cooper, c. 1986; Joseph, c. 1993 (with Holmberg)
Major Awards: Emmy, Best Writing in a Comedy Series, *The Mary Tyler Moore Show,* 1971, 1977; Emmy, Best Comedy Series, *The Mary Tyler Moore Show,* 1975, 1976, 1977; Emmy, Best Comedy Series, *Taxi,* 1979, 1980, 1981; Oscar, Best Director, *Terms of Endearment,* 1983; Oscar, Best Adapted Screenplay, *Terms of Endearment,* 1983; Emmy, Outstanding Variety, Music, or Comedy Program, *The Tracey Ullman Show,* 1989; Emmy, Outstanding Animated Program, *The Simpsons,* 1990, 1991

MEL BROOKS

Real Name: Melvin Kaminsky
Birthplace: Brooklyn, NY
Birthdate: 6/28/26
Occupation: Actor, writer, director, producer
Education: Boston College
Debut: (Stage) *Broadway Revue,* 1949; (TV) *Your Show of Shows,* 1950
Signature: *Blazing Saddles,* 1974
Facts: Fought in Battle of the Bulge during World War II.

Co-creator of the TV series *Get Smart.*
Original Job: Drummer
Marriages: Florence Baum, 1950 (divorced); Anne Bancroft, 1964
Children: Stephanie; 1951; Nicholas, 1952; Edward, 1953; (with Florence Baum). Maximillian, 1972
Major Awards: Emmy, Best Writing in a Variety or Music Program, *Howard Morris Special,* 1967; Oscar, Best Original Screenplay, *The Producers,* 1968; Emmy, Best Guest Actor in a Comedy Series, *Mad About You,* 1997; Grammy, Best Comedy Album, *The 2000 Year Old Man In The Year 2000* (with Carl Reiner), 1998; Tony, Best Musical, *The Producers,* 2001; Tony, Best Book of a Musical, *The Producers,* 2001;

Tony, Best Original Score, *The Producers*, 2001

PIERCE BROSNAN

Birthplace: Navan, County Meath, Ireland
Birthdate: 5/16/52
Occupation: Actor
Debut: (Stage) *Wait Until Dark*, 1976; (Film) *The Mirror Crack'd*, 1980; (TV) *Remington Steele*, 1982
Signature: *Tomorrow Never Dies*, 1997
Facts: Wife, Cassandra (best known for playing Countess Lisl in *For Your Eyes Only*, 1981), introduced Brosnan to Albert Broccoli, producer of the 007 series. Brosnan almost replaced Roger Moore as James Bond, but couldn't get out of his contract with NBC's *Remington Steele*.

In 1995, he finally played Bond in *Goldeneye*, and is credited with helping to revive the then-ailing series.

Ran away with the circus as a fire eater in his teens.
Original Job: Commercial artist
Marriages: Cassandra Harris, 1977 (deceased, 1991); Keely Shaye Smith, 2001
Children: Charlotte, 1971 (step-daughter); Christopher, 1972 (stepson); Sean William, 1984; (with Cassandra Harris). Dylan Thomas, 1997; Paris Beckett, 2001
Quote: "I'd like to see him killed off. I want to have a death scene with Bond. Now that would be something."

MELANIE BROWN

Birthplace: Leeds, Yorkshire, England
Birthdate: 5/29/75
Occupation: Singer
Debut: (Album) *Spice*, 1996; (Movie) *Spice World*, 1997 (American release, 1998)
Signature: "Wannabe," (1996) / Scary Spice
Facts: Tensions between Brown and Geri Halliwell were cited for Halliwell's departure from the group.

Her ex-husband was a dancer on a Spice Girls tour.

During downtime from her music career, has worked as a VJ for Pure Naughty on BBC2.

Her favorite movie star is Wesley Snipes.
Marriage: Jimmy Gulzar, 1998 (divorced, 2000)
Child: Phoenix Chi, 1999
Quote: "You can make life what you want it to be."

JOY BROWNE

Birthplace: New Orleans, LA
Birthdate: 10/24/50
Occupation: On-air psychologist
Education: Rice University; Northeastern University, Ph.D.
Facts: In 1982, she hit the Boston airwaves, and in 1984 moved to San Francisco where she was an on-air psychologist.

Author of *Dating for Dummies* (1998), *9 Fantasies That Will Ruin Your Life* (1998), *It's a Jungle Out There, Jane! Understanding the Male Animal* (1999)
Relationship: Divorced
Child: Daughter, 1977, marine biologist
Quote: "I want Oprah's warmth, Donahue's energy, Springer's excitement, Geraldo's IQ, Ricki Lake's exuberance, Sally's caring, and Montel's baldness."

KOBE BRYANT

Birthplace: Philadelphia, PA
Birthdate: 8/23/78
Occupation: Basketball player
Education: High school
Debut: (N.B.A.) Los Angeles Lakers, 1996
Facts: Was named for the Kobe steak house in suburban Philadelphia.

His family moved to Italy for eight years when he was six; there his father played pro ball.

In high school, shattered all of Wilt Chamberlain's Pennsylvania school scoring records by more than 500 points.

Took *Moesha*'s Brandy to his prom.

Has written "spiritual rap" with the rap group Cheizaw. His hip-hop name is "Kobe One Kenobe the Eighth."
Marriage: Vanessa Laine (married, 2001)
Famous Relative: Joe "Jelly Bean" Bryant, basketball player, father

JIMMY BUFFETT

Birthplace: Pascagoula, MS
Birthdate: 12/25/46
Occupation: Singer, songwriter
Education: University of Southern Mississippi
Debut: (Album) *Down to Earth*, 1970
Signature: "Margaritaville"
Facts: Has chaired Florida's Save the Manatee Club since its inception in 1981. In 1992, sued the parent Florida Audubon Society for independent control of the club, arguing that the society was "too cozy" with many of the businesses he felt were polluters.

Wrote a children's book, *The Jolly Man*, with his eight-year-old daughter in 1987. Also wrote two novels, including *Tales from Margaritaville* (1989) and a bestselling memoir, *A Pirate Looks at Fifty*. Received a $3-million advance for a collection of tropical short stories.

In 1991, four Cuban exiles seeking political asylum swam to Buffett's Florida house. He handed them over to the authorities after offering them refreshments.

Also owns the Margaritaville Cafe franchise.
Original Job: Reviewer for *Billboard* magazine and freelance writer for *Inside Sports* and *Outside* magazines
Marriage: Jane Slagsvol, 1977
Children: Savannah Jane, 1979; Sarah, 1992; Cameron Marley (adopted).

SANDRA BULLOCK

Birthplace: Arlington, VA
Birthdate: 7/26/64
Occupation: Actor
Education: East Carolina University, Neighborhood Playhouse with Sanford Meisner
Debut: (TV) *Bionic Showdown: The Six Million Dollar Man and the Bionic Woman*, 1989; (Film) *Hangmen*, 1987 [see page 64 for a complete filmography]
Signature: *Speed*, 1994
Facts: Her mother was a European opera singer, so as a child Bullock shuttled between Austria, Germany, and the U.S.

Was a cheerleader in high school.

Played lead actress in the short-lived TV series *Working Girl*.

Her role in *While You Were Sleeping* was originally offered to Demi Moore, whose salary demands were out of reach.

Formerly involved in a relationship with Matthew McConaughey.

Spent time at a Rehabilitation Clinic in 2000 to prepare for her role in *28 Days*.
Original Job: Waitress
Famous Relative: Helga Bullock, mother, opera singer

GISELE BUNDCHEN

Birthplace: Brazil
Birthdate: 7/20/80
Occupation: Model
Education: High school dropout
Debut: Alexander McQueen's *Rain*, 1997
Facts: As a child, her nickname was Oli, short for Olive Oil, because she was so tall and skinny.

Originally aspired to be a professional volleyball player.

Is terrified of public speaking.

Discovered by a modeling scout while eating a Big Mac during a school trip to Sao Paulo in 1994.

Owns over 200 belts.

At home the press calls her the "Boobs from Brazil." One newspaper report blamed her for the 36,000 breast enhancements in Brazil in 2000.
Relationship: Leonardo DiCaprio
Quote: "It's not easy, choosing between 50 pants and 50 tops."

EMMA BUNTON

Birthplace: North Finchley, North London, England
Birthdate: 1/21/76
Occupation: Singer
Debut: (Album) *Spice*, 1996; (Movie) *Spice World*, 1997 (American release, 1998)
Signature: "Wannabe," (1996) / Baby Spice
Facts: Was not an original member of the band that became Spice Girls; one of the singers chosen left the group early, and Ms. Bunton stepped in.

Prince William designated her his favorite Spice.

Describes herself as part "mummy's girl" and part "hot, sexy bitch."

Writes poetry.

Her debut solo single, released in England, was a remake of Edie Brickell's "What I Am."
Infamy: When the band fired their manager in 1997, rumors put the blame on his "nasty affair" with Bunton.

ED BURNS

Birthplace: Valley Stream, NY
Birthdate: 1/29/68
Occupation: Director, actor, writer
Education: Attended Hunter College
Debut: (Film) *The Brothers McMullen*, 1995
Signature: *The Brothers McMullen*
Facts: His first seven screenplays were rejected by agents and producers.

The Brothers McMullen was shot in eight months for around $20,000 (primarily a loan from dad), with Burns's parents' home the principal set.

Won the Catholic Daughters of America Poetry Award in sixth grade for a poem "about Jesus and a tree."

Bought JFK Jr.'s Tribeca loft for an estimated $2 million plus.

Formerly involved in a relationship with Heather Graham.
Relationship: Christy Turlington
Original Job: Production assistant, *Entertainment Tonight*
Quote: "I try not to read reviews unless they're absolutely glowing. I don't read mixed or negative at all, because life's too short."

ELLEN BURSTYN

Real Name: Edna Rae Gillooly
Birthplace: Detroit, MI
Birthdate: 12/7/32
Occupation: Actor
Education: High school dropout
Debut: (TV) *The Jackie Gleason Show*, 1956; (Broadway) *Fair Game*, 1957; (Film) *Alex in Wonderland*, 1970
Signature: *The Exorcist*, 1973
Facts: Used several stage names including Edna Rae, Keri Flynn, Erica Dean and Ellen McRae until finally settling on Ellen Burstyn in 1970.

Nominated 5 times for Academy Awards.

Named the first female President of Actor's Equity Association in 1982. She resigned from the position in 1985.

Was co-artistic director of the Actors Studio with Al Pacino from 1982–84.

Is an ordained cheraga (minister) in the Sufi Order in the West.
Original jobs: Dancer, model, photographer, soda jerk, short order cook, fashion coordinator
Marriages: William C. Alexander, 1950 (divorced, 1955); Paul Roberts, 1957 (divorced, 1959); Neil Burstyn, 1960 (divorced, 1971)
Child: Jefferson, 1962 (adopted)
Major Awards: Oscar, Best Actress, *Alice Doesn't Live Here Anymore*, 1974; Tony, Best Actress, *Same Time Next Year*, 1975

Quote: "I refuse to die. I will hang on, by a little finger if necessary."

STEVE BUSCEMI

Birthplace: Brooklyn, NY
Birthdate: 12/13/57
Occupation: Actor, director
Education: Attended Nassau Community College and Lee Strasberg Institute
Debut: (Film) *The Way It Is, or Eurydice in the Avenues,* 1984; (TV) *Miami Vice,* 1988
Signature: *Fargo,* 1996
Facts: Was hit by a bus when he was a child and received a settlement that he later used to finance acting lessons.

His wife, a performance artist-choreographer-filmmaker, has cast him in several of her performances.

Directed and starred in *Trees Lounge* in 1996, a film based on what his life on Long Island would have been be like if he'd never moved to Manhattan to pursue acting. Also directed TV commercials for Nike, and a 1998 episode of *Homicide,* and a series of episodes of HBO's *Oz* for the 1999–2000 season.

In 2001, suffered stab wounds to the head, throat and arm and received 35 stitches after intervening in a bar scuffle between Vince Vaughn and some college students in a Wilmington, N.C. bar

Was a firefighter in Manhattan for five years in the '80s and after the World Trade Center terrorist attack, he joined his former colleagues in the search and rescue efforts.
Infamy: When he was 16, he was arrested for trespassing in a Burger King parking lot.

He used to squeeze through the back window of a bar to steal crates of beer for his friends.
Original Jobs: Ice cream truck driver, comedian, firefighter
Marriage: Jo Andres
Child: Lucian, 1991
Famous Relatives: Michael Buscemi, actor, brother

Quote: "I guess I sometimes get frustrated about having played too many seedy, ratty guys. But, I'm working."

GABRIEL BYRNE

Birthplace: Dublin, Ireland
Birthdate: 5/12/50
Occupation: Actor, producer, director, screenwriter
Education: University College, Dublin
Debut: (TV) *The Riordans,* 1981; (Film) *Excalibur,* 1981; (Book) *Pictures in My Head*
Signature: *Miller's Crossing,* 1990
Facts: When he was 8, he played the accordion in a local pub with his uncle.

Began studying at an English seminary at age 12 and was expelled at age 16 after being caught smoking in a graveyard.

Founded the Irish-based production company Mirabilis Films in 1990.
Original Job: author, archaeologist, teacher, messenger, toy factory worker, plumber's assistant, apprentice chef
Marriage: Ellen Barkin, 1988 (divorced, 1999)
Children: Jack, 1989; Romey Marion, 1992

NICOLAS CAGE

Real Name: Nicholas Coppola
Birthplace: Long Beach, CA
Birthdate: 1/7/64
Occupation: Actor
Education: High school dropout
Debut: (TV) *The Best of Times,* 1980; (Film) *Valley Girl,* 1983 [see pages 64–65 for a complete filmography]
Signature: *Con Air,* 1997
Facts: Was expelled from elementary school.

Changed his last name to have an identity independent of his famous uncle. He assumed the name Cage in admiration of the avant-garde composer John Cage and comic-book character Luke Cage.

His method-acting techniques have involved having wisdom teeth removed without Novocaine for his role as a wounded war veteran in *Birdy,* slashing his arm with a knife in *Racing with the Moon,* and consuming a live cockroach for *Vampire's Kiss.*

Eight years before marrying Patricia Arquette, Cage proposed to her by volunteering to go on "a quest" for her. When he came up with a few of her chosen items— including J. D. Salinger's signature and a (spray-painted) black orchid— Arquette called off the deal to wed.

Then, according to court papers from his 2000 divorce filing, he and his wife separated only 9 months after their marriage. But in April 2000, they got back together again and Cage asked the court to dismiss the case. Finally, later in 2000, Arquette filed for divorce.
Infamy: In 1999 was criticized by friend Sean Penn, who said Cage "is no longer an actor . . . now he's more like a . . . performer." Nick Nolte and Stephen Baldwin added their own complaints about Cage's recent oeuvre.
Marriage: Kirsten Zang (engaged, never married); Patricia Arquette, 1995 (separated, 1996; reconciled, 2000; separated, 2000; Lisa Marie Presley (relationship)
Child: Weston, 1990 (by ex-girlfriend Kristina Fulton)
Famous Relatives: Francis Ford Coppola, director, uncle; Talia Shire, actor, aunt
Major Award: Oscar, Best Actor, *Leaving Las Vegas,* 1995.
Quote: "I've seen a lot of actors get high on their own importance with the Academy Award, and they snob themselves right out of the industry."

MICHAEL CAINE

Name: Maurice Joseph Micklewhite Jr.
Birthplace: Bermondsey, England
Birthdate: 3/14/33

Occupation: Actor, producer
Debut: (Film) *A Hill in Korea*, 1956; (U.S. Film) *Gambit*, 1966
Signature: *The Cider House Rules*, 1999
Facts: When he was a child, his mother pasted his ears to his head to prevent them from sticking out.

In his 1992 autobiography, Caine revealed that his mother concealed another son in a mental institution for forty years.

In 1951, he was drafted for National Service and spent two years in West Berlin and in combat in Korea.

His original stage name was Michael Scott, but when joining Actors Equity that name was taken. Seeing a marquee announcing *The Caine Mutiny*, he took Caine as his surname.

Saw his wife Shakira for the first time in a coffee commercial and called her for 12 days before she agreed to go out with him. She was Miss Guyana 1967.

In 1976, opened Langen's Brasserie, a London restaurant. He now owns six restaurants worldwide.

Knighted by Queen Elizabeth II in 2000.

He is an avid gardener.
Original Job: Production office assistant, cement mixer, driller
Marriages: Patricia Haines, 1955 (divorced, 1957); Shakira Baksh, 1973
Children: Dominique, 1956 (with Patricia Haines); Natasha, 1973
Major Awards: Oscar, Best Supporting Actor, *Hannah and Her Sisters*, 1986; Oscar, Best Supporting Actor, *Cider House Rules*, 1999
Quote: "I used to do films where I got the girl. Now I just get the part."

JAMES CAMERON

Birthplace: Kapuskasing, Ontario
Birthdate: 8/16/54
Occupation: Director, producer, screenwriter, editor
Education: Attended California

State University
Debut: (Film) *Piranha II: The Spawning*, 1981
Signature: *Titanic*, 1997
Facts: After seeing *Star Wars*, the physics-majoring college dropout knew what he wanted for his career. Following frequent trips to the USC library, he acquired camera equipment, built a dolly track in his living room, and began making a film.

When the Italian producers who hired him to direct his first film prepared the final cut without him, he flew to Rome, broke into the editing room, and secretly recut the film himself.

Co-founded his own special effects company, Digital Domain.

Went so far over budget for *Terminator 2* that distributor Carolco had to file for bankruptcy. When he again vastly exceeded his budget for *Titanic,* he voluntarily relinquished all pay except for screenwriting. After it became the biggest box-office grosser of all time, studio executives reinstated his original contract terms.
Infamy: A perfectionist, is known to be verbally abusive to his crew during filming, which frequently runs months behind schedule and tens of millions over budget.
Original Jobs: Machinist, truck driver, school-bus driver
Marriages: first wife (divorced); Gale Anne Hurd (divorced); Kathryn Bigelow (divorced); Linda Hamilton, 1981 (filed for divorce, 1999); Suzy Amis, 2000
Children: Dalton Abbott, 1989 (stepson); Josephine Archer, 1993 (with Linda Hamilton); baby, 2001 (details not released)
Major Award: Oscar, Best Director, *Titanic*, 1997

BILLY CAMPBELL

Birthplace: Charlottesville, VA
Birthdate: 7/7/59
Education: American Academy of Art
Debut: *Family Ties*, 1982; (Film) *Call*

From Space, 1989; (TV) (Broadway) *Hamlet*, 1993
Signature: *Once and Again*
Facts: Repeated senior year in high school.

An heir to the Champion spark plug fortune, he received an inheritance at age 18.

Originally wanted to be a comic-book artist.

Had a recurring role as a gay man on *Dynasty* in the 1984—85 season. Stands 6' 4".

Was once engaged to actor Jennifer Connelly, but they never married.

Still has a plus Pooh bear in his bedroom from when he was child.
Famous Relatives: David, brother, actor; John, brother, screenwriter

NAOMI CAMPBELL

Birthplace: London, England
Birthdate: 5/22/70
Occupation: Supermodel
Education: London School of Performing Arts
Debut: (Magazine) *British Elle*, 1985
Facts: In an effort to extend her talents beyond her modeling career, she wrote a novel, *Swan*, starred in the movie *Miami Rhapsody*, and recorded an album for Epic Records.

Has been romantically involved with Mike Tyson, Robert De Niro, and U2's Adam Clayton.

Opened the now-defunct Fashion Cafe in 1995 in New York City with fellow supermodels Elle MacPherson and Claudia Schiffer.
Infamy: Staged an impromptu stripping episode during lesbian night at a Manhattan bar.

Pleaded guilty in 2000 to misdemeanor assault for roughing up former assistant Georgina Galanis in 1998, and was let off with a warning. In 1999, Campbell settled a related case with Galanis for undisclosed terms.
Relationship: Muhammad Al Habtoor

NEVE CAMPBELL

Birthplace: Guelph, Ontario
Birthdate: 10/3/73
Occupation: Actor
Education: National Ballet School of Canada
Debut: (Stage) Toronto production, *Phantom of the Opera*, 1988; (TV) *Catwalk*, 1992
Signature: *Party of Five*
Facts: Beat out 300 other actors for her *Po5* role.

At age 9, joined the prestigious National Ballet of Canada. Is also trained in jazz, modern, flamenco, and hip-hop.

Drama may be in her blood: her mother once owned a dinner theater and her father was a high school drama teacher. They divorced when she was a toddler.

Her first name is her mother's Dutch maiden name and means "snow."

Auditioned for *Baywatch*. The casting director turned her down, in part, because "she is pale."
Original Job: Ballerina, model
Marriage: Jeff Colt, 1995 (divorced, 1997); John Cusack (relationship)
Famous Relative: Christian, actor, brother

JENNIFER CAPRIATI

Birthplace: Long Island, NY
Birthdate: 3/29/76
Occupation: Professional tennis player
Education: High school dropout
Debut: Virginia Slims tournament, Boca Raton, Florida, 1990
Facts: Her father and coach, Stefano, trained her to be a tennis player, practicing crib-side calisthenics and sit-ups with her from birth.

Held her first racket at age 3.

Became the youngest tennis player ever to turn pro at age 13.

In 1991, reached the semifinals of the U.S. Open and Wimbledon and became the youngest woman ever ranked in the Top 10.

A rebellious teenager, she quit playing tennis for five years before making her comeback.

Named 1999's Comeback Player of the Year by Tennis Magazine.
Infamy: Cited for shoplifting a $34.99 marcasite ring at a kiosk in a Tampa mall in 1993. The case was dismissed.

In 1994, was arrested in a Coral Gables hotel room and charged with possession of marijuana. She spent 23 days in a Miami Beach rehabilitation center.
Major Awards: Gold Medal, Women's Tennis, Barcelona Olympics, 1992; Australian Open champion, singles, 2001; French Open champion, singles, 2001
Quote: "I don't get into that whole bad-girl-makes-good hype. I just hope people who are down or don't feel good about themselves can see this and use it as inspiration."

DREW CAREY

Birthplace: Cleveland, OH
Birthdate: 5/23/58
Occupation: Actor, comedian, writer
Education: Attended Kent State University
Debut: (TV) *Star Search*, 1987
Signature: *The Drew Carey Show*
Facts: Served in the marines for six years.

Got into comedy when a DJ friend paid him to write some comedy material; Carey decided to try out the jokes himself on stage.

Battled depression for years, stemming from his grief over his father's death from a brain tumor when Drew was 8. Attempted suicide on several occasions.

Raised $500,000 for the Ohio Library Foundation by appearing as a contestant on *Who Wants to Be a Millionaire*.
Original Job: Waiter at Las Vegas Denny's

MARIAH CAREY

Birthplace: New York, NY
Birthdate: 3/27/69
Occupation: Singer
Education: High school
Debut: (Album) *Mariah Carey*, 1990; (Film) *The Bachelor*, 1999
Signature: "Vision of Love," 1990
Facts: Her vocal range spans five octaves.

Her wedding cost half a million dollars. She watched tapes of the 1981 wedding of Charles and Diana in preparation.

Bought Marilyn Monroe's white lacquered baby grand piano (it originally belonged to Marilyn's mother) at auction for $662,500.

In 1999, her $20 million former mansion in Westchester County, NY was completely destroyed by fire in what an insurance official termed "the most expensive single-family-home fire ever."

Claims a rude remark by Joan Rivers at the 1999 Oscars inspired her to diet.

Is fascinated with Guam—she started a recent world tour there, and named one of her Jack Russell terriers after the island.

Signed a multi-album deal with Virgin Records for an estimated $80 million in 2001.

Hospitalized in 2001 after suffering from an emotional and physical breakdown.
Infamy: Sued by her stepfather in 1992 for failing to share profits from her 1990 album.
Original Jobs: Waitress, hat checker, restaurant hostess
Marriage: Tommy Mottola, 1993 (divorced, 1998); Luis Miguel (relationship)
Major Awards: Grammy, Best Pop Vocal—Female, "Vision of Love," 1990; Grammy, Best New Artist, 1990

MARY CHAPIN CARPENTER

Birthplace: Princeton, NJ
Birthdate: 2/21/58
Occupation: Singer, songwriter, guitarist
Education: Brown University
Debut: (Album) *Hometown Girl*, 1988
Signature: "He Thinks He'll Keep Her"
Facts: Father, Chapin Carpenter, was a high-level *Life* magazine executive, so she spent her youth in Princeton, Tokyo, and Washington, DC.

Goes by the name Chapin, not Mary.

After college, considered music something to do for extra cash until she found her real career. Only after landing a nine-to-five job did she realize how much music meant to her, and began to focus on it.

Wrote Wynonna Judd's hit "Girls with Guitars" and co-wrote Cyndi Lauper's "Sally's Pigeon."
Infamy: Became an alcoholic after performing for years in bars.
Major Awards: Grammy, Best Country Vocal—Female, "Down at the Twist and Shout," 1991; Grammy, Best Country Vocal—Female, "I Feel Lucky," 1992; Grammy, Best Country Vocal—Female, "Passionate Kisses," 1993; Grammy, Best Country Vocal—Female, "Shut Up and Kiss Me," 1994; Grammy, Best Country Album, *Stones in the Road*, 1994

JIM CARREY

Birthplace: Jacksons Point, Canada
Birthdate: 1/17/62
Occupation: Actor
Debut: (TV) *The Duck Factory*, 1984; (Film) *Finders Keepers*, 1984
Signature: *Ace Ventura: Pet Detective*, 1994 [see page 65 for a complete filmography]
Fact: When his accountant father was laid off, he quit high school to make money doing janitorial work.

His $20 million paycheck for *The Cable Guy* was the highest salary yet paid to a comedian.

A coalition of fire prevention groups demanded that his Fire Marshall Bill sketches on *In Living Color* be taken off the air because of the negative effect they were having on children.

Gave Renee Zellwegger a $200,000 "friendship" ring in early 2000 when they were dating.
Marriages: Melissa Womer, 1987 (divorced, 1993); Lauren Holly, 1996 (divorced, 1997)
Child: Jane, 1987 (with Melissa Womer).
Quote: "I'm the Tom Hanks of the Golden Globes."

JOHNNY CARSON

Birthplace: Corning, IA
Birthdate: 10/23/25
Occupation: Talk show host
Education: University of Nebraska
Debut: (TV) *Carson's Cellar*, 1951
Signature: *The Tonight Show*
Facts: Declined role to play lead in the series that became *The Dick Van Dyke Show*.

As a 12-year-old, performed at local parties as "The Great Carsoni."

His son Richard was killed when his car plunged off a road.

Third wife Joanna Holland received $20 million in cash and property in a 1983 divorce settlement.

Served with the U.S. Naval Reserve during World War II.

Suffered a heart attack and underwent quadruple-bypass surgery in 1999.
Original Job: Radio announcer, ventriloquist, magician
Marriages: Jody Wolcott, 1949 (divorced, 1963); Joanne Copeland, 1963 (divorced, 1972); Joanna Holland, 1972 (divorced, 1983); Alexis Maas, 1987
Children: Christopher, 1950; Richard, 1952 (deceased, 1991); Cory, 1953; (with Jody Wolcott).
Major Awards: Elected to the Emmy Hall of Fame in 1987; Kennedy Center honoree, 1993

NICK CARTER

Birthplace: Jamestown, NY
Birthdate: 1/28/80
Occupation: Singer
Debut: (Single) "We've Got It Goin' On," 1995; (Album) *Backstreet Boys*, 1995 (American version, 1997)
Signature: "Everybody (Backstreet's Back),"1997
Facts: One of his early idols was Steve Perry from Journey.

Turned down *Mickey Mouse Club* for Backstreet Boys.

The band is named after Orlando, Florida's Backstreet Market, a popular teen hangout.

The group's debut was a hit in 26 countries before *Backstreet Boys* was released in the U.S.

Collects Beanie Babies.

Bandmates consider his attention span the shortest.

With Stan "Spider-man" Lee, has created a comic featuring the band as superheroes.

Is a certified scuba diver.
Famous relative: Aaron, brother
Infamy: Band filed suit against former manager Lou Pearlman, claiming he had made $10 million from their labor while they had received $300,000.
Quote: "Each one of us is extremely talented. A lot of groups might utilize one or two of the group's voices for the lead vocals. We use every single one."

JOHNNY CASH

Real Name: J. R. Cash
Birthplace: Kingsland, AR
Birthdate: 2/26/32
Occupation: Singer, songwriter
Debut: (Song) "Hey Porter," 1955
Signature: "I Walk The Line," 1955
Facts: Cash is one-fourth Cherokee Indian.

He cannot read music.

Created 75 cuts for his 1994 album, produced by Rick Rubin (of Beastie Boys fame), which included songs written for him by Red Hot Chili Pepper Flea and Glenn Danzig.

Known as "the Man in Black," which is the title of his 1975 autobiography. Cash adopted this persona while working in a trio that only wore matching black outfits.

Wrote a novel, *Man in White,* in 1986.

He chose John as a first name when the military wouldn't accept initials.

Has Parkinson's disease.

Infamy: Cash was addicted to Dexadrine in the '60s.

Original Job: Door-to-door appliance salesman, factory worker

Marriages: Vivian Liberto, 1954 (divorced, 1967); June Carter, 1968

Children: Rosanne, 1955; Kathleen, 1956; Cindy, 1958; Tara, 1961; (with Vivian Liberto). John Carter, 1970; Rebecca Carlene (stepdaughter); Rozanna Lea (stepdaughter).

Major Awards: Grammy, Best Country Performance—Duo or Group, "Jackson" (with June Carter), 1967; Grammy, Best Country Vocal—Male, "Folsom Prison Blues," 1968; Grammy, Best Country Vocal—Male, "A Boy Named Sue," 1969; Grammy, Best Country Performance—Duo or Group, "If I Were a Carpenter" (with June Carter), 1970; elected to Country Music Hall of Fame, 1980; Grammy, Best Spoken Word Recording, *Interviews from the Class of '55* (with others), 1986; Grammy, Legend Award, 1991; elected to the Rock and Roll Hall of Fame, 1992; Grammy, Best Contemporary Folk Album, *American Recordings,* 1994; Grammy, Best Country Album, *Unchained,* 1997; Grammy, Best Country Vocal—Male, "Solitary Man," 2000

ROSANNE CASH

Birthplace: Memphis, TN
Birthdate: 5/24/55
Occupation: Singer, songwriter
Education: State Community College; Vanderbilt University and Lee Strasberg Theatre Institute

Debut: (Song) "Blue Moon with Heartache," 1979
Signature: "I Don't Know Why You Don't Want Me," 1985
Fact: Never intended to become a musician. Her original ambition was to become a serious fiction writer.
Infamy: In 1982, entered a drug rehabilitation program for a cocaine dependency she had developed in 1979.
Original Job: Worked in wardrobe department during her father's tour. One day the tour managers asked her to come on stage and sing harmony.
Marriage: Rodney J. Crowell, 1979 (divorced, 1992); John Leventhal
Children: Caitlin Rivers, c. 1980; Chelsea Jane, 1982; Carrie Kathleen, 1988 (with Rodney J. Crowell). Jakob William, 1999
Famous Relatives: Johnny Cash, country singer, father; June Carter Cash, country singer, stepmother; Carlene Carter, country singer, step-sister
Major Award: Grammy, Best Country Vocal—Female, "I Don't Know Why You Don't Want Me," 1985

KIM CATTRALL

Birthplace: Liverpool, England
Birthdate: 8/21/56
Occupation: Actor
Education: American Academy of Dramatic Arts
Debut: (Film) *Rosebud,* 1975; (Stage) *The Rocky Horror Show,* 1975; (TV) *Good Against Evil,* 1977; (Broadway) *Wild Honey,* 1986
Signature: *Sex and the City*
Facts: Originally turned down her role in *Sex and the City* because she was afraid that it would interfere with her film career.
Marriages: Andreas Lyson, 1982 (divorced 1989); Daniel Benzali (engaged, never married); Mark Levinson, 1998.
Quote: "I love my curves and my softness and my breasts. I think they're beautiful, so I don't have a problem showing them."

JACKIE CHAN

Real Name: Chan Kwong-Sang
Birthplace: Hong Kong
Birthdate: 4/7/54
Occupation: Actor, writer, producer, director
Education: Chinese Opera Research Institute
Debut: *Big and Little Wong Tin Bar,* 1962; American debut, *The Big Brawl,* 1980
Signature: *Rumble in the Bronx,* 1995
Facts: Considered the biggest non-Hollywood movie star in the world; has been in more than 40 Asian action comedies. His fan club once topped 10,000 mostly young-girl members, one of whom killed herself when she read Chan was involved with someone.

His first attempts to break into Hollywood in the early '80s led to movie flops.

Nearly died making a 1986 film, when, leaping from a castle to a tree, he fell nearly 40 feet and broke his skull. He's also broken his jaw, shoulder, fingers and nose three times making movies.

To perfect his comic approach, studied old Hollywood Buster Keaton movies.

Impoverished parents left him at the Chinese Opera Institute at age 7 when they moved to Australia. During this militaristic-type training, he was beaten nearly every day.

Original Job: Stuntman
Marriage: Lin Feng-Chiao, 1983 (separated)
Child: Chan Cho-Ming, 1982
Quote: "I have a few rules that I tell my manager: No sex scenes! No make love! The kids who like me don't need to see it. It would gross them out."

J. C. CHASEZ

Real Name: Joshua Scott Chasez
Birthplace: Washington, DC
Birthdate: 8/8/76
Occupation: Singer
Debut: (Single) "I Want You Back," 1996; (Album) *NSYNC,* 1996

(American release, 1998)
Signature: *No Strings Attached*, 2000
Facts: As a boy, wanted to be a carpenter.

Claims he didn't start listening to music until he was "13 or 14."

After his years on TV's *Mickey Mouse Club*, waited tables to make ends meet.

His nickname is "Mr. Sleepy."

Is viewed as the most serious of the 'N Sync personalities.
Infamy: 'N Sync broke with their original record label and management over compensation. Suits and countersuits flew before a settlement was reached, allegedly favoring the band.
Quote: "I wouldn't go on TV grabbing this, that or the other and have my parents looking at that. That's just the way I was raised."

DON CHEADLE

Birthplace: Kansas City, MO
Birthdate: 11/29/64
Occupation: Actor
Education: California Institute of the Arts
Debut: (Film) *Moving Violations*, 1985; (TV) *Hill Street Blues*, 1987
Signature: *Devil in a Blue Dress*, 1995
Facts: Was offered scholarships to four arts colleges; two in art and two in theater.

Once acted in a production of *Hamlet* staged in a skid row parking lot.

Founded Elemental Prose, a company of artists aiming to pass down oral history through words and music.

An accidental meeting with director Carl Franklin in a doctor's office landed him an audition for *Devil in a Blue Dress*.

A trained jazz musician, he plays the saxophone and writes his own music. Learned to play the drums and the trumpet and to twirl a gun for his role as Sammy Davis Jr. in

1998's *The Rat Pack*.

Has been trying to develop a film version of *Groomed*, a play he wrote. He's also written the screenplay for an updated version of the 1973 film, *Cleopatra Jones*
Relationship: Bridgid Coulter, actor
Children: daughter, c. 1995; daughter, c. 1997
Famous relative: Colin Cheadle, brother, actor
Quote: "I'm not hot, I'm lukewarm. I'm making money and I'm saving my money and trying to be good in everything I do."

KENNY CHESNEY

Birthplace: Luttrell, TN
Birthdate: 3/26/68
Occupation: Country singer, songwriter
Education: East Tennessee State University
Debut: (Album) *In My Wildest Dreams*, 1994
Signature: "You Had Me from Hello," 2000
Facts: Majored in advertising and marketing, moved to Nashville.

Used to be a full-time songwriter and first hit the charts in country music in the early 1990s with "When I Close My Eyes."

His tour manager and concert sales director are childhood friends.
Infamy: A minor police altercation ensued after Chesney rode off on a policeman's horse in Erie County, NY while there for his concert tour. He had permission to sit in the saddle, but not to ride off. Tim McGraw went to his music friend's aid and tried to hold back the officers as they attempted to pull Chesney off the horse.
Relationship: Mandy Weals
Quote: "There's still tons of people, millions of people out there who don't know who I am."

CHER

Real Name: Cherilyn Sarkisian La Piere
Birthplace: El Centro, CA
Birthdate: 5/20/46
Occupation: Actor, singer
Education: High school dropout
Debut: (Film) *Wild on the Beach*, 1965; (TV) *The Sonny and Cher Comedy Hour*, 1971; (Stage) *Come Back to the Five and Dime, Jimmy Dean, Jimmy Dean*, 1981
Signature: "I Got You Babe," 1965
Facts: Abandoned by father when she was a few months old and placed in a home until her mother, who is part Cherokee, could save money to support her, she was eventually adopted by her mother's fifth husband, Gilbert La Piere.

Quit school as a teenager, ran away from home, and landed in L.A.

In 1964 began performing with Sonny Bono as Caesar & Cleo. The following year they changed their names to Sonny and Cher.

At one point, sold hair products by infomercial, was the spokesperson for the sweetener Equal, and started her own mail-order home decor business.

Has been linked to many famous men, including David Geffen, Mark Hudson, Gene Simmons, Val Kilmer, and Richie Sambora.

Nine days after her marriage to Gregg Allman, she filed for divorce.

Nominated for Best Supporting Actress Oscar for her role in 1983's *Silkwood*, she formed Isis, her own film production company, two years later and soon found herself in acclaimed roles in *Mask* (1985) and *Moonstruck* (1987).

Her daughter, Chastity Bono, a lesbian activist, was outed in 1990 by a tabloid and later wrote a book, *Family Outing*.

Enjoyed yet another comeback with her 1999 hit single "Believe."

Is seeking a share of Sonny's estate, claiming he owed her back alimony payments.
Original Job: Background vocalist

for the Crystals and Ronettes
Marriage: Sonny Bono, 1964 (divorced,1975); Gregg Allman, 1975 (divorced,1977)
Children: Chastity, 1969 (with Bono); Elijah Blue, 1976 (with Allman)
Major Awards: Oscar, Best Actress, *Moonstruck,* 1987; Grammy, Best Dance Recording, "Believe," 1999
Quote: "I still feel pretty kick-ass. I'm pretty vital. I have my truck and my motorcycle."

MELANIE CHISHOLM

Birthplace: Widnes, Cheshire, England
Birthdate: 1/12/74
Occupation: Singer
Debut: (Album) *Spice*, 1996; (Movie) *Spice World*, 1997 (American release, 1998)
Signature: "Wannabe," (1996) / Sporty Spice
Facts: As a child, imitated Madonna and studied ballet.

Regarded as the Spice Girl with the best vocal chops, she contests barbs that claim her bandmates can't sing.

The Chinese characters tattooed on her arm translate to "girl power."

Surfs, kick-boxes, practices yoga, and can do a backward somersault from a standing start.

Favorite film is *Toy Story*.

Owns over 200 pairs of sneakers.

Her solo album *Northern Star* (2000) veered from Spice Girls pop by including jazz balladry and industrial rock. The following year she left the group to concentrate on her solo career.

Infamy: A British tabloid ran an old photo of her at a party where other guests could be seen taking drugs.
Quote: "I think I'm pretty good, especially compared to some of the crap that's out there. And everyone likes Spice Girls records when they are drunk."

DEEPAK CHOPRA

Birthplace: India
Birthdate: April 1947
Occupation: Author
Education: All-India Institute of Medicine
Signature: *Ageless Body, Timeless Mind*
Facts: Was a mainstream endocrinologist and chief of staff at New England Memorial Hospital before embracing alternative healing methods.

Dr. Chopra practices a form of Ayurvedic medicine called Maharishi Ayur-Veda, named after the Indian spiritual leader who taught transcendental meditation to the Beatles. The system is based on a 5,000-year-old Indian holistic health system involving herbal remedies, massage, yoga, and transcendental meditation. (Ayur-Veda is derived from the Sanskrit roots for "life" and "knowledge.")
Marriage: Rita, c. 1970
Children: Gautama, Mallika

CHARLOTTE CHURCH

Birthplace: Cardiff, Wales
Birthdate: 2/21/86
Occupation: Singer
Debut: (Album) *Voice of an Angel*, 1999
Signature: *Voice of an Angel*
Facts: At 13, was the youngest classical artist to ever achieve a gold record, and the youngest solo recording artist to receive platinum status according to the Record Industry Association of America.

CHYNA

Real Name: Joanie Laurer
Birthplace: Rochester, NY
Birthdate: 12/27/69
Occupation: Wrestler
Education: University of Tampa (Florida)
Signature: WWF

Facts: Majored in Spanish literature in college.

While growing up with an alcoholic father, Chyna began following Jane Fonda's workout tapes, then moved on to weight lifting at a gym.

A basement kennel for her two schnauzers served as a makeshift wrestling ring for Chyna's older brother and wrestling soon became a source of inspiration.

She starred in high school productions of *Die Fledermaus* and *Grease*. Had reconstructive surgery on her jaw because of an underbite. Initially inspired to be an actor, she worked out too hard and developed a very muscular body.

After winning a United Nations scholarship for students with special abilities in languages, she spent her senior year in Madrid before entering University of Tampa.

Stands 6' 3", weighing in at some 200 pounds, Chyna likes to describe herself as "an empowered woman who kicks guys in the nuts for a living."
Original Job: Waitress, beeper salesperson
Relationship: Paul "Hunter Hearst Helmsley" Levesque, wrestler
Quote: "Chyna didn't just happen overnight. I took years to literally mold this character into this beautiful kick-ass woman."

TOM CLANCY

Birthplace: Baltimore, MD
Birthdate: 4/12/47
Occupation: Author
Debut: (Book) *The Hunt for Red October*, 1984
Facts: First short story was rejected by *Analog* science fiction magazine. Had just one article (on the MX missile system) to his credit when *Hunt for Red October* was published.

In the U.S. Army Reserve Officers' Training Corps, his poor eyesight kept him from serving in the Vietnam War.

Part-owner of the Baltimore Orioles, he also led the effort to bring an NFL expansion team to Baltimore for the 1994 season. He was successful, and is now part-owner of the Baltimore Ravens.

Clear and Present Danger was the bestselling book of the '80s.
Original Job: Insurance agent
Marriage: Wanda Thomas (divorced, 1999); Alexandra Llewellyn, 1999
Children: Michelle, 1973; Christine, 1974; Tom, c. 1983; Kathleen, 1985
Quote: "What do I care if someone reads my books a hundred years from now? I will be dead. And it's kind of hard to make money when you're dead."

ERIC CLAPTON

Real Name: Eric Clapp
Birthplace: Ripley, England
Birthdate: 3/30/45
Occupation: Singer, guitarist, songwriter
Education: Kingston Art School
Debut: (Album) *The Yardbirds,* 1963
Signature: "Layla," 1992
Facts: At the Ealing Club in London, occasionally substituted for lead singer Mick Jagger in Blues, Inc.

Earned the nickname "Slowhand" because his powerful playing regularly broke his guitar strings, which he then changed onstage to the accompaniment of a slow handclap from listeners.

The song "Layla" was reportedly inspired by an affair that Clapton had at the time with George Harrison's wife Patti, and was dedicated "to the wife of my best friend."

Tragedy struck in 1991, when his 4-year-old son died in a fall from Clapton's ex-girlfriend's apartment. The song "Tears in Heaven" is a tribute to him.

Was among 1,080 Britons recognized on Queen Elizabeth's honors list at the end of 1994.

In 1999, sold 100 of his guitars at auction for over $5 million, to benefit Crossroads Center, a clinic he founded in Antigua to treat drug and alcohol abuse.

Infamy: After release of *Layla and Other Assorted Love Songs* (1970), dropped out of sight for two-and-a-half years because of a heroin addiction. He was brought out of seclusion by Pete Townshend of The Who. A bout with alcoholism followed. Now, he says he hasn't touched a drink since 1987.
Original Job: Construction worker
Marriage: Patricia Anne Boyd-Harrison (divorced, 1988); Melia McEnery (relationship)
Children: Ruth, 1985; Conor, 1987 (deceased) (with Patricia Boyd-Harrison); Julie Rose, 2001
Major Awards: Grammy, Album of the Year, *The Concert for Bangladesh* (with George Harrison and Friends), 1972; Grammy, Best Rock Vocal—Male, "Bad Love," 1990; Grammy, Album of the Year, *Unplugged,* 1992; Grammy, Best Rock Vocal—Male, "Layla," 1992; Grammy, Record of the Year, Song of the Year, and Best Pop Vocal—Male, "Tears in Heaven," 1992; Grammy, Best Traditional Blues Album, *From the Cradle,* 1994; Grammy, Record of the Year, "Change the World," 1996; Grammy, Best Pop Vocal—Male, "Change the World," 1996; Grammy, Best Pop Vocal—Male, "My Father's Eyes," 1998; Grammy, Best Rock Instrumental Performance, "The Calling" (with Santana), 1999; Grammy, Best Traditional Blues Album, *Riding With the King,* 2000 (with B. B. King)

GEORGE CLOONEY

Birthplace: Lexington, KY
Birthdate: 5/6/61
Occupation: Actor
Education: Northern Kentucky University
Debut: (TV) *E/R,* 1984
Signature: *ER*
Facts: In high school, was on the basketball team.

Got his Hollywood break playing a medical intern on the short-lived CBS comedy series *E/R,* set in a

Chicago hospital emergency room. On NBC's *ER,* also set in a Chicago hospital emergency room, he graduated to full-fledged doctor.

Appeared as Roseanne's boss and Jackie's boyfriend during the first season of *Roseanne.*
Original Jobs: Sold insurance door to door; cut tobacco
Marriage: Talia Balsam, 1989 (divorced, 1992); Lisa Snowdon, model (relationship)
Famous Relatives: Rosemary Clooney, singer, aunt; Nick Clooney, TV host, father; Miguel Ferrer, actor, cousin

GLENN CLOSE

Birthplace: Greenwich, CT
Birthdate: 3/19/47
Occupation: Actor
Education: The College of William and Mary
Debut: (Stage) *Love for Love,* 1974; (TV) *Too Far To Go,* 1979; (Film) *The World According to Garp,* 1982 [see page 65 for a complete filmography]
Signature: *Fatal Attraction,* 1987
Facts: When she was 13, her father opened a clinic in the Belgian Congo (now Zaire) and ran it for 16 years. During most of that time, the Close children lived alternately in Africa and at boarding schools in Switzerland.

Her voice was dubbed over that of Andie MacDowell in the her starring role in *Greystroke: The Legend of Tarzan, Lord of the Apes.* Fifteen years later, Close's voice was used in Disney's animated *Tarzan* (1999).

Chosen by Andrew Lloyd Webber to replace Patti LuPone in *Sunset Boulevard,* 1994.

Collects costumes from her films.
Infamy: When she went on a two-week vacation from *Sunset Boulevard* in 1995, the production company released erroneous box-office figures implying that Close's absence had no effect on ticket sales. Close sent a scathing letter of complaint to composer-producer Andrew Lloyd Webber, which was

obtained and published in the media.

Original Job: Toured Europe and the U.S. as a member of Up With People
Marriages: Cabot Wade, 1969 (divorced, 1971); James Marlas, 1984 (divorced, 1987); Steve Beers (engaged, 1995)
Child: Annie Maude Starke, 1988 (from relationship with John Starke)
Major Awards: Tony, Best Actress (Dramatic), *The Real Thing*, 1984; Tony, Best Actress (Dramatic), *Death and the Maiden*, 1992; Tony, Best Actress (Musical), *Sunset Boulevard*, 1995; Emmy, Best Actress in a Miniseries or Special, *Serving in Silence: The Margarethe Cammermeyer Story*, 1995

PAULA COLE

Birthplace: Manchester, CT
Birthdate: 4/5/68
Occupation: Singer, songwriter
Education: Berklee College of Music
Debut: (Album) *Harbinger*, 1994
Signature: "Where Have All the Cowboys Gone?" 1996
Facts: In high school, was a self-proclaimed "goody two-shoes," holding posts as three-time class president and junior prom queen.

Had a nervous breakdown and contemplated suicide while in college. Wrote "Bethlehem" during that period.

This Fire's seven Grammy nominations included one for best producer, the first ever for a woman.
Relationship: Seyi Sonuga
Major Award: Grammy, Best New Artist, 1997

SHAWN COLVIN

Birthplace: Vermillion, SD
Birthdate: 1/10/56
Occupation: Singer, songwriter, guitarist
Education: Southern Illinois University
Debut: Shawn Colvin Band, 1976
Signature: "Sunny Came Home," 1997

Facts: At a young age, she sang in the church choir, learned guitar, and designed album covers.

Played folk and rock during her college years, and later played small clubs in California and with the country rock group Dixie Diesels in Texas.

Had to quit in 1978 to let her throat heal after years of singing hard rock with the Shawn Colvin Band.

Sang back-up on Suzanne Vega's 1987 hit "Luka," which led to a tour and signing with Vega's manager.
Marriage: Simon Tassano (divorced, 1995); Mario Erwin, 1997
Child: Caledonia Jean-Marie, 1998
Major Awards: Grammy, Best Contemporary Folk Recording, *Steady On*, 1991; Grammies, Song of the Year and Record of the Year, "Sunny Came Home," 1998
Quote: "I think at best my voice sounds honest."

SEAN "P. DIDDY" COMBS

Birthplace: New York, NY
Birthdate: 11/4/69
Occupation: Rap singer, producer, executive
Education: Attended Howard University
Debut: (Album) *No Way Out*, 1997; (Film) *Made*, 2001
Signature: Puff Daddy
Facts: His father died when Combs was 3; until age 14, he believed it was in a car accident, but later discovered it likely resulted from involvement in illegal street activities.

While in college in Washington, D.C., would ride a four-hour train to New York on weekends to intern at Uptown Records. Was named VP there at age 21. Became CEO of Bad Boy Entertainment at age 24.

Got the nickname "Puffy" as a child because he would huff and puff when angry. Changed his nickname to "P. Diddy" after his trial in 2001.

His clothes label, Sean John, is monikered after his first and middle names.
Infamy: Nine people died during a stampede at a hip-hop celebrity basketball game Combs organized in 1991; he was later cleared of criminal charges but settled private lawsuits with the families after a report revealed he had delegated most of the arrangements to inexperienced assistants.

In 1996, was found guilty of criminal mischief after threatening a *New York Post* photographer.

Was arrested in April 1999 on charges that he and his bodyguards beat up Interscope Records executive Steve Stoute. He pleaded guilty to a reduced violation, and was sentenced to a day of "anger management." A civil suit settlement is being negotiated.

Indicted in 2000 for allegedly trying to bribe his driver, Wardell Fenderson, to claim ownership of a gun police say was discovered in Combs's car shortly after a Dec. 27, 1999 nightclub shooting. Combs is found innocent of all charges.
Children: Justin Dior, 1993 (with ex–girlfriend Tanieka Misa Hylton); Christian Casey, 1998 (with Kim Porter)
Major Awards: Grammy, Best Rap Album, *No Way Out*, 1997; Grammy, Best Rap Performance By Duo Or Group, "I'll Be Missing You," 1997
Quote: "I need some time with my name out of print."

SEAN CONNERY

Real Name: Thomas Connery
Birthplace: Edinburgh, Scotland
Birthdate: 8/25/30
Occupation: Actor
Debut: (Stage) *South Pacific*, 1951 [see page 65 for a complete filmography]
Signature: James Bond
Facts: Connery grew up in a poor, industrial district of Scotland. At age 7, he took a job delivering milk

before school, and by age 13 he quit school.

Served in the British Navy from 1947 to 1950. Was discharged due to ulcers.

In 1950, represented Scotland in London's Mr. Universe competition.

Was denied for knighthood in 1998.

New Woman voted him sexiest man of the century.

Knighted by Queen Elizabeth II in Scotland in 2000.

Original Jobs: Lifeguard, milkman, bricklayer, plasterer, coffin polisher, and usher

Marriages: Diane Cilento, 1962 (divorced, 1973); Micheline Roque-brune, 1975

Child: Jason Joseph, 1963 (with Diane Cilento)

Major Awards: Oscar, Best Supporting Actor, *The Untouchables*, 1987; Tony, Best Play, *Art* (coproducer), 1997

HARRY CONNICK JR.

Birthplace: New Orleans, LA
Birthdate: 9/11/67
Occupation: Singer
Education: Loyola University, Hunter College, Manhattan School of Music
Debut: (Album) *Harry Connick, Jr.*, 1987
Signature: "It Had To Be You"
Facts: Performed annually at the New Orleans Jazz & Heritage Festival from the time he was 8.

He also recorded two albums of Dixieland music on little-known labels—the first when he was nine and the second when he was 10.

Learned jazz music from Ellis Marsalis, the patriarch of the Marsalis family at the New Orleans Center for the Creative Arts.
Infamy: Arrested for having a gun in his luggage at New York's JFK airport.
Marriage: Jill Goodacre, 1994
Children: Georgia Tatom, 1996; Sara Kate, 1997
Major Awards: Grammy, Best Jazz Vocal—Male, *When Harry Met Sally*,

1989; Grammy, Best Jazz Vocal—Male, "We Are in Love," 1990

DAVID COPPERFIELD

Real Name: David Kotkin
Birthplace: Metuchen, NJ
Birthdate: 9/16/56
Occupation: Magician
Education: Fordham University
Debut: (TV) *The Magic of ABC*, 1977
Facts: In his act, has levitated a Ferrari, walked through the Great Wall of China, and made the Statue of Liberty disappear. He has also extricated himself from a safe in a building about to be demolished by explosives and a steel box on a raft heading for Niagara Falls.

By age 12, had performed at local birthday parties for a fee of five dollars, under the name "Davino, the Boy Magician."

In 1982 developed Project Magic, a program designed to help people with physical and mental disabilities by teaching them magic.

Was engaged to Claudia Schiffer, but they never married.

Honored as a Living Legend by the Library of Congress in 2000. The library owns half of Harry Houdini's original library while Copperfield owns the other half—80,000 different items which he keeps in a "secret location" near his Las Vegas home.
Relationship: Amber Frisque, model

FRANCIS FORD COPPOLA

Birthplace: Detroit, MI
Birthdate: 4/7/39
Occupation: Director and writer
Education: Hofstra University, UCLA Film School
Debut: (Film) *Dementia 13*, 1963
Signature: *The Godfather*, 1972
Facts: First dreamed of becoming a filmmaker at age 10, while bedridden with polio. He put on shows for himself using puppets, a

tape recorder, a film projector, and a television set.

Coppola's interest in producing a film about the automaker Preston Tucker—*Tucker: The Man and His Dream* (1988)—began when his father invested and lost $5,000 in the automaker's company.

Directed Michael Jackson in the 15-minute Epcot Center feature *Captain EO*.

First son, Gian Carlo, was killed in a boating accident in 1986.

Built a very successful vineyard in California's Napa Valley, which he says "has now taken over supporting our family." Also owns a restaurant in San Francisco and property in Belize; he hopes to make that country the hub for a huge telecommunications center.

Successfully sued Warner Bros. for thwarting his attempts to develop "dream project," a new version of *Pinocchio*, at another studio; Coppola was awarded $20 million. But in 2001, an Appeals Court ruled in favor of Warner Bros.

Filed a lawsuit against the late science writer Carl Sagan and Warner Bros. for a portion of the earnings of the 1997 movie version of Sagan's 1985 book "Contact," claiming that it was based upon an idea of his. The case was dismissed in 2000 on the grounds that it was filed too late.
Original Job: Worked for famous B-movie producer/director Roger Corman as dialogue director, sound man, and associate producer
Marriage: Eleanor Neil, 1962
Children: Gian Carlo, 1963 (deceased, 1986); Roman, 1965; Sofia, 1971
Famous Relatives: Talia Shire, actor, sister; Nicholas Cage, actor, nephew; Jason Schwartzman, actor/musician, nephew; Spike Jonze, director/actor, son-in-law
Major Awards: Oscar, Best Original Screenplay, *Patton* (with Edmund H. North), 1970; Oscar, Best Adapted Screenplay, *The Godfather* (with Mario Puzo), 1972; Oscar, Best

Director, *The Godfather Part II,* 1974; Oscar, Best Adapted Screenplay, *The Godfather Part II* (with Mario Puzo), 1974

PATRICIA CORNWELL

Real Name: Patricia Daniels
Birthplace: Miami, FL
Birthdate: 6/9/56
Occupation: Author
Education: Davidson College
Signature: Kay Scarpetta, hero of her medical examiner–crime series
Facts: After her father had abandoned her and her siblings, her mother sought help from neighbors—evangelist Billy Graham and his wife, Ruth—who placed the children with Christian missionaries.

Her first book was an authorized biography of Ruth Graham, which strained their friendship for several years because of a "misunderstanding."

As a teenager, Cornwell was hospitalized for anorexia.

She married her English professor, 16 years her senior, after college.

Was a cartoonist for her college newspaper.

She travels with at least two bodyguards and hires armed, off-duty police officers for book signings.

She owns a .357 Colt Python, a .380 Walther semi-automatic, and a .38 Smith & Wesson.

Has a history of impulse buying and once spent $27,000 on a furniture shopping spree.

Was rescued by a jaws of life tool after her Mercedes crashed into a stalled van and flipped over three times.

She was known to behave erratically and suffered manic depression, which went undiagnosed for several years. In 1993, she checked into a clinic for recovering alcoholics.

Thoroughly researches technical details for her novels. Has attended approximately 600 autopsies for these purposes.

Gave $1.5 million to help the state of Virginia create an institute to train forensic scientists and pathologists.
Infamy: In 1992, had a lesbian affair with a married F.B.I. agent whose husband, also with the F.B.I., tried to ambush and kill his estranged wife.
Original Jobs: Police reporter for the *Charlotte Observer;* computer analyst in Richmond, Virginia, morgue
Marriage: Charles Cornwell (divorced, 1990)
Famous Relatives: Descendant of Harriet Beecher Stowe, author
Major Award: Mystery Writers of America, for *Post Mortem,* 1990
Quote: "I have this very cagey way of worming myself in; I'm an infection. You try to pacify me, and before you know it, you can't get me out of your system."

BILL COSBY

Birthplace: Philadelphia, PA
Birthdate: 7/12/37
Occupation: Actor, comedian, producer, author
Education: Temple University; Doctor of Education, University of Massachusetts at Amherst
Debut: (TV) *I Spy,* 1965; (Film) *Hickey and Boggs,* 1971
Signature: *The Cosby Show*
Facts: Grew up in a housing project in Philadelphia.

A gifted athlete, he was noticed by a scout for the Green Bay Packers.

Has played the drums since he was 11. A jazz aficionado, is president of the Rhythm and Blues Hall of Fame.
Infamy: In 1997, Cosby admitted having an adulterous "rendezvous" with Shawn Thompson in the early 1970s. The one-night stand came to light when Thompson's daughter, Autumn Jackson, threatened to tell the media that Cosby was her father unless he gave her $40 million. Jackson, whose education was financed by the entertainer, was convicted of extortion and sentenced to 26 months in jail, though a federal appeals court subsequently over- turned the conviction. Unlike Cosby, Jackson reportedly never submitted DNA samples, thereby procluding a conclusive paternity test.
Original Job: Shined shoes, delivered groceries
Marriage: Camille Hanks
Children: Erika Ranee, 1965; Erinn Charlene, 1966; Ennis William, 1969 (deceased); Ensa Camille, 1973; Evin Harrah, 1976
Major Awards: Grammy, Best Comedy Recording, *I Started Out as a Child,* 1964; Grammy, Best Comedy Recording, *Why Is There Air,* 1965; Grammy, Best Comedy Recording, *Wonderfulness,* 1966; Grammy, Best Comedy Recording, *Revenge,* 1967; Emmy, Best Actor in a Drama Series, *I Spy,* 1966, 1967, 1968; Grammy, Best Comedy Recording, *To Russell, My Brother, Whom I Slept With,* 1968; Grammy, Best Comedy Recording, *Bill Cosby,* 1969; Emmy, *Bill Cosby Special,* 1969; Grammy, Best Recording for Children, *Bill Cosby Talks to Kids About Drugs,* 1971; Grammy, Best Recording for Children, *The Electric Company* (with Lee Chamberlin and Rita Moreno), 1972; NAACP Image Award, 1976; Emmy, *The New Fat Albert Show,* 1981; Emmy, Best Comedy Series, *The Cosby Show,* 1985; Grammy, Best Comedy Recording, *Those of You with or without Children, You'll Understand,* 1986; elected to the Emmy Hall of Fame, 1991

ELVIS COSTELLO

Real Name: Declan Patrick McManus
Birthplace: London, England
Birthdate: 8/25/54
Occupation: Singer, songwriter
Education: High school dropout
Debut: (Album) *My Aim Is True,* 1977
Signature: "Alison"
Facts: "Costello" is his mother's maiden name.

Began playing guitar at age 15 after testing out the violin, among other instruments.

Strongly influenced by American

songwriters John Prine and Lowell George.

Got his first contract with CBS Records by performing on the sidewalk in front of the hotel where the label's sales conference was in progress. Was arrested for disturbing the peace but achieved his purpose.

From 1977 to 1986, he performed with the Attractions, including a tour in the U.S. and a spot on *Saturday Night Live*. He was asked on the show to perform "Less Than Zero" after the Sex Pistols cancelled. Instead, he played "Radio, Radio," a song that comments on media manipulation. Many thought the appearance would end his career.

His album *King of America* identifies him by his real name, adding on the imaginary second middle name "Aloysius."

Composed "She," the Charles Aznavour ballad from *Notting Hill*.

Infamy: In a drunken argument in 1979, used racial epithets in referring to Ray Charles and James Brown. American disc jockeys took his records off their playlists, and he received numerous death threats.
Original Job: Computer programmer at Elizabeth Arden's factory in England
Marriage: Mary, 1974 (divorced, c. 1985); Caitlin O'Riordan, 1986
Child: Matthew, c. 1973 (with Mary)
Famous Relatives: Ross McManus, jazz singer with Joe Loss Band, father
Major Awards: Grammy Pop Collaboration with Vocals (with Burt Bacharach) "I Still Have That Other Girl," 1998
Quote: "I'm not interested in courting people. If people don't like me, there's no way I'm going to be nice to them so they do like me. All I want is for the records to be heard. I'm not out there saying, 'Love me, love me.'"

KEVIN COSTNER

Birthplace: Lynwood, CA
Birthdate: 1/18/55
Occupation: Actor, director, producer
Education: California State University at Fullerton
Debut: (Film) *Sizzle Beach,* 1979 [see pages 65–66 for a complete filmography]
Signature: *The Untouchables*, 1987
Facts: At 18, built a canoe and paddled down the same rivers that Lewis and Clark had navigated on their way to the Pacific.

As a teenager, he sang in the church choir.

Turned down the leading role in *War Games* (played by Matthew Broderick) to play Alex, the character who commits suicide, in *The Big Chill*. Only two weeks before the film's release, Alex's part was cut. But director Lawrence Kasdan promised Costner that he would write a part for him in another film, and tailored the role of Jake in *Silverado* (1985) for Costner.
Infamy: In February 1995, Costner and his brother Dan began building an entertainment complex in the Black Hills of South Dakota, on land that the Lakota Indians consider sacred and have been trying to recover since 1887. Costner had been made an honorary Lakota in 1990 after working with them on *Dances with Wolves*.
Original Job: Worked in marketing, stage-managed Raleigh Studios in L.A.
Marriage: Cindy Silva (divorced, 1995); Christine Baumgartner (relationship)
Children: Anne, c. 1984; Lily, c. 1986; Joe, c. 1988; (with Cindy Silva). Liam, 1996 (with Bridget Rooney).
Major Awards: Oscar, Best Director, *Dances with Wolves*, 1990; Oscar, Best Picture, *Dances with Wolves* (produced with Jim Wilson), 1990.

KATIE COURIC

Birthplace: Arlington, VA
Birthdate: 1/7/57
Occupation: Broadcast journalist
Education: University of Virginia
Signature: *Today*
Fact: Was a cheerleader in high school.

After hearing Couric read a report on the air, the president of CNN banned the young assignment editor from further television appearances, complaining about her high-pitched, squeaky voice. Keeping her spirits, Couric began working with a voice coach.
Original Job: Desk assistant at ABC News in Washington, DC
Marriage: Jay Monahan, 1989 (deceased, 1998); Tom Werner, television producer (relationship)
Children: Elinor Tully, 1991; Caroline, 1996
Quote: "My smile is gummy and lopsided, but there's a naturalness to it that's appreciated in some quarters."
Major Awards: Daytime Emmy Outstanding Special Class Program, *Macy's Thanksgiving Day Parade*, 1996, 1997, 1998 (shared awards)

CINDY CRAWFORD

Birthplace: De Kalb, IL
Birthdate: 2/20/66
Occupation: Supermodel
Education: Northwestern University
Debut: (Film) *Fair Game,* 1995
Facts: Crawford was the valedictorian of her high school class, and received a full scholarship to study chemical engineering in college. There, a professor accused Crawford of cheating after she received a perfect score on a calculus midterm exam.

Supports P-FLAG (Parents and Friends of Lesbians and Gays) and leukemia research (her brother died of the disease at age 3).

Had LASIK eye surgery (to correct nearsightedness).
Infamy: Posed for the cover of *Vanity*

Fair shaving lesbian singer k.d. lang, prompting a renewal of international rumors she and then-husband Richard Gere were each homosexual and maintained the marriage for appearances only. In May 1994, the couple took out a $30,000 ad in the *Times* of London denying the rumors.
Original Job: Spent summers during high school detasseling corn in fields
Marriages: Richard Gere (divorced, 1994); Rande Gerber, 1998
Children: Presley Walker Gerber, 1999; Kaia Jordan Gerber, 2001

MICHAEL CRICHTON

Real Name: John Michael Crichton
Birthplace: Chicago, IL
Birthdate: 10/23/42
Occupation: Writer, director, producer
Education: Harvard, Harvard Medical School
Debut: (Book) *Odds On* (under the pseudonym John Lange), 1966; (Film) *Westworld,* 1973
Signature: *Jurassic Park*
Facts: Published a travel article in *The New York Times* when he was 14.

Developed FilmTrak, a computer program for film production, and is creator of the computer game Amazon.

As a college student, turned in a paper written by George Orwell to test whether or not a professor was grading him fairly. The professor, who had been giving Crichton C-plusses, gave the Orwell paper in Crichton's name a B-minus.
Infamy: In 1974 was fired as screenwriter of the film adaptation of *The Terminal Man* when his screenplay deviated too much from the book.
Original Job: Anthropology professor
Marriages: Joan Radam, 1965 (divorced, 1970); Kathy St. Johns, 1978 (divorced, 1980); Suzanne Childs (divorced); Anne–Marie Martin, 1987
Child: Taylor, 1989

SHERYL CROW

Birthplace: Kennett, MO
Birthdate: 2/11/62
Occupation: Singer, songwriter
Education: University of Missouri
Debut: (Album) *Tuesday Night Music Club,* 1994
Signature: "All I Wanna Do," 1994
Facts: Her mother and father played piano and trumpet, respectively, with a big band on weekends. Their four children were encouraged to learn music and often practiced on the four pianos in the house simultaneously.

In high school, she ran the hurdles in the Missouri state track meet.

Sang backup for Michael Jackson's 18-month *Bad* tour and, later, for Don Henley.

Went through a severe depression in the late '80s and didn't get out of bed for six months.

Played at Woodstock '94.
Relationship: Owen Wilson
Major Awards: Grammy, Record of the Year, "All I Wanna Do," 1994; Grammy, Best New Artist, 1994; Grammy, Best Pop Vocal—Female, "All I Wanna Do," 1994; Grammy, Best Rock Vocal—Female, "If It Makes You Happy," 1996; Grammy, Best Rock Album, *The Globe Sessions,* 1998; Grammy, Best Rock Vocal–Female, "Sweet Child O' Mine," 1999; Grammy, Best Rock Vocal—Female, "There Goes the Neighborhood," 2000

RUSSELL CROWE

Birthplace: Wellington, New Zealand
Birthdate: 4/7/64
Occupation: Actor, musician
Debut: (TV) *Spyforce,* 1970; (Film) *Blood Oath,* 1990; (Album) *The Photograph Kills,* 1996
Signature: *Gladiator,* 2000
Facts: He is one-sixteenth Maori.

In 1980, he recorded a single "I Want to Be Like Marlon Brando," billing himself as Rus La Roq, and formed the band Roman Antix. That band later became 30 Odd Foot of Grunts, in which he still plays.

Had a tooth knocked out at age 10 and did not replace it until he was 25.

His grandfather was a cinematographer of war documentaries. Crowe wore his grandfather's Member of the Order of the British Empire medal to the 2001 Oscars to honor his memory, but apparently the honor can technically be worn only by those upon whom it was bestowed.

Gained 48 pounds to play Dr. Jeffrey Wigand for 1999's *The Insider.*

Lives on a 560-acre farm north of Sydney, Australia. He recently purchased 129 cows.

Was the target of an abduction threat in early 2001, during which he received protection from the FBI.
Original Job: Street performer, waiter, bingo caller, fruit picker, bartender
Major Award: Oscar, Best Actor, *Gladiator,* 2001

TOM CRUISE

Real Name: Thomas Cruise Mapother IV
Birthplace: Syracuse, NY
Birthdate: 7/3/62
Occupation: Actor
Education: High school dropout
Debut: (Film) *Endless Love,* 1981 [see page 66 for a complete filmography]
Signature: *Jerry Maguire,* 1996
Facts: Dyslexia put him in remedial reading courses in school, but Cruise proved himself in sports.

At age 14, enrolled in a seminary to become a priest. Dropped out after one year.

Took up acting after losing his place on a high school wrestling team due to a knee injury.

Member of the Church of Scientology.

Developed an ulcer while filming *Eyes Wide Shut.*

Has saved three lives, rescuing people in Santa Monica, London, and off the island of Capri.

Likes to skydive and pilot his Pitts Special S-2B stunt plane.

Infamy: Author Anne Rice publicly criticized David Geffen for casting Cruise in *Interview with a Vampire* in 1994. After Rice saw the film she admitted Geffen had been right.

Won $580,000 in libel damages in 1998 from Britain's *Express on Sunday* for a story that claimed Cruise and his wife might be closet gays in a sham marriage.

Sued the *Star* in 1999 for claiming that sex experts had to coach Cruise and his wife in the art of lovemaking for *Eyes Wide Shut*.

In 2001, filed a $100 million lawsuit against Bold publisher Michael Davis, alleging that he wrote news outlets saying he'd found a videotape of Cruise having sex with a man. Davis claims he "only alerted certain media that there is potentially a tape and we're investigating it."

Original Job: Busboy
Marriages: Mimi Rogers (divorced), Nicole Kidman, 1990 (divorced, 2001); Penelope Cruz (relationship)
Children: Isabella Jane, 1993; Connor Antony, 1995; (both adopted)
Quote: "I'm not the Stanislavski kind of actor. I just want to communicate with the people in the scene."

PENELOPE CRUZ

Birthplace: Madrid, Spain
Birthdate: 4/28/74
Occupation: Actor
Education: National Conservatory, Madrid
Debut: (Film) *The Greek Labyrinth*, 1991; (TV) *Framed*, 1993
Signature: *All About My Mother*, 1999
Facts: Donated her salary from 1998's *The Hi-Lo Country* to Mother Theresa's children's sanctuary in Calcutta after volunteering there for a week.

Became a vegetarian in 2000

after filming *All the Pretty Horses*.

Her sister, Monica, is professional flamenco dancer.

Original Job: Ballet dancer, model
Relationship: Tom Cruise
Quote: "It is impossible to sustain an acting career longer than two or three years when you are known only for your beauty."

BILLY CRYSTAL

Birthplace: New York, NY
Birthdate: 3/14/48
Occupation: Comedian, actor
Education: Marshall University, Nassau Community College; New York University
Debut: (TV) *Soap*, 1977; (Film) *Rabbit Test*, 1978
Signature: *When Harry Met Sally...*, 1989
Facts: Went to college on a baseball scholarship and hosted a campus-radio talk show.

First theater job as a house manager for *You're a Good Man Charlie Brown*, 1968.

Studied directing under Martin Scorsese at New York University.

Daughter Jennifer is now an actor.
Infamy: Walked off the set of his first *Saturday Night Live* appearance after his seven-minute monologue was cut from the show.
Original Job: Substitute teacher, writer
Marriage: Janice Goldfinger, 1970
Children: Jennifer, 1973; Lindsay, 1977
Famous Relative: Milt Gabler, founded Commodore Records and later headed Decca Records, uncle
Major Awards: Emmy, Best Writing in a Variety or Music Program, *Midnight Train to Moscow*, 1990; Emmy, Best Individual Performance in a Variety or Music Program, *The 63rd Annual Oscars*, 1991, *The 70th Annual Academy Awards, 1998*; Emmy, Best Writing in a Variety or Music Program, *The 63rd Annual Oscars*, 1991; Emmy, Best Writing in a Variety or Music Program, *The 64th Annual Oscars*, 1992

Quote: "My father used to bring home jazz musicians at Passover. We had swinging seders."

JAMIE LEE CURTIS

Birthplace: Los Angeles, CA
Birthdate: 11/22/58
Occupation: Actor
Education: Choate; University of the Pacific
Debut: (TV) *Operation Petticoat*, 1977; (Film) *Halloween*, 1978
Signature: *A Fish Called Wanda*, 1988
Facts: Very athletic, Curtis was trained as a dancer and appeared on *Circus of the Stars* as an acrobat.

Curtis became interested in her husband Christopher Guest when she saw his picture in *Rolling Stone*. She gave him her home number through an agent.

When her husband inherited his grandfather's English peerage title, Curtis earned the right to be addressed as "Lady Haden-Guest."

She has authored several best-selling children's books, including *When I Was Little: A 4-Year-Old's Memoir of Her Youth* and *Today I Feel Silly and Other Moods That Make My Day.*
Infamy: Admitted to using cocaine, even with her father, although not abusing it. She quit completely in 1983.
Marriage: Christopher Guest, 1983
Children: Annie, 1986; Thomas Haden, 1996 (adopted)
Famous Relatives: Tony Curtis, actor, father; Janet Leigh, actor, mother

JOHN CUSACK

Birthplace: Evanston, IL
Birthdate: 6/28/66
Occupation: Actor, writer, producer
Education: Attended New York University

Debut: (Film) *Class*, 1983
Signature: *Grosse Pointe Blank*, 1997
Facts: Grew up in a tightknit Irish Catholic family, always putting on neighborhood plays. Four of the five kids appear in *Grosse Pointe Blank*, which Cusack wrote and produced.

His parents were active in the anti-war and social protest movements; today he chooses most roles with an eye towards their social statements. During the Gulf War, he even wrote an op-ed for the *Chicago Sun-Times* protesting "police brutality" during an anti-war rally outside a rap concert.

At 20, started his own Chicago theater group, New Crime Productions.
Relationship: Neve Campbell
Famous Relative: Joan Cusack, actor, sister
Quote: "I was a teen star. That's disgusting enough."

JOAN CUSACK

Birthplace: Evanston, IL
Birthdate: 10/11/62
Occupation: Actor
Education: University of Wisconsin
Debut: (Film) *My Bodyguard*, 1980; (TV) *Saturday Night Live*, 1985; (Off-Broadway) *Brilliant Traces*, 1989
Signature: *In & Out*, 1997
Facts: Trained at Evanston's Piven Theater Workshop.

Was a member of The Ark, an improv comedy troupe at the University of Wisconsin.

Received two Best Supporting Actress Oscar nominations for her comedic roles in 1989's *Working Girl* and 1997's *In and Out*.

Has appeared in eight films with brother John Cusack.
Marriage: Richard Burke, 1993
Children: Dylan John, 1997; Miles, 2000
Famous Relative: John Cusack, actor, brother
Quote: "There are way more different character roles for men than there are for women. With

women, it's usually you're the babe or you're the supportive friend, sort of brassy and obnoxious, cracking jokes. I'm not the babe."

WILLEM DAFOE

Real Name: William Dafoe
Birthplace: Appleton, WI
Birthdate: 7/22/55
Occupation: Actor
Education: Attended University of Wisconsin
Debut: (Stage) *Nayatt School*, 1977; (Film) *The Loveless*, 1981
Signature: *Platoon*, 1986
Facts: Given the nickname Willem as a child.

Toured the USA and Europe with experimental theater group Theater X before moving to New York in 1977 to join the Wooster Group, led by live-in girlfriend Elizabeth LeCompte.

Does not believe in marriage.

The role of Max Schreck in *Shadow of a Vampire* was written specifically for him by screenwriter Stephen Katz.
Original Job: Model, carpenter, electrician
Relationship: Elizabeth LeCompte
Children: Jack, 1982
Quote: "Weirdness is not my game. I'm just a square boy from Wisconsin."

CARSON DALY

Birthplace: Santa Monica, CA
Birthdate: 6/22/73
Occupation: MTV veejay
Education: Attended Loyola Marymount University
Signature: *Total Request Live* (*TRL*)
Facts: A devout Catholic, he contemplated priesthood.

Once played with Tiger Woods in the American Junior Golf Association. He received a partial scholarship to college, but left the following year hoping to turn pro.

Landed a job at KROQ-FM, L.A.'s leading modern-rock station. Previ-

ously host of *MTV Live* and *Total Request*, Daly became the host of *TRL*, a combination of the two, in 1998.

He learned of his breakup with Jennifer Love Hewitt while listening to the *Howard Stern Show*.

Reported to have dated pop star Christina Aguilera. Was engaged to actor Tara Reid, but they broke up.
Original Job: Radio deejay, KROQ-FM
Quote: "I'm nothing more than the Willy Wonka of MTV."

MATT DAMON

Birthplace: Cambridge, MA
Birthdate: 10/8/70
Occupation: Actor, screenwriter
Education: Attended Harvard University
Debut: (Film) *Mystic Pizza*, 1988
Signature: *Good Will Hunting*, 1997
Facts: As a teenager, occasionally break-danced for money in Harvard Square.

Left Harvard two semesters shy of an English degree.

Good Will Hunting, co-written with Ben Affleck, grew out of a scene Damon wrote for a Harvard playwriting class.

Lost 40 pounds in three months to play heroin addict in *Courage Under Fire*, creating an anorexia-like medical condition that injured his adrenal glands, requiring months of medication.

Formerly involved in a relationship with Winona Ryder for two years.
Major Award: Oscar, Best Original Screenplay, *Good Will Hunting*, 1997

CLAIRE DANES

Birthplace: New York, NY
Birthdate: 4/12/79
Occupation: Actor
Education: Attending Yale University
Debut: (TV) *Law & Order*, 1992; (Film) *Little Women*, 1995
Signature: *My So-Called Life*
Facts: Winona Ryder was so taken with Danes's portrayal of Angela

Chase on *My So-Called Life* that she called her director on *Little Women* to suggest Danes for the part of Beth.

First auditioned for *My So-Called Life* when she was 13, but it took two more years for the show to get a firm commitment from ABC.

Relationship: Ben Lee, musician

D'ANGELO

Real name: Michael D'Angelo Archer
Birthplace: Richmond, VA
Birthdate: 1974
Occupation: R&B singer
Debut: (Single) "U Will Know," 1994; (Album) *Brown Sugar*, 1995
Signature: *Voodoo*, 2000
Facts: His father and grandfather were both Pentecostal Ministers.

Played piano at age 3 and learned the organ at age 4.

Started his first band, Michael Archer and Precise, when he was 16 and learned the drums, sax, guitar, bass, and keyboards.

In 1992, he was a three-time winner at Amateur Night at Harlem's Apollo Theater.

By 19, having moved to New York, he gave a three-hour impromptu piano recital for an EMI records executive, who signed him to a record deal.

The mother of his first child was his writing partner on his inaugural album.

Children: Michael, Jr. (with Angie Stone); Imani, 1999 (mother unreported)

JEFF DANIELS

Real Name: Jeffrey Daniels
Birthplace: Athens, GA
Birthdate: 2/19/55
Occupation: Actor
Education: Attended Central Michigan University
Debut: (Stage) *Fifth of July*, 1980; (TV) *A Rumor of War*, 1980; (Film) *Ragtime*, 1981
Signature: *Dumb and Dumber*, 1995
Facts: Starred in McDonald's

commercials as a child.

He married his high school sweetheart on Friday the 13th because he used to wear the number 13 on his baseball uniform.

He won an Obie in 1982 for his one-man show, *Johnny Got His Gun*.

Worked four summers in his dad's lumber company in Chelsea, Michigan, and eventually moved there with his family. In 1990, he founded and financed Purple Rose Theater Company in Chelsea, where several of his original plays have been produced.

Learned how to moonwalk for the high school reunion scene in *Something Wild*.

During *The Fifth of July*, he shared a stage kiss, in successive productions, with William Hurt and Christopher Reeve.

His most prized possessions are an autographed Al Kaline–Norm Cash baseball and a 1968 Kaline trading card.

Marriage: Kathleen Traedo, 1979
Children: Benjamin, 1984; Lucas, 1987; Nellie, 1990
Quote: "Sometimes you have to do things that will put the kids through college, in an industry that will spit you out tomorrow and forget your name."

TED DANSON

Real Name: Edward Bridge Danson III
Birthplace: San Diego, CA
Birthdate: 12/29/47
Occupation: Actor
Education: Stanford University, Carnegie-Mellon University
Debut: (TV) *Somerset*, 1975; (Film) *The Onion Field*, 1979
Signature: *Cheers*
Facts: Father was the director of a local Native American museum.

In 1981, was the Aramis man on TV ads for cologne and men's toiletry products.

While at Stanford, followed a good-looking waitress to an audition

"just to be near her" and ended up winning a part.

Tap dances.

Infamy: Appeared at then-companion Whoopi Goldberg's 1993 Friars Club roast in blackface.
Marriages: Randall Lee Gosch (divorced), Casey Coates (divorced), Mary Steenburgen, 1995
Children: Kate, 1979 (with Casey Coates). Alexis, 1985
Major Awards: Emmy, Best Actor in a Comedy Series, *Cheers*, 1990, 1993; Golden Globe, Best Actor in a Comedy Series, *Cheers*, 1990, 1991

GEENA DAVIS

Real Name: Virginia Davis
Birthplace: Wareham, MA
Birthdate: 1/21/56
Occupation: Actor
Education: Boston University
Debut: (Film) *Tootsie*, 1982; (TV) *Buffalo Bill*, 1983
Signature: *Thelma & Louise*, 1991
Facts: Six-foot Davis, two inches taller than the cutoff established by professional modeling agencies, worked as a waitress to pay her bills. Finally she lied about her height and was accepted by the Zoli agency.

While working as a saleswoman at Anne Taylor, Davis got a job as a human mannequin in the store window.

Tried to qualify for the U.S. women's Olympic archery team in 1999.

Marriages: Richard Emmolo (divorced); Jeff Goldblum (divorced); Renny Harlin, 1993 (divorced, 1997); Reza Jarrahy, doctor, 2001
Major Award: Oscar, Best Supporting Actress, *The Accidental Tourist*, 1988

KRISTIN DAVIS

Birthplace: Boulder, CO
Birthdate: 2/23/65
Occupation: Actor
Education: Rutgers University
Debut: (Film) *Doom Asylum*, 1987; (TV) *Another World*, 1987 (TV movie)

N.Y.P.D. Mounted, 1991.
Signature: *Sex and the City*
Facts: Played a recurring role on *General Hospital*. Gained notice in 1995 for her recurring role as Brooke Armstrong on *Melrose Place*.

Appeared in numerous commercials, including one for Odor-Eaters (her most embarrassing).

Guest starred on *Seinfeld* as the girl whose toothbrush Jerry drops in the toilet.

Does yoga.
Relationship: Alec Baldwin
Original Job: Waitress
Quote: "I don't want to be taking my clothes off as an actress. My mother wouldn't be very happy."

DANIEL DAY-LEWIS

Birthplace: London, England
Birthdate: 4/29/57
Occupation: Actor
Education: Old Vic Theatre School
Debut: (Film) *Sunday, Bloody Sunday*, 1971
Signature: *My Left Foot*, 1989
Fact: At 16, accidentally overdosed on migraine medicine and suffered from two weeks of hallucinations. Because of this, he was mistakenly diagnosed as a heroin addict and placed in a mental hospital. To escape, he had to put on his "greatest performance of sanity."
Original Job: Loaded trucks
Marriage: Rebecca Miller, 1996
Child: Gabriel Kane, 1995 (with Isabelle Adjani). son, 1998
Famous Relatives: C. Day-Lewis, former poet laureate of Britain, father; Sir Michael Balcon, producer, grandfather; Jane Balcon, actress, mother
Major Award: Oscar, Best Actor, *My Left Foot*, 1989

ELLEN DEGENERES

Birthplace: New Orleans, LA
Birthdate: 1/26/58
Occupation: Actor, comedian
Signature: *Ellen*
Facts: Considered becoming a professional golfer.

In the 1980s the Showtime cable network, looking to name someone Funniest Person in America, found DeGeneres at a comedy club in New Orleans. She was given the title, and toured the country in a Winnebago with a big nose above the front bumper. It earned her the scorn of other comics, who thought she received the title undeservedly.

Was the first female comic ever to be invited to sit on Carson's couch in her first appearance on *The Tonight Show*.

Ellen's title character became the first uncloseted TV lead when she declared herself a lesbian; weeks before the "coming out" episode aired, DeGeneres herself did the same.

Formerly involved in a relationship with Anne Heche.
Original Job: Vacuum cleaner saleswoman, waitress
Major Award: Emmy, Best Writing in a Comedy Series, *Ellen*, 1997

BENICIO DEL TORO

Birthplace: Santurce, Puerto Rico
Birthdate: 2/19/67
Occupation: Actor
Education: Attended University of California, San Diego; Stella Adler Conservatory
Debut: (Film) *Big Top Pee-Wee*, 1988; (TV) *Drug Wars: The Camarena Story*, 1990
Signature: *Traffic*, 2000
Facts: Moved with his family to Pennsylvania at age 12 after his mother's death.

Stands 6' 4" and hails from a family of lawyers.

Was co-captain of his high school basketball team.

Originally studied business at UCSD until an acting class inspired him.

Has been linked with Clare Forlani, Alicia Silverstone and Chiara Mastroianni.

Gained two or three pounds a day with a diet of doughnuts and fried chicken for his role in *Fear and Loathing in Las Vegas*.
Major Award: Academy Award, Best Supporting Actor, *Traffic*, 2000.

JUDY DENCH

Real Name: Judith Olivia Dench
Birthplace: York, England
Birthdate: 12/9/34
Occupation: Actor, director
Education: Central School of Speech and Drama, London
Debut: (London stage) *Hamlet*, 1957; (Broadway) *Henry V*, 1958; (Film) *The Third Secret*, 1964
Signature: *Shakespeare in Love*, 1998
Facts: A much heralded actress, a member of the Old Vic Theatre Company since 1957 and the Royal Shakespeare Company since 1969, she has received numerous awards in England for her performances.

When she was young, she attended the Mount School and became a Quaker, a decision that she stands by to this day.

She has portrayed a wide range of characters, from Shakespeare's Ophelia and Lady Macbeth to historic queens Victoria and Elizabeth I to M, James Bond's boss in *GoldenEye* and *Tomorrow Never Dies*.

In 1980, she was awarded an Order of the British Empire and in 1987, named a Dame Commander of the British Empire.

Was the original choice to play Grizabella in *Cats*.

Was on screen for only eight minutes in *Shakespeare in Love*, for which she won an Academy Award.

She, along with Audrey Hepburn, is one of only a few actresses who have won an Oscar and a Tony in the

same year.
Marriage: Michael Williams, actor, 1971
Child: Finty, a.k.a. Tara Cressida Frances, actor, 1972
Famous Relatives: Jeffrey Dench, actor, brother
Major Awards: Oscar, Best Supporting Actress, *Shakespeare In Love,* 1999; Tony, Best Actress (Dramatic), *Amy's View,* 1999
Quote: "If anyone called me Judith they'd get a black eye. Judi, Judi, I like best."

ROBERT DE NIRO

Birthplace: New York, NY
Birthdate: 8/17/43
Occupation: Actor
Education: Attended the High School of Music and Art and dropped out, studied at the Dramatic Workshop, the Luther James Studio, the Stella Adler Studio, and the Actor's Studio
Debut: (Film) *Greetings,* 1969
Signature: *Taxi Driver,* 1976
Facts: Although commonly regarded as Italian-American, De Niro is more Irish in ancestry.

First acting experience was playing the Cowardly Lion in a Public School 41 production of *The Wizard of Oz.*

Co-owns Rubicon, a San Francisco restaurant, with Francis Ford Coppola.

The pop group Bananarama recorded a song (1984) called "Robert De Niro's Waiting." They originally wanted to use Al Pacino's name, but Pacino refused to let them.

De Niro grew up in New York City's Little Italy, just a few blocks away from his future friend, Martin Scorsese.

Three years after their breakup, De Niro was sperm donor for his ex-girlfriend Toukie Smith; a surrogate mother delivered her twin boys, Aaron and Julian

Was questioned by French police for nine hours regarding an international prostitution ring. Charging

that the detectives' only reason for interrogating him was to heighten their profile, De Niro won a defamation case against the paper that printed the investigators' leak, returned his Legion of Honor medal, and vowed never to return to France.
Marriages: Diahnne Abbott (divorced, 1988), Grace Hightower, 1997 (filed for divorce, 1999)
Children: Drena, 1967; Raphael, c. 1976 (with Diahnne Abbott). Aaron, 1995; Julian, 1995; (with Toukie Smith). Elliot, 1998
Major Awards: Oscar, Best Supporting Actor, *The Godfather Part II,* 1974; Oscar, Best Actor, *Raging Bull,* 1980.

BRIAN DENNEHY

Birthplace: Bridgeport, CT
Birthdate: 7/9/38
Occupation: Actor
Education: Columbia University; attended Yale University, graduate program
Debut: (Stage) *Streamers,* 1976; (Film) *Semi-Tough,* 1977; (TV) *It Happened at Lakewood Manor,* 1977
Signature: *Death of a Salesman,* 1999
Facts: Was in the Marines for over five years and served eight months in Vietnam before returning home because of shrapnel wounds and a concussion.

He made his TV screenwriting-directing debut in 1994, with *Jack Reed: A Search for Justice.*

Attended college on football scholarship and, although he loved the theater, never auditioned because he was a member of the team.

Admits to being a "functional alcoholic" in the beginning of his career.

Owns a cottage on the coast of Ireland.

Collects art and enjoys sailing.
Infamy: Arrested for drunk driving while with actor Steve Guttenberg.
Original Jobs: Meat truck driver, bartender, salesman
Marriage: Judy (divorced); Jennifer

Arnott, 1988
Children: Elizabeth, 1960; Kathleen, 1962; Deirdre, 1964 (with Judy). Cormack, 1993 (adopted; with Arnott); Sarah, 1995 (adopted, biological sister of Cormack; with Arnott).
Famous Relatives: Edward Dennehy Jr., acting teacher, theater director, brother
Major Award: Tony, Best Actor (Dramatic), *Death of a Salesman,* 1999
Quote: "People always ask me if my size has helped or hurt me in this business. It's pretty much an even split."

JOHNNY DEPP

Birthplace: Owensboro, KY
Birthdate: 6/9/63
Occupation: Actor
Education: High school dropout
Debut: (Film) *Nightmare on Elm Street,* 1984
Signature: *21 Jump Street*
Facts: Dropped out of school at age 16 and joined a series of garage bands, one of which (The Kids) opened for Iggy Pop. Moved to L.A., where his ex-wife introduced him to actor Nicolas Cage, who spawned Depp's career.

Once owned a painting of a clown by executed serial killer John Wayne Gacy; now Depp has a pathological fear of clowns.

Tattoos: "Betty Sue" and "Wino Forever" (formerly "Winona Forever").

Co-owns the Viper Room, the '30s-style nightclub in L.A., outside of which River Phoenix died (1994).

Member of the band P, with ex-Sex Pistol Steve Jones and Red Hot Chili Pepper Flea.
Infamy: Charged with trashing a $1,200/night hotel room in New York City in September 1994. He agreed to pay the $9,767.12 in damages.
Original Jobs: Rock guitarist, sold pens over the phone
Marriages: Lori Anne Allison (divorced); Sherilyn Fenn (engaged,

never married); Jennifer Grey (engaged, never married); Winona Ryder (engaged, never married); Vanessa Paradis (relationship)
Child: Lily-Rose Melody, 1999
Quote: "I've built a career at being a failure. I'm always shocked when I get a job."

PORTIA DE ROSSI

Real Name: Amanda Rogers
Birthplace: Melbourne, Australia
Birthdate: 1/31/73
Occupation: Actor
Education: Attended Melbourne University
Debut: (Film) *Sirens*, 1994
Signature: *Ally McBeal*
Facts: Began modeling at 11 and took professional name at 14.

Attended college as law major but dropped out to pursue career. She still holds on to *Black's Law Dictionary* for reference.

Modeled and appeared in TV commercials in Melbourne to pay tuition when a local film producer suggested she audition for *Sirens*.

Nicknamed "Portia de Froggy" after an episode of *Ally McBeal* where she had several scenes involving frogs.
Original Job: Model
Quote: "I think playing a lawyer alleviates some of my guilt at not becoming one."

DANNY DEVITO

Birthplace: Neptune, NJ
Birthdate: 11/17/44
Occupation: Actor, director, producer
Education: American Academy of Dramatic Arts
Debut: (Stage) *The Man with a Flower in His Mouth*, 1969
Signature: *Taxi*
Facts: After high school he worked in his sister's hair salon and was known as "Mr. Danny."

Got his part in *One Flew Over the Cuckoo's Nest* (1975) through producer Michael Douglas, whom

DeVito had met in summer stock a few years before. Kirk Douglas had directed DeVito in *Scalawag* in 1973. At one point, the two were roommates in New York City.
Original Jobs: Hairdresser, theatrical makeup artist, valet
Marriage: Rhea Perlman, 1982
Children: Lucy Chet, 1983; Gracie Fan, 1985; Jake Daniel Sebastian, 1987
Major Award: Emmy, Best Supporting Actor in a Comedy Series, *Taxi*, 1981

CAMERON DIAZ

Birthplace: San Diego, CA
Birthdate: 8/30/72
Occupation: Actor, model
Education: High school
Debut: (Film) *The Mask*, 1994
Signature: *There's Something About Mary*, 1998
Facts: The 5' 9" beauty signed with the Elite Modeling Agency at age 16; as a teen, made up to $2,000 a day.

Was a cheerleader in high school.

Says she "nearly killed herself" with her excessive drinking as she traveled the world as a successful —and fun-loving—model.

Nicknamed "Skeletor" as a child for being so skinny.

Competed in the Long Beach celebrity Grand Prix.

Since her only acting experience was in a school play, she originally auditioned for the smaller part of a reporter in *The Mask*; she was called back 12 times before snaring the lead.

Her looks spring from a combination of her dad's Cuban ethnicity and her mother's heritage of German, English, and American Indian. First name means "crooked stream" in Gaelic.

Her favorite authors are Charles Bukowski and Raymond Carver.
Relationship: Jared Leto
Quote: " 'Model turned actress' is a silly phrase. People just assume you don't have the capacity to think."

LEONARDO DICAPRIO

Birthdate: 11/11/74
Occupation: Actor
Debut: (TV) *Romper Room;* (Film) *Poison Ivy,* 1992
Signature: *Titanic*, 1997
Facts: Rejected by a talent agent when he was 10 years old for having a bad haircut.

First memory is of wearing red-and-yellow tap shoes and being lifted onto a stage by his father to entertain people waiting for a concert.

First acting experience was in a Matchbox car commercial.

Successfully sued *Playgirl* to block publication of unauthorized nude photos.

Under a 1999 settlement with director R. D. Robb, it was agreed *Don's Plum*, a film he made in 1995–96, could be released internationally, but not in the U. S. and Canada. It debuted at the Berlin Film Festival in 2001.

Plays pick-up basketball with Tobey Maguire, Freddie Prinze Jr., Will Smith, and Mark Wahlberg.

Interviewed President Clinton about the state of the environment for an Earth Day 2000 special.
Relationship: Gisele Bundchen
Famous Relative: Adam Farrar, actor, stepbrother
Quote: "I used to think that famous people were so full of crap."

VIN DIESEL

Birthplace: New York, NY
Birthdate: 7/18/67
Occupation: Actor, director, screenwriter, producer
Education: Attended Hunter College
Signature: *The Fast and the Furious* (2001)
Facts: His first name is Vincent; he hasn't revealed his true last name.

Started acting at age 7 with the Theatre for New York City.

In 1992 he began writing scripts, and directed the film short *Multi-*

Facial, which was shown in 1995 at the Cannes Film Festival. Two years later, his first full-length feature (which he wrote, coproduced and starred in), *Strays*, premiered in the Sundance Film Festival competition.

His script *Doorman* is based on his experiences as a New York City bouncer.

Original Job: Bouncer
Famous relative: Paul Vincent, film editor, twin brother
Quote: "I don't think I'm a man yet. I'm learning and I'm getting a little bit closer every day, but I'm not there yet."

TAYE DIGGS

Birthplace: Essex County, NJ
Birthdate: 1/2/71
Occupation: Actor
Education: Syracuse University
Debut: (Stage) *Carousel*, 1994; (TV) *New York Undercover*, 1996; (Film) *How Stella Got Her Groove Back*, 1998
Signature: *How Stella Got Her Groove Back*, 1998
Facts: Spent nine months singing and dancing in the *Caribbean Revue* at Tokyo's Disneyland.

Landed feature role in Broadway's *Rent* and continued TV spots in *Guiding Light*.

Upon learning he landed the *Stella* role, he ran naked through the aisles of *Rent*'s theater.

Costarred in the 1999 films *Go* and *The Wood*.

Relationship: Idina Menzel, singer
Quote: "If you could have seen me in high school, you would laugh. I loved sports and I loved women, but I was always a little too small and geeky."

CELINE DION

Birthplace: Charlemagne, Canada
Birthdate: 3/30/68
Occupation: Singer
Education: High school dropout
Signature: "My Heart Will Go On," 1997
Fact: Celine had nine best-selling

French albums behind her before she recorded *Unison* in 1990.

She has over 500 pairs of shoes, with not letup in sight.

Announced she would retire after her 1999 tour, in part to focus on having children. She plans to return to performing in March 2003, headlining at a $65 million, 4,000-seat amphitheater at Las Vegas's Caesars Palace where she will perform 200 nightsper year in the venue for at least three years.

Renewed her vows with husband Rene Angelil in 2000 at Caesars Palace. The ballroom was transformed into a scene from "1001 Arabian Nights" with camels, exotic birds, singers, belly dancers jugglers and Berber tents.

Infamy: In 1990, refused to accept a Quebec music award as anglophone artist of the year, declaring she was "proud to be Quebecoise." The anglophone press criticized her harshly for exploiting the incident for its publicity value.

Marriage: Rene Angélil, 1994 (renewed their vows in 2000)
Child: Rene-Charles, 2001
Major Awards: Grammy, Best Pop Performance—Duo or Group, "Beauty and the Beast" (with Peabo Bryson), 1992; Grammy, Best Song Written Specifically for a Movie, "Beauty and the Beast" (with Peabo Bryson), 1992; Grammy, Record of the Year, "My Heart Will Go On," 1998; Grammy, Best Pop Vocal— Female, "My Heart Will Go On," 1998.

SHANNEN DOHERTY

Birthplace: Memphis, TN
Birthdate: 4/12/71
Occupation: Actor
Education: High school
Debut: (Film) *Night Shift*, 1982; (TV) *Father Murphy*, 1982
Signature: *Beverly Hills, 90210*
Facts: Before her role on *90210*, she starred in *Little House on the Prairie* with Melissa Gilbert and *Our House*

with Wilfred Brimley.

Gained attention as a teen lead in *90210* for her temperamental behavior.

Subject of *I Hate Brenda* newsletter.

Reteamed with Aaron Spelling for *Charmed* in 1998.

Led the Pledge of Allegiance at the Republican National Convention in 1992.

Was asked to audition for *The Class of Beverly Hills* (a.k.a. *Beverly Hills, 90210*) based on her performance in *Heathers*.

She has three dogs.

Met ex-husband, Ashley Hamilton, only two weeks before they were married.

At her backyard wedding, Doherty wore a silk bathrobe and went barefoot.

Infamy: Highly volatile, she engaged in a bar fight with an aspiring actress and several public brawls with boyfriends.

Cited for thousands of dollars in unpaid rent.

Admits to abusing drugs and alcohol.

Pleaded no contest to charges of drunken driving and driving with a blood-alcohol level above the legal limit in 2001, and was sentenced to three years probation and a $1,500 fine.

Marriage: Dean Factor (engaged, 1990; never married); Chris Foufas (engaged, 1991; never married); Ashley Hamilton (divorced, 1994); Rob Weiss (engaged, never married).
Quote: "Don't judge me for who I am, because everybody makes mistakes."

HEATHER DONAHUE

Birthplace: Upper Darby, PA
Birthdate: 12/22/73
Occupation: Actor
Education: University of the Arts, Philadelphia
Debut: (Film) *The Blair Witch Project*, 1999

Signature: *The Blair Witch Project,* 1999

Facts: After growing up in Philadelphia, Donahue landed a role in the spooky hit independent film *Blair Witch*. Left to their own devices, with their own handheld cameras, the cast had little contact with the film's directors.

Original Job: Office temp

Relationship: Gregor Hrynisdak, writer-photographer

Quote: "When you know you look like crap, you roll with it after a while. What was I going to do? Start putting on mascara?"

HOWIE DOROUGH

Birthplace: Orlando, FL

Birthdate: 8/22/73

Occupation: Singer

Education: Valencia Community College

Debut: (Single) "We've Got It Goin' On," 1995; (Album) *Backstreet Boys,* 1995 (American version, 1997)

Signature: "Everybody (Backstreet's Back),"1997

Facts: Took jazz, tap, and ballet classes as a child.

Missed the final cut to be a member of Menudo.

'N Sync's Chris Kirkpatrick was in his college graduating class.

The band is named after Orlando, Florida's Backstreet Market, a popular teen hangout.

The group's debut was a hit in 26 countries before *Backstreet Boys* was released in the U.S.

Backstreet's very first gig was at Sea World.

Labeled the "friendliest," "sweetest" Backstreet Boy.

Develops condos on the east coast of Florida.

Established the Caroline Dorough-Cochran Lupus Memorial Foundation in memory of his late sister.

Acted in an episode of *Roswell*.

Infamy: Band filed suit against former manager Lou Pearlman, claiming he had made $10 million from their labor while they had received $300,000.

Original Job: Actor in commercials

Quote: "We want [our music] to be for everybody. Our audience is not just teenagers—it's mothers and daughters, boyfriends and girlfriends, people my age and older than me."

ILLEANA DOUGLAS

Birthplace: Massachusetts

Birthdate: 7/25/65

Occupation: Actor, screenwriter, director, producer

Education: American Academy of Dramatic Art, NY

Debut: (Film) *New York Stories,* 1989; (TV) *Homicide: Life on the Street,* 1995

Signature: *To Die For,* 1995

Facts: As a child, she created anti-pollution shows while in the third grade. Also sent sketches to *Saturday Night Live* on spec, and tape-recorded movies on TV to replay and mimic.

Had a relationship with Martin Scorsese from 1988 to 1997. First auditioned for him while working as an assistant for PR maven Peggy Siegal.

Loves to drive by famous people's houses.

Original Job: Comic, publicist

Marriage: Jonathan Axelrod, producer, 1998

Child: Sam Axelrod (stepson), 1990

Famous relatives: Melvyn Douglas, actor, grandfather; Rosalind Hightower, actor, grandmother

Quote: "When you're an actress in Hollywood, playing a hooker is the highest form of flattery. I'm serious. It's like when men get asked to play Hamlet."

MICHAEL DOUGLAS

Birthplace: New Brunswick, NJ

Birthdate: 9/25/44

Occupation: Actor, producer, director

Education: University of California, Santa Barbara

Debut: (TV) *The Experiment,* 1969; (Film) *Hail, Hero!,* 1969

Signature: *Fatal Attraction,* 1987

Facts: His film company produced *One Flew over the Cuckoo's Nest* (1975) and *The China Syndrome* (1979), in which he starred.

Directed two episodes of TV show *The Streets of San Francisco,* in which he costarred.

Flunked out of college during his freshman year.

Shared an apartment in New York City with Danny DeVito when both were struggling actors.

Is a UN Ambassador on nuclear disarmament.

Marriage: Diandra Luker, 1977 (separated, 1995); Catherine Zeta-Jones

Children: Cameron, 1978 (with Diandra Luker); Dylan Michael, 2000

Famous Relatives: Kirk Douglas, actor, father; Diana Dill, actress, mother; Eric Douglas, comedian, half brother

Major Award: Oscar, Best Actor, *Wall Street,* 1987

ROBERT DOWNEY JR.

Birthplace: New York, NY

Birthdate: 4/4/65

Occupation: Actor

Education: High school dropout

Debut: (Film) *Pound,* 1970; (TV) *Mussolini: The Untold Story,* 1985

Signature: *Chaplin,* 1992

Facts: His middle name is John.

At age 5, he played a puppy in his father's film *Pound*.

Was the live-in companion of Sarah Jessica Parker for seven years.

In 1985, he took a turn as a regular cast member on *Saturday Night Live*.

To play the part of Charlie Chaplin, Downey learned to pantomime, speak two British dialects, and play left-handed tennis.

An avid musician, Downey plays the piano and sings opera. He composed the closing theme song for *Two Girls and a Guy* as well as recording a version of "Smile" for *Chaplin*.

Infamy: In 1987, he began therapy at a substance rehabilitation center.

Arrested in 1996 on charges of driving while under the influence, carrying a concealed weapon, and drug possession.

Arrested a month later for criminal trespass and leaving a court-ordered rehab, he spent time in a drug clinic and, in 1997, was sentenced to time served and three years' probation.

Arrested again in June 1999 for admitting that he was still doing drugs, he was sentenced to 3 years in prison for violating his probation. With credit for time spent in county jail and treatment centers, he was released just over a year later.

Arrested in 2000 on felony drug possession charges. In a plea bargain, he was ordered to spend up to a year in a rehabilitation program and sentenced to three years of probation.

Arrested in April 2001 on misdemeanor charges of being under the influence of a controlled substance after his behavior led police to believe he was under the influence of drugs. Prosecutors decided to treat it as a parole violation rather than filing new charges. He is fired from the cast of *Ally McBeal*.

His stepmother says he was diagnosed with bipolar disorder syndrome and has not received help for it, which she blames for his trouble in staying clean.

Marriage: Deborah Falconer, 1992 (filed for divorce, 2001)
Child: Indio, 1993
Famous Relatives: Robert Downey, actor, director, screenwriter, father; Elsie Downey, actor, singer, mother; Laura Downey, screenwriter, stepmother
Quote: "Stopping isn't hard. Not starting again is."

ROMA DOWNEY

Birthplace: Derry, Northern Ireland
Birthdate: 5/6/60
Occupation: Actor
Education: London Drama Studio
Debut: (Stage) *The Circle*, 1989; (TV) *A Woman Named Jackie*, 1991
Signature: *Touched by an Angel*
Facts: An Irish Catholic, was raised in war-torn Northern Ireland, where she sometimes heard gunshots in the night.

Her mother collapsed from a heart attack in front of her when she was 10. Her father died from a heart attack 11 years later.

Turned down for a grant to attend drama school; her tuition was paid by a local theater director and two other teachers who believed in her talent.

Angel costar Della Reese, a minister, officiated at her Salt Lake City wedding, then entertained guests with a jazzy, romantic set.
Marriage: One prior marriage; David Anspaugh, 1995 (divorced, 1998); Michael Nouri, actor, relationship
Child: Reilly Marie, 1996

FRAN DRESCHER

Birthplace: Queens, NY
Birthdate: 9/30/57
Occupation: Actor
Education: Queens College
Debut: (Film) *Saturday Night Fever*, 1977
Signature: *The Nanny*
Facts: Her husband (since 1979) is a writer and executive producer of *The Nanny*.

Her five-line part in *Saturday Night Fever* included memorably asking John Travolta, "Are you as good in bed as you are on the dance floor?"

Before pursuing acting, went to beauty school to have a profession to fall back on. Uses that knowledge to do her own "AstroTurf of hairdos—nothing can hurt it": first mousse, then gel, then voluminize.

Studied with a vocal coach to lose her accent, but gave that up when she stopped getting acting work.

During the writer's strike in the late '80s, started a gourmet crouton business, a product that recently grossed seven figures annually.
Marriage: Peter Marc Jacobson, 1978 (separated, 1997); Michael Angelo (relationship).

MINNIE DRIVER

Real Name: Amelia Driver
Birthplace: Barbados
Birthdate: 1/31/70
Occupation: Actor
Education: England's Webber-Douglas Academy of Dramatic Art
Debut: (Film) *Circle of Friends*, 1995
Signature: *Good Will Hunting*, 1997
Facts: Grew up in the Caribbean until age 9, when she was sent to an English boarding school.

Gained over 20 pounds for *Circle of Friends*, then shed every ounce to play a thin Bond woman in *Goldeneye*.

Stands 5'10".

Broke off engagement to Josh Brolin in 2001.
Original Jobs: Jazz singer, guitarist

MATT DRUDGE

Birthplace: Tacoma Park, MD
Birthdate: 10/27/66
Occupation: Cybercolumnist, television commentator
Education: High school
Signature: *Drudge Report*
Facts: He reportedly graduated 325th of 350 in his high school class.

When he was younger, he watched television talk shows, listened to talk radio, and sat in his bedroom with a microphone and tape recorder, narrating his own show.

After moving to L.A., he managed a CBS Studio Center gift shop, and in 1995 began his Internet column with tidbits garnered from trashcans.

He works out of his Hollywood apartment.

In 1997, he posted items about Kathleen Willey, the former Clinton campaign worker who would later allege unwanted sexual advances from the Oval Office, and the following year he reported that *Newsweek* held back on a story about intimacies between Clinton and Monica Lewinsky.

Infamy: In 1997, his unsubstantiated report accusing White House aide Sidney Blumenthal of wife-beating was retracted, but because Drudge would not divulge his sources, he was slapped with a $30 million defamation suit, which remains unresolved.

Original Job: Night shift manager at 7-Eleven.

Quote: "I know it's unethical as hell, but it's fun."

DAVID DUCHOVNY

Birthplace: New York, NY
Birthdate: 8/7/60
Occupation: Actor
Education: Princeton; master's degree from Yale
Debut: (Film) *Working Girl*, 1988
Signature: *The X-Files*
Facts: As a six-year-old, Duchovny wanted to be a bathtub.

Duchovny was working on his Ph.D. dissertation, "Magic and Technology in Contemporary Fiction," when he got his first acting job in a Lowenbrau beer commercial.

Played Denise the transvestite detective on *Twin Peaks*, 1990–91.

America Online has two separate folders devoted to messages about him; as one fan explained, "the drool is too heavy to be confined to one."

Infamy: In 1999, filed suit against 20th Century Fox, alleging that the studio has cheated him out of millions of dollars in profits from his TV series, of which he owns a percentage. The lawsuit was settled in 2000.

Original Jobs: Teaching assistant at Yale, bartender
Marriage: Téa Leoni, 1997

Child: Madelaine West, 1999
Quote: "Seven years of trying to find my sister is enough already. For me as an actor, there's nothing left."

KIRSTEN DUNST

Name: Kirsten Caroline Dunst
Birthplace: Point Pleasant, NJ
Birthdate: 4/30/82
Occupation: Actor, model
Debut: (Film) *Oedipus Wrecks* of *New York Stories*, 1989; (TV) *Darkness Before Dawn*, 1993
Signature: *Interview with the Vampire*, 1994
Facts: While growing up in New York City, she appeared in TV commercials (eventually appearing in more than 70) and signed with a modeling agency.

Was 10 when she played Claudia in *Interview with the Vampire*, which brought a Golden Globe nomination.

Plans on starting her own production company, with her mother, to be named Wooden Spoon Productions (because her grandmother always carried one to keep the grandkids in line). Also aspires to have a fashion and makeup line.

Relationship: Jake Hoffman, actor (son of Dustin Hoffman)
Quote: "On my down time, I am a clean fanatic. I love to clean. It's a sick thing. I clean more than my mom. Scrubbing helps me get out my stress. I love Windex."

ROBERT DUVALL

Birthplace: San Diego, CA
Birthdate: 1/5/31
Occupation: Actor, director, producer, screenwriter
Education: Principia College
Debut: (Off-Broadway) *Mrs. Warren's Profession*, 1958; (Film) *To Kill a Mockingbird*, 1962; (Broadway) *Wait Until Dark*, 1966
Signature: *The Godfather*, 1972
Facts: Served two years in the Army in Korea before becoming an actor.

Worked with Dustin Hoffman,

James Caan and Gene Hackman under famed drama coach Sanford Meisner for several years.

Has a passion for the tango, which he practices every day.

Turned down $1 million to reprise his role in *The Godfather, Part III*.

Wrote and performed his own songs for his role in *Tender Mercies*.

Original Jobs: Truck driver, dishwasher, postal clerk
Marriage: Barbara Benjamin, 1964 (divorced); Gail Youngs, 1982 (divorced, 1986); Sharon Brophy, 1991 (divorced); Luciana Pedraza (relationship)
Child: Nancy Horne (stepdaughter)
Major Award: Academy Award, Best Actor, *Tender Mercies*, 1983

BOB DYLAN

Real Name: Robert Zimmerman
Birthplace: Duluth, MN
Birthdate: 5/24/41
Occupation: Singer, songwriter
Education: University of Minnesota
Debut: (Album) *Bob Dylan*, 1961
Signature: "Blowin' in the Wind," 1963
Facts: Took stage name from Dylan Thomas.

His backup band, The Hawks, later evolved into The Band.

Motorcycle crash in July 1966 led to a brief retirement.

Became a born-again Christian in 1979.

Infamy: Sued by Ruth Tryangiel in 1994. She claims she was his lover on and off for 19 years, and that she cowrote much of his music and helped manage his career. The lawsuit asks for $5 million plus damages and palimony.

His marriage to Dennis, and news of their child together, was not revealed until the publication of an unauthorized biography in 2001.

Original Job: Performed with a Texas carnival
Marriage: Sarah Lowndes (divorced, 1977); Carol Dennis, 1986 (divorced, 1992)

Children: Jesse, 1966; Maria, 1961 (stepdaughter, adopted); Samuel, 1968; Anna, 1967; Jakob, 1969; Desiree Gabrielle Dennis-Dylan, 1986 (with Carol Dennis)
Major Awards: Grammy, Album of the Year, *The Concert for Bangladesh* (with George Harrison and Friends), 1972; Grammy, Best Rock Vocal—Male, "Gotta Serve Somebody," 1979; Grammy, Lifetime Achievement Award, 1991; Grammy, Best Traditional Folk Album, *World Gone Wrong*, 1994; Grammy, Album of the Year, *Time Out of Mind*, 1997; Grammy, Best Rock Vocal—Male, "Cold Irons Bound," 1997; Grammy, Best Contemporary Folk Album, *Time Out of Mind*, 1997; Oscar, Best Original Song, "Things Have Changed (from *WonderBoys*), 2001

JAKOB DYLAN

Birthplace: New York, NY
Birthdate: 12/9/69
Occupation: Singer, songwriter
Education: Attended Parsons School of Design
Debut: (Album) *The Wallflowers*, 1992
Signature: The Wallflowers
Facts: The youngest of five children, is rumored to be the inspiration for his father's classic "Forever Young." As a child, often went on the road with dad.

Lived with his mother, Sarah Lowndes, after parents' bitter 1977 divorce. In an incident during a custody suit, Sarah tried to take Jakob and his siblings out of school, chasing them down the halls and even assaulting an uncooperative teacher.

Had a D average in high school. Began career wearing anonymous knit caps for seven years, playing L.A.'s clubs and delis without identifying himself as Dylan's son.

Having grown up the protected child of a famous celebrity, Dylan says privacy and security are crucial

to his own family as well: he won't even reveal his son's first name.

Debut album bombed at only 40,000 copies, causing Virgin Records to drop him; took more than a year to find a new label.
Marriage: Paige
Child: Son
Famous Relative: Bob Dylan, singer, songwriter, father
Major Awards: Grammy, Best Rock Vocal—Duo or Group, "One Headlight" (with the Wallflowers), 1997; Grammy, Best Rock Song, "One Headlight," 1997

CLINT EASTWOOD

Birthplace: San Francisco, CA
Birthdate: 5/31/30
Occupation: Actor, director
Education: Los Angeles City College
Debut: (Film) *Revenge of the Creature*, 1955 [see page 66 for a complete filmography]
Signature: *Dirty Harry*, 1972
Facts: He was drafted in 1951 but en route to Korea his plane crashed. He swam miles to shore and was made swimming instructor at a boot camp, where he met actors Martin Milner and David Janssen, who sparked his acting career.

Elected mayor of Carmel, CA, in 1986; reelected in 1988.

Jazz musician and self-taught piano player, he plays three songs in the movie *In the Line of Fire*. Also composed two Cajun-inspired instrumentals for *A Perfect World*.

Has own beer "Pale Rider Ale," named for his 1985 Western *Pale Rider*.

Reportedly had a son and a daughter with Jacelyn Reeves. Names were not released.

Is a part-owner of the famed golf courses at Pebble Beach.
Infamy: Slapped with palimony suit by former lover Sondra Locke.
Original Job: Lumberjack, forest-fire fighter, steelworker
Marriages: Maggie Johnson (divorced); Dina Ruiz, 1996

Children: Kimber, 1964 (with Roxanne Tunis). Kyle, 1968; Alison, 1972; (with Maggie Johnson). Francesca, 1993 (with Frances Fisher). Morgan, 1996
Major Awards: Oscar, Best Picture, *Unforgiven*, 1992, Academy of Motion Pictures Arts and Sciences, Irving G. Thalberg Memorial Award, 1995

ROGER EBERT

Birthplace: Urbana, IL
Birthdate: 6/18/42
Occupation: Film critic, writer
Education: University of Illinois; University of Cape Town, South Africa; University of Chicago
Debut: Film critic for the *Chicago Sun-Times*, 1967
Signature: Siskel & Ebert
Facts: While at the University of Illinois, was editor of the *Daily Illini* and president of the U.S. Student Press Association, 1963–64.

Wrote the screenplay for *Beyond the Valley of the Dolls*, 1970. Also wrote a novel, *Behind the Phantom's Mask*, which was released in 1993.

Is a member of the Studebaker Drivers' Club.
Marriage: Chaz Hammel-Smith, 1993
Major Award: Pulitzer Prize for Distinguished Criticism, 1975

KENNETH "BABYFACE" EDMONDS

Birthplace: Indianapolis, IN
Birthdate: 4/10/58
Occupation: Singer, songwriter, producer
Debut: (Album) *Lovers*, 1989
Facts: While in ninth grade, phoned concert promoters pretending to be his teacher, asking if musicians would grant his gifted young charge—actually himself—an interview. Through this ruse, chatted with Stevie Wonder, the Jackson 5, and Earth, Wind and Fire.

Given his moniker in the early '80s

by funk guitarist Bootsy Collins because of his youthful looks.

Has written or produced hits for Mariah Carey, Whitney Houston, Bobby Brown, TLC, Boyz II Men, and Toni Braxton.

Produced the movie *Soul Food* with his wife; they both cameo as film executives in *Hav Plenty*.

Marriages: Denise (divorced); Tracey McQuarn, 1992

Child: Brandon, 1997; Dylan Michael, 2001

Major Awards: Grammy, Best R&B Song, "End of the Road" (with L.A. Reid and Daryl Simmons), 1992; Grammy, Producer of the Year (with L.A. Reid), 1992; Grammy, Album of the Year (producer), *The Bodyguard*, 1993; Grammy, Best R&B Song, "I'll Make Love to You," 1994; Grammy, Best R&B Vocal—Male, "When Can I See You," 1994; Grammy, Producer of the Year, 1995; Grammy, Record of the Year, "Change the World," 1996; Best R&B Song, "Exhale (Shoop Shoop)," 1996; Grammy, Producer of the Year, 1996; Grammy, Producer of the Year, 1997

ANTHONY EDWARDS

Birthplace: Santa Barbara, CA
Birthdate: 7/19/62
Occupation: Actor
Education: University of Southern California
Debut: (TV) *The Killing of Randy Webster*, 1981; (Film) *Heart Like a Wheel*, 1982
Signature: *ER*
Facts: His classmates at USC included Forest Whitaker and Ally Sheedy.

Played a burnt-out surfer in 1982's *Fast Times at Ridgemont High*, and one of the two head nerds in 1984's *Revenge of the Nerds.*

Somewhat bored with acting, he was planning to direct a low-budget children's feature, *Charlie's Ghost Story*, when he was called for *ER*. Originally turned down the *ER* role

when production dates for the two projects initially overlapped.

Original Job: Actor in commercials for McDonald's and Country Time Lemonade
Marriage: Jeanine Lobell, 1995
Child: Bailey, 1994; Esme, 1997

CARMEN ELECTRA

Real Name: Tara Leigh Patrick
Birthplace: Cincinnati, OH
Birthdate: 4/20/72
Occupation: Actor, model, singer, dancer
Education: High school
Debut: (Album) *Carmen Electra*, 1992; (TV) *Baywatch Nights*, 1994
Signature: *Baywatch*
Facts: As a protégé of The Artist Formerly Known As Prince, she changed her name and flopped with her debut album. She later scored with *Playboy*, replaced Jenny McCarthy in 1997 as cohost of *Singled Out*, then played a *Baywatch* lifeguard when Pamela Anderson left the hit show, and is now a regular on *Hyperion Bay.*

She's the youngest of five children.

She lost her mother and her sister within a week of each other.

Wore Capri pants, a black Mark Wong Nark shirt, and black high-heel platform shoes to her wedding.

After marrying her in Las Vegas, Dennis Rodman sought an annulment of their marriage, issuing a statement that claimed he was drunk at the time. They remained married for months thereafter, though. Even after Rodman filed for divorce, the two were still linked.

Infamy: Posed nude for *Playboy* in 1996 and appeared in the video *Playboy Cheerleaders*
Original Job: Model
Marriage: Dennis Rodman, 1998 (divorced, 2000); Dave Navarro, musician (engaged, 2001)
Quote: "I love being in front of an audience. It's so stimulating. You get that adrenaline rush in your

body and there's nothing like it in the world. I also love to barbecue."

JENNA ELFMAN

Real name: Jenna Butala
Birthplace: Los Angeles, CA
Birthdate: 9/30/71
Occupation: Actor, dancer
Education: Attended Cal State University and Beverly Hills Playhouse
Debut: (Film) *Grosse Pointe Blank*, 1997
Signature: *Dharma & Greg*
Facts: Became a member of the Church of Scientology in 1991.

Trained in classical dance from age 5, she considered joining Seattle's Pacific Northwest Ballet.

Was a chorus line tap dancer at the 1991 Academy Awards and a "Legs Girl" in ZZ Top's 1994 World Tour.

Marriage: Bodhi Elfman, 1994
Famous Relative: Danny Elfman, composer, rocker, uncle-in-law

MISSY ELLIOTT

Real Name: Melissa Elliott
Birthplace: Portsmouth, VA
Birthdate: 7/1/71
Occupation: Musician
Debut: (Album) *Brand New*, 1995 (with Sista); (Solo album) *Supa Dupa Fly*, 1997
Signature: *Supa Dupa Fly*
Facts: Got her break in 1991 when Sista, a group comprising some of her junior high school friends, performed for Devante Swing of Jodeci. They did a set of original songs written by Elliott and were signed immediately.

Dressed in giant plastic garbage bags in the video for "Supa Dupa Fly."

Spends an estimated four hours a day on her hair.

Wrote to Michael and Janet Jackson every day in high school, asking them to come and save her.

Dr. Seuss is her favorite author.

In 1997, founded The Gold Mind,

Inc., a label on Elektra Records.

Has her own lipstick, Misdemeanor Lipstick.

In 1999, after going public about her father's domestic abuse, became a spokesperson for Break the Cycle, a national foundation that educates kids about domestic violence.

Quote: "If there was a party and everybody had to wear white, I'll come in with purple on."

EMINEM

Name: Marshall Mathers III
Birthplace: Kansas City, MO
Birthdate: 10/17/72
Occupation: Rap artist
Education: High school dropout
Debut: (Album) *Infinite*, 1997
Signature: "The Real Slim Shady," 2000
Facts: Never knew his father.

Failed the ninth grade three times.

His 2000 album *The Marshall Mathers LP* is the fastest-selling rap CD ever.

Musicians ribbed in his music include Christina Aguilera, Britney Spears, 'N Sync, the Spice Girls, and Vanilla Ice.

Infamy: Sued by his mother for depicting her in interviews as "pill-popping" and "lawsuit-happy." She's also a subject of his song "Kill You."

The Gay and Lesbian Alliance Against Defamation announced that his lyrics may provoke hate crimes against gays.

Police reports state Eminem threatened Insane Clown Posse rapper Douglas Dali with an unloaded revolver.

Had a rocky eight-year relationship with his ex-wife Kim. Eminem sports a "Kim: Rot in Pieces" tattoo on his chest, and his songs "97 Bonnie and Clyde" and "Kim" present tales of killing her.

In 2000, Eminem was charged with pistol-whipping a man he claims he found kissing his wife. Soon after, his wife attempted suicide. In a matter of weeks, Eminem filed for divorce; his wife then filed civil suit, seeking $10 million and charging "intentional infliction of emotional distress."

Pleaded no contest to a 2000 concealed-weapons charge and in 2001 was sentenced to two years' probation. Later in the year, he pleaded no contest to charges of carrying a concealed weapon and of brandishing a firearm in public in connection with a June 3, 2000 argument with the road manager of the band Insane Clown Posse, and was sentenced to one year of probation.

In 2001, a judge required his mother to settle a pair of defamation lawsuits against him for $25,000.

Marriage: Kimberly, 1999 (divorced, 2001)
Child: Hallie Jade, 1995
Major Awards: Grammy, Best Rap Album, *The Slim Shady LP*, 1999; Grammy, Best Rap Solo Performance, "My Name Is," 1999; Grammy, Best Rap Album, *The Marshall Mathers LP*, 2000; Grammy, Best Rap Solo Performance, "The Real Slim Shady," 2000
Quote: "I do feel like I'm coming from a standpoint where people don't realize there are a lot of poor white people."

NORA EPHRON

Birthplace: New York, NY
Birthdate: 5/19/41
Occupation: Screenwriter, director
Education: Wellesley College
Debut: (Book) *Wallflower at the Orgy*, 1970; (TV) *Perfect Gentleman*, 1978
Signature: *Sleepless in Seattle*, 1993
Facts: She was the subject of the play *Take Her, She's Mine*, written by her parents.

Her autobiographical novel *Heartburn* was adapted into a 1986 movie starring Jack Nicholson and Meryl Streep. Wrote screenplays for *Silkwood* and *When Harry Met Sally...*

Marriages: Dan Greenburg, 1967 (divorced); Carl Bernstein, 1976 (divorced, 1979); Nicholas Pileggi, 1987
Children: Jacob, 1978; Max, 1979; (with Carl Bernstein).
Famous Relatives: Henry Ephron, screenwriter, father; Phoebe Ephron, screenwriter, mother; Delia Ephron, writer, sister
Quote: "No matter how cynical I get, I just can't keep up."

MELISSA ETHERIDGE

Birthplace: Leavenworth, KS
Birthdate: 5/29/61
Occupation: Singer, songwriter, guitarist
Education: Berklee College of Music
Debut: *Melissa Etheridge*, 1988
Facts: Played in women's bars around L.A. for six years beginning in 1982.

Came out by leaping onstage at one of Bill Clinton's presidential inaugural bashes, kissing cult figure Elvira, and proclaiming herself a proud lifelong lesbian.

David Crosby was the sperm donor for her children.

Her former partner, Julie Cypher, was once married to Lou Diamond Phillips.

Relationship: Tammy Lynn Michaels, actor
Children: Bailey Jean, 1997; Beckett, 1998
Major Awards: Grammy, Best Rock Vocal—Female, "Ain't It Heavy," 1992; Grammy, Best Rock Vocal—Female, "Come to My Window," 1994
Quote: "I like to bring the sexual energy out by seducing the audience, and, when it's there, building on it. I would like to say that, maybe, going to a concert of mine is like foreplay."

RUPERT EVERETT

Birthplace: Norfolk, England
Birthdate: 5/29/59
Occupation: Actor
Education: High school dropout
Debut: (Film) *A Shocking Accident*, 1982; (TV) *Princess Daisy*, 1983; (American stage) *The Vortex*, 1991
Signature: *My Best Friend's Wedding*, 1997
Facts: As a child, he was very thin with huge buck teeth.

Was expelled for insubordination from Central School of Speech and Drama.

At his all-male, Catholic boarding schools, he was often cast in female roles in plays.

While a struggling actor, he supported himself as a male prostitute. Everett publicly disclosed his homosexuality in 1989.

Scenes from *My Best Friend's Wedding* were reshot to give him more screen time after focus groups praised his performance.

In 1991, he published his first novel, *Hello Darling, Are You Working?*
Original Job: Model
Quote: "I don't think anyone's particularly shocked by anything any more. Are they? We are all such old sluts now."

EDIE FALCO

Birthplace: Brooklyn, NY
Birthdate: 7/5/63
Occupation: Actor
Education: SUNY, Purchase
Debut: (Film) *The Unbelievable Truth*, 1989; (TV) *Homicide: Life on the Street*, 1993 (Stage) *Side Man*, 1999
Signature: *The Sopranos*
Facts: Her full name is Edith.

In college, she studied with fellow drama majors Parker Posey, Wesley Snipes, Stanley Tucci, and Sherry Stringfield.

Played Sheriff Marge Gunderson in a pilot based on the film *Fargo*, directed by Kathy Bates.

Has her own Aunt Carmela.
Relationship: John Devlin, actor/director
Major award: Emmy, Best Actress in a Drama Series, *The Sopranos*, 1999

MIA FARROW

Birthplace: Los Angeles, CA
Birthdate: 2/9/45
Occupation: Actor
Education: Marymount in Los Angeles and Cygnet House in London
Debut: (Stage) *The Importance of Being Earnest*, 1963
Signature: *Rosemary's Baby*, 1968
Facts: Mother—biological or adoptive—of 15 kids.

Was on first cover of PEOPLE, March 4, 1974.

At age 12, son Seamus became the youngest student at Simon's Rock College of Bard.
Infamy: Was awarded custody of the two children she and Woody Allen adopted, as well as their biological son, after a highly publicized case involving allegations of molestation by Allen.
Marriages: Frank Sinatra, 1966 (divorced, 1968); André Previn 1970 (divorced, 1977).
Children: Matthew, 1970; Sascha, 1970; Soon-Yi, 1970 (adopted); Lark, 1973 (adopted); Fletcher, 1974; Daisy, 1974 (adopted); (with André Previn).

Moses, 1978 (adopted); Tam, c. 1981 (adopted by Mia alone; deceased 2000); Malone, 1985 (originally Dylan, changed to Eliza, changed again; adopted); Seamus (formerly Satchel), 1987; (with Woody Allen).
Thaddeus, c. 1989 (adopted); Frankie-Minh, c. 1991 (adopted); Isaiah Justus, 1992 (adopted); Kaeli-Shea, 1994 (adopted); Gabriel Wilk (adopted); (by Mia alone)
Famous Relatives: Maureen O'Sullivan, actor, mother; John Farrow, director, father

JOEY FATONE

Birthplace: Brooklyn, NY
Birthdate: 1/28/77
Occupation: Singer
Debut: (Single) "I Want You Back," 1996; (Album) **NSYNC*, 1996 (American release, 1998)
Signature: *No Strings Attached*, 2000
Facts: Had a bit part in the 1993 film *Matinee*.

Was a singing star in high school in a quartet named The Big Guys.

Worked as the Wolfman at Universal Studios Florida.

His dancing clinched his invitation to join 'N Sync.

When in public, he and his bandmates wear matching bracelets engraved with "WWJD"—standing for "What Would Jesus Do?"

Describes self as the "ladies' man" of the five.

Along with Lance Bass, has written a screenplay for the band's movie debut.

His father's group Not So Boy Band opened for 'N Sync at some of their 2001 concerts.
Infamy: 'N Sync broke with their original record label and management over compensation. Suits and countersuits flew before a settlement was reached, allegedly favoring the band.
Quote: "You'll never find an ad in some old newspaper saying, 'Looking for a group.' We put this group together ourselves."

JON FAVREAU

Birthplace: Queens, NY
Birthdate: 10/19/66
Occupation: Actor, screenwriter
Education: Attended Queens College
Debut: (Film) *Folks!*, 1992
Signature: *Swingers*, 1996
Facts: Once overweight (he's since lost 75 pounds), he was inspired by Chris Farley when he was at Second City. He wrote his first script, *Swingers*, in two weeks and eventu-

ally sold the rights with the provision that he and friend, actor Vince Vaughn, would play leading roles.

His TV guest appearances include *Seinfeld, Chicago Hope, Friends,* and *The Sopranos.*

Wrote the script for *The Marshal of Revelation,* about an Hasidic gunslinger.

Original Job: Maintenance worker
Quote: "Write an inexpensive movie, get famous friends to be in it, and you get to do whatever you want."

WILL FERRELL

Real Name: John William Ferrell
Birthplace: Irvine, CA
Birthdate: 7/16/67
Occupation: Comedian
Education: University of Southern California
Debut: (TV) *A Bucket of Blood,* 1995; (Film) *Austin Powers: International Man of Mystery,* 1997
Signature: *Saturday Night Live*
Facts: In high school, was the captain of the basketball team, played varsity football and soccer, and was a member of the student council.

Stands 6' 3".

His father was a longtime keyboard player for the Righteous Brothers.

Majored in sports journalism in college.

Joined L.A.'s Groundlings comedy troupe in 1991, where he met future SNL castmates Chris Kattan, Cheri Oteri and Ana Gasteyer.

Original Job: Sportscaster
Marriage: Viveca Paulin, 2000
Famous Relatives: Lee Ferrell, father, musician
Quote: "Sometimes I feel like I'm continuously letting people down by being normal."

SALLY FIELD

Birthplace: Pasadena, CA
Birthdate: 11/6/46
Occupation: Actor

Education: Columbia Pictures Workshop, Actor's Studio
Debut: (TV) *Gidget,* 1965
Signature: *The Flying Nun*
Facts: Was a cheerleader in high school.

Won the lead role in *Gidget* from among 150 other finalists.

Though entertaining, *The Flying Nun* discouraged people from thinking of her as a serious actress; the producers of the movie *True Grit* refused even to give her an audition. She was paid $4,000 a week for the television show.

According to PEOPLE's Pop Profiles for 3 consecutive years, Field was among the top three female celebrities most appreciated by the public.
Marriages: Steve Craig (divorced); Alan Greisman (divorced, 1994)
Children: Peter, 1969; Elijah, 1972; (with Steve Craig). Samuel, 1987
Famous Relatives: Mary Field Mahoney, actor, mother; Jock Mahoney, actor, stepfather
Major Awards: Emmy, *Sybil,* 1977; Oscar, Best Actress, *Norma Rae,* 1979; Oscar, Best Actress, *Places in the Heart,* 1984

JOSEPH FIENNES

Birthplace: Wiltshire, England
Birthdate: 5/27/70
Occupation: Actor
Education: Guildhall School of Music and Drama
Debut: (Stage) *A Month in the Country,* 1994; (TV) *The Vacillations of Poppy Carew,* 1995; (Film) *Stealing Beauty,* 1996
Signature: *Shakespeare in Love,* 1998
Facts: His middle name is Alberic.

He has a fraternal twin.

He began his career on stage with Helen Mirren and the Royal Shakespeare Company.
Original Job: Dresser, National Theatre
Famous Relatives: Ralph Fiennes, actor, brother; Martha Fiennes, director, sister; Magnus Hubert

Fiennes, musician, brother; Sophie Victoria Fiennes, producer, sister; Jennifer Lash, mother, novelist (deceased)

RALPH FIENNES

Birthplace: Suffolk, England
Birthdate: 12/22/62
Education: London's Royal Academy of Dramatic Art
Debut: (Film) *Wuthering Heights,* 1992
Signature: *Schindler's List,* 1993
Facts: Fiennes gained 28 pounds to play Amon Goeth in *Schindler's List,* 1993. He was chosen for the role after director Steven Spielberg saw Fiennes's performance in the British TV movie *A Dangerous Man: Lawrence After Arabia.*

His name is pronounced "Rafe."
Marriage: Alex Kingston (divorced, 1997); Francesca Annis (relationship)
Famous Relative: Joseph, actor, brother; Martha Fiennes, director, sister; Magnus Hubert Fiennes, musician, brother; Sophie Victoria Fiennes, producer, sister; Jennifer Lash, mother, novelist (deceased)
Major Award: Tony, Best Actor (Dramatic), *Hamlet,* 1995

COLIN FIRTH

Birthplace: Grayshot, Hampshire, England
Birthdate: 9/10/60
Occupation: Actor
Education: Attended The Drama Centre, London
Debut: (London Stage) *Another Country,* 1983; (Film) *Another Country,* 1984; (TV) *Camille,* 1984
Signature: *Pride and Prejudice,* 1995
Facts: Lived in Nigeria until the age of 4.

His portrayal of Mr. Darcy in *Pride and Prejudice* was the model for Helen Fielding's character Mark Darcy in her novel *Bridget Jones's Diary.* Was cast in the film version in

2001.

Is afraid of his "sex-symbol" status, claiming to avoid "attractive" roles whenever possible.

Marriage: Livia Giuggioli, 1997
Children: Will, 1990 (with actress Meg Tilly); Luca, 2001
Quote: "I would love to dazzle. I just don't have a great capacity for it."

LAURENCE FISHBURNE

Birthplace: Augusta, GA
Birthdate: 7/30/61
Occupation: Actor
Education: Lincoln Square Academy
Debut: (Stage) *Section D*, 1975; (Film) *Cornbread, Earl and Me*, 1975
Signature: *Boyz N the Hood*, 1991
Facts: Appeared regularly on soap opera *One Life to Live* for four years starting when he was 9.

At 14, went with his mother to the Philippines for what was supposed to be a three-month shoot for *Apocalypse Now*; the shoot lasted 18 months.

A theater buff, he wrote, directed, and starred in a play, *Riff Raff*, in 1994.

Marriage: Hanja Moss, 1985 (divorced, c. 1993); Gina Torres, actor, (engaged, 2001)
Children: Langston, 1987; Montana, 1991
Major Awards: Tony, Featured Actor (Dramatic), *Two Trains Running*, 1992; Emmy, Best Guest Actor in a Drama, *Tribeca*, 1993

CARRIE FISHER

Birthplace: Burbank, CA
Birthdate: 10/21/56
Occupation: Actor, novelist, screenwriter
Education: Dropped out of Beverly Hills High School, attended Sarah Lawrence College and Central School of Speech and Drama, London
Debut: (Stage) *Irene*, 1972; (Book) Postcards from the Edge
Signature: *Star Wars*, 1977
Facts: Sang in her mother's Las Vegas nightclub act.

Her first public appearance was in a *Life* magazine photograph with her mother shortly after her father had run off to marry Elizabeth Taylor.

Previous owners of her house in Beverly Hills include Bette Davis and Edith Head.

At one point, a "psychotic break" tied to her long battle with manic depression landed her in a mental ward.

Infamy: Was a user of LSD and Percodan; almost overdosed, 1985.
Marriage: Paul Simon, 1983 (divorced, 1984)
Child: Billie Catherine Lourd, 1992
Famous Relatives: Debbie Reynolds, actress, mother; Eddie Fisher, singer, father
Quote: "You find me a kid that thinks he got enough affection and attention as a child and I'll show you Dan Quayle."

CALISTA FLOCKHART

Birthplace: Freeport, IL
Birthdate: 11/11/64
Occupation: Actor
Education: Rutgers University
Debut: (TV) *Darrow*, 1991
Signature: *Ally McBeal*
Facts: Named after her great-grandmother, "Calista" means "most beautiful" in Greek.

Was a cheerleader in high school.

Has performed in several lead roles on Broadway.

In 1992, she joined Malaparte, a small Manhattan theater group headed by Ethan Hawke.

Turned down an audition for *Ally McBeal* because she was busy with theater and reluctant to do TV. The producers were persistent and she eventually agreed, flying to L.A. between the Sunday-matinee and Monday-evening performances. She was hired on the spot.

After a local TV station aired an unconfirmed report that she was anorexic, a flurry of rumors led her to publicly declare, "Am I anorexic?...No."

Previously dated Ben Stiller and director Sam Mendes.
Child: Liam, 2001 (adopted)
Quote: "I live vicariously through my rumors."

BRIDGET FONDA

Birthplace: Los Angeles, CA
Birthdate: 1/27/64
Occupation: Actor
Education: New York University, studied at the Lee Strasberg Institute and with Harold Guskin
Debut: (Film) *Aria*, 1987; (TV) *21 Jump Street*, 1989
Signature: *Singles*, 1992
Facts: Named after Bridget Hayward, a woman her father had loved who had committed suicide.

Her movie debut was in *Aria*, in which she stripped naked, had sex, then committed suicide during her eight minutes on screen with no dialogue.

Dated Eric Stoltz for eight years.
Relationship: Dwight Yoakam
Famous Relatives: Peter Fonda, actor, father; Susan Brewer, actor, mother; Henry Fonda, actor, grandfather; Jane Fonda, actor, aunt

JANE FONDA

Birthplace: New York, NY
Birthdate: 12/21/37
Occupation: Actor, political activist, fitness instructor
Education: Vassar College, studied method acting in Lee Strasberg's Actors Studio
Debut: (Film) *Tall Story*, 1960
Signature: *Barbarella*, 1968
Facts: Mother committed suicide in a sanitarium in 1953.

Jane Fonda's Workout is the best-selling nondramatic video in history.

Spent much of the '70s speaking for the Black Panthers and against the Vietnam War and was almost arrested for treason, earning her the nickname "Hanoi Jane."

Reportedly has an adopted daughter whom she refuses to speak about.

Marriages: Roger Vadim, 1965 (divorced, 1973); Tom Hayden, 1973 (divorced, 1990); Ted Turner, 1991 (divorced, 2001)
Children: Vanessa, 1968 (with Vadim); Troy Garrity, 1973 (with Hayden)
Famous Relatives: Henry Fonda, actor, father; Peter Fonda, actor, brother; Bridget Fonda, actor, niece
Major Awards: Oscar, Best Actress, *Klute*, 1971; Oscar, Best Actress, *Coming Home*, 1978; Emmy, Lead Actress in a Limited Series or Special, *The Dollmaker*, 1983
Quote: "The disease to please a man goes deep. I had to reach my sixties to find my voice again.... If you're not convinced of your self-worth, you won't be respected."

HARRISON FORD

Birthplace: Chicago, IL
Birthdate: 7/13/42
Occupation: Actor, director
Education: Ripon College
Debut: (Film) *Dead Heat on a Merry-Go-Round*, 1966 [see page 66 for a complete filmography]
Signature: Indiana Jones
Fact: Scar beneath his lower lip is from losing control of his car.

Ford had his ear pierced at age 54, explaining that he had always wanted one; he was accompanied by already-pierced old friends Jimmy Buffett and Ed Bradley.

Owns a Bell 206 helicopter and three planes. In 1999, he crashed his chopper while practicing emergency landings and, in 2000, he missed the runway when landing his Beech Bonanza plane.

Used his helicopter to rescue a dehydrated mountain climber in 2000, and a lost Boy Scout in 2001.
Original Job: Carpenter
Marriages: Mary Marquardt (divorced), Melissa Mathison, 1983 (filed for divorce, 2001)
Children: Benjamin, 1966; Willard, 1969; (with Mary Marquardt). Malcolm, 1987; Georgia, 1990

Quote: "I feel physically fit—and capable of pretending to be fitter."

CLARE FORLANI

Birthplace: London, England
Birthdate: 7/1/71
Occupation: Actor
Education: High school
Debut: (Film) *C.I.A. Trackdown*, 1992; (TV) *JFK: Reckless Youth*, 1993
Signature: *Meet Joe Black*, 1998
Facts: Dated Benicio Del Toro, John Cusack, and Ben Stiller.

Took two years off after *Meet Joe Black* to attend to her terminally ill mother.

Every one of her film characters has been American.

Loves to sleep.
Quote: "Yes, I'm single. I encourage all men to try. Don't be afraid!"

JODIE FOSTER

Real Name: Alicia Christian Foster
Birthplace: Los Angeles, CA
Birthdate: 11/19/62
Occupation: Actor, director
Education: Yale University
Debut: (TV) *Mayberry RFD*, 1968; (Film) *Napoleon and Samantha*, 1972 [see pages 66–67 for a complete filmography]
Signature: *The Silence of the Lambs*, 1991
Facts: Started at 3 years old as the bare-bottomed Coppertone child in the then ubiquitous advertisement. She got the job when, too young to wait in the car, she was noticed at her brother's casting call. By age 8, she had appeared in over 40 commercials.

At 13, played a hooker in *Taxi Driver*. Because she was so young, the film's producers hired her sister Constance to double for her in a nude scene. Before she got the role, she had to pass psychological tests. "I spent four hours with a shrink to prove I was normal enough to play a hooker. Does that make sense?"

As valedictorian in high school, she gave her graduation speech in French.

Object of would-be presidential assassin John Hinckley's obsession.

Has not identified the father of her children.
Children: Charles, 1998; Kit, 2001
Famous Relative: Buddy Foster, actor, brother
Major Awards: Oscar, Best Actress, *The Accused*, 1988; Oscar, Best Actress, *The Silence of the Lambs*, 1991

MATTHEW FOX

Birthplace: Crowheart, WY
Birthdate: 7/14/66
Occupation: Actor
Education: Columbia University
Debut: (TV) *Freshman Dorm*, 1992
Signature: *Party of Five*
Facts: Grew up on a 120-acre Wyoming ranch, attending a one-room schoolhouse until the fourth grade.

Pondered becoming a farmer like his father, but dad suggested he go east for college. During a year of prep at Massachusetts' Deerfield Academy, snooty classmates voted him "Most Likely to Appear on *Hee-Haw*."

Played football at college, where he was wide receiver and an economics major.
Original Job: Model
Marriage: Margherita Ronchi, 1992
Child: Kyle Allison, 1997

MICHAEL J. FOX

Birthplace: Edmonton, Canada
Birthdate: 6/9/61
Occupation: Actor
Education: High school dropout
Debut: (TV) *Palmerstown, U.S.A*, 1980; (Film) *Midnight Madness*, 1980
Signature: *Family Ties*
Facts: When he got the audition for *Family Ties*, he was $35,000 in debt, living on macaroni and cheese, and had been forced to sell off a sectional couch piece by piece to raise money.

Eric Stoltz was first cast in *Back to the Future*, but when he proved to be "too intense for the comedy," Fox got the role. For seven weeks he played Alex on *Family Ties* by day, then transformed himself into Marty McFly for the film.

Heavy smoker, but asks not to be photographed smoking to avoid becoming a negative role model for his younger fans.

Announced in 1998 that he suffers from Parkinson's Disease. First diagnosed seven years prior, he underwent brain surgery to alleviate his tremors.

Purchased two of Eric Clapton's guitars at auction for $79,300.

In 2000, he left TV show *Spin City* to spend time with his family and to head the Michael J. Fox Foundation for Parkinson's Research which is merging with the Parkinson's Action Network.

Is eligible to vote for the first time in 2000, having recently become a U.S. citizen.
Marriage: Tracy Pollan, 1988
Children: Sam Michael, 1989; Aquinnah Kathleen, 1995; Schuyler Frances, 1995
Major Awards: Emmy, Best Actor in a Comedy Series, *Family Ties,* 1985, 1986, 1987, 1988, *Spin City,* 1999

VIVICA A. FOX

Birthplace: Indianapolis, IN
Birthdate: 7/30/64
Occupation: Actor
Education: High school
Debut: (TV) *Days of Our Lives*; (Film) *Born on the Fourth of July,* 1989
Signature: *Independence Day,* 1996
Facts: She was a cheerleader in high school.

Her nickname for her husband is "Big Daddy."

Her middle name is Agnetta.

She has two cats named Tiger and Snookie.

She got her first big break in 1988 when a producer saw her in a restaurant and recommended an agent.

Appeared in *Days of Our Lives; Family Matters; Matlock; Beverly*

Hills, 90210; The Fresh Prince of Bel-Air; and *The Young and the Restless* before being tapped to play Will Smith's girlfriend in *Independence Day.*

She and Christopher Harvest arrived at their wedding in a horse-drawn carriage. She wore a diamond tiara and was presented with a thousand red roses from her husband.
Original Job: Model, waitress
Marriage: Christopher Harvest (a.k.a. Sixx-Nine), 1998

JAMIE FOXX

Real Name: Eric Bishop
Birthplace: Terrell, TX
Birthdate: 12/13/67
Occupation: Actor, comedian, singer
Education: attended U.S. International University
Debut: (TV) *In Living Color,* 1991; (Film) *Toys,* 1992; (Album) *Peep This,* 1994
Signature: *The Jamie Foxx Show,* 1996
Facts: His college major was classical music.

First tried stand-up on a dare from his girlfriend.

Chose his androgynous stage name when he saw female comics getting preference at open-microphone nights.

Doing stand-up after *In Living Color* was cancelled, Foxx talked up his next project, *The Jamie Foxx Show*—even though it existed only as a name in his head.

His show was initially branded as stereotypical by the NAACP; since then, however, Foxx has earned three nominations for NAACP Image Awards in three years.

Won acclaim for his dramatic turn in *Any Given Sunday.*
Original Job: Shoe salesman
Child: Corinne, 1995

ARETHA FRANKLIN

Birthplace: Memphis, TN
Birthdate: 3/25/42
Occupation: Singer
Education: High school dropout
Debut: (Song) "Rock-A-Bye Your Baby with a Dixie Melody," 1961
Signature: "Respect," 1967
Facts: Started out as a gospel singer in her father's Baptist church in Detroit in the '50s. Her father was minister of the New Bethel Baptist Church, one of the largest pastorates in the U.S., until 1979, when he went into a coma after being shot in his home by a burglar.
Infamy: Was sued for breach of contract in 1984 when she was unable to open in the Broadway musical *Sing, Mahalia, Sing,* mainly because of her fear of flying.
Marriages: Ted White (divorced), Glynn Turman, 1978 (divorced, 1984).
Children: Edward, 1957; Clarence, c. 1958;(father undisclosed). Theodore Jr., 1963 (with Ted White). Kecalf, 1970 (with Ken Cunningham).
Major Awards: Grammy, Best Rhythm and Blues Song, "Respect," 1967; Grammy, Best R&B Vocal—Female, "Respect," 1967; Grammy, Best R&B Vocal—Female, "Chain of Fools," 1968; Grammy, Best R&B Vocal—Female, "Share Your Love with Me," 1969; Grammy, Best R&B Vocal—Female, "Don't Play That Song," 1970; Grammy, Best R&B Vocal—Female, "Bridge over Troubled Water," 1971; Grammy, Best R&B Vocal—Female, *Young, Gifted, & Black,* 1972; Grammy, Best R&B Vocal—Female, "Master of Eyes," 1973; Grammy, Best R&B Vocal—Female, "Ain't Nothing Like the Real Thing," 1974; Grammy, Best R&B Vocal—Female, "Hold On I'm Comin'," 1981; Grammy, Best R&B Vocal—Female, "Freeway of Love," 1985; Grammy, Best R&B Vocal—Female, *Aretha,* 1987; Grammy, Best R&B Duo or Group, "I Knew You Were Waiting (For Me)" (with George Michael), 1987; Grammy Legend

Award, 1991; inducted into the Rock and Roll Hall of Fame, 1987; NARAS Lifetime Achievement Award, 1994

DENNIS FRANZ

Birthplace: Chicago, IL
Birthdate: 10/28/44
Occupation: Actor
Debut: (TV) *Chicago Story,* 1981
Signature: *NYPD Blue*
Facts: Claims he was the "worst postman in the history of the post office" before becoming an actor. "I used to start my route at daybreak, and I would finish long after dark. I'd stop for donuts, I'd play with animals, I'd go home with my bag of mail and just lay around the house a bit."

Served 11 months in Vietnam with an elite Airborne division.
Marriage: Joanie Zeck, 1995
Children: Tricia, 1974 (step-daughter); Krista, 1976 (stepdaughter)
Major Awards: Emmy, Best Actor in a Drama Series, *NYPD Blue,* 1994, 1996, 1997, 1999

BRENDAN FRASER

Birthplace: Indianapolis, IN
Birthdate: 12/3/68
Occupation: Actor
Education: Cornish College of the Arts
Debut: (Film) *Dogfight,* 1991
Signature: *The Mummy,* 1999
Facts: His Canadian-tourism-exec father had the family moving every three years. As a child, lived in Cincinnati, Detroit, Ottawa, Holland and Toronto, among others.

Stands 6' 3".

Underwent six months of intensive weight training and a strict high-protein, low carb diet to beef up for his *George of the Jungle* role.
Marriage: Afton Smith, 1998
Quote: "Rather than dumb, I think these characters [the ones he plays] are more of an exploration of wide-eyed availableness."

MORGAN FREEMAN

Birthplace: Memphis, TN
Birthdate: 6/1/37
Occupation: Actor, director
Education: Attended Los Angeles City College
Debut: (Stage, Broadway) *Hello, Dolly,* 1967; (Film) *Brubaker,* 1980
Signature: *Driving Miss Daisy,* 1989
Facts: Got his show business start as a dancer at the 1964 New York World's Fair. He had studied ballet, tap, and jazz.

Played Easy Reader for five years in the 1970s on the PBS series *Electric Company.*

Moved from New York City, where he lived for 25 years, to a Mississippi farm. Is raising one of his nine grandchildren there.
Marriage: Jeanette Adair Bradshaw (divorced), Myrna Colley-Lee, 1984
Children: Alphonse; Saifoulaye; Deena (adopted); Morgana

LIAM GALLAGHER

Birthplace: Manchester, England
Birthdate: 9/21/72
Occupation: Musician
Education:
Debut: (Album) *Definitely Maybe,* 1994
Signature: Oasis
Facts: With the British pop band Oasis, Gallagher, famous for a quick temper, is wont to stalk the stage and glare at his audience.

Known as a drinker, along with his brother and bandmate Noel, Gallagher went on the wagon while recording *Standing on the Shoulder of Giants.*

Was voted Best Dressed Man in Britain by *GQ* magazine.
Infamy: Cathay Pacific airlines banned Liam Gallagher and his brother Neil in 1998 after rowdy behavior on a 747 flying from Hong Kong to Australia.

Was sued in civil court by a man who alleged he suffered a broken nose after being butted in the head by Gallagher while taking his photograph.
Marriage: Patsy Kensit, 1997 (divorced, 2000); Nicole Appleton, musician
Children: Lennon (with Patsy Kensit); Gene Appleton, 2001
Famous relative: Noel Gallagher, brother, fellow bandmate
Quote: "To be really big in America, to tell you the truth, mate, you've got to f- - -ing put a lot of work into it. You've gotta spend a lot of time there, y'know, and I don't personally want to."

JAMES GANDOLFINI

Birthplace: Westwood, NY
Birthdate: 9/18/61
Occupation: Actor
Education: Rutgers University
Debut: (Broadway) *A Streetcar Named Desire,* 1992; (Film) *A Stranger Among Us,* 1992; (TV) *The Sopranos,* 1999
Signature: *The Sopranos*
Facts: Began as a theater actor before Hollywood found him.

He plays the trumpet and saxophone.

Got a late start as an actor when a friend took him to his first acting class in the late 1980s.

Having never been in therapy, he struggles with the therapy scenes of his character, Tony Soprano.
Original Jobs: Bouncer, night club manager, truck driver
Major Award: Emmy, Best Actor in a Drama Series, *The Sopranos,* 1999
Quote: "Human frailty and confusion are what interest me. The more sensitive the character and the more he's in touch with things, the more confusion there is."

ANDY GARCIA

Real Name: Andres Arturo Garcia-Menendez
Birthplace: Havana, Cuba
Birthdate: 4/12/56

Occupation: Actor, director, songwriter
Education: Florida International University
Debut: (TV) *Hill Street Blues*, 1981; (Film) *Blue Skies Again*, 1983
Signature: *The Godfather Part III*, 1990
Facts: His family moved to Florida from Cuba after the Bay of Pigs invasion. He was 5 years old at the time and claims to have vivid memories of the event.

He was athletic as a child, until he was sidelined by a case of mononucleosis and began to take an interest in performing.

After college, he went to L.A. and waited tables while working improv and the Comedy Store.

In 1993, he produced and directed a documentary about Cuban mambo artist Cachao, called *Cachao: Like His Rhythm, There Is No Other*.

He wrote and performed several songs for 1995's *Steal Little, Steal Big*. His daughter Dominik made an appearance in this film.

He proposed to his wife on the first night he met her. They were married seven years later.

He produced, helped score, and starred in 1999's *Just the Ticket*.

Owns 25 conga drums, collects hats, and wears a beret in the winter.

Wore his father's pearl tie-pin, his most personal keepsake from Cuba, in *When a Man Loves a Woman*.
Original Job: Waiter
Marriage: Maria (Marvi) Victoria Lorido, 1982
Children: Dominik, 1984; Daniella, 1988; Alessandra, 1991
Quote: "First and foremost, I am a father—who just happens to act."

JANEANE GAROFALO

Birthplace: New Jersey
Birthdate: 9/28/64
Occupation: Actor, comedian
Education: Providence College

Debut: (TV) *The Ben Stiller Show*, 1992; (Film) *Reality Bites*, 1994
Signature: *The Truth About Cats and Dogs*, 1996
Facts: Has "Think" tattooed on her arm.

Does the voice for the never-seen character Sally on *Felicity*.
Original Jobs: Bike messenger, receptionist
Marriage: Rob Cohn (divorced); Craig Bierko (relationship)
Quote: "I really am not full of self-loathing. People think that because the name of my company is I Hate Myself Productions."

BILL GATES

Birthplace: Seattle, WA
Birthdate: 10/28/55
Occupation: Computer software entrepreneur-executive
Education: Harvard University
Signature: Microsoft Windows
Facts: After learning how to crash an operating system while a high school student, did it to the Control Data Corporation. Their reprimand caused him to abandon computers for a year.

Formed a company to sell a computerized traffic counting system to cities, which made $20,000 its first year. Business fell off when customers learned Gates was only 14.

Became the youngest billionaire ever at age 31.

As head of fast-growing Microsoft, took a total of six vacation days in the company's first six years.

Owns the Bettmann Archive, one of the world's greatest collections of documentary images.

His $100 million "smart house" in Lake Washington features a 20-vehicle garage; dining space for 100; and music, artwork, lighting, and TV shows that follow individuals from room to room.
Infamy: Accused by competitors of using clout from operating systems software to quash other software .
Marriage: Melinda French, 1994

Child: Jennifer Katharine, 1996; Rory John, 1999

SARAH MICHELLE GELLAR

Birthplace: New York, NY
Birthdate: 4/14/77
Occupation: Actor, model
Education: Professional Children's High School
Debut: (TV movie) *Invasion of Privacy*, 1983
Signature: *Buffy the Vampire Slayer*
Facts: At age 4, she chided McDonald's for their skimpy patties in a Burger King ad, for which BK was sued for libel. Gellar appeared in court, though the case was soon settled. Has appeared in more than100 commercials.

Has five holes in each earlobe and one for a navel ring. Tattooed the Chinese character for integrity on her lower back.

Possesses a brown belt in tae kwon do, and was a competitive figure skater as a child.
Marriage: Freddie Prinze Jr. (engaged, 2001)
Major Award: Emmy, Outstanding Younger Actress, *All My Children*, 1994
Quote: "It's really hard to be a vampire slayer if you're scared of cemeteries."

RICHARD GERE

Birthplace: Philadelphia, PA
Birthdate: 8/31/49
Occupation: Actor
Education: attended University of Massachusetts, Amherst
Debut: (Film) *Report to the Commissioner*, 1975
Signature: *Pretty Woman*, 1990
Facts: Won a gymnastics scholarship to the University of Massachusetts.

In 1973, first studied the "middle way" of Siddhartha Gotama Buddha as preached by a Japanese sect. In 1982, switched faith to the Tibetan school of Buddhism. In 1986, became a student of the exiled Dalai Lama.

First three big film roles (*Days of Heaven*, 1978, *American Gigolo*, 1980, and *An Officer and a Gentleman*, 1982) were roles turned down by John Travolta.

His photographs of Tibetans were published in the book *Pilgrims*.

His son's middle name, Jigme, means "fearless" in Tibetan.

Girlfriend Lowell was formerly married to Griffin Dunne, father of their daughter, Hannah.

Infamy: Took out a $30,000 ad with then-wife Cindy Crawford in the *Times* of London in May 1994 denying rumors of their homosexuality.
Original Job: Rock musician
Marriage: Cindy Crawford (divorced, 1994); Carey Lowell (relationship)
Child: Homer James Jigme, 2000
Quote: "I think most actors go into acting because there's a lot of self-loathing and confusion."

MEL GIBSON

Birthplace: Peekskill, NY
Birthdate: 1/3/56
Occupation: Actor, director
Education: University of New South Wales
Debut: (Film) *Summer City*, 1977 [see page 67 for a complete filmography]
Signature: *Lethal Weapon*, 1987
Facts: Father moved the family from New York to Australia in the '60s so his sons wouldn't be drafted.

The night before his audition for *Mad Max*, he got into a barroom fight in which his face was badly beaten, an accident that won him the role.

Took up acting only because his sister submitted an application to the National Institute of Dramatic Art behind his back.

For *Lethal Weapon 4*, was dragged on a freeway at 35 mph.
Marriage: Robyn Moore, 1980
Children: Hannah, c. 1980; Edward, 1982; Christian, 1982; Will, 1984;

Louis, 1987; Milo, 1989; Tommy, 1999
Famous Relative: Eva Mylott, opera singer, grandmother
Major Awards: Oscars for Best Director and Best Picture, *Braveheart*, 1995

KATHIE LEE GIFFORD

Real Name: Kathie Epstein
Birthplace: Paris, France
Birthdate: 8/16/53
Occupation: Talk show host, singer
Education: Oral Roberts University
Debut: (TV) *$100,000 Name That Tune*, 1976
Signature: *Live with Regis and Kathie Lee*
Facts: Despite having a Jewish father, became a born-again Christian at age 11.

Won the Maryland Junior Miss Pageant at age 17.

Organized a folk singing group while at Oral Roberts University.

Was a cheerleader in high school.

Named her dog Regis.

In 2000, decided to leave "Live with Regis & Kathie Lee" after 11 years.
Infamy: A human rights crusader accused Gifford's Honduran-manufactured clothing line of using exploitative child labor.
Original Job: Gospel singer
Marriages: Paul Johnson (divorced); Frank Gifford, 1986
Children: Cody Newton, 1990; Cassidy Erin, 1993
Quote: "I am irreverent, I am opinionated, but I'm not perky."

VINCE GILL

Birthplace: Norman, OK
Birthdate: 4/12/57
Occupation: Singer, songwriter, guitarist
Education: High school
Debut: (Song) "Turn Me Loose," 1984
Signature: "When I Call Your Name," 1990
Facts: After high school, contem-

plated a career as a pro golfer, but dropped that idea when offered a spot in a top progressive bluegrass group, Bluegrass Alliance.

Joined the band Sundance to play with its great fiddler, Bryon Berline; later joined The Cherry Bombs to be with singer-songwriter Rodney Crowell.

Lead singer for Pure Prairie League in the late '70s.

In the 1980s, worked in Nashville as a studio session vocalist and musician with such stars as Bonnie Raitt, Rosanne Cash, and Patty Loveless.

Dubbed "The Benefit King," he sponsors his own pro-celebrity golf tournament and annual celebrity basketball game and concert.
Marriage: Janis Oliver, 1980 (divorced, 1997); Amy Grant 2000
Children: Jennifer, 1982 (with Janis Oliver); Corrina, 2001
Major Awards: Grammy, Best Country Vocal—Male, "When I Call Your Name," 1990; Grammy, Best Country Vocal Collaboration (with Steve Wariner and Ricky Skaggs), "Restless," 1991; Grammy, Best Country Song, "I Still Believe in You" (with John Barlow Jarvis), 1992; Grammy, Best Country Vocal—Male, "I Still Believe in You," 1992; Grammy, Best Country Instrumental "Red Wing" (with Asleep at the Wheel), 1993; Grammy, Best Country Vocal—Male, "When Love Finds You," 1994; Grammy, Best Country Vocal—Male, "Go Rest High on That Mountain," 1995; Grammy, Best Country Song, "Go Rest High on That Mountain," 1995; Grammy, Best Country Vocal—Male, "Worlds Apart," 1996; Grammy, Best Country Vocal—Male, "Pretty Little Adriana," 1997; Grammy, Best Country Vocal—Male, "If You Ever Have Forever In Mind," 1998; Grammy, Best Country Instrumental Performance, "A Soldier's Joy" (with Randy Scruggs), 1998, Grammy, Best Country Instrumental Performance, "Bob's

Breakdowns" (with Asleep at the Wheel), 1999

SAVION GLOVER

Birthplace: Newark, NJ
Birthdate: 11/19/73
Occupation: Dancer, choreographer
Education: Newark Arts High School
Debut: (Stage) *The Tap Dance Kid*, 1984; (Film) *Tap*, 1989
Signature: *Bring In 'Da Noise, Bring in 'Da Funk*, 1996
Facts: At age 7, played drums in a band.

Made choreography debut at age 16 at New York's Apollo Theater.

Began a featured run on *Sesame Street* in 1990 as a character also named Savion.

His name is his mother's variation on the word "savior."
Infamy: Arrested in late 1995 for driving under the influence of marijuana and criminal possession of bags of marijuana, hidden in his socks. Pled guilty to the reduced charge of disorderly conduct.
Famous Relatives: Yvette Glover, actress and singer, mother
Major Award: Tony, Best Choreography, *Bring In 'Da Noise, Bring in 'Da Funk*, 1996

GOLDBERG

Real Name: Bill Goldberg
Birthplace: Tulsa, OK
Birthdate: 12/27/66
Occupation: Wrestler
Education: University of Georgia
Debut: (Film) *Universal Soldier, the Return*, 1999
Facts: Attended World Championship Wrestling Power Plant training school.

On scholarship at University of Georgia, he majored in psychology and was an all-conference nose tackle before going into pro football.

An eleventh round draft pick in 1990 for the Los Angeles Rams, he was cut after pulling a hamstring muscle and spent three seasons as a defensive lineman for the Atlanta

Falcons. He finally opted for wrestling after an abdominal injury. He dips snuff.

He weighs in at some 285 pounds.

He enjoys fishing and collects vintage muscle cars.

His signature finishing move is the "Jackhammer," in which he drives his opponent headfirst into the mat.

His girlfriend of six years is a former "Diamond Doll," who used to escort wrestler Diamond Dallas Page to and from the ring.
Original Job: Bouncer
Relationship: Lisa Shekter
Famous Relatives: Ethel Goldberg, concert violinist with Oklahoma City Philharmonic, mother
Quote: "I never aspired to wrestle. But here I am, wearing my underwear on national television in front of millions of people."

WHOOPI GOLDBERG

Real Name: Caryn Johnson
Birthplace: New York, NY
Birthdate: 11/13/49
Occupation: Actor, comedian
Education: School for the Performing Arts, New York
Debut: (Film) *The Color Purple*, 1985 [see page 67 for a complete filmography]
Signature: *Ghost*, 1990
Facts: Kicked a heroin addiction in the '70s.

Began performing at age 8 with the Helena Rubenstein Children's Theater and later enrolled in the Hudson Guild children's arts program.

Co-owns the West Hollywood restaurant Eclipse with Steven Seagal and Joe Pesci.

She hates to fly and travels on a customized bus.
Infamy: Was roasted by black-faced companion Ted Danson at a Friars Club event, 1993.
Original Jobs: Bricklayer, hairdresser, bank teller, and makeup artist for a funeral parlor
Marriages: One prior marriage,

David Claessen (divorced); Lyle Trachtenberg (divorced, 1995)
Child: Alexandrea Martin, 1974
Major Awards: Grammy, Best Comedy Recording, *Whoopi Goldberg*, 1985; Oscar, Best Supporting Actress, *Ghost*, 1990

JEFF GOLDBLUM

Birthplace: Pittsburgh, PA
Birthdate: 10/22/52
Occupation: Actor
Education: Trained at Sanford Meisner's Neighborhood Playhouse
Debut: (Stage) *Two Gentlemen of Verona*, 1971; (Film) *Death Wish*, 1974
Signature: *The Big Chill*, 1983
Facts: Brother Rick died at 23 from a rare virus picked up on a North African trip.

Starred as a stockbroker-turned-P.I. with Ben Vereen in the TV series *Tenspeed and Brownshoe*, 1980.
Marriages: Patricia Gaul (divorced), Geena Davis (divorced)

CUBA GOODING JR.

Birthplace: Bronx, NY
Birthdate: 1/2/68
Occupation: Actor
Education: High school dropout
Debut: (Film) *Coming to America*, 1988
Signature: *Jerry Maguire*, 1996
Facts: His first professional job was at age 16, breakdancing with Lionel Richie at the 1984 Olympic Games.

Big money came to his family when Cuba was a child, after his father's band (The Main Ingredient) hit it big with "Everybody Plays the Fool," but dad split two years later (they have since reunited), leaving mom and the kids on welfare.

Became a born-again Christian at age 13.
Original Jobs: Construction worker, busboy
Marriage: Sara Kapfer, 1994
Children: Spencer, 1994; Mason, 1996
Famous Relative: Cuba Gooding,

singer, father; Omar Gooding, actor, brother

Quote: "The first time I saw myself naked in a school locker room, I was like, 'Wow.' After that, everything had to be trimmed, oiled, and together."

Major Awards: Oscar, Best Supporting Actor, *Jerry Maguire*, 1996

JOHN GOODMAN

Birthplace: Afton, MO
Birthdate: 6/20/52
Occupation: Actor
Education: Southwest Missouri State University
Debut: (Film) *Eddie Macon's Run*, 1983
Signature: *Roseanne*
Facts: Made a living doing dinner and children's theater before Broadway debut in 1979 in *Loose Ends*.

Acted in college with Kathleen Turner and Tess Harper.

Appeared in commercials for Coors beer, Crest toothpaste, and 7UP.
Original Job: Bouncer
Marriage: Anna Beth Hartzog, 1989
Child: Molly, 1990
Major Award: Golden Globe, Best Actor in a Comedy Series, *Roseanne*, 1993

JEFF GORDON

Birthplace: Vallejo, CA
Birthdate: 8/4/71
Occupation: Race car driver
Education: High school
Facts: Began racing at age five when his stepfather bought him a race car. By age eight he was a national champion. By age 11, he won 25 of 25 races in the go-cart division.

After donning his racing suit, he always puts right glove on first.
In 1993 Gordon, the first rookie in 30 years to win Daytona's 125-mile qualifying race, went on to become Rookie of the Year in the Winston

Cup Series, and the first driver to win rookie honors in NASCAR's two top divisions.

Polite, slim, and slight, Gordon loses some eight pounds during a race. After races, his eye sockets ache.

Major Awards: Three-time NASCAR Winston Cup winner
Marriage: Brooke

HEATHER GRAHAM

Birthplace: Milwaukee, WI
Birthdate: 1/29/70
Occupation: Actor, model
Education: Attended UCLA
Debut: (Film) *License to Drive*, 1988
Signature: *Boogie Nights*, 1997
Facts: Raised in a religious Catholic household; her parents once encouraged her to become a nun.

Had a year-long romance with actor James Woods, who was twice her age at the time. Also was involved with Ed Burns.

Regularly practices Transcendental Meditation.
Original Job: Usher at Hollywood Bowl
Relationship: Heath Ledger
Famous Relative: Aimee Graham, actor, sister
Quote: "I see myself as this nerdy geek that people find attractive."

KELSEY GRAMMER

Birthplace: St. Thomas, Virgin Islands
Birthdate: 2/21/55
Occupation: Actor
Education: Juilliard School
Debut: (TV) *Another World*, 1983
Signature: *Frasier*
Facts: Father and sister were murdered; his two half brothers died in a scuba accident.

His unborn child died when his ex-wife attempted suicide.

Was nominated five times before finally winning an Emmy in 1994.
Infamy: Arrested for driving under the influence of drugs in 1987;

failed to show up for two arraignments for a cocaine arrest in 1988; sentenced to community service and 30 days in prison in 1990.

In 1995, faced allegations of sexual assault by a 17-year-old, who claimed they had had sex when she was 15. The New Jersey grand jury declined to charge him.

In 1996, crashed his Viper and wound up in the Betty Ford Clinic.
Original Job: Theatrical painter
Marriages: Doreen Alderman (divorced), Leigh-Anne Csuhany (divorced), Camille Donatucci, 1997
Children: Spencer,1985 (with Doreen Alderman). Greer, 1992 (with Barrie Buckner)
Major Awards: Emmy, Best Actor in a Comedy, *Frasier*, 1994, 1995, 1998

HUGH GRANT

Birthplace: London, England
Birthdate: 9/9/60
Occupation: Actor
Education: New College, Oxford University
Debut: (Film) *Privileged*, 1982
Signature: *Four Weddings and a Funeral*, 1994
Facts: Grant opted not to do a nude scene with Andie MacDowell in *Four Weddings and a Funeral* when a makeup artist asked if he wanted definition painted on his body.

While at Oxford, formed a revue group, The Jockeys of Norfolk.

Grant is very popular in Japan, and there are two books on him published there, *Hugh Grant Vol. 1* and *Hugh Grant Vol. 2*.

Split with girlfriend Elizabeth Hurley after 13 years in 2000. The two continue to co-own Simian Films and maintain their two London homes.
Infamy: Arrested in June 1995 in Hollywood for picking up a prostitute. Was sentenced to two years' probation, fined $1,180 (which included court costs), and ordered to complete an AIDS education program.
Quote: "So many dogs have their

day. I'm having mine now—and though I'd love it to go on and on, I suspect I'll be back doing BBC radio drama next spring."

MACY GRAY

Real Name: Natalie McIntyre
Birthplace: Canton, OH
Birthdate: 9/6/67
Occupation: Singer
Education: attended USC
Debut: (Album) *On How Life Is,* 1999; (Single) "Do Something," 1999
Signature: "I Try"
Facts: Was kicked out of boarding school—she says it was because she reported a Dean who made improper physical contact.

Played basketball, volleyball, swam, and ran track in high school. She wears size 11 shoes.

Left film school a few credits short of a degree.

Made a Super-8 film of a strait-jacketed woman in a psychiatric ward.

A classmate asked her to write some lyrics for his music, then asked her to sing the song for his demo recording. The publisher liked her voice. She eventually signed with Epic.

Was dropped from her original recording contract and moved home, planning to become a teacher.

Sang "Winter Wonderland" for the BabyGap ad in 1998.

Wrote all the lyrics for her debut album. Also wrote songs for Fatboy Slim, Rod Stewart, and Guru.

Worked behind the scenes on videos by Tupac Shakur and others.

Took her stage name from a neighbor who played pool with her father.
Marriage: Married 1993, divorced 1998
Children: Happy, 1995; Aanisah, 1995; Mel, 1997
Quote: "I won't say that I've had a bad life, but I've definitely gone through a lot."

TOM GREEN

Birthplace: Pembroke, Ontario, Canada
Birthdate: 7/71
Occupation: Comedian
Education: Algonquin College of Applied Arts and Technology
Debut: (TV) MTV's *Tom Green Show,* 1999; (Video) *Something Smells Funny,* 1999, (Film) *Charlie's Angels,* 2000
Signature: *Tom Green Show*
Facts: At 15, began performing on amateur night at a comedy club. He dropped out of a college radio and TV program to form his rap-spoof group Organized Rhyme. The group won an A&M record deal.

In 1990, became a cohost on a nighttime college radio show. Five years later he launched the *Tom Green Show* on community access cable.

Notorious for his sometimes cruel and grotesque pranks and his taste-less humor, which frequently targets his parents. Green has painted their house plaid, brought animals into their home, and had a pornographic picture airbrushed on their car. He also put a severed cow's head in their bed. He once conned his grandmother into licking a sex toy on television.

In March 2000, he had surgery for testicular cancer and taped the procedure for *the Tom Green Cancer Special*. Then started the Tom Green's Nuts Cancer Fund
Original Job: Musician
Marriage: Drew Barrymore, 2001
Quote: "I think people under the age of 30 get this. Once you get over 40, there are people who really don't understand why it's funny. It just doesn't register as comedy to them, which to me is hilarious. That's what it's all about, confusing conservative people

MELANIE GRIFFITH

Birthplace: New York, NY
Birthdate: 8/9/57
Occupation: Actor
Education: Pierce College
Debut: (Film) *Night Moves,* 1975
Signature: *Working Girl,* 1988
Facts: Alfred Hitchcock, who was in love with Griffith's mother, gave Melanie a tiny wooden coffin containing a wax replica of her mother, outfitted in the same clothes she had worn in *The Birds,* on her sixth birthday.

At 14, left home to move in with Don Johnson, who was then 22. She married him at 18 and was divorced a year later. In 1988, on her way to the Hazelden Clinic for rehab, she called Don from the plane and renewed their love.

Was clawed in the face by a lioness in the filming of *Roar* (1981).
Infamy: Was addicted to drugs and alcohol in the late '70s and early '80s, and studio executives refused to speak with her. In 1980, she was hit by a car while crossing Sunset Boulevard. She suffered a broken leg and arm, but her doctor said that if she hadn't been so drunk she probably would have been killed.
Original Job: Model
Marriages: Don Johnson (divorced), Steven Bauer (divorced), Don Johnson (divorced), Antonio Banderas, 1996
Children: Alexander, 1985 (with Steven Bauer). Dakota, 1989 (with Don Johnson). Stella del Carmen, 1996
Famous Relatives: Tippi Hedren, actor, mother; Tracy Griffith, actor, half-sister
Quote: "I'm done with stupid movies—I want to be taken seriously again."

JOHN GRISHAM

Birthplace: Arkansas
Birthdate: 2/8/55
Occupation: Author

Education: Mississippi State, University of Mississippi Law School
Debut: (Book) *A Time To Kill*, 1989
Signature: *The Firm*
Facts: Little League baseball coach.

Wife edits his books as he writes them.

Was inspired to write *A Time To Kill* by testimony he heard at the De Soto County courthouse from a 10-year-old girl who was testifying against a man who had raped her and left her for dead.

Served as a Democrat in the Mississippi State Legislature for seven years (1983–90).

Shaves only once a week, before church on Sunday.

In 1989 formed Bongo Comics Group.

A 16th cousin of Bill Clinton.
Original Job: Attorney
Marriage: Renee Jones, 1981
Children: Ty, c. 1983; Shea, c. 1986

CHARLES GRODIN

Real Name: Charles Grodinsky
Birthplace: Pittsburgh, PA
Birthdate: 4/21/35
Occupation: Actor, writer
Education: University of Miami, Pittsburgh Playhouse School, studied with Lee Strasberg and Uta Hagen
Debut: (Stage) *Tchin-Tchin*, 1962
Signature: *Midnight Run*, 1988
Facts: Grodin was almost cast in the lead role in *The Graduate* but lost it due to an argument with the producers over salary.

Only leases white or gray Cadillac DeVille sedans because he doesn't like to attract attention.

Took his "self-parodying loutishness," as one reviewer called it, to his own cable TV talk show in 1995, to entertaining results.
Marriages: Julia (divorced), Elissa, 1985
Children: Marion, 1960 (with Julia). Nicky, c. 1987
Quote: On a *Tonight Show* appearance, Grodin told Johnny Carson,

"It's hard for me to answer a question from someone who really doesn't care about the answer." Carson banned Grodin from the show.

MATT GROENING

Birthplace: Portland, OR
Birthdate: 2/15/54
Occupation: Cartoonist
Education: Evergreen College
Debut: (Comic Strip) *Life in Hell* (in the *Los Angeles Reader)*, April 1980
Signature: *The Simpsons*
Facts: Elected student-body president in high school. Once elected, tried to rewrite the student government constitution to switch absolute power to himself.

In Los Angeles, ghostwrote the autobiography of an elderly film director who also employed him as a chauffeur, and worked as a landscaper for a sewage treatment plant.

The members of the Simpson family bear the same names as members of Groening's family (although Bart is an anagram for brat).

Groening's home in Venice, CA, is near a canal so he can canoe easily.
Original Job: Writer, rock critic
Marriage: Deborah Caplin, 1986 (separated, 1999)
Children: Homer, 1989; Abraham, 1991
Major Award: Emmy, Outstanding Animated Program, *The Simpsons*, 1990, 1991

BRYANT GUMBEL

Birthplace: New Orleans, LA
Birthdate: 9/29/48
Occupation: TV host, newscaster, sportscaster
Education: Bates College
Debut: (sportscaster) KNBC-TV Los Angeles, 1972
Signature: *Today*
Facts: Likes to cook, golf, and shop.

Received News Emmy for interview

with Ted Kennedy after 1994 Palm Beach family scandal.

His nickname was "No-Stumble Gumbel."
Infamy: In 2000, June Gumbel went public with her filing for a separation and for emergency financial relief, saying Bryant left her "practically destitute" and stopped paying some bills for her and their son and daughter. In January 2001, she attempted to amend her divorce petition to add adultery as grounds, claiming he was a "serial adulterer." The couple reportedly arrived at a divorce settlement in April 2001.
Original Job: Magazine editor
Marriage: June Gumbel, 1973 (divorced, 2001); Hilary Quinlan (relationship)
Children: Bradley Christopher, 1978; Jillian Beth, 1984
Famous Relative: Greg Gumbel, sportscaster
Major Awards: Sports Emmy, 1988; News Emmy, 1994
Quote: "I'm not a guy who enjoys taped TV...By the time I put it on the air, I didn't feel anything for it. So the work may have been as flat as my emotions."

GENE HACKMAN

Birthplace: San Bernardino, CA
Birthdate: 1/30/30
Occupation: Actor
Education: Pasadena Playhouse, University of Illinois, School of Radio Technique in NY
Debut: (Stage) *Any Wednesday,* 1964; (Film) *Lillith,* 1964; (Novel) *Wake of the Perdido Star*, 1999
Signature: *The French Connection*, 1971
Facts: Did his own driving in the car-chase scenes in *The French Connection.*

At the Pasadena Playhouse, he and classmate Dustin Hoffman were voted the two least likely to succeed.
Original Jobs: Doorman, truck driver,

shoe salesman, soda jerk, furniture mover, dog license-checker
Marriages: Faye Maltese (divorced, 1986), Betsy Arakawa, 1991
Children: Christopher, 1960;Elizabeth, 1962; Leslie, 1966; (with Faye Maltese)
Major Awards: Oscar, Best Actor, *The French Connection,* 1971; Oscar, Best Supporting Actor, *Unforgiven,* 1992

GERI HALLIWELL

Real Name: Geraldine Estolle Halliwell
Birthplace: Watford, England
Birthdate: 8/6/72
Education: College graduate, UK
Debut: (Album) *Spice,* 1997; (Solo album) *Schizophonic,* 1999
Signature: Ginger Spice
Facts: After leaving the Spice Girls, auctioned her performance clothing, earning $246,000 for charity.

Had a benign lump in her breast when she was 18, which inspired in part her current role as a Goodwill Ambassador of the United Nations Population Fund, promoting population control and reproductive health care.

At Prince Charles's 50th birthday party, she sang in a manner reminiscent of Marilyn Monroe's famous serenade of John F. Kennedy.

Lived with friend George Michael and his boyfriend for three months after leaving the Spice Girls.

Was a game-show host on Turkish television.

Vandals broke into her West London home in 2001 and stole electronics and jewelry, including a necklace once owned by Elizabeth Taylor.
Infamy: Was first photographed nude by Sebastian Amengual when she was 17, and subsequently posed nude for numerous other photographers. She also appeared nude in *Playboy.*
Relationship: Chris Evans, television host

Quote: "I am more creative when I don't have sex."

DARRELL HAMMOND

Birthplace: Melbourne, FL
Birthdate: 10/8/55
Occupation: Comedian
Education: Attended University of Florida at Gainesville
Debut: (TV) *Saturday Night Live,* 1995; (Film) *Celtic Pride,* 1996
Signature: *Saturday Night Live*
Facts: Best known for his Bill Clinton and Al Gore impressions on *Saturday Night Live.*

Bought George W. Bush a baseball glove as an act of friendship when they met in 2001.

As head of the Washington, D.C. based charity KaBOOM, he made building playgrounds for poor kids his mission in 1999.
Original Job: Waiter
Child: Mia, 1998

TOM HANKS

Birthplace: Concord, CA
Birthdate: 7/9/56
Occupation: Actor
Education: Chabot College, California State University–Sacramento
Debut: (Film) *He Knows You're Alone,* 1980 [see page 67 for a complete filmography]
Signature: *Forrest Gump,* 1994
Facts: Attended at least five different elementary schools.

In high school, became a born-again Christian for a couple of years. Converted to Greek Orthodox after marrying Wilson.

After a one-shot guest spot on *Happy Days,* producer Ron Howard asked him to read for a secondary part in *Splash,* but he got the lead instead.

Played Michael J. Fox's alcoholic uncle on the sitcom *Family Ties.*

Doesn't like to talk on the phone, is a bit of a hermit at times.

Collects 1940s typewriters.

Marriages: Samantha Lewes (divorced), Rita Wilson, 1988
Children: Colin, 1977; Elizabeth, 1982; (with Samantha Lewes). Chester, 1990; Truman Theodore, 1995
Major Awards: Oscar, Best Actor, *Philadelphia,* 1993; Oscar, Best Actor, *Forrest Gump,* 1994

MARCIA GAY HARDEN

Birthplace: La Jolla, CA
Birthdate: 8/14/59
Occupation: Actress
Education: Attended University of Maryland; University of Texas, Austin (BA); Tisch School of the Arts, NYU (MFA)
Debut: (Film) *Miller's Crossing,* 1990; (Off-Broadway) *The Years,* 1993; (Broadway) *Angels in America,* 1993
Signature: *Pollock,* 2000
Facts: At age 13, posed as a boy for a period in Japan.

Spent first year of college in Greece and continued her studies in Germany before returning to the U. S. to study drama.

A casting agent said that her "flaring nostril look" would prevent her from being successful.

Recognized in 1989 by a casting director during a performance at NYU in which she played a character called Lucy the Fat Pig, following the male lead around and snorting.

Trained in various circus skills including trapeze, tightrope and juggling.

Her father brother are both named Thaddeus; her husband has the same name, with a different spelling.
Original jobs: Dancer, babysitter, waitress, caterer
Marriage: Thaddaeus Scheel, 1996
Child: Eulala Grace, 1998
Major Award: Academy Award, Best Supporting Actress, *Pollock,* 2001
Quote: "I was always an exhibitionist. I liked it when everyone laughed."

ANGIE HARMON

Birthplace: Dallas, TX
Birthdate: 8/10/72
Occupation: Actor, model
Education: High school graduate
Debut: (TV) *Baywatch Nights*, 1995; (Film) *Lawn Dogs*, 1997
Signature: *Law & Order*
Facts: Began her career as a newborn, in *How to Give Your Baby a Bath*, a hospital-made film. Both of her parents were models.

After working as a child model, she won a *Seventeen* magazine cover model contest at age 17, beating out 63,000 contestants.

Was a runway model for major designers, including Calvin Klein, Giorgio Armani, and Donna Karan.

Was cast in *Baywatch Nights* after being discovered on an airplane by David Hasselhoff.

Organizes her 75 boxes of shoes by taping Polaroid pictures on the boxes.

Her fiancé proposed to her on *The Tonight Show* with Jay Leno.
Original Job: Model
Marriage: Jason Sehorn, professional football player, 2001
Quote: "This life is so much fun. I keep waiting, like in the cartoons, for an anvil to drop on my head."

WOODY HARRELSON

Real Name: Woodrow Tracy Harrelson
Birthplace: Midland, TX
Birthdate: 7/23/61
Occupation: Actor
Education: Hanover College
Debut: (Film) *Wildcats*, 1986
Signature: *Cheers*
Facts: A hyperactive child, sometimes prone to violence, he was placed in a school for problem students. "Violence was almost an aphrodisiac for me." Took Ritalin.

His absent father was convicted of murdering a federal judge and sentenced to life in prison when Woody was a freshman in college.

Sang and composed for a 10-piece "blues-a-billy" band, Manly Moondog and the Three Kool Kats.

Dated Brooke Shields, Carol Kane, Glenn Close, and Moon Unit Zappa.
Infamy: Admits to having been a sex addict.

Arrested for marijuana possession when he planted four hemp seeds in July 1996 to challenge a state law making it illegal to grow industrial hemp. After a four-year court battle, a Kentucky jury cleared him.

Arrested November 1996 for climbing the Golden Gate Bridge. Harrelson was intending to hang banners calling for federal protection for 60,000 acres of redwood trees in Northern California. He was charged with trespassing, being a public nuisance, and failing to obey a peace officer. Agreed to pay a $1,000 fine and spend 25 hours teaching children about the environment.
Original Job: Claims he had over 17 different jobs in one year, including waiting tables and short-order cooking, and was fired from almost all of them
Marriages: Nancy Simon (divorced), Laura Louie, 1998
Children: Deni Montana, 1993; Zoe, 1996
Major Award: Emmy, Best Supporting Actor in a Comedy Series, *Cheers,* 1989

ED HARRIS

Birthplace: Tenafly, NJ
Birthdate: 11/28/50
Occupation: Actor
Education: California Institute of the Arts
Debut: (Film) *Coma*, 1978
Signature: *Apollo 13*, 1995
Facts: Twelve years before *Apollo 13*, appeared in the space film *The Right Stuff*.

His highly lauded *Apollo* scene where he reacts to the astronauts' splashing down was perfected in a single take.

Played more than 20 film roles in 17 years.

Marriage: Amy Madigan, 1983
Child: Lily, 1993

THOMAS HARRIS

Birthplace: Jackson, TN
Birthdate: 9/22/40
Occupation: Author
Education: Baylor University
Debut: (Novel) *Black Sunday*, 1973
Signature: *Silence of the Lambs*, 1988
Facts: As a seemingly shy crime reporter for the *Waco Herald Tribune* after college, he tooled off to assignments on his motorcycle. One such story involved a Mexican child-prostitution racket, which some consider the beginning of his interest in the darker side.

While working at the Associated Press in New York, he and two colleagues came up with a premise for a thriller about terrorists, which soon became *Black Sunday*.

A reclusive perfectionist, he meticulously researches his material.

He refuses to lecture, promote his books, or grant interviews. (He stopped giving interviews in the early '80s after he was asked if you had to be a homicidal psycho to write about serial killers.)
Original Job: Newspaper copy boy
Marriage: One prior marriage (divorced); Pace Barnes (relationship)
Child: Anne, c. 1962
Quote: "I think really everything that I know is in my books."

MELISSA JOAN HART

Birthplace: Sayville, NY
Birthdate: 4/18/76
Occupation: Actor
Education: Attended New York University
Debut: (TV) *The Lucie Arnaz Show*, 1984
Signature: *Sabrina, the Teenage Witch*
Facts: By age five, had already

appeared in 22 commercials. In the next few years she would star in more than a hundred.

She was so young at the time of her 1984 performance on *Saturday Night Live* that she couldn't stay up for the entire show.

Her mom developed *Sabrina*, and became its executive producer.

Relationship: Bryan Kirkwood, soap opera actor

Famous Relatives: Emily, actor, half-sister; Alexandra Hart-Gilliams, actor, half-sister

Quote: "If your butt looks good, your outfit looks good."

JOSH HARTNETT

Birthplace: San Francisco, CA
Birthdate: 7/21/78
Occupation: Actor
Education: Attended State University of New York, Purchase
Debut: (TV) *Cracker*, 1997; (Film) *Halloween: H2O*, 1998
Signature: *Pearl Harbor*, 2001
Facts: When torn ligaments sidelined him from football, followed his aunt's advice and tried out for a Minneapolis production of *Tom Sawyer*, where he landed the role of Huckleberry Finn.

Was cut from the acting program in college after his first year.

His hobby is oil painting.

Auditioned six times for a role on *Dawson's Creek*.

Original Job: Video store clerk
Quote: "I see movies all the time that manipulate you by playing a high note on the piano or some string instrument, and suddenly you're crying. I'm sick of being told what to think."

STEVE HARVEY

Birthplace: Cleveland, OH
Birthdate: 10/20/60
Occupation: Comedian
Education: Attended Kent State University

Debut: (TV) *It's Showtime at the Apollo*
Signature: *The Steve Harvey Show*
Facts: Hosts the syndicated TV series *It's Showtime at the Apollo*, and used to host a morning radio show in Chicago.

Has criticized his network, the WB, for not supporting his show and others that appeal to black audiences. His show is the highest-rated on the network.

His own show, in which he stars as Steve Hightower, a former '70s R&B singer who became a high school music teacher, is the top-rated sitcom in African-American homes. He signed a book deal for his autobiography.

The Kings of Comedy tour, featuring Harvey, D. L. Hughley, Bernie Mac, and Cedric "The Entertainer," is the highest grossing comedy tour ever, and has taken in tens of millions of dollars. Spike Lee made a feature film of a performance.

Marriage: One prior marriage; Mary Lee
Child: Twin daughters, c. 1982 (from first marriage); Wynton, 1997
Quote: "America is not yet where it needs to be in race relations for all of us, toward one another. If you had to explain to your children why their faces aren't on television or why we're not in many movies, then you would feel the exact same way yourself."

DAVID HASSELHOFF

Birthplace: Baltimore, MD
Birthdate: 7/17/52
Occupation: Actor
Education: California Institute of the Arts
Debut: (TV) *The Young and the Restless*, 1975
Signature: *Baywatch*
Facts: Hasselhoff is a successful recording star in Europe, and has toured Germany and Austria. He

performed a concert in front of 500,000 people at the Berlin Wall.

Baywatch was the first American show to appear in mainland China. It is the most watched show on the planet, seen by almost a billion people every day.

Marriages: Catherine Hickland (divorced), Pamela Bach, 1989
Children: Taylor Ann, 1990; Hayley Amber, 1992

ETHAN HAWKE

Birthplace: Austin, TX
Birthdate: 11/6/70
Occupation: Actor, director, writer
Education: New York University, studied acting at the McCarter Theatre in Princeton, the British Theatre Association, and Carnegie-Mellon University
Debut: (Film) *Explorers*, 1985; (Stage) *The Seagull*, 1992
Signature: *Dead Poets Society*, 1989
Facts: Was seen out drinking and dancing with the married Julia Roberts in April 1994. He claims they were just discussing a possible movie project.

Starred in *Explorers* when he was 14 with River Phoenix.

His own singing was featured in the *Reality Bites* soundtrack.

Dropped out of Carnegie Mellon after two months to act in *Dead Poets Society*.

Co-founded the New York theater company Malaparte.

Raised eyebrows when *The Hottest State*, his first published novel, attracted advance payments much higher than other novice authors'.

Marriage: Uma Thurman, 1998
Child: Maya Ray Thurman-Hawke, 1998
Quote: "I didn't realize how selfish I was until I had a baby."

GOLDIE HAWN

Birthplace: Takoma Park, MD
Birthdate: 11/21/45
Occupation: Actor

Education: American University
Debut: (Film) *The One and Only Genuine Family Band,* 1968
Signature: *Private Benjamin,* 1980
Facts: Discovered while dancing in the chorus of an Andy Griffith TV special in 1967. Became a regular on *Laugh-In.*

Father performed as a musician at the White House.

Hobbies include knitting.
Original Job: Go-go dancer
Marriages: Gus Trikonis (divorced, 1976); Bill Hudson (divorced, 1982); Kurt Russell (relationship)
Children: Oliver Rutledge, 1976; Kate Garry, 1979; (with Bill Hudson). Wyatt, 1986
Major Award: Oscar, Best Supporting Actress, *Cactus Flower,* 1969

SALMA HAYEK

Birthplace: Coastzacoalcos, Veracruz, Mexico
Birthdate: 9/2/66
Occupation: Actor
Education: Attended National University of Mexico and Stella Adler Conservatory
Debut: (TV) *Nurses,* 1992; (TV movie) *Roadracers,* 1994; (Film) *Mi vida loca ("My Crazy Life"),* 1993
Signature: *Desperado,* 1995
Facts: Attained stardom on Mexican TV, then moved to L.A. in 1991 to study English and acting.

She is of Lebanese descent.

As a child, her grandmother frequently shaved Salma's head and clipped her eyebrows, believing that it would add body to her dark, thick hair.

She finished high school in two years, but her mother was afraid of "college boys" and made her live in Houston until the age of 17.

Discovered by director Robert Rodriguez on a Spanish-language cable-access talk show while he was channel surfing.

Has two pet monkeys, a gift from friend Antonio Banderas.

Infamy: Expelled from a boarding school in Louisiana for setting alarm clocks back three hours.
Relationship: Ed Norton
Famous Relatives: Diana Hayek, opera singer, mother
Quote: "When I was a little girl, they told me I couldn't wear tiaras to school. Now I get to wear whatever I want!"

SEAN HAYES

Birthplace: Glen Ellyn, IL
Birthdate: 6/26/70
Occupation: Actor
Education: Illinois State University
Debut: (TV) *Silk Stalkings,* 1991; (Film) *Billy's Hollywood Screen Kiss,* 1998
Signature: *Will & Grace*
Facts: As a teenager, he was an extra in *Lucas,* Winona Ryder's first movie.

In college he played in the pop band Sounds from the Stairs and also worked as a classical pianist.

Hasn't seen his father, who allegedly abandoned his wife and five children, in over 10 years.

Composed original music for a Steppenwolf production of *Antigone.*

Was a member of Chicago's Second City improv group.

Toured as an elf in the Kenny Rogers' Christmas Show.

Prefers his Toyota Camry to the silver Porsche NBC gave the *Will & Grace* stars.
Major Award: Emmy, Supporting Actor in a Comedy Series, 1999–2000
Quote: "Being an actor, the less people know about my personal life, the more open-minded they can be about each role I play."

ANNE HECHE

Birthplace: Aurora, OH
Birthdate: 5/25/69
Occupation: Actor
Education: High school
Debut: (TV) *Another World,* 1988;

(Film) *The Adventures of Huck Finn,* 1993
Signature: *Volcano,* 1969
Facts: Her father was a Baptist church choir director who was secretly gay; Heche found out at age 12 when he was dying of AIDS. In her memoir, she says that she spent the first 31 years of her life suffering from mental illness that she says was triggered by sexual abuse at the hands of her father.

The same year her father died, her brother was killed in a car accident. To help support her family while in junior high school, Heche sang in a local dinner theater.

Was asked to be in a soap opera by a Procter & Gamble talent scout who happened to see her in a high school play.

Dated Steve Martin, costar of her film *A Simple Twist of Fate* for two years until she broke it off.

Formerly involved in a relationship with Ellen DeGeneres.
Infamy: Shortly after her relationship with Ellen DeGeneres was announced, the pair was criticized for nuzzling and hugging during the annual White House Correspondents' Dinner.
Marriage: Coleman Laffoon, cameraman, 2001
Quote: "I put a very high premium on honesty. If you don't accept your own sexuality, it will kill you."
Major Awards: Emmy, Outstanding Younger Actress, *Another World,* 1990

KATHARINE HEPBURN

Birthplace: Hartford, CT
Birthdate: 5/12/07
Occupation: Actor
Education: Bryn Mawr College
Debut: (Stage) *The Czarina,* 1928; (Film) *A Bill of Divorcement,* 1932
Signature: *The African Queen,* 1951
Facts: In her strict New England home, where her father was a surgeon and her mother a militant

suffragette, Hepburn and her siblings took cold showers every morning.

Since she was considered too much of a tomboy, she was educated by home tutors.

Decided to take up acting once she realized there was little opportunity for a woman to become a doctor.

According to a 1995 biography, she settled for Tracy after her true love, Catholic director John Ford, couldn't get a divorce from his wife.

Original Job: Sold balloons
Marriages: Ludlow Ogden Smith (divorced, 1934), Spencer Tracy (relationship, deceased)
Major Awards: Oscar, Best Actress, *Morning Glory*, 1933; Oscar, Best Actress, *Guess Who's Coming to Dinner*, 1967; Oscar, Best Actress, *The Lion in Winter*, 1968; Emmy, Best Actress in a Drama Special, *Love Among the Ruins*, 1975; Oscar, Best Actress, *On Golden Pond*, 1981; Kennedy Center Honor for Lifetime Achievement, 1990
Quote: "I am revered rather like an old building."

JENNIFER LOVE HEWITT

Birthplace: Waco, TX
Birthdate: 2/21/79
Occupation: Actor, dancer, singer
Education: High school
Debut: (Film) *Sister Act 2*, 1993
Signature: *Party of Five*
Facts: Made her acting debut at age 6 in a pig barn at a Texas livestock show.

Her debut CD, *Love Songs*, was released in Japan, but not the U.S., when she was 13.

The "starstruck" star has a large celebrity autograph collection.

She sang "How Do I Deal" on the soundtrack for *I Still Know What You Did Last Summer*.

Sent Gwyneth Paltrow, who she looks up to, three dozen roses the night she won an Oscar.

Relationship: Rich Cronin, musician in the group LFO

TOMMY HILFIGER

Birthplace: Elmira, NY
Birthdate: 3/24/51
Occupation: Designer
Education: High school
Debut: (Clothes line) Tommy Hilfiger, 1985
Facts: As a child, struggled with dyslexia and, consequently, was a poor student.

Opened his first store, People's Place, selling bell bottoms and other trendy clothes, at age 18. After expanding to several cities, the chain went bankrupt.

Sales of his clothes went up $90 million in 1994, the year Snoop Dogg wore his oversized jersey on *Saturday Night Live*.

Bought a blimp in 1998.
Marriage: Susie, 1980 (separated, 2000)
Children: Alexandra, c. 1985; Richard; Elizabeth; Kathleen Anne, 1995
Major Award: Council of Fashion Designers of America, Menswear Designer of the Year, 1995

FAITH HILL

Real Name: Audrey Faith Hill
Birthplace: Jackson, MI
Birthdate: 9/21/67
Occupation: Country singer
Education: High school
Debut: (Album) *Take Me As I Am*, 1993
Signature: *This Kiss*, 1998
Facts: Adopted and raised in Star, Mississippi, she sang in church and formed her first country band by age 16, performing first at a Tobacco Spit competition and eventually at rodeos and country fairs.

Her break came when a talent scout heard her sing harmony with Gary Burr at the Bluebird Cafe.

After some 150 performances in 1994, she endured vocal surgery, followed by three weeks of complete silence.

At the last minute, she was asked

to join Tina Turner, Elton John, Cher, and Whitney Houston for the *VH1 Divas Live* concert event.

Husband Tim McGraw proposed to her in his trailer during 1996's "Spontaneous Combustion" tour. She responded by scrawling "I'm going to be your wife" on the mirror while he was performing on stage.
Marriage: Dan Hill (divorced); Scott Hendricks (engaged, 1995; never married); Tim McGraw, 1996
Children: Gracie Katherine, 1997; Maggie Elizabeth, 1998
Major Awards: Grammy, Best Country Vocal - Female, "Breathe," 2000; Grammy, Best Country Collaboration with Vocals, "Let's Make Love," (with Tim McGraw); Grammy, Best Country Album, *Breathe*, 2001
Quotes: "I'm not even sure I know what a diva is. But I'm very glad I was there."

LAURYN HILL

Birthplace: South Orange, NJ
Birthdate: 5/25/75
Occupation: Singer
Education: Attended Columbia University
Debut: (Album) *Blunted on Reality*, 1993
Signature: *The Miseducation of Lauryn Hill*, 1998
Facts: Originally called Tranzlator Crew, the group changed their name to The Fugees when a long-forgotten 1980s new-wave act called Translator objected.

The Fugees sprang from the trio's feeling of being refugees from mainstream culture and even hip-hop, and from their sense that they found refuge in the music they made.

Hill met fellow group member Pras Michel when the two attended the same high school. Wyclef Jean, who soon joined forces with them, is Michel's cousin.

Her five-Grammy haul for *The Miseducation of Lauryn Hill* tied her with Carole King for most trophies by a female artist in a single year.

Her fiancé is an ex-college football star and the son of the late Bob Marley.

Relationship: Rohan Marley (engaged)

Children: Zion David, 1997; Selah Louise, 1998

Major Award: Grammy, Best R&B Group with Vocal, "Killing Me Softly," 1996; Grammy, Album of the Year, *The Miseducation of Lauryn Hill,* 1998; Grammy, Best New Artist, 1998; Grammy, Best R&B Song, "Doo Wop (That Thing)," 1998; Grammy, Best R&B Vocal—Female, "Doo Wop (That Thing)," 1998; Grammy, Best R&B Album, *The Miseducation of Lauryn Hill,* 1998.

DUSTIN HOFFMAN

Birthplace: Los Angeles, CA
Birthdate: 8/8/37
Occupation: Actor
Education: Los Angeles Conservatory of Music, Santa Monica City College; studied at the Pasadena Playhouse and the Actor's Studio
Debut: (Stage) *Yes Is for a Very Young Man,* 1960; (Film) *Tiger Makes Out,* 1967
Signature: *The Graduate,* 1967
Facts: Played Tiny Tim in junior high school.

Slept on Gene Hackman's kitchen floor while looking for work.

Achieved Ratso's distinctive walk in *Midnight Cowboy* by putting pebbles in his shoe.

When taking the screen test for *The Graduate,* Hoffman said, "I don't think I'm right for the role. He's a kind of Anglo-Saxon, tall, slender, good-looking chap. I'm short and Jewish." During the screen test he forgot his lines and was nervous and clumsy.

Hoffman originally wanted to be a concert pianist. Also studied to be a doctor.

The $3 million verdict he won in 1999 against Los Angeles magazine for running a computer–altered image of him in an evening dress and high heels was thrown out on appeal.

Original Job: Washing dishes, checking coats, waiting tables, cleaning a dance studio, selling toys at Macy's, attendant in a psychiatric institution

Marriages: Anne Byrne (divorced); Lisa Gottsegen, 1980

Children: Karina, 1966; Jenna, 1970; (with Anne Byrne). Jacob, 1981; Rebecca, 1983; Max, 1984; Alexandra, 1987

Major Awards: Oscar, Best Actor, *Kramer vs. Kramer,* 1979; Oscar, Best Actor, *Rain Man,* 1988; Emmy, Best Actor in a Made-for-TV Movie, *Death of a Salesman,* 1986

Quote: "I kept all the dresses from Tootsie. I wear them every Thursday night."

LAUREN HOLLY

Birthplace: Geneva, NY
Birthdate: 10/28/63
Occupation: Actor
Education: Sarah Lawrence College
Debut: (Film) *Band of the Hand,* 1986
Signature: *Picket Fences* (TV series)
Facts: Personal tragedy struck in 1992 when her parents ended their 30-year marriage and, a short time later, her 14-year-old brother died in a house fire.

Her very public 1994 divorce from Anthony Quinn's struggling actor son, Danny, had him claiming that her careless spending squandered their fortune and her accusing him of having affairs and refusing to work.

Roomed with Robin Givens in college.

Marriages: Danny Quinn, 1991 (divorced, 1993); Jim Carrey 1996 (divorced, 1997); Francis Greco, 2001

Child: son (adopted, 2001)

KATIE HOLMES

Real Name: Kate Noelle Holmes
Birthplace: Toledo, OH
Birthdate: 12/18/78
Occupation: Actor
Education: High school

Debut: (Film) *The Ice Storm,* 1997; (TV) *Dawson's Creek,* 1998
Signature: *Dawson's Creek*
Facts: Was cast as Joey Potter on *Dawson's Creek* based on a video-tape that she made in her basement.

She grew up in a strict Catholic household as the youngest of five children.

The Ice Storm was the first movie she ever auditioned for.

Her mother sent her to modeling school at age 10 to expose her to the field and to teach her how to be graceful. At 16 she attended a modeling convention in New York City, but she never pursued the career.

Earned a 4.0 average in high school and graduated in 1997, deferring enrollment twice at Columbia University.

Relationship: Chris Klein
Quote: "It isn't my fault that I come from a really normal, dream family."

ANTHONY HOPKINS

Birthplace: Port Talbot, South Wales
Birthdate: 12/31/37
Occupation: Actor
Education: Welsh College of Music and Drama, Royal Academy of Dramatic Art, London
Debut: (Stage) *Julius Caesar,* 1964; (Film) *The Lion in Winter,* 1968 [see page 67 for a complete filmography]
Signature: *The Silence of the Lambs,* 1991
Facts: Debuted as conductor with the New Symphony Orchestra at Royal Albert Hall, 1982.

Was knighted by Queen Elizabeth in 1993.

Understudied for Laurence Olivier in *Dance Of Death,* 1966.

Wrote the music for his 1996 film *August.*

Became a U.S. citizen in 2000.

Infamy: Had a long bout with alcohol addiction.
Original Job: Steelworker
Marriages: Petronella Barker, 1967

(divorced, 1972); Jennifer Ann Lynton, 1973
Child: Abigail, 1968 (with Petronella Barker)
Major Awards: Emmy, Best Actor in a Drama or Comedy Special, *The Lindbergh Kidnapping Case,* 1976; Emmy, Best Actor in a Miniseries, *The Bunker,* 1981; Oscar, Best Actor, *The Silence of the Lambs,* 1991
Quote: "I don't like slow movies. I don't like *Masterpiece Theater.*"

WHITNEY HOUSTON

Birthplace: Newark, NJ
Birthdate: 8/9/63
Occupation: Singer
Education: High school
Debut: (Album) *Whitney Houston,* 1985
Signature: "The Greatest Love of All," 1987
Facts: Got her start at age 8 singing in the New Hope Baptist Junior Choir.

Sang backup for Chaka Khan, Lou Rawls, and Dionne Warwick.

As a model, appeared on the cover of *Seventeen.*

Was an actress in her early days, appearing on *Silver Spoons* and *Gimme a Break.*

Signed a multi-album deal with Arista worth in excess of $100 million in 2001.
Infamy: In 2000 was found with 15.2 grams of marijuana in her pocketbook at a Hawaii airport security checkpoint. She departed before local police arrived, but was later charged with a misdemeanor. After pleading no contest, the charge was dismissed and a small fine levied.
Original Job: Model
Marriage: Bobby Brown, 1992
Child: Bobbi Kristina, 1993
Famous Relatives: Cissy Houston, singer, mother; Thelma Houston, singer, aunt; Dionne Warwick, singer, cousin
Major Awards: Emmy, Best Individual Performance in a Variety or Music Program, *The 28th Annual*

Grammy Awards, 1986; Grammy, Best Pop Vocal—Female, "Saving All My Love for You," 1985; Grammy, Best Pop Vocal—Female, "I Wanna Dance with Somebody," 1987; Grammy, Best Pop Vocal—Female, "I Will Always Love You," 1993; Grammy, Record of the Year, "I Will Always Love You," 1993; Grammy, Album of the Year, *The Bodyguard Soundtrack,* 1993; Grammy, Best R&B Vocal—Female, "It's Not Right But It's Okay," 1999

RON HOWARD

Birthplace: Duncan, OK
Birthdate: 3/1/54
Occupation: Actor, director, producer
Education: University of Southern California
Debut: (Film) *Frontier Woman,* 1956; (TV) *Playhouse 90, 1959*
Signature: *Cocoon,* 1985
Facts: Starred on *The Andy Griffith Show* as Opie when just 6 years old.

The long-running hit *Happy Days* actually struggled in the ratings when it focused mostly on the misadventures of Howard's teenage character; it took off a year later when Henry Winkler's Fonzie became the star.

First directing effort, 1977's *Grand Theft Auto,* was shot in 20 days for $602,000; grossed $15 million.

True to his All-American persona, married his high school sweetheart.
Marriage: Cheryl Alley, 1975
Children: Bryce, 1980; Jocelyn, 1985; Paige, 1985; Reed, 1987
Famous Relatives: Rance Howard, actor, father; Jean Howard, actor, mother; Clint Howard, actor, brother

KATE HUDSON

Birthplace: Los Angeles, CA
Birthdate: 4/19/79
Education: High school graduate
Occupation: Actor
Debut: (TV) *Party of Five,* 1996; (Film) *Desert Blue,* 1999

Signature: *Almost Famous,* 2000
Facts: Her middle name is Garry. Brother Oliver calls her Hammerhead Shark (because of the space between her eyes) and Dumbo.

Turned down the title role in *Felicity* to continue her education.

Was in a relationship with Eli Craig, son of Sally Field.

Is estranged from her natural father.
Marriage: Chris Robinson, musician, 2000
Famous relatives: Goldie Hawn, mother, actor; Bill Hudson, father, comedian-musician; Kurt Russell, "adoptive father," actor; Wyatt Russell, half-brother, actor; Oliver Hudson, brother, actor,
Quote: "I'm not the cool, hard, independent-movie-chick—the grungy outfit, reading Dostoyevsky. I like to look nice and dress nice. I'm very Betty Crocker."

D. L. HUGHLEY

Real Name: Darryl Lynn Hughley
Birthplace: Los Angeles, CA
Birthdate: 3/6/63
Occupation: Comedian
Education: High school
Debut: (TV) *Def Comedy Jam*
Signature: *The Hughleys*
Facts: Urged by his barber to enter a stand-up comedy contest, then booked on the so-called "Chitlin Circuit." Big break came after 10 years and a million frequent-flyer miles as a stand-up comic.

Expelled from high school in tenth grade for fighting, he later completed his GED.

Sitcom *The Hughleys* is based on his personal experiences living in a white neighborhood.
Infamy: One-time member of the notorious L.A. gang the Bloods, he turned his life around after his cousin, a member of rival gang the Crips, was murdered.
Original Job: Telemarketer for *Los Angeles Times*
Marriage: LaDonna, 1986

Children: Ryan, 1987; Kyle, 1989; Tyler, 1991

Quote: "I don't sing, I don't dance, I don't do impressions. I'm just a guy who gets up there and talks trash."

SAMMO HUNG

Real Name: Samo Hung Kam-Bo
Birthplace: Hong Kong
Birthdate: 1/7/52
Occupation: Actor, director, producer, fight choreographer
Education: Chinese Opera Research Institute
Debut: (Film) *Education of Love*, 1961; (Directorial) *The Iron-Fisted Monk*, 1978; (TV) *Martial Law*, 1998
Signature: *Martial Law*
Facts: Inspired to be an actor, he studied at the Beijing Opera School, combining physical conditioning with dramatic study, and became star member of the Seven Little Fortunes children's troupe, performing in local nightclubs.

Instructed younger classmates, including Jackie Chan, in Opera-style martial arts, earning him the nickname of "Big Brother."

He's completely colorblind.

His wife, who also acts as his dialogue coach, is a former Miss Hong Kong.

His trademark scar, that runs from the side of his nose to the top of his lip, is the result of being slashed with a cracked soda bottle at age 16.

With some 140 films to his credit in Hong Kong, he is best known in America for his fight with Bruce Lee at the beginning of 1973's *Enter the Dragon*.

Marriages: Jo Yuen Ok, 1973 (divorced,1994); Joyce Mina Godenzi, 1995
Children: Timmy, c. 1974; Jimmy, c. 1975; Sammy, c. 1979; Stephanie, c. 1983 (with Jo Yuen Ok)
Quote: "A sprained ankle to me is like a paper cut to you."

HELEN HUNT

Birthplace: Los Angeles, CA
Birthdate: 6/15/63
Occupation: Actor
Education: UCLA
Debut: (TV) *The Mary Tyler Moore Show*, 1970; (Film) *Rollercoaster*, 1977 [see pages 67–68 for a complete filmography]
Signature: *Mad About You*
Facts: Hunt studied acting, got an agent, and got a part in the TV movie *Pioneer Woman* by age 9.

Began a two-year romance with actor Matthew Broderick while working on *Project X* (1986).

Played Murray Slaughter's daughter on *The Mary Tyler Moore Show*.

Autograph Collector named her as 1999's Worst Signer. If she does give you an autograph, complains the publication, it's "just an H with a sloppy line after it."
Marriage: Hank Azaria, 1999 (separated, 2000)
Famous Relatives: Gordon Hunt, director, father; Peter Hunt, director, uncle
Major Awards: Emmy, Best Actress in a Comedy Series, *Mad About You*, 1996, 1997, 1998, 1999; Oscar, Best Actress, *As Good As It Gets*, 1997

HOLLY HUNTER

Birthplace: Conyers, GA
Birthdate: 3/20/58
Occupation: Actor
Education: Carnegie Mellon University
Debut: (Film) *The Burning*, 1981; (Stage) *Crimes of the Heart*, 1981
Signature: *Broadcast News*
Facts: Director Jane Campion was originally looking for a tall, statuesque Sigourney Weaver type for the lead in *The Piano*.

Youngest of seven children, grew up on a cattle and hay farm in Georgia, where she drove a tractor.

Appeared in pilot for television series *Fame* (1982).
Marriage: Janusz Kaminski, 1995

Major Awards: Emmy, Best Actress in a Miniseries, *Roe vs. Wade*, 1989; Emmy, Best Actress in a Miniseries, *The Positively True Adventures of the Alleged Texas Cheerleader-Murdering Mom*, 1993; Oscar, Best Actress, *The Piano*, 1993

ELIZABETH HURLEY

Birthplace: Hampshire, England
Birthdate: 6/10/65
Occupation: Actor, model
Education: London Studio Centre
Debut: (Stage) *The Man Most Likely To...*, (Film) *Rowing in the Wind*, 1986
Signature: *Austin Powers: International Man of Mystery*, 1997
Facts: Long recognized only as actor Hugh Grant's girlfriend. In 1995 when she accompanied Grant on a guest appearance on *The Joan Rivers Show*, Rivers asked, "And who are you?" The two broke up in 2000 after dating for 13 years.

At the opening of Grant's movie *Four Weddings and a Funeral*, she wore a Versace dress held together by 24 safety pins.

Replaced Paulina Porizkova as the face of Estée Lauder cosmetics. Defied conventional stardom by beginning as an actor and becoming a supermodel at age 29.

Characterizes herself as an army brat; her father was a major.

Notorious in her early 20s for her punk-rock phase. She pierced her nose, spiked and painted her hair pink and frequented punk rock bars.

Needlepoint is one of her favorite pastimes.

Was a candidate for the position of ambassador for the United Nations High Commissioner for Refugees.

Won a libel suit against a London paper that claimed she could be "hired" for private functions. Money she has been awarded from such suits has funded an island preserve for abandoned or abused chimpanzees.

Infamy: Was expelled from the London Studio Centre after leaving school and going to a Greek Island.

Angered SAG members in 2000 by shooting a non-union commercial for Estee Lauder during a strike. She apologized to the union, claiming that she was unaware of the situation because she does not live in the country.

Quote: "I've always wanted to be a spy, and frankly I'm a little surprised that British intelligence has never approached me."

ICE CUBE

Real Name: O'Shea Jackson
Birthplace: Los Angeles, CA
Birthdate: 6/15/69
Occupation: Rap artist, actor
Education: Phoenix Institute of Technology
Debut: (Album) *Boyz N the Hood* (with N.W.A.), 1986; (Album) *Amerikkka's Most Wanted* (solo), 1990
Signature: *Boyz N the Hood*, 1991
Facts: Former lyricist of the rap group N.W.A. His 1991 album, *Death Certificate*, stirred controversy because it contained racist attacks on Koreans and called for the murder of a Jewish man.

Began writing rap lyrics at age 14.
Marriage: Kim
Child: Darrell, 1986 (stepson); O'Shea Jackson Jr., 1991; Kareema, 1994
Quote: "Rap is the network newscast black people never had."

ENRIQUE IGLESIAS

Birthplace: Madrid, Spain
Birthdate: 5/8/75
Occupation: Singer
Education: Attended University of Miami
Debut: (Album) *Enrique Iglesias*, 1995; (Single) "Si Tu Te Vas," 1995
Facts: After parents divorced in 1979 and his grandfather had been kidnapped in Spain, he went to Miami

to live with his father, Julio, not only to learn English but also for safety.

Began singing and writing music at 15 with a couple of older musicians in a Morales basement studio. He kept these meetings secret from his family.

He hates to have his picture taken.

When he first began performing, he was known only as Enrique because he wanted to succeed (or fail) on his own. Walked out of a New York radio interview because he was introduced as Julio's son, and, for the same reason, turned down a spot on Oprah's scheduled show about sons of famous fathers.

Dubbed Sexiest Man by *PEOPLE en Español.*

He loves to windsurf.

Booked himself on Howard Stern's radio show in 2000 after hearing Stern suggest that he could not sing. After appearing on the show, Stern changed his mind and agreed to play Iglesias's songs for several days.
Major Awards: Grammy, Best Latin Pop Performer, 1997
Famous Relatives: Julio Iglesias, singer, father; Julio Jose, actor, model, brother; Chabelli, Spanish television personality, sister
Quote: "I say stuff in my music that I would never dare say face-to-face; I'd be too embarrassed."

NATALIE IMBRUGLIA

Birthplace: Campsie, Sydney, Australia
Birthdate: 2/4/75
Occupation: Singer, actor
Education: High school dropout
Debut: (TV, Australia) *Neighbours*, 1992; (Album) *Left of the Middle*, 1998
Signature: "Torn," 1998
Facts: Started dance lessons at age 2 and attended six days a week.

At 14 she turned down the offer of an Australian entrepreneur for a solo recording act.

She left parochial high school at 16, did some commercials, attended a performing arts college in Sydney, and landed a role in *Neighbours,* an Australian teen-oriented soap.

"Torn" was originally recorded by Ednaswap, an L.A. punk band, though it received no airplay.

DON IMUS

Real Name: John Donald Imus Jr.
Birthplace: Riverside, CA
Birthdate: 7/23/40
Occupation: Radio talk-show host
Education: High school dropout
Debut: KUTY, Palmdale, CA, 1968
Signature: "Imus in the Morning"
Facts: Fired from an early window dressing job for staging striptease shows with mannequins to amuse passersby.

Once called a fast-food restaurant while on the air and ordered 1,200 specially-prepared hamburgers to go, an incident that contributed to an FCC ruling that DJs must identify themselves when phoning listeners.

Wrote the novel *God's Other Son,* based on his lecherous evangelist radio character. Originally published in 1981, it was reissued in 1994 and hit the bestseller list for 13 weeks.

Hospitalized in 2000 with numerous broken bones and a punctured lung after being thrown by his horse.
Infamy: Caused a stir among media members when his jokes insulted Bill and Hillary Clinton during a televised correspondents' dinner.

Had a severe alcohol and cocaine abuse problem, for which he was fired from his New York station in 1977. Finally kicked the habit in 1987, after a nine-day drinking binge scared him into a treatment center.
Original Job: Department store window dresser
Marriage: Harriet (divorced, 1979); Deirdre Coleman, 1994
Children: Nadine, 1960 (stepdaughter); Antoinette, 1962

(stepdaughter); Elizabeth, 1966; Ashleigh, 1967; (with Harriet). Fredric Wyatt, 1998
Major Award: Inducted into the Broadcast Hall of Fame, 1996

JEREMY IRONS

Birthplace: Isle of Wight, England
Birthdate: 9/19/48
Occupation: Actor
Education: Bristol Old Vic Theatre School
Debut: (Stage) Godspell, 1972
Signature: The French Lieutenant's Woman, 1982
Facts: At school, excelled at rugby, the fiddle, and clarinet and headed the cadet corps.

Made his mark with the BBC series Brideshead Revisited, 1981.

Played a dual role as twin brothers in Dead Ringers, a 1988 movie he considers his best work.
Original Job: Housecleaner, gardener, assistant stage manager, busker (singing and playing guitar outside movie theaters)
Marriage: Sinéad Moira Cusack, 1978
Children: Samuel James, 1978; Maximilian Paul, 1985
Major Awards: Tony, Best Actor (Dramatic), The Real Thing, 1984; Oscar, Best Actor, Reversal of Fortune, 1990

JOHN IRVING

Birthplace: Exeter, NH
Birthdate: 3/2/42
Education: University of New Hampshire, BA; University of Iowa, MFA
Occupation: Novelist, screenwriter, actor, college instructor
Debut: (Novel) Setting Free the Bears, 1969
Signature: The World According to Garp, 1978
Facts: His father taught at Phillips Exeter Academy.

Was dyslexic as a child.

Studied under Günter Grass for a year at the Institute of European Studies in Vienna, Austria. Also studied with Kurt Vonnegut

Played a wrestling referee in the movie version of The World According to Garp.

When starting a new novel, he typically writes the last line first.

His son Colin, an actor, appeared in the movie versions of The Cider House Rules and The Hotel New Hampshire.
Was so unhappy with changes made in the 1998 film Simon Birch that he demanded the credit, "suggested by A Prayer for Owen Meany."

The Cider House Rules was his screenwriting debut. His grandfather, a noted obstetrician at Boston's Lying-In Hospital, was one of the models for Dr. Larch. (He had a cameo as the stationmaster in the film.)

In 1999, Irving published My Movie Business: A Memoir, about his film experiences.
Original Job: English instructor
Marriages: Shyla Leary Irving, 1964 (divorced 1981); Janet Turnbull, 1987
Children: Colin, c. 1965; Brendan, c. 1969 (with Shyla Irving); Everett, 1991
Quote: "I write about characters I love. I want the readers or the audience to love them or at least to sympathize with them, too. If that's sentimental, then I'm guilty."
Major Award: Oscar, Best Adapted Screenplay, The Cider House Rules, 1999

CHRIS ISAAK

Birthplace: Stockton, CA
Birthdate: 6/26/56
Occupation: Musician, actor
Education: University of the Pacific
Debut: (Album) Silvertone, 1985; (Film) Married to the Mob, 1988; (TV) Friends, 1996
Signature: "Wicked Game," 1991
Facts: Played the role of a fast-food clown in his film debut.

Drives a 1964 Chevy Nova.

Stands 6' 1".

Got his first guitar at age 13 and taught himself to play.

Furnished his San Francisco home with thrift-store furniture and turned his bedroom into a replica of the bedroom he grew up in as a child.

In 2001, launched the cable comedy series The Chris Isaak Show, loosely based on his own life.
Original Job: Funeral parlor assistant

ALAN IVERSON

Birthplace: Hampton, VA
Birthdate: 6/7/75
Occupation: Basketball player
Education: Attended Georgetown University
Facts: Nicknamed "Bubba Chuck" after his two uncles, Bubba and Chuck.

Growing up, there were times when his family went without electricity or water. When he was 14, his family was evicted from their home.

Draws caricatures and portraits of sports figures in his spare time.

Has 21 tattoos, all about loyalty and strength.

During the 1998–99 season switched from point guard to shooting guard and led the NBA in scoring with 26.8 points per game.
Infamy: Arrested and convicted in 1993 after a bowling alley brawl for allegedly throwing a chair at a young woman. Tried as an adult and sentenced to five years in prison. Served for four months before Virginia governor commuted his sentence under the condition that he would not play organized sports until he graduated from high school.

On the way to record a rap song at a local Richmond recording studio in 1997, was pulled over going 93 miles per hour; marijuana and a handgun were allegedly found inside his car. Charges were dropped after he was given two years probation with monthly drug tests and 100

hours of community service.
Children: Tiara, c.1995; Allen II, c.1998
Major Award: NBA Rookie of the Year, 1997
Quote: "I'm not perfect, but I am trying every day to concentrate on being a better basketball player and a better person."

HUGH JACKMAN

Birthplace: Sydney, Australia
Birthdate: 10/12/68
Occupation: Actor, singer, TV host
Education: University of Technology, Sydney; Attended School of Practical Philosophy, Melbourne
Debut: (Film) *Paperback Hero*, 1999; (U.S. TV) *Hey, Mr. Producer*, 1998
Signature: *Erskineville Kings*, 1999
Facts: Majored in radio journalism at Sydney's University of Technology.

Met his wife when they co-starred on the Australian TV series *Corelli*.

Starred in the Australian productions of *Beauty and the Beast* (1995) and *Sunset Boulevard* (1996–97).

Won a Best Actor Olivier, the British Tony, for his portrayal of Curly in a 1999 National Theatre revival of *Oklahoma!*

Got the role of Wolverine in *X-Men* when actor Dougray Scott opted to make *Mission: Impossible 2* instead.
Original job: Health club cashier
Marriage: Deborra-Lee Furness, 1996
Child: Oscar Maximillian, 2000 (adopted)

ALAN JACKSON

Birthplace: Newnan, GA
Birthdate: 10/17/58
Occupation: Singer, songwriter
Education: South Georgia College
Debut: (Album) *Here in the Real World*, 1989
Signature: "Neon Rainbow"
Facts: In 1985, his wife got Jackson his big break. A flight attendant, she cornered Glen Campbell in the

Atlanta airport and asked him to listen to her husband's tape.

Started wearing his trademark white Stetson to hide scars above his left eyebrow (a result of a childhood accident with a coffee table).
Original Job: Forklift operator, car salesman, home builder
Marriage: Denise, 1979
Children: Mattie, 1990; Alexandra, 1993; Dani Grace, 1997

JANET JACKSON

Birthplace: Gary, IN
Birthdate: 5/16/66
Occupation: Singer, actor
Debut: (TV) *Good Times,* 1977
Signature: *Control*, 1986
Facts: With 1986 song "When I Think of You," she and brother Michael became the first siblings in the rock era to have No. 1 songs as soloists.

Paula Abdul was Janet's choreographer before starting her own career.

Played Charlene DuPrey on the TV series *Diff'rent Strokes*.

Estranged husband Elizondo sued her in 2001, claiming that she broke a 1987 promise to divide property acquired before their marriage in 1991, and seeking proceeds from her 1989 album *Janet Jackson's Rhythm Nation 1814* among other assets
Marriages: James DeBarge, 1984 (annulled, 1985); Rene Elizondo Jr., 1991 (separated, 1999)
Famous Relatives: Michael, singer, brother; La Toya, singer, sister; Tito, singer, brother; Randy, singer, brother; Marlon, singer, brother; Jermaine, singer, brother; Jackie, singer, brother
Major Awards: Grammy, Best Music Video—Long Form, *Rhythm Nation 1814*, 1989; Grammy, Best R&B Song, "That's the Way Love Goes," 1993; Grammy, Best Short Form Music Video, "Got 'Till It's Gone," 1997
Quote: "It was always my dream for no one to know I was a Jackson."

JOSHUA JACKSON

Real name: Joshua Carter Jackson
Birthplace: British Columbia, Canada
Birthdate: 6/11/78
Education: High school equivalency
Occupation: Actor
Debut: (Film) *Crooked Hearts*, 1991
Signature: *Dawson's Creek*
Facts: By age nine, Jackson had lived in Vancouver, the U.S. and in Dublin, Ireland, moving 10 different times.

Was expelled from two different high schools, once for poor attendance and once for "being mouthy."

His mother is a casting director. In 1987, he begged her to send him out on auditions and he soon landed a commercial for British Columbia Tourism. She also cast him in his movie debut.

In 1999, he and a friend saved two girls from drowning; the girls then sold the story to *The Star*.

He would eventually like to find time for college. Philosophy is his favorite subject.

Briefly dated Katie Holmes.

Has been estranged from his father for years.
Relationship: Brittany Daniel, actor
Quote: "I'm really a normal guy with an abnormal job."

MICHAEL JACKSON

Birthplace: Gary, IN
Birthdate: 8/29/58
Occupation: Singer, songwriter, actor
Debut: (Stage) Mr. Lucky's, Gary, IN (with Jackson 5), 1966
Signature: *Thriller*, 1983
Facts: Built amusement park on property and maintains a menagerie of animals including Bubbles the Chimp.

In 1985 bought rights to most of the Beatles' songs in a $47.5 million deal.

Gave Elizabeth Taylor away at her marriage to Larry Fortensky in 1991.

Surgery includes four nose jobs, two

nose adjustments, and cleft put in his chin. J. Randy Taraborrelli's unauthorized biography claims that Michael had the surgery to avoid resembling his abusive father as much as possible.

Bought the Best Picture statuette awarded by the Academy for *Gone with the Wind* at auction for $1.54 million.

Plans to build a $500 million dollar amusement park in Warsaw, Poland were stalled when the local citizenry protested the proposed site of the park. After planning to visit Warsaw to discuss the location, he cancelled his trip and financial discussions with a private investor have reportedly stalled.

Infamy: Settled out of court a civil lawsuit alleging child molestation. The boy then refused to testify in a criminal proceeding, so prosecutors declined to press charges.

Accused of including anti-Semitic lyrcs in his song "They Don't Care About Us" on *HIStory;* to stem the controversy, the offending lines were altered on later pressings.

In 1999, an Italian judge ruled that he plagiarized the work of songwriter Al Bano when composing the 1991 song, "Will You Be There," but appeals courts ruled in Jackson's favor in 2000 and 2001.

Famous Relatives: Janet, singer, sister; LaToya, singer, sister; Tito, singer, brother; Randy, singer, brother; Marlon, singer, brother; Jermaine, singer, brother; Jackie, singer, brother

Marriage: Lisa Marie Presley (divorced); Debbie Rowe, 1997 (separated, 1999)

Children: Prince Michael Jr, 1997; Paris Michael Katherine, 1998

Major Awards: Grammy, Best R&B Vocal—Male, "Don't Stop Till You Get Enough," 1979; Grammy, Album of the Year, *Thriller,* 1983; Grammy, Best Pop Vocal—Male, *Thriller,* 1983; Grammy, Best R&B Song, "Billie Jean," 1983; Grammy, Best R&B Vocal—Male, "Billie Jean," 1983; Grammy, Best Recording for Children, *E.T., the Extra-Terrestrial,* 1983; Grammy, Record of the Year, "Beat It," 1984; Grammy, Best Pop Vocal—Male, "Beat It," 1984; Grammy, Song of the Year, "We Are the World" (with Lionel Richie), 1985; Grammy, Best Music Video, Short Form, *Leave Me Alone,* 1989; Grammy, Legend Award, 1993; Grammy, Best Music Video, "Scream," 1995

Quote: "The press exaggerated the plastic surgery. It's just my noes, you know. Elvis had his nose done—Lisa Marie told m.

SAMUEL L. JACKSON

Birthplace: Chattanooga, TN
Birthdate: 12/21/48
Occupation: Actor
Education: Morehouse College
Debut: (Film) *Ragtime,* 1981
Signature: *Pulp Fiction,* 1994
Facts: Angry at Morehouse College's lack of African-American studies and its control by a white governing body, he participated in a protest involving locking up the school's board of trustees, and was expelled in 1969. He later returned to graduate.

In 1991's *Jungle Fever,* Jackson's performance as crackhead Gator won him the first-ever supporting actor award given by the Cannes Film Festival.

Was Bill Cosby's stand-in for three years on *The Cosby Show.*

Infamy: Had a problem with drugs and alcohol for several years. Ironically, his first role after taking a vow of sobriety was as the crack addict Gator.

Original Job: Security guard
Marriage: LaTanya Richardson, 1980
Child: Zoe, 1982

MICK JAGGER

Birthplace: Dartford, England
Birthdate: 7/26/43
Occupation: Singer, songwriter
Education: London School of Economics
Debut: (Song) "Come On" (cover of Chuck Berry original), 1963
Signature: The Rolling Stones
Facts: Went to elementary school with guitarist Keith Richards but lost touch with him until they met again on a London train in 1960.

Sang backup on Carly Simon's 1973 hit, "You're So Vain."

Co-owned the Philadelphia Furies, a soccer team, with Peter Frampton, Rick Wakeman, and Paul Simon.

In agreeing to an annullment, Hall capitulated to Jagger's claim that their 1990 Hindu wedding on Bali was invalid due to incomplete paperwork. She received a reported settlement of $15 million and ownership of their $8 million, 26-room London mansion.

In 2001, London's *Sunday Times* estimated his fortune at $216 million.

Marriages: Bianca Perez Morena de Macias (divorced); Jerry Hall, 1990 (annulled, 1999); Vanessa Neumann (relationship)

Children: Karis, 1970 (with Marsha Hunt). Jade, 1971 (with Bianca Jagger). Elizabeth Scarlett, 1984; James Leroy Augustine, 1985; Georgia May Ayeesha, 1992; Gabriel Luke Beauregard, 1997 (with Jerry Hall). Lucas Maurice, 1999 (with Luciana Morad)

Major Awards: Grammy, Best Album Package, *Tattoo You* (with the Rolling Stones), 1981; Grammy, NARAS Lifetime Achievement Award, 1986; inducted into the Rock and Roll Hall of Fame (with the Rolling Stones), 1989; Grammy, Best Rock Album, *Voodoo Lounge* (with the Rolling Stones), 1994

Quote: "It's a good way of making a living. I think we'll just keep right on doing it."

ALLISON JANNEY

Birthplace: Dayton, OH
Birthdate: 11/19/59
Occupation: Actor
Education: Attended Kenyon College
Debut: (Film) *The Cowboy Way*, 1994; (Off-Broadway) *Fat Men in Skirts*, 1994; (TV) *Guiding Light*, 1994; (Broadway) *Present Laughter*, 1996
Signature: *The West Wing*
Facts: Aspired to be a competitive figure skater before a freak accident in her senior year of high school dashed her plans.

Began acting in college when Kenyon College alumnus Paul Newman cast her in one of his plays.

Stands 6' and is addicted to shopping.

She is a board game fanatic.
Original jobs: Waitress, ice cream scooper
Relationship: Dennis Gagomiros
Major Award: Emmy, Outstanding Supporting Actress, *The West Wing*, 1999–2000
Quote: "I like to have a good time. I love to dance. I love all kinds of music, from salsa to punk, acid rock. My trailer is the most fun to hang out in."

JAY-Z

Real name: Shawn Carter
Birthplace: Brooklyn, NY
Birthdate: 12/4/70
Occupation: Rap artist
Debut: (Single) "In My Lifetime," 1995; (Album) *Reasonable Doubt*, 1996
Signature: "Money Ain't a Thang," 1998
Facts: Grew up in the Marcy Projects in Brooklyn, near the J and Z subway lines.

Was a high-school friend of the late Notorious B.I.G.

Began producing albums for other artists in 1994, and has collaborated with Puff Daddy, Timbaland, and Jermaine Dupri.

Was featured on Mariah Carey's "Heartbreaker."

In 1997, released *Vol. 1…In My Lifetime*—his second album, title notwithstanding.

The chorus of his song "Hard Knock Life," describing life in the ghetto, samples singing children from the family musical *Annie*.

Co-headlined the Hard Knock Life tour, which became rap's biggest-grossing ever—and surprised naysayers by proceeding without any violent incidents.

Is preparing his Roc-a-Wear clothing line.
Infamy: Was a crack cocaine dealer.

In December, 1999, was charged with first-degree assault in a stabbing incident in a New York City nightclub. He was also charged with two earlier assaults at other nightclubs. After turning himself in and pleading not guilty, he was released on $50,000 bail. He and his attorney later claimed to have a videotape taken at the time of the stabbing that would clear Jay-Z of the charge. As of press time, details of any resolution have not been made public.

Was charged with gun possession in New York in 2001.
Major Awards: Grammy, Best Rap Album, *Vol. 2… Hard Knock Life*, 1998
Quote: "When you're part of rap, anything that happens definitely is going to be related back to rap, which is unfair."

WYCLEF JEAN

Real Name: Nelust Wyclef Jean
Birthplace: Port-au-Prince, Haiti
Birthdate: 10/17/69
Education: High school
Occupation: Rap artist, guitarist
Debut: (Album) *Blunted on Reality*, 1993; (Solo Album) *The Carnival*, 1997
Signature: The Fugees
Facts: At age nine, he came to the U.S. with his family, as his Baptist preacher father fled the reign of "Baby Doc" Duvalier.

His mother bought him an acoustic guitar to keep him off the streets. He mastered it—along with the organ, drums, and bass.

Learned English by listening to rap music.

His devout parents would not allow him to listen to any music that was not religious.

Bandmate Prakazrel "Pras" Michel is his cousin; Lauryn Hill he knew from high school.

Originally called Tranzlator Crew, the group changed their name to The Fugees when a long-forgotten 1980s new-wave act called Translator objected.

The Fugees sprang from the trio's feeling of being refugees from mainstream culture and even hip-hop, and from their sense that they found refuge in the music they made.

At one performance, he played the guitar with his teeth, then put on a hockey mask (like Jason from *Friday the 13th*) to thrill the crowd.

Sang at the memorial service for John F. Kennedy Jr. in 1999.
Major Awards: Grammy Award, R&B Vocal by a Duo or Group, "Killing Me Softly with His Song," 1997; Grammy Award, Best Rap Album, 1997
Quote: "My father would whup my ass for playing rap."

PETER JENNINGS

Birthplace: Toronto, Canada
Birthdate: 7/29/38
Occupation: Anchor, senior editor
Education: Carleton University and Rider College
Debut: At age nine, hosted *Peter's People*, a CBC radio show for children, 1947
Signature: *ABC's World News Tonight*
Facts: At 26, was the youngest network anchor ever. ABC removed him after three years. Took over as permanent anchor in 1983.

Original Job: Bank teller and late-night radio host
Marriages: First marriage (divorced); Valerie Godsoe (divorced); Kati Marton (divorced); Kayce Freed, 1997
Children: Elizabeth, 1979; Christopher, c. 1982; (with Kati Marton).
Famous Relative: Charles Jennings, vice president of programming at CBC, father
Awards: 12 News and Documentary Emmys: 7 as correspondent, 3 as anchor, 1 as interviewer, 1 as reporter

JEWEL

Real Name: Jewel Kilcher
Birthplace: Payson, UT
Birthdate: 5/23/74
Occupation: Singer, songwriter
Education: Interlochen Arts Academy High School
Debut: (Album) *Pieces of You,* 1995; (TV) *The Wizard of Oz in Concert;* (Film) *Ride With the Devil,* 1999
Signature: *Pieces of You*
Facts: Was raised by her father in a log cabin on an 800-acre farm near Homer, Alaska, with no running water, an outhouse for a bathroom, and only a coal stove for heat.

At one point, she lived across a canyon from her dad, who yodeled when he wanted her to visit.

Before they divorced, her parents, Atz and Nedra Kilcher, recorded two LPs as a folk duo.

Jewel has been a crackerjack yodeler since she was a small child; experts told her parents it was supposed to be impossible for someone so young to yodel, since the vocal cords aren't well developed.

As a teenager, she spelled her name, "Juel."

When she began singing at coffeehouses, she and her mom lived in adjacent vans, surviving on fruit from nearby orchards and free happy-hour fare from bars.

Ex-boyfriend Sean Penn directed the video for "You Were Meant for Me"; Jewel had it refilmed after their breakup.

Still suffers from a past kidney infection that hospitals refused to treat due to Jewel's then-low income.
Infamy: Is being sued by former manager, Inga Vainshtein, for $10 million. The suit includes charges that Jewel's mother and current manager, Nedra Carroll, consulted channeler Jackie Snyder on business decisions. Snyder, a friend of Jewel's, died of cancer in 1998.
Original Job: Restaurant worker
Relationship: Ty Murray, rodeo champion
Quote: "I'm just this cute blonde folk singer who should be patted on the head. My motto is, 'Candy bars for everybody.'"

BILLY JOEL

Birthplace: Bronx, NY
Birthdate: 5/9/49
Occupation: Singer, songwriter, piano player
Education: High school
Debut: (Song) "You Got Me Hummin'" (cover of Sam and Dave original, with The Hassles), 1965
Signature: "Piano Man," 1973
Facts: Had a suicidal period when he was in his early 20s; after taking pills and swallowing furniture polish, he spent three weeks in Meadowbrook Hospital.

As a Long Island teenager, was a local welterweight boxing champion.

Wrote "New York State of Mind" within 20 minutes of returning home from California in 1975.
Original Job: Rock critic for *Changes* magazine
Marriages: Elizabeth Weber (divorced); Christie Brinkley (divorced, 1994)
Child: Alexa Ray, 1985
Major Awards: Grammy, Record of the Year, "Just the Way You Are," 1978; Grammy, Song of the Year, "Just the Way You Are," 1978; Grammy, Album of the Year, *Billy Joel,* 1979; Grammy, Best Pop Vocal—Male, *52nd Street,* 1979; Grammy, Best Rock Vocal—Male, *Glass Houses,* 1980; Grammy, Best

Recording for Children, *In Harmony 2* (with others), 1982; Grammy, Legend Award, 1991; inducted into Rock and Roll Hall of Fame, 1999

ELTON JOHN

Real Name: Reginald Kenneth Dwight
Birthplace: Pinner, England
Birthdate: 3/25/47
Occupation: Singer, songwriter, piano player
Education: Royal Academy of Music, London
Debut: (Album) *Come Back Baby* (with Bluesology), 1965
Signature: "Candle in the Wind"
Facts: Took his name from first names of Bluesology members Elton Deal and John Baldry.

Wrote "Philadelphia Freedom" in 1975 for Billie Jean King.

Is godfather to Sean Lennon.

Attended London's Royal Academy of Music but quit three weeks before final exams.

Has donated more than $5.5 million—profits from his singles—to his nonprofit care and education foundation.

"Candle in the Wind" is the best-selling single of all time, having sold over 35 million copies.

Had a pacemaker installed in 1999.

Was knighted by Queen Elizabeth in 1998.

In 2000, sued his former accountacts at Pricewaterhouse-Coopers and the management company of John Reid, charging mismanagement of funds and claiming they owed him $28.5 million for tour expenses dating back to the 1980s. The suit was unsuccessful.

In 2001, London's *Sunday Times* estimated his fortune at $216 million."I am not a nest-egg person." His possessions include $13 million worth of homes in Atlanta, London, Nice, and Windsor, and $42 million for clothes, jewelry, art, and "14 or 15 Bentleys."
Infamy: In 1994, *Star* magazine

alleged that he was in a romantic relationship with an Atlanta man. He denied being involved with the man and sued the magazine over the article.

Original Job: Worked at Mills Music Publishers

Marriage: Renate Blauer (divorced, 1988); David Furnish (relationship)

Major Awards: Grammy, Best Pop Performance—Duo or Group, "That's What Friends Are For" (with Dionne & Friends), 1986; Grammy, Best Pop Vocal Performance—Male, "Can You Feel the Love Tonight," 1994; inducted into the Rock and Roll Hall of Fame, 1994; Oscar, Best Original Song, "Can You Feel the Love Tonight," 1994; Grammy, Best Pop Vocal—Male, "Candle in the Wind 1997," 1997; Tony, Best Score, *Aida*, 2000

DON JOHNSON

Birthplace: Flat Creek, MO

Birthdate: 12/15/49

Occupation: Actor

Education: University of Kansas, studied at the American Conservatory Theater in San Francisco

Debut: (Stage) *Fortunes and Men's Eyes*, 1969; (Film) *The Magic Garden of Stanley Sweetheart*, 1970

Signature: *Nash Bridges*

Facts: At age 12, seduced his babysitter. At 16, moved out of his dad's place and moved in with a 26-year-old cocktail waitress. At the University of Kansas, became romantically involved with a drama professor.

Owns a successful race horse, Penny Blues.

Infamy: When he was 12, was caught stealing a car and sent to a juvenile detention home.

Admits to having been addicted to alcohol and cocaine. Says he was sober for ten years, but was treated again for a drinking problem in 1994.

Original Job: Worked in a meat-packing plant

Marriages: a first and second

marriage; Melanie Griffith (divorced, remarried, divorced); Kelley Phleger, 1999

Children: Jesse, 1982 (with Patti D'Arbanville). Dakota, 1989 (with Melanie Griffith). Atherton Grace, 1999.

MAGIC JOHNSON

Real Name: Earvin Johnson

Birthplace: Lansing, MI

Birthdate: 8/14/59

Occupation: Basketball player (retired)

Education: Michigan State University

Facts: On November 7, 1991, announced that he was retiring from basketball after being diagnosed HIV positive. Was diagnosed only months after marrying longtime friend Earleatha "Cookie" Kelly, who was in the early stages of pregnancy. Neither Cookie nor the child have tested positive for the disease.

After his diagnosis, became one of the world's major fundraisers and spokesmen for AIDS.

Given his nickname in high school by a local sportswriter after a game in which he scored 36 points and had 18 rebounds.

Hosted short-lived late-night talk show in 1998.

Now a leading businessman, he has helped launch movie theaters in urban locations in Los Angeles and other cities; owns Starbucks and TGIFriday's franchises, has a music management agency with such clients as Boys II Men and Mase, and a music label with MCA Records.

Infamy: In 1992, admitted he caught the AIDS virus from "messing around with too many women."

Marriage: Earleatha "Cookie" Kelly, 1991

Children: Andre, 1982; Earvin III, 1992; Elisa, 1995 (adopted)

Major Awards/Titles: MVP, National Collegiate Athletic Association Final Four playoff tournament, 1979; MVP, NBA Finals, 1980, 1982, 1987; 3

Time NBA Regular Season MVP; 9 Time All-NBA First Team; 11 Time NBA All-Star; Olympic Gold Medal 1992; Grammy, Best Spoken Word Album, *What You Can Do To Avoid AIDS* (with Robert O'Keefe), 1992

ANGELINA JOLIE

Real Name: Angelina Jolie Voight

Birthplace: Los Angeles, CA

Birthdate: 6/4/75

Occupation: Actor

Education: Attended New York University

Debut: (Film) *Lookin' to Get Out*, 1982. (Stage) *Room Service*

Signature: *Girl Interrupted*, 1999

Facts: Collects daggers, reads about Vlad the Impaler, and has the Japanese word for death tattooed on her shoulder. Other tatoos include a cross, a dragon, the letter H, and the newest, "Billy Bob."

Six years after film debut, began studying acting at age 11.

Originally wanted to be a funeral director.

Dropped last name to develop individual identity.

Appeared in numerous music videos, including some by Meat Loaf, The Lemonheads, and the Rolling Stones.

First lead in a theatrical release was *Hackers,* which costarred her future husband, Jonny Lee Miller.

For her first wedding, she wore black rubber pants and a white shirt with Miller's name written in blood across the back.

Nominated for an Emmy for her roles in *George Wallace* and *Gia*.

She never goes anywhere without Blistex lip balm.

Gave husband Thornton his-and-her cemetery plots as an anniversary present. She carries drops of his blood in a pendant around her neck, and they signed their wills in blood.

Named a United Nations goodwill ambassador for refugees in 2001.

Original Job: Model

Marriages: Jonny Lee Miller

(divorced, 1999); Billy Bob Thornton, 2000

Famous Relatives: Jon Voight, actor, father; Marcheline Bertrand, actor, mother; James Haven Voight, director, brother

Major Award: Oscar, Best Supporting Actress, *Girl Interrupted*, 1999

Quote: "I'm never concerned about going too far. I don't even care if I'm judged."

JAMES EARL JONES

Birthplace: Arkabutla, MS
Birthdate: 1/17/31
Occupation: Actor
Education: Attended University of Michigan
Debut: (Broadway) *The Egghead*, 1957 (understudy); (Film) *Dr. Strangelove*, 1964; (TV) *As the World Turns*, 1966
Facts: Raised by his maternal grandparents after his father left home before he was born and his mother left when he was very young.

He developed a serious stutter at age six, which necessitated communication through written notes in school.

Was drawn to acting after seeing a magazine photo of his father appearing in a Broadway play.

One of his favorite roles was in 1989's *Field of Dreams*.

He was one of the first black regulars on a daytime drama.

Original Jobs: Floor waxer, janitor
Marriages: Julienne Marie Hendricks (divorced); Cecilia Hart, 1982
Child: Flynn Earl Jones, 1983
Famous Relatives: Robert Earl Jones, prizefighter (known as "Battling Bill Stovall") and actor, father
Major Awards: Tony, Outstanding Actor in a Play, *The Great White Hope*, 1969; Grammy, Best Spoken Word Recording, *Great American Documents*, 1976 (with Orson Welles, Helen Hayes, and Henry Fonda); Tony, Best Actor in a Play, *Fences*, 1987; Emmy, *Gabriel's Fire*,

1990; Emmy, Outstanding Supporting Actor in a Miniseries or Special, *Heatwave*, 1990.

Quote: "I was a stutterer, a stammerer, totally impaired vocally, and I still am. I worked on it all my life and I still do. From the beginning of high school through the end of college, my extracurricular activity was using my voice."

QUINCY JONES

Birthplace: Chicago, IL
Birthdate: 3/14/33
Occupation: Composer, producer
Education: Seattle University; Berklee College of Music, Boston Conservatory
Debut: Trumpeter, arranger, for Lionel Hampton Orchestra, 1950
Signature: Produced *Off the Wall*, *Thriller*, and *Bad*
Facts: Established his own label, Qwest, in 1981 and founded *Vibe* magazine.

Scored the TV series *Roots* in 1977.

Has worked with many prominent pop and jazz artists, including Ray Charles, Miles Davis, Ella Fitzgerald, Dizzy Gillespie, Ice-T, Chaka Khan, and Sarah Vaughan.

Middle name is Delight.
Marriages: Jeri Caldwell (divorced); Ulla Anderson (divorced); Peggy Lipton (divorced, 1989); Donya Fiorentino (relationship)
Children: Jolie, 1953 (with Jeri Caldwell). Martina, 1966; Quincy III, 1968 (with Ulla Anderson). Kidada, 1974; Rashida, 1976 (with Peggy Lipton). Kenya, 1993 (with Nastassja Kinski)
Major Award: Grammy, Album of the Year, *Back on the Block*, 1991; Oscar, Jean Hersholt Humanitarian Award, 1995

TOMMY LEE JONES

Birthplace: San Saba, TX
Birthdate: 9/15/46
Occupation: Actor
Education: Harvard University

Debut: (Stage) *A Patriot for Me*, 1969; (TV) *One Life To Live*, 1969; (Film) *Love Story*, 1970
Signature: *The Fugitive*, 1993
Facts: Roomed with Vice President Al Gore while attending Harvard.

Is a champion polo player.

Raises Black Angus cattle on his ranch in San Antonio.
Original Job: Worked in oil fields
Marriages: Katherine Lardner (divorced); Kimberlea Gayle Cloughley (divorced, 1995); Dawn Maria Laurel, 2001
Children: Austin, c. 1992; Victoria, c. 1991 (with Cloughley)
Major Awards: Emmy, Best Actor in a Miniseries, *The Executioner's Song*, 1983; Oscar, Best Supporting Actor, *The Fugitive*, 1993
Quote: "I like to cook. I'm really interested in killing things and eating them."

MICHAEL JORDAN

Birthplace: Brooklyn, NY
Birthdate: 2/17/63
Occupation: Basketball player
Education: University of North Carolina
Signature: Ability to fly.
Facts: He was cut from the varsity basketball team in high school.

Though he said, "This is my dream," after hitting his first homer playing professional baseball in the minor leagues, he soon left baseball to return to basketball.

In his first game back as a Bull against archrival Knicks in 1995, some fans paid scalpers more than $1,000 a ticket. They were not disappointed; he scored 55 points.

Took control of the Washington Wizards' basketball operations in 2000. Sold back his stake and resigned his position to play basketball for the team in 2001.

Launched Hidden Beach Recordings, a new record label, in 2000.
Marriage: Juanita Vanoy, 1989
Children: Jeffrey Michael, 1988;

Marcus James, 1990; Jasmine Mickael, 1992

Major Awards/Titles: NCAA College Player of the Year 1984; MVP NBA Finals, 1991, 1992, 1993, 1996, 1998; four-time NBA Regular Season MVP; eight-time All NBA First Team; ten-time NBA All-Star; eight-time Winner of NBA Scoring Title; Gold Medal at 1984 and 1992 Olympics.

ASHLEY JUDD

Birthplace: Los Angeles, CA
Birthdate: 4/19/68
Occupation: Actor
Education: University of Kentucky
Debut: (Film) *Kuffs*, 1992; (TV) *Sisters*, 1995
Signature: *Double Jeopardy*, 1999
Facts: Grew up dirt poor in various Kentucky homes lacking electricity, running water or a telephone. Was shuttled around to 12 different schools while Naomi and Wynonna tried to make it in the music business.

As a teenager she cleaned her sister and mother's tour bus for $10 a day.

Graduated Phi Beta Kappa from college.

Suffered a severe depression in 1996 that lasted for several months.

Used to date Matthew McConaughey and Michael Bolton.
Relationship: Dario Franchitti, race car driver (engaged, 2000)
Famous Relatives: Naomi Judd, singer, mother; Wynonna, singer, sister

MIKE JUDGE

Birthplace: Guayaqyuil, Ecuador
Birthdate: 10/17/62
Occupation: Animator, voice actor
Education: University of California at San Diego
Debut: (Film short) *Office Space* 1991; (TV) *Beavis and Butt-head*, 1993; (Film) *Beavis and Butt-head Do America*, 1996
Signature: *Beavis and Butt-head*
Facts: Grew up in Albuquerque, New Mexico, with his father, an archaeology professor, and his school librarian mother.

Was employee of the month at Whataburger, a fast-food emporium, in June 1979. He drew on his early experiences in such jobs to form Beavis and Butt-head.

While studying physics in college, he took a year off to play bass. After receiving his degree and suffering tedium of two engineering jobs, he moved to Texas to briefly try his hand as a blues musician.

After its 1993 debut, *Beavis and Butt-head* was blamed for several destructive acts committed by young people. MTV eventually responded by moving the program to a later time slot and requesting that Judge tone down references to pyromania and animal cruelty.

He taught himself animation, drawing on books from the library and using an old Bolex 16mm movie camera with his own system of track reading.
Original Jobs: Electrical engineer, professional musician
Marriage: Francesca Morocco, 1989

Children: Julia, 1991; daughter, 1994
Quote: "Sometimes the truth comes out if you let yourself be simpleminded."

MELINA KANAKAREDES

Birthplace: Akron, OH
Birthdate: 4/23/67
Occupation: Actor
Education: Attended Ohio State University, Point Park College
Debut: (Film) *Bleeding Hearts*, 1994; (TV) *One Life to Live*, 1989
Signature: *Providence*
Facts: Growing up, she spent many hours in her family's candy store.

First performed at age 8 in a local community theater and was a runner-up in the Miss Ohio beauty pageant.

Had a recurring role as Jimmy Smits's reporter girlfriend on *NYPD Blue* before landing *Providence*.

Known for researching her projects, she visited a coroner's office for *Leaving L.A.* and plastic surgeons for *Providence*.

Her extended family is so large that she and her husband invited 550 guests to their wedding.

She was cast for *Providence* without an audition and the other members of the cast were chosen on the basis of their chemistry with her.

She never leaves home without her Braun electric toothbrush.

Met her husband at Ohio State in Sigma Epsilon Phi, a group that tried to get Greek-American kids to socialize with the hope that they will eventually marry.
Original Jobs: Singer, dancer, model, waitress on World Yacht
Marriage: Peter Constantinides, 1992
Child: Zoe, 2000
Quote: "My sanity is my family. Actually, my sanity and my insanity is my family. I'm Greek, and togetherness is a big part of our culture."

DONNA KARAN

Real Name: Donna Faske
Birthplace: Forest Hills, NY
Birthdate: 10/2/48
Occupation: Fashion designer
Education: Parsons School of Design
Signature: DKNY clothes
Facts: While in college, worked for designers Chuck Howard and Liz Claiborne.

After serving a long apprenticeship with the Anne Klein collection, at age 26 was given full creative control by the principal owner of the firm after Anne Klein died of cancer in 1974.

Close personal friend to many stars including Barbra Streisand.
Original Job: Sales clerk at a Long Island dress shop
Marriages: Mark Karan (divorced), Stephen Weiss, 1983
Child: Cory, 1955 (stepson); Lisa,

1957 (stepdaughter); Gabrielle, 1974 (with Mark Karan)
Major Awards: Coty Award, 1977, 1981; named to Coty Hall of Fame, 1984

DIANE KEATON

Real Name: Diane Hall
Birthplace: Los Angeles, CA
Birthdate: 1/5/46
Occupation: Actor, director, producer
Education: Santa Ana College
Debut: (Broadway) *Hair*, 1968; (Film) *Lovers and Other Strangers*, 1970; (as Director) *Heaven*, 1987
Signature: *Annie Hall*, 1977
Facts: When starting out as an actress, she used her sister's name, Dorrie Hall.

After making her Broadway debut in *Hair*, became known as the girl who would not remove her clothes in the finale.

Has been linked with Woody Allen, Warren Beatty, and Al Pacino.

Her college named a street after her in 2000.

Directed music videos for Belinda Carlisle's "Heaven is a Place on Earth" and "I Get Weak."

Has published three collections of photography.
Original job: Photographer
Children: Dexter, 1995 (adopted); Duke, 2001 (adopted)
Major Award: Academy Award, Best Actress, *Annie Hall*, 1977
Quote: "It's my nature to be cautious and a little bit...leery."

CATHERINE KEENER

Birthplace: Miami, FL
Birthdate: 3/23/59
Occupation: Actor
Education: Wheaton College
Debut: (Film) *About Last Night*, 1986; (TV) *The Alan King Show*, 1986
Signature: *Being John Malkovich*, 1999
Facts: Appeared in a 1992 episode of *Seinfeld* as Jerry's girlfriend.

Met her husband in 1987 on the set of *Survival Quest*. He saved her when she got caught in a heavy current and was carried out into the river during filming.

Was temporarily expelled in the eleventh grade and considered the chief instigator of her crowd of high school friends.
Original job: Secretary
Marriage: Dermot Mulroney, 1991
Child: Clyde, 1999
Quote: "When people are scrutinizing how you look and what you sound like or how big or small you are, you have to know that it's not personal."

HARVEY KEITEL

Birthplace: Brooklyn, NY
Birthdate: 5/13/39
Occupation: Actor, producer
Education: Studied with Lee Strasberg at the Actor's Studio and Stella Adler
Debut: (Film) *Who's That Knocking at My Door?*, 1968
Signature: *The Piano*
Facts: Joined the U.S. Marine Corps at age 16 and served in Lebanon.

Answered a newspaper ad placed by Martin Scorsese, then an NYU student director, seeking actors for his first film in 1965, which started their professional relationship.

Was cast as the lead in *Apocalypse Now*, but had a falling out with director Francis Ford Coppola and was fired on location in the Philippines. He was replaced by Martin Sheen.

As a child, Keitel had a severe stutter.

Unusual among Hollywood actors for his willingness to show frontal nudity in his films *(The Piano, Bad Lieutenant)*.
Infamy: Was asked to leave the Alexander Hamilton Vocational School in Brooklyn because of truancy.

His ex-wife filed for Chapter 11 protection in 1999, and claimed that her protracted custody battle (she was awarded sole custody in 1996, now being challenged) with Keitel was the cause after paying nearly $2 million in legal fees.
Original Job: Shoe salesman
Marriages: Lorraine Bracco (divorced, 1992); Daphna Kastner, actor-filmmaker
Child: Stella, 1986

DAVID E. KELLEY

Birthplace: Waterville, ME
Birthdate: 4/4/56
Occupation: Producer, scriptwriter
Education: Princeton University, Boston University Law School
Debut: (TV writing) *L.A. Law*, 1986
Signature: *Ally McBeal*
Facts: While working at a law firm, wrote a screenplay about young lawyers which an agent sent to Steven Bochco. Soon hired for the then-fledgling *L.A. Law*, he took a leave from his firm rather than resign.

Simultaneously wrote every episode of *Chicago Hope* and *Picket Fences* in 1994 and *Ally McBeal* and *The Practice* several years later.

Signed a deal with Fox TV in 2000 that will make him the highest-paid TV producer ever. His gross over a 6-year contract will be over $300 million.
Original Job: Attorney
Marriage: Michelle Pfeiffer, 1993
Children: Claudia Rose, 1993 (adopted); John Henry, 1994
Major Awards: Emmy, Outstanding Drama Series, *L.A. Law*, 1989; Emmy, Outstanding Drama Series, *L.A. Law*, 1990; Emmy, Outstanding Writing in a Drama Series, *L.A. Law*, 1990; Emmy, Outstanding Drama Series, *L.A. Law*, 1991; Emmy, Outstanding Writing in a Drama Series, *L.A. Law*, 1991; Emmy, Outstanding Drama Series, *Picket Fences*, 1993; Emmy, Outstanding Drama Series, *Picket Fences*, 1994; Emmy, Outstanding Drama Series, *The Practice*, 1998, 1999; Emmy, Outstanding Comedy Series, *Ally McBeal*, 1999

KID ROCK

Real Name: Robert James Ritchie
Birthplace: Rome, MI
Birthdate: c. 1972
Occupation: Rapper, rock musician
Debut: Grit Sandwiches for Breakfast, 1990
Signature: Devil Without a Cause, 1998
Facts: Despite his act's celebration of "white trash," Rock grew up in a lakefront home with six acres of land.

Learned to scratch with turntables at urban house parties. The mostly black crowds gave him his stage name by crying, "Look at that white kid rock!"

His mother kicked him out of the house when he wouldn't support his brother in rehab.

When preparing Devil Without a Cause, clashed with record labels executives over his emphasis on rap, his disposition toward ballads, and the title cut's "I'm going platinum" boast.

Has a contract rider demanding Pabst Blue Ribbon in his dressing room.

His stage show featured an eight-foot-tall middle finger.

Describes his cleanliness as "anal."
Infamy: Sold crack as a teen.

The FCC declared "Yodeling in the Valley" from his debut "obscene, indecent and profane."
Child: Robert Jr., 1993 (with Kelly Russell)
Quote: "I've been into this music since I was eleven years old—purchased it, played it, loved it. If people are going to have a problem with me performing it, I'm like, 'F—you and your black and white s—.' "

NICOLE KIDMAN

Birthplace: Hawaii
Birthdate: 6/20/67
Occupation: Actor

Education: St. Martin's Youth Theatre, Melbourne, Australia
Debut: (Film) Bush Christmas, 1983 [see page 68 for a complete filmography]
Signature: To Die For, 1995
Facts: Became an overnight star in Australia with her performance in the miniseries Vietnam, 1988.

Joined the Church of Scientology, of which husband Cruise is a devoted member.

Had a miscarriage in mid-March of 2001, after husband Cruise filed for divorce the month before.
Infamy: Won $580,000 in libel damages in 1998 from Britain's Express on Sunday for a story that claimed Kidman and her husband might be closet gays in a sham marriage.

Appeared nude on stage (for approximately 14 seconds) in a limited-run Broadway production of David Hare's The Blue Room in 1999.

Sued the Star in 1999 for claiming that sex experts had to coach Kidman and her husband in the art of lovemaking for Eyes Wide Shut.
Marriage: Tom Cruise, 1990 (divorced, 2001)
Children: Isabella Jane, 1993; Connor Antony, 1995; (both adopted)
Quote: "Well, I can wear heels now." (on the bright side of her divorce)

CRAIG KILBORN

Birthplace: Hastings, MN
Birthdate: 8/24/62
Occupation: Comedian, sports announcer
Education: Montana State University
Debut: (TV) Salinas, CA's KCBA-TV sports anchor, 1987
Signature: The Daily Show
Facts: After college, was offered a spot on a professional basketball team in Luxembourg. Turned down the $600/month job to try his luck in Hollywood.

Stands 6' 4".

Daily Show's "5 Questions" was inspired by a failed pickup line he once used in a Manhattan bar.

Infamy: Long-running feud with Daily Show female head writer resulted in his one-week suspension after he called her and other female staffers a derogatory name in Esquire magazine and suggested that she would perform a sex act on him if requested.

In 1999, admitted to having an 11-year-old son after a tabloid prepared to break the story.
Original Job: Traffic school instructor
Child: son

VAL KILMER

Birthplace: Los Angeles, CA
Birthdate: 12/31/59
Occupation: Actor
Education: Hollywood Professional School, Juilliard
Debut: (Stage) Slab Boys, 1983; (TV) One Too Many, 1985; (Film) Top Secret!, 1984
Signature: The Doors, 1991
Facts: Grew up in Chatsworth, CA, across the road from the Roy Rogers ranch. Was the middle child of three boys.

His younger brother, Wesley, drowned right before he left for Juilliard.

At 17, was the youngest person ever accepted to Juilliard's drama school. Cowrote a play with Juilliard classmates, How It All Began; starred in an off-Broadway production at the New York Shakespeare Festival.

Met Joanne Whalley on the set of Willow in 1988. Pursued her persistently until she finally agreed to marry him.

Provided much of the vocals for the film The Doors.

Lives in a cabin in Tesuque, NM. Is part Cherokee and spends his leisure time exploring the Southwest.
Infamy: On the set of The Island of Dr. Moreau, Kilmer burned a cameraman's face with a cigarette.
Marriage: Joanne Whalley (divorced, 1995)

Children: Mercedes, 1991; Jack, 1995
Famous Relatives: Joyce Kilmer, poet, second cousin twice removed
Quote: "I don't make any pretense about being normal. I'm not."

LARRY KING

Real Name: Lawrence Harvey Zeiger
Birthplace: Brooklyn, NY
Birthdate: 11/19/33
Occupation: Talk show host
Facts: Father died of a heart attack when he was 10, and he grew up on public assistance.

As a teenager, ran away to get married. Had the ceremony annulled shortly thereafter.

Graduated from high school just one point above passing.

In February of 1992, Ross Perot announced his bid for the presidency on *Larry King Live*.
Infamy: In December of 1971, he was arrested for stealing money a financier had given him for the New Orleans D.A.'s investigation into the death of John F. Kennedy. King had used the money to pay taxes after he had blown his own money on Cadillacs, expensive restaurants, and gambling debts. The charge was eventually dropped.
Original Job: Janitor at a local AM radio station in Florida
Marriages: Frada Miller, c. 1953 (annulled); Alene Akins, c. 1961 (divorced, remarried, divorced, 1963); Mickey Sutphin, 1964 (divorced, 1968); Sharon Leporte, 1976 (divorced, 1983); Julie Alexander, 1989 (divorced, 1992); Rama Fox (engaged, 1992; never married); Deanna Lund (engaged, 1995; never married); Shawn Southwick, 1997
Children: Andy (adopted); Chaia, 1967; (with Alene Akins). Larry Jr., 1961 (mother unknown). Kelly (with Mickey Sutphin). Chance Armstrong, 1999; Cannon Edward, 2000
Major Award: One News and Documentary Emmy, as interviewer

STEPHEN KING

Birthplace: Portland, ME
Birthdate: 9/21/47
Occupation: Author
Education: University of Maine
Debut: (Book) *Carrie*, 1974
Signature: *The Shining*
Facts: Family was deserted by father, who went out for a pack of cigarettes and never returned.

Wrote first short story at age 7.

Had his first story published in a comic book fan magazine, *Comics Review*, in 1965.

Was working as a high school English teacher at Hampden Academy, in Maine, when his first book was published.

Used the pseudonym Richard Bachman for five novels, including *The Running Man* (made into an Arnold Schwarzenegger film, 1987).

His tales have been turned into seven TV movies and 27 feature films.

Rob Reiner's production company Castle Rock is named after the fictional Maine town in which many King tales are set.

Underwent 5 operations to set broken bones after he was hit by Bryan Smith, an out-of-control motorist, in 1999 while walking alongside the road in Maine. Criticized prosecutors in 2000 for allowing Smith to plead guilty to a lesser charge of driving to endanger, calling the plea agreement "irresponsible public business."

His e-book, "Riding the Bullet," racked up 400,000 orders during its first 24 hours for sale.

In 2000, he started posting installments of a rewritten serialized novel, *The Plant*, on his Web site and asked readers to pay for each installment onthe honor system.
Original Job: Laborer in an industrial laundry
Marriage: Tabitha Spruce, 1971
Children: Naomi, 1970; Joe, 1972; Owen, 1977

GREG KINNEAR

Birthplace: Logansport, IN
Birthdate: 6/17/63
Occupation: Actor
Education: University of Arizona
Debut: (TV) *Movietime*, 1987; (Film) *Sabrina*, 1995
Signature: *As Good As It Gets*, 1997
Facts: Lived in Beirut, Lebanon, with family and then evacuated to Athens, Greece, when the Lebanese civil war broke out.

Worked on the advertising campaigns for such films as *Space Sluts in the Slammer, The Imp*, and the *Ghoulies* series.

Hosted syndicated action game show, *College Mad House*.
Marriage: Helen Labdon, 1999

CHRIS KIRKPATRICK

Birthplace: Clarion, PA
Birthdate: 10/17/71
Occupation: Singer
Education: Valencia Community College
Debut: (Single) "I Want You Back," 1996; (Album) **NSYNC*, 1996 (American release, 1998)
Signature: *No Strings Attached*, 2000
Facts: Grew up in near-poverty.

Graduated from college with Backstreet Boy Howie Dorough.

When the band switched record labels, they scrapped months' worth of work to make a completely new beginning.

No Strings Attached smashed CD sales records, moving 1.13 million copies on the day of its release and 2.4 million within a week.

Would like to launch a clothing line.
Infamy: 'N Sync broke with their original record label and management over compensation. Suits and countersuits flew before a settlement was reached, allegedly favoring the band.
Original Job: Performer at Universal Studios Florida theme park

Quote: "We're not going to pierce everything that we have and paint our faces trying to get a different market."

CALVIN KLEIN

Real Name: Richard Klein
Birthplace: New York, NY
Birthdate: 11/19/42
Occupation: Fashion designer
Education: Fashion Institute of Technology
Facts: Rescued his daughter from kidnappers in 1978.

As a boy in the Bronx, grew up around the corner from Ralph Lifshitz (now Ralph Lauren).

Former junk bond czar Michael Milken issued $80 million in high-interest Klein bonds in the '80s.
Infamy: Was addicted to valium and alcohol in the '80s, and attended a Minnesota rehabilitation center for 31 days in 1988.
Marriages: Jayne Centre, 1964 (divorced, 1974); Kelly Rector, 1986 (separated, 1996)
Child: Marci, 1966 (with Jayne Centre)
Major Awards: Coty Award, 1973, 1974, 1975; elected to American Fashion Critics Circle Hall of Fame, 1975; Council of Fashion Designers of America Award, 1994
Quote: "Anything I've ever wanted to do, I've done. Anyone I've wanted to be with, I've had."

HEIDI KLUM

Birthplace: Germany
Birthdate: 1973
Occupation: Model
Facts: She was the 1998 *Sports Illustrated* swimsuit-issue cover girl.

Has been nicknamed "The Body." She's 5'9".

Her husband proposed to her atop the Empire State Building.
Marriage: Ric Pipino, 1997
Quote: "On the runway you always wish your body was a little tighter,

and you worry that if you walk too fast things start to jiggle."

JOHNNY KNOXVILLE

Real Name: Philip John Clapp
Birthplace: Knoxville, TN
Birthdate: 3/11/71
Occupation: Actor
Education: Attended the American Academy of Dramatic Arts
Debut: (Film) *Desert Blues*, 1995; (TV) *Jackass*, 2000
Signature: *Jackass*
Facts: Received attention from television networks after a videotape of him testing self-defense weapons on himself made the rounds in Hollywood.

He has asthma; as a child, he almost died when he got the flu, pneumonia, and bronchitis all at the same time.

Performed stunts in the 1993 film *Robin Hood: Men in Tights*.

In one episode of *Jackass*, he had the contents of a Porta-John poured over him.
Infamy: Imitating stunts on *Jackass*, two 12-year-olds tried to emulate the human BBQ and wound up with second and third degree burns. A 17-year-old drove a 1983 Honda Civic into a 16-year-old friend while their other friend was videotaping it. In another incident, a 19-year-old wearing a hospital gown and waving a chainsaw ran into Sunday afternoon traffic.
Original Job: Writer for skateboard magazine *Big Brother*
Marriage: Melanie
Child: Madison, 1996

BEYONCE KNOWLES

Birthplace: Houston, TX
Birthdate: 9/4/81
Occupation: Singer
Debut: (Album) *Destiny's Child*, 1998
Signature: Destiny's Child
Facts: Formed her first group, Girls Tyme, at age 9 with fellow Destiny's

Child singer Kelly Rowland.

Her father manages her group and her mother is their stylist.

Destiny's Child's second album, *The Writing's on the Wall* (1999), sold more than 9 million copies.

Starred in MTV's hip-hop update of the opera *Carmen* in 2001.
Quote: "I just hope people don't get sick of us. I'm sick of us, and I'm in Destiny's Child."

TED KOPPEL

Birthplace: Lancashire, England
Birthdate: 2/8/40
Occupation: Broadcast journalist
Education: Syracuse University, Stanford University
Debut: (Radio) WMCA radio
Signature: *Nightline*
Facts: Author, *Adlai Stevenson: In the National Interest*.

When he joined ABC in 1963, he was the youngest news reporter ever to join a network.

Emigrated to the U.S. from England in 1953.
Marriage: Grace Anne Dorney, 1963
Children: Andrea, 1963; Deidre, 1965; Andrew, 1970; Tara, 1971
Major Awards: 32 News and Documentary Emmys: 22 as Anchor/Managing Editor, 7 as correspondent, 2 as interviewer, 1 as reporter; elected to the Emmy Hall of Fame, 1991

ANNA KOURNIKOVA

Birthplace: Moscow, Russia
Birthdate: 6/7/81
Occupation: Tennis player
Facts: At age nine, she left Russia for Florida, to live and train at Nick Bollettieri's Tennis Academy. She broke away from Bollettieri in 1997, made the semifinals in her Wimbledon debut and became the No. 1 junior player in the world.

Her father was a Greco-Roman wrestling champion, and her mother ran the 400 meters.

Won the doubles title with Martina

Hingis at the Australian Open in 1999, her only major title.

Has not cut her waist-length hair since she was seven.

Is the most downloaded athlete on the Web, far outpacing Michael Jordan. There are an estimated 18,000 Web pages devoted to her.

With multiple endorsement deals, she earns an estimated $10 to $14 million a year (less than a million of which is from playing tennis).

Formerly involved with hockey player Sergei Fedorov.

Relationship: Pavel Bure, hockey player

Quote: "I'm still a virgin. I do not let anyone even have a peep in my bed…not for love [or] affection."

JANE KRAKOWSKI

Birthplace: Parsippany, NJ
Birthdate: 9/11/68
Occupation: Actor, singer, dancer
Education: Professional Children's School
Debut: (Film) *National Lampoon's Vacation,* 1983; (TV) *Search for Tomorrow,* 1984; (Stage) *Starlight Express,* 1987
Signature: *Ally McBeal*
Facts: Twice nominated for a Daytime Emmy for her role in *Search for Tomorrow,* which she landed at age 14.

Made her broadway debut in *Starlight Express* at the age of 18. She was one of only four cast members to stay for its two-year run.

Earned a Tony nomination for her role in *Grand Hotel* in 1990.

She has recorded music by Sondheim, Burt Bacharach, and Paul Simon, and recently signed a contract for a new solo album.
Original Job: Performing at industrial fashion shows
Relationship: Charles Hart

DIANA KRALL

Birthplace: Nanaimo, Canada
Birthdate: 4/16/64
Occupation: Singer, pianist
Education: Berklee School of Music
Debut: (Album) *Stepping Out,* 1993; (Movie) *At First Sight,* 1999
Signature: "Peel Me a Grape," 1997
Facts: Major influences include Shirley Horn, Willie Nelson, and her father's record collection.

Regularly played lounge piano jobs in Nanaimo at 15.

As a student in Boston, had a moonlighting gig playing "to nobody" for four years. "They didn't care. They just wanted to have someone in there, playing."

Made recurring appearances on *Melrose Place.*

Music video "Why Should I Care?" was directed by Clint Eastwood.

Her album *When I Look Into Your Eyes* is one of the few jazz albums to ever be nominated for an Album of the Year Grammy.

Is currently the bestselling jazz artist in the world.
Major Award: Grammy, Jazz Vocal Album of the Year, 1999
Quote: "Hey, I'm a cowgirl who loves to ride horses on the beach, but I'm also a girl who likes clothes and likes to look nice. So why shouldn't I have a beautiful [album] cover? I'm confident enough in my music that I don't have to apologize for that."

LENNY KRAVITZ

Birthplace: Brooklyn, NY
Birthdate: 5/24/64
Occupation: Singer, songwriter, musician
Debut: *Let Love Rule,* 1989
Signature: "It Ain't Over 'Til It's Over"
Facts: As a child, sang in the California Boys Choir.

Though he jams with musicians on tour, in the studio he prefers to play all parts himself.

Cowrote Madonna's "Justify My Love" and Aerosmith's "Line Up."

Cut off his distinctive long dreadlocks "to change my energy… It had to do with getting rid of that baggage from the last 10 years."
Marriage: Lisa Bonet (divorced)
Children: Zoe, 1988
Famous Relative: Roxie Roker, actor, mother, deceased 1995
Major Award: Grammy, Best Rock Vocal—Male, "Fly Away," 1998; Grammy, Best Rock Vocal—Male, "Again," 2001
Quote: "Maybe someday I'll do something that no one's heard, I don't know. But at least I'm doing what God put in me to come out."

LISA KUDROW

Birthplace: Encino, CA
Birthdate: 7/30/63
Occupation: Actor
Education: Vassar College
Debut: (TV) *Cheers,* 1982
Signature: *Friends*
Facts: Earned her B.S. in sociobiology, intent on being a doctor like her father, a renowned headache expert. Decided to become a comic actor when she saw Jon Lovitz, her brother's childhood friend, make it on *Saturday Night Live.*

Was on the tennis team in college.

Her movie debut in 1990's *Impulse* ended up completely cut from the film. Later, she was hired but soon fired as Roz on the pilot for *Frasier.*

Grew up with a pool table in her house and is something of a pool shark, able to perform many difficult trick shots.

In 2000, along with *Friends* costars, received a salary increase from $125,000 to $750,000 per episode.
Marriage: Michel Stern, 1995
Child: Julian Murray, 1998
Major Award: Emmy, Best Supporting Actress in a Comedy Series, *Friends,* 1998

EMERIL LAGASSE

Birthplace: Fall River, MA
Birthdate: 10/15/59
Occupation: Chef, television show host
Education: Johnson and Wales University
Debut: (TV) *Essence of Emeril*, 1993
Signature: "Whoo!" "Bam!" "Pow!"
Facts: Interest in cooking began when he was growing up with his French-Canadian father and Portuguese mother.

Had taught himself how to play trombone, trumpet, flute, and drums, played in a Portuguese band, but turned down a scholarship to the New England Conservatory of Music to pursue culinary arts.

Raises hogs to produce farm-fresh andouille sausage, bacon, and ham, and is a firm believer in organically grown produce.
Original Job: Dishwasher in a Portuguese bakery
Marriages: Elizabeth (divorced, c. 1982); Tari Hohn (divorced, 1996); Alden Lovelace, 2000
Children: Jessica, c. 1980; Jillian, c. 1982 (with Elizabeth)
Quote: "I've been a big Spam fan for a long time."

RICKI LAKE

Birthplace: New York, NY
Birthdate: 9/21/68
Occupation: Actor, talk show host
Education: Ithaca College
Debut: (Film) *Hairspray*, 1988
Signature: *The Ricki Lake Show*
Facts: This once-dumpy star of John Waters' cult films like *Cry Baby* lost 125 pounds over a three-year period.

Plays the flute, piccolo, clarinet, and piano.
Infamy: Arrested in 1994 for criminal mischief for her part in a People for the Ethical Treatment of Animals attack on the offices of designer Karl Lagerfeld.
Original Job: Cabaret singer, appeared off-Broadway in 1983
Marriage: Rob Sussman, 1994

Children: Milo Sebastian, 1997; Owen Tyler, 2001

NATHAN LANE

Real Name: Joseph Lane
Birthplace: Jersey City, NJ
Birthdate: 2/3/56
Occupation: Actor
Education: High school
Debut: (Stage) *A Midsummer Night's Dream*, 1978; (Film) *Ironweed*, 1987
Signature: *The Birdcage*, 1996
Facts: Took the name Nathan at age 22 after playing Nathan Detroit in a *Guys and Dolls* dinner-theater show, since there was another Joe Lane in Actors' Equity.

His truckdriver father drank himself to death when Lane was 11. Lane, too, had a drinking problem for two decades, one he kicked only a few years ago.

Playwright Terrence McNally wrote several plays specifically for him.

Played the voice of Timon, the wisecracking meerkat in *The Lion King.*
Original Job: Police bail interviewer
Major Award: Tony, Best Actor (Musical), *A Funny Thing Happened on the Way to the Forum*, 1996; Emmy, Outstanding Performer in an Animated Program, *Disney's Teacher's Pet*, 2000; Tony, Best Actor (Musical), *The Producers*, 2001

K.D. LANG

Real Name: Katherine Dawn Lang
Birthplace: Consort, Canada
Birthdate: 11/2/61
Occupation: Singer, songwriter
Education: Attended college in Red Deer, Alberta, Canada
Debut: (Album) *A Truly Western Experience*, 1984
Signature: "Constant Craving," 1992
Facts: Acted in the movie *Salmonberries,* 1991.

Recorded a duet with Roy Orbison on a remake of his song "Crying" in 1988, shortly before he died.

Her recordings have been boycotted in the conservative areas of the South and cattle ranching areas of central Canada because she is a lesbian and an animal rights activist.
Original Job: Performance artist
Relationship: Leisha Hailey
Major Awards: Grammy, Best Country Vocal—Collaboration, "Crying" (with Roy Orbison), 1988; Grammy, Best Country Vocaynl—Female, "Absolute Torch and Twang," 1989; Grammy, Best Pop Vocal—Female, "Constant Craving," 1992
Quote: "I have a little bit of penis envy. They're ridiculous, but they're cool."

JESSICA LANGE

Birthplace: Cloquet, MN
Birthdate: 4/20/49
Occupation: Actor
Education: University of Minnesota
Debut: (Film) *King Kong*, 1976
Signature: *Frances*, 1982
Facts: Raised in a depression-prone family with an alcoholic father who moved the family repeatedly, Lange adopted a full-blown, travel-and-party lifestyle as a young adult.

Had a relationship (and a child) with Mikhail Baryshnikov.

The 1994 film *Blue Sky*, for which she won a best actress Academy Award (after four previous nominations), languished in a bank vault after it was made in 1991 because its studio, Orion Pictures, had declared bankruptcy.
Original Jobs: Dancer, model
Marriage: Paco Grande (divorced, 1982); Sam Shepard (relationship)
Children: Alexandra,1981 (with Mikhail Baryshnikov). Hannah Jane, 1985; Samuel Walker, 1987
Major Awards: Oscar, Best Supporting Actress, *Tootsie*, 1982; Oscar, Best Actress, *Blue Sky*, 1994
Quote: "I did bail on the glamor thing early. And now I look back and think oh, hell, I should have done it for another five or 10 years…I'm

tired of thinking I have to rip my heart out for every character."

ANGELA LANSBURY

Birthplace: London, England
Birthdate: 10/16/25
Occupation: Actor
Education: Webber-Douglas School of Singing and Dramatic Art, Feagin School of Drama and Radio
Debut: (Film) *Gaslight*, 1944
Signature: *Murder, She Wrote*
Facts: Immigrated with her family to the U.S. when the Germans began to bomb London in World War II.

In 1943, went to MGM to audition for *The Picture of Dorian Gray* and was told the studio was looking for someone to play the role of the maid in *Gaslight*. She auditioned and got it.

In the seven years she was under contract to MGM, she appeared in 70 films.
Original Job: Ticket-taker in the theater in which her mother worked, clerk in department store
Marriages: Richard Cromwell (divorced); Peter Pullen Shaw, 1949
Children: David, 1944 (stepson); Anthony Peter, 1952; Deidre Angela, 1953
Famous Relatives: Moyna McGill, actor, mother; David Lansbury, actor, nephew
Major Awards: Tony, Best Actress (Musical), *Mame*, 1966; Tony, Best Actress (Musical), *Dear World*, 1969; Tony, Best Actress (Musical), *Gypsy*, 1975; Tony, Best Actress (Musical), *Sweeney Todd*, 1979

ERIQ LASALLE

Birthplace: Hartford, CT
Birthdate: 7/23/62
Occupation: Actor, director
Education: New York University; attended Julliard
Debut: (Film) *Coming to America*, 1988
Signature: *ER*
Facts: Was once a competitor in martial arts.

After four years of unsuccessfully shopping a screenplay he wrote and wanted to direct, he borrowed $140,000 and some equipment and filmed a short version of the work himself.

Along with the four other original, continuing *ER* cast members, received a $1 million bonus in 1998 from Warner Bros. Television.
Marriage: Angela Johnson (engaged; never married)

MATT LAUER

Birthplace: New York, NY
Birthdate: 12/30/57
Occupation: Newscaster, producer
Education: Ohio University
Debut: (TV) WOWK-TV, Huntington, WV, 1980
Signature: *Today*
Facts: Quit college for a TV job four credits shy of graduation in 1979; finally got the degree 18 years later by writing a paper on his work experience.

Hosted *9 Broadcast Plaza*, a low-budget tabloid talk show, for two years, but was fired when he refused to do live commercials during the program. Months later, desperate for a job, he applied for a tree-trimming position in upstate New York. When the phone rang, however, it was NBC, asking him to host a local news show.

Appeared 150 times as guest-host of *Today* before landing the permanent slot.

Has an impressive 8 handicap in golf.
Marriages: Nancy Alspaugh (divorced); Annette Roque, 1998
Child: Jack Matthew, 2001

RALPH LAUREN

Real Name: Ralph Lifshitz
Birthplace: Bronx, NY
Birthdate: 10/14/39
Occupation: Designer
Education: Attended City College of New York

Facts: Growing up in the Moshulu Park area of New York, Lauren lived two blocks from Calvin Klein.

As a youth, he was drawn to movies and the novels of F. Scott Fitzgerald.

While attending high school in the Bronx, he worked part-time as a department store stockboy and spent most of his earnings on clothes.

After a stint in the army, he was hired as a designer by Beau Brummell Ties. His unusual, wider products sold well, and within a year he formed his own company—Polo—with a loan of $50,000.

He is the only American designer who manufactures and licenses his own designs.

Met his wife when he went to get his eyes tested—she was the optician's receptionist.
Original Job: Salesman
Marriage: Ricky Low Beer, 1964
Children: Andrew, 1969; David, 1971; Dylan, 1974
Quote: "Being comfortable is more important than being slinky."

JUDE LAW

Real Name: David Jude Law
Birthplace: Lewisham, London, England
Birthdate: 12/29/72
Occupation: Actor
Education: Attended Alleyns, Dulwich, England
Debut: (TV) *The Tailor of Gloucester*, 1990; (Film) *Shopping*, 1994
Signature: *The Talented Mr. Ripley*, 1998
Facts: He decided on an acting career at age 4.

Began six years of National Youth Music Theater training at age 12. Played lead in their production of *Joseph and the Amazing Technicolor Dreamcoat*.

Met pal Ewen McGregor at a 1990 audition when, to see how the actors would get along, the director paid them to get drunk together.

Has "Sexy Sadie" tattooed on his arm.

Appeared nude on Broadway during the 1995 run of *Indiscretions*.

Made his directorial debut in 1999 with a segment of the TV movie *Tube Tales*.

Is one of the British actors who formed the film production company Natural Nylon.

He and his wife's film contracts specify they must be released on days of their children's school events.

Marriage: Sadie Frost, 1997
Children: Finlay, c.1990 (stepson); Rafferty, c.1996
Quote: "I model each character on me, really."

LUCY LAWLESS

Birthplace: Mount Albert, Auckland, New Zealand
Birthdate: 3/28/68
Occupation: Actor
Education: Attended Auckland University
Debut: (TV) *Funny Business,* 1988
Signature: *Xena: Warrior Princess*
Facts: Got the part of Xena when the original actor became ill and the producers needed someone to fill in quickly. They turned to Lawless, who had been cast in bit parts in the show.

Stands at 5' 11".

Original Jobs: Picking grapes along Germany's Rhine River, working a gold mine in Australia.
Marriages: Garth Lawless (divorced); Rob Tapert, 1998
Children: Daisy, 1988 (with Garth Lawless); Julius Robert Bay, 1999

MARTIN LAWRENCE

Birthplace: Frankfurt, Germany
Birthdate: 4/16/65
Occupation: Actor
Education: High school
Debut: (TV) *What's Happening Now,* 1985; (Film) *Do the Right Thing,* 1989

Signature: *Martin*
Facts: He was a *Star Search* winner, a street performer in Washington Square Park, and a stand-up comedian at the Improv's open-mike night.

Worked at Sears in Queens with Salt-N-Pepa and Kid 'N Play.

Infamy: After a 1994 appearance on *Saturday Night Live* in which he told women to "put a Tic-Tac in your ass" to remain clean, Lawrence was banned from all NBC productions.

Yelled at passersby and brandished a pistol in the middle of a busy L.A. intersection. Tried to board a plane while carrying a Baretta.

In 1997, former *Martin* costar Tisha Campbell filed a suit claiming that he groped and kissed her, among other things, in front of the cast and crew.

Original Jobs: Gas station attendant, store clerk
Marriage: Patricia Southall, 1995 (divorced, 1996)
Child: Jasmine Page, 1996

DENIS LEARY

Birthplace: Worcester, MA
Birthdate: 8/18/57
Occupation: Actor
Education: Emerson College
Debut: (Off-Broadway) *No Cure for Cancer,* 1991; (Film) *Strictly Business,* 1992
Signature: *Dennis Leary: Lock 'n' Load,* 1997
Facts: Co-founded Comedy Workshop in Boston before moving to New York City in 1990, where he formed Apostle Productions.

Made Fiona Apple cry with a joke about her MTV Awards speech in his HBO special *Lock 'n' Load*.

Known as a "bad boy of comedy" for his aggressive smoking and politically incorrect jokes.

To make extra money while teaching drama, he drove a delivery truck and worked in a sulfuric-acid plant.

During a weekend trip to London with his wife, their first son was

born prematurely and they were forced to live there for five months.
Original Job: Acting teacher
Marriage: Ann Lembeck, c. 1990
Children: Jack, c. 1990; Devin, c. 1992
Famous Relative: Conan O'Brien, talk-show host, cousin
Quote: "I have a lot of anger about the loss of the way things used to be. Like how you can't get coffee-flavored coffee anymore because everything is frappuccino or mochaccino."

MATT LEBLANC

Birthplace: Newton, MA
Birthdate: 7/25/67
Occupation: Actor
Education: Wentworth Institute of Technology
Debut: (TV) *TV 101,* 1988
Signature: *Friends*
Facts: First big breaks were in TV commercials, including an award-winning Heinz spot that ran four years.

Actually of mixed heritage—Italian, French, English, Irish, and Dutch—though usually cast as Italian.

After receiving his first motorcycle at age 8, began entering amateur competitions with hopes of racing professionally, a dream his mother quickly quashed.

A passion for landscape photography has taken him all over the world.

Before *Friends,* starred in three TV flops; interest in him soon cooled, and he sold his truck and motorcycle and moved to a smaller apartment to stay afloat financially.

In 2000, along with *Friends* costars, received a salary increase from $125,000 to $750,000 per episode.
Marriage: Melissa McKnight (engaged, 1999)

HEATH LEDGER

Real Name: Heathcliff Andrew Ledger
Birthplace: Perth, Australia
Birthdate: 4/4/79
Occupation: Actor
Education: High school
Debut: (Australian TV) *Sweat,* 1996; (U.S. TV) *Roar,* 1997; (Film) *Two Hands,* 1998
Signature: *The Patriot,* 2000
Facts: Stands 6' 4".

Hobbies include painting, tap dancing and collecting old Mustangs.

Named after Bronte's character Heathcliff of *Wuthering Heights.*

Dated actress Heather Graham, 9 years his senior, in 2001.

Turned down the role of Spider-Man in the upcoming movie which eventually went to Tobey Maguire.

Quote: "I don't want to do this for the rest of my life. I don't. There's so much more I want to discover."

VIRGINIE LEDOYEN

Birthplace: Aubervilliers, France
Birthdate: 11/15/76
Occupation: Actor, model
Education: L'Ecole des Enfants du Spectacle
Debut: (Stage) *L'affaire du courrier de Lyon,* c. 1987; (Film) *The Exploits of a Young Don Juan,* 1987
Signature: *The Beach,* 2000
Facts: Did TV commercials as a child.

Likes the subway, existential literature, Agnes B. clothes, and Leonard Cohen's music.

Her idol is Jeanne Moreau.

Secretary General of "Pour le Tibet," a charity that brings medical aid to Tibetan centers in the Himalayas and North India.

Quote: "I do like to play girls who are independent, who have a lot of character and a story to tell. They aren't there just to be pretty."

SPIKE LEE

Real Name: Shelton Lee
Birthplace: Atlanta, GA
Birthdate: 3/20/57
Occupation: Filmmaker, director
Education: Morehouse College, New York University
Debut: (Film) *She's Gotta Have It,* 1986 [see page 68 for a complete filmography]
Signature: *Do the Right Thing,* 1989
Facts: Known as an unofficial New York Knick, sitting courtside and shouting out to players on both teams. During the 1994 Eastern Conference Championships, some fans felt that his harassment of an Indiana Pacer caused the player to score the most points in the game and defeat the Knicks.

Taught at Harvard as a visiting professor in 1992.

A film he made at NYU, *Joe's Barbershop: We Cut Heads,* was the first student work ever selected for Lincoln Center's "New Directors, New Films" showcase and won a student award from the Academy of Motion Pictures Arts and Sciences.

Infamy: Accused by the Anti-Defamation League of B'Nai Brith of fostering anti-Semitism through his films, most notably via his portrayal of two Jewish nightclub owners in *Mo' Better Blues.*

Original Job: Advertising copywriter
Marriage: Tonya Linette Lewis, 1993
Children: Satchel Lewis, 1994; Jackson Lewis, 1997

TOMMY LEE

Real Name: Thomas Lee Bass
Birthplace: Athens, Greece
Birthdate: 10/3/62
Occupation: Rock drummer, singer
Debut: *Too Fast for Love,* 1981 (with Mötley Crüe)
Signature: *Dr. Feelgood,* 1989 (with Mötley Crüe)
Facts: His band Mötley Crüe was an early target of Tipper Gore's music watchdog group, the PMRC.

Proposed to Pamela Anderson after four days of dating.

He and Anderson once unwound by water-skiing nude on Lake Mead.

Spent a night in jail with Robert Downey, Jr.

Among his tattoos are "eather"—a now-defaced tribute to his first wife—and "mayhem," which marks his stomach.

Credits prison stint with helping him break substance abuse habits.

Now playing in the rock-rap hybrid Methods of Mayhem.

Infamy: In a failed attempt to get high, once injected Jack Daniels into his arm.

Arrested in 1993 for possession of a semiautomatic weapon.

Arrested in 1994 for injuring his then live-in fiancée, Bobbi Brown.

In 1996, a homemade video of Lee and then-wife Pamela Anderson enjoying their honeymoon made its way to the public.

In 1998, pleaded no contest to kicking Lee once in the buttocks and once in the back; served four months in prison.

In 2000, jailed for five days for violating his probation by drinking alcohol.

A five-year-old boy drowned in Lee's pool in 2001 while attending a birthday party for son Brandon.

Marriages: Heather Locklear, 1984 (divorced, 1994); Pamela Anderson, 1995 (divorced, 1998; reunited, 1999; separated, 2000)
Children: Brandon Thomas, 1996; Dylan Jagger, 1998
Quote: "You see everything thrown on stage: money, shoes, bottles of pee. I thought I'd pretty much seen it all until this cow's eye came up and stuck in my drum riser."

JOHN LEGUIZAMO

Birthplace: Bogota, Colombia
Birthdate: 7/22/64
Occupation: Actor, comedian, playwright, producer
Education: Attended New York University
Debut: (Film) *Mixed Blood,* 1984;

(Television) *Miami Vice*, 1984; (One man show) *Mambo Mouth*, 1990
Signature: *To Wong Foo, Thanks for Everything, Julie Newmar* 1995
Facts: Named after actor John Saxon (now best known for *Enter the Dragon* and *A Nightmare on Elm Street*).
Grew up in Jackson Heights, Queens. Would imitate TV comics to make his "painfully serious" father laugh.
Voted "Most Talkative" in high school.
His leading inspirations are Lily Tomlin, Jonathan Winters, and especially Richard Pryor.
Attracted note in *Casualties of War*, but got few meaty roles until he created *Freak* and *Spic-o-Rama*, solo shows drawing from his stand-up experience and eye on Hispanic culture.
Created, executive produced, wrote for, and starred in "House of Buggin' ", a Latino-oriented sketch comedy show.
Infamy: Arrested at 15 for broadcasting a comedy routine about his sex life over a subway public address system. Was also once arrested for truancy.
Major Award: Emmy, Individual Performance—Variety or Music Program, *Freak*, 1999
Marriages: Yelba Matamoros, 1994 (filed for divorce, 1996); Justine Maurer (relationship)
Children: Allegra Sky, 1999
Quote: "As long as a director or an actor understands and observes life, you can capture anybody."

JENNIFER JASON LEIGH

Real Name: Jennifer Leigh Morrow
Birthplace: Los Angeles, CA
Birthdate: 2/5/62
Occupation: Actor
Education: High school dropout
Debut: (TV) *The Young Runaways*, 1978; (Film) *Eyes of a Stranger*, 1980; (Off Broadway) *Sunshine*, 1989
Signature: *Single White Female*, 1992

Facts: Dropped out of high school six weeks before graduation to act in her debut film.
Since another Jennifer Leigh was already registered with the Screen Actors Guild, she added Jason in honor of family friend Jason Robards.
For her role in 1981 as an anorexic teen in TV's *The Best Little Girl in the World*, she dropped her weight to 86 pounds.
Her father was killed in a helicopter accident on the set of *Twilight Zone: The Movie*.
She is very shy and dreads parties. As a result, she spends her free time reading or going to movies.
Famous Relatives: Barbara (Freedman) Turner, TV scriptwriter, mother; Vic Morrow, actor, father; Mina Badie, actor, half-sister
Quote: "I like the idea of being able to play anything from waif to prostitute."

JAY LENO

Real Name: James Leno
Birthplace: New Rochelle, NY
Birthdate: 4/28/50
Occupation: Talk show host, comedian
Education: Emerson College
Debut: (TV) *The Marilyn McCoo & Billy Davis Jr. Show*, 1977; (Film) *Silver Bears*, 1978
Signature: *The Tonight Show*
Facts: Collects antique cars and motorcycles.
Made his first appearance on *The Tonight Show* in 1977.
While in grade school, Leno executed such pranks as flushing tennis balls down the toilet and hiding a dog in his locker. His fifth grade teacher wrote on his report card, "If Jay spent as much time studying as he does trying to be a comedian, he'd be a big star."
Once failed an employment test at Woolworth's.
Was made a contributing editor at *Popular Mechanics* magazine in

1999. He pens the "Jay Leno's Garage" column.
Original Jobs: Rolls-Royce mechanic, deliveryman
Marriage: Mavis Nicholson, 1980

TÉA LEONI

Real name: Elizabeth Téa Pantaleoni
Birthplace: New York, NY
Birthdate: 2/25/66
Occupation: Actor
Education: Sarah Lawrence College
Debut: (TV) *Santa Barbara*, 1984; (Film) *Switch*, 1994
Signature: *Deep Impact*, 1998
Facts: A sufferer of stage fright, was so nervous shooting the pilot for *The Naked Truth* she threw up five times.
Got into acting when, on a dare, entered a mass audition for the remake of *Charlie's Angels* and was chosen, although the show never aired.
Caused a stir when *The Naked Truth* producer Chris Thompson left his wife and children to date her.
Original Job: Teaching Japanese men how to interact with American women
Marriages: Neil Tardio, 1991 (divorced, 1993); David Duchovny, 1997
Child: Madelaine West, 1999

DAVID LETTERMAN

Birthplace: Indianapolis, IN
Birthdate: 4/12/47
Occupation: Talk show host
Education: Ball State University
Debut: (TV) *The Starland Vocal Band Show*, 1977
Signature: *Late Show with David Letterman*
Facts: While working as a weather announcer at a local TV station, he congratulated a tropical storm on being upgraded to a hurricane.
Was the announcer for the late-night movie program *Freeze Dried Movies*. On the program, he blew up

a model of the television station at which he was working.

Margaret Ray stalked him at his New Canaan, Conn., home. She was caught at or in his home eight times from 1988 to 1993.

Underwent quintuple bypass surgery at age 52. When he returned to the Late Show he received his best ratings in six years.

Original Jobs: TV announcer, weatherman

Marriage: Michelle Cook (divorced, 1977); Regina Lasko (relationship)

Major Awards: Emmy, Best Host of a Daytime Variety Series, *The David Letterman Show*, 1981; Emmy, Writing in a Variety or Music Show, *Late Night with David Letterman*, 1984, 1985, 1986, 1987

JET LI

Real Name: Li Lian-jie
Birthplace: Beijing, China
Birthdate: 4/26/63
Occupation: Actor, martial artist
Education: Beijing Martial Art Troupe
Debut: *Shaolin Temple*, 1982
Signature: *Romeo Must Die*, 2000
Facts: Began his study of martial arts at age 7 to overcome a sickly childhood.

At 11, performed at the Nixon White House. When warned that his hotel room might be bugged, he told the furnishings what kinds of foods he liked—and found them waiting upon his return.

Won China's gold medal for *wu shu* (a type of martial art he performs) four times.

Has directed (*Born to Defend*) and produced (*Bodyguard from Beijing*).

For Hong Kong film fans, Li's signature is the recent *Once Upon a Time in China* films. Li made the lead role of real-life folk hero Wong Fei-hung his own—even though it had previously been played by others onscreen nearly a hundred times.

Was initially left off the *Lethal Weapon 4* print ads and posters.

When his fans deluged the movie's web site with complaints, he was included with the five heroes—even though he played the villain.

Marriages: Qiuyan Huang, 1987 (divorced, c. 1989); Nina Li, 1999
Children: Two daughters (with Qiuyan Huang); Jane, 2000
Quote: "I want to give a smart and positive image to martial arts, not this bloody, fight-for-no-reason image."

RUSH LIMBAUGH

Birthplace: Cape Girardeau, MO
Birthdate: 1/12/51
Occupation: Political commentator, radio and TV broadcaster, author
Education: Elkins Institute of Radio and Technology; attended Southeastern Missouri State University
Facts: After dropping out of college, he left home in 1971 in pursuit of a big-time radio career. Fired from various stations, he left radio seven years later and worked in the public relations office of the Kansas City Royals baseball team.

He targets radical-liberals, environmentalists, do-gooders, and anyone further left than he.

More than 300 "Rush rooms" have opened in restaurants nationwide for the purpose of broadcasting Rush Limbaugh's programs to patrons.

Met his wife, Marta, via electronic mail on CompuServe Information Service. They were married by Supreme Court Justice Clarence Thomas.

He named his radio web The Excellence in Broadcasting Network, which began with 56 AM stations and 250,000 listeners. Within three years, his broadcast had an estimated 2 million listeners at any given moment

Signed a new contract in 2001 reportedly worth in the vicinity of $250 million.

Infamy: His recurring AIDS Update enraged activists. He ultimately

apologized, withdrew the segment, and donated $10,000 to the Pediatric AIDS Foundation.

In February 1994, the Florida Citrus Commission advertised orange juice on Limbaugh's show. The ads generated 7,500 calls to the commission protesting their choice of such a controversial figure to promote their product. The National Organization for Women, as well as various gay and lesbian groups, urged people to boycott Florida orange juice. Meanwhile, about 30 Rush supporters bought out the entire supply of orange juice at an Orlando, Florida, store in counterprotest.

Original job: Apprentice at KGMO radio station
Marriages: Roxie Maxine McNeely (divorced); Michelle Sixta (divorced); Marta Fitzgerald
Famous Relatives: Rush Limbaugh Sr., President Eisenhower's ambassador to India, grandfather; Stephen Limbaugh, federal judge appointed by Ronald Reagan, uncle.
Quote: "My first real interest in radio can be traced to a dislike for school."

LAURA LINNEY

Birthplace: New York, NY
Birthdate: 2/5/64
Occupation: Actor
Education: Attended Northwestern University, Brown University, Juilliard School
Debut: (Stage) *Six Degrees of Separation*, 1990; (Film) *Lorenzo's Oil*, 1992; (TV) *Class of '61*, 1993
Signature: *The Truman Show*, 1998
Facts: First recognized in 1994 for her portrayal of Mary Ann Singleton in *Armistead Maupin's Tales of the City.*

Her middle name is Legett.

During her years at Juilliard, she suffered from severe stage fright.

She is afraid to fly.

In elementary school she tried to con her teachers into letting her act out book reports instead of writing them.

Based on her performance in *Primal Fear,* she was handpicked by Clint Eastwood to star in 1997's *Absolute Power.*

Reportedly received less than $10,000 for her Oscar-nominated role in *You Can Count on Me.*

Original Job: Backstage hand in New England theaters

Marriage: David Adkins, 1995

Famous Relative: Romulus Linney, playwright

Quote: "I have the Cindy Brady complex. You know that episode of *The Brady Bunch* where Cindy goes catatonic when she appears on a TV show? That was me."

TARA LIPINSKI

Birthplace: Sewell, NJ
Birthdate: 6/10/82
Occupation: Ice skater
Debut: (TV) *The Young and the Restless,* 1999
Facts: At age 11, she and her mother left Texas so she could train year-round with prestigious coaches.

Practiced only two weeks before landing her signature triple-loop combination—the first ice skater ever to do so.

Stood 4'10" and weighed 82 pounds when she won her Olympic medal.

At age 14, she was the youngest-ever winner of the U.S. Figure Skating Championship.

Major Award: Olympics, Gold medal, women's figure skating, 1998

JOHN LITHGOW

Birthplace: Rochester, NY
Birthdate: 10/19/45
Occupation: Actor
Education: Harvard University, London Academy of Music and Dramatic Arts
Debut: (Film) *Dealing: or The Berkeley-to-Boston Forty-Brick Lost-*

Bag Blues, 1972; (TV) *Mom, the Wolfman and Me,* 1980
Signature: *3rd Rock from the Sun*
Facts: His father ran the Antioch Shakespeare Festival, and John had small parts in the plays from early childhood.

Stars in a children's videotape, *John Lithgow's Kid-Size Concert.*

Some years ago he read the book *Forrest Gump* and wanted to acquire the movie rights so he could play the lead, but he didn't get around to it.

Known as a serious dramatic actor, but actually did more than 40 comedies on stage.

Son Ian appears in *3rd Rock* as Professor Solomon's slowest student.
Marriage: Jean Taynton, 1966 (divorced); Mary Yeager, 1981
Children: Ian, 1972 (with Jean Taynton). Phoebe, 1982; Nathan, c. 1984
Major Awards: Tony, Best Supporting Actor (Dramatic), *The Changing Room,* 1973; Emmy, Outstanding Guest Performance in a Drama Series, *Amazing Stories,* 1986; Emmy, Best Actor in a Comedy Series, *3rd Rock from the Sun,* 1996, 1997, 1999
Quote: "God bless television."

BRIAN LITTRELL

Birthplace: Lexington, KY
Birthdate: 2/20/75
Occupation: Singer
Education: High school dropout
Debut: (Single) "We've Got It Goin' On," 1995; (Album) *Backstreet Boys,* 1995 (American version, 1997)
Signature: "Everybody (Backstreet's Back),"1997
Facts: Is cousin to Backstreet Boy Kevin Richardson.

Before joining the band, was planning to attend Cincinnati Bible College.

Got the call to join the band while sitting in history class during the last hour of his junior year.

The band is named after Orlando, Florida's Backstreet Market, a popular teen hangout.

The group's debut was a hit in 26 countries before *Backstreet Boys* was released in the U.S.

Underwent surgery to fix a congenital hole in his heart at the age of 22. Was onstage again in eight weeks, with oxygen tents waiting in the wings.

Wrote the song "The Perfect Fan" for his mother.

Has a chihuahua named Little Tyke.

Plays basketball, tennis, and golf to relax.

Infamy: Band filed suit against former manager Lou Pearlman, claiming he had made $10 million from their labor while they had received $300,000.

Original Job: Employee of Long John Silver's

Marriage: Leighanne Wallace, 2000

Quote: "I don't want a Backstreet Boys cereal."

LUCY LIU

Birthplace: New York, NY
Birthdate: 12/2/67
Occupation: Actor
Education: Attended New York University; University of Michigan
Debut: (TV) *Beverly Hills, 90210,* 1991; (Film) *Jerry Maguire,* 1996
Signature: *Ally McBeal*
Facts: Her middle name is Alexis.

While earning her B.A. in Chinese language and culture, Liu became serious about acting when she played the lead in a campus production of *Alice in Wonderland.*

Her mixed-media photo collages have been exhibited frequently in New York and Los Angeles. After her show at SoHo's Cast Iron Gallery, she was awarded a grant in 1994 to study in China.

She was originally signed on to *Ally McBeal* for only six episodes but her popularity among audiences won her a recurring role.

She practices martial arts.

She treats her long hair with olive oil and lavender.

Nickname among friends is "Curious George."
Original Job: Artist, caterer, aerobics instructor
Quote: "I wanted to be Barbie and I was as opposite to Barbie as you could get."

HEATHER LOCKLEAR

Birthplace: Los Angeles, CA
Birthdate: 9/25/61
Occupation: Actor
Education: UCLA
Debut: (TV) *Dynasty,* 1981
Signature: *Melrose Place*
Facts: Served over six years as the spokesperson for the Health and Tennis Corporation of America.

Played officer Stacy Sheridan on the crime drama series *T.J. Hooker* with William Shatner, 1982–87.

When she joined the cast of *Melrose Place,* the series's audience jumped 50 percent.
Marriage: Tommy Lee (divorced), Richie Sambora, 1994
Child: Ava Elizabeth, 1997
Quote: "Having to sit like a lady isn't my favorite thing. So I like pants. It's nicer to be comfy."

LISA LOPES

Birthplace: Philadelphia, PA
Birthdate: 5/27/71
Occupation: Singer, songwriter
Debut: *Ooooooohhh…On the TLC Tip,* 1992
Signature: "Waterfalls," 1995 / "Left Eye"
Facts: Taught herself to play piano by age five.

Grew up with a physically abusive father who beat her and introduced her to alcohol.

Her nickname comes from the condom she regularly wore over the left lens of her glasses.

Hosted MTV fashion show, *The Cut.*

When third album *Fanmail* was released, Lopes repeatedly aired misgivings about TLC's musical and business decisions. When her bandmates counterattacked with charges of unprofessional behavior, Lopes challenged them to produce solo albums in order to compete against the one she was planning
Infamy: In 1993, was arrested in Atlanta for fighting with police.

Charged with disorderly conduct at the Georgia Dome football stadium.

Turned herself in for burning down boyfriend Andre Rison's mansion. She entered an alcohol rehab clinic soon after, and intimated that she was being battered by Rison.
Relationship: Andre Rison, ex-football player (engaged, 2001)
Major Awards: Grammy, Best R&B Album, *Crazysexycool,* 1995; Grammy, Best R&B Vocal—Duo or Group, "Creep," 1995; Grammy, Best R&B Album, *Fanmail,* 1999; Grammy, Best R&B Vocal—Duo or Group, "No Scrubs," 1999

JENNIFER LOPEZ

Birthplace: Bronx, NY
Birthdate: 7/24/69
Occupation: Actor, singer
Debut: (TV) *In Living Color,* 1990; (Film) *Mi Familia ("My Family"),* 1995; (Album) *On the 6,* 1999
Signature: *The Cell,* 2000; "If You Had My Love," 1999
Facts: The daughter of Puerto Rican parents, she danced for music videos and on stage, and then was selected to be a Fly Girl for TV's *In Living Color.*

Her role as Selena was protested by some Latinos because she is of Puerto Rican rather than Mexican descent.

She is the highest paid Latina actress in history.

When she was younger she wanted to be a hairstylist.

On the 6 is named for the subway line that she took to Manhattan when she was growing up.

Formerly involved with Sean Combs.

Launched her own "sporty chic" women's wear line in 2001, backed in part by Tommy Hilfiger's brother Andy, saying "From little to voluptuous everybody gets to be sexy."
Original Job: Dancer
Marriages: Ojani Noa, 1997 (divorced, 1998); Cris Judd, 2001
Quote: "I'm a typical Latino. I scream and shout about things. Some men can't handle that."

SOPHIA LOREN

Real Name: Sophia Villani Scicolone
Birthplace: Rome, Italy
Birthdate: 9/20/34
Education: Catholic parochial school, Teachers' Institute
Occupation: Actor
Debut: (Film) *Variety Lights,* 1950; (TV) *The World of Sophia Loren,* 1962
Signature: *Two Women,* 1961
Facts: Although her parents never married, her father, Ricardo Scicolone, granted her the legal right to use his last name.

Growing up poor with her sister and mother in Pozzuoli, a small industrial town near Naples, Italy, she attended a Catholic school, where she has said she was plain, thin, and nicknamed *"Stecchetto"* ("the stick") or *"Stuzzicadenti"* ("toothpick").

At age 12, she enrolled in the Teachers' Institute, where she studied teaching for three years.

Met producer and future husband Carlo Ponti during a beauty contest where he was a judge and she was a contestant. She was 15 years old.

She and her mother worked as extras in *Quo Vadis,* earning a total income of $33.

Sophia began modeling for Italian magazines and in 1952 was given the name Sophia Loren by a director.

She did her famous striptease in 1963 in the film *Yesterday, Today and Tomorrow,* which she reprised in 1994's *Ready to Wear* at age 59.

Suffered two miscarriages and two difficult pregnancies.

Her marriage to Ponti was annulled due to charges by the Italian government that Ponti was a bigamist, claiming that his divorce from a previous wife was invalid. They were married again in 1966.

She is the only actress to have won an Oscar for a foreign-language film.

Infamy: Spent 17 days in jail in 1982 for underpaying her taxes in Italy.
Original Job: Model
Marriage: Carlo, 1957 (annulled in 1962; remarried, 1966)
Children: Carlo Ponti Jr., 1968; Eduardo, 1972
Major Awards: Academy Award, Best Actress, *Two Women*, 1961; Honorary Academy Award, as "one of the genuine treasures of world cinema," 1990
Quote: "I am not a sexy pot."

JULIA LOUIS-DREYFUS

Birthplace: New York, NY
Birthdate: 1/13/61
Occupation: Actor
Education: Northwestern University
Debut: (TV) *Saturday Night Live*, 1982; (Film) *Hannah and Her Sisters*, 1986
Signature: *Seinfeld*
Facts: Parents were divorced when she was only 1 year old.

Met husband in college and worked with him on *Saturday Night Live*.

Her role in *Seinfeld* was not in the original mix created by Jerry Seinfeld and Larry David, but was imposed by the network, which felt a female perspective was needed.
Original Job: Member of the Second City comedy troupe
Marriage: Brad Hall, 1987
Child: Henry, 1992; Charles, 1997
Major Award: Emmy, Best Supporting Actress, *Seinfeld*, 1996

COURTNEY LOVE

Real Name: Love Michelle Harrison
Birthplace: San Francisco, CA
Birthdate: 7/9/64
Occupation: Singer, songwriter, actor
Education: High school dropout
Debut: (Film) *Sid and Nancy*, 1986 (Album) *Pretty on the Inside*, 1991
Signature: Hole
Facts: Ran away to Europe at 15; her grandfather's death left her a millionaire.

Mother was the psychologist who examined Katherine Anne Power ('60s radical and fugitive who recently confessed to being an accessory to bank robbery).

Appeared in the film *Straight to Hell*, 1987.

Before founding Hole, Love was lead vocalist for the rock band Faith No More in the early '80s "for about a week" (before they found Chuck Mosely). She also played with Kat Bjelland of the Minneapolis all-girl band Babes in Toyland and future L7 member Jennifer Finch in Sugar Baby Doll.

Named daughter after the '30s actress Frances Farmer, who is the subject of Nirvana song "Frances Farmer Will Have Her Revenge on Seattle."
Infamy: In her early teens, was sent to a juvenile detention center after stealing a Kiss T-shirt from a department store.

A *Vanity Fair* article described Love as shooting heroin while pregnant. Though she denied the charge, child-welfare authorities temporarily removed the baby after she was born.

Arrested in 1995 for verbally abusing a flight attendant aboard an Australian flight. She was not convicted, but ordered to remain on good behavior for one month.

Sued by David Geffen of Geffen Records for breach of contract in 2000. Geffen is claiming that Hole still owes his company 5 albums and is seeking unspecified damages

as well as an injunction barring Hole from recording for any other label.
Original Job: Danced in strip joints in L.A. and Alaska
Marriages: James Moreland, 1989 (divorced, 1989); Kurt Cobain, 1992 (deceased, 1994)
Child: Frances Bean, 1992
Famous Relatives: Linda Carroll, psychologist, mother; Hank Harrison, author, father
Quote: "Once you've cleared a million bucks, excuse me, you're not a punk anymore"

LYLE LOVETT

Birthplace: Klein, TX
Birthdate: 11/1/57
Occupation: Singer, songwriter
Education: Texas A&M
Debut: (Album) *Lyle Lovett*, 1986
Facts: Played guitar in coffee shops while in college.

Lives in a clapboard house built by his grandparents.

Is afraid of cows.
Marriage: Julia Roberts, 1993 (divorced, 1995)
Major Awards: Grammy, *Lyle Lovett and His Large Band*, 1989; Grammy, Best Pop Vocal Collaboration, "Funny How Time Slips Away" (with Al Green), 1994; Grammy, Best Country Group Performance with Vocal, "Blues for Dixie" (with Asleep at the Wheel), 1994

ROB LOWE

Birthplace: Charlottesville, VA
Birthdate: 3/17/64
Occupation: Actor
Education: High school
Debut: (TV) *A New Kind of Family*, 1978; (Film) *The Outsiders*, 1983; (Broadway) *A Little Hotel on the Side*, 1992
Signature: *The West Wing*, 1999
Facts: His middle name is Helper.

While in high school, he appeared in Super 8 movies made by classmates Sean Penn and Charlie Sheen.

He is deaf in his right ear.

As the "crown prince" of the Brat Pack, he was romantically linked to Melissa Gilbert, Chynna Phillips, and Princess Stephanie of Monaco.

Wears a gold cross and a gold medallion around his neck with the Serenity Prayer used in 12-step recovery programs, both given to him by his wife.

Infamy: After being caught on videotape with two young women, one of whom was only 16, while attending 1988's Democratic National Convention in Atlanta, he avoided prosecution by agreeing to perform 20 hours of community service.

During the 1989 Academy Awards, in a disastrously bad number, he crooned "Proud Mary" with a Snow White impostor. The Academy apologized to the Walt Disney Company for the potential trademark infringement.

Original Job: Actor in TV commercials

Marriage: Sheryl Berkoff, 1991

Children: Matthew Edward, 1993; John Owen, 1995

Famous Relative: Chad Lowe, actor, brother; Hilary Swank, actor, sister-in-law

Quote: "I drank too much. I had no sense of what should be private and what should be public. And I was very unfocused and not even aware of how the onrush of really being a *man*—as opposed to a young man—was scaring me."

GEORGE LUCAS

Birthplace: Modesto, CA
Birthdate: 5/14/44
Occupation: Director, producer, screenwriter
Education: University of Southern California
Debut: (Film) *THX-1138*, 1971
Signature: *Star Wars*, 1977
Facts: Has sold more than $3 billion in licensed *Star Wars* merchandise, money Lucas got to keep because

licensing rights were thrown into his contract in exchange for his having given up an extra director's fee (he forfeited the higher fee to ensure that 20th Century Fox would bankroll his sequel).

His empire includes the Industrial Light & Magic special effects firm, LucasArts interactive media, and a group selling his advanced THX theater sound system.

Still writes scripts in longhand, using the same three-ring binder he used in college.

As an 18-year-old, nearly killed himself while joyriding on a country road when his Fiat hit a car, flipped over, and crashed into a tree. He survived only because his seat belt broke and threw him from the car before impact.

Has received permission from the government to develop 23 acres of land at the former Presidio Army base in San Francisco for his Letterman Digital Arts Center, which will house part of Lucas's film and technology empire.

Marriage: Marcia Griffin (divorced, 1983)

Children: Amanda, 1981; Katie, 1988; Jett, 1993; (all adopted).

Major Award: Academy of Motion Pictures Arts and Sciences, Irving Thalberg Award, 1992

SUSAN LUCCI

Birthplace: Scarsdale, NY
Birthdate: 12/23/46
Occupation: Actor
Education: Marymount College
Debut: (TV) *All My Children*, 1969
Signature: *All My Children*
Facts: Was nominated 19 times for the best actress in a daytime series Emmy, and finally won in 1999. In 2000, she was overlooked for a nomination but served as the event's host.

Was a cheerleader in high school.

Made the semifinals in New York State Miss Universe pageant, 1968.

Dropped out of the competition to finish her college exams.

As Erica Kane, Lucci has impersonated a nun, been kidnapped, rescued a lover from prison using a helicopter, and stared down a grizzly bear.

Daughter Liza appears on the new daytime drama, *Passions*.

Original Job: "Color girl" for CBS, sitting for cameras as a new lighting system for color TV was being developed

Marriage: Helmut Huber, 1969

Children: Liza Victoria, actor, 1975; Andreas Martin, 1980

Major Award: Emmy, Best Actress in a Daytime Drama Series, *All My Children*, 1998–99

LORETTA LYNN

Real Name: Loretta Webb
Birthplace: Butcher Hollow, KY
Birthdate: 4/14/35
Occupation: Singer, songwriter
Debut: (Single) "Honky Tonk Girl," 1960
Signature: "Coal Miner's Daughter"
Facts: First woman to earn a certified gold country album.

While her kids were still young, her husband gave her a guitar to accompany the singing she did around the house. She taught herself to play.

Her first No. 1 single, "Don't Come Home A-Drinkin' (With Lovin' on Your Mind)" was banned from several stations. Many of her songs have been banned, including "Rated X" and "The Pill."

Married when she was 13. "By the time I was 17, I had four kids, and I had never been anywhere." She was a grandmother at 31, one year after her twins (her last children) were born.

Marriage: Oliver Vanetta Lynn Jr., 1948 (deceased, 1996)

Children: Betty Sue Lynn Markworth, c. 1948; Jack Benny, 1949 (deceased, 1984); Ernest Ray, 1953;

Clara Marie Lynn Lyell, 1954; Peggy, 1964; Patsy, 1964
Famous Relative: Crystal Gayle, singer, sister
Major Awards: Grammy, Best Country Performance—Duo or Group, "After the Fire Is Gone" (with Conway Twitty), 1971; Grammy, Best Recording for Children, *Sesame Country* (with others), 1981; inducted into the Country Music Hall of Fame, 1988

SHELBY LYNNE

Birthplace: Quantico, VA
Birthdate: 10/22/68
Occupation: Country-soul singer
Debut: (Album) *Sunrise,* 1988
Signature: *I AM Shelby Lynne,* 1999
Facts: Raised by a grandmother after her father killed her mother before turning the gun on himself.

Married her high school sweetheart at 18. She and her then-husband moved to Nashville, where a cable-TV appearance encouraged Tammy Wynette's retired writer-producer to help Lynne's career.

Sang with George Jones on her debut single.

Made five albums with three different labels by 1997. Now disavows her Nashville hits.

When branded a complainer and a troublemaker, Lynne left Nashville to work on new songs in Alabama. She re-emerged with fresh music that became *I AM Shelby Lynne.* It was first released in England, where her musical and personal differences with Nashville would less of an obstacle to creating buzz. The strategy worked.

Drives a 1968 Cadillac Coupe de Ville.
Marriage: One marriage (divorced)
Famous Relative: Allison Moorer, singer-songwriter, sister
Major Award: Grammy, Best New Artist, 2000
Quote: "I am proud of all my albums, but I'm not gonna sit around and study them or anything, man. They're just not that good, and it's not where I

am any more. Those hairstyles haunt me, but hey, what are you gonna do?"

NORM MACDONALD

Birthplace: Quebec, Canada
Birthdate: 10/4/62
Occupation: Comedian, actor, screenwriter
Debut: (TV) *Saturday Night Live,* 1993; (Film) *Billy Madison,* 1995
Signature: *The Norm Show,* 1999
Facts: Once conned reporters into believing that he played pro hockey in Ottowa.

Was removed from his *SNL* "Weekend Update" post in 1998. Speculation attributed it to his constant on-air jabs at O. J. Simpson, a friend of NBC West Coast president Don Ohlmeyer. Macdonald disputes the theory, offering that NBC brass simply didn't find him funny. Soon after Macdonald's ousting, NBC refused to air advertisements for *Dirty Work,* written by and starring Macdonald.

Declined an offer to host his own late-night show out of deference to his idol, David Letterman.

Played Michael "Kramer" Richards in *Man on the Moon.*
Infamy: Used the F-word in an April 1997 live *SNL* broadcast.

His off-color stand-up show shocked the University of Iowa so much it apologized to its students. A similar response followed his hosting an ESPN awards ceremony.
Original Job: Stand-up comic, writer for *The Dennis Miller Show* and *Roseanne*
Marriage: Connie (separated)
Child: Dylan, 1992
Quote: "I'm not a versatile actor. I have no idea how to act. I can specifically write for myself and be funny."

ANDIE MACDOWELL

Real Name: Rosalie Anderson MacDowell
Birthplace: Gaffney, SC

Birthdate: 4/21/58
Occupation: Actor
Education: Attended Winthrop College
Debut: (Film) *Greystoke: The Legend of Tarzan, Lord of the Apes,* 1984
Signature: *Sex, Lies and Videotape,* 1989
Facts: After *Greystoke* was filmed, MacDowell's part was overdubbed with a British accent provided by Glenn Close.

Played Jimi Hendrix's "Angel" at her wedding.
Original Job: McDonald's, Elite model
Marriage: Paul Qualley, 1986 (separated, 1999)
Children: Justin, 1986; Rainey, 1989; Sarah Margaret, 1994

SHIRLEY MACLAINE

Real Name: Shirley MacLean Beaty
Birthplace: Richmond, VA
Birthdate: 4/24/34
Occupation: Actor, author
Education: Washington School of Ballet
Debut: (Stage) *Oklahoma!,* 1950
Signature: *Terms of Endearment,* 1983
Facts: Starred in her own TV series, *Shirley's World* (1971–72).

Was performing with the Washington School of Ballet by the time she was 12, but soon grew too tall to be a ballerina.

Following a showbiz cliché, she got the lead in the 1954 Broadway show *The Pajama Game* when the lead hurt her ankle.

As a young girl, often had to come with fists blazing to the aid of her bookish and picked-on younger brother.
Infamy: Ridiculed for her oft-expressed beliefs in reincarnation, detailed in her best-selling books *Out on a Limb* and *Dancing in the Light.* Satirized herself in the "Pavilion of Former Lives" in the film *Defending Your Life* (1991).

Had an open marriage with husband Parker, but was stunned to learn from a channeler (later confirmed by a private eye) that he had transferred millions of dollars to his girlfriend's account.

Wrote a tell-all book in 1995, detailing how Debra Winger mooned her and broke wind, and describing Frank Sinatra as "a perpetual kid" and "someone who muscled others." Sinatra's response to the book: "It's amazing what a broad will do for a buck."

Original Job: Dancer
Marriage: Steve Parker (divorced, 1983); Andrew Peacock (relationship)
Child: Stephanie Sachiko, 1956
Famous Relative: Warren Beatty, actor, brother
Major Awards: Emmy, Outstanding Comedy-Variety or Musical Special, *Shirley MacLaine: If They Could See Me Now*, 1974; Emmy, Outstanding Comedy-Variety or Musical Special, *Gypsy in My Soul*, 1976; Emmy, Outstanding Writing of Variety or Music Program, *Shirley MacLaine... Every Little Movement*, 1980; Oscar, Best Actress, *Terms of Endearment*, 1983

PETER MACNICOL

Birthplace: Texas
Birthdate: 4/10/58
Education: Attended University of Minnesota
Occupation: Actor
Debut: (Film) *Dragonslayer*, 1981; (Stage) *Crimes of the Heart*
Signature: *Ally McBeal*
Facts: Originally planned a career in paleontology.

After his first movie experience, he left New York and traveled around Europe and the United States without telling anyone where he was going. When he finally called his agent, he found out that he had an audition for *Sophie's Choice*.
Marriage: Marsue Cumming

ELLE MACPHERSON

Real Name: Eleanor Gow
Birthplace: Sydney, Australia
Birthdate: 3/29/64
Occupation: Supermodel, actor
Debut: *Sports Illustrated* swimsuit model, (Film) *Sirens*, 1994
Facts: Appeared in every issue of *Elle* magazine from 1982 to 1988.

Launched a designer lingerie line in Australia and New Zealand in 1991.

Opened Fashion Cafe in New York City in 1995 with supermodels Claudia Schiffer and Naomi Campbell.

Named the world's wealthiest model by *Business Age* in 1998.
Marriage: Gilles Bensimon (divorced, 1989); Arpad Busson (relationship)
Children: Arpad Flynn, 1998

WILLIAM H. MACY

Birthplace: Miami, FL
Birthdate: 3/13/50
Occupation: Actor, stage director, screenwriter
Education: Goddard College
Debut: (Broadway) *Our Town*, 1988; (TV) *The Awakening Land*, 1978; (Film) *House of Games*, 1987
Signature: *Fargo*, 1996
Facts: Initially planning on a career in veterinary medicine, he transferred from Bethany College to major in theater at Goddard, where he studied under David Mamet.

Moved to Chicago with Mamet and Steven Schacter and founded the St. Nicholas Theater, where he appeared in 1975 in its first production, *American Buffalo*, and landed small roles in TV.

Is actively involved with Boy Scout Troop 184 in L.A.

His middle name is Hall.

During the 1980s, he performed in more than 50 Broadway and Off-Broadway productions. He and Mamet founded the Atlantic Theatre Company in New York in 1983.
Original Jobs: Musician, acting teacher

Marriage: Felicity Huffman, actor, 1997
Child: Sofia Grace, 2000
Quote: "I'm sort of an odd duck. I look really odd sometimes, then other times I look okay. I tend to get cast for who I am, which is a white guy who can talk a good game."

MADONNA

Real Name: Madonna Louise Veronica Ciccone
Birthplace: Bay City, MI
Birthdate: 8/16/58
Occupation: Singer
Education: University of Michigan
Debut: Dancer, Alvin Ailey Dance Company, 1979
Signature: "Material Girl"
Facts: Was a cheerleader in high school.

She starred in an exploitation film called *A Certain Sacrifice* in 1980.

Early in her career, posed nude for a New York photographer. Those photos later appeared in *Playboy*.

She appears in a nightclub scene from the 1983 movie *Vision Quest*, singing "Crazy for You" in the background.

Her hobby is making scrapbooks.

Has been drinking "kabbalah water," blessed by a rabbi versed in the Jewish mystical tradition, to help with her insomnia.

In 2001, London's *Sunday Times* estimated her fortune at $260 million.
Infamy: In 1994, swore 14 times while on *The Late Show with David Letterman*, to get revenge for his many jokes at her expense. She also handed Letterman a pair of her panties and told him to smell them.

Her video for "Justify My Love" (1990) was banned from MTV.

Her book *Sex* (1992) was originally banned in Japan, where it is against the law to show pubic hair. Officials eventually relented since the book was being distributed anyway.
Original Jobs: Model, worked in a doughnut shop

Marriage: Sean Penn (divorced, 1988); Guy Ritchie, director, 2000
Child: Lourdes Maria Ciccone Leon, 1996 (with Carlos Leon); Rocco Ritchie, 2000
Major Awards: Grammy, Best Music Video—Long Form, *Madonna—Blonde Ambition World Tour Live,* 1991; Grammy, Best Dance Recording, "Ray of Light," 1998; Grammy, Best Shortform Music Video, "Ray of Light," 1998; Grammy, Best Pop Album, *Ray of Light,* 1998; Grammy, Best Song written for a Motion Picture/Television, "Beautiful Stranger" (with William Orbit), *Austin Powers: The Spy Who Shagged Me,* 1999
Quote: "I don't think that having a child has made me unsexy. There's nothing sexier than a mother."

TOBEY MAGUIRE

Birthplace: Santa Monica, CA
Birthdate: 6/27/75
Occupation: Actor
Education: High school dropout; earned a GED
Debut: (TV) *On Location: Rodney Dangerfield—"Opening Night at Rodney's Place";* (Film) *This Boy's Life,* 1995
Signature: *The Cider House Rules,* 2000
Facts: Grew up "super-duper poor." Was planning to take culinary arts in school until his mother offered him $100 to try the drama elective.

Auditioned for the lead in *This Boy's Life,* but choked over acting with Robert DeNiro; pal Leonardo DiCaprio got the part.

Played Joan Allen's son in both *The Ice Storm* and *Pleasantville.*

Does not drink, smoke, take drugs, or eat meat. Does do yoga.

Under a 1999 settlement with director R. D. Robb, it was agreed *Don's Plum,* a film he made with Leonardo DiCaprio in 1995–96, could be released internationally, but not in the U. S. and Canada. It debuted at the Berlin Film Festival in 2001.
Relationship: Rashida Jones
Quote: "I think I'm going somewhere between Tom Hanks and John Malkovich."

BILL MAHER

Birthplace: New York, NY
Birthdate: 1/20/56
Occupation: Comedian, talk show host
Education: Cornell University
Debut: *The Tonight Show,* 1982
Signature: *Politically Incorrect*
Facts: Says the most politically incorrect thing he ever did was to say "f--k" in front of the president.

Originally did stand-up on the New York club circuit with other up-and-coming comics, including Jerry Seinfeld and Paul Reiser.

Wrote *True Story: A Comedy Novel.*

JOHN MALKOVICH

Birthplace: Christopher, IL
Birthdate: 12/9/53
Occupation: Actor
Education: Eastern Illinois University, Illinois State University
Debut: (Stage) *True West,* 1982
Signature: *Dangerous Liaisons,* 1988
Facts: Played football and tuba in high school.

Took up acting in college when he fell for a female drama student.

Co-founded the Steppenwolf Theatre in Chicago, in 1976.
Original Job: Enrolled in Eastern Illinois University with plans of becoming an environmentalist
Marriages: Glenne Headly, 1982 (divorced, c. 1988); Nicoletta Peyran (relationship)
Children: Amandine, 1990; Lowey, 1992
Major Award: Emmy, Best Supporting Actor in a Made-for-TV Movie, *Death of a Salesman,* 1986

DAVID MAMET

Birthplace: Chicago, IL
Birthdate: 11/30/47
Occupation: Writer, director
Education: Goddard College, studied at the Neighborhood Playhouse in New York
Debut: (Stage) *The Duck Variations,* 1972
Signature: *Glengarry Glen Ross,* 1984
Facts: Has written several books and children's plays, including *Revenge of the Space Pandas, or Binky Rudich and the Two-Speed Clock.*

Has worked as a busboy, driven a cab, worked at *Oui* magazine, and waited tables. Was an assistant office manager for a real estate company and taught drama at Yale, New York University, and the University of Chicago.

Wrote the screenplays for *The Postman Always Rings Twice* (1981), *The Verdict* (1982), and *The Untouchables* (1987).

Published his first novel, *The Village,* in 1994.

Still writes on a '70s manual typewriter and uses a pencil.

Co-founded the Atlantic Theater Company as a summer workshop in Vermont for his NYU students.
Original Job: Worked backstage at the Hull House Theatre in Chicago
Marriages: Lindsay Crouse, 1977 (divorced); Rebecca Pidgeon, 1991
Children: Willa, 1982; Zosia, 1988; (with Lindsay Crouse). Clara, 1994; Noah, 1999
Major Award: Pulitzer Prize, *Glengarry Glen Ross,* 1984

CAMRYN MANHEIM

Real Name: Debra Manheim
Birthplace: Caldwell, NJ
Birthdate: 3/8/61
Occupation: Actor
Education: Cabrillo Junior College; University of California at Santa Cruz; New York University (MFA)

Debut: (Stage) *Hydriotaphia*, 1987; (Film) *The Bonfire of the Vanities*, 1990; (TV) *Law & Order*, 1991
Signature: *The Practice*
Facts: While at NYU she took crystal methedrine to lose weight, became addicted, and accidentally overdosed.

Between sporadic acting gigs in New York, she was a sign language interpreter for the deaf in theaters and hospitals.

The success in 1993 of her one-woman Off-Broadway show, *Wake Up, I'm Fat!*, caught the eye of David E. Kelley, who cast her in the series pilot of *The Practice*.

Has 12 piercings in her right ear, a tattoo of Pegasus above her ankle, and drives a motorcycle.

Accepting her Emmy Award in 1998, she held it up and said, "This is for all the fat girls!"

Influenced by her activist parents, she was once arrested for marching in a pro-choice demonstartion.
Child: Milo Jacob, 2001
Original Job: Sign language interpreter, improvisation teacher
Major Award: Emmy Award, Outstanding Supporting Actress in Drama Series, *The Practice*, 1998
Quote: "I'm a five-foot-ten Amazon who isn't afraid to be naked or to kiss men or to be sexual anymore."

AIMEE MANN

Birthplace: Richmond, VA
Birthdate: 8/9/60
Occupation: Singer, songwriter
Education: Attended Berklee School of Music
Debut: *Voices Carry*, 1985 (with 'Til Tuesday)
Signature: *Magnolia* soundtrack
Facts: Was abducted to Europe at age 4 by her mother. After a year, Mann's father tracked down his ex-wife and regained their daughter.

Took up music when recovering from mononucleosis.

Majored in bass at Berklee. Says that "no one could teach me how to sing."

Her first band was a postpunk group called the Young Snakes. She quit when she realized her attraction to melodic music.

When her record label went bankrupt, Warner Bros. offered to release her upcoming solo album as a personal favor to her old label head. Mann declined, citing lack of commitment to her and her music.

Her song "Deathly" inspired the screenplay of *Magnolia*.
Marriage: Michael Penn, 1998
Famous Relatives: Sean Penn, actor, brother-in-law; Chris Penn, actor, brother-in-law
Quote: "I think the role of artists and songwriters is to say, 'Maybe you can't do this, but I'll do it for you…' I'll try to sing, out loud, the truth."

MARILYN MANSON

Real Name: Brian Hugh Warner
Birthplace: Canton, OH
Birthdate: 1/5/69
Occupation: Singer, band leader
Education: High school
Debut: (Album) *Portrait of an American Family*, 1994
Facts: An only child, he was sent to a private conservative Christian school for the best possible education, but he resented the restrictions and the warnings about evil rock music. He eventually caused sufficient trouble to be expelled and finished his last two years in a public school.

He formed his band in 1990 and created his alter ego based on Marilyn Monroe and Charles Manson, considering them the most popular personalities of the 1960s.

For his music and stage show, he drew from pornography, horror films, and Satanism because they were the forbidden items of youth.

The title of his album *Antichrist Superstar* is a twist on Andrew Lloyd Webber's *Jesus Christ Superstar*.

He proposed to Rose on Valentine's Eve with an antique diamond ring.

After candlelight vigils and bomb threats at some venues, Manson had a hard time getting booked in certain cities.
Infamy: His group was banned in Salt Lake City after he ripped apart a Mormon Bible on stage.

He sold T-shirts imprinted "Kill God…Kill Your Mom and Dad…Kill Yourself."

During a 1998 rampage in Poughkeepsie, NY, he trashed and burned his dressing room and destroyed four hotel rooms.

Charged with criminal sexual conduct in 2001 after allegedly assaulting a security guard during a concert.
Relationship: Rose McGowan (engaged; never married)
Quote: "To the people who are afraid of things like me, the answer is to raise your kids to be more intelligent."

SHIRLEY MANSON

Birthplace: Edinburgh, Scotland
Birthdate: 8/26/66
Education: High school dropout
Occupation: Singer, guitarist
Debut: (Album) *Garbage*, 1995
Signature: *Version 2.0*, 1998
Facts: Learned to play violin, clarinet and piano.

Left school at 16 to work in a clothing store.

Joined the band Goodbye Mr. McKenzie after she had a crush on the lead singer. Ten years later, around 1994, she left the band to form her own group, Angelfish.
Marriage: Eddie Farrell, sculptor, 1996
Quote: "I was born with rage. What can I say? Under the Chinese calendar I'm a fire horse."

JULIANNA MARGULIES

Birthplace: Spring Valley, NY
Birthdate: 6/8/66
Occupation: Actor
Education: Sarah Lawrence College
Debut: (Film) *Out for Justice*, 1991
Signature: *ER*
Facts: Her father was the ad execu-

tive who wrote the Alka Seltzer "Plop, plop, fizz, fizz" jingle.

Her parents divorced early, and her mother, a former dancer with the American Ballet Theatre, moved her to Paris and then London.

A perfectionist in high school, once threw a 50-page, illustrated research report into the mud because it got an A-minus.

While waiting for an acting break, waitressed at some of New York's trendiest restaurants.

Turned down a $27 million two-year contract offer when she left *ER*.
Relationship: Ron Eldard
Major Award: Emmy, Best Supporting Actress (Drama), *ER*, 1995

WYNTON MARSALIS

Birthplace: New Orleans, LA
Birthdate: 10/18/61
Occupation: Trumpeter
Education: Attended Juilliard on a full scholarship
Debut: (Band) Art Blakey's Jazz Messengers, 1980
Facts: His first trumpet was a hand-me-down from bandleader Al Hirt.

Played with New Orleans Philharmonic at age 14.

Released his first classical album, *Trumpet Concertos,* in 1983. Was first artist ever to receive—or be nominated for—awards in both jazz and classical categories in a single year.

Was named a United Nations peace messenger in 2001.
Children: Wynton, 1990; Simeon, 1992; Jasper Armstrong, 1996
Famous Relatives: Ellis Marsalis, musician, father; Branford Marsalis, musician, brother
Major Awards: Grammy, Best Jazz Performance—Soloist, "Think of One," 1983; Grammy, Best Jazz Performance—Soloist, "Hot House Flowers," 1984; Grammy, Best Jazz Performance—Soloist, "Black Codes from the Underground," 1985; Grammy, Best Jazz Performance—Group, "Black Codes from the

Underground," 1985; Grammy, Best Jazz Performance—Group, "J Mood," 1986; Grammy, Best Jazz Performance—Group, *Marsalis Standard Time Volume I,* 1987; Pulitzer Prize, *Blood on the Fields,* 1997; Grammy, Best Spoken Word Album for Children, *Listen to the Storyteller* (with Graham Greene and Kate Winslet), 1999

PENNY MARSHALL

Real Name: Carole Penny Marshall
Birthplace: New York, NY
Birthdate: 10/15/43
Occupation: Actor, director
Education: University of New Mexico
Debut: (TV) *The Danny Thomas Hour,* 1967
Signature: *Laverne and Shirley*
Facts: Even though the family was Congregationalist, Marshall's mother was convinced that Jewish men make the best husbands, so she sent Penny to a Jewish summer camp each year.

Lost the part of Gloria on TV's *All in the Family* to Sally Struthers.

Was first woman director to have a film take in more than $100 million at the box office (*Big*).
Original Jobs: Dance instructor, secretary
Marriages: Michael Henry (divorced); Rob Reiner, 1971 (divorced, 1979)
Child: Tracy Lee, 1964
Famous Relatives: Garry Marshall, director, producer, brother; Tony Maschiarelli, producer, father

RICKY MARTIN

Real Name: Enrique José Martin Morales
Birthplace: San Juan, PR
Birthdate: 12/24/71
Occupation: Singer
Education: High school
Debut: (Solo Album) *Ricky Martin,* 1988; (Solo English-Language Album) *Ricky Martin,* 1999; (TV)

Getting By, 1993; (Broadway) *Les Misérables,* 1996
Signature: "Livin' La Vida Loca"
Facts: At age six, he began appearing in local television commercials.

When he first tried out the singing group Menudo, he was considered too short. By 1984, he joined as its youngest member, and took "mandatory retirement" before turning 18.

In 1985, legally changed his name from Enrique to Ricky

Played a singing bartender in the soap *General Hospital* in 1993 and by 1994, he had a regular role.

Considers himself a "spiritual" person, is a student of yoga and Buddhism, and shaved his head in India in December, 1998.

Sang the Spanish-language version of the theme to Disney's *Hercules.*

Ricky Martin (1999) has sold over 5 million copies in the U.S. and is the best-selling album ever by a Latin artist.
Relationship: Ines Misan
Major Award: Grammy, Best Latin Pop Performance, *Vuelve,* 1999
Quote: "I have no butt. Everybody tells me that. It's tiny…not even rock climbing helps."

STEVE MARTIN

Birthplace: Waco, TX
Birthdate: 8/14/45
Occupation: Actor, writer
Education: Long Beach State College, UCLA
Debut: (TV) *The Smothers Brothers Comedy Hour,* 1967
Signature: "A wild and crazy guy"
Facts: Lived behind Disneyland and got his start there performing magic tricks and playing the banjo.

Was a cheerleader in high school.

Is a dedicated art collector.

Dated Anne Heche for two years before she broke it off.

Has published sophisticated satirical pieces in *The New Yorker* and the book *Pure Drivel*.

Original Job: Sold guidebooks at Disneyland

Marriage: Victoria Tennant (divorced, 1993); Ellen Ladowsky, writer (relationship)

Major Awards: Emmy, Best Writing in a Comedy, Variety, or Music Program, *The Smothers Brothers Comedy Hour,* 1969; Grammy, Best Comedy Recording, *Let's Get Small,* 1977; Grammy, Best Comedy Recording, *A Wild and Crazy Guy,* 1978

Quote: "I became an actor because I was fearful of becoming a has-been standup comic working Las Vegas. And I became a standup comic because I was fearful of becoming a has-been TV writer. Fear is a very constructive force."

MASTER P

Real Name: Percy Miller
Birthplace: New Orleans, LA
Birthdate: 2/9/69
Occupation: Rapper, actor, movie producer, record and film company executive
Education: Junior college
Debut: (Album) *The Ghetto's Tryin' to Kill Me,* 1994
Signature: No Limit
Facts: The eldest of five children, he grew up in a housing project in an area with a high crime rate and a reputation for violence.

Attended University of Houston on a basketball scholarship but left when he was sidelined with a leg injury.

Moved to Richmond, Virginia, opened a small record store, No Limits, which has become a very successful independent record company and has made him a multi-millionaire.

He sold his debut album out of the trunk of his car in Oakland and New Orleans. It became an underground hit, selling 200,000 copies without radio play.

His film, *I'm 'Bout It,* which he produced, directed, and acted in, was a fictionalized version of his brother's murder.

He tried out for the Continental Basketball Association's team in 1998 and signed on as a free agent, earning $1,000 per week with a $15 per day allowance. Several months later, he tried out for the Charlotte Hornets, an NBA team, but did not make the cut.

In 1997 he started No Limit Sports Management, a company that represented young NBA players, including Ron Mercer (Boston Celtics) and Derek Anderson (Cleveland Cavaliers).

In 1998 *Forbes* ranked him as the tenth highest paid entertainer.

Original Job: Record store owner
Marriage: Sonya Miller
Children: Four children
Quote: "What I learned in the ghetto is that everybody wants more for their money. You gotta be able to give your customers more for their money, 'cause that's how you're going to keep them coming back to you."

PAUL McCARTNEY

Real Name: James Paul McCartney
Birthplace: Liverpool, England
Birthdate: 6/18/42
Occupation: Singer, songwriter, bassist
Education: High school
Debut: Formed the Quarry Men, Moondogs, and the Silver Beatles with John Lennon and George Harrison, 1956–1962
Signature: The Beatles
Facts: When he wanted to use "Yesterday" in his 1984 film *Give My Regards to Broad Street,* he had to apply to the publishers for its use; he no longer owned the copyright of the most recorded song in history (over 2,500 cover versions exist).

Was the first Beatle to quit in 1970, releasing his solo album *McCartney* almost simultaneously with the band's release of *Let It Be.*

His version of "Mary Had a Little Lamb" hit No. 9 on the British charts in June 1972.

In the Paul McCartney Kindergarten in Krakow, Poland, children are taught English through McCartney's songs.

Was knighted by Queen Elizabeth in 1996.

Inherited his wife's fortune after her death and, although no monetary value was placed on the trust, it is estimated that he is now worth over $1 billion.

Infamy: Admitted to taking LSD and was arrested numerous times with Linda for possession of marijuana and for growing it at their Scotland farmhouse. Because of this, his application for a U.S. passport was refused many times.

Marriage: Linda Eastman, 1969 (deceased, 1998); Heather Mills (engaged, 2001)

Children: Heather, 1962 (stepdaughter); Mary, 1969; Stella, 1971; James, 1977

Major Awards: Grammy, Best New Artist (with The Beatles), 1964; Grammy, Best Pop Vocal—Duo or Group, *A Hard Day's Night* (with The Beatles), 1964; Grammy, Song of the Year, "Michelle" (with John Lennon), 1966; Grammy, Best Rock Vocal, "Eleanor Rigby," 1966; Grammy, Album of the Year, *Sgt. Pepper's Lonely Hearts Club Band* (with The Beatles), 1967; Grammy, Best Score, *Let It Be* (with The Beatles), 1970; Grammy, Best Pop Performance—Duo or Group, *Band on the Run* (with Wings), 1974; Grammy, Hall of Fame Winner, *Sgt. Pepper's Lonely Hearts Club Band* (with The Beatles), 1992; Oscar, Best Score, *Let It Be* (with The Beatles), 1970; inducted into the Rock and Roll Hall of Fame (with The Beatles), 1988; NARAS Lifetime Achievement Award, 1990; Grammy, Best Pop Vocal, Duo or Group with Vocal, "Free as a Bird" (with the Beatles), 1996; inducted into Rock and Roll Hall of Fame, 1999.

STELLA MCCARTNEY

Birthplace: England
Birthdate: 9/13/71
Occupation: Fashion designer
Education: Central St. Martin's College of Art and Design
Facts: At 15 she worked at Patou, the French couture house, but left because she was opposed to the use of fur in fashion.

Apprenticed with a Savile Row tailor, enabling her to sew as well as to design.

Her graduation fashion show for St. Martin's featured a song by her father, and her clothes were modeled by friends Kate Moss, Yasmin Le Bon, and Naomi Campbell.

A brief stint running her own company failed, and she was hired by Chloe where she became head designer and revitalized the house's line. In 2001 she left Chloe to run her own line at Gucci.

Like her parents, she is an active member of PETA, and narrated a video about animal cruelty at fur ranches.

Her father advised her, "Nobody is Beatle-proof."
Famous Relatives: Linda Eastman McCartney, photographer/musician, mother (deceased 1998); Paul McCartney, ex-Beatle, father
Quote: "Of course my name opens doors. But they can close just as quickly if I don't deliver."

MATTHEW MCCONAUGHEY

Birthplace: Uvalde, TX
Birthdate: 11/4/69
Occupation: Actor
Education: University of Texas
Debut: (Film) *Dazed and Confused*, 1993
Signature: *A Time To Kill*, 1996
Facts: College friend of Rene Zellweger's, they appeared together in school productions.

Endlessly rereads the motivational book, *The Greatest Salesman in the*

World. Used its techniques to sell his talents to get acting parts.

Was cast in *Kill* after executives vetoed Kevin Costner, Keanu Reeves, Val Kilmer and others in a year-long search. Received just $200,000 to play the part.
Quote: "There are certain nights you and your image just aren't in the same bed."

ERIC MCCORMACK

Birthplace: Toronto, Canada
Birthdate: 4/18/63
Occupation: Actor
Education: Ryerson Polytechnic University; Banff Center for the Arts
Debut: (TV) *The Boys from Syracuse*, 1986; (Film) *Holy Man*, 1998; (Broadway) *The Music Man*, 2001
Signature: *Will & Grace*
Fact: Realized he wanted to be an actor after starring as Jesus in a high-school production of *Godspell*.

Honed his acting skills at the Stratford Shakespeare Theatre Festival in Ontario, Canada where he performed for five seasons.

Met his wife on the set of *Lonesome Dove: The Outlaw Years*, where she was an assistant director.

Has three dogs and a cat.

Learned to play the trombone for his role as Harold Hill in 2001's Broadway revival of *The Music Man*.
Marriage: Janet Holden, 1997
Quote: "The great irony in this is people asking me how it feels to play a gay character. But the weird thing is this is the closest character to me I've ever played."

DYLAN MCDERMOTT

Birthplace: Waterbury, CT
Birthdate: 10/26/61
Occupation: Actor
Education: Fordham University; also trained under Sanford Meisner at the Neighborhood Playhouse
Debut: (Theater) *Biloxi Blues*, 1985; (Film) *Hamburger Hill*, 1987
Signature: *The Practice*

Facts: Moved to Greenwich Village as a teen to live with his father. His playwright-stepmother soon wrote a part for him.

Engagement to Julia Roberts was broken off by her after she fell for Kiefer Sutherland on a movie set.
Original job: Busboy
Marriage: Shiva Afshar, 1995
Child: Colette, 1996
Famous Relative: Eve Ensler, playwright, stepmother
Quote: "My theory about actors is, we're all walking milk cartons. Expiration dates everywhere."

FRANCES MCDORMAND

Birthplace: Illinois
Birthdate: 6/23/57
Occupation: Actor
Education: Bethany College, Yale Drama School
Debut: (Film) *Blood Simple*, 1984
Signature: *Fargo*, 1996
Facts: Born to a Disciples of Christ preacher. The family moved repeatedly throughout the Midwest when she was a child.

Met Holly Hunter when the two studied at Yale. After graduation, Hunter told her she had auditioned for "two weird guys" (the Coen brothers) and that McDormand should too. After repeated failed attempts to get an audition, McDormand finally succeeded. *Blood Simple* not only launched her (and Hunter's) career, it introduced her to future husband Joel.

Was nominated in 1988 for Oscar's best supporting actress (for *Mississippi Burning*), the same year she was also nominated for a Tony for *A Streetcar Named Desire*.
Marriage: Joel Coen, 1994
Child: Pedro, c. 1994 (adopted)
Famous Relative: Ethan Coen, writer, director, producer, brother-in-law
Major Award: Oscar, Best Actress, *Fargo*, 1996

REBA MCENTIRE

Birthplace: Chockie, OK
Birthdate: 3/28/55
Occupation: Singer, songwriter
Education: Southeastern State University
Debut: (Song) "I Don't Want To Be a One-Night Stand," 1976
Signature: "Is There Life Out There?"
Facts: As a teenager, performed with her siblings in the Singing McEntires. Their first single was a tribute to her grandfather, rodeo rider John McEntire.

Appeared in the 1990 movie *Tremors*, as well as other film and TV roles.

Her longtime tour manager and seven of her band members died in a plane crash in 1991.
Original Job: Cattle rancher, rodeo barrel racer
Marriages: Charlie Battles (divorced), Narvel Blackstock, 1989
Child: Shelby, 1990 (with Blackstock)
Major Awards: Grammy, Best Country Vocal—Female, "Whoever's in New England," 1986; Grammy, Best Country Female Vocalist, 1987; Grammy, Best Country Vocal—Collaboration, "Does He Love You" (with Linda Davis), 1993

TIM MCGRAW

Birthplace: Jacksonville, FL
Birthdate: 5/11/66
Occupation: Singer
Education: Attended Northeast Louisiana University
Debut: (Album) *Tim McGraw,* 1993
Signature: *Not a Moment Too Soon*
Facts: Mom Betty was an 18-year-old dancer when she and then bachelor Tug consummated their summer romance while Tug was in baseball camp. Tim learned who his father was only when he found his birth certificate at age 11. Tim met Tug but had little contact until high school, when Tug agreed to help pay for his son's college education.

Started his own management company, Breakfast Table Management, to launch other groups.

The lyrics to his "Indian Outlaw" outraged some Native American groups, who had it banned from radio stations in several states. Infamy: Charged with a felony count of second degree assault after attacking officers who were trying to remove fellow performer Kenny Chesney from a police horse after a concert in Buffalo, NY.
Marriage: Faith Hill, 1996
Child: Gracie Katherine, 1997; Maggie Elizabeth, 1998
Famous Relative: Tug McGraw, baseball player, father
Major Award: Grammy, Best Country Collaboration with Vocals, "Let's Make Love," (with Faith Hill), 2001

EWAN MCGREGOR

Birthplace: Crieff, Scotland
Birthdate: 3/31/71
Occupation: Actor
Education: Attended London's Guildhall School of Music and Drama
Debut: (Film) *Being Human,* 1993
Signature: *Star Wars: Episode 1—The Phantom Menace,* 1999
Facts: Inspired by his uncle, knew he wanted to be in theater at age 9. Left home at 16 to work backstage at Scotland's Perth Repertory Theatre.

Lost nearly 30 pounds and shaved his head for his role in *Trainspotting.* Debated trying to shoot heroin but decided that it would be disrespectful to the recovering addicts acting as technical advisors to the film.
Marriage: Eve Maurakis, 1995
Child: Clara Mathilde, 1996
Famous Relative: Dennis Lawson, actor, uncle

MARK MCGWIRE

Birthplace: Pomona, CA
Birthdate: 10/1/63
Occupation: Baseball player
Education: University of Southern California
Debut: (Major League Baseball) Oakland Athletics, 1986
Signature: Record-setting home-run hitter
Facts: Began playing Little League baseball at 8. Hit a home run in his first at-bat, against a 12-year-old pitcher.

Has 4 brothers, all of whom are over 6 feet tall and weigh more than 200 pounds.

His ex-wife was a bat girl at USC.

Brother Dan played quarterback for the Seattle Seahawks and the Miami Dolphins.

Was drafted by the Montreal Expos out of high school, but when they offered a signing bonus of only $8,500, he opted for college, where he intended to be a pitcher.

Was rookie of the year in 1987, hitting 49 home runs, the most ever for a rookie.

In 1998 smashed Roger Maris's legendary record of 61 home runs in a season, finishing with a total of 70.

His biceps are 20 inches wide.

Hit 500 home runs sooner in his career than any other slugger.

Loves classical music and watching the Learning Channel.

His on-again, off-again girlfriend runs the Mark McGwire Foundation.

Very close to his son, who fills in as a St. Louis Cardinal's batboy and is contractually guaranteed a seat on the team plane with his father.
Infamy: Has admitted to taking androstenedione pills. Though legal and allowed in baseball, this testosterone-producing substance is banned by the NFL and IOC. Also took creatine, a muscle-building substance.
Marriage: Kathy Williamson (divorced, 1988); Ali Dickson (relationship)
Child: Matthew, 1987

SARAH MCLACHLAN

Birthplace: Halifax, Nova Scotia, Canada
Birthdate: 1/28/68
Occupation: Singer, songwriter, concert promoter
Education: Attended Nova Scotia College of Art and Design
Debut: (Album) *Touch*, 1988
Signature: Lilith Fair
Facts: She and two brothers were adopted; at age 19, met her birth mother by coincidence.

Offered a chance to record demo tapes for a Vancouver independent label while in high school, but her parents refused to let her.

Was harassed for years by an obsessive fan, with his letters inspiring the song "Possession." Recognizing his words, he sued, but committed suicide before the matter was resolved.

Named the Lilith concert after Adam's first wife in Jewish mythology, a woman tossed out of Eden for being too independent and forced to make it alone.
Marriage: Ashwin Sood, 1997
Major Awards: Grammy, Best Female Pop Vocal Performance, "Building a Mystery," 1997; Grammy, Best Pop Instrumental Performance, "Last Dance," 1997; Grammy, Best Pop Vocal Performance–Female, "I Will Remember You," 1999
Quote: "Don't think I don't count the horseshoes on my ass daily."

A. J. MCLEAN

Real Name: Alexander James McLean
Birthplace: West Palm Beach, FL
Birthdate: 1/9/78
Occupation: Singer
Debut: (TV) *Hi Honey, I'm Home*, 1991; (Single) "We've Got It Goin' On," 1995; (Album) *Backstreet Boys*, 1995 (American version, 1997)
Signature: "Everybody (Backstreet's Back),"1997

Facts: Has a strong background in theater.

The band is named after Orlando, Florida's Backstreet Market, a popular teen hangout.

The group's debut was a hit in 26 countries before *Backstreet Boys* was released in the U.S.

The "edgy" Backstreet Boy.

Has at least eight tattoos.

His lucky number is 69.

His favorite restaurant is McDonald's.

Spends a half-hour each morning sculpting his goatee.

Has never blown his nose: "When it comes to anything mucus-oriented or phlegm or someone spitting, I gag."

His mother manages his career.

Sometimes performs solo as his British alter ego "Johnny No Name," who covers songs by Stone Temple Pilots and the Commodores.

Entered a rehabilitation hospital in July, 2001 to get treatment for "depression, anxiety, and excessive consumption of alcohol," forcing a delay in the group's summer tour.
Infamy: Band filed suit against former manager Lou Pearlman, claiming he had made $10 million from their labor while they had received $300,000.
Original Job: Actor
Quote: "I'm the complete opposite of every clean-cut, decent-looking guy you could think of, yet I have the biggest heart in the world."

JANET MCTEER

Birthplace: Newcastle, England
Birthdate: 5/8/61
Occupation: Actor
Education: Royal Academy of Dramatic Art
Debut: (Stage) *Mother Courage and Her Children*, 1984; (Film) *Half Moon Street*, 1984
Signature: *Tumbleweeds*, 1999
Facts: Was "tiny" until she was 13, when she shot up six inches in a year; her knees were bandaged to cope with the growing pains. She now stands 6' 1".

Became a British celebrity when she played Virginia Woolf's lover in a BBC made-for-television movie.

While shooting in North Africa, caught a virus which robbed her right eye of its central vision.

Despite her size, is such a chameleon that she was brushed aside by theatergoers waiting for her outside *A Doll's House*.

To nail her *Tumbleweeds* accent, spent three months in South Carolina and watched *Coal Miner's Daughter* "32 million times."
Original Job: Coffee seller at Theatre Royal
Major Award: Tony, Best Actress (Dramatic), *A Doll's House*, 1997
Quote: "Let's face it, there aren't many wonderful scripts for women over the age of 10."

NATALIE MERCHANT

Birthplace: Jamestown, NY
Birthdate: 10/26/63
Occupation: Singer
Education: High school dropout
Debut: (Album, with 10,000 Maniacs) *Human Conflict No. 5*; (Solo album) *Tigerlily*, 1995
Signature: "Carnival"
Facts: After her mother remarried, the family moved to a commune: "I fell in love with those people."

At 16 she dropped out of high school, took college courses, and worked three jobs, including one at a whole foods bakery.

Frequently in the audience for 10,000 Maniacs' performances, she was suddenly invited up to sing, and at 17 joined the group as lead singer. Quit the group in 1992 to go solo.

Dated R.E.M.'s Michael Stipe on and off for three years.
Quote: "People need to change within first, with their hearts before their minds. Now, instead of wanting to change people, I just want to move them."

DEBRA MESSING

Birthplace: Brooklyn, NY
Birthdate: 8/15/68
Occupation: Actor
Education: Brandeis University, New York University (MFA)
Debut: (Off-Broadway) *Four Dogs and a Bone;* (TV) *NYPD Blue,* 1994; (Film) *A Walk in the Clouds,* 1995
Signature: *Will & Grace*
Facts: Graduated summa cum laude from college.

She won her own series, *Ned and Stacey,* after four episodes of *NYPD Blue.*

Appeared twice on *Seinfeld* as Jerry's unavailable crush.

Is allergic to flowers and perfume.
Marriage: Daniel Zelman, 2000
Major Award: Emmy, Best Actress in a Comedy Series, *Will & Grace,* 2000

BETTE MIDLER

Birthplace: Honolulu, HI
Birthdate: 12/1/45
Occupation: Singer, comedian, actor, producer
Education: Attended University of Hawaii
Debut: (Album) *The Divine Miss M,* 1972; (Film) *Hawaii,* 1966
Signature: "Wind Beneath My Wings," 1989
Facts: Named after Bette Davis, which her mother mistakenly thought was pronounced "Bet."

Spent her first 21 years in Hawaii, then worked carefully to cultivate a New Yorker image.

Was married in a Las Vegas chapel by an Elvis impersonator.

Wrote a best-selling children's book, *The Saga of Baby Divine.*
Infamy: Became a gay icon in the 1970s by singing at New York's bath houses, often with then-unknown Barry Manilow as her pianist.
Original Jobs: Pineapple cannery worker, radio station secretary, go-go dancer
Marriage: Martin Von Haselburg, 1984

Child: Sophie, 1986
Major Awards: Grammy, Best New Artist, 1973; Grammy, Best Contemporary/Pop Female Solo Vocal, *The Rose,* 1980; Grammy, Best Children's Recording, *In Harmony, A Sesame Street Record,* 1980; Grammy, Record of the Year, "Wind Beneath My Wings,"1989; Grammy, Song of the Year, "Wind Beneath My Wings," 1989; Grammy, Song of the Year, "From a Distance," 1990; Emmy, Best Individual Performance—Variety or Music Show, *The Tonight Show Starring Johnny Carson,* 1992; Emmy, Outstanding Special — Comedy, Variety, or Music, *Ol' Red Hair Is Back,* 1978; Emmy, Best Individual Performance—Variety or Music Show, *Diva Las Vegas,* 1997; Tony, special award, 1974

ALYSSA MILANO

Birthplace: Brooklyn, NY
Birthdate: 12/19/72
Occupation: Actor
Education: High school dropout
Debut: (Stage) *Annie,* 1980; (Film) *Old Enough,* 1982; (TV) *Who's the Boss,* 1984
Signature: *Who's the Boss*
Facts: Began acting at age eight, as Molly in a national touring company production of *Annie.*

Made an exercise video, *Teen Steam,* and released three albums in Japan.

Says she is "obsessed with religious art" and has an impressive collection of Madonnas, cruicifixes, statues, and rosaries. Also collects Barbie and Madame Alexander dolls.

Her tattoos include an angel, a sacred heart, a garland of flowers, a fairy kneeling in grass, and rosary beads.
Infamy: Successfully sued multiple parties to get images of herself, including both real and fake nude photos, removed from the Internet, and contributed the settlements toward funding Web site www.safe-searching.com, which she developed

with her mother to direct surfers to celebrity sites.
Marriage: Scott Wolf (engaged; never married); Cinjun Tate, singer and guitarist for rock band Remy Zero, 1999 (separated, 1999)
Quote: "Every part I play, I change my hair."

MATTHEW MODINE

Birthplace: Loma Linda, CA
Birthdate: 3/22/59
Occupation: Actor
Education: Attended Brigham Young University
Debut: (TV) *Amy and the Angel,* 1982; (Film) *Baby, It's You,* 1983; (Stage) *Breaking Up,* 1990
Signature: *Married to the Mob,* 1988
Facts: Was raised as a Mormon.

He and his siblings worked at their father's drive-in movie theaters.

Feeling connected to the characters in the musical *Oliver!,* he took up tapdancing.

Was kicked out of at least two high schools.

Married his wife at a Halloween-night costume ceremony at New York City's Plaza Hotel.

Played Vietnam vets in *Birdy* and *Full Metal Jacket,* but turned down the lead in *Top Gun* because of its cold-warrior worldview.

Passionate about horticulture, he is planting hundreds of trees at his upstate NY farm.
Original Job: Drive-in theater worker, electrician, rock band gofer, macrobiotic chef
Marriage: Caridad Rivera, 1980
Children: Ruby, 1990; Boman, c. 1996

JAY MOHR

Real Name: Jon Ferguson Mohr
Birthplace: Verona, NJ
Birthdate: 8/23/71
Occupation: Actor, comedian
Education: High school
Debut: (TV) MTV's *Lip Service,* 1991;

(Film) *For Better or Worse,* 1995
Signature: *Jerry Maguire* (1996)
Facts: After graduating from high school in 1988, Mohr spent two years racking up 10 national comedy shows.

In 1993 he began a two-year stint on *Saturday Night Live,* known for his impersonations of Tony Bennett and Christopher Walken. Though well known for his time on the show, he complains about "All that waiting around for a glimmer of stage time, just getting angry every week...It was just an oppressive, horrible, horrible place to be. I went to work feeling nauseous."

The inside of his left arm is tattooed with "Will 12-27," in honor of his cousin who was killed by a drunk driver in 1995, two days after Christmas.
Wife: Nicole Chamberlain, model, actor, 1998
Quote: "Hey, I'm no nancy boy. I've got my bitchin' truck and my rottweiler. I'm a dude...But I still admit to my girlfriend when I'm wrong."

MONICA

Real Name: Monica Arnold
Birthplace: College Park, GA
Birthdate: 12/24/80
Occupation: Singer
Education: High school
Debut: (Single) "Don't Take It Personal," 1995; (Album) *Miss Thang,* 1995; (TV) *Living Single*
Signature: "The Boy Is Mine" (1998)
Facts: Began to sing publicly in church at age 2, and at 12 was discovered at a talent show.

At age 14 with her debut single became the youngest artist to top the Billboard charts. Her 1998 album, *The Boy Is Mine,* produced three consecutive No. 1 singles.

Had a 4.0 average at Atlanta County Day School.

Rapper Queen Latifah is her manager.
Major Award: Grammy, R&B Perfor-

mance—Duo or Group with vocal, "The Boy Is Mine" (with Brandy), 1998

DEMI MOORE

Real Name: Demetria Guynes
Birthplace: Roswell, NM
Birthdate: 11/11/62
Occupation: Actor
Education: Left high school to model in Europe, studied with Zina Provendie
Debut: (Film) *Choices,* 1981; (TV) *General Hospital,* 1981 [see page 68 for a complete filmography]
Signature: *Ghost,* 1990
Facts: Was cross-eyed as a child and had an operation to correct it, wearing a patch over one eye.

Decided to become an actor in high school when she lived in the same building as Nastassja Kinski.

In order to play coke addict Jules in the 1985 movie *St. Elmo's Fire,* she had to sign a contract stipulating that she would stop her own alcohol and drug abuse, an agreement that caused her to turn her life around.

Was engaged to Emilio Estevez.

She and Bruce Willis were married by singer Little Richard.
Infamy: Posed nude and pregnant on the cover of *Vanity Fair.*
Original Job: Model
Marriages: Freddy Moore (divorced), Bruce Willis, 1987 (separated, 1998); Oliver Whitcomb (relationship)
Children: Rumer Glenn, 1988; Scout Larue, 1991; Tallulah Belle, 1994

JULIANNE MOORE

Real Name: Julie Anne Smith
Birthplace: Fort Bragg, NC
Birthdate: 12/3/60
Occupation: Actor
Education: Boston University
Debut: (TV) *Edge of Night,* 1983; (Film) *Tales from the Darkside: The Movie,* 1990
Signature: *Boogie Nights,* 1997
Facts: Was an Army brat.

Played good and evil twins Frannie

and Sabrina on *As the World Turns.*

Has vowed not to gorge or starve for a part after weight loss for *Safe* left her sick for a year.

Is a self-described "library girl" and "magazine addict."

Credits her love of reading with providing an eye for good scripts.
Original Job: Waitress
Marriages: John Gould Rubin, c. 1984 (divorced, 1995); Bart Freundlich (relationship)
Child: Caleb, 1997
Quote: "I like falling down and into walls. I like physical comedy.

MANDY MOORE

Birthplace: Nashua, NH
Birthdate: 4/10/84
Occupation: Singer
Debut: *So Real,* 1999
Signature: "Candy"
Facts: Decided to become a performer after seeing a stage revival of *Oklahoma!* at age 6.

Was Orlando's "National Anthem Girl" because of her frequent gigs opening sporting matches.

Was discovered by a FedEx man who had a friend at Epic Records.

Aims to do Broadway.

Is learning to play guitar.

Is friends with Jessica Simpson.
Relationship: Wilmer Valderrama, actor
Quote: "I don't think I have to dress sexy or provocative to get my point across. I don't sing about stuff I haven't experienced yet."

ALANIS MORISSETTE

Birthplace: Ottawa, Canada
Birthdate: 6/1/74
Occupation: Singer, songwriter
Education: High school
Debut: (Album) *Alanis,* 1991
Signature: "You Oughta Know," 1995
Facts: At age 10, appeared as a sweet little girl on Nickelodeon's *You Can't Do That on Television.* At 17,

was a Queen of Disco, dubbed the Canadian Debbie Gibson.

During her dance pop days, toured with Vanilla Ice.

Has a twin brother, Wade.

Claimed it took 15 to 45 minutes to write most of the songs on *Jagged Little Pill.*

Major Awards: Grammy, Album of the Year, *Jagged Little Pill,* 1995; Grammy, Best Rock Album, *Jagged Little Pill,* 1995; Grammy, Best Female Rock Vocalist, "You Oughta Know," 1995; Grammy, Best Rock Song, "You Oughta Know," 1995; Grammy, Best Long Form Music Video, *Jagged Little Pill Live,* 1997; Grammy, Best Rock Song, "Uninvited," 1998

TONI MORRISON

Real Name: Chloe Anthony Wofford
Birthplace: Lorain, OH
Birthdate: 2/18/31
Occupation: Author
Education: Howard University, Cornell University
Debut: (Book) *The Bluest Eye,* 1969
Signature: *Beloved*
Facts: Has served as an editor at Random House, helping to publish the works of other black Americans like Toni Cade Bambara, Angela Davis, and Muhammad Ali.

Has taught at Harvard, Yale, and Princeton.

Original Job: Textbook editor
Marriage: Harold Morrison, 1958 (divorced, 1964)
Children: Harold Ford, 1961; Slade Kevin, 1965
Major Awards: National Book Critics Circle Award, *Song of Solomon,* 1977; Pulitzer Prize, *Beloved,* 1988; Nobel Prize for Literature, 1993
Quote: "Although we women are coming into our own, we still love you men for what you are, just to let you know."

VAN MORRISON

Real Name: George Ivan Morrison
Birthplace: Belfast, Northern Ireland
Birthdate: 8/31/45
Occupation: Singer, songwriter
Education: High school dropout
Debut: (Song) "Don't Start Crying" (with Them), 1964
Signature: "Brown Eyed Girl"
Facts: Was lead singer of Them from 1964 to 1967 and has worked solo ever since.

In 1965, wrote "Gloria," which achieved moderate success but didn't hit the U.S. top ten until it was covered by The Shadows of Knight in 1966.

Marriage: Janet Planet, 1968 (divorced, 1973)
Child: Shana, 1970
Major Award: Grammy, Best Pop Vocal Collaboration (with Sinead O'Connor and the Chieftains), "Have I Told You Lately That I Love You," 1995

MEGAN MULLALY

Birthplace: Los Angeles, CA
Birthdate: 11/12/58
Occupation: Actor
Education: Attended Northwestern University
Debut: (TV movie) *The Children Nobody Wanted,* 1981; (Film) *Risky Business,* 1983; (Broadway) *Grease,* 1994
Signature: *Will & Grace*
Facts: Raised in Oklahoma City and as a child performed with the Oklahoma Ballet.

Her mother was a model.

Her first TV series role was playing Ellen Burstyn's daughter on *The Ellen Burstyn Show.*

Played guest roles on many well-known sitcoms, including *Seinfeld, Frasier* and *Mad About You.*
Marriage: Michael Katcher (married and divorced in the early '90s)
Famous relative: Carter Mullaly Jr., actor (contract player for

Paramount)
Major Award: Emmy, Best Supporting Actress in a Comedy Series, 1999–2000
Quote: "I should have my 'girl citizenship' revoked. I never get facials. I never get my nails done. I'm so busy,"

FRANKIE MUNIZ

Birthplace: Wood Ridge, NJ
Birthdate: c. 1985
Occupation: Actor
Debut: (TV) *To Dance with Olivia,* 1997; (Film) *My Dog Skip,* 2000
Signature: *Malcolm in the Middle,* 2000
Facts: When money from *Malcolm* came in, Muniz rewarded himself with golf clubs and a new computer.

Is keeping a video record of his life and career.

Counts his appearance on the cover of *Super Teen* magazine as the culmination of a dream.
Quote: "Acting classes, I guess, are good, and I would like to maybe sometime take one, but I would feel like I'm learning someone else's technique. I like mine."

EDDIE MURPHY

Birthplace: Hempstead, NY
Birthdate: 4/3/61
Occupation: Actor
Education: Nassau Community College
Debut: (TV) *Saturday Night Live,* 1980
Signature: *Beverly Hills Cop,* 1984
Facts: Father was a policeman who died when Eddie was 5.

Was voted most popular at Roosevelt Jr.-Sr. High School in Roosevelt, NY.

Created and produced the TV series *The Royal Family,* which was cut short upon the sudden death of the star Redd Foxx.

Co-created the controversial animated comedy *The PJ's* (complaints, from Spike Lee among others, arose about its racial depictions, though TV reviewers found it hilarious)and provides the voice of lead character Thurgood Stubbs

Co-owns the L.A. restaurant Georgia with Denzel Washington. **Infamy:** In May 1997, police tracking a transvestite prostitute pulled Murphy's Toyota over at 4:45 a.m.; police arrested the prostitute and immediately released Murphy, who explained he was only giving the streetwalker a lift. In the aftermath Murphy sued the *National Enquirer* for publishing interviews with transvestite prostitutes claiming to have had sex with Murphy; the suit was eventually dropped.
Original Job: Shoe store clerk

Marriage: Nicole Mitchell, 1992
Children: Ashlee, 1987; Bria, 1989; (with Nicolle Rader). Eddie Jr., c. 1989; (with Paulette McNeeley). Christian Edward, 1990 (with Tamara Hood). Miles Mitchell, 1992; Shayne Audra, 1994; Zola Ivy, 1999
Major Award: Grammy, Best Comedy Recording, *Eddie Murphy—Comedian,* 1983
Quote: "You get born only once in this business, but you can die over and over again. Then you make comebacks."

BILL MURRAY

Birthplace: Wilmette, IL
Birthdate: 9/21/50
Occupation: Actor, writer
Education: Loyola Academy, Regis College, Second City Workshop in Chicago
Debut: (TV) *Saturday Night Live,* 1977
Signature: *Ghostbusters,* 1984
Facts: Was a pre-med student at St. Regis College.

Provided the voice of Johnny Storm, the Human Torch, on Marvel Comics' radio show, *The Fantastic Four.* This is where he was heard by the producers of *Saturday Night Live.*

Bill's son, Homer Banks, is named after legendary Chicago Cub Ernie Banks.

In 1981, performed the song "The Best Thing (Love Song)" for John Waters' *Polyester.*
Original Job: Pizza maker
Marriage: Margaret Kelly (divorced, 1996)
Children: Homer, 1982; Luke, 1985
Famous Relative: Brian Doyle-Murray, actor, brother
Major Award: Emmy, Best Writing in a Comedy Series, *Saturday Night Live,* 1977

MIKE MYERS

Birthplace: Scarborough, Canada
Birthdate: 5/25/63
Occupation: Actor, writer
Education: High school
Debut: (TV) *Mullarkey & Myers,* 1984; (Film) *Elvis Stories,* 1989
Signature: Austin Powers
Facts: When he was a child, Myers's comedy-loving father would wake his three sons at night to watch *Monty Python.*

First appeared in TV commercials when he was 4, and at 8 he did a commercial with Gilda Radner. Also appeared as a kid on Canadian TV programs such as the dance show, *Boogie Junior.*

Modeled his *Saturday Night Live* character Linda "Coffee Talk" Richman on his mother-in-law.

Wrote the script for the original *Austin Powers* in three weeks.

Started a retro-mod band, Ming Tea.

Hobbies include watching old war footage and painting toy soldiers.

Chris Farley originally recorded nearly all the voices for the lead character in *Shrek* before he died in 1977. And Myers first recorded *Shrek* in a Canadian voice, before redoing it with a Scottish accent.
Marriage: Robin Ruzan, 1993
Major Awards: Emmy, Outstanding Writing in a Comedy Series, *Saturday Night Live,* 1989

LIAM NEESON

Birthplace: Ballymena, Northern Ireland
Birthdate: 6/7/52
Occupation: Actor
Debut: (Stage) *In the Risen,* 1976; (Film) *Excalibur,* 1981
Signature: *Schindler's List,* 1993
Facts: At age 9, joined a boxing team run by a priest. Nose was broken during an early match, and had it set on site by his manager. Quit boxing at age 17.

First starring role was the disfigured hero of the film *Darkman,* 1990.

Chipped his pelvis in 2000 after hitting a deer while riding his motorcycle.
Original Job: Forklift operator, architect's assistant, amateur boxer
Marriage: Natasha Richardson, 1994
Children: Micheál, 1995; Daniel Jack N., 1996
Quote: "You have these people in therapy 25 years because, what, their moms didn't cuddle them? I'm sorry. Get a f---in' life."

WILLIE NELSON

Birthplace: Abbott, TX
Birthdate: 4/30/33
Occupation: Singer, songwriter, guitarist, actor
Education: Baylor University
Debut: (Album) *...And Then I Wrote,* 1962; (Film) *The Electric Horseman,* 1979
Signature: "Mamas, Don't Let Your Babies Grow Up To Be Cowboys," 1978
Facts: Nelson taught at Baptist Sunday school until officials objected to him playing in seedy bars.

Sold his first song, "Family Bible," for $50 to feed his family; it became a huge hit, performed by more than 70 country artists.

Organized Farm Aid concerts to help midwestern farmers stricken by drought and threatened with fore-closure.

Began writing songs at age 7.
Infamy: In 1991, after a seven-year dispute with the IRS over $16.7 million in back taxes, the government seized most of Nelson's possessions (country club, recording studio, 44-acre ranch, 20 other properties in four states, instruments, recordings, and memorabilia).

Arrested in 1994 for possession of marijuana. Charges were later dismissed.
Original Jobs: Janitor, door-to-door salesman (Bibles, encyclopedias, vacuum cleaners, sewing machines), hosted country music shows on Texas radio stations
Marriages: Martha Matthews, 1952 (divorced, 1962); Shirley Collie, 1963 (divorced, 1971); Connie Koepke (divorced, 1989); Annie D'Angelo, 1991
Children: Lana, 1953; Susie, 1957; Billy, 1958 (deceased, 1991); (with Martha Matthews). Paula Carlene, 1969; Amy, 1973; (with Connie Koepke). Lukas Autry, 1988; Jacob Micah, 1990
Major Awards: Grammy, Best Country Vocal—Male, "Blue Eyes Cryin' in the Rain," 1975; Grammy, Best Country Vocal—Male, "Georgia on My Mind," 1978; Grammy, Best Country Performance—Duo or Group, "Mamas Don't Let Your Babies Grow Up To Be Cowboys" (with Waylon Jennings), 1978; Grammy, Best Country Song, "On the Road Again," 1980; Grammy, Best Country Vocal—Male, "Always on My Mind," 1982; Grammy, Best Country Song, "Always on My Mind," 1982; Grammy, Legend Award, 1990; inducted into the Country Music Hall of Fame in 1993

PAUL NEWMAN

Birthplace: Cleveland, OH
Birthdate: 1/26/25
Occupation: Actor, director, producer

Education: Kenyon College, Yale School of Drama, Actors Studio
Debut: (Film) *The Silver Chalice*, 1954
Signature: *The Hustler*, 1961
Facts: Briefly attended Ohio University and was allegedly asked to leave for crashing a beer keg into the president's car.

The Newman's Own food company he founded in 1987 with writer friend A.E. Hochner has donated more than $100 million to charity.

Has worked on more than nine movies with actor wife Joanne Woodward.

A die-hard, marching liberal, he invested in the leftist opinion-making magazine, *The Nation*.

Is a professional race car driver.
Marriages: Jacqueline Witte (divorced), Joanne Woodward, 1958
Children: Scott, 1950 (deceased); Susan, 1953; Stephanie, 1955; (with Jacqueline Witte). Elinor "Nell" Teresa, 1959; Melissa Steward, 1961; Claire Olivia, 1965
Major Awards: Oscar, Jean Hersholt Humanitarian Award, 1993; Oscar, Lifetime Achievement, 1985; Oscar, Best Actor, *The Color of Money*, 1986

THANDIE NEWTON

Real Name: Thandiwe Newton
Birthplace: Zambia
Birthdate: 11/6/72
Occupation: Actor
Education: Cambridge University
Debut: (Film) *Flirting*, 1991
Signature: *Beloved*, 1999
Fact: First name is pronounced "Tandie" and is Zulu for "beloved."

Dated Australian director John Duigan, 25 years her senior, when she was 17.

At 18, was cast by Michael Douglas in *Made in America* but walked out when she was treated badly by the crew.

Majored in anthropology at Cambridge.

Turned down a lead role in the big-screen version of *Charlie's*

Angels to work on low-budget thriller *It Was an Accident*, written by her husband.
Marriage: Oliver Parker, 1998
Child: Ripley, 2000
Quote: "Rather than walk into an audition and spend 20 minutes convincing people that you're more than tits and arse, you say you've got a degree from Cambridge, and it's amazing how it cuts through the crap."

WAYNE NEWTON

Birthplace: Norfolk, VA
Birthdate: 4/3/42
Occupation: Entertainer
Education: High school dropout
Debut: (TV) *Jackie Gleason and His American Scene Magazine*, 1962; (Film) *80 Steps to Jonah*, 1969
Signature: "Danke Schoen"
Facts: Protégé of Jackie Gleason.

Partly Native American.

In 1999, signed a multimillion-dollar deal to perform seven shows a week, 40 weeks a year, for up to 10 years in a new showroom bearing his name at the Stardust Hotel in Las Vegas.
Infamy: In 1992, declared bankruptcy, listing debts of more than $20 million.

In 1994 his creditors again went to court, charging that, despite millions in current earnings, he continued spending lavishly on himself (including a reported $75,000 repairing his home pond for his pet penguins) and made little effort to pay what he owed them.
Marriages: Elaine Okamura (divorced, 1985); Kathleen McCrone, 1994
Child: Erin, 1976 (with Elaine Okamura)

JACK NICHOLSON

Birthplace: Neptune, NJ
Birthdate: 4/22/37
Occupation: Actor, director, producer, screenwriter

Education: Studied with the Players Ring acting group
Debut: (Stage) *Tea and Sympathy*, 1957; (Film) *Cry-Baby Killer*, 1958
Signature: *One Flew Over the Cuckoo's Nest*, 1975 [see page 68 for a complete filmography]
Facts: Recorded *The Elephant's Child*, a children's record, with Bobby McFerrin (1987).

Abandoned by his father in childhood, he was raised believing his grandmother was his mother and his real mother was his older sister. The truth was revealed to him years later when a *Time* magazine researcher uncovered the truth while preparing a story on the star.

Has been nominated 11 times for the Academy Award.

Infamy: Known for being a ladies' man, Nicholson had a 17-year relationship with actress Anjelica Huston that ended in 1990 when Nicholson revealed that actor Rebecca Broussard, his daughter's best friend, was carrying his child.

During a later two-year falling out period with Broussard, he dated a 20-year-old and allegedly fathered her baby girl.

Was accused of using a golf club to strike the windshield of a '69 Mercedes that had cut him off in traffic in 1994. The driver's civil suit was settled out of court.

Admitted the paternity of Caleb Goddard, an adult New York City producer and writer. The public acknowledgment arose out of a messy civil battle between Nicholson and Goddard's mother, actress Susan Anspach.
Original Job: Office boy in MGM's cartoon department
Marriage: Sandra Knight, 1961 (divorced, 1966)
Children: Jennifer Norfleet, c. 1964 (with Sandra Knight). Caleb Goddard, 1970 (with Susan Anspach). Lorraine, 1990; Raymond, 1992 (with Rebecca Broussard)
Major Awards: Oscar, Best Actor, *One Flew over the Cuckoo's Nest*, 1975; Oscar, Best Supporting Actor, *Terms*

of Endearment, 1983; Grammy, Best Recording for Children, *The Elephant's Child,* 1987; Oscar, Best Actor, *As Good As It Gets,* 1997
Quote: "More good times—that's my motto."

LESLIE NIELSEN

Real Name: Leslie Nielsen
Birthplace: Regina, Saskatchewan
Birthdate: 2/11/26
Occupation: Actor
Education: Lorne Greene's Academy of Radio Arts, Toronto
Debut: (TV) *Studio One's Battleship Bismarck,* 1950; (Film) *The Vagabond King,* 1956
Signature: *The Naked Gun*
Facts: Spent his childhood 100 miles from the Arctic Circle.

Father was a Royal Canadian Mountie.

A prolific actor, he appeared on countless television programs—over 45 live dramas in 1950 alone, and over 1,500 shows to date—including everything from *Playhouse 90, Wagon Train, Dr. Kildare,* and *Bonanza* to *M*A*S*H* and *The Love Boat.*

Comedic career was launched with *Airplane!*

Author of *The Naked Truth* (1993) and *Bad Golf My Way* (1996).
Original Job: Royal Canadian Air Force; D.J. and radio announcer
Marriages: Monica Boyer, singer (1950; divorced 1955); Alisand "Sandy" Ullman (1958; divorced, 1974); Brooks Nielsen (divorced, 1982); Barbaree Earl (relationship, since 1981)
Children: Thea, 1961; Maura, 1963 (with Ullman)
Famous Relative: Jean Hersholt, character actor, uncle.
Quote: "At this stage of my life, I don't give a damn. If they want to type me, let 'em. I just want to maintain whatever celebrity status I have, so they'll keep inviting me to golf tournaments."

CYNTHIA NIXON

Birthplace: New York, NY
Birthdate: 4/9/66
Occupation: Actor
Education: Barnard College; Yale Drama School
Debut: (TV) *The Seven Wishes of a Rich Kid,* 1979; (Film) *Little Darlings,* 1980; (Stage) *The Philadelphia Story,* 1980
Signature: *Sex and the City*
Facts: Met her husband in junior high school.

When filming *Amadeus* in Prague, flew back and forth five times so she wouldn't miss high school classes.

In 1984, appeared on Broadway at the same time in both *The Real Thing* and *Hurlyburly,* two blocks apart.

Co-founded The Drama Dept., whose members include Billy Crudup and Sarah Jessica Parker.
Marriage: Danny Mozes
Child: Samantha, 1996
Quote: "I have very nice men in my life. But I see men all around me who shock and horrify me."

NICK NOLTE

Real Name: Nicholas King Nolte
Birthplace: Omaha, NE
Birthdate: 2/8/41
Occupation: Actor, producer
Debut: (TV) *The Framing of Billy the Kid,* 1973; (Film) *Return to Macon County,* 1975
Signature: *Prince of Tides,* 1991
Facts: Did runway and print modeling and appeared on Clairol box for many years.

Was 35 before gaining attention for his role in *Rich Man, Poor Man.*

Known to show up in public wearing pajama bottoms.

Has openly admitted lying to the press to create a persona. He has lied about his educational background, claiming that he won football scholarships to several different universities, and once told a reporter, as a lark, that his ex-wife had been a high-wire circus performer.

Infamy: Convicted in 1962 for selling fake draft cards.

Was sued for palimony by longtime companion Karen Louise Eklund; suit was settled out of court.

Original Jobs: Model, ironworker
Marriages: Sheila Page (divorced 1971); Sharon Haddad (divorced 1983); Rebecca Linger (divorced 1991); Vicki Lewis (relationship)
Children: Brawley King, 1986 (with Linger)
Quote: "Early on I decided that I was going to lie to the press. The best approach to talking about my personal life was to lie."

EDWARD NORTON

Birthplace: Columbia, MD
Birthdate: 8/18/69
Occupation: Actor
Education: Yale University
Debut: (Film) *Primal Fear*, 1996
Signature: *Primal Fear*
Facts: Was on the baseball team in high school.

When Leonardo DiCaprio dropped out of *Primal Fear*, Paramount launched an international search of 2,100 actors with no success. Costar Richard Gere was ready to walk from the project until Norton read for the part.

Grandfather James Rouse designed Boston's Faneuil Hall and New York's South Street Seaport. Father Ed Sr., a lawyer, was a federal prosecutor under Jimmy Carter.

Studied astronomy and Japanese (he's fluent) in college before getting a degree in history.

Original Jobs: Proofreader, waiter, low-income housing worker
Relationship: Salma Hayek
Famous Relative: James Rouse, architect, grandfather

CONAN O'BRIEN

Birthplace: Brookline, MA
Birthdate: 4/18/63
Occupation: Talk show host
Education: Harvard University
Debut: (TV) *Not Necessarily the News*, 1985
Signature: *NBC's Late Night with Conan O'Brien*
Facts: Has written for *Saturday Night Live* and *The Simpsons*.

While at Harvard, served as president of *The Harvard Lampoon* for two years, the first person to do so since Robert Benchley in 1912.

First TV producing credit was *Lookwell* (1991), a sitcom pilot starring Adam West as a former TV detective who becomes a real cop.

Once dated Lisa Kudrow, who he met while performing with the Groundlings.

Famous Relative: Denis Leary, actor, cousin
Major Award: Emmy, Best Writing in a Variety or Music Program, *Saturday Night Live*, 1989
Quote: "The nightmare is that you spend the rest of your life being funny at parties and people say, 'Why didn't you do *that* when you were on television?'"

CHRIS O'DONNELL

Birthplace: Chicago, IL
Birthdate: 6/26/70
Occupation: Actor
Education: Boston College, UCLA
Debut: (TV) *Jack and Mike*, 1986; (Film) *Men Don't Leave*, 1990
Signature: *Scent of a Woman*, 1992
Facts: Youngest of seven children (four sisters and two brothers), grew up in Winnetka, IL.

Began modeling and appearing in commercials in 1983, at age 13. Appeared in a McDonald's commercial opposite Michael Jordan.

Was 17 when he auditioned for *Men Don't Leave*. His mother had to promise him a new car to get him to try out. He is still waiting for that car.

Originally cast as Barbra Streisand's son in *Prince of Tides*, but she decided to have her real-life son play the role instead.

Took time off from pursuing a degree in marketing from Boston College in order to work with Al Pacino on *Scent of a Woman*.

Marriage: Caroline Fentress, 1997
Child: Lily Anne, 1999

ROSIE O'DONNELL

Birthplace: Commack, NY
Birthdate: 3/21/62
Occupation: Actor, comedian
Education: Dickinson College and Boston University
Debut: (TV) *Gimme a Break*, 1986; (Film) *A League of Their Own*, 1992; (Stage) *Grease*, 1994
Signature: *The Rosie O'Donnell Show*
Facts: Won the *Star Search* comedy competition five times.

Fascinated with the blue-collar mundane, she began extensively collecting McDonald's Happy Meal figurines.

Against her agent's advice, she auditioned for—and won—the role of Betty Rizzo in the Broadway revival of *Grease* in 1994. She had no theater experience and says she'd never sung in public before.

In a 1999 interview with Tom Selleck, who once filmed a commercial for the NRA, she began a heated debate about gun control. Selleck finally declared, "I didn't come on your show to have a debate, I came on your show to plug a movie."

In 2000, her producers sued radio station Rosie 105 (KRSK-FM) in Portland, Ore. over the name and a logo they said is similar to theirs.

Helped contestant Jerry Halpin win $32,000 as a phone friend on *Who Wants to Be a Millionaire*. Before giving her final answer, she promised Halpin that if she were wrong, she would pay him the money out of guilt.

Appearing on *Millionaire* as a contestant, she raised $500,000 for the For All Kids Foundation.

Admitted in her magazine Rosie (started in 2001) that she's been in therapy on and off since she was 16 and has used anti-depressants for the last two years to alleviate her depression.

Children: Parker Jaren, 1995; Chelsea Belle, 1997; Blake Christopher, 1999; Maria, c. 1997 (all adopted).

Major Awards: Emmy, Best Host—Talk or Service Show, *The Rosie O'Donnell Show*, 1995–96; Emmy, Best Host—Talk or Service Show, *The Rosie O'Donnell Show*, 1996–97; Emmy, Best Host—Talk or Service Show, *The Rosie O'Donnell Show*, 1997–98; 1998–99; 1999-00; 2000-01

ASHLEY OLSEN

Birthdate: 6/13/86
Occupation: Actor
Debut: (TV) *Full House*, 1987
Facts: Two minutes older than fraternal twin sister Mary-Kate and has a freckle under her nose.

Their mother says, "When they need someone to be more active or emotional, they let Ashley do it."

The twins' commercial empire includes Olsen Twins books (100-plus titles), videos (over 20), game cartridges for Nintendo and Playstation, and a popular Web site, www.marykateandashley.com, plus a pair of Olsen Barbie dolls and a clothing line from Wal-Mart. How is she different from her twin? "My voice is deeper."

Famous Relative: Jamie Olsen, former dancer with the Los Angeles Ballet, mother

MARY-KATE OLSEN

Birthdate: 6/13/86
Occupation: Actor
Debut: (TV) *Full House*, 1987
Facts: Wants to be a candymaker or a cowgirl when she grows up.

The twins' commercial empire includes Olsen Twins books (100-plus titles), videos (over 20), game cartridges for Nintendo and Playsta-

tion, and a popular Web site, www.marykateandashley.com, plus a pair of Olsen Barbie dolls and a clothing line from Wal-Mart.

"Mary-Kate is more serious, so she gets the serious lines to do," says her mother.

Famous Relative: Jamie Olsen, former dancer with the Los Angeles Ballet, mother

SHAQUILLE O'NEAL

Birthplace: Newark, NJ
Birthdate: 3/6/72
Occupation: Basketball player
Education: Louisiana State University
Facts: His rap album, *Shaq Diesel*, sold more than one million copies. Got his rap start by singing on "What's Up Doc," a song put out in 1993 by his favorite rap group, FU-Schnickens.

He stands seven feet one inch, weighs 303 pounds, and wears size 21 triple-E shoes.

His first name translates, ironically, to "little one."

Spent most of his adolescence in Germany, where his stepfather was an army sergeant.

Relationship: Arnetta (engaged)
Children: Taheara, 1996
Major Awards: NBA Rookie of the Year, 1993;Winner of NBA Scoring Title 1995; Gold Medal at 1996 Olympics

SUZE ORMAN

Real Name: Suzie Orman
Birthdate: 6/5/51
Occupation: Author, financial guru
Education: University of Illinois at Urbana-Champaign
Signature: *Nine Steps to Financial Freedom* (1997)
Facts: As a child, her parents lost their boardinghouse in a liability suit, and 10 years later her father's deli burned down. He suffered third-degree burns on his arms after he ran inside to save the cash register. She claims that incident taught her that money is "more important than life."

During college, she roomed with John Belushi and his wife, Judy. "I told Judy he'd never amount to anything. Shows you what I know about picking husbands."

Her degree is in social work.

After college, she waitressed at the Buttercup Bakery in Berkeley, Califoria, for seven years before talking her way into a stockbroker's job at Merrill Lynch. One of the first female brokers in northern California, she sought out unusual clients, like truck drivers and waitresses, and consulted a crystal on investment decisions.

In 1987 opened her own investment/financial advisory firm, which failed in six months because of an employee dispute over commissions, which was finally settled in court.

Receives up to $20,000 for lecture appearances. Is the most successful personality ever on PBS pledge drives.

She lives alone in the same one-bedroom, one-story home she bought 23 years ago, and drives a 1987 BMW.

Quote: "I don't care that I don't look like a hotshot and my English isn't always proper. People can relate to that. I've helped people realize their dreams."

JULIA ORMOND

Birthplace: Epsom, Surrey, England
Birthdate: 1/4/65
Occupation: Actor
Education: Attended West Surrey College of Art and Design; Webber-Douglas Academy of Dramatic Art, London
Debut: (Stage) *Faith, Hope and Charity*, 1989; (TV) *Traffik*, 1990; (Film) *The Baby of Macon*, 1993
Signature: *Legends of the Fall*, 1994
Fact: Her first acting job was a commercial for cottage cheese.

Middle name is Karin.

Father is a millionaire software designer.

Formerly dated Gabriel Byrne.

Original Job: Waitress
Marriages: Rory Edwards (divorced, 1993); Jon Rubin, 1999
Major Award: Emmy, Investigative Journalism, *Calling the Ghosts: A Story About Rape, War and Women*, 1997–98

OZZY OSBOURNE

Real Name: John Michael Osbourne
Birthplace: Birmingham, England
Birthdate: 12/3/48
Occupation: Singer
Debut: (Album) *Black Sabbath*, 1969; (Solo album) *Blizzard of Oz, 1980*
Signature: Godfather of heavy metal
Facts: Was the vocalist with Black Sabbath until he was kicked out of the band in 1979.

The original band members reunited in 1997 for a series of concerts in Birmingham and to record an album.

Gave a facelift to his favorite bulldog Baldrick, whose face wrinkles produced sores.

Collects art, particularly Victorian nudes.

A member of the Church of England, he kneels to pray backstage before performances.

Has 15 tattoos.
Infamy: He spent years on various drugs, was often in a clinic to kick his addictions. Doctors determined he has a chemical imbalance resulting from years of alcohol and drugs, and he has been drug- and alcohol-free since 1991.

In 1982 he bit off the head of a live bat, thinking it was made of rubber, but when it bit him back and lashed his face with its wings, he rushed for a rabies shot.

Bit the head off a white dove in front of American businessmen.

Shot his ex-wife's 17 cats.

Was arrested in San Antonio for urinating on the Alamo (he was drunk and wearing a dress).

In 1989 he was charged with attempted manslaughter after allegedly trying to strangle his wife, Sharon, but she later dropped the charges.

In the mid-'80s, he was taken to court by parents who accused him of recording subliminal messages urging teens to commit suicide.
Original Jobs: Car-horn assembly-line worker; slaughterhouse worker
Marriages: Thelma (divorced 1981); Sharon Arden, 1982
Children: Elliott, c. 1966; Jessica, c. 1972; Louis, c. 1975 (with Thelma; Elliott was her son from a previous relationship but took Osbourne's name). Aimee, 1983; Kelly, c. 1984; Jack, c. 1985.
Major Award: Grammy, Best Heavy Metal Performance, "I Don't Want to Change the World," 1994
Quote: "I used to be an alcoholic drug addict, now I'm a workaholic. I've gotta keep moving all the time."

DONNY OSMOND

Real Name: Donald Clark Osmond
Birthplace: Ogden, Utah
Birthdate: 12/9/57
Occupation: Singer, keyboardist, actor, TV host
Education:
Debut: (TV) *The Andy Williams Show*, 1963; (Album) *One Bad Apple*, 1971; (Film) *Goin' Coconuts*, 1978; (Stage) *Little Johnny Jones*, 1982
Signature: "One Bad Apple," 1971
Facts: Joined his singing brothers on *The Andy Williams Show* at age six.

Had his first solo gold record with 1971's *Go Away Little Girl*, and his 1972 single, "Puppy Love," also went gold.

In 1989 had a comeback hit with his somewhat edgier rock recording "Soldier of Love."

In the 90s, toured as the lead in *Joseph and the Amazing Technicolor Dreamcoat*.

Joked about Rosie O'Donnell's weight on her talk show in 1996, and came back to apologize dressed in dog suit, serenading her with "Puppy Love."

Provided the singing voice in *Mulan* and teamed with sister Marie for a syndicated daily talk show.

In 1999, he published his autobiography *Life Is Just What You Make It: My Life So Far*.
Marriage: Debra Glenn, 1978
Children: Donald, 1979; Jeremy, 1981; Brandon, 1985; Christopher, 1990; Joshua, 1998
Famous relatives: Alan, Wayne, Merrill, Jay, entertainers, brothers (The Osmond Brothers); Marie, singer, sister
Quote: "We've had life experiences. Now, granted, we may not have been in the ditches like a lot of people who had drug problems or were fired from jobs. But when I quit the old *Donny and Marie* show, that was the toughest time in my life. I couldn't even get arrested."

MARIE OSMOND

Real Name: Olive Marie Osmond
Birthplace: Ogden, Utah
Birthdate: 10/13/59
Occupation: Singer, actor, TV host
Debut: (TV) *The Andy Williams Show*, 1963; (Film) *Goin' Coconuts*, 1978; (Stage) *The King and I*, 1998
Signature: "Paper Roses," 1975
Facts: The only girl in a family of nine children, she made her TV debut at age three, and by 12, had recorded her first No. 1 hit on the country charts, "Paper Roses."

Toured as Maria in *The Sound of Music* from 1994–95, and made her Broadway debut in 1998. That same year, she and bother Donny co-hosted a daily talk show, *Donny & Marie*.

Has had her own line of cosmetics, issued a line of clothing patterns and published *Marie Osmond's Guide to Beauty, Health and Style*. Since 1991, she has also marketed own line of porcelain dolls on QVC, with total sales of over 1 million units.

Reportedly turned down the role of

Sandy in the film version of *Grease* because she thought the script was too racy.

She suffered a severe bout of postpartum depression, which she openly discussed on *Oprah Winfrey* in 1999.

Is the cofounder of the Children's Miracle Network, which has raised $1.5 billion for children's hospitals across the country.

Marriages: Steve Craig, 1982 (divorced, 1985); Brian Blosil, record producer, 1986 (separated, then reconciled, 2000)

Children: Stephen (with Steve Craig), 1983; Jessica, adopted, c. 1988; Rachel, 1989; Michael, c. 1991; Brandon, c. 1996; Brianna, daughter, c. 1997; Matthew, 1999

Famous relatives: Alan, Wayne, Merrill, Jay and Donny, entertainers, brothers (The Osmond Brothers)

Quote: "I learned early on that choices have consequences. You can either plan for the long-term or grab the short-term fix."

AL PACINO

Real Name: Alfredo James Pacino
Birthplace: New York, NY
Birthdate: 4/25/40
Occupation: Actor
Education: attended High School of the Performing Arts, Actor's Studio
Debut: (Stage) *The Peace Creeps*, 1966; (Film) *Me, Natalie*, 1969
Signature: *The Godfather*, 1972
Facts: Has been involved with actresses Jill Clayburgh, Marthe Keller, and Diane Keaton.

Is so shy that in 1999 he appeared on the *Rosie O'Donnell Show* only on the condition that no audience be present.

Original Jobs: Mail deliverer at *Commentary* magazine, messenger, movie theater usher, building superintendent
Relationship: Beverly D'Angelo
Child: Julie Marie, 1989 (with Jan Tarrant); Anton, 2001; Olivia, 2001
Major Awards: Tony, Best Supporting

Actor (Dramatic), *Does a Tiger Wear a Necktie?*, 1969; Tony, Best Actor (Dramatic), *The Basic Training of Pavlo Hummel*, 1977; Oscar, Best Actor, *Scent of a Woman*, 1992

SE RI PAK

Birthplace: Taejon, South Korea
Birthdate: 9/28/77
Occupation: Golfer
Education: Student at David Leadbetter Golf Academy
Facts: Was avid track athlete before turning to golf at age 14.

Her father, who admits to being a thug in his past, occasionally left her alone in a dark cemetery to develop her courage.

At 20, was the youngest winner of a major women's golf tournament in 30 years.

Major Awards: Winner, U.S. Women's Open, 1998; Winner, McDonald's LPGA Championship, 1998

GWYNETH PALTROW

Birthplace: Los Angeles, CA
Birthdate: 9/27/72
Occupation: Actor
Education: University of California, Santa Barbara
Debut: (Film) *Shout*, 1991 [see pages 69–70 for a complete filmography]
Signature: *Shakespeare in Love*, 1998
Facts: Nude pictures of her and former beau Brad Pitt that were taken with a telephoto lens while the couple vacationed in privacy in St. Bart's were circulated on the Internet and published in the tabloids. Pitt filed suit against the photographer. The couple split in 1997 after more than two years together.

Says a major goal for her life is to have babies.

Infamy: Was named in a personal injury lawsuit in 2000, alleging that a year prior Paltrow's rental car collided with the plaintiff's vehicle.

The plaintiff is allegedly seeking $62,000 from Paltrow and Midway Rent-a-Car to cover medical expenses and repairs.

Relationship: Luke Wilson, actor
Famous Relatives: Blythe Danner, actor, mother; Bruce Paltrow, producer, father; Jake Paltrow, actor, director, brother; Hillary Danner, actor, cousin
Major Award: Academy Award, Best Actress, *Shakespeare In Love*, 1998
Quote: "I'm so sick of myself, my boring voice and my stupid sound bites."

SARAH JESSICA PARKER

Birthplace: Nelsonville, OH
Birthdate: 3/25/65
Occupation: Actor
Education: American Ballet Theater, Professional Children's School in New York
Debut: (TV) *The Little Match Girl*, 1973; (Stage) *The Innocents*, 1976
Signature: *Sex in the City*
Facts: Sang in Metropolitan Opera productions of *Hansel and Gretel*, *Cavalleria Rusticana*, *Pagliacci*, and *Parade*.

Starred as nerdy Patty Green on the CBS TV sitcom *Square Pegs*, 1982–83.

Played Annie in the Broadway musical, 1979–80.

Lived with Robert Downey Jr. for seven years.

Wears a size two.

Original Job: Dancer with Cincinnati Ballet and the American Ballet Theatre
Marriage: Matthew Broderick, 1997

DOLLY PARTON

Birthplace: Sevierville, TN
Birthdate: 1/19/46
Occupation: Singer, songwriter
Education: High school
Debut: (Song) "Puppy Love," 1956
Signature: "9 to 5," 1981
Facts: Met her husband in the Wishy Washy laundromat.

Has her own theme park, Dollywood, located in Gatlinburg at the edge of the Smoky Mountains. In her hometown of Sevierville, Tennessee, there is a statue of her on the Sevier County Courthouse lawn.

Marriage: Carl Dean, 1966
Major Awards: Grammy, Best Country Vocal—Female, *Here You Come Again,* 1978; Grammy, Best Country Vocal—Female, "9 to 5," 1981; Grammy, Best Country Performance—Duo or Group, *Trio* (with Linda Rondstadt and Emmylou Harris), 1987; Grammy, Best Country Vocal—Collaboration, *After the Gold Rush* (with Linda Ronstadt and Emmylou Harris), 1999
Quote: "Left to my own, I'd rather look like trash. I love tacky clothes. My look came from a very serious honest place, and that was a country girl's idea of what glamour was."

JANE PAULEY

Real Name: Margaret Jane Pauley
Birthplace: Indianapolis, IN
Birthdate: 10/31/50
Occupation: Broadcast journalist
Education: Indiana University
Debut: (TV) WISH-TV, Indiana, 1972
Signature: *Dateline NBC*
Facts: Succeeded Barbara Walters on the *Today* show two weeks shy of her 26th birthday in 1976; left 13 years later in a controversy over Deborah Norville's role that generated enormous sympathy for Pauley.

Limited her children's TV viewing to one hour a day.
Marriage: Garry Trudeau, 1980
Children: Richard Ross, 1983; Rachel Grandison, 1983; Thomas Moore, 1986
Major Awards: 3 News and Documentary Emmys: 2 as correspondent, 1 as writer

LUCIANO PAVAROTTI

Birthplace: Modena, Italy
Birthdate: 10/12/35
Occupation: Singer
Education: Istituto Magistrale Carlo Sigonio
Debut: (Stage) *La Bohème,* 1961
Facts: Established Opera Company of Philadelphia/ Luciano Pavarotti Vocal Company, 1980.

Makes at least $100,000 per concert. His fortune is estimated to be between $25 and $50 million.

Dreads the anticipation of singing more than singing itself. "The 10 minutes before the performance you wouldn't wish on your worst enemies."

Half a billion people saw the televised "Three Tenors" concert (with Placido Domingo and José Carreras) in 1990.

In 1990, the only musicians who sold more recordings than Pavarotti were Madonna and Elton John.
Infamy: He was sued by the BBC when it found out that a 1992 Pavarotti concert it had bought for broadcast had really been lip-synched.

An ongoing affair with his 26-year old secretary, Nicoletta Mantovani, led to his separation.

In 2000, agreed to pay nearly $12 million in back taxes and interest to the Italian government. He still faced trial in 2001 for allegedly failing to declare another $19 million in income.
Original Jobs: Elementary school teacher, salesman
Marriage: Adua Veroni (separated, 1996); Nicoletta Mantovani (relationship)
Children: Lorenza, Cristina, Giuliana
Major Awards: Grammy, Best Classical Vocal Performance, *Luciano Pavarotti—Hits from London Center,* 1978; Grammy, Best Classical Vocal Performance, *O Sole Mio (Favorite Neapolitan Songs),* 1979; Grammy, Best Classical Vocal Performance, *Live from Lincoln Center—Sutherland—Horne—Pavarotti* (with Joan Sutherland and Marilyn Horne), 1981; Grammy, Best Classical Vocal Performance, *Luciano Pavarotti in Concert,* 1988; Grammy, Best Classical Vocal Performance, *Carreras, Domingo, Pavarotti in Concert* (with José Carreras and Placido Domingo), 1990

BILL PAXTON

Birthplace: Ft. Worth, TX
Birthdate: 5/17/55
Occupation: Actor
Education: New York University
Debut: (Film) *Mortuary,* 1981
Signature: *Twister,* 1996
Facts: Spent much of his career making B-grade movies like *Pass the Ammo* and *Brain Dead.*

For his *Mortuary* character's wardrobe, Paxton bought second-hand sweaters, from which he caught scabies.

Directed *Fishheads,* a cult music video that aired on MTV in the early 1980s.

Has had several long bouts of depression that sometimes took months to shake.

Wife is 10 years younger than he is. They met when he followed her onto a bus.
Original Job: Set dresser
Marriages: First wife (divorced), Louise Newbury, 1985
Children: James, 1994; Lydia, 1997

AMANDA PEET

Birthplace: New York, NY
Birthdate: 1/11/72
Occupation: Actor
Education: Columbia University, 1995
Debut: (TV) *One Life to Live,* 1994; (Film) *Grind,* 1994
Signature: *The Whole Nine Yards,* 2000
Facts: While a junior in college, she began studying theater with actor Uta Hagen.

Is able to recite the entire dialogue from *Tootsie* and *A Chorus Line.*
Relationship: Brian Van Holt, actor
Quote: "I'm a perennial stress ball. I find it really hard to be Zen and take a deep breath."

ROBIN WRIGHT PENN

Real Name: Robin Wright
Birthplace: Dallas, TX
Birthdate: 4/8/66
Occupation: Actor
Education: High school
Debut: (TV) *The Yellow Rose,* 1984; (Film) *Hollywood Vice Squad,* 1986
Signature: *Forrest Gump,* 1994
Facts: Began modeling after a talent scout spotted her roller-skating.

She was waiting tables in Hawaii when she found out that she had won the role of Kelly on NBC soap opera *Santa Barbara*; received two daytime Emmy nominations for her work on the show.

Met future husband, Sean Penn, at a coffee shop where he bummed a cigarette off of her. He was married to Madonna at the time.

Paired with Sean in 1990's *State of Grace,* directed by him in 1995 in *The Crossing Guard,* then costarred with him again in *She's So Lovely,* 1997.

Was the victim of a carjacking in front of her home in 1996.

On Oscar night, 1996, she needed emergency gall bladder surgery and Sean skipped the ceremony to be with her.

Son, Hopper Jack, is named after Dennis Hopper and Jack Nicholson.
Original Job: Model
Marriages: Dane Witherspoon (divorced); Sean Penn, 1996
Children: Dylan Frances, 1991; Hopper Jack, 1993
Quote: "I don't want my daughter to think she should go to the front of the line just because her daddy is Sean Penn. I want us to wait like everybody else."

SEAN PENN

Birthplace: Burbank, CA
Birthdate: 8/17/60
Occupation: Actor, director, writer
Education: High school
Debut: (Film) *Taps,* 1981

Signature: *Dead Man Walking,* 1995
Facts: In high school, was on the tennis team. Rob Lowe and Charlie Sheen were his classmates.

His lavish house burned to the ground in the 1993 Malibu brush-fires. Rather than rebuilding, he put a 27 1/ foot trailer on the land and moved in there.

Wears a tattoo saying "NOLA deliver me!," a reference to a frightening night spent in New Orleans (the NOLA) after drinking a glass of water spiked with seven hits of acid.

While growing up, his director father was blacklisted as a Communist, and had trouble getting work for years.
Infamy: Punched several photographers attempting to take his picture, and allegedly fired a gun at a hovering helicopter covering his first wedding. Spent 34 days in jail in 1987 for smacking a film extra while on probation for hitting someone who tried to kiss then wife Madonna.

Was so volatile during his marriage to Madonna she called a SWAT team to help her retrieve her possessions. Now says he "was drunk all the time" during their marriage.
Marriages: Elizabeth McGovern (engaged, never married); Madonna, 1985 (divorced,1989); Robin Wright, 1996
Children: Dylan Frances, 1991; Hopper Jack, 1993
Famous Relatives: Leo Penn, director, father; Eileen Ryan, actor, mother; Christopher Penn, actor, brother; Aimee Mann, sister-in-law
Quote: "I'm not an alcoholic. I'm just a big drinker, and there's a difference."

MATTHEW PERRY

Birthplace: Williamstown, MA
Birthdate: 8/19/69
Occupation: Actor, writer
Education: High school
Debut: (Film) *A Night in the Life of Jimmy Reardon,* 1988

Signature: *Friends*
Facts: His father is best known for Old Spice commercials.

Moved to his mother's native Ottawa after his parents split when he was a year old. His journalist mother became press aide to Canadian Prime Minister Pierre Trudeau.

An avid tennis player, at 13 was ranked the No. 2 junior player in Ottawa.

Frustrated by the lack of good parts, he and a friend wrote a sitcom about six twentysomethings, which interested NBC. When the network ultimately decided to go with a similar sitcom, *Friends,* Perry decided since he couldn't beat 'em, he'd join 'em.

In 2000, along with *Friends* costars, received a salary increase from $125,000 to $750,000 per episode.

Withdrew his name from the Emmy ballot in 2000 after learning that he had been placed in the leading man column rather than in the supporting category with the rest of the cast of *Friends.*
Infamy: Checked into rehab to overcome addiction to prescription painkillers.

In 2001 battling an unspecified addiction, again checked himself into a rehabilitation hospital.
Relationship: Jennifer Keohane, producer
Famous Relative: John Bennett Perry, actor, father
Quote: "I describe my dating style as 'basic stupidity.' I'll take a woman and try to impress her with my sense of humor to the level that my head will almost implode. I also juggle if all else fails."

JOE PESCI

Birthplace: Newark, NJ
Birthdate: 2/9/43
Occupation: Actor
Education: High school dropout

Debut: (Radio) *Star Kids,* 1947; (Film) *Hey, Let's Twist!,* 1961
Signature: *My Cousin Vinny* , 1992
Facts: Played guitar for Joey Dee and The Starliters.

At age 5 appeared in Broadway musicals and Eddie Dowling plays. At age 10 became a regular on TV's *Star Time Kids* doing impersonations and singing.

Was managing a restaurant in the Bronx when called by Robert De Niro and Martin Scorsese to play Jake LaMotta's brother in *Raging Bull,* 1978.

He appears in some of his films under the psuedonym Joe Ritchie.
Original Jobs: Nightclub singer, stand-up comedian, barber, postal worker, delivery boy, produce manager, answering service worker, and restaurant manager
Marriages: Two prior marriages; Martha Haro, 1988 (divorced, 1991).
Child: Tiffany, 1966
Major Award: Oscar, Best Supporting Actor, *GoodFellas,* 1990

BERNADETTE PETERS

Real Name: Bernadette Lazzara
Birthplace: Ozone Park, Queens, NY
Birthdate: 2/28/48
Occupation: Actress, comedian, singer, dancer
Education: Quintano's School for Young Professionals, New York City
Debut: (TV) *Juvenile Jury,* 1951; (Stage) *Most Happy Fella,* 1959; (Broadway) *Johnny No Trump,* 1967; (Film) *Ace Eli and Rodger of the Skies,* 1973
Signature: *Sunday in the Park with George*
Facts: At age 3 appeared on a TV game show; two years later, won $800 on *Name That Tune.*

At 9, joined Actors' Equity, and when she was 10, she changed her name (after her father's first name); by 15 she was in a national tour of *Gypsy.*

Her Broadway debut closed after one performance.

First attained success in *Dames at Sea,* a 1967 Off-Broadway spoof.

In 1999, after a five-year absence from the theater, she returned to the stage to star in a remake of the 1946 Irving Berlin classic *Annie Get Your Gun.*
Marriage: Michael Wittenberg, 1997
Major Awards: Tony Award, *Song and Dance,* 1985
Quotes: "I've done it all—everything but circus acrobatics."

TOM PETTY

Birthplace: Gainesville, FL
Birthdate: 10/20/50
Occupation: Singer, songwriter, guitarist
Education: High school dropout
Debut: *Tom Petty and the Heartbreakers,* 1977
Signature: "Free Fallin' "
Facts: Toured for two years as Bob Dylan's backing band.

Recorded two albums with The Traveling Wilburys, comprised of George Harrison, Bob Dylan, Roy Orbison, Jeff Lynne, and Petty.
Marriages: Jane (divorced, 1996); Dana York, 2001
Children: Adria, Anna Kim (with Jane Petty)

MICHELLE PFEIFFER

Birthplace: Santa Ana, CA
Birthdate: 4/29/58
Occupation: Actor
Education: Golden West College and Whitley College for Court Reporting
Debut: (TV) *Delta House,* 1979; (Film) *The Hollywood Knights,* 1980 [see page 69 for a complete filmography]
Signature: *The Fabulous Baker Boys,* 1989
Facts: Had one line on TV show *Fantasy Island.*

Got her first break by winning the Miss Orange County Beauty Pageant.

In 1993, she decided to be a single mother and adopted a baby girl, who was given the last name Kelley after Pfeiffer married.

Had the leading role in *Grease 2,* 1982.
Original Job: Supermarket cashier, court reporter, model
Marriages: Peter Horton (divorced); David E. Kelley, 1993
Children: Claudia Rose, 1993 (adopted); John Henry, 1994
Famous Relatives: DeDee Pfeiffer, actor, sister

REGIS PHILBIN

Birthplace: New York, NY
Birthdate: 8/25/31
Occupation: Talk show host
Education: University of Notre Dame
Debut: (TV) KOGO news anchor, San Diego, 1960
Signature: *Live With Regis and Kathie Lee*
Facts: Named after Regis High, a Manhattan Catholic boys' school and his father's alma mater.

Son Dan was born with two malformed legs, which were later amputated.

Between 1970 and 1990, hosted nearly a dozen talk and game shows and went through a series of co-hosts before clicking with Kathie Lee.

Finished last twice on *Celebrity Jeopardy!.*

Closed a deal with ABC in 2000 that yielded him $20 million a year for hosting *Who Wants to Be a Millionaire.*

In 2001, claimed his first (and second) Daytime Emmys, after 11 prior nominations.
Marriages: Kay Faylan, 1955 (divorced,1968); Joy Senese, 1970
Children: Amy, 1958; Dan, 1965; (with Kay Faylan). Joanna, 1973; Jennifer, 1974
Major Awards: Emmy, Outstanding Game Show Host, *Who Wants to Be a Millionaire,* 2000; Emmy, Outstanding Talk Show Host, *Live With Regis,* 2000
Quote: "I've worked with Kathie Lee for 15 years. That builds stamina

and endurance. A lesser man would be in his grave by now."

RYAN PHILLIPPE

Birthplace: Iowa
Birthdate: 9/10/74
Occupation: Actor
Education: High school
Debut: (TV) *One Life to Live,* 1992; (Film) *Crimson Tide,* 1995
Signature: *54,* 1998
Facts: Was getting a haircut when a stranger approached him and suggested that he consider an acting career. The man gave him the name of an agent whom Phillippe met and signed with shortly afterward. He had no acting experience at the time.

Played first openly gay male on daytime TV in *One Life to Live.*
Marriage: Reese Witherspoon, 1999
Child: Ava Elizabeth, 1999

BIJOU PHILLIPS

Birthplace: Greenwich, CT
Birthdate: 4/1/80
Occupation: Actor, model, singer, songwriter
Debut: (Film) *Sugar Town,* 1999; (Album) *I'd Rather Eat Glass,* 1999
Signature: *Black and White,* 2000
Facts: When her musician father was touring, he placed her in foster homes.

Began modeling at 13; a year later she declared herself emancipated and began living on her own. At 15, participated in the controversial Calvin Klein ads featuring underage models and was a regular on the party scene. At 17, she entered rehab.

Had a very public affair with Evan Dando when she was 16. Also was formerly involved with Elijah Blue Allman, daughter of Cher.

In the film *Black and White,* she is featured in a same-sex scene. Posed in a *Playboy* pictorial, and appeared on the cover in April 2000.

Claims to have "Daddy" tattooed

on her behind.

Wrote a song called "When I Hated Him" about her father, and another called "Little Dipper" about her mother.
Infamy: At 20, she "borrowed" a car from a Miss USA winner and cut off a lounge patron's fingertip with a cigar cutter, later saying it was a magic trick.
Famous relatives: John Phillips, musician, founding member of the pop group The Mamas and the Papas, father; Genevieve Waite, actor, painter, mother; Mackenzie Phillips, actor, half-sister; Chynna Phillips, actor, singer, half-sister
Quote: "I don't regret anything that I did. If I had stayed home and gone to school and done the normal *Brady* [*Bunch*] thing, I would have been a total idiot. My whole thing is that I was stupid, but I was 14 and everybody's stupid at that age, so it's fine."

JOAQUIN PHOENIX

Real Name: Joaquin Rafael Bottom
Birthplace: Puerto Rico
Birthdate: 10/28/74
Occupation: Actor
Education: Dropped out of ninth grade; home-schooled
Signature: *Gladiator* (2000)
Debut: (TV musical) *Seven Brides for Seven Brothers,* (with brother River) 1982; (Film) *Space Camp,* 1986
Facts: The son of missionaries for the Children of God, he traveled throughout Puerto Rico, Mexico, South America, Venezuela, and, returning to the U.S., lived in Florida. When siblings Rainbow and River won talent contests, the family moved to Los Angeles.

Changed his name to Leaf around age 6 or 7; changed it back to Joaquin as a teenager.

Has been a strict vegan since he was 3. (He turned down a part as a bullfighter.)

Drives a yellow '72 Pontiac LeMans.

Was in a relationship with Liv Tyler.
Infamy: Made the 911 call as his brother River suffered a drug overdose on Sunset Strip.
Original Job: Model
Famous Relatives: River Phoenix, a.k.a. River Jude Bottom, who died of a drug overdose in 1993, actor, brother; Rain Joan of Arc Phoenix, a.k.a. Rainbow Phoenix, actor, sister; Liberty Butterfly Phoenix, former actor, sister; Summer Joy Phoenix, actor, sister
Quote: "The reason why I keep making movies—which is the reason why I keep doing interviews—is because I hate the last thing that I did. I'm always trying to rectify my wrongs."

DAVID HYDE PIERCE

Birthplace: Saratoga Springs, NY
Birthdate: 4/3/59
Occupation: Actor
Education: Yale University
Debut: (Stage) *Beyond Therapy,* 1982; (Film) *The Terminator,* 1984; (TV) *Powers That Be,* 1991
Signature: *Frasier*
Facts: Realized he had a strong resemblance to his TV brother Frasier (Kelsey Grammer) after being mistaken for Grammer many times before he even accepted the role. In the original storyline for *Frasier,* Pierce's character (Niles) didn't exist but was added after producers, who saw Pierce in *The Powers That Be,* noticed the resemblance.
Original Job: Clothing salesman, church organist
Major Award: Emmy, Best Supporting Actor in a Comedy Series, *Frasier,* 1995, 1998, 1999

BRAD PITT

Real Name: William Bradley Pitt
Birthplace: Shawnee, OK
Birthdate: 12/18/63
Occupation: Actor
Education: University of Missouri at

Columbia, studied acting with Roy London
Debut: (TV) *Dallas*; (Film) *Cutting Class*, 1989 [see page 69 for a complete filmography]
Signature: *Legends of the Fall*, 1994
Facts: Graduated from Kickapoo High, where he was on the tennis team.

Got his big break when he was seen in a sexy Levi's TV ad in 1989. Was cast as the hitchhiker in the 1991 movie *Thelma and Louise* only after William Baldwin turned down the role, choosing to star in *Backdraft* instead.

Dated Robin Givens for six months when they both acted in the TV series *Head of the Class*. Also lived with Juliette Lewis for several years; was engaged to Gwyneth Paltrow.

While at college, posed shirtless for a campus fundraising calendar.

His earliest movie work was filmed in Yugoslavia and lost during its civil war; eight years later, in 1996, the producer finally found all the scattered footage.

In 1997, sued *Playgirl* to force them to recall an issue that contained nude photos of him.

Had LASIK eye surgery (to correct nearsightedness).
Infamy: Aspiring actress Athena Marie Rolando, 19, broke into his home in 1999. A three-year restraining order bars any communication with Pitt and requires that she stay at least 100 yards away from him.
Marriage: Jennifer Aniston, 2000
Original Job: Chauffeur for Strip-O-Gram women, dressed up as the El Pollo Loco restaurant chicken
Quote: "Being a sex symbol all the time hampers my work."

SARA POLLEY

Birthplace: Toronto, Ontario, Canada
Birthdate: 1/8/79
Occupation: Actor, singer
Education: High School drop-out

Debut: (Film) *One Magic Christmas*, 1985; (TV) *Ramona/The Ramona Series*, 1988
Signature: *The Sweet Hereafter*, 1997
Facts: Began acting at age five, and made her film debut in 1985.

From 1990 to 1996, she costarred in the Canadian TV series *The Road to Avonlea*, which also aired in the U.S. as *Avonlea*.

At 14, she moved out of her parents' home, with their blessings.

In 1994, she had major surgery for scoliosis, during which a steel rod was inserted into her back.

Dropped out of high school in her senior year to devote all her time to political activism, joining the Ontario Coalition Against Poverty.

Wrote, coproduced, and directed a film short, *Don't Think Twice*, which was shown at Sundance in 2000.
Famous relatives: Michael Polley, actor, father; Diane Polley, actor and casting director, mother (deceased)
Quote: "When people ask me what I do, acting is usually the furthest thing from my mind."

NATALIE PORTMAN

Real Name: Has been kept from the press
Birthplace: Jerusalem, Israel
Birthdate: 6/9/81
Occupation: Actor, model
Education: High school
Debut: (Film) *The Professional*, 1994; (Broadway) *The Diary of Anne Frank*, 1997
Signature: *Star Wars: Episode I— The Phantom Menace* (1999)
Facts: After spending her first four years in Israel, she and her parents moved to the U.S., eventually settling on Long Island.

Was discovered by a Revlon scout in a pizza parlor in 1991.

Her first professional acting job was as an understudy in the Off-Broadway show *Ruthless*.

Turned down the title role in the *Lolita* remake, heeding her father's

advice to do on screen only what she had experienced in real life.

A high school honor student, she is fluent in Hebrew and has studied French and Japanese.

Calls acting her "extra-curricular activity."

Role models include the late AIDS activist Elisabeth Glaser and the late prime minister of Israel Yitzhak Rabin. Favorite actor is Ben Kingsley.

Her last name has been kept from the press to protect the privacy of her and her family.

Is committed to play Queen Amidala in Episodes II and III of *Star Wars*.
Relationship: Lukas Haas, actor
Quote: "I'm going to college. I don't care if it ruins my career. I'd rather be smart than a movie star."

PARKER POSEY

Birthplace: Baltimore, MD
Birthdate: 11/8/68
Occupation: Actor
Education: Attended North Carolina School for the Arts and State University of New York, Purchase
Debut: (Film) *Dazed and Confused*, 1993
Signature: *House of Yes*
Facts: Was named after the supermodel Suzy Parker.

Roomed with *ER*'s Sherry Stringfield while at SUNY. Left school three weeks short of graduation to appear on *As the World Turns*.

Appeared in more than 20 films, the vast majority independents, in a five-year period.

Has a twin brother.

MAURY POVICH

Birthplace: Washington, D.C.
Birthdate: 1/17/39
Occupation: Talk show host, newscaster
Education: University of Pennsylvania
Debut: (TV) *Panorama*, 1969; (Film) *The Imagemaker*, 1986

Signature: *A Current Affair*
Facts: His father Shirley was a well-known sports writer for the *Washington Post*.

Started in broadcasting as as a general assignment and sports reporter in Washington, D.C.,

Briefly worked as a coanchor with Connie Chung in 1977.

In 1986, Povich was the first anchor of a TV tabloid show when he began *A Current Affair*.

In 1989, Povich hosted the prime-time, tongue-in-cheek show *Confessions of Mr. Tabloid*. In 1991, he began the daytime talk show, *The Maury Povich Show*, which aired until 1998.

In 1991, he coauthored a book, *Current Affairs: Life on the Edge*, with Ken Gross.
Marriages: Phyllis Minkoff, c. 1962; Connie Chung, 1984
Children: Susan, c. 1964; Amy, c. 1967 (with Phyllis Minkoff); Matthew Jay, c. 1995 (adopted)
Quote: "Connie has always made a lot more money. There have been times when I would have pangs about it, but whenever they surfaced, I would just put a stake in them."

LISA MARIE PRESLEY

Birthplace: Memphis,TN
Birthdate: 2/1/68
Facts: Daughter of Elvis and Priscilla Presley

Inherited an estate of upwards of $100 million from her father.

When Lisa Marie once said she had never seen snow, Elvis flew her to Utah. She also received a tiny mink coat from her father and $100 bills from the Tooth Fairy.

Is a devoted follower of the Church of Scientology.
Marriages: Danny Keough (divorced); Michael Jackson (divorced, 1996); John Oszajca (engaged, never married); Nicolas Cage (relationship)
Children: Danielle, 1989; Benjamin, 1992

PRINCE

Real Name: Prince Rogers Nelson
Birthplace: Minneapolis, MN
Birthdate: 6/7/58
Occupation: Singer, songwriter, actor
Education: High school dropout
Debut: (Album) *For You*, 1978
Signature: *Purple Rain*, 1984
Facts: Named after the Prince Roger Trio, a jazz group led by his father.

Can play over two dozen instruments.

Returned to using the name Prince in 2000, after his publishing contract with Warner-Chappell expired. He had previously been known as a symbol, or referred to as "The Artist Formerly Known as Prince," sometimes abbreviated to "TAFKA," in order to free himself from "undesirable relationships."

After annulling his marriage, he said he believes marriage contracts "guarantee the possibility of divorce," though he did remain with his Mayte.

On his 43rd birthday, Prince declares that he has found religion and will rewrite many of his songs to eliminate the "cuss words."
Marriage: Mayte Garcia, 1996 (annulled, 1999; relationship)
Child: deceased (name unreported)
Major Awards: Grammy, Best Rock Performance—Duo or Group, *Purple Rain* (with The Revolution), 1984; Grammy, Best Rhythm and Blues Song, "I Feel for You," 1984; Grammy, Best Soundtrack Album, *Purple Rain* (with The Revolution, John L. Nelson, Lisa & Wendy), 1984; Oscar, Best Original Song Score, *Purple Rain*, 1984; Grammy, Best R&B Duo or Group, "Kiss" (with The Revolution), 1986

FREDDIE PRINZE JR.

Birthplace: Los Angeles, CA
Birthdate: 3/8/76
Occupation: Actor
Education: High school
Debut: (TV) *Family Matters*, 1994; (Film) *To Gillian on Her 37th Birthday*, 1996
Signature: *She's All That* (1999)
Facts: His father committed suicide when Freddie was 10 months old (his father nicknamed him "Pie").

His mother is of English, Irish, and Native American descent.
Marriage: Sarah Michelle Gellar (engaged, 2001)
Famous Relative: Freddie Prinze, comedian, actor (*Chico and the Man*), father; high on prescription drugs and despondent over divorce from his wife, he committed suicide in 1977.
Quote: "I know one day I'm going to be the best father in the world. Me not having a father makes me want to be a great one. I have so much love I wanted to give him, and I'll be damned if I don't give it to a child of mine."

JEFF PROBST

Birthplace: Wichita, KS
Birthdate: 11/1/61
Occupation: TV Host, writer, director
Education: Attended Seattle Pacific University
Debut: (TV movie) *Face of a Stranger*, 1991; (TV series) *Access Hollywood*, 1996 (Screenwriter/director) *Finder's Fee*, 2001
Signature: *Survivor*
Facts: Grew up mostly in Seattle, where he was active in school plays and sung in a rock band. Hosted local television garden and car shows there in 1991.

Enjoys softball and golf.

Lost 15 pounds on location during the filming of the first *Survivor*.

Hosts VH1's *Rock and Roll Jeopardy*.
Original Job: Produced and narrated

sales/marketing videos
Marriage: Shelly Wright, 1996 (separated, 2001)

DENNIS QUAID

Birthplace: Houston, TX
Birthdate: 4/9/54
Occupation: Actor
Education: University of Houston
Debut: (Film) *September 30, 1955,* 1978
Signature: *The Big Easy,* (1987)
Fact: Wrote songs for three of his films: *The Night the Lights Went Out in Georgia* in 1981, *Tough Enough* in 1983, and *The Big Easy* in 1987.

Shed 47 pounds over a three-month period before playing the scrawny Doc Holliday in 1994's *Wyatt Earp.*

In 2000, filed for divorce from Meg Ryan after nine years, citing irreconcilable differences and asking for joint custody of their son, Jack.
Infamy: Admitted to having a cocaine addiction, a problem he overcame with help from then girlfriend Meg Ryan.
Marriages: Pamela Jayne Soles (divorced), Meg Ryan, 1991 (filed for divorce, 2000); Shanna Moakler, former Miss USA (relationship)
Child: Jack Henry, 1992
Famous Relative: Randy Quaid, actor, brother

QUEEN LATIFAH

Real Name: Dana Owens
Birthplace: East Orange, NJ
Birthdate: 3/18/70
Occupation: Rap artist, actor
Education: High school
Debut: (Album) *All Hail the Queen,* 1989; (TV) *The Fresh Prince of Bel-Air,* 1991; (Film) *Jungle Fever,* 1991
Facts: Was a power forward on two state championship basketball teams in high school.

Trained in karate and use of firearms by her policeman father.

CEO of Flavor Unit, a management and production company whose

clients have included Naughty by Nature and FU-Schnickens.

Brother Lance Owens Jr. died at age 24 in a motorcycle accident in 1992; "Winky's Theme" on the album *Black Reign* was dedicated to him.

Starred in sitcom *Living Single.*
Infamy: Charged in a municipal misdemeanor complaint in 1995 after 240 illegally copied tapes were found in a video store she had sold in 1994.

Arrested by California Highway Patrolman in west L.A. and cited for speeding, driving under the influence, carrying a concealed firearm, carrying a loaded firearm, and possession of marijuana.
Original Jobs: Worked at Burger King, cashier at the Wiz
Major Award: Grammy, Best Rap Solo Performance, "U.N.I.T.Y.", 1994

KATHLEEN QUINLAN

Birthplace: Pasadena, CA
Birthdate: 11/19/54
Occupation: Actor
Education:
Debut: (Film) *American Graffiti,* 1973; (TV) *Where Have All the People Gone?,* 1974
Signature: *Family Law*
Facts: Suffered allergy-induced asthma as a child.

Her original aspiration was to each gymnastics. She's a longtime surfer.

Appeared as a diving double for Trish Van Devere in 1972's *One Is a Lonely Number.*

George Lucas spotted her at high school and cast her a very small part in 1973's *American Graffiti.*

Had a three-year relationship with Al Pacino in the late '70s and early '80s.
Marriages: One previous marriage; Bruce Abbott, actor, 1994
Children: Dalton Abbott, stepson, 1989; Tyler Abbott, 1990
Famous relative: Robert Quinlan, TV sportscaster, father (deceased)
Quote: "I was not ambitious. Never have been."

BONNIE RAITT

Birthplace: Burbank, CA
Birthdate: 11/8/49
Occupation: Singer, songwriter
Education: Radcliffe College
Debut: (Album) *Bonnie Raitt,* 1971
Signature: "Something To Talk About," 1991
Facts: Grew up in a Quaker family in L.A.

Got her first guitar for Christmas when she was eight.

Founded the annual Rhythm & Blues Awards, to provide money to deserving R&B stars who may have been cheated in the early days by managers and/or record labels.
Infamy: Was an avid drinker until giving up all alcohol and drugs a decade ago.
Marriage: Michael O'Keefe, 1991 (separated, 1999)
Child: One son
Famous Relative: John Raitt, actor, father
Major Awards: Grammies, Album of the Year, Best Rock Vocal—Female, and Best Pop Vocal—Female, "Nick of Time," 1989; Grammy, Best Pop Vocal—Female, "Something To Talk About," 1991; Grammy, Best Rock Vocal—Female, "Luck of the Draw," 1991; Grammy, Best Rock Duo with Vocal, "Good Man, Good Woman" (with Delbert McClinton), 1991; Grammy, Best Pop Album, *Longing in Their Hearts,* 1994

DAN RATHER

Birthplace: Wharton, TX
Birthdate: 10/31/31
Occupation: Anchor, correspondent, editor
Education: Sam Houston State College
Debut: (TV) KHOU-TV, Houston, 1960
Signature: *CBS Evening News with Dan Rather*
Facts: Succeeded Walter Cronkite in anchoring the evening news upon Cronkite's retirement in 1981.

In his 1994 book, *The Camera Never Blinks Twice,* he devotes less than a page to his former co-anchor Connie Chung.

Was attacked on the street by two men who called him "Kenneth" and repeatedly demanded "What's the frequency?" R.E.M. used the cryptic phrase as a song title and later performed the tune with Rather on *Late Show with David Letterman.*
Infamy: Angry over a delay in the start of the news, he walked off the set, leaving TV screens blank for six minutes. He also had a stormy pre-election interview with then vice-president George Bush in 1988.
Marriage: Jean Goebel, 1958
Children: Robin, 1958; Danjack, 1960
Major Awards: 28 News and Documentary Emmys: 19 as correspondent, 9 as anchor

ROBERT REDFORD

Real Name: Charles Robert Redford Jr.
Birthplace: Santa Monica, CA
Birthdate: 8/18/36
Occupation: Actor, director, producer
Education: University of Colorado, Pratt Institute of Design, the American Academy of Dramatic Arts
Debut: (Stage) *Tall Story,* 1959; (Film) *War Hunt,* 1962
Signature: *Butch Cassidy and the Sundance Kid,* 1969
Facts: In 1959, his first child died of Sudden Infant Death Syndrome.

Went to college on a baseball scholarship but lost it due to alcohol abuse. Left school in 1957 to go to Europe; lived in Paris and Florence as a painter.

Was burned in effigy in 1976 for opposing a $3.5 billion power plant.

Founded the nonprofit Sundance Institute in Park City, UT, which sponsors an annual film festival and provides support for independent film production.
Infamy: As a teenager, Redford stole and resold hubcaps.
Original Job: Carpenter, shop assistant, oil field worker
Marriage: Lola Van Wagenen

(divorced, 1985); Sibylle Szaggars (relationship)
Children: Shauna, 1960; James, 1962; Amy, 1970
Major Awards: Oscar, Best Director, *Ordinary People,* 1980; Cecil B. DeMille Lifetime Achievement Award, 1994

CHRISTOPHER REEVE

Birthplace: New York, NY
Birthdate: 9/25/52
Occupation: Actor
Education: Cornell University, Juilliard graduate program
Debut: (Film) *Gray Lady Down,* 1977
Signature: *Superman,* 1978
Facts: While studying at Juilliard under John Houseman, shared an apartment with then-unknown Robin Williams.

Turned down a lucrative offer to do cigarette commericals in Japan in 1990.

Says the accident that fractured his first and second vertebrae happened on an easy jump, when his Thoroughbred Eastern Express suddenly halted and his hands became entangled in the bridle so he couldn't break his fall.

Completely paralyzed, though with some sensation in his left leg, he gets around by motorized wheelchair, which he directs by puffing air through a tube.

A television ad featuring a computer generated Reeves walking, which debuted on the 2000 Super Bowl broadcast, caused considerable controversy.
Marriage: Dana Morosini, 1992
Children: Matthew, 1979; Alexandra, 1983; (with Gae Exton); Will, 1992
Major Award: Grammy, Best Spoken Word Album, *Still Me,* 1998

KEANU REEVES

Birthplace: Beirut, Lebanon
Birthdate: 9/2/64
Occupation: Actor

Education: High school dropout; studied with Jasper Deeter
Debut: (Film) *Youngblood,* 1986; (Album) *Happy Ending,* 2000
Signature: *The Matrix,* 1999
Facts: His father is Chinese-Hawaiian and his mother is English.

Hasn't seen his father, who is currently serving a ten-year prison term in Hawaii for cocaine possession, since he was 13.

His first name means "cool breeze over the mountains" in Hawaiian.

Had traveled around the world by the time he was 2 years old.

Was the MVP on his high school hockey team in Toronto. A skilled goalie, Reeves earned the name "The Wall."

Turned down the Al Pacino/Robert De Niro film *Heat* to play Hamlet on stage in Winnipeg, Canada. The February 1995 sold-out run was critically acclaimed.

He plays bass in the band Dogstar.

His mother was a costume designer for rock stars.

His child with Jennifer Syme was reportedly stillborn in late 1999. Syme was killed in a car accident in 2001.

PAUL REISER

Birthplace: New York, NY
Birthdate: 3/30/56
Occupation: Actor, comedian
Education: SUNY-Binghamton
Debut: (Film) *Diner,* 1982
Signature: *Mad About You*
Facts: Has appeared in several hit films, including *Beverly Hills Cop* (1984), *Aliens* (1986), and *Beverly Hills Cop II* (1987).

Dubbed by reporters as part of the Four Funniest Men in the World Club, which includes Jerry Seinfeld, Larry Miller, and Mark Schiff. The members meet every New Year's Day for lunch (once they even met in London when Reiser was there filming *Aliens*).
Original Job: Health food distributor
Marriage: Paula, 1988
Child: Ezra Samuel, 1995

GLORIA REUBEN

Birthplace: Toronto, Canada
Birthdate: 6/9/65
Occupation: Actor
Education: Attended Canadian Royal Conservatory
Debut: (TV) *The Round Table*, 1988
Signature: *ER*
Facts: Her father, who died when she was 11, was a white Jamaican while her mother is a black Jamaican.

Studied ballet and jazz dancing at a prestigious music college, and plays classical piano.

In 2000, toured with Tina Turner as a backup singer.
Original Job: Model
Marriage: Wayne Isaak, VH1 executive, 1999
Famous Relative: Denis Simpson, brother, actor

BURT REYNOLDS

Birthplace: Waycross, GA
Birthdate: 2/11/36
Occupation: Actor, director
Education: Attended Florida State University, Palm Beach Junior College and Hyde Park Playhouse
Debut: (Stage) *Mister Roberts*, 1956; (Film) *Angel Baby*, 1961
Signature: *Smokey and the Bandit*, 1977
Facts: Was signed to play football with the Baltimore Colts, but a car accident derailed that career and led him to acting.

Has dated Dinah Shore (19 years his senior), Chris Evert, and Sally Field.

Is part Cherokee, part Italian.
Infamy: Appeared nude in *Cosmopolitan* magazine centerfold in 1972.

Untrue rumors circulated in the late 1980s that Reynolds had AIDS; he was actually suffering from a joint disorder.

Ugly divorce from Loni Anderson cost him fans and product endorsement contracts, partly contributing to a 1996 bankruptcy filing.
Original Jobs: Bouncer, dishwasher, stuntman
Marriages: Judy Carne (divorced); Loni Anderson (divorced, 1993); Pam Seals (engaged)
Child: Quentin, c. 1988 (adopted)
Major Award: Emmy, Best Actor in a Comedy Series, *Evening Shade*, 1991

TRENT REZNOR

Birthplace: Mercer, PA
Birthdate: 5/17/65
Occupation: Singer, keyboardist
Education: Allegheny College
Debut: (Album) *Pretty Hate Machine*, 1989
Signature: Nine Inch Nails
Facts: Reznor makes all Nine Inch Nails albums himself, using a band only for live shows.

In 1990, misplaced video footage of a half-naked Reznor being thrown from a building landed in the hands of the FBI, who thought it was an actual murder. They led an investigation and found Reznor, alive and well and on tour. The publicity helped put Nine Inch Nails in the spotlight.

Mixed the soundtrack LP for Oliver Stone's film *Natural Born Killers* in 1994.

Lived for a year in the Benedict Canyon, CA, house where Sharon Tate and others were murdered by Charles Manson followers.

In what he says was possibly an unconscious attempt to identify with Woodstock '94 fans, he tripped his guitar player on the way to the stage, who fell flat in the mud and started the whole band in a mud match. They performed covered in the stuff.
Original Job: Odd jobs—including cleaning toilets—at a recording studio
Major Awards: Grammy, Best Metal Performance, "Wish," 1992

BUSTA RHYMES

Real Name: Trevor Smith
Birthplace: Brooklyn, NY
Birthdate: 5/20/72
Occupation: Musician, actor
Education: High school dropout
Debut: (Album) *A Future Without a Past...*, 1991 (Leaders of the New School); (Film) *Who's the Man?*, 1993; (Solo Album) *The Coming*, 1996
Signature: "Woo Hah!! Got You All In Check," 1996
Facts: Entered a performing contest in tenth grade sponsored by Chuck D and Public Enemy which eventually led to a contract with Elektra Records with his band Leaders of the New School.

Is a member of the Five Percent sect of Islam.

Made three platinum albums in five years.

Is a pitchman for Mountain Dew and the head of Flipmode, his own entertainment company.

Launched his Bushi clothing line in 2001, whose products he modeled in the film *Shaft*.
Infamy: In 1999, pled guilty to a felony charge of criminal possession of a weapon and received five years probation.
Children: Tahiem, 1993 (deceased); T'Ziah (1994)
Quote: "I don't just represent a 20-block radius known as my 'hood,' I represent the universe."

CHRISTINA RICCI

Birthplace: Santa Monica, CA
Birthdate: 2/12/80
Occupation: Actor
Education: Professional Children's School
Debut: (Film) *Mermaids*, 1990
Signature: *The Opposite of Sex*, 1998
Facts: While starring in her second-grade pageant, she caught the eye of a local movie critic in the audience, who told her parents to get her an agent.

Was a schoolmate of Macaulay Culkin.

Fellow teen actress Natalie Portman was initially approached for the role in *The Ice Storm,* but her parents decided it was too sexual.

Quote: "Basically, I'm like a whore. I'll give people whatever they want so they'll like me."

ANNE RICE

Real Name: Howard Allen O'Brien
Birthdate: 10/4/41
Occupation: Writer
Education: North Texas State University, San Francisco State College
Debut: (Book) *Interview with a Vampire,* 1976
Facts: Is the author of a series of pornographic novels under the name A. N. Roquelaure (which means "cloak").

Is afraid of the dark.

Was originally named after her father and mother's maiden name; changed name to Anne by the time she was in first grade.

In 1972 her six-year-old daughter died of leukemia.

Son Christopher is now also a bestselling novelist.

Original Job: Waitress, cook, insurance claims adjuster
Marriage: Stan Rice, 1961
Children: Michelle, 1966 (deceased, 1972); Christopher, 1978

DENISE RICHARDS

Birthplace: Downers Grove, IL
Birthdate: 2/17/71
Occupation: Actor
Education: High school
Debut: (TV) *Life Goes On,* 1990; (Film) *National Lampoon's Loaded Weapon 1,* 1993
Signature: *Wild Things,* 1998
Facts: Was called Fish Lips in junior high school.

Played a recurring role (beauty contestant Brandy Carson) in *Melrose Place.*

Original Job: Model
Relationship: Patrick Muldoon, actor
Quote: "It's always fun to be a bad girl and get away with it."

MICHAEL RICHARDS

Birthplace: Culver City, CA
Birthdate: 7/24/49
Occupation: Actor
Education: Los Angeles Valley College, California Insitute of the Arts
Debut: (TV) *Fridays,* 1980
Signature: *Seinfeld*
Facts: Has appeared in guest spots on *Hill Street Blues* and *Miami Vice.*

Starred with Weird Al Yankovic in the film *UHF,* 1989.

He was drafted at the height of the Vietnam War in 1970: "When the drill sergeant yelled at me on the first day, I tried to explain the duffel bag was too heavy."

Original Job: Postal worker, schoolbus driver
Marriages: Cathleen (divorced, 1993); Ann Talman (relationship)
Child: Sophia, 1975
Major Award: Emmy, Best Supporting Actor in a Comedy Series, *Seinfeld,* 1992, 1993, 1997

KEVIN RICHARDSON

Birthplace: Lexington, KY
Birthdate: 10/3/72
Occupation: Singer
Debut: (Single) "We've Got It Goin' On," 1995; (Album) *Backstreet Boys,* 1995 (American version, 1997)
Signature: "Everybody (Backstreet's Back),"1997
Facts: Is cousin to Backstreet Boy Kevin Littrell.

Has played the piano since he was 9.

Was football captain at Estill County High in Lexington.

Spent eight years of his life in a log cabin.

After high school, played piano and sang in a band named Paradise. Their covers included Journey

and Bobby Brown tunes.

Played a Ninja Turtle at the Disney-MGM Studios theme park. Met his wife in the park's cafeteria.

The band is named after Orlando, Florida's Backstreet Market, a popular teen hangout.

The group's debut was a hit in 26 countries before *Backstreet Boys* was released in the U.S.

Seen as the most business-minded Backstreet Boy.

Since PEOPLE named him "Sexiest Pop Star" in 1999, his bandmates call him "Mr. Sexy."

Infamy: Band filed suit against former manager Lou Pearlman, claiming he had made $10 million from their labor while they had received $300,000.
Original Job: MGM Studios guide
Marriage: Kristin Willits, 2000
Quote: "You know, we do more than just sing and dance. We've got a brain, too."

NATASHA RICHARDSON

Birthplace: London, England
Birthdate: 5/11/63
Occupation: Actor
Education: Central School for Speech and Drama
Debut: (Stage) *On the Razzle,* 1983
Signature: *The Handmaid's Tale,* 1990
Facts: At age 4, appeared as a bridesmaid of Vanessa Redgrave in *The Charge of the Light Brigade.*

Was named after the heroine in Tolstoy's *War and Peace.*

Marriages: Robert Fox (divorced); Liam Neeson, 1994
Children: Micheál, 1995; Daniel Jack N., 1996
Famous Relatives: Vanessa Redgrave, actor, mother; Tony Richardson, director, father; Joely Richardson, actor, sister; Lynn Redgrave, actor, aunt
Quote: "I've spent half my life trying to get away from being Vanessa Redgrave's daughter, and now I've

got to get away from being Liam Neeson's wife."

Major Award: Tony, Best Actress (Musical), *Cabaret*, 1998

LEANN RIMES

Birthplace: Flowood, MS
Birthdate: 8/28/82
Occupation: Singer
Debut: (Album) *Blue*, 1996
Signature: *Blue*
Facts: Was singing songs like "Jesus Loves Me"—on pitch—at 18 months. Appeared on *Star Search* at age 8 and signed a major record deal at 11.

"Blue" was actually written for Patsy Cline in 1963 but was never recorded because she died that year. When songwriter Bill Mack heard Rimes sing the "Star-Spangled Banner" at a Texas Rangers game he was so impressed he sent her the tune.

Filed a lawsuit against her father and former co-manager in 2000, claiming that the two are responsible for spending more than $7 million of her earnings.

Formerly dated actor Andrew Keegan.

Relationship: Dean Sheremet, dancer
Major Awards: Grammy, Best New Artist, 1996; Grammy, Best Country Vocal—Female, "Blue," 1996

KELLY RIPA

Birthplace: Berlin, NJ
Birthdate: 10/2/70
Occupation: TV Host, soap opera star
Education: Attended Camden Community College
Debut: (TV) *All My Children*
Signature: *Live with Regis and Kelly*
Facts: As a teenager, had a regular part on a Philadelphia TV dance show.

Landed her role as Hayley Vaughan Cortlandt McIntyre Santos on *All My Children* after auditioning

at age 20 with just a few credits.

Began dating her on-and-off-screen husband Mark Consuelos a few weeks after he arrived on the set of *AMC*. In 1996 they eloped to Las Vegas.

Has a 4-inch-long tattoo of a flower on the inside of her left ankle.
Marriage: Mark Consuelos, 1996
Children: Michael Joseph, 1997; Lola Grace, 2001
Quote: "In the world of daytime, everyone is beautiful. Even in a fiery explosion on *All My Children*, I wonder if I'm wearing enough lip gloss."

GERALDO RIVERA

Birthplace: New York, NY
Birthdate: 7/4/43
Occupation: Broadcast journalist, talk show host
Education: University of Arizona; J.D., Brooklyn School of Law; Columbia Journalism School post-graduate
Debut: (TV) *Eyewitness News*, WABC-TV, New York, 1968
Signature: *Geraldo!*
Facts: In the late '60s was involved with a Latino activist group, the Young Lords. Appeared so many times on the evening news the station eventually hired him as a temporary reporter—a good way to satisfy federal minority hiring quotas.

Was fired from ABC-TV in 1985 when the network tired of his sensationalist style and arrogance. At the time, was making $800,000 a year.

In the late '80s, promised a junior high school class he would pay for their college education. Five years later paid $180,000 for nine of the graduates' schooling.

In 1993, opened the Broadcast Boxing Club fitness center in New York.
Infamy: Arrested several times at demonstrations, as well as at a TV filming of a rally, when he got into a scuffle with a Ku Klux Klansman.

Accused of leading talk shows into the gutter. Once even had his nose broken during a brawl on his show.

Original Job: Attorney
Marriage: Linda Coblentz, c. 1965 (divorced); Edith Bucket Vonnegut, 1971 (divorced); Sherryl Raymond, 1976 (divorced, 1984); C. C. Dyer, 1987 (separated, 1999)
Children: Gabriel Miguel, 1979 (with Sherryl Raymond); Cruz, 1987 (born after a brief liaison); Isabella Holmes, 1992; Simone Cruickshank, 1994 (with Dyer)
Major Awards: 3 national and 4 local Emmy Awards

JOAN RIVERS

Real Name: Joan Alexandra Molinsky
Birthplace: Brooklyn, NY
Birthdate: 6/8/33
Occupation: Talk show host
Education: Connecticut College for Women, Barnard College
Debut: (TV) *The Tonight Show*, 1965
Facts: Wrote for *Candid Camera* and *The Ed Sullivan Show*.
Original Job: Publicist at Lord & Taylor, fashion coordinator for Bond Clothing Stores, temporary office secretary, syndicated columnist
Marriage: Edgar Rosenberg, 1965 (deceased); Orin Lehman (relationship)
Child: Melissa, 1968
Major Award: Emmy, Best Host of a Talk Show, *The Joan Rivers Show*, 1990

TIM ROBBINS

Birthplace: West Covina, CA
Birthdate: 10/16/58
Occupation: Writer, director, actor
Education: New York University, SUNY-Plattsburgh, and UCLA
Debut: (Film) *No Small Affair*, 1984
Signature: *The Player*, 1992
Facts: Was kicked off the hockey team in high school for fighting.

Founded Los Angeles theater group Actors' Gang.

Has been an outspoken political activist and peace advocate.
Original Job: Factory worker
Relationship: Susan Sarandon

Children: Jack Henry, 1989; Miles, 1992

JULIA ROBERTS

Birthplace: Smyrna, GA
Birthdate: 10/28/67
Occupation: Actor
Education: High school
Debut: (TV) *Crime Story*, 1986 [see page 69 for a complete filmography]
Signature: *Pretty Woman*, 1990
Facts: Originally wanted to be a veterinarian.

Her middle name is Fiona.

In 1986, she played opposite her brother (actor Eric Roberts) in the film *Blood Red*.

Was set to marry Kiefer Sutherland in 1991, but canceled the wedding at the last minute with virtually no explanation. And she had taken up with Sutherland after breaking off an engagement to Dylan McDermott.

Has also been linked to Liam Neeson, Jason Patric, Daniel Day-Lewis, Ethan Hawke, Matthew Perry, and Benjamin Bratt.

Hobbies include knitting.

Has a 51-acre ranch in Taos. N.M.

Filed a lawsuit against entrepreneur Russell Boyd, who had been the first to register juliaroberts.com as an Internet domain, in 2000 and won back her own name.

Is the first actress to star in movies that grossed more than $1 billion at the box office.
Original Job: Worked in a shoe store and an ice cream shop
Marriage: Lyle Lovett, 1993 (divorced, 1995)
Famous Relatives: Eric Roberts, actor, brother; Lisa Roberts, actor, sister; Emma Roberts, actor, niece
Major Award: Oscar, Best Actress, *Erin Brockovich*, 2001
Quote: "I used to think I was weird. Now I think I'm just interesting."

ANNE ROBINSON

Birthplace: Liverpool, England
Birthdate: 9/26/44
Occupation: TV game show host
Education: High school
Debut: (TV) *Points of View*, BBC
Signature: *The Weakest Link*
Facts: Voted "Rudest Woman on TV" by *TV Times* in Britain in 2000.

A recovering alcoholic, her consumption of cigarettes rose to 60 per day in 1979 after she quit drinking.

Was the first woman to serve as a high-ranking editor on Fleet Street.
Infamy: In 1973, daughter Emma was sent by court order to live with her father due to Robinson's alcoholism.
Original Jobs: Editor, columnist, TV journalist
Marriage: Charlie Wilson, 1968 (divorced, 1973); John Penrose, 1980 (separated, 1990; reconciled, 1992)
Child: Emma, c. 1970 (with Charlie Wilson)

CHRIS ROCK

Birthplace: Brooklyn, NY
Birthdate: 2/7/65
Occupation: Actor, comedian
Education: High school dropout (later got his GED)
Debut: (Film) *Beverly Hills Cop II*, 1987; (TV) *Saturday Night Live*, 1990
Signature: *The Chris Rock Show*
Facts: Grew up in Brooklyn's Bedford-Stuyvesant but was bused to an all-white grade school in Bensonhurst, where he was often the victim of racial violence and discrimination.

Discovered by Eddie Murphy at age 18 during open-mike night at a New York comedy club.

Created the voice of the Little Penny puppet on the Penny Hardaway Nike ads.
Marriage: Malaak Compton
Major Awards: Emmy, Best Writing in a Variety or Music Program, *Chris Rock: Bring the Pain*, 1997; Grammy,

Best Spoken Comedy Album, *Roll With the New*, 1997; Emmy, Best Writing in a Variety or Music Program, *The Chris Rock Show*, 1999; Grammy, Best Comedy Album, *Bigger and Blacker*, 1999
Quote: "Cool is comedy's biggest enemy."

AL ROKER

Birthplace: Queens, NY
Birthdate: 8/20/54
Occupation: TV host, weatherman
Education: SUNY, Oswego
Debut: (TV) WTVH in Syracuse, NY, 1974
Signature: *Today*
Facts: While a sophomore in college, Roker worked as a weatherman for a Syracuse station and found his calling. After graduation, he was a weathercaster in Washington, D.C., (where he befriended Willard Scott), then Cleveland, where he was a pioneer in the use of computer graphics for weather forcasts.

Has hosted *Remember This?*, a college quiz show (MSNBC) and *The Al Roker Show*. His production company produced *Savage Skies* (PBS), a weather documentary series, and *Going Places* (PBS), a series on time- and cost-efficient vacations.

Received the American Meteorological Society's Seal of Approval, awarded to fewer than 2 percent of TV weather reporters.

Won Cleveland's "International Rib Burn-Off" cooking contest twice.

Has served on the board of Outward Bound.

For his website, roker.com, he creates "Rokertoon of the Day" cartoons.

His wife used to think he was "kind of annoying, overly chatty."

His ancestors were slaves on a plantation on the Caribbean island of Exuma, which he has visited. Relatives still live on the island.
Marriages: Alice (divorced); second wife (divorced); Deborah Ann Roberts, NY correspondent for ABC's *20/20*, 1995

Children: Courtney Roker, c. 1988 (with Alice); Leila Ruth, 1998
Major Awards: Daytime Emmys, Outstanding Special Class Program, *Macy's Thanksgiving Day Parade*, 1996, 1997, 1998
Quote: "I really wanted to write comedy or direct. But my college professors told me that I had the perfect face for radio."

RAY ROMANO

Birthplace: Queens, NY
Birthdate: 12/21/57
Occupation: Actor, comedian
Education: High school
Debut: (TV, stand-up) *The Tonight Show Starring Johnny Carson*, 1991; (TV) *Dr. Katz: Professional Therapist*, cartoon voice, 1995
Signature: *Everybody Loves Raymond*
Facts: While working a variety of jobs, he appeared at clubs as a stand-up comic.

Lived in the basement of his parents' home in Forest Hills, New York, until he was 29.

Was replaced by Joe Rogan after two days of rehearsal on *NewsRadio*.

David Letterman's production company developed the sitcom *Everybody Loves Raymond*.

Published his autobiography, *Everything and a Kite,* in 1998.
Original Job: Gas station attendant, futon delivery man
Marriage: Anna Scarpulla, 1987
Children: Alexandra, 1990; twins Matthew and Gregory, 1993; Joseph, 1998
Quote: "Whenever my wife complains about material we use on the show, I tell her to go cry on a bag of money."

REBECCA ROMIJN-STAMOS

Birthdate: 11/6/72
Occupation: Model, actor
Education: University of California, Santa Cruz
Debut: (TV) *House of Style*

Signature: *Sports Illustrated* swimsuit issue cover
Facts: Was nicknamed "Jolly Blonde Giant" in high school.

Likes craft projects, including building an elaborate dollhouse.
Marriage: John Stamos, actor, 1998
Quote: "Fashion is intimidating, and I'm intimidated by most designers I meet. It's a scary thing, and I think other women are intimidated too."

ROSEANNE

Birthplace: Salt Lake City, UT
Birthdate: 11/3/52
Occupation: Actor
Education: High school dropout
Debut: (TV) *Funny*, 1983; (Film) *She-Devil*, 1989
Signature: *Roseanne*
Facts: Dropped out of high school to hitchhike cross country, landing in a Colorado artists' colony at age 18.

Had cosmetic surgery and weight reduction in 1993. Breasts were reduced from 40DD to 38C.

Had a tattoo on her upper right thigh that read: "Property of Tom Arnold." When the pair split, she tattooed over it with a flying fairy and flowers.

Claims she was physically and sexually abused as a child and that she suppressed memory of the abuse until an adult.

Gave up first baby girl, Brandi, for adoption at age 18.

Born to Jewish parents but raised as a Mormon in Salt Lake City. Her dad sold crucifixes door to door.

In 1999, four of her children developed an animated autobiographical comedy pilot: "The kids live off her money and have to do what she says," described ringleader Jenny.
Infamy: Grabbed her crotch, spat, and screeched while singing the national anthem at a San Diego baseball game in 1990.
Original Job: Window dresser, cocktail waitress
Marriages: Bill Pentland, 1974 (divorced, 1990); Tom Arnold

(divorced); Ben Thomas, 1995 (separated, 1998)
Children: Brandi Brown, 1971. Jessica, 1975; Jennifer, 1976; Jake, c. 1978; (with Bill Pentland). Buck, 1995
Major Award: Emmy, Best Actress in a Comedy Series, *Roseanne*, 1993

DIANA ROSS

Real Name: Diane Ernestine Ross
Birthplace: Detroit, MI
Birthdate: 3/26/44
Occupation: Singer, actor
Education: High school
Debut: *The Primettes*, 1959; (TV) *Tarzan*, 1968; (Film) *Lady Sings the Blues*, 1972
Signature: *Ain't No Mountain High Enough*, 1970
Facts: Sung with the Primettes as a teenager until the group was reformed as the Supremes in 1961 and signed on with Motown. Six years later the group, then called Diana Ross and the Supremes, became the most successful black recording artists of their time. Nominated for an Oscar for her first feature film role in 1972's *Lady Sings the Blues,* she went on to appear in 1978's *The Wiz*, which proved unsuccessful and ended her movie career.

She often insists that subordinates address her as "Miss Ross."

Received rave reviews in 1994 for her role as a paranoid schizophrenic in the TV movie *Out of Darkness*.

In the late 1970s, she turned down the role that would become Whitney Houston's in *The Bodyguard*.

Her 2000 "Return to Love" concert tour, without the other two original Supremes, was cut short due to lackluster ticket sales.
Infamy: Kept secret the fact that Motown mogul Berry Gordy fathered her first child.
Original Job: Fashion designer, cafeteria busgirl
Marriage: Robert Ellis Silberstein (divorced, 1976); Arne Naess, 1986

(divorced, 2000)
Children: Rhonda Suzanne, 1971 (with Berry Gordy). Tracee Joy, 1972; Chudney Lane, 1975 (with Silberstein). Ross Arne, 1987; Evan, 1988 (with Naess).
Major Awards: Grammy, Best Vocal (Contemporary) Performance by a Female, "Ain't No Mountain High Enough," 1970; Special Tony for *An Evening with Diana Ross,* 1977
Quote: "I never thought this little Detroit girl would ever go to Nepal, climb the Himalayas, or be in the bush country in Africa".

GAVIN ROSSDALE

Birthplace: London, England
Birthdate: 10/30/67
Occupation: Singer, songwriter, guitarist
Education: High school
Debut: (Album) *Sixteen Stone,* 1994
Signature: Bush
Facts: His parents divorced when he was eleven. He lived with his physician father in the well-heeled North London Kilburn district, attending the posh Westminster high school. After graduating, became a regular party animal at London's clubs.

As a teen, played semi-pro soccer in London and even tried out for a top pro team, Chelsea.

His former band, the pop-oriented Midnight, had a record deal in the mid-1980s but produced no hits.

Originally signed by Disney's Hollywood Records, but exec Frank G. Wells, a major fan, was killed in a helicopter crash just as *Sixteen Stone* was completed. Other execs deemed the album unacceptable, so it went into limbo until being rescued by Interscope.
Original Job: Music video production assistant
Relationship: Gwen Stefani

J. K. ROWLING

Real Name: Joanne Kathleen Rowling
Birthplace: Bristol, England
Birthdate: 7/31/65
Occupation: Author
Education: Exeter University
Debut: (UK) *Harry Potter and the Philosopher's Stone,* 1997 (*Harry Potter and the Sorcerer's Stone,* 1998, in U.S.)
Signature: Harry Potter
Facts: Wanted to be a writer from age six.

Her last name is pronounced "ROE-ling."

Originally worked in London at Amnesty International, then at the Chamber of Commerce in Manchester.

Following her divorce from a Portuguese journalist, Rowling returned to England in 1993 with no money, no job, and a young child. She qualified for public assistance, but not for child care, so she was forced to remain unemployed.

Wrote her first book in a coffee shop as her daughter napped. She first thought of the series in 1990, and conceived portions of all seven books from the start.

Received an advance of $4,000 for the first Harry Potter book.

Harry Potter and the Goblet of Fire was the fastest-selling book of all time in the U.S., practically selling out its 3-million copy first printing in its first week on sale. Her books have been translated into at least 28 languages.
Original Job: Teacher
Marriage: Jorge Arantes, 1992 (divorced, 1995)
Children: Jessica, 1993
Quote: "It's going to break my heart when I stop writing about Harry."

GEOFFREY RUSH

Birthplace: Toowoomba, Queensland, Australia
Birthdate: 7/6/51
Occupation: Actor, theater director, playwright, musician
Education: University of Queensland
Debut: (Film) *Hoodwink,* 1981
Signature: *Shine,* 1996
Facts: Played Snoopy in *You're a Good Man, Charlie Brown.* ("One of my first big hits. I was a very good dog.")

Studied for two years at Jacques Lecoq School of Mime, Movement and Theater in Paris.

Made his stage directing debut in 1978 with the Queensland Theatre Company.

Appeared with Mel Gibson in *Waiting for Godot.* They were roommates for four months in 1980 during the production.

In 1992, he suffered a breakdown, which was attributed to his hectic schedule.
Marriage: Jane Menelaus, actor, 1988
Children: Angelica, c. 1992; James, c. 1995
Quote: "My career has been in theater for 23 years, with spits and coughs in bits and pieces of films."
Major award: Oscar, Best Actor, *Shine,* 1996

KERI RUSSELL

Birthplace: Fountain Valley, CA
Birthdate: 3/23/76
Occupation: Actor
Education: High school
Debut: (TV) Disney Channel's *All New Mickey Mouse Club,* 1991; (Film) *Honey, I Blew Up the Kid,* 1992
Signature: *Felicity*
Facts: A successful audition in Denver led to her three-year stint as a Mouseketeer, launching her career and her long romance with Tony Lucca, with whom she also costarred in TV's 1996 *Malibu Shores.*

Her middle name is Lynn.

At age 17 she set off on her own to L.A. and got a role right away on Dudley Moore's sitcom *Daddy's Girl.*

Producers originally thought she

was too pretty for the role of Felicity—even though she dressed down for the audition to make herself look plain.

Her favorite things are massages, fresh flowers, live music, and trips to Ireland and Big Sur.
Original Job: Model
Relationship: Scott Speedman
Quote: "You gotta be low maintenance."

KURT RUSSELL

Birthplace: Springfield, MA
Birthdate: 3/17/51
Occupation: Actor, screenwriter, producer
Education: High school
Debut: (Film) *The Absent-Minded Professor,* 1960
Signature: *Stargate,* 1994
Facts: At 12, starred in his own Western series, *The Travels of Jaimie McPheeters,* featuring Charles Bronson and the very young Osmond brothers.

Left acting in 1971 to play minor league baseball. Returned to acting two years later after tearing a shoulder muscle.

His actor father played the sheriff for 14 years on *Bonanza.*
Marriages: Season Hubley, 1979 (divorced, 1983); Goldie Hawn (relationship)
Children: Boston, 1980 (with Season Hubley). Wyatt, 1986
Famous Relatives: Bing Russell, actor, father

RENE RUSSO

Birthplace: Burbank, CA
Birthdate: 2/17/54
Occupation: Actor
Education: High school dropout
Debut: (Film) *Major League,* 1989
Signature: *Lethal Weapon 3,* 1992
Facts: Considered herself unattractive as a teen because she wore a body cast to correct a curved spine from ages 10 to 14. Shy and uninterested in school (where high school classmates included Ron Howard), she dropped out in 10th grade and worked in an eyeglass factory.

Was discovered by a modeling agent in the parking lot following a Rolling Stones concert. A few weeks later, she was in New York shooting a Revlon ad with Richard Avedon.

At age 30, depressed by being too old to model, she discovered Christian theology, which she spent the next three years studying. Religion gave her the confidence to try an acting career.

Met her future husband on the set of *Freejack,* a film for which she had originally turned down an acting role and for which Gilroy had originally rejected the job of script rewriting.
Original Job: Supermodel
Marriage: Danny Gilroy (divorced)
Child: Rose, 1993
Quote: (on her nude scenes in *The Thomas Crown Affair*): "It never really dawned on me that, gee, I'm 45 and I'm taking off my clothes."

JERI RYAN

Real Name: Jeri Lynn Zimmerman
Birthplace: Munich, Germany
Birthdate: 2/22/68
Occupation: Actor
Education: Northwestern University
Debut: (TV movie) *Nightmare in Columbia County,* 1991
Signature: Seven of Nine in *Star Trek: Voyager*
Facts: From 1993 to 1997, she appeared in episodes of *Who's the Boss, Murder, She Wrote, Diagnosis Murder, Melrose Place,* and the short-lived *Dark Skies.*

Was a National Merit Scholar.

Her original *Voyager* suit was so tight that she passed out four times and required oxygen on the set.
Marriage: Jack Ryan (John Clemens Ryan), 1991 (separated, 1998)
Child: Alex Ryan, c. 1994
Quote: "I don't mind being called a babe. It's better than being called a dog."

MEG RYAN

Real Name: Margaret Hyra
Birthplace: Fairfield, CT
Birthdate: 11/19/61
Occupation: Actor
Education: New York University
Debut: (Film) *Rich and Famous,* 1981; (TV) *As the World Turns, 1983* [see page 69 for a complete filmography]
Signature: *When Harry Met Sally...,* 1989
Fact: Became high school homecoming queen when the original queen was suspended.

Her strained relationship with her mother became tabloid-show fodder when her stepfather wrote an article about the pair's discord in a magazine in 1992. Ryan subsequently ended all contact with them.

Met husband Quaid on the set of the comedy film, *Innerspace,* in 1987. A year later, they professionally reunited for the unsuccessful film *D.O.A.*
Marriage: Dennis Quaid, 1991 (filed for divorce, 2000);
Child: Jack Henry, 1992
Quote: "I have remained consistently and nauseatingly adorable. In fact, I have been known to cause diabetes."

WINONA RYDER

Real Name: Winona Laura Horowitz
Birthplace: Winona, MN
Birthdate: 10/29/71
Occupation: Actor
Education: High school
Debut: (Film) *Lucas,* 1986 [see page 69 for a complete filmography]
Signature: *Beetlejuice,* 1988
Facts: Her childhood home in Elk, CA, had no electricity.

In junior high school, was attacked and beaten by fellow students during her first week at a new school, apparently because they mistook her for a boy.

Her natural hair color is blond.

She's been a brunette since she auditioned for *Lucas* in 1986.

Has read *The Catcher in the Rye* countless times, and travels with a copy.

Dated Christian Slater, David Pirner, and Matt Damon; was engaged to Johnny Depp. Is rumored to have also dated Daniel Day-Lewis, Stephan Jenkins, and Evan Dando.

Timothy Leary, the famous psychologist and countercultural philosopher, was her godfather.

ADAM SANDLER

Birthplace: Brooklyn, NY
Birthdate: 9/9/66
Occupation: Comedian, actor
Education: New York University
Debut: (TV) *The Cosby Show*, 1987; (Film) *Shakes the Clown*, 1992
Signature: *Big Daddy*, 1999
Facts: Became a writer for *Saturday Night Live* in 1990, but his sketches were often too eccentric for others to make their own. He soon became a "featured player" doing those skits and, after the success of his Opera Man, became a regular cast member.

As a developing comic, was so taken by Rodney Dangerfield he memorized many of Dangerfield's routines.

Original Job: Stand-up comedian
Relationship: Margaret Ruden (engaged, never married); Jackie Titone
Quote: "If you don't get the best grades, don't fret—I didn't do too well in school and I'm a multimillionaire."

CARLOS SANTANA

Birthplace: Autlan de Navarro, Mexico
Birthdate: 7/20/47
Occupation: Musician, bandleader
Debut: (Album) *Santana*, 1969
Signature: "Smooth," 1999

Facts: His father, a traditional violinist, played mariachi music, and began teaching music theory to his son, then five.

Began playing in night clubs when he was just 11.

Five years later, the family moved to San Francisco.

Was mentored by the Grateful Dead's Jerry Garcia before forming the Santana Blues Band. The band played at Woodstock in 1969, even though they didn't have an album out at the time. Their appearance on *The Ed Sullivan Show* landed them a deal with Columbia Records.

In the early '70s he became a follower of Sri Chimnoy, and in 1973 changed his name to Devadip (meaning the light of the lamp of the Supreme). He discontinued the association in 1982.

In 1988, helped organize the "Blues for Salvador" concert in California, to benefit children of El Salvador.

Founded a record label, Guts and Grace, in 1994.

The eight Grammy wins for *Supernatural* tied it with Michael Jackson's 1983 *Thriller* for most awards in a single night.

Launched a line of women's shoes that "radiate rhythm, passion and energy," as well as his own handbags and neckties, in 2001.
Original Job: Dishwasher
Marriage: Deborah King, 1973
Children: Salvador, 1984; Stella, 1985; Angelica, 1990
Major Awards: Grammy, Best Rock Instrumental Performance of Blues, *Salvador*, 1988; Grammy, Record of the Year, "Smooth," 1999; Grammy, Song of the Year, "Smooth," 1999; Grammy, Pop Collaboration with Voals, "Smooth," 1999; Grammy, Album of the Year, *Supernatural*, 1999; Grammy, Rock Album, *Supernatural*, 1999; Grammy, Pop Instrumental Performance, "El Farol," 1999; Grammy, Rock Performance by a Due or Group with Vocal, "Put Your Lights on," 1999; Grammy, Rock Instrumental Performance,

"The Calling," 1999
Quote: "A lot of people didn't want to work with be because I'm too old."

SUSAN SARANDON

Real Name: Susan Abigail Tomaling
Birthplace: New York, NY
Birthdate: 10/4/46
Occupation: Actor
Education: Catholic University of America
Debut: (Film) *Joe*, 1970 [see pages 69–70 for a complete filmography]
Signature: *Thelma & Louise*, 1991
Facts: Her background is Welsh-Italian. Was one of nine children, and attended Catholic school.

Is 12 years older than beau Tim Robbins.

An activist for numerous political, cultural, and health causes, she digressed during her 1991 Academy Awards presentation to speak for a half-minute on behalf of Haitian refugees with AIDS.

Starred in cult classic *The Rocky Horror Picture Show*.

She and Robbins keep all their awards in the "famous bathroom."
Original Job: While in college, worked in the drama department, modeled, and cleaned apartments.
Marriages: Chris Sarandon, 1967 (divorced, 1979); Tim Robbins (relationship)
Children: Eva Maria Livia, 1985 (with Franco Amurri). Jack Henry, 1989; Miles, 1992 (with Tim Robbins)
Major Awards: Oscar, Best Actress, *Dead Man Walking*, 1995

DIANE SAWYER

Birthplace: Glasgow, KY
Birthdate: 12/22/45
Occupation: Broadcast journalist
Education: Wellesley College
Debut: (TV) WLKY-TV, Louisville, 1967
Signature: *Primetime Live*
Facts: Was national Junior Miss, largely on the strength of her interview and essays.

Dated Bill Bradley in college.

As a weathercaster in Louisville, KY, she spruced up forecasts with quotes from her favorite poems.

Served as staff assistant to former President Nixon and helped him research his memoirs.

Marriage: Mike Nichols, 1988
Major Awards: 11 News and Documentary Emmys: 9 as correspondent, 1 as anchor, 1 as interviewer

CLAUDIA SCHIFFER

Birthplace: Dusseldorf, Germany
Birthdate: 8/25/70
Occupation: Supermodel
Education: High school
Facts: Tripped during her runway modeling debut in 1990.

Earns as much as $50,000 a day.

Opened Fashion Cafe in New York City in 1995 with fellow supermodels Elle MacPherson and Naomi Campbell.

Was engaged to David Copperfield, but they never married.

Marriage: Tim Jeffries (engaged, 2000)
Quote: "I actually don't meet very many men because they are, I guess, afraid to approach me or think that I'm from another planet."

LAURA SCHLESSINGER

Birthdate: 1947
Occupation: Radio talk show host
Education: SUNY, Stony Brook; Columbia University, Ph.D. in physiology; University of Southern California, post-doctoral certificate in marriage and family therapy
Debut: (Radio) *The Dr. Laura Schlessinger Show,* 1990
Signature: "Dr. Laura"
Facts: Had a tubal ligation at age 30, which she later had reversed.

Has been estranged from her mother since before the birth of her son.

Converted to Judaism in 1994.

Her house burned almost entirely in an electrical fire in 1992.

Has a black belt in Karate.

Her radio call-in show now has an audience of some 18 million listeners on 450 U.S. stations and 30 Canadian stations, and is even heard in South Africa.

In addition to her adult bestsellers, recently began writing children's picture books, her first entitled *Why Do You Love Me?*

Owns a Harley and a rose-colored Mercedes-Benz.

Her radio show was sold in 1997 for $71.5 million, 40 percent more than an earlier deal for Rush Limbaugh's show.

It's estimated that 60,000 people call into to her show every day.

She encountered a firestorm of protest in 2000 after making comments on the air that characterized homosexuality as deviant behavior and a biological error. A successful boycott pressured advertisers to stay away from her television talk show, launched in the fall, prompting her to run a full-page apology in *Variety.* By the next year, the TV show was cancelled.

Infamy: In 1998 tried unsuccessfully to have a court keep a dozen nude photos of her, taken by a former lover decades earlier, from being posted on the Internet.
Marriages: First husband (divorced, 1978); Lewis Bishop, 1984
Child: Deryk Schlessinger, 1986
Quotes: "I do not see it as my mission to make anybody feel better. I want them to get better."

RICK SCHRODER

Birthplace: Staten Island, NY
Birthdate: 4/13/70
Occupation: Actor
Education: Mesa State College
Debut: (Film) *The Champ,* 1979; (TV) *Silver Spoons,* 1982
Signature: *Silver Spoons*
Facts: "Ricky" began making TV commercials as a toddler, appearing

in some 60 by age 7.

Won a Golden Globe when he was 9 for his role as boxer Jon Voight's son in *The Champ,* directed by Franco Zeffirelli.

Following his youthful sitcom run, he landed his first starring role in the TV movie *Something So Right* in 1982. He later won a key role in the miniseries *Lonesome Dove* and its sequel.

Owns 800 head of cattle, quarter horses, 2,000 deer, and 3 trout lakes on his 45,000-acre Colorado ranch.

He takes time out of his days to indulge in yoga and receives weekly massages.

He wishes he were taller.

Original Job: Model
Marriage: Andrea Bernard, 1992
Children: Holden, 1992; Luke, 1993; Cambrie, 1996; Faith Anne, 2001
Major Awards: Golden Globe Award, New Star of the Year, *The Champ,* 1979
Quote: "I guess I've come to terms with myself and what I look like. These are the cards I was dealt, so I play 'em the best I know how."

ARNOLD SCHWARZENEGGER

Birthplace: Graz, Austria
Birthdate: 7/30/47
Occupation: Actor, director, body-builder
Education: University of Wisconsin
Debut: (Film) *Hercules in New York,* 1969 [see page 70 for a complete filmography]
Signature: *The Terminator,* 1984
Facts: After coming to the U.S. in the '60s, founded a bricklaying business, Pumping Bricks, to finance his body-building career.

Won the Austrian Junior Olympic weightlifting championship as well as Junior Mr. Europe and several curling titles.

In 1974, acted in *Happy Anniversary and Goodbye,* an unsold CBS sitcom pilot starring Lucille Ball and Art Carney.

Has killed over 275 people on screen.
Infamy: Named in a 1995 paternity suit by a Texas woman who claims he fathered her daughter 12 years earlier.
Original Job: Managed a Munich health club
Marriage: Maria Owings Shriver, 1986
Children: Katherine Eunice, 1989; Christina Maria Aurelia, 1991; Patrick, 1993; Christopher, 1997
Quote: "Everything I have ever done in my life has always stayed. I've just added to it...But I will not change. Because when you are successful and you change, you are an idiot."

DAVID SCHWIMMER

Birthplace: Queens, NY
Birthdate: 11/2/66
Occupation: Actor
Education: Northwestern University
Debut: (TV movie) *A Deadly Silence*, 1989; (Film) *Crossing the Bridge*, 1992
Signature: *Friends*
Facts: His mother is the attorney who handled Roseanne's first divorce. Since his father is also an attorney, he flirted with becoming one before settling into acting.
Appeared in the 1994 Henry Winkler flop, *Monty*.
Started Chicago's Lookingglass Theater Company in 1988 with seven other Northwestern graduates.
In 2000, along with *Friends* costars, received a salary increase from $125,000 to $750,000 per episode.
Relationship: Mili Avital

MARTIN SCORSESE

Birthplace: New York, NY
Birthdate: 11/17/42
Occupation: Director
Education: New York University
Debut: (Film) *Boxcar Bertha*, 1972

[see page 70 for a complete filmography]
Signature: *Taxi Driver*, 1976
Facts: Collaborated on the production of Michael Jackson's *Bad* video in 1987.
Was originally enrolled as an English major before switching to film.
Original Job: Faculty assistant and instructor in film department at NYU
Marriages: Larraine Marie Brennan, 1965 (divorced); Julia Cameron, 1975 (divorced); Isabella Rosellini, 1979 (divorced, 1983); Barbara DeFina, 1985 (divorced); Helen Morris, 1999
Children: Catherine Terese, 1965 (with Larraine Marie Brennan). Domenica Elizabeth, 1976 (with Julia Cameron). Francesca, 1999 (with Helen Morris).
Major Award: Cannes Film Festival, Palme d'Or, *Taxi Driver*, 1976

STEVEN SEAGAL

Birthplace: Lansing, MI
Birthdate: 4/10/52
Occupation: Actor, producer
Education: Orange Coast College
Debut: (Film) *Above the Law*, 1988
Signature: *Hard To Kill*, 1990
Facts: Founder, Aikido Ten Shin Dojo, Los Angeles.
First non-Asian to successfully open a martial arts academy in Japan.
In 1968, moved to Japan, where he taught English and wrote articles for Japanese magazines and newspapers.
Organized security for the departure of the Shah's family from Iran.
Commands the title of Shihan (Master of Masters).
The high lama of the Nyingma school of Buddhism ceremonially recognized Seagal as a *tulku*—a reincarnated holy man.
Infamy: Was sued by a film assistant for sexual harassment. Paid money to settle out of court in 1990.

Was married to both his first and second wives simultaneously.
Scriptwriter Lars Hansson claimed in 1994 that Seagal threatened him with death after he refused to sell him film rights to a CIA hit-man story.
In 1995, was accused by ex-girlfriend Cheryl Shuman of harassing her. A judge threw out her lawsuit, calling it unintelligible.
Original Job: Martial arts instructor, bodyguard
Marriages: Miyako Fujitani (divorced); Adrienne LaRussa (annulled); Kelly LeBrock, 1994; Arissa Wolf (relationship)
Children: Justice (a.k.a. Kentaro), 1975; Ayako, c. 1980; (with Miyako Fujitani). Anna-lisa, c. 1987; Dominick San Rocco, 1990; Arissa, 1993; (with Kelly LeBrock). Savannah, 1996
Quote: "I just care about bringing joy into this world in my little way."

SEAL

Real Name: Sealhenry Samuel
Birthplace: Paddington, England
Birthdate: 2/19/63
Occupation: Singer, songwriter
Education: High school dropout
Debut: (Album) *Seal*, 1991
Signature: "Kiss from a Rose," 1995
Facts: His name comes from his Brazilian father's custom of having the grandparents select the name (they chose Seal) coupled with his parents' fascination with British royalty (they wanted Henry).
As an infant, lived with a white foster family until his Nigerian mother reclaimed him. When she became ill several years later, went to his father's, whom he says beat him mercilessly.
Plays a six-string guitar upside down; left-handed, learned on guitars borrowed from studios and they were all right-handed.
The scars on his face are remnants of lupus contracted at age 23.
Major Awards: Grammy, Record of the Year, "Kiss from a Rose," 1995;

Grammy, Song of the Year, "Kiss from a Rose," 1995; Grammy, Best Male Pop Vocal Performance, "Kiss from a Rose," 1995

JERRY SEINFELD

Birthplace: Brooklyn, NY
Birthdate: 4/29/54
Occupation: Actor, comedian
Education: Queens College
Debut: (Stand-up) Catch a Rising Star, Manhattan, 1976
Signature: Seinfeld
Facts: At his first stage appearance, he was so nervous he forgot his routine and only mumbled the words "The beach. Driving. Shopping. Parents," and walked off.

Owns several dozen pairs of sneakers, including a custom pair of "Air Seinfelds."

Has practiced yoga for 20 years and is a strict vegetarian.

His TV series Seinfeld was one of 15 stamps depicting 90s pop culture issued in 2000.
Infamy: Created a stir when he began dating 18-year-old Shoshanna Lonstein in 1993. They broke up in 1997.

His relationship with newlywed Jessica Sklar, 27, broke up her marriage
Marriage: Jessica Sklar, 1999
Child: Sascha, 2000
Original Job: Sought the worst jobs possible, including selling light bulbs over the phone and costume jewelry on the streets of New York, to force himself to succeed at comedy
Major Award: Emmy, Best Comedy Series, Seinfeld, 1993
Quote: "I'm hardly interested in my own life. I don't know how you could be interested."

CHLOE SEVIGNY

Birthplace: Darien, CT
Birthdate: 11/18/74
Occupation: Actor
Education: High School
Debut: (Film) Kids, 1994

Signature: Boys Don't Cry, 1999
Facts: Met screenwriter Harmony Korine as a teenager while hanging out in New York City's Washington Square park. They dated for a while, and she lives next door to Korine in Darien, CT now.

Interned at Sassy magazine.

Jay McInerney heralded her as Manhattan's It girl in a 1994 New Yorker profile, prior to the release of Kids.

She likes to sail.
Original Job: Salesgirl, model
Quote: "I've questioned issues of gender and sexuality since I was a teenager, and I did some experimenting. Its not my thing now, but I've always questioned it."

JANE SEYMOUR

Real Name: Joyce Frankenberg
Birthplace: Hillingdon, England
Birthdate: 2/15/51
Occupation: Actor
Education: Arts Educational School, London
Debut: (Film) Oh, What a Lovely War, 1968
Signature: Dr. Quinn, Medicine Woman
Facts: Danced with the London Festival Ballet at 13.

Named Honorary Citizen of Illinois by Governor Thompson in 1977.
Original Job: Ballet dancer
Marriages: Michael Attenborough (divorced); Geoffrey Planer (divorced); David Flynn (divorced); James Keach, 1993
Children: Kalen; 1977 (stepson, with James Keach). Jennifer, 1980; Katie, 1982; Sean, 1985 (with David Flynn). John, 1995; Kristopher, 1995
Major Awards: Emmy, Best Supporting Actress in a Miniseries, Onassis, 1988

SHAGGY

Real Name: Orville Richard Burrell
Birthplace: Kingston, Jamaica
Birthdate: 10/22/68

Occupation: Musician
Education: High School
Debut: (Album) Pure Pleasure, 1993
Signature: "It Wasn't Me," 2001
Facts: Joined the Marines in 1988 and served 5 months in the Persian Gulf War.

Made two hit albums with Virgin Records but was dropped from the label when his third album, 1997's Midnite Lover, bombed. Signed with MCA in 2000 and went to work on his fourth album, the quadruple-platinum Hot Shot.

Was the first dance hall artist to perform in South Africa following the abolition of apartheid.

Nicknamed Shaggy by friends after the popular cartoon character on Scooby Doo because of his wild hair.

In 2001, launched a record label, Big Yard, with MCA.
Children: Richie, 1995; Tyler, 1999 (with Carol Johnson)
Major Award: Grammy, Best Reggae Album, Boombastic, 1996
Quote: "If you don't know me yet, come to a Shaggy concert. I guarantee, when you leave, you'll be a Shaggy fan."

GARRY SHANDLING

Birthplace: Chicago, IL
Birthdate: 11/29/49
Occupation: Actor, writer, comedian
Education: University of Arizona
Debut: (TV) Sanford & Son, 1976
Signature: The Larry Sanders Show
Fact: Wrote for Sanford & Son, Welcome Back, Kotter, and Three's Company.

Named The Tonight Show's permanent guest host in 1986 and was widely expected to be Johnny Carson's successor, but decided he didn't enjoy it enough so he left.
Infamy: A former co-star sued Shandling for sexual harassment; she claimed her firing from Sanders was tied to the break-up of their relationship.

In 1998, Shandling sued his 18-

year friend and manager, Brad Grey, for $100 million, claiming that Grey didn't protect his interests and built a management/production empire on Shandling's talents. Grey counter-sued for $10 million, alleging breach of contract and fiduciary duty. They settled their respective suits in 1999 by exchanging "certain interests in various television properties."

Major Award: Emmy, Writing for a Comedy Series, *The Larry Sanders Show*, 1998

Quote: "It's really to the point now, when I envision myself walking down the aisle with a woman in white, it's a nurse."

WILLIAM SHATNER

Birthplace: Montreal, Canada
Birthdate: 3/22/31
Occupation: Actor, author, producer, director
Education: McGill University
Debut: (TV) *Goodyear TV Playhouse*, 1956
Signature: *Star Trek*
Facts: Has written a series of books, beginning with *TekWar,* which were turned into movies in which he stars.

Most celebrated pre-*Trek* experience was as a guest on one of the most famous *Twilight Zone* episodes, "Nightmare at 20,000 Feet," in 1963.

One of his leisure activities is breeding horses.

Became CEO of a special effects company, CORE Digital Pictures, in 1995.

Original Job: Novelist
Marriages: Gloria Rand (divorced); Marcy Lafferty, 1973 (divorced, 1996); Nerine Kidd, 1997 (deceased, 1999); Elizabeth J. Martin, 2001
Children: Leslie, 1958; Lisabeth, 1961; Melanie, 1964; (with Gloria Rand).

CHARLES SHEEN

Real name: Carlos Irwin Estevez
Birthplace: Los Angeles CA
Birthdate: 9/3/65
Occupation: Actor, screenwriter, producer, poet
Education: High school dropout
Debut: (TV) *Silence of the Heart*, 1984; (Film) *Grizzly II-The Predator*, 1984; (Book) *A Peace of Mind*, poetry, 1991
Signature: *Platoon*, 1986
Facts: The third son of actor Martin Sheen, he lost his college baseball scholarship because of poor grades, and failed to graduate high school.

At age 9 appeared as extra in a TV movie, *The Execution of Private Slovik*, starring his father. Appeared as an extra in *Apocalypse Now*.

Since childhood, has created over 200 Super-8 and video film shorts, and the 16mm film *R.P.G.*

Was friendly in high school with classmates Sean Penn and Rob Lowe.

Had a child out of wedlock with his high school girlfriend.

In 1990, he checked into a drug and alcohol rehab center after reportedly suffering from exhaustion.

Has his own $1.5 million custom-designed bus with a full-size master bedroom and three satellite TVs to take on the set with him.

Told *Maxim* magazine that he guesses he's slept with 5,000 women.

Has 12 tattoos.

Infamy: While in high school, he was arrested for marijuana possession and credit card forgery.

In 1995, he admitted paying Heidi Fleiss more than $53,000 for 27 trysts with her employees.

Assault charges were filed against him by companion Brittany Ashland in 1996; he pleaded no contest and received a one-year suspended sentence with two years probation.

In 1998, he was hospitalized following a drug overdose. After walking out of rehab, his father asked prosecutors to file probation violation charges. A judge extended his probation and ordered him into rehab.

In 1999, he was sued by two female adult movie actors who claimed his bodyguard had assaulted them.

Marriages: Kelly Preston (engaged, never married); Donna Peele, 1995 (divorced 1996)
Child: Cassandra Sheen, 1984 (with Paula Profitt)
Famous relatives: Martin Sheen, actor, director, father; Renee Pilar Estevez, actor, sister; Emilio Estevez, actor, director, screenwriter, brother; Ramon Estevez, actor, brother
Quote: "What do you do when you've got studio heads that won't hire you, even though you screwed the same whores? Yet they pull you aside at a party and say that you're their hero for the things that you do…. I feel like Vicarious Man. I am Vicarious Man!"

MARTIN SHEEN

Real Name: Ramon G. Estevez
Birthplace: Dayton, OH
Birthdate: 8/3/40
Occupation: Actor, producer, director
Education: High school
Debut: (Stage) *The Connection*, 1959; (TV) *The Defenders*, 1961; (Film) *The Incident*, 1967
Signature: *Apocalypse Now*, 1979
Facts: His father was Spanish and his mother Irish (she was sent to the U.S. as a child for safety, since her father and brothers were very involved with the IRA).

A forceps delivery crushed his left shoulder, and he is still handicapped by it.

At 11, he worked as a caddy at a local country club, but was fired when he tried to start a union.

Read poetry and scripture on a local Dayton TV program and won a trip to New York for an audition.

Took his stage name from the last names of CBS's casting director

Robert Dale Martin and Bishop Fulton Sheen.

Was featured on *As the World Turns* in the early 60s.

A play he wrote, *Down the Morning Line*, was performed at New York City's Public Theater in 1969.

Sons Charlie Sheen and Emilio Estevez both became fathers at young ages, and out of wedlock. He bought houses for both mothers and set up trusts for the grandchildren.

Was made honorary mayor of Malibu, California in 1989.

Made his feature film screenwriting and directing debut in 1990's *Cadence*, which starred his sons Charlie Sheen and Ramon Estevez.

A longtime activist, he was arrested in 1996 for trespassing at a New York think tank which was thought to be contributing to nuclear weapons programs.

Marriage: Janet, 1961
Children: Emilio Estevez, actor, son, 1962; Ramon Estevez, actor, son, 1963; Charlie Sheen, actor, son, 1965; Renee Estevez, actor, daughter, 1967
Famous Relative: Joe Estevez, brother, actor
Major Awards: Daytime Emmy for Outstanding Direction in Children's Programming for *Babies Having Babies*, 1986; Emmy, guest appearance, *Murphy Brown*, 1993
Quote: "I'm not a purist. I've been at this for 31 years, and most of the work I've done has been crap.... But I did it for the money. I'm not proud of it."

JUDITH SHEINDLIN

Real Name: Judy Blum
Birthplace: Brooklyn, NY
Birthdate: 10/21/42
Occupation: TV judge
Education: American University, New York Law School
Signature: *Judge Judy*
Facts: Married while in law school and the only woman in the gradu-

ating class of 1965, she practiced law for a few years before staying home to care for her young children.

Returned to work in 1972 as a prosecutor in New York's family court, then served as family court judge in New York for 24 years.

Following publication of her 1996 book, *Don't Pee on My Leg and Tell Me It's Raining*, she began her successful courtroom TV show.
Original Job: Lawyer
Marriage: Ronald Levy, 1964 (divorced, 1976); Jerry Sheindlin, 1978
Children: Adam (with Levy); Jamie Hartwright (with Sheindlin)
Quote: "I'm rough on people. I say what's on my mind. If that's not the law in your jurisdiction, it ought to be."

BROOKE SHIELDS

Birthplace: New York, NY
Birthdate: 5/31/65
Occupation: Actor
Education: Princeton University
Debut: (Film) *Alice, Sweet Alice*, 1978
Signature: *Suddenly Susan*
Facts: Began her career as an Ivory Snow baby when she was 11 months old. Appeared on more than 30 magazine covers at age 16.

Says now that her overbearing ex-manager stage-mother, Teri, was an alcoholic. Shields was conceived out of wedlock and her father was around only for the first few months of her life.

Has previously been linked romantically to Liam Neeson, Prince Albert of Monaco, George Michael, Michael Bolton, and Michael Jackson.

Her divorce papers cited "incompatible tastes [and] temperament."
Infamy: As the 12-year-old star of *Pretty Baby*, played a prostitute in various states of undress.
Original Job: Model
Marriage: André Agassi, 1997 (separated, 1999); Chris Henchy, 2001

Quote: "Every time I go to the doctor I say, 'Can I still make a baby?... How much time do I have? What am I going to have to do, find a sire?'"

MARTIN SHORT

Birthplace: Hamilton, Ontario, Canada
Birthdate: 3/26/50
Occupation: Actor
Education: McMaster University
Debut: (Stage) *Godspell*, 1972; (Movie) *Lost and Found*, 1979
Signature: *Saturday Night Live*, 1984
Facts: As a child, used to produce his own mock talk show in his family's attic; he had his own syndicated talk show in 1999.

Majored in social work in college.

His first acting job was as a giant Visa card for a television commercial.

A lively talk-show guest, he once did his Bette Davis imitation while the actress was next to him on Johnny Carson's couch.

Has received the Order of Canada, which is the equivalent of Britain's knighthood.
Marriage: Nancy Dolman, 1980
Children: Oliver, c. 1986; Henry, c. 1990
Major Awards: Emmy, Outstanding Writing in a Variety or Music Program, *SCTV Network*, 1983; Tony, Best Actor (Musical), *Little Me*, 1999
Quote: "I am a timeless imp with endless energy."

ELISABETH SHUE

Birthplace: Wilmington, DE
Birthdate: 10/6/63
Occupation: Actor
Education: attended Wellesley College, Harvard University
Debut: (Film) *The Karate Kid*, 1984
Signature: *Leaving Las Vegas*, 1995
Facts: Admits to drinking heavily and going to class stoned while in high school.

Encouraged her baby brother Andrew to join her in acting.

Broke into show business as a teenager appearing on a series of 20 Burger King commercials.

Older brother Will died in a swimming accident on a family vacation at age 27.

In 2000, returned to Harvard to finish course work toward a political science degree (she left school one semester shy of graduation in the 1980s).

Marriage: Davis Guggenheim, 1994
Children: Miles William, 1997; Stella, 2001
Famous Relatives: Andrew Shue, actor, brother

ALICIA SILVERSTONE

Birthplace: San Francisco, CA
Birthdate: 10/4/76
Occupation: Actor
Education: High school equivalency
Debut: (Film) *The Crush*, 1993
Signature: *Clueless*, 1995
Facts: Filed for emancipation from her parents at 15 so she could work in films as an adult.

Was a cheerleader in high school.

Won MTV's Villain of the Year award in 1993 for her performance as the lovestruck psychopath in *The Crush.*

Relationship: Chris Jarecki, musician
Quote: "People who say I'm sexy don't really understand what sexy means. I'm always dirty and always in sweats. That's the real me."

NEIL SIMON

Real Name: Marvin Neil Simon
Birthplace: Bronx, NY
Birthdate: 7/4/27
Occupation: Playwright, screen-writer, producer
Education: New York University
Debut: (Stage) *Adventures of Marco Polo: A Musical Fantasy,* 1959; (Film) *After the Fox,* 1966
Signature: *The Odd Couple,* 1965

Facts: Flew in the U.S. Air Force, 1945–46.

Met his third wife in 1985 when she was handing out perfume samples at the Beverly Hills Neiman Marcus store.

Owns Eugene O'Neill Theatre in New York.

Has written nearly 30 Broadway shows.

Was nicknamed Doc by older brother Danny after Simon took to a toy doctor's kit.

Original Job: Mail room clerk
Marriages: Joan Baim (deceased); Marsha Mason (divorced, 1983); Diane Lander (divorced, remarried, divorced, 1998); Elaine Joyce, 1999
Children: Ellen, 1957; Nancy, 1963; (with Joan Biam). Bryn, c. 1984 (stepdaughter)
Major Awards: Tony, Best Author (Dramatic), *The Odd Couple,* 1965; Tony, Special Award, 1975, Tony, Best Play, *Biloxi Blues,* 1985; Tony, Best Play, *Lost in Yonkers,* 1991; Pulitzer Prize, Best Play, *Lost in Yonkers,* 1991

PAUL SIMON

Birthplace: Newark, NJ
Birthdate: 10/13/41
Occupation: Singer, songwriter
Education: Queens College, Brooklyn Law School
Debut: (Song) "Hey Schoolgirl" (with Art Garfunkel, under the name Tom and Jerry), 1957
Signature: *Graceland,* 1986
Facts: In sixth grade, he played the White Rabbit to Garfunkel's Cheshire Cat in *Alice in Wonderland.*

Co-owned the Philadelphia Furies, a soccer team, with Mick Jagger, Peter Frampton, and Rick Wakeman.

Composed music and cowrote book for *The Capeman,* a Broadway show that played briefly in 1998.

Marriages: Peggy Harper (divorced); Carrie Fisher (divorced); Edie Brickell, 1992
Children: Harper,1992; Adrian Edward, 1993; Lulu, 1995

Famous Relative: Louis Simon, bassist, father
Major Awards: Grammy, Record of the Year, "Mrs. Robinson" (with Simon & Garfunkel), 1968; Grammy, Best Pop Performance—Duo or Group, "Mrs. Robinson" (with Simon & Garfunkel), 1968; Grammy, Best Soundtrack Album, *The Graduate* (with Dave Grusin), 1968; Grammy, Record of the Year, "Bridge over Troubled Water" (with Simon & Garfunkel), 1970; Grammy, Album of the Year, *Bridge over Troubled Water* (with Simon & Garfunkel), 1970; Grammy, Song of the Year, "Bridge over Troubled Water," 1970; Grammy, Best Rock/Contemporary Song, "Bridge over Troubled Water," 1970; Grammy, Album of the Year, *Still Crazy After All These Years,* 1975; Grammy, Best Pop Vocal—Male, "Still Crazy After All These Years," 1975; Grammy, Album of the Year, *Graceland,* 1986; Emmy, Best Writing in a Comedy, Variety, or Music Special, *The Paul Simon Special,* 1978; inducted into the Rock and Roll Hall of Fame (with Art Garfunkel), 1990

JESSICA SIMPSON

Birthplace: Dallas, TX
Birthdate: 7/10/80
Education: High school
Debut: (Album) *Sweet Kisses,* 1999
Signature: "I Wanna Love You Forever"''
Facts: Auditioned for *The New Mickey Mouse Club* at age 12 but lost out to Christina Aguilera and Britney Spears.

Performed in her church choir was discovered at a church summer camp. Her initial success came on the Christian Youth Conference circuit.

Her father was a Baptist minister; now he's her manager.

Is friends with Mandy Moore.
Quote: "My virginity is something I stand strong in."

SINBAD

Real Name: David Adkins
Birthplace: Benton Harbor, MI
Birthdate: 11/10/56
Occupation: Actor, comedian
Education: University of Denver
Debut: (TV) *Comedy Tonight*, 1985; (Film) *That's Adequate*, 1989
Signature: *A Different World*
Facts: Finalist in the comedy competition on *Star Search* in 1984.

Original dream was to play pro basketball.

Infamy: While in the Air Force, impersonated officers and went AWOL.
Marriage: Meredith Adkins (divorced, 1992)
Children: Paige, c. 1986; Royce, c. 1989

GARY SINISE

Birthplace: Blue Island, IL
Birthdate: 3/17/55
Occupation: Actor, director, producer
Education: High school graduate
Debut: (TV) *Knots Landing*, 1980; (Film) *A Midnight Clear*, 1992; (Film, as director) *Miles from Home*, 1988
Signature: *Forrest Gump*, 1994
Facts: Co-founded Steppenwolf Theater in 1974 (at age 18) in the basement of a church with John Malkovich, Terry Kinney, Jeff Perry, and Moira Harris (whom he later married).

First appeared on TV as an extra in *General Hospital*.

His TV directorial debut came in 1987, with a two-part episode of *Crime Story*. Two years later he directed a couple of episodes of *thirtysomething*.

In 1997, formed the band The Bonsoir Boys, playing bass and singing.

Marriage: Moira Harris, 1981
Children: Sophie, c. 1988; McCanna, c. 1990; Ella, c. 1992
Major Award: Emmy, Lead Actor in a Miniseries or Movie, for *George Wallace*, 1997

SISQO

Real Name: Mark Andrews
Birthplace: Baltimore, MD
Birthdate: 11/9/75
Occupation: Singer
Debut: (Album) *Dru Hill*, 1996; (Solo Album) *Unleash the Dragon*, 2000
Signature: "Thong Song," 2000
Facts: His Baltimore-based R&B group Dru Hill, which includes high school friends Woody (James Green), Nokio (Tamir Ruffin) and Jazz (Larry Anthony Jr.) was spotted at a talent show when Sisqó was a high school junior.

His name is pronounced "SIS-co."

Fans regularly throw Victoria's Secret g-strings at him when he performs.

Now hosts his own MTV dance competition show.

Designs his own clothes with Jonathan Logan. The dragon, which he calls his alter ego, always appears on his clothes. Also has a penchant for exotic belt buckles.

Sprays his hair every day to make it platinum.

Infamy: He was jailed twice as a teenager for fight-related incidents.
Child: Shaione, 1995 (with Tera Thomas); Shaione appears in his "Thong Song" video
Quote: "I'm still looking for that celebrity chick that's gonna take my career to the next level."

CHRISTIAN SLATER

Real Name: Christian Hawkins
Birthplace: New York, NY
Birthdate: 8/18/69
Occupation: Actor
Education: Dalton School, Professional Children's School
Debut: (TV) *One Life To Live*, 1976; (Film) *The Legend of Billie Jean*, 1985
Signature: *Heathers*, 1989
Facts: Began his career in the stage revival of *The Music Man*, at the age of 9.

Dated Winona Ryder, Christy Turlington, and Samantha Mathis.

Was born on the final day of Woodstock.

Infamy: Arrested twice for drunk driving, served ten days in jail in 1990.

Arrested in 1994 for attempting to carry a 9mm pistol through an airport metal detector. He was ordered to spend three days working with homeless children on a plea-bargained misdemeanor charge in 1995.

Was sued in 1995 for palimony seeking $100,000 plus property worth $2 million by ex-fiancée Nina Peterson Huang, who claims she had an agreement with Slater to put her career on hold during their five years of living together. Four months after they got engaged, Huang left the volatile actor and broke off the relationship.

Was arrested in 1997 for assault and battery for acts which encompassed stomach-biting; later admitted to being on alcohol, heroin, and cocaine at the time. He served 59 days in jail and 90 days of community service.

Marriage: Ryan Haddon, 2000
Children: Jaden Christopher, 1999; Eliana Sophia, 2001
Famous Relatives: Mary Jo Slater, casting director, mother; Michael Gainsborough, stage and soap actor, father

JADA PINKETT SMITH

Birthplace: Baltimore, MD
Birthdate: 9/18/71
Occupation: Actor
Education: Attended North Carolina School for the Arts
Debut: (TV) *A Different World*, 1991; (Film) *Menace II Society*, 1993
Signature: *The Nutty Professor*
Facts: Her parents divorced around the time of her birth. She was raised in a rough Baltimore neighborhood by her mother and grandmother.

In addition to acting, has directed rap music videos, performed poetry readings, appeared at inner-city schools as a motivational speaker, and started a mail-order clothing line of T-shirts and dresses bearing feminist slogans.

Five feet tall and just 100 pounds, she often buys her clothes from stores' children's departments.

Reportedly gave $100,000 bail to rapper/actor friend Tupac Shakur to gain his release from jail while awaiting an appeal on a sexual abuse conviction.

Marriage: Will Smith, 1997
Child: Jaden Christopher Syre, 1998

WILL SMITH

Birthplace: Philadelphia, PA
Birthdate: 9/25/68
Occupation: Actor, rap artist
Debut: Rapper as part of DJ Jazzy Jeff & The Fresh Prince
Signature: Men In Black, 1997
Facts: Turned down a scholarship to MIT to pursue music.

By 1989 had made and lost his first million dollars, the latter due to excessive spending.

Earned his nickname, the Prince, from a teacher in Overbrook High School because of his regal attitude and ability to talk his way out of difficult situations.

Original Job: Rap artist
Marriages: Sheree Zampino (divorced); Jada Pinkett, 1997
Children: Willard C. "Trey" III, 1992 (with Sheree Zampino). Jaden Christopher Syre, 1998
Major Awards: Grammy, Best Rap Performance—Solo, "Parents Just Don't Understand" (with D.J. Jazzy Jeff & The Fresh Prince), 1988; Grammy, Best Rap Performance—Duo or Group, "Summertime" (with D.J. Jazzy Jeff & The Fresh Prince), 1991; Grammy, Best Rap Performance—Solo, "Men in Black," 1997; Grammy, Best Rap Performance—Solo, "Gettin' Jiggy Wit It," 1998
Quote: "I have no idea what my limits are. I believe that if I set my mind to it, within the next 15 years, I would be the President of the United States."

JIMMY SMITS

Birthplace: New York, NY
Birthdate: 7/9/55
Occupation: Actor
Education: Brooklyn College, 1980; Cornell University, MFA in theater, 1982
Debut: (Off-Broadway) Hamlet, 1982; (TV) Miami Vice, 1984; (Film) Running Scared, 1986
Signature: NYPD Blue
Facts: His mother is Puerto Rican; his father is from the former Dutch colony of Suriname.

Played linebacker on his high school football team.

Was producer Steven Bochco's original choice for the costarring role in NYPD Blue first filled by David Caruso, but the timing was not right for Smits. (Smits appeared in Bochco's earlier hit, L.A. Law.)

Is an investor in L.A.'s dance club and restaurant, The Conga Room, along with Jennifer Lopez, Paul Reiser, and others.

Original Job: Community organizer
Marriage: Barbara, 1981 (divorced 1987); Wanda De Jesus, actor (engaged)
Children: Taiana, c. 1973; Joaquin, c. 1983
Major Award: Emmy, Best Supporting Actor, L.A. Law, 1990

WESLEY SNIPES

Birthplace: Orlando, FL
Birthdate: 7/31/62
Occupation: Actor
Education: New York City's High School of the Performing Arts, SUNY-Purchase
Debut: (Film) Wildcats, 1985
Signature: New Jack City, 1991
Facts: Has studied martial arts, including the African/Brazilian version Capoeira, since his youth.

Was "in the Girl Scouts when I was 9 or 10"—in a helper capacity.

"I sold cookies like anybody else, so I could get to go on the field trip."

Appeared in commercials for Levi's 501 Jeans and Coca-Cola Classic.

Snipes came to director Spike Lee's attention when he played a young punk who threatens Michael Jackson in the Martin Scorsese–directed video Bad, 1987.

Infamy: Arrested in 1994 for reckless driving for speeding at up to 120 mph on his motorcycle in Florida, leading state troopers on a 30-mile chase. Sentenced to eighty hours of community service, six months' probation, and $7,000 in fines and court costs.
Original Jobs: Street and puppet theater in his troupe, Struttin' Street Stuff, telephone installer, parking attendant
Marriages: One marriage (divorced), Donna Wong (relationship)
Child: Jelani Asar, 1988
Quote: "What I may be lacking in terms of my physical beauty, I make up for in personality and experience."

SNOOP DOGG

Real Name: Cordozar "Calvin" Broadus
Birthplace: Long Beach, CA
Birthdate: 10/20/71
Occupation: Rap artist
Education: High school
Debut: (Album) Doggystyle, 1993
Facts: Nickname "Snoop" was given to him by his mother; "Doggy Dogg" came from a cousin who used to call himself Tate Doggy Dog. In 1999 he shortened his moniker, dropping the "Doggy."

Says his musical heroes are Al Green, Curtis Mayfield, and L. J. Reynolds of the Dramatics.

He's 6' 4".
Infamy: One month after graduating from Long Beach Polytechnic High School, was arrested and incarcerated on a drug charge.

Dogg went on trial for the murder of L.A. gang member Phil Woldemariam; Snoop was driving the Jeep from which his bodyguard fired two fatal gunshots. The two were found not guilty of murder; the jury deadlocked on manslaughter charges and a mistrial was declared.

In 1994, was arrested in Lake Charles, La., when deputies attempting to deliver civil court papers smelled marijuana outside his hotel room. Charged with possession of marijuana and drug paraphernalia.
Original Job: Sold candy, delivered newspapers, bagged groceries
Marriage: Shanté Taylor, 1997
Child: Cordé, c. 1994; Cordell, 1997

TOM SNYDER

Birthplace: Milwaukee, WI
Birthdate: 5/12/36
Occupation: Talk show host
Education: Marquette University
Debut: (Radio) WRIT-AM, Milwaukee; (TV) KNBC-TV News, Los Angeles, 1970
Signature: Late Late Show with Tom Snyder
Facts: David Letterman, whose company produces Snyder's new late-night talk show, Late Late Show with Tom Snyder, is the one who took over Snyder's time slot when NBC dropped Tomorrow in 1982.
Marriage: One marriage (divorced)
Child: Anne Marie, 1964
Major Award: Emmy, Best Host, Tomorrow, 1974

LEELEE SOBIESKI

Real Name: Liliane Rudabet Gloria Elsveta Sobieski
Birthplace: New York, NY
Birthdate: 6/10/82
Occupation: Actor, model
Debut: (TV) Reunion, 1994; (Film) Jungle2Jungle, 1997
Signature: Joan of Arc, 1999 (TV version)
Facts: Born to French painter Jean and novelist Elizabeth, Leelee grew up on a ranch in the Carmarque region of France and in New York.

Her father once acted in Westerns; her mother is working on a script for her.

Was spotted in her school by a casting director when she was 10.

Claimed to be the first virgin to play virgin Joan of Arc.

Plans to attend college every other semester to continue her education and her acting career.
Quote: "[My opinions are] the opinions of a teenage girl whose ideas have been borrowed or stolen from others and infiltrated by those of her parents."

STEPHEN SONDHEIM

Birthplace: New York, NY
Birthdate: 3/22/30
Occupation: Composer, lyricist
Education: Williams College
Debut: (Stage) Girls of Summer, 1956
Signature: West Side Story
Facts: In May 1992, turned down the NEA's Medal of Arts Award, claiming the agency is "a symbol of censorship and repression rather than encouragement and support."

When Sondheim left home at age 15, he was taken in by Oscar Hammerstein II (lyricist of Oklahoma!), who taught him how to structure songs.
Original Jobs: Wrote for Topper TV series, 1953, crossword puzzle writer
Major Awards: Grammy, Best Cast Show Album, Company, 1970; Tony, Best Score, Company, 1971; Tony, Best Score, Follies, 1972; Tony, Best Score, A Little Night Music, 1973; Grammy, Best Cast Show Album, A Little Night Music, 1973; Grammy, Song of the Year, "Send in the Clowns," 1975; Tony, Best Score, Sweeney Todd, 1979; Grammy, Best Cast Show Album, Sweeney Todd, 1979; Grammy, Best Cast Show Album, Sunday in the Park with George, 1984; Pulitzer Prize, Best Play, Sunday in the Park with George, 1985; Grammy, Best Cast Show Album, West Side Story, 1985;

Grammy, Best Cast Show Album Follies in Concert, 1986; Tony, Best Score, Into the Woods, 1988; Grammy, Best Cast Show Album, Into the Woods, 1988; Oscar, Best Song, "Sooner or Later (I Always Get My Man)," 1990; Tony, Best Score, Passion, 1994
Quote: "I like neurotic people. I like troubled people. Not that I don't like squared away people, but I prefer neurotic people...Songs can't develop uncomplicated characters or unconflicted people. You can't just tell the sunny side and have a story with any richness to it."

KEVIN SORBO

Real Name: Kevin Sorbo
Birthplace: Bound, MN
Birthdate: 9/24/58
Occupation: Actor
Education: Attended University of Minnesota
Debut: (TV) Murder, She Wrote, 1993; (Film) Kull, the Conqueror
Signature: Hercules
Facts: Sorbo, who aspired to act from age 11, joined a theater group in Dallas after dropping out of college.

During the 1980s he filmed numerous TV commercials, including Diet Coke, Budweiser, BMW, and Lexus, before heading for Hollywood in 1987.

Lost the role of Superman in Lois and Clark: The New Adventures of Superman after seven auditions.
Original Job: Model
Marriage: Sam Jenkins, actor, 1998
Child: Braeden, 2001
Quote: "I've paid my dues. It's not like I was an accountant and all of a sudden I said, 'Hey, I want a series.'"

MIRA SORVINO

Birthplace: Tenafly, NJ
Birthdate: 9/28/67
Occupation: Actor
Education: Harvard University
Debut: (Film) Amongst Friends, 1993

Signature: *Mighty Aphrodite*, 1995
Facts: The East Asian Studies major speaks fluent Chinese Mandarin.

Discouraged from acting by her father, took up ballet and performed in a professional production of *The Nutcracker* at age 12.

In addition to playing the female in *Amongst Friends*, was casting director and third assistant director.
Original Job: Script reader
Relationship: Olivier Martinez
Famous Relative: Paul Sorvino, actor, father
Major Award: Oscar, Best Supporting Actress, *Mighty Aphrodite*, 1995

SAMMY SOSA

Birthplace: San Pedro de Macoris, Dominican Republic
Birthdate: 11/10/68
Occupation: Baseball player
Debut: (Major League Baseball) Texas Rangers, 1989
Signature: record-breaking home-run hitter
Facts: As a child, after his father died when he was 7, Sosa sold oranges, shined shoes, and worked as a janitor to help support his family.

His first "baseball glove" was made out of a milk carton.

Signed with the Philadelphia Phillies when he was 15, but the contract was voided because he was too young. Signed the following year with the Texas Rangers, and gave the $3,500 bonus to his mother after buying himself a bicycle.

In 1993, was the first Chicago Cubs players to have 30 home runs and 30 stolen bases in a season.

His hometown was also produced major leaguers George Bell, Pedro Guererro, and Tony Fernandez.

Wears number 21 on his jersey in honor of Roberto Clemente.

In 1998 smashed Roger Maris's legendary record of 61 home runs in a season, hitting 66, but lost the record to Mark McGwire, who hit 70.
Marriage: Sonia

Children: Keysha; Kenia; Sammy; Michael
Major Award: National League Most Valuable Player, 1998
Quote: "My life is kind of like a miracle."

KEVIN SPACEY

Birthplace: South Orange, NJ
Birthdate: 7/26/59
Occupation: Actor
Education: Los Angeles Valley College, Juilliard
Debut: (Film) *Heartburn*, 1986
Signature: *American Beauty*, 1999
Facts: Kicked out of a military academy as a kid for hitting a classmate with a tire.

Worked in New York theater in classic Shakespeare, Chekhov, and O'Neill roles before coming to Hollywood.

Was once considered not talented enough to appear on *The Gong Show*.

Bought composer George Stoll Oscar for 1945's *Anchors Aweigh* auction in order to donate it back to the Academy.
Major Awards: Tony, Best Featured Actor (Dramatic), *Lost in Yonkers*, 1991; Oscar, Best Supporting Actor, *The Usual Suspects*, 1995; Oscar, Best Actor, *American Beauty*, 1999

DAVID SPADE

Birthplace: Birmingham, MI
Birthdate: 7/22/64
Occupation: Comedian, actor
Education: Attended Arizona State University
Debut: (Film) *Police Academy 4*, 1987
Signature: *Just Shoot Me*
Facts: His father abandoned the family when he was 5.

In his debut year on *Saturday Night Live* he appeared on camera just three times.
Infamy: Many criticized his decision not to attend friend Chris Farley's funeral.
Original Job: Skateboard shop worker

Famous Relative: Kate Spade, handbag designer, sister-in-law

BRITNEY SPEARS

Birthplace: Kentwood, LA
Birthdate: 12/2/81
Occupation: Singer
Education: home-schooled
Debut: (Album) *[Hit Me]...Baby One More Time*, 1998; (Song) "[Hit Me]...Baby One More Time," 1998
Signature: "[Hit Me]...Baby One More Time"
Facts: Was turned away from *The Mickey Mouse Club* at age 9 as too young, but admitted 2 years later, joining such future stars as 'N Sync's JC Chasez and Justin Timberlake, Christina Aguilera, and *Felicity*'s Keri Russell.

In 1991, was in the off-Broadway show *Ruthless*.

Was a *Star Search* champion in 1992.

Had arthroscopic surgery on her left knee in 1999 to remove cartilage damaged while rehearsing for a video.

Misses eating crawfish when she is on tour.

Favorite authors include Danielle Steel and Jackie Collins.

Her hometown has a population of approximately 2,500.

Has a pierced belly-button.

A Baptist, she jots her daily prayers in a journal she calls her Bible Book.

Plans for the Spears Museum, an addition to the existing Kentwood Museum, have been proposed by two fans in Kentwood, LA as a means of boosting tourism in their town.

Set a new benchmark in 2000 for first week sales for a single female artist or group with *Oops! I Did It Again*.
Relationship: Justin Timberlake
Quote: "I have really strong morals, and just because I look sexy on the cover of *Rolling Stone* doesn't mean that I'm a naughty girl."

AARON SPELLING

Birthplace: Dallas, TX
Birthdate: 4/22/23
Occupation: Producer, writer
Education: The Sorbonne, Southern Methodist University
Signature: *Beverly Hills 90210*
Facts: Served in U.S. Army Air Force, 1942–45; awarded the Bronze Star and Purple Heart with Oak Leaf Cluster.

In 1969, founded Thomas-Spelling Productions with actor Danny Thomas.

Has produced network hit series such as *The Mod Squad, Starsky and Hutch, S.W.A.T., Charlie's Angels, Family, Dynasty, Beverly Hills 90210,* and *Melrose Place.*
Original Job: Actor
Marriage: Carole Gene Marer, 1968
Children: Victoria "Tori" Davey, 1973; Randall Gene, 1976
Famous Relative: Tori Spelling, actor, daughter
Major Awards: Emmy, Outstanding Drama/Comedy Special, *Day One,* 1989; Emmy, Outstanding Made-for-TV Movie, *And the Band Played On,* 1993
Quote: "I just got tired of the critics saying that I was the master of schlock. It didn't bother me until my kids began growing up and reading it. Well, I'm proud of those entertainment shows they call schlock."

STEVEN SPIELBERG

Birthplace: Cincinnati, OH
Birthdate: 12/18/46
Occupation: Director, producer
Education: California State College at Long Beach
Debut: (TV) *Night Gallery,* 1969 [see page 70 for a complete filmography]
Signature: *E.T., the Extra-Terrestrial,* 1982
Facts: Made the film *Firelight* at age 16, about the reflecting telescope he made himself, and his father hired a Phoenix, AZ, movie house to show it.

Became a TV director at Universal Pictures at age 20 after finding an empty office and pretending he belonged there.

Was not accepted by the University of Southern California's film department.

Co-owns the Las Vegas restaurant Dive! with Jeffrey Katzenberg.

A 22-minute film he made in college, *Amblin',* brought him the attention of Sidney Sheinberg, at the time head of Universal Television. It also provided the name for his production company.

Directed the first episode of *Columbo,* as well as installments of *Marcus Welby, M.D.*

Was given an honorary knighthood by Britain in 2001.

Resigned from the Boy Scouts advisory board over dismay from their "actively and publicly participating in discrimination."

Bought Bette Davis's Oscar for *Jezebel* at auction for nearly $600,000 and donated it back to the Academy.
Marriages: Amy Irving (divorced); Kate Capshaw, 1991
Children: Jessica, 1976 (stepdaughter); Max, 1985 (with Amy Irving); Theo, 1988 (adopted); Sasha, 1990; Sawyer, 1992; Mikaela George, 1996 (adopted); Destry Allyn, 1996
Famous Relative: Anne Spielberg, screenwriter, sister
Major Awards: Academy of Motion Picture Arts and Sciences, Irving G. Thalberg Award, 1986; Oscar, Best Director, *Schindler's List,* 1993; American Film Institute Lifetime Achievement Award, 1995; Oscar, Best Director, *Saving Private Ryan,* 1998

JERRY SPRINGER

Birthplace: London, England
Birthdate: 2/13/44
Occupation: Talk-show host
Education: Tulane University, Northwestern Law School
Signature: *The Jerry Springer Show*

Facts: His family emigrated from London when he was 5.

Elected mayor of Cincinnati at age 33; later ran for governor of Ohio but lost.

Was a serious news anchor and commentator before hosting his talk show.

His daughter was born without nasal passages and is legally blind and deaf in one ear.
Infamy: Early in his career while vice mayor of Cincinnati, police found his check to a whorehouse and he resigned in disgrace.

A Chicago TV station's offer that he do commentaries for the news prompted the resignation of two esteemed anchors.

Several ex-guests accused his show of staging dialogue, situations, and those notorious fights —charges Springer denied.
Original Job: Presidential campaign worker for Robert Kennedy
Marriage: Micki Velton, 1973 (divorced 1994)
Child: Katie, 1976
Major Awards: Seven local Emmys for nightly news commentaries

BRUCE SPRINGSTEEN

Birthplace: Freehold, NJ
Birthdate: 9/23/49
Occupation: Singer, songwriter
Education: Ocean City Community College
Debut: (Album) *Greetings from Asbury Park,* 1973
Signature: *Born in the USA*
Facts: E Street Band, formed in 1973, was named after the road in Belmar, NJ, where keyboardist David Sancious's mother lives.

After a 1976 Memphis concert, was caught climbing over the wall to Graceland.

Gave the song "Because the Night" to Patti Smith's producer, who was working in the adjacent recording studio.

In 1986, he rejected a $12-million

offer from Lee Iacocca to use "Born in the U.S.A." for Chrysler commercials.
Marriages: Julianne Phillips (divorced); Patti Scialfa, 1991
Children: Evan, 1990; Jessica, 1991; Sam, 1994
Major Awards: Grammy, Best Recording for Children, *In Harmony 2* (with others), 1982; Grammy, Best Rock Vocal, "Dancing in the Dark," 1984; Grammy, Best Rock Vocal, "Tunnel of Love," 1987; Oscar, Best Song, "Streets of Philadelphia," 1993; Grammy, Song of the Year, "Streets of Philadelphia," 1994; Grammy, Best Rock Vocal—Male, "Streets of Philadelphia," 1994; Grammy, Best Rock Song, "Streets of Philadelphia," 1994; Grammy, Best Song Written for a Motion Picture, "Streets of Philadelphia," 1994; Grammy, Best Contemporary Folk Recording, *The Ghost of Tom Joad*, 1996; inducted into Rock and Roll Hall of Fame, 1999

SYLVESTER STALLONE

Birthplace: Hell's Kitchen, New York
Birthdate: 7/6/46
Occupation: Actor, writer, director
Education: American School of Switzerland, University of Miami
Debut: (Film) *Bananas*, 1971 [see page 70 for a complete filmography]
Signature: *Rocky*, 1976
Facts: When he was born, the forceps severed a nerve in his face and partially paralyzed his lip, chin, and half of his tongue.

Had rickets as a child.

In high school he played football, fenced, and threw discus.

His paintings have been featured in galleries.

In *Bananas* (1971), played a goon who was thrown off a subway by Woody Allen.

As a boy was kicked out of fourteen schools in eleven years.

In 1971 appeared in a soft-core porn film, *A Party at Kitty & Stud's.*

Finally completed his degree at the University of Miami nearly 30 years after he dropped out.
Infamy: In March 1994, dumped longtime girlfriend Jennifer Flavin via letter sent FedEx. They have since reconciled.

Romanced Janice Dickinson, until DNA tests revealed that her newborn daughter wasn't his. She claimed to be pregnant by him again, then miscarried.
Original Jobs: Usher, fish salesman, zoo attendant, bookstore detective, teacher at American School of Switzerland.
Marriages: Sasha Czack (divorced); Brigitte Nielsen (divorced); Jennifer Flavin, 1997
Children: Sage, 1976; Seargeoh, 1979; (with Sasha Czack) Sophia Rose, 1996; Sistine Rose, 1998
Famous Relative: Frank Stallone, musician, brother; Jacqueline Stallone, astrologer, mother

DANIELLE STEEL

Real Name: Danielle Schuelein-Steel
Birthplace: New York, NY
Birthdate: 8/14/47
Occupation: Writer
Education: Lycée Français, Parsons School of Design, New York University
Debut: (Book) *Going Home*, 1973
Facts: Wrote over 30 best-selling novels in 20 years, including *The Ring* (1980), *Secrets* (1985), and *Daddy* (1989).

Vowed to wear only black until the one-year anniversary of her son's death.
Infamy: Two of her ex-husbands were convicts; she married one while he was still in prison, the other when she was eight months pregnant with his child.
Original Job: Vice president of public relations and new business for Supergirls, Ltd., a PR and ad agency
Marriages: Claude-Eric Lazard (divorced); Danny Zugelder (divorced); Bill Toth (divorced); John

Traina (divorced); Tom Perkins, 1998 (separated, 1999)
Children: Beatrix, 1968 (with Claude-Eric Lazard). Nicholas, 1978 (deceased, 1997); (with Bill Toth). Samantha, 1982; Victoria, 1983; Vanessa, 1984; Max, 1986; Zara, 1987 (with John Traina).

GWEN STEFANI

Birthplace: Anaheim, CA
Birthdate: 10/3/69
Occupation: Singer, songwriter
Education: Attended California State—Fullerton
Debut: (Album) *No Doubt*, 1992
Signature: No Doubt
Facts: Older brother Eric recruited her in 1986 to sing in the band he formed with his Dairy Queen coworker John Spence, their flamboyant front man who the following year fatally shot himself in a local park. Gwen was eventually encouraged to step out front so the group could continue.

The bouncy group gave away kazoos at the album-release party for their first record. Released at the height of grunge's popularity, the album bombed.

Started wearing the stick-on *pottu* dots, the jewel-like Hindi forehead decoration, when she dated fellow band member Tony Kanal, whose parents are Indian. Many of the songs on *Tragic Kingdom* reflect her distress about their breakup after seven years.
Relationship: Gavin Rossdale

HOWARD STERN

Birthplace: New York, NY
Birthdate: 1/12/54
Occupation: Radio DJ
Education: Boston University
Signature: *The Howard Stern Show*
Facts: 1994 Libertarian gubernatorial candidate in New York but dropped out of race before the elections.

Once fired for referring to station management as "scumbags" on the air during a salary dispute.

Practices transcendental meditation each morning in the limo ride to work.

Infamy: After angry listeners provided the FCC with transcripts of Stern's show about masturbating to thoughts of Aunt Jemima and having rough sex with actress Michelle Pfeiffer, the commission fined Infinity Broadcasting, which owns WNBC-New York, $600,000.

Stern made fun of singer Selena Quintanilla Perez after her murder in April 1995, playing her music with sounds of gunfire in the background and parodying her mourners. The League of United Latin American Citizens said it intended to drive Stern's program off the air. Stern later apologized for his conduct.

Refusing to apologize for calling French-speakers "scumbags," Stern reasoned, "I can't imagine anybody would take what I say seriously."

In 1999, he signed a deal to produce his own animated cartoon series about people in motor homes searching for family values in post–apocalyptic America.

Marriage: Alison Berns, 1978 (separated, 1999)
Children: Emily, Debra, Ashley Jade, 1993

JON STEWART

Real Name: Jon Stuart Leibowitz
Birthplace: Lawrence, NJ
Birthdate: 11/28/62
Occupation: Comedian, actor
Education: College of William and Mary
Debut: (TV) *Short Attention Span Theater*, 1991
Signature: *The Daily Show, with Jon Stewart*
Facts: Got the idea to do stand-up at age 24, when using puppets to teach schoolkids about disabled people—a gig that honed his prop-wielding skills. Went on the road doing stand-up for the next six years.

His parents divorced when he was 9, and his relationship with his dad

became increasingly strained over the years as Stewart gleefully aired the family's dirty laundry in his club acts.

Original Jobs: Bartender, bike mechanic, porter in a bakery, research lab assistant
Quote: "As long as I can remember, I wanted to sleep late, stay up late, and do nothing in between."

MARTHA STEWART

Birthplace: Nutley, NJ
Birthdate: 8/3/41
Occupation: Entertainment and lifestyle consultant
Education: Barnard College
Debut: (Book) *Entertaining*, 1981
Signature: *Martha Stewart Living*
Facts: Has published nearly 30 books on entertaining.

Discovered her love for decorating, gardening, and cooking when she and her husband bought a Connecticut farmhouse and fixed it up themselves in 1971. Over the years, she added a barn-turned-party-room, a greenhouse, pool, vegetable gardens, orchards, an English border garden, and beehives, turkeys, chickens, and cats.

Sleeps four hours a night with the lights on so when she wakes up she can get right to work.

Has filed an extortion, coercion, and defamation suit against a landscaper who claims she and her car pinned him against a security box.

After the IPO of her company Martha Stewart Living Omnimedia in 1999 (and before the stock slid the following year) was worth over $1 billion on paper.

Infamy: Ordered by NY Division of Tax Appeals to pay $221,677 in back homeowner's taxes for 1991 and 1992. She plans to appeal, claiming that she has been a resident of Connecticut since 1971.
Original Jobs: Model, stockbroker, take-out gourmet food store owner

Marriage: Andy Stewart (divorced, 1990)
Child: Alexis, 1965

PATRICK STEWART

Birthplace: Mirfield, England
Birthdate: 7/13/40
Occupation: Actor, writer
Education: Bristol Old Vic Theatre School
Debut: (Stage) *Treasure Island*, 1959
Signature: *Star Trek: The Next Generation*
Facts: Was so sure that he was going to be fired from the initial season of *Star Trek: The Next Generation* that he didn't unpack his bags for six weeks.

In 2000, complained from the stage after a performance of Arthur Miller's *The Ride Down Mt. Morgan* that his producers, the Shuberts, weren't supporting the show. After receiving a complaint, Actors Equity ordered him to make a public apology to the Shuberts.

A doll based on his Professor X character in *X-Men* was "resculpted to add to the realism" after he complained that it looked nothing like him.

Original Job: Journalist
Marriage: Sheila Falconer, 1966 (divorced, 1990); Wendy Neuss, 2000
Children: Daniel Freedom, 1968; Sophie Alexandra, 1973
Quote: "I was brought up in a very poor and very violent household. I spent much of my childhood being afraid."

JULIA STILES

Birthplace: New York, NY
Birthdate: 3/28/81
Occupation: Actor
Education: Professional Children's School, New York, NY; attends Columbia University (enrolled, 2000)
Debut: (Film) *I Love You, I Love You Not* (1996); (TV) *Promised Land*, 1997

Signature: *10 Things I Hate About You*, 1999

Fact: At age 11, wrote a letter in crayon to the director of an avant-guard theater company begging for a part. Was cast in his next production.

Co-wrote a screenplay entitled *The Anarchist's Daughter* when she was 16.

Trained in hip-hop and ballet four hours a day for three months for her role in 2000's *Save the Last Dance*.

Relationship: Ben Foster

Quote: "I tend to gravitate toward the more powerful roles. As opposed to the doe-eyed girl who bats her eyelashes and runs around in towels, you know what I mean? Because that kind of makes me want to vomit."

BEN STILLER

Birthplace: New York, NY
Birthdate: 11/30/65
Occupation: Actor, director
Education: UCLA
Debut: (Film) *Empire of the Sun*, 1987
Signature: *Reality Bites*, 1994
Facts: At age 10, began making Super-8 movies about getting revenge on bullies in his neighborhood.

Learned swimming from the Pips, Gladys Knight's backup vocalists.

His short film parody of *The Color of Money* landed him a job at *Saturday Night Live* and his own show on MTV.

Was once engaged to Jeanne Tripplehorn.

Marriage: Christine Taylor, actress
Famous Relatives: Jerry Stiller, comedian, father; Anne Meara, comedian, mother; Amy Stiller, actor, sister
Major Award: Emmy, Best Writing in Variety or Music Program, *The Ben Stiller Show* (with others), 1992

R. L. STINE

Real Name: Robert Lawrence Stine
Birthplace: Columbus, OH
Birthdate: 10/8/43
Occupation: Writer

Education: Ohio State University, New York University
Signature: The Goosebumps series
Facts: Noted author of the Goosebumps and Fear Street series of books for children among others, he has sold over 170 million books.

Before hitting it big, wrote everything from coloring books to bubble gum cards.

Types only with his left index finger.

In 1997 he published his autobiography, *It Came from Ohio*.

Has written under the pseudonyms Eric Affabee, Zachary Blue, Jovial Bob Stine.

Original Jobs: Social studies teacher; magazine editor
Marriage: Jane Waldhorn, 1969
Children: Matthew, 1980
Quote: "I've been called a literary training bra for Stephen King."

STING

Real Name: Gordon Matthew Sumner
Birthplace: Newcastle upon Tyne, England
Birthdate: 10/2/51
Occupation: Singer, songwriter, actor
Education: Warwick University
Debut: (Song) "Fall Out" (with The Police), 1977
Signature: The Police
Facts: Rejected the villain role in James Bond film *A View to a Kill*.

He gained his nickname by wearing a black-and-yellow striped shirt, like a bee.

Received a seaman's card and worked as a bass player with The Ronnie Pierson Trio on Princess Cruise Lines at age 17.

Claimed in a 1993 *Rolling Stone* interview that by practicing meditation, he can make love for more than five hours at a time.

In 2000, he was unable to gain ownership of the Internet address www.sting.com because he had never registered the name Sting as

a trademark. He is the first celebrity to lose such a case at the World Intellectual Property Organization.

Original Jobs: Teacher, construction worker, clerk for Inland Revenue
Marriages: Frances Eleanor Tomelty (divorced); Trudie Styler, 1996
Children: Joseph, 1977; Katherine "Kate," 1982 (with Tomelty); Michael "Mickey," 1984; Jake, 1985; Eliot Pauline "Coco," 1990; Giacomo Luke, 1995 (with Styler)
Major Awards: Grammy, Best Rock Performance—Duo or Group, "Don't Stand So Close to Me" (with The Police), 1981; Grammy, Song of the Year, "Every Breath You Take," 1983; Grammy, Best Pop Performance—Duo or Group, "Every Breath You Take" (with The Police), 1983; Grammy, Best Pop Vocal—Male, "Bring On the Night," 1987; Grammy, Best Rock Song/Vocal Performance, "Soul Cages," 1991; Grammy, Best Pop Vocal—Male, "If I Ever Lose My Faith in You," 1993; Grammy, Best Music Video—Long Form, *Ten Summoner's Tales*, 1993; Grammy, Best Pop Vocal—Male, "Brand New Day," 1999; Grammy, Best Pop Album, *Brand New Day*, 1999

MICHAEL STIPE

Birthplace: Decatur, GA
Birthdate: 1/4/60
Occupation: Singer, songwriter
Education: Southern Illinois University, University of Georgia
Debut: *Chronic Town* (with R.E.M.), 1982
Signature: R.E.M.
Facts: In the early years of R.E.M., traveled to 49 states by the time he was 24.

Planned to record with friend Kurt Cobain. Cobain had tickets to come to Stipe's in Atlanta but called to cancel, and committed suicide soon after.

Was rumored to have AIDS because, he says, he is thin, has bad skin, and is sexually ambiguous. He denies being HIV-positive.

Major Awards: Grammy, Best Alternative Performance, *Out of Time*, 1991; Grammy, Best Pop Vocal—Group, "Losing My Religion," 1991

OLIVER STONE

Birthplace: New York, NY
Birthdate: 9/15/46
Occupation: Director, writer, producer
Education: Yale University, New York University film school
Debut: (Film) *Seizure,* 1974
Signature: *Platoon,* 1986
Facts: Served in the U.S. Merchant Marine, 1966; in the Army in Vietnam, 1967–68. Awarded Bronze Star and Purple Heart with Oak Leaf Cluster.

Made acting debut as a bum in *The Hand* (1981), which he wrote and directed.

Infamy: At least 10 real killings were linked to his ode to violence, *Natural Born Killers,* with one 14-year-old decapitator even telling friends he wanted to be famous like the killers in the movie.

Was arrested in 1999 for allegedly driving under the influence and possession of hashish. Plead no contest on the DUI count and guilty to possession, and was ordered to enter drug and alchohol treatment programs.

Original Jobs: Taxi driver in New York City, teacher at Free Pacific Institute in South Vietnam
Marriages: Majwa Sarkis (divorced); Elizabeth Burkit Cox (divorced, 1993)
Children: Sean, 1984; Michael, 1991; (with Elizabeth Cox Stone). Tara, 1995 (with Chong Son Chong).
Major Awards: Oscar, Best Adapted Screenplay, *Midnight Express,* 1978; Oscar, Best Director, *Platoon,* 1986; Oscar, Best Director, *Born on the Fourth of July,* 1991

SHARON STONE

Birthplace: Meadville, PA
Birthdate: 3/10/58
Occupation: Actor
Education: Edinboro State University
Debut: (Film) *Stardust Memories,* 1981 [see page 71 for a complete filmography]
Signature: *Basic Instinct,* 1992
Facts: She has an I.Q. of 154.

Between 1977 and 1980, became one of the top 10 models at the Ford Agency.

Infamy: Posed nude for *Playboy* just days after finishing *Total Recall,* 1990.

Original Job: Model
Marriages: Michael Greenburg (divorced), Phil Bronstein, 1998
Child: Roan Joseph, 2000 (adopted)
Famous Relative: Michael Stone, actor, brother
Quote: "I'm naked at the drop of a hat.... Why not? Why pretend? Be happy they're interested."

JOHN STOSSEL

Birthplace: Illinois
Birthdate: 3/47
Occupation: News correspondent, producer
Education: Princeton University
Debut: KGW, Portland, Oregon
Signature: (TV series) *20/20,* 1981; (TV Special) *Are We Scaring Ourselves to Death?,* 1994
Facts: Was a stutterer. The disability was severe enough to earn him a draft deferment.

Finally found a successful treatment for his stutter—but only after he struggling through on-camera news work.

His transition from a consumer activist who supported government regulation into a challenger of alarmist reporting and overintervention has provoked former allies like Ralph Nader to castigate him as "lazy and dishonest."

Surfs and coaches soccer.
Infamy: ABC News made him apologize on *20/20* for citing a nonexistent study stating that the level of pesticide residue on organic foods was no less than that on conventionally grown foods.

Original Job: Television newsroom researcher
Marriage: One marriage
Children: Two children
Major Awards: Nineteen Emmy awards for reporting
Quote: "When I started consumer reporting I was a typical left-wing, Ivy League graduate. Now I lean toward liberty."

GEORGE STRAIT

Birthplace: Pearsall, TX
Birthdate: 5/18/52
Occupation: Singer, songwriter
Education: Southwest Texas State
Debut: (Album) *Let's Get Down To It,* 1976
Signature: "Carrying Your Love With Me"
Facts: Grew up on a Texas ranch his family owned for decades.

Before joining the army, eloped with his high school sweetheart.

Frustrated by his lack of success, gave up singing in 1979 and went back to his agriculture roots. Returned soon after to give it one more try.

Original Job: Cattle-pen employee
Marriage: Norma
Children: Jenifer (deceased); George Jr.

MERYL STREEP

Real Name: Mary Louise Streep
Birthplace: Summit, NJ
Birthdate: 6/22/49
Occupation: Actor
Education: Vassar College; MFA, Yale University
Debut: (Stage) *Trelawny of the Wells,* NY Shakespeare Festival, 1975; (Film) *Julia,* 1977 [see page 71 for a complete filmography]
Signature: *Sophie's Choice,* 1982
Facts: When she was 12, began

studying with vocal coach Estelle Liebling, who had also taught diva Beverly Sills.

In high school, was a cheerleader and homecoming queen.

Formed a child support group with Annette Bening, Carrie Fisher, and Tracey Ullman, in which they watch each other's children.

When New York theater giant Joseph Papp—who ran New York's Public Theater and Shakespeare in the Park—knew he was dying, he asked Streep to succeed him; she turned him down so she could devote more time to her family.

Is tied with Katharine Hepburn for most Oscar nominations for acting.
Original Job: Waitress
Marriage: Don Gummer, 1978
Children: Henry, 1979; Mary Willa, 1983; Grace Jane, 1986; Louisa Jacobson, 1991
Major Awards: Emmy, Best Actress in a Miniseries, *Holocaust*, 1978; Oscar, Best Supporting Actress, *Kramer vs. Kramer*, 1979; Oscar, Best Actress, *Sophie's Choice*, 1982
Quote: "My own kids haven't seen most of my movies. Too upsetting: Mommy dies."

BARBRA STREISAND

Real Name: Barbara Streisand
Birthplace: Brooklyn, NY
Birthdate: 4/24/42
Occupation: Singer, actor, director
Education: Yeshiva University
Debut: (Stage) *Another Evening with Harry Stoones*, 1961; (Film) *Funny Girl*, 1968
Signature: "The Way We Were"
Facts: Her father died when she was 15 months old.

She graduated from high school two years early.

Although she had never sung before an audience before, she won a talent contest in a Greenwich Village bar and won a singing job at another bar.

Her Academy Award for *Funny Girl* (1968) was shared with Katharine

Hepburn for *A Lion in Winter;* it's only tie for the Best Actress Oscar to date.

Reportedly has a pet name from her husband: "Beezer."

She's only the second artist (after Elvis Presley) to claim 40 gold albums. Her *Christmas Album* is the only vocal holiday album to sell over 5 million copies.

Her 1999/2000 New Year's Eve sell-out show at MGM Grand in Las Vegas set a U.S. box-office record for a single concert, grossing $14.7 million.
Original Jobs: Theater usher, switchboard operator, waitress
Marriages: Elliot Gould (divorced); James Brolin, 1998
Child: Jason Emanuel, 1966 (with Elliot Gould)
Famous Relative: Roslyn Kind, singer, sister
Major Awards: Grammy, Best Female Pop Vocalist 1963–65; Emmy, Outstanding Program Achievements in Entertainment, *My Name Is Barbra*, 1965; Oscar, Best Actress, *Funny Girl*, 1968; Tony, Special Award, 1970; Oscar, Best Song, "Evergreen" (with Paul Williams), 1976; Grammy, Best Songwriter (with Paul Williams), 1977; Grammy, Best Female Pop Vocalist, 1977, 1986; Grammy, Legend Award, 1992; Emmy, Best Individual Performance in a Variety or Music Program, *Barbra Streisand: The Concert*, 1995
Quote: "I don't like performing. I feel like I'm in a beauty pageant, like I'm 18 and strutting around on stage."

MENA SUVARI

Birthplace: Newport, RI
Birthdate: 2/13/79
Occupation: Actor
Education: High school
Debut: (TV) *Boy Meets World*, 1996; (Film) *Nowhere*, 1997
Signature: *American Beauty*, 1999
Facts: She is of Estonian and Greek descent.

Signed with Wilhelmina modeling

agency in seventh grade and modeled for five years.

Has three brothers, all of whom went to the Citadel and joined the U.S. Army.

Did her own singing when playing a chorus member in *American Pie*.
Original Job: Model
Marriage: Robert Brinkmann, cinematographer, 2000
Quote: "Early on, I told my agent, 'I'm not interested in being popular, the flavor of the week. I want meaty, challenging parts.'"

HILARY SWANK

Birthplace: Lincoln, NB
Birthdate: 7/30/74
Occupation: Actor
Education: Santa Monica City College
Debut: (TV) *Harry and the Hendersons*, 1990; (Film) *Buffy the Vampire Slayer*, 1992.
Signature: *Boys Don't Cry*, 1999
Facts: She is part Spanish, part Native American.

Competed in the Junior Olympics and the Washington State championships in swimming, and ranked fifth in her state's gymnastics competitions.

After her parents separated, she and her mother endured hardship, at times living out of their car.

She played recurring roles in *Growing Pains* and *Evening Shade*.

To prepare for her role in *Boys Don't Cry*, she spent almost a month living as a man in Los Angeles.
Marriage: Chad Lowe, actor,1997
Major award: Oscar, Best Actress, *Boys Don't Cry*, 1999
Quote: "It's so boring to play the pretty girl."

AMY TAN

Birthplace: Oakland, CA
Birthdate: 2/19/52
Occupation: Author
Education: Attended Linfield College; San Jose State University (BA and MA)
Signature: *The Joy Luck Club*, 1989
Facts: At age 8, wrote an essay titled "What the Library Means to Me" which won first prize in an elementary school contest.

Has written four acclaimed best-selling novels.

Has a family history of depression.

Moved to Switzerland with her mother after the deaths of her brother and father of brain tumors in 1967.

Attempted suicide at age 6 by dragging a butter knife across her wrists and went through a period in her 20s when she thought about suicide every day. Began taking antidepressant medication in 1993.

Is a member of the band Rock Bottom Remainders, performing charity concerts with fellow members including Stephen King, Dave Barry and Ridley Pearson.

Original Jobs: Language consultant, freelance business writer
Marriage: Louis DeMattei, 1974
Quote: "In a way, I'm grateful to bad psychotherapy for my start in fiction."

QUENTIN TARANTINO

Birthplace: Knoxville, TN
Birthdate: 3/27/63
Occupation: Director, writer, actor
Education: High school dropout
Debut: (Film) *Reservoir Dogs*, 1992 (writer, director, and actor)
Signature: *Pulp Fiction*, 1994
Facts: Studied movies while working at an L.A. video store for four years. Got the idea for *Reservoir Dogs* when he saw that no one had made a heist movie in a long time.

Once played an Elvis impersonator on *The Golden Girls*.

Is said to have an I.Q. of 160.

Had already tried his hand at screenwriting as a teenager, penning *Captain Peachfuzz and the Anchovy Bandit*.
Infamy: Once went to jail for failing to pay his parking tickets.

Physically attacked *Natural Born Killers* producer Don Murphy in an L.A. restaurant; recounted the episode on Keenan Ivory Wayans's talk show as a "bitch-slap." Got into another bar brawl in the spring of 1998.
Original Job: Video sales clerk
Major Awards: Cannes Film Festival, Palme d'Or, *Pulp Fiction*, 1994; Oscar, Best Original Screenplay, *Pulp Fiction*, 1994
Quote: "People ask me if I went to film school. And I tell them, 'No, I went to films.'"

ELIZABETH TAYLOR

Birthplace: London, England
Birthdate: 2/27/32
Occupation: Actor
Education: Byron House, Hawthorne School, Metro-Goldwyn-Mayer School
Debut: (Film) *There's One Born Every Minute*, 1942
Signature: *Cleopatra*
Facts: Almost died from pnuemonia and had an emergency tracheotomy in 1961.

When she was three years old she danced before Queen Elizabeth and Princess Margaret.

After friend Rock Hudson died from AIDS, became the founding chair of the American Foundation for AIDS Research (AMFAR) in 1985.

She met construction worker Larry Fortensky, whom she married in 1992, at the Betty Ford Clinic.

Was made a Dame by Queen Elizabeth in 2000 in a London ceremony.
Infamy: Checked herself into the Betty Ford Clinic to overcome alcohol dependency, 1983. Returned in 1988 to overcome painkiller dependency.
Marriages: Nicholas Conrad Hilton Jr. (divorced); Michael Wilding (divorced); Mike Todd (deceased);

Eddie Fisher (divorced); Richard Burton (divorced, remarried, divorced); John Warner (divorced); Larry Fortensky (divorced, 1996)
Children: Michael, 1953; Christopher, 1955; (with Michael Wilding). Liza, 1957 (with Mike Todd). Maria Carson, c. 1961 (adopted with Richard Burton).
Major Awards: Oscar, Best Actress, *Butterfield 8*, 1960; Oscar, Best Actress, *Who's Afraid of Virginia Woolf*, 1966; Oscar, Jean Hersholt Humanitarian Award, 1992; American Film Institute Lifetime Achievement Award, 1993
Quote: "I've been known to swim in my emeralds."

JOHN TESH

Birthplace: Garden City, NY
Birthdate: 7/9/52
Occupation: Television host, composer, pianist
Education: Attended Juilliard during high school, North Carolina State University
Signature: *Entertainment Tonight*
Facts: Anchored local TV news in Durham, N.C.; Orlando; Nashville; and New York before signing with CBS Sports and, in 1986, *Entertainment Tonight*.

An incurable romantic, he proposed to Selleca by reserving an entire Monterey restaurant; hiring a string quartet to serenade her with a song he had written, "Concetta"; and arranging for a fireworks display outside the window.

He and Selleca, who pledged to avoid premarital sex during their year-long courtship, starred in a late-night infomercial for a series of videos about relationships.

Composed songs for sporting events he was covering for CBS, including the Tour de France and the Pan-American Games, both of which won Emmys.

His own recording label, GTS Records, has sold more than two million of his CDs. His *Romantic*

Christmas, with Selleca, went gold, selling more than 500,000 copies.

Whenever Tesh performs a concert, the event's promoters are contractually bound to provide at least one World Wrestling Foundation action figure for his dressing room.

In 1998 he graced 12 million Kellogg's Complete Oat Bran Flakes cereal boxes (his late parents both suffered from heart-related ailments).

Original Job: TV reporter
Marriages: Julie Wright (divorced); Connie Selleca, 1992
Child: Prima, 1994
Major Awards: Emmy, Best Musical Composition for a Sports Program, Pan-American Games, 1983; Emmy, Best Musical Score, Tour de France, 1987

CHARLIZE THERON

Birthplace: Benoni, South Africa
Birthdate: 8/7/75
Occupation: Actor, model
Debut: (Film) *Two Days in the Valley,* 1996
Signature: *The Cider House Rules,* 1999
Facts: Had a pet goat as a child.

Afrikaans was her first language. She mastered English by watching television.

Her father was French, her mother German.

At 16 entered a modeling contest on a whim and won. After a brief modeling stint, she studied with the Joffrey Ballet until a knee injury halted her career.

By 1994 she settled in Los Angeles and caught the attention of a personal manager when she caused a fuss because a bank would not cash her check.

She and her mother have matching fish tattoos.
Original Job: Model
Relationships: Stephan Jenkins, musician with Third Eye Blind, 1998
Quotes: "A nice pair of pumps, a skirt that goes to your knees, that

Vargas-red-lipstick glamour—to me, that's what a girl is."

JONATHAN TAYLOR THOMAS

Real Name: Jonathan Weiss
Birthplace: Bethlehem, PA
Birthdate: 9/8/81
Occupation: Actor
Debut: (TV) *The Bradys,* 1990
Signature: *Home Improvement*
Facts: Was the voice of Simba in *The Lion King,* as well as several other characters in kids' cartoons.

Got straight A's when attending public school during breaks in filming.

At one point received nearly 50,000 pieces of fan mail a month.
Original Job: Model
Quote: "On occasion, I've taken the test that's been in the teen magazines about me and I've failed. Isn't that scary?"

KRISTIN SCOTT THOMAS

Birthplace: Redruth, Cornwall, England
Birthdate: 5/24/60
Occupation: Actor
Education: Attended London's Central School of Speech and Drama and Paris's Ecole Nationale des Arts et Techniques de Theatre
Debut: (Film) *Under the Cherry Moon,* 1986
Signature: *The English Patient,* 1996
Facts: Her father, a naval pilot, was killed in a flying accident when she was 5. Some years later her stepfather, another naval pilot, was killed in a nearly identical crash.

At 16, enrolled in a convent school with aspirations to be a nun.

Was married in Dorset, a beautiful part of England made famous by novelist Thomas Hardy. Two days of ceremonies included one civil and one before a rabbi and a priest (she's Catholic).
Marriage: François Oliviennes

Children: Hannah, c. 1989; Joseph, 1991; George, 2000
Famous Relative: Serena Scott Thomas, model, actor, sister

ROB THOMAS

Birthplace: Germany
Birthdate: 2/14/72
Occupation: Musician
Education: High school (G.E.D.)
Debut: (Album) *Yourself Or Someone Like You,* 1996 (with Matchbox Twenty)
Signature: "Smooth," 1999 (with *Santana*)
Facts: Was born on a military base in Germany.

Spent three years wandering about the southeast after dropping out of high school at age 17. Slept on park benches and entertained at parties in exchange for a place to spend the night.

Settled in Florida and formed the band Tabitha's Secret. Two members, Paul Doucette and Brian Yale, would later be part of Matchbox 20 with Thomas.

Has collaborated with Mick Jagger, Willie Nelson and Carlos Santana.
Marriage: Marisol Maldonaldo, 1999
Major Awards: Grammy, Record of the Year, "Smooth", 1999 (with Carlos Santana); Grammy, Best Pop Collaboration with Vocals, "Smooth", 1999 (with Santana); Grammy, Song of the Year, "Smooth", 1999 (with Santana).
Quote: "The best thing that ever happened to me was that I never learned the value of being a man. Because I'm not concerned with 'manly' things. I guess I've always been more sensitive or girly."

ROZONDA THOMAS

Birthplace: Atlanta, GA
Birthdate: 2/27/71
Occupation: Singer, songwriter
Education: Attended Georgia Southern University

Debut: *Oooooohhh...On the TLC Tip,* 1992
Signature: "Waterfalls," 1995 / "Chilli"
Facts: Wanted to be in fashion, but when given the choice between managing a clothing store and dancing for hip-hop artist Damian Dane, she tried the latter.

Was a replacement for TLC's original "C," named Crystal.

Choreographs the band's videos and live performances.

In 1997, met her father for the first time as part of the *Sally Jessy Raphael Show.*

After researching breast implants, decided against them—as dramatized in the "Unpretty" video.

Appeared in the movies *House Party 3, Hav Plenty,* and *Snow Day.*
Relationship: Dallas Austin
Child: Tron, 1997
Major Awards: Grammy, Best R&B Album, *Crazysexycool,* 1995; Grammy, Best R&B Vocal—Duo or Group, "Creep," 1995; Grammy, Best R&B Album, *Fanmail,* 1999; Grammy, Best R&B Vocal—Duo or Group, "No Scrubs," 1999

EMMA THOMPSON

Birthplace: London, England
Birthdate: 4/15/59
Occupation: Actor
Education: Cambridge University
Debut: (Film) *Henry V,* 1989
Signature: *Howards End,* 1992
Facts: Wrote screenplay adaptation of *Sense and Sensibility* by Jane Austen, whose novels she began reading at age 9.

When first met her ex-husband, Kenneth Branagh, she "thought he had strange hair."

Lives on the street on which she was raised, opposite her mother and down the street from her younger sister, Sophie.
Marriage: Kenneth Branagh (divorced, 1996); Greg Wise (relationship)

Child: Gaia Romilly Wise, 1999 (with Greg Wise)
Famous Relatives: Eric Thompson, producer, father; Phyllida Law, actor, mother; Sophie Thompson, actor, sister
Major Awards: Oscar, Best Actress, *Howards End,* 1992; Oscar, Best Adapted Screenplay, *Sense and Sensibility,* 1995

COURTNEY THORNE-SMITH

Birthplace: San Francisco, CA
Birthdate: 11/8/67
Occupation: Actor
Education: High school
Debut: (Film) *Lucas,* 1986; (TV) *Fast Time,* 1986
Signature: *Melrose Place*
Facts: Her hyphenated name is a combination of her mother's maiden name, Thorne, and her father's name, Smith.

Drew attention with her recurring role in *L.A. Law* in 1990.

Used to date actor Andrew Shue.

Hobbies include knitting.
Marriage: Andrew Conrad, 2000 (separated, 2001)

BILLY BOB THORNTON

Birthplace: Alpine, AR
Birthdate: 8/4/55
Occupation: Actor, screenwriter, director
Education: Attended Henderson State University
Debut: (Film) *Hunter's Blood,* 1986
Signature: *Sling Blade,* 1996
Facts: Grew up in a rural area with coal-oil lamps and an outhouse, where supper was whatever grandpa happened to shoot.

Mother Virginia was a psychic, who once predicted that Thornton would work with Burt Reynolds, which he did on *Evening Shade* in 1990.

Broke for years in L.A., he ate nothing but potatoes during a particularly bleak period in 1984,

which resulted in nearly fatal heart failure.

Sling Blade's character Karl came to Thornton in 1985 while in a B-movie trailer awaiting his four-line part. The character later appeared in his 1994 short film *Some Folks Call It a Sling Blade,* a forerunner to the feature.

Terrified of flying, he got distributor Miramax to drive him to the New York Film Festival from L.A. in a limousine.
Original Job: Drummer (one of his bands, Tres Hombres, once opened for Hank Williams Jr.), singer, screen-door factory worker, pizza maker
Marriage: Melissa Lee Gatlin, 1978 (divorced, 1980); Toni Lawrence, 1986 (divorced, 1988); Cynda Williams (divorced, 1992); Pietra Dawn Cherniak, 1993 (divorced, 1997); Angelina Jolie, 2000
Children: Amanda, 1979 (with Melissa Lee Gatlin). William Langston, 1993; Harry James, 1994; (with Pietra Dawn Cherniak).
Major Award: Oscar, Best Adapted Screenplay, *Sling Blade,* 1996
Quote: "I prefer eating with plastic—I can't use real silver. Swear to God. I think some big old mad king used to use it or something."

UMA THURMAN

Birthplace: Boston, MA
Birthdate: 4/29/70
Occupation: Actor
Education: Professional Children's School
Debut: (Film) *Kiss Daddy Good Night,* 1987
Signature: *Pulp Fiction,* 1994
Facts: Her father, Robert, an eminent professor of Asian religion, named her Uma after a Hindu goddess.

Her Swedish mother, a psychotherapist, was once married to Timothy Leary.

The nearly six-foot actress quit

school and headed for New York at age 16. Modeling jobs and movies quickly followed.
Original Job: Model, dishwasher
Marriages: Gary Oldman (divorced); Ethan Hawke, 1998
Child: Maya Ray Thurman-Hawke, 1998

MAURA TIERNEY

Birthplace: Boston, MA
Birthdate: 2/3/65
Occupation: Actor
Education: New York University
Debut: (TV) *Student Exchange*, 1987; (Film) *Dead Women in Lingerie*, 1990;
Signature: *ER*
Facts: Made guest appearances on *Family Ties, Growing Pains* and *Law & Order* in the '80s.

Was fired from her *Growing Pains* guest spot because she wasn't "working out."

Her pug's name is Rose, after her hometown's matriarch, Rose Kennedy.

Travels cross-country with her husband and has visited every state but Iowa and Kansas.
Marriage: Billy Morrissette, 1994
Quote: "In a lot of my roles, I'm sort of the facilitator, the straight man—or whatever you call it."

JUSTIN TIMBERLAKE

Birthplace: Memphis, TN
Birthdate: 1/31/81
Occupation: Singer
Debut: (Single) "I Want You Back," 1996; (Album) **NSYNC*, 1996 (American release, 1998)
Signature: *No Strings Attached*, 2000
Facts: Lost on *Star Search* at the age of 4.

Like bandmate J C Chasez, is a former Mouseketeer.

His mother came up with 'N Sync's name.

The band was successful in Europe before its first album was released in America.

Set up the Justin Timberlake Foundation to support arts programs in U.S. public schools.

Acted in 2000 TV movie *Model Behavior.*

Is so popular that a piece of french toast that he didn't finish eating was auctioned on eBay. It went for $1,025.

Though Eminem rails against 'N Sync, Timberlake loves him, saying: "He's a supertalented artist."
Infamy: 'N Sync broke with their original record label and management over compensation. Suits and countersuits flew before a settlement was reached, allegedly favoring the band.
Relationship: Britney Spears
Quote: "We're like Frosted Flakes. The parents don't like to admit they enjoy the music."

JOHN TRAVOLTA

Birthplace: Englewood, NJ
Birthdate: 2/18/54
Occupation: Actor
Education: High school dropout
Debut: (Stage) *Who Will Save the Plow*, 1966; (Film) *The Devil's Rain*, 1975; (TV) *Welcome Back, Kotter*, 1975 [see page 71 for a complete filmography]
Signature: *Saturday Night Fever*, 1977
Facts: Holds the record for the most *Rolling Stone* covers for an actor: four.

An avid flyer since the age of 16, he turned down the lead in *An Officer and a Gentleman*, a part reportedly written for him, because the shooting conflicted with his attendance of American Airlines' month-long jet pilot training school. In 1995, a plane he owns and was piloting lost electrical power over Washington, DC, and had a mid-air near-miss with a commercial jetliner.

His first love, actor Diana Hyland, was 18 years older than the then 22-year-old Travolta. Nine months into the romance she died of cancer—in Travolta's arms.

Languished for nearly a decade in forgettable and/or unpopular films until *Pulp Fiction* restored him to Hollywood's A-list. He earned just $140,000 for his part in the film, far less than the millions-per-picture he once commanded and now receives again.

Has been a member of the Church of Scientology for more than 20 years.
Marriage: Kelly Preston, 1991
Child: Jett, 1992; Ella Bleu, 2000
Famous Relatives: Ellen Travolta, actor, sister; Joey Travolta, actor, brother

CHRIS TUCKER

Birthplace: Atlanta, GA
Birthdate: 8/31/71
Occupation: Comedian, actor
Education: High school
Debut: (Film) *House Party 3*, 1994
Signature: *Rush Hour*, 1999
Facts: Is the youngest of six children.

Was voted Most Humorous in his high school, dubbed a Little Eddie Murphy.

Personally rewrote or improvised most of his trademark quick dialogue in *Money Talks*.

TANYA TUCKER

Birthplace: Seminole, TX
Birthdate: 10/10/58
Occupation: Singer
Education: High school dropout
Debut: (Album) *Delta Dawn*, 1972
Signature: "Delta Dawn"
Facts: Her family moved to Las Vegas when she was 12, on the theory that it was a good city to launch a new entertainer. Within two years she had a hit in "Delta Dawn," a $1.5 million record deal, and a cover story in *Rolling Stone.*

High-profile romances included Merle Haggard, Don Johnson, the late Andy Gibb, and Glen Campbell.

Has released more than 30 country albums.

A reported $700,000 advance and the prodding of friends convinced her to write the tell-all, *Nickel Dreams*.

Infamy: Began drinking in her late teens and quickly developed a reputation as a wild party girl. The cocaine, alcohol, and violence that was integral to her 1980 relationship with Glen Campbell became a national symbol of celebrity excess (the pair split in 1981, and Tucker continued her drinking and drugging until entering the Betty Ford clinic in 1988).

In 1997, with a TV crew in attendance to film a *Dateline* profile segment, Tucker flashed her breasts to a roomful of Nashville music-industry partygoers.

Relationship: Jerry Laseter (engaged)

Children: Presley Tanita, 1989; Beau Grayson, 1991 (both with Ben Reed)

CHRISTY TURLINGTON

Birthplace: Walnut Creek, CA
Birthdate: 1/2/69
Occupation: Supermodel
Education: New York University
Facts: Her face was used on mannequins at the Metropolitan Museum of Art's costume galleries.

Dated screenwriter Roger Wilson for seven years; they had a Buddhist service together, though they were never officially married. Also dated Jason Patric.

Has early-stage emphysema, a chronic lung disease. She quit smoking six years prior to the diagnosis, and helped crusade against smoking after her father died of lung cancer in 1997.

Relationship: Edward Burns

TED TURNER

Real Name: Robert Edward Turner III
Birthplace: Cincinnati, OH
Birthdate: 11/19/38
Occupation: Media executive, owner of Atlanta Braves and Hawks
Education: Brown University

Debut: In 1970, bought failing Atlanta TV station, which he turned into WTBS
Signature: CNN
Facts: Won the America's Cup in his yacht, *Courageous,* in 1977.

Interested in owning a major TV network, he made a failed bid for CBS in 1985, and launched negotiations with NBC in 1994 that ultimately broke down.

Owns four bison ranches out west, making him America's largest private bison rancher.

Infamy: Was "asked to leave" Brown University in 1967 for having a girl in his room after hours; was later awarded an honorary degree.
Original Job: Selling space on billboards in family business
Marriages: Judy Nye (divorced), Janie Shirley Smith (divorced), Jane Fonda, 1991 (divorced, 2001)
Children: Laura Seydel, 1961; Robert Edward IV, 1963; (with Judy Nye). Rhett, 1965; Beau, 1968; Sara Jean "Jennie," 1969; (with Janie Shirley Smith).
Major Award: Elected to the Emmy Hall of Fame, 1991
Quote: "You don't have to be smart to make a lot of money."

TINA TURNER

Real Name: Anna Mae Bullock
Birthplace: Nutbush, TN
Birthdate: 11/26/39
Occupation: Singer, actor
Debut: (Song) "Fool in Love," 1960
Signature: "What's Love Go to Do with It?" 1984
Facts: "River Deep, Mountain High" (1966) was No. 1 in Britain and earned The Ike and Tina Turner Revue the chance to open for The Rolling Stones in 1969.

Became a Buddhist in the early '80s.

Endured years of physical abuse and extramarital affairs by then husband Ike.
Marriages: Ike Turner, 1956

(divorced, 1978); Erwin Bach (relationship)
Children: Raymond Craig Hill, 1958 (with Raymond Hill); Ronald Renelle "Ronnie," 1960 (with Ike Turner)
Major Awards: Grammy, Best R&B Duo or Group, "Proud Mary" (with Ike Turner), 1972; Grammy, Record of the Year and Best Pop Vocal—Female, "What's Love Got to Do with It?," 1984; Grammy, Best Rock Vocal of the Year, "Better Be Good to Me," 1985; Grammy, Best Rock Vocal of the Year, "One of the Living," 1986; Grammy, Best Rock Vocal of the Year, "Back Where You Started," 1986; Grammy, Best Rock Vocal of the Year, *Tina Live in Europe,* 1988; inducted into Rock and Roll Hall of Fame, 1991

SHANIA TWAIN

Real name: Eileen Regina Twain
Birthplace: Windsor, Ontario
Birthdate: 8/28/65
Occupation: Singer, songwriter
Education: High school
Debut: (Album) *Shania Twain,* 1993
Signature: *Come on Over,* 1997
Facts: Grew up so poor her Canadian family often went without heat.

Says she's of Ojibwa Indian ancestry, but was actually adopted by her Indian stepfather. Shania means "I'm on my way" in Ojibwa dialect.

Raised her three younger siblings after her parents died in an auto accident when she was 21.

Come on Over is the best-selling album by a female artist ever, as well as the top country album of all time.
Original job: secretary
Marriage: Robert "Mutt" Lange, 1993
Child: son Eja, 2001
Major Awards: Grammy, Best Country Album, *The Woman in Me,* 1995; Best Country Song, "You're Still The One" (with Robert John "Mutt" Lange), 1998; Grammy, Best Country Vocal—Female, "You're Still The One," 1998; Grammy, Best

Country Song, "Come on Over" (with Robert John "Mutt" Lange), 1999; Grammy, Best Country Vocal—Female, "Man! I Feel Like A Woman," 1999

LIV TYLER

Birthplace: New York, NY
Birthdate: 7/1/77
Occupation: Actor
Education: High school
Debut: (Film) *Silent Fall*, 1994
Signature: *Armageddon*, 1998
Facts: First came to the world's attention as the girl wearing a silver bra in the Aerosmith's 1994 video "Crazy," which also starred Alicia Silverstone.

As a child, believed her father was rocker Todd Rundgren, who was married to her mother, '70s Playboy Playmate Bebe Buell. But at an Aerosmith concert at age 11, she realized she greatly resembled Steven Tyler.

Likes to shop with her father: "We both wear the same size, and we'll just try on clothes for hours."

Was in a relationship with Joaquin Phoenix.
Relationship: Royston Langton, musician
Original Job: Model
Famous Relative: Steve Tyler, Aerosmith lead singer, father
Quote: "It's important to surround yourself with beautiful friends and family who will say, 'You are a dork today.'"

STEVEN TYLER

Real Name: Steven Tallarico
Birthplace: Boston, MA
Birthdate: 3/26/48
Education: High school dropout
Debut: (Album) *Aerosmith*, 1973
Signature: Aerosmith
Facts: Met future Aerosmith members Joe Perry and Tom Hamilton at Lake Sunapee, NH, where their families had vacation houses.

Seriously injured in a motorcycle accident in 1981, capping a long period of discord and debauchery among band members. "I lay there in the hospital crying and flipping out, knowing some other group was going to step into our space. Through the stupor of my medication, I pictured a spotlight. We walked out of it."

When the band reformed in 1984, they got a contract with Geffen but had to audition first.

Aerosmith co-owns the West Hollywood restaurant House of Blues with Dan Aykroyd and Jim Belushi.
Infamy: Alcohol and drug use including heroin addiction.

Sued his ex-wife in 1999 in an attempt to get her to return photographs taken of him in the nude after reading that she intended to publish them.
Marriages: Cyrinda Fox (divorced); Kathleen Tallarico (divorced, 1987); Theresa Barrick
Children: Liv, 1977 (with Bebe Buell). Mia, 1978 (with Cyrinda Fox). Chelsea, 1988; Taj, 1992.
Major Awards: Grammy, Best Rock Performance by a Duo or Group with Vocal, "Janie's Got a Gun," 1990; Grammy, Best Rock Performance by a Duo or Group with Vocal, "Crazy," 1994; Grammy, Best Rock Performance by a Duo or Group with Vocal, "Pink," 1998
Quote: On what is left for his band to accomplish: "I'm looking to be the lounge act on the space shuttle so I can sing 'Walk This Way' on the ceiling."

JOHN UPDIKE

Birthplace: Shillington, PA
Birthdate: 3/18/32
Occupation: Writer
Education: Harvard College, Oxford University
Debut: (Book) *The Carpentered Hen and Other Tame Creatures*, 1958
Signature: *Rabbit, Run*
Fact: Collects Walt Disney comic books.

Marriages: Mary Entwhistle Pennington, 1953 (divorced, 1974); Martha R. Bernhard, 1977
Children: Elizabeth, c. 1955; David, c. 1957; Michael, c. 1959; Miranda, c. 1960; (with Pennington). Three stepchildren
Major Awards: Pulitzer Prize, *Rabbit Is Rich*, 1982, *Rabbit at Rest*, 1991; American Book Award, *Rabbit Is Rich*, 1982

USHER

Real Name: Usher Raymond IV
Birthplace: Chattanooga, TN
Birthdate: 10/14/78
Occupation: Singer, songwriter, actor
Education: High school
Debut: (Album) *Usher*, 1994
Signature: *My Way*
Facts: Appeared on *Star Search* at age 13 and won as best teen vocalist.

Was signed by a record label while still in high school.

When he travels, decoys dressed like the singer head for packs of screaming fans so he can quietly escape.

Does up to 1,000 stomach crunches a day.
Quote: "I'm a ladies' man. But it really shocks me how attached women are to their emotions, whereas a man thinks more in terms of realities."

JAMES VAN DER BEEK

Birthplace: Cheshire, CT
Birthdate: 3/8/77
Occupation: Actor
Education: Attended Drew University
Debut: (Film) *Angus*, 1995
Signature: *Dawson's Creek*
Facts: Was identified as dyslexic in kindergarden and learned to read in a special class. Later became an honors student.

In eighth grade, he was sidelined from football with a concussion and discovered acting in community theater.

Depressed after reading about successful up-and-comers when he was unemployed, he went backpacking in Europe for six weeks. Upon returning, was offered a movie, play, and *Dawson's Creek.*

LUTHER VANDROSS

Birthplace: New York, NY
Birthdate: 4/20/51
Occupation: Singer, songwriter
Education: Attended Western Michigan University
Debut: (Song) "Everybody Rejoice (A Brand New Day)" from *The Wiz,* 1978
Signature: "Here and Now," 1990
Facts: Started playing the piano at age 3.

Sister was a member of the '50s group The Crests.

His first group, Listen My Brother, formed while he was a high school student, played at the Apollo and appeared on the first episode of *Sesame Street.*

He fights a continuous battle with his weight; he has seesawed between189 and 340 pounds.

His middle name is Ronzoni, the only food his mother could keep down during a diffcult pregnancy.

At one point, supported himself singing jingles for Pepsi-Cola, Juicy Fruit gum, and the U.S. Army.
Original Job: S&H Green Stamp defective-merchandise clerk
Major Awards: Grammy, Best R&B Vocal—Male, "Here and Now," 1990; Grammy, Best R&B Song, "Power of Love/Love Power," 1991; Grammy, Best R&B Vocal—Male, *Power of Love,* 1991; Grammy, Best R&B Vocal—Male, "Your Secret Love," 1996

VINCE VAUGHN

Birthplace: Buffalo Grove, IL
Birthdate: 3/28/70
Occupation: Actor
Education: High school
Debut: (TV) *China Beach,* 1989; (Film) *Rudy,* 1993

Signature: *Swingers*
Facts: First film role was a sex-education short, in which he played a guy trying to persuade his girlfriend to have sex with him.

Met *Swingers* writer and star Jon Favreau while filming *Rudy.* Favreau based the script on his late-night adventures in L.A. with Vaughn.

His father is named Vernon, and both of his sisters and all three family dogs have names beginning with "V."

Stands 6' 5".
Infamy: In 2001 was arrested in a scuffle with college students in a Wilmington, N.C. bar. He agrees to testify against another defendant, and is ordered to stay out the city's bars and to undergo alcohol counseling.
Relationship: Jody Lauren Adams, actor
Quote: "I made an independent movie thinking I'll have chicks crawling all over me. Instead, I got guys who emulate me because they—wrongly—think I'm some kind of real swinger."

DONATELLA VERSACE

Birthplace: Reggio di Calabria, Italy
Birthdate: 5/2/55
Occupation: Designer, businessperson
Education: University of Florence
Facts: Began working with her brother Gianni's rising fashion business in 1978. Her contributions include the design of ad campaigns and the introduction of a rock-and-roll sensibility to the clothes.

In the 1990s she created Versace's youthful Versus line and led the making of the perfume Blonde; she was the face in the fragrance's advertisements.

Became chief designer of the Versace empire upon her brother's murder; she had 12 weeks to finish a spring collection and mount the show.

Her influence has resulted in softer, sleeker business suits, with a greater emphasis on shape and color.

Has been recruited to spruce up the image of Prince Charles's companion, Camilla Parker Bowles.

Chain smokes.

Never eats until noon.
Marriage: Paul Beck, c. 1982
Children: Allegra, c. 1986; Daniel, c. 1991
Famous Relative: Gianni Versace, brother, deceased 1997
Quote: "For me, there's no middle way—I live my life in extremes.... If [a skirt is] tight, it should be super-tight. If I want to be blonde, it has to be platinum!"

GORAN VISNJIC

Birthplace: Sibenik, Croatia
Birthdate: 9/9/72
Occupation: Actor
Education: Academy of Dramatic Arts, Zagreb, Croatia
Debut: (TV) *Alistair MacLean's Night Watch,* 1995; (Film) *The Peacemaker,* 1997
Signature: *ER*
Facts: Served a mandatory tour in the Yugoslavian army as a paratrooper, and volunteered for another three months in the Croatian army during the Balkan conflict.

Is widely known in Croatia for playing Hamlet on the stage for years (he won the Croatian equivalent of a Tony award when he was 21).

His name is pronounced "GOR-an VISH-nick."

He is 6' 4".
Marriage: Ivana, sculptor

MARK WAHLBERG

Birthplace: Dorchester, MA
Birthdate: 6/5/71
Occupation: Actor, model, rap artist
Education: High school dropout
Debut: (Album) *Music for the People,* 1991; (Film) *Renaissance Man,* 1994

Signature: *Boogie Nights*, 1997
Facts: Left school at 14 to hustle on the street.

An original member with older brother in New Kids on the Block, he dropped out after six months.

Debut album under nom de rap Marky Mark was produced by his brother with his brother's money.

Has a third nipple, which was airbrushed out of Calvin Klein underwear ads.

Wore a 13-inch prosthetic penis and lost 30 pounds for his role in *Boogie Nights*.
Infamy: Convicted at age 16 for his involvement in the beating of two Vietnamese men during a robbery. Served 45 days in jail.

Was arrested on two occasions for yelling racial epithets at black schoolchildren. Gays and Asian-Americans also accused him of bias.

His public misconduct included a catfight with Madonna and an alleged assault on a security guard.
Famous Relative: Donnie Wahlberg, singer (original New Kids on the Block member), brother

CHRISTOPHER WALKEN

Real Name: Ronald Walken
Birthplace: New York
Birthdate: 3/31/43
Occupation: Actor
Education: Attended Hofstra University
Debut: (TV) *The Guiding Light*, 1954; (Film) *Me and My Brother*, 1968
Signature: *The Deer Hunter*, 1978
Facts: Studied dance as a child.

Spent the summer of 1960 as an assistant lion tamer.

Changed his name when a singer remarked, "I see you more as a Christopher."

Tested for the lead in *Love Story* and played Romeo in 1970.

Made a splash—and started his creepy public image—as Diane Keaton's mild yet deranged brother in *Annie Hall*.

In 1995, performed in one-man stage play he wrote, *Him,* about Elvis Presley.

A Christopher Walken mask outsold the Freddy Krueger mask in Halloween, 1996.

Is scared of guns and does not like to use them as props.
Original Job: Catalog model
Marriage: Georgianne, 1968
Major Award: Oscar, Best Supporting Actor, *The Deer Hunter,* 1978
Quote: "I'm such a pussycat in real life. I'm a song-and-dance man who played a few scary parts and got mistaken for the characters he plays."

BARBARA WALTERS

Birthplace: Boston, MA
Birthdate: 9/25/31
Occupation: Broadcast journalist
Education: Sarah Lawrence College
Debut: (TV) *The Today Show,* 1974
Signature: *20/20*
Facts: In 1957, Don Hewitt, now executive producer of *60 Minutes,* told Walters: "You're marvelous, but stay out of television."

Walters was the only woman reporter in the press group that accompanied President Nixon on his historic trip to China in 1972.
Original Job: Intent on becoming a teacher, went for her master's in education while working as a secretary
Marriages: Robert Henry Katz (annulled); Lee Guber (divorced); Merv Adelson (divorced, 1992); Sen. John Warner (relationship)
Child: Jacqueline Dena, 1968
Major Awards: Emmy, Best Host on a Talk Show, *Today,* 1975; Emmy, Best Interviewer, *The Barbara Walters Show,* 1982; 5 News and Documentary Emmys as correspondent; elected to the Television Hall of Fame, 1990

VERA WANG

Birthplace: New York, NY
Birthdate: 6/27/49
Occupation: Designer
Education: Sarah Lawrence College
Signature: Mariah Carey's wedding dress
Facts: Her parents emigrated from China and built a multimillion-dollar oil and pharmaceutical company in the U.S.

Competed in figure skating at the U.S. national championship in 1968.

Began designing bridal gowns after she saw a niche when she couldn't find anything mature and elegant for her own nuptials. Has designed wedding-wear for Sharon Stone, Holly Hunter, Uma Thurman and Chynna Phillips.
Original Job: *Vogue* fashion editor
Marriage: Arthur Becker, 1989
Children: Cecilia, 1990; Josephine, 1993; (both adopted).

SELA WARD

Birthplace: Meridian, MS
Birthdate: 7/11/56
Occupation: Actress
Education: University of Alabama
Debut: (Film) *The Man Who Loved Women,* 1983
Signature: *Once and Again,* 1999
Facts: Her name is from the Bible; it means "hallelujah" or "amen."

Was a cheerleader and homecoming queen in college.

Modeled before studying acting.

Was engaged to Peter "Robocop" Weller.

Appeared as Harrison Ford's murdered wife in *The Fugitive.*

Her favorite thing in life: a candle-lit bubblebath with her husband.
Original Job: Advertising art director
Marriage: Howard Sherman, 1992
Children: Austin Ward, 1994; Anabella Raye, 1998
Major Awards: Emmy, Best Actress in a Drama Series, *Sisters,* 1994; Emmy, Best Actress in a Drama

Series, *Once and Again,* 2000
Quote: "At the age of 43, I have never felt better in my life. Much more grounded, and very sexy. I feel like a juicy piece of fruit."

ESTELLA WARREN

Birthplace: Peterborough, Canada
Birthdate: 12/23/78
Occupation: Model, actor
Education: Attended high school
Debut: (Film) *Perfume,* 2001
Signature: *Sports Illustrated* swimsuit issue, *Planet of the Apes* (2001)
Facts: Started synchronized swimming at age 8 and won three Canadian national championships and a bronze medal at the Junior World Championships before giving up a shot at the Olympics for a career in modeling.
Quote: "Coming from a barely clothed childhood as a swimmer makes me really comfortable with my body. But a nude photo has to be taken in good taste, not like, 'Hey, here's my breast!'"

DENZEL WASHINGTON

Birthplace: Mt. Vernon, NY
Birthdate: 12/28/54
Occupation: Actor
Education: Fordham University, studied acting at the American Conservatory Theatre, San Francisco
Debut: (Film) *Carbon Copy,* 1981
Signature: *Malcolm X,* 1992 [see page 71 for a complete filmography]
Facts: Played Malcolm X in *When The Chickens Come Home To Roost* on Broadway, as well as in the 1992 Spike Lee movie.

In college, played football and basketball and wrote poetry before deciding to try acting.
Original Job: Drama instructor
Marriage: Pauletta Pearson, 1983
Children: John David, 1984; Katia, 1987; Malcolm, 1991; Olivia, 1991
Major Award: Oscar, Best Supporting Actor, *Glory,* 1989

WENDY WASSERSTEIN

Birthplace: Brooklyn, NY
Birthdate: 10/18/50
Occupation: Playwright
Education: Mount Holyoke College, City College of New York, Yale University School of Drama
Debut: (Stage) *Any Woman Can't,* 1973
Signature: *The Heidi Chronicles*
Facts: Almost enrolled in business school rather than pursuing drama.

Brother sent her a note prior to a premiere: "Can't come to play tonight. Am buying Nabisco."
Child: Lucy Jane, 1999
Famous Relative: Bruce Wasserstein, investment banking star, brother
Major Awards: Pulitzer Prize, *The Heidi Chronicles,* 1988; Tony, Best Play, *The Heidi Chronicles,* 1989

TIONNE WATKINS

Birthplace: Des Moines, IA
Birthdate: 4/26/70
Occupation: Singer, songwriter
Debut: (Album) *Oooooooohhh ... On the TLC Tip,* 1992; (Book) *Thoughts,* 1999
Signature: "Waterfalls," 1995 / "T-Boz"
Facts: TLC's original look featured colorful, baggy clothes, a hip-hop style previously reserved for men.

Suffers from sickle cell anemia; her bandmates didn't know until she collapsed during a 1995 concert.

The band's sophomore effort, *Crazysexycool,* is the bestselling album ever by a female group.

Soon after *Crazysexycool,* the band declared bankruptcy, blaming a low royalty clause in their contract.

Appeared in the movies *House Party 3* and *Belly.*

Thoughts contains her poetry and essays.
Original Jobs: Hair model, shampoo girl, manicurist
Marriage: D'Mon Rolison, 2000 (aka Mack 10, rap artist)
Child: Chase Rolison, 2000

Major Awards: Grammy, Best R&B Album, *Crazysexycool,* 1995; Grammy, Best R&B Vocal—Duo or Group, "Creep," 1995; Grammy, Best R&B Album, *Fanmail,* 1999; Grammy, Best R&B Vocal—Duo or Group, "No Scrubs," 1999
Quote: "We stand up for the girl groups who always wanted to dress like this, but couldn't. We didn't show a stitch of our skin and we made it."

EMILY WATSON

Birthplace: London, England
Birthdate: 1/14/67
Occupation: Actress
Education: Bristol University, England; London Drama Studio
Debut: (Film) *Breaking the Waves,* 1996
Signature: *Breaking the Waves,* 1996
Facts: At age 4, modeled for Laura Ashley.

Her parents didn't allow television in her childhood home.

Was a member of the Royal Shakespeare Company, which is where she met her husband.

For her role as Jacqueline du Pre in *Hilary and Jackie,* Watson first learned to play the cello, then to physically mimic du Pre's playing.

Is a devoted Londoner.
Original Jobs: Waitress; photocopier
Marriage: Jack Waters, 1995
Quote: "To be famous for pretending to be someone else is quite anonymous, in a way."

DAMON WAYANS

Birthplace: New York, NY
Birthdate: 9/4/60
Occupation: Comedian, actor, writer, director
Education: High school
Debut: (Film) *Beverly Hills Cop,* 1984; (TV) *Saturday Night Live,* 1985
Signature: *In Living Color*
Facts: Grew up poor as one of 11 children.

Began career performing stand-up in clubs.

Marriage: Lisa

Children: Damon Jr., 1983; Michael, 1985; Cara Mia, c. 1987; Kyla, c. 1990

Famous Relatives: Keenan Ivory Wayans, actor/producer/writer/director, brother; Kim Wayans, actor, sister; Marlon Wayans, actor, brother; Shawn Wayans, actor, brother

SIGOURNEY WEAVER

Real Name: Susan Weaver
Birthplace: New York, NY
Birthdate: 10/8/49
Occupation: Actor
Education: Stanford University; Yale University (MFA)
Debut: (Stage) *The Constant Wife* (with Ingrid Bergman), 1974
Signature: *Alien*
Facts: Took her name from a character in *The Great Gatsby*.

As a senior at Stanford, she dressed as an elf and lived in a treehouse with her boyfriend.

Accepted at Yale Drama School as "Mr." Sigourney Weaver.

Marriage: Jim Simpson, 1984
Child: Charlotte, 1990
Famous Relatives: Sylvester "Pat" Weaver, president of NBC, father; Elizabeth Inglis, actor, mother

VERONICA WEBB

Birthplace: Detroit, MI
Birthdate: 2/25/65
Occupation: Model, writer, actor
Education: Attended New School for Social Research
Signature: *Veronica Webb Sight*
Facts: Was a cashier in a SoHo boutique when spotted by a makeup artist for the Click modeling agency. Fearing he was a fraud, she resisted calling him back until she was fired from her job.

While a top model for Chanel and Revlon, wrote articles for *Esquire*, *Details*, and other magazines.

Broke the color barrier in modeling when she became a multimillion-dollar Revlon model.

Original Job: Cashier

ANDREW LLOYD WEBBER

Birthplace: London, England
Birthdate: 3/22/48
Occupation: Composer, producer
Education: Magdelen College of Oxford University, Royal Academy of Music, Oxford, Guildhall School of Music, Royal College of Music
Debut: (Stage) *Joseph and the Amazing Technicolor Dreamcoat*, 1968
Signature: *The Phantom of the Opera*
Fact: In 1969, was commissioned by RCA to write an opera based on a single, "Jesus Christ Superstar."

By *2001*, Cats had grossed over $1.4 billion worldwide and ranked as London's longest-running musical.

Infamy: After firing Faye Dunaway from the play *Sunset Boulevard* in 1994 because, he said, she couldn't sing, Webber wrote a confidential letter of apology that he then allowed the *London Standard* to print in its entirety. Dunaway, claiming she could indeed sing, sued, and settled for a reported $1.5 million.

Marriages: Sarah Jane Tudor Hugill (divorced); Sarah Brightman (divorced); Madeleine Astrid Gurdon, 1991
Children: Nicholas; Imogen; Alastair, 1992; Richard, 1993; Billy, 1994; Isabella Aurora, 1996
Famous Relative: William Webber, London College of Music director, father
Major Awards: Grammy, Best Cast Show Album, *Evita* (with Tim Rice), 1980; Grammy, Best Cast Show Album, *Cats*, 1983; Grammy, Legend Award, 1990; New York Drama Critics Award, *Evita*, 1980; Tony, Best Score, *Evita* (music; Tim Rice,

lyrics), 1980; Tony, Best Score, *Cats* (music; T. S. Eliot, lyrics), 1983; Tony, Best Musical, *The Phantom of the Opera*, 1988; Academy Award, Best Song, "You Must Love Me," (music; Tim Rice, lyrics), 1996

FOREST WHITAKER

Birthplace: Longview, TX
Birthdate: 7/15/61
Occupation: Actor, director, producer
Education: USC
Debut: (Film) *Fast Times at Ridgemont High*, 1982; (TV) *North and South*, 1985; (Film, directing) *Waiting to Exhale*, 1995
Signature: *The Crying Game*, 1992
Facts: Growing up in the Compton area of south central Los Angeles, he was an All-league defensive tackle on his high school football team.

First attended college on a full sports scholarship; then switched schools, intending to be a classical tenor, on a Levar Burton Scholarship.

Marriage: Keisha Nash, 1996
Children: Ocean Alexander, c. 1990 (from a previous relationship); Autumn, stepdaughter, c. 1991; Sonnet Noel, 1996; True Isabella Summer, 1998
Famous relative: Damon Whitaker, actor, brother

BARRY WHITE

Birthplace: Galveston, TX
Birthdate: 9/12/44
Occupation: Singer, songwriter
Education: High school dropout
Debut: "Love's Theme" (with the Love Unlimited Orchestra, 1971)
Signature: "Can't Get Enough of Your Love, Babe," 1974
Facts: His birth certificate read "Barry Eugene Carter," but when White's unmarried father caught a look at his son's birth certificate, he had the name changed.

Credits his mother, who taught him how to harmonize at age 4, with providing his core of personal values.

According to his autobiography, White was an amateur couples therapist at the age of 14.

Went to jail for stealing tires at 14; claimed hearing Elvis's "It's Now or Never" in his cell convinced him to turn his life around.

After singing in vocal groups and a drumming stint, teenage White toiled as a songwriter, record producer, and label A&R man.

Wrote two songs for the kids show *The Banana Splits*.

His nicknames include The Maestro, The Prince of Pillow Talk, and Dr. Love.

Designs his own clothes and handpicks the tailors.

Original Jobs: News vendor, fry cook, construction worker
Marriages: Mary Smith (divorced); Glodean James, 1973 (divorced, 1988); Katherine Denton (relationship, 1994)
Children: Eight children
Major Awards: Grammy, Best R&B Vocal—Male, *Staying Power*, 1999
Quote: "Once my voice changed, there was no escaping its power."

LUCINDA WILLIAMS

Birthplace: Lake Charles, LA
Birthdate: 1/26/53
Occupation: Musician
Education: Attended the University of Arkansas
Debut: (Album) *Ramblin' on My Mind*, 1979
Signature: *Car Wheels on a Gravel Road*, 1998
Facts: Raised by her poet father after her parents' divorce.

Family friends including writers James Dickey, Allen Ginsberg and Charles Bukowski inspired her to write songs.

Suspended from high school for refusing to say the Pledge of Allegiance in a one-woman Vietnam protest.

Dropped out of college after freshman year and began playing in New Orleans clubs for tips.

Collects what she calls "hillbilly hoodoo"—stones, chips, dirt, and snakeskin from important musical sites, like a part of the roof from the Carter Family's store and some wood from Dock Boggs' front porch.
Marriage: Greg Sowders, 1986 (divorced, 1988)
Major Award: Grammy, Best Country Song, "Passionate Kisses," 1994
Quote: "I'm always going to be tortured, no matter how much money I make."

MICHELLE WILLIAMS

Birthplace: Kalispell, Montana
Birthdate: 9/9/80
Occupation: Actor
Education: High school
Debut: (TV) *Baywatch*, 1989; (Film) *Lassie*, 1994
Signature: *Dawson's Creek*
Facts: At 16, was legally emancipated from her parents so she could live on her own in Burbank, Calif.

Her father, a Republican, ran for the U.S. Senate twice in Montana.

Her favorite authors are Ayn Rand and Fyodor Dostoyevsky.

Cowrote a feature script set in a brothel with two friends.
Relationship: Morgan J. Freeman, director, screenwriter
Quote: "I can't imagine why anyone would want to be a sex symbol. It's so surface, so uninteresting and so boring. Sex symbols are a dime a dozen; you can find one on any street in Los Angeles."

ROBIN WILLIAMS

Birthplace: Chicago, IL
Birthdate: 7/21/51
Occupation: Actor
Education: Claremont Men's College, College of Marin, Juilliard
Debut: (TV) *Laugh-In*, 1977 [see page 71 for a complete filmography]
Signature: *Mork and Mindy*

Facts: Grew up on a 30-room estate in Bloomfield Hills, MI.

Spent most of childhood playing with his 2,000 toy soldiers.

Second wife was a former nanny of Robin's children and his personal assistant. She served as a producer for *Mrs. Doubtfire*, 1994.

In 2000, launched a weekly web-based show at RobinWilliams@audible.com.
Infamy: Sued for $6.2 million in 1986 by former companion Michelle Tish Carter, who claimed that he gave her herpes during their two-year relationship. Williams countersued for extortion. The suits were settled out of court for an undisclosed amount.

Shared cocaine with John Belushi only a few hours before Belushi's death.
Original Job: Street mime
Marriages: Valeri Velardi (divorced, 1978); Marsha Garces, 1989
Children: Zachary, 1983 (with Valeri Velardi). Zelda, 1989; Cody Alan, 1991
Major Awards: Grammy, Best Comedy Recording, *Reality…What a Concept,* 1979; Emmy, Best Individual Performance in a Variety or Music Program, *A Carol Burnett Special,* 1987; Grammy, Best Comedy Recording, *A Night at the Met,* 1987; Emmy, Best Individual Performance in a Variety or Music Program, *ABC Presents a Royal Gala,* 1988; Grammy, Best Comedy Recording, *Good Morning, Vietnam,* 1988; Grammy, Best Recording for Children, *Pecos Bill,* 1988; Oscar, Best Supporting Actor, *Good Will Hunting,* 1997

VANESSA WILLIAMS

Birthplace: New York, NY
Birthdate: 3/18/63
Occupation: Singer, actor
Education: Syracuse University
Debut: (Album) *The Right Stuff*, 1988; (Film) *The Pick-Up Artist,* 1987

Signature: *Kiss of the Spider Woman*
Facts: Was the first black Miss America. Got hate mail from white-supremacist groups and also from blacks claiming she was too white.

Her debut album sold more than 500,000 copies.
Infamy: Forced to resign as Miss America in 1984, after *Penthouse* printed nude photos of her in leather bondage gear with another woman that had been taken several years earlier.
Marriage: Ramon Hervey, 1988 (divorced, 1996); Rick Fox, professional basketball player, 1999
Children: Melanie, 1987; Jillian, 1989; Devin, 1993 (with Ramon Hervey). Sasha Gabriella, 2000
Quote: "I've had four children. Going topless is no longer an option."

KEVIN WILLIAMSON

Birthplace: Bern, NC
Birthdate: 3/14/65
Occupation: Screenwriter, director, executive producer
Education: Attended East Carolina State University
Debut: (Filmwriting) *Scream*, 1996
Signature: *Dawson's Creek*
Facts: In high school, an English teacher told him he had little talent and shouldn't consider a writing career.

The real Dawson's Creek is located a few miles from his childhood home and was a favored hangout.

Like Dawson, Williamson has memorized many lines from *Jaws*.
Original Jobs: Actor, music-video director's assistant, dog-walker

BRUCE WILLIS

Real Name: Walter Bruce Willis
Birthplace: Idar-Oberstein, Germany
Birthdate: 3/19/55
Occupation: Actor
Education: Montclair State College
Debut: (Stage) *Heaven and Earth*, 1977
Signature: *Die Hard*, 1988

Facts: Was student council president in high school.

The stammer he'd had since childhood disappeared whenever he performed.

Willis and Demi Moore were married by singer Little Richard.

Has his own band, Bruno.

He and his family live in once sleepy Hailey, Idaho, in the Rockies. Attempting to revitalize the town, Willis bought nearly every building on Main Street.
Infamy: During his senior year in high school, was expelled after a racial disturbance and was only permitted to graduate because his father hired an attorney to get him reinstated.
Original Jobs: Du Pont plant worker, bartender, commercial actor for Levi's 501 jeans
Marriage: Demi Moore, 1987 (separated, 1998); Maria Bravo, model (relationship)
Children: Rumer Glenn, 1988; Scout Larue, 1991; Tallulah Belle, 1994
Major Award: Emmy, Best Actor in a Drama Series, *Moonlighting*, 1987; Emmy, Guest Actor, *Friends*, 2000
Quote: "Being famous, it's like alcohol—whatever you are, it's just a little more of that. If you're an ---hole, you're more of an ---hole; if you're a nice guy, you're more of a nice guy."

AUGUST WILSON

Real Name: Frederick August Kittel
Birthplace: Pittsburgh, PA
Birthdate: 4/27/45
Education: High school dropout
Occupation: Playwright
Debut: (Play) *Ma Rainey's Black Bottom*, 1981
Signature: *The Piano Lesson*, 1990
Fact: Founded the black activist theater company Black Horizon on the Hill in the 1960s.
Marriages: One prior marriage, Judy Oliver (divorced), Constanza Romero, 1994
Child: Sakina Ansari, 1970

Major Awards: Tony, Best Play, *Fences*, 1987; Pulitzer Prize, Best Play, *Fences*, 1987; Pulitzer Prize, Best Play, *The Piano Lesson*, 1990

CASSANDRA WILSON

Birthplace: Jackson, Mississippi
Birthdate: 12/4/55
Occupation: Jazz singer, composer
Education: attended Millsaps College; Jackson State University
Debut: (Album) *Point of View*, 1985
Signature: *New Moon Daughter*, 1995
Facts: Widely considered one of the top jazz singers of the 1990s, she studied classical piano for six years, then learned acoustic guitar. By age 15, she had written some 20 songs.

After moving to New York, joined forces with the Brooklyn-based M-Base movement (stands for macro-basic array of structured extemporizations), which tried to create music inspired from jazz and the contemporary urban scene.

Was selected by Wynton Marsalis for the lead vocal role in his jazz oratorio *Blood on the Fields,* which won the 1997 Pulitzer Prize for Music.
Original Job: Television station public-affairs assistant
Marriage: Bruce Lincoln (divorced); Isaach de Bankole, actor (engaged)
Child: Jeris, 1990
Major Award: Grammy, Best Jazz Vocal Recording, *New Moon Daughter,* 1995
Quote: "People don't see things in streams, they don't see what tends to connect us all together. That's what I see. That's what I try to get to."

OPRAH WINFREY

Birthplace: Kosciusko, MS
Birthdate: 1/29/54
Occupation: Talk show host
Education: Tennesee State University
Debut: (Radio Reporter) WVOL, Nashville, 1971–72
Signature: *The Oprah Winfrey Show*

Facts: Delivered Easter sermon to congregation when she was 2 years old.

Once approached Aretha Franklin as she was stepping out of a limo and convinced Franklin that she had been abandoned. Aretha gave her $100, which Oprah used to stay in a hotel.

After being sexually abused at age 9 by an older cousin and later by a family friend, she ran away from home at age 13.

She bore a child when she was 14, though the baby died as an infant.

As a college sophomore, was the first African-American news co-anchor on a local TV station.

In college, won the title of Miss Tennessee and competed in the Miss Black America contest.

She left college in 1975, just a few credits shy of her degree. She finally received a B.S. in communications and theater in 1987, at age 33.

Formed Oxygen Media with Marcy Carsey and Geraldine Laybourne. She says she'll give up her talk show in 2002 and focus on the female-oriented channel.

First taught a course on "Dynamics of Leadership" to graduate students at Northwestern University in 1999.

In 2001, bought a 42-acre estate in Montecito, Calif. for an estimated $50 million (the previous owners, who were renovating, bought the mansion in 1998 for $14 million). Winfrey also has owns a Chicago penthouse, a 160-acre Indiana farm, a house in Tennessee, and a Wisconsin condo.
Original Jobs: News reporter, WVOL radio, WTVF television, Nashville, TN
Relationship: Stedman Graham (engaged)
Major Awards: Emmy, Best Host of a Talk Show, *The Oprah Winfrey Show*, 1986, 1990, 1991, 1992, 1993, 1994, 1997

KATE WINSLET

Birthplace: Reading, England
Birthdate: 10/5/75
Occupation: Actor
Education: High school
Debut: (Film) *Heavenly Creatures*, 1994
Signature: *Titanic*, 1997
Facts: Her grandparents ran a local repertory theater, where uncle Robert Bridges and father Roger Winslet both worked as actors.

Appeared in a breakfast cereal commercial frolicking with a "honey monster" creature at age 11. By age 17, starred in her first feature film.

Weighing 180 pounds in high school, she had the unhappy nickname Blubber. Went on Weight Watchers to drop 50 pounds.
Original Job: Delicatessen worker
Marriage: Jim Threapleton, 1998 (separated, 2001)
Child: Mia, 2000
Major Award: Grammy, Best Spoken Word Album for Children, *Listen to the Storyteller* (with Wynton Marsalis and Graham Greene), 1999

REESE WITHERSPOON

Real Name: Laura Jean Reese Witherspoon
Birthplace: New Orleans, LA
Birthdate: 3/22/76
Occupation: Actor
Education: Attended Stanford University
Debut: (Film) *The Man in the Moon*, 1991; (TV) *Wildflower*, 1991
Signature: *Election*, 1999
Facts: She began acting and modeling at age 7.

Won a 10-state talent search and, at age 15 debuted in *The Man in the Moon*. By 23 she had appeared in 10 films.

Met future husband, Ryan Phillippe, at her twenty-first birthday party before they became an on-screen couple in 1999's *Cruel Intentions*.
Original Job: Model

Marriage: Ryan Phillippe, 1999
Child: Ava Elizabeth, 1999
Quote: "Thank God none of my movies have made any money. God forbid they should ever make any money."

SCOTT WOLF

Birthplace: Boston, MA
Birthdate: 6/4/68
Occupation: Actor
Education: George Washington University
Debut: (TV) *Evening Shade*, 1990
Signature: *Party of Five*
Facts: Majored in finance in college.

Played doubles tennis with Tony the Tiger in a long-running early 1990s Frosted Flakes commercial.

Proposed to actress Alyssa Milano by hiding a 1940s-vintage diamond engagement ring in a pumpkin, getting down on one knee to pop the question, then carving the gourd with a big heart. The pair subsequently broke off their engagement. For a time after, Wolf dated fellow *Po5* costar Paula Devicq.

ELIJAH WOOD

Birthplace: Cedar Rapids, IA
Birthdate: 1/28/81
Occupation: Actor
Debut: (Film) *Back to the Future II*, 1989
Signature: *The War*, 1994
Facts: His first acting role was when he was seven, playing the pint-sized executive in Paula Abdul's "Forever Your Girl" video.

Has appeared in more than 15 national commercials.

Gets more than 700 fan letters every week from adoring teenage girls.

Favorite actors include Tim Roth and Gary Oldman.
Original Job: Model, commercial actor

JAMES WOODS

Birthplace: Vernal, UT
Birthdate: 4/18/47
Occupation: Actor
Education: Massachusetts Institute of Technology
Debut: (Film) *The Visitors,* 1972
Signature: *Ghosts of Mississippi*
Facts: Majored in political science in college. His mother was also interested in politics and was once asked to run for lieutenant governor of Rhode Island, though she declined.

Modeled his voice as Hades for Disney's *Hercules* after an oily William Morris agent he knows.

Was formerly involved in a relationship with Heather Graham.
Infamy: He and then fiancé Sarah Owen were allegedly the objects of harassment in the late 1980s by actress Sean Young, with whom Woods supposedly had an affair. Hate mail and gifts of mutilated dolls arrived, though nothing was ever proven. After Owen split with Woods following their four-month marriage, she accused him in the tabloids of spousal abuse. Woods countered by saying that Owen had been the one staging the earlier harassment.
Marriage: Kathryn Greko, 1980 (divorced, 1983); Sarah Owen, 1989 (divorced, 1990); Missy Crider (twice engaged, never married); Alexis Thorpe (relationship)
Major Awards: Emmy, Best Actor in a Miniseries, *The Promise,* 1986; Emmy, Best Actor in a Special, *My Name Is Bill W,* 1988

TIGER WOODS

Real Name: Eldrick Woods
Birthplace: Cypress, CA
Birthdate: 12/30/75
Occupation: Golfer
Education: Attended Stanford University
Facts: Was introduced to golf by his athletic father at nine months; by age 2 had outputt Bob Hope on *The Mike Douglas Show,* by 6 had hit his first hole-in-one, and by 8 had broken 80.

Began listening to subliminal tapes at age 6, featuring such messages as "I believe in me," and "My will moves mountains."

A gifted athlete, is also a switch-hitter in baseball, plays shooting guard in basketball, runs 400-meter track, and has played wide receiver in football.

His ethnicity includes parts African-American, Thai, Chinese, and Indian. On applications requesting ethnic identity, he has described himself as Asian.

The nickname Tiger comes from father Earl's Green Beret army past; it was the moniker of a South Vietnamese officer who saved Earl's life on several occasions.

In 2000, won his sixth consecutive tournament, tying Ben Hogan for the second-longest winning streak. He finished in a tie for second in his seventh outing, but did claim the all-time money-winning crown.

Also in 2000, won the U.S. Open by a record-setting 15 strokes, and captured the British Open and the PGA championship as well. He is the first player to win three straight majors since Ben Hogan in 1953, and the first golfer to win back-to-back PGA titles since Denny Shute repeated in 1937.

Later in 2000, he signed a new five-year contract with Nike said to be worth $85 million or more. By one estimate he earns more than $50 million a year in endorsements.

Was fined $100,000 by SAG for shooting a comercial during their strike in 2000.

In 2001 became the first player to sweep modern golf's four major championships in a row.
Major Awards: U.S. Golf Association National Junior Amateur Champion, 1991-1993; U.S. Amateur Golf Champion, 1994-1996; Masters Tournament winner, 1997; PGA Championship winner, 1999; U.S. Open winner, 2000; British Open winner, 2000; PGA Championship winner, 2000; Masters Tournament winner, 2001

NOAH WYLE

Birthplace: Los Angeles, CA
Birthdate: 6/4/71
Occupation: Actor
Education: High school
Debut: (TV) *Blind Faith,* 1990
Signature: *ER*
Facts: Is a Civil War buff.

Was given George Clooney's 1960 Oldsmobile Dynamic 88, with the hope that his so-called makeoutmobile would be as lucky for him as it had been for Clooney.

Plays billiards like a pool shark at the Hollywood Athletic Club and at his pool table at home.
Marriage: Tracy Warbin, 2000

WYNONNA

Real Name: Christina Claire Ciminella
Birthplace: Ashland, KY
Birthdate: 5/3/64
Occupation: Singer
Education: High school
Debut: (Song) "Had a Dream" (with The Judds), 1984
Signature: *Wynonna*
Facts: Drives a 1957 Chevy and a turquoise Harley-Davidson.

Had asthma as a child.

Adopted her name after the town of Wynona, OK, mentioned in the song "Route 66."

The Judds got their first recording contract when mother Naomi, a nurse, gave a tape to patient Diana Maher, daughter of record producer Brent Maher.
Marriage: Arch Kelley III, 1996 (divorced, 1999); D.R. Roach (engaged, 2001)
Children: Elijah, 1995; Pauline Grace, 1996
Famous Relatives: Naomi Judd, country singer, mother; Ashley Judd, actor, sister

Major Awards: Best Country Performance by a Group or Duo, "Mama He's Crazy," 1984; "Why Not Me," 1985; "Grandpa (Tell Me 'Bout the Good Old Days)," 1986; "Give a Little Love," 1988; "Love Can Build a Bridge," 1991; Grammy, Best Country Song, "Love Can Build a Bridge," 1991

YANNI

Real Name: Yanni Chrysomallis
Birthplace: Kalamata, Greece
Birthdate: 11/4/54
Occupation: Musician, pianist
Education: University of Minnesota
Debut: (Album) *Optimystique*, 1986
Facts: Former member of the Greek National Swimming Team.

Toured with the cult rock band Chameleon.

His music has been used on broadcasts of numerous sporting events, including the Tour de France, the Olympic Games, and the World Series.

Spent nine years as Linda Evans's signficant other.

RENEE ZELLWEGER

Birthplace: Katy, TX
Birthdate: 4/25/69
Occupation: Actor
Education: University of Texas
Debut: (Film) *The Texas Chainsaw Massacre 2*, 1986

Signature: *Bridget Jones's Diary*, 2001
Facts: Her Texas hometown was so small it had neither a movie theater nor cable television.

Signed up for her first drama class in college simply because she needed the credit to complete her English degree. Fell in love with acting and declared herself a professional actor upon graduation.

Was a star cheerleader in high school.

Was a college friend of Matthew McConaughey; they appeared together in school productions.

Though practically every well-known actress under age 35 auditioned during a four-month hunt for the *Jerry Maguire* part, the relatively obscure Zellweger impressed Tom Cruise and writer Cameron Crowe with her freshness and offbeat quality—and the fact that she wasn't intimidated by her sizzling co-star.

Recevied a $200,000 "friendship" ring from Jim Carrey, her boyfriend at the time.
Original Job: Bartender assistant
Quote: "Those were my boobs. I have the bras to prove it." (on her role in *Bridget Jones's Diary*)

CATHERINE ZETA-JONES

Birthplace: Swansea, Wales
Birthdate: 9/25/69
Occupation: Actor
Signature: *The Mask of Zorro*, 1998
Debut: (Film) *Sheherazade/Les 1001 Nuits*, 1990; (TV) *The Young Indiana Jones Chronicles*, 1992
Facts: As an infant, she contracted a virus which caused difficulty breathing, and has a tracheotomy scar.

As a child, she appeared on the stage in various British musicals, starting with Annie.

Was a major television star in the U.K. in the early '90s for her role in *The Darling Buds of May.* Moved to Hollywood to avoid the British press.

Zeta, her grandmother's Christian name, was added to distinguish herself from another Catherine Jones in Actors Equity.

Reportedly turned down producer and former studio chief Jon Peters' marriage proposal in 1996 because "I want to be known as an actress rather than a Hollywood wife."

Douglas gave her a vintage 1920s 10-carat, marquis-cut diamond engagement ring.
Relationship: Angus Macfadyen, actor (engaged, never married); Michael Douglas (engaged, 2000)
Child: Dylan Michael Douglas, 2000
Quote: "I think I came out of the womb loving makeup."

THE REGISTER OF THOUSANDS

Here's a celebrity database covering the multitudes of shakers and shapers, the near-great and notorious, those who grace the screen and the tube, the page and the stage—a resource to discover the real names, birthdates, birthplaces, occupations, and claims to fame of a large slice of pop culture. Those who are coy about their birthdates or are too new on the scene to be sufficiently well documented have been passed over for this year's list—but stay tuned.

AAMES, WILLIE (Willie Upton). Los Angeles, CA, 7/15/60. Actor. *Eight Is Enough.*

ABBOTT, JIM. Flint, MI, 9/19/67. One-handed baseball pitcher.

ABDUL, PAULA. Los Angeles, CA, 6/19/62. Singer, dancer, choreographer, divorced from Emilio Estevez. "Straight Up."

ABRAHAM, F. MURRAY. Pittsburgh, PA, 10/24/39. Actor. *Amadeus.*

ABRAHAMS, JIM. Milwaukee, WI, 5/10/44. Producer, writer, director. *Airplane!; The Naked Gun.*

ABRAHAMS, MICK. Luton, England, 4/7/43. Guitarist. Jethro Tull.

AD-ROCK, KING (Adam Horovitz). New York, NY, 10/31/66. Rap artist. The Beastie Boys.

ADAMS, BROOKE. New York, NY, 2/8/49. Actor. *Invasion of the Body Snatchers.*

ADAMS, BRYAN. Kingston, Canada, 11/5/59. Singer, songwriter. "(Everything I Do) I Do It for You."

ADAMS, DON. New York, NY, 4/19/26. Actor. Maxwell Smart on *Get Smart.*

ADAMS, EDIE (Elizabeth Edith Enke). Kingston, PA, 4/16/29. Actor. *The Ernie Kovacs Show.*

ADAMS, MAUD (Maud Wikstrom). Lulea, Sweden, 2/12/45. Actor. *Octopussy.*

ADAMS, VICTORIA. 4/7/74. Singer. Posh Spice of the Spice Girls.

ADAMSON, STUART (William Adamson). Manchester, England, 4/11/58. Guitarist, singer. Big Country.

ADJANI, ISABELLE. Paris, France, 6/27/55. Actor. *Camille Claudel.*

AGAR, JOHN. Chicago, IL, 1/31/21. Actor, formerly married to Shirley Temple. *The Sands of Iwo Jima.*

AGASSI, ANDRÉ Las Vegas, NV, 4/29/70. Tennis Player.

AGNEW, PETE. Scotland, 9/14/46. Bassist, singer. Nazareth.

AGUTTER, JENNY. Taunton, England, 12/20/52. Actor. *Logan's Run.*

AIELLO, DANNY. New York, NY, 6/20/33. Actor, writer. *Moonstruck.*

AIKMAN, TROY KENNETH. Cerritos, CA, 11/21/66. Football player. Quarterback for the Dallas Cowboys.

AIMEE, ANOUK (Françoise Soyra Dreyfus). Paris, France, 4/27/32. Actor. *A Man and a Woman.*

AKERS, KAREN. New York, NY, 10/13/45. Cabaret singer.

ALBERT, EDDIE (Eddie Albert Heimberger). Rock Island, IL, 4/22/08. Actor, father of Edward. Oliver Wendell Douglas on *Green Acres.*

ALBERT, EDWARD. Los Angeles, CA, 2/20/51. Actor, son of Eddie. *Midway.*

ALBERT, MARV. 6/12/41. Sportscaster.

ALBRECHT, BERNIE (Bernard Dicken). Salford, England, 1/4/56. Guitarist. Joy Division; New Order.

ALDA, ALAN (Alphonso D'Abruzzo). New York, NY, 1/28/36. Actor, writer, director, son of Robert Alda. Benjamin Franklin "Hawkeye" Pierce on *M*A*S*H.*

ALDRIN, BUZZ (Edwin Eugene Aldrin Jr.). Montclair, NJ, 1/20/30. Astronaut, businessman.

ALEXANDER, GARY. Chattanooga, TN, 9/25/43. Singer, guitarist. The Association.

ALEXANDER, JANE (Jane Quigley). Boston, MA, 10/28/39. Actor. *All the President's Men.* Head of the National Endowment for the Arts.

ALI, MUHAMMAD (Cassius Clay). Louisville, KY, 1/17/42. Boxing great.

ALLEN, DEBBIE. Houston, TX, 1/16/50. Choreographer, actor, sister of Phylicia Rashad. *Fame.*

ALLEN, DUANE. Taylortown, TX, 4/29/43. Singer. The Oak Ridge Boys.

ALLEN, KAREN. Carrollton, IL, 10/5/51. Actor. *Raiders of the Lost Ark.*

ALLEN, NANCY. New York, NY, 6/24/50. Actor. *Robocop.*

ALLEN, PAPA DEE (Thomas Allen). Wilmington, DE, 7/18/31. Keyboardist, singer. War.

ALLEN, RICK. Sheffield, England, 11/1/63. One-armed drummer. Def Leppard.

ALLEN, ROD (Rod Bainbridge). Leicester, England, 3/31/44. Bassist, singer. The Fortunes.

ALLEN, STEVE. New York, NY, 12/26/21. Writer, performer, variety show host, husband of Jayne Meadows. *The Steve Allen Show.*

ALLEN, VERDEN. Hereford, England, 5/26/44. Keyboardist. Mott The Hoople.

ALLEY, KIRSTIE. Wichita, KS, 1/12/51. Actor. Formerly married to Parker Stevenson. Rebecca Howe on *Cheers.*

ALLISON, JERRY. Hillsboro, TX, 8/31/39. Drummer. Buddy Holly & The Crickets.

ALLMAN, GREGG. Nashville, TN, 12/8/47. Keyboardist, guitarist, singer, formerly married to Cher. The Allman Brothers Band.

ALLSUP, MIKE. Modesto, CA, 3/8/47. Guitarist. Three Dog Night.

ALLYSON, JUNE (Ella Geisman). Westchester, NY, 10/7/17. Actor. *The Dupont Show Starring June Allyson; Lassie.*

ALMOND, MARC (Peter Almond). Southport, England, 7/9/59. Singer. Soft Cell.

ALONSO, MARIA CONCHITA. Cuba, 6/29/56. Actor. *The Running Man.*

ALPERT, HERB. Los Angeles, CA, 3/31/35. Trumpeter, band leader, cofounder of A&M Records. The Tijuana Brass.

ALSTON, BARBARA. Brooklyn, NY, 1945. Singer. The Crystals.

ALSTON, SHIRLEY (Shirley Owens). Passaic, NJ, 6/10/41. Singer. The Shirelles.

ALT, CAROL. Queens, NY, 8/18/60. Supermodel.

ALTMAN, ROBERT. Kansas City, MO, 2/20/25. Director, writer, producer. *The Player.*

ALVARADO, TRINI. New York, NY, 1/10/67. Actor. *Rich Kids.*

AMIS, SUZY. Oklahoma City, OK, 1/5/61. Actor. *Titanic.*

AMOS, JOHN. Newark, NJ, 12/27/41. Actor. James Evans on *Good Times.*

AMOS, WALLY JR. Tallahassee, FL, 7/1/36. Business executive. Famous Amos chocolate chip cookies.

ANDERSON, ALFA. 9/7/46. Singer. Chic.

ANDERSON, HARRY. Newport, RI, 10/14/52. Actor. Judge Harry Stone on *Night Court.*

ANDERSON, IAN. Edinburgh, Scotland, 8/10/47. Singer, flautist. Jethro Tull.

ANDERSON, JON. Lancashire, England, 10/25/44. Singer, drummer. Yes.

ANDERSON, KEVIN. Illinois, 1/13/60. Actor. *Sleeping with the Enemy.*

ANDERSON, LAURIE. Chicago, IL, 6/5/47. Singer, performance artist.

ANDERSON, LONI. St. Paul, MN, 8/5/45. Actor. Receptionist Jennifer Marlowe on *WKRP in Cincinnati.*

ANDERSON, MELISSA SUE. Berkeley, CA, 9/26/62. Actor. Mary Ingalls Kendall on *Little House on the Prairie.*

ANDERSON, MELODY. Edmonton, Canada, 1/3/55. Actor. Dale Arden in *Flash Gordon.*

ANDERSON, RICHARD. Long Branch, NJ, 8/8/26. Actor. Oscar Goldman on *The Six Million Dollar Man* and *The Bionic Woman.*

ANDERSON, RICHARD DEAN. Minneapolis, MN, 1/23/50. Actor. *MacGyver.*

ANDERSON, RICK. St. Paul, MN, 8/1/47. Bassist. The Tubes.

ANDERSON, TERRY. 10/27/47. Journalist, former hostage.

ANDERSSON, BENNY (Goran Andersson). Stockholm, Sweden, 12/16/46. Keyboards, singer. Abba.

ANDERSSON, BIBI. Stockholm, Sweden, 11/11/35. Actor. *The Seventh Seal.*

ANDES, MARK. Philadelphia, PA, 2/19/48. Bassist. Spirit.

ANDRESS, URSULA. Berne, Switzerland, 3/19/36. Actor. *Dr. No.*

ANDRETTI, MARIO. Montona Trieste, Italy, 2/28/40. Auto racer.

ANDREW, PRINCE. London, England, 2/19/60. British royalty, son of Queen Elizabeth II.

ANDREWS, ANTHONY. London, England, 1/12/48. Actor. *Brideshead Revisited.*

ANDREWS, BARRY. London, England, 9/12/56. Keyboardist. XTC.

ANKA, PAUL. Ottawa, Canada, 7/30/41. Singer, songwriter. "Diana."

ANN-MARGRET (Ann-Margret Olsson). Valsjobyn, Sweden, 4/28/41. Actor, singer. *Viva Las Vegas.*

ANNAUD, JEAN-JACQUES. Draveil, France, 10/1/43. Writer, director. *Quest for Fire; The Lover.*

ANNE, PRINCESS. London, England, 8/15/50. British royalty, daughter of Queen Elizabeth II.

ANSPACH, SUSAN. New York, NY, 11/23/42. Actor. *Five Easy Pieces.*

ANT, ADAM (Stewart Goddard). London, England, 11/3/54. Singer. Adam & The Ants.

ANTHONY, MICHAEL. Chicago, IL, 6/20/55.

Bassist. Van Halen.

ANTON, SUSAN. Oak Glen, CA, 10/12/50. Actor, singer. *Goldengirl.*

ANWAR, GABRIELLE. Laleham, England, 2/4/70. Actor. Tangoed with Al Pacino in *Scent of a Woman.*

APPICE, CARMINE. New York, NY, 12/15/46. Drummer. Vanilla Fudge.

AQUINO, CORAZON. Tarlac, Philippines, 1/25/33. Political leader. Former president of the Philippines.

ARAFAT, YASIR. Cairo, Egypt, 8/24/29. Political leader. Head of the PLO.

ARCHER, ANNE. Los Angeles, CA, 8/25/47. Actor. Wife of Michael Douglas in *Fatal Attraction.*

ARENHOLZ, STEPHEN. The Bronx, NY, 4/29/69. Actor.

ARGENT, ROD. St. Albans, England, 6/14/45. Keyboardist. The Zombies.

ARKIN, ALAN. New York, NY, 3/26/34. Actor, director, writer, folk singer, member of Second City, father of Adam Arkin (*Chicago Hope*). *The In-Laws.*

ARMATRADING, JOAN. Basseterre, West Indies, 12/9/50. Singer, songwriter. "Me, Myself, I."

ARMSTRONG, BESS. Baltimore, MD, 12/11/53. Actor. Julia Peters on *On Our Own.*

ARMSTRONG, BILLIE JOE. Rodeo, CA, 2/17/72, Singer, songwriter, guitarist, Green Day.

ARMSTRONG, NEIL. Wapakoneta, OH, 8/5/30. Astronaut.

ARNAZ, DESI JR. Los Angeles, CA, 1/19/53. Actor, singer, son of Lucille Ball and Desi Arnaz. *Here's Lucy.*

ARNAZ, LUCIE. Los Angeles, CA, 7/17/51. Actor, daughter of Lucille Ball and Desi Arnaz, married to Laurence Luckinbill. *Here's Lucy.*

ARNESS, JAMES (James Aurness). Minneapolis, MN, 5/26/23. Actor, brother of Peter Graves. *Gunsmoke.*

ARNOLD, TOM Ottumwa, IA, 3/6/59. Actor, ex-husband of Roseanne. *Roseanne, True Lies.*

ARQUETTE, PATRICIA. New York, NY, 4/8/68. Actor, granddaughter of Cliff Arquette, sister of Rosanna, David and Alexis. *True Romance.*

ARQUETTE, ROSANNA. New York, NY, 8/10/59. Actor, granddaughter of Cliff Arquette, sister of Patricia, and inspiration for Toto song "Rosanna." *Desperately Seeking Susan.*

ARTHUR, BEATRICE (Bernice Frankel). New York, NY, 5/13/26. Actor. *Maude.*

ASH, DANIEL. 7/31/57. Guitarist, singer. Bauhaus; Love and Rockets.

ASHER, PETER. London, England, 6/22/44. Singer. Peter and Gordon.

ASHFORD, NICKOLAS. Fairfield, SC, 5/4/42. Singer. Ashford and Simpson.

ASHFORD, ROSALIND. Detroit, MI, 9/2/43. Singer. Martha & The Vandellas.

ASHLEY, ELIZABETH (Elizabeth Ann Cole). Ocala, FL, 8/30/39. Actor. *Evening Shade.*

ASNER, EDWARD. Kansas City, KS, 11/15/29. Actor. *Lou Grant.*

ASSANTE, ARMAND. New York, NY, 10/4/49. Actor. *The Doctors.*

ASTBURY, IAN. Heswall, England, 5/14/62. Singer. The Cult.

ASTIN, JOHN. Baltimore, MD, 3/30/30. Actor, formerly married to Patty Duke, father of Sean Astin. Gomez Addams on *The Addams Family.*

ASTIN, SEAN. Santa Monica, CA, 2/25/71. Actor, son of John Astin and Patty Duke. *Encino Man.*

ASTLEY, RICK. Warrington, England, 2/6/66. Singer, songwriter. "Never Gonna Give You Up."

ASTON, JAY. London, England, 5/4/61. Singer. Bucks Fizz.

ASTON, JOHN. England, 11/30/57. Guitarist. Psychedelic Furs.

ATKINS, CHRISTOPHER. Rye, NY, 2/21/61. Actor. *The Blue Lagoon.*

ATKINSON, PAUL. Cuffley, England, 3/19/46. Guitarist. The Zombies.

ATTENBOROUGH, RICHARD. Cambridge, England, 8/29/23. Actor, producer, director. *Gandhi.*

ATWOOD, MARGARET. Ottawa, Canada, 11/18/39. Author, poet. *The Handmaid's Tale.*

AUBERJONOIS, RENE. New York, NY, 6/1/40. Actor. Security Chief Odo on *Deep Space Nine.*

AUERMANN, NADJA. Berlin, Germany, 1971. Supermodel.

AUTRY, ALAN. Shreveport, LA, 7/31/52. Actor. Bubba Skinner on *In the Heat of the Night.*

AVALON, FRANKIE (Francis Thomas Avallone). Philadelphia, PA, 9/18/40. Singer, actor. *Beach Blanket Bingo.*

AVORY, MICK. London, England, 2/15/44. Drummer. The Kinks.

AZARIA, HANK. 4/25/64. Actor. *The Simpsons.*

AZNAVOUR, CHARLES (Shahnour Varenagh Aznourian). Paris, France, 5/22/24. Singer, songwriter, actor. *Shoot the Piano Player.*

BACALL, LAUREN (Betty Perske). New York, NY, 9/16/24. Actor, widow of Humphrey Bogart, formerly married to Jason Robards. *Key Largo.*

BACH, BARBARA. Queens, NY, 8/27/47. Actor, married to Ringo Starr. *The Spy Who Loved Me.*

BACHMAN, RANDY. Winnipeg, Canada, 9/27/43. Guitarist, singer. Bachman-Turner Overdrive; The Guess Who.

BACHMAN, ROBBIE. Winnipeg, Canada, 2/18/53. Drummer. Bachman-Turner Overdrive.

BADANJEK, JOHN. 1948. Drummer. Mitch Ryder & The Detroit Wheels.

BAEZ, JOAN. Staten Island, NY, 1/9/41. Folk singer and songwriter, peace and civil rights activist.

BAILEY, PHILIP. Denver, CO, 5/8/51. Singer, conga player, percussionist. Earth, Wind & Fire.

BAILEY, TOM. Halifax, England, 6/18/57. Singer, keyboardist. Thompson Twins.

BAIN, BARBARA. Chicago, IL, 9/13/31. Actor. *Mission: Impossible.*

BAIO, SCOTT. Brooklyn, NY, 9/22/61. Actor. Charles "Chachi" Arcola on *Happy Days.*

BAIUL, OKSANA. 11/16/77. Figure skater. Olympic Gold Medalist.

BAKER, ANITA. Detroit, MI, 12/20/57. R&B singer.

BAKER, CARROLL. Johnstown, PA, 5/28/31. Actor. *Kindergarten Cop.*

BAKER, CHERYL (Rita Crudgington). London, England, 3/8/54. Singer. Bucks Fizz.

BAKER, GINGER (Peter Baker). Lewisham, England, 8/19/40. Drummer. Cream; Blind Faith.

BAKER, JOE DON. Groesbeck, TX, 2/12/36. Actor. *Walking Tall.*

BAKER, KATHY. Midland, TX, 6/8/50. Actor. *Picket Fences.*

BAKER, MICKEY (McHouston Baker). Louisville, KY, 10/15/25. Singer. Mickey & Sylvia.

BAKKER, JIM. Muskegon, MI, 1/2/40. TV evangelist, participant in the PTL scandal.

BAKSHI, RALPH. Haifa, Palestine, 10/29/38. Animator, writer, director. *Fritz the Cat.*

BAKULA, SCOTT. St. Louis, MO, 10/9/55. Actor. *Quantum Leap.*

BALABAN, BOB. Chicago, IL, 8/16/45. Actor. *Midnight Cowboy, Little Man Tate.*

BALDWIN, ADAM. Chicago, IL, 2/27/62. Actor. *My Bodyguard.*

BALDWIN, DANIEL.. Massapequa, NY, 10/5/60. Actor. *Homicide.*

BALDWIN, STEPHEN. Massapequa, NY, 5/12/66. Actor. *Threesome.*

BALDWIN, WILLIAM. Massapequa, NY, 2/21/63. Actor, married to Chynna Phillips. *Backdraft.*

BALIN, MARTY (Martyn Jerel Buchwald). Cincinnati, OH, 1/30/43. Singer. Jefferson Airplane/Starship.

BALL, DAVID. Blackpool, England, 5/3/59. Keyboardist. Soft Cell.

BALL, ROGER. Dundee, Scotland, 6/4/44. Alto and baritone saxophonist. Average White Band.

BALLARD, HANK. Detroit, MI, 11/18/36. Singer/songwriter. "Work with Me Annie."

BALLARD, KAYE (Catherine Gloria Balotta). Cleveland, OH, 11/20/26. Actor, singer.

BALSLEY, PHILIP. 8/8/39. Singer. Kingsmen; Statler Brothers.

BAMBAATAA, AFRIKA. The Bronx, NY, 1958. Rap/hip-hop DJ.

BAN BREATHNACH, SARAH. 5/5/47. Author. *Simple Abundance.*

BANALI, FRANKIE. 11/14/55. Musician. Quiet Riot.

BANANA (Lowell Levinger). Cambridge, MA, 1946. Keyboardist, guitarist. The Youngbloods.

BANCROFT, ANNE (Anna Maria Italiano). The Bronx, NY, 9/17/31. Actor. Mrs. Robinson in *The Graduate.*

BANKS, TONY. East Heathly, England, 3/27/51. Keyboardist. Genesis.

BARANSKI, CHRISTINE Buffalo, NY, 5/2/52. Actor. *Cybill.*

BARBATA, JOHN. 4/1/45. Drummer. The Turtles; Jefferson Starship.

BARBEAU, ADRIENNE. Sacramento, CA, 6/11/45. Actor. Carol on *Maude.*

BARBIERI, RICHARD. 11/30/57. Keyboardist. Japan.

BARDOT, BRIGITTE (Camille Javal). Paris, France, 9/28/34. Sex goddess. *And God Created Woman.*

BARGERON, DAVE. Massachusetts, 9/6/42. Trombonist. Blood, Sweat and Tears.

BARKER, BOB. Darrington, WA, 12/12/23. Game show host. *The Price Is Right.*

BARKER, CLIVE. Liverpool, England, 10/5/52. Author. *The Inhuman Condition.*

BARKIN, ELLEN. The Bronx, NY, 4/16/54. Actor. Separated from Gabriel Byrne. *Sea of Love.*

BARNES, LEO. 10/5/55. Musician. Hothouse Flowers.

BARRE, MARTIN. 11/17/46. Guitarist. Jethro Tull.

BARRERE, PAUL. Burbank, CA, 7/3/48. Lead guitarist. Little Feat.

BARRETT, ASTON. Kingston, Jamaica, 11/22/46. Bassist. Bob Marley & The Wailers.

BARRETT, MARCIA. St. Catherine's, Jamaica, 10/14/48. Singer. Boney M.

BARRETT, RONA. New York, NY, 10/8/36. News correspondent, columnist.

BARRETT, SYD (Roger Barrett). Cambridge, England, 1/6/46. Singer, guitarist. Pink Floyd.

BARRY, DAVE. 7/3/47. Columnist, author. *Dave's World.*

BARRY, MARION. Itta Bena, MS, 3/6/36. Mayor of Washington, served six-month prison term for cocaine possession.

BARRYMORE, JOHN DREW. Beverly Hills, CA, 6/4/32. Actor, father of Drew Barrymore.

BARSON, MIKE. England, 5/21/58. Keyboardist. Madness.

BARTHOL, BRUCE. Berkeley, CA, 1947. Bassist. Country Joe & The Fish.

BARYSHNIKOV, MIKHAIL. Riga, Latvia, 1/28/48. Dancer, actor. *White Nights.*

BATEMAN, JASON. Rye, NY, 1/14/69. Actor, brother of Justine. David on *The Hogan Family.*

BATEMAN, JUSTINE. Rye, NY, 2/19/66. Actor, sister of Jason. Mallory Keaton on *Family Ties.*

BATES, ALAN. Allestree, England, 2/17/34. Actor. *An Unmarried Woman.*

BATTLE, KATHLEEN. Portsmouth, OH, 8/13/48. Opera singer.

BAUER, JOE. Memphis, TN, 9/26/41. Drummer. The Youngbloods.

BAUER, STEVEN (Steven Echevarria). Havana, Cuba, 12/2/56. Actor, formerly married to Melanie Griffith. *Wiseguy.*

BAUMGARTNER, STEVE. Philadelphia, PA, 10/28/67. Writer. *The Rogue Element.*

BAXTER, JEFF "SKUNK." Washington, DC, 12/13/48. Lead Guitarist. Steely Dan; The Doobie Brothers.

BAXTER, KEITH. Monmouthshire, Wales, 4/29/33. Actor.

BAXTER, MEREDITH. Los Angeles, CA, 6/21/47. Actor, formerly married to David Birney. Elyse Keaton on *Family Ties.*

BAY, WILLOW. 12/28/63. Model, television journalist.

BEACHAM, STEPHANIE. Hertfordshire, England, 2/28/47. Actor. Sable Scott Colby on *The Colbys.*

BEAKY (John Dymond). Salisbury, England, 7/10/44. Guitarist. Dave Dee, Dozy, Beaky, Mick and Tich.

BEALS, JENNIFER. Chicago, IL, 12/19/63. Actor. *Flashdance.*

BEARD, FRANK. Dallas, TX, 12/10/49. Drummer. ZZ Top.

BEASLEY, ALLYCE. Brooklyn, NY, 7/6/54. Actor. Agnes Dipesto on *Moonlighting.*

BEATRICE, PRINCESS. London, England, 8/8/88. British royalty, daughter of Prince Andrew and the Duchess of York.

BEATTY, NED. Lexington, KY, 7/6/37. Actor. *Deliverance.*

BECK, JEFF. Wallington, England, 6/24/44. Guitarist. The Yardbirds; The Jeff Beck Group; The Jan Hammer Group.

BECK, JOHN. Chicago, IL, 1/28/43. Actor. Mark Graison on *Dallas.*

BECK, MICHAEL. Memphis, TN, 2/4/49. Actor. *The Warriors.*

BECKER, BORIS. Liemen, Germany, 11/22/67. Tennis player.

BECKER, WALTER. New York, NY, 2/20/50. Bassist. Steely Dan.

BECKLEY, GERRY. Texas, 9/12/52. Singer, guitarist. America.

BEDELIA, BONNIE. New York, NY, 3/25/48. Actor. *Presumed Innocent.*

BEDFORD, MARK. London, England, 8/24/61. Bassist. Madness.

BEEFHEART, CAPTAIN (Don Van Vliet). Glendale, CA,

1/15/41. Singer, high school friend of Frank Zappa. Captain Beefheart & The Magic Band.

BEERS, GARY. 6/22/57. Bassist, singer. INXS

BEGLEY, ED JR. Los Angeles, CA, 9/16/49. Actor. Dr. Victor Ehrlich on *St. Elsewhere.*

BEL GEDDES, BARBARA New York, NY, 10/31/22. Actor. *Dallas.*

BELAFONTE, HARRY. New York, NY, 3/1/27. Actor, singer, father of Shari. "The Banana Boat Song."

BELAFONTE, SHARI. New York, NY, 9/22/54. Actor, daughter of Harry. *Hotel.*

BELL, ANDY. Peterborough, England, 4/25/64. Singer. Erasure.

BELL, RICKY. Boston, MA, 9/18/67. Singer. New Edition.

BELL, ROBERT. Youngstown, OH, 10/8/50. Bassist. Kool & The Gang.

BELL, RONALD. Youngstown, OH, 11/1/51. Saxophonist. Kool & The Gang.

BELLADONNA, JOEY. Oswego, NY. Singer. Anthrax.

BELLAMY, GEORGE. Sunderland, England, 10/8/41. Guitarist. The Tornados.

BELLAMY, TONY. Los Angeles, CA, 9/12/40. Singer, guitarist. Redbone.

BELLO, FRANK. 7/9/65. Bassist. Anthrax.

BELMONDO, JEAN-PAUL. Paris, France, 4/9/33. Actor. *Breathless.*

BELUSHI, JIM. Chicago, IL, 6/15/54. Actor, brother of late John Belushi. *K-9.*

BENATAR, PAT (Pat Andrzejewski). Brooklyn, NY, 1/10/53. Singer. "Heartbreaker."

BENBEN, BRIAN. Newburgh, NY. Actor. Dream On. Married to Madeline Stowe.

BENEDICT, DIRK (Dirk Niewoehner). Helena, MT, 3/1/45. Actor. Lt. Templeton

Peck on *The A-Team.*

BENJAMIN, RICHARD. New York, NY, 5/22/38. Actor, director. *Love at First Bite; Goodbye, Columbus.*

BENNETT, BRIAN. London, England, 2/9/40. Drummer. The Shadows.

BENNETT, ESTELLE. New York, NY, 7/22/44. Singer. The Ronettes.

BENNETT, PATRICIA. New York, NY, 4/7/47. Singer. The Chiffons.

BENSON, GEORGE. Pittsburgh, PA, 3/22/43. Singer, guitarist. "Give Me the Night."

BENSON, RENALDO. Detroit, MI, 1947. Singer. The Four Tops.

BENSON, ROBBY (Robby Segal). Dallas, TX, 1/21/56. Actor, writer, director. *Ice Castles.*

BERENDT, JOHN. 12/5/39. Author. *Midnight in the Garden of Good and Evil.*

BERENGER, TOM. Chicago, IL, 5/31/49. Actor. *Platoon.*

BERENSON, MARISA. New York, NY, 2/15/47. Actor. *Barry Lyndon.*

BERGEN, POLLY (Nellie Paulina Burgin). Knoxville, TN, 7/14/30. Singer, actor. *The Winds of War.*

BERGER, ALAN. 11/8/49. Bassist. Southside Johnny & The Asbury Jukes.

BERGMAN, INGMAR. Uppsala, Sweden, 7/14/18. Writer, director. *The Silence.*

BERKLEY, ELIZABETH. 7/28/72. Actor. *Showgirls.*

BERKOWITZ, DAVID. New York, NY, 6/1/53. Serial killer. Son of Sam.

BERLE, MILTON (Milton Berlinger). New York, NY, 7/12/08. Actor. *The Milton Berle Show.*

BERNHARD, SANDRA. Flint, MI, 6/6/55. Actor, singer. *Roseanne.*

BERNSEN, CORBIN. Los Angeles, CA, 9/7/54. Actor, married to Amanda Pays.

Arnie Becker on *L.A. Law.*

BERRI, CLAUDE (Claude Langmann). Paris, France, 7/1/34. Actor, director, producer of films.

BERRY, BILL. Hibbing, MN, 7/31/58. Drummer. R.E.M.

BERRY, CHUCK. San Jose, CA, 10/18/26. Rock and Roll legend, singer and guitarist. "Johnny B. Goode."

BERRY, JAN. Los Angeles, CA, 4/3/41. Singer. Jan & Dean.

BERTINELLI, VALERIE. Wilmington, DE, 4/23/60. Actor, married to Eddie Van Halen. Barbara Cooper Royer on *One Day at a Time.*

BETTS, DICKEY. West Palm Beach, FL, 12/12/43. Guitarist, singer. The Allman Brothers Band.

BIALIK, MAYIM. San Diego, CA, 12/12/75. Actor. *Blossom.*

BIEHN, MICHAEL. Anniston, AL, 7/31/56. Actor. *The Terminator.*

BIG FIGURE, THE (John Martin). 1947. Drummer. Dr. Feelgood.

BILLINGSLEY, BARBARA. Los Angeles, CA, 12/22/22. Actor. June Cleaver on *Leave It to Beaver.*

BILLINGSLEY, PETER. New York, NY, 1972. Child actor. *A Christmas Story.*

BILLINGSLEY, RAY. Wake Forest, NC, 7/25/57. Cartoonist. *Curtis.*

BIRD, LARRY. West Baden, IN, 12/7/56. Basketball great. Boston Celtics.

BIRNEY, DAVID. Washington, DC, 4/23/39. Actor, formerly married to Meredith Baxter. *St. Elsewhere.*

BIRRELL, PETE. Manchester, England, 5/9/41. Bassist. Freddie & The Dreamers.

BIRTLES, BEEB (Gerard Birtlekamp). Amsterdam, the Netherlands, 11/28/48. Guitarist. The Little River Band.

BISHOP, JOEY (Joseph Gotlieb). The Bronx, NY, 2/3/18. Actor. *The Joey Bishop Show.*

BISSET, JACQUELINE. Waybridge, England, 9/13/44. Actor. *The Deep.*

BISSET, JOSIE. Seattle, WA, 10/5/70. Actor. *Melrose Place.*

BIVINS, MICHAEL. 8/10/68. Singer. New Edition, Bell Biv DeVoe.

BLACK, CILLA (Cilla White). Liverpool, England, 5/27/43. Singer, TV personality.

BLACK, JET (Brian Duffy). England, 8/26/58. Drummer. The Stranglers.

BLACK, KAREN (Karen Ziegler). Park Ridge, IL, 7/1/42. Actor. *Easy Rider.*

BLACK, LISA HARTMAN. 6/1/56. Actor, married to Clint Black. *Knot's Landing.*

BLACKMON, LARRY. New York, 5/29/56. Singer, drummer. Cameo.

BLACKMORE, RITCHIE. Weston-Super-Mare, England, 4/14/45. Guitarist. Deep Purple; Rainbow.

BLADD, STEPHEN JO. Boston, MA, 7/13/42. Drummer, singer. The J. Geils Band.

BLADES, RUBEN. Panama City, Panama, 7/16/48. Actor, singer. *The Milagro Beanfield War.*

BLAIR, BONNIE. Cornwall, NY, 3/18/64. Speed skater.

BLAIR, LINDA. Westport, CT, 1/22/59. Actor. *The Exorcist.*

BLAKE, ROBERT (Michael Gubitosi). Nutley, NJ, 9/18/33. Actor. *Baretta.*

BLAKELY, SUSAN. Frankfurt, Germany, 9/7/50. Actor. *Rich Man, Poor Man.*

BLAKLEY, ALAN. Bromley, England, 4/1/42. Guitarist. Brian Poole & The Tremeloes.

BLAND, BOBBY. Rosemark, TN, 1/27/30. Singer.

BLASS, BILL. Ft. Wayne, IN, 6/22/22. Fashion designer.

BLEDSOE, TEMPESTT. Chicago, IL, 8/1/73. Actor. Vanessa Huxtable on *The Cosby Show.*

BLEETH, YASMINE. 6/14/68. Actor. *Baywatch.*

BLOOM, CLAIRE. London, England, 2/15/31. Actor. *Richard III.*

BLOOM, ERIC. Long Island, NY, 12/1/44. Lead guitarist, keyboardist. Blue Öyster Cult.

BLOW, KURTIS (Kurtis Walker). New York, NY, 8/9/59. DJ, rapper. "The Breaks."

BLUECHEL, TED JR. San Pedro, CA, 12/2/42. Singer, drummer. The Association.

BLUME, JUDY. Elizabeth, NJ, 2/12/38. Novelist. *Are You There God? It's Me Margaret.*

BLUNSTONE, COLIN. Hatfield, England, 6/24/45. Singer. The Zombies.

BOBBY G. (Bobby Gubby). London, England, 8/23/53. Singer. Bucks Fizz.

BOGERT, TIM. Richfield, NJ, 8/27/44. Bassist. Vanilla Fudge.

BOGLE, BOB. Portland, OR, 1/16/37. Guitarist, bassist. The Ventures.

BOGOSIAN, ERIC. Woburn, MA, 4/24/53. Actor, writer. *Talk Radio.*

BOLDER, TREVOR. 6/9/50. Bassist. Spiders from Mars; Uriah Heep.

BOLOGNA, JOSEPH. Brooklyn, NY, 12/30/34. Actor. *Chapter Two.*

BONADUCE, DANNY. 8/13/59. Actor, radio personality. Danny on *The Partridge Family.*

BOND, RONNIE (Ronnie Bullis). Andover, England, 5/4/43. Drummer. The Troggs.

BONDS, GARY (Gary Anderson). Jacksonville, FL, 6/6/39. Singer.

BONET, LISA. San Francisco, CA, 11/16/67. Actor, for-

merly formerly married to Lenny Kravitz. Denise Huxtable on *The Cosby Show.*

BONNER, FRANK. Little Rock, AR, 2/28/42. Actor. Herb Tarlek on *WKRP in Cincinnati.*

BONO, CHASTITY. Los Angeles, CA, 3/4/69. Daughter of Sonny and Cher.

BONSALL, BRIAN. 12/3/82. Child actor. *Family Ties.*

BONSALL, JOE. Philadelphia, PA, 5/18/48. Singer. The Oak Ridge Boys.

BOONE, PAT. Jacksonville, FL, 6/1/34. Singer, actor. *The Pat Boone Show.*

BOONE, STEVE. North Carolina, 9/23/43. Bassist, singer. The Lovin' Spoonful.

BOOTHE, POWERS. Snyder, TX, 6/1/49. Actor. *Guyana Tragedy: The Story of Jim Jones.*

BORGNINE, ERNEST (Ernest Borgnino). Hamden, CT, 1/24/17. Actor. *McHale's Navy.*

BOSSON, BARBARA. Charleroi, PA, 11/1/39. Actor, formerly married to producer Steven Bochco. Fay Furillo on *Hill Street Blues.*

BOSTWICK, BARRY. San Mateo, CA, 2/24/45. Actor. *The Rocky Horror Picture Show.*

BOTTOMS, JOSEPH. Santa Barbara, CA, 4/22/54. Actor. *The Black Hole.*

BOTTOMS, SAM. Santa Barbara, CA, 10/17/55. Actor. *Apocalypse Now.*

BOTTOMS, TIMOTHY. Santa Barbara, CA, 8/30/51. Actor. *Johnny Got His Gun.*

BOTTUM, RODDY. Los Angeles, CA, 7/1/63. Keyboardist. Faith No More.

BOUCHARD, JOE. Long Island, NY, 11/9/48. Bassist, singer. Blue Öyster Cult.

BOWE, RIDDICK. New York, NY, 8/10/67. Boxer, former

heavyweight champion of the world.

BOWERS, TONY. 10/31/56. Bassist. Simply Red.

BOX, MICK. London, England, 6/8/47. Guitarist, songwriter. Uriah Heep.

BOXLEITNER, BRUCE. Elgin, IL, 5/12/50. Actor, married to Melissa Gilbert. *Scarecrow and Mrs. King.*

BOY GEORGE (George O'Dowd). Eltham, England, 6/14/61. Singer. Culture Club.

BOYLE, LARA FLYNN. Davenport, IA, 3/24/70. Actor. *Twin Peaks.*

BOYLE, PETER. Philadelphia, PA, 10/18/33. Actor. *Young Frankenstein.*

BRACCO, LORRAINE. Brooklyn, NY, 10/2/54. Actor. *GoodFellas.*

BRADBURY, RAY. Waukegan, IL, 8/22/20. Novelist. *The Martian Chronicles.*

BRAGG, BILLY (Steven Bragg). Barking, England, 12/20/57. Punk/R&B singer, songwriter.

BRAID, LES (William Braid). Liverpool, England, 9/15/41. Bassist. The Swinging Blue Jeans.

BRAMLETT, BONNIE. Acton, IL, 11/8/44. Singer. Delaney & Bonnie.

BRAMLETT, DELANEY. Pontotoc County, MS, 7/1/39. Guitarist, singer. Delaney & Bonnie.

BRANDAUER, KLAUS MARIA. Altaussee, Austria, 6/22/44. Actor. *Out of Africa.*

BRATTON, CREED. Sacramento, CA, 2/8/43. Guitarist. The Grass Roots.

BRAUNN, ERIK. Boston, MA, 8/11/50. Guitarist, singer. Iron Butterfly.

BREATHED, BERKE. Encino, CA, 6/21/57. Cartoonist. *Bloom County.*

BRENNAN, EILEEN. Los Angeles, CA, 9/3/34. Actor. *Private Benjamin.*

BRENNER, DAVID. Philadelphia, PA, 2/4/45. Stand-up comedian. *Nightlife.*

BREWER, DONALD. Flint, MI, 9/3/48. Drummer. Grand Funk Railroad.

BRICKELL, EDIE. Oak Cliff, TX, 1966. Singer, songwriter, married to Paul Simon. Edie Brickell and New Bohemians.

BRIDGES, BEAU (Lloyd Vernet Bridges III). Los Angeles, CA, 12/9/41. Actor, director, brother of Jeff. *The Fabulous Baker Boys.*

BRIDGES, TODD. San Francisco, CA, 5/27/65. Actor. Willis Jackson on *Diff'rent Strokes.*

BRIGATI, EDDIE. Garfield, NJ, 10/22/46. Singer, percussionist. The (Young) Rascals.

BRIGGS, DAVID. Melbourne, Australia, 1/26/51. Guitarist. The Little River Band.

BRILEY, ALEX. 4/12/56. Singer. The Village People.

BRIMLEY, WILFORD. Salt Lake City, UT, 9/27/34. Actor. *Cocoon.*

BRINKLEY, DAVID. Wilmington, NC, 7/10/20. Pioneer news journalist and anchor. *This Week with David Brinkley.*

BRIQUETTE, PETE (Patrick Cusack). Ireland, 7/2/54. Bassist, singer. The Boomtown Rats.

BRITTANY, MORGAN (Suzanne Cupito). Los Angeles, CA, 12/5/51. Actor. Katherine Wentworth on *Dallas.*

BRITTON, CHRIS. Watford, England, 6/21/45. Guitarist. The Troggs.

BROLIN, JAMES (James Bruderlin). Los Angeles, CA, 7/18/40. Actor, father of Josh. Dr. Steven Kiley on *Marcus Welby, M.D.*

BRONSON, CHARLES (Charles Buchinsky). Ehrenfield, PA, 11/3/21. Actor,

widower of Jill Ireland. *Death Wish.*

BROOKER, GARY. Southend, England, 5/29/45. Singer, keyboardist. Procol Harum.

BROOKS, ALBERT (Albert Einstein). Los Angeles, CA, 7/22/47. Actor, writer, director. *Defending Your Life.*

BROOKS, LALA. Brooklyn, NY, 1946. Singer. The Crystals.

BROTHERS, JOYCE (Joyce Bauer). New York, NY, 10/20/27. Psychologist.

BROWN, BLAIR. Washington, DC, 1948. Actor. *The Days and Nights of Molly Dodd.*

BROWN, BOBBY. Boston, MA, 2/5/69. Singer, dancer. "My Perogative."

BROWN, BRYAN. Panania, Australia, 6/23/47. Actor, married to Rachel Ward. *FX.*

BROWN, DAVID. Houston, TX, 2/15/47. Bassist. Santana.

BROWN, ERROL. Kingston, Jamaica, 11/12/48. Singer. Hot Chocolate.

BROWN, GEORG STANFORD. Havana, Cuba, 6/24/43. Actor. *Colossus: The Forbin Project.*

BROWN, GEORGE. Jersey City, NJ, 1/5/49. Drummer. Kool and The Gang.

BROWN, HAROLD. Long Beach, CA, 3/17/46. Drummer. War.

BROWN, IAN. Sale, England, 2/20/63. Singer. Stone Roses.

BROWN, JAMES. Augusta, GA, 5/3/33. The Godfather of Soul.

BROWN, JIM. St. Simons Island, GA, 2/17/36. Football player, actor. *The Dirty Dozen.*

BROWN, JIMMY. Birmingham, England, 11/20/57. Drummer. UB40.

BROWN, MELANIE. 5/29/75. Singer. Scary Spice of the Spice Girls.

BROWN, MICHAEL (Michael Lookofsky). New York, NY, 4/25/49. Keyboardist. The Left Banke.

BROWNE, JACKSON. Heidelberg, Germany, 10/9/48. Singer, songwriter.

BRUCE, JACK. Glasgow, Scotland, 5/14/43. Singer, bassist. Cream.

BRUCE, MICHAEL. 3/16/48. Guitarist, keyboardist. Alice Cooper.

BRUFORD, BILL. London, England, 5/17/48. Drummer. Yes.

BRYAN, DAVID (David Rashbaum). New Jersey, 2/7/62. Keyboardist. Bon Jovi.

BRYON, DENNIS. Cardiff, Wales, 4/14/49. Drummer. Amen Corner.

BRYSON, PEABO (Robert Peabo Bryson), Greenville, SC, 4/13/51, Singer.

BRZEZICKI, MARK. Slough, England, 6/21/57. Drummer. Big Country.

BUCHANAN, PAUL. Scotland. Singer, synthesizer player. Blue Nile.

BUCHHOLZ, FRANCIS. 2/19/50. Guitarist. Scorpions.

BUCK, PETER. Athens, GA, 12/6/56. Guitarist. R.E.M.

BUCK, ROBERT. Guitarist. 10,000 Maniacs.

BUCKINGHAM, LINDSEY. Palo Alto, CA, 10/3/47. Guitarist, singer. Fleetwood Mac.

BUCKLER, RICK (Paul Buckler). 12/6/56. Drummer, singer. The Jam.

BUCKLEY, BETTY. Big Spring, TX, 7/3/47. Actor. *Eight Is Enough.*

BUJOLD, GENEVIEVE. Montreal, Canada, 7/1/42. Actor. *Dead Ringers.*

BUNKER, CLIVE. Blackpool, England, 12/12/46. Drummer. Jethro Tull.

BUNNELL, DEWEY. Yorkshire, England, 1/19/51. Singer, guitarist. America.

BUNTON, EMMA. 1/21/76. Singer. Baby Spice of the Spice Girls.

BURCHILL, CHARLIE. Glasgow, Scotland, 11/27/59. Guitarist. Simple Minds.

BURDEN, IAN. 12/24/57. Synthesizer player. Human League.

BURDON, ERIC. Walker-on-Tyne, England, 5/11/41. Singer, songwriter. The Animals; War.

BURGHOFF, GARY. Bristol, CT, 5/24/43. Actor. Radar O'Reilly on *M*A*S*H*.

BURKE, DELTA. Orlando, FL, 7/30/56. Actor, married to Gerald McRaney. *Designing Women*.

BURKE, SOLOMON. Philadelphia, PA, 1936. Country-gospel-R&B singer, songwriter.

BURNEL, JEAN-JACQUES. London, England, 2/21/52. Bassist. The Stranglers.

BURNETT, CAROL. San Antonio, TX, 4/26/33. Actor. *The Carol Burnett Show*.

BURNS, BOB. Drummer. Lynyrd Skynyrd.

BURR, CLIVE. 3/8/57. Drummer. Iron Maiden.

BURRELL, BOZ (Raymond Burrell). Lincoln, England, 1946. Bassist. Bad Company.

BURROWS, DARREN E. Winfield, KS, 9/12/66. Actor. Ed Chigliak on *Northern Exposure*.

BURT, HEINZ. Hargin, Germany, 7/24/42. Bassist. The Tornados.

BURTON, LEVAR. Landstuhl, Germany, 2/16/57. Actor. Geordi LaForge on *Star Trek: The Next Generation*.

BURTON, TIM. 8/25/58. Director. *Edward Scissorhands*.

BURTON, TREVOR. Aston, England, 3/9/44. Lead guitarist. The Move.

BUSEY, GARY. Goose Creek, TX, 6/29/44. Actor. *The Buddy Holly Story*.

BUSFIELD, TIMOTHY. Lansing, MI, 6/12/57, Actor, *thirtysomething*.

BUSH, BARBARA. Rye, NY, 6/8/25. Former First Lady, married to George Bush.

BUSH, GEORGE. Milton, MA, 6/12/24. Political leader, husband of Barbara. Forty-first president of the U.S.

BUSH, KATE. Bexleyheath, England, 7/30/58. Singer, songwriter.

BUSHY, RONALD. Washington, DC, 9/23/45. Drummer. Iron Butterfly.

BUTKUS, DICK. Chicago, IL, 12/9/42. Football player, actor. *My Two Dads*.

BUTLER, GEEZER (Terry Butler). Birmingham, England, 7/17/49. Bassist. Black Sabbath.

BUTLER, JERRY. Sunflower, MS, 12/8/39. Singer. The Impressions.

BUTLER, BRETT Montgomery, AL, 1/30/58. Actor, comedian. *Grace Under Fire*.

BUTLER, JOE. Glen Cove, NY, 9/16/43. Drummer, singer. The Lovin' Spoonful.

BUTLER, RICHARD. Surrey, England, 6/5/56. Singer, lyricist. Psychedelic Furs.

BUTLER, TONY. Ealing, England, 2/13/57. Bassist. Big Country.

BUTTAFUOCO, JOEY. Massapequa, NY. 3/11/56. Mechanic. Had affair with Amy Fisher.

BUXTON, GLEN. Akron, OH, 11/10/47. Guitarist. Alice Cooper.

BUZZI, RUTH. Westerly, RI, 7/24/36. Actor. *Laugh-In*.

BYRNE, DAVID. Dumbarton, Scotland, 5/14/52, Singer, songwriter, director, Talking Heads.

BYRON, DAVID. Essex, England, 1/29/47. Singer. Uriah Heep.

CAAN, JAMES. The Bronx, NY, 3/26/40. Actor. *The Godfather*.

CADDY, ALAN. London, England, 2/2/40. Guitarist. The Tornados; Johnny Kidd & The Pirates.

CAFFEY, CHARLOTTE. Santa Monica, CA, 10/21/53. Singer. The Go-Gos.

CAIN, DEAN Mt. Clemens, MI, 7/31/66. Actor. *Lois & Clark: The New Adventures of Superman*.

CAIN, JONATHAN. Chicago, IL, 2/26/50. Keyboardist. Journey.

CALABRO, THOMAS. 2/3/59. Actor. Michael Mancini on *Melrose Place*.

CALE, JOHN. Garnant, Wales, 3/9/42. Bassist, keyboardist, violist, singer. The Velvet Underground.

CALIFORNIA, RANDY (Randy Wolfe). Los Angeles, CA, 2/20/51. Guitarist, singer. Spirit.

CALLOW, SIMON. London, England, 6/15/49. Actor. *A Room with a View*.

CALVERT, BERNIE. Burnley, England, 9/16/43. Bassist. The Hollies.

CAMERON, KIRK. Panorama City, CA, 10/12/70. Actor, brother of Candace. Mike Seaver on *Growing Pains*.

CAMP, COLLEEN. San Francisco, CA, 1953. Actor. Kristin Shepard on *Dallas*.

CAMPBELL, ALI (Alastair Campbell). Birmingham, England, 2/15/59. Lead singer, guitarist. UB40.

CAMPBELL, BRUCE. Royal Oak, MI, 6/22/58. Actor, producer, screenwriter. *The Adventures of Briscoe County Jr.*

CAMPBELL, GLEN. Delight, AR, 4/22/36. Actor, singer. *The Glen Campbell Goodtime Hour.*

CAMPBELL, MIKE. Panama City, FL, 2/1/54. Guitarist. Tom Petty & The Heartbreakers.

CAMPBELL, ROBIN. Birmingham, England, 12/25/54. Lead guitarist, singer. UB40.

CAMPBELL, TISHA. Oklahoma City, OK, 10/13/70. Actor. *Martin*.

CAMPION, JANE. Wellington, New Zealand, 4/30/54. Director, screenwriter, daughter of Richard and Edith. *The Piano*.

CANN, WARREN. Victoria, Canada, 5/20/52. Drummer. Ultravox.

CANNON, DYAN (Samille Diane Friesen). Tacoma, WA, 1/4/39. Actor. *Bob & Carol & Ted & Alice*.

CAPALDI, JIM. Evesham, England, 8/24/44. Drummer, singer. Traffic.

CAPRIATI, JENNIFER. Long Island, NY, 3/29/76. Tennis player

CAPSHAW, KATE (Kathleen Sue Nail). Ft. Worth, TX, 11/3/53. Actor, married to Steven Spielberg. *Indiana Jones and the Temple of Doom.*

CARA, IRENE. New York, NY, 3/18/59. Actor, singer. *Fame*.

CARDINALE, CLAUDIA. Tunis, Tunisia, 4/15/39. Actor. *The Pink Panther*.

CAREY, TONY. 10/16/53. Keyboardist. Rainbow.

CARLIN, GEORGE. New York, NY, 5/12/37. Actor. "Seven Dirty Words."

CARLISLE, BELINDA. Hollywood, CA, 8/17/58. Singer, songwriter.

CARLOS, BUN (Brad Carlson). Rockford, IL, 6/12/51. Drummer. Cheap Trick.

CARMEN, ERIC. Cleveland, OH, 8/11/49. Singer. The Raspberries.

CARNE, JUDY (Joyce Botterill). Northampton, England, 3/27/39. Actor. *Laugh-In*.

CARNEY, ART. Mt. Vernon, NY, 11/4/18. Actor and comedian. Ed Norton on *The Honeymooners*.

CAROLINE, PRINCESS. Monte Carlo, Monaco, 1/23/57. Daughter of Princess Grace of Monaco.

CARON, LESLIE. Paris, France, 7/1/31. Actor. *Lili.*

CARPENTER, JOHN. Carthage, NY, 1/16/48. Director, writer. *Halloween.*

CARPENTER, RICHARD. New Haven, CT, 10/15/46. Keyboardist, singer. The Carpenters.

CARR, DAVID. Leyton, England, 8/4/43. Keyboardist. The Fortunes.

CARRACK, PAUL. Sheffield, England, 4/21/51. Singer, songwriter. Squeeze; Ace; Mike and the Mechanics.

CARRADINE, DAVID. Hollywood, CA, 12/8/36. Actor, son of John Carradine, brother of Keith and Robert. *Kung Fu.*

CARRADINE, KEITH. San Mateo, CA, 8/8/49. Actor, son of John, brother of David and Robert, father of Martha Plimpton. *The Will Rogers Follies.*

CARRADINE, ROBERT. Hollywood, CA, 3/24/54. Actor, son of John, brother of David and Keith. *Revenge of the Nerds.*

CARRERA, BARBARA. Managua, Nicaragua, 12/31/47. Model, actor. *Dallas.*

CARROLL, DIAHANN (Carol Diahann Johnson). New York, NY, 7/17/35. Actor, singer, married to Vic Damone. *I Know Why the Caged Bird Sings.*

CARRY, JULIUS. Actor. Mitchell Baldwin on *Murphy Brown.*

CARTER, DIXIE. McLemoresville, TN, 5/25/39. Actor. Julia Sugarbaker on *Designing Women.*

CARTER, JIMMY. Plains, GA, 10/1/24. Political leader. Thirty-ninth president of the U.S.

CARTER, LYNDA. Phoenix, AZ, 7/24/51. Actor. *Wonder Woman.*

CARTER, NELL. Birmingham, AL, 9/13/48. Actor, singer. *Gimme a Break.*

CARTERIS, GABRIELLE. 1/2/61. Actor. Andrea Zuckerman on *Beverly Hills 90210.*

CARTWRIGHT, VERONICA. Bristol, England, 1950. Actor. *Alien.*

CARVEY, DANA. Missoula, MT, 4/2/55. Actor. *Saturday Night Live, Wayne's World.*

CARUSO, DAVID. Queens, NY, 1/17/56, Actor, *NYPD Blue.*

CASADY, JACK. Washington, DC, 4/13/44. Bass guitarist. Jefferson Airplane/Starship.

CASEY, HARRY WAYNE (Harold Casey). Hialeah, FL, 1/31/51. Singer, keyboardist. KC & The Sunshine Band.

CASS, PEGGY (Mary Margaret Cass). Boston, MA, 5/21/24. Actor. Panelist on *To Tell the Truth.*

CASSIDY, DAVID. New York, NY, 4/12/50. Actor, half brother of Shaun, son of Jack, step-son of Shirley Jones. Keith in *The Partridge Family.*

CASSIDY, ED. Chicago, IL, 5/4/31. Drummer. Spirit.

CASSIDY, JOANNA. Camden, NJ, 8/2/44. Actor. Jo Jo White on *Buffalo Bill.*

CASTRO, FIDEL (Fidel Ruz). Mayari, Cuba, 8/13/26. Political leader. President of Cuba.

CATES, PHOEBE. New York, NY, 7/16/63. Actor, married to Kevin Kline. *Fast Times at Ridgemont High.*

CATHERALL, JOANNE. Sheffield, England, 9/18/62. Singer. Human League.

CATTINI, CLEM. 8/28/39. Drummer. Johnny Kidd & The Pirates; Tornados.

CAVALIERE, FELIX. Pelham, NY, 11/29/44. Singer, keyboardist. The (Young) Rascals.

CAVETT, DICK. Gibbon, NE, 11/19/36. Actor, talk show host. *The Dick Cavett Show.*

CEASE, JEFF. Nashville, TN, 6/24/67. Guitarist. The Black Crowes.

CETERA, PETER. Chicago, IL, 9/13/44. Singer, songwriter. Chicago.

CHABERT, LACEY. 9/30/82. Actor. *Party of Five.*

CHADWICK, LES (John Chadwick). Liverpool, England, 5/11/43. Bassist. Gerry & The Pacemakers.

CHAMBERLAIN, RICHARD (George Chamberlain). Los Angeles, CA, 3/31/34. Actor. *Dr. Kildare.*

CHAMBERS, GEORGE. Flora, MS, 9/26/31. Bassist, singer. The Chambers Brothers.

CHAMBERS, JOE. Scott County, MS, 8/24/42. Guitarist, singer. The Chambers Brothers.

CHAMBERS, LESTER. Flora, MS, 4/13/40. Harmonicist, singer. The Chambers Brothers.

CHAMBERS, MARTIN. Hereford, England, 9/4/51. Drummer. The Pretenders.

CHAMBERS, TERRY. England, 7/18/55. Drummer. XTC.

CHAMBERS, WILLIE. Flora, MS, 3/3/38. Guitarist, singer. The Chambers Brothers.

CHANDLER, GENE (Gene Dixon). Chicago, IL, 7/6/37. Singer, songwriter.

CHANNING, CAROL. Seattle, WA, 1/31/21. Actor. *Hello, Dolly!*

CHANNING, STOCKARD (Susan Williams Antonia Stockard). New York, NY, 2/13/44. Actor. *Grease.*

CHAO, ROSALIND. Los Angeles, CA. Actor. Soon-Lee on *M*A*S*H.*

CHAPLIN, GERALDINE. Santa Monica, CA, 7/31/44. Actor. *Dr. Zhivago.*

CHAPMAN, ROGER. Leicester, England, 4/8/44. Singer. Family.

CHAPMAN, TRACY. Cleveland, OH, 3/30/64. Folk singer, songwriter.

CHAQUICO, CRAIG. 9/26/54. Singer, guitarist. Jefferson Starship.

CHARISSE, CYD (Tula Ellice Finklea). Amarillo, TX, 3/8/22. Actor. *Brigadoon.*

CHARLES, RAY (Ray Robinson). Albany, GA, 9/23/30. Singer, songwriter. "Georgia on My Mind."

CHARLTON, MANUEL. 7/25/41. Guitarist, singer, songwriter. Nazareth.

CHARO. Murcia, Spain, 1/15/41. Actor, singer. *The Love Boat.*

CHASE, CHEVY (Cornelius Crane Chase) New York, NY, 10/8/43. Actor, *National Lampoon's Vacation* movies.

CHECKER, CHUBBY (Ernest Evans). Spring Gulley, SC, 10/3/41. Singer, songwriter. Popularized the Twist and Limbo.

CHERRY, NENEH. Stockholm, Sweden, 3/10/64. Rap/pop singer, songwriter.

CHILD, JULIA. Pasadena, CA, 8/15/12. TV chef, author. *Mastering the Art of French Cooking.*

CHILES, LOIS. Alice, TX, 4/15/47. Model, actor. *The Way We Were.*

CHILTON, ALEX. Memphis, TN, 12/28/50. Guitarist, singer. The Box Tops; Big Star.

CHISHOLM, MELANIE. 1/12/74. Singer. Sporty Spice of the Spice Girls.

CHONG, RAE DAWN. Vancouver, Canada, 1962. Actor, daughter of Thomas Chong. *The Color Purple.*

CHONG, THOMAS. Edmonton, Canada, 5/24/38. Singer, actor, writer, director, former partner of Cheech Marin, father of Rae Dawn Chong. *Up in Smoke.*

CHRISTIAN, GARRY. Merseyside, England, 2/27/55. Singer. The Christians.

CHRISTIAN, ROGER. 2/13/50. Singer. The Christians.

CHRISTIAN, RUSSELL. 6/8/56. Singer. The Christians.

CHRISTIE, JULIE. Chukua, India, 4/14/41. Actor. *Dr. Zhivago.*

CHRISTIE, LOU (Lugee Sacco). Glenwillard, PA, 2/19/43. Singer, songwriter. "Lightnin' Strikes."

CHRISTO (Christo Javacheff). Gabrovo, Bulgaria, 6/13/35. Artist. The Umbrellas.

CHRISTOPHER, WILLIAM. Evanston, IL, 10/20/32. Actor. Father Francis Mulcahy on *M*A*S*H.*

CHUCK D. (Charles Ridenhour). 1960. Rap artist. Public Enemy.

CHUNG, CONNIE (Constance Yu-Hwa Chung) Washington, DC, 8/20/46, TV journalist, CBS.

CHURCHILL, CHICK. Mold, Wales, 1/2/49. Keyboardist. Ten Years After.

CIPOLLINA, JOHN. Berkeley, CA, 8/24/43. Guitarist. Quicksilver Messenger Service.

CLAIBORNE, LIZ (Elisabeth Claiborne). Brussels, Belgium, 3/31/29. Fashion designer.

CLARK, ALAN. Durham, NC, 3/5/52. Keyboardist. Dire Straits.

CLARK, DAVE. Tottenham, England, 12/15/42. Drummer. The Dave Clark Five.

CLARK, DICK. Mt. Vernon, NY, 11/30/29. Producer, music/game show host. *American Bandstand.*

CLARK, GRAEME. Glasgow, Scotland, 4/15/66. Bassist. Wet Wet Wet.

CLARK, NEIL. 7/3/55. Guitarist. Lloyd Cole & The Commotions.

CLARK, PETULA. Surrey, England, 11/15/32. Actor, singer. *Downtown.*

CLARK, ROY. Meherrin, VA, 4/15/33. Country singer, songwriter. *Hee Haw.*

CLARK, STEVE. Hillsborough, England, 4/23/60. Guitarist. Def Leppard.

CLARKE, ALLAN (Harold Clarke). Salford, England, 4/5/42. Singer. The Hollies.

CLARKE, EDDIE. 10/5/50. Guitarist. Motörhead.

CLARKE, MICHAEL (Michael Dick). New York, NY, 6/3/44. Drummer. The Byrds.

CLARKE, VINCE. Basildon, England, 7/3/61. Keyboardist. Erasure.

CLAY, ANDREW DICE. Brooklyn, NY, 1958. Actor. *The Adventures of Ford Fairlaine.*

CLAYBURGH, JILL. New York, NY, 4/30/44. Actor. *An Unmarried Woman.*

CLAYTON, ADAM. Ireland, 3/13/60. Bassist. U2.

CLAYTON-THOMAS, DAVID (David Thomsett). Surrey, England, 9/13/41. Lead singer. Blood, Sweat & Tears.

CLEESE, JOHN. Weston-Super-Mare, England, 10/27/39. Actor. *Monty Python's Flying Circus.*

CLIFF, JIMMY (Jimmy Chambers). Somerton, Jamaica, 1949. Reggae singer, songwriter.

CLIFFORD, DOUG. Palo Alto, CA, 4/24/45. Drummer. Creedence Clearwater Revival.

CLINTON, BILL. Hope, AK, 8/19/46. Husband of Hillary Rodham, father of Chelsea. 42nd President of the United States.

CLINTON, CHELSEA. Arkansas, 2/27/80. Daughter of Bill and Hillary.

CLINTON, GEORGE. Kannapolis, NC, 7/22/41. Funk pioneer, singer. Parliament; Funkadelic.

CLINTON, HILLARY RODHAM. Park Ridge, IL, 10/26/47. Wife of Bill,

mother of Chelsea. First Lady.

CLOONEY, NICK. 1/13/35. Actor, father of George Clooney. American Movie Classics.

CLOONEY, ROSEMARY. Maysville, KY, 5/23/28. Actor, singer, aunt of George Clooney.

CLYDE, JEREMY. England, 3/22/44. Singer, guitarist. Chad & Jeremy.

COBURN, JAMES. Laurel, NE, 8/31/28. Actor. *The Magnificent Seven.*

COCA, IMOGENE. Philadelphia, PA, 11/18/08. Actor. *Your Show of Shows.*

COCHRANE, TOM. 5/14/53. Singer, guitarist. Red Rider.

COCKER, JOE (John Cocker). Sheffield, England, 5/20/44. Singer.

COEN, ETHAN. St. Louis Park, MN, 1958. Director, writer. Brother of Joel. *Raising Arizona.*

COEN, JOEL. St. Louis Park, MN, 1955. Director, writer. Brother of Ethan. *Fargo.*

COGHLAN, JOHN. Dulwich, England, 9/19/46. Drummer. Status Quo.

COHEN, DAVID. Brooklyn, NY, 1942. Keyboardist. Country Joe & The Fish.

COHEN, LEONARD. Montreal, Canada, 9/21/34. Singer, songwriter, poet.

COLE, BRIAN. Tacoma, WA, 9/8/42. Singer, bassist. The Association.

COLE, LLOYD. Derbyshire, England, 1/31/61. Singer, guitarist. Lloyd Cole & The Commotions.

COLE, NATALIE (Stephanie Natalie Maria Cole). Los Angeles, CA, 2/6/50. Singer. *Unforgettable.*

COLEMAN, DABNEY. Austin, TX, 1/3/32. Actor. *Buffalo Bill.*

COLEMAN, GARY. Zion, IL, 2/8/68. Actor. Arnold Jackson on *Diff'rent Strokes.*

COLEY, DORIS. Passaic, NJ, 8/2/41. Singer. The Shirelles.

COLLA, JOHNNY. California, 7/2/52. Saxophonist, guitarist. Huey Lewis & The News.

COLLEN, PHIL. London, England, 12/8/57. Guitarist. Def Leppard.

COLLINS, ALLEN. Jacksonville, FL, 7/19/52. Guitarist. Lynyrd Skynrd.

COLLINS, GARY. Boston, MA, 4/30/38. Actor, talk show host. *Home.*

COLLINS, JACKIE. 10/4/39. Author. *Lucky.*

COLLINS, JOAN. London, England, 5/23/33. Actor. Alexis Carrington Colby on *Dynasty.*

COLLINS, JUDY. Seattle, WA, 5/1/39. Folk/rock guitarist, singer, songwriter. "Send in the Clowns."

COLLINS, PHIL. Chiswick, England, 1/30/51. Singer, drummer. Genesis.

COLLINS, STEPHEN. Des Moines, IA, 10/1/47. Actor. *Tales of the Gold Monkey.*

COLOMBY, BOBBY. New York, NY, 12/20/44. Drummer, singer. Blood, Sweat & Tears.

COLT, JOHNNY. Cherry Point, NC, 5/1/66. Bassist. The Black Crowes.

COLUMBUS, CHRIS. Spangler, PA, 9/10/58. Director. *Home Alone.*

CONAWAY, JEFF. New York, NY, 10/5/50. Actor. Bobby Wheeler on *Taxi.*

CONNELLY, JENNIFER. New York, NY, 12/12/70. Actor. *The Rocketeer.*

CONNOLLY, BRIAN. Hamilton, Scotland, 10/5/49. Singer. Sweet.

CONNORS, JIMMY. Belleville, IL, 9/2/52. Tennis player.

CONNORS, MIKE (Krekor Ohanian). Fresno, CA, 8/15/25. Actor. *Mannix.*

CONROY, KEVIN. Westport, CT, 11/30/55. Actor. Voice of Batman in *Batman: The Animated Series.*

CONROY, PAT. 10/26/45. Author. *Prince of Tides.*

CONSTANTINE, MICHAEL (Constantine Joanides). Reading, PA, 5/22/27. Actor. *Room 222.*

CONTI, TOM. Paisley, Scotland, 11/22/41. Actor. *Reuben Reuben.*

CONWAY, KEVIN. New York, NY, 5/29/42. Actor. *Slaughterhouse Five.*

CONWAY, TIM (Thomas Daniel Conway). Willoughby, OH, 12/15/33. Actor. *The Carol Burnett Show.*

COODER, RY (Ryland Cooder). Los Angeles, CA, 3/15/47. Folk blues guitarist, composer.

COOK, JEFF. Fort Payne, AL, 8/27/49. Singer, fiddler, guitarist, keyboardist. Alabama.

COOK, NORMAN (Quentin Cook). Sussex, England, 7/31/63. Singer. The Housemartins.

COOK, PAUL. London, England, 7/20/56. Drummer. The Sex Pistols.

COOK, STU. Oakland, CA, 4/25/45. Bassist. Creedence Clearwater Revival.

COOLIO Los Angeles,CA, 8/1/63. Rap Artist. "Gangsta's Paradise."

COONCE, RICKY. Los Angeles, CA, 8/1/47. Drummer. The Grass Roots.

COOPER, ALICE (Vincent Furnier). Detroit, MI, 2/4/48. Singer, songwriter. Alice Cooper.

COOPER, JACKIE (John Cooper Jr.). Los Angeles, CA, 9/15/22. Actor, director. *Superman.*

COPE, JULIAN. Bargoed, Wales, 10/21/57. Singer, bassist. The Teardrop Explodes.

COPELAND, STEWART. Alexandria, Egypt, 7/16/52.

Drummer, singer. The Police.

CORBIN, BARRY. Dawson County, TX, 10/16/40. Actor. Maurice Minnifield on *Northern Exposure.*

CORGAN, BILLY. Chicago, IL, 3/17/67. Singer, songwriter, guitarist. Smashing Pumpkins.

CORLEY, PAT. Dallas, TX, 6/1/30. Actor. Phil the bartender on *Murphy Brown.*

CORNELL, CHRIS. Seattle, WA, 7/20/64. Singer, songwriter, drummer. Soundgarden.

CORNICK, GLENN. Barrow-in-Furness, England, 4/24/47. Bassist. Jethro Tull.

CORNISH, GENE. Ottowa, Canada, 5/14/45. Guitarist. The (Young) Rascals.

CORNWELL, HUGH. London, England, 8/28/49. Singer, guitarist. The Stranglers.

CORT, BUD (Walter Edward Cox). New Rochelle, NY, 3/29/48. Actor. *Harold and Maude.*

COSTELL, DAVID. Pittsburgh, PA, 3/15/44. Bassist. Gary Lewis and the Playboys.

COULIER, DAVID. Detroit, MI. Actor. Joey Gladstone on *Full House.*

COVERDALE, DAVID. Saltburn-by-the-Sea, England, 9/22/49. Singer. Whitesnake.

COWSILL, BARRY. Newport, RI, 9/14/54. Bassist, singer. The Cowsills.

COWSILL, BILL. Newport, RI, 1/9/48. Guitarist, singer. The Cowsills.

COWSILL, BOB. Newport, RI, 8/26/49. Guitarist, singer. The Cowsills.

COWSILL, JOHN. Newport, RI, 3/2/56. Drummer. The Cowsills.

COWSILL, PAUL. Newport, RI, 11/11/52. Keyboardist, singer. The Cowsills.

COWSILL, SUE. Newport, RI, 5/20/60. Singer. The Cowsills.

COX, ANDY. Birmingham, England, 1/25/60. Guitarist. Fine Young Cannibals.

COX, RONNY. Cloudcroft, NM, 8/23/38. Actor. *Beverly Hills Cop.*

COYOTE, PETER (Peter Cohon). New York, NY, 1942. Actor. *Jagged Edge.*

CRAIG, MIKEY. Hammersmith, England, 2/15/60. Bassist. Culture Club.

CRAVEN, WES. Cleveland, OH, 8/2/39. Director, novelist. *A Nightmare on Elm Street.*

CRAWFORD, JOHN. 1/17/60. Bassist, singer. Berlin.

CRAWFORD, MICHAEL (Michael Dumble-Smith). Salisbury, England, 1/19/42. Actor, singer. *The Phantom of the Opera.*

CRAWFORD, RANDY (Veronica Crawford). Macon, GA, 2/18/52. Rock-R&B singer, songwriter.

CRAY, ROBERT. Columbus, GA, 8/1/53. Contemporary blues singer, songwriter. "Smoking Gun."

CREGAN, JIM. 3/9/46. Guitarist. Steve Harley & Cockney Rebel.

CREME, LOL. Manchester, England, 9/19/47. Singer, guitarist. 10cc; Godley & Creme.

CRENNA, RICHARD. Los Angeles, CA, 11/30/27. Actor. *Rambo: First Blood Part II.*

CREWSDON, ROY. Manchester, England, 5/29/41. Guitarist. Freddie & The Dreamers.

CRISS, PETER (Peter Crisscoula). Brooklyn, NY, 12/27/47. Drummer, singer. Kiss.

CROFTS, DASH. Cisco, TX, 8/14/40. Singer, guitarist, mandolinist. Seals & Crofts.

CRONIN, KEVIN. Evanston, IL, 10/6/51. Singer. REO Speedwagon.

CRONKITE, WALTER. St. Joseph, MO, 11/4/16. News

journalist and anchor. *CBS Evening News.*

CRONYN, HUME. London, Canada, 7/18/11. Actor, writer, director, widower of Jessica Tandy. *The Postman Always Rings Twice.*

CROPPER, STEVE. Willow Springs, MO, 10/21/41. Guitarist. Booker T. & The MG's.

CROSBY, CATHY LEE. Los Angeles, CA, 12/2/49. Actor. *That's Incredible!*

CROSBY, DAVID (David Van Cortland). Los Angeles, CA, 8/14/41. Singer, guitarist. The Byrds; Crosby, Stills, Nash & Young.

CROSBY, DENISE. Hollywood, CA, 1958. Actor, granddaughter of Bing Crosby. *Star Trek: The Next Generation.*

CROSBY, HARRY. Los Angeles, CA, 8/8/58. Actor, singer.

CROSS, BEN. London, England, 12/16/48. Actor. *Chariots of Fire.*

CROSS, CHRIS (Chris St. John). London, England, 7/14/52. Bassist, synthesizer player. Ultravox.

CROSS, CHRISTOPHER (Christopher Geppert). San Antonio, TX, 5/3/51. Guitarist, singer, songwriter. "Ride Like the Wind."

CROUSE, LINDSAY. New York, NY, 5/12/48. Actor. *The Verdict.*

CRYER, JON. New York, NY, 4/16/65. Actor. *Pretty in Pink.*

CULKIN, MACAULAY. New York, NY, 8/26/80. Actor. *Home Alone, My Girl.*

CULLIMORE, STAN. Hull, England, 4/6/62. Bassist. The Housemartins.

CULLUM, JOHN. Knoxville, TN, 3/2/30. Actor. Holling Vincoeur on *Northern Exposure.*

CULP, ROBERT. Oakland, CA, 8/16/30. Actor. *I Spy.*

CUMMINGS, BURTON. Winnipeg, Canada, 12/31/47.

494

Singer, keyboardist. The Guess Who.

CUMMINGS, GEORGE. Meridian, MS, 7/28/38. Lead guitarist. Dr. Hook.

CUNNINGHAM, BILL. Memphis, TN, 1/23/50. Bassist, pianist. The Box Tops; Big Star.

CUNNINGHAM, TOM. Glasgow, Scotland, 6/22/65. Drummer. Wet Wet Wet.

CUOMO, MARIO. Queens, NY, 6/15/32. Political leader. Former Governor of New York.

CURRIE, ALANNAH. Auckland, New Zealand, 9/20/59. Singer, saxophonist, percussionist. Thompson Twins.

CURRIE, BILLY. Huddersfield, England, 4/1/52. Synthesizer player, keyboardist. Ultravox.

CURRIE, CHERIE. Los Angeles, CA, 1960. Singer, married to Robert Hays. The Runaways.

CURRY, TIM. Cheshire, England, 4/19/46. Actor. *The Rocky Horror Picture Show*.

CURTIN, JANE. Cambridge, MA, 9/6/47. Actor. *Kate & Allie*.

CURTIS, CHRIS (Chris Crummy). Oldham, England, 8/26/41. Singer, drummer. The Searchers.

CURTIS, SONNY. Meadow, TX, 5/9/37. Guitarist. Buddy Holly & The Crickets.

CURTIS, TONY (Bernard Schwartz). New York, NY, 6/3/25. Actor, father of Jamie Lee Curtis, formerly married to Janet Leigh. *Some Like It Hot*.

CUSACK, SINEAD. Ireland, 2/18/48. Actor, formerly married to Jeremy Irons, daughter of Cyril Cusack.

CYRUS, BILLY RAY. Flatwoods, NY, 8/25/61. Singer, son of politician Ronald Ray Cyrus. "Achy-Breaky Heart."

D'ABO, OLIVIA. 1/22/69. Actor. *The Wonder Years*.

D'ALEO, ANGELO. The Bronx, NY, 2/3/41. Singer. Dion & The Belmonts.

D'ANGELO, BEVERLY. Columbus, OH, 11/15/51. Actor. *Hair*.

D'ARBANVILLE, PATTI. 5/25/51. Actress

D'ARBY, TERENCE TRENT. New York, NY, 3/15/62. R&B singer, songwriter. "Wishing Well."

D'ONOFRIO, VINCENT. 6/30/59. Actor. *The Newton Boys*.

DALE, GLEN (Richard Garforth). Deal, England, 4/2/43. Guitarist, singer. The Fortunes.

DALEY, ROSIE. South Seaville, NJ, 1961. Chef. *In the Kitchen with Rosie*.

DALLIN, SARAH. Bristol, England, 12/17/61. Singer. Bananarama.

DALTON, TIMOTHY. Colwyn Bay, Wales, 3/21/44. Actor. James Bond in *The Living Daylights*.

DALTREY, ROGER. London, England, 3/1/44. Lead singer. The Who.

DALY, GARY. Merseyside, England, 5/5/62. Singer. China Crisis.

DALY, TIMOTHY. New York, NY, 3/1/56. Actor. *Wings*.

DALY, TYNE (Ellen Tyne Daly). Madison, WI, 2/21/46. Actor. *Cagney & Lacey*.

DAMMERS, JERRY (Jerry Dankin). 5/22/54. Keyboardist. The Specials.

DAMONE, VIC (Vito Farinola). Brooklyn, NY, 6/12/28. Singer, married to Diahann Caroll. *The Vic Damone Show*.

DANCE, CHARLES. Worcestershire, England, 10/10/46. Actor. *The Jewel in the Crown*.

DANDO, EVAN. 3/4/67. Musician. The Lemonheads.

DANELLI, DINO. New York, NY, 7/23/45. Drummer. The (Young) Rascals.

DANGERFIELD, RODNEY (Jacob Cohen). Babylon, NY, 11/22/21. Actor. *Back to School*.

DANIEL, JEFFREY. Los Angeles, CA, 8/24/55. Singer. Shalamar.

DANIELS, WILLIAM. Brooklyn, NY, 3/31/27. Actor. *St. Elsewhere*.

DANNER, BLYTHE. Philadelphia, PA, 2/3/43. Actor. *The Prince of Tides*.

DANTE, MICHAEL (Ralph Vitti). Stamford, CT, 1935. Actor. Crazy Horse in *Custer*.

DANZA, TONY. Brooklyn, NY, 4/21/51. Actor. Tony Micelli on *Who's the Boss?*

DAVIDOVICH, LOLITA. Ontario, Canada, 7/15/61. Actor. *Blaze*.

DAVIDSON, JAYE. Riverside, CA, 1967. Actor. *The Crying Game*.

DAVIDSON, JOHN. Pittsburgh, PA, 12/13/41. Game show host. *Hollywood Squares*.

DAVIDSON, LENNY. Enfield, England, 5/30/44. Guitarist. The Dave Clark Five.

DAVIES, DAVE. Muswell Hill, England, 2/3/47. Singer, guitarist. The Kinks.

DAVIES, IVA. Australia, 5/22/55. Guitarist, singer. Icehouse.

DAVIES, RAY. Muswell Hill, England, 6/21/44. Singer, guitarist. The Kinks.

DAVIES, RICHARD. England, 7/22/44. Singer, keyboardist. Supertramp.

DAVIS, BILLY JR. St. Louis, MO, 6/26/38. Singer. The 5th Dimension.

DAVIS, CLIFTON. Chicago, IL, 10/4/45. Actor, singer, composer. *Never Can Say Goodbye*.

DAVIS, JIM. Marion, IN, 7/28/45. Cartoonist. *Garfield*.

DAVIS, MAC (Morris Mac Davis). Lubbock, TX, 1/21/42. Singer, songwriter, actor. *The Mac Davis Show*.

DAVIS, MARTHA. Berkeley, CA, 1/15/51. Singer. The Motels.

DAVIS, OSSIE. Cogdell, GA, 12/18/17. Actor, writer. *Evening Shade*.

DAVIS, PAUL. Manchester, England, 3/7/66. Keyboardist. Happy Mondays.

DAVIS, ROB. Carshalton, England, 10/1/47. Lead guitarist, singer. Mud.

DAVIS, SPENCER. Swansea, Wales, 7/17/42. Guitarist. The Spencer Davis Group.

DAVIS, WILLIE. 1940. Drummer. Joey Dee and the Starliters.

DAWBER, PAM. 10/18/50. Actor. Married to Mark Harmon. *Mork and Mindy*.

DAY, DORIS (Doris von Kappelhoff). Cincinnati, OH, 4/3/24. Actor, performer. *The Doris Day Show*.

DAY, MARK. Manchester, England, 12/29/61. Guitarist. Happy Mondays.

DE BURGH, CHRIS (Chris Davidson). Argentina, 10/15/48. Singer, songwriter. "Lady in Red."

DE HAVILLAND, OLIVIA. Tokyo, Japan, 7/1/16. Actor. *Gone with the Wind*.

DE LAURENTIS, DINO. Torre Annunziata, Italy, 8/8/19. Producer. *King Kong; Conan the Barbarian*.

DEACON, JOHN. Leicester, England, 8/19/51. Bassist. Queen.

DEAN, JIMMY. Plainview, TX, 8/10/28. Performer. *The Jimmy Dean Show*.

DEBARGE, EL (Eldra DeBarge). Grand Rapids, MI, 6/4/61. Singer, keyboardist, record producer.

DEE, DAVE (Dave Harman). Salisbury, England, 12/17/43. Lead singer, tambourinist. Dave Dee, Dozy, Beaky, Mick and Tich.

DEE, JOEY (Joey DiNicola). Passaic, NJ, 6/11/40. Singer. Joey Dee and the Starliters.

DEE, KIKI. Bradford, England, 3/6/47. Pop singer.

DEE, RUBY. Cleveland, OH, 10/27/24. Actor. *Do the Right Thing*.

DEE, SANDRA (Alexandra Zuck). Bayonne, NJ, 4/23/42. Actor. *Gidget*.

DEFOREST, CALVERT. Brooklyn, NY, 1923. Actor, Larry "Bud" Melman.

DEKKER, DESMOND (Desmond Dacris). Kingston, Jamaica, 7/16/42. Reggae singer, songwriter.

DELANEY, KIM. 11/29/61. Actress. *NYPD Blue*.

DELANY, DANA. New York, NY, 3/11/56. Actor. *China Beach*.

DELON, ALAIN. Sceaux, France, 11/8/35. Actor. *Le Samourai*.

DELP, BRAD. Boston, MA, 6/12/51. Guitarist, singer. Boston.

DELUISE, DOM. Brooklyn, NY, 8/1/33. Actor. *The Dom DeLuise Show*.

DELUISE, PETER. Hollywood, CA, 1967. Actor. Doug Penhall on *21 Jump Street*.

DEMME, JONATHAN. Rockville Centre, MD, 2/22/44. Director, producer, writer. *The Silence of the Lambs*.

DEMORNAY, REBECCA. Santa Rosa, CA, 8/29/59. Actor. *The Hand That Rocks the Cradle*.

DEMPSEY, PATRICK. Lewiston, ME, 1/13/66. Actor. *Loverboy*.

DENEUVE, CATHERINE (Catherine Dorleac). Paris, France, 10/22/43. Actor. *Belle de Jour*.

DENSMORE, JOHN. Los Angeles, CA, 12/1/44. Drummer. The Doors.

DENVER, BOB. New Rochelle, NY, 1/9/35. Actor. Gilligan on *Gilligan's Island*.

DEPARDIEU, GERARD. Chateauroux, France, 12/27/48. Actor. *Green Card*.

DEREK, BO (Mary Cathleen Collins). Long Beach, CA, 11/20/56. Actor, married to John Derek. *10*.

DERN, BRUCE. Chicago, IL, 6/4/36. Actor, father of Laura. *Coming Home*.

DERN, LAURA. Los Angeles, CA, 2/10/67. Actor, daughter of Bruce Dern and Diane Ladd, engaged to Jeff Goldblum. *Jurassic Park*.

DERRINGER, RICK (Richard Zehringer). Fort Recovery, OH, 8/5/47. Singer, songwriter, producer. The McCoys.

DESTRI, JIMMY. 4/13/54. Keyboardist. Blondie.

DEVANE, WILLIAM. Albany, NY, 9/5/39. Actor. Greg Sumner in *Knots Landing*.

DEVITO, TOMMY. Montclair, NJ, 6/19/36. Singer, guitarist. The Four Seasons.

DEVOE, RONALD. 11/17/67. Singer. New Edition; Bell Biv DeVoe.

DEY, SUSAN. Pekin, IL, 12/10/52. Actor. *L.A. Law*.

DEYOUNG, CLIFF. Inglewood, CA, 2/12/45. Actor. *The Hunger*.

DEYOUNG, DENNIS. Chicago, IL, 2/18/47. Singer, keyboardist. Styx.

DIAMOND, NEIL (Noah Kaminsky). New York, NY, 1/24/41. Singer, songwriter. *The Jazz Singer*.

DIAMONDE, DICK (Dingeman Van Der Sluys). Hilversum, Holland, 12/28/47. Bassist. The Easybeats.

DICKEN (Jeff Pain). 4/4/50. Singer. Mr. Big.

DICKERSON, B. B. (Morris Dickerson). Torrance, CA, 8/3/49. Bassist, singer. War.

DICKINSON, ANGIE (Angie Brown). Kulm, ND, 9/30/32. Actor. *Police Woman*.

DICKINSON, BRUCE (Paul Dickinson). Worksop, England, 8/7/58. Singer. Iron Maiden.

DIDDLEY, BO (Otha Bates). McComb, MS, 12/30/28.

Legendary blues guitarist, singer, songwriter.

DIFFORD, CHRIS. London, England, 11/4/54. Singer, guitarist. Squeeze.

DILLER, PHYLLIS (Phyllis Driver). Lima, OH, 7/17/17. Actor. *The Phyllis Diller Show*.

DILLON, KEVIN. Mamaroneck, NY, 8/19/65. Actor. *The Doors*.

DILLON, MATT. New Rochelle, NY, 2/18/64. Actor. *The Outsiders*.

DIMUCCI, DION. The Bronx, NY, 7/18/39. Lead singer. Dion & The Belmonts.

DIO, RONNIE JAMES. Cortland, NY, 7/10/48. Singer. Rainbow; Black Sabbath.

DITKA, MIKE. Carnegie, PA, 10/18/39. NFL football player, coach.

DIXON, DONNA. Alexandria, VA, 7/20/57. Actor, married to Dan Aykroyd. *Bosom Buddies*.

DOBSON, KEVIN. New York, NY, 3/18/43. Actor. *Knots Landing*.

DOHERTY, DENNY. Halifax, Canada, 11/29/41. Singer. The Mamas and the Papas.

DOLENZ, MICKEY (George Dolenz). Los Angeles, CA, 3/8/45. Singer, drummer. The Monkees.

DOMINO, FATS (Antoine Domino). New Orleans, LA, 2/26/28. Legendary singer, songwriter.

DONAHUE, PHIL. Cleveland, OH, 12/21/35. Talk show host.

DONAHUE, TROY (Merle Johnson). New York, NY, 1/27/36. Actor. *Hawaiian Eye*.

DONALDSON, SAM. El Paso, TX, 3/11/34. News reporter and anchor. *Prime Time Live*.

DONEGAN, LAWRENCE. 7/13/61. Bassist. Lloyd Cole & The Commotions.

DONEGAN, LONNIE (Anthony Donegan). Glasgow, Scot-

land, 4/29/31. Folk/blues guitarist, banjoist, and singer.

DONOVAN (Donovan Leitch). Glasgow, Scotland, 2/10/46. Folk/psychedelic singer, songwriter, father of Ione Skye and Donovan Leitch. "Mellow Yellow."

DONOVAN, JASON. Malvern, Australia, 6/1/68. Singer, actor.

DORMAN, LEE. St. Louis, MO, 9/19/45. Bassist. Iron Butterfly.

DOUGHTY, NEAL. Evanston, IL, 7/29/46. Keyboardist. REO Speedwagon.

DOUGLAS, BUSTER (James Douglas). Columbus, OH, 4/7/60. Boxer. Defeated Mike Tyson.

DOUGLAS, DONNA (Dorothy Bourgeois). Baywood, LA, 9/26/35. Actor. Elly May Clampett on *The Beverly Hillbillies*.

DOUGLAS, KIRK (Issur Danielovitch). Amsterdam, NY, 12/9/16. Actor, producer, father of Michael. *Spartacus*.

DOW, TONY. Hollywood, CA, 4/13/45. Actor. Wally Cleaver on *Leave It to Beaver*.

DOWN, LESLEY-ANN. London, England, 3/17/54. Actor. *Dallas*.

DOWNEY, BRIAN. Dublin, Ireland, 1/27/51. Drummer. Thin Lizzy.

DOWNS, HUGH. Akron, OH, 2/14/21. Host, actor, commentator. *20/20*.

DOZY (Trevor Davies). Enford, England, 11/27/44. Bassist. Dave Dee, Dozy, Beaky, Mick and Tich.

DRAGON, DARYL. Los Angeles, CA, 8/27/42. Keyboardist. The Captain & Tennille.

DR. DRE. Compton, CA, 1965. Rap artist, record producer. *The Chronic*.

DREJA, CHRIS. Surbiton, England, 11/11/44. Guitarist. The Yardbirds.

DREYFUSS, RICHARD. Brooklyn, NY, 10/29/47. Actor. *Close Encounters of the Third Kind.*

DRYDEN, SPENCER. New York, NY, 4/7/38. Drummer. Jefferson Airplane/Starship.

DUBROW, KEVIN. 10/29/55. Lead singer. Quiet Riot.

DUDIKOFF, MICHAEL. Redondo Beach, CA, 10/8/54. Actor. *American Ninja.*

DUFFY, BILLY. 5/12/61. Lead guitarist. The Cult.

DUFFY, JULIA. Minneapolis, MN, 6/27/51. Actor. *Newhart.*

DUFFY, KAREN. 5/23/61. TV personality. MTV.

DUFFY, PATRICK. Townsend, MT, 3/17/49. Actor. Bobby Ewing on *Dallas.*

DUKAKIS, OLYMPIA. Lowell, MA, 6/20/31. Actor. *Moonstruck.*

DUKE, DAVID. Tulsa, OK, 1951. White supremacist, politician.

DUKE, PATTY (Anna Marie Duke). New York, NY, 12/14/46. Actor, formerly married to John Astin, mother of Sean Astin. *The Patty Duke Show.*

DUKES, DAVID. San Francisco, CA, 6/6/45. Actor. *Sisters.*

DULLEA, KEIR. Cleveland, OH, 5/30/36. Actor. *2001: A Space Odyssey.*

DUNAWAY, DENNIS. Cottage Grove, OR, 12/9/48. Bassist. Alice Cooper.

DUNAWAY, FAYE. Bascom, FL, 1/14/41. Actor. *Mommie Dearest.*

DUNCAN, GARY (Gary Grubb). San Diego, CA, 9/4/46. Guitarist. Quicksilver Messenger Service.

DUNCAN, SANDY. Henderson, TX, 2/20/46. Actor. *Funny Face.*

DUNN, DONALD. Memphis, TN, 11/24/41. Bassist. Booker T. & The MG's.

DUNN, LARRY. Colorado, 6/19/53. Keyboardist. Earth, Wind & Fire.

DUNNE, GRIFFIN. New York, NY, 6/8/55. Actor, director, son of Dominick. *After Hours.*

DUNST, KIRSTEN. 4/30/82. Actor. *Interview With A Vampire.*

DURBIN, DEANNA (Edna Durbin). Winnipeg, Canada, 12/4/21. Actor. *One Hundred Men and a Girl.*

DURNING, CHARLES. Highland Falls, NY, 2/28/23. Actor. *Evening Shade.*

DUTTON, CHARLES. Baltimore, MD, 1/30/51. Actor. *Roc.*

DUVALL, SHELLEY. Houston, TX, 7/7/49. Actor, producer. *The Shining.*

DYSART, RICHARD. Brighton, MA, 3/30/29. Actor. Leland McKenzie on *L.A. Law.*

EARLE, STEVE. Fort Monroe, VA, 1/17/55. Country/rock singer, songwriter. Guitar Town.

EASTON, ELLIOT (Elliot Shapiro). Brooklyn, NY, 12/18/53. Guitarist. The Cars.

EASTON, SHEENA (Sheena Orr). Bellshill, Scotland, 4/27/59. Rock/R&B singer.

EBSEN, BUDDY (Christian Ebsen Jr.). Belleville, IL, 4/2/08. Actor. Jed Clampett on *The Beverly Hillbillies.*

ECHOLS, JOHN. Memphis, TN, 1945. Lead guitarist. Love.

EDDY, DUANE. Corning, NY, 4/26/38. Legendary rock guitarist.

EDEN, BARBARA (Barbara Huffman). Tucson, AZ, 8/23/34. Actor. Jeannie in *I Dream of Jeannie.*

EDGE, GRAEME. Rochester, England, 3/30/42. Drummer. The Moody Blues.

EDGE, THE (David Evans). Wales, 8/8/61. Guitarist. U2.

EDMONTON, JERRY. Canada, 10/24/46. Drummer. Steppenwolf.

EDWARD, PRINCE. London, England, 3/10/64. British royalty, son of Queen Elizabeth II.

EDWARDS, BERNARD. Greenville, NC, 10/31/52. Bassist. Chic.

EDWARDS, BLAKE (William Blake McEdwards). Tulsa, OK, 7/26/22. Writer, director. The *Pink Panther* series. Married to Julie Andrews.

EDWARDS, NOKIE. Washington, DC, 5/9/39. Lead guitarist. The Ventures.

EGGAR, SAMANTHA. London, England, 3/5/39. Actor. *The Collector.*

EIKENBERRY, JILL. New Haven, CT, 1/21/47. Actor. Ann Kelsey on *L.A. Law.*

EKBERG, ANITA. Malmo, Sweden, 9/29/31. Actor. *La Dolce Vita.*

EKLAND, BRITT. Stockholm, Sweden, 10/6/42. Actor. *After the Fox.*

ELIZONDO, HECTOR. New York, NY, 12/22/36. Actor. *Pretty Woman.*

ELLERBEE, LINDA. Bryan, TX, 8/15/44. News commentator. *Our World.*

ELLIOTT, BOBBY. Burnley, England, 12/8/42. Drummer. The Hollies.

ELLIOTT, CHRIS. New York, NY, 1960. Comedy writer, actor. *Get a Life.*

ELLIOTT, DENNIS. London, England, 8/18/50. Drummer. Foreigner.

ELLIOTT, JOE. Sheffield, England, 8/1/59. Singer. Def Leppard.

ELLIOTT, SAM. Sacramento, CA, 8/9/44. Actor. *Tombstone.*

ELLIS, RALPH. Liverpool, England, 3/8/42. Guitarist, singer. The Swinging Blue Jeans.

ELMORE, GREG. San Diego, CA, 9/4/46. Drummer.

Quicksilver Messenger Service.

ELSWIT, RIK. New York, NY, 7/6/45. Guitarist, singer. Dr. Hook.

ELVIRA (Cassandra Peterson). Manhattan, KS, 9/17/51. Horror film hostess.

ELWES, CARY. London, England, 10/26/62. Actor. *The Princess Bride.*

EMERSON, KEITH. Todmorden, England, 11/1/44. Keyboardist. Emerson, Lake & Palmer.

ENGEL, SCOTT (Noel Engel). Hamilton, OH, 1/9/44. Singer. The Walker Brothers.

ENGLUND, ROBERT. Hollywood, CA, 6/6/49. Actor. Freddie Krueger in *Nightmare on Elm Street* series.

ENNIS, RAY. Liverpool, England, 5/26/42. Lead guitarist, singer. The Swinging Blue Jeans.

ENO, BRIAN. Woodbridge, England, 5/15/48. Synthesizer player, producer. Cofounder of Roxy Music.

ENTNER, WARREN. Boston, MA, 7/7/44. Singer, guitarist. The Grass Roots.

ENTWISTLE, JOHN. Chiswick, England, 10/9/44. Bassist. The Who.

ENYA (Eithne Ni Bhraona). Gweedore, Ireland, 1962. Singer, composer.

ERRICO, GREG. San Francisco, CA, 9/1/46. Drummer. Sly & The Family Stone.

ERVING, JULIUS. Roosevelt, NY, 2/22/50. Basketball great. Philadelphia 76ers.

ESIASON, BOOMER (Norman Julius Esiason Jr.). West Islip, NY, 4/17/61. NFL football player.

ESPOSITO, GIANCARLO. Copenhagen, Denmark, 4/26/61. Actor. *Do the Right Thing.*

ESSEX, DAVID (David Cook). Plaistow, England, 7/23/47. Drummer, singer, songwriter, actor. *Stardust.*

ESTEFAN, GLORIA (Gloria Fajardo). Havana, Cuba, 9/1/57. Latin pop singer. The Miami Sound Machine.

ESTEVEZ, EMILIO. New York, NY, 5/12/62. Actor, writer, divorced from Paula Abdul, son of Martin Sheen. *Repo Man.*

ESTRADA, ERIK. New York, NY, 3/16/49. Actor. Frank "Ponch" Poncherello on *CHiPS.*

EUGENIE, PRINCESS. London, England, 3/23/90. British royalty, daughter of Prince Andrew and the Duchess of York.

EVANGELISTA, LINDA. Canada, 5/10/65. Supermodel.

EVANS, LINDA (Linda Evanstad). Hartford, CT, 11/18/42. Actor. *Dynasty.*

EVANS, MARK. Melbourne, Australia, 3/2/56. Bassist. AC/DC.

EVANS, MIKE (Michael Jonas Evans). Salisbury, NC, 11/3/49. Actor. Lionel on *The Jeffersons.*

EVERETT, CHAD (Raymond Lee Cramton). South Bend, IN, 6/11/36. Actor. *Medical Center.*

EVERLY, DON (Isaac Everly). Brownie, KY, 2/1/37. Singer, guitarist. The Everly Brothers.

EVERLY, PHIL. Chicago, IL, 1/19/39. Singer, guitarist. The Everly Brothers.

EVERT, CHRIS. Ft. Lauderdale, FL, 12/21/54. Tennis player.

EVIGAN, GREG. South Amboy, NJ, 10/14/53. Actor. *B.J. and the Bear.*

FABARES, SHELLEY (Michelle Marie Fabares). Santa Monica, CA, 1/19/44. Actor, married to Mike Farrell, niece of Nanette Fabray. Christine Armstrong on *Coach.*

FABIAN (Fabian Forte). Philadelphia, PA, 2/6/43. Singer, actor. *American Bandstand.*

FABIO (Fabio Lanzoni). Milan, Italy, 3/15/61. Model.

FABRAY, NANETTE (Ruby Nanette Fabares). San Diego, CA, 10/27/20. Actor, aunt of Shelley Fabares. *One Day at a Time.*

FAGEN, DONALD. Passaic, NJ, 1/10/48. Singer, keyboardist. Steely Dan.

FAHEY, SIOBHAN. 9/10/60. Singer. Bananarama.

FAIRCHILD, MORGAN (Patsy McClenny). Dallas, TX, 2/3/50. Actor. *Falcon Crest.*

FAIRWEATHER-LOW, ANDY. Ystrad Mynach, Wales, 8/8/50. Singer, guitarist. Amen Corner.

FAITH, ADAM (Terence Nelhams). Acton, England, 6/23/40. Singer, actor, financial adviser.

FAITHFULL, MARIANNE. Hampstead, England, 12/29/46. Folk/rock singer.

FAKIR, ABDUL. Detroit, MI, 12/26/35. Singer. The Four Tops.

FALANA, LOLA (Loletha Elaine Falana). Philadelphia, PA, 9/11/43. Singer.

FALCONER, EARL. Birmingham, England, 1/23/59. Bassist. UB40.

FALK, PETER. New York, NY, 9/16/27. Actor. *Columbo.*

FALTSKOG, AGNETHA. Jonkoping, Sweden, 4/5/50. Singer. Abba.

FAMBROUGH, HENRY. 5/10/38. Singer. The (Detroit) Spinners.

FAME, GEORGIE (Clive Powell). Leigh, England, 9/26/43. Singer, keyboardist. Georgie Fame & The Blue Flames.

FARENTINO, JAMES. Brooklyn, NY, 2/24/38. Actor. *Dynasty.*

FARINA, DENNIS. Chicago, IL, 2/29/44. Actor. *Crime Story.*

FARNER, MARK. Flint, MI, 9/29/48. Singer, guitarist. Grand Funk Railroad.

FARR, JAMIE (Jameel Joseph Farah). Toledo, OH, 7/1/34. Actor. Maxwell Klinger on *M*A*S*H.*

FARRAKHAN, LOUIS (Louis Eugene Walcott). New York, NY, 5/11/33. Controversial Muslim minister.

FARRELL, BOBBY. Aruba, West Indies, 10/6/49. Singer. Boney M.

FARRELL, MIKE. St. Paul, MN, 2/6/39. Actor, writer, director, married to Shelley Fabares. B. J. Hunnicutt on *M*A*S*H.*

FARRIS, STEVE. 5/1/57. Guitarist. Mr. Mister.

FARRISS, ANDREW. Perth, Australia, 3/27/59. Keyboardist. INXS.

FARRISS, JON. Perth, Australia, 8/10/61. Drummer, singer. INXS.

FAULKNER, ERIC. Edinburgh, Scotland, 10/21/55. Guitarist. The Bay City Rollers.

FAWCETT, FARRAH. Corpus Christi, TX, 2/2/47. Actor. Jill Munroe on *Charlie's Angels.*

FELDMAN, COREY. Reseda, CA, 7/16/71. Actor. *Stand By Me.*

FELDON, BARBARA (Barbara Hall). Pittsburgh, PA, 3/12/41. Actor. Agent 99 on *Get Smart.*

FELDSHUH, TOVAH. New York, NY, 12/27/53. Actor. *The Idolmaker.*

FELICIANO, JOSE. Lares, Puerto Rico, 9/10/45. Singer, guitarist. *Chico and the Man.*

FENN, SHERILYN. Detroit, MI, 2/1/65. Actor. *Twin Peaks.*

FERGUSON, JAY (John Ferguson). Burbank, CA, 5/10/47. Singer. Spirit.

FERGUSON, LARRY. Nassau, Bahamas, 4/14/48. Keyboardist. Hot Chocolate.

FERGUSON, SARAH. London, England, 10/15/59. Duchess of York. Formerly married to Prince Andrew.

FERRARO, GERALDINE. Newburgh, NY, 8/26/35. Politician, first woman vice-presidential candidate.

FERRER, MEL (Melchor Gaston Ferrer). Elberon, NJ, 8/25/12. Producer, director, actor, formerly married to Audrey Hepburn. *Falcon Crest.*

FERRER, MIGUEL. Santa Monica, CA, 2/7/54. Actor, son of Jose Ferrer and Rosemary Clooney. *Twin Peaks.*

FERRIGNO, LOU. Brooklyn, NY, 11/9/52. Actor, bodybuilder. *The Incredible Hulk.*

FERRIS, BARBARA. London, England, 10/3/40. Actor. *The Strauss Family.*

FERRY, BRYAN. Durham, England, 9/26/45. Singer, songwriter. Roxy Music.

FIEGER, DOUG. Detroit, MI, 8/20/52. Singer, guitarist. The Knack.

FIELDER, JIM. Denton, TX, 10/4/47. Bassist. Blood, Sweat & Tears.

FIELDS, KIM. Los Angeles, CA, 5/12/69. Actor. Dorothy "Tootie" Ramsey on *The Facts of Life.*

FIERSTEIN, HARVEY. Brooklyn, NY, 6/6/54. Actor, writer. *Mrs. Doubtfire.*

FILIPOVIC, ZLATA. Sarajevo, Bosnia-Herzegovina, 12/3/81. Author. *Zlata's Diary.*

FINCH, RICHARD. Indianapolis, IN, 1/25/54. Bassist. KC & The Sunshine Band.

FINER, JEM. Ireland. Banjoist. The Pogues.

FINGERS, JOHNNIE (Johnnie Moylett). Ireland, 9/10/56. Keyboardist, singer. The Boomtown Rats.

FINN, TIM (Te Awamutu). New Zealand, 6/25/52. Singer, keyboardist. Split Enz.

FINNEY, ALBERT. Salford, England, 5/9/36. Actor. *Tom Jones.*

FIORENTINO, LINDA (Clorinda Fiorentino). Philadelphia, PA, 3/9/58. Actor. *The Last Seduction.*

FIRTH, COLIN. Grayshott, England, 9/10/60. Actor. *Another Country.*

FISH (Derek Dick). Dalkeith, Scotland, 4/25/58. Singer. Marillion.

FISHER, AMY. New York, NY, 1974. The "Long Island Lolita."

FISHER, EDDIE. Philadelphia, PA, 8/10/28. Singer, formerly married to Debbie Reynolds, Elizabeth Taylor, and Connie Stevens, father of Carrie Fisher. *The Eddie Fisher Show.*

FISHER, JOELY. 10/29/67. Actor, daughter of Eddie Fisher. *Ellen.*

FISHER, MATTHEW. Croydon, England, 3/7/46. Keyboardist. Procol Harum.

FISHER, ROGER. Seattle, WA, 2/14/50. Guitarist. Heart.

FITZGERALD, GERALDINE. Dublin, Ireland, 11/24/14. Actor. *Wuthering Heights.*

FLACK, ROBERTA. Black Mountain, NC, 2/10/40. Pop singer. "The First Time Ever I Saw Your Face."

FLATLEY, MICHAEL. 7/16/58. Dancer. *Lord of the Dance.*

FLEA (Michael Balzary). Melbourne, Australia. Singer, bassist. The Red Hot Chili Peppers.

FLEETWOOD, MICK. London, England, 6/24/42. Drummer. Fleetwood Mac.

FLEMING, PEGGY. San Jose, CA, 7/27/48. Ice skater. Olympic gold medalist.

FLETCHER, ANDY. Basildon, England, 7/8/60. Keyboardist. Depeche Mode.

FLETCHER, LOUISE. Birmingham, AL, 7/22/34. Actor. *One Flew over the Cuckoo's Nest.*

FLOYD, EDDIE. Montgomery, AL, 6/25/35. R&B singer, songwriter.

FOGELBERG, DAN. Peoria, IL, 8/13/51. Guitarist, singer, songwriter.

FOGERTY, JOHN. Berkeley, CA, 5/28/45. Singer, guitarist. Creedence Clearwater Revival.

FOLLOWS, MEGAN. Toronto, Canada, 3/14/68. Actor. *Anne of Green Gables.*

FONDA, PETER. New York, NY, 2/23/40. Actor, son of Henry Fonda, brother of Jane, father of Bridget. *Easy Rider.*

FONTAINE, JOAN (Joan de Havilland). Tokyo, Japan, 10/22/17. Actor, sister of Olivia de Havilland. *Suspicion.*

FONTANA, WAYNE (Glyn Ellis). Manchester, England, 10/28/40. Singer. Wayne Fontana & The Mindbenders.

FORD, FAITH. Alexandria, LA, 9/14/64. Actor. Corky Sherwood Forrest on *Murphy Brown.*

FORD, FRANKIE (Frankie Guzzo). Gretna, LA, 8/4/40. Singer.

FORD, LITA. London, England, 9/23/59. Lead guitarist. The Runaways.

FOREMAN, CHRIS. England, 8/8/58. Guitarist. Madness.

FOREMAN, GEORGE. Marshall, TX, 1/10/49. Boxer, actor. *George.*

FORSSI, KEN. Cleveland, OH, 1943. Bassist. Love.

FORSTER, ROBERT. Rochester, NY, 7/13/41. Actor. *Jackie Brown.*

FORSYTHE, JOHN (John Freund). Penns Grove, NJ, 1/29/18. Actor. Blake Carrington on *Dynasty.*

FORTUNE, JIMMY. Newport News, VA, 3/1/55. Musician. Statler Brothers.

FORTUNE, NICK (Nick Fortuna). Chicago, IL, 5/1/46. Bassist. The Buckinghams.

FOSTER, MEG. Reading, PA, 5/14/48. Actor. *Cagney and Lacey.*

FOX, JACKIE. California, 1960. Bassist. The Runaways.

FOX, JAMES. London, England, 5/19/39. Actor. *The Loneliness of the Long Distance Runner.*

FOX, SAMANTHA. England, 4/15/66. Singer. "Naughty Girls (Need Love Too)."

FOX, TERRY (Terrance Stanley Fox). Winnipeg, Canada, 7/28/58. Track athlete, fund-raiser.

FOXTON, BRUCE. Woking, Surrey England, 9/1/55. Guitarist. The Jam.

FOXWORTH, ROBERT. Houston, TX, 11/1/41. Actor. Chase Gioberti on *Falcon Crest.*

FOXWORTHY, JEFF Hapeville, GA, 9/6/58. Comedian, actor. "You Might Be a Redneck If…"

FRAKES, JONATHAN. Bethlehem, PA, 8/19/52. Actor. Commander William Riker on *Star Trek: The Next Generation.*

FRAME, RODDY. East Kilbride, Scotland, 1/29/64. Singer, guitarist. Aztec Camera.

FRAMPTON, PETER KENNETH. Beckenham, England, 4/22/50. Guitarist, singer, songwriter.

FRANCIOSA, ANTHONY (Anthony Papaleo). New York, NY, 10/25/28. Actor. *The Long Hot Summer.*

FRANCIS, ANNE. Ossining, NY, 9/16/30. Actor, former child model.

FRANCIS, BILL. Mobile, AL, 1/16/42. Keyboardist, singer. Dr. Hook.

FRANCIS, CONNIE (Concetta Franconero). Newark, NJ, 12/12/38. Singer. "Where the Boys Are."

FRANCIS, GENIE. 5/26/62. Actor. *General Hospital.*

FRANKEN, AL. 5/21/51. Actor, author. *Rush Limbaugh's a Big Fat Idiot.*

FRANKLIN, BONNIE. 1/6/44. Actor. *One Day At A Time.*

FRANTZ, CHRIS (Charlton Frantz). Fort Campbell, KY, 5/8/51. Drummer. Talking Heads.

FRASER, ANDY. London, England, 8/7/52. Bassist. Free.

FRAZIER, JOE. Beaufort, SC, 1/17/44. Boxer, former heavyweight champ.

FREDRIKSSON, MARIE. Sweden, 5/30/58. Singer. Roxette.

FREEMAN, BOBBY. San Francisco, CA, 6/13/40. Singer, songwriter.

FREEMAN, MORGAN. Memphis, TN, 6/1/37. Actor. *Driving Miss Daisy.*

FREHLEY, ACE (Paul Frehley). The Bronx, NY, 4/22/51. Guitarist, singer. Kiss.

FREIBERG, DAVID. Boston, MA, 8/24/38. Bassist. Quicksilver Messenger Service.

FREWER, MATT. Washington, DC, 1/4/58. Actor. *Max Headroom.*

FREY, GLENN. Detroit, MI, 11/6/48. Singer, songwriter. The Eagles.

FRICKER, BRENDA. Dublin, Ireland, 2/17/45. Actor. *My Left Foot.*

FRIPP, ROBERT. Wimborne Minster, England, 1946. Guitarist. King Crimson.

FROST, CRAIG. Flint, MI, 4/20/48. Keyboardist. Grand Funk Railroad.

FRY, MARTIN. Manchester, England, 3/9/58. Singer. ABC.

FUNICELLO, ANNETTE. Utica, NY, 10/22/42. Actor, Mouseketeer. *Beach Blanket Bingo.*

FURAY, RICHIE. Yellow Springs, OH, 5/9/44. Singer, guitarist. Buffalo Springfield; Poco.

FURUHOLMEN, MAGS. Oslo, Norway, 11/1/62. Keyboardist, singer. a-ha.

G, KENNY. 6/5/56. Musician. *Breathless*.

GABLE, JOHN CLARK. Los Angeles, CA, 3/20/61. Actor. Son of Clark Gable.

GABOR, ZSA ZSA (Sari Gabor). Budapest, Hungary, 2/6/17. Actor. *Moulin Rouge*.

GABRIEL, PETER. Cobham, England, 2/13/50. Singer, songwriter. Genesis.

GAHAN, DAVE. Epping, England, 5/9/62. Singer. Depeche Mode.

GAIL, MAXWELL. Derfoil, MI, 4/5/43. Actor. Sergeant Stanley Wojohowicz on *Barney Miller*.

GALLAGHER, PETER. Armonk, NY, 8/19/55. Actor. *sex, lies and videotape*.

GARDNER, CARL. Tyler, TX, 4/29/27. Lead singer. The Coasters.

GARFAT, JANCE. California, 3/3/44. Bassist, singer. Dr. Hook.

GARFUNKEL, ART. New York, NY, 11/5/41. Singer, actor, former partner of Paul Simon. *Carnal Knowledge*.

GARLAND, BEVERLY. Santa Cruz, CA, 10/17/26. Actor. *My Three Sons*.

GARNER, JAMES (James Baumgarner). Norma, OK, 4/7/28. Actor, producer. *The Rockford Files*.

GARR, TERI. Lakewood, OH, 12/11/44. Actor. *Tootsie*.

GARRETT, BETTY. St. Joseph, MO, 5/23/19. Actor. *All in the Family*.

GARRITY, FREDDIE. Manchester, England, 11/14/40. Singer. Freddie & The Dreamers.

GARTH, JENNIE. Champaign, IL, 4/3/72. Actor. Kelly Taylor on *Beverly Hills 90210*.

GARTSIDE, GREEN (Green Strohmeyer-Gartside). Cardiff, Wales, 6/22/56. Singer. Scritti Politti.

GARY, BRUCE. Burbank, CA, 4/7/52. Drummer. The Knack.

GATES, DAVID. Tulsa, OK, 12/11/40. Keyboardist, singer. Bread.

GATLIN, RUDY. 8/20/52. Singer. The Gatlin Brothers.

GATLIN, STEVE. 4/4/51. Singer. The Gatlin Brothers.

GAUDIO, BOB. The Bronx, NY, 11/17/42. Singer, organist. The Four Seasons.

GAYLE, CRYSTAL (Brenda Webb). Paintsville, KY, 1/9/51. Country singer.

GAYLORD, MITCH. Van Nuys, CA, 1961. Gymnast.

GAYNOR, MITZI (Francesca Marlene Von Gerber). Chicago, IL, 9/4/31. Actor. *Anything Goes*.

GAZZARA, BEN (Biago Gazzara). New York, NY, 8/28/30. Actor. *Inchon*.

GEARY, ANTHONY. Coalville, UT, 5/29/47. Actor. Luke Spencer on *General Hospital*.

GEARY, CYNTHIA. Jackson, MS, 3/21/66. Actor. *Northern Exposure*.

GEFFEN, DAVID Brooklyn, NY, 2/21/43. Procucer, executive. Geffen Records, Dreamworks SKG.

GEILS, J. (Jerome Geils). New York, NY, 2/20/46. Guitarist. The J. Geils Band.

GELDOF, BOB. Dublin, Ireland, 10/5/54. Singer. The Boomtown Rats.

GERARD, GIL. Little Rock, AR, 1/23/43. Actor. *Buck Rogers in the 25th Century*.

GERARDO. Ecuador, 1965. Rap artist. "Rico Suave."

GERTZ, JAMI. Chicago, IL, 10/28/65. Actor. *Less Than Zero; Twister*.

GESSLE, PER. 1/12/59. Guitarist, singer. Roxette.

GETTY, BALTHAZAR. 1/22/75. Actor, grandson of J. Paul Getty. *Where the Day Takes You*.

GETTY, ESTELLE. New York, NY, 7/25/23. Actor. Sophia Petrillo on *The Golden Girls*.

GHOSTLEY, ALICE. Eve, MO, 8/14/26. Actor. *Bewitched*.

GIAMMARESE, CARL. Chicago, IL, 8/21/47. Guitarist. The Buckinghams.

GIANNINI, GIANCARLO. Spezia, Italy, 8/1/42. Actor. *Seven Beauties*.

GIBB, BARRY. Isle of Man, England, 9/1/46. Singer, guitarist. The Bee Gees.

GIBB, CYNTHIA. Bennington, VT, 12/14/63. Actor. *Madman of the People*.

GIBB, MAURICE. Manchester, England, 12/22/49. Singer, bassist. The Bee Gees.

GIBB, ROBIN. Manchester, England, 12/22/49. Singer. The Bee Gees.

GIBBINS, MIKE. Swansea, Wales, 3/12/49. Drummer. Badfinger.

GIBBONS, BILLY. Houston, TX, 12/16/49. Guitarist, singer. ZZ Top.

GIBBONS, LEEZA. 3/26/57. TV personality. *Entertainment Tonight*.

GIBBS, MARLA (Margaret Bradley). Chicago, IL, 6/14/31. Actor. Florence Johnston on *The Jeffersons*.

GIBSON, DEBORAH. Long Island, NY, 8/31/70. Singer, songwriter, actor. "Foolish Beat."

GIBSON, HENRY. Germantown, PA, 9/21/35. Actor. Poet from *Laugh-In*.

GIFFORD, FRANK. Santa Monica, CA, 8/16/30. Football player turned sports commentator, married to Kathie Lee Gifford. *Monday Night Football*.

GIFT, ROLAND. Birmingham, England, 5/28/62. Singer. Fine Young Cannibals.

GIGUERE, RUSS. Portsmouth, NH, 10/18/43. Singer, guitarist. The Association.

GILBERT, GILLIAN. Manchester, England, 1/27/61. Keyboardist. New Order.

GILBERT, MELISSA. Los Angeles, CA, 5/8/64. Actor, daughter of Robert and Barbara Crane. *Little House on the Prairie*.

GILBERT, SARA (Rebecca Sara MacMahon). Santa Monica, CA, 1/29/75. Actor, sister of Melissa and Jonathan Gilbert. Darlene Conner on *Roseanne*.

GILES, MIKE. Bournemouth, England, 1942. Drummer. King Crimson.

GILL, PETER. Liverpool, England, 3/8/64. Drummer. Frankie Goes to Hollywood.

GILLAN, IAN. Hounslow, England, 8/19/45. Singer. Deep Purple.

GILLIAM, TERRY. Minneapolis, MN, 11/22/40. Writer, director, actor. *Monty Python and the Holy Grail*.

GILMORE, JIMMIE DALE. Tulia, TX, 1945. Country singer. "Dallas."

GILMOUR, DAVID. Cambridge, England, 3/6/44. Singer, guitarist. Pink Floyd.

GINTY, ROBERT. New York, NY, 11/14/48. Actor. *Baa Baa Black Sheep*.

GILPIN, PERI. 5/27/61. Actor. *Frasier*.

GIVENS, ROBIN. New York, NY, 11/27/64. Actor, formerly married to Mike Tyson. *Head of the Class*.

GLASER, PAUL MICHAEL. Cambridge, MA, 3/25/43. Actor, director. Det. Dave Starsky on *Starsky and Hutch*.

GLASS, RON. Evansville, IN, 7/10/45. Actor. *Barney Miller*.

GLEASON, JOANNA. Winnipeg, Canada, 6/2/50. Actor, daughter of Monty Hall. *Into the Woods*.

GLENN, SCOTT. Pittsburgh, PA, 1/26/42. Actor. *Urban Cowboy*.

GLESS, SHARON. Los Angeles, CA, 5/31/43. Actor. Chris Cagney on *Cagney and Lacey*.

GLITTER, GARY (Paul Gadd). Banbury, England, 5/8/40. Singer, songwriter.

GLOVER, CRISPIN. New York, NY, 9/20/64. Actor. George McFly in *Back to the Future.*

GLOVER, DANNY. San Francisco, CA, 7/22/47. Actor. *Lethal Weapon.*

GLOVER, JOHN. Kingston, NY, 8/7/44. Actor. *Shamus.*

GLOVER, ROGER. Brecon, Wales, 11/30/45. Bassist. Deep Purple.

GOBLE, GRAHAM. Adelaide, Australia, 5/15/47. Guitarist. Little River Band.

GODLEY, KEVIN. Manchester, England, 10/7/45. Singer, drummer. 10cc; Godley & Creme.

GOLD, TRACEY. New York, NY, 5/16/69. Actor. *Growing Pains.*

GOLDEN, WILLIAM LEE. Brewton, AL, 1/12/39. Singer. The Oak Ridge Boys.

GOLDING, LYNVAL. Coventry, England, 7/24/51. Guitarist. The Specials.

GOLDTHWAIT, BOBCAT. Syracuse, NY, 5/26/62. Actor. *Police Academy* series.

GOLDWYN, TONY. Los Angeles, CA, 5/20/60. Actor. *Ghost.*

GOLINO, VALERIA. Naples, Italy, 10/22/66. Actor. *Rain Man.*

GOODALL, JANE. London, England, 4/3/34. Author, anthropologist. *In the Shadow of Man.*

GOODEN, SAM. Chattanooga, TN, 9/2/39. Singer. The Impressions.

GORBACHEV, MIKHAIL. Privolnoye, Russia, 3/2/31. Former leader of the USSR.

GORE, ALBERT JR. Washington, DC, 3/31/48. Vice president of the United States.

GORE, LESLEY. New York, NY, 5/2/46. Singer. "It's My Party."

GORE, MARTIN. Basildon, England, 7/23/61. Keyboardist. Depeche Mode.

GORHAM, SCOTT. Santa Monica, CA, 3/17/51. Guitarist. Thin Lizzy.

GORMAN, STEVE. Hopkinsville, KY, 8/17/65. Drummer. The Black Crowes.

GORME, EYDIE. New York, NY, 8/16/32. Singer. Steve and Eydie.

GORRIE, ALAN. Perth, Scotland, 7/19/46. Singer, bassist. Average White Band.

GORSHIN, FRANK. Pittsburgh, PA, 4/5/33. Actor. The Riddler on *Batman.*

GOSSETT, LOUIS JR. Brooklyn, NY, 5/27/37. Actor. *An Officer and a Gentleman.*

GOTTI, JOHN. New York, NY, 10/27/41. Reputed mob leader.

GOUDREAU, BARRY. Boston, MA, 11/29/51. Guitarist. Boston.

GOULD, BILLY. Los Angeles, CA, 4/24/63. Bassist. Faith No More.

GOULD, BOON. 3/14/55. Guitarist. Level 42.

GOULD, ELLIOTT (Elliott Goldstein). Brooklyn, NY, 8/29/38. Actor. Formerly married to Barbra Streisand. *Bob & Carol & Ted & Alice.*

GOULD, PHIL. 2/28/57. Drummer. Level 42.

GOULDMAN, GRAHAM. Manchester, England, 5/10/45. Singer, guitarist. 10cc.

GOULET, ROBERT (Stanley Applebaum). Lawrence, MA, 11/26/33. Singer, actor. *Blue Light.*

GRAF, STEFFI. Bruhl, Germany, 6/14/69. Tennis player, youngest woman to win French Open.

GRAHAM, BILLY. Charlotte, NC, 11/7/18. Evangelist. *Billy Graham Crusades.*

GRAHAM, LARRY. Beaumont, TX, 8/14/46. Bass guitarist. Sly & The Family Stone.

GRAMM, LOU. Rochester, NY, 5/2/50. Singer. Foreigner.

GRANDMASTER FLASH (Joseph Saddler). New York, NY, 1958. Rap artist. Grandmaster Flash; Melle Mel & The Furious Five.

GRANDY, FRED. Sioux City, IA, 6/29/48. Actor, politician. Burl "Gopher" Smith on *The Love Boat.*

GRANGER, FARLEY. San Jose, CA, 7/1/25. Actor. *Strangers on a Train.*

GRANT, AMY. Augusta, GA, 11/25/60. Singer. *Age to Age.*

GRANT, EDDY (Edmond Grant). Plaisance, Guyana, 3/5/48. Reggae singer, songwriter.

GRANT, LEE (Lyova Rosenthal). New York, NY, 10/31/27. Actor, mother of Dinah Manoff. *Peyton Place.*

GRANTHAM, GEORGE. Cordell, OK, 11/20/47. Drummer, singer. Poco.

GRATZER, ALAN. Syracuse, NY, 11/9/48. Drummer. REO Speedwagon.

GRAVES, PETER (Peter Aurness). Minneapolis, MN, 3/18/26. Actor, brother of James Arness. Jim Phelps on *Mission: Impossible.*

GRAY, EDDIE. 2/27/48. Guitarist. Tommy James & The Shondells.

GRAY, LES. Carshalton, England, 4/9/46. Singer. Mud.

GRAY, LINDA. Santa Monica, CA, 9/12/40. Actor. *Dallas.*

GRAY, SPALDING. Barrington, RI, 6/5/41. Actor, writer, performance artist. *The Killing Fields.*

GREBB, MARTY. Chicago, IL, 9/2/46. Keyboardist. The Buckinghams.

GREEN, AL (Al Greene). Forrest City, AR, 4/13/46. R&B singer, songwriter.

GREEN, BRIAN AUSTIN. 7/15/73. Actor. *Beverly Hills 90210.*

GREEN, KARL. Salford, England, 7/31/47. Bassist. Herman's Hermits.

GREENAWAY, PETER. Newport, Wales, 4/5/42. Director, writer. *The Cook, the Thief, His Wife and Her Lover.*

GREENFIELD, DAVE. Keyboardist. The Stranglers.

GREENSPOON, JIMMY. Los Angeles, CA, 2/7/48. Organist. Three Dog Night.

GREENWOOD, ALAN. New York, NY, 10/20/51. Keyboardist. Foreigner.

GREGG, BRIAN. Bassist. Johnny Kidd & The Pirates.

GREGORY, GLENN. Sheffield, England, 5/16/58. Singer. Heaven 17.

GRETZKY, WAYNE. Brantford, Canada, 1/26/61. Hockey player.

GREY, JENNIFER. New York, NY, 3/26/60. Actor, daughter of Joel. *Dirty Dancing.*

GREY, JOEL (Joel Katz). Cleveland, OH, 4/11/32. Musical comedy performer, father of Jennifer. *Cabaret.*

GRIER, DAVID ALAN. Detroit, MI, 6/30/55. Actor. *In Living Color.*

GRIER, PAM. 5/26/49. Actor. *Jackie Brown.*

GRIER, ROSEY (Roosevelt Grier). Cuthbert, GA, 7/14/32. Football player, actor.

GRIFFEY, KEN JR. 11/21/69. Baseball player.

GRIFFITH, ANDY. Mt. Airy, NC, 6/1/26. Actor, writer, producer. *The Andy Griffith Show.*

GRIFFITH, NANCI. Austin, TX, 7/6/53. Singer, songwriter. "From a Distance."

GRILL, ROB. Los Angeles, CA, 11/30/44. Bassist, singer. The Grass Roots.

GROSS, MARY. Chicago, IL, 3/25/53. Actor, sister of Michael. *Saturday Night Live.*

GROSS, MICHAEL. Chicago, IL, 6/21/47. Actor, brother of Mary. Steven Keaton on *Family Ties*.

GRUNDY, HUGH. Winchester, England, 3/6/45. Drummer. The Zombies.

GUCCIONE, BOB. New York, NY, 12/17/30. Publisher, founder of *Penthouse*.

GUEST, CHRISTOPHER. New York, NY, 2/5/48. Actor, writer, married to Jamie Lee Curtis. *This Is Spinal Tap*.

GUEST, LANCE. Saratoga, CA, 7/21/60. Actor. *Knots Landing*.

GUEST, WILLIAM. Atlanta, GA, 6/2/41. Singer. Gladys Knight & The Pips.

GUILLAUME, ROBERT (Robert Williams). St. Louis, MO, 11/30/27. Actor. Benson DuBois on *Soap*.

GUISEWITE, CATHY. 9/5/50. Cartoonist. *Cathy*.

GULAGER, CLU. Holdenville, OK, 11/16/28. Actor. *The Last Picture Show*.

GUMBEL, BRYANT. New Orleans, LA, 9/29/48. News show host and sportscaster. *Today*.

GUSTAFSON, KARIN. Miami, FL, 6/23/59. Actor. *Taps*.

GUSTAFSON, STEVEN. Bassist. 10,000 Maniacs.

GUTHRIE, ARLO. New York, NY, 7/10/47. Folk singer, songwriter. "Alice's Restaurant."

GUTTENBERG, STEVE. Brooklyn, NY, 8/24/58. Actor. *Three Men and a Baby*.

GUY, BILLY. Attasca, TX, 6/20/36. Baritone. The Coasters.

GUY, BUDDY (George Guy). Lettsworth, LA, 7/30/36. Blues guitarist.

GUY, JASMINE. Boston, MA, 3/10/62. Actor. Whitley Gilbert on *A Different World*.

HAAS, LUKAS. West Hollywood, CA, 4/16/76. Actor. *Witness*.

HACK, SHELLEY. Greenwich, CT, 7/6/52. Actor. *Charlie's Angels*.

HACKETT, BUDDY (Leonard Hacker). Brooklyn, NY, 8/31/24. Actor. *It's a Mad Mad Mad Mad World; The Love Bug*.

HADLEY, TONY. Islington, England, 6/2/59. Singer. Spandau Ballet.

HAGAR, SAMMY. Monterey, CA, 10/13/47. Singer, guitarist. Van Halen.

HAGERTY, JULIE. Cincinnati, OH, 6/15/55. Actor. *Airplane!*

HAGMAN, LARRY (Larry Hageman). Fort Worth, TX, 9/21/31. Actor, son of Mary Martin. J. R. Ewing on *Dallas*.

HAHN, JESSICA. Massapequa, NY, 7/7/59. *Playboy* model, involved in PTL/Jim Bakker scandal.

HAID, CHARLES. San Francisco, CA, 6/2/43. Actor, director, producer. Andrew Renko on *Hill Street Blues*.

HAIM, COREY. Toronto, Canada, 12/23/71. Actor. *The Lost Boys*.

HALE, BARBARA. DeKalb, IL, 4/18/22. Actor, mother of William Katt. Della Street on *Perry Mason*.

HALFORD, ROB. Birmingham, England, 8/25/51. Singer. Judas Priest.

HALL, ANTHONY MICHAEL. Boston, MA, 4/14/68. Actor. *Sixteen Candles*.

HALL, ARSENIO. Cleveland, OH, 2/12/56. Actor. *The Arsenio Hall Show*.

HALL, BRIDGET. Dallas, TX, 12/14/77. Supermodel.

HALL, BRUCE. Champaign, IL, 5/3/53. Bassist. REO Speedwagon.

HALL, DARYL (Daryl Hohl). Pottstown, PA, 10/11/46. Singer, guitarist. Hall & Oates.

HALL, DEIDRE. 10/31/47. Actor. Marlena Evans on *Days of Our Lives*.

HALL, FAWN. Annandale, VA, 9/4/59. Secretary for Oliver North. Iran-Contra scandal.

HALL, JERRY. 7/2/56. Model, formerly married to Mick Jagger.

HALL, MONTY. Winnipeg, Canada, 8/25/21. TV personality. *Let's Make a Deal*.

HALL, TERRY. Coventry, England, 3/19/59. Singer. The Specials.

HAM, GREG. Australia, 9/27/53. Saxophonist, keyboardist, flautist. Men at Work.

HAM, PETE. Swansea, Wales, 4/27/47. Guitarist, pianist, singer. Badfinger.

HAMEL, VERONICA. Philadelphia, PA, 11/20/43. Actor. Joyce Davenport on *Hill Street Blues*.

HAMILL, DOROTHY. Chicago, IL, 7/26/56. Ice skater. Olympic gold medalist.

HAMILL, MARK. Oakland, CA, 9/25/51. Actor. Luke Skywalker in *Star Wars* trilogy.

HAMILTON, GEORGE. Memphis, TN, 8/12/39. Actor. *Love at First Bite*.

HAMILTON, LINDA. Salisbury, MD, 9/26/56. Actor. Sarah Connor in *The Terminator*. Separated from James Cameron.

HAMILTON, SCOTT. Haverford, PA, 8/28/58. Ice skater.

HAMILTON, TOM. Colorado Springs, CO, 12/31/51. Bassist. Aerosmith.

HAMLIN, HARRY. Pasadena, CA, 10/30/51. Actor. *L.A. Law*.

HAMLISCH, MARVIN. New York, NY, 6/2/44. Composer. *The Way We Were; The Sting*.

HAMMER, MC. (Stanley Kirk Burrell). Oakland, CA, 3/30/62. Rap artist, dancer. *Please Hammer Don't Hurt 'Em*.

HAMMETT, KIRK. 11/18/62. Guitarist. Metallica.

HAMPSHIRE, SUSAN. London, England, 5/12/41. Actor. *The Forsythe Saga*.

HANCOCK, HERBIE. Chicago, IL, 4/12/40. Jazz pianist, composer. "Rockit."

HANNAH, DARYL. Chicago, IL, 12/3/60. Actor. *Splash*.

HANSON, ISAAC. 11/17/80. Singer. "MMMbop."

HANSON, TAYLOR. 3/14/83. Singer. "MMMbop."

HANSON, ZAC. 10/22/85. Singer. "MMMbop."

HARDING, TONYA. Portland, OR, 11/12/70. Figure skater. Pled guilty to hindering prosecution in Nancy Kerrigan attack.

HARDISON, KADEEM. Brooklyn, NY, 7/24/66. Actor. Dwayne Wayne on *A Different World*.

HAREWOOD, DORIAN. Dayton, OH, 8/6/50. Actor. *Roots—The Next Generation*.

HARKET, MORTEN. Konigsberg, Norway, 9/14/59. Lead singer. a-ha.

HARLEY, STEVE (Steve Nice). London, England, 2/27/51. Singer. Steve Harley & Cockney Rebel.

HARLIN, RENNY. 3/15/58. Director, formerly married to Geena Davis.

HARMON, MARK. Los Angeles, CA, 9/2/51. Actor. *Chicago Hope*. Married to Pam Dawber.

HARPER, JESSICA. Chicago, IL, 10/10/49. Actor.

HARPER, TESS (Tessie Jean Washam). Mammoth Spring, AR, 8/15/50. Actor. *Crimes of the Heart*.

HARPER, VALERIE. Suffern, NY, 8/22/39. Actor. Rhoda Morgenstern on *The Mary Tyler Moore Show*.

HARRINGTON, PAT. New York, NY, 8/13/29. Actor. Dwayne Schneider on *One Day at a Time*.

HARRIS, BARBARA (Sandra Markowitz). Evanston, IL, 7/25/35. Actor. *Family Plot*.

HARRIS, JULIE. Grosse Point, MI, 12/2/25. Actor.

Knots Landing.

HARRIS, EMMYLOU. 4/2/47. Singer.

HARRIS, MEL (Mary Ellen Harris). Bethlehem, PA, 7/12/56. Actor. Hope Murdoch Steadman on *thirtysomething.*

HARRIS, RICHARD. Limerick, Ireland, 10/1/33. Actor. *A Man Called Horse.*

HARRISON, BILLY. Belfast, Ireland, 10/14/42. Lead guitarist. Them.

HARRISON, GEORGE. Liverpool, England, 2/25/43. Singer, lead guitarist. The Beatles.

HARRISON, GREGORY. Catalina Island, CA, 5/31/50. Actor. *Trapper John, MD.*

HARRISON, JENILEE. Northridge, CA, 6/12/59. Actor. Jamie Ewing Barnes on *Dallas.*

HARRISON, JERRY. Milwaukee, WI, 2/21/49. Keyboardist. Talking Heads.

HARRISON, NOEL. London, England, 1/29/34. Singer, actor. *The Girl from U.N.C.L.E.*

HARRY, DEBORAH. Miami, FL, 7/1/45. Singer. Blondie.

HART, MARY. Sioux Falls, SD, 11/8/51. TV hostess. *Entertainment Tonight.*

HART, MICKY (Michael Hart). New York, NY, 9/11/44. Drummer, songwriter. Grateful Dead.

HARTLEY, MARIETTE. New York, NY, 6/21/40. Actor. *Peyton Place.*

HARTMAN, DAVID. Pawtucket, RI, 5/19/35. Actor, talk show host. *Good Morning America.*

HARTMAN, JOHN. Falls Church, VA, 3/18/50. Drummer. The Doobie Brothers.

HASSAN, NORMAN. Birmingham, England, 11/26/57. Percussionist. UB40.

HATCHER, TERI. 12/8/64. Actor. *Lois and Clark: The New Adventures of Superman.*

HATFIELD, BOBBY. Beaver Dam, WI, 8/10/40. Singer. The Righteous Brothers.

HATTON, BILLY. Liverpool, England, 6/9/41. Bassist. The Fourmost.

HAUER, RUTGER. Breukelen, Netherlands, 1/23/44. Actor. *Blade Runner.*

HAVENS, RICHIE. Brooklyn, NY, 1/21/41. Folk/blues guitarist, singer, songwriter.

HAWKING, STEPHEN. Oxford, England, 1/8/42. Theoretical physicist, author of *A Brief History of Time.*

HAY, COLIN. Scotland, 6/29/53. Singer. Men at Work.

HAY, ROY. Southend, England, 8/12/61. Guitarist, keyboardist. Culture Club.

HAYDOCK, ERIC. Stockport, England, 2/3/42. Bassist. The Hollies.

HAYES, CHRIS. California, 11/24/57. Lead guitarist. Huey Lewis & The News.

HAYES, ISAAC. Covington, TN, 8/20/42. R&B/rock saxophonist, keyboardist, singer, songwriter, radio personality, actor. *South Park.*

HAYS, ROBERT. Bethesda, MD, 7/24/47. Actor, married to Cherie Currie. *Airplane!*

HAYWARD, JUSTIN. Wiltshire, England, 10/14/46. Singer, songwriter. The Moody Blues.

HEADLY, GLENNE. New London, CT, 3/13/55. Actor, formerly married to John Malkovich. *Dirty Rotten Scoundrels.*

HEADON, NICKY. Bromley, England, 5/30/55. Drummer. The Clash.

HEALEY, JEFF. Toronto, Canada, 1966. Singer, songwriter, guitarist.

HEARD, JOHN. Washington, DC, 3/7/46. Actor. Father in *Home Alone.*

HEATON, PAUL. Birkenhead, England, 5/9/62. Singer, guitarist. The Housemartins.

HEDREN, TIPPI (Natalie Kay Hedren). New Ulm, MN, 1/19/35. Actor. Mother of Melanie Griffith. *The Birds.*

HEFNER, HUGH. Chicago, IL, 4/9/26. Publisher, founder of *Playboy.*

HELL, RICHARD (Richard Myers). Lexington, KY, 10/2/49. Bassist. Television.

HELLIWELL, JOHN. England, 2/15/45. Saxophonist. Supertramp.

HELM, LEVON. Marvell, AR, 5/26/42. Drummer, singer. The Band.

HELMSLEY, LEONA. New York, NY, 7/4/20. Hotel executive. Convicted of tax evasion.

HEMINGWAY, MARIEL. Ketchum, ID, 11/22/61. Actor, granddaughter of Ernest Hemingway, sister of Margaux. *Manhattan.*

HEMSLEY, SHERMAN. Philadelphia, PA, 2/1/38. Actor. George on *The Jeffersons.*

HENDERSON, ALAN. Belfast, Ireland, 11/26/44. Bassist. Them.

HENDERSON, BILLY. Detroit, MI, 8/9/39. Singer. The (Detroit) Spinners.

HENDERSON, FLORENCE. Dale, IN, 2/14/34. Actor. Carol Brady on *The Brady Bunch.*

HENLEY, DON. Linden, TX, 7/22/47. Singer, songwriter, drummer, guitarist. The Eagles.

HENNER, MARILU. Chicago, IL, 4/6/52. Actor. Elaine Nardo on *Taxi.*

HENRIKSEN, LANCE. New York, NY, 5/5/40. Actor. *Aliens.*

HENRY, BUCK (Buck Zuckerman). New York, NY, 12/9/30. Actor, writer. *Get Smart; That Was the Week That Was.*

HENRY, CLARENCE. Algiers, LA, 3/19/37. Singer. "Ain't Got No Home."

HENRY, JUSTIN. Rye, NY, 5/25/71. Actor. *Kramer vs. Kramer.*

HENRY, PRINCE. London, England, 8/15/84. British royalty, son of Prince Charles and Princess Diana.

HENSLEY, KEN. England, 8/24/45. Keyboardist, guitarist, singer, percussionist. Uriah Heep.

HENSLEY, PAMELA. Los Angeles, CA, 10/3/50. Actor. C. J. Parsons on *Matt Houston.*

HENSTRIDGE, NATASHA. 8/15/74. Actor. *Species.*

HERMAN, PEE-WEE (Paul Reubens). Peekskill, NY, 8/27/52. Children's performer. *Pee-Wee's Playhouse.*

HERRMANN, EDWARD. Washington, DC, 7/21/43. Actor. *The Paper Chase.*

HERSHEY, BARBARA (Barbara Herzstein). Hollywood, CA, 2/5/48. Actor. *Hannah and Her Sisters.*

HERVEY, JASON. Los Angeles, CA, 4/6/72. Actor. Wayne Arnold on *The Wonder Years.*

HESSEMAN, HOWARD. Salem, OR, 2/27/40. Actor. Dr. Johnny Fever on *WKRP in Cincinnati.*

HESTON, CHARLTON (Charles Carter). Evanston, IL, 10/4/24. Actor. *The Ten Commandments.*

HETFIELD, JAMES. 8/3/63. Singer, guitarist. Metallica.

HEWETT, HOWARD. Akron, OH, 10/1/55. Singer. Shalamar.

HEYWARD, NICK. Kent, England, 5/20/61. Guitarist, singer. Haircut 100.

HICKS, CATHERINE. New York, NY, 8/6/51. Actor. *7th Heaven.*

HICKS, TONY. Nelson, England, 12/16/43. Guitarist. The Hollies.

HILL, ANITA. Tulsa, OK, 7/30/56. Lawyer, law professor. Accused Supreme Court nominee Clarence Thomas of sexual harrassment.

HILL, ARTHUR. Saskatchewan, Canada, 8/1/22. Actor. *Owen Marshall, Counsellor at Law.*

HILL, DAVE. Fleet Castle, England, 4/4/52. Guitarist. Slade.

HILL, DUSTY. Dallas, TX, 5/19/49. Bassist, singer. ZZ Top.

HILL, STEVEN. Seattle, WA, 2/24/22. Actor. *Law and Order.*

HILLERMAN, JOHN. Denison, TX, 12/20/32. Actor. Jonathan Quayle Higgins III on *Magnum P.I.*

HILLERMAN, TONY. Sacred Heart, OK, 5/27/25. Novelist.

HILLMAN, CHRIS. Los Angeles, CA, 12/4/42. Singer, bassist. The Byrds.

HINES, GREGORY. New York, NY, 2/14/46. Actor, dancer. *The Cotton Club.*

HINGLE, PAT (Martin Patterson Hingle). Denver, CO, 7/19/23. Actor. *Gunsmoke.*

HINSLEY, HARVEY. Northampton, England, 1/19/48. Guitarist. Hot Chocolate.

HIRSCH, GARY "CHICKEN." England, 1940. Drummer. Country Joe & The Fish.

HIRSCH, JUDD. New York, NY, 3/15/35. Actor. Alex Rieger on *Taxi.*

HITCHCOCK, RUSSELL. Melbourne, Australia, 6/15/49. Singer. Air Supply.

HO, DON. Kakaako, HI, 8/13/30. Singer. "Tiny Bubbles."

HOBBS, RANDY. 3/22/48. Bassist. The McCoys.

HODGE, PATRICIA. Lincolnshire, England, 9/29/46. Actor. *The Elephant Man.*

HODGSON, ROGER. Portsmouth, England,

3/21/50. Guitarist. Supertramp.

HODO, DAVID. 7/7/50. Singer. The Village People.

HOFFS, SUSANNA. Newport Beach, CA, 1/17/57. Guitarist, singer. The Bangles.

HOGAN, HULK (Terry Gene Bollea). Augusta, GA, 8/11/53. Wrestler, former World Federation heavyweight champion.

HOGAN, PAUL. Lightning Ridge, Australia, 10/8/39. Actor. *Crocodile Dundee.*

HOLBROOK, HAL. Cleveland, OH, 2/17/25. Actor. *All the President's Men.*

HOLDER, NODDY (Neville Holder). Walsall, England, 6/15/50. Guitarist, singer. Slade.

HOLLAND, JOOLS (Julian Holland). 1/24/58. Keyboardist. Squeeze.

HOLLIMAN, EARL. Delhi, LA, 9/11/28. Actor. *Police Woman.*

HOLLIS, MARK. Tottenham, England, 1955. Singer, guitarist, keyboardist. Talk Talk.

HOLM, CELESTE. New York, NY, 4/29/19. Actor. *All About Eve.*

HOLMES, LARRY. Cuthbert, GA, 11/3/49. Boxer. Former heavyweight champ.

HOOK, PETER. Salford, England, 2/13/56. Bassist. Joy Division; New Order.

HOOKER, JOHN LEE. Clarksdale, MS, 8/22/17. Legendary blues guitarist, singer, songwriter.

HOOKS, JAN. Decatur, GA, 4/23/57. Actor. Carlene Frazier Dobber on *Designing Women.*

HOPE, BOB (Leslie Hope). Eltham, England, 5/29/03. Actor, performer for overseas troops. *The Road* movies with Bing Crosby.

HOPE, DAVE. Kansas, 10/7/49. Bassist. Kansas.

HOPKIN, MARY. Pontardawe, Wales, 5/3/50.

Singer, discovered by the Beatles. "Those Were the Days."

HOPKINS, TELMA. Louisville, KY, 10/28/48. Singer, actor, former member of Tony Orlando & Dawn. *Family Matters.*

HOPPER, DENNIS. Dodge City, KS, 5/17/36. Actor, director. *Easy Rider.*

HOPPER, SEAN. California, 3/31/53. Keyboardist. Huey Lewis & The News.

HOPWOOD, KEITH. Manchester, England, 10/26/46. Guitarist. Herman's Hermits.

HORNE, LENA. Brooklyn, NY, 6/30/17. Singer, actor.

HORNSBY, BRUCE. Williamsburg, VA, 11/23/54. Singer, keyboardist, accordionist. Bruce Hornsby & The Range.

HOSKINS, BOB. Bury St. Edmunds, England, 10/26/42. Actor. *Who Framed Roger Rabbit.*

HOWARD, ALAN. Dagenham, England, 10/17/41. Bassist. Brian Poole & The Tremeloes.

HOWARD, ARLISS. Independence, MO, 1955. Actor. *Full Metal Jacket.*

HOWARD, KEN. El Centro, CA, 3/28/44. Actor. *The White Shadow.*

HOWE, STEVE. London, England, 4/8/47. Guitarist, singer. Yes; Asia.

HUCKNALL, MICK "RED." Manchester, England, 6/8/60. Singer. Simply Red.

HUDLIN, REGINALD. Centerville, IL, 12/15/61. Director, writer, producer, brother of Warrington. *House Party.*

HUDLIN, WARRINGTON. East St. Louis, IL, 1952. Producer, director, brother of Reginald. *House Party.*

HUDSON, GARTH. London, Canada, 8/2/37. Organist. The Band.

HUGG, MIKE. Andover, England, 8/11/42. Drummer.

Manfred Mann.

HULCE, TOM. White Water, WI, 12/6/53. Actor. *Amadeus.*

HUMPERDINCK, ENGELBERT (Arnold Dorsey). Madras, India, 5/2/36. Pop singer. *The Engelbert Humperdinck Show.*

HUMPHREYS, PAUL. London, England, 2/27/60. Keyboardist. Orchestral Manoeuvres in the Dark (OMD).

HUNT, BILL. 5/23/47. Keyboardist. Electric Light Orchestra (ELO).

HUNT, LINDA. Morristown, NJ, 4/2/45. Actor. *The Year of Living Dangerously.*

HUNTER, IAN. Shrewsbury, England, 6/3/46. Singer, guitarist. Mott The Hoople.

HUNTER, TAB (Arthur Gelien). New York, NY, 7/11/31. Actor. *Damn Yankees.*

HUPPERT, ISABELLE. Paris, France, 3/16/55. Actor. *Entre Nous.*

HURT, JOHN. Shirebrook, England, 1/22/40. Actor. *The Elephant Man.*

HURT, MARY BETH (Mary Beth Supinger). Marshalltown, IA, 9/26/48. Actor, formerly married to William Hurt. *The World According to Garp.*

HURT, WILLIAM. Washington, DC, 3/20/50. Actor, formerly married to Mary Beth Hurt. *Children of a Lesser God.*

HUSSEIN, SADDAM. Tikrit, Iraq, 4/28/37. Leader of Iraq.

HUSSEY, WAYNE. Bristol, England, 5/26/59. Guitarist, singer. The Mission.

HUSTON, ANJELICA. Santa Monica, CA, 7/8/51. Actor, daughter of John Huston. *Prizzi's Honor.*

HUTTER, RALF. Krefeld, Germany, 1946. Keyboardist, drummer, singer. Kraftwerk.

HUTTON, DANNY. Buncrana, Ireland, 9/10/42. Singer. Three Dog Night.

HUTTON, LAUREN (Mary Hutton). Charleston, SC, 11/17/43. Actor, model. *American Gigolo.*

HUTTON, TIMOTHY. Malibu, CA, 8/16/60. Actor, director. *Ordinary People.*

HUXLEY, RICK. Dartford, England, 8/5/42. Guitarist. The Dave Clark Five.

HYNDE, CHRISSIE. Akron, OH, 9/7/51. Singer, divorced from Jim Kerr. The Pretenders.

IACOCCA, LEE (Lido Anthony Iacocca). Allentown, PA, 10/15/24. Auto executive, author. *Iacocca.*

IAN, JANIS (Janis Fink). New York, NY, 4/7/51. Folk/rock singer, songwriter.

ICE-T Newark, NJ, 2/16/58. Rap artist, actor. *New Jack City, Breakin'.*

IDLE, ERIC. Durham, England, 3/29/43. Actor. *Monty Python's Flying Circus.*

IDOL, BILLY (Billy Broad). Stanmore, England, 11/30/55. Singer, songwriter.

IGLESIAS, JULIO. Madrid, Spain, 9/23/43. Pop singer, songwriter.

ILLSLEY, JOHN. Leicester, England, 6/24/49. Bassist. Dire Straits.

IMAN. Mogadishu, Somalia, 7/25/55. Model, married to David Bowie.

INGELS, MARTY. Brooklyn, NY, 3/9/36. Actor, agent, married to Shirley Jones. *The Pruitts of Southampton.*

INGLE, DOUG. Omaha, NE, 9/9/46. Singer, keyboardist. Iron Butterfly.

INGRAM, JAMES. Akron, OH, 2/16/56. R&B singer, songwriter.

INNES, NEIL. Essex, England, 12/9/44. Singer, keyboardist. The Bonzo Dog Doo-Dah Band.

INNIS, ROY. Saint Croix, Virgin Islands, 6/6/34. Civil rights leader.

IOMMI, TONY. Birmingham, England, 2/19/48. Guitarist. Black Sabbath.

IRELAND, KATHY. Santa Barbara, CA, 3/20/63. Model, sister of Mary and Cynthia. *Sports Illustrated* swimsuit cover girl.

IRELAND, PATRICIA. Oak Park, IL, 10/19/45. Political activist. President of NOW.

IRVING, AMY. Palo Alto, CA, 9/10/53. Actor. *Yentl.*

IRWIN, BILL. Santa Monica, CA, 4/11/50. Actor. *Eight Men Out.*

ISLEY, O'KELLY. Cincinnati, OH, 12/25/37. Singer. The Isley Brothers.

ISLEY, RONALD. Cincinnati, OH, 5/21/41. Lead singer. The Isley Brothers.

ISLEY, RUDOLPH. Cincinnati, OH, 4/1/39. Singer. The Isley Brothers.

IVEY, JUDITH. El Paso, TX, 9/4/51. Actor. *Designing Women.*

IVORY, JAMES. Berkeley, CA, 6/7/28. Director, producer. *Howards End.*

JABS, MATTHIAS. 10/25/56. Guitarist. Scorpions.

JACKEE (Jackee Harry). Winston-Salem, NC, 8/14/56. Actor. *227.*

JACKSON, BO. Bessemer, AL, 11/30/62. Pro football, baseball player.

JACKSON, EDDIE. 1/29/61. Bassist, singer. Queensryche.

JACKSON, FREDDIE. New York, NY, 10/2/56. R&B singer, songwriter.

JACKSON, GLENDA. Birkenhead, England, 5/9/36. Actor, member of British Parliament. *Women in Love.*

JACKSON, JACKIE (Sigmund Jackson). Gary, IN, 5/4/51. Singer, brother of Michael and Janet Jackson. The Jacksons.

JACKSON, JERMAINE. Gary, IN, 12/11/54. Singer, brother of Michael and Janet. The Jacksons.

JACKSON, JESSE. Greenville, SC, 10/8/41. Civil rights leader, politician. Founded the Rainbow Coalition.

JACKSON, JOE. Burton-on-Trent, England, 8/11/55. Singer, songwriter.

JACKSON, KATE. Birmingham, AL, 10/29/48. Actor. Sabrina Duncan on *Charlie's Angels.*

JACKSON, LATOYA. 5/29/56. Sister of Michael and Janet.

JACKSON, MARLON. Gary, IN, 3/12/57. Singer, brother of Michael and Janet. The Jacksons.

JACKSON, PERVIS. 5/17/38. Singer. The (Detroit) Spinners.

JACKSON, TITO (Toriano Jackson). Gary, IN, 10/15/53. Singer, brother of Michael and Janet. The Jacksons.

JACKSON, TONY. Liverpool, England, 7/16/40. Singer, bassist. The Searchers.

JACKSON, VICTORIA. Miami, FL, 8/2/59. Actor. *Saturday Night Live.*

JACOBI, DEREK. London, England, 10/22/38. Actor. *The Day of the Jackal.*

JACOBI, LOU. Toronto, Canada, 12/28/13. Actor. *Irma La Douce.*

JAGGER, BIANCA. Managua, Nicaragua, 5/2/45. Socialite, actor. Divorced from Mick Jagger.

JAM MASTER JAY (Jason Mizell). New York, NY, 1965. DJ. Run-D.M.C.

JAMES, CLIFTON. Portland, OR, 5/29/25. Actor. *Cool Hand Luke.*

JAMES, ETTA. Los Angeles, CA, 1/25/38. Singer. Bridged R&B and rock.

JAMES, RICK (James Johnson). Buffalo, NY, 2/1/48. Funk singer, songwriter. "Super Freak."

JAMES, TOMMY (Tommy Jackson). Dayton, OH, 4/29/47. Singer. Tommy James & The Shondells.

JANIS, CONRAD. New York, NY, 2/11/28. Actor, musician. Frederick McConnell on *Mork and Mindy.*

JARDINE, AL. Lima, OH, 9/3/42. Guitarist, singer. The Beach Boys.

JARREAU, AL. Milwaukee, WI, 3/12/40. Jazz singer, sang theme song to *Moonlighting.*

JAZZIE B. (Beresford Romeo). London, England, 1/26/63. Rap artist. Soul II Soul.

JEFFRIES, LIONEL. London, England, 6/10/26. Actor, director. *The Water Babies.*

JENNER, BRUCE. Mount Kisco, NY, 10/28/49. Track athlete, sportscaster. Olympic gold medalist.

JENNINGS, WAYLON. Littlefield, TX, 6/15/37. Country singer, songwriter. *The Dukes of Hazzard* theme song.

JETER, MICHAEL. Lawrenceburg, TN, 8/26/52. Actor. *Evening Shade.*

JETT, JOAN. Philadelphia, PA, 9/22/58. Singer, guitarist. "I Love Rock 'n' Roll."

JILLIAN, ANN (Anne Nauseda). Cambridge, MA, 1/29/51. Actor. *It's a Living.*

JOHANSEN, DAVID. Staten Island, NY, 1/9/50. Actor, singer, a.k.a. Buster Poindexter. *Scrooged.*

JOHN, DR. (Malcolm Rebennack). New Orleans, LA, 11/21/41. Rock/cajun/blues singer, songwriter. "Right Place Wrong Time."

JOHN PAUL II, POPE. Wadowice, Poland, 5/18/20. First non-Italian pope since the Renaissance.

JOHNS, GLYNIS. Durban, South Africa, 10/5/23. Actor. *Glynis.*

JOHNSON, ARTE. Benton Harbor, MI, 1/20/29. Actor.

Laugh-In.

JOHNSON, BEVERLY. Buffalo, NY, 10/13/52. Model, actor.

JOHNSON, HOLLY (William Johnson). Khartoum, Sudan, 2/19/60. Singer. Frankie Goes to Hollywood.

JOHNSON, HOWIE. Washington, DC, 1938. Drummer. The Ventures.

JOHNSON, LADY BIRD. Karnack, TX, 12/22/12. Former First Lady, wife of Lyndon.

JOHNSON, MATT. 8/15/61. Singer, guitarist. The The.

JOHNSON, VAN. Newport, RI, 8/25/16. Actor. *The Caine Mutiny.*

JOHNSON, WILKO (John Wilkinson). 1947. Guitarist. Dr. Feelgood.

JON, JOHN. 2/26/61. Musician. Bronski Beat.

JONES, ALAN. Swansea, Wales, 2/6/47. Baritone saxophonist. Amen Corner.

JONES, BOOKER T. Memphis, TN, 12/11/44. Keyboardist. Booker T. & The MG's.

JONES, DAVY. Manchester, England, 12/30/45. Singer, actor. The Monkees.

JONES, DEAN. Decatur, AL, 1/25/31. Actor. *The Shaggy D.A.*

JONES, GRACE. Spanishtown, Jamaica, 5/19/52. Singer, actor. *A View to a Kill.*

JONES, GRAHAM. North Yorkshire, England, 7/8/61. Guitarist. Haircut 100.

JONES, HOWARD. Southampton, England, 2/23/55. Singer, songwriter.

JONES, JEFFREY. Buffalo, NY, 9/28/47. Actor. Principal Ed Rooney in *Ferris Bueller's Day Off.*

JONES, JENNIFER (Phyllis Isley). Tulsa, OK, 3/2/19. Actor. *The Song of Bernadette.*

JONES, JOHN PAUL (John Paul Baldwin). Sidcup, England, 1/31/46. Bassist. Led Zeppelin.

JONES, KENNY. London, England, 9/16/48. Drummer. The Small Faces.

JONES, MICK. Brixton, England, 6/26/55. Guitarist, singer. The Clash; Big Audio Dynamite.

JONES, MICK. London, England, 12/27/44. Guitarist. Foreigner.

JONES, NEIL. Llanbradach, Wales, 3/25/49. Guitarist. Amen Corner.

JONES, PAUL (Paul Pond). Portsmouth, England, 2/24/42. Singer, harmonicist. Manfred Mann.

JONES, RANDY. 9/13/52. Singer. The Village People.

JONES, RAY. Oldham, England, 10/22/39. Bassist. Billy J. Kramer & The Dakotas.

JONES, RICKIE LEE. Chicago, IL, 11/8/54. Rock/jazz singer, songwriter.

JONES, SAM J. Chicago, IL, 8/12/54. Actor. *Flash Gordon.*

JONES, SHIRLEY. Smithton, PA, 3/31/34. Actor, married to Marty Ingels. *The Partridge Family.*

JONES, STAR. 3/24/62. TV host. *The View.*

JONES, STEVE. London, England, 9/3/55. Guitarist. The Sex Pistols.

JONES, TERRY. Colwyn Bay, Wales, 2/1/42. Actor, director, writer. *Monty Python's Life of Brian.*

JONES, TOM (Tom Woodward). Pontypridd, Wales, 6/7/40. Pop singer.

JORDAN, LONNIE (Leroy Jordan). San Diego, CA, 11/21/48. Keyboardist, singer. War.

JOURARD, JEFF. 1955. Guitarist. The Motels.

JOURDAN, LOUIS (Louis Gendre). Marseilles, France, 6/19/19. Actor. *Gigi.*

JOVOVICH, MILLA. 12/17/75. Actor. *The Fifth Element.*

JOYCE, MIKE. Manchester, England, 6/1/63. Drummer. The Smiths.

JOYNER-KERSEE, JACKIE. St. Louis, IL, 3/3/62. Track athlete. Olympic gold medalist.

JUDD, NAOMI (Diana Judd). Ashland, KY, 1/11/46. Country singer, mother of Wynonna and Ashley. The Judds.

JUMP, GORDON. Dayton, OH, 4/1/32. Actor. Arthur Carlson on *WKRP in Cincinnati.*

JUSTMAN, SETH. Washington, DC, 1/27/51. Keyboardist, singer. The J. Geils Band.

KALE, JIM. 8/11/43. Bassist. The Guess Who.

KANE, BIG DADDY. New York, NY, 9/10/68. Rap artist, songwriter. "Long Live the Kane."

KANE, CAROL. Cleveland, OH, 6/18/52. Actor. Simka Graves on *Taxi.*

KANTNER, PAUL. San Francisco, CA, 3/12/42. Guitarist. Jefferson Airplane; Starship.

KAPRISKY, VALERIE. Paris, France, 1963. Actor. *Breathless.*

KARPOV, ANATOLY. Zlatoust, Russia, 5/23/51. Chess player. International grandmaster, world champion.

KARRAS, ALEX. Gary, IN, 7/15/35. Former football player, actor. *Webster.*

KASPAROV, GARRY. Baku, Russia, 4/13/63. Chess player. International grandmaster, world champion.

KATH, TERRY. Chicago, IL, 1/31/46. Guitarist. Chicago.

KATT, WILLIAM. Los Angeles, CA, 2/16/55. Actor, son of Barbara Hale. *The Greatest American Hero.*

KATZ, STEVE. New York, NY, 5/9/45. Guitarist, harmonicist, singer. Blood, Sweat & Tears.

KATZENBERG, JEFFREY. New York, NY, 12/21/50. Studio executive.

KAUKONEN, JORMA. Washington, DC, 12/23/40. Guitarist. Jefferson Airplane; Hot Tuna.

KAVNER, JULIE. Los Angeles, CA, 9/7/50. Actor. Voice of Marge Simpson on *The Simpsons; Rhoda.*

KAY, JOHN (Joachim Krauledat). Tilsit, Germany, 4/12/44. Guitarist, singer. Steppenwolf.

KAYLAN, HOWARD (Howard Kaplan). New York, NY, 6/22/47. Singer, saxophonist. The Turtles.

KAZURINSKY, TIM. Johnstown, PA, 3/3/50. Actor. *Saturday Night Live.*

KEACH, STACY (William Keach Jr.). Savannah, GA, 6/2/41. Actor. *Mickey Spillane's Mike Hammer.*

KEANE, BIL. Philadelphia, PA, 10/5/22. Cartoonist. *The Family Circus.*

KEATON, MICHAEL (Michael Douglas). Coraopolis, PA, 9/9/51. Actor. *Batman.*

KEEBLE, JON. London, England, 7/6/59. Drummer. Spandau Ballet.

KEEL, HOWARD (Harold Leek). Gillespie, IL, 4/13/17. Actor. Clayton Farlow on *Dallas.*

KEENAN, BRIAN. New York, NY, 1/28/44. Drummer. The Chambers Brothers; Manfred Mann.

KEESHAN, BOB (Robert James Keeshan). Lynbrook, NY, 6/27/27. TV personality, author. *Captain Kangaroo.*

KEFFORD, ACE (Christopher Kefford). Mosely, England, 12/10/46. Bassist. The Move.

KEILLOR, GARRISON. 8/7/42. Author, radio personality. *Lake Wobegon Days.*

KEITH, DAVID. Knoxville, TN, 5/8/54. Actor. *An Officer and a Gentleman.*

KELLER, MARTHE. Basel, Switzerland, 1/28/45. Actor. *Marathon Man.*

KELLERMAN, SALLY. Long Beach, CA, 6/2/37. Actor. Hot Lips in the movie *M*A*S*H*.

KELLEY, DEFOREST. Atlanta, GA, 1/20/20. Actor. Dr. Leonard "Bones" McCoy on *Star Trek*.

KELLEY, KITTY. Spokane, WA, 4/4/42. Unauthorized biographer.

KELLING, GRAEME. Paisley, Scotland, 4/4/57. Guitarist. Deacon Blue.

KELLY, MARK. Dublin, Ireland, 4/9/61. Keyboardist. Marillion.

KELLY, MOIRA. 1968. Actor. *The Cutting Edge*.

KEMP, GARY. Islington, England, 10/16/60. Guitarist, brother of Martin. Spandau Ballet.

KEMP, MARTIN. London, England, 10/10/61. Bassist, brother of Gary. Spandau Ballet.

KENDRICKS, EDDIE. Birmingham, AL, 12/17/39. Singer. The Temptations.

KENNEDY, GEORGE. New York, NY, 2/18/25. Actor. *Cool Hand Luke*.

KENNEDY, TED. Brookline, MA, 2/22/32. Politician, brother of John and Robert.

KENNIBREW, DEE DEE (Dolores Henry). Brooklyn, NY, 1945. Singer. The Crystals.

KENNY G (Kenneth Gorelick). Seattle, WA, 6/5/56. Jazz saxophone player.

KENSIT, PATSY. London, England, 3/4/68. Actor, formerly married to Jim Kerr; married to Liam Gallagher. *Lethal Weapon 2*.

KERNS, JOANNA (Joanna De Varona). San Francisco, CA, 2/12/53. Actor. Maggie Seaver on *Growing Pains*.

KERR, DEBORAH. Helensburg, Scotland, 9/30/21. Actor. *The King and I*.

KERR, JIM. Glasgow, Scotland, 7/9/59. Singer. Simple Minds.

KERRIGAN, NANCY. Stoneham, MA, 10/13/69. Figure skater. Olympic silver medalist, victim of knee attack.

KHAN, CHAKA (Yvette Marie Stevens). Great Lakes, IL, 3/23/53. Singer. Rufus.

KIDD, JOHNNY (Frederick Heath). London, England, 12/23/39. Singer. Johnny Kidd & The Pirates.

KIDDER, MARGOT. Yellow Knife, Canada, 10/17/48. Actor. Lois Lane in *Superman*.

KIEDIS, ANTHONY. Grand Rapids, MI, 11/1/62. Singer. Red Hot Chili Peppers.

KIEL, RICHARD. Detroit, MI, 9/13/39. Actor. Jaws in *The Spy Who Loved Me*.

KILPATRICK, JAMES JR. Oklahoma City, OK, 11/1/20. Journalist. *60 Minutes*.

KIMBALL, BOBBY (Bobby Toteaux). Vinton, LA, 3/29/47. Lead singer. Toto.

KING, ALAN (Irwin Kniberg). Brooklyn, NY, 12/26/27. Producer, comedian. *The Andersen Tapes*.

KING, B. B. (Riley King). Itta Bena, MS, 9/16/25. Legendary blues guitarist, singer, songwriter.

KING, BEN E. (Ben E. Nelson). Henderson, NC, 9/23/38. Singer. The Drifters.

KING, BILLIE JEAN. Long Beach, CA, 11/22/43. Tennis player.

KING, CAROLE (Carole Klein). Brooklyn, NY, 2/9/42. Singer, songwriter.

KING, CORETTA SCOTT. Marion, AL, 4/29/27. Author, lecturer, widow of Martin Luther King Jr.

KING, DON. Cleveland, OH, 8/20/31. Boxing promoter.

KING, MARK. Isle of Wight, England, 10/20/58. Singer, bassist. Level 42.

KING, PERRY. Alliance, OH, 4/30/48. Actor. Cody Allen on *Riptide*.

KING, WILLIAM. Alabama, 1/30/49. Trumpeter, keyboardist. The Commodores.

KINGSLEY, BEN (Krishna Bhanji). Snaiton, England, 12/31/43. Actor. *Gandhi*.

KINSKI, NASTASSJA (Nastassja Nakszynski). Berlin, Germany, 1/24/61. Actor, daughter of Klaus Kinski. *Cat People*.

KIRBY, BRUNO (Bruce Kirby Jr.). New York, NY, 4/28/49. Actor. *City Slickers*.

KIRKE, SIMON. Wales, 7/28/49. Drummer. Bad Company; Free.

KIRKLAND, SALLY. New York, NY, 10/31/41. Actor. *Anna*.

KIRKMAN, TERRY. Salina, KS, 12/12/41. Singer, keyboardist. The Association.

KIRKPATRICK, JEANE. Duncan, OK, 11/19/26. Diplomat. Former U.S. representative to the U.N.

KISSINGER, HENRY. Fuerth, Germany, 5/27/23. Richard Nixon's secretary of state.

KITT, EARTHA. North, SC, 1/17/27. Actor, singer. *The Mark of the Hawk*.

KLEIN, DANNY. New York, NY, 5/13/46. Bassist. The J. Geils Band.

KLEIN, ROBERT. New York, NY, 2/8/42. Actor. *Comedy Tonight*.

KLEMPERER, WERNER. Cologne, Germany, 3/22/20. Actor. Colonel Wilhelm Klink on *Hogan's Heroes*.

KLINE, KEVIN. St. Louis, MO, 10/24/47. Actor, married to Phoebe Cates. *The Big Chill*.

KLUGMAN, JACK. Philadelphia, PA, 4/27/22. Actor. Oscar Madison on *The Odd Couple*.

KNIGHT, GLADYS. Atlanta, GA, 5/28/44. Singer. Gladys Knight & The Pips.

KNIGHT, JONATHAN. Boston, MA, 11/29/69. Singer. New Kids on the Block.

KNIGHT, JORDAN. Boston, MA, 5/17/71. Singer. New Kids on the Block.

KNIGHT, MERALD. Atlanta, GA, 9/4/42. Singer. Gladys Knight & The Pips.

KNIGHT, MICHAEL E. Princeton, NJ, 5/7/59. Actor. Tad Martin on *All My Children*.

KNIGHT, SHIRLEY. Goessell, KS, 7/5/36. Actor. *The Dark at the Top of the Stairs*.

KNIGHT, SUGE. 4/19/65. Musician.

KNIGHTS, DAVE. Islington, England, 6/28/45. Bassist. Procol Harum.

KNOPFLER, DAVID. Glasgow, Scotland, 12/27/52. Guitarist. Dire Straits.

KNOPFLER, MARK. Glasgow, Scotland, 8/12/49. Singer, guitarist. Dire Straits.

KNOTTS, DON. Morgantown, WV, 7/21/24. Actor. Barney Fife on *The Andy Griffith Show*.

KNUDSEN, KEITH. Ames, IA, 10/18/52. Drummer, singer. The Doobie Brothers.

KOCH, ED. New York, NY, 12/12/24. Former mayor of New York.

KOENIG, WALTER. Chicago, IL, 9/14/36. Actor, writer, director, producer. Pavel Chekov on *Star Trek*.

KOOL ROCK (Damon Wimbley). 11/4/66. Rap artist. Fat Boys.

KOPELL, BERNIE. New York, NY, 6/21/33. Actor. Dr. Adam Bricker on *The Love Boat*.

KORMAN, HARVEY. Chicago, IL, 2/15/27. Actor. *The Carol Burnett Show*.

KOSSOFF, PAUL. London, England, 9/14/50. Guitarist. Free.

KOTTO, YAPHET. New York, NY, 11/15/39. Actor. *Live and Let Die*.

KRABBE, JEROEN. Amsterdam, The Netherlands, 12/5/44. Actor. *The Fugitive*.

KRAMER, BILLY J. (Billy J. Ashton). Bootle, England, 8/19/43. Singer. Billy J. Kramer & The Dakotas.

KRAMER, JOEY. New York, NY, 6/21/50. Drummer. Aerosmith.

KRANTZ, JUDITH. New York, NY, 1/9/28. Novelist. *Scruples.*

REUTZMANN, BILL JR. Palo Alto, CA, 5/7/46. Drummer. Grateful Dead.

KRIEGER, ROBBIE. Los Angeles, CA, 1/8/46. Guitarist. The Doors.

KRIGE, ALICE. Upington, South Africa, 6/28/55. Actor. *Chariots of Fire.*

KRISTOFFERSON, KRIS. Brownsville, TX, 6/22/36. Singer, songwriter, actor. *Amerika.*

KUHLKE, NORMAN. Liverpool, England, 6/17/42. Drummer. The Swinging Blue Jeans.

KURTZ, SWOOSIE. Omaha, NE, 9/6/44. Actor. *Sisters.*

KWAN, NANCY. Hong Kong, 5/19/39. Actor. *The World of Suzie Wong.*

LABELLE, PATTI (Patricia Holt). Philadelphia, PA, 10/4/44. Pop/soul singer.

LADD, CHERYL (Cheryl Stoppelmoor). Huron, SD, 7/12/51. Actor. Kris Munroe on *Charlie's Angels.*

LADD, DIANE (Diane Ladner). Meridian, MS, 11/29/39. Actor, mother of Laura Dern. *Alice Doesn't Live Here Anymore.*

LAGASSE, EMERIL. 10/15/59. Chef, author, TV personality.

LAGERFELD, KARL Hamburg, Germany, 9/10/38. Fashion designer. Chanel.

LAHTI, CHRISTINE. Birmingham, MI, 4/4/50. Actor. *Swing Shift.*

LAINE, DENNY (Brian Hines). Jersey, England, 10/29/44. Singer, guitarist. The Moody Blues.

LAKE, GREG. Bournemouth, England, 11/10/48. Bassist, singer. Emerson, Lake & Palmer; King Crimson.

LAMAS, LORENZO. Los Angeles, CA, 1/20/58. Actor. Lance Cumson on *Falcon Crest.*

LAMBERT, CHRISTOPHER. New York, NY, 3/29/57. Actor. *Greystoke: The Legend of Tarzan, Lord of the Apes.*

LAMM, ROBERT. New York, NY, 10/13/44. Singer, keyboardist. Chicago.

LANCASTER, ALAN. London, England, 2/7/49. Bassist. Status Quo.

LANDAU, MARTIN. Brooklyn, NY, 6/20/28. Actor. *Mission: Impossible.*

LANDERS, AUDREY. Philadelphia, PA, 7/18/59. Actor. Afton Cooper on *Dallas.*

LANDESBERG, STEVE. The Bronx, NY, 11/3/45. Actor. Detective Arthur Dietrich on *Barney Miller.*

LANDIS, JOHN. Chicago, IL, 8/3/50. Director. *Twilight Zone—The Movie.*

LANE, ABBE. Brooklyn, NY, 12/14/34. Actor, formerly married to Xavier Cugat. *Xavier Cugat Show.*

LANE, CHARLES. New York, NY, 12/5/53. Director. *Sidewalk Stories.*

LANE, DIANE. New York, NY, 1/22/65. Actor. *Rumble Fish.*

LANG, BOB. Manchester, England, 1/10/46. Bassist. Wayne Fontana & The Mindbenders.

LANGE, HOPE. Redding Ridge, CT, 11/28/31. Actor. *The Ghost and Mrs. Muir.*

LANGE, TED. Oakland, CA, 1/5/47. Actor. Isaac Washington on *The Love Boat.*

LANGELLA, FRANK. Bayonne, NJ, 1/1/38. Actor. *Dracula.*

LANIER, ALLEN. 6/25/46. Guitarist, keyboardist. Blue Öyster Cult.

LANSING, ROBERT (Robert Brown). San Diego, CA, 6/5/29. Actor. *The Man Who Never Was.*

LAPREAD, RONALD. Alabama, 9/4/50. Bassist, trumpeter. The Commodores.

LARDIE, MICHAEL. 9/8/58. Musician. Great White.

LARROQUETTE, JOHN. New Orleans, LA, 11/25/47. Actor. *Night Court.*

LARUE, FLORENCE. Pennsylvania, 2/4/44. Singer. The 5th Dimension.

LASSER, LOUISE. New York, NY, 4/11/39. Actor, formerly married to Woody Allen. *Bananas.*

LAUDER, ESTEE. New York, NY, 7/1/08. Fashion designer.

LAUPER, CYNDI. New York, NY, 6/22/53. Singer, actor, professional wrestling promoter. *She's So Unusual.*

LAURIE, PIPER (Rosetta Jacobs). Detroit, MI, 1/22/32. Actor. Mother in *Carrie.*

LAVERN, ROGER (Roger Jackson). Kidderminster, England, 11/11/38. Keyboardist. The Tornados.

LAVIN, LINDA. Portland, ME, 10/15/37. Actor, singer. *Alice.*

LAWRENCE, CAROL (Carol Laraia). Melrose Park, IL, 9/5/34. Actor, singer. *West Side Story.*

LAWRENCE, JOEY. Montgomery, PA, 4/20/76. Actor, singer. *Blossom.*

LAWRENCE, VICKI. Inglewood, CA, 3/26/49. Actor. *Mama's Family.*

LAWSON, LEIGH. Atherston, England, 7/21/45. Actor. *Tess.*

LAWTON, JOHN. 6/11/46. Singer. Uriah Heep.

LEA, JIMMY. Melbourne Arms, England, 6/14/52. Bassist, keyboardist, violinist. Slade.

LEACH, ROBIN. London, England, 8/29/41. TV host. *Lifestyles of the Rich and Famous.*

LEACHMAN, CLORIS. Des Moines, IA, 4/30/26. Actor. Phyllis Lyndstrom on *The Mary Tyler Moore Show.*

LEADON, BERNIE. Minneapolis, MN, 7/19/47. Guitarist, singer. The Eagles.

LEAR, NORMAN. New Haven, CT, 7/27/22. Producer, director, formerly married to Frances. *All in the Family.*

LEARNED, MICHAEL. Washington, DC, 4/9/39. Actor. Olivia on *The Waltons.*

LEBON, SIMON. Bushey, England, 10/27/58. Lead singer. Duran Duran.

LEBROCK, KELLY. 3/22/60. Actor, formerly married to Steven Seagal. *Weird Science.*

LEE, ALVIN. Nottingham, England, 12/19/44. Guitarist, singer. Ten Years After.

LEE, ARTHUR. Memphis, TN, 1945. Guitarist, singer. Love.

LEE, BARBARA. New York, NY, 5/16/47. Singer. The Chiffons.

LEE, BEVERLY. Passaic, NJ, 8/3/41. Singer. The Shirelles.

LEE, BRENDA (Brenda Tarpley). Lithonia, GA, 12/11/44. Singer.

LEE, GEDDY. Willowdale, Canada, 7/29/53. Singer, bassist. Rush.

LEE, JASON SCOTT. Los Angeles, CA, 1966. Actor. *Dragon: The Bruce Lee Story.*

LEE, JOHNNY. Texas City, TX, 7/3/46. Singer. "Lookin' for Love."

LEE, MICHELE (Michele Dusiak). Los Angeles, CA, 6/24/42. Actor. Karen Fairgate MacKenzie on *Knots Landing.*

LEE, PEGGY (Norma Delores Egstrom). Jamestown, ND, 5/26/20. Actor, singer. *The Jazz Singer.*

LEE, RIC. Cannock, England, 10/20/45. Drummer. Ten Years After.

LEE, STAN. New York, NY, 12/28/22. Artist, writer, Marvel Comics legend.

LEEDS, GARY. Glendale, CA, 9/3/44. Drummer. The Walker Brothers.

LEESE, HOWARD. Los Angeles, CA, 6/13/51. Keyboardist, guitarist. Heart.

LEEVES, JANE. East Grinstead, England, 4/18/61. Actor. Daphne Moon on *Frasier*.

LEEWAY, JOE. London, England, 1957. Percussionist. Thompson Twins.

LEIBMAN, RON. New York, NY, 10/11/37. Actor. *Kaz*.

LEIFER, CAROL. 7/27/56. Comic. *Alright Already*.

LEIGH, JANET (Jeannette Helen Morrison). Merced, CA, 7/6/27. Actor, mother of Jamie Lee Curtis. *Psycho*.

LEIGHTON, LAURA (Laura Miller). Iowa City, IA, 7/24/68. Actor. *Melrose Place*.

LEITCH, DONOVAN. 8/16/67. Actor, son of folk singer Donovan, brother of Ione Skye.

LEMAT, PAUL. Rahway, NJ, 9/22/52. Actor. *American Graffiti*.

LEMIEUX, MARIO. Montreal, Canada, 10/5/65. NHL hockey player. Pittsburgh Penguins.

LEMMON, CHRIS. Los Angeles, CA, 1/22/54. Actor, son of Jack Lemmon. *Swing Shift*.

LEMMY (Ian Kilmister). Stoke-on-Trent, England, 12/24/45. Bassist, singer. Motorhead.

LEMON, MEADOWLARK. Wilmington, NC, 4/25/32. Basketball player. Harlem Globetrotters.

LENNON, JULIAN (John Charles Julian Lennon). Liverpool, England, 4/8/63. Singer, songwriter, son of John Lennon. Half brother of Sean.

LENNON, SEAN. 10/9/75. Musician. Son of John Lennon and Yoko Ono. Half brother of Julian Lennon.

LENNOX, ANNIE. Aberdeen, Scotland, 12/25/54. Singer, songwriter. Eurythmics.

LEONARD, ROBERT SEAN. Westwood, NJ, 2/28/69. Actor. *Dead Poets Society*.

LEONARD, SUGAR RAY. Wilmington, NC, 5/17/56. Boxer.

LERNER, MICHAEL. Brooklyn, NY, 6/22/41. Actor. *Barton Fink*.

LESH, PHIL (Phil Chapman). Berkeley, CA, 3/15/40. Bassist. Grateful Dead.

LESTER, ROBERT "SQUIRREL." 1/13/30. Singer. The Chi-Lites.

LEVERT, EDDIE. Canton, OH, 6/16/42. Singer. The O'Jays.

LEVIN, DRAKE. Guitarist. Paul Revere & The Raiders.

LEVY, EUGENE. Hamilton, Canada, 12/17/46. Actor, writer. *SCTV*.

LEWINSKY, MONICA. 7/23/73. Former White House intern, had "inappropriate" relationship with Bill Clinton.

LEWIS, AL (Alexander Meister). New York, NY, 4/30/10. Actor. *The Munsters*.

LEWIS, CARL (Carl Frederick Carlton). Birmingham, AL, 7/1/61. Track athlete. Olympic gold medalist.

LEWIS, EMMANUEL. New York, NY, 3/9/71. Actor. Webster Long on *Webster*.

LEWIS, GARY (Gary Levitch). New York, NY, 7/31/46. Singer, drummer, son of Jerry Lewis. Gary Lewis & The Playboys.

LEWIS, HUEY (Hugh Cregg III). New York, NY, 7/5/50. Singer. Huey Lewis & The News.

LEWIS, JERRY (Joseph Levitch). Newark, NJ, 3/16/26. Actor, father of Gary Lewis. *The Nutty Professor*.

LEWIS, JERRY LEE. Ferriday, LA, 9/29/35. Legendary rock keyboardist, singer, songwriter.

LEWIS, JULIETTE. San Fernando Valley, CA, 6/21/73. Actor. *Cape Fear*.

LEWIS, PETER. Los Angeles, CA, 7/15/45. Guitarist, singer. Moby Grape.

LEWIS, RICHARD. 6/29/47. Comic. *Anything But Love*.

LIDDY, G. GORDON. New York, NY, 11/30/30. Watergate participant, talk show host. *The G. Gordon Liddy Show*.

LIFESON, ALEX. Fernie, Canada, 8/27/53. Guitarist. Rush.

LIGHT, JUDITH. Trenton, NJ, 2/9/49. Actor. Angela on *Who's the Boss?*

LIGHTFOOT, GORDON. Orillia, Canada, 11/17/38. Folk guitarist, singer, songwriter.

LINCOLN, ABBEY (Anna Marie Woolridge). Chicago, IL, 8/6/30. Singer, actor. *For Love of Ivy*.

LINDEN, HAL (Hal Lipschitz). The Bronx, NY, 3/20/31. Actor. *Barney Miller*.

LINDES, HAL. Monterey, CA, 6/30/53. Guitarist. Dire Straits.

LINDSAY, MARK. Eugene, OR, 3/9/42. Singer, saxophonist. Paul Revere & The Raiders.

LINDUP, MIKE. 3/17/59. Keyboardist, singer. Level 42.

LINKLETTER, ART. Moose Jaw, Canada, 7/17/12. TV personality. *People Are Funny*.

LINN-BAKER, MARK. St. Louis, MO, 6/17/54. Actor. Cousin Larry Appleton on *Perfect Strangers*.

LIOTTA, RAY. Newark, NJ, 12/18/54. Actor. *GoodFellas*.

LIPNICKI, JONATHAN. 10/22/90. Actor. *Jerry Maguire*.

LITTLE EVA (Eva Narcissus Boyd). Bellhaven, NC, 6/29/45. Singer. "The Loco-Motion."

LITTLE RICHARD (Richard Penniman). Macon, GA, 12/5/32. Legendary singer, songwriter.

LIVGREN, KERRY. Kansas, 9/18/49. Guitarist. Kansas.

L.L. COOL J (James Todd Smith). New York, NY, 1/14/68. Rap artist.

LLOYD, CHRISTOPHER. Stamford, CT, 10/22/38. Actor. "Reverend Jim" Ignatowski on *Taxi*.

LLOYD, EMILY. London, England, 9/29/70. Actor. *Wish You Were Here*.

LOCKE, JOHN. Los Angeles, CA, 9/25/43. Keyboardist. Spirit.

LOCKE, SONDRA. Shelbyville, TN, 5/28/47. Actor. *The Gauntlet*.

LOCKHART, JUNE. New York, NY, 6/25/25. Actor. *Lost in Space*.

LOCKWOOD, GARY. Van Nuys, CA, 2/21/37. Actor. *2001: A Space Odyssey*.

LOCORRIERE, DENNIS. Union City, NJ, 6/13/49. Lead singer. Dr. Hook.

LODGE, JOHN. Birmingham, England, 7/20/45. Bassist. The Moody Blues.

LOEB, LISA. 3/11/68. Singer. "Stay."

LOFGREN, NILS. Chicago, IL, 6/21/51. Guitarist, keyboardist, singer, songwriter.

LOGGIA, ROBERT. Staten Island, NY, 1/3/30. Actor. *Mancuso, FBI*.

LOGGINS, KENNY. Everett, WA, 1/7/48. Singer, songwriter.

LOLLOBRIGIDA, GINA. Subiaco, Italy, 7/4/27. Actor. *Circus*.

LOM, HERBERT. Prague, Czechoslovakia, 1/9/17. Actor. *Spartacus*.

LONG, SHELLEY. Ft. Wayne, IN, 8/23/49. Actor. Diane Chambers on *Cheers*.

LONGMUIR, ALAN. Edinburgh, Scotland, 6/20/53. Bassist. The Bay City Rollers.

LONGMUIR, DEREK. Edinburgh, Scotland, 3/19/55. Drummer. The Bay City Rollers.

LORD, JON. Leicester, England, 6/9/41. Keyboardist. Deep Purple.

LORDS, TRACI (Norma Kuzma). Steubenville, OH, 5/7/68. Actor, former porn star. Melrose Place.

LOUGANIS, GREG. El Cajon, CA, 1/29/60. Diver. Olympic gold medalist.

LOUGHNANE, LEE. Chicago, IL, 10/21/46. Trumpeter. Chicago.

LOUISE, TINA (Tina Blacker). New York, NY, 2/11/34. Actor. Ginger Grant on Gilligan's Island.

LOVE, MIKE. Baldwin Hills, CA, 3/15/41. Singer. The Beach Boys.

LOVELADY, DAVE. Liverpool, England, 10/16/42. Drummer. The Fourmost.

LOVELESS, PATTY. Belcher Holler, KY, 1/4/57 Singer.

LOVITZ, JON. Tarzana, CA, 7/21/57. Actor. Saturday Night Live.

LOWE, CHAD. Dayton, OH, 1/15/68. Actor, brother of Rob Lowe. Life Goes On.

LOWE, CHRIS. Blackpool, England, 10/4/59. Keyboardist. Pet Shop Boys.

LUCIA, PETER. 2/2/47. Drummer. Tommy James & The Shondells.

LUCKINBILL, LAURENCE. Fort Smith, AR, 11/21/34. Actor, married to Lucie Arnaz. The Boys in the Band.

LUFT, LORNA. Los Angeles, CA, 11/21/52. Actor, half-sister of Liza Minnelli, daughter of Judy Garland. Where the Boys Are.

LUKATHER, STEVE. Los Angeles, CA, 10/21/57. Lead guitarist. Toto.

LULU (Marie Lawrie). Glasgow, Scotland, 11/3/48. Singer, actor. To Sir with Love.

LUNDEN, JOAN. Fair Oaks, CA, 9/19/50. Host. Good Morning America.

LUNDGREN, DOLPH. Stockholm, Sweden, 11/3/59. Actor. Rocky IV.

LUPONE, PATTI. Northport, NY, 4/21/49. Actor. Life Goes On.

LUPUS, PETER. Indianapolis, IN, 6/17/37. Actor. Willie Armitage on Mission: Impossible.

LWIN, ANNABELLA (Myant Aye). Rangoon, Burma, 10/31/65. Singer. Bow Wow Wow.

LYDON, JOHN. London, England, 1/31/56. Singer, a.k.a. Johnny Rotten. The Sex Pistols; Public Image Ltd.

LYNCH, STAN. Gainesville, FL, 5/21/55. Drummer. Tom Petty & The Heartbreakers.

LYNGSTAD, FRIDA (Anni-Frid Lyngstad). Narvik, Sweden, 11/15/45. Singer. Abba.

LYNNE, JEFF. Birmingham, England, 12/30/47. Singer, guitarist. Electric Light Orchestra (ELO).

LYNOTT, PHIL. Dublin, Ireland, 8/20/51. Singer, bassist. Thin Lizzy.

LYONS, LEO. Standbridge, England, 11/30/43. Bassist. Ten Years After.

LYTE, MC. New York, NY, 1971. Rap artist.

MA, YO-YO. Paris, France, 10/7/55. Cello virtuoso.

MACARTHUR, JAMES. Los Angeles, CA, 12/8/37. Actor, son of Helen Hayes. Danny Williams on Hawaii Five-O.

MACCHIO, RALPH. Long Island, NY, 11/4/62. Actor. The Karate Kid.

MACCORKINDALE, SIMON. Cambridge, England, 2/12/52. Actor. Falcon Crest.

MACDONALD, EDDIE. St. Asaph, Wales, 11/1/59. Bassist. The Alarm.

MACDONALD, ROBIN. Nairn, Scotland, 7/18/43. Guitarist. Billy J. Kramer & The Dakotas.

MACGOWAN, SHANE. Kent, England, 12/25/57. Guitarist, singer. The Pogues.

MACGRAW, ALI. Pound Ridge, NY, 4/1/38. Actor. Love Story.

MACKAY, ANDY. London, England, 7/23/46. Saxophonist, woodwindist. Roxy Music.

MACKAY, DUNCAN. 7/26/50. Keyboardist. Steve Harley & Cockney Rebel.

MACLACHLAN, KYLE. Yakima, WA, 2/22/59. Actor. Twin Peaks.

MACLEAN, BRYAN. Los Angeles, CA, 1947. Guitarist, singer. Love.

MACLEOD, GAVIN. Mt. Kisco, NY, 2/28/31. Actor. Captain Stubing of The Love Boat.

MACNAUGHTON, ROBERT. New York, NY, 12/19/66. Actor. E.T., the Extra-Terrestrial.

MACNEE, PATRICK. London, England, 2/6/22. Actor. The Avengers.

MACNEIL, ROBERT. Montreal, Canada, 1/19/31. Broadcast journalist. MacNeil/Lehrer Report.

MACNELLY, JEFF. New York, NY, 9/17/47. Cartoonist. Shoe.

MADDEN, JOHN. Austin, MN, 4/10/36. Sportscaster, football analyst.

MADIGAN, AMY. Chicago, IL, 9/11/51. Actor. Places in the Heart.

MADSEN, MICHAEL. Chicago, IL, 1959. Actor, brother of Virginia. Reservoir Dogs.

MADSEN, VIRGINIA. Winnetka, IL, 9/11/61. Actor, sister of Michael. Electric Dreams.

MAGNUSON, ANN. Charleston, WV, 1/4/56. Actor. Catherine Hughes on Anything but Love.

MAGUIRE, LES. Wallasey, England, 12/27/41. Keyboardist, saxophonist. Gerry & The Pacemakers.

MAHONEY, JOHN. Manchester, England, 6/20/40. Actor. Father of Dr. Crane on Cheers and Frasier.

MAJORS, LEE (Harvey Lee Yeary II). Wyandotte, MI, 4/23/39. Actor, formerly married to Farrah Fawcett. The Six Million Dollar Man.

MAKEPEACE, CHRIS. Montreal, Canada, 4/22/64. Actor. My Bodyguard.

MAKO (Makoto Iwamatsu). Kobe, Japan, 12/10/33. Actor. The Sand Pebbles.

MALDEN, KARL (Mladen Sekulovich). Gary, IN, 3/22/12. Actor, American Express spokesperson. The Streets of San Francisco.

MALONE, DOROTHY. Chicago, IL, 1/30/25. Actor. Written on the Wind.

MALTIN, LEONARD. New York, NY, 12/18/50. Film critic. Entertainment Tonight.

MANDEL, HOWIE. Toronto, Canada, 11/29/55. Actor. Dr. Wayne Fiscus on St. Elsewhere.

MANDELA, NELSON. Umtata, South Africa, 7/18/18. President of South Africa.

MANDELA, WINNIE. Transkei, South Africa, 9/26/34. Political activist, formerly married to Nelson Mandela.

MANDRELL, BARBARA. Houston, TX, 12/25/48. Country singer. Barbara Mandrell & The Mandrell Sisters.

MANETTI, LARRY. Chicago, IL, 7/23/47. Actor. Rick on Magnum, P. I.

MANILOW, BARRY (Barry Alan Pincus). Brooklyn, NY, 6/17/43. Singer, songwriter. I Write the Songs.

MANN, MANFRED (Michael Lubowitz). Johannesburg, South Africa, 10/21/40. Keyboardist. Manfred Mann.

MANN, TERRENCE. Kentucky, 1945. Actor. Les Misérables.

MANOFF, DINAH. New York, NY, 1/25/56. Actor, daughter of Lee Grant. Carol Weston on *Empty Nest.*

MANSON, CHARLES. Cincinnati, OH, 11/12/34. Murderer, cult leader.

MANTEGNA, JOE. Chicago, IL, 11/13/47. Actor. *The Godfather, Part III.*

MANZANERA, PHIL. London, England, 1/31/51. Guitarist. Roxy Music.

MANZAREK, RAY. Chicago, IL, 2/12/39. Keyboardist. The Doors.

MARCEAU, MARCEL. Strasbourg, France, 3/22/23. Actor, pantomimist. *Bip.*

MARCOS, IMELDA. Talcoban, the Philippines, 7/2/31. Wife of late Ferdinand Marcos.

MARCOVICCI, ANDREA. New York, NY, 11/18/48. Actor, singer. *Trapper John, MD.*

MARGO, MITCH. Brooklyn, NY, 5/25/47. Tenor singer. The Tokens.

MARGO, PHIL. Brooklyn, NY, 4/1/42. Bass singer. The Tokens.

MARIN, CHEECH (Richard Marin). Los Angeles, CA, 7/13/46. Actor, writer, former partner of Tommy Chong. *Up in Smoke.*

MARINARO, ED. New York, NY, 3/31/50. Actor, football player. *Hill Street Blues.*

MARLEY, ZIGGY (David Marley). Jamaica, 10/17/68. Singer, songwriter, son of Bob Marley. Ziggy Marley & The Melody Makers.

MARR, JOHNNY. Manchester, England, 10/31/63. Guitarist. The Smiths.

MARRIOTT, STEVE. Bow, England, 1/30/47. Singer, guitarist. The Small Faces.

MARS, MICK (Bob Deal). Terre Haute, IN, 4/4/55. Guitarist. Mötley Crüe.

MARSALIS, BRANFORD. Breaux Bridge, LA, 8/26/60. Jazz musician, bandleader, saxophonist. Brother of Wynton Marsalis. Former musical director of *The Tonight Show.*

MARSDEN, FREDDIE. Liverpool, England, 10/23/40. Drummer. Gerry & The Pacemakers.

MARSDEN, GERRY. Liverpool, England, 9/24/42. Singer, lead guitarist. Gerry & The Pacemakers.

MARSH, IAN. Sheffield, England, 11/11/56. Keyboardist. The Human League; Heaven 17.

MARSHALL, PETER (Pierre La Cock). Huntington, WV, 3/30/30. TV personality. Host of *The Hollywood Squares.*

MARTELL, VINCE. New York, NY, 11/11/45. Guitarist. Vanilla Fudge.

MARTIN, ANDREA. Portland, ME, 1/15/47. Writer, actor. *SCTV.*

MARTIN, DEWEY. Chesterville, Canada, 9/30/42. Singer, drummer. Buffalo Springfield.

MARTIN, DICK. Battle Creek, MI, 1/30/22. Actor. Cohost of *Laugh-In.*

MARTIN, JIM. Oakland, CA, 7/21/61. Guitarist. Faith No More.

MARTIN, PAMELA SUE. Westport, CT, 1/15/53. Actor. *Dynasty.*

MARTINDALE, WINK (Winston Conrad Martindale). Bells, TN, 12/4/34. TV personality. Host of *Tic Tac Dough* and *Debt.*

MARTINI, JERRY. Colorado, 10/1/43. Saxophonist. Sly & The Family Stone.

MARVIN, HANK (Brian Rankin). Newcastle, England, 10/28/41. Lead guitarist. The Shadows.

MARX, RICHARD. Chicago, IL, 9/16/63. Singer, songwriter.

MASON, DAVE. Worcester, England, 5/10/47. Singer, guitarist. Traffic.

MASON, JACKIE. Sheboygan, WI, 6/9/34. Actor. *Chicken Soup.*

MASON, MARSHA. St. Louis, MO, 4/3/42. Actor. *The Goodbye Girl.*

MASON, NICK. Birmingham, England, 1/27/45. Drummer. Pink Floyd.

MASSI, NICK (Nick Macioci). Newark, NJ, 9/19/35. Singer, bassist. The Four Seasons.

MASTELOTTO, PAT. 9/10/55. Drummer. Mr. Mister.

MASTERSON, MARY STUART. Los Angeles, CA, 6/28/66. Actor, daughter of Peter. *Fried Green Tomatoes.*

MASTERSON, PETER. Houston, TX, 6/1/34. Actor, writer, director, father of Mary Stuart. *The Exorcist.*

MASTRANGELO, CARLO. The Bronx, NY, 10/5/39. Bass singer. Dion & The Belmonts.

MASTRANTONIO, MARY ELIZABETH. Oak Park, IL, 11/17/58. Actor. *The Color of Money.*

MASUR, RICHARD. New York, NY, 11/20/48. Actor, Screen Actors Guild president. *One Day at a Time.*

MATHERS, JERRY. Sioux City, IA, 6/2/48. Actor. Theodore "Beaver" Cleaver on *Leave It to Beaver.*

MATHESON, TIM. Glendale, CA, 12/31/47. Actor. *National Lampoon's Animal House.*

MATHEWS, DENISE (formerly Vanity). Niagara, Canada, 1/3/63. Former singer and actor (a.k.a. D.D. Winters), now Christian Evangelist, bible student, married to L.A. Raiders defensive end Anthony Smith. *The Last Dragon.*

MATHIS, JOHNNY. San Francisco, CA, 9/30/35. Pop singer.

MATLOCK, GLENN. 8/27/56. Bassist. The Sex Pistols.

MATTHEWS, IAN (Ian McDonald). Lincolnshire, England, 6/16/45. Singer, guitarist. Matthew's Southern Comfort.

MAUS, JOHN. New York, NY, 11/12/43. Singer. The Walker Brothers.

MAXFIELD, MIKE. Manchester, England, 2/23/44. Lead guitarist. Billy J. Kramer & The Dakotas.

MAY, BRIAN. Twickenham, England, 7/19/47. Guitarist. Queen.

MAY, ELAINE (Elaine Berlin). Philadelphia, PA, 4/21/32. Actor, director, writer. *Ishtar.*

MAY, PHIL. Dartford, England, 11/9/44. Singer. The Pretty Things.

MAYALL, JOHN. Macclesfield, England, 11/29/33. Singer, keyboardist, harmonicist. The Bluesbreakers.

MAYS, WILLIE. Fairfield, AL, 5/6/31. Baseball player. San Francisco Giants.

MAZAR, DEBI. Queens, NY, 1964. Actor. *Civil Wars; L.A. Law.*

MAZURSKY, PAUL. Brooklyn, NY, 4/25/30. Producer, director, writer, actor. *Down and Out in Beverly Hills.*

M.C. ERIC. 8/19/70. Rap artist. Technotronic.

MCA (Adam Yauch). Brooklyn, NY, 8/15/67. Rap artist. The Beastie Boys.

MCBRIDE, MARTINA. Sharon, KS, 7/29/66. Singer.

MCCALLUM, DAVID. Glasgow, Scotland, 9/19/33. Actor. *The Great Escape.*

MCCARTHY, ANDREW. Westfield, NJ, 11/29/62. Actor. *Less Than Zero.*

MCCARTHY, JENNY Chicago, IL, 11/1/72. *Singled Out.*

MCCARTHY, KEVIN. Seattle, WA, 2/15/14. Actor. *Invasion of the Body Snatchers.*

MCCARTY, JIM. Liverpool, England, 7/25/44. Drummer. The Yardbirds; Mitch Ryder & The Detroit Wheels.

MCCAULEY, JACKIE. Coleraine, Ireland, 12/14/46. Keyboardist. Them.

MCCAULEY, PATRICK. Northern Ireland, 3/17/44. Drummer. Them.

MCCLANAHAN, RUE. Healdton, OK, 2/21/34. Actor. Blanche Devereaux on *The Golden Girls.*

MCCLARY, THOMAS. 10/6/50. Lead guitarist. The Commodores.

MCCLINTON, DELBERT. Lubbock, TX, 11/4/40. Singer, songwriter.

MCCLURG, EDIE. Kansas City, MO, 7/23/50. Actor. *The Hogan Family.*

MCCLUSKEY, ANDY. Wirral, England, 6/24/59. Singer. Orchestral Manoeuvres in the Dark (OMD).

MCCOO, MARILYN. Jersey City, NJ, 9/30/43. Singer, cohost of *Solid Gold*. The 5th Dimension.

MCCREADY, MIKE. 4/5/66. Guitarist. Pearl Jam.

MCCULLOCH, IAN. Liverpool, England, 5/5/59. Singer. Echo & The Bunnymen.

MCDANIELS, DARRYL D. New York, NY, 1964. Rap artist. Run-D.M.C.

MCDONALD, COUNTRY JOE. El Monte, CA, 1/1/42. Guitarist, singer. Country Joe & The Fish.

MCDONALD, IAN. London, England, 6/25/46. Saxophonist. King Crimson.

MCDONALD, MICHAEL. St. Louis, MO, 12/2/52. Singer, songwriter, keyboardist. The Doobie Brothers.

MCDONALD, PAT. 8/6/52. Musician. Timbuk 3.

MCDONNELL, MARY. Ithaca, NY, 1952. Actor. *Dances with Wolves.*

MCDOWELL, MALCOLM. Leeds, England, 6/19/43. Actor. *A Clockwork Orange.*

MCENROE, JOHN JR. Wiesbaden, Germany, 2/16/59. Tennis player. Formerly married to Tatum O'Neal, relationship with Patty Smyth.

MCFADDEN, CYNTHIA. 5/27/56. Television journalist.

MCFERRIN, BOBBY. New York, NY, 3/11/50. Singer. "Don't Worry, Be Happy."

MCGAVIN, DARREN. Spokane, WA, 5/7/22. Actor. *The Night Stalker.*

MCGEOCH, JOHN. Guitarist. Siouxsie & The Banshees.

MCGILLIS, KELLY. Newport Beach, CA, 7/9/57. Actor. *Witness.*

MCGOVERN, ELIZABETH. Evanston, IL, 7/18/61. Actor. *Ragtime.*

MCGOVERN, MAUREEN. Youngstown, OH, 7/27/49. Singer, actor. "The Morning After."

MCGUINN, ROGER "JIM" (James Joseph McGuinn). Chicago, IL, 7/13/42. Singer, guitarist. The Byrds.

MCGUINNESS, TOM. Wimbledon, England, 12/2/41. Bassist. Manfred Mann.

MCINTOSH, LORRAINE. Glasgow, Scotland, 5/13/64. Singer. Deacon Blue.

MCINTYRE, FRITZ. 9/2/58. Keyboardist. Simply Red.

MCINTYRE, JOE. Needham, MA, 12/31/73. Singer. New Kids on the Block.

MCINTYRE, ONNIE. Lennox Town, Scotland, 9/25/45. Guitarist. Average White Band.

MCJOHN, GOLDY. 5/2/45. Organist. Steppenwolf.

MCKAGAN, DUFF ROSE (Michael McKagan). Seattle, WA. Bassist. Guns N' Roses.

MCKEAN, MICHAEL. New York, NY, 10/17/47. Actor, writer. Lenny Kosnowski on *Laverne & Shirley.*

MCKELLAR, DANICA. 1/3/75. La Jolla, CA. Actor. Winnie Cooper on *The Wonder Years.*

MCKELLEN, IAN. Burnley, England, 5/25/39. Shakespearian actor.

MCKEON, NANCY. Westbury, NY, 4/4/66. Actor. Jo Polniaczek on *The Facts of Life.*

MCKEOWN, LESLIE. Edinburgh, Scotland, 11/12/55. Singer. The Bay City Rollers.

MCKUEN, ROD. Oakland, CA, 4/29/33. Poet. *Laugh-In.*

MCLAGAN, IAN. England,

5/12/46. Keyboardist. The Faces.

MCLEAN, DON. New Rochelle, NY, 10/2/45. Singer, songwriter.

MCLEMORE, LAMONTE. St. Louis, MO, 9/17/39. Singer. The 5th Dimension.

MCMAHON, ED. Detroit, MI, 3/6/23. Announcer and host. *The Tonight Show; Star Search.*

MCNALLY, JOHN. Liverpool, England, 8/30/41. Singer, guitarist. The Searchers.

MCNEIL, MICK. Scotland, 7/20/58. Keyboardist. Simple Minds.

MCNICHOL, KRISTY. Los Angeles, CA, 9/11/62. Actor. Barbara Weston on *Empty Nest.*

MCPHERSON, GRAHAM. Hastings, England, 1/13/61. Singer. Madness.

MCVIE, CHRISTINE (Christine Perfect). Birmingham, England, 7/12/44. Keyboardist, singer. Fleetwood Mac.

MCVIE, JOHN. London, England, 11/26/45. Bassist. Fleetwood Mac.

MEADOWS, JAYNE (Jayne Cotter). Wu Chang, China, 9/27/24. Actor, quiz show regular, married to Steve Allen, sister of Audrey.

MEANEY, COLM. Dublin, Ireland, 1953. Actor. Miles O'Brien on *Star Trek: The Next Generation.*

MEARA, ANNE. Brooklyn, NY, 9/20/29. Actor, partner/married to Jerry Stiller, mother of Ben Stiller. *The Out-of-Towners.*

MEAT LOAF (Marvin Lee Aday). Dallas, TX, 9/27/51. Singer. *Bat out of Hell.*

MEDLEY, BILL. Santa Ana, CA, 9/19/40. Singer. The Righteous Brothers.

MEDRESS, HANK. Brooklyn, NY, 11/19/38. Tenor singer. The Tokens.

MEHTA, ZUBIN. Bombay, India, 4/29/36. Conductor.

MEINE, KLAUS. 5/25/48. Singer. Scorpions.

MEISNER, RANDY. Scottsbluff, NE, 3/8/47. Bassist, singer. The Eagles; Poco.

MELLENCAMP, JOHN. Seymour, IN, 10/7/51. Guitarist, singer, songwriter.

MENDOZA, MARK. Long Island, NY, 6/13/54. Bassist. Twisted Sister.

MENKEN, ALAN. New Rochelle, NY, 1949. Composer. *Beauty and the Beast.*

MERCHANT, JIMMY. New York, NY, 2/10/40. Singer. Frankie Lymon & The Teenagers.

MESSINA, JIM. Maywood, CA, 12/5/47. Guitarist, singer. Poco.

MESSNER, TAMMY FAYE. International Falls, MN, 3/7/42. Former wife of PTL founder Jim Bakker.

METCALF, LAURIE. Edwardsville, IL, 6/16/55. Actor. Jackie Conner Harris on *Roseanne.*

METHENY, PAT. Lee's Summit, MO, 8/12/54. Jazz guitarist. "Offramp."

MEYERS, ARI. San Juan, Puerto Rico, 4/6/69. Actor. Emma McArdle on *Kate & Allie.*

MEYERS, AUGIE. San Antonio, TX, 5/31/40. Keyboardist. Texas Tornados.

MIALL, TERRY LEE. England, 11/8/58. Drummer. Adam & The Ants.

MICHAEL, GEORGE (Georgios Kyriacou Panayiotou). London, England, 6/25/63. Singer, songwriter. Wham!

MICHAELS, LORNE Toronto, Canada, 11/17/44. Producer, writer. *Saturday Night Live.*

MICK (Michael Wilson). Amesbury, England, 3/4/44. Drummer. Dave Dee, Dozy, Beaky, Mick and Tich.

MIDORI. Osaka, Japan, 10/25/71. Violinist.

MIKE D. (Mike Diamond). New York, NY, 11/20/65. Rap artist. The Beastie Boys.

MILANO, FRED. The Bronx, NY, 8/26/40. Tenor singer. Dion & The Belmonts.

MILES, SARAH. Ingatestone, England, 12/31/41. Actor. *Ryan's Daughter.*

MILES, SYLVIA. New York, NY, 9/9/34. Actor. *Midnight Cowboy.*

MILES, VERA (Vera Ralston). Boise City, OK, 8/23/30. Actor. *Psycho.*

MILKEN, MICHAEL. Van Nuys, CA, 1946. Financier. Convicted of securities violations.

MILLER, ANN (Lucille Ann Collier). Chireno, TX, 4/12/23. Actor. *On the Town.*

MILLER, CHARLES. Olathe, KS, 6/2/39. Saxophonist, clarinetist. War.

MILLER, DENNIS. Pittsburgh, PA, 11/3/53. TV personality. *Saturday Night Live.*

MILLER, JERRY. Tacoma, WA, 7/10/43. Guitarist. Moby Grape.

MILLER, PENELOPE ANN. Santa Monica, CA, 1/13/64. Actor. *Carlito's Way.*

MILLER, STEVE. Milwaukee, WI, 10/5/43. Singer, guitarist. The Steve Miller Band.

MILLS, HAYLEY. London, England, 4/18/46. Actor, daughter of John Mills, sister of Juliet Mills. *The Parent Trap.*

MILLS, JOHN. Suffolk, England, 2/22/08. Actor, father of Hayley and Juliet Mills. *Ryan's Daughter.*

MILLS, JULIET. London, England, 11/21/41. Actor, daughter of John Mills, sister of Hayley Mills. *Nanny and the Professor.*

MILLS, MIKE. 12/17/58. Bassist. R.E.M.

MILLS, STEPHANIE. New York, NY, 3/22/57. Actor, singer. *The Wiz.*

MILLWARD, MIKE. Bromborough, England, 5/9/42. Guitarist, singer. The Fourmost.

MIMIEUX, YVETTE. Los Angeles, CA, 1/8/42. Actor. *The Black Hole.*

MINNELLI, LIZA. Los Angeles, CA, 3/12/46. Singer, actor, daughter of Vincente Minnelli and Judy Garland, half-sister of Lorna Luft. *Cabaret; The Sterile Cuckoo.*

MINOGUE, KYLIE. Melbourne, Australia, 5/28/68. Actor, singer.

MIOU-MIOU (Sylvette Hery). Paris, France, 2/22/50. Actor. *Going Places.*

MIRABELLA, GRACE. Maplewood, NJ, 6/10/29. Fashion editor, publishing executive. *Mirabella.*

MIRREN, HELEN. 7/26/45. Actor. *Prime Suspect.*

MITCHELL, JONI (Roberta Anderson). Fort McLeod, Canada, 11/7/43. Folk singer, songwriter.

MITCHELL, LIZ. Clarendon, Jamaica, 7/12/52. Singer. Boney M.

MITCHELL, MITCH (John Mitchell). Middlesex, England, 7/9/46. Drummer. The Jimi Hendrix Experience.

MITCHELL, NEIL. Helensborough, Scotland, 6/8/67. Keyboardist. Wet Wet Wet.

MITCHUM, JAMES. Los Angeles, CA, 5/8/41. Actor, son of Robert. *Thunder Road.*

MOFFAT, DONALD. Plymouth, England, 12/26/30. Actor. *Clear and Present Danger.*

MOL, GRETCHEN. 11/8/72. Actor. *Rounders.*

MOLL, RICHARD. Pasadena, CA, 1/13/43. Actor, stands 6' 8". Nostradamus "Bull" Shannon on *Night Court.*

MOLLAND, JOEY. Liverpool, England, 6/21/48. Guitarist, keyboardist, singer. Badfinger.

MONARCH, MICHAEL. Los Angeles, CA, 7/5/50. Guitarist. Steppenwolf.

MONDALE, WALTER "FRITZ." Ceylon, MN, 1/5/28. Politician, former Vice President of the United States, former presidential candidate. Father of Eleanor.

MONEY, EDDIE (Eddie Mahoney). Brooklyn, NY, 3/21/49. Singer.

MONTALBAN, RICARDO. Mexico City, Mexico, 11/25/20. Actor. *Fantasy Island.*

MONTANA, JOE. New Eagle, PA, 6/11/56. Football great.

MONTGOMERY, GEORGE (George Letz). Brady, MT, 8/29/16. Actor. *The Texas Rangers.*

MONTGOMERY, JOHN MICHAEL. Lexington, KY, 1/20/65. Country singer.

MOODY, MICKY. 8/30/50. Guitarist. Whitesnake.

MOONEY, KEVIN. England, 5/5/62. Bassist. Adam & The Ants.

MOORE, DUDLEY. Dagenham, England, 4/19/35. Actor. *Arthur.*

MOORE, MARY TYLER. Brooklyn, NY, 12/29/36. Actor. *The Mary Tyler Moore Show.*

MOORE, MELBA (Beatrice Hill). New York, NY, 10/29/45. R&B singer, actor. *Purlie.*

MOORE, ROGER. London, England, 10/14/27. Actor, replaced Sean Connery as James Bond. *Live and Let Die.*

MOORE, SAM. Miami, FL, 10/12/35. Singer. Sam & Dave.

MORAN, ERIN. Burbank, CA, 10/18/61. Actor. Joanie Cunningham on *Happy Days.*

MORANIS, RICK. Toronto, Canada, 4/18/54. Actor, writer. *Honey, I Shrunk the Kids.*

MOREAU, JEANNE. Paris, France, 1/23/28. Actor. *Jules et Jim.*

MORENO, RITA (Rosita Dolores Alverio). Humacao, PR, 12/11/31. Actor. *West Side Story.*

MORGAN, LORRIE (Loretta Lynn Morgan). Nashville, TN, 6/27/59. Singer.

MORIARTY, CATHY. The Bronx, NY, 11/29/60. Actor. *Raging Bull.*

MORIARTY, MICHAEL. Detroit, MI, 4/5/41. Actor. *Law and Order.*

MORITA, NORIYUKI "PAT." Isleton, CA, 6/28/32. Actor. *The Karate Kid.*

MORRIS, STEPHEN. Macclesfield, England, 10/28/57. Drummer. New Order.

MORRISSEY (Stephen Morrissey). Manchester, England, 5/22/59. Singer. The Smiths.

MORROW, ROB. New Rochelle, NY, 9/21/62. Actor. *Northern Exposure.*

MORSE, DAVID. Hamilton, MA, 10/11/53. Actor. *St. Elsewhere.*

MORTON, JOE. New York, NY, 10/18/47. Actor. *Terminator 2: Judgment Day.*

MORVAN, FABRICE. Guadeloupe, 5/14/66. "Singer." Milli Vanilli.

MOSLEY, BOB. Paradise Valley, CA, 12/4/42. Bassist. Moby Grape.

MOSS, JON. Wandsworth, England, 9/11/57. Drummer. Culture Club.

MOSS, KATE. London, England, 1/16/74. Supermodel.

MOST, DONNY. New York, NY, 8/8/53. Actor. Ralph Malph on *Happy Days.*

MOSTEL, JOSH. New York, NY, 12/21/46. Actor. *City Slickers.*

MOULDING, COLIN. Swindon, England, 8/17/55. Bassist, singer. XTC.

MOUNT, DAVE. Carshalton, England, 3/3/47. Drummer, singer. Mud.

MOYERS, BILL. Hugo, OK, 6/5/34. Journalist, commentator. *Bill Moyers' Journal.*

MOYET, ALISON (Genevieve Moyet). Basildon, England, 6/18/61. Singer. Yazoo.

MUDD, ROGER. Washington, DC, 2/9/28. Broadcast journalist, newscaster.

MULDAUR, DIANA. New York, NY, 8/19/38. Actor. *L.A. Law; Star Trek: The Next Generation.*

MULGREW, KATE. Dubuque, IA, 4/29/55. Actor. Capt. Kathryn Janeway on *Star Trek: Voyager.*

MULHERN, MATT. Philadelphia, PA, 7/21/60. Actor. 2nd Lt. Gene Holowachuk on *Major Dad.*

MULL, MARTIN. Chicago, IL, 8/18/43. Actor. *Mary Hartman, Mary Hartman.*

MULLEN, LARRY JR. Dublin, Ireland, 10/31/61. Drummer. U2.

MULLIGAN, RICHARD. New York, NY, 11/13/32. Actor. Dr. Harry Weston on *Empty Nest.*

MUMY, BILLY. El Centro, CA, 2/1/54. Actor. *Lost in Space.*

MURPHY, MICHAEL. Los Angeles, CA, 5/5/38. Actor. *Manhattan.*

MURPHY, PETER. 7/11/57. Singer. Bauhaus.

MURRAY, DAVE. London, England, 12/23/58. Lead guitarist. Iron Maiden.

MUSIC, LORENZO. Brooklyn, NY, 5/2/37. Actor, writer. Carlton the Doorman on *Rhoda.*

NABORS, JIM. Sylacauga, GA, 6/12/32. Actor. Gomer Pyle on *The Andy Griffith Show.*

NADER, RALPH. Winsted, CT, 2/27/34. Political activist, author. *Unsafe at Any Speed.*

NAMATH, JOE. Beaver Falls, PA, 5/31/43. Football great, endorser.

NASH, BRIAN. Liverpool, England, 5/20/63. Guitarist. Frankie Goes to Hollywood.

NASH, GRAHAM. Blackpool, England, 2/2/42. Guitarist. The Hollies; Crosby, Stills, Nash & Young.

NAUGHTON, DAVID. West Hartford, CT, 2/13/51. Actor, brother of James. *An American Werewolf in London.*

NAUGHTON, JAMES. Middletown, CT, 7/6/45. Actor, brother of David. *The Good Mother.*

NAVRATILOVA, MARTINA. Prague, Czechoslovakia, 10/18/56. Tennis player.

NEAL, PATRICIA. Packard, KY, 1/20/26. Actor. *Hud.*

NEGRON, CHUCK. The Bronx, NY, 6/8/42. Singer. Three Dog Night.

NEIL, VINCE (Vince Wharton). Hollywood, CA, 2/8/61. Singer. Mötley Crüe.

NEILL, SAM. Ireland, 9/14/47. Actor. *Jurassic Park.*

NELLIGAN, KATE. London, Canada, 3/16/51. Actor. *The Prince of Tides.*

NELSON, CRAIG T. Spokane, WA, 4/4/46. Actor, writer. Hayden Fox on *Coach.*

NELSON, DAVID. New York, NY, 10/24/36. Actor, son of Ozzie and Harriet, brother of Ricky. David Nelson on *The Adventures of Ozzie and Harriet.*

NELSON, JUDD. Portland, ME, 11/28/59. Actor. *The Breakfast Club.*

NELSON, SANDY. Santa Monica, CA, 12/1/38. Rock/jazz drummer.

NELSON, TRACY. Santa Monica, CA, 10/25/63. Actor, daughter of Rick Nelson. *Father Dowling Mysteries.*

NEMES, LES. Surrey, England, 12/5/60. Bassist. Haircut 100.

NESMITH, MIKE (Robert Nesmith). Houston, TX, 12/30/42. Singer, guitarist, actor. The Monkees.

NEVILLE, AARON. New Orleans, LA, 1/24/41. Singer. The Neville Brothers.

NEVILLE, ART. New Orleans, LA, 12/17/37. Singer, keyboardist. The Neville Brothers.

NEVILLE, CHARLES. New Orleans, LA, 12/28/38. Saxophonist. The Neville Brothers.

NEVILLE, CYRIL. 1/10/48. Singer, percussionist. The Neville Brothers.

NEWHART, BOB (George Newhart). Chicago, IL, 9/5/29. Actor, comedian. *The Bob Newhart Show.*

NEWMAN, RANDY. Los Angeles, CA, 11/28/43. Singer, songwriter.

NEWTON, JUICE. Lakehurst, NJ, 2/18/52. Country singer. "Angel of the Morning."

NEWTON-JOHN, OLIVIA. Cambridge, England, 9/26/48. Singer, actor. *Grease.*

NGUYEN, DUSTIN. Saigon, Vietnam, 1962. Actor. *21 Jump Street.*

NICHOL, AL. Winston-Salem, NC, 3/31/46. Guitarist, keyboardist, singer. The Turtles.

NICKS, STEVIE. Phoenix, AZ, 5/26/48. Singer. Fleetwood Mac.

NIELSEN, RICK. Rockford, IL, 12/22/46. Singer, guitarist. Cheap Trick.

NIELSEN, BRIGITTE. Denmark, 7/15/63. Actor, formerly married to Sylvester Stallone. *Red Sonja.*

NIMOY, LEONARD. Boston, MA, 3/26/31. Actor, director. Mr. Spock on *Star Trek.*

NOIRET, PHILIPPE. Lille, France, 10/1/31. Actor. *Cinema Paradiso.*

NOLAN, MIKE. Dublin, Ireland, 12/7/54. Singer. Bucks Fizz.

NOONAN, PEGGY. New York, NY, 9/7/50. Author, presidential speechwriter. Responsible for phrase "a kinder, gentler nation."

NOONE, PETER. Manchester, England, 11/5/47. Singer. Herman's Hermits.

NORRIS, CHUCK (Carlos Ray). Ryan, OK, 3/10/40. Karate champion, actor. *Good Guys Wear Black.*

NORTH, OLIVER. San Antonio, TX, 10/7/43. Presidential aide, senatorial candidate. Iran-Contra.

NORTON, KEN. Jacksonville, IL, 8/9/45. Boxer, actor. *The Gong Show.*

NOURI, MICHAEL. Washington, DC, 12/9/45. Actor. *Flashdance.*

NOVAK, KIM (Marilyn Novak). Chicago, IL, 2/13/33. Actor. *Vertigo.*

NOVELLO, DON. Ashtabula, OH, 1/1/43. Actor. Father Guido Sarducci.

NUGENT, TED. Detroit, MI, 12/13/48. Hard rock guitarist, actor.

NUMAN, GARY (Gary Webb). Hammersmith, England, 3/8/58. Singer. "Cars."

O'CONNOR, CARROLL. New York, NY, 8/2/24. Actor. Archie Bunker on *All in the Family.*

O'CONNOR, DONALD. Chicago, IL, 8/28/25. Actor. *Singin' in the Rain.*

O'CONNOR, SANDRA DAY. El Paso, TX, 3/26/30. Supreme Court Justice.

O'CONNOR, SINEAD. Dublin, Ireland, 12/8/66. Singer.

O'HARA, BRIAN. Liverpool, England, 3/12/42. Guitarist, singer. The Fourmost.

O'HARA, CATHERINE. Toronto, Canada, 3/4/54. Actor. Mother in *Home Alone.*

O'HARA, MAUREEN (Maureen FitzSimons). Dublin, Ireland, 8/17/21. Actor. *How Green Was My Valley.*

O'NEAL, ALEXANDER. 11/14/53. Singer, songwriter.

O'NEAL, RYAN (Patrick Ryan O'Neal). Los Angeles, CA,

4/20/41. Actor, father of Tatum O'Neal. *Love Story.*

O'NEAL, TATUM. Los Angeles, CA, 11/5/63. Actor, daughter of Ryan, formerly married to John McEnroe. *Paper Moon.*

O'NEILL, ED. Youngstown, OH, 4/12/46. Actor. Al Bundy on *Married … with Children.*

O'NEILL, JENNIFER. Rio de Janeiro, Brazil, 2/20/48. Actor, former model. *Summer of '42.*

O'NEILL, JOHN. 8/26/57. Guitarist. The Undertones.

O'SHEA, MILO. Dublin, Ireland, 6/2/26. Actor. *The Verdict.*

O'SULLIVAN, GILBERT (Raymond O'Sullivan). Waterford, Ireland, 12/1/46. Singer, songwriter.

O'TOOLE, ANNETTE (Annette Toole). Houston, TX, 4/1/53. Actor. *Superman III.*

O'TOOLE, MARK. Liverpool, England, 1/6/64. Bassist. Frankie Goes to Hollywood.

O'TOOLE, PETER. Connemara, Ireland, 8/2/32. Actor. *Lawrence of Arabia.*

OAKEY, PHILIP. Sheffield, England, 10/2/55. Singer. The Human League.

OAKLEY, BERRY. Chicago, IL, 4/4/48. Bassist. The Allman Brothers Band.

OATES, JOHN. New York, NY, 4/7/48. Singer, guitarist. Hall & Oates.

OCASEK, RIC (Ric Otcasek). Baltimore, MD, 3/23/49. Singer, guitarist, married to Paulina Porizkova. The Cars.

OCEAN, BILLY (Leslie Charles). Fyzabad, Trinidad, 7/21/50. Rock/R&B singer, songwriter.

OLDFIELD, MIKE. Reading, England, 5/15/53. Bassist, composer. "Tubular Bells."

OLDMAN, GARY. New Cross, England, 3/21/58. Actor, formerly married to Uma Thurman. *Bram Stoker's Dracula.*

OLIN, KEN. Chicago, IL, 7/30/54. Actor, director. Michael Steadman on *thirtysomething.*

OLIN, LENA. Stockholm, Sweden, 3/22/55. Actor. *Havana.*

OLMOS, EDWARD JAMES. East Los Angeles, CA, 2/24/47. Actor. Martin Castillo on *Miami Vice.*

ONO, YOKO. 2/18/33. Singer, wife of John Lennon, mother of Julian Lennon and Sean.Lennon.

ONTKEAN, MICHAEL. Vancouver, Canada, 1/24/46. Actor. *Twin Peaks.*

OPPENHEIMER, ALAN. New York, NY, 4/23/30. Actor. Gene Kinsella on *Murphy Brown.*

ORANGE, WALTER. Florida, 12/10/47. Singer, drummer. The Commodores.

ORBACH, JERRY. The Bronx, NY, 10/20/35. Actor. *Law and Order.*

ORLANDO, TONY (Michael Cassivitis). New York, NY, 4/3/44. Singer. Tony Orlando & Dawn.

ORR, BENJAMIN (Benjamin Orzechowski). Cleveland, OH, 8/9/55. Singer, bass guitarist. The Cars.

ORZABAL, ROLAND (Roland Orzabal de la Quintana). Portsmouth, England, 8/22/61. Guitarist, keyboardist. Tears for Fears.

OSBORNE, JEFFREY. Providence, RI, 3/9/48. Singer, songwriter, drummer. L.T.D.

OSGOOD, CHARLES. New York, NY, 1/8/33. Broadcast journalist, author.

OSKAR, LEE (Oskar Hansen). Copenhagen, Denmark, 3/24/46. Harmonicist. War.

OSMOND, ALAN. Ogden, UT, 6/22/49. Singer, member of the Osmond family. The Osmonds.

OSMOND, JAY. Ogden, UT, 3/2/55. Singer, member of the Osmond family. The Osmonds.

OSMOND, MERRILL. Ogden, UT, 4/30/53. Singer, member of the Osmond family. The Osmonds.

OSMOND, WAYNE. Ogden, UT, 8/28/51. Singer, member of the Osmond family. The Osmonds.

OTIS, CARRE. 9/28/68. Model, actor, formerly married to Mickey Rourke.

OTIS, JOHNNY (John Veliotes). Vallejo, CA, 12/28/21. R&B drummer, pianist, and songwriter.

OWEN, RANDY. Fort Payne, AL, 12/13/49. Singer, guitarist. Alabama.

OWENS, SHIRLEY. Passaic, NJ, 6/10/41. Lead singer. The Shirelles.

OVITZ, MICHAEL. Encino, CA, 12/14/46. Studio executive.

OXENBERG, CATHERINE. New York, NY, 9/21/61. Actor. Amanda Carrington on *Dynasty.*

OZ, FRANK. Hereford, England, 5/25/44. Puppeteer, film director. *The Muppet Show.*

PACULA, JOANNA. Tamaszow Lubelski, Poland, 1/2/57. Actor. *Gorky Park.*

PAGE, JIMMY. Heston, England, 1/9/44. Guitarist. Led Zeppelin.

PAICE, IAN. Nottingham, England, 6/29/48. Drummer. Deep Purple.

PAICH, DAVID. Los Angeles, CA, 6/25/54. Keyboardist, singer. Toto.

PALANCE, JACK (Walter Palanuik). Lattimer, PA, 2/18/20. Actor. *City Slickers.*

PALIN, MICHAEL. Sheffield, England, 5/5/43. Actor, writer. *Monty Python's Flying Circus.*

PALMER, BETSY. East Chicago, IN, 11/1/26. Actor, panelist on *I've Got a Secret.*

PALMER, CARL. Birmingham, England, 3/20/51. Drummer. Emerson, Lake &

Palmer; Asia.

PALMER, JOHN. 5/25/43. Keyboardist. Family.

PALMER, ROBERT (Alan Palmer). Batley, England, 1/19/49. Singer, songwriter. "Addicted to Love."

PALMINTERI, CHAZZ (Chalogero Lorenzo Palminteri). Bronx, NY, 5/15/51. Actor, playwright, screenwriter. *A Bronx Tale.*

PANKOW, JAMES. Chicago, IL, 8/20/47. Trombonist. Chicago.

PANOZZO, CHUCK. Chicago, IL, 9/20/47. Bassist. Styx.

PAQUIN, ANNA. Wellington, New Zealand, 7/24/82. Actor. *The Piano.*

PARAZAIDER, WALTER. Chicago, IL, 3/14/45. Saxophonist. Chicago.

PARE, MICHAEL. Brooklyn, NY, 10/9/59. Actor. *Eddie and the Cruisers.*

PARFITT, RICK (Richard Harrison). Redhill, England, 10/25/43. Guitarist, singer. Status Quo.

PARILLAUD, ANNE. France, 1961. Actor. *La Femme Nikita.*

PARKER, FESS. Fort Worth, TX, 8/16/24. Actor. *Daniel Boone.*

PARKER, GRAHAM. Deepcut, England, 11/18/50. Singer. Graham Parker & The Rumour.

PARKER, JAMESON. Baltimore, MD, 11/18/47. Actor. *Simon and Simon.*

PARKER, MARY-LOUISE. Ft. Jackson, SC, 8/2/64. Actor. *Fried Green Tomatoes.*

PARKER, RAY JR. Detroit, MI, 5/1/54. Singer, songwriter. "Ghostbusters."

PARKER, TREY. 10/19/69. Actor, cartoonist. *South Park.*

PARSONS, ESTELLE. Lynn, MA, 11/20/27. Actor. *Roseanne.*

PARTRIDGE, ANDY. Malta, 11/11/53. Guitarist, singer. XTC.

PASTORELLI, ROBERT. 6/21/54. Actor. *Murphy Brown*.

PATERSON, GERRY. Winnepeg, Canada, 5/26/45. Drummer. The Guess Who.

PATINKIN, MANDY (Mandel Patinkin). Chicago, IL, 11/30/52. Actor. *Yentl*.

PATRIC, JASON (Jason Patrick Miller). Queens, NY, 6/17/66. Actor. *Rush*.

PATRICK, ROBERT. Marietta, GA, 1959. Actor. Evil T-1000 in *Terminator 2: Judgment Day*.

PATTEN, EDWARD. Atlanta, GA, 8/2/39. Singer. Gladys Knight & The Pips.

PATTERSON, LORNA. Whittier, CA, 6/1/57. Actor. *Private Benjamin*.

PATTERSON, MELODY. Los Angeles, CA, 1947. Actor. Wrangler Jane on *F Troop*.

PATTINSON, LES. Ormskirk, England, 4/18/58. Bassist. Echo & The Bunnymen.

PATTON, MIKE. Eureka, CA, 1/27/68. Lead singer. Faith No More.

PATTON, WILL. Charleston, SC, 6/14/54. Actor. *No Way Out*.

PAYCHECK, JOHNNY (Donald Eugene Lytle). Greenfield, OH, 5/31/41. Singer. "Take This Job and Shove It."

PAYNE, BILL. Waco, TX, 3/12/49. Keyboardist. Little Feat.

PAYS, AMANDA. Berkshire, England, 6/6/59. Actor, married to Corbin Bernsen. *The Flash*.

PAYTON, DENIS. Walthamstow, England, 8/11/43. Saxophonist. The Dave Clark Five.

PAYTON, WALTER. Columbia, MS, 6/25/54. Football player.

PEARSON, DELROY. Romford, England, 4/11/70. Singer. Five Star.

PEARSON, DENIECE. Romford, England, 6/13/68. Lead singer. Five Star.

PEARSON, DORIS. Romford, England, 6/8/66. Singer. Five Star.

PEARSON, LORRAINE. Romford, England, 8/10/67. Singer. Five Star.

PEARSON, STEDMAN. Romford, England, 6/29/64. Singer. Five Star.

PEART, NEIL. Hamilton, Canada, 9/12/52. Drummer. Rush.

PECK, GREGORY (Eldred Peck). La Jolla, CA, 4/5/16. Actor, producer. *To Kill a Mockingbird*.

PEEK, DAN. Panama City, FL, 11/1/50. Singer, guitarist. America.

PELE, PEROLA NEGRA (Edson Arantes do Nascimento). Tres Coracoes, Brazil, 10/23/40. Soccer legend.

PELLOW, MARTI (Mark McLoughlin). Clydebank, Scotland, 3/23/66. Singer. Wet Wet Wet.

PENA, ELIZABETH. Elizabeth, NJ, 9/23/61. Actor. *La Bamba*.

PENDER, MIKE (Michael Prendergast). Liverpool, England, 3/3/42. Singer, lead guitarist. The Searchers.

PENDERGRASS, TEDDY. Philadelphia, PA, 3/26/50. R&B singer, songwriter, drummer.

PENDLETON, AUSTIN. Warren, OH, 3/27/40. Actor. *What's Up Doc?*

PENDLETON, BRIAN. Wolverhampton, England, 4/13/44. Guitarist. The Pretty Things.

PENGILLY, KIRK. 7/4/58. Guitarist, saxophonist, singer. INXS.

PENNY, JOE. London, England, 9/14/56. Actor. Jake Styles on *Jake and the Fatman*.

PEPA (Sanda Denton). Queens, NY, 9/9/64. Rap artist. Salt-N-Pepa.

PEREZ, ROSIE. Brooklyn, NY, 9/4/66. Actor, choreographer. *Do the Right Thing*.

PERKINS, ELIZABETH. Queens, NY, 11/18/61. Actor. *Big*.

PERLMAN, RHEA. Brooklyn, NY, 3/31/48. Actor, married to Danny DeVito. Carla Tortelli LeBec on *Cheers*.

PERLMAN, RON. New York, NY, 4/13/50. Actor. The Beast in *Beauty and the Beast*.

PEROT, HENRY ROSS. Texarkana, TX, 6/27/30. Self-made billionaire businessman, former presidential candidate.

PERRINE, VALERIE. Galveston, TX, 9/3/43. Actor. *Lenny*.

PERRY, JOE. Boston, MA, 9/10/50. Guitarist. Aerosmith.

PERRY, LUKE (Perry Coy III). Fredericktown, OH, 10/11/66. Actor. *Beverly Hills 90210*.

PERRY, STEVE. Hanford, CA, 1/22/53. Singer. Journey.

PERRY, WILLIAM "THE REFRIGERATOR." Aiken, SC, 12/16/62. Very large football player. Chicago Bears.

PESCOW, DONNA. Brooklyn, NY, 3/24/54. Actor. *Saturday Night Fever*.

PETERS, BROCK. New York, NY, 7/2/27. Actor, singer. *To Kill a Mockingbird*.

PETERS, MIKE. Prestatyn, Wales, 2/25/59. Guitarist, singer. The Alarm.

PETERSEN, WILLIAM. Chicago, IL, 1953. Actor. *To Live and Die in L.A.*

PETERSON, DEBBI. Los Angeles, CA, 8/22/61. Drummer, singer. The Bangles.

PETERSON, SYLVIA. New York, NY, 9/30/46. Singer. The Chiffons.

PETERSON, VICKI. Los Angeles, CA, 1/11/58. Guitarist, singer. The Bangles.

PETERSSON, TOM. Rockford, IL, 5/9/50. Singer, bassist. Cheap Trick.

PETTY, LORI. Chattanooga, TN. Actor. *A League of Their Own*.

PFEIFFER, DEDEE. 1/1/64. Actor, sister of Michelle Pfeiffer. *Cybill*.

PFISTERER, ALBAN. Switzerland, 1947. Drummer, keyboardist. Love.

PHANTOM, SLIM JIM (Jim McDonnell). 3/20/61. Drummer. The Stray Cats.

PHAIR, LIZ. New Haven, CT, 4/17/67. Singer, songwriter. *Exile in Guyville*.

PHILIP, PRINCE (Philip Mountbatten). Corfu, Greece, 6/10/21. Husband of Queen Elizabeth II, Duke of Edinburgh.

PHILLIPS, CHYNNA. Los Angeles, CA, 1/12/68. Singer, half-sister of Mackenzie, daughter of John and Michelle, married to Billy Baldwin. Wilson Phillips.

PHILLIPS, LOU DIAMOND (Lou Upchurch). Philippines, 2/17/62. Actor. *La Bamba*.

PHILLIPS, MACKENZIE (Laura Mackenzie Phillips). Alexandria, VA, 11/10/59. Actor, daughter of John Phillips, half-sister of Chynna. Julie Cooper Horvath on *One Day at a Time*.

PHILLIPS, MICHELLE (Holly Gilliam). Santa Ana, CA, 6/4/44. Actor, formerly married to John, mother of Chynna. Anne Matheson on *Knots Landing*.

PHILTHY ANIMAL (Philip Taylor). Chesterfield, England, 9/21/54. Drummer. Motorhead.

PICKETT, WILSON. Prattville, AL, 3/18/41. Singer, songwriter. "In the Midnight Hour."

PIERSON, KATE. Weehawken, NJ, 4/27/48. Organist, singer. The B-52's.

PINCHOT, BRONSON. New York, NY, 5/20/59. Actor. Balki Bartokomous on *Per-*

fect Strangers.

PINDER, MIKE. Birmingham, England, 12/12/42. Keyboardist. The Moody Blues.

PINKNEY, BILL. Sumter, NC, 8/15/25. Bassist. The Drifters.

PIRNER, DAVE. Green Bay, WI, 4/16/64. Singer, songwriter, guitarist. Soul Asylum.

PIRRONI, MARCO. England, 4/27/59. Guitarist. Adam & The Ants.

PISCOPO, JOE. Passaic, NJ, 6/17/51. Actor. *Saturday Night Live.*

PITNEY, GENE. Hartford, CT, 2/17/41. Singer, songwriter. "Town Without Pity."

PLACE, MARY KAY. Tulsa, OK, 9/23/47. Actor. *The Big Chill.*

PLANT, ROBERT. Bromwich, England, 8/20/48. Singer. Led Zeppelin.

PLATT, OLIVER. 1/12/60. Actor. *Flatliners.*

PLESHETTE, JOHN. New York, NY, 7/27/42. Actor. Richard Avery on *Knots Landing.*

PLESHETTE, SUZANNE. New York, NY, 1/31/37. Actor. Emily Hartley on *The Bob Newhart Show.*

PLOWRIGHT, JOAN. Brigg, England, 10/28/29. Actor, widow of Laurence Olivier. *Enchanted April.*

PLUMB, EVE. Burbank, CA, 4/29/58. Actor. Jan Brady on *The Brady Bunch.*

PLUMMER, AMANDA. New York, NY, 3/23/57. Actor, daughter of Christopher Plummer. *The Fisher King.*

PLUMMER, CHRISTOPHER. Toronto, Canada, 12/13/27. Actor, father of Amanda Plummer. Baron von Trapp in *The Sound of Music.*

POINTER, ANITA. East Oakland, CA, 1/23/48. Singer. Pointer Sisters.

POINTER, BONNIE. East Oakland, CA, 6/11/51.

Singer. Pointer Sisters.

POINTER, JUNE. East Oakland, CA, 11/30/54. Singer. Pointer Sisters.

POINTER, RUTH. East Oakland, CA, 3/19/46. Singer. Pointer Sisters.

POITIER, SIDNEY. Miami, FL, 2/20/27. Actor. *Guess Who's Coming to Dinner.*

POLANSKI, ROMAN. Paris, France, 8/18/33. Director, writer. *Rosemary's Baby.*

POLLAK, KEVIN. 10/30/57. Actor.

POLLACK, SYDNEY. South Bend, Indiana, 7/1/34. Director, producer, actor. *The Way We Were.*

POLLAN, TRACY. New York, NY, 6/22/60. Actor, married to Michael J. Fox. *Family Ties.*

POOLE, BRIAN. Barking, England, 11/2/41. Singer. Brian Poole & The Tremeloes.

POP, IGGY (James Osterburg). Ann Arbor, MI, 4/21/47. Singer, songwriter.

POPCORN, FAITH. New York, NY, 5/11/43. Trend analyst, consultant.

PORCARO, STEVE. Los Angeles, CA, 9/2/57. Keyboardist, singer. Toto.

PORTZ, CHUCK. Santa Monica, CA, 3/28/45. Bassist. The Turtles.

POST, MARKIE. Palo Alto, CA, 11/4/50. Actor. Christine Sullivan on *Night Court.*

POTTER, CAROL. Tenafly, NJ, 5/21/48. Actor. *Beverly Hills 90210.*

POTTS, ANNIE. Nashville, TN, 10/28/52. Actor. Mary Jo Shively on *Designing Women.*

POUNDSTONE, PAULA. Alabama, 12/29/60. Comedian, actor.

POVICH, MAURY. Washington, DC, 1/17/39. Talk show host, married to Connie Chung. *A Current Affair.*

POWELL, BILLY. Florida, 6/3/52. Keyboardist. Lynyrd

Skynyrd.

POWELL, COLIN. New York, NY, 4/5/37. Military leader.

POWELL, DON. 9/10/50. Drummer. Slade.

POWERS, STEPHANIE (Stefania Federkiewicz). Hollywood, CA, 11/12/42. Actor. Jennifer on *Hart to Hart.*

POWTER, SUSAN. Sydney, Australia, 1957. Weight-loss expert. *Stop the Insanity!*

PRENTISS, PAULA (Paula Ragusa). San Antonio, TX, 3/4/38. Actor. *What's New Pussycat?*

PRESLEY, PRISCILLA. Brooklyn, NY, 5/24/45. Actor, producer, married and divorced Elvis Presley.

PRESLEY, REG (Reginald Ball). Andover, England, 6/12/43. Singer. The Troggs.

PRESTON, KELLY. Honolulu, HI, 10/13/62. Actor, married to John Travolta. *52 Pick-Up.*

PRICE, ALAN. Fairfield, Durham, 4/19/41. Keyboardist. The Animals.

PRICE, LLOYD. Kenner, LA, 5/9/33. Singer, songwriter.

PRICE, RICK. 6/10/44. Bassist. Wizzard.

PRIDE, CHARLEY. Sledge, MS, 3/18/38. Country singer, songwriter.

PRIEST, STEVE. London, England, 2/23/50. Bassist. Sweet.

PRIESTLEY, JASON. Vancouver, Canada, 8/28/69. Actor. Brandon Walsh on *Beverly Hills 90210.*

PRIESTMAN, HENRY. 7/21/58. Singer. The Christians.

PRIME, JAMES. Kilmarnock, Scotland, 11/3/60. Keyboardist. Deacon Blue.

PRINCE MARK D. 2/19/60. Rap artist. Fat Boys.

PRINCIPAL, VICTORIA. Fukuoka, Japan, 1/3/50. Actor. Pam Ewing on *Dallas.*

PRITCHARD, BARRY. Birmingham, England, 4/3/44.

Guitarist, singer. The Fortunes.

PROBY, P. J. (James Smith). Houston, TX, 11/6/38. Singer, actor.

PRYCE, JONATHAN. North Wales, 6/1/47. Actor. *Miss Saigon.*

PRYOR, NICHOLAS. Baltimore, MD, 1/28/35. Actor. *Risky Business.*

PRYOR, RICHARD. Peoria, IL, 12/1/40. Actor. *Stir Crazy.*

PUERTA, JOE. 7/2/51. Bassist, singer. Bruce Hornsby & The Range.

PULLMAN, BILL. Hornell, NY, 12/17/53. Actor. *While You Were Sleeping.*

PURCELL, SARAH. Richmond, IN, 10/8/48. TV personality. Cohost on *Real People.*

QADDAFI, MUAMMAR. Sirta, Libya, 1942. Political leader. Libyan head of state.

QUAID, RANDY. Houston, TX, 10/1/50. Actor, brother of Dennis. *The Last Picture Show.*

QUAIFE, PETE. Tavistock, England, 12/31/43. Bassist. The Kinks.

QUATRO, SUZI (Suzi Quatrocchio). Detroit, MI, 6/3/50. Singer, songwriter, actor.

QUAYLE, DAN. Indianapolis, IN, 2/4/47. Vice president under George Bush.

QUAYLE, MARILYN. Indianapolis, IN, 7/29/49. Lawyer, author, married to Dan. *Embrace the Serpent.*

QUEEN LATIFAH. 3/18/70. Singer, actor. *Living Single.*

QUINLAN, KATHLEEN. Mill Valley, CA, 11/19/54. Actor. *Apollo 13.*

QUINN, AIDAN. Chicago, IL, 3/8/59. Actor. *The Playboys.* Married to Elizabeth Bracco.

QUINN, DEREK. Manchester, England, 5/24/42. Lead guitarist. Freddie & The Dreamers.

QUIVERS, ROBIN. 8/8/52. Radio personality, author. *The Howard Stern Show.*

RAFFERTY, GERRY. Paisley, Scotland, 4/16/47. Singer, songwriter. "Baker Street."

RAFFI. Cairo, Egypt, 7/8/48. Singer, songwriter, children's performer. *Everything Grows.*

RAFFIN, DEBORAH. Los Angeles, CA, 3/13/53. Actor. *Once Is Not Enough.*

RALPH, SHERYL LEE. Waterbury, CT, 12/30/56. Actor. *The Distinguished Gentleman.*

RALPHS, MICK. Hereford, England, 3/31/44. Guitarist. Mott The Hoople; Bad Company.

RAMIS, HAROLD. Chicago, IL, 11/21/44. Writer, director, actor. Egon Spengler in *Ghostbusters.*

RAMONE, DEE DEE (Douglas Colvin). Fort Lee, VA, 9/18/52. Bassist. The Ramones.

RAMONE, JOHNNY (John Cummings). Long Island, NY, 10/8/48. Guitarist. The Ramones.

RAMONE, TOMMY (Thomas Erdelyi). Budapest, Hungary, 1/29/49. Drummer. The Ramones.

RAMOS, LARRY JR. (Hilario Ramos Jr.). Kauai, HI, 4/19/42. Singer, guitarist. The Association.

RAMPLING, CHARLOTTE. Surmer, England, 2/5/46. Actor. *The Verdict.*

RAMSEY, AL. New Jersey, 7/27/43. Guitarist. Gary Lewis & The Playboys.

RANDALL, TONY (Leonard Rosenberg). Tulsa, OK, 2/26/20. Actor. Felix Unger on *The Odd Couple.*

RAPHAEL, SALLY JESSY. Easton, PA, 2/25/43. talk show hostess. *Sally Jessy Raphäel.*

RAPP, DANNY. Philadelphia, PA, 5/10/41. Lead singer. Danny & The Juniors.

RAREBELL, HERMAN. 11/18/49. Drummer. Scorpions.

RASCHE, DAVID. St. Louis, MO, 8/7/44. Actor. *Sledge Hammer.*

RASHAD, AHMAD. Portland, OR, 11/19/49. Football player, sportscaster, husband of Phylicia.

RASHAD, PHYLICIA. Houston, TX, 6/19/48. Actor, sister of Debbie Allen, wife of Ahmad. Clair Huxtable on *The Cosby Show.*

RATZENBERGER, JOHN. Bridgeport, CT, 4/6/47. Actor. Cliff Claven on *Cheers.*

RAWLS, LOU. Chicago, IL, 12/1/36. R&B singer. "You'll Never Find Another Love Like Mine."

RAY, JAMES EARL. Alton, IL, 3/10/28. Assassin. Killed Martin Luther King Jr.

REA, CHRIS. Middlesbrough, England, 3/4/51. Singer, songwriter, guitarist. "Fool (If You Think It's Over)."

REAGAN, NANCY. New York, NY, 7/6/21. Former First Lady, married to president Ronald Reagan.

REAGAN, RONALD. Tampico, IL, 2/6/11. Politician, actor, father of Ron Jr., husband of Nancy. Fortieth U.S. president. *Bedtime for Bonzo.*

REAGAN, RONALD JR. Los Angeles, CA, 5/20/58. Performer, son of former president Ronald Reagan.

REASON, REX. Berlin, Germany, 11/30/28. Actor. *This Island Earth.*

RECORD, EUGENE. 12/23/40. Lead singer. The Chi-Lites.

REDDING, NOEL. Folkestone, England, 12/25/45. Bassist. The Jimi Hendrix Experience.

REDDY, HELEN. Melbourne, Australia, 10/25/41. Pop singer. *The Helen Reddy Show.*

REDGRAVE, CORIN. London, England, 6/16/39. Actor,

brother of Lynn and Vanessa. *A Man for All Seasons.*

REDGRAVE, LYNN. London, England, 3/8/43. Actor, sister of Corin and Vanessa. *House Calls.*

REDGRAVE, VANESSA. London, England, 1/30/37. Actor, sister of Corin and Lynn. *Playing for Time.*

REED, LOU (Louis Firbank). Long Island, NY, 3/2/43. Singer, songwriter. The Velvet Underground.

REED, PAMELA. Tacoma, WA, 4/2/53. Actor. *The Right Stuff.*

REEMS, HARRY (Herbert Streicher). The Bronx, NY, 8/27/47. Actor. *Deep Throat.*

REESE, DELLA. 7/6/32. Actor. *Touched By An Angel.*

REEVES, STEVE. Glasgow, MT, 1/21/26. Actor. *Hercules.*

REGALBUTO, JOE. Brooklyn, NY. Actor. Frank Fontana on *Murphy Brown.*

REID, DON. Staunton, VA, 6/5/45. Musician, brother of Harold. Statler Brothers.

REID, HAROLD. Staunton, VA, 8/21/39. Musician, brother of Don. Statler Brothers.

REID, JIM. East Kilbride, Scotland, 1961. Guitarist, singer. The Jesus & Mary Chain.

REID, TIM. Norfolk, VA, 12/19/44. Actor, producer. Gordon "Venus Flytrap" Sims on *WKRP in Cincinnati.*

REID, WILLIAM. East Kilbride, Scotland, 1958. Guitarist, singer. The Jesus & Mary Chain.

REINER, CARL. New York, NY, 3/20/22. Actor, writer, and director. *The Dick Van Dyke Show.*

REINER, ROB. New York, NY, 3/6/45. Actor, writer, producer, director, son of Carl, formerly married to Penny Marshall. Mike Stivic on *All*

in the Family.

REINHOLD, JUDGE (Edward Ernest Reinhold Jr.). Wilmington, DE, 5/21/57. Actor. Rosewood in *Beverly Hills Cop.*

REINKING, ANN. Seattle, WA, 11/10/49. Actor, dancer. *Annie.*

REITMAN, IVAN. Komarno, Czechoslovakia, 10/26/46. Director, producer. *Ghostbusters.*

REVERE, PAUL. Harvard, NE, 1/7/38. Keyboardist. Paul Revere & The Raiders.

REYNOLDS, DEBBIE (Mary Frances Reynolds). El Paso, TX, 4/1/32. Actor, formerly married to Eddie Fisher, mother of Carrie Fisher. *Singin' in the Rain.*

RHAMES, VING. 5/12/59. Actor. *Only in America: The Don King Story.*

RHODES, NICK (Nicholas Bates). Mosely, England, 6/8/62. Keyboardist. Duran Duran.

RIBEIRO, ALFONSO. New York, NY, 9/21/71. Actor, dancer. *Fresh Prince of Bel Air.*

RICH, ADAM. New York, NY, 10/12/68. Actor. Nicholas Bradford on *Eight Is Enough.*

RICHARD, CLIFF (Harry Webb). Lucknow, India, 10/14/40. Singer, drummer. The Shadows.

RICHARDS, KEITH. Dartford, England, 12/18/43. Guitarist. The Rolling Stones.

RICHARDSON, MIRANDA. Lancashire, England, 3/3/58. Actor. *The Crying Game.*

RICHARDSON, SUSAN. Coatesville, PA, 3/11/52. Actor. Susan Bradford on *Eight Is Enough.*

RICHIE, LIONEL. Tuskegee, AL, 6/20/49. Singer, songwriter. The Commodores.

RICHRATH, GARY. Peoria, IL, 10/18/49. Guitarist. REO Speedwagon.

RICKLES, DON. New York, NY, 5/8/26. Actor. *The Don Rickles Show.*

RICKMAN, ALAN. Hammersmith, England, 1946. Actor. *Die Hard.*

RIDGELEY, ANDREW. Windlesham, England, 1/26/63. Guitarist. Wham!

RIEGERT, PETER. New York, NY, 4/11/47. Actor. *Crossing Delancey.*

RIGBY, CATHY. Long Beach, CA, 12/12/52. Gymnast, actor.

RIGG, DIANA. Doncaster, England, 7/20/38. Actor. Emma Peel on *The Avengers.*

RIGGS, BOBBY. Los Angeles, CA, 2/25/18. Tennis player, defeated by Billie Jean King.

RILEY, PAT. Rome, NY, 3/20/45. Basketball coach. Former New York Knicks coach.

RINGWALD, MOLLY. Sacramento, CA, 2/18/68. Actor. *Sixteen Candles.*

RITTER, JOHN. Burbank, CA, 9/17/48. Actor, producer. Jack Tripper on *Three's Company.*

RIVERA, CHITA. Washington, DC, 1/23/33. Singer.

RIVERS, JOHNNY (John Ramistella). New York, NY, 11/7/42. Soul/rock singer, songwriter.

RIZZUTO, PHIL. New York, NY, 9/25/18. Baseball great, sports announcer.

ROBERTS, ERIC. Biloxi, MS, 4/18/56. Actor, brother of Julia. *The Pope of Greenwich Village.*

ROBERTS, ORAL. Ada, OK, 1/24/18. Evangelist. Oral Roberts University.

ROBERTS, TANYA (Tanya Leigh). The Bronx, NY, 10/15/55. Actor. *Charlie's Angels.*

ROBERTS, TONY. New York, NY, 10/22/39. Actor. *Play It Again, Sam.*

ROBERTS, XAVIER. Cleveland, GA, 10/31/55. Businessman. Creator of Cabbage Patch Kids.

ROBERTSON, BRIAN. Glasgow, Scotland, 9/12/56. Guitarist. Thin Lizzy.

ROBERTSON, CLIFF. La Jolla, CA, 9/9/23. Actor. *Charly.*

ROBERTSON, PAT (Marion Gordon Robertson). Lexington, VA, 3/22/30. Evangelist, TV personality. Founder of Christian Broadcasting Network.

ROBERTSON, ROBBIE (Jaime Robertson). Toronto, Canada, 7/5/44. Guitarist, singer. The Band.

ROBINSON, CHRIS. Atlanta, GA, 12/20/66. Singer. The Black Crowes.

ROBINSON, CYNTHIA. Sacramento, CA, 1/12/46. Trumpeter. Sly & The Family Stone.

ROBINSON, JAY. New York, NY, 4/14/30. Actor. *The Robe.*

ROBINSON, RICH. Atlanta, GA, 5/24/69. Guitarist. The Black Crowes.

ROBINSON, SMOKEY (William Robinson). Detroit, MI, 2/19/40. Motown singer, songwriter. Smokey Robinson & The Miracles.

ROCKER, LEE (Leon Drucher). 1961. Double bassist. The Stray Cats.

ROCKWELL (Kenneth Gordy). Detroit, MI, 3/15/64. Singer, son of Berry Gordy. "Somebody's Watching Me."

RODGERS, NILE. New York, NY, 9/19/52. Guitarist. Chic.

RODGERS, PAUL. Middlesbrough, England, 12/17/49. Singer. Free; Bad Company.

RODMAN, DENNIS Trenton, NJ, 5/13/61. Basketball player. Formerly married to Carmen Electra.

ROE, TOMMY. Atlanta, GA, 5/9/42. Singer, songwriter.

ROGERS, KENNY. Houston, TX, 8/21/38. Country singer, actor. "The Gambler."

ROGERS, MIMI. Coral Gables, FL, 1/27/55. Actor. Formerly married to Tom Cruise. *Someone To Watch Over Me.*

ROGERS, FRED. Latrobe, PA, 3/20/28. Children's host, producer. *Mr. Rogers' Neighborhood.*

ROGERS, ROY (Leonard Slye). Cincinnati, OH, 11/5/12. TV cowboy, singer. *Happy Trails with Roy and Dale.*

ROGERS, WAYNE. Birmingham, AL, 4/7/33. Actor. Trapper John on *M*A*S*H.*

ROGERS, WILL JR. New York, NY, 10/20/12. Actor, lecturer. *The Story of Will Rogers.*

RONSTADT, LINDA. Tucson, AZ, 7/15/46. Singer, actor. *The Pirates of Penzance.*

ROONEY, ANDY. Albany, NY, 1/14/19. News commentator. *60 Minutes.*

ROONEY, MICKEY (Joe Yule Jr.). Brooklyn, NY, 9/23/20. Actor. *National Velvet.*

ROSE, AXL (William Bailey). Lafayette, IN, 1962. Singer. Guns N' Roses.

ROSE, PETE. Cincinnati, OH, 4/14/41. Baseball player and manager. Cincinnati Reds.

ROSS, KATHARINE. Hollywood, CA, 1/29/43. Actor. *The Graduate.*

ROSS, MARION. Albert Lea, MN, 10/25/28. Actor. Marion Cunningham on *Happy Days.*

ROSS, RICKY. Dundee, Scotland, 12/22/57. Singer. Deacon Blue.

ROSSELLINI, ISABELLA. Rome, Italy, 6/18/52. Actor, formerly married to Martin Scorsese. *Blue Velvet.*

ROSSI, FRANCIS. Forest Hill, England, 4/29/49. Guitarist, singer. Status Quo.

ROSSINGTON, GARY. Jacksonville, FL, 12/4/51. Guitarist. Lynyrd Skynyrd.

ROTH, DAVID LEE. Bloomingtom, IN, 10/10/54. Singer. Van Halen.

ROTH, TIM. London, England, 1961. Actor. *Reservoir Dogs.*

ROTHERY, STEVE. Brampton, England, 11/25/59. Guitarist. Marillion.

ROTHWELL, RIC. Stockport, England, 3/11/44. Drummer. Wayne Fontana & The Mindbenders.

ROUNDTREE, RICHARD. New Rochelle, NY, 9/7/42. Actor. *Shaft.*

ROURKE, MICKEY. Schenectady, NY, 9/16/56. Actor, formerly married to Carre Otis. *9 1/2 Weeks.*

ROWLAND, KEVIN. Wolverhampton, England, 8/17/53. Singer, guitarist. Dexy's Midnight Runners.

ROWLANDS, GENA. Cambria, WI, 6/19/30. Actor. *Gloria.*

RUCKER, DARIUS Charleston, SC, 5/13/66. Singer, songwriter, guitarist. Hootie & The Blowfish.

RUDD, PHILIP. Australia, 5/19/46. Drummer. AC/DC.

RUDNER, RITA. Miami, FL, 9/11/55. Actor, comedian.

RUEHL, MERCEDES. Queens, NY, 2/28/52. Actor. *Lost in Yonkers.*

RUFFIN, DAVID. Meridian, MS, 1/18/41. Singer. The Temptations.

RUNDGREN, TODD. Philadelphia, PA, 6/22/48. Singer, songwriter.

RUSHDIE, SALMAN. Bombay, India, 6/19/47. Author. *The Satanic Verses.*

RUSSELL, GRAHAM. Nottingham, England, 6/1/50. Singer. Air Supply.

RUSSELL, JACK. 12/5/60. Singer. Great White.

RUSSELL, JANE. Bemidji, MN, 6/21/21. Actor, pinup girl. *The Outlaw.*

RUSSELL, LEON (Hank Wilson). Lawton, OK, 4/2/41. Country/blues singer, songwriter.

RUSSELL, NIPSEY. Atlanta, GA, 10/13/24. Actor. *Car 54, Where Are You?*

RUSSELL, THERESA (Theresa Paup). San Diego, CA, 3/20/57. Actor. *Black Widow.*

RUTHERFORD, MIKE. Guildford, England, 10/2/50. Guitarist. Genesis; Mike & The Mechanics.

RUTHERFORD, PAUL. Liverpool, England, 12/8/59. Singer. Frankie Goes to Hollywood.

RUTTAN, SUSAN. Oregon City, OR, 9/16/48. Actor. Roxanne on *L.A. Law.*

RYAN, TOM. Anderson, IN, 6/6/26. Cartoonist. *Tumbleweeds.*

RYDER, MITCH (William Levise Jr.). Detroit, MI, 2/26/45. Singer. Mitch Ryder & The Detroit Wheels.

RYDER, PAUL. Manchester, England, 4/24/64. Bassist. Happy Mondays.

RYDER, SHAUN. Little Hulton, England, 8/23/62. Singer. Happy Mondays.

SABATINI, GABRIELA. Buenos Aires, Argentina, 5/16/70. Tennis player.

SADE (Helen Folasade Adu). Ibadan, Nigeria, 1/16/59. Singer.

SAGAL, KATEY. Los Angeles, CA, 1/19/54. Actor. Peg on *Married … with Children.*

SAGET, BOB. Philadelphia, PA, 5/17/56. Actor. *Full House.*

SAHM, DOUG. San Antonio, TX, 11/6/41. Singer, guitarist. Sir Douglas Quintet.

SAINT, EVA MARIE. Newark, NJ, 7/4/24. Actor. *On the Waterfront.*

SAINT JAMES, SUSAN (Susan Miller). Los Angeles, CA, 8/14/46. Actor. Kate on *Kate & Allie.*

SAJAK, PAT. Chicago, IL, 10/26/46. Game show host. *Wheel of Fortune.*

SALAZAR, ALBERTO. Havana, Cuba, 8/7/58. Track athlete, won New York City Marathon.

SALES, SOUPY (Milton Supman). Franklinton, NC, 1/8/26. TV personality. *The Soupy Sales Show.*

SALINGER, J. D. (Jerome David Salinger). New York, NY, 1/1/19. Author. *The Catcher in the Rye.*

SALT (Cheryl James). Brooklyn, NY, 3/8/64. Rap artist. Salt-N-Pepa.

SALT, JENNIFER. Los Angeles, CA, 9/4/44. Actor. *Midnight Cowboy.*

SAMBORA, RICHIE. 7/11/59. Guitarist, married to Heather Locklear. Bon Jovi.

SAMMS, EMMA. London, England, 8/28/60. Actor. Fallon Carrington Colby on *Dynasty* and *The Colbys.*

SAMPRAS, PETE. Washington, DC, 8/12/71. Tennis player.

SAMWELL-SMITH, PAUL. Richmond, England, 5/8/43. Bassist. The Yardbirds.

SAN GIACOMO, LAURA. Denville, NJ, 11/14/61. Actor. *Just Shoot Me.*

SANDERS, RICHARD. Harrisburg, PA, 8/23/40. Actor. Les Nessman on *WKRP in Cincinnati.*

SANDS, JULIAN. Yorkshire, England, 1/15/58. Actor. *A Room with a View.*

SANDY, GARY. Dayton, OH, 11/3/46. Actor. Andy Travis on *WKRP in Cincinnati.*

SANFORD, ISABEL. New York, NY, 8/29/17. Actor. Louise on *The Jeffersons.*

SANTANA, CARLOS. Autlan de Navarro, Mexico, 7/20/47. Guitarist, singer. Santana.

SANTIAGO, HERMAN. New York, NY 2/18/41. Singer. Frankie Lymon & The Teenagers.

SARANDON, CHRIS. Beckley, WV, 7/24/42. Actor, former husband of Susan. Leon in *Dog Day Afternoon.*

SASSOON, VIDAL. London, England, 1/17/28. Hairstylist.

SAVAGE, FRED. Highland Park, IL, 7/9/76. Actor, brother of Ben. Kevin Arnold on *The Wonder Years.*

SAVAGE, JOHN (John Youngs). Long Island, NY, 8/25/49. Actor. *The Deer Hunter.*

SAVAGE, RICK. Sheffield, England, 12/2/60. Bassist. Def Leppard.

SAVANT, DOUG. 6/21/64. Actor. *Melrose Place.*

SAWYER, RAY. Chickasaw, AL, 2/1/37. Lead singer. Dr. Hook.

SAYER, LEO (Gerard Sayer). Shoreham-by-Sea, England, 5/21/48. Singer, songwriter. "You Make Me Feel Like Dancing."

SAYLES, JOHN. 9/28/50. Director.

SCABIES, RAT (Chris Miller). Kingston-upon-Thames, England, 7/30/57. Drummer. The Damned.

SCACCHI, GRETA. Milan, Italy, 2/18/60. Actor. *Presumed Innocent.*

SCAGGS, BOZ (William Scaggs). Ohio, 6/8/44. Guitarist, singer, songwriter. "Lowdown."

SCALIA, JACK. Brooklyn, NY, 11/10/51. Actor. *Dallas.*

SCARPELLI, GLENN. Staten Island, NY, 7/6/68. Actor. Alex Handris on *One Day at a Time.*

SCAVULLO, FRANCESCO. 1/16/29. Photographer.

SCHACHER, MEL. Flint, MI, 4/3/51. Bassist. Grand Funk Railroad.

SCHEIDER, ROY. Orange, NJ, 11/10/32. Actor. Chief Brody in *Jaws.*

SCHELL, MAXIMILIAN. Vienna, Austria, 12/8/30. Actor. *Judgment at Nuremberg.*

SCHENKER, RUDOLPH. 8/31/48. Guitarist. Scorpions.

SCHERMIE, JOE. Madison, WI, 2/12/45. Bassist. Three Dog Night.

SCHNEIDER, FRED. Newark, GA, 7/1/51. Keyboardist, singer. The B-52's.

SCHNEIDER, MARIA. Paris, France, 3/27/52. Actor. *Last Tango in Paris.*

SCHNEIDER-ESLEBEN, FLORIAN. Dusseldorf, Germany, 1947. Keyboardist, drummer, singer, woodwindist. Kraftwerk.

SCHOLZ, TOM. Toledo, OH, 3/10/47. Guitarist, keyboardist. Boston.

SCHON, NEAL. San Mateo, CA, 2/27/54. Guitarist. Journey.

SCHORR, DANIEL. New York, NY, 8/31/16. Broadcast journalist. NPR.

SCHULTZ, DWIGHT. Baltimore, MD, 11/24/47. Actor. H. M. "Howling Mad" Murdock on *The A-Team.*

SCHWARZKOPF, NORMAN. Trenton, NJ, 8/22/34. Retired army general, Gulf War hero.

SCHYGULLA, HANNA. Katlowitz, Germany, 12/25/43. Actor. *Dead Again.*

SCIORRA, ANNABELLA. New York, NY, 3/24/64. Actor. *The Hand That Rocks the Cradle.*

SCOLARI, PETER. New Rochelle, NY, 9/12/54. Actor. *Bosom Buddies.*

SCOTT, ANDY. Wrexham, Wales, 6/30/51. Guitarist. Sweet.

SCOTT, BON (Ronald Scott). Kirriemuir, Scotland, 7/9/46. Singer. AC/DC.

SCOTT, GORDON (Gordon Werschkul). Portland, OR, 8/3/27. Actor. *Tarzan's Hidden Jungle.*

SCOTT, HOWARD. San Pedro, CA, 3/15/46. Guitarist, singer. War.

SCOTT, MIKE. Edinburgh, Scotland, 12/14/58. Singer, guitarist. The Waterboys.

SCOTT, RIDLEY. South Shields, England, 11/30/37. Director, brother of director Tony. *Thelma and Louise.*

SCOTT, WILLARD. Alexandria, VA, 3/7/34. Weatherman. *Today.*

SEAL, ELIZABETH. Genoa, Italy, 8/28/33. Actor. *Irma La Douce.*

SEALE, BOBBY. Dallas, TX, 10/20/36. Political activist, author. Cofounder of the Black Panthers.

SEALS, JIM. Sidney, TX, 10/17/41. Singer, guitarist, saxophonist, violinist. Seals & Crofts.

SEAVER, TOM. Fresno, CA, 11/17/44. Baseball pitcher.

SEBASTIAN, JOHN. New York, NY, 3/17/44. Singer, guitarist, harmonicist, autoharpist. "The Lovin' Spoonful."

SEDAKA, NEIL. Brooklyn, NY, 3/13/39. Pop singer, songwriter. "Laughter in the Rain."

SEDGWICK, KYRA. New York, NY, 8/19/65. Actor, married to Kevin Bacon. *Phenomenon.*

SEEGER, PETE. New York, NY, 5/3/19. Folk singer, songwriter, guitarist, social activist. Founded The Weavers.

SEGAL, ERICH. 6/16/37. Author. *Love Story.*

SEGAL, GEORGE. New York, NY, 2/13/34. Actor. *Look Who's Talking.*

SEGER, BOB. Dearborn, MI, 5/6/45. Singer, songwriter. The Silver Bullet Band.

SELLECCA, CONNIE (Concetta Sellecchia). The Bronx, NY, 5/25/55. Actor, married to John Tesh. *Hotel.*

SELLECK, TOM. Detroit, MI, 1/29/45. Actor. *Magnum, P.I.*

SENDAK, MAURICE. New York, NY, 1/10/28. Author, illustrator. *Where the Wild Things Are.*

SENSIBLE, CAPTAIN (Ray Burns). England, 4/23/55. Bassist. The Damned.

SERAPHINE, DANNY. Chicago, IL, 8/28/48. Drummer. Chicago.

SERGEANT, WILL. Liverpool, England, 4/12/58. Guitarist. Echo & The Bunnymen.

SETZER, BRIAN. 4/10/60. Guitarist, singer. The Stray Cats.

SEVERIN, STEVE. 9/25/55. Bassist. Siouxsie & The Banshees.

SEYMOUR, STEPHANIE. San Diego, CA, 7/23/68. Supermodel.

SHAFFER, PAUL. Toronto, Canada, 11/28/49. Musician, bandleader. *Late Show with David Letterman.*

SHALIT, GENE. New York, NY, 1932. Critic. *Today.*

SHAPIRO, HELEN. Bethnal Green, England, 9/28/46. Singer, actor, cabaret performer.

SHARIF, OMAR (Michel Shalhoub). Alexandria, Egypt, 4/10/32. Actor. *Dr. Zhivago.*

SHARKEY, FEARGAL. Londonderry, Northern Ireland, 8/13/58. Singer. The Undertones.

SHARP, DAVE. Salford, England, 1/28/59. Guitarist. The Alarm.

SHARPTON, AL. Brooklyn, NY, 1954. Politician, activist, clergyman.

SHAVER, HELEN. St. Thomas, Canada, 2/24/51. Actor. *The Amityville Horror.*

SHAW, SANDIE (Sandra Goodrich). Dagenham, England, 2/26/47. Pop singer.

SHAW, TOMMY. Montgomery, AL, 9/11/52. Lead guitarist. Styx.

SHAWN, WALLACE. New York, NY, 11/12/43. Playwright, actor. *My Dinner with Andre.*

SHEA, JOHN. North Conway, NH, 4/14/49. Actor. *Lois & Clark.*

SHEARER, HARRY. Los Angeles, CA, 12/23/43. Actor. *This Is Spinal Tap.*

SHEEDY, ALLY. New York, NY, 6/13/62. Actor. *WarGames.*

SHEEHAN, FRAN. Boston, MA, 3/26/49. Bassist. Boston.

SHEEN, CHARLIE Los Angeles, CA, 9/3/65. Actor. *Platoon.*

SHEILA E. (Sheila Escovedo). Oakland, CA, 12/12/57. Drummer, singer.

SHELDON, SIDNEY. Chicago, IL, 2/11/17. Novelist, producer. *The Other Side of Midnight.*

SHELLEY, CAROLE. London, England, 8/16/39. Actor. *The Elephant Man.*

SHELLEY, PETE (Peter McNeish). Lancashire, England, 4/17/55. Guitarist, singer. The Buzzcocks.

SHEPARD, SAM (Sam Rogers). Ft. Sheridan, IL, 11/5/43. Playwright, actor. *True West; The Right Stuff.*

SHEPHERD, CYBILL Memphis, TN, 2/18/50. Actor. *Cybill.*

SHERIDAN, JIM. Dublin, Ireland, 1949. Director, writer. *My Left Foot.*

SHERIDAN, NICOLLETTE. Worthington, England, 11/21/63. Actor, model. *The Sure Thing.*

SHIRE, TALIA (Talia Rose Coppola). Lake Success, NY, 4/25/45. Actor, sister of Francis Ford Coppola. *Rocky I–V.*

SHORE, PAULY. 2/1/68. Actor. "The Weez."

SHORROCK, GLENN. Rochester, England, 6/30/44. Singer. The Little River Band.

SHOW, GRANT. Detroit, MI, 2/27/62. Actor. *Melrose Place.*

SHRIVER, MARIA. Chicago, IL, 11/6/55. Broadcast journalist, married to Arnold Schwarzenegger. *First Person with Maria Shriver.*

SHUE, ANDREW. South Orange, NJ, 2/20/67. Actor, brother of Elizabeth Shue. *Melrose Place.*

SIEGEL, JAY. Brooklyn, NY, 10/20/39. Baritone singer. The Tokens.

SIKKING, JAMES B. Los Angeles, CA, 3/5/34. Actor. Lt. Howard Hunter on *Hill Street Blues.*

SILLS, BEVERLY. New York, NY, 5/25/29. Opera singer.

SILVER, RON. New York, NY, 7/2/46. Actor, director. *Reversal of Fortune.*

SILVERMAN, JONATHAN. Los Angeles, CA, 8/5/66. Actor. *The Single Guy.*

SIMMONS, GENE (Chaim Witz). Haifa, Israel, 8/25/49. Long-tongued bassist, singer. Kiss.

SIMMONS, JEAN. London, England, 1/31/29. Actor. *The Thorn Birds.*

SIMMONS, JOSEPH. Queens, NY, 1964. Rap artist. Run-D.M.C.

SIMMONS, PATRICK. Aberdeen, WA, 1/23/50. Guitarist, singer. The Doobie Brothers.

SIMMONS, RICHARD. New Orleans, LA, 7/12/48. Health guru. *Sweatin' to the Oldies.*

SIMON, CARLY. New York, NY, 6/25/45. Singer, songwriter, childrens' book author.

SIMONE, NINA. Tryon, NC, 2/21/33. Singer. Soundtrack for *The Crying Game.*

SIMONON, PAUL. Brixton, England, 12/15/55. Bassist. The Clash.

SIMPSON, O.J. San Francisco, CA, 7/9/47. Football player, actor, indicted for murder of ex-wife, guilty in a civil trial but not the criminal one.

SINGER, LORI. Corpus Christi, TX, 5/6/62. Actor. *Fame.*

SINGLETON, JOHN. Los Angeles, CA, 1/6/68. Director, writer. *Boyz N the Hood.*

SINGLETON, STEPHEN. Sheffield, England, 4/17/59. Saxophonist. ABC.

SIOUX, SIOUXSIE (Susan Dallon). Chiselhurst, Eng

land, 5/27/57. Singer. Siouxsie & The Banshees.

SIXX, NIKKI (Frank Ferrano). Seattle, WA, 12/11/58. Bassist. Mötley Crüe.

SKERRITT, TOM. Detroit, MI, 8/25/33. Actor. *Picket Fences.*

SKYE, IONE (Ione Leitch). London, England, 9/4/71. Actor, daughter of folk singer Donovan, sister of Donovan Leitch. *Say Anything.*

SLASH (Saul Hudson). Stoke-on-Trent, England, 1965. Guitarist. Guns N' Roses.

SLATER, HELEN. New York, NY, 12/15/65. Actor. *Supergirl.*

SLATER, RODNEY. Lincolnshire, England, 11/8/44. Saxophonist, trumpeter. The Bonzo Dog Doo-Dah Band.

SLEDGE, DEBBIE. Philadelphia, PA, 7/9/54. Singer. Sister Sledge.

SLEDGE, JONI. Philadelphia, PA, 9/13/56. Singer. Sister Sledge.

SLEDGE, KATHY. Philadelphia, PA, 1/6/59. Singer. Sister Sledge.

SLEDGE, KIM. Philadelphia, PA, 8/21/57. Singer. Sister Sledge.

SLEDGE, PERCY. Leighton, AL, 11/25/41. Singer. "When a Man Loves a Woman."

SLICK, GRACE (Grace Wing). Chicago, IL, 10/30/39. Singer. Jefferson Airplane/Starship.

SLIWA, CURTIS. New York, NY, 3/26/54. Founder of the Guardian Angels.

SMIRNOFF, YAKOV (Yakov Pokhis). Odessa, Russia, 1/24/51. Actor. *What a Country!*

SMITH, ADRIAN. Huckney, England, 2/27/57. Guitarist. Iron Maiden.

SMITH, BOBBIE. 4/10/36. Singer. The (Detroit) Spinners.

SMITH, CHARLES MARTIN. Los Angeles, CA, 10/30/53. Actor. *American Graffiti.*

SMITH, CLAYDES (Charles Smith). Jersey City, NJ, 9/6/48. Guitarist. Kool & The Gang.

SMITH, CURT. Bath, England, 6/24/61. Singer, bassist. Tears for Fears.

SMITH, JACLYN. Houston, TX, 10/26/45. Actor. Kelly Garrett on *Charlie's Angels.*

SMITH, JEFF. Seattle, WA, 1/22/39. TV personality, chef, author. *The Frugal Gourmet.*

SMITH, LARRY. Oxford, England, 1/18/44. Drummer. The Bonzo Dog Doo-Dah Band.

SMITH, LIZ. Fort Worth, TX, 2/2/23. Gossip columnist.

SMITH, MAGGIE. Ilford, England, 12/28/34. Actor. *Sister Act.*

SMITH, MIKE. Neath, Wales, 11/4/47. Tenor saxophonist. Amen Corner.

SMITH, MIKE. Edmonton, England, 12/12/43. Singer, keyboardist. The Dave Clark Five.

SMITH, PATTI. Chicago, IL, 12/30/46. Singer, songwriter.

SMITH, PHIL. 5/1/59. Saxophonist. Haircut 100.

SMITH, ROBERT. Crawley, England, 4/21/59. Guitarist, singer. The Cure.

SMOTHERS, DICK. New York, NY, 11/20/38. Actor, singer, brother of Tom. *The Smothers Brothers Comedy Hour.*

SMOTHERS, TOM. New York, NY, 2/2/37. Actor, singer, brother of Dick. *The Smothers Brothers Comedy Hour.*

SMYTH, PATTY. New York, NY, 6/26/57. Singer, relationship with John McEnroe. "The Warrior."

SNEED, FLOYD. Calgary, Canada, 11/22/43. Drummer. Three Dog Night.

SNODGRESS, CARRIE. Chicago, IL, 10/27/46.

Actor. *Diary of a Mad Housewife.*

SOMERS, SUZANNE (Suzanne Mahoney). San Bruno, CA, 10/16/46. Actor. *Three's Company.*

SOMERVILLE, JIMMY. Glasgow, Scotland, 6/22/61. Dance/rock singer, keyboardist.

SOMMER, ELKE (Elke Schletz). Berlin, Germany, 11/5/40. Actor. *A Shot in the Dark.*

SORVINO, PAUL. New York, NY, 4/13/39. Actor, father of Mira. *GoodFellas.*

SOTHERN, ANN (Harriet Lake). Valley City, ND, 1/22/09. Actor. *The Ann Sothern Show.*

SOUL, DAVID (David Solberg). Chicago, IL, 8/28/43. Actor. Kevin "Hutch" Hutchinson on *Starsky and Hutch.*

SOUTH, JOE. Atlanta, GA, 2/28/40. Rock/country guitarist, singer, songwriter.

SOUTHSIDE JOHNNY (Johnny Lyon). Neptune Park, NJ, 12/4/48. Singer. Southside Johnny & The Asbury Jukes.

SPACEK, SISSY (Mary Elizabeth Spacek). Quitman, TX, 12/25/49. Actor. *Coal Miner's Daughter.*

SPADER, JAMES. Boston, MA, 2/7/60. Actor. *sex, lies, and videotape.*

SPANO, JOE. San Francisco, CA, 7/7/46. Actor. Henry Goldblume on *Hill Street Blues.*

SPANO, VINCENT. New York, NY, 10/18/62. Actor. *Rumble Fish.*

SPEAR, ROGER. London, England, 6/29/43. Saxophonist, kazooist. The Bonzo Dog Doo-Dah Band.

SPECTOR, PHIL. New York, NY, 12/26/39. Music producer. Wall of sound.

SPECTOR, RONNIE (Veronica Bennett). New York, NY, 8/10/43. Lead singer. The Ronettes.

SPELLING, TORI. Los Angeles, CA, 5/16/73. Actor, daughter of Aaron Spelling. Donna on *Beverly Hills, 90210.*

SPENCE, ALEXANDER. Windsor, Canada, 4/18/46. Guitarist, lead singer. Moby Grape.

SPENCER, JEREMY. West Hartlepoole, England, 7/4/48. Guitarist. Fleetwood Mac.

SPILLANE, MICKEY (Frank Morrison). New York, NY, 3/9/18. Author. Mike Hammer detective stories.

SPINKS, LEON. St. Louis, MO, 7/11/53. Boxer, former heavyweight champion, brother of Michael.

SPINKS, MICHAEL. St. Louis, MO, 7/29/56. Boxer. Olympic gold medalist, brother of Leon.

SPOONER, BILL. Phoenix, AZ, 4/16/49. Guitarist. The Tubes.

SPRINGFIELD, DUSTY (Mary O'Brien). Hampstead, England, 4/16/39. Folk/pop singer.

SPRINGFIELD, RICK (Richard Spring Thorpe). Sydney, Australia, 8/23/49. Singer, actor. *General Hospital.*

SQUIER, BILLY. Wellesley, MA, 5/12/50. Singer. "Everybody Wants You."

SQUIRE, CHRIS. London, England, 3/4/48. Bassist. Yes.

SQUIRE, JOHN. Sale, England, 11/24/62. Lead guitarist. The Stone Roses.

ST. JOHN, JILL (Jill Oppenheim). Los Angeles, CA, 8/19/40. Actor, married to Robert Wagner. *Diamonds Are Forever.*

STACK, ROBERT. Los Angeles, CA, 1/13/19. Actor. Eliot Ness on *The Untouchables.*

STAFFORD, JIM. Eloise, FL, 1/16/44. Singer, songwriter. "Spiders and Snakes."

STAMOS, JOHN. Cypress, CA,

8/19/63. Actor. *Full House.*

STAMP, TERENCE. London, England, 7/23/38. Actor. *Superman II.*

STANLEY, PAUL (Paul Eisen). Queens, NY, 1/20/50. Guitarist, singer. Kiss.

STANSFIELD, LISA. Rochdale, England, 4/11/66. Singer, songwriter. "All Around the World."

STANTON, HARRY DEAN. West Irvine, KY, 7/14/26. Actor. *Paris, Texas.*

STAPLES, NEVILLE. 4/11/56. Singer, percussionist. The Specials.

STAPLES, PETE. Andover, England, 5/3/44. Bassist. The Troggs.

STAPLETON, JEAN (Jeanne Murray). New York, NY, 1/19/23. Actor. Edith Bunker on *All in the Family.*

STAPLETON, MAUREEN. Troy, NY, 6/21/25. Actor. *Airport.*

STARR, RINGO (Richard Starkey). Liverpool, England, 7/7/40. Drummer, singer, actor, married to Barbara Bach. The Beatles.

STAUBACH, ROGER. Cincinnati, OH, 2/5/42. NFL football player. Dallas Cowboys.

STAX, JOHN (John Fullegar). London, England, 4/6/44. Bassist. The Pretty Things.

STEEL, JOHN. Gateshead, England, 2/4/41. Drummer. The Animals.

STEELE, DAVID. Birmingham, England, 9/8/60. Keyboardist, bassist. Fine Young Cannibals.

STEELE, MICHAEL. 6/2/54. Bassist, singer. The Bangles; The Runaways.

STEELE, TOMMY (Thomas Hicks). Bermondsey, England, 12/17/36. Guitarist, singer, actor.

STEENBURGEN, MARY. Newport, AR, 2/8/53. Actor, married to Ted Danson. *Parenthood.*

STEIGER, ROD. Westhampton, NY, 4/14/25. Actor. *In the Heat of the Night.*

STEIN, CHRIS. Brooklyn, NY, 1/5/50. Guitarist. Blondie.

STEIN, MARK. Bayonne, NJ, 3/11/47. Singer, organist. Vanilla Fudge.

STEINBERG, DAVID. Winnipeg, Canada, 8/9/42. Actor, director. *Paternity.*

STEINEM, GLORIA. Toledo, OH, 3/25/34. Women's rights activist.

STERBAN, RICHARD. Camden, NJ, 4/24/43. Singer, bassist. The Oak Ridge Boys.

STERN, DANIEL. Bethesda, MD, 8/28/57. Actor, narrator of *The Wonder Years. City Slickers.*

STERN, ISAAC. Kreminiecz, Russia, 7/21/20. Violinist.

STERNHAGEN, FRANCES. Washington, DC, 1/13/30. Actor. *Driving Miss Daisy.*

STEVENS, ANDREW. Memphis, TN, 6/10/55. Actor, son of Stella. *Dallas.*

STEVENS, CAT (Steven Georgiou). Soho, England, 7/21/47. Folk singer, songwriter—left recording upon conversion to Islam.

STEVENS, CONNIE (Concetta Ann Ingolia). Brooklyn, NY, 8/8/38. Actor. *Hawaiian Eye.*

STEVENS, FISHER. Chicago, IL, 11/27/63. Actor. *Short Circuit.*

STEVENS, RAY (Ray Ragsdale). Clarksdale, GA, 1/24/39. Singer. *Andy Williams Presents Ray Stevens.*

STEVENS, SHAKIN' (Michael Barratt). Ely, Wales, 3/4/48. Singer, actor.

STEVENS, STELLA (Estelle Eggleston). Hot Coffee, MS, 10/1/36. Actor, mother of Andrew. *Santa Barbara.*

STEVENSON, DON. Seattle, WA, 10/15/42. Drummer. Moby Grape.

STEVENSON, PARKER. Philadelphia, PA, 6/4/52. Actor. Formerly married to Kirstie Alley. *Falcon Crest.*

STEWART, AL. Glasgow, Scotland, 9/5/45. Guitarist, singer, songwriter.

STEWART, DAVE. Sunderland, England, 9/9/52. Keyboardist, guitarist. Eurythmics.

STEWART, ERIC. Manchester, England, 1/20/45. Singer, guitarist. 10cc.

STEWART, MARTHA (Martha Haworth). Bardwell, KY, 10/7/22. Actor. *Holocaust.*

STEWART, ROD. Highgate, England, 1/10/45. Singer, songwriter.

STIERS, DAVID OGDEN. Peoria, IL, 10/31/42. Actor. Dr. Charles Emerson Winchester on *M*A*S*H.*

STILES, RAY. Carshalton, England, 11/20/46. Bassist, singer. Mud.

STILLER, JERRY. New York, NY, 6/8/27. Actor, partner/married to Anne Meara, father of Ben. *Seinfeld.*

STILLS, STEPHEN. Dallas, TX, 1/3/45. Singer, guitarist. Buffalo Springfield; Crosby, Stills, Nash & Young.

STOCKDALE, JAMES. Abington, IL, 12/23/23. Vietnam POW, running mate of presidential candidate Ross Perot.

STOCKWELL, DEAN. Hollywood, CA, 3/5/36. Actor. Al Calavicci on *Quantum Leap.*

STOCKWELL, JOHN (John Samuels). Galveston, TX, 3/25/61. Actor. *My Science Project.*

STOLTZ, ERIC. American Samoa, 9/30/61. Actor. *Mask.*

STONE, DEE WALLACE (Deanna Bowers). Kansas City, MO, 12/14/48. Actor. Mother in *E.T., the Extra-Terrestrial.*

STONE, FREDDIE. Dallas, TX, 6/5/46. Guitarist. Sly & The Family Stone.

STONE, MATT. 5/26/71. Actor, cartoonist. *South Park.*

STONE, ROSIE. Vallejo, CA, 3/21/45. Singer, keyboardist. Sly & The Family Stone.

STONE, SLY (Sylvester Stewart). Dallas, TX, 3/15/44. Singer, keyboardist, guitarist. Sly & The Family Stone.

STORCH, LARRY. New York, NY, 1/8/23. Actor. *F Troop.*

STORM, GALE (Josephine Cottle). Bloomington, TX, 4/5/22. Actor. *My Little Margie.*

STOWE, MADELEINE. Los Angeles, CA, 8/18/58. Actor. *The Last of the Mohicans.*

STRASSMAN, MARCIA. New York, NY, 4/28/48. Actor. Julie Kotter on *Welcome Back Kotter.*

STRATHAIRN, DAVID. San Francisco, CA, 1949. Actor. *Matewan.*

STRATTON, DENNIS. London, England, 11/9/54. Guitarist. Iron Maiden.

STRAUSS, PETER. Croton-on-Hudson, NY, 2/20/47. Actor. *The Jericho Mile.*

STRINGFIELD, SHERRY. Colorado Springs, CO, 6/24/67. Actor. *ER.*

STRICKLAND, KEITH. Athens, GA, 10/26/53. Drummer. The B-52's.

STRITCH, ELAINE. Detroit, MI, 2/2/25. Actor. *September.*

STRUMMER, JOE (John Mellors). Ankara, Turkey, 8/21/52. Singer, guitarist. The Clash.

STRUTHERS, SALLY. Portland, OR, 7/28/47. Actor. Gloria Bunker Stivic on *All in the Family.*

STRYKERT, RON. Australia, 8/18/57. Guitarist. Men at Work.

STUART, CHAD. England, 12/10/43. Singer, guitarist. Chad & Jeremy.

STUART, HAMISH. Glasgow, Scotland, 10/8/49. Singer, guitarist. Average White Band.

STUBBS, LEVI (Levi Stubbles). Detroit, MI, 6/6/36. Lead singer. The Four Tops.

SUCH, ALEC. 11/14/56. Bassist. Bon Jovi.

SULLIVAN, SUSAN. New York, NY, 11/18/44. Actor. Maggie Gioberti Channing on *Falcon Crest.*

SULLIVAN, TOM. Boston, MA, 3/27/47. Singer, actor, composer. "If You Could See What I Hear."

SUMMER, DONNA (LaDonna Gaines). Boston, MA, 12/31/48. Disco/pop singer. "Love To Love You Baby."

SUMMERS, ANDY (Andrew Somers). Poulton le Fylde, France, 12/31/42. Guitarist, singer. The Police.

SUMNER, BARNEY (Bernard Dicken). Salford, England, 1/4/56. Guitarist, singer. New Order.

SUTHERLAND, DONALD. St. John, Canada, 7/17/35. Actor, father of Kiefer. *Ordinary People.*

SUTHERLAND, KIEFER. Los Angeles, CA, 12/21/66. Actor, son of Donald. *Flatliners.*

SUZMAN, JANET. Johannesburg, South Africa, 2/9/39. Actor. *Nicholas and Alexandra.*

SVENSON, BO. Goreborg, Sweden, 2/13/41. Actor. *North Dallas Forty.*

SWAGGART, JIMMY. Ferriday, LA, 3/15/35. Evangelist.

SWAIN, DOMINIQUE. 8/12/80. Actor. *Lolita.*

SWANN, LYNN. Alcoa, TN, 3/7/52. NFL football player.

SWAYZE, PATRICK. Houston, TX, 8/18/52. Actor, dancer. *Dirty Dancing.*

SWEENEY, D. B. (Daniel Bernard Sweeney). Shoreham, NY, 11/14/61. Actor. *The Cutting Edge.*

SWEET, DERRELL. 5/16/47. Drummer, percussionist, singer. Nazareth.

SWEET, MATTHEW. Lincoln, NE, 10/6/64. Singer, song-writer, guitarist. "Girlfriend."

SWENSON, INGA. Omaha, NE, 12/29/32. Actor. Gretchen Kraus on *Benson.*

SWIT, LORETTA. Passaic, NJ, 11/4/37. Actor. Margaret "Hot Lips" Houlihan on *M*A*S*H.*

SYLVIAN, DAVID (David Batt). Lewisham, England, 2/23/58. Singer, guitarist. Japan.

T, MR. (Lawrence Tero). Chicago, IL, 5/21/52. Actor and wrestler. Bosco "B.A." Baracus on *The A-Team.*

TAJ MAHAL. New York, NY, 5/17/42. Singer, songwriter, composer. "Sounder."

TAKEI, GEORGE. Los Angeles, CA, 4/20/39. Mr. Sulu on *Star Trek.*

TALBOT, MICK. London, England, 9/11/58. Keyboardist. The Style Council.

TALLEY, GARY. Memphis, TN, 8/17/47. Guitarist. The Box Tops/Big Star.

TALLEY, NEDRA. New York, NY, 1/27/46. Singer. The Ronettes.

TAMBLYN, RUSS. Los Angeles, CA, 12/30/34. Actor. *West Side Story.*

TAMBOR, JEFFREY. San Francisco, CA, 7/8/44. Actor. *The Larry Sanders Show.*

TANDY, RICHARD. Birmingham, England, 3/26/48. Bassist. Electric Light Orchestra (ELO).

TARKENTON, FRAN. Richmond, VA, 2/3/40. Football player, sportscaster. *Monday Night Football.*

TAUPIN, BERNIE. Sleaford, England, 5/22/50. Lyricist. Wrote for Elton John.

TAYLOR, ANDY. Tynemouth, England, 2/16/61. Guitarist. Duran Duran.

TAYLOR, CLIVE. Cardiff, Wales, 4/27/49. Bassist. Amen Corner.

TAYLOR, DICK. Dartford, England, 1/28/43. Lead guitarist. The Pretty Things.

TAYLOR, JAMES. South Carolina, 8/16/53. Lead singer. Kool & The Gang.

TAYLOR, JAMES. Boston, MA, 3/12/48. Folk-oriented singer, songwriter.

TAYLOR, JOHN. Birmingham, England, 6/20/60. Bassist. Duran Duran.

TAYLOR, LARRY. Brooklyn, NY, 6/26/42. Bassist. Canned Heat.

TAYLOR, LILI. Chicago, IL, 1967. Actor. *Mystic Pizza.*

TAYLOR, ROD. Sydney, Australia, 1/11/30. Actor. *The Time Machine.*

TAYLOR, ROGER. King's Lynn, England, 7/26/49. Drummer. Queen.

TENCH, BENMONT. Gainesville, FL, 9/7/54. Keyboardist. Tom Petty & The Heartbreakers.

TENNANT, NEIL. Gosforth, England, 7/10/54. Singer. Pet Shop Boys.

TENNANT, VICTORIA. London, England, 9/30/50. Actor, formerly married to Steve Martin. *L.A. Story.*

TENNILLE, TONI. Montgomery, AL, 5/8/43. Singer. The Captain & Tennille.

TERRANOVA, JOE. 1/30/41. Baritone. Danny & The Juniors.

THICKE, ALAN. Ontario, Canada, 3/1/47. Actor. *Growing Pains.*

THISTLETHWAITE, ANTHONY. Leicester, England, 8/31/55. Saxophonist. The Waterboys.

THOMAS, B. J. (Billy Joe Thomas). Hugo, OK, 8/7/42. Pop singer. "Raindrops Keep Fallin' on My Head."

THOMAS, BETTY. Saint Louis, MO, 7/27/47. Actor, director. Lucy Bates on *Hill Street Blues.*

THOMAS, DAVE. Saint Catharines, Canada, 6/20/49. Actor. Doug MacKenzie on *SCTV.*

THOMAS, HENRY. San Antonio, TX, 9/8/72. Actor. Elliot in *E.T., the Extra-Terrestrial.*

THOMAS, JAY. New Orleans, LA, 7/12/48. Actor, radio personality. *Murphy Brown.*

THOMAS, MARLO (Margaret Thomas). Detroit, MI, 11/21/37. Actor, married to Phil Donahue, daughter of Danny Thomas. *That Girl.*

THOMAS, MARY. Brooklyn, NY, 1946. Singer. The Crystals.

THOMAS, PHILIP MICHAEL. Columbus, OH, 5/26/49. Actor. Ricardo Tubbs on *Miami Vice.*

THOMAS, RAY. Stourport-on-Severn, England, 12/29/42. Flautist, harmonicist, singer. The Moody Blues.

THOMAS, RICHARD. New York, NY, 6/13/51. Actor. John Boy on *The Waltons.*

THOMPKINS, RUSSELL JR. Philadelphia, PA, 3/21/51. Lead singer. The Stylistics.

THOMPSON, LEA. Rochester, MN, 5/31/61. Actor. *Caroline in the City.*

THOMPSON, PAUL. Jarrow, England, 5/13/51. Drummer. Roxy Music.

THOMPSON, SADA. Des Moines, IA, 9/27/29. Actor. *Family.*

THOMSON, DOUGIE. Glasgow, Scotland, 3/24/51. Bassist. Supertramp.

THORN, TRACEY. Hartfordshire, England, 9/26/62. Singer. Everything but the Girl.

THORNTON, BLAIR. Vancouver, Canada, 7/23/50. Guitarist. Bachman-Turner Overdrive.

THOROGOOD, GEORGE. Wilmington, DE, 1951. Singer, guitarist. George Thorogood and the Delaware Destroyers.

TICH (Ian Amey). Salisbury, England, 5/15/44. Lead guitarist. Dave Dee, Dozy, Beaky, Mick and Tich.

TIEGS, CHERYL. Alhambra, CA, 9/25/47. Model, author. *The Way to Natural Beauty.*

TIFFANY (Tiffany Renee Darwish). Norwalk, CA, 10/2/71. Singer.

TILBROOK, GLENN. London, England, 8/31/57. Singer, lead guitarist. Squeeze.

TILLIS, MEL. Pahokee, FL, 8/8/32. Singer, songwriter, father of Pam Tillis.

TILLIS, PAM. Plant City, FL, 7/24/57. Singer, daughter of Mel Tillis.

TILLY, MEG. Texada, Canada, 2/14/60. Actor, sister of Jennifer. *The Big Chill*.

TILTON, CHARLENE. San Diego, CA, 12/1/58. Actor. Lucy Ewing Cooper on *Dallas*.

TIPTON, GLENN. Birmingham, England, 10/25/48. Guitarist. Judas Priest.

TOLHURST, LOL (Laurence Tolhurst). 2/3/59. Keyboardist. The Cure.

TOLKAN, JAMES. Calumet, MI, 6/20/31. Actor. Principal in *Back to the Future*.

TOMEI, MARISA. Brooklyn, NY, 12/4/64. Actor. *My Cousin Vinny*.

TOMLIN, LILY (Mary Jean Tomlin). Detroit, MI, 9/1/39. Actor. *Rowan & Martin's Laugh-In*.

TONE-LOC. Los Angeles, CA, 3/3/66. Rap artist. "Wild Thing."

TOPHAM, ANTHONY "TOP." England, 1947. Guitarist. The Yardbirds.

TORK, PETER (Peter Halsten Thorkelson). Washington, DC, 2/13/44. Keyboardist, bassist, actor. The Monkees.

TORN, RIP. (Elmore Rual Torn Jr). Temple, TX, 2/6/31. Actor. *Blind Ambition*.

TORRENCE, DEAN. Los Angeles, CA, 3/10/40. Singer. Jan & Dean.

TOWNSEND, ROBERT. Chicago, IL, 2/6/57. Actor. *Hollywood Shuffle*.

TOWNSHEND, PETE. Chiswick, England, 5/19/45. Guitarist. The Who.

TOWNSON, RON. St. Louis, MO, 1/20/33. Singer. The 5th Dimension.

TRAVANTI, DANIEL J. Kenosha, WI, 3/7/40. Actor. Captain Frank Furillo on *Hill Street Blues*.

TRAVERS, BRIAN. Birmingham, England, 2/7/59. Saxophonist. UB40.

TRAVIS, NANCY. 9/21/61. Actor. *Three Men and a Baby*.

TRAVIS, RANDY (Randy Traywick). Marshville, NC, 5/4/59. Country singer, songwriter.

TREBEK, ALEX. Sudbury, Canada, 7/22/40. Game show host. *Jeopardy!*

TRESVANT, RALPH. Boston, MA, 5/16/68. Singer. New Edition.

TREWAVAS, PETER. Middlesborough, England, 1/15/59. Keyboardist. Marillion.

TRIPPLEHORN, JEANNE. Tulsa, Oklahoma, 1963. Actor. *The Firm*.

TRITT, TRAVIS. Marietta, GA, 2/9/63. Country singer, songwriter.

TROWER, ROBIN. Southend, England, 3/9/45. Guitarist. Procol Harum.

TRUDEAU, GARRY (Garretson Beckman Trudeau). New York, NY, 1948. Cartoonist, married to Jane Pauley. *Doonesbury*.

TRUGOY THE DOVE (David Jolicoeur). 9/21/68. Musician. De La Soul.

TRUMP, DONALD. New York, NY, 6/14/46. Real estate developer, author. Married to Marla Maples, formerly married to Ivana Winkelmayr Trump.

TRUMP, MARLA MAPLES. 10/27/63. Actor. Formerly married to Donald Trump. *The Will Rogers Follies*.

TUCKER, JIM. Los Angeles, CA, 10/17/46. Guitarist. The Turtles.

TUCKER, MICHAEL. Baltimore, MD, 2/6/45. Actor, married to Jill Eikenberry. *L.A. Law*.

TUCKER, MICK. Harlesden, England, 7/17/49. Drummer. Sweet.

TUFANO, DENNIS. Chicago, IL, 9/11/46. Guitarist, lead singer. The Buckinghams.

TUNE, TOMMY. Wichita Falls, TX, 2/28/39. Actor, director, choreographer, dancer.

TURBO B.(Durron Maurice Butler). Pittsburgh, PA, 4/30/67. Rap artist. Snap.

TURNER, C. F. Winnipeg, Canada, 10/16/43. Bassist, singer. Bachman-Turner Overdrive.

TURNER, IKE. Clarksdale, MS, 11/5/31. Singer, songwriter, formerly married to Tina Turner. Ike & Tina Turner.

TURNER, JANINE (Janine Gauntt). Lincoln, NE, 12/6/63. Actor. *Northern Exposure*.

TURNER, KATHLEEN Springfield, MO, 6/19/54. Actor. *Romancing the Stone*.

TURNER, LONNIE. Berkeley, CA, 2/24/47. Bassist, singer. The Steve Miller Band.

TUROW, SCOTT. Chicago, IL, 4/12/49. Author. *The Burden of Proof*.

TURTURRO, JOHN. Brooklyn, NY, 2/28/57. Actor. *Barton Fink*.

TWIGGY (Lesley Hornby). London, England, 9/19/49. Model, actor. *The Boy Friend*.

TWIST, NIGEL. Manchester, England, 7/18/58. Drummer. The Alarm.

TYLER, BONNIE (Gaynor Hopkins). Swansea, Wales, 6/8/53. Singer. "Total Eclipse of the Heart."

TYLER, RICHARD. Sunshine, Australia, 1948. Designer.

TYSON, CICELY. New York, NY, 12/19/24. Actor. *The Autobiography of Miss Jane Pittman*.

TYSON, MIKE New York, NY, 6/30/66. Boxer, convicted of rape.

UECKER, BOB. Milwaukee, WI, 1/26/35. Actor. *Mr. Belvedere*.

UGGAMS, LESLIE. New York, NY, 5/25/43. Singer, actor. Kizzy in *Roots*.

ULLMAN, TRACEY. Hackbridge, England, 12/30/59. Actor. *The Tracey Ullman Show*.

ULLMANN, LIV. Tokyo, Japan, 12/16/39. Actor. *Persona*.

ULVAEUS, BJORN. Gothenburg, Sweden, 4/25/45. Guitarist, singer. Abba.

UNDERWOOD, BLAIR. Tacoma, WA, 8/25/64. Actor. *L.A. Law*.

URICH, ROBERT. Toronto, Canada, 12/19/46. Actor. *Spenser: For Hire*.

VACCARO, BRENDA. Brooklyn, NY, 11/18/39. Actor. *Midnight Cowboy*.

VALE, JERRY. New York, NY, 7/8/32. Pop singer. "Innamorata."

VALE, MIKE. 7/17/49. Bassist. Tommy James & The Shondells.

VALENTINE, HILTON. North Shields, England, 5/21/43. Guitarist. The Animals.

VALENTINE, SCOTT. Saratoga Springs, NY, 6/3/58. Actor. Nick Moore on *Family Ties*.

VALLI, FRANKIE (Frank Castelluccio). Newark, NJ, 5/3/37. Lead singer. The Four Seasons.

VALLONE, RAF (Raffaele Vallone). Tropea, Italy, 2/17/18. Actor. *Obsession*.

VALORY, ROSS. San Francisco, CA, 2/2/49. Bassist. Journey.

VAN ARK, JOAN. New York, NY, 6/16/43. Actor. Val Ewing *Knots Landing*.

VAN DAMME, JEAN-CLAUDE. Brussels, Belgium, 10/18/60. Actor, martial arts expert. *Kickboxer*.

VAN DEVERE, TRISH (Patricia Dressel). Englewood Cliffs, NJ, 3/9/45. Actor, married to George C. Scott.

The Day of the Dolphin.

VAN DOREN, MAMIE (Joan Lucile Olander). Rowena, SD, 2/6/31. Actor. *High School Confidential!*

VAN DYKE, DICK. West Plains, MO, 12/13/25. Actor and performer, brother of Jerry. *The Dick Van Dyke Show.*

VAN DYKE, JERRY. Danville, IL, 7/27/31. Actor, brother of Dick. *Coach.*

VAN HALEN, ALEX. Nijmegen, Holland, 5/8/55. Drummer. Van Halen.

VAN HALEN, EDDIE Nijmegen, Holland, 1/26/55. Singer, guitarist. Van Halen.

VAN PATTEN, DICK. New York, NY, 12/9/28. Actor. *Eight Is Enough.*

VAN PEEBLES, MARIO. New York, NY, 1/15/57. Actor, director, writer, son of Melvin. *Posse.*

VAN PEEBLES, MELVIN. Chicago, IL, 8/21/32. Actor, writer, composer, father of Mario. *Sweet Sweetback's Badasssss Song.*

VAN ZANDT, DONNIE. Florida, 6/11/52. Singer, guitarist. .38 Special.

VAN ZANDT, STEVIE. Boston, MA, 11/22/50. Bassist. E Street Band.

VANDA, HARRY (Harry Vandenberg). The Hague, The Netherlands, 3/22/47. Guitarist. The Easybeats.

VANDERBILT, GLORIA. New York, NY, 2/20/24. Fashion designer. Gloria Vanderbilt Jeans.

VANIAN, DAVE (David Letts). 10/12/56. Singer. The Damned.

VANNELLI, GINO. Montreal, Canada, 6/16/52. Singer, songwriter. "Living Inside Myself."

VAUGHN, ROBERT. New York, NY, 11/22/32. Actor. *The Man from U.N.C.L.E.*

VEDDER, EDDIE Chicago, IL, 12/23/64. Pearl Jam.

VEE, BOBBY (Robert Velline). Fargo, ND, 4/30/43. Singer, songwriter.

VEGA, SUZANNE. New York, NY, 8/12/59. Folk-oriented guitarist, singer, songwriter. "Luka."

VELEZ, EDDIE (Edwin Velez). New York, NY, 6/4/58. Actor. *Extremities.*

VELJOHNSON, REGINALD. Queens, NY, 8/16/52. Actor. *Family Matters.*

VENDELA (Vendela Kirsebom). Sweden, 1/12/67. Supermodel.

VERDON, GWEN. Culver City, CA, 1/13/25. Actor, dancer, choreographer. *The Cotton Club.*

VEREEN, BEN. Miami, FL, 10/10/46. Actor, performer. Chicken George Moore on *Roots.*

VERLAINE, TOM (Thomas Miller). Mt. Morris, NJ, 12/13/49. Singer, lead guitarist. Television.

VERUSCHKA. 1943. Model, actor. *Blow Up.*

VESTINE, HENRY. Washington, DC, 12/25/44. Guitarist. Canned Heat.

VICKERS, MIKE. Southampton, England, 4/18/41. Guitarist. Manfred Mann.

VIDAL, GORE (Eugene Luther Vidal). West Point, NY, 10/3/25. Author, dramatist. *Lincoln: A Novel.*

VINCENT, JAN-MICHAEL. Denver, CO, 7/15/45. Actor. *The Mechanic.*

VINTON, BOBBY. Canonsburg, PA, 4/16/35. Singer, songwriter.

VIRTUE, MICKEY. Birmingham, England, 1/19/57. Keyboardist. UB40.

VOIGHT, JON. Yonkers, NY, 12/29/38. Actor. *Midnight Cowboy.*

VOLMAN, MARK. Los Angeles, CA, 4/19/47. Singer, saxophonist. The Turtles.

VON BULOW, CLAUS. Copenhagen, Denmark, 8/11/26. Businessman. Subject of the motion picture *Reversal of Fortune.*

VON SYDOW, MAX. Lund, Sweden, 7/10/29. Actor. *The Greatest Story Ever Told.*

VONNEGUT, KURT JR. Indianapolis, IN, 11/11/22. Author. *Slaughterhouse Five.*

WAAKTAAR, PAUL. Oslo, Norway, 9/6/61. Guitarist, singer. a-ha.

WAGGONER, LYLE. Kansas City, KS, 4/13/35. Actor. *Wonder Woman.*

WAGNER, JACK. Washington, MO, 10/3/59. Actor, singer. Frisco Jones on *General Hospital.*

WAGNER, LINDSAY. Los Angeles, CA, 6/22/49. Actor. *The Bionic Woman.*

WAGNER, ROBERT. Detroit, MI, 2/10/30. Actor, widower of Natalie Wood, married to Jill St. John. Jonathan Hart on *Hart to Hart.*

WAHL, KEN. Chicago, IL, 2/14/57. Actor. Vinnie Terranova on *Wiseguy.*

WAHLBERG, DONNIE. Dorchester, MA, 8/17/69. Singer, brother of Mark. New Kids on the Block.

WAILER, BUNNY (Neville O'Riley Livingston). Kingston, Jamaica, 4/10/47. Singer, percussionist. Bob Marley & The Wailers.

WAITE, JOHN. Lancaster, England, 7/4/54. Singer, songwriter.

WAITS, TOM. Pomona, CA, 12/7/49. Singer, actor, composer. *Short Cuts.*

WALKER, ALICE. Eatonton, GA, 2/9/44. Author. *The Color Purple.*

WALKER, CLINT. Hartford, IL, 5/30/27. Actor. *Cheyenne.*

WALKER, DAVID. Montgomeryville, AL, 5/12/43. Keyboardist. Gary Lewis & The Playboys.

WALKER, JIMMIE. New York, NY, 6/25/48. Actor. J. J. Evans on *Good Times.*

WALKER, JUNIOR (Autry DeWalt II). Blytheville, AR, 1942. Saxophonist, singer. Junior Walker & The All-Stars.

WALKER, MORT. El Dorado, KS, 9/3/23. Cartoonist. *Beetle Bailey.*

WALLACE, MIKE (Myron Leon Wallace). Brookline, MA, 5/9/18. News reporter and interviewer, anchor. *60 Minutes.*

WALLACH, ELI. Brooklyn, NY, 12/7/15. Actor. *The Good, the Bad and the Ugly.*

WALLER, GORDON. Braemar, Scotland, 6/4/45. Singer. Peter and Gordon.

WALLER, ROBERT JAMES. Rockford, IA, 8/1/39. Author. *The Bridges of Madison County.*

WALLINGER, KARL. Prestatyn, Wales, 10/19/57. Keyboardist, guitarist. World Party.

WALSH, JOE. Cleveland, OH, 11/20/47. Guitarist, singer. The Eagles; The James Gang.

WALSH, M. EMMET. Ogdensburg, NY, 3/22/35. Actor. *Blood Simple.*

WALTER, JESSICA. Brooklyn, NY, 1/31/41. Actor. *Play Misty for Me.*

WALTER, TRACEY. Jersey City, NJ. Actor. Bob the Goon in *Batman.*

WARD, BILL. Birmingham, England, 5/5/48. Drummer. Black Sabbath.

WARD, BURT. Los Angeles, CA, 7/6/46. Actor. *Batman.*

WARD, FRED. San Diego, CA, 12/30/42. Actor. *Henry and June.*

WARD, RACHEL. London, England, 1957. Actor. *Against All Odds.*

WARDEN, JACK (Jack Warden Lebzelter). Newark, NJ, 9/18/20. Actor. Harry Fox on *Crazy Like a Fox.*

WARE, MARTYN. Sheffield, England, 5/19/56. Synthesizer player. The Human

League; Heaven 17.

WARFIELD, MARSHA. Chicago, IL, 3/5/55. Actor. Roz Russell on *Night Court*.

WARNER, DAVID. Manchester, England, 7/29/41. Actor. *The Omen*.

WARNER, JULIE. New York, NY, 1965. Actor. *Doc Hollywood*.

WARNER, MALCOLM-JAMAL. Jersey City, NJ, 8/18/70. Actor. Theo Huxtable on *The Cosby Show*.

WARNES, JENNIFER. Orange County, CA, 1947. Pop singer.

WARREN, LESLEY ANN. New York, NY, 8/16/46. Actor. *Mission: Impossible*.

WARRICK, RUTH. St. Joseph, MO, 6/29/15. Actor. Phoebe Wallingford on *All My Children*.

WARWICK, CLINT (Clinton Eccles). Birmingham, England, 6/25/40. Bassist. The Moody Blues.

WARWICK, DIONNE (Marie Warrick). East Orange, NJ, 12/12/40. Gospel/pop singer.

WATERS, JOHN. Baltimore, MD, 4/22/46. Director, writer, actor. *Hairspray; Pink Flamingos; Serial Mom*.

WATERS, ROGER. Great Bookham, England, 9/9/44. Singer, bassist. Pink Floyd.

WATERSTON, SAM. Cambridge, MA, 11/15/40. Actor. *The Killing Fields*.

WATLEY, JODY. Chicago, IL, 1/30/59. Singer. Shalamar.

WATSON, BRUCE. Ontario, Canada, 3/11/61. Guitarist. Big Country.

WATT, BEN. 12/6/62. Guitarist, keyboardist, singer. Everything but the Girl.

WATTS, CHARLIE. Islington, England, 6/2/41. Drummer. The Rolling Stones.

WATTS, OVEREND (Peter Watts). Birmingham, England, 5/13/49. Bassist. Mott The Hoople.

WAXMAN, AL. Toronto, Canada, 3/2/34. Actor. Bert Samuels on *Cagney and Lacey*.

WAYANS, KEENEN IVORY. New York, NY, 6/8/58. Actor, director, writer. *In Living Color*.

WAYBILL, FEE (John Waldo). Omaha, NE, 9/17/50. Singer. The Tubes.

WAYNE, CARL. Mosely, England, 8/18/44. Singer. The Move.

WAYNE, PATRICK. Los Angeles, CA, 7/15/39. Actor, son of John. *McClintock!*

WEATHERS, CARL. New Orleans, LA, 1/14/48. Actor. Apollo Creed in *Rocky*.

WEAVER, BLUE (Derek Weaver). Cardiff, Wales, 3/3/49. Organist. Amen Corner.

WEAVER, DENNIS. Joplin, MO, 6/4/24. Actor. *McCloud*.

WEAVER, FRITZ. Pittsburgh, PA, 1/19/26. Actor. *Marathon Man*.

WEBB, PAUL. 1/16/62. Bassist. Talk Talk.

WEIDER, JOHN. England, 4/21/47. Bassist. Family.

WEIR, BOB. San Francisco, CA, 10/6/47. Guitarist. Grateful Dead.

WEITZ, BRUCE. Norwalk, CT, 5/27/43. Actor. Mick Belker on *Hill Street Blues*.

WELCH, BRUCE (Bruce Cripps). Bognor Regis, England, 11/2/41. Guitarist. The Shadows.

WELCH, RAQUEL (Raquel Tejada). Chicago, IL, 9/5/40. Actor. *One Million Years B.C.*

WELD, TUESDAY (Susan Weld). New York, NY, 8/27/43. Actor. *Looking for Mr. Goodbar*.

WELLER, PAUL. 5/25/58. Singer, bassist. The Jam.

WELLER, PAUL. Woking, England, 5/25/58. Singer, guitarist. The Style Council.

WELLER, PETER. Stevens Point, WI, 6/24/47. Actor. *Robocop*.

WELLS, CORY. Buffalo, NY, 2/5/42. Singer. Three Dog Night.

WELLS, KITTY (Muriel Deason). Nashville, TN, 8/30/19. Country singer.

WELNICK, VINCE. Phoenix, AZ, 2/21/51. Keyboardist. The Tubes.

WENDT, GEORGE. Chicago, IL, 10/17/48. Actor. Norm Peterson on *Cheers*.

WEST, ADAM (William Anderson). Walla Walla, WA, 9/19/28. Actor. *Batman*.

WEST, JOHN. Uhrichsville, OH, 7/31/39. Guitarist. Gary Lewis & The Playboys.

WEST, RICK. Dagenham, England, 5/7/43. Lead guitarist. Brian Poole & The Tremeloes.

WESTHEIMER, RUTH (Karola Ruth Siegel). Frankfurt, Germany, 6/4/28. Sex therapist. *Ask Dr. Ruth*.

WETTON, JOHN. Derbyshire, England, 7/12/49. Lead singer, bassist. Asia.

WEYMOUTH, TINA. Coronado, CA, 11/22/50. Bassist. Talking Heads.

WHALEY, FRANK. Syracuse, NY, 1963. Actor. *The Doors*.

WHALLEY, JOANNE. Manchester, England, 8/25/64. Actor, formerly married to Val Kilmer. *Willow*.

WHELCHEL, LISA. Fort Worth, TX, 5/29/63. Actor. Blair Warner on *The Facts of Life*.

WHITAKER, JOHNNY. Van Nuys, CA, 12/13/59. Actor. Jody on *Family Affair*.

WHITE, BETTY. Oak Park, IL, 1/17/22. Actor. Rose Nylund on *The Golden Girls*.

WHITE, CHRIS. Barnet, England, 3/7/43. Bassist. The Zombies.

WHITE, DAVE (David Tricker). Philadelphia, PA, 9/1/40. Singer. Danny & The Juniors.

WHITE, JALEEL. Los Angeles, CA, 11/27/76. Actor. Steve Urkel on *Family Matters*.

WHITE, MARK. Sheffield, England, 4/1/61. Guitarist. ABC.

WHITE, MAURICE. Memphis, TN, 12/19/41. Singer, drummer, kalimba player. Earth, Wind & Fire.

WHITE, VANNA (Vanna Rosich). North Myrtle Beach, SC, 2/18/57. Letter turner extraordinaire. *Wheel of Fortune*.

WHITE, VERDINE. Illinois, 7/25/51. Singer, bassist. Earth, Wind & Fire.

WHITELAW, BILLIE. Coventry, England, 6/6/32. Actor. *Charlie Bubbles*.

WHITFORD, BRAD. Winchester, MA, 2/23/52. Guitarist. Aerosmith.

WHITMORE, JAMES. White Plains, NY, 10/1/21. Actor. *Will Rogers, USA*.

WHITNEY, CHARLIE. Leicester, England, 6/4/44. Guitarist. Family.

WIEST, DIANNE. Kansas City, MO, 3/28/46. Actor. *Hannah and Her Sisters*.

WILCOX, LARRY. San Diego, CA, 8/8/47. Actor. Officer Jon Baker on *CHiPs*.

WILDE, KIM (Kim Smith). London, England, 11/18/60. Singer, songwriter.

WILDER, ALAN. 6/1/59. Singer, synthesizer player. Depeche Mode.

WILDER, GENE (Jerome Silberman). Milwaukee, WI, 6/11/33. Actor, director, writer, widower of Gilda Radner. *Young Frankenstein*.

WILLIAM, PRINCE. London, England, 6/21/82. British royalty, son of Prince Charles and Princess Diana.

WILLIAMS, ANDY. Wall Lake, IA, 12/3/27. Pop singer. "Where Do I Begin?"

WILLIAMS, BARRY. Santa Monica, CA, 9/30/54. Actor. Greg on *The Brady Bunch*.

WILLIAMS, BILLY DEE. New York, NY, 4/6/37. Actor. *Lady Sings the Blues*.

WILLIAMS, CINDY. Van Nuys, CA, 8/22/47. Actor. Shirley Feeney on *Laverne & Shirley*.

WILLIAMS, CLARENCE III. New York, NY, 8/21/39. Actor. Lincoln Hayes on *The Mod Squad*.

WILLIAMS, CLIFF. Rumford, England, 12/14/29. Bass guitarist. AC/DC.

WILLIAMS, DENIECE (Deniece Chandler). Gary, IN, 6/3/51. Gospel/pop singer.

WILLIAMS, ESTHER. Los Angeles, CA, 8/8/21. Actor, swimmer, widow of Fernando Lamas. *Bathing Beauty*.

WILLIAMS, HANK JR (Randall Hank). Shreveport, LA, 5/26/49. Country singer, songwriter. "Texas Women."

WILLIAMS, JOBETH. Houston, TX, 12/6/48. Actor. *The Big Chill*.

WILLIAMS, JOHN TOWNER. Queens, NY, 2/8/32. Composer, conductor. *Jaws; Star Wars*.

WILLIAMS, MAISIE. Montserrat, West Indies, 3/25/51. Singer. Boney M.

WILLIAMS, MILAN. Mississippi, 3/28/48. Keyboardist, trombonist, guitarist, drummer. The Commodores.

WILLIAMS, MONTEL. Baltimore, MD, 7/3/56. Talk show host. *The Montel Williams Show*.

WILLIAMS, OTIS (Otis Miles). Texarkana, TX, 10/30/49. Singer. The Temptations.

WILLIAMS, PAUL. Birmingham, AL, 7/2/39. Singer. The Temptations.

WILLIAMS, TREAT (Richard Williams). Rowayton, CT, 12/1/51. Actor. *Prince of the City*.

WILLIAMS, WALTER. 8/25/42. Singer. The O'Jays.

WILLIAMS, WENDY O. (Wendy Orlean Williams). Rochester, NY, 1946. Entertainer, singer.

WILLIAMSON, NICOL. Hamilton, Scotland, 9/14/38. Actor. *Excalibur*.

WILLIG, GEORGE. New York, NY, 6/11/49. Actor, stuntman. Climbed World Trade Center.

WILSON, AL "BLIND OWL." Boston, MA, 7/4/43. Guitarist, singer, harmonicist. Canned Heat.

WILSON, ANN. San Diego, CA, 6/19/51. Lead singer. Heart.

WILSON, BARRY J. London, England, 3/18/47. Drummer. Procol Harum.

WILSON, BRIAN. Inglewood, CA, 6/20/42. Bassist, keyboardist, singer, father of Wendy and Carnie. The Beach Boys.

WILSON, CARNIE. Los Angeles, CA, 4/29/68. Singer, daughter of Brian, sister of Wendy. Wilson Phillips.

WILSON, CINDY. Athens, GA, 2/28/57. Guitarist, singer. The B-52's.

WILSON, DEMOND. Valdosta, GA, 10/13/46. Actor. *Sanford and Son*.

WILSON, DON. Tacoma, WA, 2/10/37. Guitarist. The Ventures.

WILSON, JOYCE. Detroit, MI, 12/14/46. Singer. Tony Orlando & Dawn.

WILSON, MARY. Greenville, MS, 3/6/44. Singer. The Supremes.

WILSON, NANCY. Chillicothe, OH, 2/20/37. R&B singer.

WILSON, NANCY. San Francisco, CA, 3/16/54. Guitarist, singer. Heart.

WILSON, TOM. Grant Town, WV, 8/1/31. Cartoonist. *Ziggy*.

WILSON, TONY. Trinidad, 10/8/47. Bassist, singer. Hot Chocolate.

WILSON, WENDY. Los Angeles, CA, 10/16/69. Singer, sister of Carnie, daughter of Brian. Wilson Phillips.

WINCHELL, PAUL. New York, NY, 12/21/22. Ventriloquist, actor. *The Paul Winchell-Jerry Mahoney Show*.

WINDOM, WILLIAM. New York, NY, 9/28/23. Actor. *Murder She Wrote*.

WINFIELD, DAVE. Saint Paul, MN, 10/3/51. Baseball player.

WINFIELD, PAUL. Los Angeles, CA, 5/22/41. Actor. *Sounder*.

WINGER, DEBRA (Mary Debra Winger). Cleveland, OH, 5/16/55. Actor. *Terms of Endearment*.

WINKLER, HENRY. New York, NY, 10/30/45. Actor, producer, director. Arthur "The Fonz" Fonzarelli on *Happy Days*.

WINNINGHAM, MARE. Phoenix, AZ, 5/6/59. Actor. *St. Elmo's Fire*.

WINSTON, JIMMY (James Langwith). London, England, 4/20/45. Organist. The Small Faces.

WINTER, EDGAR. Beaumont, TX, 12/28/46. Blues/rock keyboardist, brother of Johnny.

WINTER, JOHNNY. Beaumont, TX, 2/23/44. Blues/rock guitarist, brother of Edgar.

WINTERS, JONATHAN. Dayton, OH, 11/11/25. Actor. *The Jonathan Winters Show*.

WINTERS, SHELLEY (Shirley Schrift). St. Louis, MO, 8/18/20. Actor. *The Poseidon Adventure*.

WINWOOD, MUFF (Mervyn Winwood). Birmingham, England, 6/14/43. Singer, songwriter, bassist. The Spencer Davis Group.

WINWOOD, STEVE. Birmingham, England, 5/12/48. Singer, songwriter. The Spencer Davis Group; Traffic; Blind Faith.

WITHERS, BILL. Slab Fork, WV, 7/4/38. Pop singer, songwriter, guitarist.

WITHERS, JANE. Atlanta, GA, 4/12/26. Actor. Josephine the Plumber on TV commercials.

WOLF, PETER (Peter Blankfield). New York, NY, 3/7/46. Singer. The J. Geils Band.

WOLTERS, JOHN. 4/28/45. Drummer, singer. Dr. Hook.

WOMACK, BOBBY. Cleveland, OH, 3/4/44. Gospel/R&B singer, songwriter, guitarist.

WONDER, STEVIE (Steveland Morris). Saginaw, MI, 5/13/50. Singer, songwriter, formerly married to Syreeta Wright.

WONG, B. D. San Francisco, CA, 10/24/62. Actor. *M. Butterfly*.

WOOD, DANNY. Boston, MA, 5/14/71. Singer. New Kids on the Block.

WOOD, RON. London, England, 6/1/47. Guitarist. The Rolling Stones.

WOOD, ROY (Ulysses Adrian Wood). Birmingham, England, 11/8/46. Singer, guitarist, cellist. Electric Light Orchestra (ELO); Wizzard; The Move.

WOOD, STUART. Edinburgh, Scotland, 2/25/57. Guitarist. The Bay City Rollers.

WOODARD, ALFRE. Tulsa, OK, 11/8/53. Actor. *Cross Creek*.

WOODWARD, EDWARD. Croydon, England, 6/1/30. Actor. *The Equalizer*.

WOODWARD, JOANNE. Thomasville, GA, 2/27/30. Actor, married to Paul Newman. *The Three Faces of Eve*.

WOODWARD, KEREN. Bristol, England, 4/2/61. Singer. Bananarama.

WORLEY, JO ANNE. Lowell, IN, 9/6/39. Actor, singer. *Laugh-In*.

WRAY, FAY. Alberta, Canada, 9/10/07. Actor. *King Kong*.

WRIGHT, ADRIAN. Sheffield, England, 6/30/56. Projector

operator for on-stage slides and films. The Human League.

WRIGHT, LITTLE STEVIE. Leeds, England, 12/20/48. Singer. The Easybeats.

WRIGHT, MAX. Detroit, MI, 8/2/43. Actor. Willie Tanner on *ALF.*

WRIGHT, PAT. Brooklyn, NY, 1945. Singer. The Crystals.

WRIGHT, RICK. London, England, 7/28/45. Keyboardist. Pink Floyd.

WRIGHT, STEVEN.Burlington, MA, 12/6/55. Comedian.

WRIGHT, SYREETA. Pittsburgh, PA, 1946. Singer, songwriter, formerly married to Stevie Wonder.

WUHL, ROBERT. Union City, NJ, 10/9/51. Actor, writer. *Bull Durham.*

WYATT, JANE. Campgaw, NJ, 8/13/12. Actor. *Father Knows Best.*

WYMAN, BILL (William Perks). London, England, 10/24/36. Bassist. The Rolling Stones.

WYMAN, JANE (Sarah Jane Fulks). St. Joseph, MO, 1/4/14. Actor, formerly married to Ronald Reagan. Angela Channing on *Falcon Crest.*

YAMAGUCHI, KRISTI. Hayward, CA, 7/12/71. Skater, Olympic gold medalist.

YANKOVIC, WEIRD AL (Alfred Matthew Yankovic). Los Angeles, CA, 10/23/59. Singer, spoof artist. "Like a Surgeon."

YANOVSKY, ZAL. Toronto, Canada, 12/19/44. Guitarist, singer. The Lovin' Spoonful.

YARROW, PETER. New York, NY, 5/31/38. Composer, author, singer. Peter, Paul and Mary.

YEARWOOD, TRISHA. Monticello, GA, 9/19/64. Singer.

YELTSIN, BORIS. Burka, Russia, 2/1/31. Russian political leader.

YESTER, JIM. Birmingham, AL, 11/24/39. Singer, guitarist. The Association.

YOAKAM, DWIGHT. Pikesville, KY, 10/23/56. Country singer. "Honky Tonk Man."

YORK, MICHAEL. Fulmer, England, 3/27/42. Actor. *Logan's Run.*

YORK, PETE. Redcar, England, 8/15/42. Drummer. The Spencer Davis Group.

YOUNG, ANGUS. Glasgow, Scotland, 3/31/59. Guitarist. AC/DC.

YOUNG, GEORGE. Glasgow, Scotland, 11/6/47. Guitarist. The Easybeats.

YOUNG, JAMES. Chicago, IL, 11/14/48. Guitarist. Styx.

YOUNG, JESSE COLIN (Perry Miller). New York, NY, 11/11/41. Guitarist, bassist, singer. The Youngbloods.

YOUNG, MALCOLM. Glasgow, Scotland, 1/6/53. Guitarist. AC/DC.

YOUNG, NEIL. Toronto, Canada, 11/12/45. Singer, songwriter, guitarist. Buffalo Springfield; Crosby, Stills, Nash & Young.

YOUNG, RUSTY. Long Beach, CA, 2/23/46. Pedal steel guitarist. Poco.

YOUNG, SEAN. Louisville, KY, 11/20/59. Actor. *No Way Out.*

YOUNG MC (Marvin Young). London, England, 1968. Rap artist.

ZADORA, PIA. New York, NY, 5/4/56. Actor. *Naked Gun 33 1/3.*

ZAHN, PAULA. Naperville, IL, 2/24/56. Broadcast journalist. *CBS This Morning.*

ZAL, ROXANA. Los Angeles, CA, 11/8/69. Actor. *Something About Amelia.*

ZANDER, ROBIN. Rockford, IL, 1/23/53. Singer, guitarist. Cheap Trick.

ZAPPA, DWEEZIL. Los Angeles, CA, 9/5/69. Guitarist, son of Frank, brother of Moon Unit.

ZAPPA, MOON UNIT. Hollywood, CA, 9/28/67. Singer, daughter of Frank, sister of Dweezil. "Valley Girl."

ZEMECKIS, ROBERT Chicago, IL, 5/14/51. Director, producer, screenwriter. *Forrest Gump.*

ZEVON, WARREN. Chicago, IL, 1/24/47. Singer, songwriter. "Werewolves of London."

ZIERING, IAN. 3/30/64. Actor. *Beverly Hills 90210.*

ZIMBALIST, STEPHANIE. Encino, CA, 10/8/56. Actor, daughter of Efrem. Laura Holt on *Remington Steele.*

ZMED, ADRIAN. Chicago, IL, 3/4/54. Actor. Vince Romano on *T. J. Hooker.*

ZUNIGA, DAPHNE. Berkeley, CA, 10/28/62. Actor. *Melrose Place.*

HAPPY BIRTHDAY! THE GREATS' NATAL DATES

JANUARY 1
Frank Langella
Don Novello
Dedee Pfeiffer
J.D. Salinger

JANUARY 2
Jim Bakker
Gabrielle Carteris
Chick Churchill
Taye Diggs
Cuba Gooding Jr.
Joanna Pacula

JANUARY 3
Melody Anderson
Dabney Coleman
Mel Gibson
Robert Loggia
Danica McKellar
Victoria Principal
Stephen Stills

JANUARY 4
Bernie Albrecht
Dyan Cannon
Matt Frewer
Ann Magnuson
Julia Ormond
Michael Stipe
Barney Sumner
Jane Wyman

JANUARY 5
Suzy Amis
George Brown
Robert Duvall
Diane Keaton
Ted Lange
Marilyn Manson
Walter Mondale
Chris Stein

JANUARY 6
Rowan Atkinson
Syd Barrett
Bonnie Franklin
Mark O'Toole
John Singleton
Kathy Sledge
Malcolm Young

JANUARY 7
Nicolas Cage
Katie Couric
Sammo Hung
Kenny Loggins
Paul Revere

JANUARY 8
David Bowie
Stephen Hawking
Robbie Krieger
Yvette Mimieux
Charles Osgood
Soupy Sales
Larry Storch

JANUARY 9
Joan Baez
Bill Cowsill
Bob Denver
Scott Engel
Crystal Gayle
David Johansen
Judith Krantz
Herbert Lom
AJ McLean
Jimmy Page

JANUARY 10
Trini Alvarado
Pat Benatar
Shawn Colvin
Donald Fagen
George Foreman
Bob Lang
Cyril Neville
Maurice Sendak
Rod Stewart

JANUARY 11
Mary J. Blige
Naomi Judd
Vicki Peterson
Rod Taylor

JANUARY 12
Kirstie Alley
Anthony Andrews
Melanie Chisholm
Per Gessle
William Lee
   Golden
Rush Limbaugh
Oliver Platt
Chynna Phillips
Cynthia Robinson
Vendela

JANUARY 13
Kevin Anderson
Nick Clooney
Patrick Dempsey
Robert "Squirrel"
   Lester
Julia Louis-Drey-
   fus
Graham McPher-
   son

Penelope Ann
   Miller
Richard Moll
Robert Stack
Frances
   Sternhagen
Gwen Verdon

JANUARY 14
Jason Bateman
Faye Dunaway
L.L. Cool J
Andy Rooney
Emily Watson
Carl Weathers

JANUARY 15
Captain Beefheart
Charo
Martha Davis
Chad Lowe
Andrea Martin
Pamela Sue Mar-
   tin
Julian Sands
Peter Trewavas
Mario Van Peebles

JANUARY 16
Debbie Allen
Bob Bogle
John Carpenter
Bill Francis
Kate Moss
Sade
Laura Schles-
   singer
Jim Stafford
Paul Webb

JANUARY 17
Muhammad Ali
Jim Carrey
David Caruso
John Crawford
Steve Earle
Joe Frazier
Susanna Hoffs
James Earl Jones
Eartha Kitt
Maury Povich
Vidal Sassoon
Betty White

JANUARY 18
Kevin Costner
David Ruffin
Larry Smith

JANUARY 19
Desi Arnaz Jr.
Dewey Bunnell

Michael Crawford
Phil Everly
Shelley Fabares
Tippi Hedren
Harvey Hinsley
Robert MacNeil
Robert Palmer
Dolly Parton
Katey Sagal
Jean Stapleton
Mickey Virtue
Fritz Weaver

JANUARY 20
Buzz Aldrin
Arte Johnson
Lorenzo Lamas
David Lynch
Bill Maher
John Michael
   Montgomery
Patricia Neal
Paul Stanley
Eric Stewart
Ron Townson

JANUARY 21
Robby Benson
Emma Bunton
Geena Davis
Mac Davis
Jill Eikenberry
Richie Havens

JANUARY 22
Linda Blair
Olivia D'Abo
Balthazar Getty
John Hurt
Diane Lane
Piper Laurie
Chris Lemmon
Steve Perry
Jeff Smith
Ann Sothern

JANUARY 23
Richard Dean
   Anderson
Princess Caroline
Bill Cunningham
Earl Falconer
Gil Gerard
Rutger Hauer
Jeanne Moreau
Anita Pointer
Chita Rivera
Patrick Simmons
Robin Zande

JANUARY 24
Ernest Borgnine
Neil Diamond
Jools Holland
Nastassja Kinski
Michael Ontkean
Oral Roberts
Yakov Smirnoff
Ray Stevens
Warren Zevon

JANUARY 25
Corazon Aquino
Andy Cox
Richard Finch
Etta James
Dean Jones
Dinah Manoff

JANUARY 26
Jazzie B
David Briggs
Ellen DeGeneres
Scott Glenn
Wayne Gretsky
Paul Newman
Andrew Ridgeley
Bob Uecker
Eddie Van Halen
Lucinda Williams

JANUARY 27
Bobby Bland
Troy Donahue
Brian Downey
Bridget Fonda
Gillian Gilbert
Seth Justman
Nick Mason
Mike Patton
Mimi Rogers
Nedra Talley

JANUARY 28
Alan Alda
Mikhail
   Baryshnikov
John Beck
Nick Carter
Joey Fatone
Brian Keenan
Marthe Keller
Sarah McLachlan
Nicholas Pryor
Dave Sharp
Dick Taylor
Elijah Wood

JANUARY 29
David Byron
Ed Burns

John Forsythe
Roddy Frame
Sara Gilbert
Heather Graham
Noel Harrison
Eddie Jackson
Anne Jillian
Greg Louganis
Tommy Ramone
Katharine Ross
Tom Selleck
Oprah Winfrey

JANUARY 30
Christian Bale
Marty Balin
Phil Collins
Charles Dutton
Gene Hackman
William King
Dorothy Malone
Steve Marriott
Dick Martin
Vanessa Redgrave
Joe Terranova
Jody Watley

JANUARY 31
John Agar
Harry Wayne
   Casey
Carol Channing
Lloyd Cole
Portia De Rossi
Minnie Driver
John Paul Jones
Terry Kath
John Lydon
Phil Manzanera
Suzanne Pleshette
Jean Simmons
Justin Timberlake

FEBRUARY 1
Mike Campbell
Don Everly
Dennis Farina
Sherilynn Fenn
Sherman Hemsley
Rick James
Terry Jones
Billy Mumy
Lisa Marie Pres-
   ley-Jackson
Ray Sawyer
Pauly Shore
Boris Yeltsin

FEBRUARY 2
Christie Brinkley
Garth Brooks
Alan Caddy

Farrah Fawcett
Gale Gordon
Peter Lucia
Graham Nash
Liz Smith
Tom Smothers
Elaine Stritch
Ross Valory

FEBRUARY 3
Joey Bishop
Thomas Calabro
Angelo D'Aleo
Blythe Danner
Dave Davies
Morgan Fairchild
Eric Haydock
Nathan Lane
Fran Tarkenton
Maura Tierney
Lol Tolhurst

FEBRUARY 4
Gabrielle Anwar
Michael Beck
Clint Black
David Brenner
Alice Cooper
Natalie Imbruglia
Florence LaRue
Dan Quayle
John Steel

FEBRUARY 5
Bobby Brown
Christopher Guest
Barbara Hershey
Jennifer Jason
 Leigh
Laura Linney
Charlotte Rampling
Roger Staubach
Cory Wells

FEBRUARY 6
Rick Astley
Tom Brokaw
Natalie Cole
Fabian
Mike Farrell
Zsa Zsa Gabor
Alan Jones
Patrick Macnee
Ronald Reagan
Rip Torn
Robert Townsend
Michael Tucker
Mamie Van Doren

FEBRUARY 7
David Bryan
Miguel Ferrer
Jimmy Greenspoon
Alan Lancaster
Chris Rock

James Spader
Brian Travers

FEBRUARY 8
Brooke Adams
Brian Bennett
Creed Bratton
Gary Coleman
John Grisham
Robert Klein
Ted Koppel
Vince Neil
Nick Nolte
Mary Steenburgen
John Williams

FEBRUARY 9
Mia Farrow
Carole King
Judith Light
Master P
Roger Mudd
Joe Pesci
Janet Suzman
Travis Tritt
Alice Walker

FEBRUARY 10
Laura Dern
Donovan
Roberta Flack
Jimmy Merchant
Mark Spitz
Robert Wagner
Don Wilson

FEBRUARY 11
Jennifer Aniston
Brandy
Sheryl Crow
Conrad Janis
Tina Louise
Leslie Nielsen
Burt Reynolds
Sidney Sheldon

FEBRUARY 12
Maud Adams
Joe Don Baker
Judy Blume
Cliff DeYoung
Arsenio Hall
Joanna Kerns
Simon
 MacCorkindale
Ray Manzarek
Christina Ricci
Joe Schermie

FEBRUARY 13
Tony Butler
Stockard Channing
Roger Christian
Peter Gabriel
Peter Hook

David Naughton
Kim Novak
George Segal
Jerry Springer
Mena Suvari
Bo Svenson
Peter Tork

FEBRUARY 14
Hugh Downs
Roger Fisher
Florence Henderson
Gregory Hines
Rob Thomas
Meg Tilly
Paul Tsongas
Ken Wahl

FEBRUARY 15
Mick Avory
Marisa Berenson
Claire Bloom
David Brown
Ali Campbell
Mikey Craig
Matt Groening
John Helliwell
Harvey Korman
Kevin McCarthy
Jane Seymour

FEBRUARY 16
LeVar Burton
James Ingram
William Katt
John McEnroe Jr.
Andy Taylor

FEBRUARY 17
Billie Joe Armstrong
Alan Bates
Jim Brown
Brenda Fricker
Hal Holbrook
Michael Jordan
Lou Diamond
 Phillips
Gene Pitney
Denise Richards
Rene Russo
Raf Vallone

FEBRUARY 18
Robbie Bachman
Randy Crawford
Sinead Cusack
Dennis DeYoung
Matt Dillon
George Kennedy
Toni Morrison
Juice Newton
Yoko Ono
Jack Palance
Molly Ringwald

Herman Santiago
Greta Scacchi
Cybill Shepherd
John Travolta
Vanna White

FEBRUARY 19
Mark Andes
Justine Bateman
Francis Buchholz
Lou Christie
Jeff Daniels
Benicio Del Toro
Tony Iommi
Holly Johnson
Smokey Robinson
Seal
Amy Tan

FEBRUARY 20
Edward Albert
Robert Altman
Charles Barkley
Walter Becker
Ian Brown
Randy California
Cindy Crawford
Sandy Duncan
J. Geils
Kelsey Grammer
Brian Littrell
Jennifer O'Neill
Sidney Poitier
Andrew Shue
Peter Strauss
Gloria Vanderbilt
Nancy Wilson

FEBRUARY 21
Christopher Atkins
William Baldwin
Jean-Jacques
 Burnel
Mary Chapin Carpenter
Charlotte Church
Tyne Daly
David Geffen
Kelsey Grammer
Jerry Harrison
Jennifer Love
 Hewitt
Gary Lockwood
Rue McClanahan
Nina Simone
Vince Welnick

FEBRUARY 22
Drew Barrymore
Jonathan Demme
Julius Erving
Ted Kennedy
Kyle MacLachlan
John Mills
Miou-Miou

FEBRUARY 23
Kristen Davis
Peter Fonda
Howard Jones
Mike Maxfield
Steve Priest
David Sylvian
Brad Whitford
Johnny Winter
Rusty Young

FEBRUARY 24
Barry Bostwick
James Farentino
Steven Hill
Paul Jones
Edward James
 Olmos
Helen Shaver
Lonnie Turner
Paula Zahn

FEBRUARY 25
Sean Astin
George Harrison
Téa Leoni
Mike Peters
Sally Jessy
 Raphael
Bobby Riggs
Veronica Webb
Stuart Wood

FEBRUARY 26
Erykah Badu
Michael Bolton
Jonathan Cain
Johnny Cash
Fats Domino
John Jon
Tony Randall
Mitch Ryder
Sandie Shaw

FEBRUARY 27
Adam Baldwin
Garry Christian
Chelsea Clinton
Eddie Gray
Steve Harley
Howard Hesseman
Paul Humphreys
Ralph Nader
Neal Schon
Grant Show
Adrian Smith
Elizabeth Taylor
Rozonda Thomas
Joanne Woodward

FEBRUARY 28
Mario Andretti
Stephanie
 Beacham
Frank Bonner
Charles Durning

Phil Gould
Robert Sean
 Leonard
Gavin MacLeod
Bernadette Peters
Mercedes Ruehl
Bubba Smith
Joe South
Tommy Tune
John Turturro
Cindy Wilson

MARCH 1
Javier Bardem
Harry Belafonte
Dirk Benedict
Roger Daltrey
Timothy Daly
Jimmy Fortune
Ron Howard
Alan Thicke

MARCH 2
Jon Bon Jovi
John Cowsill
John Cullum
Mark Evans
Mikhail Gorbachev
John Irving
Jennifer Jones
Jay Osmond
Lou Reed
Al Waxman

MARCH 3
Jessica Biel
Willie Chambers
Jance Garfat
Jackie Joyner-
 Kersee
Tim Kazurinsky
Dave Mount
Mike Pender
Miranda
 Richardson
Tone-Loc
Blue Weaver

MARCH 4
Chastity Bono
Evan Dando
Patsy Kensit
Catherine O'Hara
Paula Prentiss
Chris Rea
Chris Squire
Shakin' Stevens
Bobby Womack
Adrian Zmed

MARCH 5
Alan Clark
Samantha Eggar
Eddy Grant
James B. Sikking
Dean Stockwell

Marsha Warfield

MARCH 6
Tom Arnold
Marion Barry
Kiki Dee
David Gilmour
Hugh Grundy
D.L. Hughley
Ed McMahon
Shaquille O'Neal
Rob Reiner
Mary Wilson

MARCH 7
Tammy Faye
 Messner
Paul Davis
Matthew Fisher
John Heard
Willard Scott
Lynn Swann
Daniel J. Travanti
Chris White
Peter Wolf

MARCH 8
Mike Allsup
Cheryl Baker
Clive Burr
Cyd Charisse
Mickey Dolenz
Ralph Ellis
Peter Gill
Camryn Manheim
Randy Meisner
Gary Numan
Aidan Quinn
Lynn Redgrave
James Van Der
 Beek

MARCH 9
Juliette Binoche
Trevor Burton
John Cale
Jim Cregan
Linda Fiorentino
Martin Fry
Marty Ingels
Emmanuel Lewis
Mark Lindsey
Jeffrey Osborne
Mickey Spillane
Robin Trower
Trish Van Devere

MARCH 10
Neneh Cherry
Prince Edward
Jasmine Guy
Chuck Norris
James Earl Ray
Tom Scholz
Sharon Stone
Dean Torrence

MARCH 11
Douglas Adams
Sam Donaldson
Johnny Knoxville
Lisa Loeb
Bobby McFerrin
Susan Richardson
Ric Rothwell
Mark Stein
Bruce Watson

MARCH 12
Barbara Feldon
Mike Gibbins
Marlon Jackson
Al Jarreau
Paul Kantner
Liza Minnelli
Brian O'Hara
Bill Payne
James Taylor

MARCH 13
Adam Clayton
Dana Delany
Glenne Headly
William H. Macy
Deborah Raffin
Neil Sedaka

MARCH 14
Jamie Bell
Michael Caine
Billy Crystal
Megan Follows
Boon Gould
Taylor Hanson
Quincy Jones
Walter Parazaider
Kevin Williamson

MARCH 15
Ry Cooder
David Costell
Terence Trent
 D'Arby
Fabio
Renny Harlin
Judd Hirsch
Phil Lesh
Mike Love
Bret Michaels
Rockwell
Howard Scott
Sly Stone
Jimmy Lee Swag-
 gart

MARCH 16
Michael Bruce
Erik Estrada
Isabelle Huppert
Jerry Lewis
Kate Nelligan
Nancy Wilson

MARCH 17
Harold Brown
Lesley-Anne Down
Patrick Duffy
Scott Gorham
Mike Lindup
Rob Lowe
Patrick McCauley
Kurt Russell
John Sebastian
Gary Sinise

MARCH 18
Bonnie Blair
Irene Cara
Kevin Dobson
Peter Graves
John Hartman
Wilson Pickett
Charley Pride
Queen Latifah
John Updike
Vanessa Williams
Barry J. Wilson

MARCH 19
Ursula Andress
Paul Atkinson
Glenn Close
Terry Hall
Clarence Henry
Derek Longmuir
Ruth Pointer
Bruce Willis

MARCH 20
John Clark Gable
Holly Hunter
William Hurt
Kathy Ireland
Spike Lee
Hal Linden
Carl Palmer
Slim Jim Phantom
Carl Reiner
Mr. Rogers
Theresa Russell

MARCH 21
Matthew Broderick
Timothy Dalton
Cynthia Geary
Roger Hodgson
Eddie Money
Rosie O'Donnell
Gary Oldman
Rosie Stone
Russell
 Thompkins Jr.

MARCH 22
George Benson
Jeremy Clyde
Randy Hobbs
Werner Klemperer
Kelly LeBrock

Andrew
 Lloyd Webber
Karl Malden
Marcel Marceau
Stephanie Mills
Matthew Modine
Lena Olin
Pat Robertson
William Shatner
Harry Vanda
M. Emmet Walsh
Reese Wither-
 spoon

MARCH 23
Princess Eugenie
Catherine Keener
Chaka Khan
Ric Ocasek
Marti Pellow
Amanda Plummer
Keri Russell

MARCH 24
Lara Flynn Boyle
Robert Carradine
Tommy Hilfiger
Star Jones
Lee Oskar
Donna Pescow
Annabella Sciorra
Dougie Thomson

MARCH 25
Bonnie Bedelia
Aretha Franklin
Paul Michael
 Glaser
Mary Gross
Jeff Healey
Elton John
Neil Jones
Sarah Jessica
 Parker
Gloria Steinem
John Stockwell
Maisie Williams

MARCH 26
Alan Arkin
James Caan
Kenny Chesney
Leeza Gibbons
Jennifer Grey
Vicki Lawrence
Leonard Nimoy
Teddy Pendergrass
Diana Ross
Fran Sheehan
Martin Short
Curtis Sliwa
Richard Tandy
Steven Tyler

MARCH 27
Tony Banks
Mariah Carey
Judy Carne
Andrew Farriss
Austin Pendleton
Maria Schneider
Tom Sullivan
Quentin Tarantino
Michael York

MARCH 28
Dirk Bogarde
Ken Howard
Lucy Lawless
Reba McEntire
Chuck Portz
Salt
Julia Stiles
Dianne Wiest
Milan Williams

MARCH 29
Jennifer Capriati
Bud Cort
Eric Idle
Bobby Kimball
Christopher Lam-
 bert
Elle Macpherson

MARCH 30
John Astin
Warren Beatty
Tracy Chapman
Eric Clapton
Richard Dysart
Graeme Edge
Hammer
Peter Marshall
Paul Reiser
Ian Ziering

MARCH 31
Rod Allen
Herb Alpert
Richard
 Chamberlain
Liz Claiborne
William Daniels
Albert Gore
Sean Hopper
Shirley Jones
Ewen McGregor
Ed Marinaro
Al Nichol
Rhea Perlman
Mick Ralphs
Christopher
 Walken
Angus Young

APRIL 1
John Barbata
Alan Blakley
Billy Currie

Rudolph Isley
Gordon Jump
Ali MacGraw
Phil Margo
Annette O'Toole
Bijou Phillips
Debbie Reynolds
Mark White

APRIL 2
Dana Carvey
Glen Dale
Buddy Ebsen
Emmylou Harris
Linda Hunt
Pamela Reed
Leon Russell
Keren Woodward

APRIL 3
Alec Baldwin
Jan Berry
Marlon Brando
Doris Day
Jennie Garth
Jane Goodall
Marsha Mason
Eddie Murphy
Wayne Newton
Tony Orlando
Barry Pritchard
Mel Schacher

APRIL 4
Maya Angelou
David Blaine
Robert Downey Jr.
Steve Gatlin
Dave Hill
David E. Kelley
Kitty Kelley
Graeme Kelling
Christine Lahti
Heath Ledger
Mick Mars
Nancy McKeon
Craig T. Nelson
Berry Oakley

APRIL 5
Allan Clarke
Paula Cole
Agnetha Faltskog
Maxwell Gail
Frank Gorshin
Peter Greenaway
Mike McCready
Michael Moriarty
Gregory Peck
Colin Powell
Gale Storm

APRIL 6
Stan Cullimore
Marilu Henner
Jason Hervey

Ari Meyers
John Ratzenberger
John Stax
Billy Dee Williams

APRIL 7
Mick Abrahams
Patricia Bennett
Jackie Chan
Francis Ford Coppola
Russell Crowe
Buster Douglas
Spencer Dryden
James Garner
Bruce Gary
Janis Ian
Elaine Miles
John Oates
Wayne Rogers

APRIL 8
Patricia Arquette
Roger Chapman
Steve Howe
Julian Lennon
Robin Wright Penn

APRIL 9
Jean-Paul Belmondo
Les Gray
Hugh Hefner
Mark Kelly
Michael Learned
Cynthia Nixon
Dennis Quaid

APRIL 10
Kenneth "Babyface" Edmonds
Peter MacNicol
John Madden
Mandy Moore
Steven Seagal
Brian Setzer
Omar Sharif
Bobbie Smith
Bunny Wailer

APRIL 11
Stuart Adamson
Joel Grey
Bill Irwin
Louise Lasser
Delroy Pearson
Peter Riegert
Richie Sambora
Lisa Stansfield
Neville Staples

APRIL 12
Alex Briley
David Cassidy
Tom Clancy
Claire Danes

Shannen Doherty
Andy Garcia
Vince Gill
Herbie Hancock
John Kay
David Letterman
Ann Miller
Ed O'Neill
Will Sergeant
Scott Turow
Jane Withers

APRIL 13
Peabo Bryson
Jack Casady
Lester Chambers
Jimmy Destri
Tony Dow
Al Green
Garry Kasparov
Howard Keel
Brian Pendleton
Ron Perlman
Rick Schroder
Paul Sorvino
Lyle Waggoner

APRIL 14
Ritchie Blackmore
Dennis Bryon
Julie Christie
Larry Ferguson
Sarah Michelle Gellar
Anthony Michael Hall
Suge Knight
Buddy Knox
Jay Robinson
Pete Rose
John Shea
Rod Steiger

APRIL 15
Claudia Cardinale
Lois Chiles
Graeme Clark
Roy Clark
Samantha Fox
Emma Thompson

APRIL 16
Edie Adams
Ellen Barkin
Jon Cryer
Lukas Haas
Diana Krall
Gerry Rafferty
Bill Spooner
Dusty Springfield
Bobby Vinton

APRIL 17
Victoria Beckham
Boomer Esiason
Liz Phair

Pete Shelley
Stephen Singleton

APRIL 18
Barbara Hale
Melissa Joan Hart
Jane Leeves
Eric McCormack
Hayley Mills
Rick Moranis
Conan O'Brien
Les Pattinson
Eric Roberts
Alexander Spence
Mike Vickers
James Woods

APRIL 19
Don Adams
Tim Curry
Kate Hudson
Ashley Judd
Dudley Moore
Alan Price
Larry Ramos Jr.
Mark Volman

APRIL 20
Carmen Electra
Craig Frost
Jessica Lange
Joey Lawrence
Ryan O'Neal
George Takei
Luther Vandross
Jimmy Winston

APRIL 21
Paul Carrack
Tony Danza
Queen Elizabeth II
Charles Grodin
Patti LuPone
Andie MacDowell
Elaine May
Iggy Pop
Anthony Quinn
Robert Smith
John Weider

APRIL 22
Eddie Albert
Joseph Bottoms
Glen Campbell
Peter Kenneth Frampton
Ace Frehley
Chris Makepeace
Jack Nicholson
Aaron Spelling
John Waters

APRIL 23
Valerie Bertinelli
David Birney
Steve Clark

Sandra Dee
Jan Hooks
Melinda Kanakaredes
Lee Majors
Alan Oppenheimer
Captain Sensible

APRIL 24
Eric Bogosian
Doug Clifford
Glenn Cornick
Billy Gould
Shirley MacLaine
Paul Ryder
Richard Sterban
Barbra Streisand

APRIL 25
Hank Azaria
Andy Bell
Michael Brown
Stu Cook
Meadowlark Lemon
Paul Mazursky
Al Pacino
Talia Shire
Bjorn Ulvaeus
Renee Zellwegger

APRIL 26
Carol Burnett
Duane Eddy
Giancarlo Esposito
Jet Li
Tionne Watkins

APRIL 27
Anouk Aimee
Sheena Easton
Pete Ham
Jack Klugman
Kate Pierson
Marco Pirroni
Clive Taylor

APRIL 28
Jessica Alba
Ann-Margret
Penelope Cruz
Saddam Hussein
Bruno Kirby
Jay Leno
Marcia Strassman
John Wolters

APRIL 29
Andre Agassi
Duane Allen
Stephen Arenholz
Keith Baxter
Daniel Day-Lewis
Lonnie Donegan
Carl Gardner
Celeste Holm
Tommy James

Coretta Scott King
Rod McKuen
Zubin Mehta
Kate Mulgrew
Michelle Pfeiffer
Eve Plumb
Francis Rossi
Jerry Seinfeld
Uma Thurman
Carnie Wilson

APRIL 30
Turbo B
Jill Clayburgh
Gary Collins
Kirsten Dunst
Perry King
Cloris Leachman
Al Lewis
Willie Nelson
Merrill Osmond
Bobby Vee

MAY 1
Judy Collins
Johnny Colt
Steve Farris
Nick Fortune
Tim McGraw
Ray Parker Jr.
Phil Smith

MAY 2
Christine Baranski
Lesley Gore
Lou Gramm
Engelbert Humperdinck
Bianca Jagger
Goldy McJohn
Lorenzo Music
Donatella Versace

MAY 3
David Ball
James Brown
Christopher Cross
Bruce Hall
Mary Hopkin
Pete Seeger
Pete Staples
Frankie Valli
Wynonna

MAY 4
Nickolas Ashford
Jay Aston
Lance Bass
Ronnie Bond
Ed Cassidy
Jackie Jackson
Randy Travis
Pia Zadora

MAY 5
Sarah Ban Breathnach
Gary Daly
Lance Henriksen
Ian McCulloch
Kevin Mooney
Cathy Moriarty
Michael Murphy
Michael Palin
Bill Ward

MAY 6
George Clooney
Roma Downey
Willie Mays
Bob Seger
Lori Singer
Mare Winningham

MAY 7
Michael Knight
Bill Kreutzmann Jr.
Traci Lords
Darren McGavin
Rick West

MAY 8
Philip Bailey
Rick Derringer
Chris Frantz
Melissa Gilbert
Gary Glitter
Enrique Iglesias
David Keith
Janet McTeer
James Mitchum
Don Rickles
Paul Samwell-Smith
Toni Tennille
Alex Van Halen

MAY 9
Candice Bergen
Pete Birrell
James L. Brooks
Sonny Curtis
Nokie Edwards
Albert Finney
Richie Furay
Dave Gahan
Paul Heaton
Glenda Jackson
Billy Joel
Steve Katz
Mike Millward
Tom Petersson
Dave Prater
Lloyd Price
Tommy Roe
Mike Wallace

MAY 10
Jim Abrahams
Bono

MAY 16
Pierce Brosnan
Tracey Gold
Glenn Gregory
Janet Jackson
Barbara Lee
Gabriela Sabatini
Derrell Sweet
Debra Winger
Ralph Tresvant

MAY 17
Bill Bruford
Dennis Hopper
Pervis Jackson
Jordan Knight
Sugar Ray
  Leonard
Bill Paxton
Trent Reznor
Bob Saget
Taj Mahal

MAY 18
Joe Bonsall
Pope John Paul II
George Strait

MAY 19
Nora Ephron
James Fox
David Hartman
Dusty Hill
Grace Jones
Nancy Kwan
Joey Ramone
Philip Rudd
Pete Townshend
Martyn Ware

MAY 20
Warren Cann
Cher
Joe Cocker
Sue Cowsill
Tony Goldwyn
Nick Heyward
Brian Nash
Bronson Pinchot
Ronald Reagan Jr.
Busta Rhymes

MAY 21
Mike Barson
Peggy Cass
Al Franken
Ronald Isley
Stan Lynch
Carol Potter
Judge Reinhold
Leo Sayer
Mr. T
Hilton Valentine

MAY 22
Charles Aznavour
Richard Benjamin
Naomi Campbell
Michael Constan-
  tine
Jerry Dammers
Iva Davies
Morrissey
Bernie Taupin
Paul Winfield

MAY 23
Drew Carey
Rosemary Clooney
Joan Collins
Betty Garrett
Bill Hunt
Jewel
Anatoly Karpov

MAY 24
Gary Burghoff
Roseanne Cash
Thomas Chong
Bob Dylan
Lenny Kravitz
Priscilla Presley
Derek Quinn
Rich Robinson
Kristin Scott
  Thomas

MAY 25
Dixie Carter
Patti D'Arbanville
Anne Heche
Justin Henry
Lauryn Hill
Mitch Margo
Ian McKellen
Klaus Meine
Mike Myers
Frank Oz
John Palmer
Connie Sellecca
Beverly Sills
Leslie Uggams
Paul Weller

MAY 26
Verden Allen
James Arness
Helena Bonham-
  Carter
Ray Ennis
Genie Francis
Bobcat Goldthwait
Pam Grier
Levon Helm
Wayne Hussey
Peggy Lee
Stevie Nicks
Gerry Paterson
Matt Stone

Philip Michael
  Thomas
Hank Williams Jr.

MAY 27
Cilla Black
Todd Bridges
Joseph Fiennes
Peri Gilpin
Louis Gossett Jr.
Tony Hillerman
Henry Kissinger
Lisa Lopes
Cynthia McFadden
Siouxsie Sioux
Bruce Weitz

MAY 28
Carroll Baker
John Fogerty
Roland Gift
Gladys Knight
Sondra Locke
Kylie Minogue

MAY 29
Annette Bening
Larry Blackmon
Gary Brooker
Melanie Brown
Kevin Conway
Roy Crewsdon
Melissa Etheridge
Rupert Everett
Anthony Geary
Bob Hope
Clifton James
Lisa Whelchel

MAY 30
Lenny Davidson
Keir Dullea
Marie Fredriksson
Nicky Headon
Ted McGinley
Clint Walker

MAY 31
Tom Berenger
Clint Eastwood
Sharon Gless
Gregory Harrison
Augie Meyers
Joe Namath
Johnny Paycheck
Brooke Shields
Lea Thompson
Peter Yarrow

JUNE 1
Rene Auberjonois
David Berkowitz
Lisa Hartman
  Black
Pat Boone
Powers Boothe

Pat Corley
Jason Donovan
Morgan Freeman
Andy Griffith
Mike Joyce
Peter Masterson
Alanis Morissette
Lorna Patterson
Jonathan Pryce
Graham Russell
Alan Wilder
Ron Wood
Edward Woodward

JUNE 2
Joanna Gleason
William Guest
Tony Hadley
Charles Haid
Marvin Hamlisch
Stacy Keach
Sally Kellerman
Jerry Mathers
Charles Miller
Milo O'Shea
Michael Steele
Charlie Watts

JUNE 3
Michael Clarke
Tony Curtis
Ian Hunter
Billy Powell
Suzi Quatro
Scott Valentine
Deniece Williams

JUNE 4
Roger Ball
John Drew
  Barrymore
El DeBarge
Bruce Dern
Angelina Jolie
Michelle Phillips
Parker Stevenson
Eddie Velez
Gordon Waller
Dennis Weaver
Ruth Westheimer
Charlie Whitney
Scott Wolf
Noah Wyle

JUNE 5
Laurie Anderson
Richard Butler
Spalding Gray
Kenny G
Robert Lansing
Marky Mark
Bill Moyers
Don Reid
Freddie Stone
Mark Wahlberg

JUNE 6
Sandra Bernhard
Gary Bonds
David Dukes
Robert Englund
Harvey Fierstein
Roy Innis
Amanda Pays
Tom Ryan
Levi Stubbs
Billie Whitelaw

JUNE 7
James Ivory
Tom Jones
Anna Kournikova
Alan Iverson
Liam Neeson
Prince

JUNE 8
Kathy Baker
Mick Box
Barbara Bush
Russell Christian
Griffin Dunne
Mick "Red"
  Hucknall
Julianna Mar-
  gulies
Neil Mitchell
Chuck Negron
Doris Pearson
Nick Rhodes
Joan Rivers
Boz Scaggs
Jerry Stiller
Bonnie Tyler
Keenen Ivory
  Wayans

JUNE 9
Trevor Bolder
Patricia Cornwell
Johnny Depp
Michael J. Fox
Billy Hatton
Jon Lord
Jackie Mason
Natalie Portman

JUNE 10
Shirley Alston
Human Beatbox
Lionel Jeffries
Tara Lipinski
Grace Mirabella
Shirley Owens
Prince Philip
Rick Price
Leelee Sobieski
Andrew Stevens

JUNE 11
Adrienne Barbeau
Joey Dee

Linda Evangelista
Henry Fambrough
Jay Ferguson
Graham
  Gouldman
Dave Mason
Danny Rapp

MAY 11
Eric Burdon
Les Chadwick
Louis Farrakhan
Faith Popcorn
Natasha
  Richardson

MAY 12
Burt Bacharach
Stephen Baldwin
Jason Biggs
Bruce Boxleitner
Gabriel Byrne
George Carlin
Lindsay Crouse
Billy Duffy
Emilio Estevez
Kim Fields
Susan Hampshire
Katharine Hep-
  burn
Ian McLagan
Ving Rhames
Tom Snyder
Billy Squier
David Walker
Steve Winwood

MAY 13
Beatrice Arthur
Harvey Keitel
Danny Klein
Lorraine McIntosh
Dennis Rodman
Darius Rucker
Paul Thompson
Overend Watts
Stevie Wonder

MAY 14
Ian Astbury
Cate Blanchett
Jack Bruce
David Byrne
Tom Cochrane
Gene Cornish
Meg Foster
George Lucas
Fabrice Morvan
Danny Wood
Robert Zemeckis

MAY 15
Brian Eno
Graham Goble
Mike Oldfield

Chad Everett
Joshua Jackson
John Lawton
Joe Montana
Bonnie Pointer
Donnie Van Zandt
Gene Wilder
George Willig

JUNE 12
Marv Albert
Timothy Busfield
George Bush
Bun Carlos
Vic Damone
Brad Delp
Jenilee Harrison
Jim Nabors
Reg Presley

JUNE 13
Tim Allen
Christo
Bobby Freeman
Howard Leese
Dennis Locorriere
Mark Mendoza
Deniece Pearson
Ally Sheedy
Richard Thomas

JUNE 14
Rod Argent
Jasmine Bleeth
Boy George
Marla Gibbs
Steffi Graf
Jimmy Lea
Will Patton
Donald Trump
Muff Winwood

JUNE 15
Jim Belushi
Simon Callow
Courteney Cox
Mario Cuomo
Julie Hagerty
Russell Hitchcock
Noddy Holder
Helen Hunt
Waylon Jennings

JUNE 16
Eddie Levert
Ian Matthews
Laurie Metcalf
Corin Redgrave
Erich Segal
Joan Van Ark
Gino Vannelli

JUNE 17
Greg Kinnear
Norman Kuhlke
Mark Linn-Baker

Peter Lupus
Barry Manilow
Jason Patric
Joe Piscopo

JUNE 18
Tom Bailey
Roger Ebert
Carol Kane
Paul McCartney
Alison Moyet
Isabella Rossellini

JUNE 19
Paula Abdul
Tommy DeVito
Larry Dunn
Malcolm McDowell
Phylicia Rashad
Gena Rowlands
Salman Rushdie
Kathleen Turner
Ann Wilson

JUNE 20
Danny Aiello
Michael Anthony
Chet Atkins
Olympia Dukakis
John Goodman
Billy Guy
Martin Landau
Alan Longmuir
Lionel Richie
John Taylor
Dave Thomas
James Tolkan
Brian Wilson

JUNE 21
Meredith Baxter
Berke Breathed
Chris Britton
Mark Brzezicki
Ray Davies
Michael Gross
Mariette Hartley
Bernie Kopell
Joey Kramer
Juliette Lewis
Nils Lofgren
Joey Molland
Robert Pastorelli
Jane Russell
Doug Savant
Maureen Staple-
ton
Prince William

JUNE 22
Peter Asher
Gary Beers
Bill Blass

Klaus Maria
Brandauer
Amy Brenneman
Bruce Campbell
Tom Cunningham
Carson Daly
Green Gartside
Howard Kaylan
Kris Kristofferson
Cyndi Lauper
Michael Lerner
Alan Osmond
Tracy Pollan
Todd Rundgren
Jimmy Somerville
Meryl Streep
Lindsay Wagner

JUNE 23
Bryan Brown
Adam Faith
Karin Gustafson
Frances McDor-
mand

JUNE 24
Nancy Allen
Jeff Beck
Colin Blunstone
Georg Stanford
Brown
Jeff Cease
Mick Fleetwood
John Illsley
Michele Lee
Andy McCluskey
Curt Smith
Sherry Stringfield
Peter Weller

JUNE 25
Tim Finn
Eddie Floyd
Allen Lanier
June Lockhart
Ian McDonald
George Michael
David Paich
Walter Payton
Carly Simon
Pearly Sweets
Jimmie Walker
Clint Warwick

JUNE 26
Billy Davis Jr.
Sean Hayes
Chris Isaak
Mick Jones
Chris O'Donnell
Larry Taylor

JUNE 27
Isabelle Adjani
Julia Duffy
Bob Keeshan

Toby Maguire
Lorrie Morgan
Henry Ross Perot
Vera Wang

JUNE 28
Kathy Bates
Gil Bellows
Mel Brooks
John Cusack
Dave Knights
Alice Krige
Mary Stuart
Masterson
Noriyuki "Pat"
Morita

JUNE 29
Maria Conchita
Alonso
Gary Busey
Fred Grandy
Colin Hay
Richard Lewis
Little Eva
Ian Paice
Stedman Pearson
Roger Spear
Ruth Warrick

JUNE 30
Vincent D'Onofrio
David Alan Grier
Lena Horne
Hal Lindes
Andy Scott
Glenn Shorrock
Mike Tyson
Adrian Wright

JULY 1
Wally Amos Jr.
Pamela Anderson
Dan Aykroyd
Claude Berri
Karen Black
Roddy Bottum
Delaney Bramlett
Genevieve Bujold
Leslie Caron
Olivia De Havil-
land
Princess Diana
Missy Elliott
Jamie Farr
Farley Granger
Deborah Harry
Estee Lauder
Carl Lewis
Alanis Morissette
Sydney Pollack
Fred Schneider
John Tesh
Liv Tyler

JULY 2
Pete Briquette
Johnny Colla
Jerry Hall
Imelda Marcos
Brock Peters
Joe Puerta
Ron Silver
Paul Williams

JULY 3
Paul Barrere
Dave Barry
Betty Buckley
Neil Clark
Vince Clarke
Tom Cruise
Johnny Lee
Montel Williams

JULY 4
Leona Helmsley
Gina Lollobrigida
Kirk Pengilly
Geraldo Rivera
Eva Marie Saint
Neil Simon
Jeremy Spencer
John Waite
Al "Blind Owl"
Wilson
Bill Withers

JULY 5
Edie Falco
Shirley Knight
Huey Lewis
Michael Monarch
Robbie Robertson

JULY 6
Allyce Beasley
Ned Beatty
Gene Chandler
Rik Elswit
Nanci Griffith
Shelley Hack
Bill Haley
Jon Keeble
Janet Leigh
James Naughton
Nancy Reagan
Della Reese
Geoffrey Rush
Glenn Scarpelli
Sylvester Stallone
Burt Ward

JULY 7
Billy Campbell
Pierre Cardin
Shelley Duvall
Warren Entner
Jessica Hahn
David Hodo
Joe Spano

Ringo Starr

JULY 8
Kevin Bacon
Beck
Andy Fletcher
Anjelica Huston
Graham Jones
Raffi
Jeffrey Tambor
Jerry Valy

JULY 9
Marc Almond
Frank Bello
Brian Dennehy
Tom Hanks
Jim Kerr
Kelly McGillis
Mitch Mitchell
Fred Savage
Bon Scott
O.J. Simpson
Debbie Sledge
Jimmy Smits
John Tesh

JULY 10
David Brinkley
Ronnie James Dio
Ron Glass
Arlo Guthrie
Jerry Miller
Neil Tennant
Max Von Sydow

JULY 11
Giorgio Armani
Tab Hunter
Peter Murphy
Leon Spinks
Sela Ward

JULY 12
Milton Berle
Bill Cosby
Mel Harris
Cheryl Ladd
Christine McVie
Liz Mitchell
Richard Simmons
Jay Thomas
John Wetton
Kristi Yamaguchi

JULY 13
Stephen Jo Bladd
Lawrence Done-
gan
Harrison Ford
Robert Forster
Cheech Marin
Roger "Jim"
McGuinn
Patrick Stewart
Spud Webb

JULY 14
Polly Bergen
Ingmar Bergman
Chris Cross
Matthew Fox
Rosey Grier
Harry Dean Stanton

JULY 15
Willie Aames
Brian Austin
  Green
Alex Karras
Peter Lewis
Brigitte Nielsen
Linda Ronstadt
Jan-Michael
  Vincent
Patrick Wayne
Forest Whitaker

JULY 16
Ruben Blades
Phoebe Cates
Stewart Copeland
Desmond Dekker
Corey Feldman
Will Ferrell
Michael Flatley
Tony Jackson

JULY 17
Lucie Arnaz
Geezer Butler
Diahann Carroll
Spencer Davis
Phyllis Diller
David Hasselhoff
Art Linkletter
Donald Sutherland
Mick Tucker
Mike Vale

JULY 18
Papa Dee Allen
James Brolin
Terry Chambers
Hume Cronyn
Vin Diesel
Dion DiMucci
Glenn Hughes
Audrey Landers
Robin MacDonald
Nelson Mandela
Elizabeth
  McGovern
Martha Reeves
Nigel Twist

JULY 19
Allen Collins
Alan Gorrie
Anthony Edwards
Pat Hingle
Bernie Leadon

Brian May

JULY 20
Gisele Bundchen
Paul Cook
Chris Cornell
Donna Dixon
John Lodge
Mike McNeil
Diana Rigg
Carlos Santana

JULY 21
Lance Guest
Josh Hartnett
Edward Herrmann
Don Knotts
Leigh Lawson
Jon Lovitz
Jim Martin
Matt Mulhern
Billy Ocean
Henry Priestman
Isaac Stern
Cat Stevens
Robin Williams

JULY 22
Estelle Bennett
Albert Brooks
George Clinton
Willem Dafoe
Richard Davies
Louise Fletcher
Danny Glover
Don Henley
John Leguizamo
David Spade
Alex Trebek

JULY 23
Dino Danelli
David Essex
Martin Gore
Woody Harrelson
Eriq LaSalle
Andy Mackay
Don Imus
Larry Manetti
Edie McClurg
Stephanie Seymour
Terence Stamp
Blair Thornton

JULY 24
Heinz Burt
Ruth Buzzi
Lynda Carter
Lynval Golding
Kadeem Hardison
Robert Hays
Laura Leighton
Jennifer Lopez
Anna Paquin
Michael Richards

Chris Sarandon

JULY 25
Ray Billingsley
Manuel Charlton
Illeana Douglas
Estelle Getty
Barbara Harris
Iman
Matt LeBlanc
Jim McCarty
Verdine White

JULY 26
Kate Beckinsale
Sandra Bullock
Blake Edwards
Dorothy Hamill
Mick Jagger
Duncan Mackay
Kevin Spacey
Roger Taylor
Peggy Fleming
Norman Lear
Carol Leifer
Maureen McGovern
Helen Mirren
John Pleshette
Al Ramsey
Betty Thomas
Jerry Van Dyke

JULY 28
Elizabeth Berkley
George Cummings
Jim Davis
Terry Fox
Simon Kirke
Sally Struthers
Rick Wright

JULY 29
Neal Doughty
Peter Jennings
Geddy Lee
Martina McBride
Marilyn Quayle
Michael Spinks
David Warner

JULY 30
Paul Anka
Delta Burke
Kate Bush
Larry Fishburne
Vivica A. Fox
Buddy Guy
Anita Hill
Lisa Kudrow
Ken Olin
Rat Scabies
Arnold Schwarzenegger
Hilary Swank

JULY 31
Daniel Ash
Alan Autry
Bill Berry
Michael Biehn
Dean Cain
Geraldine Chaplin
Norman Cook
Karl Green
Gary Lewis
J.K. Rowling
Wesley Snipes
John West

AUGUST 1
Rick Anderson
Tempestt Bledsoe
Coolio
Ricky Coonce
Robert Cray
Dom DeLuise
Joe Elliott
Giancarlo Giannini
Arthur Hill
Robert James
  Waller
Tom Wilson

AUGUST 2
Joanna Cassidy
Doris Coley
Wes Craven
Garth Hudson
Victoria Jackson
Carroll O'Connor
Peter O'Toole
Mary-Louise
  Parker
Edward Patten
Max Wright

AUGUST 3
Tony Bennett
B.B. Dickerson
James Hetfield
John Landis
Beverly Lee
Gordon Scott
Martin Sheen
Martha Stewart

AUGUST 4
David Carr
Frankie Ford
Jeff Gordon
Billy Bob Thornton

AUGUST 5
Loni Anderson
Neil Armstrong
Rick Derringer
Rick Huxley
Jonathan Silverman

AUGUST 6
Paul Bartel
Geri Halliwell
Dorian Harewood
Catherine Hicks
Abbey Lincoln
Pat McDonald

AUGUST 7
Bruce Dickinson
Andy Fraser
John Glover
Garrison Keillor
David Rasche
Alberto Salazar
B. J. Thomas

AUGUST 8
Richard Anderson
Philip Balsley
Princess Beatrice
Keith Carradine
JC Chasez
Harry Crosby
Dino De Laurentiis
The Edge
Andy Fairweather-
  Low
Chris Foreman
Dustin Hoffman
Donny Most
Robin Quivers
Connie Stevens
Mel Tillis
Larry Dee Wilcox
Esther Williams

AUGUST 9
Gillian Anderson
Kurtis Blow
Sam Elliott
Melanie Griffith
Billy Henderson
Whitney Houston
Aimee Mann
Ken Norton
Benjamin Orr
David Steinberg

AUGUST 10
Ian Anderson
Rosanna Arquette
Antonio Banderas
Veronica Bennett
Michael Bivins
Riddick Bowe
Jimmy Dean
Jon Farriss
Eddie Fisher
Angie Harmon
Bobby Hatfield
Lorraine Pearson

AUGUST 11
Erik Braunn
Eric Carmen

Hulk Hogan
Mike Hugg
Joe Jackson
Jim Kale
Denis Payton
Claus Von Bulow

AUGUST 12
George Hamilton
Roy Hay
Sam J. Jones
Mark Knopfler
Pat Metheny
Pete Sampras
Dominique Swain
Suzanne Vega
Jane Wyatt

AUGUST 13
Kathleen Battle
Danny Bonaduce
Fidel Castro
Dan Fogelberg
Pat Harrington
Don Ho
Feargal Sharkey

AUGUST 14
Halle Berry
Dash Crofts
David Crosby
Alice Ghostley
Larry Graham
Marcia Gay
  Harden
Jackee
Magic Johnson
Steve Martin
Susan Saint
  James
Danielle Steel

AUGUST 15
Princess Anne
Ben Affleck
Julia Child
Mike Connors
Linda Ellerbee
Tess Harper
Natasha Henstridge
Matt Johnson
MCA
Debra Messing
Bill Pinkney
Rose-Marie
Pete York

AUGUST 16
Bob Balaban
Angela Bassett
James Cameron
Robert Culp
Frank Gifford
Kathie Lee Gifford
Eydie Gorme

Timothy Hutton
Madonna
Fess Parker
Carole Shelley
James Taylor
Reginald
 Veljohnson
Lesley Ann Warren

AUGUST 17

Belinda Carlisle
Robert De Niro
Steve Gorman
Colin Moulding
Maureen O'Hara
Sean Penn
Kevin Rowland
Gary Talley
Donnie Wahlberg

AUGUST 18

Carol Alt
Dennis Elliott
Dennis Leary
Martin Mull
Edward Norton
Roman Polanski
Robert Redford
Christian Slater
Madeleine Stowe
Ron Strykert
Patrick Swayze
Malcolm-Jamal
 Warner
Carl Wayne
Shelley Winters

AUGUST 19

Ginger Baker
Bill Clinton
John Deacon
Kevin Dillon
Jonathan Frakes
Peter Gallagher
Ian Gillan
Billy J. Kramer
M.C. Eric
Diana Muldaur
Matthew Perry
Jill St. John
John Stamos

AUGUST 20

Joan Allen
Connie Chung
Doug Fieger
Rudy Gatlin
Isaac Hayes
Don King
Phil Lynott
James Pankow
Robert Plant
Al Roker

AUGUST 21

Kim Cattrall
Carl Giammarese
Kenny Rogers
Kim Sledge
Joe Strummer
Melvin Van
 Peebles
Clarence
 Williams III

AUGUST 22

Ray Bradbury
Howie Dorough
Valerie Harper
John Lee Hooker
Roland Orzabal
Debbi Peterson
Norman
 Schwarzkopf
Cindy Williams

AUGUST 23

Kobe Bryant
Ronny Cox
Barbara Eden
Bobby G.
Shelley Long
Vera Miles
Shaun Ryder
Richard Sanders
Rick Springfield

AUGUST 24

Yasir Arafat
Mark Bedford
Jim Capaldi
Joe Chambers
John Cipollina
Jeffrey Daniel
David Freiberg
Steve Guttenberg
Ken Hensley
Craig Kilborn
Marlee Matlin
Claudia Schiffer

AUGUST 25

Anne Archer
Sean Connery
Elvis Costello
Billy Ray Cyrus
Mel Ferrer
Rob Halford
Monty Hall
Van Johnson
Regis Philbin
John Savage
Gene Simmons
Tom Skerritt
Blair Underwood
Joanne Whalley
Walter Williams

AUGUST 26

Jet Black
Bob Cowsill
Macaulay Culkin
Chris Curtis
Geraldine Ferraro
Michael Jeter
Shirley Manson
Branford Marsalis
Fred Milano
John O'Neill

AUGUST 27

Barbara Bach
Tim Bogert
Jeff Cook
Daryl Dragon
Pee-Wee Herman
Alex Lifeson
Glenn Matlock
Harry Reems
Tuesday Weld

AUGUST 28

Clem Cattini
Hugh Cornwell
Ben Gazzara
Scott Hamilton
Donald O'Connor
Wayne Osmond
Jason Priestley
LeAnn Rimes
Emma Samms
Elizabeth Seal
Danny Seraphine
David Soul
Daniel Stern

AUGUST 29

Richard
 Attenborough
Tim Burton
Rebecca DeMor-
nay
Elliott Gould
Michael Jackson
Robin Leach
George Mont-
gomery
Isabel Sanford

AUGUST 30

Elizabeth Ashley
Timothy Bottoms
Cameron Diaz
John McNally
Micky Moody
John Phillips
Kitty Wells

AUGUST 31

Jerry Allison
James Coburn
Richard Gere
Debbie Gibson

Buddy Hackett
Van Morrison
Harold Reid
Rudolph Schenker
Daniel Schorr
Anthony
 Thistlethwaite
Glenn Tilbrook
Chris Tucker

SEPTEMBER 1

Billy Blanks
Greg Errico
Gloria Estefan
Bruce Foxton
Barry Gibb
Lily Tomlin
Dave White

SEPTEMBER 2

Rosalind Ashford
Jimmy Connors
Sam Gooden
Marty Grebb
Mark Harmon
Salma Hayek
Fritz McIntyre
Steve Porcaro
Keanu Reeves

SEPTEMBER 3

Eileen Brennan
Donald Brewer
Al Jardine
Steve Jones
Gary Leeds
Valerie Perrine
Charles Sheen
Mort Walker

SEPTEMBER 4

Martin Chambers
Gary Duncan
Greg Elmore
Mitzi Gaynor
Fawn Hall
Judith Ivey
Merald Knight
Beyonce Knowles
Ronald LaPread
Rosie Perez
Jennifer Salt
Ione Skye
Damon Wayans

SEPTEMBER 5

William Devane
Cathy Guisewhite
Carol Lawrence
Bob Newhart
Al Stewart
Raquel Welch
Dweezil Zappa

SEPTEMBER 6

Dave Bargeron
Jane Curtin
Jeff Foxworthy
Macy Gray
Swoosie Kurtz
Claydes Smith
Paul Waaktaar
Jo Anne Worley

SEPTEMBER 7

Alfa Anderson
Corbin Bernsen
Susan Blakely
Chrissie Hynde
Julie Kavner
Peggy Noonan
Richard Roundtree
Benmont Tench

SEPTEMBER 8

Brian Cole
Michael Lardie
David Steele
Henry Thomas
Jonathan Taylor
 Thomas

SEPTEMBER 9

Doug Ingle
Michael Keaton
Sylvia Miles
Cliff Robertson
Adam Sandler
Dave Stewart
Goran Visnjic
Roger Waters
Michelle Williams

SEPTEMBER 10

Chris Columbus
Siobhan Fahey
Jose Feliciano
Johnnie Fingers
Colin Firth
Danny Hutton
Amy Irving
Big Daddy Kane
Pat Mastelotto
Joe Perry
Ryan Phillippe
Don Powell
Fay Wray

SEPTEMBER 11

Maria Bartiromo
Harry Connick Jr.
Lola Falana
Mickey Hart
Earl Holliman
Jane Krakowski
Amy Madigan
Virginia Madsen
Kristy McNichol
Jon Moss
Tommy Shaw

Mick Talbot
Dennis Tufano

SEPTEMBER 12

Barry Andrews
Gerry Beckley
Tony Bellamy
Darren E. Burrows
Linda Gray
Neil Peart
Brian Robertson
Peter Scolari
Barry White

SEPTEMBER 13

Fiona Apple
Barbara Bain
Jacqueline Bisset
Nell Carter
Peter Cetera
David Clayton-
 Thomas
Randy Jones
Richard Kiel
Joni Sledge

SEPTEMBER 14

Pete Agnew
Barry Cowsill
Faith Ford
Morten Harket
Walter Koenig
Paul Kossoff
Sam Neill
Joe Penny
Nicol Williamson

SEPTEMBER 15

Les Braid
Jackie Cooper
Prince Henry
Tommy Lee Jones
Oliver Stone

SEPTEMBER 16

Marc Antony
Lauren Bacall
Ed Begley Jr.
Joe Butler
Bernie Calvert
David Copperfield
Peter Falk
Anne Francis
Kenny Jones
B.B. King
Richard Marx
Mickey Rourke
Susan Ruttan

SEPTEMBER 17

Anne Bancroft
Elvira
Jeff MacNelly
Lamonte
 McLemore
John Ritter

Fee Waybill

SEPTEMBER 18
Frankie Avalon
Ricky Bell
Robert Blake
Joanne Catherall
James Gandolfini
Kerry Livgren
Dee Dee Ramone
Jada Pinkett
 Smith
Jack Warden

SEPTEMBER 19
Jim Abbott
John Coghlan
Lol Creme
Lee Dorman
Jeremy Irons
Joan Lunden
Nick Massi
David McCallum
Bill Medley
Nile Rodgers
Twiggy
Adam West

SEPTEMBER 20
Alannah Currie
Crispin Glover
Sophia Loren
Anne Meara
Chuck Panozzo

SEPTEMBER 21
Leonard Cohen
Henry Gibson
Liam Gallagher
Larry Hagman
Faith Hill
Stephen King
Ricki Lake
Rob Morrow
Bill Murray
Catherine
 Oxenberg
Philthy Animal
Alfonso Ribeiro
Nancy Travis
Trugoy the Dove

SEPTEMBER 22
Scott Baio
Shari Belafonte
Andrea Bocelli
David Coverdale
Thomas Harris
Joan Jett
Paul LeMat

SEPTEMBER 23
Jason Alexander
Steve Boone
Ronald Bushy
Ray Charles
Lita Ford
Julio Iglesias

Ben E. King
Elizabeth Pena
Mary Kay Place
Mickey Rooney
Bruce Springsteen

SEPTEMBER 24
Gerry Marsden
Kevin Sorbo

SEPTEMBER 25
Gary Alexander
Michael Douglas
Mark Hamill
John Locke
Heather Locklear
Onnie McIntyre
Christopher Reeve
Phil Rizzuto
Steve Severin
Will Smith
Cheryl Tiegs
Barbara Walters

SEPTEMBER 26
Melissa Sue
 Anderson
Joe Bauer
George Chambers
Craig Chaquico
Donna Douglas
Georgie Fame
Bryan Ferry
Linda Hamilton
Mary Beth Hurt
Winnie Mandela
Olivia Newton-
 John
Anne Robinson
Tracey Thorn

SEPTEMBER 27
Randy Bachman
Wilford Brimley
Greg Ham
Jayne Meadows
Gwyneth Paltrow
Meat Loaf
Sada Thompson

SEPTEMBER 28
Brigitte Bardot
Jeffrey Jones
Carre Otis
Se Ri Pak
John Sayles
Helen Shapiro
Mira Sorvino
William Windom
Moon Unit Zappa

SEPTEMBER 29
Anita Ekberg
Mark Farner
Bryant Gumbel
Patricia Hodge
Jerry Lee Lewis
Emily Lloyd

SEPTEMBER 30
Angie Dickinson
Lacey Chabert
Fran Drescher
Jenna Elfman
Deborah Kerr
Dewey Martin
Johnny Mathis
Marilyn McCoo
Sylvia Peterson
Victoria Tennant
Barry Williams

OCTOBER 1
Julie Andrews
Jean-Jacques
 Annaud
Jimmy Carter
Stephen Collins
Rob Davis
Richard Harris
Howard Hewett
Jerry Martini
Walter Matthau
Mark McGwire
Philippe Noiret
Randy Quaid
Stella Stevens
James Whitmore

OCTOBER 2
Lorraine Bracco
Richard Hell
Freddie Jackson
Donna Karan
Don McLean
Philip Oakey
Kelly Ripa
Mike Rutherford
Sting
Tiffany

OCTOBER 3
Lindsey Bucking-
 ham
Neve Campbell
Chubby Checker
Barbara Ferris
Pamela Hensley
Tommy Lee
Kevin Richardson
Gwen Stefani
Gore Vidal
Jack Wagner
Dave Winfield

OCTOBER 4
Armand Assante
Jackie Collins
Clifton Davis
Jim Fielder
Charlton Heston
Patti LaBelle
Chris Lowe
Norm MacDonald
Anne Rice
Susan Sarandon

Alicia Silverstone

OCTOBER 5
Karen Allen
Daniel Baldwin
Clive Barker
Leo Barnes
Josie Bissett
Eddie Clarke
Jeff Conaway
Brian Connolly
Bob Geldof
Glynis Johns
Bil Keane
Mario Lemieux
Carlo Mastrangelo
Steve Miller
Kate Winslet

OCTOBER 6
Kevin Cronin
Britt Ekland
Bobby Farrell
Thomas McClary
Elizabeth Shue
Matthew Sweet
Bob Weir

OCTOBER 7
June Allyson
Toni Braxton
Kevin Godley
Dave Hope
Yo-Yo Ma
John Mellencamp
Oliver North

OCTOBER 8
Rona Barrett
Robert Bell
George Bellamy
Chevy Chase
Matt Damon
Michael Dudikoff
Darrell Hammond
Paul Hogan
Jesse Jackson
Sarah Purcell
Johnny Ramone
R.L. Stine
Hamish Stuart
Sigourney Weaver
Tony Wilson
Stephanie
 Zimbalist

OCTOBER 9
Scott Bakula
Jackson Browne
John Entwistle
Sean Lennon
Michael Pare
Robert Wuhl

OCTOBER 10
Charles Dance
Jessica Harper
Martin Kemp

Alan Rachins
David Lee Roth
Tanya Tucker
Ben Vereen

OCTOBER 11
Joan Cusack
Daryl Hall
Ron Leibman
David Morse
Luke Perry
Grant Shaud

OCTOBER 12
Susan Anton
Kirk Cameron
Hugh Jackman
Sam Moore
Luciano Pavarotti
Adam Rich
Dave Vanian

OCTOBER 13
Karen Akers
Tisha Campbell
Sammy Hagar
Beverly Johnson
Nancy Kerrigan
Robert Lamm
Marie Osmond
Kelly Preston
Nipsey Russell
Demond Wilson

OCTOBER 14
Harry Anderson
Marcia Barrett
Greg Evigan
Billy Harrison
Justin Hayward
Ralph Lauren
Roger Moore
Cliff Richard
Usher

OCTOBER 15
Mickey Baker
Richard Carpenter
Chris De Burgh
Sarah Ferguson
Lee Iacocca
Tito Jackson
Emeril Lagasse
Linda Lavin
Penny Marshall
Tanya Roberts
Don Stevenson

OCTOBER 16
Tony Carey
Barry Corbin
Gary Kemp
Angela Lansbury
Dave Lovelady
Tim Robbins
Suzanne Somers
C.F. Turner
Wendy Wilson

OCTOBER 17
Sam Bottoms
Eminem
Beverly Garland
Alan Howard
Wyclef Jean
Mike Judge
Margot Kidder
Chris Kirkpatrick
Ziggy Marley
Michael McKean
Howard Rollins Jr.
Jim Seals
Jim Tucker
George Wendt

OCTOBER 18
Chuck Berry
Peter Boyle
Pam Dawber
Mike Ditka
Russ Giguere
Keith Knudsen
Melina Mercouri
Erin Moran
Joe Morton
Martina
 Navratilova
Gary Richrath
Vincent Spano

OCTOBER 19
Richard Dreyfuss
Jon Favreau
Patricia Ireland
John Lithgow
Trey Parker
Karl Wallinger

OCTOBER 20
Joyce Brothers
William Christo-
 pher
Snoop Dogg
Alan Greenwood
Steve Harvey
Mark King
Ric Lee
Jerry Orbach
Tom Petty
Will Rogers Jr.
Bobby Seale
Jay Siegel

OCTOBER 21
Charlotte Caffey
Julian Cops
Steve Cropper
Eric Faulkner
Lee Loughnane
Steve Lukather
Manfred Mann
Judith Sheindlin

OCTOBER 22

Eddie Brigati
Catherine Deneuve
Joan Fontaine
Annette Funicello
Jeff Goldblum
Valeria Golino
Zac Hanson
Derek Jacobi
Ray Jones
Jonathan Lipnicki
Christopher Lloyd
Shelby Lynne
Tony Roberts
Shaggy

OCTOBER 23

Johnny Carson
Michael Crichton
Freddie Marsden
Perola Negra Pele
Weird Al Yankovic
Dwight Yoakam

OCTOBER 24

F. Murray Abraham
Joy Browne
Jerry Edmonton
Kevin Kline
David Nelson
B.D. Wong
Bill Wyman

OCTOBER 25

Jon Anderson
Anthony Franciosa
Matthias Jabs
Midori
Tracy Nelson
Rick Parfitt
Helen Reddy
Marion Ross
Glenn Tipton

OCTOBER 26

Hillary Rodham Clinton
Pat Conroy
Cary Elwes
Keith Hopwood
Bob Hoskins
Dylan McDermott
Ivan Reitman
Pat Sajak
Jaclyn Smith
Keith Strickland

OCTOBER 27

Terry Anderson
Roberto Benigni
John Cleese
Ruby Dee
Matt Drudge
Nanette Fabray
John Gotti
Simon LeBon

Marla Maples
Carrie Snodgress

OCTOBER 28

Jane Alexander
Steve Baumgartner
Wayne Fontana
Dennis Franz
Bill Gates
Jami Gertz
Lauren Holly
Telma Hopkins
Bruce Jenner
Hank Marvin
Stephen Morris
Joan Plowright
Annie Potts
Julia Roberts
Daphne Zuniga

OCTOBER 29

Ralph Bakshi
Kevin Dubrow
Joely Fisher
Kate Jackson
Denny Laine
Melba Moore
Winona Ryder

OCTOBER 30

Harry Hamlin
Kevin Pollak
Gavin Rossdale
Grace Slick
Charles Martin Smith
Otis Williams
Henry Winkler

OCTOBER 31

King Ad-Rock
Barbara Bel Geddes
Tony Bowers
Bernard Edwards
Dale Evans
Lee Grant
Deidre Hall
Sally Kirkland
Annabella Lwin
Johnny Marr
Larry Mullen Jr.
Jane Pauley
Dan Rather
Xavier Roberts
David Ogden Stiers
Chris Tucker

NOVEMBER 1

Rick Allen
Ronald Bell
Barbara Bosson
Keith Emerson
Robert Foxworth
Mags Furuholmen

James Kilpatrick Jr.
Lyle Lovett
Eddie MacDonald
Jenny McCarthy
Betsy Palmer
Dan Peek
Jeff Probst

NOVEMBER 2

k.d. lang
Brian Poole
David Schwimmer
Ray Walston
Bruce Welch
Alfre Woodard

NOVEMBER 3

Adam Ant
Roseanne Arnold
Charles Bronson
Kate Capshaw
Mike Evans
Larry Holmes
Steve Landesberg
Lulu
Dolph Lundgren
Dennis Miller
James Prime
Gary Sandy

NOVEMBER 4

Art Carney
Sean "Puffy" Combs
Walter Cronkite
Chris Difford
Ralph Macchio
Delbert McClinton
Matthew McConaughey
Markie Post
Kool Rock
Mike Smith
Loretta Swit

NOVEMBER 5

Bryan Adams
Art Garfunkel
Peter Noone
Tatum O'Neal
Roy Rogers
Sam Shepard
Paul Simon
Elke Sommer
Ike Turner

NOVEMBER 6

Sally Field
Glenn Frey
Ethan Hawke
Thandie Newton
P.J. Proby
Rebecca Romijn
Doug Sahm
Maria Shriver
George Young

NOVEMBER 7

Billy Graham
Joni Mitchell
Johnny Rivers

NOVEMBER 8

Alan Berger
Bonnie Bramlett
Alain Delon
Mary Hart
Rickie Lee Jones
Terry Lee Miall
Gretchen Mol
Parker Posey
Bonnie Raitt
Rodney Slater
Courtney Thorne-Smith
Roy Wood
Roxana Zal

NOVEMBER 9

Joe Bouchard
Lou Ferrigno
Alan Gratzer
Phil May
Pepa
Sisqó
Dennis Stratton

NOVEMBER 10

Glen Buxton
Greg Lake
MacKenzie Phillips
Ann Reinking
Jack Scalia
Roy Scheider
Sammy Sosa

NOVEMBER 11

Bibi Andersson
Paul Cowsill
Chris Dreja
Calista Flockhart
Roger Lavern
Ian Marsh
Vince Martell
Demi Moore
Andy Partridge
Kurt Vonnegut Jr.
Jonathan Winters
Jesse Colin Young

NOVEMBER 12

Errol Brown
Tonya Harding
Charles Manson
John Maus
Leslie McKeown
Megan Mullaly
Stephanie Powers
Wallace Shawn
Neil Young

NOVEMBER 13

Whoopi Goldberg
Joe Mantegna

Richard Mulligan

NOVEMBER 14

Frankie Banali
Prince Charles
Freddie Garrity
Robert Ginty
Alexander O'Neal
Laura San Giacomo
Alec Such
D. B. Sweeney
Yanni
James Young

NOVEMBER 15

Edward Asner
Petula Clark
Beverly D'Angelo
Yaphet Kotto
Frida Lyngstad
Sam Waterston

NOVEMBER 16

Oksana Baiul
Lisa Bonet
Dwight Gooden
Clu Gulager

NOVEMBER 17

Martin Barre
Danny DeVito
Ronald DeVoe
Bob Gaudio
Isaac Hanson
Lauren Hutton
Gordon Lightfoot
Mary Elizabeth Mastrantonio
Lorne Michaels
Martin Scorsese
Tom Seaver

NOVEMBER 18

Margaret Atwood
Hank Ballard
Imogene Coca
Linda Evans
Kirk Hammett
Allison Janney
Andrea Marcovicci
Graham Parker
Jameson Parker
Elizabeth Perkins
Herman Rarebell
Chloë Sevigny
Susan Sullivan
Brenda Vaccaro
Kim Wilde

NOVEMBER 19

Dick Cavett
Jodie Foster
Savion Glover
Larry King
Jeane Kirkpatrick
Calvin Klein
Hank Medress

Kathleen Quinlan
Ahmad Rashad
Meg Ryan
Ted Turner

NOVEMBER 20

Kaye Ballard
Jimmy Brown
Mike D
Bo Derek
George Grantham
Veronica Hamel
Richard Masur
Estelle Parsons
Dick Smothers
Ray Stiles
Joe Walsh
Sean Young

NOVEMBER 21

Bjork
Ken Griffey Jr.
Goldie Hawn
Dr. John
Lonnie Jordan
Laurence Luckinbill
Lorna Luft
Juliet Mills
Harold Ramis
Nicollette Sheridan
Marlo Thomas

NOVEMBER 22

Aston Barrett
Boris Becker
Tom Conti
Jamie Lee Curtis
Rodney Dangerfield
Terry Gilliam
Mariel Hemingway
Billie Jean King
Floyd Sneed
Stevie "Little Steven" Van Zandt
Robert Vaughn
Tina Weymouth

NOVEMBER 23

Susan Anspach
Bruce Hornsby

NOVEMBER 24

Donald Dunn
Geraldine Fitzgerald
Chris Hayes
Dwight Schultz
John Squire
Jim Yester

NOVEMBER 25

Christina Applegate
Amy Grant

John Larroquette
Ricardo Montal-
ban
Steve Rothery
Percy Sledge

NOVEMBER 26
Cyril Cusack
Robert Goulet
Norman Hassan
Alan Henderson
John McVie
Tina Turner

NOVEMBER 27
Charlie Burchill
Dozy
Robin Givens
Fisher Stevens
Jaleel White

NOVEMBER 28
Beeb Birtles
Ed Harris
Hope Lange
Judd Nelson
Randy Newman
Jon Stewart

NOVEMBER 29
Felix Cavaliere
Don Cheadle
Kim Delaney
Denny Doherty
Barry Goudreau
Jonathan Knight
Diane Ladd
Howie Mandel
John Mayall
Andrew McCarthy
Garry Shandling

NOVEMBER 30
John Aston
Richard Barbieri
Dick Clark
Kevin Conroy
Richard Crenna
Roger Glover
Rob Grill
Robert Guillaume
Billy Idol
Bo Jackson
G. Gordon Liddy
Leo Lyons
Mandy Patinkin
June Pointer
Rex Reason
Ridley Scott
Ben Stiller

DECEMBER 1
Woody Allen
Eric Bloom
John Densmore
Bette Midler
Sandy Nelson
Gilbert O'Sullivan

Richard Pryor
Lou Rawls
Charlene Tilton
Treat Williams

DECEMBER 2
Steven Bauer
Ted Bluechel Jr.
Cathy Lee Crosby
Julie Harris
Lucy Liu
Michael McDonald
Tom McGuinness
Rick Savage
Howard Stern

DECEMBER 3
Brian Bonsall
Brendan Fraser
Julianne Moore
Ozzy Osbourne
Andy Williams

DECEMBER 4
Tyra Banks
Jeff Bridges
Deanna Durbin
Chris Hillman
Jay-Z
Wink Martindale
Bob Mosley
Gary Rossington
Southside Johnny
Marisa Tomei

DECEMBER 5
John Berendt
Morgan Brittany
Gabriel Byrne
Jeroen Krabbe
Charles Lane
Little Richard
Jim Messina
Les Nemes
Jack Russell

DECEMBER 6
Peter Buck
Rick Buckler
Tom Hulce
Janine Turner
Ben Watt
JoBeth Williams
Steven Wright

DECEMBER 7
Larry Bird
Ellen Burstyn
Mike Nolan
Tom Waits
Eli Wallach

DECEMBER 8
Gregg Allman
Kim Basinger
Jerry Butler
David Carradine
Phil Collen

Bobby Elliott
Teri Hatcher
James MacArthur
Sinead O'Connor
Paul Rutherford
Maximilian Schell

DECEMBER 9
Joan Armatrading
Beau Bridges
Dick Butkus
Judi Dench
Kirk Douglas
Morton Downey Jr.
Dennis Dunaway
Buck Henry
Neil Innes
John Malkovich
Michael Nouri
Donny Osmond
Dick Van Patten

DECEMBER 10
Frank Beard
Kenneth Branagh
Susan Dey
Ace Kefford
Mako
Walter Orange
Chad Stuart

DECEMBER 11
Bess Armstrong
Teri Garr
David Gates
Jermaine Jackson
Booker T. Jones
Brenda Lee
Rita Moreno
Nikki Sixx

DECEMBER 12
Bob Barker
Dickey Betts
Mayim Bialik
Clive Bunker
Jennifer Connelly
Sheila E.
Connie Francis
Terry Kirkman
Ed Koch
Rush Limbaugh
Mike Pinder
Cathy Rigby
Mike Smith
Dionne Warwick

DECEMBER 13
Jeff "Skunk" Bax-
ter
Steve Buscemi
John Davidson
Jamie Foxx
Ted Nugent
Randy Owen
Christopher
Plummer
Dick Van Dyke

Tom Verlaine
Johnny Whitaker

DECEMBER 14
Patty Duke
Cynthia Gibb
Bridget Hall
Abbe Lane
Jackie McCauley
Mike Scott
Dee Wallace Stone
Cliff Williams
Joyce Wilson

DECEMBER 15
Carmine Appice
Dave Clark
Tim Conway
Reginald Hudlin
Don Johnson
Paul Simonon
Helen Slater

DECEMBER 16
Benny Andersson
Benjamin Bratt
Steven Bochco
Ben Cross
Billy Gibbons
Tony Hicks
William Perry
Liv Ullmann

DECEMBER 17
Sarah Dallin
Dave Dee
Bob Guccione
Milla Jovovich
Eddie Kendricks
Eugene Levy
Mike Mills
Art Neville
Bill Pullman
Paul Rodgers
Tommy Steele

DECEMBER 18
Christina Aguilera
Steve Austin
Ossie Davis
Elliot Easton
Katie Holmes
Ray Liotta
Leonard Maltin
Brad Pitt
Keith Richards
Steven Spielberg

DECEMBER 19
Jennifer Beals
Alvin Lee
Robert Mac-
Naughton
Alyssa Milano
Tim Reid
Cicely Tyson
Robert Urich
Maurice White

Zal Yanovsky

DECEMBER 20
Jenny Agutter
Anita Baker
Billy Bragg
Bobby Colomby
John Hillerman
Chris Robinson
Little Stevie
Wright

DECEMBER 21
Phil Donahue
Chris Evert
Jane Fonda
Samuel L. Jackson
Jeffrey Katzenberg
Josh Mostel
Ray Romano
Kiefer Sutherland
Kurt Waldheim
Paul Winchell

DECEMBER 22
Barbara Billings-
ley
Hector Elizondo
Maurice Gibb
Robin Gibb
Lady Bird Johnson
Rick Nielsen
Ricky Ross
Diane Sawyer

DECEMBER 23
Corey Haim
Jorma Kaukonen
Johnny Kidd
Susan Lucci
Dave Murray
Eugene Record
Ruth Roman
Harry Shearer
James Stockdale
Eddie Vedder
Estella Warren

DECEMBER 24
Ian Burden
Lemmy

DECEMBER 25
Jimmy Buffett
Robin Campbell
O'Kelly Isley
Annie Lennox
Shane MacGowan
Barbara Mandrell
Noel Redding
Hanna Schygulla
Sissy Spacek
Henry Vestine

DECEMBER 26
Steve Allen
Abdul Fakir

Alan KingDonald
Moffat
Phil Spector

DECEMBER 27
John Amos
Chyna
Goldberg
Peter Criss
Gerard Depardieu
Tovah Feldshuh
Mick Jones
David Knopfler
Les Maguire

DECEMBER 28
Willow Bay
Alex Chilton
Dick Diamonde
Lou Jacobi
Stan Lee
Charles Neville
Johnny Otis
Maggie Smith
Denzel Washing-
ton
Edgar Winter

DECEMBER 29
Ted Danson
Mark Day
Marianne Faithfull
Jude Law
Mary Tyler Moore
Paula Poundstone
Inga Swenson
Ray Thomas
Jon Voight

DECEMBER 30
Joseph Bologna
Bo Diddley
Davy Jones
Matt Lauer
Jeff Lynne
Mike Nesmith
Sheryl Lee Ralph
Russ Tamblyn
Tracey Ullman
Fred Ward
Tiger Woods

DECEMBER 31
Barbara Carrera
Rosalind Cash
Burton Cummings
Tom Hamilton
Anthony Hopkins
Val Kilmer
Ben Kingsley
Tim Matheson
Joe McIntyre
Sarah Miles
Pete Quaife
Patti Smith
Donna Summer
Andy Summers

2002'S WATERSHED BIRTHDAYS

The following folks will have reason to celebrate (or toast themselves) a little harder this year as they reach birthday milestones.

TURNING 95
Ossie Davis
Katharine Hepburn

TURNING 90
Julia Child
Lady Bird Johnson
Art Linkletter
Karl Malden
Will Rogers, Jr.

TURNING 80
Barbara Billingsley
Bill Blass
Blake Edwards
Barbara Hale
Arthur Hill
Steven Hill
Bil Keane
Jack Klugman
Norman Lear
Stan Lee
Patrick MacNee
Dick Martin
Darren McGavin
Carl Reiner
Gale Storm
Kurt Vonnegut, Jr.
Betty White
Paul Winchell

TURNING 75
Harry Belafonte
Joyce Brothers
Michael Constantine
Richard Crenna
William Daniels
Peter Falk
Carl Gardener
Lee Grant
Robert Guillaume
Alan King
Coretta Scott King
Eartha Kitt
Janet Leigh
Gina Lollobrigida
Roger Moore
Estelle Parsons
Brock Peters
Christopher Plummer
Sidney Poitier
Gordon Scott
Neil Simon
Jerry Stiller
Clint Walker

Andy Williams

TURNING 70
Anouk Aimee
John Barrymore
Ellen Burstyn
Johnny Cash
William Christopher
Petula Clark
Dabney Coleman
Mario Cuomo
Angie Dickinson
Joel Grey
Rosey Grier
John Hillerman
Gordon Jump
Ted Kennedy
Piper Laurie
Meadowlark Lemon
Little Richard
Elaine May
Noriyuki "Pat" Morita
Jim Nabors
Peter O'Toole
Della Reese
Debbie Reynolds
Roy Scheider
Gene Shalit
Omar Sharif
Inga Swenson
Elizabeth Taylor
Mel Tillis
John Updike
Jerry Vale
Melvin Van Peebles
Robert Vaughn
Billie Whitelaw
John Towner Williams

TURNING 65
Ned Beatty
Bob Bogle
Bill Cosby
Sonny Curtis
Jane Fonda
Morgan Freeman
Louis Gossett, Jr.
Dustin Hoffman
Anthony Hopkins
O'Kelly Isley
Waylon Jennings
Sally Kellerman

Ron Leibman
Gary Lockwood
Peter Lupus
James MacArthur
Jack Nicholson
Vanessa Redgrave
Ridley Scott
Erich Segal
Tom Smothers
Marlo Thomas
Frankie Valli
Billy Dee Williams

TURNING 60
Muhammad Ali
Susan Anspach
Nickolas Ashford
Dave Bargeron
Karen Black
Stephen Jo Bladd
Ted Bluechel, Jr.
Frank Bonner
Genevieve Bujold
Heinz Burt
Dick Butkus
John Cale
Joe Chambers
Dave Clark
Allan Clarke
David Cohen
Brian Cole
Kevin Conway
Peter Coyote
Michael Crawford
Michael Crichton
Mac Davis
Spencer Davis
Sandra Dee
Desmond Dekker
Daryl Dragon
Roger Ebert
Graeme Edge
Britt Ekland
Bobby Elliott
Ralph Ellis
Ray Ennis
Linda Evans
Mick Fleetwood
Harrison Ford
Bill Francis
Aretha Franklin
Annette Funicello
Bob Gaudio
Giancarlo Giannini
Mike Giles
Scott Glenn
Peter Greenaway

Billy Harrison
Stephen Hawking
Eric Haydock
Isaac Hayes
Levon Helm
Chris Hillman
Bob Hoskins
Mike Hugg
Danny Hutton
Rick Huxley
John Irving
Al Jardine
Paul Jones
Terry Jones
Paul Kantner
Garrison Keillor
Kitty Kelly
Carole King
Calvin Klein
Robert Klein
Merald Knight
Norman Kuhlke
Michelle Lee
Eddie Levert
Mark Lindsay
Dave Lovelady
Phil Margo
Gerry Marsden
Dewey Martin
Marsha Mason
Paul McCartney
Roger "Jim" McGuinn
Tammy Faye Messner
Mike Millward
Yvette Mimieux
Bob Mosley
Graham Nash
Chuck Negron
Mike Nesmith
Wayne Newton
Brian O'Hara
Mike Pender
John Pleshette
Muammar Qaddafi
Derek Quinn
Larry Ramos Jr.
Johnny Rivers
Tommy Roe
Richard Roundtree
Martin Scorsese
Judith Sheindlin
Roger Staubach
David Steinberg
Don Stevenson

David Ogden Stiers
Barbra Streisand
Andy Summers
Taj Mahal
Larry Taylor
B. J. Thomas
Ray Thomas
Junior Walker
Fred Ward
Cory Wells
Walter Williams
Brian Wilson
Michael York
Pete York

TURNING 50
Jenny Agutter
Harry Anderson
Alan Autry
Dan Aykroyd
Christine Baranski
Clive Barker
Gerry Beckley
Roberto Benigni
Pierce Brosnan
Jean-Jaques Burnel
David Byrne
Warren Cann
Alan Clark
Johnny Colla
Allen Collins
Jimmy Connors
Stewart Copeland
Paul Coswill
Chris Cross
Billy Currie
Susan Dey
Bernard Edwards
Lou Ferrigno
Doug Fieger
Tim Finn
Jonathan Frakes
Andy Fraser
Bruce Gary
Rudy Gatlin
Jeff Goldblum
John Goodman
Shelley Hack
David Hasselhoff
Marilu Henner
Dave Hill
Warrington Hudlin
Sammo Hung
Michael Jeter
Beverly Johnson

Grace Jones
Randy Jones
Carol Kane
David Knopfler
Keith Knudsen
Jimmy Lea
Paul Lemat
Lorna Luft
Simon MacCorkindale
Michael McDonald
Mary McDonnell
Liz Mitchell
Liam Neeson
Juice Newton
Mandy Patinkin
Neil Peart
Annie Potts
Billy Powell
Robin Quivers
DeeDee Ramone
Christopher Reeve
Susan Richardson
Cathy Rigby
Roseanne
Nile Rodgers
Isabella Rossallini
Mercedes Ruehl
Steven Seagal
Maria Schneider
Tommy Shaw
Parker Stevenson
Dave Stewart
George Strait
Lynn Swann
Patrick Swayze
Mr. T
Amy Tan
John Tesh
Donnie Van Zandt
Gino Vannelli
Reginald VelJohnson
Brad Whitford

TURNING 40
Paula Abdul
Ian Astbury
Adam Baldwin
Jon Bon Jovi
Matthew Broderick
Garth Brooks
David Bryan
Jim Carrey
Joanne Catherall
Rae Dawn Chong
Sheryl Crow

Tom Cruise
Stan Cullimore
Joan Cusack
Terence Trent
 D'Arby
Gary Daly
Anthony Edwards
Cary Elwes
Enya
Emilio Estevez
Ralph Fiennes
Jodie Foster
Mags Furuholmen
Dave Gahan
Roland Gift
Bobcat Goldthwait
Jasmine Guy
MC Hammer
Kirk Hammett
Paul Heaton
Bo Jackson
Star Jones

Jackie Joyner-
 Kersee
Mike Judge
Anthony Kiedis
Craig Kilborn
Eriq LaSalle
Tommy Lee
Jennifer Jason
 Leigh
Ralph Macchio
Norm MacDonald
Andrew McCarthy
Kristy McNichol
Kevin Mooney
Demi Moore
Rob Morrow
Dustin Nguyen
Rosie O'Donnell
William "The
 Refrigerator"
 Perry
Lou Diamond
 Phillips

Kelly Preston
Nick Rhodes
Axl Rose
Shaun Ryder
Ally Sheedy
Grant Show
Lori Singer
Wesley Snipes
Vincent Spano
John Squire
Jon Stewart
Tracey Thorn
Ben Watt
Paul Webb
B. D. Wong
Daphne Zuniga

TURNING 30

Ben Affleck
Billie Joe Arm-
 strong
Elizabeth Berkley
Peter Billingsley

Cameron Diaz
Carmen Electra
Eminem
Liam Gallagher
Jennie Garth
Geri Halliwell
Angie Harmon
Jason Hervey
Jude Law
Alyssa Milano
Gretchen Mol
Thandie Newton
Shaquille O'Neal
Gwyneth Paltrow
Amanda Peet
Busta Rhymes
Kevin Richardson
Rebecca Romijn-
 Stamos
Henry Thomas
Rob Thomas
Goran Visnjic

TURNING 21

Anna Kournikova
Natalie Portman
Britney Spears
Jonathan Taylor
 Thomas
Justin Timberlake
Elijah Wood

TURNING 20

Jessica Biel
Brian Bonsall
Lacey Chabert
Kirsten Dunst
Tara Lipinski
Anna Paquin
Leann Rimes
Leelee Sobieski
Prince William